W9-CTF-647

SOFTWARE ENGINEERING

A PRACTITIONER'S APPROACH

THIRD EDITION

Roger S. Pressman, Ph.D.

McGraw-Hill, Inc.
New York St. Louis San Francisco Auckland Bogotá
Caracas Lisbon London Madrid Mexico Milan
Montreal New Delhi Paris San Juan Singapore
Sydney Tokyo Toronto

To my parents

SOFTWARE ENGINEERING

A PRACTITIONER'S APPROACH

Copyright © 1992, 1987, 1982 by McGraw-Hill, Inc. All rights reserved. Printed in the United States of America. Except as permitted under the United States Copyright Act of 1976, no part of this publication may be reproduced or distributed in any form or by any means, or stored in a data base or retrieval system, without the prior written permission of the publisher.

4 5 6 7 8 9 0 DOH DOH 9 0 9 8 7 6 5 4 3 2

ISBN 0-07-050814-3

This book was set in New Century Schoolbook
by Beacon Graphics Corporation.
The editors were Eric M. Munson and Bernadette Boylan;
the designer was Jo Jones.
New drawings were done by Fine Line Illustrations, Inc.
Cover painting by Joseph Gillians.
R. R. Donnelley & Sons Company was printer and binder.

Library of Congress Cataloging-in-Publication Data

Pressman, Roger S.
Software engineering: a practitioner's approach / by Roger S. Pressman
p. cm.
Includes bibliographical references and index.
ISBN 0-07-050814-3
1. Software engineering. I. Title.
QA76.758.P75 1992 91-11321
005.1—dc20

ABOUT THE AUTHOR

Roger S. Pressman is an internationally recognized consultant and author in software engineering. He received a B.S.E. (cum laude) from the University of Connecticut, an M.S. from the University of Bridgeport, and a Ph.D. in engineering from the University of Connecticut, and has over two decades of industry experience, holding both technical and management positions with responsibility for the development of software for engineered products and systems.

As an industry practitioner and manager, Dr. Pressman worked on the development of CAD/CAM systems for advanced engineering and manufacturing in aerospace applications. He has also held positions with responsibility for scientific and systems programming.

In addition to his industry experience, Dr. Pressman was Bullard Associate Professor of Computer Engineering at the University of Bridgeport and Director of the University's Computer-Aided Design and Manufacturing Center. His research interests included software engineering methods and tools.

Dr. Pressman is President of R.S. Pressman & Associates, Inc., a consulting firm specializing in software engineering methods and training. He serves as principal consultant, specializing in helping companies establish effective software engineering practices. In addition to consulting services rendered to many Fortune 500 clients, the company markets a wide variety of software engineering training products and services. Dr. Pressman has authored three videotape training series, *Software Engineering Training Curriculum*, *A CASE Curriculum*, and *Essential Software Engineering*, that are distributed worldwide.

Dr. Pressman has written many technical papers, is a regular contributor to industry newsletters, and is the author of five books. In addition to *Software Engineering: A Practitioner's Approach,* he has written *Making Software Engineering Happen* (Prentice-Hall), a book that addresses the management problems associated with implementing software engineering technology, *Software Engineering: A Beginner's Guide* (McGraw-Hill), an introductory text, and *Software Shock* (Dorset House), a book that focuses on software and its impact on business and society. Dr. Pressman is a member of the ACM, IEEE and Tau Beta Pi, Phi Kappa Phi, Pi Tau Sigma, and Eta Kappa Nu.

CONTENTS

PART THREE THE DESIGN AND IMPLEMENTATION OF SOFTWARE

PREFACE

Over the past two decades, software engineering has come of age. Today, it is recognized as a legitimate discipline, one worthy of serious research, conscientious study, and tumultuous debate. Throughout the industry, "software engineer" has replaced "programmer" as the job title of preference. Software engineering methods, procedures, and tools have been adopted successfully across a broad spectrum of industry applications. Managers and practitioners alike recognize the need for a more disciplined approach to software development.

But the problems discussed in the first and second editions of this book remain with us. Many individuals and companies still develop software haphazardly. Many professionals and students are unaware of modern methods. And as a result, the quality of the software that we produce suffers. In addition, debate and controversy about the true nature of the software engineering approach continue. The status of software engineering is a study in contrasts. Attitudes have changed, progress has been made, but much remains to be done before the discipline reaches full maturity.

The third edition of *Software Engineering: A Practitioner's Approach* is intended to provide one element of a foundation from which a bridge from adolescence to maturity can be constructed. The third edition, like the two editions that have preceded it, is intended for both students and practitioners, and maintains the same format and style as its predecessors. The book retains its appeal as a guide to the industry professional and a comprehensive introduction to the student at the upper-level undergraduate or first-year graduate level.

Like in the earlier editions, software engineering methods are presented in the chronological sequence that they are applied during software development. However, the third edition is more than a simple update. The book has been restructured to accommodate the dramatic growth in the field and to emphasize new and important software engineering methods and tools. Rather than maintaining a strict life-cycle view, this edition presents generic activities that are performed regardless of the software engineering paradigm that has been chosen.

Chapters that have been retained from earlier editions have been revised and updated to reflect current trends and techniques. Major new sections have been added to chapters on computer system engineering, requirements analysis fundamentals, data flow-oriented design, object-oriented design, real-time design, software quality assurance, software testing techniques, and maintenance. In addition to these revisions, eight new chapters have been added to the third edition.

The original chapter on software project management has been removed and replaced by three new chapters on software metrics, estimation, and project planning. A new chapter on structured analysis presents the notation and approach for both conventional and real-time applications. A chapter on object-oriented analysis and data modeling provides a detailed treatment of these new and important modeling techniques.

The five existing chapters on software design have been further bolstered with a new chapter on user interface design. Software configuration management—a topic that has become pivotal to successful software development—is now treated in a separate chapter. The role of automation in software engineering is considered in two new chapters on computer-aided software engineering (CASE). One chapter emphasizes software tools and their application and the other discusses integrated CASE environments and the repository. The final chapter (also new) looks toward the twenty-first century and examines changes that will affect our approach to software engineering.

Many new examples, problems, and points to ponder have been added, and the "Further Readings" sections (one of the more popular tidbits in earlier editions) have been expanded and updated for every chapter.

The 24 chapters of the third edition have been divided into five parts. This has been done to compartmentalize topics and assist instructors who may not have the time to complete the entire book in one term. Part I—"Software—the Process and Its Management"—presents a thorough treatment of software project management issues. Part II— "System and Software Requirements Analysis"—contains five chapters that cover analysis fundamentals and requirements modeling methods and notation. Part III—"The Design and Implementation of Software"—presents a thorough treatment of software design, emphasizing fundamental design criteria that lead to high-quality systems and design methods that translate an analysis model into a software solution. Part IV— "Ensuring, Verifying, and Maintaining Software Integrity"—emphasizes the activities that are applied to ensure quality throughout the software engineering process. Part V— "The Role of Automation"—discusses the impact of CASE on the software development process.

The five-part organization of the third edition enables an instructor to "cluster" topics based on available time and student need. An entire one-term course can be built around one or more of the five parts. For example, a "design course" might emphasize only part III; a "methods course" might present selected chapters in parts II, III, IV, and V; and a "management course" would stress parts I and IV. By organizing the third edition in this way, I have attempted to provide an instructor with a number of teaching options.

An *Instructor's Guide* for the third edition of *Software Engineering: A Practitioner's Approach* is available from McGraw-Hill. The *Instructor's Guide* presents suggestions for conducting various types of software engineering courses, recommendations for a variety of software projects to be conducted in conjunction with a course, solutions to selected problems, and reference to a variety of complementary teaching materials that form a "system" for teaching software engineering.

The software engineering literature continues to expand at an explosive rate. Once again, my thanks to the many authors of books, papers, and articles who have provided me with additional insight, ideas, and commentary over the past decade. Many have been referenced within the pages of each chapter. All deserve credit for their contribution to this rapidly evolving field. I also wish to thank the reviewers of the third edition, James Cross, Auburn University; Mahesh Dodani, University of Iowa; William S. Junk, University of Idaho; and Laurie Werth, University of Texas. Their comments and criticism have been invaluable.

The content of the third edition of *Software Engineering: A Practitioner's Approach* has been shaped by hundreds of industry professionals, university professors, and students who have used the first and second editions of the book and have taken the time to communicate their suggestions, criticisms, and ideas. In addition, my personal thanks go to our many industry clients throughout North America and Europe, who certainly teach me as much or more than I can teach them.

Finally, to Barbara, Mathew, and Michael, my love and thanks for tolerating my travel schedule, understanding the evenings at the office, and encouraging still another edition of "the book."

Roger S. Pressman

PART 1

SOFTWARE— THE PROCESS AND ITS MANAGEMENT

CHAPTER 1

SOFTWARE AND SOFTWARE ENGINEERING

As the decade of the 1980s began, a front page story in *Business Week* magazine trumpeted the following headline: "Software: The New Driving Force." Software had come of age—it had become a topic for management concern. During the mid-1980s, a cover story in *Fortune* lamented "A Growing Gap in Software," and at the close of the decade, *Business Week* warned managers about "The Software Trap—Automate or Else." As the 1990s dawned, a feature story in *Newsweek* asked "Can We Trust Our Software?" and *The Wall Street Journal* related a major software company's travails with a front page article entitled "Creating New Software Was an Agonizing Task. . . ." These headlines, and many others like them, were a harbinger of a new understanding of the importance of computer software—the opportunities that it offers and the dangers that it poses.

Software has now surpassed hardware as the key to the success of many computer-based systems. Whether a computer is used to run a business, control a product, or enable a system, software is the factor that *differentiates.* The completeness and timeliness of information provided by software (and related databases) differentiate one company from its competitors. The design and "human friendliness" of a software product differentiate it from competing products with an otherwise similar function. The intelligence and function provided by embedded software often differentiate two similar industrial or consumer products. It is software that can make the difference.

1.1 THE IMPORTANCE OF SOFTWARE

During the first three decades of the computing era, the primary challenge was to develop computer hardware that reduced the cost of processing and storing data. Throughout the decade of the 1980s, advances in microelectronics resulted in more computing power at increasingly lower cost. Today, the problem is different. The primary challenge during the 1990s is to improve the quality (and reduce the cost) of computer-based solutions—solutions that are implemented with software.

The power of a 1980s-era mainframe computer is available now on a desk top. The awesome processing and storage capabilities of modern hardware represent computing potential. Software is the mechanism that enables us to harness and tap this potential.

1.1.1 The Evolving Role of Software

The context in which software has been developed is closely coupled to almost five decades of computer system evolution. Better hardware performance, smaller size, and lower cost have precipitated more sophisticated computer-based systems. We've moved from vacuum tube processors to microelectronic devices that are capable of processing 200 million instructions per second. In popular books on "the computer revolution," Osborne [OSB79] characterized a "new industrial revolution," Toffler [TOF80] called the advent of microelectronics part of "the third wave of change" in human history, and Naisbitt [NAI82] predicted that the transformation from an industrial society to an "information society" will have a profound impact on our lives. Feigenbaum and McCorduck [FEI83] suggested that information and knowledge (controlled by computers) will be the focal point for power in the twenty-first century, and Stoll [STO89] argued that the "electronic community" created by networks and software is the key to knowledge interchange throughout the world. As the 1990s began, Toffler [TOF90] described a "power shift" in which old power structures (governmental, educational, industrial, economic, and military) will disintegrate as computers and software lead to a "democratization of knowledge."

Figure 1.1 depicts the evolution of software within the context of computer-based system application areas. During the early years of computer system development, hardware underwent continual change while software was viewed by many as an afterthought. Computer programming was a "seat-of-the-pants" art for which few systematic methods existed. Software development was virtually unmanaged—until schedules slipped or costs began to escalate. During this period, a batch orientation was used for most systems. Notable exceptions were interactive systems such as the early American Airlines reservation system and real-time defense-oriented systems such as SAGE. For the most part, however, hardware was dedicated to the execution of a single program that in turn was dedicated to a specific application.

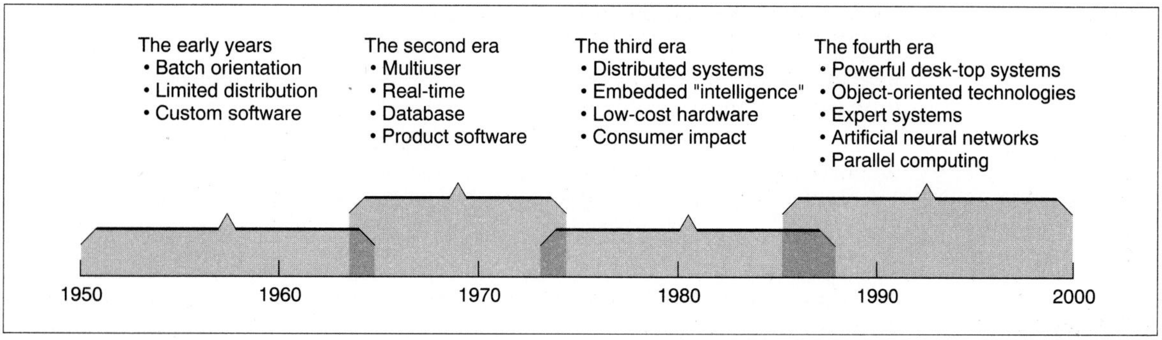

FIGURE 1.1. Evolution of software.

During the early years, general-purpose hardware became commonplace. Software, on the other hand, was custom-designed for each application and had a relatively limited distribution. Product software (i.e., programs developed to be sold to one or more customers) was in its infancy. Most software was developed and ultimately used by the same person or organization. You wrote it, you got it running, and if it failed, you fixed it. Because job mobility was low, managers could rest assured that you'd be there when bugs were encountered.

Because of this personalized software environment, design was an implicit process performed in one's head, and documentation was often nonexistent. During the early years we learned much about the implementation of computer-based systems, but relatively little about computer system engineering. In fairness, however, we must acknowledge the many outstanding computer-based systems that were developed during this era. Some of these remain in use today and provide landmark achievements that continue to justify admiration.

The second era of computer system evolution (Figure 1.1) spanned the decade from the mid-1960s to the late 1970s. Multiprogramming and multiuser systems introduced new concepts of human-machine interaction. Interactive techniques opened a new world of applications and new levels of hardware and software sophistication. Real-time systems could collect, analyze, and transform data from multiple sources, thereby controlling processes and producing output in milliseconds rather than minutes. Advances in on-line storage led to the first generation of database management systems.

The second era was also characterized by the use of product software and the advent of "software houses." Software was developed for widespread distribution in a multidisciplinary market. Programs for mainframes and minicomputers were distributed to hundreds and sometimes thousands of users. Entrepreneurs from industry, government, and academia broke away to "develop the ultimate software package" and earn a bundle of money.

As the number of computer-based systems grew, libraries of computer software began to expand. In-house development projects produced tens of thousands of program source statements. Software products purchased from the outside added hundreds of thousands of new statements. A dark cloud appeared on the horizon. All of these programs—all of these source statements—had to be corrected when faults were detected, modified as user requirements changed, or adapted to new hardware that was purchased. These activities were collectively called *software maintenance*. Effort spent on software maintenance began to absorb resources at an alarming rate.

Worse yet, the personalized nature of many programs made them virtually unmaintainable. A "software crisis" loomed on the horizon.

The third era of computer system evolution began in the mid-1970s and continues today. The distributed system—multiple computers, each performing functions concurrently and communicating with one another—greatly increased the complexity of computer-based systems. Global and local area networks, high-bandwidth digital communications, and increasing demands for 'instantaneous' data access put heavy demands on software developers.

The third era has also been characterized by the advent and widespread use of microprocessors, personal computers, and powerful desk-top workstations. The microprocessor has spawned a wide array of intelligent products—from automobiles to microwave ovens, from industrial robots to blood serum diagnostic equipment. In many cases, software technology is being integrated into products by technical staff who understand hardware but are often novices in software development.

The personal computer has been the catalyst for the growth of many software companies. While the software companies of the second era sold hundreds or thousands of copies of their programs, the software companies of the third era sell tens and even hundreds of thousands of copies. Personal computer hardware is rapidly becoming a commodity, while software provides the differentiating characteristic. In fact, as the rate of personal computer sales growth flattened during the mid-1980s, software product sales continued to grow. Many people in industry and at home spent more money on software than they did to purchase the computer on which the software would run.

The fourth era in computer software is just beginning. Object-oriented technologies (Chapters 8 and 12) are rapidly displacing more conventional software development approaches in many application areas. Authors such as Feigenbaum and McCorduck [FEI83] and Allman [ALL89] predict that "fifth-generation" computers, radically different computing architectures, and their related software will have a profound impact on the balance of political and industrial power throughout the world. Already, "fourth-generation" techniques for software development (discussed later in this chapter) are changing the manner in which some segments of the software community build computer programs. Expert systems and artificial intelligence software has finally moved from the laboratory into practical application for wide-ranging problems in the real world. Artificial neural network software has opened exciting possibilities for pattern recognition and human-like information processing abilities.

As we move into the fourth era, the problems associated with computer software continue to intensify:

1. Hardware sophistication has outpaced our ability to build software to tap hardware's potential.
2. Our ability to build new programs cannot keep pace with the demand for new programs.
3. Our ability to maintain existing programs is threatened by poor design and inadequate resources.

In response to these problems, software engineering practices—the topic to which this book is dedicated—are being adopted throughout the industry.

1.1.2 An Industry Perspective

In the early days of computing, computer-based systems were developed using hardware-oriented management. Project managers focused on hardware because it was the single largest budget item for system development. To control hardware costs, managers instituted formal controls and technical standards. They demanded thorough analysis and design before something was built. They measured the process to determine where improvements could be made. Stated simply, they applied the controls, methods, and tools that we recognize as hardware engineering. Sadly, software was often little more than an afterthought.

In the early days, programming was viewed as an "art form." Few formal methods existed and fewer people used them. The programmer often learned his or her craft by trial and error. The jargon and challenges of building computer software created a mystique that few managers cared to penetrate. The software world was virtually undisciplined—and many practitioners of the day loved it!

Today, the distribution of costs for the development of computer-based systems has changed dramatically. Software, rather than hardware, is often the largest single cost item. For the past decade managers and many technical practitioners have asked the following questions:

- Why does it take so long to get programs finished?
- Why are costs so high?
- Why can't we find all errors before we give the software to our customers?
- Why do we have difficulty in measuring progress as software is being developed?

These, and many other questions, are a manifestation of the concern about software and the manner in which it is developed—a concern that has led to the adoption of software engineering practices.

1.1.3 An Aging Software Plant[1]

In the 1950s and 1960s many commentators criticized the steel industry in the United States for lack of investment in its physical plant. Factories had begun to deteriorate, modern methods were rarely applied, the quality and cost of the end product suffered, and competition began to win substantial market share. Management in these industries decided against making the capital investment that was required to remain competitive in their core business. Over time, the steel industry suffered, losing significant market share to foreign competition—competition that had newer plants, used more modern technology, and was provided with government subsidies to make it extremely cost-competitive.

During that period, many of us in the fledgling computer industry looked at the steel industry with contempt. "If they're unwilling to invest in their own business," we said, "they deserve to lose market share." Those words may come back to haunt us.

At the risk of sounding melodramatic, the software industry today is in a position that is quite similar to the steel industry of the 1950s and 1960s. Across companies large and small, we have an aging "software plant"—there are thousands of critical software-based applications that are in dramatic need of refurbishing:

- Information system applications written 20 years ago that have undergone 40 generations of changes and are now virtually unmaintainable. Even the smallest modification can cause the entire system to fail.
- Engineering applications that are used to produce critical design data, and yet, because of their age and state of repair, are not really understood. No one has detailed knowledge of the internal structure of their programs.
- Embedded systems (used to control power plants, air traffic, and factories, among thousands of applications) that exhibit strange and sometimes unexplained behavior, but that cannot be taken out of service because there's nothing available to replace them.

It will not be enough to "patch" what is broken and give these applications a modern look. Many components of the software plant require significant re-engineering, or they will not be competitive during the 1990s and beyond. Unfortunately, many business managers are unwilling to commit the resources to undertake this re-engineering effort. "The applications still work," they say, "and it is 'uneconomic' to commit the resources to make them better."

Some might argue that the preceding metaphor is weak. "Where will the competition come from?" they ask.

---

[1]This section has been adapted from the book *Software Shock* by Pressman and Herron [PRE91].

The fact is that competition is forming right now. It will be intense, it will be competent, and it will be here sooner than many think. Countries in the Far East (Japan, Korea, Singapore), in Asia (India, China), and in Eastern Europe all offer a large pool of highly motivated, competently educated, and relatively low-cost professionals. This workforce will move rapidly to adopt state-of-the-art software engineering methods and tools and may very well become a force to be reckoned with during the late 1990s.

Some companies have already thrown in the towel and have begun "outsourcing."[2] A company cuts its information systems staff to the bone and contracts with a third party to handle all new software development, much of its on-going system maintenance, and all of its computer operations. To date, outsourcing is generally restricted to local service bureaus. But because this trend has one primary goal—to save money—it won't be long before outsourcing goes off-shore. Recall that, in the 1960s, companies such as RCA and Motorola attempted to cut television costs by outsourcing only a few electronic components to off-shore manufacturers. The core industry would remain in the United States, they said. Today, there are no major television manufacturers left in the United States.

In their book on the impact of information services on the United States and the world, Feigenbaum and McCorduck [FEI83, p. 1] state the following:

> Knowledge is power, and the computer is an amplifier of that power.... The American computer industry has been innovative, vital, successful. It is, in a way, the ideal industry. It creates value by transforming the brainpower of knowledge workers, with little consumption of energy and raw materials. Today [1983], we dominate the world's ideas and markets in this most important of all modern technologies. But what about tomorrow?

Indeed, what about tomorrow? Already, computer hardware is becoming a commodity, available from many sources. But software remains an industry where the United States has been "innovative, vital, successful." Will we maintain our place at the top?

Feigenbaum and McCorduck may be closer to the mark than many of us want to believe. There are economic, political, technological, and national security reasons why the United States cannot afford to lose its leadership in software development technologies. Yet, we do nothing about our aging software plant. There may come a time when it will be less costly to outsource software development and maintenance to third parties located halfway around the world. These third parties will be supported by their governments, will be extremely competent, and, therefore, very competitive. Software is not steel, but foreign competition may make them look very much alike.

---

[2]The pros and cons of outsourcing are discussed in "Outsourcing: The Great Debate," *Computerworld*, December 11, 1989, p. 69.

1.2 SOFTWARE

Twenty years ago, less than 1 percent of the public could have intelligently described what "computer software" meant. Today, most professionals and many members of the public at large feel that they understand software. But do they?

A textbook description of software might take the following form: "Software is: (1) instructions (computer programs) that when executed provide desired function and performance, (2) data structures that enable the programs to adequately manipulate information, and (3) documents that describe the operation and use of the programs." There is no question that other, more complete definitions could be offered. But we need more than a formal definition.

1.2.1 Software Characteristics

To gain an understanding of software (and ultimately an understanding of software engineering), it is important to examine the characteristics of software that make it different from other things that human beings build. When hardware is built, the human creative process (analysis, design, construction, testing) is ultimately translated into a physical form. If we build a new computer, our initial sketches, formal design drawings, and breadboarded prototype evolve into a physical product (VLSI chips, circuit boards, power supplies, etc.).

Software is a logical rather than a physical system element. Therefore, software has characteristics that are considerably different than those of hardware:

1. *Software is developed or engineered, it is not manufactured in the classical sense.*

Although some similarities exist between software development and hardware manufacture, the two activities are fundamentally different. In both activities, high quality is achieved through good design, but the manufacturing phase for hardware can introduce quality problems that are nonexistent (or easily corrected) for software. Both activities are dependent on people, but the relationship between people applied and work accomplished is entirely different (see Chapter 3). Both activities require the construction of a "product," but the approaches are different.

Software costs are concentrated in engineering. This means that software projects cannot be managed as if they were manufacturing projects.

Over the past decade, the concept of the "software factory" had been discussed in the literature (e.g., [MAN84], [TAJ84]). It is important to note that this term does not imply that hardware manufacturing and software development are equivalent. Rather, the software factory concept recommends the use of automated tools (see Part 5) for software development.

2. *Software doesn't "wear out."*

Figure 1.2 depicts failure rate as a function of time for hardware. The relationship, often called the "bathtub curve," indicates that hardware exhibits relatively high failure rates early in its life (these failures are often attributable to design or manufacturing defects); defects are corrected and the failure rate drops to a steady-state level (hopefully, quite low) for some period of time. As time passes, however, the failure rate rises again as hardware components suffer from the cumulative effects of dust, vibration, abuse, temperature extremes and many other environmental maladies. Stated simply, the hardware begins to wear out.

Software is not susceptible to the environmental maladies that cause hardware to wear out. In theory, therefore, the failure rate curve for software should take the form shown in Figure 1.3. Undiscovered defects will cause high failure rates early in the life of a program. However, these are corrected (hopefully without introducing other errors) and the curve flattens as shown. Figure 1.3 is a gross oversimplification of actual failure models (see Chapter 17 for more information) for software. However, the implication is clear—software doesn't wear out. But it does deteriorate!

This seeming contradiction can best be explained by considering Figure 1.4. During its life, software will undergo change (maintenance). As changes are made, it is likely that some new defects will be introduced, causing the failure rate curve to spike as shown in Figure 1.4. Before the curve can return to the original steady-state failure rate, another change is requested, causing the curve to spike again. Slowly, the minimum failure rate level begins to rise—the software is deteriorating due to change.

Another aspect of wear illustrates the difference between hardware and software. When a hardware component wears out, it is replaced by a "spare part." There are no software spare parts. Every software failure indicates

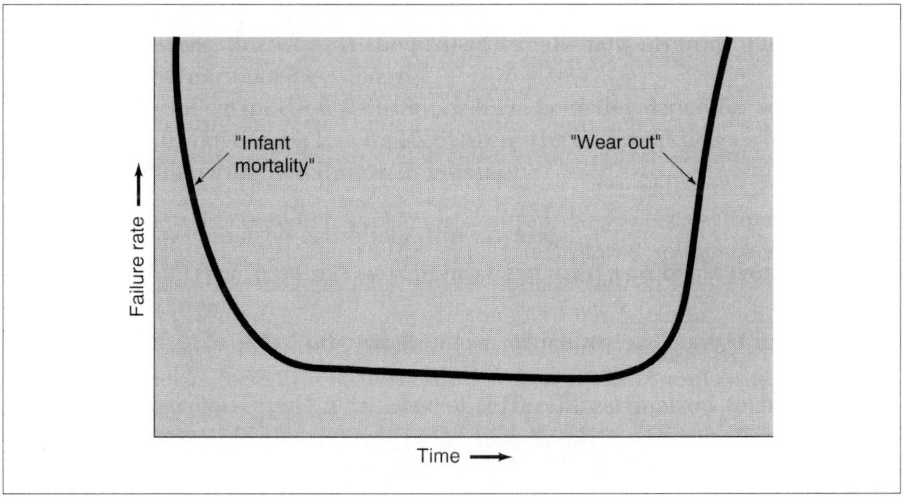

FIGURE 1.2. Failure curve for hardware.

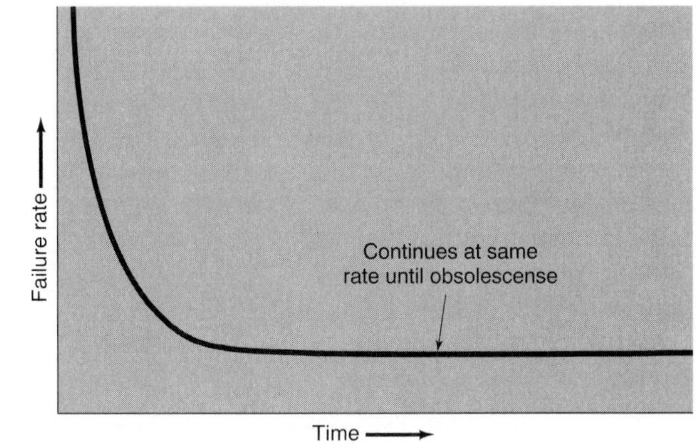

FIGURE 1.3.
Failure curve for software (idealized).

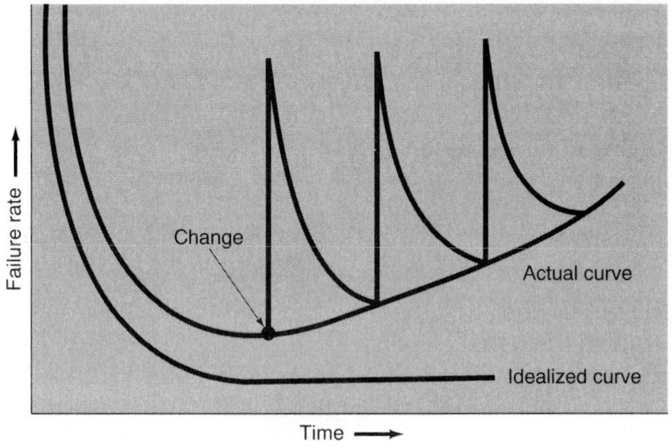

FIGURE 1.4.
Actual failure curve for software.

an error in design or in the process through which design was translated into machine-executable code. Therefore, software maintenance involves considerably more complexity than hardware maintenance.

3. *Most software is custom-built, rather than being assembled from existing components.*

Consider the manner in which the control hardware for a microprocessor-based product is designed and built. The design engineer draws a simple schematic of the digital circuitry, does some fundamental analysis to assure that the proper function will be achieved, and then goes to the shelf where catalogs of digital components exist. Each integrated circuit (often called an

"IC" or a "chip") has a part number, a defined and validated function, a well-defined interface, and a standard set of integration guidelines. After each component is selected, it can be ordered off-the-shelf.

Sadly, software designers are not afforded the luxury described above. With few exceptions, there are no catalogs of software components. It is possible to order off-the-shelf software, but only as a complete unit, not as components that can be re-assembled into new programs.[3] Although much has been written about "software reusability" (e.g., [TRA88]), we are only beginning to see the first successful implementations of the concept.

1.2.2 Software Components

Computer software is information that exists in two basic forms: non-machine-executable components and machine-executable components. For the purposes of our discussion in this chapter, only those software components that directly lead to machine-executable instructions are presented. All software components comprise a *configuration* that is discussed in later chapters.

Software components are created through a series of translations that map customer requirements to machine-executable code. A requirements model (or prototype) is translated into a design. The software design is translated into a language form that specifies software data structure, procedural attributes, and related requirements. The language form is processed by a translator that converts it into machine-executable instructions.

Reusability is an important characteristic of a high-quality software component [BIG84]. That is, the component should be designed and implemented so that it can be reused in many different programs. In the 1960s, we built scientific subroutine libraries that were reusable in a broad array of engineering and scientific applications. These subroutine libraries reused well-defined algorithms in an effective manner, but had a limited domain of application. Today, we have extended our view of reuse to encompass not only algorithms, but also data structures. A reusable component of the 1990s encapsulates both data and processing in a single package (often called a *class* or *object*), enabling the software engineer to create new applications from reusable parts.[4] For example, today's interactive interfaces are often built using reusable components that enable the creation of graphics windows, pull-down menus, and a wide variety of interaction mechanisms. The

---

[3] This situation is changing rapidly. The widespread use of object-oriented programming has resulted in the creation of "software IC's." These are discussed in Chapter 12.

[4] In later chapters we examine the use of object-oriented technologies and their impact on component reuse.

data structures and processing detail required to build the interface are contained within a library of reusable components for interface construction.

Software components are built using a programming language that has a limited vocabulary, an explicitly defined grammar, and well-formed rules of syntax and semantics. These attributes are essential for machine translation. The language forms in use today are machine-level languages, high-order languages, and nonprocedural languages.

Machine-level language is a symbolic representation of the central processing unit (CPU) instruction set. When a good software developer produces a maintainable, well-documented program, machine-level language can make extremely efficient use of memory and "optimize" program execution speed. When a program is poorly designed and has little documentation, machine language is a nightmare.

High-order languages allow the software developer and the program to be machine-independent. When a more sophisticated translator is used, the vocabulary, grammar, syntax, and semantics of a high-order language can be much more sophisticated than machine-level languages. In fact, high-order language compilers and interpreters produce machine-level language as output.

Although hundreds of programming languages are in use today, fewer than 10 high-order programming languages are widely used in the industry. Languages such as COBOL and FORTRAN remain in widespread use nearly 30 years after their introduction. Modern programming languages (languages that directly support modern design practices for procedural and data design) such as Pascal, C, and Ada are being used widely. Object-oriented languages such as C++, Object Pascal, Eiffel and others are gaining an enthusiastic following.

Specialized languages (designed for specific application domains), such as APL, LISP, OPS5, Prolog, and descriptive languages for artificial neural networks are gaining wider acceptance as new application approaches move from the laboratory to practical use.

Machine code, assembly (machine-level) languages, and high-order programming languages are often referred to as the "first three generations" of computer languages. With any of these languages, the programmer must be concerned both with the specification of the information structure and the control of the program itself. Hence, languages in the first three generations are termed *procedural languages*.

Over the past decade, a group of fourth-generation or *non-procedural* languages have been introduced. Rather than requiring the software developer to specify procedural detail, the nonprocedural language implies a program by "specifying the desired result, rather than specifying action required to achieve that result" [COB85]. Support software translates the specification of result into a machine-executable program. To date, fourth-generation languages have been used in database applications and other business data processing areas. Further discussion of their application within the context of software engineering is presented later in this chapter.

1.2.3 Software Applications

Software may be applied in any situation for which a prespecified set of procedural steps (i.e., an algorithm) has been defined (notable exceptions to this rule are expert system software and neural network software). Information content and determinacy are important factors in determining the nature of a software application. *Content* refers to the meaning and form of incoming and outgoing information. For example, many business applications make use of highly structured input data (a database) and produce formatted "reports." Software that controls an automated machine (e.g., a numerical controlled lathe) accepts discrete data items with limited structure and produces individual machine commands in rapid succession.

Information determinacy refers to the predictability of the order and timing of information. An engineering analysis program accepts data that has a predefined order, executes the analysis algorithm(s) without interruption, and produces resultant data in report or graphical format. Such applications are determinate. A multiuser operating system, on the other hand, accepts inputs that have varied content and arbitrary timing, executes algorithms that can be interrupted by external conditions, and produces output that varies as a function of environment and time. Applications with these characteristics are indeterminate.

It is somewhat difficult to develop meaningful generic categories for software applications. As software complexity grows, neat compartmentalization disappears. The following software areas indicate the breadth of potential applications:

System Software System software is a collection of programs written to service other programs. Some system software (e.g., compilers, editors, and file management utilities) process complex, but determinate, information structures. Other system applications (e.g., operating system components, drivers, telecommunications processors) process largely indeterminate data. In either case, the system software area is characterized by heavy interaction with computer hardware; heavy usage by multiple users; concurrent operation that requires scheduling, resource sharing, and sophisticated process management; complex data structures; and multiple external interfaces.

Real-Time Software Software that monitors/analyzes/controls real-world events as they occur is called *real-time*. Elements of real-time software include a data gathering component that collects and formats information from an external environment, an analysis component that transforms information as required by the application, a control/output component that responds to the external environment, and a monitoring component that coordinates all other components so that real-time response (typically ranging from 1 millisecond to 1 minute) can be maintained. It should be noted that the term "real-time" differs from "interactive" or "time-sharing." A real-time system must respond within strict time constraints. The response time of an interactive (or time-sharing) system can normally be exceeded without disastrous results.

Business Software Business information processing is the largest single software application area. Discrete "systems" (e.g., payroll, accounts receivable/payable, inventory, etc.) have evolved into management information system (MIS) software that accesses one or more large databases containing business information. Applications in this area restructure existing data in a way that facilitates business operations or management decision-making. In addition to conventional data processing application, business software applications also encompass interactive computing (e.g., point-of-sale transaction processing).

Engineering and Scientific Software Engineering and scientific software has been characterized by "number crunching" algorithms. Applications range from astronomy to volcanology, from automotive stress analysis to space shuttle orbital dynamics, and from molecular biology to automated manufacturing. However, new applications within the engineering/scientific area are moving away from conventional numerical algorithms. Computer-aided design (CAD), system simulation, and other interactive applications have begun to take on real-time and even system software characteristics.

Embedded Software Intelligent products have become commonplace in nearly every consumer and industrial market. Embedded software resides in read-only memory and is used to control products and systems for the consumer and industrial markets. Embedded software can perform very limited and esoteric functions (e.g., keypad control for a microwave oven) or provide significant function and control capabilities (e.g., digital functions in an automobile such as fuel control, dashboard displays, braking systems, etc.).

Personal Computer Software The personal computer software market has burgeoned over the past decade. Word processing, spreadsheets, computer graphics, entertainment, database management, personal and business financial applications, external network, or database access are only a few of hundreds of applications. In fact, personal computer software continues to represent some of the most innovative human-interface designs of all software.

Artificial Intelligence Software Artificial intelligence (AI) software makes use of nonnumerical algorithms to solve complex problems that are not amenable to computation or straightforward analysis. Currently, the most active AI area is *expert systems,* also called *knowledge-based systems* [WAT85]. However, other application areas for AI software are pattern recognition (image and voice), theorem proving, and game playing. In recent years, a new branch of AI software, called *artificial neural networks* [WAS89], has evolved. A neural network simulates the structure of brain processes (the functions of the biological neuron) and may ultimately lead to a new class of software that can recognize complex patterns and learn from past "experience."

1.3 SOFTWARE: A CRISIS ON THE HORIZON

Many industry observers (including this author in earlier editions of this book) have characterized the problems associated with software development as a "crisis." Yet, what we really have may be something rather different.

The word "crisis" is defined in *Webster's Dictionary* as "a turning point in the course of anything; decisive or crucial time, stage or event." Yet, for software there has been no "turning point," no "decisive time," only slow, evolutionary change. In the software industry, we have had a "crisis" that has been with us for close to 30 years, and that is a contradiction in terms.

Anyone who looks up the word "crisis" in the dictionary will find another definition: "the turning point in the course of a disease, when it becomes clear whether the patient will live or die." This definition may give us a clue about the real nature of the problems that have plagued software development.

We have yet to reach the stage of crisis in computer software. What we really have is a *chronic affliction.*[5] The word "affliction" is defined in Webster's as "anything causing pain or distress." But it is the definition of the adjective "chronic" that is the key to our argument: "lasting a long time or recurring often; continuing indefinitely." It is far more accurate to describe what we have endured for the past three decades as a chronic affliction rather than a crisis. There are no miracle cures, but there are many ways that we can reduce the pain as we strive to discover a cure.

Whether we call it a software crisis or a software affliction, the term alludes to a set of problems that are encountered in the development of computer software. The problems are not limited to software that "doesn't function properly." Rather, the affliction encompasses problems associated with how we develop software, how we maintain a growing volume of existing software, and how we can expect to keep pace with a growing demand for more software. Although reference to a crisis or even an affliction can be criticized for being melodramatic, the phrases do serve a useful purpose by encompassing real problems that are encountered in all areas of software development.

---

[5]This terminology was suggested by Professor Daniel Tiechrow of the University of Michigan in a talk presented in Geneva, Switzerland, April 1989.

1.3.1 Problems

The problems that afflict software development can be characterized from a number of different perspectives, but managers responsible for software development concentrate on the "bottom line" issues: (1) Schedule and cost estimates are often grossly inaccurate, (2) the "productivity" of software people hasn't kept pace with the demand for their services, and (3) the quality of software is sometimes less than adequate. Cost overruns of an order of magnitude have been experienced. Schedules slip by months or years. Little has been done to improve the productivity of software practitioners. Error rates for new programs cause customer dissatisfaction and lack of confidence. These problems are the most visible manifestation of other software difficulties:

- We haven't taken the time to collect data on the software development process. With little historical data as a guide, estimation has been by "seat of the pants" with predictably poor results. With no solid indication of productivity, we can't accurately evaluate the efficacy of new tools, methods, or standards.
- Customer dissatisfaction with the "completed" system is encountered too frequently. Software development projects are frequently undertaken with only a vague indication of customer requirements. Communication between customer and software developer is often poor.
- Software quality is often suspect. We have only recently begun to understand the importance of systematic, technically complete software testing. Solid quantitative concepts of software reliability and quality assurance are only beginning to emerge [IAN84, EVA87].
- Existing software can be very difficult to maintain. The software maintenance task devours the majority of all software dollars. Software maintainability has not been emphasized as an important criteria for software acceptance.

We have presented the bad news first. Now for the good news. Each of the problems described above can be corrected. An engineering approach to the development of software, coupled with continuing improvement of techniques and tools, provides the key.

One problem (we could call it a fact of life) will remain. Software will absorb a larger and larger percentage of the overall development cost for computer-based systems. In the United States, we spend close to $200 billion each year on the development, purchase, and maintenance of computer software. We had better take the problems associated with software technology seriously.

1.3.2 Causes

Problems associated with the software crisis have been caused by the character of software itself and by the failings of the people charged with software development responsibility. It is possible, however, that we have expected too much in too short a period of time. After all, our experience spans little more than 40 years.

The character of computer software was discussed briefly in the preceding section. To review, software is a logical rather than a physical system element; therefore, success is measured by the quality of a single entity rather than by the quality of many manufactured entities. Software does not wear out. If faults are encountered, there is a high probability that each was inadvertently introduced during development and went undetected during testing. We replace "defective parts" during software maintenance, but we have few, if any, spare parts, i.e., maintenance often includes correction or modification to design.

The logical nature of software provides a challenge to the people who develop it. For the first time we have accepted the task of communicating with an alien intelligence—a machine. The intellectual challenge of software development is certainly one cause of the affliction that affects software, but the problems discussed above have been caused by more mundane human failings.

Middle- and upper-level managers with no background in software are often given responsibility for software development. There is an old management axiom that states: "A good manager can manage any project." We should add: "...if he or she is willing to learn the milestones that can be used to measure progress, apply effective methods of control, disregard mythology, and become conversant in a rapidly changing technology." The manager must communicate with all constituencies involved with software development—customers, software developers, support staff, and others. Communication can break down because the special characteristics of software and the problems associated with its development are misunderstood. When this occurs, the problems associated with the software crisis are exacerbated.

Software practitioners (the past generation has been called *programmers;* this generation is earning the title *software engineer*) have had little formal training in new techniques for software development. In some organizations a mild form of anarchy still reigns. Each individual approaches the task of "writing programs" with experience derived from past efforts. Some people develop an orderly and efficient approach to software development by trial and error, but many others develop bad habits that result in poor software quality and maintainability.

We all resist change. It is truly ironic, however, that while computing potential (hardware) experiences enormous change, the software people responsible for tapping that potential often oppose change when it is discussed and resist change when it is introduced. Maybe that's the real cause for some of our problems with software.

1.4 SOFTWARE MYTHS

Many of our problems with software can be traced to a mythology that arose during the early history of software development. Unlike ancient myths that often provide human lessons that are well worth heeding, software myths propagated misinformation and confusion. Software myths had a number of attributes that made them insidious; for instance, they appeared to be reasonable statements of fact (sometimes containing elements of truth), they had an intuitive feel and were often promulgated by experienced practitioners who "knew the score."

Today, most knowledgeable professionals recognize myths for what they are—misleading attitudes that have caused serious problems for managers and technical people alike. However, old attitudes and habits are difficult to modify, and remnants of software myths are still believed as we move toward the fifth decade of software.

Management Myths Managers with software responsibility, like managers in most disciplines, are often under pressure to maintain budgets, keep schedules from slipping, and improve quality. Like a drowning person who grasps at a straw, a software manager often grasps at belief in a software myth, if that belief will lessen the pressure (even temporarily).

Myth: We already have a book that's full of standards and procedures for building software. Won't that provide my people with everything they need to know?

Reality: The book of standards may very well exist, but is it used? Are software practitioners aware of its existence? Does it reflect modern software development practice? Is it complete? In many cases, the answer to all of these questions is "no."

Myth: My people do have state-of-the-art software development tools; after all, we buy them the newest computers.

Reality: It takes much more than the latest model mainframe, workstation, or PC to do high-quality software development. Computer-aided software engineering (CASE) tools are more important than hardware for achieving good quality and productivity, yet the majority of software developers still do not use them.

Myth: If we get behind schedule, we can add more programmers and catch up (sometimes called the "Mongolian horde concept").

Reality: Software development is not a mechanistic process like manufacturing. In the words of Brooks [BRO75]: "... adding people to a late software project makes it later." At first, this statement may seem counterintuitive. However, as new people are added, people who were working must spend time educating the newcomers, thereby reducing the amount of time spent on productive development effort. People can be added, but only in a planned and well-coordinated manner.

Customer Myths A customer who requests computer software may be a person at the next desk, a technical group down the hall, the marketing/sales department, or an outside company that has requested software under contract. In many cases, the customer believes myths about software because software responsible managers and practitioners do little to correct misinformation. Myths lead to false expectations (by the customer) and, ultimately, to dissatisfaction with the developer.

Myth: A general statement of objectives is sufficient to begin writing programs—we can fill in the details later.

Reality: Poor up-front definition is the major cause of failed software efforts. A formal and detailed description of information domain, function, performance, interfaces, design constraints, and validation criteria is essential. These characteristics can be determined only after thorough communication between customer and developer.

Myth: Project requirements continually change, but change can be easily accommodated because software is flexible.

Reality: It is true that software requirements do change, but the impact of change varies with the time at which it is introduced. Figure 1.5 illustrates the impact of change. If serious attention is given to up-front definition, early requests for change can be accommodated easily. The customer can review requirements and recommend modifications with

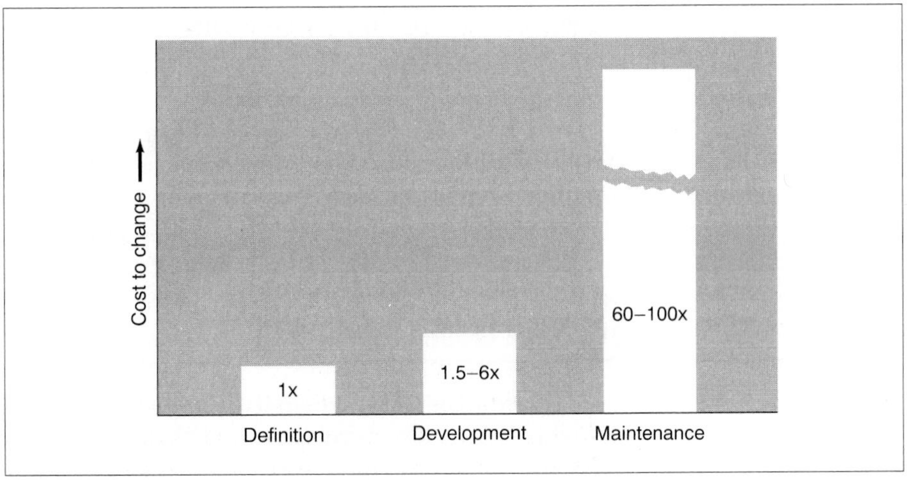

FIGURE 1.5. The impact of change.

relatively little impact on cost. When changes are requested during software design, cost impact grows rapidly. Resources have been committed and a design framework has been established. Change can cause upheaval that requires additional resources and major design modification, i.e., additional cost. Changes in function, performance, interfaces, or other characteristics during implementation (code and test) have a severe impact on cost. Change, when requested late in a project, can be more than an order-of-magnitude more expensive than the same change requested early.

Practitioner's Myths Myths that are still believed by software practitioners have been fostered by four decades of programming culture. As we noted earlier in this chapter, during the early days of software, programming was viewed as an art form. Old ways and attitudes die hard.

Myth: Once we write the program and get it to work, our job is done.

Reality: Someone once said that "the sooner you begin 'writing code,' the longer it'll take you to get done." Industry data [LIE80] indicate that between 50 and 70 percent of all effort expended on a program will be expended after it is delivered to the customer for the first time.

Myth: Until I get the program "running" I really have no way of assessing its quality.

Reality: One of the most effective software quality assurance mechanisms can be applied from the inception of a project—the *formal technical review.* Software reviews (described in Chapter 17) are a "quality filter" that have been found to be more effective than testing for finding certain classes of software defects.

Myth: The only deliverable for a successful project is the working program.

Reality: A working program is only one part of a *software configuration* that includes all the elements illustrated in Figure 1.6. Documentation forms the foundation for successful development and, more importantly, provides guidance for the software maintenance task.

Many software professionals recognize the fallacy of the myths described above. Regrettably, habitual attitudes and methods foster poor management and technical practices even when reality dictates a better approach. Recognition of software realities is the first step toward formulation of practical solutions for software development.

1.5 SOFTWARE ENGINEERING PARADIGMS

The affliction that has infected software development will not disappear overnight. Recognizing problems and their causes and debunking software myths are the first steps toward solutions. But solutions themselves must provide practical assistance to the software developer, improve software

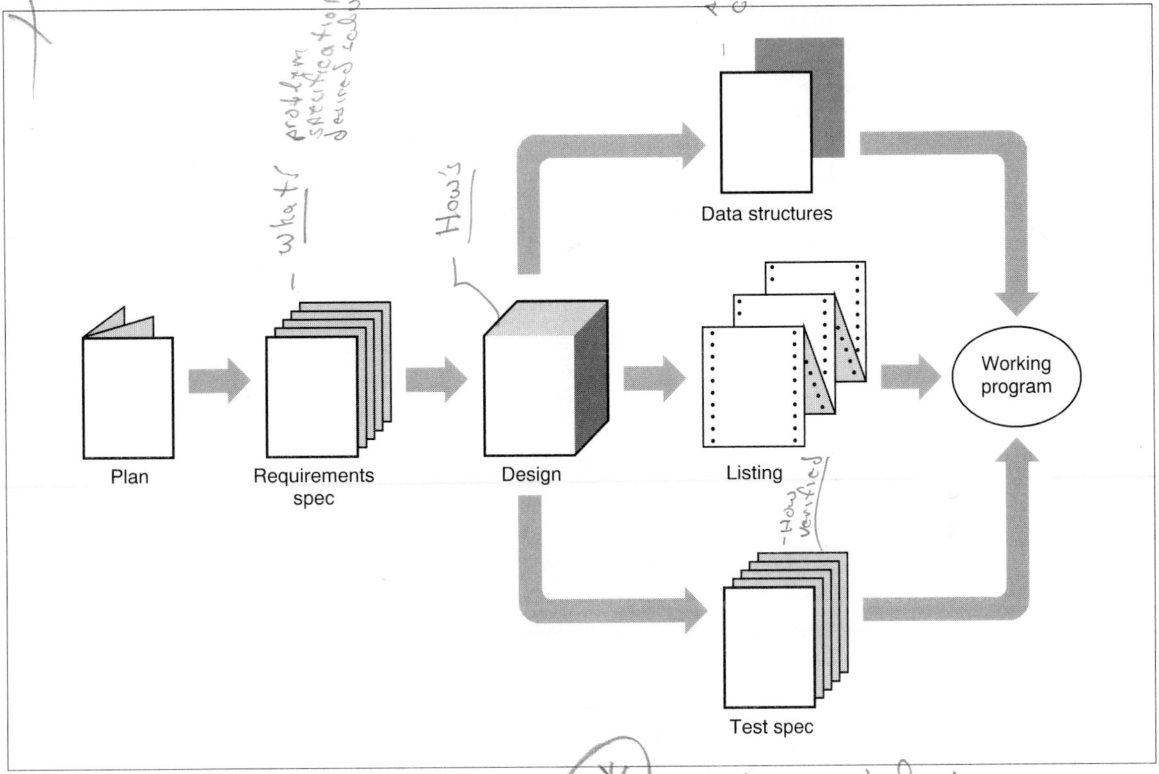

FIGURE 1.6. The software configuration.

quality, and, finally, allow the software world to keep pace with the hardware world.

There is no single best approach to a solution for the software affliction. However, by combining comprehensive methods for all phases in software development, better tools for automating these methods, more powerful building blocks for software implementation, better techniques for software quality assurance, and an overriding philosophy for coordination, control, and management, we can achieve a discipline for software development—a discipline called *software engineering.*

1.5.1 Software Engineering: A Definition

An early definition of software engineering was proposed by Fritz Bauer at the first major conference [NAU69] dedicated to the subject:

> The establishment and use of sound engineering principles in order to obtain economically software that is reliable and works efficiently on real machines.

Although many more comprehensive definitions have been proposed, all reinforce the requirement for engineering discipline in software development.

Software engineering is an outgrowth of hardware and system engineering. It encompasses a set of three key elements—methods, tools, and procedures—that enable the manager to control the process of software development and provide the practitioner with a foundation for building high-quality software in a productive manner. In the paragraphs that follow, we briefly examine each of these elements.

Software engineering *methods* provide the technical "how to's" for building software. Methods encompass a broad array of tasks that include: project planning and estimation, system and software requirements analysis, design of data structure, program architecture and algorithm procedure, coding, testing, and maintenance. Methods for software engineering often introduce a special language-oriented or graphical notation and introduce a set of criteria for software quality.

Software engineering *tools* provide automated or semiautomated support for methods. Today, tools exist to support each of the methods noted above. When tools are integrated so that information created by one tool can be used by another, a system for the support of software development, called *computer-aided software engineering* (CASE), is established. CASE combines software, hardware, and a software engineering database (a data structure containing important information about analysis, design, code, and testing) to create a software engineering environment (e.g., [BRE88]) that is analogous to computer-aided design/computer-aided engineering (CAD/CAE) for hardware.

Software engineering *procedures* are the glue that holds the methods and tools together and they enable rational and timely development of computer software. Procedures define the sequence in which methods will be applied, the deliverables (documents, reports, forms, etc.) that are required, the controls that help ensure quality and coordinate change, and the milestones that enable software managers to assess progress.

Software engineering is comprised of a set of steps that encompass methods, tools, and procedures discussed above. These steps are often referred to as *software engineering paradigms*. A paradigm for software engineering is chosen based on the nature of the project and application, the methods and tools to be used, and the controls and deliverables that are required. Four paradigms have been widely discussed (and debated) and are described in the following sections.

1.5.2 The Classic Life Cycle

Figure 1.7 illustrates the classic life-cycle paradigm for software engineering. Sometimes called the "waterfall model," the life-cycle paradigm demands a systematic, sequential approach to software development that begins at the system level and progresses through analysis, design, coding,

model is honored in a failure to follow
But you must do them all

successon

Sets context

Requirements (what to produce)

How solve it

implmintation

meets requirements

modification

to device to study to develope

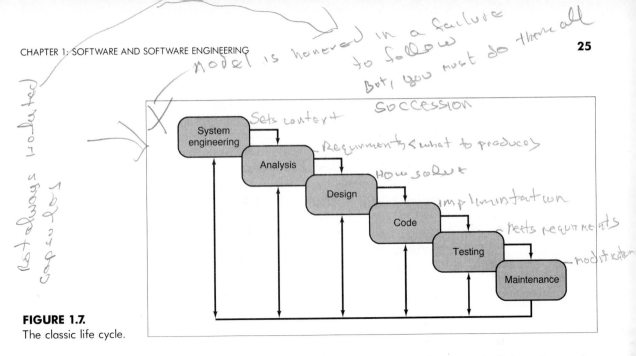

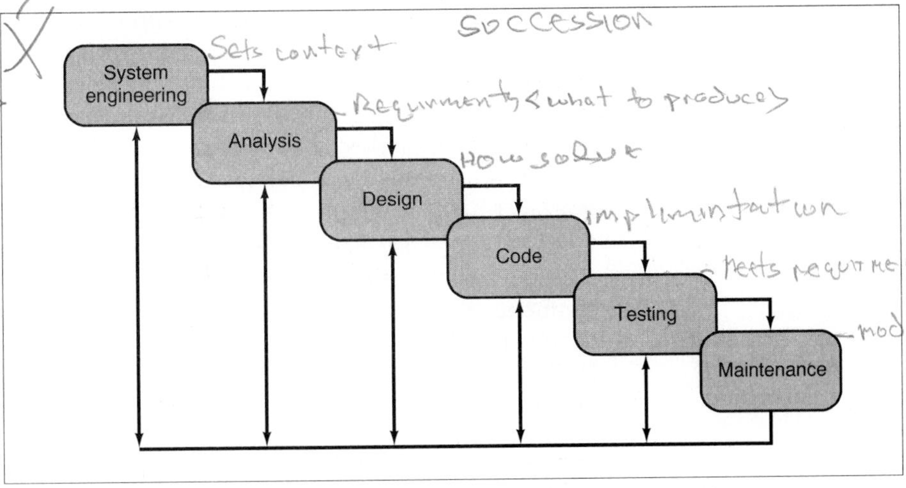

FIGURE 1.7.
The classic life cycle.

testing, and maintenance. Modeled after the conventional engineering cycle, the life-cycle paradigm encompasses the following activities:

System engineering and analysis. Because software is always part of a larger system, work begins by establishing requirements for all system elements and then allocating some subset of these requirements to software. This system view is essential when software must interface with other elements such as hardware, people, and databases. System engineering and analysis encompasses requirements gathering at the system level with a small amount of top-level design and analysis.

Software requirements analysis. The requirements gathering process is intensified and focused specifically on software. To understand the nature of the program(s) to be built, the software engineer ("analyst") must understand the information domain (described in Chapter 6) for the software, as well as the required function, performance, and interfacing. Requirements for both the system and the software are documented and reviewed with the customer.

Design. Software design is actually a multistep process that focuses on four distinct attributes of the program: data structure, software architecture, procedural detail, and interface characterization. The design process translates requirements into a representation of the software that can be assessed for quality before coding begins. Like requirements, the design is documented and becomes part of the software configuration.

Coding. The design must be translated into a machine-readable form. The coding step performs this task. If design is performed in a detailed manner, coding can be accomplished mechanistically.

Testing. Once code has been generated, program testing begins. The testing process focuses on the logical internals of the software, ensuring that all statements have been tested, and on the functional externals, that is, conducting tests to uncover errors and ensure that defined input will produce actual results that agree with required results.

Maintenance. Software will undoubtedly undergo change after it is delivered to the customer (a possible exception is embedded software). Change will occur because errors have been encountered, because the software must be adapted to accommodate changes in its external environment (e.g., a change required because of a new operating system or peripheral device), or because the customer requires functional or performance enhancements. Software maintenance reapplies each of the preceding life-cycle steps to an existing program rather than a new one.

The classic life cycle is the oldest and the most widely used paradigm for software engineering. However, over the past decade, criticism of the paradigm has caused even active supporters to question its applicability in all situations. Among the problems that are sometimes encountered when the classic life-cycle paradigm is applied are:

1. Real projects rarely follow the sequential flow that the model proposes. Iteration always occurs and creates problems in the application of the paradigm.
2. It is often difficult for the customer to state all requirements explicitly. The classic life cycle requires this and has difficulty accommodating the natural uncertainty that exists at the beginning of many projects.
3. The customer must have patience. A working version of the program(s) will not be available until late in the project timespan. A major blunder, if undetected until the working program is reviewed, can be disastrous.

Each of these problems is real. However, the classic life-cycle paradigm has a definite and important place in software engineering work. It provides a template into which methods for analysis, design, coding, testing, and maintenance can be placed. In addition, we shall see that the steps of the classic life-cycle paradigm are very similar to the generic steps (Section 1.6) that are applicable to all software engineering paradigms. The classic life cycle remains the most widely used procedural model for software engineering. While it does have weaknesses, it is significantly better than a haphazard approach to software development.

1.5.3 Prototyping

Often, a customer has defined a set of general objectives for software, but has not identified detailed input, processing, or output requirements. In other cases, the developer may be unsure of the efficiency of an algorithm, the adaptability of an operating system, or the form that human-machine interaction should take. In these, and many other situations, a prototyping approach to software engineering may offer the best approach.

Prototyping is a process that enables the developer to create a model of the software that must be built. The model can take one of three forms: (1) a paper prototype or PC-based model that depicts human-machine interaction in a form that enables the user to understand how such interaction will occur, (2) a working prototype that implements some subset of the function required of the desired software, or (3) an existing program that performs part or all of the function desired but has other features that will be improved upon in the new development effort.

The sequence of events for the prototyping paradigm is illustrated in Figure 1.8. Like all approaches to software development, prototyping begins with requirements gathering. Developer and customer meet and define the overall objectives for the software, identify whatever requirements are known, and outline areas where further definition is mandatory. A "quick design" then occurs. The quick design focuses on a representation of those aspects of the software that will be visible to the user (e.g., input approaches and output formats). The quick design leads to the construction of a prototype. The prototype is evaluated by the customer/user and is used to refine requirements for the software to be developed. A process of iteration occurs

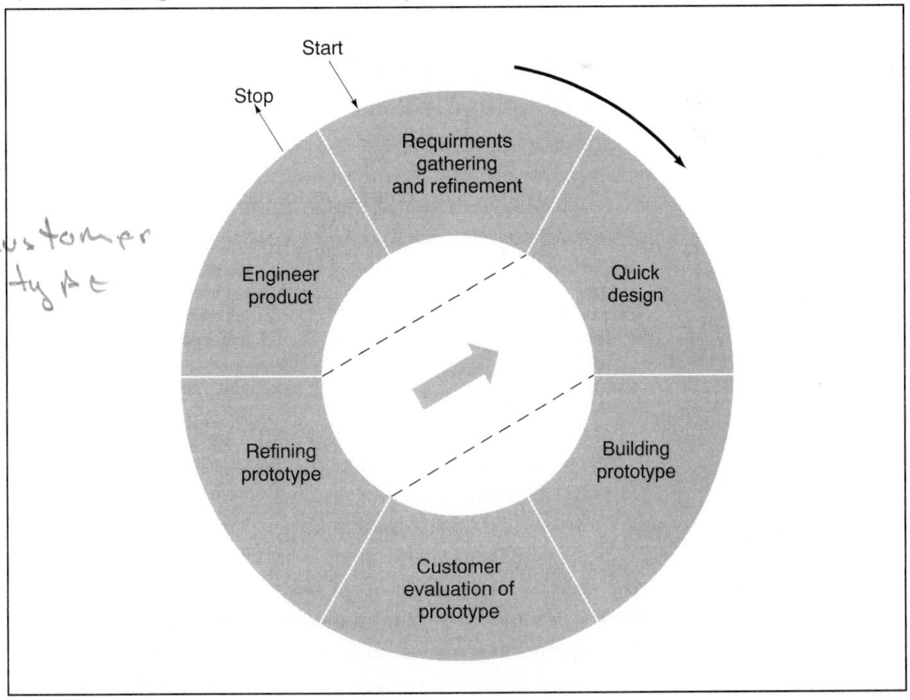

FIGURE 1.8.
Prototyping.

as the prototype is "tuned" to satisfy the needs of the customer while at the same time enabling the developer to better understand what needs to be done.

Ideally, the prototype serves as a mechanism for identifying software requirements. If a working prototype is built, the developer attempts to make use of existing program fragments or applies tools (e.g., report generators, window managers, etc.) that enable working programs to be generated quickly.

But what do we do with the prototype when it has served the purpose described above? Brooks [BRO75, p. 116] provides an answer:

> In most projects, the first system built is barely usable. It may be too slow, too big, awkward in use or all three. There is no alternative but to start again, smarting but smarter, and build a redesigned version in which these problems are solved.... When a new system concept or new technology is used, one has to build a system to throw away, for even the best planning is not so omniscient as to get it right the first time. The management question, therefore, is not whether to build a pilot system and throw it away. You will do that. The only question is whether to plan in advance to build a throwaway, or to promise to deliver the throwaway to customers....

The prototype can serve as "the first system"—the one that Brooks recommends we throw away. But this may be an idealized view. Like the classic life cycle, prototyping as a paradigm for software engineering can be problematic for the following reasons:

1. The customer sees what appears to be a working version of the software, unaware that the prototype is held together "with chewing gum and baling wire," unaware that in the rush to get it working we haven't considered overall software quality or long-term maintainability. When informed that the product must be rebuilt, the customer cries foul and demands that "a few fixes" be applied to make the prototype a working product. Too often, software development management relents.
2. The developer often makes implementation compromises in order to get a prototype working quickly. An inappropriate operating system or programming language may be used simply because it is available and known; an inefficient algorithm may be implemented simply to demonstrate capability. After a time, the developer may become familiar with these choices and forget all the reasons why they were inappropriate. The less-than-ideal choice has now become an integral part of the system.

Although problems can occur, prototyping is an effective paradigm for software engineering. The key is to define the rules of the game at the beginning; that is, the customer and developer must both agree that the prototype is built to serve as a mechanism for defining requirements. It is then discarded (at least in part) and the actual software is engineered with an eye toward quality and maintainability.

1.5.4 The Spiral Model

The spiral model for software engineering [BOE88] has been developed to encompass the best features of both the classic life cycle and prototyping, while at the same time adding a new element—risk analysis—that is missing in these paradigms. The model, represented by the spiral in Figure 1.9, defines four major activities represented by the four quadrants of the figure:

1. *Planning*—determination of objectives, alternatives and constraints
2. *Risk analysis*—analysis of alternatives and identification/resolution of risks
3. *Engineering*—development of the "next-level" product
4. *Customer evaluation*—assessment of the results of engineering

An intriguing aspect of the spiral model becomes apparent when we consider the radial dimension depicted in Figure 1.9. With each iteration around the spiral (beginning at the center and working outward), progressively more complete versions of the software are built. During the first circuit around the spiral, objectives, alternatives, and constraints are defined

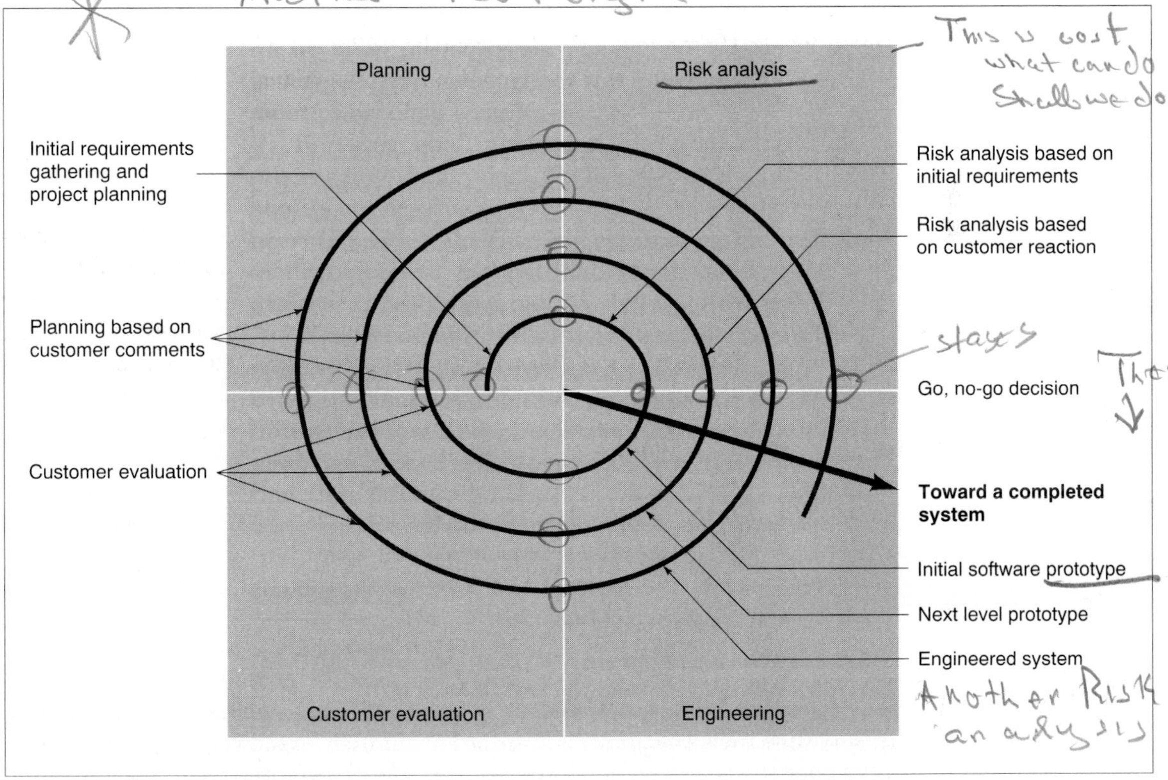

FIGURE 1.9. The spiral model.

and risks are identified and analyzed. If risk analysis (see Chapter 4 for details) indicates that there is uncertainty in requirements, prototyping may be used in the engineering quadrant to assist both the developer and the customer. Simulations and other models may be used to further define the problem and refine requirements.

The customer evaluates the engineering work (the customer evaluation quadrant) and makes suggestions for modifications. Based on customer input, the next phase of planning and risk analysis occur. At each loop around the spiral, the culmination of risk analysis results in a "go, no-go" decision. If risks are too great, the project can be terminated.

In most cases, however, flow around a spiral path continues, with each path moving the developers outward toward a more complete model of the system, and, ultimately, to the operational system itself. Every circuit around the spiral requires engineering (lower right quadrant) that can be accomplished using either the classic life-cycle or prototyping approaches. It should be noted that the number of development activities occurring in the lower right quadrant increases as activities move further from the center of the spiral.

The spiral model paradigm for software engineering is currently the most realistic approach to the development for large scale systems and software. It uses an "evolutionary" approach [GIL88] to software engineering, enabling the developer and customer to understand and react to risks at each evolutionary level. It uses prototyping as a risk reduction mechanism, but, more importantly, enables the developer to apply the prototyping approach at any stage in the evolution of the product. It maintains the systematic stepwise approach suggested by the classic life cycle, but incorporates it into an iterative framework that more realistically reflects the real world. The spiral model demands a direct consideration of technical risks at all stages of the project, and if properly applied, should reduce risks before they become problematic.

But like other paradigms, the spiral model is not a panacea. It may be difficult to convince large customers (particularly in contract situations) that the evolutionary approach is controllable. It demands considerable risk assessment expertise, and relies on this expertise for success. If a major risk is not discovered, problems will undoubtedly occur. Finally, the model itself is relatively new and has not been used as widely as the life cycle or prototyping. It will take a number of years before efficacy of this important new paradigm can be determined with absolute certainty.

1.5.5 Fourth-Generation Techniques

The term "fourth-generation techniques" (4GT) encompasses a broad array of software tools that have one thing in common: Each enables the software developer to specify some characteristic of software at a high level. The tool then automatically generates source code based on the developer's specification. There is little debate that the higher the level at which software can be specified to a machine, the faster a program can be built. The 4GT paradigm for software engineering focuses on the ability to specify software to a machine at a level that is close to natural language or using a notation that imparts significant function.

Currently, a software development environment that supports the 4GT paradigm includes some or all of the following tools: nonprocedural languages for database query, report generation, data manipulation, screen interaction and definition, code generation, high-level graphics capability, spreadsheet capability. Each of these tools does exist, but only for very specific application domains. There is no 4GT environment available today that may be applied with equal facility to each of the software application categories described in Section 1.2.3.

The 4GT paradigm for software engineering is depicted in Figure 1.10. Like other paradigms, 4GT begins with a requirements gathering step. Ideally, the customer would describe requirements and these would be directly translated into an operational prototype. But this is unworkable. The customer may be unsure of what is required, may be ambiguous in specifying facts that are known, and may be unable or unwilling to specify information in a manner that a 4GT tool can consume. In addition, current 4GT tools are not sophisticated enough to accommodate truly "natural language" and won't be for some time. At this time, the customer-developer dialog described for other paradigms remains an essential part of the 4GT approach.

For small applications, it may be possible to move directly from the requirements gathering step to implementation using a non-procedural *fourth-generation language* (4GL). However, for larger efforts, it is necessary to develop a design strategy for the system, even if a 4GL is to be used. The use of 4GT without design (for large projects) will cause the same difficulties (poor quality, poor maintainability, poor customer acceptance) that we have encountered when developing software using conventional approaches.

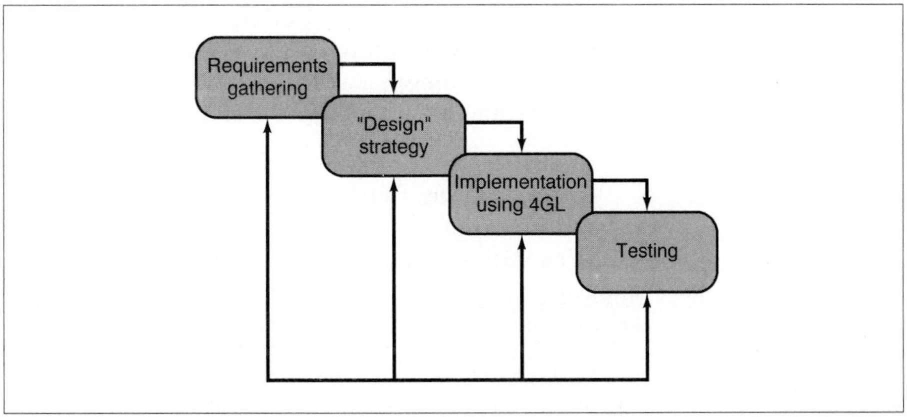

FIGURE 1.10. Fourth-generation techniques.

Implementation using a 4GL enables the software developer to represent desired results in a manner that results in automatic generation of code to generate those results. Obviously, a data structure with relevant information must exist and be readily accessible by the 4GL. A more detailed description of 4GL is contained in Chapter 16.

To transform a 4GT implementation into a product, the developer must conduct thorough testing, develop meaningful documentation, and perform all other "transition" activities that are also required in other software engineering paradigms. In addition, the 4GT developed software must be built in a manner that enables maintenance to be performed expeditiously.

There has been much hyperbole and considerable debate surrounding the use of the 4GT paradigm (e.g., see [COB85] and [GRA85]). Proponents claim dramatic reduction in software development time and greatly improved productivity for people who build software. Opponents claim that current 4GT tools are not all that much easier to use than programming languages, that the resultant source code produced by such tools is "inefficient," and that the maintainability of large software systems developed using 4GT is open to question.

There is some merit in the claims of both sides. Although it is somewhat difficult to separate fact from fancy (few controlled studies have been done to date), it is possible to summarize the current state of 4GT approaches:

1. With very few exceptions, the current application domain for 4GT is limited to business information systems applications, specifically, information analysis and reporting that is keyed to large databases. However, new CASE tools (see Chapter 22) now support the use of 4GT for the automatic generation of "skeleton code" for engineering and real-time applications.
2. Preliminary data collected from companies that are using 4GT seems to indicate that time required to produce software is greatly reduced for small and intermediate applications and that the amount of design and analysis for small applications is also reduced.
3. However, the use of 4GT for large software development efforts demands as much or more analysis, design, and testing (software engineering activities) to achieve substantial time savings that can be achieved through the elimination of coding.

To summarize, fourth-generation techniques have already become an important part of software development in the information systems application area and will likely become widely used in engineering and real-time applications during the middle to late 1990s. As Figure 1.11 illustrates, the demand for software will continue to escalate throughout the remainder of this century, but software produced using conventional methods and

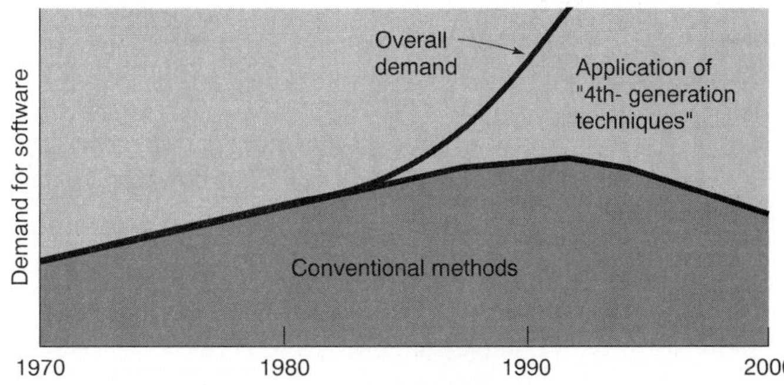

FIGURE 1.11. The changing nature of software development.

paradigms is likely to contribute less and less to all software developed. Fourth-generation techniques will fill the gap.

1.5.6 Combining Paradigms

The software engineering paradigms discussed in the preceding sections are often described as alternative approaches to software engineering rather than complementary approaches. In many cases, however, the paradigms can and should be combined so that the strengths of each can be achieved on a single project. The spiral model paradigm accomplishes this directly, combining prototyping and elements of the classic life cycle in an evolutionary approach to software engineering. But any one of the paradigms can serve as a foundation into which others are integrated.

Figure 1.12 illustrates how software engineering paradigms can be combined during a single software development effort. In all cases, work begins with a determination of objectives, alternatives and constraints—a step that is sometimes called *preliminary requirements gathering*. From this point, any one of the paths indicated in Figure 1.12 can be taken. For example, the classic life-cycle steps (far left-hand path) can be followed, if the system can be fully specified at the beginning. If requirements are uncertain, a prototype can be used to define requirements more fully. Using the prototype as a guide, the developer can then return to the steps of the classic life cycle (design, code, and test). Alternatively, the prototype can evolve toward the production system, with a return to the life cycle paradigm for testing. Fourth-generation techniques can be used to implement the prototype or to implement the production system during the coding step of the life cycle. 4GT can also be used in conjunction with the spiral model for prototyping or coding steps.

There is no need to be dogmatic about the choice of paradigms for software engineering. The nature of the application should dictate the approach

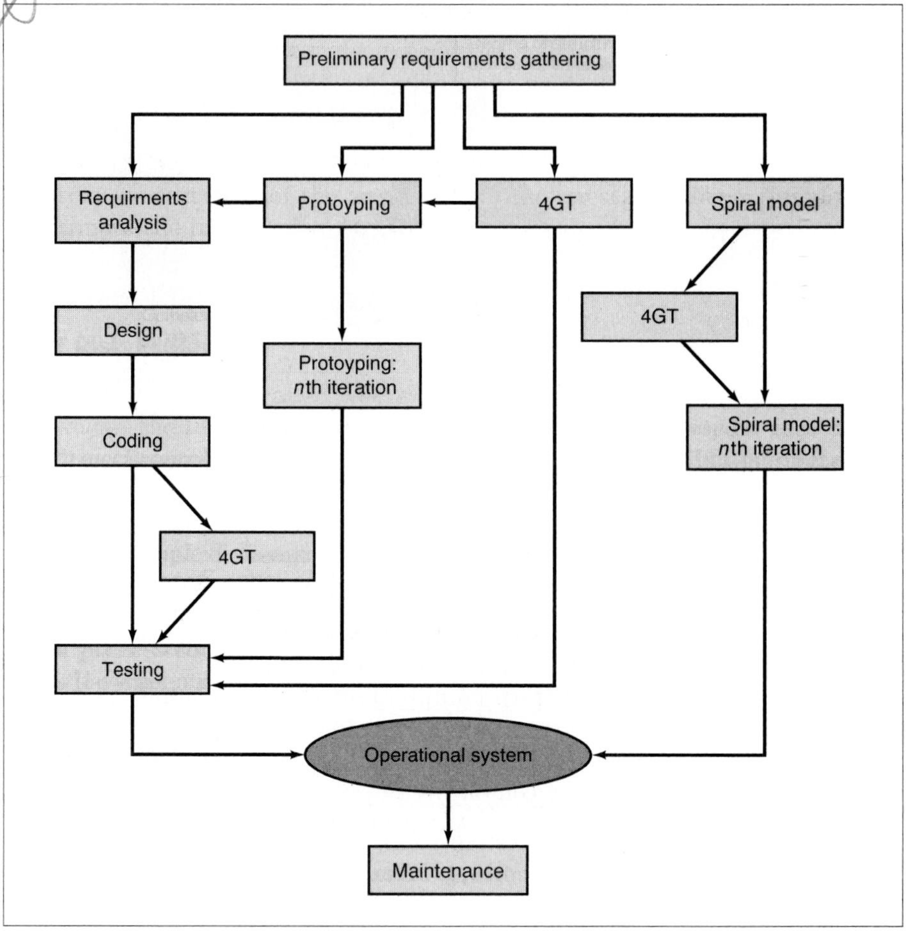

FIGURE 1.12. Combining paradigms.

to be taken. By combining approaches, the whole can be greater than the sum of the parts.

1.6 A GENERIC VIEW OF SOFTWARE ENGINEERING

The software development process contains three generic phases regardless of the software engineering paradigm that is chosen. The three phases, *definition, development,* and *maintenance,* are encountered in all software development, regardless of application area, project size, or complexity.

The definition phase focuses on *what.* That is, during definition, the software developer attempts to identify what information is to be processed, what function and performance are desired, what interfaces are to be established, what design constraints exist, and what validation criteria are required to define a successful system. The key requirements of the system and the software are identified. Although the methods applied during the definition phase will vary depending upon the software engineering paradigm (or combination of paradigms) that is applied, three specific steps will occur in some form:

System analysis. Already described in our discussion of the classic life cycle (Section 1.5.2), system analysis defines the role of each element in a computer-based system, ultimately allocating the role that software will play.

Software project planning. Once the scope of the software is established, risks are analyzed, resources are allocated, costs are estimated, and work tasks and schedule are defined.

Requirements analysis. The scope defined for the software provides direction, but a more detailed definition of the information domain and function of the software is necessary before work can begin.

The development phase focuses on *how.* That is, during definition the software developer attempts to define how data structure and software architecture are to be designed, how procedural details are to be implemented, how the design will be translated into a programming language (or nonprocedural language), and how testing will be performed. The methods applied during the development phase will vary, but three specific steps will always occur in some form:

Software design. Design translates the requirements for the software into a set of representations (some graphical, others tabular or language-based) that describe data structure, architecture, algorithmic procedure, and interface characteristics.

Coding. Design representations must be translated into an artificial language (the language may be a conventional programming language or a nonprocedural language used in the context of the 4GT paradigm) that results in instructions that can be executed by the computer. The coding step performs this translation.

Software testing. Once the software is implemented in machine-executable form, it must be tested to uncover defects in function, in logic, and in implementation.

The maintenance phase focuses on *change* that is associated with error correction, adaptations required as the software's environment evolves, and enhancements brought about by changing customer requirements. The maintenance phase reapplies the steps of the definition and development phases, but does so in the context of existing software. Three types of change are encountered during the maintenance phase:

Correction. Even with the best quality assurance activities, it is likely that the customer will uncover defects in the software. *Corrective maintenance* changes the software to correct defects.

Adaptation. Over time, the original environment (e.g., CPU, operating system, peripherals) for which the software was developed is likely to change. *Adaptive maintenance* results in modification to the software to accommodate changes to its external environment.

Enhancement. As software is used, the customer/user will recognize additional functions that will provide benefit. *Perfective maintenance* extends the software beyond its original function requirements.

In addition to these basic maintenance activities, the "aging software plant" (discussed in Section 1.1.3) is forcing some companies to consider *reverse engineering* [CHI90]. Using a specialized set of CASE tools, old software is reverse-engineered so that its internal working can be understood and improved (see Chapter 20).

Umbrella
Review
Documentation
Change Control

The phases and related steps described in our generic view of software engineering are complemented by a number of "umbrella activities": Reviews are conducted to ensure that quality is maintained as each step is completed. Documentation is developed and controlled to ensure that complete information about the system and software will be available for later use. Change control is instituted so that changes can be approved and tracked. In the classic life-cycle and spiral model paradigms, the phases and steps described in this section are explicitly defined. In the prototyping and 4GT paradigms, some of the steps are implied, but not explicitly identified. The approach to each step may vary from paradigm to paradigm, but an overall approach that demands definition, development, and maintenance remains invariant. You can conduct each phase with discipline and well-defined methods, or you can muddle through each haphazardly. But you will perform them nonetheless. The remainder of this book is dedicated to an approach to software development that emphasizes discipline and well-defined methods—an approach that we have already learned to call software engineering.

1.7 SUMMARY

Software has become the key element in the evolution of computer-based systems and products. Over the past four decades, software has evolved from a specialized problem-solving and information analysis tool to an industry in itself. But early "programming" culture and history have created a set of problems that persist today. Software has become a limiting factor in the evolution of computer-based systems.

Software engineering is a discipline that integrates methods, tools, and procedures for the development of computer software. A number of different paradigms for software engineering have been proposed, each exhibiting strengths and weaknesses, but all having a series of generic phases in common. It is the steps of these generic phases and the methods that are applied with each step that comprise the remainder of this book.

REFERENCES

[ALL89] Allman, W. F., *Apprentices of Wonder,* Bantam, 1989.

[BIG84] Biggerstaff, T. J., and A. J. Perlis (eds.), Special Issue on Software Reusability, *IEEE Trans. Software Engineering,* vol. SE-10, no. 5, September 1984.

[BOE88] Boehm, B., "A Spiral Model for Software Development and Enhancement," *Computer,* vol. 21, no. 5, May 1988, pp. 61–72.

[BRE88] Brereton, P. (ed.), *Software Engineering Environments,* Wiley, 1988.

[BRO75] Brooks, F., *The Mythical Man-Month,* Addison-Wesley, 1975.

[CHI90] Chikofsky, E. J., and J. H. Cross, II, "Reverse Engineering and Design Recovery: A Taxonomy," *IEEE Software,* January 1990, pp. 13–18.

[COB85] Cobb, R. H., "In Praise of 4GLs," *Datamation,* July 15, 1985, p. 92.

[EVA87] Evans, M.W., and J. J. Marciniak, *Software Quality Assurance and Management,* Wiley-Interscience, 1987.

[FEI83] Feigenbaum, E. A., and P. McCorduck, *The Fifth Generation,* Addison-Wesley, 1983.

[GIL88] Gilb, T., *Principles of Software Engineering Management,* Addison-Wesley, 1988.

[GRA85] Grant, F.J., "The Downside of 4GLs," *Datamation,* July 15, 1985, pp. 99–104.

[IAN84] Iannino, A., et al., "Criteria for Software Reliability Model Comparisons," *IEEE Trans. Software Engineering,* vol. SE-10, no. 6, November 1984, pp. 687–691.

[LIE80] Lientz, B., and E. Swanson, *Software Maintenance Management,* Addison-Wesley, 1980.

[MAN84] Manley, J. H., "CASE: Foundation for Software Factories," *COMPCON Proceedings,* IEEE, September 1984, pp. 84–91.

[NAI82] Naisbitt, J., *Megatrends,* Warner Books, 1982.

[NAU69] Naur, P., and B. Randell (eds.), *Software Engineering: A Report on a Conference sponsored by the NATO Science Committee,* NATO, 1969.

[OSB79] Osborne, A., *Running Wild—The Next Industrial Revolution,* Osborne/McGraw-Hill, 1979.

[PRE91] Pressman, R. S., and S. R. Herron, *Software Shock,* Dorset House, 1991.

[STO89] Stoll, C., *The Cuckoo's Egg,* Doubleday, 1989.

[TAJ84] Tajima, D., and T. Matsubara, "Inside the Japanese Software Factory," *Computer,* vol. 17, no. 3, March 1984, pp. 34–43.

[TOF80] Toffler, A., *The Third Wave,* Morrow, 1980.

[TOF90] Toffler, A., *Powershift,* Bantam, 1990.

[TRA88] Tracz, W., *Software Reuse: Emerging Technology,* IEEE Computer Society Press, 1988.

[WAS89] Wasserman, P. D., *Neural Computing: Theory and Practice,* Van Nostrand Reinhold, 1989.

[WAT85] Waterman, D. A., *A Guide to Expert Systems,* Addison-Wesley, 1985.

PROBLEMS AND POINTS TO PONDER

1.1 Software is the differentiating characteristic in many computer-based products and systems. Provide examples of two or three products and at least one system in which software, not hardware, is the differentiating element.

1.2 In the 1950s and 1960s computer programming was an art form learned in an apprentice-like environment. How have the early days affected software development practices today?

1.3 Toffler [TOF80] and Naisbitt [NAI82] have discussed the impact of the "information era." (a) Provide a number of examples (both positive and negative) that indicate the impact of software on our society. (b) Their work is now 10 years old. Review one of the references and indicate where the author was right and where he was wrong.

1.4 Research the early history of software engineering, starting with early papers on program design and continuing with attempts to develop a broader methodology.

1.5 The myths described in this chapter are only the tip of the iceberg. List additional myths for each of the categories presented in Section 1.4.

1.6 Computer-aided software engineering is a growing industry. Research three commercially available CASE products and provide a comparison using criteria that you develop. Revisit this problem after you've read the remaining chapters.

1.7 Which of the software engineering paradigms presented in this chapter would be most applicable for your software applications? Why?

1.8 Provide five examples of software development projects that would be amenable to prototyping. Name two or three applications that would be more difficult to prototype.

1.9 Develop a paper prototype for a video game of your own invention.

1.10 Research two or three fourth-generation languages and present a summary discussion. How broad is their applicability?

1.11 Many people argue that the term "maintenance" is incorrectly applied to software—that the activities associated with software maintenance aren't "maintenance" at all. What do you think?

1.12 Is there ever a case when the generic phases of the software engineering process don't apply? If so, describe it.

1.13 Research the popular media (e.g., newspapers, magazines, TV that is directed at the masses) over the past 12 months and find at least five major features where software was the prevailing theme. Note any errors in the presentation.

FURTHER READINGS

The current state of the art in software engineering can best be determined from monthly publications such as *IEEE Software, Computer,* and the *IEEE Transactions on Software Engineering.* The discipline is "summarized" every 12 months in the *Proceedings of the International Conference on Software Engineering,* sponsored by the IEEE and ACM.

Many software engineering books have been published in recent years. Some present an overview of the entire process while others delve into a few important topics to the exclusion of others. Recent additions to the literature include:

Ince, D., *Software Engineering,* Van Nostrand Reinhold, 1991.

Macro, A., *Software Engineering: Concepts and Management,* Prentice-Hall, 1990.

Ng, P., and R.T. Yeh, *Modern Software Engineering,* Van Nostrand Reinhold, 1990.
Sommerville, I., *Software Engineering,* 3d ed., Addison-Wesley, 1989.
von Mayrhauser, A., *Software Engineering: Methods and Management,* Academic Press, 1990.

To gain insight into software engineering as it is practiced by a major technology competitor, the interested reader should review Matsumoto and Ohno *(Japanese Perspectives in Software Engineering,* Addison-Wesley, 1989), who provide a worthwhile collection of essays.

On the lighter side, a book by Robert Glass *(Software Conflict,* Yourdon Press, 1991) presents amusing and controversial essays on software and the software engineering process. The role of computers and software in a broader societal context is discussed by Stoll [STO89] and Toffler [TOF90]. Pressman and Herron *(Software Shock,* Dorset House, 1991) consider software and its impact on individuals, businesses, and government. Written for the nontechnical professional, their book makes good reading for nontechnical managers who must understand software people, the software engineering process, and the software products that affect our world.

The Software Engineering Institute (located at Carnegie-Mellon University) has been chartered with the responsibility of sponsoring a software engineering monograph series. Practitioners from industry, government, and academia are contributing important new work. Additional software engineering research is conducted by the Software Productivity Consortium—an industry sponsored "think tank" that addresses software-related issues.

A wide variety of software engineering standards and procedures have been published over the past decade. *Software Engineering Standards,* 3d ed., (IEEE, 1989) contains 17 different standards that cover many important aspects of the technology. Other software engineering standards can be obtained from the Department of Defense, the Federal Aviation Administration, and other government and nonprofit agencies.

CHAPTER 2

PROJECT MANAGEMENT: SOFTWARE METRICS

In the preface to his book on software project management, Meiler Page-Jones [PAG85, p. 1] makes a statement that can be echoed by many software engineering consultants:

> I've visited dozens of commercial shops, both good and bad, and I've observed scores of data processing managers, again, both good and bad. Too often, I've watched in horror as these managers futilely struggled through nightmarish projects, squirmed under impossible deadlines, or delivered systems that outraged their users and went on to devour huge chunks of maintenance time.

What Page-Jones describes are symptoms that result from an array of management and technical problems. However, if a post mortem were to be conducted for every project, it is very likely that a consistent theme would be encountered: Project management was weak.

In this chapter and the two that follow we will consider the key concepts that lead to effective software project management. This chapter considers the role of measurement and software metrics and their impact on project management. The techniques that are used to estimate cost and resource requirements (using the measurements that have been made) are presented in Chapter 3. Finally, Chapter 4 discusses the planning activities that are required to assess risk, define project tasks, and establish a workable project schedule.

2.1 THE PROJECT MANAGEMENT PROCESS

Software project management is the first layer of the software engineering process. We call it a *layer,* rather than a step or activity, because it overlays the entire development process from beginning to end.

In order to conduct a successful software project we must understand the scope of work to be done, the risks to be incurred, the resources to be required, the tasks to be accomplished, the milestones to be tracked, the effort (cost) to be expended, and the schedule to be followed. Software project management provides that understanding. It begins before technical work starts, continues as the software evolves from concept to reality, and culminates only when the software is retired.

Because software project management is so important to the success of a project, it would seem reasonable to assume that all project leaders understand how to do it, and all practitioners understand how to work within the bounds established by it. Unfortunately, many do not. In the paragraphs that follow, an overview[1] of the key elements of software project management is presented.

2.1.1 Beginning a Software Project

Before a project can be planned, objectives and scope should be established, alternative solutions should be considered, and technical and management constraints should be identified. Without this information, it is impossible to define reasonable (and accurate) estimates of the cost, a realistic breakdown of project tasks, or a manageable project schedule that provides a meaningful indication of progress.

The software developer and customer must meet to define project objectives and scope. In many cases, this activity occurs as part of the system engineering process (Chapter 5). Objectives identify the overall goals of the project without considering how these goals will be achieved. Scope identifies the primary functions that software is to accomplish, and more importantly, attempts to *bound* these functions in a quantitative manner.

Once the project objectives and scope are understood, alternative solutions are considered. Although very little detail is discussed, the alternatives enable managers and practitioners to select a "best" approach, given the constraints imposed by delivery deadlines, budgetary restrictions, personnel availability, technical interfaces, and a myriad of other factors.

[1]A detailed discussion of these topics is presented in this and the two chapters that follow.

2.1.2 Measures and Metrics

In most technical endeavors, measurement and metrics help us to understand the technical process that is used to develop a product and the product itself. The process is measured in an effort to improve it. The product is measured in an effort to increase its quality.

At first, it would seem that measurement is self-evident. After all, measurement enables us to quantify and therefore manage more effectively. But reality can be somewhat different. Measurement often leads to controversy and argument. What are appropriate metrics for the process and the product? How should the data that are collected be used? Is it fair to use measurements to compare people, processes, or products? These questions and dozens of others always surface when an attempt is made to measure something that has not been measured in the past. Such is the case with software engineering (the process) and software (the product).

In Sections 2.2 through 2.4 software metrics are considered. These metrics have been developed to provide managers and technical practitioners with insight into the software engineering process and the product that it produces.

2.1.3 Estimation

One of the pivotal activities in the software project management process is *planning*. When a software project is planned, estimates of required human effort (usually in person-months), chronological project duration (in calendar time), and cost (in dollars) must be derived. But how is this done?

In many cases estimates are made using past experience as the only guide. If a new project is quite similar in size and function to a past project, it is likely that the new project will require approximately the same amount of effort, take the same calendar time, and cost the same number of dollars as the older work. But what if the project breaks new ground? Then past experience alone may not be enough.

A number of estimation techniques have been developed for software development. Although each has its own strengths and weaknesses (Chapter 3), all have the following attributes in common:

- Project scope must be established in advance.
- Software metrics (past measurements) are used as a basis from which estimates are made.
- The project is broken into small pieces which are estimated individually.

Many managers apply a number of different estimation techniques, using one as a cross-check for another. In Chapter 3, a number of popular software estimation techniques are considered.

2.1.4 Risk Analysis

Whenever a computer program is to be built, there are areas of uncertainty. Are the needs of the customer really understood? Can the functions that must be implemented be accomplished before the project deadline? Will there be difficult technical problems that are currently hidden from view? Will the changes that invariably occur during any project cause the schedule to slip badly?

Risk analysis is crucial to good software project management, and yet many projects are undertaken with no specific consideration of risk. In his book on software engineering management [GIL88], Tom Gilb says, "If you don't actively attack [project and technical] risks, they will actively attack you." Risk analysis is actually a series of risk management steps that enable us to "attack" risk: risk identification, risk assessment, risk prioritization, risk management strategies, risk resolution, and risk monitoring. These steps are applied throughout the software engineering process (see the discussion of the spiral model in Chapter 1) and are described in Chapter 4.

2.1.5 Scheduling

Every software project has a schedule, but not all schedules are created equal. Did the schedule evolve on its own or was it planned in advance? Was work done "by the seat of our pants" or was a set of well-defined tasks identified? Have managers focused solely on the deadline date or has a critical path been identified and monitored to be sure the deadline is achieved? Has progress been measured by "Are we done yet?" or has a set of evenly spaced milestones been established?

Software project scheduling is really no different than scheduling for any engineering project. A set of project tasks is identified. Interdependencies among tasks are established. The effort associated with each task is estimated. People and other resources are assigned. A "task network" is created. A time-line schedule is developed. Each of these activities is described in detail in Chapter 4.

2.1.6 Tracking and Control

Once the development schedule has been established, tracking and control activity commences. Each task noted in the schedule is tracked by the project manager. If the task falls behind schedule, the manager can use an automated project scheduling tool to determine the impact of schedule slippage on intermediate project milestones and the overall delivery date. Resources can be redirected, tasks can be reordered, or (as a last resort) delivery commitments can be modified to accommodate the problem that has been uncovered. In this way, software development can be better controlled.

2.2 METRICS FOR SOFTWARE PRODUCTIVITY AND QUALITY

Measurement is fundamental to any engineering discipline and software engineering is no exception. Lord Kelvin once said:

> When you can measure what you are speaking about and express it in numbers, you know something about it; but when you cannot measure, when you cannot express it in numbers, your knowledge is of a meager and unsatisfactory kind: it may be the beginning of knowledge, but you have scarcely, in your thoughts, advanced to the stage of a science.

Over the past decade, the software engineering community has taken Lord Kelvin's words to heart. But not without frustration and more than a little controversy!

Software metrics refers to a broad range of measures for computer software (e.g., [ART85], [GRA87]). Within the context of software project management, we are concerned primarily with productivity and quality metrics—measures of software development "output" as a function of effort applied and measures of the "fitness for use" of the output that is produced. For planning and estimating purposes, our interest is historical. What was software development productivity on past projects? What was the quality of the software that was produced? How can past productivity and quality data be extrapolated to the present? How can it help us plan and estimate more accurately?

In the sections that follow we first consider the broad range of software metrics to understand where productivity and quality measures fit. Next, two important (and opposing) views on the measurement of software productivity and quality are presented. Finally, we examine the practical problems of collecting metrics and using them for software project estimation.

2.3 MEASURING SOFTWARE

Measurement is commonplace in the engineering world. We measure power consumption, weight, physical dimensions, temperature, voltage, signal-to-noise ratio... the list is almost endless. Unfortunately, measurement is far from commonplace in the software engineering world. We have trouble agreeing on what to measure and trouble evaluating measurements that are collected.

Software is measured for many reasons: (1) to indicate the quality of the product; (2) to assess the productivity of the people who produce the product; (3) to assess the benefits (in terms of productivity and quality) derived from new software engineering methods and tools; (4) to form a baseline for estimation; (5) to help justify requests for new tools or additional training.

Measurements in the physical world can be categorized in two ways: *direct measures* (e.g., the length of a bolt) and *indirect measures* (e.g., the "quality" of bolts produced, measured by counting rejects). Software metrics can be categorized similarly.

Direct measures of the software engineering process include cost and effort applied. Direct measures of the product include lines of code (LOC) produced, execution speed, memory size, and defects reported over some set period of time. Indirect measures of the product include functionality, quality, complexity, efficiency, reliability, maintainability, and many other "-abilities" that are discussed in Chapter 17.

The cost and effort required to build software, the number of lines of code produced, and other direct measures are relatively easy to collect, as long as specific conventions for measurement are established in advance. However, the quality and functionality of software, or its efficiency or maintainability, are more difficult to assess and can only be measured indirectly.

We can further categorize the software metrics domain as shown in Figure 2.1. As we have already noted, *productivity metrics* focus on the output of the software engineering process, *quality metrics* provide an indication of how closely software conforms to implicit and explicit customer requirements (software's fitness for use), and *technical metrics* focus on the character of the software (e.g, logical complexity, degree of modularity) rather than the process through which the software was developed. Referring again to Figure 2.1, we note that a second categorization can also be developed. *Size-oriented metrics* are used to collect direct measures of software engineering output and quality. *Function-oriented metrics* provide indirect measures, and human-oriented measures collect information about the manner in which people develop computer software and human perceptions about the effectiveness of tools and methods.

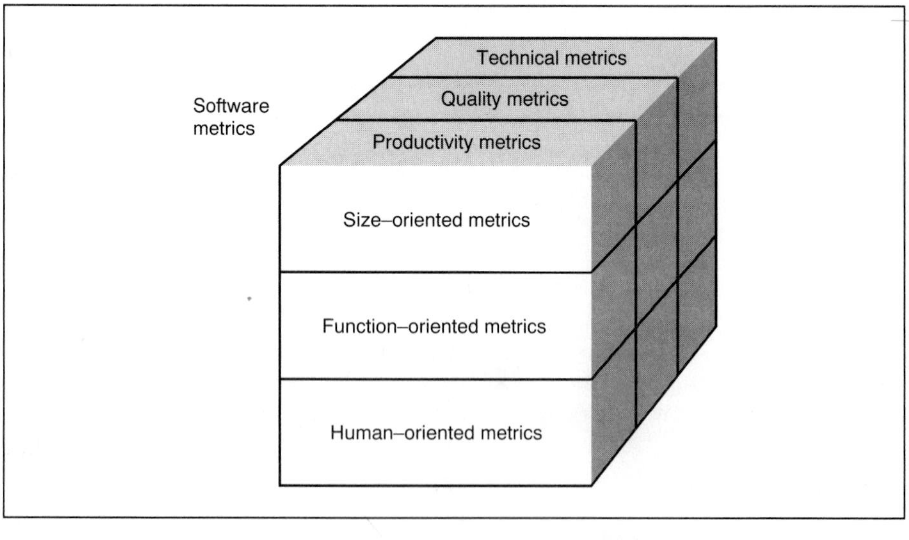

FIGURE 2.1. Metrics categorization.

2.3.1 Size-Oriented Metrics

Size-oriented software metrics are direct measures of software and the process by which it is developed. If a software organization maintains simple records, a table of size-oriented data, such as the one shown in Figure 2.2, can be created. The table lists each software development project that has been completed over the past few years and corresponding size-oriented data for that project. Referring to the table entry (Figure 2.2) for project aaa-01: 12.1 KLOC (thousand lines of code) were developed with 24 person-months of effort at a cost of $168,000. It should be noted that the effort and cost recorded in the table represent all software engineering activities (analysis, design, code, and test), not just coding. Further information for project aaa-01 indicates that 365 pages of documentation were developed, and 29 errors were encountered after release to the customer within the first year of operation. Three people worked on the development of software for project aaa-01.

From the rudimentary data contained in the table, a set of simple size-oriented productivity and quality metrics can be developed for each project. Averages can be computed for all projects. From Figure 2.2:

$$\text{Productivity} = \text{KLOC/person-month}$$

$$\text{Quality} = \text{defects/KLOC}$$

In addition, other interesting metrics may be computed:

$$\text{Cost} = \$/\text{LOC}$$

$$\text{Documentation} = \text{pages of documentation/KLOC}$$

project	effort	$	KLOC	pgs.doc.	errors	people
aaa–01	24	168	12.1	365	29	3
ccc–04	62	440	27.2	1224	86	5
fff–03	43	314	20.2	1050	64	6
⋮	⋮	⋮	⋮	⋮		

FIGURE 2.2.
Size-oriented metrics.

Size-oriented metrics are controversial and are not universally accepted as the best way to measure the process of software development [JON86a]. Most of the controversy swirls around the use of lines of code as a key measure. Proponents of the LOC measure claim that LOC is an "artifact" of all software development projects that can be easily counted, that many existing software estimation models use LOC or KLOC as a key input, and that a large body of literature and data predicated on LOC already exists. On the other hand, opponents claim that LOC measures are programming-language-dependent, that they penalize well-designed but shorter programs, that they cannot easily accommodate nonprocedural languages, and that their use in estimation requires a level of detail that may be difficult to achieve (i.e., the planner must estimate the LOC to be produced long before analysis and design have been completed).

2.3.2 Function-Oriented Metrics

Function-oriented software metrics are indirect measures of software and the process by which it is developed. Rather than counting LOC, function-oriented metrics focus on program "functionality" or "utility." Function-oriented metrics were first proposed by Albrecht [ALB79], who suggested a productivity measurement approach called the *function point* method. Function points (FPs) are derived using an empirical relationship based on countable measures of software's information domain and assessments of software complexity.

Function points are computed by completing the table shown in Figure 2.3. Five information domain characteristics are determined and counts are provided in the appropriate table location. Information domain values are defined in the following manner:

Number of user inputs. Each user input that provides distinct application oriented data to the software is counted. Inputs should be distinguished from inquiries which are counted separately.

Number of user outputs. Each user output that provides application-oriented information to the user is counted. In this context "output" refers to reports, screens, error messages, etc. Individual data items within a report are not counted separately.

Number of user inquiries. An inquiry is defined as an on-line input that results in the generation of some immediate software response in the form of an on-line output. Each distinct inquiry is counted.

Number of files. Each logical master file, i.e., a logical grouping of data that may be one part of a large database or a separate file, is counted.

Number of external interfaces. All machine-readable interfaces (e.g., data files on tape or disk) that are used to transmit information to another system are counted.

Measurement parameter	Count		Weighting factor Simple	Average	Complex		
Number of user inputs	☐	×	3	4	6	=	☐
Number of user outputs	☐	×	4	5	7	=	☐
Number of user inquiries	☐	×	3	4	6	=	☐
Number of files	☐	×	7	10	15	=	☐
Number of external interfaces	☐	×	5	7	10	=	☐
Count - total →							☐

FIGURE 2.3. Computing function-point metrics.

Once the above data have been collected, a complexity value is associated with each count. Organizations that use function point methods develop criteria for determining whether a particular entry is simple, average, or complex. Nonetheless, the determination of complexity is somewhat subjective.

To compute function points, the following relationship is used:

$$\text{FP} = \text{count-total} \times [0.65 + 0.01 \times \text{SUM}(F_i)] \qquad (2.1)$$

where count-total is the sum of all FP entries obtained from the table in Figure 2.3. F_i ($i = 1$ to 14) are "complexity adjustment values" based on responses to questions [ART85] noted in Table 2.1. The constant values in the above equation and the weighting factors that are applied to information domain counts are determined empirically.

Once function points have been calculated, they are used in a manner analogous to LOC as a measure of software productivity, quality, and other attributes:

$$\text{Productivity} = \text{FP/person-month}$$

$$\text{Quality} = \text{defects/FP}$$

$$\text{Cost} = \$/\text{FP}$$

$$\text{Documentation} = \text{pages of documentation/FP}$$

among others.

TABLE 2.1

COMPUTING FUNCTION POINTS

Rate each factor on a scale of 0 to 5:

0	1	2	3	4	5
No influence	Incidental	Moderate	Average	Significant	Essential

F_i:

1. Does the system require reliable backup and recovery?
2. Are data communications required?
3. Are there distributed processing functions?
4. Is performance critical?
5. Will the system run in an existing, heavily utilized operational environment?
6. Does the system require on-line data entry?
7. Does the on-line data entry require the input transaction to be built over multiple screens or operations?
8. Are the master files updated on-line?
9. Are the inputs, outputs, files, or inquiries complex?
10. Is the internal processing complex?
11. Is the code designed to be reusable?
12. Are conversion and installation included in the design?
13. Is the system designed for multiple installations in different organizations?
14. Is the application designed to facilitate change and ease of use by the user?

The function point measure was originally designed to be applied to business information systems applications. However, extensions proposed by Jones [JON86b], called *feature points,* may enable this measure to be applied to systems and engineering software applications. The feature point measure accommodates applications in which algorithmic complexity is high. Real-time, process control, and embedded software applications tend to have high algorithmic complexity and are therefore amenable to the feature point.

To compute the feature point, information domain values are again counted and weighted as described above. In addition, the feature point metric counts a new software characteristic, *algorithms.* An algorithm is defined as "a bounded computational problem that is included within a specific computer program." Inverting a matrix, decoding a bit string, or handling an interrupt are all examples of algorithms.

To compute feature points, the table shown in Figure 2.4 is used. A single weight value is used for each of the measurement parameters and the overall feature point value is computed using equation (2.1).

Measurement parameter	Count		Weight		
Number of user inputs		×	4	=	
Number of user outputs		×	5	=	
Number of user inquiries		×	4	=	
Number of files		×	7	=	
Number of external interfaces		×	7	=	
Algorithms		×	3	=	
Count - total →					

FIGURE 2.4. Computing feature-point metrics.

It should be noted that feature points and function points represent the same thing—"functionality" or "utility" delivered by software. In fact, both measures result in the same value of FP for conventional engineering computation or information systems applications. For more complex real-time systems, the feature point count is often between 20 and 35 percent higher than the count determined using function points alone.

The function point (or feature point) metric, like LOC, is controversial. Proponents claim that FP is programming-language-independent, making it ideal for applications using conventional and nonprocedural languages; they also claim that it is based on data that are more likely to be known early in the evolution of a project, making FP more attractive as an estimation approach. Opponents claim that the method requires some "sleight of hand" in that computation is based in part on subjective, rather than objective, data; that information domain information can be difficult to collect after-the-fact; and that FP has no direct physical meaning—it's just a number.

2.4 METRICS FOR SOFTWARE QUALITY

Quality can be measured throughout the software engineering process and after the software has been released to the customer and users. Metrics derived before the software is delivered provide a quantitative basis for making design and testing decisions. Quality metrics in this category include *program complexity* (Chapter 18), *effective modularity* (Chapter 10), and overall *program size*. Metrics used after delivery focus on the number of defects uncovered in the field and the *maintainability* of the system. It is important to emphasize that *after-delivery measures* of software quality present managers and technical staff with a post mortem indication of the effectiveness of the software engineering process.

In Chapter 17, the use of quality metrics is described as the key component of *statistical quality assurance*. That is, by adding additional information about the types of defects uncovered and their causes, we can provide a mechanism for planning actions to correct the elements of the software process that "introduce" defects in the first place.

2.4.1 An Overview of Factors that Affect Quality

Over two decades ago, McCall and Cavano [MCC78] defined a set of quality factors that were a first step toward the development of metrics for software quality. These factors assessed software from three distinct points of view: (1) product operation (using it), (2) product revision (changing it), and (3) product transition (modifying it to work in a different environment, i.e., "porting" it). In their work, the authors describe the relationship between these quality factors (what they call a "framework") and other aspects of the software engineering process [MCC78, p. 137]:

> First, the framework provides a mechanism for the project manager to identify what qualities are important. These qualities are attributes of the software in addition to its functional correctness and performance which have life cycle implications. Such factors as maintainability and portability have been shown in recent years to have significant life cycle cost impact....
>
> Secondly, the framework provides a means for quantitatively assessing how well the development is progressing relative to the quality goals established....
>
> Thirdly, the framework provides for more interaction of QA personnel throughout the development effort....
>
> Lastly,...quality assurance personnel can use indications of poor quality to help identify [better] standards to be enforced in the future.

A detailed discussion of McCall and Cavano's framework, as well as other quality factors, is presented in Chapter 17.

2.4.2 Measuring Quality

Although there are many measures of software quality, the after-the-fact measures discussed earlier are the most widely used. These include: *correct-*

ness, maintainability, integrity, and *usability.* Gilb [GIL88] has suggested definitions and measures for each.

Correctness. A program must operate correctly or it provides little value to its users. Correctness is the degree to which the software performs its required function. The most common measure for correctness is *defects per KLOC,* where a defect is defined as a verified lack of conformance to requirements. Defects are reported by a user of the program after the program has been released for general use and are counted over a standard period of time, typically 1 year.

Maintainability. Software maintenance accounts for more effort than any other software engineering activity. Maintainability is the ease with which a program can be corrected if an error is encountered, adapted if its environment changes, or enhanced if the customer desires a change in requirements. There is no way to measure maintainability directly; therefore, we must use indirect measures. A simple time-oriented metric is *mean-time-to-change* (MTTC), the time it takes to analyze the change request, design an appropriate modification, implement the change, test it, and distribute the change to all users. On average, programs that are maintainable will have a lower MTTC (for equivalent types of changes) than programs that are not maintainable.

Hitachi [TAJ81] has used a cost-oriented metric for maintainability which they call "spoilage"—the cost to correct defects encountered after the software has been released to its end-users. When the ratio of spoilage to overall project cost (for many projects) is plotted as a function of time, a manager can determine whether the overall maintainability of software produced by a software development organization is improving. Actions can then be taken in response to the insight gained from this information.

Integrity. Software integrity has become increasingly important in the age of hackers and viruses. This attribute measures a system's ability to withstand attacks (both accidental and intentional) to its security. Attacks can be made on all three components of software: programs, data, and documents.

To measure integrity, two additional attributes must be defined: threat and security. *Threat* is the probability (which can be estimated or derived from empirical evidence) that an attack of a specific type will occur within a given time. *Security* is the probability (which can be estimated or derived from empirical evidence) that the attack of a specific type will be repelled. The integrity of a system can then be defined as:

$$\text{Integrity} = \sum [1 - \text{threat} \times (1 - \text{security})]$$

where threat and security are summed over each type of attack.

Usability. The catch-phrase "user friendliness" has become ubiquitous in discussions of software products. If a program is not "user friendly," it is often doomed to failure, even if the functions that it performs are valuable. Usability is an attempt to quantify "user friendliness" and can be measured in terms of four characteristics: (1) the physical and/or intellectual skill required to learn the system, (2) the time required to become moderately efficient in the use of the system, (3) the net increase in productivity (over the approach that the system replaces) measured when the system is used by someone who is moderately efficient, and (4) a subjective assessment (sometimes obtained through a questionnaire) of users' attitudes toward the system. Further discussion of this topic is contained in Chapter 14.

The four factors described above are only a sampling of those that have been proposed as measures for software quality. Chapter 17 considers this topic in additional detail.

2.5 RECONCILING DIFFERENT METRICS APPROACHES

The relationship between lines of code and function points depends upon the programming language (Chapter 16) that is used to implement the software and the quality of the design. A number of studies have attempted to relate FP and LOC measures. To quote Albrecht and Gaffney [ALB83]:

> The thesis of this work is that the amount of function to be provided by the application (program) can be estimated from the itemization of the major components of data to be used or provided by it. Furthermore, this estimate of function should be correlated to both the amount of LOC to be developed and the development effort needed.

The following list [ALB83, JON92] provides rough estimates of the average number of lines of code required to build one function point in various programming languages:

Programming Language	*LOC/FP (Average)*
Assembly language	300
COBOL	100
FORTRAN	100
Pascal	90
Ada	70
Object-oriented languages	30
Fourth-generation languages (4GL)	20
Code generators	15

A review of the above data indicates that one LOC of Ada provides approximately 1.4 times the "functionality" (on average) as one LOC of FORTRAN.

Furthermore, one LOC of a 4GL provides between three and five times the functionality of a LOC for a conventional programming language. More precise data on the relationship between FP and LOC are presented by Jones [JON92] and can be used to "backfire" (i.e., to compute the number of function points when the number of delivered LOC are known) existing programs to determine the FP measure for each.

Any discussion of software productivity measurement invariably leads to a debate about the use of such data. Should the LOC/person-month (or FP/person-month) of one group be compared to similar data from another? Should managers appraise the performance of individuals by using these metrics? The answers to these questions is an emphatic NO! The reason for this response is that many factors influence productivity, making for "apples and oranges" comparisons that can be easily misinterpreted.

Basili and Zelkowitz [BAS78] define five important factors that influence software productivity:

People factors: The size and expertise of the development organization

Problem factors: The complexity of the problem to be solved and the number of changes in design constraints or requirements

Process factors: Analysis and design techniques that are used, languages and CASE tools available, and review techniques

Product factors: Reliability and performance of the computer-based system

Resource factors: Availability of CASE tools, hardware and software resources

The effect of these and other factors are illustrated by the results of a landmark study conducted by Walston and Felix [WAL77]. If one of the above factors is above average (highly favorable) for a given project, software development productivity will be significantly higher than if the same factor is below average (unfavorable). For the five factors noted above, changes from highly favorable to unfavorable conditions will affect productivity in the following manner[2]:

Factor	*Approximate % Variation*
People factors	90
Problem factors	40
Process factors	50
Product factors	140
Resource factors	40

[2]The factors noted by Walston and Felix have been placed into one of the five categories specified by Basili and Zelkowitz and average variation has been computed. This is done to illustrate the relative impact of variations in people, problem, process, product, and resources.

To understand the meaning of these numbers, assume that two software engineering teams have people with equal skills who use the same resources and process. One of the teams is working on a relatively simple problem with average reliability and performance requirements. The other team is working on a complex problem with extremely high reliability and performance goals. Based on the numbers in the list on page 55, the first team might exhibit software development productivity that is between 40 and 140 percent better than that of the second team. Problem and product factors make a productivity comparison between the two teams meaningless.

Function points and LOC have been found to be relatively accurate predictors of software development effort and cost. However, in order to use LOC and FP in the estimation techniques described in Chapter 3, an historical baseline of information must be established. In the next section guidelines for metrics data collection are presented.

2.6 INTEGRATING METRICS WITHIN THE SOFTWARE ENGINEERING PROCESS

Most software developers do not measure, and, sadly, most have little desire to begin. The problem is cultural. Attempting to collect measures where none have been collected in the past often precipitates resistance. "Why do we need to do this?" asks a harried project manager. "I don't see the point," complains an overworked practitioner.

In this section, we consider some arguments for software metrics and present an approach for instituting a metrics collection program within a software engineering organization. But before we begin, some words of wisdom suggested by Grady and Caswell [GRA87, p. 1]:

> Some of the things we describe here will sound quite easy. Realistically, though, establishing a successful company-wide software metrics program is hard work. When we say that you must wait at least three years before broad organizational trends are available, you get some idea of the scope of such an effort.

The caveat suggested by these authors is well worth heeding, but the benefits of measurement are so compelling that the hard work is worth it.

2.6.1 Arguments for Software Metrics

Why is it so important to measure the process of software engineering and the product (software) that it produces? The answer is relatively obvious. If we do not measure, there is no real way of determining whether we are improving. And if we are not improving, we are lost.

Measurement is one of a number of "medications" that may help cure the software affliction described in Chapter 1. It provides benefits at the strategic level, at the project level, and at the technical level.

By requesting and evaluating productivity and quality measures, senior management can establish meaningful goals for improvement of the software engineering process. In Chapter 1 we noted that software is a strategic business issue for many companies. If the process through which it is developed can be improved, a direct impact on the bottom line can result. But to establish goals for improvement, the current status of software development must be understood. Hence, measurement is used to establish a process baseline from which improvements can be assessed.

The day-to-day rigors of software project work leave little time for strategic thinking. Software project managers are concerned with more mundane (but equally important) issues: developing meaningful project estimates; producing higher-quality systems; getting product out the door on time. By using measurement to establish a project baseline, each of these issues becomes more manageable. We have already noted that the baseline serves as a basis for estimation. Additionally, the collection of quality metrics enables an organization to "tune" its software engineering process to remove the "vital few" causes of defects that have the greatest impact on software development.[3]

At the technical level (in the trenches), software metrics, when they are applied to the product, provide immediate benefits. As the software design is completed, most developers would be anxious to obtain answers to the questions such as:

- Which user requirements are most likely to change?
- Which modules in this system are most errorprone?
- How much testing should be planned for each module?
- How many errors (of specific types) can I expect when testing commences?

Answers to these questions can be determined if metrics have been collected and used as a technical guide. In later chapters we will examine how this is done.

2.6.2 Establishing a Baseline

By establishing a metrics baseline, benefits can be obtained at the strategic, project, and technical level. Yet the information that is collected need not be

---

[3]These ideas have been formalized into an approach called *statistical software quality assurance* and are discussed in detail in Chapter 17.

fundamentally different to satisfy each of the different constituencies discussed above. The manner in which the information is presented will be different, but the metrics themselves can serve many masters.

The baseline consists of data collected from past software development projects and can be as simple as the table presented in Figure 2.2 or as complex as the template illustrated in Figure 2.6. In addition to simple size- or function-oriented measures, the baseline can be supplemented with quality metrics such as the ones described in Section 2.4.2.

To be an effective aid in strategic planning and/or cost and effort estimation, baseline data must have the following attributes: (1) Data must be reasonably accurate—"guesstimates" about past projects are to be avoided; (2) data should be collected for as many projects as possible; (3) measurements must be consistent, e.g., a line of code must be interpreted consistently across all projects for which data are collected; (4) applications should be similar to work that is to be estimated—it makes little sense to use a baseline for batch information systems work to estimate a real-time microprocessor application.

2.6.3 Metrics Collection, Computation, and Evaluation

The process for establishing a baseline is illustrated in Figure 2.5. Ideally, data needed to establish a baseline has been collected in an on-going manner. Sadly, this is rarely the case. Therefore, *data collection* requires an historical investigation of past projects to reconstruct required data. Once data have been collected (unquestionably the most difficult step), *metrics computation* is possible. Depending on the breadth of data collected, metrics can span a broad range of LOC or FP measures. Finally, computed data must be evaluated and applied in estimation. *Data evaluation* focuses on the underlying reasons for the results obtained. Are the computed averages relevant to the project at hand? What extenuating circumstances invalidate certain data for use in this estimate? These and other questions must be addressed so that metrics data are not used blindly.

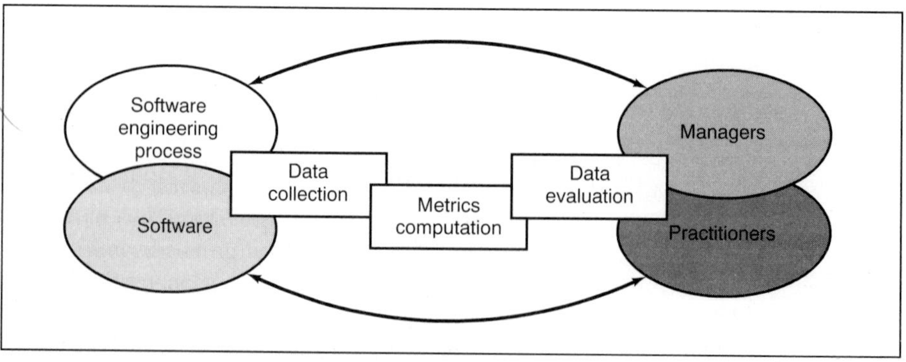

FIGURE 2.5.
Software metrics collection process.

KSLOC

↑

Slip but deep *Thousand Lines of Code*

```
COST DATA INPUT

                                                          Example
DESCRIPTION                              UNITS               Data

labor cost                               $/person-month    $7,744
labor year                               hrs/year            1560

DATA FOR METRICS COMPUTATION

                                                          Example
DESCRIPTION                              UNITS               Data

project name or identifier               alphanumeric      Proj#1
release type (development/maint)         alphanumeric   maintenance
number of project staff                  people               3
effort                                   person-hours      4800
effort, computed                         person-months     36.9
elapsed time to completion               months            13.0
source lines newly developed             KLOC              11.5
source lines modified (existing code)    KLOC               0.4
source lines delivered (includes existing LOC)  KLOC       33.4
source lines reused (from other programs/libraries)  KLOC  0.8
number of separate programs              programs             1
technical documentation                  pages              265
user documentation                       pages              122
number of errors (1st year after release)  errors            26
maintenance effort-modifications (1st year)  person-hours  3550
maintenance effort-errors (1st year)     person-hours      1970

PROJECT DATA
Percentage of total project time spent on:
   problem analysis & specification      %                  18%
   design                                %                  20%
   coding                                %                  23%
   testing                               %                  25%
   other_describe                        %                  14%

FUNCTION-ORIENTED DATA INPUT

DESCRIPTION                              UNITS              DATA

Information Domain
   1. no. user inputs                    inputs              24
   2. no. user outputs                   outputs             46
   3. no. use inquiries                  inquiries            8
   4. no. files                          files                4
   5. no. external interfaces            interfaces           2

Weighting Values
Use first number for simple, second for
average, and last for complex
   1. input weights                      3, 4, 6              4
   2. outputs                            4, 5, 7              4
   3. inquiries                          3, 4, 6              6
   4. files                              7, 10, 15           10
   5. interfaces                         5, 7, 10             5

Processing Complexity Factors
Factors rated from 0 to 5 where:
no influence (0); incidental (1); moderate (2);
average (3); significant (4); essential (5)
   1. backup and recovery required       0,1,2,3,4,5          4
   2. data communication required        0,1,2,3,4,5          1
```

FIGURE 2.6.
Software metrics:
collection,
computation, and
evaluation.

3. distributed processing function	0,1,2,3,4,5	0
4. performance critical	0,1,2,3,4,5	3
5. heavily utilized operating environment	0,1,2,3,4,5	3
6. online data entry	0,1,2,3,4,5	5
7. input transcation with multiple screens	0,1,2,3,4,5	4
8. master files updated online	0,1,2,3,4,5	4
9. input, output, files, inquiries complex	0,1,2,3,4,5	3
10. internal processing complex	0,1,2,3,4,5	3
11. code designed to be reusable	0,1,2,3,4,5	2
12. conv./installation included in design	0,1,2,3,4,5	2
13.system design for multiple installations	0,1,2,3,4,5	4
14. maintainability/ease of use	0,1,2,3,4,5	5

SIZE-ORIENTED METRICS

DESCRIPTION	UNITS	DATA
Productivity and Cost Metrics:		
project name	alphanumeric	Proj #1
output	KLOC/p-m	0.905
cost-all maintained code	$/KLOC	$22,514
cost excluding reused	$/KLOC	$24,028
elapsed time	months/KLOC	1.0
documentation	pages/KLOC	30
documentation	pages/p-m	10
documentation	$/page	$739
Quality Metrics:		
defects	errors/KLOC	2.0
cost of errors	$/error	$376
maint. errors/total maint.	ratio	0.36
maint. mods./total maint.	ratio	0.64
maint. effort/dev.effort	ratio	1.15

Note: Size oriented metrics computed above use "KLOC maintained," that is, source lines newly developed, modified and reused only.

FUNCTION-ORIENTED METRICS

DESCRIPTION	UNITS	DATA
Function-Point Computations		
unadjusted function points		378
total degree of influence		43
complexity adjustment		1.08
function points (FP)		408
Productivity and Cost Metrics FP		
project name	alphanumeric	Proj # 1
output	FP/p-m	11.1
cost	$/FP	$700
elapsed time	FP/month	31.4
documentation	pages/FP	0.9
Functionality		
program size	FP/program	408
function to size	FP/KLOC-maintained	32
Quality Metrics		
defects	errors/FP	0.064
maint. effort-errors	person-days/FP	0.817
maint. effort-mods.	person-days/FP	1.472

FIGURE 2.6. (continued)

Figures 2.6 presents a spreadsheet model for collection and computation of historical software baseline data. Note that the model includes cost data, size-oriented data, and function-oriented data, enabling computation of both LOC- and FP-oriented metrics. It should be noted that it is not always possible to collect all data requested in this model. If we apply such a model to a number of past projects, a software metrics baseline will have been established.

2.7 SUMMARY

Software project management represents the first layer of the software engineering process. Project management is comprised of activities that include measurement, estimation, risk analysis, scheduling, tracking, and control.

Measurement enables managers and practitioners to better understand the software engineering process and the product (software) that it produces. Using direct and indirect measures, metrics for productivity and quality can be defined.

Both size- and function-oriented metrics are used throughout the industry. Size-oriented metrics make use of the line of code as a normalizing factor for other measures such as person-months or defects. The function point is derived from measures of the information domain and a subjective assessment of problem complexity.

Software quality metrics, like productivity metrics, focus on both the process and the product. By developing and analyzing a metrics baseline for quality, an organization can act to correct those areas of the software engineering process that are the cause of software defects. In this chapter, four quality metrics—correctness, maintainability, integrity, and usability—are discussed. Additional quality metrics are described later in this book.

Measurement results in cultural change. Data collection, metrics computation, and data evaluation are the three steps that must be implemented to begin a metrics program. By creating a metrics baseline—a database containing process and product measurements—software engineers and their managers can gain better insight into the work that they do and the product that they produce.

REFERENCES

[ALB79] Albrecht, A. J., "Measuring Application Development Productivity," *Proc. IBM Applic. Dev. Symposium*, Monterey, CA, October 1979, pp. 83–92.

[ALB83] Albrecht, A. J., and J. E. Gaffney, "Software Function, Source Lines of Code and Development Effort Prediction: A Software Science Validation," *IEEE Trans. Software Engineering*, Vol. SE-9, no. 6 November 1983, pp. 639–648.

[ART85] Arthur, L. J., *Measuring Programmer Productivity and Software Quality,* Wiley-Interscience, 1985.

[BAS78] Basili, V., and M. Zelkowitz, "Analyzing Medium Scale Software Development," *Proc. 3rd Intl. Conf. Software Engineering,* IEEE, 1978, pp. 116–123.

[GIL88] Gilb, T., *Principles of Software Project Management,* Addison-Wesley, 1988.

[GRA87] Grady, R. B., and D. L. Caswell, *Software Metrics: Establishing a Company-Wide Program,* Prentice-Hall, 1987.

[JON86a] Jones, C., *Programming Productivity,* McGraw-Hill, 1986.

[JON86b] Jones, C., *A Short History of Function Points and Feature Points,* Software Productivity Research, Inc., Burlington, MA, June 1986.

[JON92] Jones, C., *Measuring Software Productivity and Quality* (to be published).

[MCC78] McCall, J. A., and J. P. Cavano, "A Framework for the Measurement of Software Quality," *ACM Software Quality Assurance Workshop,* November 1978.

[PAG85] Page-Jones, M., *Practical Project Management,* Dorset House, 1985.

[TAJ81] Tajima, D., and T. Matsubara, "The Computer Software Industry in Japan," *Computer,* vol. 14, no. 5, May 1981, p. 96.

[WAL77] Walston, C., and C. Felix, "A Method for Programming Measurement and Estimation," *IBM Systems Journal,* vol. 16, no. 1, 1977, pp. 54–73.

PROBLEMS AND POINTS TO PONDER

2.1 Assume that you are the project manager for a company that builds software for consumer products. You have been contracted to build the software for a sophisticated home security system. Using the information discussed in Section 2.1, develop a detailed outline (be as specific as possible) of the steps that you would perform to manage this project. Assume that you have yet to meet with your customer. What software engineering paradigm would you choose?

2.2 Suggest three direct and three indirect productivity and quality metrics for software documentation.

2.3 Present an argument against lines of code as a measure for software productivity. Will your case hold up when dozens or hundreds of projects are considered?

2.4 Compute the function point value for a project with the following information domain characteristics:

Number of user inputs: 32
Number of user outputs: 60
Number of user inquiries: 24
Number of files: 8
Number of external interfaces: 2

Assume that all complexity adjustment values are average. Assume that 14 algorithms have been counted. Compute the feature point value under the same conditions.

2.5 McCall and Cavano [MCC78] (see Section 2.4.1) define a "framework" for software quality. Using information contained in this and other books, expand each of the three major "points of view" into a set of quality factors and metrics.

2.6 Develop your own metrics (do not use those presented in this chapter) for correctness, maintainability, integrity, and usability. Be sure that they can be translated into quantitative values.

2.7 Write a paragraph that describes your view of "user-friendliness."

2.8 Is it possible for spoilage to increase while at the same time defects/KLOC decrease? Explain.

2.9 Does the LOC measure make any sense when fourth-generation languages are used? Explain.

2.10 The Walston and Felix study [WAL77] is only one of a number of sources for software productivity data. Write a paper outlining the results of other studies (see Further Readings). Is there commonality among the results?

2.11 Collect software productivity data for two to five projects on which you have worked. Basic information should include cost (if applicable), LOC, effort (person-months), a complexity indicator (scale 1 to 10), and chronological time to completion. Combine your data with information from other students/colleagues. Do the data correlate well?

2.12 Put together a presentation that could be used to convince management that measurement would be a worthwhile activity. Be sure to use a quantitative argument. Present it to your class.

FURTHER READINGS

Dozens of books and hundreds of technical papers have been written about software project management. Books by Gilb [GIL88] and Simpson (*New Techniques in Software Project Management,* Wiley, 1987) and a tutorial by Reifer (*Software Management,* 3d ed., IEEE Computer Society Press, 1986) are worth examining. A relatively recent paper by Boehm and Ross (*IEEE Trans. Software Engineering,* July 1989) presents an intriguing "theory" of software project management whose underlying philosophy is to "make everyone [developers, users, customers, maintainers, managers] a winner."

Software metrics can be used not only to "tune" an existing software development process, but also to assist an organization in implementing new software engineering practices. Bouldin (*Agents of Change,* Yourdon Press, 1989), Humphrey (*Managing the Software Process,* Addison-Wesley, 1989), and Pressman (*Making Software Engineering Happen,* Prentice-Hall, 1988) have written books that discuss the use of software metrics as a catalyst for change.

A quasi-expert system for software project planning is described by Capers Jones [JON86]. Jones' automated tool, CHECKPOINT [JON92], may be used for metrics evaluation as well as project estimation. Books on productivity by Arthur (*Programmer Productivity,* Wiley, 1983) and Parikh (*Programmer Productivity,* Reston, 1984) treat aspects of this broad subject. Schulmeyer and McManus (*Handbook of Software Quality Assurance,* Van Nostrand Reinhold, 1987) present useful information on quality metrics and the statistical methods that result in an improved process.

A major source for software productivity data is a large database maintained by the Rome Air Development Center (RADC) at Griffiss Air Force Base in New York. Data from hundreds of software development projects have been entered in the database. Software metrics data have also been collected by the Software Engineering Institute at Carnegie Mellon University and the Software Productivity Consortium, an industry-sponsored software engineering think tank located in Herndon, Virginia.

Software metrics has become a popular research topic and many papers appearing in major technical publications focus on the subject. A special issue of *IEEE Software* (March 1990) is dedicated to software metrics and contains seven worthwhile papers on both management and technical measurement. Gorla et al. ("Debugging Effort Estimation using Software Metrics," *IEEE Trans. Software Engineering,* February 1990) present one of the first quantitative evaluations of this important debugging effort. Dreger (*Function Point Analysis,* Prentice-Hall, 1989) presents a thorough treatment of the function point metric.

CHAPTER 3

PROJECT MANAGEMENT: ESTIMATION

The software project management process begins with a set of activities that are collectively called *project planning*. The first of these activities is *estimation*. Whenever estimates are made, we look into the future and accept some degree of uncertainty as a matter of course. To quote Frederick Brooks [BRO75, p. 14]:

> . . . our techniques of estimating are poorly developed. More seriously, they reflect an unvoiced assumption that is quite untrue, i.e., that all will go well. . . . because we are uncertain of our estimates, software managers often lack the courteous stubbornness to make people wait for a good product.

Although estimating is as much art as it is science, this important activity need not be conducted in a haphazard manner. Useful techniques for time and effort estimation do exist. And because estimation lays a foundation for all other project planning activities, and project planning provides the road map for successful software engineering, we would be ill-advised to embark without it.

3.1 OBSERVATIONS ON ESTIMATING

A leading executive was once asked what single characteristic was most important in a project manager. His response: ". . . a person with the ability to know what will go wrong before it actually does. . . ." We might add: ". . . and the courage to estimate when the future is cloudy. . . ."

Estimation of resources, cost, and schedule for a software development effort requires experience, access to good historical information, and the courage to commit to quantitative measures when qualitative data are all that exist. Estimation carries inherent risk[1] and factors that increase risk are illustrated in Figure 3.1. The axes shown in the figure represent characteristics of the project to be estimated.

[1]Systematic techniques for risk analysis are presented in Chapter 4.

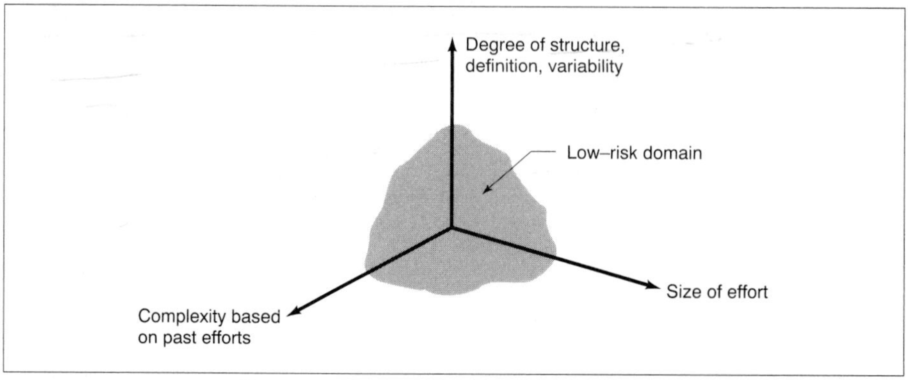

FIGURE 3.1.
Estimation and risk.

Project complexity has a strong effect on uncertainty that is inherent in planning. Complexity, however, is a relative measure that is affected by familiarity with past effort. A real-time application might be perceived as "exceedingly complex" to a software group that has previously developed only batch applications. The same real-time application might be perceived as "run-of-the-mill" for a software group that has been heavily involved in high-speed process control. A number of quantitative software complexity measures have been proposed (e.g., [MCC76]). Such measures are applied at the design or code level and are therefore difficult to use during software planning (before a design and code exist). However, other, more subjective assessments of complexity (e.g., the function-point complexity adjustment factors described in Chapter 2) can be established early in the planning process.

Project size is another important factor that can affect the accuracy and efficacy of estimates. As size increases, the interdependency among various elements of the software grows rapidly. Problem decomposition, an important approach to estimating, becomes more difficult because decomposed elements may still be formidable. To paraphrase Murphy's law: "What can go wrong will go wrong"—and if there are more things that can fail, more things will fail.

The degree of *project structure* also has an effect on estimation risk. In this context, structure refers to the ease with which functions can be compartmentalized and the hierarchical nature of information that must be processed. Figure 3.1 uses the reciprocal measure of structure, i.e., as the degree of structure increases, the ability to accurately estimate is improved and risk decreases.

The availability of historical information also determines estimation risk. Santayana once said, "Those who cannot remember the past are condemned to repeat it." By looking back, we can emulate things that worked and improve areas where problems arose. When comprehensive software metrics (Chapter 2) are available for past projects, estimates can be made with greater assurance; schedules can be established to avoid past difficulties, and overall risk is reduced.

Risk is measured by the degree of uncertainty in the quantitative estimates established for resources, cost, and schedule. If project scope is poorly understood or project requirements are subject to change, uncertainty and risk become dangerously high. The software planner should demand completeness of function, performance, and interface definitions (contained in a *System Specification*). The planner and, more importantly, the customer should recognize that variability in software requirements means instability in cost and schedule.

As a final observation on estimating, we consider the words of Aristotle (330 B.C.):

> . . . it is the mark of an instructed mind to rest satisfied with the degree of precision which the nature of a subject admits, and not to seek exactness when only an approximation of the truth is possible. . . .

3.2 PROJECT PLANNING OBJECTIVES

The software project manager is confronted with a dilemma at the very beginning of a development effort. Quantitative estimates are required but solid information is unavailable. A detailed analysis of software requirements would provide necessary information for estimates, but analysis often takes weeks or months to complete. Estimates are needed "now!"

The objective of software project planning is to provide a framework that enables the manager to make reasonable estimates of resources, cost, and schedule. These estimates are made within a limited time frame at the beginning of a software project and should be updated regularly as the project progresses.

As noted above, the planning objective is achieved through a process of information discovery that leads to reasonable estimates. In the following sections, each of the activities associated with software project planning is discussed.

3.3 SOFTWARE SCOPE

The first activity in software project planning is the determination of *software scope*. Function and performance allocated to software during computer system engineering (Chapter 5) should be assessed to establish a project scope that is unambiguous and understandable at management and technical levels. A statement of software scope must be *bounded*. That is, quantitative data (e.g., number of simultaneous users, size of mailing list, maximum allowable response time) are stated explicitly, constraints and/or limitations (e.g., product cost that restricts memory size) are noted, and mitigating factors (e.g., desired algorithms that are well understood and available in Ada) are described.

Software scope describes function, performance, constraints, interfaces, and reliability. *Functions* described in the statement of scope are evaluated and in some cases refined to provide more detail prior to the beginning of estimation. Because both cost and schedule estimates are functionally oriented, some degree of decomposition is often useful. *Performance* considerations encompass processing and response time requirements. *Constraints* identify limits placed on the software by external hardware, available memory, or other existing systems.

As an example of function, performance, and constraints, consider software that must be developed to drive a conveyor line sorting system (CLSS). The statement of scope for CLSS follows:

> The conveyor line sorting system (CLSS) sorts boxes moving along a conveyor line. Each box will be identified by a bar code that contains a part number and is sorted into one of six bins at the end of the line. The boxes will pass by a sorting station that contains a bar code reader and a PC. The sorting station PC is connected to a shunting mechanism that sorts the boxes into the bins. Boxes pass in random order and are evenly spaced. The line is moving at five feet per minute. CLSS is depicted schematically in Figure 3.2.
>
> CLSS software will receive input information from a bar code reader at time intervals that conform to the conveyor line speed. Bar code data will be decoded into box identification format. The software will do a look-up in a part number database containing a maximum of 1000 entries to determine proper bin location for the box currently at the reader (sorting station). The proper bin location will be passed to a sorting shunt that will position boxes in the appropriate bin. A list will be used to keep track of shunt positions for each box as it moves past the sorting station. CLSS software will also receive input from a pulse tachometer that will be used to synchronize the control signal to the

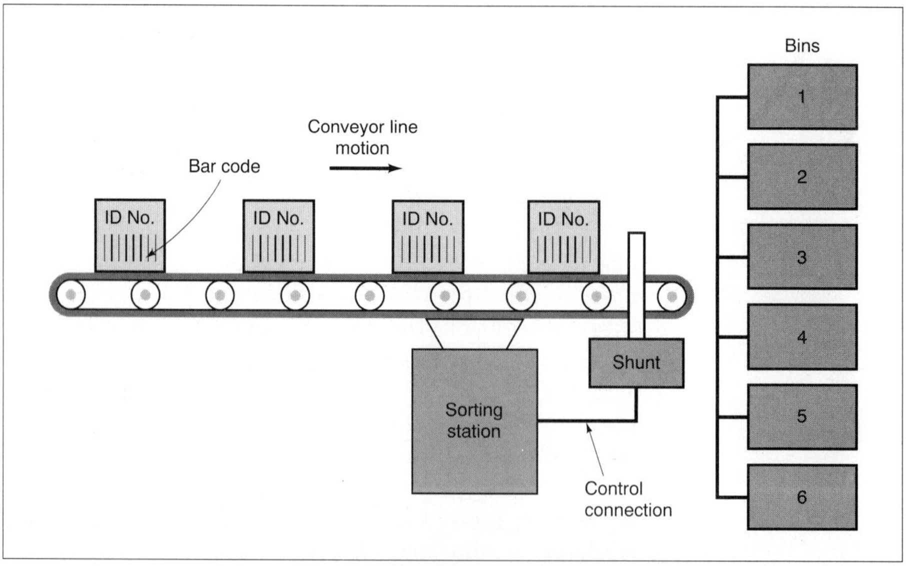

FIGURE 3.2. Example: a conveyor line sorting system.

> shunting mechanism. Based on the number of pulses that will be generated between the sorting station and the shunt, the software will produce a control signal to the shunt to properly position the box....

The project planner examines the statement of scope and extracts all important software functions. This process, called *decomposition*, is discussed later in this chapter and results in the following[2]:

- Read bar code input
- Read pulse tachometer
- Decode part code data
- Do database lookup
- Determine bin location
- Produce control signal for shunt

In this case, performance is dictated by conveyor line speed. Processing for each box must be completed before the next box arrives at the bar code reader. The CLSS software is constrained by the hardware it must access [the bar code reader, the shunt, the personal computer (PC)], the available memory, and the overall conveyor line configuration (evenly spaced boxes).

Function, performance, and constraints must be evaluated together. The same function can precipitate an order-of-magnitude difference in development effort when considered in the context of different performance bounds. The effort and cost required to develop CLSS software would be dramatically different if the function remained the same (i.e., the conveyor line still put boxes into bins) but performance varied. For instance, if conveyor line average speed increased by a factor of 10 (performance) and boxes were no long spaced evenly (a constraint), software would become considerably more complex—thereby requiring more developmental effort. Function, performance, and constraints are intimately connected.

Software interacts with other elements of a computer-based system. The planner considers the nature and complexity of each interface to determine any effect on development resources, cost, and schedule. The concept of an interface is interpreted to mean: (1) hardware (e.g., processor, peripherals) that executes the software and devices (e.g., machines, displays) that are indirectly controlled by the software; (2) software that already exists (e.g., database access routines, subroutine packages, operating system) and must be linked to the new software; (3) people that make use of the software via terminals or other input/output (I/O) devices; (4) procedures that precede or succeed the software as a sequential series of operations. In each case the information transfer across the interface must be clearly understood.

---

[2]In reality, the functional decomposition is performed during system engineering (Chapter 5). The planner uses information derived from the *System Specification* to define software functions.

The least precise aspect of software scope is the discussion of reliability. Software reliability measures do exist (see Chapter 17) but they are rarely used at this stage of a project. Classic hardware reliability characteristics such as mean time between failure (MTBF) are difficult to translate to the software domain. However, the general nature of the software may dictate special considerations to insure its reliability. For example, software for an air traffic control system or the Space Shuttle (both human-rated systems) must not fail or human life may be lost. An inventory control system or word processor software should not fail, but the impact of failure is considerably less dramatic. Although it may not be possible to quantify software reliability as precisely as we would like in the statement of scope, we can use the nature of the project to aid in formulating estimates of effort and cost to ensure reliability.

If a *System Specification* (see Chapter 5) has been properly developed, nearly all the information required for a description of software scope is available and documented before software project planning begins. In cases where a specification has not been developed, the planner must take on the role of system analyst to determine attributes and bounds that will influence estimation tasks.

3.4 RESOURCES

The second task of software planning is the estimation of resources required to accomplish the software development effort. Figure 3.3 illustrates development resources as a pyramid. At the foundation, tools—hardware and software—must exist to support the development effort. At a higher level, the primary resource—people—is always required. Each resource is specified with four characteristics: description of the resource, a statement of availability, chronological time that the resource will be required, duration of time that the resource will be applied. The last two characteristics can be viewed as a *time window*. Availability of the resource for a specified window must be established at the earliest practical time.

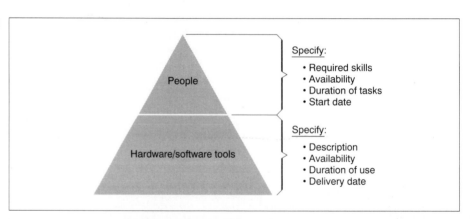

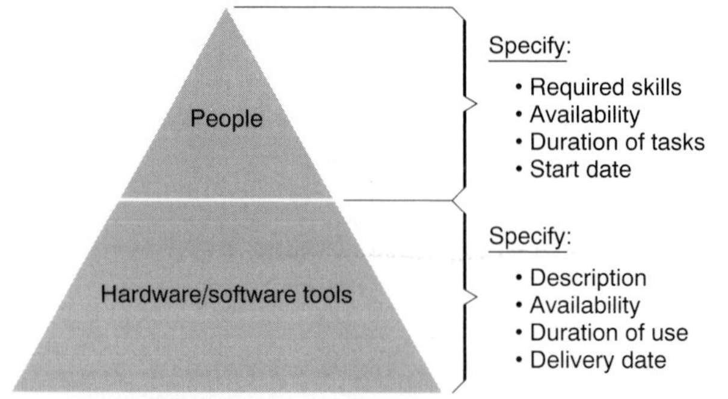

FIGURE 3.3. Resources.

3.4.1 Human Resources

The planner begins by evaluating scope and selecting the skills required to complete development. Both organizational position (e.g., manager, senior software engineer, etc.) and specialty (e.g., telecommunications, database, microprocessor) are specified. For relatively small projects (1 person-year or less) a single individual may perform all software engineering steps, consulting with specialists as required.

The number of people required for a software project can be determined only after an estimate of development effort (e.g., person-months or person-years) is made. Techniques for estimating effort are discussed in Sections 3.6, 3.7, and 3.8.

3.4.2 Hardware Resources

Earlier in this book, we referred to hardware as computing potential. Within the resource context, hardware is also a tool for software development.

Three hardware categories should be considered during software project planning: the development system, the target machine, and other hardware elements of the new system. The *development system* (also called the *host system)* is a computer and related peripherals that will be used during the software development. For example, a 32-bit computer may serve as the development system for a 16-bit microprocessor—the *target machine*—on which the software will eventually be executed. The development system is used because it can support multiple users,[3] maintain large volumes of information that can be shared by software development team members, and support a rich assortment of software tools (to be discussed in the next section). Because most development organizations have multiple constituencies that require development system access, the planner must carefully prescribe the time window required and verify that the resource will be available.

Other hardware elements of the computer-based system may be specified as resources for software development. For example, software for a numerical control (NC) used on a class of machines tools may require a specific machine tool (e.g., an NC lathe) as part of the validation test step; a software project for automated typesetting may need a photo-typesetter at some point during development. Each hardware element must be specified by the planner.

3.4.3 Software Resources

Just as we use hardware as a tool to build new hardware, we use software to aid in the development of new software. The earliest application of software

[3]Networked engineering workstations are often used as a development system, even though each workstation supports only a single developer.

in software development was bootstrapping. A primitive assembly language translator was written in machine language and used to develop a more sophisticated assembler. Building on the capabilities of the previous version, software developers eventually bootstrapped high-level language compilers and other tools.

Today, software engineers use a tool set that is analogous in many ways to the computer-aided design and computer-aided engineering (CAD/CAE) tools used by hardware engineers. The tool set, called *computer-aided software engineering* (CASE), is depicted in Figure 3.4. Part 5 of this book is dedicated to CASE technologies, and a complete description of the technology is reserved until later chapters. For now, a brief overview of the primary tool categories is presented.

Business Systems Planning Tools By modeling the strategic information requirements of an organization, business systems planning tools provide a "meta-model" from which specific information systems are derived. These tools answer simple but important questions: Where do business-critical data originate? Where does such information go? How is it used? How is it transformed as it moves through the business? What new information is added? Business systems planning tools help software developers to create information systems that route data to those that need the information and that resist burying staff members with information that is extraneous. In the final analysis, the transfer of data is improved and decision making is expedited.

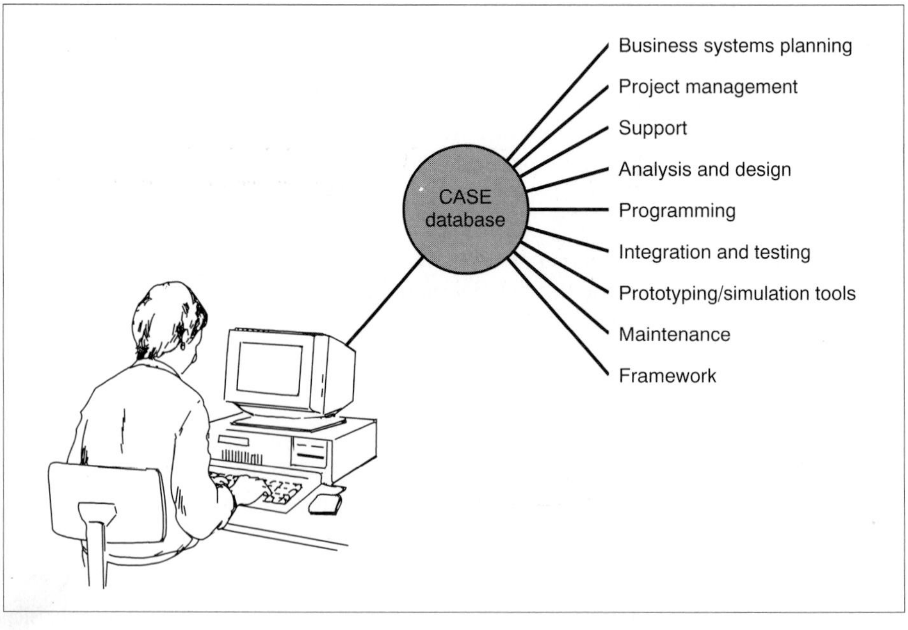

FIGURE 3.4. Computer-aided software engineering.

Project Management Tools Using these management tools, a project manager can generate useful estimates of effort, cost, and duration of a software project; define a work breakdown structure (WBS); plan a workable project schedule; and track projects on a continuing basis. In addition, the manager can use tools to collect metrics that will establish a baseline for software development productivity and product quality.

Support Tools The support tools category encompasses document production tools, network system software, databases, electronic mail, bulletin boards, and *configuration management* tools (Chapter 21) that are used to control and manage the information that is created as software is developed.

Analysis and Design Tools Analysis and design tools enable a software engineer to create a model of the system to be built. These tools assist in the creation of the model and also in an evaluation of the model's quality. By performing consistency and validity checking on each model, analysis and design tools provide a software engineer with insight and help to eliminate errors before they propagate into the program.

Programming Tools System software utilities, editors, compilers, and debuggers are a legitimate part of CASE. But in addition to these tools, new and more powerful programming tools can be added. Object-oriented programming tools, fourth-generation programming languages, advanced database query systems, and a wide array of PC tools (e.g., spreadsheets) all fall into this CASE tool category.

Integration and Testing Tools Testing tools provide a variety of different levels of support for the software testing steps that are applied as part of the software engineering process. Some tools, such as path coverage analyzers, provide direct support for the design of test cases and are used during early stages of testing. Other tools, such as automatic regression testing and test data generation tools, are used during integration and validation testing and can help reduce the amount of effort applied to the testing process.

Prototyping and Simulation Tools Prototyping and simulation tools span a large tool set that ranges in sophistication from simple screen painters to simulation products for timing and sizing analysis of real-time embedded systems. At their most fundamental, prototyping tools focus on the creation of screens and reports that will enable a user to understand the input and output domain of an information system or engineering application. At their most sophisticated, simulation tools are used to create system models for embedded real-time applications (e.g., modeling a process control system for a refinery or the avionics system for an aircraft). The models created by a simulation tool can then be analyzed, and in some cases executed, so that the run-time performance of a proposed system can be evaluated *before* the system is built.

Maintenance Tools Maintenance tools can help to decompose an existing program and provide the engineer with insight; however, the engineer must apply intuition, design sense, and human intelligence to complete the reverse engineering process and/or to re-engineer the application. This human component is an integral part of reverse engineering and re-engineering tools and is unlikely to be replaced by full automation in the foreseeable future.

Framework Tools These tools provide a framework from which an integrated project support environment (IPSE)[4] can be created. In most cases, framework tools actually provide database management and configuration management capabilities along with utilities that enable tools from different vendors to be integrated into the IPSE.

3.4.4 Reusability

Any discussion of the software resource would be incomplete without recognition of *reusability*—that is, the creation and reuse of software building blocks [FRE87, TRA88]. Such building blocks must be catalogued for easy reference, standardized for easy application, and validated for easy integration.

Most industry observers agree that improved product quality and software development productivity will bring an end to the "affiction" that sometimes besets software. In such a world, reusable software would abound. Software building blocks would be available to allow construction of large programs with minimum "from scratch" development. Unfortunately, we have not as yet achieved this ideal. Libraries of reusable software do exist for commercial applications, systems and real-time work, and engineering and scientific problems. However, few systematic techniques exist for making additions to a library, standard interfaces for reusable software are difficult to enforce, quality and maintainability issues remain unresolved, and lastly, the developer is often unaware that appropriate software building blocks even exist!

Two "rules" should be considered by the software planner when reusable software is specified as a resource:

1. If existing software meets requirements, acquire it. The cost for acquisition of existing software will almost always be less than the cost to develop equivalent software.
2. If existing software requires "some modification" before it can be properly integrated with the system, proceed carefully. The cost to modify existing software can sometimes be greater than the cost to develop equivalent software.

---

[4]Chapter 23 is dedicated to integrated CASE (I-CASE) environments.

Ironically, software resources are often neglected during planning, only to become a paramount concern during the development phase of the software engineering process. It is far better to specify software resource requirements early. In this way technical evaluation of alternatives can be conducted and timely acquisition can occur.

3.5 SOFTWARE PROJECT ESTIMATION

In the early days of computing, software costs comprised a small percentage of overall computer-based system cost. An order-of-magnitude error in estimates of software cost had relatively little impact. Today, software is the most expensive element in many computer-based systems. Large cost estimation errors can make the difference between profit and loss. Cost overruns can be disastrous for the developer.

Software cost and effort estimation will never be an exact science. Too many variables—human, technical, environmental, political—can affect the ultimate cost of software and effort applied to develop it. However, software project estimation can be transformed from a black art to a series of systematic steps that provide estimates with acceptable risk.

To achieve reliable cost and effort estimates, a number of options arise:

1. Delay estimation until late in the project (obviously, we can achieve 100 percent accurate estimates after the project is complete!).
2. Use relatively simple decomposition techniques to generate project cost and effort estimates.
3. Develop an empirical model for software cost and effort.
4. Acquire one or more automated estimation tools.

Unfortunately, the first option, however attractive, is not practical. Cost estimates must be provided "up front." However, we should recognize that the longer we wait, the more we know, and the more we know, the less likely we are to make serious errors in our estimates.

The remaining three options are viable approaches to software project estimation. Ideally, the techniques noted for each option should be applied in tandem, each used as a cross-check for the others. *Decomposition techniques* take a "divide and conquer" approach to software project estimation. By decomposing a project into major functions and related software engineering tasks, cost and effort estimation can be performed in a stepwise fashion. *Empirical estimation models* can be used to complement decomposition techniques and offer a potentially valuable estimation approach in their own right. A model is based on experience (historical data) and takes the form:

$$d = f(v_i)$$

where d is one of a number of estimated values (e.g., effort, cost, project duration) and v_i are selected independent parameters (e.g., estimated LOC or

FP). *Automated estimation tools* implement one or more decomposition techniques or empirical models. When combined with an interactive human-machine interface, automated tools provide an attractive option for estimating. In such systems, the characteristics of the development organization (e.g., experience, environment) and the software to be developed are described. Cost and effort estimates are derived from these data.

Each of the viable software cost estimation options is only as good as the historical data used to seed the estimate. If no historical data exist, costing rests on a very shaky foundation. In Chapter 2, we examined the characteristics of software productivity data and how they can be used as an historical bases for estimation.

3.6 DECOMPOSITION TECHNIQUES

Humans have developed a natural approach to problem solving: If the problem to be solved is too complicated, we tend to subdivide it until manageable problems are encountered. We then solve each of the latter individually and hope that their solutions can be combined to form a whole.

Software project estimation is a form of problem solving, and in most cases, the problem to be solved (i.e., developing a cost and effort estimate for a software project) is too complex to be considered in one piece. For this reason, we decompose the problem, recharacterizing it as a set of smaller (and, hopefully, more manageable) problems.

3.6.1 LOC and FP Estimation

In Chapter 2, lines of code and function points were described as basic data from which productivity metrics can be computed. LOC and FP data are used in two ways during software project estimation: (1) as *estimation variables* that are used to "size" each element of the software, and (2) as *baseline metrics* collected from past projects and used in conjunction with estimation variables to develop cost and effort projections.

LOC and FP estimation are distinct estimation techniques. Yet both have a number of characteristics in common. The project planner begins with a bounded statement of software scope and from this statement attempts to decompose software into small subfunctions that can each be estimated individually. LOC or FP (the estimation variable) is then estimated for each subfunction. Baseline productivity metrics (e.g., LOC/pm or FP/pm[5]) are then applied to the appropriate estimation variable and cost or effort for the subfunction is derived. Subfunction estimates are combined to produce an overall estimate for the entire project.

[5]Throughout the rest of this book, pm will be used as an acronym for person-month.

The LOC and FP estimation techniques differ in the level of detail required for decomposition. When LOC is used as the estimation variable, functional decomposition is absolutely essential and is often taken to considerable levels of detail. Because the data required to estimate function points are more macroscopic, the level of decomposition used when FP is the estimation variable is considerably less detailed. It should also be noted that LOC is estimated directly, while FP is determined indirectly by estimating the number of inputs, outputs, data files, inquiries, and external interfaces, as well as the 14 *complexity adjustment values* described in Section 2.3.2.

Regardless of the estimation variable that is used, the project planner typically provides a range of values for each decomposed function. Using historical data or (when all else fails) intuition, the planner estimates an optimistic, most likely, and pessimistic LOC or FP value for each function. An implicit indication of the degree of uncertainty is provided when a range of values is specified.

The *expected value* for LOC or FP is then computed. The expected value for the estimation variable, E, can be computed as a weighted average of the optimistic (a), most likely (m), and pessimistic (b) LOC or FP estimates. For example,

$$E = \frac{a + 4m + b}{6}$$

gives heaviest credence to the most likely estimate and follows a beta probability distribution.

We assume that there is a very small probability that the actual LOC or FP result will fall outside the optimistic or pessimistic values. Using standard statistical techniques, we can compute the deviation of the estimates. However, it should be noted that a deviation based on uncertain (estimated) data must be used judiciously.

Once the expected value for the estimation variable has been determined, LOC or FP productivity data are applied. At this stage, the planner can apply one of two different approaches:

1. The total estimation variable value for all subfunctions can be multiplied by the average productivity metric corresponding to that estimation variable. For example, if we assume that 310 FP are estimated in total and that average FP productivity based on past projects is 5.5 FP/pm, then the overall effort for the project is:

$$\text{Effort} = \frac{310}{5.5} = 56 \text{ person-months}$$

2. The estimation variable value for each subfunction can be multiplied by an *adjusted productivity value* that is based on the perceived level of complexity of the subfunction. For functions of average complexity, the

> average productivity metric is used. However, the average productivity metric is adjusted up or down (somewhat subjectively) based on higher or lower than average complexity for a particular subfunction. For example, if average productivity is 490 LOC/pm, subfunctions that are considerably more complex than average might reflect an estimated productivity of only 300 LOC/pm and simple functions, 650 LOC/pm.

It is important to note that average productivity metrics should be corrected to reflect inflationary effects, increased project complexity, new people, or other development characteristics.

Are the estimates correct? The only reasonable answer to this question is: We can't be sure. Any estimation technique, no matter how sophisticated, must be cross-checked with another approach. Even then, common sense and experience must prevail. Other approaches to estimation are presented in later sections, but first it is worthwhile to consider a brief example.

3.6.2 An Example

As an example of LOC and FP estimation techniques, let us consider a software package to be developed for a computer-aided design (CAD) application. A review of the *System Specification* indicates that the software is to execute on an engineering workstation and must interface with various computer graphics peripherals including a mouse, digitizer, high-resolution color display, and laser printer.

For the purposes of this example, LOC will be used as the estimation variable. It should be noted, however, that FP could also be used and would require estimates of the information domain values discussed in Section 2.3.2.

Using a *System Specification* as a guide, a preliminary statement of software scope can be developed:

> The CAD software will accept two- and three-dimensional geometric data from an engineer. The engineer will interact and control the CAD system through a user interface that will exhibit characteristics of good human-machine interface design. All geometric data and other supporting information will be maintained in a CAD database. Design analysis modules will be developed to produce required output which will be displayed on a variety of graphics devices. The software will be designed to control and interact with peripheral devices that include a mouse, digitizer, laser printer, and plotter.

The above statement of scope is preliminary—it is *not* bounded. Every sentence would have to be expanded to provide concrete detail and quantitative bounding. For example, before estimation can begin the planner must determine what "characteristics of good human-machine interface design" means or what the size and sophistication of the "CAD database" is to be.

For our purposes, we assume that further refinement has occurred and that the following major software functions are identified:

- User interface and control facilities (UICF)
- Two-dimensional geometric analysis (2DGA)
- Three-dimensional geometric analysis (3DGA)
- Database management (DBM)
- Computer graphics display facilities (CGDF)
- Peripheral control (PC)
- Design analysis modules (DAM)

Following the decomposition technique, an estimation table, shown in Figure 3.5, is developed. A range of LOC estimates is developed. Viewing the first three columns of the table, it can be seen that the planner is fairly certain of LOC required for the peripheral control function (only 450 lines of code separate optimistic and pessimistic estimates). On the other hand, the three-dimensional geometric analysis function is a relative unknown, as indicated by the 4000-LOC difference between optimistic and pessimistic values.

Calculations for expected value are performed for each function and placed in the fourth column of the table (Figure 3.6). By summing vertically in the expected value column, an estimate of 33,360 lines of code is established for the CAD system.[6]

[6]It should be noted that the estimation precision implied by the three low-order significant digits (i.e., 360) is not attainable. Rounding off to the nearest 1000 LOC would be far more realistic. Low-order digits are maintained for calculation accuracy only.

Function	Optimistic	Most Likely	Pessimistic	Expected	$/line	Line/month	Cost	Months
User interface control	1800	2400	2650					
2–D geometric analysis	4100	5200	7400					
3–D geometric analysis	4600	6900	8600					
Data structure management	2950	3400	3600					
Computer graphics display	4050	4900	6200					
Peripheral control	2000	2100	2450					
Design analysis	6600	8500	9800					

FIGURE 3.5. Estimation table.

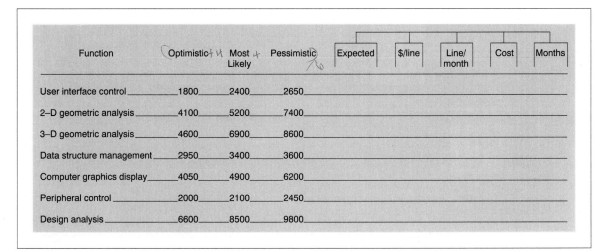

Function	Optimistic	Most Likely	Pessimistic	Expected	$/line	Line/ month	Cost	Months
User interface control	1800	2400	2650	2340				
2–D geometric analysis	4100	5200	7400	5380				
3–D geometric analysis	4600	6900	8600	6800				
Data structure management	2950	3400	3600	3350				
Computer graphics display	4050	4900	6200	4950				
Peripheral control	2000	2100	2450	2140				
Design analysis	6600	8500	9800	8400				
Total				33360				

FIGURE 3.6. Estimation table.

The remainder of the estimation table required for the decomposition technique is shown in Figure 3.7. Productivity metrics (derived from an historical baseline) are acquired for $/LOC and LOC/person-month. In this case the planner uses different values of productivity metrics for each func-

Function	Optimistic	Most likely	Pessimistic	Expected	$/line	Line/ month	Cost	Months
User interface control	1800	2400	2650	2340	14	315	32,760	7.4
2–D geometric analysis	4100	5200	7400	5380	20	220	107,600	24.4
3–D geometric analysis	4600	6900	8600	6800	20	220	136,000	30.9
Data structure management	2950	3400	3600	3350	18	240	60,300	13.9
Computer graphics display	4050	4900	6200	4950	22	200	108,900	24.7
Peripheral control	2000	2100	2450	2140	28	140	59,920	15.2
Design analysis	6600	8500	9800	8400	18	300	151,200	28.0
				33360 (Estimated LOC)			$656,680 (Estimated project cost ($))	144.5 (Estimated effort required (PM))

FIGURE 3.7. Estimation table.

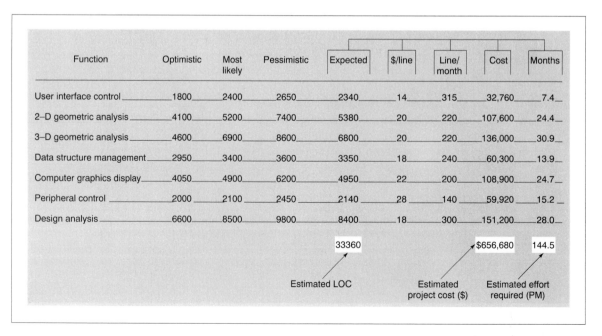

tion based on the degree of complexity. Values contained in the cost and months columns of the table are determined by taking the products of expected LOC and $/LOC and LOC/person-month, respectively.

From the estimation table, the total estimated project cost is $657,000 and the estimated effort is 145 person-months. In Section 3.7, we will see how the estimated effort can be used with an empirical model to derive an estimate for project duration (in chronological months).

3.6.3 Effort Estimation

Effort estimation is the most common technique for costing any engineering development project. A number of person-days, months, or years is applied to the solution of each project task. A dollar cost is associated with each unit of effort and an estimated cost is derived.

Like the LOC or FP technique, effort estimation begins with a delineation of software functions obtained from the project scope. A series of software engineering tasks—requirements analysis, design, code and test—must be performed for each function. Functions and related software engineering tasks may be represented as part of a table illustrated in Figure 3.8.

The planner estimates the effort (e.g., person-months) that will be required to accomplish each software engineering task for each software function. These data comprise the central matrix of the table in Figure 3.8. Labor rates (i.e., cost/unit effort) are applied to each of the software engineering tasks. It is very likely the labor rate will vary for each task. Senior staff are heavily involved in requirements analysis and early design tasks; junior staff (who are inherently less costly) are involved in later design tasks, code, and early testing.

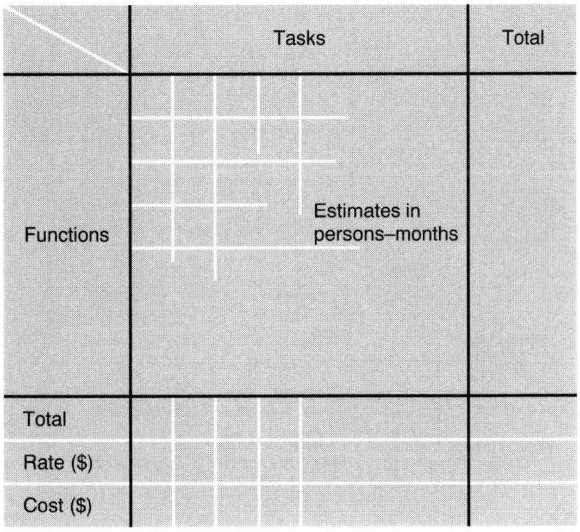

FIGURE 3.8. Developing an effort matrix.

Cost and effort for each function and software engineering task are computed as the last step. If effort estimation is performed independently of LOC or FP estimation, we now have two estimates for cost and effort that may be compared and reconciled. If both sets of estimates show reasonable agreement, there is good reason to believe that the estimates are reliable. If, on the other hand, the results of these decomposition techniques show little agreement, further investigation and analysis must be conducted.

3.6.4 An Example

To illustrate the use of effort estimation, we again consider the CAD software introduced in Section 3.6.2. The system configuration and all software functions remain unchanged and are indicated by project scope.

Referring to the completed effort estimation table shown in Figure 3.9, estimates of effort (in person-months) for each software engineering task are provided for each CAD software function (abbreviated for brevity). Horizontal and vertical totals provide an indication of effort required. It should be noted that 75 person-months are expended on "front-end" development tasks (requirements analysis and design), indicating the relative importance of this work.

Functions \ Tasks	Requirements analysis	Design	Code	Test	Total
UICF	1.0	2.0	0.5	3.5	7
2DGA	2.0	10.0	4.5	9.5	26
3DGA	2.5	12.0	6.0	11.0	31.5
DSM	2.0	6.0	3.0	4.0	15
CGDF	1.5	11.0	4.0	10.5	27
PCF	1.5	6	3.5	5	16
DAM	4	14	5	7	30
Total*	14.5	61	26.5	50.5	152.5 (Estimated effort for all tasks)
Rate ($)	5200	4800	4250	4500	
Cost ($)	75,400	292,800	112,625	227,250	708,075 (Estimated cost for all tasks)

*All estimates are in person–months except where otherwise noted.

FIGURE 3.9. Effort estimation table.

Labor rates are associated with each software engineering task and entered in the Rate($) row of the table. These data reflect "burdened" labor costs, i.e., labor costs that include company overhead. In this example it is assumed that labor costs for requirements analysis ($5200/person-month) will be 22 percent greater than costs for code and unit test.

Total estimated cost and effort for the CAD software are $708,000 and 153 person-months, respectively. Comparing these values to data derived using the lines-of-code technique, a cost variance of 7 percent and effort variance of 5 percent are found. We have achieved extremely close agreement.

What happens when agreement between estimates is poor? The answer to this question requires a re-evaluation of information used to make the estimates. Widely divergent estimates can often be traced to one of two causes:

1. The scope of the project is not adequately understood or has been misinterpreted by the planner.
2. Productivity data used in the lines-of-code technique is inappropriate for the application, obsolete (in that it no longer accurately reflects the software development organization), or has been misapplied.

The planner must determine the cause of divergence and reconcile the estimates.

3.7 EMPIRICAL ESTIMATION MODELS

An *estimation model* for computer software uses empirically derived formulas to predict data that are a required part of the software project planning step. The empirical data that support most models are derived from a limited sample of projects. For this reason, no estimation model is appropriate for all classes of software and in all development environments. Therefore, the results obtained from such models must be used judiciously.

Resource models consist of one or more empirically derived equations that predict effort (in person-months), project duration (in chronological months), or other pertinent project data. Basili [BAS80] describes four classes of resource models: static single-variable models, static multivariable models, dynamic multivariable models, and theoretical models.

The *static single-variable model* takes the form:

$$\text{Resource} = c_1 \times (\text{estimated characteristic})^{c_2}$$

where the resource could be effort, project duration, staff size, or requisite lines of software documentation. The constants c_1 and c_2 are derived from data collected from past projects. The estimated characteristic is lines of source code, effort (if estimated), or other software characteristics. Models taking the form described above can be derived for a local environment if sufficient historic data are available. The basic version of the *Constructive Cost Model*, or COCOMO, presented in Section 3.7.1, is an example of a static single-variable model.

Static multivariable models, like their single-variable counterpart, make use of historical data to derive empirical relationships. A typical model in this category takes the form

$$\text{Resource} = c_{11}e_1 + c_{21}e_2 + \cdots$$

where e_i is the ith software characteristic and c_{i1}, c_{i2} are empirically derived constants for the ith characteristic.

A *dynamic multivariable model* projects resource requirements as a function of time. If the model is derived empirically, resources are defined in a series of time steps that allocate some percentage of effort (or other resource) to each step in the software engineering process. Each step may be further subdivided into tasks. A theoretical approach to dynamic multivariable modeling hypothesizes a continuous "resource expenditure curve" [BAS80] and, from it, derives equations that model the behavior of the resource. The Putnam Estimation Model, a theoretical dynamic multivariable model, is discussed in Section 3.7.2.

Each of the models discussed above addresses macroscopic issues in software project development. The last resource model category examines software from the microscopic viewpoint, that is, the characteristics of the source code (e.g., number of operators and operands). A number of theoretical models are discussed in Chapter 17.

3.7.1 COCOMO

In his book on software engineering economics, Barry Boehm [BOE81] introduces a hierarchy of software estimation models bearing the name COCOMO, for *COnstructive COst MOdel.* Boehm's hierarchy of models takes the following form:

Model 1. Basic COCOMO is a static single-valued model that computes software development effort (and cost) as a function of program size expressed in estimated lines of code.

Model 2. Intermediate COCOMO computes software development effort as a function of program size and a set of "cost drivers" that include subjective assessments of product, hardware, personnel, and project attributes.

Model 3. Advanced COCOMO incorporates all characteristics of the intermediate version with an assessment of the cost driver's impact on each step (analysis, design, etc.) of the software engineering process.

To illustrate COCOMO, we present an overview of the basic and intermediate versions. For a more detailed discussion, the reader is urged to study Boehm [BOE81].

COCOMO may be applied to three classes of software projects. Using Boehm's terminology these are: (1) *organic mode*—relatively small, simple software projects in which small teams with good application experience work to a set of less than rigid requirements (e.g., a thermal analysis program developed for a heat transfer group); (2) *semi-detached mode*—an intermediate (in size and complexity) software project in which teams with mixed experience levels must meet a mix of rigid and less than rigid requirements (e.g., a transaction processing system with fixed requirements for terminal hardware and database software); (3) *embedded mode*—a software project that must be developed within a set of tight hardware, software, and operational constraints (e.g., flight control software for aircraft).

The basic COCOMO equations take the form

$$E = a_b(\text{KLOC})\ \exp(b_b)$$

$$D = c_b(E)\ \exp(d_b)$$

where E is the effort applied in person-months, D is the development time in chronological months, and KLOC is the estimated number of delivered lines of code for the project (express in thousands). The coefficients a_b and c_b and the exponents b_b and d_b are given in Table 3.1.

The basic model is extended to consider a set of "cost driver attributes" [BOE81] that can be grouped into four major categories:

1. Product attributes
   a. Required software reliability
   b. Size of application database
   c. Complexity of the product
2. Hardware attributes
   a. Run-time performance constraints
   b. Memory constraints
   c. Volatility of the virtual machine environment
   d. Required turnaround time

TABLE 3.1

BASIC COCOMO

Software project	a_b	b_b	c_b	d_b
Organic	2.4	1.05	2.5	0.38
Semidetached	3.0	1.12	2.5	0.35
Embedded	3.6	1.20	2.5	0.32

3. Personnel attributes
  a. Analyst capability
  b. Software engineer capability
  c. Applications experience
  d. Virtual machine experience
  e. Programming language experience
4. Project attributes
  a. Use of software tools
  b. Application of software engineering methods
  c. Required development schedule

Each of the 15 attributes is rated on a 6-point scale that ranges from "very low" to "extra high" (in importance or value). Based on the rating, an effort multiplier is determined from tables published by Boehm [BOE81], and the product of all effort multipliers results is an *effort adjustment factor* (EAF). Typical values for EAF range from 0.9 to 1.4.

The intermediate COCOMO equation takes the form:

$$E = a_i(\text{LOC})\ \exp(b_i) \times \text{EAF}$$

where E is the effort applied in person-months and LOC is the estimated number of delivered lines of code for the project. The coefficient a_i and the exponent b_i are given in Table 3.2.

COCOMO represents a comprehensive empirical model for software estimation. However, Boehm's own comments [BOE81, p. 32] about COCOMO (and by extension all models) should be heeded:

> Today, a software cost estimation model is doing well if it can estimate software development costs within 20% of actual costs, 70% of the time, and on its own turf (that is, within the class of projects to which it has been calibrated).... This is not as precise as we might like, but it is accurate enough to provide a good deal of help in software engineering economic analysis and decision making.

To illustrate the use of COCOMO, we apply the basic model to the CAD software example described earlier in this chapter. Using the LOC estimate

TABLE 3.2

INTERMEDIATE COCOMO

Software project	a_i	b_i
Organic	3.2	1.05
Semidetached	3.0	1.12
Embedded	2.8	1.20

developed in Figure 3.7 and the coefficients noted in Table 3.1, we use the semidetached model to get

$$\begin{aligned} E &= 3.0(\text{LOC})\ \exp(1.12) \\ &= 3.0(33.3)^{1.12} \\ &= 152 \text{ person-months} \end{aligned}$$

This value compares quite favorably to the estimates derived in Sections 3.6.2 and 3.6.4. To compute recommended project duration, we use the effort estimate described above:

$$\begin{aligned} D &= 2.5(E)\ \exp(0.35) \\ &= 2.5(152)^{0.35} \\ &= 14.5 \text{ months} \end{aligned}$$

The value for project duration enables the planner to determine a recommended number of people, N, for the project:

$$\begin{aligned} N &= E/D \\ &= 152/14.5 \\ &\sim 11 \text{ people} \end{aligned}$$

In reality, the planner may decide to use only four people and extend the project duration accordingly.

3.7.2 Putnam Estimation Model

The Putnam Estimation Model [PUT78] is a dynamic multivariable model that assumes a specific distribution of effort over the life of a software development project. The model has been derived from labor distributions encountered on large projects (total effort of 30 person-years or more). However, extrapolation to smaller software projects is possible.

The distribution of effort for large software projects can be characterized as shown in Figure 3.10. The curves shown in the figure take on a classic shape that was first described analytically by Lord Rayleigh. Empirical data on system development, collected by Norden [NOR80], have been used to substantiate the curves. Hence, the distribution of effort shown in Figure 3.10 is called the *Rayleigh-Norden curve.*

The Rayleigh-Norden curve may be used to derive [PUT78] a "software equation" that relates the number of delivered lines of code (source statements) to effort and development time:

$$L = C_k K^{1/3} t_d^{4/3}$$

where C_k is a state-of-technology constant and reflects "throughput constraints that impede the progress of the programmer." Typical values might be: C_k = 2000 for a poor software development environment (e.g., no methodology, poor documentation and reviews, a batch execution mode); C_k =

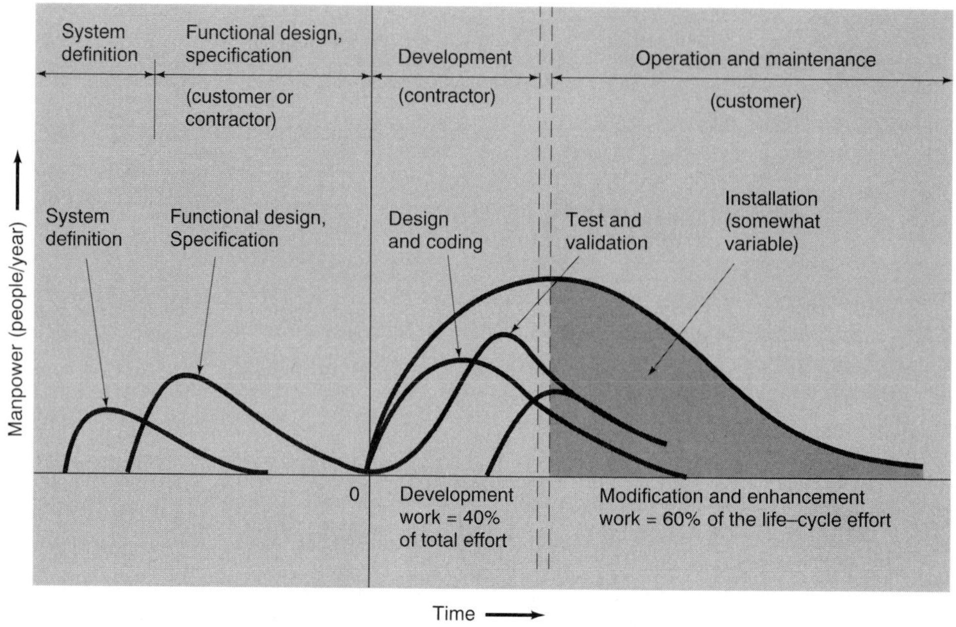

FIGURE 3.10. Effort distribution—large points. *(Source: Software Cost Estimating and Life Cycle Control, IEEE Computer Society Press, 1980, p. 15. Reproduced with permission.)*

8000 for a good software development environment (e.g., methodology in place, adequate documentation/reviews, interactive execution mode); C_k = 11,000 for an 'excellent' environment (e.g., automated tools and techniques). The constant C_k can be derived for local conditions using historical data collected from past development efforts. Rearranging the software equation (above), we can arrive at an expression for development effort K:

$$K = \frac{L^3}{C_k^3 t_d^4}$$

where K is the effort expended (in person-years) over the entire life cycle for software development and maintenance, and t_d is the development time in years. The equation for development effort can be related to development cost by the inclusion of a burdened labor rate factor ($/person-year).

Because of the high-order power relationship exhibited by the software equation, it can be shown [PUT78] that relatively small extensions in delivery date can result in (projected) substantial savings in human effort applied to the project. Stated another way, the relationship between effort applied and chronological time to delivery is highly nonlinear.

3.7.3 Function-Point Models

Both COCOMO and the Putnam model are predicated on estimates of the number of lines of code. A number of researchers (e.g., [ALB83], [LOW90]) have examined estimation models based on the function-point metric for software productivity. However, the number of completed projects that served as a basis for the models preclude their use in a general context.

To date, little detailed information about empirical models for function-point estimation have been published. However, proprietary function-point-oriented estimation models have been developed and are being used by many large software developers, and automated estimation tools (Section 3.8) based on the function-point approach are being offered in the marketplace.

3.8 AUTOMATED ESTIMATION TOOLS

The decomposition techniques and empirical estimation models described in the preceding sections can be implemented in software. These automated estimation tools allow the planner to estimate cost and effort and to perform "what if" analyses for important project variables such as delivery date or staffing. Although many automated estimation tools exist, all exhibit the same general characteristics and all require one or more of the following data categories:

1. A quantitative estimate of project size (e.g., LOC) or functionality (function-point data)
2. Qualitative project characteristics such as complexity, required reliability, or business criticality
3. Some description of the development staff and/or development environment

From these data, the model implemented by the automated estimation tool provides estimates of the effort required to complete the project, costs, staff loading, and, in some cases, development schedule and associated risk. In the paragraphs that follow we examine six representative tools.

BYL (Before You Leap) developed by the Gordon Group, *WICOMO* (Wang Institute Cost Model) developed at the Wang Institute, and *DECPlan* developed by Digital Equipment Corporation are automated estimation tools that are based on COCOMO (described in Section 3.7.1). Each of the tools requires the user to provide preliminary LOC estimates. These estimates are categorized by programming language and type (i.e., adapted code, reused code, new code). The user also specifies values for the cost driver attributes described in Section 3.7.1.

Each of the tools produces estimated elapsed project duration (in months), effort in person-months, average staffing per month, average productivity in LOC/pm, and cost per month. These data can be developed for each phase in the software engineering process individually or for the entire project.

SLIM [PUT80] is an automated costing system that is based on the Rayleigh-Norden curve for the software life cycle and the Putnam Estimation Model (described in Section 3.7.2). SLIM applies the Putnam software model, linear programming, statistical simulation, and program evaluation and review technique, or PERT (a scheduling method) techniques to derive software project estimates. The system enables a software planner to perform the following functions in an interactive session: (1) *calibrate* the local software development environment by interpreting historical data supplied by the planner; (2) create an *information model* of the software to be developed by eliciting basic software characteristics, personal attributes, and environmental considerations; and (3) conduct software *sizing*—the approach used in SLIM is a more sophisticated, automated version of the LOC costing technique described in Section 3.7.2.

Once software size (i.e., LOC for each software function) has been established, SLIM computes size deviation (an indication of estimation uncertainty), a *sensitivity profile* that indicates potential deviation of cost and effort, and a consistency check with data collected for software systems of similar size.

The planner can invoke a linear programming analysis that considers development constraints on both cost and effort. Using the Rayleigh-Norden curve as a model, SLIM also provides a month-by-month distribution of effort, and a *consistency check* with data collected for software systems of similar size.

ESTIMACS [RUB83] is a "macro-estimation model" that uses a function-point estimation method enhanced to accommodate a variety of project and personnel factors. The ESTIMACS tool contains a set of models that enable the planner to estimate (1) system development effort, (2) staff and cost, (3) hardware configuration, (4) risk, and (5) the effects of "development portfolio."

The system development effort model combines data about the user, the developer, the project geography (i.e., the proximity of developer and customer), and the number of "major business functions" to be implemented with information domain data (see Section 3.5.3) required for function-point computation. In addition, the overall nature of the proposed system (e.g., on-line, batch, etc.), the application complexity, performance, and reliability are taken into account.

Using data from the system development effort model, ESTIMACS can develop staffing and costs using "a customizable life cycle data base to provide work distribution and deployment information" [RUB83]. The target hardware configuration is sized (i.e., processor power and storage capacity are estimated) using answers to a series of questions that help the planner evaluate transaction volume, windows of application, and other data. The level of risk associated with the successful implementation of the proposed system is determined based on responses to a questionnaire that examines project factors such as size, structure, and technology. Finally, ESTIMACS takes the effects of other concurrent work, called the *development portfolio,* into account.

SPQR/20, developed by Software Productivity Research, Inc., and based on work by Jones [JON86], has the user complete a simple set of multiple-choice questions that address project type (e.g., new program, maintenance), project scope (e.g., prototype, reusable module), goals (e.g., minimum duration, highest quality), project class (e.g., personal program, product), application type (e.g., batch, expert system), novelty (e.g., repeat of a previous application), office facilities (e.g., open office environment, crowded bullpen), program requirements (e.g., clear, hazy), design requirements (e.g., informal design with no automation), user documentation (e.g., informal, formal), response time, staff experience, percent source code reuse, programming language, logical complexity of algorithms, code, and data complexity. Project related cost data (e.g., length of work week, average salary) are also input.

In addition to output data described for other tools, SPQR/20 estimates total pages of project documentation, total defects potential for the project, cumulative defect removal efficiency (see Chapter 17), total defects at delivery, and number of defects per KLOC.

Each of the automated estimating tools conducts a dialog with the planner, obtaining appropriate project and supporting information and producing both tabular and (in some cases) graphical output. All of the tools described above have been implemented on personal computers or engineering workstations.

An interesting comparison of some of the tools described above has been done by Martin [MAR88]. Each of the tools was applied to the same project. Not surprisingly, a relatively large variation in estimated results was encountered. More importantly, the predicted values sometimes were significantly different than actual values. This reinforces the notion that the output of estimation tools should be used as one "data point" from which estimates are derived—not as the only source for an estimate.

3.9 SUMMARY

The software project planner must estimate three things before a project begins: how long it will take, how much effort will be required, and how many people will be involved. In addition, the planner must predict the resources (hardware and software) that will be required and the risk involved.

The statement of scope helps the planner to develop estimates using one or more of the following techniques: decomposition, empirical modeling, and automated tools. Decomposition techniques require a delineation of major software functions, followed by estimates of either the number of LOC or FP, or the number of person-months required to implement each function. Empirical techniques use empirically derived expressions for effort and time to predict these project quantities. Automated tools implement a specific empirical model.

Accurate project estimates generally make use of at least two of the three techniques noted above. By comparing and reconciling estimates derived using different techniques, the planner is more likely to derive an accurate estimate. Software project estimation can never be an exact science, but a combination of good historical data and systematic techniques can improve estimation accuracy.

REFERENCES

[ALB79] Albrecht, A. J., "Measuring Application Development Productivity," *Proc. IBM Applic. Dev. Symposium,* Monterey, CA, October, 1979, pp. 83–92.

[ALB83] Albrecht, A. J., and J. E. Gaffney, "Software Function, Source Lines of Code and Development Effort Prediction: A Software Science Validation," *IEEE Trans. Software Engineering,* vol. SE-9, no. 6, November 1983, pp. 639–648.

[BAS78] Basili, V., and M. Zelkowitz, "Analyzing Medium Scale Software Development," *Proc. 3rd Intl. Conf. Software Engineering,* IEEE, 1978, pp. 116–123.

[BAS80] Basili, V., *Models and Metrics for Software Management and Engineering,* IEEE Computer Society Press, 1980, pp. 4–9.

[BOE81] Boehm, B., *Software Engineering Economics,* Prentice-Hall, 1981.

[BRO75] Brooks, F., *The Mythical Man-Month,* Addison-Wesley, 1975.

[FRE87] Freeman, P., *Tutorial: Software Reusability,* IEEE Computer Society Press, 1987.

[JON86] Jones, C., *Programming Productivity,* McGraw-Hill, 1986.

[LOW90] Low, G.C., and D.R. Jeffrey, "Function Points in Estimation and Evaluation of the Software Process," *IEEE Trans. Software Engineering,* vol. 16, no. 1, January 1990, pp. 64–71.

[MAR88] Martin, R., "Evaluation of Current Software Costing Tools," *ACM Sigsoft Notes,* vol. 13, no. 3, July 1988, pp. 49–51.

[MCC76] McCabe, T., "A Complexity Measure," *IEEE Trans. Software Engineering,* vol. SE-2, no. 6, December 1976, pp. 308–320.

[NOR80] Norden, P., "Useful Tools for Project Management," in *Software Cost Estimating and Life Cycle Control,* IEEE Computer Society Press, 1980, pp. 216–225.

[PUT78] Putnam, L., "A General Empirical Solution to the Macro Software Sizing and Estimating Problem," *IEEE Trans. Software Engineering,* vol. 4, no. 4, 1978, pp. 345–361.

[RUB83] Rubin, H. A., "Macro-estimation of Software Development Parameters: The Estimacs System," *Softfair Proceedings,* IEEE, July, 1983, pp. 109–118.

[TRA88] Tracz, W., *Software Reuse: Emerging Technology,* IEEE Computer Society Press, 1988.

PROBLEMS AND POINTS TO PONDER

3.1 Software project complexity is discussed briefly in Section 3.1. Develop a list of software characteristics (e.g., concurrent operation, graphical output, etc.) that affect the complexity of a program. Prioritize the list.

3.2 Consider a software project on which you have recently worked. Write a bounded description of the software scope and present it for criticism. Can the scope you have established be misinterpreted? Have you bounded the system?

3.3 Performance is an important consideration during planning. Discuss how performance can be interpreted differently depending upon the software application area.

3.4 In Section 3.4, we discuss human, software, and hardware resources. Are there others?

3.5 Using reference [PUT78] as a guide, write a brief paper outlining the derivation of the Putnam's "software equation" discussed in Section 3.6.2.

3.6 How well do the data collected as part of Problem 2.11 fit the Putnam model? The COCOMO model?

3.7 Specify, design, and develop a program that implements COCOMO. Using reference [BOE81] as a guide, extend the program so that it can be used as a planning tool.

3.8 Given a project on which you are currently working or a project description assigned by your instructor, apply the lines-of-code costing technique described in Section 3.6. Develop a complete cost table using derived productivity data or "average data" specified by your instructor (e.g., $18.00/LOC average, 400-LOC/person-month average).

3.9 Using the results obtained in Problem 3.8, indicate potential deviation in cost and end date; assign a probability estimate to these numbers.

3.10 For the project noted in Problem 3.12, apply the effort/task costing technique. Develop a table similar to the one shown in Figure 3.9. Use a burdened rate structure for wages that averages $5000/person-month.

3.11 Use the COCOMO model to recompute the estimate developed in Problem 3.8. How do the results compare to one another?

3.12 Use the Putnam model to compute development effort from the LOC estimates derived in Problem 3.8. How do decomposition, COCOMO, and Putnam compare? Can you suggest reasons for any variation?

3.13 Given a project on which you are currently working or a project description assigned by your instructor, compute function-point information and use the function-point costing technique, described in Section 3.6. Assume $900/FP and 8-FP/person-month average.

3.14 Specify, design, and implement an abbreviated interactive software costing system. The system should incorporate models and techniques described in Sections 3.6 and 3.7.

3.15 It seems odd that cost and schedule estimates are developed during software project planning—before detailed software requirements analysis or design has been conducted. Why do you think this is done? Are there circumstances when it should not be done?

FURTHER READINGS

Putnam's tutorial on software cost estimating [PUT78] and Boehm's book on software engineering economics [BOE81], respectively, describe the SLIM and COCOMO estimation techniques. Boehm's book presents detailed project data and provides excellent quantitative insight into the process of estimation. An excellent book by DeMarco (*Controlling Software Projects,* Yourdon Press, 1982) provides valuable insight into the management, measurement, and estimation of software projects. Londiex (*Cost Estimation for Software Development,* Addison-Wesley, 1987) is dedicated to the subject and provides a number of useful examples. Sneed (*Software Engineering Management,* Wiley, 1989) and Macro (*Software Engineering: Concepts and Management,* Prentice-Hall, 1990) consider software project estimation in considerable detail.

Lines-of-code cost estimation is the most commonly used approach in the industry. However, the impact of the object-oriented paradigm (see Chapters 8, 12, and 16) may invalidate some estimation models. Laranjeira ("Software Size Estimation of Object-Oriented Systems," *IEEE Trans. Software Engineering,* May 1990) explores this issue in considerable detail.

Each of the techniques described in this chapter can help us to derive project duration. In theory, these techniques apply to projects of any size. Ware Myers ("Allow Plenty of Time for Large Scale Software," *IEEE Software,* July 1989) discusses the impact and accuracy of estimation techniques when they are applied to mega-projects (multimillion LOC efforts).

CHAPTER 4

PROJECT MANAGEMENT: PLANNING

Time is the most valuable commodity available to a software engineer. If enough of it is available, a problem can be properly analyzed, a solution can be comprehensively designed, source code can be carefully implemented, and the program can be thoroughly tested. But we never seem to have enough time.

Every software engineer (and every software engineering student) has learned to work under significant time pressure. Part of the pressure comes from arbitrary and sometimes unrealistic deadlines that are established by those who don't have to build the product. But part of the pressure is created by the people who must ultimately endure it. A project is planned and scheduled in a haphazard fashion; risks are considered only after they have blossomed into full-fledged problems; people aren't organized in a way that expedites progress. Sometimes it seems that in our anxiety to get started we don't spend the time to "get our act together." Software project planning forces managers and practitioners to spend the time.

The first step of software project planning—estimation—was introduced in the preceding chapter. Estimation provides the project planner with the information necessary to complete the remaining project planning activities. In this chapter the remaining activities—risk analysis, scheduling, acquisition decision making, re-engineering, and organizational planning—are presented.

4.1 PROJECT PLANNING—REVISITED

Upon gaining an understanding of software's functional requirements, performance characteristics, system constraints, and reliability concerns, the planner applies techniques and tools to derive effort and time estimates. But these estimates provide us with useful information only if they are integrated into a more complete planning framework.

In Chapter 3, a CAD software project was discussed. Using a number of different estimating techniques, we determined that the project would require approximately 150 person-months of effort to complete. Using an empirical model, we estimated that the project duration would span approximately 15 calendar months. Now what? Do we just "get started?" The answer, of course, is *no.*

Before we can get started, we must answer some important questions about risk, develop a strategy for attacking the problem, establish a mechanism for assessing progress, and organize the staff members who have been selected to build the product. Each of these activities is part of project planning, and in the sections that follow each will be considered in some detail.

4.2 RISK ANALYSIS

In his book on risk analysis and management, Robert Charette [CHA89, p. 49] presents the following conceptual definition of risk:

> First, risk concerns future happenings. Today and yesterday are beyond active concern, as we are already reaping what was previously sowed by our past actions. The question is, can we, therefore, by changing our actions today, create an opportunity for a different and hopefully better situation for ourselves tomorrow. This means, second, that risk involves change, such as in changes of mind, opinion, actions, or places.... [Third,] risk involves choice, and the uncertainty that choice itself entails. Thus paradoxically, risk, like death and taxes, is one of the few certainties of life.

When risk is considered in the context of software engineering, Charette's three conceptual underpinnings are always in evidence. The future is our concern—what risks might cause the software project to go awry? Change is our concern—how will changes in customer requirements, development technologies, target computers, and all other entities connected to the project affect timeliness and overall success? Last, we must grapple with choices—what methods and tools should we use, how many people should be involved, how much emphasis on quality is enough?

Risk analysis is actually four distinct activities: risk identification, risk projection, risk assessment, and risk management. Each of these activities are described in the paragraphs that follow.

4.2.1 Risk Identification

Peter Drucker [DRU75] once said, "While it is futile to try to eliminate risk, and questionable to try to minimize it, it is essential that the risks taken be the right risks." Before we can identify the "right risks" to be taken during a software project, it is important to identify all the risks that are obvious to both managers and practitioners.

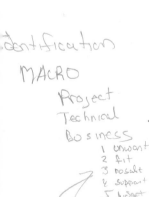

It is possible to categorize risks in many different ways. At a macroscopic level, project risks, technical risks and business risks can be defined.[1] *Project risks* identify potential budgetary, schedule, personnel (staffing and organization), resource, customer, and requirements problems and their impact on the software project. In Chapter 3, project complexity, size, and structure were also defined as risk factors. *Technical risks* identify potential design, implementation, interfacing, verification, and maintenance problems. In addition, specification ambiguity, technical uncertainty, technical obsolescence, and "leading edge" technology are also risk factors. Technical risks occur because a problem is harder to solve than we thought it would be. *Business risks* are insidious because they can unravel the results of even the best software projects. Candidates for the top five business risks are: (1) building an excellent product that no one really wants (market risk); (2) building a product that no longer fits into the overall product strategy for the company; (3) building a product that the sales force doesn't understand how to sell; (4) losing the support of senior management due to a change in focus or a change in people (management risk); (5) losing budgetary or personnel commitment (budget risk). It is extremely important to note that simple categorization won't always work. Some risks are simply impossible to predict in advance.

Risk identification lists the specific project risks within the broad categories outlined above. One of the best methods for understanding each of the risks is to use a set of questions that will help the project planner to understand the risk in project or technical terms. Boehm [BOE89] suggests the use of a "risk item checklist"—a set of questions that are relevant to each risk factor. For example, the planner could attain a feeling for staffing risk by answering the following questions [BOE89]:

- Are the best people available?
- Do the people have the right combination of skills?
- Are enough people available?
- Is the staff committed for the entire duration of the project?

---

[1]It should be noted that many of the factors that comprise these risk categories are similar to the "cost driver attributes" defined for COCOMO (other empirical models have similar attributes) in Chapter 3. Therefore, some risks can be translated to influence project estimates directly.

- Will some project staff members be working only part time on this project?
- Does the staff have the right expectations about the job at hand?
- Have staff members received necessary training?
- Will turnover among staff members be low enough to allow continuity?

The relative certainty of the answers to these questions allows the planner to estimate the impact of risk.

4.2.2 Risk Projection

Risk projection, also called *risk estimation,* attempts to rate each risk in two ways—the *likelihood* that the risk is real and the *consequences* of the problems associated with the risk, should it occur. The project planner, along with other managers and technical staff, performs four risk projection activities [CHA89]: (1) establishing a scale that reflects the perceived likelihood of a risk, (2) delineating the consequences of the risk, (3) estimating the impact of the risk on the project and the product, and (4) noting the overall accuracy of the risk projection so that there will be no misunderstandings.

A scale can be defined in either boolean, qualitative, or quantitative terms. In the extreme, each question in the risk item checklist (Section 4.2.1) can be answered with a "yes" or "no" response, but this is highly unrealistic. It is rarely possible to assess risk in such absolute terms. A better approach might be to answer on a qualitative *probability scale* that has the following values: highly improbable, improbable, moderate, likely, highly likely. Alternatively, the planner can estimate the mathematical probability that the risk will be realized (e.g., a probability of 0.90 implies a highly likely risk). Numerical probabilities can be estimated using statistical analysis of metrics collected from past projects, intuition, or other information. For example, if metrics (Chapter 2) collected for 45 projects indicate that 37 projects experienced twice the number of customer changes as predicted, the probability that a new project will experience excessive numbers of changes is 37/45 = 0.82, very likely.

Finally, risks are weighted by perceived impact (on the project) and then prioritized. Three factors affect impact: its nature, its scope, and its timing. The *nature* of the risk indicates the problems that are likely if it occurs. For example, a poorly defined external interface to customer hardware (a technical risk) will preclude early design and testing and will likely lead to system integration problems late in a project. The *scope* of a risk combines the severity (just how serious is it?) with its overall distribution (how much of the project will be affected or how many customers are harmed?). Finally, the *timing* of a risk considers when and for how long the impact will be felt. In most cases, a project manager might want the "bad news" to occur as soon as possible, but in some cases, the longer the delay, the better.

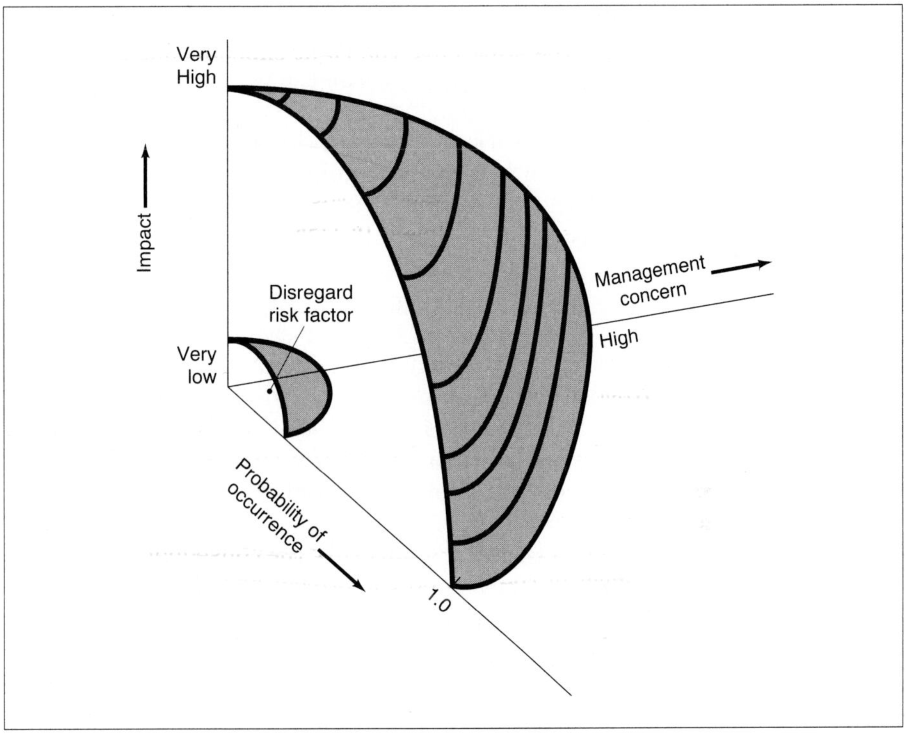

FIGURE 4.1. Risk and management concern.

Referring to Figure 4.1, risk impact and probability have a distinct impact on management concern. A risk factor that has a high-impact weight but a very low probability of occurrence should not absorb a significant amount of management time. However, high-impact risks with moderate to high probability and low-impact risks with high probability should be carried forward into the risk analysis steps that follow.

4.2.3 Risk Assessment

At this point in the risk analysis process, we have established a set of triplets of the form [CHA89]:

$$[r_i, l_i, x_i]$$

where r_i is risk, l_i is the likelihood (probability) of the risk, and x_i is the impact of the risk. During *risk assessment,* we further examine the accuracy of the estimates that were made during risk projection, attempt to prioritize the risks that have been uncovered, and begin thinking about ways to control and/or avert risks that are likely to occur.

For assessment to be useful, a *risk referent level* [CHA89] must be defined. For most software projects, cost, schedule, and performance represent three typical risk referent levels. That is, there is a level for cost overrun, schedule slippage, or performance degradation (or any combination of the three) that will cause the project to be terminated. If a combination of risks create problems that cause one or more of these referent levels to be exceeded, work will stop. In the context of software risk analysis, a risk referent level has a single point, called the *referent point* or *break point,* at which the decision to proceed with the project or terminate it (problems are just too great) are equally acceptable.

Figure 4.2 represents this situation graphically. If a combination of risks leads to problems that cause cost and schedule overruns, there will be a level, represented by the curve in the figure, that (when exceeded) will cause project termination (the darkly shaded region). At a referent point, the decisions to proceed or terminate are equally weighted.

In reality, the referent level can rarely be represented as a smooth line on a graph. In most cases it is a region in which there are areas of uncertainty, i.e., attempting to predict a management decision based on the combination of referent values is often impossible.

Therefore, during risk assessment, we perform the following steps:

1. Define the risk referent levels for the project
2. Attempt to develop a relationship between each $[r_i, l_i, x_i]$ and each of the referent levels
3. Predict the set of referent points that define a region of termination, bounded by a curve or areas of uncertainty
4. Try to predict how compound combinations of risks will affect a referent level

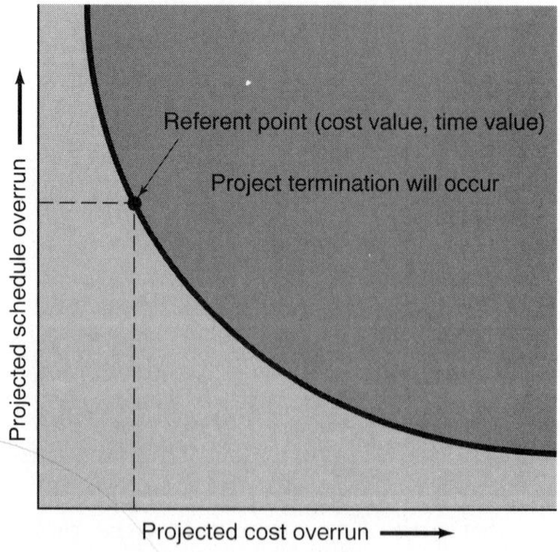

FIGURE 4.2.
Risk referent level.

A detailed discussion of the mathematics that can be used to support these steps is beyond the scope of this book. For further information, see Charette [CHA89] and Rowe [ROW88].

4.2.4 Risk Management and Monitoring

The risk management and monitoring activity is illustrated schematically in Figure 4.3. The triplet (risk description, likelihood, and impact) associated with each risk is used as the basis from which *risk management* (also called *risk aversion) steps* are developed. For example, assume that high staff turnover is noted as a project risk, r_1. Based on past history and management intuition, the likelihood, l_1, of high turnover is estimated to be 0.70 (70 percent, rather high), and the impact, x_1, is projected to increase project duration by 15 percent and overall cost by 12 percent. Given these data, the following risk management steps are proposed:

- Meet with current staff to determine causes for turnover (e.g., poor working conditions, low pay, competitive job market)
- Act to mitigate those causes that are under our control before the project starts
- Once the project commences, *assume turnover will occur* and develop techniques to ensure continuity when people leave
- Organize project teams so that information about each development activity is widely dispersed
- Define documentation standards and establish mechanisms to be sure that documents are developed in a timely manner
- Conduct peer reviews of all work (so that more than one person is "up to speed")
- Define a backup staff member for every critical technologist

It is important to note that these risk management steps incur additional project cost. For example, spending the time to "back up" every criti-

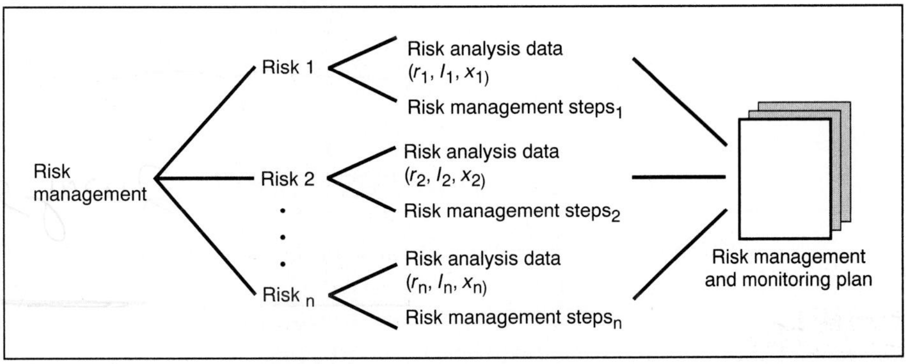

FIGURE 4.3. Risk management and monitoring.

cal technologist costs money. Part of risk management, therefore, is to evaluate when the benefits accrued by the risk management steps are outweighed by the costs associated with implementing them. In essence, the project planner performs a classic cost-benefit analysis. If risk aversion steps for high turnover will increase project cost and duration by an estimated 15 percent, and the predominant cost factor is backup, management may decide not to implement this risk management step. On the other hand if the risk aversion steps are projected to increase costs by 5 percent and duration by only 3 percent, management will likely put all of them into place.

For a large project, 30 or 40 risks may be identified. If between three and seven risk management steps are identified for each, risk management may become a project in itself! For this reason, we adapt the Pareto 80/20 rule to software risk. Experience indicates that 80 percent of the overall project risk (i.e., 80 percent of the potential for project failure) can be accounted for by only 20 percent of the identified risks. The work performed during earlier risk analysis steps will help the planner to determine which of the risks reside in that 20 percent. For this reason, some of the risks identified, assessed, and projected may not make it into the risk management plan—they don't comprise the critical 20 percent (the risks with highest project priority).

Referring again to Figure 4.3, the risk management steps are organized into a *Risk Management and Monitoring Plan* (RMMP). The RMMP documents all work performed as part of risk analysis and is used by the project manager as part of the overall *Project Plan* (Section 4.7). An outline for the RMMP [CHA89] is presented in Table 4.1.

Once the RMMP has been developed and the project has begun, *risk monitoring* commences. Risk monitoring is a project tracking activity (Section 4.3.6) with three primary objectives: (1) to assess whether a predicted risk does, in fact, occur, (2) to ensure that risk aversion steps defined for the risk are being properly applied, and (3) to collect information that can be used for future risk analysis. In many cases, the problems that occur during a project can be traced to many risks. Another job of risk monitoring is to attempt to allocate "blame" [what risk(s) caused which problems] throughout the project.

Risk analysis can absorb a significant amount of project planning effort. Identification, projection, assessment, management, and monitoring all take time. But the effort is worth it. To quote Sun Tzu [CLA83], a Chinese general who lived 2500 years ago, "If you know the enemy and know yourself, you need not fear the result of a hundred battles."

4.3 SOFTWARE PROJECT SCHEDULING

Scheduling for software development projects can be viewed from two rather different perspectives. In the first, an end date for release of a computer-based system has already (and irrevocably) been established. The software organization is constrained to distribute effort within the prescribed

TABLE 4.1

RISK MANAGEMENT AND MONITORING PLAN OUTLINE [CHA89]

RMMP

- **I.** Introduction
  - **1.** Scope and purpose of document
  - **2.** Overview
    - **a.** Objectives
    - **b.** Risk aversion priorities
  - **3.** Organization
    - **a.** Management
    - **b.** Responsibilities
    - **c.** Job descriptions
  - **4.** Aversion program description
    - **a.** Schedule
    - **b.** Major milestones and reviews
    - **c.** Budget
- **II.** Risk analysis
  - **1.** Identification
    - **a.** Survey of risks
      - **(i)** Sources of risk
    - **b.** Risk taxonomy
  - **2.** Risk estimation
    - **a.** Estimate probability of risk
    - **b.** Estimate consequence of risk
    - **c.** Estimation criteria
    - **d.** Possible sources of estimation error
  - **3.** Evaluation
    - **a.** Evaluation methods to be used
    - **b.** Evaluation method assumptions and limitations
    - **c.** Evaluation risk referents
    - **d.** Evaluation results
- **III.** Risk management
  - **1.** Recommendations
  - **2.** Risk aversion options
  - **3.** Risk aversion recommendations
  - **4.** Risk monitoring procedures
- **IV.** Appendices
  - **1.** Risk estimate of the situation
  - **2.** Risk abatement plan

time frame. The second view of software scheduling assumes that rough chronological bounds have been discussed but that the end date is set by the software engineering organization. Effort is distributed to make the best use of resources and an end date is defined after careful analysis of the software. Unfortunately, the first perspective is encountered far more frequently than the second.

Accuracy in scheduling can sometimes be more important than accuracy in costing. In a product-oriented environment, added cost can be absorbed by repricing or amortization over a large number of sales. A missed schedule, however, can reduce market impact, create dissatisfied customers, and raise internal costs by creating additional problems during system integration.

When we approach software project scheduling, a number of questions must be asked. How do we correlate chronological time with human effort? What tasks and parallelism are to be expected? What milestones can be used to show progress? How is effort distributed throughout the software engineering process? Are scheduling methods available? How do we physically represent a schedule and then track progress as the project commences? Each of these questions is addressed in the following sections.

4.3.1 People-Work Relationships

In a small software development project, a single person can analyze requirements, perform design, generate code, and conduct tests. As the size of a project increases, more people must become involved. (We can rarely afford the luxury of approaching a 10-person-year effort with one person working for 10 years!)

There is a common myth that is still believed by many managers who are responsible for software development effort: "...if we fall behind schedule, we can always add more programmers and catch up later in the project...." Unfortunately, adding people late in a project often has a disruptive effect on a project, causing schedules to slip even further. We noted the reason for this in Chapter 1. To reiterate: The people who are added must learn the system, and the people who teach them are the same people who were doing the work. While teaching, no work is done and the project falls further behind.

In addition to the time it takes to learn the system, more people increase the number of communication paths and the complexity of communication throughout a project. Although communication is absolutely essential to successful software development, every new communication path requires additional effort and therefore additional time.

As an example, consider four software engineers, each capable of producing 5000 LOC/year when working on an individual project. When these four engineers are placed on a team project, six potential communication paths are possible. Each communication path requires time that could otherwise be spent developing software. We shall assume that team productivity (when measured in LOC) will be reduced by 250 LOC/year for each communication path, due to the overhead associated with communication. Therefore, team productivity is 20,000 − (250 × 6) = 18,500 LOC/year—7.5 percent less than what we might expect.

The 1-year project on which the above team is working falls behind schedule and, with two months remaining, two additional people are added to the team. The number of communication paths escalates to 14. The productivity input of the new staff is the equivalent of 840 × 2 = 1680 LOC for the 2 months remaining before delivery. Team productivity now is 20,000 + 1680 − (250 × 14) = 18,180 LOC/year.

Although the above example is a gross oversimplification of real-world circumstances, it does serve to illustrate the contention that the relationship between the number of people working on a software project and overall productivity is not linear.

Based on the people-work relationship, are teams counterproductive? The answer is an emphatic *no* if communication serves to improve software quality and maintainability. In fact, formal technical reviews (see Chapter 17) conducted by software development teams can lead to better software analysis and design and, more importantly, can reduce the number of errors that go undetected until testing (thereby reducing testing effort). Hence, productivity and quality, when measured by time to project completion and customer satisfaction, can actually improve.

The Rayleigh-Norden model for large projects (Chapter 3) predicts a highly nonlinear relationship between chronological time to complete a project and effort. This leads to some interesting results. Recalling the CAD software example (Section 3.6.2), an estimated 33,000 LOC, 12-person-year effort could be accomplished with eight people working for 1.3 years. If, however, we extend the end date to 1.75 years, from Putnam's software equation:

$$K = L^3/(C_k^3 \times t_d^4) \sim 3.8 \text{ person-years}$$

This implies that by extending the end date 6 months, we can reduce the number of people from eight to four! The validity of such results is suspect, but the implication is clear: Benefits can be gained by using fewer people over a somewhat longer time span to accomplish the same objective.

4.3.2 Task Definition and Parallelism

When more than one person is involved in a software engineering project, it is likely that development activities will be performed in parallel. Figure 4.4 shows a schematic *task network* for a typical multiperson software engineering project. The network represents the all project tasks, their sequential order, and their dependencies.

Analysis and specification and the resultant requirements review are the first tasks to be performed and lay the foundation for parallel tasks that follow. Once requirements have been identified and reviewed, design activities (architectural and data design) and test planning commence in parallel.

The modular nature of well-designed software lends itself to parallel development tracks for procedural design, coding, and unit testing, illustrated in Figure 4.4. As components of the software are completed, the integration testing task commences. Finally, validation testing readies the software for release to the customer.

Referring to Figure 4.4, it is important to note that *milestones* are spaced at regular intervals through the software engineering process, providing a manager with a regular indication of progress. A milestone is reached once documentation produced as part of a software engineering task has been successfully reviewed.

The concurrent nature of software engineering activities leads to a number of important scheduling requirements. Because parallel tasks occur asynchronously, the planner must determine intertask dependencies to ensure continuous progress toward completion. In addition, the project manager should be aware of those tasks that lie on the *critical path,* that is, tasks that must be completed on schedule if the project as a whole is to be completed on schedule. These issues are discussed in more detail in Section 4.3.4.

4.3.3 Effort Distribution

Each of the software project estimation techniques discussed in Chapter 3 leads to estimates of person-months (or person-years) required to complete software development. Figure 4.5 illustrates a recommended distribution of

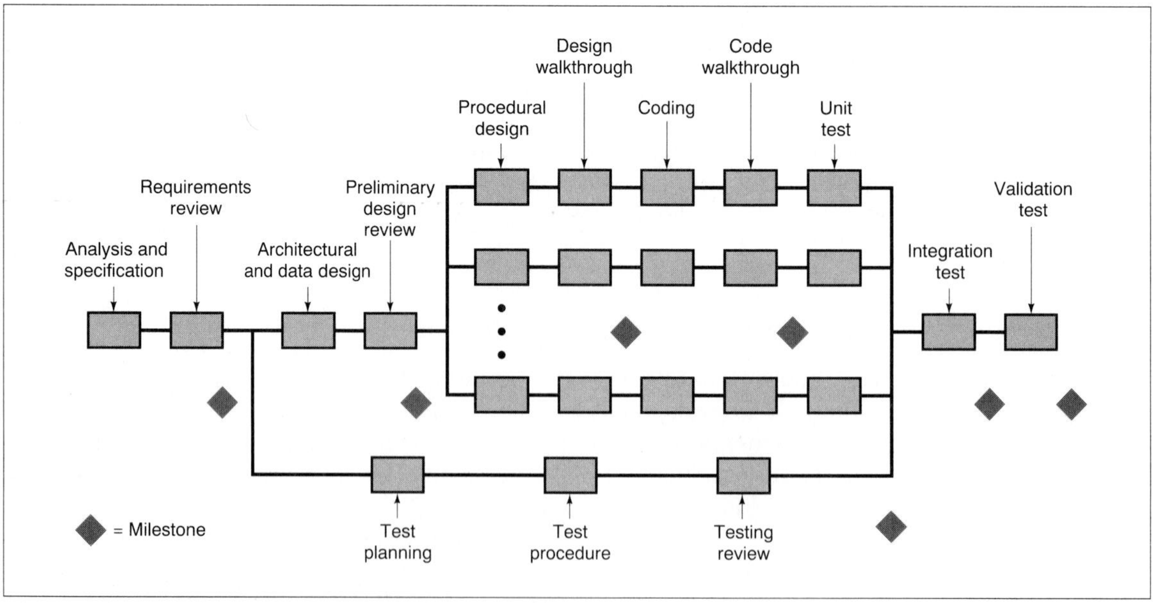

FIGURE 4.4. Task network and parallelism.

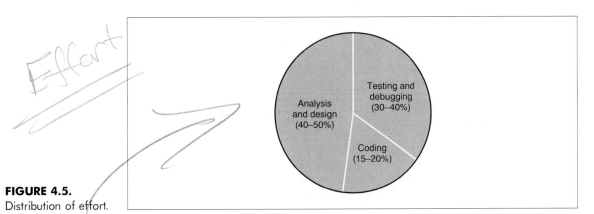

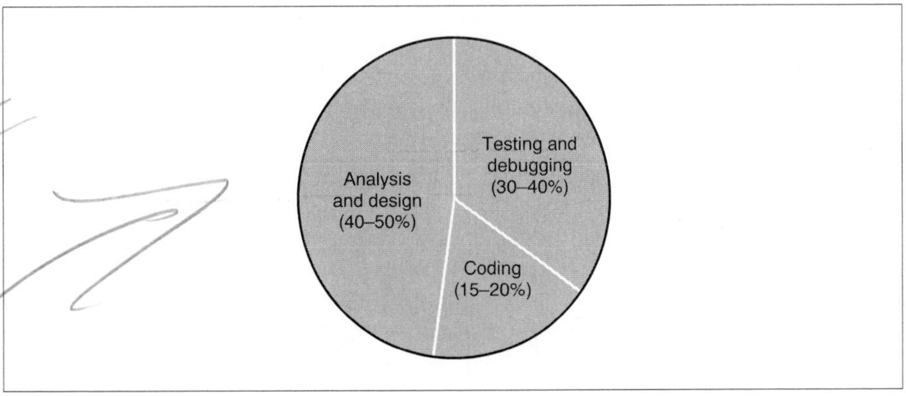

FIGURE 4.5.
Distribution of effort.

effort across the definition and development phases. This distribution, once called the *40-20-40 rule*,[2] emphasizes front-end analysis and design tasks and back-end testing. The reader can correctly infer that coding (20 percent of effort) is de-emphasized.

The effort distribution shown in Figure 4.5 should be used as a guideline only. The characteristics of each project must dictate the distribution of effort. Effort expended on project planning rarely accounts for more than 2 to 3 percent of effort, unless the plan commits an organization to large expenditures with high risk. Requirements analysis may comprise 10 to 25 percent of project effort. Effort expended on analysis or prototyping should increase in direct proportion with project size and complexity. A range of 20 to 25 percent of effort is normally applied to software design. Time expended for design review and subsequent iteration must also be considered.

Because of the effort applied to software design, code should follow with relatively little difficulty. A range of 15 to 20 percent of overall effort can be achieved. Testing and subsequent debugging can account for 30 to 40 percent of software development effort. The criticality of the software often dictates the amount of testing that is required. If software is human-rated (i.e., software failure can result in loss of life), higher percentages may be considered.

4.3.4 Scheduling Methods

Scheduling of a software project does not differ greatly from scheduling of any multitask development effort. Therefore, generalized project scheduling tools and techniques can be applied to software with little modification.

The *Program evaluation and review technique* (PERT) and the *critical-path method* (CPM) are two project scheduling methods [WIE77] that can

---

[2]Today, more than 40 percent of all project effort is often recommended for analysis and design tasks for large software development projects. Hence, the name "40-20-40" no longer applies in a strict sense.

be applied to software development. Both techniques develop a task network description of a project, that is, a pictorial or tabular representation of tasks that must be accomplished from beginning to end of a project (Figure 4.4). The network is defined by developing a list of all tasks, sometimes called the project *work breakdown structure* (WBS), associated with a specific project and a list of orderings (sometimes called a *restriction list*) that indicates in what order tasks must be accomplished.

Both PERT and CPM provide quantitative tools that allow the software planner to: (1) determine the *critical path*—the chain of tasks that determines the duration of the project; (2) establish *most likely* time estimates for individual tasks by applying statistical models; (3) calculate *boundary times* that define a time "window" for a particular task.

Boundary time calculations can be very useful in software project scheduling. Slippage in the design of one function, for example, can retard further development of other functions. Riggs [RIG81] describes important boundary times that may be discerned from a PERT or CPM network: (1) the earliest time that a task can begin when all preceding tasks are completed in the shortest possible time; (2) the latest time for task initiation before the minimum project completion time is delayed; (3) the earliest finish—the sum of the earliest start and the task duration; (4) the latest finish—the latest start time added to task duration; (5) the total float—the amount of surplus time or leeway allowed in scheduling tasks so that the network critical path is maintained on schedule. Boundary time calculations lead to a determination of critical path and provide the manager with a quantitative method for evaluating progress as tasks are completed.

As a final comment on scheduling, we recall the Rayleigh-Norden curve representation of effort expended during the software life cycle (Figure 3.10). The planner must recognize that effort expended on software does not terminate at the end of development. Maintenance effort, although not easy to schedule at this stage, will ultimately become the largest cost factor. A primary goal of software engineering is to help reduce this cost.

4.3.5 A Scheduling Example

The scheduling techniques described in the preceding section can be implemented with automated project scheduling tools that are available for virtually all personal computers [WOO88]. Such tools are relatively easy to use and make the analysis methods described above available to every software project manager.

This section presents a project scheduling example developed using an automated scheduling tool, *MacProject II* (Claris), available for the Apple Macintosh personal computer. The *project task network,* shown in Figure 4.6*a* to *e*, is drawn interactively by the project planner. Rectangular boxes represent software engineering tasks and boxes with rounded edges are milestones. The critical path is computed by the tool and is displayed

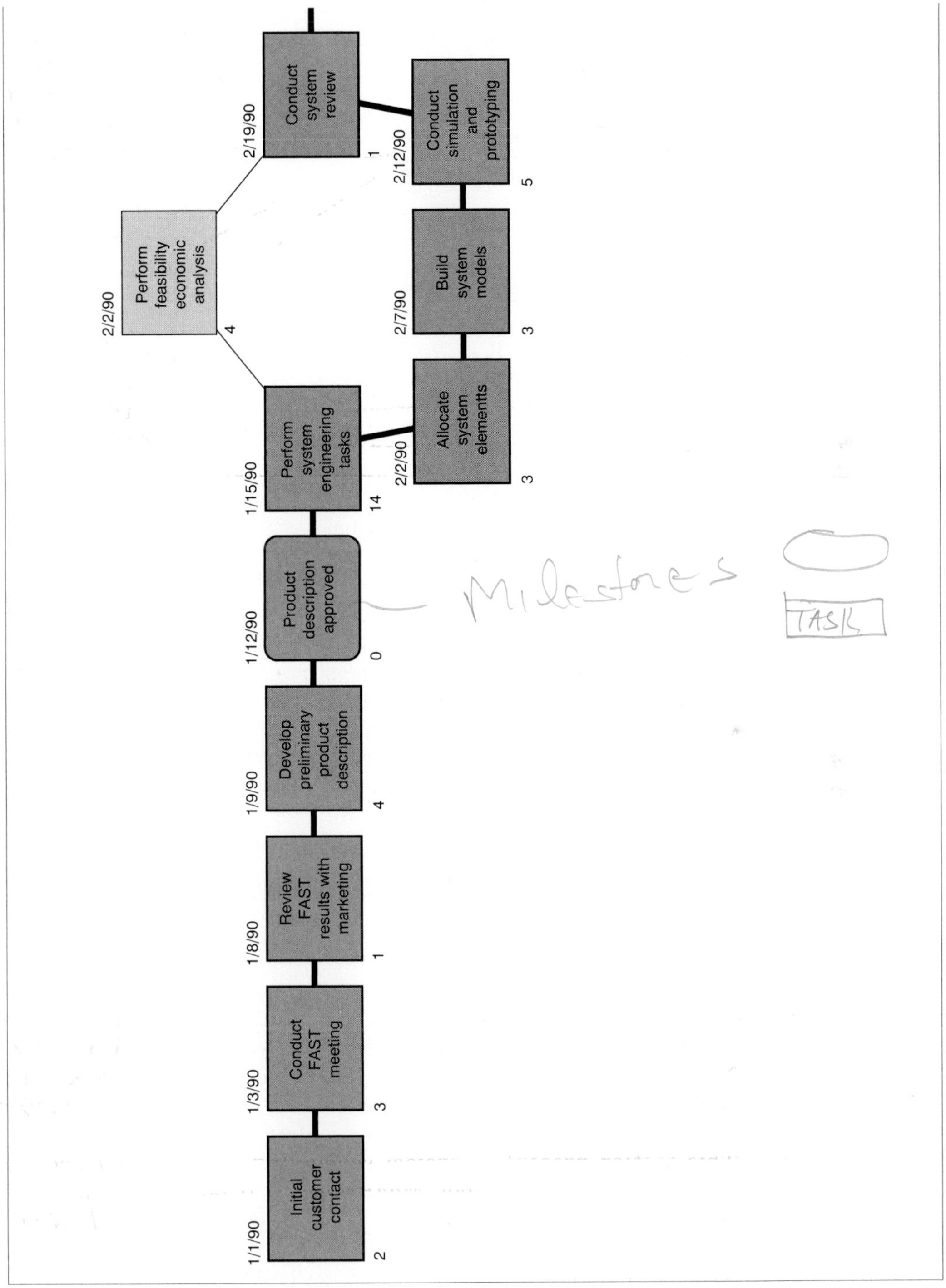

FIGURE 4.6. A typical task network (bold lines and boxes represent the critical path).

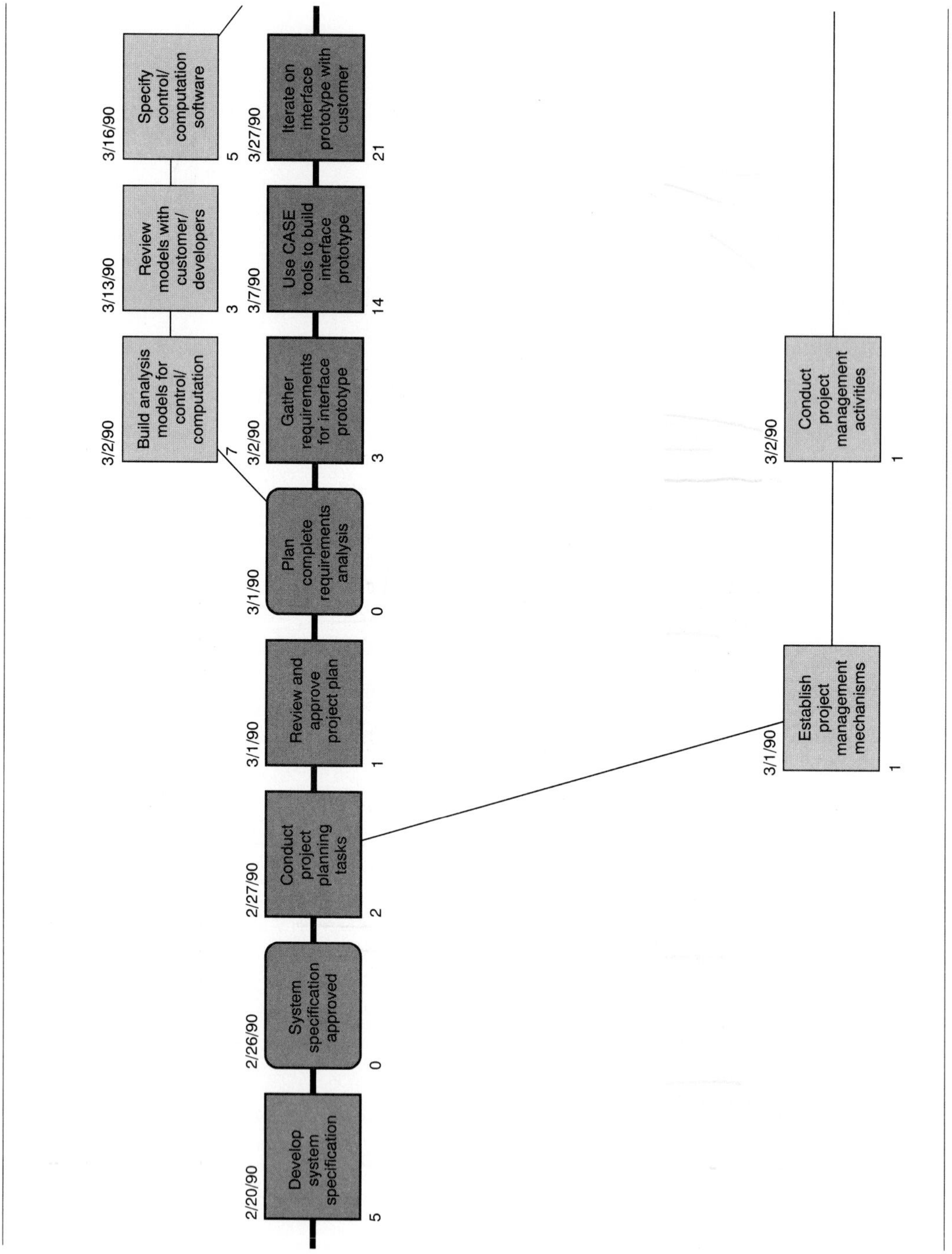

FIGURE 4.6. A typical task network (*continued*).

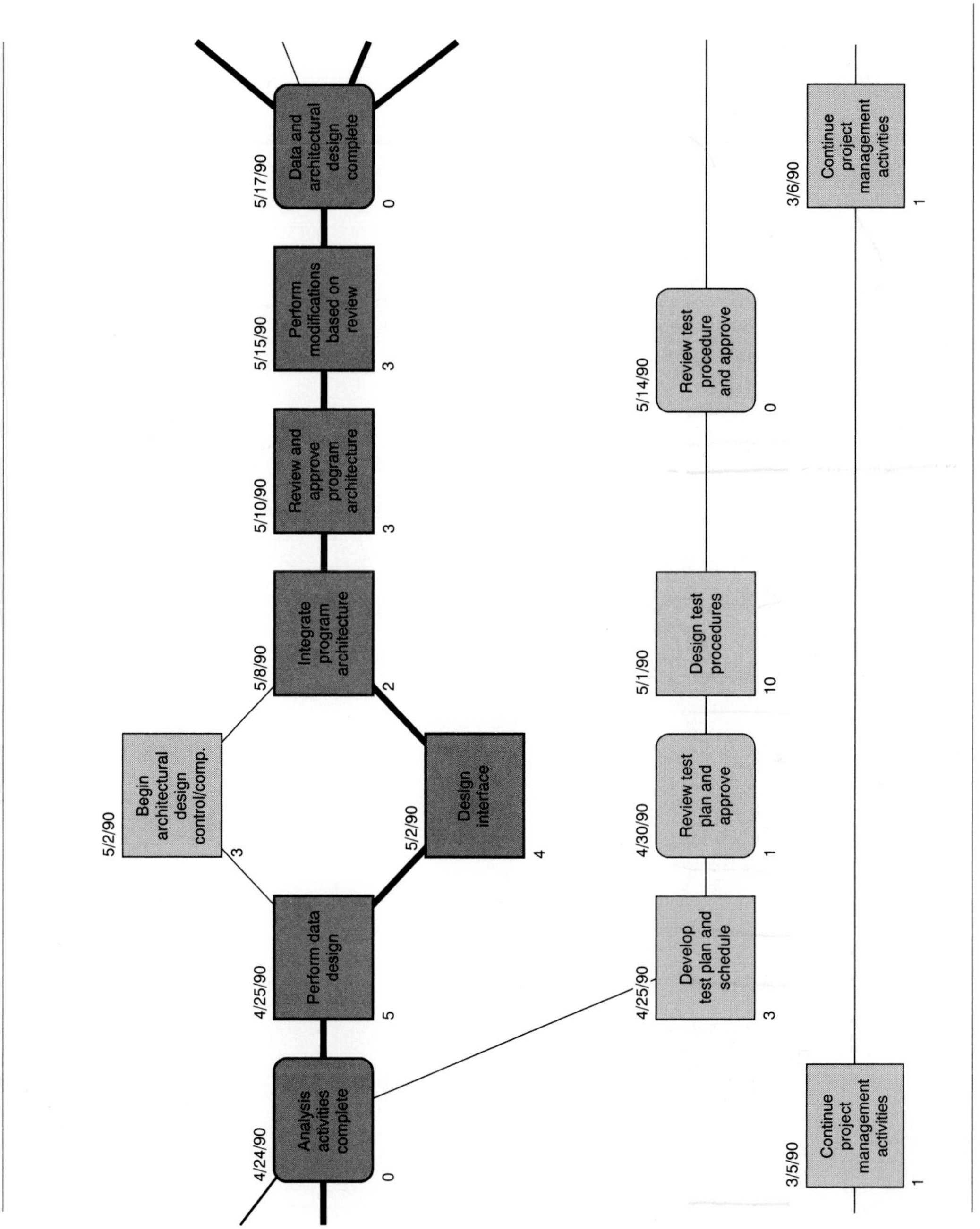

FIGURE 4.6. A typical task network (*continued*).

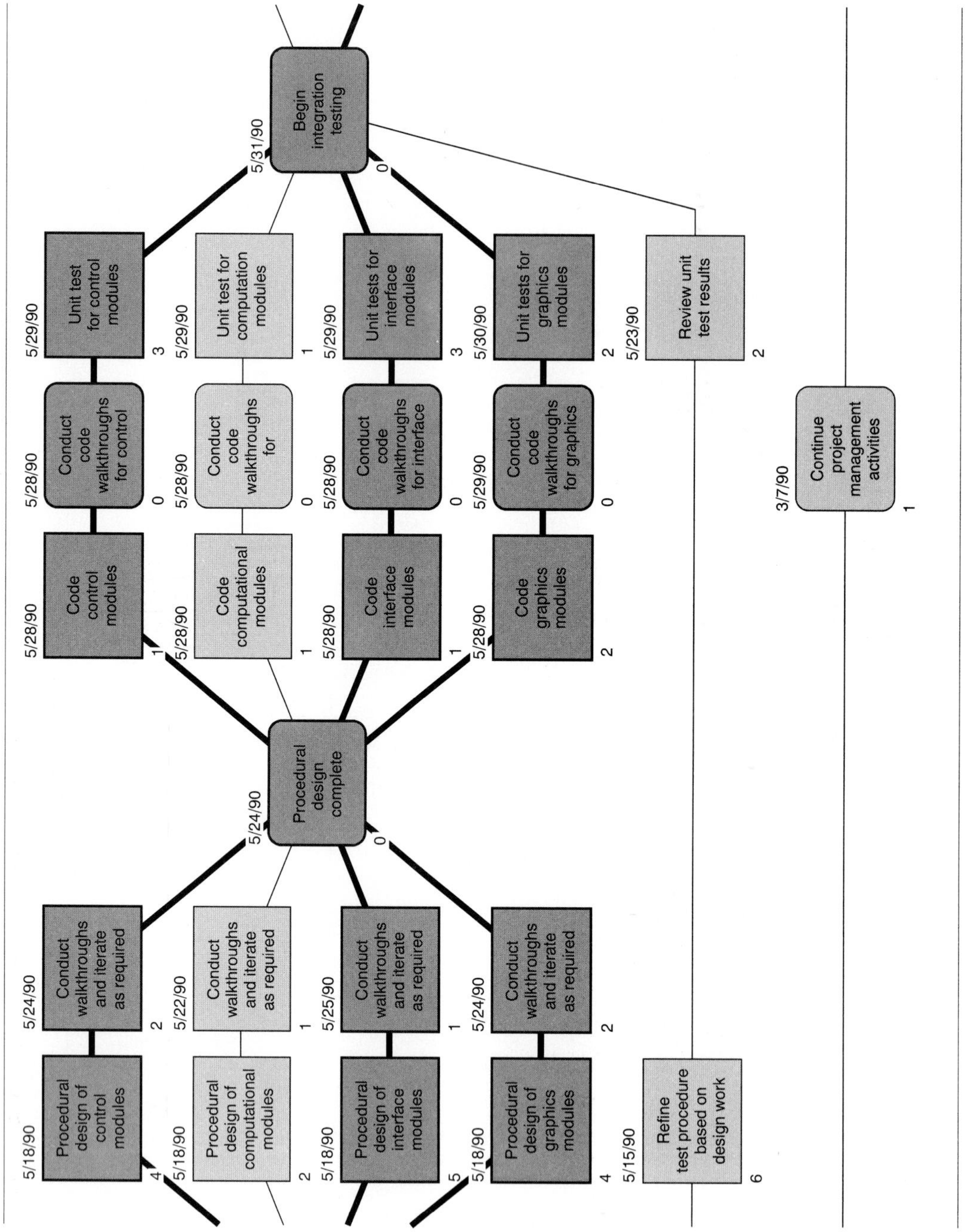

FIGURE 4.6. A typical task network (*continued*).

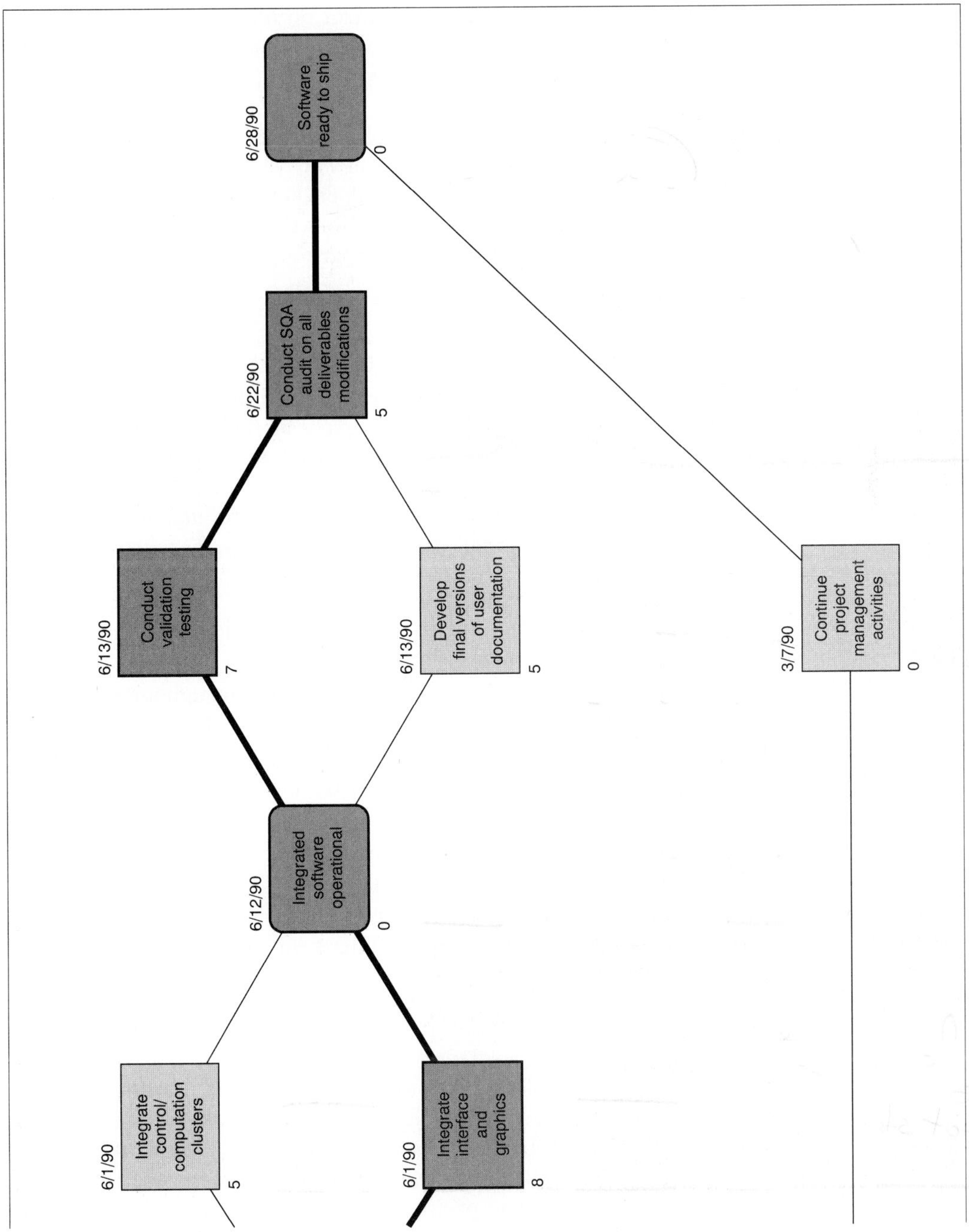

FIGURE 4.6. A typical task network (*continued*).

with bold lines. The starting date and duration for each task are specified. In addition, the planner specifies the resources (people) who will be working on each task and the costs of these resources.

Once project data are entered (in the form of the network diagram shown in Figure 4.6), *MacProject II* automatically generates the following information: (1) a timeline chart (Figure 4.7) that describes tasks as a function of chronological date; (2) a resource allocation table (Figure 4.8) that contains task start and finish times, work effort to be applied, and other data that enable a project manager to track progress as the project commences.

4.3.6 Project Tracking and Control

There's an old saying that "software projects fall behind schedule one day at a time." A 1-day slip in schedule will rarely be fatal to a project. But the days add up, and over the length of a project small delays can result in big problems.

We have already noted that one role of project management is to track and control the software project once it is underway. *Tracking* can be accomplished in a number of different ways:

- Conducting periodic project status meetings in which each team member reports progress and problems
- Evaluating the results of all reviews conducted throughout the software engineering process
- Determining whether formal project milestones (the rectangles with rounded corners shown in Figure 4.6) have been accomplished by the scheduled date
- Comparing the actual start date to the planned start date for each project task listed in the resource table (Figure 4.8)
- Meeting informally with practitioners to obtain their subjective assessments of the progress to date and problems on the horizon

In reality, all of these tracking techniques are used by experienced project managers.

Control is employed by a software project manager to administer project resources, cope with problems, and direct project staff. If things are going well (i.e., the project is on schedule and within budget, reviews indicate real progress, and milestones are being reached), control is light. But when problems occur, the project manager must exercise control to reconcile them as quickly as possible. After the problem has been diagnosed,[3] additional re-

[3]It is important to note that schedule slippage is a symptom of some underlying problem. The role of the project manager is to diagnose what the underlying problem is and then act to correct it.

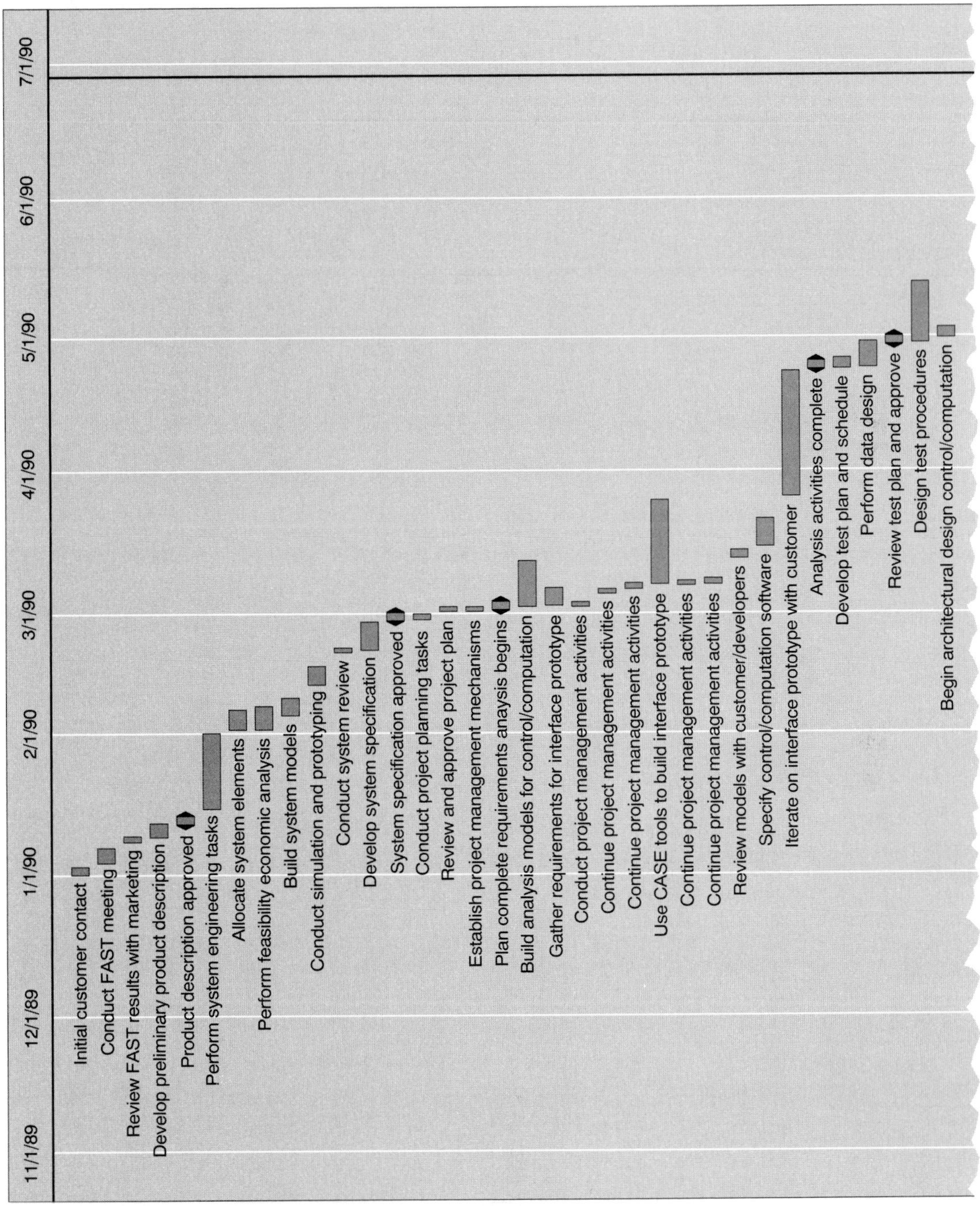

FIGURE 4.7. Partial task time line for a typical project (diamonds represent milestones, rectangles are tasks).

Name	Earliest Start	Earliest Finish	Latest Start	Latest Finish	Type	Elapsed Time	Resource	Work-Days	Resource	Work-Days	Resource	Work-Days
Initial customer contact	1/1/90	1/2/90	1/1/90	1/2/90	Starting Task	2	Jennifer	1.50				
Conduct FAST meeting	1/3/90	1/5/90	1/3/90	1/5/90	Task	3	Jennifer	1	Matt	1	Mike	1
Review FAST results with marketing	1/8/90	1/8/90	1/8/90	1/8/90	Task	1	Jennifer	0.50				
Develop preliminary product description	1/9/90	1/12/90	1/9/90	1/12/90	Task	4	Jennifer	2	Matt	2		
Product description approved	1/12/90	1/12/90	1/15/90	1/15/90	Milestone	0						
Perform system engineering tasks	1/15/90	2/1/90	1/15/90	2/1/90	Task	18	Matt	6	Carolyn	3	Brian	3
Allocate system elements	2/2/90	2/6/90	2/2/90	2/6/90	Task	5	Matt	1	Carolyn	1	Jennifer	1
Perform feasibility economic analysis	2/2/90	2/7/90	2/13/90	2/16/90	Task	6	Mike	3				
Build system models	2/7/90	2/9/90	2/7/90	2/9/90	Task	3	Matt	3				
Conduct simulation and prototyping	2/12/90	2/16/90	2/12/90	2/16/90	Task	5	Matt	3	Carolyn	2		
Conduct system review	2/19/90	2/19/90	2/19/90	2/19/90	Task	1	Staff	1				
Develop system specification	2/20/90	2/26/90	2/20/90	2/26/90	Task	7	Matt	4	Jennifer	1		
System specification approved	2/26/90	2/26/90	2/27/90	2/27/90	Milestone	0						
Conduct project planning tasks	2/27/90	2/28/90	2/27/90	2/28/90	Task	2	Norm	1.50	Jennifer	1		
Review and approve project plan	3/1/90	3/1/90	3/1/90	3/1/90	Task	1	Staff	1				
Establish project management mechanisms	3/1/90	3/1/90	6/22/90	6/22/90	Task	1	Norm	1				
Plan complete requirements analysis begins	3/1/90	3/1/90	3/2/90	3/2/90	Milestone	0						
Build analysis models for control/computation	3/2/90	3/12/90	4/4/90	4/12/90	Task	11	Matt	5	Carolyn	5	Mike	5
Gather requirements for interface prototype	3/2/90	3/6/90	3/2/90	3/6/90	Task	5	Brian	3				
Conduct project management activities	3/2/90	3/2/90	6/25/90	6/25/90	Task	1	Staff	1				
Review models with customer/developers	3/13/90	3/15/90	4/13/90	4/17/90	Task	3	Staff	2				
Use CASE tools to build interface prototype	3/7/90	3/26/90	3/7/90	3/26/90	Task	20	Brian	10	Mike	2		
Specify control/computation software	3/16/90	3/22/90	4/18/90	4/24/90	Task	7	Matt	3	Carolyn	3		
Iterate on interface prototype with customer	3/27/90	4/24/90	3/27/90	4/24/90	Task	29	Brian	10				
Analysis activities complete	4/24/90	4/24/90	4/25/90	4/25/90	Milestone	0						
Develop test plan and schedule	4/25/90	4/27/90	5/4/90	5/8/90	Task	3	Andy	2				
Continue project management activities	3/5/90	3/5/90	6/26/90	6/26/90	Task	1	Staff	1				
Perform data design	4/25/90	5/1/90	4/25/90	5/1/90	Task	7	Matt	4	Carolyn	4		
Review test plan and approve	4/27/90	4/27/90	5/9/90	5/9/90	Milestone	0	Andy	0.50	Matt	0.50	Brian	0.50
Begin architectural design control/comp.	5/2/90	5/4/90	5/3/90	5/7/90	Task	3	Matt	1	Carolyn	1	Jennifer	1
Conduct architectural design interface	5/2/90	5/7/90	5/2/90	5/7/90	Task	6	Brian	4	Carolyn	2		
Design test procedures	4/30/90	5/11/90	5/9/90	5/22/90	Task	12	Andy	7	Matt	1	Jennifer	1
Integrate program architecture	5/8/90	5/9/90	5/8/90	5/9/90	Task	2	Matt	1	Brian	1		
Review test procedure and approve	5/11/90	5/11/90	5/23/90	5/23/90	Milestone	0						
Review and approve program architecture	5/10/90	5/14/90	5/10/90	5/14/90	Task	5	Staff	2				
Perform modifications based on review	5/15/90	5/17/90	5/15/90	5/17/90	Task	3	Matt	1	Brian	1		
Data and architectural design complete	5/17/90	5/17/90	5/18/90	5/18/90	Milestone	0						
Continue project management activities	3/6/90	3/6/90	6/27/90	6/27/90	Task	1	Staff	1				
Procedural design of control modules	5/18/90	5/23/90	5/18/90	5/23/90	Task	6	Matt	4				
Procedural design of computational modules	5/18/90	5/21/90	5/23/90	5/24/90	Task	4	Carolyn	2				
Procedural design of interface modules	5/18/90	5/24/90	5/18/90	5/24/90	Task	7	Brian	4				
Procedural design of graphics modules	5/18/90	5/23/90	5/18/90	5/23/90	Task	6	Jennifer	3				
Refine test procedure based on design work	5/14/90	5/18/90	5/23/90	5/29/90	Task	5	Andy	3				
Conduct walkthroughs and iterate as required	5/24/90	5/25/90	5/24/90	5/25/90	Task	2	Staff	1				
Conduct walkthroughs and iterate as required	5/22/90	5/22/90	5/25/90	5/25/90	Task	1	Staff	1				
Conduct walkthroughs and iterate as required	5/25/90	5/25/90	5/25/90	5/25/90	Task	1	Staff	1				

FIGURE 4.8. Partial project table.

sources may be focused on the problem area; staff may be re-deployed or the project schedule can be redefined.

4.4 SOFTWARE ACQUISITION

In many software application areas, it is often more cost-effective to acquire, rather than develop, computer software. Software engineering managers are faced with a *make-buy decision* that can be further complicated by a number of acquisition options: (1) software may be purchased (or licensed) *off-the-shelf,* (2) off-the-shelf software may be purchased and then modified to meet specific needs, or (3) software may be custom-built by an outside contractor to meet the purchaser's specifications.

The steps involved in the acquisition of software are defined by the criticality of the software to be purchased and the end cost. In some cases (e.g., low-cost PC software), it is less expensive to purchase and experiment than to conduct a lengthy evaluation. For more expensive software packages, the following guidelines can be applied:

1. Develop a specification for function and performance of the desired software. Define measurable characteristics whenever possible.
2. Estimate the internal cost to develop and the delivery date.
3. Select three or four candidate software packages that best meet your specifications.
4. Develop a comparison matrix that presents a head-to-head comparison of key functions. Alternatively, conduct benchmark tests to compare candidate software.
5. Evaluate each software package based on past product quality, vendor support, product direction, reputation, etc.
6. Contact other users of the software and ask for opinions.

In the final analysis, the make-buy decision is made based on the following conditions: (1) Will the delivery date of the software product be sooner than that for internally developed software? (2) Will the cost of acquisition plus the cost of customization be less than the cost of developing the software internally? (3) Will the cost of outside support (e.g., a maintenance contract) be less than the cost of internal support? These conditions apply for each of the acquisition options noted above.

The steps described above can be augmented using statistical techniques such as *decision tree analysis* [BOE89]. For example, Figure 4.9 depicts a decision tree for a software-based system X. In this case, the software engineering organization can (1) build system X from scratch, (2) reuse an existing system by making modifications to it, (3) buy an available software product and modify it to meet local needs, or (4) contract the software development to an outside vendor.

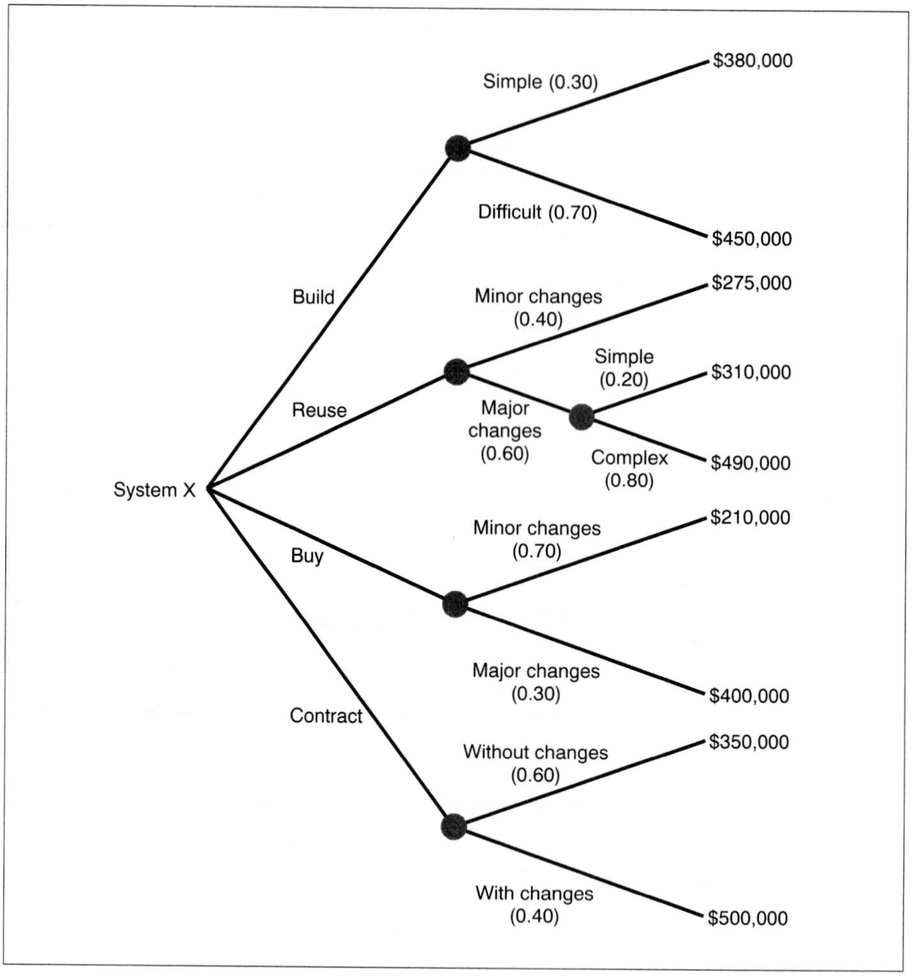

FIGURE 4.9. A decision tree to support the make-buy decision.

If the system is to be built from scratch, there is a 70 percent probability that the job will be difficult. Using the estimation techniques discussed in Chapter 3, the project planner projects that a difficult development effort will cost \$450,000. A "simple" development effort is estimated to cost \$380,000. The expected value for cost, computed along any branch of the decision tree, is

$$\text{Expected cost} = \sum(\text{path probability})_i \times (\text{estimated path cost})_i$$

where i is the decision tree path. For the *build* path,

$$\text{Expected cost}_{\text{build}} = 0.30(\$380\text{K}) + 0.70(\$450\text{K}) = \$429\text{K}$$

Following other paths of the decision tree, the projected costs for reuse, purchase, and contract, under a variety of circumstances, are also shown. The expected costs for these paths are:

$$\text{Expected cost}_{\text{reuse}} = 0.40(\$275\text{K}) + 0.60[0.20(\$310\text{K}) + 0.80(\$490\text{K})]$$
$$= \$382\text{K}$$
$$\text{Expected cost}_{\text{buy}} = 0.70(\$210\text{K}) + 0.30(\$400\text{K}) = \$267\text{K}$$
$$\text{Expected cost}_{\text{contract}} = 0.60(\$350\text{K}) + 0.40(\$500\text{K}) = \$410\text{K}$$

Based on the probability and projected costs that have been noted in Figure 4.9, the lowest expected cost is the "buy" option.

It is important to note, however, that many criteria—not just cost—must be considered during the decision-making process. Delivery/availability, experience of the developer/vendor/contractor, conformance to requirements, local "politics," and the likelihood of change are but a few of the criteria that may affect the ultimate decision to build, reuse, buy, or contract.

4.5 SOFTWARE RE-ENGINEERING

Almost all companies that use information systems or build computer-based products will face an "aging software plant" during the 1990s.[4] Many programs that are pivotal to business operations are becoming more and more difficult to maintain. Patches are placed on top of patches, resulting in programs that work inefficiently, fail too often, and do not respond to user's needs. In fact, the maintenance of aging programs has become prohibitively expensive for many information systems, manufacturing, and engineering organizations. Yet, many managers think that the cost to re-engineer all of these programs is also prohibitively expensive.

At first, it would appear that few acceptable options exist. But this is not the case. A strategy for re-engineering existing software can be developed, if company management is willing to "pay now," rather than waiting to "pay (much more) later." In reality, re-engineering may be a "low-cost" alternative to software maintenance. The following steps are recommended:

1. Select those programs that are used heavily at the present time and are likely to be used for the next 5 to 10 years.
2. Estimate the yearly cost of maintaining the programs selected in step 1. Maintenance cost should include error correction, environmental adaptation, and functional enhancements.

[4]The notion of an aging software plant was discussed in Chapter 1, Section 1.1.3.

3. Prioritize the programs selected in step 1 by importance and cost to maintain.
4. Estimate (using methods suggested in Chapter 3) the cost to re-engineer (rebuild) the programs selected in step 1. [Note: Because a prototype exists (the old program), re-engineering costs may be less than first imagined.] Estimate the annual cost to maintain these re-engineered programs.
5. For each program selected, compare the cost of maintaining it to the cost of re-engineering it.
6. Compute the time required to show a return on the re-engineering investment.
7. Consider intangible issues such as improved responsiveness to change, better system reliability, superior system performance, and improved user interfaces.
8. Gain management approval to begin the re-engineering of a single program.
9. Using lessons learned from the first re-engineering effort, develop a strategy for the re-engineering of other programs.

By the latter part of the 1990s, it is likely that advanced CASE tools for re-engineering will greatly reduce the costs associated with this activity. For now, however, a combination of existing *reverse engineering tools* (Chapters 20 and 22) and human effort still make re-engineering a cost-effective option.

4.6 ORGANIZATIONAL PLANNING

There are almost as many human organizational structures for software development as there are organizations that develop software. For better or worse, organizational structure cannot be easily modified. Concern with the practical and political consequences of organizational change is not within the software project planner's scope of responsibilities. However, organization of the people directly involved in a new software project can be considered at this time.

The following options are available for applying human resources to a project that will require n people working for k years:

1. n individuals are assigned to m different functional tasks; relatively little combined work occurs; coordination is the responsibility of a software manager who may have six other projects to be concerned with.
2. n individuals are assigned to m different functional tasks ($m < n$) so that informal "teams" are established; an ad hoc team leader may be appointed; coordination among teams is the responsibility of a software manager.

3. n individuals are organized into t teams; each team is assigned one or more functional tasks; each team has a specific organization; coordination is controlled by both the team and a software manager.

Although it is possible to voice pro and con arguments for each of the above approaches, there is a growing body of evidence (e.g., [SHN80], [ABD89]) that indicates that a formal team organization (option 3) is most productive.

The software development team approach has its origins in the *chief programmer team* concept first proposed by Harlan Mills and described by Baker [BAK72]. The organization of the software development team is illustrated in Figure 4.10. The nucleus of the team is composed of a *senior engineer* ("the chief programmer") who plans, coordinates, and reviews all technical activities of the team; *technical staff* (normally two to five people) who conduct analysis and development activities; and a *backup engineer* who supports the senior engineer in his or her activities and can replace the senior engineer with minimum loss in project continuity.

The software development team may be served by one or more specialists (e.g., telecommunications expert, database designer), support staff (e.g., technical writers, clerical personnel), and a *software librarian*. The librarian serves many teams and performs the following functions: maintains and controls all elements of the software configuration, i.e., documentation, source listings, data, magnetic media; helps collect and format software productivity data; catalogs and indexes reusable software modules; assists the teams in research, evaluation, and document preparation. The importance of a librarian cannot be overemphasized. The librarian acts as a controller, coordinator and, potentially, an evaluator of the software configuration.

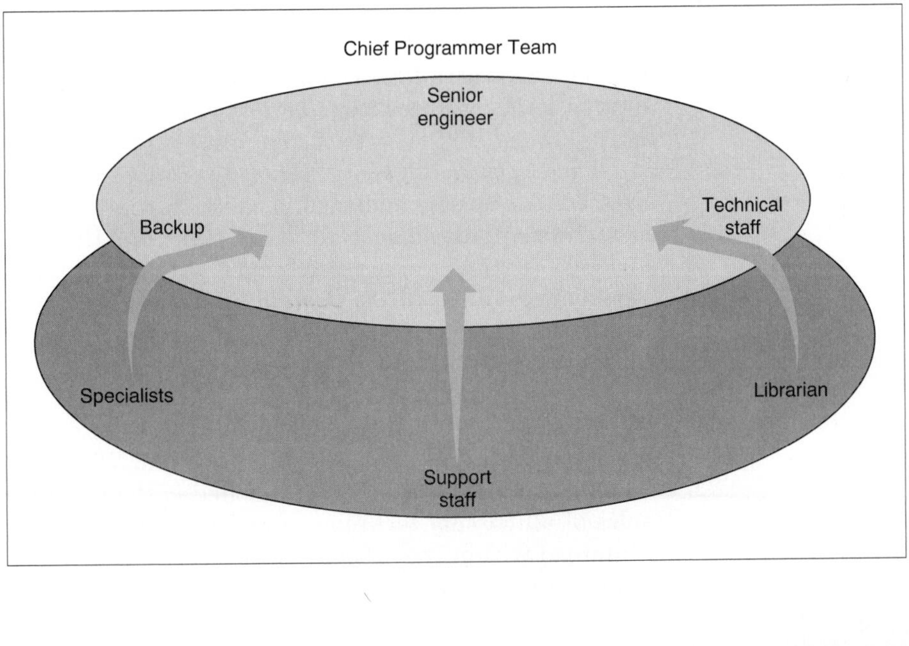

FIGURE 4.10. Software development team.

Other approaches to software engineering teams are also being used. Rettig [RET90] describes a "structured open team" which defines somewhat different roles for the participants but has the same goal—to build higher quality software.

The primary goal of the software development team is to approach a project as a joint effort. The team fosters the concept of *egoless programming* [WEI71] in that "my program" becomes "our program." By helping to eliminate ego attachment to software, the team can foster more thorough review, increased learning through side-by-side work, and improved software quality.

In Section 4.3.1 we discussed people-work relationships. The increased communication that is inherent in any team project would seem to militate against improved development productivity when software teams are used. However, a significant percentage of effort in the software engineering process must be expended on communication (e.g., planning, analysis, reviews) regardless of project organization. The team organization reduces communication effort and eliminates many time-consuming misunderstandings that occur when people work independently. In addition, the team organization encourages review, thereby improving software product quality.

Although it is not always practical to use software development teams (e.g., for small one-person projects or for large highly compartmentalized efforts), the underlying concepts are sound and should be applied whenever needs warrant.

4.7 THE SOFTWARE PROJECT PLAN

Each step in the software engineering process should produce a deliverable that can be reviewed and that can act as a foundation for the steps that follow. The *Software Project Plan* is produced at the culmination of the planning tasks. It provides baseline cost and scheduling information that will be used throughout the software engineering process.

The *Software Project Plan* is a relatively brief document that is addressed to a diverse audience. It must (1) communicate scope and resources to software management, technical staff, and the customer; (2) define risks and suggest risk aversion techniques; (3) define cost and schedule for management review; and (4) provide an overall approach to software development for all people associated with the project. An outline of the plan is presented in Table 4.2.

A presentation of cost and schedule will vary with the audience to whom it is addressed. If the plan is used only as an internal document, the results of each costing technique can be presented. When the plan is disseminated outside the organization, a reconciled cost breakdown (combining the results of all costing techniques) is provided. Similarly, the degree of detail contained within the schedule section may vary with the audience and formality of the plan.

TABLE 4.2

SOFTWARE PROJECT PLAN

- **I.** Introduction
  - **A.** Scope and purpose of document
  - **B.** Project objectives
    - **1.** Objectives
    - **2.** Major functions
    - **3.** Performance issues
    - **4.** Management and technical constraints
- **II.** Project estimates
  - **A.** Historical data used for estimates
  - **B.** Estimation techniques
  - **C.** Estimates
- **III.** Project risks (RMMP may be included by reference)
  - **A.** Risk analysis
    - **1.** Identification
    - **2.** Risk estimation
    - **3.** Evaluation
  - **B.** Risk management
    - **1.** Risk aversion options
    - **2.** Risk monitoring procedures
- **IV.** Schedule
  - **A.** Project work breakdown structure
  - **B.** Task network
  - **C.** Time-line chart (Gantt chart)
  - **D.** Resource table
- **V.** Project resources
  - **A.** People
  - **B.** Hardware and software
  - **C.** Special resources
- **VI.** Staff organization
  - **A.** Team structure (if applicable)
  - **B.** Management reporting
- **VII.** Tracking and control mechanisms
- **VIII.** Appendices

The *Software Project Plan* need not be a lengthy, complex document. Its purpose is to help establish the viability of the software development effort. The plan concentrates on a general statement of what and a specific statement of how much and how long. Subsequent steps in the software engineering process will concentrate on definition, development, and maintenance.

4.8 SUMMARY

Planning is a software project management activity that combines the measurement techniques and estimation methods discussed in earlier chapters with risk analysis, scheduling, and other decision-making activities.

Risk is an inherent part of all software projects and, for this reason, project risks must be analyzed and managed. The analysis of risk begins with identification and is followed by projection and assessment. These activities define each risk, its likelihood of occurrence, and its projected impact. Once this information is known, risk management and monitoring activities can be conducted to help control the risks that do actually occur.

Using the human effort that has been estimated for a project, scheduling begins with the creation of a network that represents each development task, its dependency on other tasks, and its projected duration. The task network is used to compute the critical project path, a time-line chart, and a variety of project information. Using the schedule as a guide, the project manager can track and control each step in the software engineering process.

In some cases, it may be possible to acquire an existing software package, or subcontract its development, rather than build it in-house. The make-buy decision can be approached using a set of simple guidelines that are augmented with statistical decision-making techniques.

The *Software Project Plan* combines information generated as a consequence of all estimating and planning activities. It provides a road map for project management.

REFERENCES

[ABD89] Abdel-Hamid, T. K., "The Dynamics of Software Project Staffing: A System Dynamics Based Simulation Approach," *IEEE Trans. Software Engineering,* vol. 15, no. 2, February 1989, pp. 109–119.

[BAK72] Baker, F.T., "Chief Programmer Team Management of Production Programming," *IBM Systems Journal,* vol. 11, no. 1, 1972, pp. 56–73.

[BOE89] Boehm, B.W., *Software Risk Management,* IEEE Computer Society Press, 1989.

[CHA89] Charette, R. N., *Software Engineering Risk Analysis and Management,* McGraw-Hill/Intertext, 1989.

[CLA83] Clavell, J. (ed.), *The Art of War* (by Sun Tzu), Dell Publishing, 1983.

[DRU75] Drucker, P., *Management,* W. Heinemann, 1975.

[RET90] Rettig, M., "Software Teams," *CACM,* vol. 33, no. 10, October 1990, pp. 23–27.

[RIG81] Riggs, J., *Production Systems Planning, Analysis and Control,* 3d ed., Wiley, 1981.

[ROW88] Rowe, W. D., *An Anatomy of Risk,* Robert E. Krieger Publishing, 1988.

[SHN80] Shniederman, B., *Software Psychology,* Winthrop Publishers, 1980, pp. 124–132.

[WEI71] Weinberg, G., *The Psychology of Computer Programming,* Van Nostrand, 1971, pp. 47–66.

[WIE77] Wiest, J., and F. Levy, *A Management Guide to PERT/CPM,* 2d ed., Prentice-Hall, 1977.

[WOO88] Wood, L., "The Promise of Project Management," *BYTE,* vol. 13, no. 12, November 1988, pp. 180–192.

PROBLEMS AND POINTS TO PONDER

4.1 Project risk is only one of many types of risk that are encountered when computer-based systems are developed and then used in the outside world. List additional generic categories of risk that should be considered when systems are used for business, personal, or governmental activities.

4.2 Why is it "futile to try to eliminate risk?" Consider this first from a technical and then from an economic point of view.

4.3 Assume that you have been contracted by a university to develop an on-line course registration system (OLCRS). First, act as the customer (if you're a student, that should be easy!) and specify the characteristics of a good system. (Alternatively, your instructor will provide you with a set of preliminary requirements for the system.) Next, perform risk identification and projection by performing the following tasks:
(a) Identify as many project risks for OLCRS as you can.
(b) Establish a scale that reflects the perceived likelihood of a risk.
(c) Delineate the consequences of the risk.
(d) Estimate the impact of the risk on the project and the product.
(e) Note the overall accuracy of the risk projection.
You should ultimately be able to list a set of triplets described in Section 4.2.3.

4.4 Attempt to perform risk assessment on the risks noted for OLCRS in Problem 4.3. Use product cost and delivery schedule as the risk referent levels. Show how you develop relationships between the risks you've identified and the risk referent levels.

4.5 How will you manage and monitor risk for the OLCRS project described in Problem 4.3?

4.6 Write a four- or five-page *Risk Management and Monitoring Plan* for OLCRS.

4.7 Although adding people to a late software project can make it later, there are circumstances in which this is not true. Describe them.

4.8 The relationship between people and time is highly nonlinear. Using Putnam's software equation (described in Chapter 3), develop a table that relates number of people to project duration for a software project requiring 50,000 LOC and 15 person-years of effort (the technology constant is 5000). Assume that the software must be delivered in 24 months plus or minus 12 months.

4.9 Using COCOMO (described in Chapter 3), develop an effort and duration estimate for OLCRS (Problem 4.3). Suggest how you would
(a) Define parallel work activities during the OLCRS project
(b) Distribute effort throughout the project
(c) Establish milestones for the project

4.10 Define a task network for OLRCS or, alternatively, for another software project that interests you. Be sure to show tasks and milestones and to attach effort and duration estimates to each task. If possible, use an automated scheduling tool to perform this work.

4.11 If an automated scheduling tool is available, determine the critical path for the network defined in Problem 4.10.

4.12 Using a scheduling tool (if available) or paper and pencil (if necessary), develop a time-line chart for the OLCRS project.

4.13 The make-buy decision is an important management prerogative. You are manager of a software organization that has an average software development cost of $20.00/LOC. You are considering the purchase of a 5000-LOC software package that will cost $50,000. Initially, your technical staff indicates that no modifications will be required for the package to meet your specifications. However, your software development group wants to develop similar software in-house. Should you make or buy? After further study, your technical group now finds that at least 1000 LOC will have to be modified or added to make the package viable. Should you now make or buy? Carefully state any assumptions you have made in making your decision.

4.14 The decision discussed in Problem 4.13 becomes more complicated when a contractor offers to build the software for $65,000. Using a modified version of the decision tree shown in Figure 4.9, consider whether you should make, buy, or contract the software. Use the same probabilities as those shown in the figure, but develop your own cost estimates.

4.15 An engineering analysis program originally developed in the late 1960s is still pivotal to your company's business. The program is 300,000 LOC and is a major source of maintenance problems. After collecting metrics for 5 years, you find that 10,000 LOC are modified each year to account for bug fixes, adaptation to changing hardware and operating systems, and user-requested enhancements. The average cost to modify one LOC for each of the 5 years has been:

Year 1	$40.00/LOC
Year 2	$42.00/LOC
Year 3	$45.00/LOC
Year 4	$53.00/LOC
Year 5	$64.00/LOC

Your software engineering staff indicates that a re-engineered version of the program can be developed using 175,000 LOC. It is estimated that development time will be 18 months. Currently, new software costs $25.00/LOC to build. Do a return-on-investment analysis to determine whether you should re-engineer the program.

4.16 Many software projects are so large that a number of software development teams must be formed. Recommend a management structure for coordinating multiple teams. What are some of the potential problems that can arise?

4.17 Suggest practical methods by which a manager can monitor compliance with costs and schedules defined in the *Software Project Plan*.

FURTHER READINGS

Boehm [BOE89] and Charette [CHA89] present comprehensive treatments of risk analysis for software engineering. Charette calls on probability theory and statistical techniques to analyze and manage risks. Boehm suggests excellent questionnaire and checklist formats that can prove invaluable in identifying risks. *Air Force Systems Command Pamphlet AFSCP 800-45* (U.S. Airforce, September 1988) describes risk identification and reduction techniques and contains tables of "risk drivers." Gilb (*Principles of Software Engineering Management,* Addison-Wesley, 1988) presents a set of "principles" (often amusing and sometimes profound) that can serve as a worthwhile guide for risk management. Every issue of the *ACM Sigsoft (Software Engineering) Notes* publishes a section entitled "Risks to the Public" (editor, P.G. Neumann). If you want the latest and best software horror stories, this is the place to go. Software tools for risk analysis include *PROMAP V* (LOG/AN, Inc.), *PROSIM* (Venture Analytical Associates), and *RISNET* (J.M. Cockerman Associates).

Many software project management books discuss scheduling. Page-Jones (*Practical Project Management,* Dorset House, 1985), Simpson (*New Techniques in Software Project Management,* Wiley, 1987), and Whitten (Managing Software Development Projects, Wiley, 1989) are representative. Although his work is somewhat dated, Gunther (*Management Methodology for Software Product Engineering,* Wiley, 1978) continues to be one of the few sources of information on the management and scheduling of software products. Bodie (*Crunch Mode,* Prentice-Hall, 1987) discusses the special concerns of managers who must "build effective systems on a [very] tight schedule." An excellent anthology of important papers has been collected by Thayer (*Software Engineering Project Management,* IEEE Computer Society Press, 1988).

Many software project managers have had little or no formal training. Weinberg (*Becoming a Technical Leader,* Dorset House, 1986) is "must" reading for every manager and every software engineer who may become a manager.

PART 2

SYSTEM AND SOFTWARE REQUIREMENTS ANALYSIS

CHAPTER 5

COMPUTER SYSTEM ENGINEERING

Four hundred and fifty years ago, Machiavelli said: "...there is nothing more difficult to take in hand, more perilous to conduct or more uncertain in its success, than to take the lead in the introduction of a new order of things...."

During the last quarter of the twentieth century, computer-based systems have introduced a new order. Although technology has made great strides since Machiavelli spoke, his words continue to ring true.

Software engineering and hardware engineering are activities within the broader category that we shall call *computer system engineering*. Each of these disciplines represents an attempt to bring order to the development of computer-based systems. Engineering techniques for computer hardware grew out of electronic design and have reached a state of relative maturity. Hardware design techniques are well-established, manufacturing methods are continually improved, and reliability is a realistic expectation rather than a modest hope. Unfortunately, computer software still suffers from the Machiavellian description stated above. In computer-based systems, software has replaced hardware as the system element that is most difficult to plan, least likely to succeed (on time and within cost), and most dangerous to manage. Yet the demand for software continues unabated as computer-based systems grow in number, complexity, and application.

Engineering techniques for computer software are gaining widespread acceptance. In Chapter 1, we discussed the evolution of a software culture that once viewed computer programming as an art form. No engineering precedent existed and no engineering approach was applied. Times are changing!

5.1 COMPUTER-BASED SYSTEMS

The word "system" is possibly the most overused and abused term in the technical lexicon. We speak of political systems and educational systems, of avionics systems and manufacturing systems, of banking systems and subway systems. The word tells us little. We use the adjective describing "system" to understand the context in which the word is used. *Webster's Dictionary* defines "system" in the following way:

> 1. a set or arrangement of things so related as to form a unity or organic whole; 2. a set of facts, principles, rules, etc., classified and arranged in an orderly form so as to show a logical plan linking the various parts; 3. a method or plan of classification or arrangement; 4. an established way of doing something; method; procedure. . . .

Five additional definitions are provided in the dictionary, yet no precise synonym is suggested. "System" is a special word.

Borrowing from Webster's definition above, we define a *computer-based system* as:

> A set or arrangement of elements that are organized to accomplish some method, procedure or control by processing information.

The elements of a computer-based system are depicted in Figure 5.1 and often include the following:

Software: Computer programs, data structures, and related documentation that serve to effect the logical method, procedure or control that is required

Hardware: Electronic devices (e.g., CPU, memory) that provide computing capability, and electromechanical devices (e.g., sensors, motors, pumps) that provide external world function

People: Users and operators of hardware and software

Database: A large, organized collection of information that is accessed via software and is an integral part of system function

Documentation: Manuals, forms, and other descriptive information that portrays the use and/or operation of the system

Procedures: The steps that define the specific use of each system element or the procedural context in which the system resides.

The elements combine in a variety of ways to *transform* information. For example, a robot transforms a command file containing specific instructions into a set of control signals that cause some specific physical action.

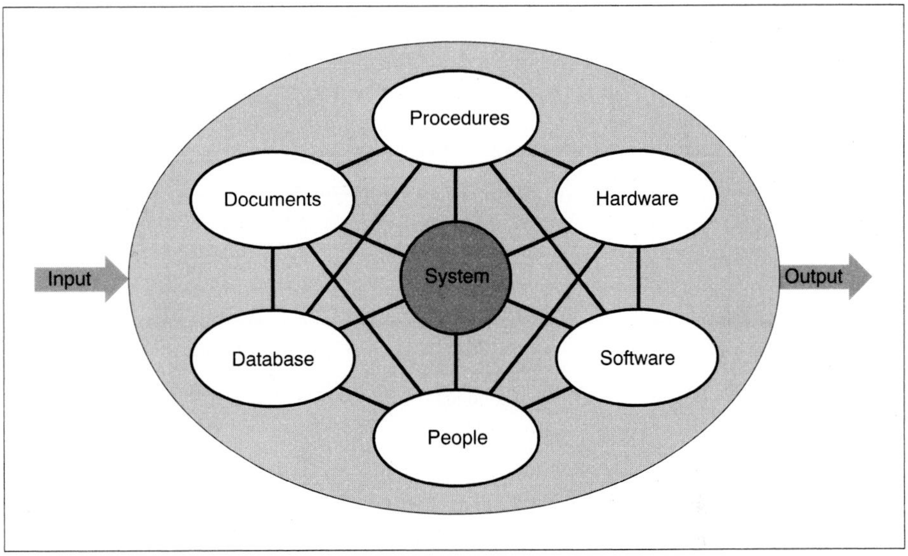

FIGURE 5.1.
System elements.

One complicating characteristic of computer-based systems is that the elements comprising one system may also represent one macro element of a still larger system. The *macro element* is a computer-based system that is one part of a larger computer-based system. As an example, we consider a factory automation system that is essentially the hierarchy of systems shown in Figure 5.2. At the lowest level of the hierarchy, we have a numerical control machine, robots, and data entry devices. Each is a computer-based system in its own right. The elements of the numerical control machine include electronic and electromechanical hardware (e.g., processor and memory, motors, sensors), software (for communications, machine control, interpolation), people (the machine operator), a database (the stored NC program), documentation, and procedures. A similar decomposition could be applied to the robot and data entry device. Each is a computer-based system.

At the next level in the hierarchy (Figure 5.2), a *manufacturing cell* is defined. The manufacturing cell is a computer-based system that may have elements of its own (e.g., computers, mechanical fixtures) and also integrates the macro elements that we have called numerical control machine, robot, and data entry device.

To summarize, the manufacturing cell and its macro elements each are comprised of system elements with the generic labels: software, hardware, people, database, procedures, and documentation. In some cases, macro elements may share a generic element. For example, the robot and the NC machine might both be managed by a single operator (the people element). In other cases, generic elements are exclusive to one system.

The role of the system engineer (or system analyst) is to define the elements for a specific computer-based system in the context of the overall

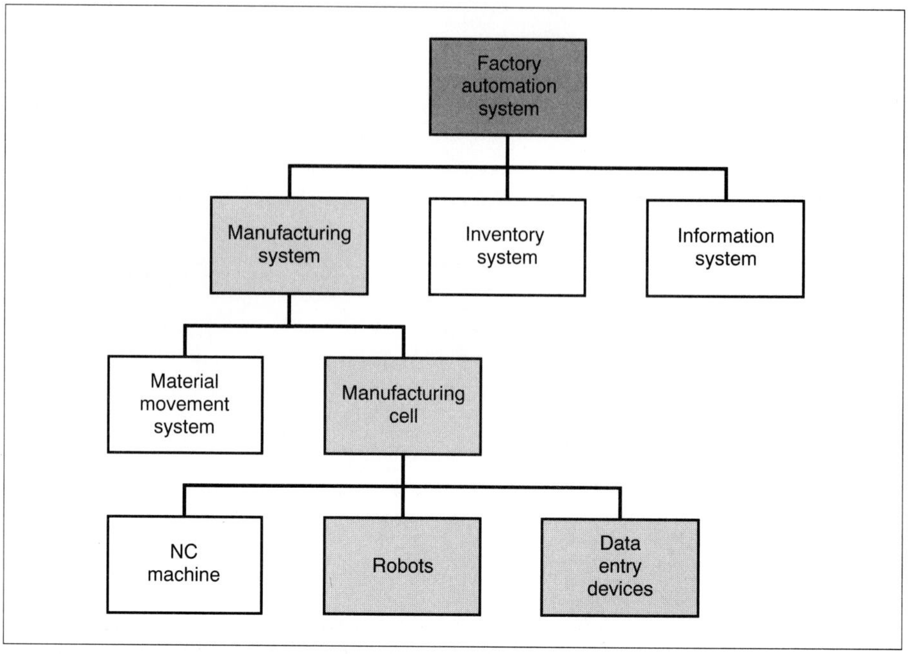

FIGURE 5.2.
A system of systems.

hierarchy of systems (macro elements). In the sections that follow, we examine the tasks that constitute computer system engineering.

5.2 COMPUTER SYSTEMS ENGINEERING

Computer system engineering[1] is a problem-solving activity. Desired system functions are uncovered, analyzed, and allocated to individual system elements. The computer system engineer (called a *system analyst* in some application domains) begins with customer-defined goals and constraints and derives a representation of function, performance, interfaces, design constraints, and information structure that can be allocated to each of the generic system elements described in the preceding section.

The genesis of most new systems begins with a rather nebulous concept of desired function. Therefore, the system engineer must *bound* the system by identifying the scope of function and performance that are desired. For example, it is not enough to say that the control software for the robot in a manufacturing automation system will "respond rapidly if a parts tray is

[1]The terms "computer system engineering" and "computer engineering" should not be confused. Computer engineering focuses exclusively on the design and implementation of computer hardware and its associated system software, while computer system engineering can be applied to all products that make use of computers.

empty." The system engineer must define (1) what indicates an empty tray to the robot; (2) the precise time bounds (in seconds) in which software response is expected; (3) what form the response must take.

Once function, performance, constraints, and interfaces are bounded, the system engineer moves on to a task that is called *allocation*. During allocation, function is assigned to one or more generic system elements (i.e., software, hardware, people, etc.). Often alternative allocations are proposed and evaluated. To illustrate the process of allocation, we consider a macro element of the factory automation system—the conveyor line sorting system (CLSS) that was introduced in Chapter 3. The system engineer is presented with the following (somewhat nebulous) statement of objectives for CLSS:

> CLSS must be developed such that boxes moving along a conveyor line will be identified and sorted into one of six bins at the end of the line. The boxes will pass by a sorting station where they will be identified. Based on an identification number printed on the side of the box (an equivalent bar code is provided), the boxes will be shunted into the appropriate bins. Boxes pass in random order and are evenly spaced. The line is moving slowly.

CLSS is depicted schematically in Figure 3.2. Before continuing, make a list of questions that you would ask if you were the system engineer.

Among the many questions that should be asked and answered are the following:

1. How many different identification numbers must be processed and what is their form?
2. What is the speed of the conveyor line in feet/second and what is the distance between boxes in feet?
3. How far is the sorting station from the bins?
4. How far apart are the bins?
5. What should happen if a box doesn't have an identification number or an incorrect number is present?
6. What happens when a bin fills to capacity?
7. Is information about box destination and bin contents to be passed elsewhere in the factory automation system? Is real-time data acquisition required?
8. What error/failure rate is acceptable?
9. What pieces of the conveyor line system currently exist and are operational?
10. What schedule and budgetary constraints are imposed?

Note that the above questions focus on function, performance, and information flow and content. The system engineer does not ask the customer *how* the task is to be done; rather, the engineer asks *what* is required.

Assuming reasonable answers, the system engineer develops a number of alternative allocations. Note that function and performance are assigned to different generic system elements in each allocation.

Allocation 1 A sorting operator is trained and placed at the sorting station location. He/she reads the box and places it into an appropriate bin.

Allocation 1 represents a purely manual (but nevertheless effective) solution to the CLSS problem. The primary system element is people (the sorting operator). The person performs all sorting functions. Some documentation (in the form of a table relating identification number to bin location and procedural description for operator training) may be required. Therefore, this allocation uses only the people and documentation elements.

Allocation 2 A bar code reader and controller are placed at the sorting station. Bar code output is passed to a programmable controller that controls a mechanical shunting mechanism. The shunt slides the box to the appropriate bin.

For allocation 2, hardware (bar code reader, programmable controller, shunt hardware, etc.), software (for the bar code reader and programmable controller), and database (a look-up table that related box identification, or ID, with bin location) elements are used to provide a fully automated solution. It is likely that each of these system elements may have corresponding manuals and other documentation, adding another generic system element.

Allocation 3 A bar code reader and controller are placed at the sorting station. Bar code output is passed to a robot arm that grasps a box and moves it to the appropriate bin location.

Allocation 3 makes use of generic system elements and one macro element—the robot. Like allocation 2, this allocation uses hardware, software, a database, and documentation as generic elements. The robot is a macro element of CLSS and itself contains a set of generic system elements.

By examining the three alternative allocations for CLSS, it should be obvious that the same function can be allocated to different system elements. In order to choose the most effective allocation, a set of trade-off criteria should be applied to each alternative.

The following trade-off criteria govern the selection of a system configuration based on a specific allocation of function and performance to generic system elements:

Project considerations. Can the configuration be built within pre-established cost and schedule bounds? What is the risk associated with cost and schedule estimates?

Business considerations. Does the configuration represent the most profitable solution? Can it be marketed successfully? Will ultimate payoff justify development risk?

Technical analysis. Does the technology exist to develop all elements of the system? Are function and performance assured? Can the configuration be adequately maintained? Do technical resources exist? What is the risk associated with the technology?

Manufacturing evaluation. Are manufacturing facilities and equipment available? Is there a shortage of necessary components? Can quality assurance be adequately performed?

Human issues. Are trained personnel available for development and manufacture? Do political problems exist? Does the customer understand what the system is to accomplish?

Environmental interfaces. Does the proposed configuration properly interface with the system's external environment? Are machine-to-machine and human-to-machine communication handled in an intelligent manner?

Legal considerations. Does this configuration introduce undue liability risk? Can proprietary aspects be adequately protected? Is there potential infringement?

We examine some of these issues in more detail later in this chapter.

It is important to note that the system engineer should also consider off-the-shelf solutions to the customer's problem. Does an equivalent system already exist? Can major parts of a solution be purchased from a third party?

The application of trade-off criteria results in the selection of a specific system configuration and the specification of function and performance allocated to hardware, software (and firmware), people, databases, documentation, and procedures. Essentially, the scope of function and performance is allocated to each system element. The role of hardware engineering, software engineering, human engineering, and database engineering is to refine scope and produce an operational system element that can be properly integrated with other system elements.

5.2.1 Hardware and Hardware Engineering

The computer system engineer selects some combination of hardware components that comprise one element of the computer-based system. Hardware selection, although by no means simple, is aided by a number of characteristics: (1) Components are packaged as individual building blocks, (2) interfaces among components are standardized, (3) numerous off-the-shelf alternatives are available, and (4) performance, cost, and availability are relatively easy to determine.

A hardware configuration evolves from a hierarchy of "building blocks." Discrete components (i.e., integrated circuits and electronic components such as resistors, capacitors, etc.) are assembled as a printed circuit board that performs a specific set of operations. Boards are interfaced with a bus (an information and control pathway) to form system components (e.g., a single board computer) that in turn are integrated to become the hardware subsystem or hardware system element. Because very-large-scale integration is now commonplace, functions that were once available on a set of PC boards with dozens of integrated circuits are available on a single chip.

Hardware engineering for digital computers grew from precedent established by decades of electronic design. The hardware engineering process can be viewed in three phases: planning and specification; design and prototype implementation; and manufacturing, distribution, and field service. The phases are illustrated in Figure 5.3*a*, *b*, and *c*.

Once system engineering (system analysis and definition) has been conducted, functions are allocated to hardware. The first phase of hardware engineering (Figure 5.3*a*) includes *development planning* and *hardware requirements analysis*. Development planning is conducted to establish the scope of the hardware effort. That is, we ask the following questions:

- What classes of hardware best address the specified functions?
- What hardware is available for purchase; what are the sources, availability, and cost?
- What kinds of interfacing are required?
- What do we have to design and build; what are the potential problems and required resources?

From these questions and others, preliminary cost and schedule estimates for the hardware system element are established. These estimates are reviewed by the appropriate managers and technical staff and modified if necessary.

Next, we must establish a "road map" for hardware design and implementation. Hardware requirements analysis is conducted to specify precise functional, performance, and interface requirements for all components of the hardware element. In addition, design constraints (e.g., size, environment) and test criteria are established. A *Hardware Specification* is often produced. Review and modification are to be encouraged at this stage.

The popular image of "shirt-sleeve" engineering is characterized by the second phase (Figure 5.3*b*). Requirements are analyzed and a preliminary hardware configuration is designed. Technical reviews are conducted as the design evolves toward detailed engineering drawings (a design specification). Today, analysis and design are conducted using *computer-aided engineering* and *computer-aided design* (CAE/CAD) tools. Off-the-shelf components are acquired; custom components are built and a prototype is assembled. The prototype is tested to ensure that it meets all requirements.

The prototype (sometimes called the "breadboard" model in electronics) often bears little resemblance to the manufactured product. Therefore, manufacturing specifications are derived. Breadboards become PC boards; (EPROM) or (PROM) become ROM; new packaging is designed; tooling and equipment are defined. Emphasis shifts from function and performance to ease of manufacture.

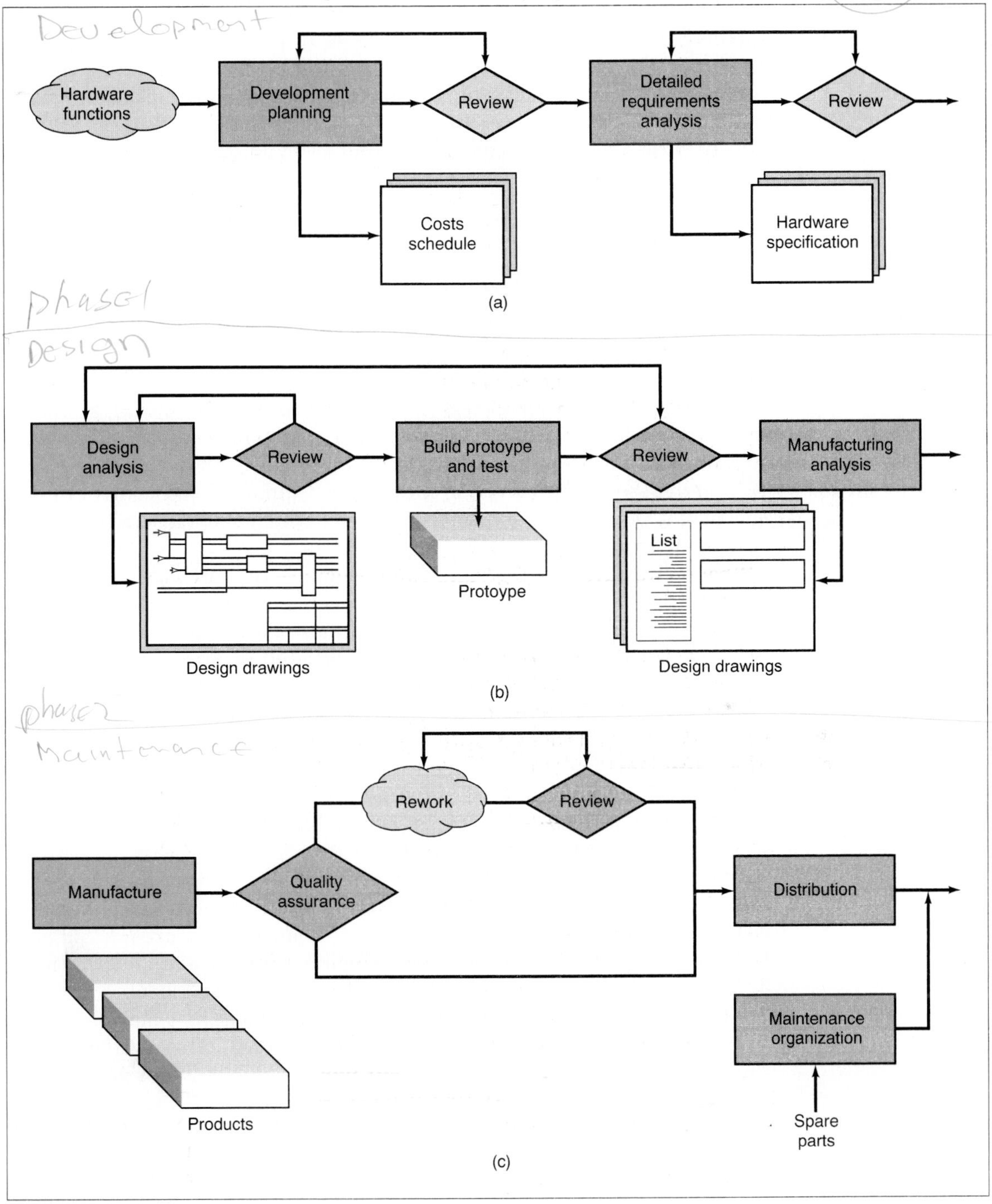

FIGURE 5.3. Hardware engineering. (a) Phase I; (b) phase II; (c) phase III.

The third phase of hardware engineering makes few direct demands on the design engineer but taxes the abilities of the manufacturing engineer. Before production begins, quality assurance methods must be established and a product distribution mechanism must be defined. Spare parts are placed in inventory and a field service organization is established for product maintenance and repair. The manufacturing phase of hardware engineering is illustrated in Figure 5.3*c*.

5.2.2 Software and Software Engineering

The characteristics of software and software engineering have been discussed in detail in Chapter 1. In this section we summarize our earlier discussion in the context of computer system engineering.

Function and performance are allocated to software during system engineering. In some cases, function is simply the implementation of a sequential procedure for data manipulation. Performance is not explicitly defined. In other cases, function is the internal coordination and control of other concurrent programs, and performance is defined explicitly in terms of response and wait times.

To accommodate function and performance, the software engineer must build or acquire a set of software components. Unlike hardware, software components are rarely standardized.[2] In most cases, the software engineer creates custom components to meet the allocated requirements for the software element of the system that is to be developed.

The software element of a computer-based system is comprised of programs, data, and documentation that is categorized as *application software* and *system software.* Application software implements the procedure that is required to accommodate information processing functions. System software implements control functions that enable application software to interface with other system elements.

Generic software application areas have been described in Section 1.2.3. Software applications in the broader context of a computer-based system are considered in this section. Regardless of its application area, a computer-based system can be represented using an input-process-output (IPO) model. The software element plays a role in each aspect of the model.

Software is used to acquire incoming information that may be provided from some source external to the system or from another system element (including macro elements). When a computer-based system requires an interactive human-machine interface, software implements the I/O "conversation." Prompting and data input mechanisms are implemented in software,

---

[2]The use of object-oriented techniques (Chapters 8 and 12) may lead to a broad array of "software ICs"—reusable software building blocks.

displays and graphics are generated with software, and the logic that leads the user through the sequence of interactive steps is accomplished through software. When data are acquired from a device, software in the form of *drivers* accommodates the special characteristics of the hardware. Finally, software is used to establish an interface to databases, enabling a program to tap a pre-existing data source.

Software implements processing algorithms that are required to accomplish system function. In general, a processing algorithm transforms input data or control information and produces data or control for output to another system element or macro element. Today, the most common type of processing is the numerical or nonnumerical procedure in which all steps, loops, and conditions are predefined in advance. However, new categories of processing algorithms, *expert system software* and *artificial neural networks,* are being introduced into some computer-based systems. Unlike conventional algorithms, expert systems software [RAE90] makes use of specified facts and rules for inference, enabling the software to exhibit human-like diagnostic abilities in a limited problem domain. Unlike expert systems software, an artificial neural network [WAS89] mimics the neural functions of the human brain and shows promise in pattern recognition and machine learning.

To be of practical use in a computer-based system, software must output data or control to another system element or an external source. To produce output, software must format data in a manner that is amenable to the output medium and interface with the output device [e.g., printer, optical disk, workstation display device].

Software engineering is a discipline for developing high-quality software for computer-based systems. In Chapter 1, we discussed software engineering in some detail and identified four software engineering paradigms—the classic life cycle, prototyping, the spiral model, and fourth-generation techniques. Each is distinct, yet all have three phases in common. We examine these phases using a flow of events that is analogous to the hardware engineering process.

Figure 5.4*a*, *b*, and *c* illustrates the generic steps in the software engineering process. The parts of the figure illustrate the steps that must be accomplished and the various representations of software that are derived as it evolves from concept to realization.

Definition Phase The definition phase of software engineering, depicted in Figure 5.4*a*, begins with the software planning step. During this step a bounded description of the scope of software effort is developed; risk analysis is conducted; resources required to develop the software are predicted; cost and schedule estimates are established. The purpose of the software project planning step is to provide a preliminary indication of project viability in relationship to cost and schedule constraints that may have already been established. A *Software Project Plan* is produced and reviewed by project management.

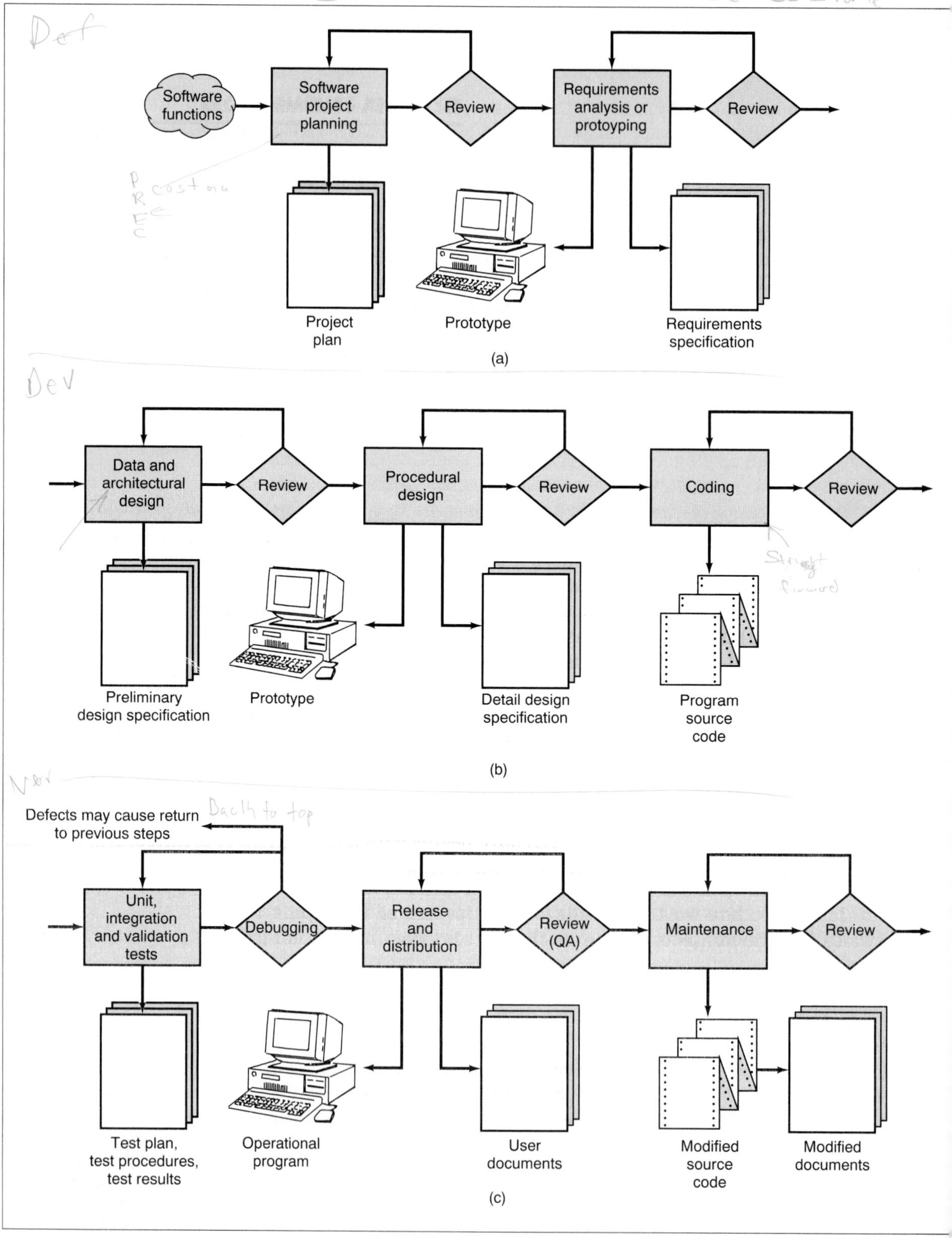

FIGURE 5.4. Software engineering—(a) Definition phase; (b) Development phase; (c) Verification, release, and maintenance phase.

The next step in the definition phase is software requirements analysis and definition. During this step, the system element allocated to software is defined in detail. Requirements are analyzed and defined in one of two ways. Formal information domain analysis may be used to establish models of information flow and structure. These models are then expanded to become a software specification. Alternatively, a prototype of the software is built and evaluated by the customer in an attempt to solidify requirements. Performance requirements or resource limitations are translated into software design characteristics. Global analysis of the software element defines validation criteria that will serve as the basis for test planning and will be used to demonstrate that requirements have been met.

Software requirements analysis and definition is a joint effort conducted by the software developer and the customer. A *Software Requirements Specification* is the deliverable document produced as a result of this step.

The definition phase culminates with a technical review of the *Software Requirements Specification* (or in lieu of the specification, a software prototype) by the developer and the customer. Once acceptable requirements have been defined, the *Software Project Plan* is re-evaluated for correctness. Information uncovered during requirements analysis may impact estimates made during the planning. Deliverables developed during the definition phase serve as the foundation for the second phase in the process—software development.

Development Phase The development phase (Figure 5.4*b*) translates a set of requirements into an operational system element that we call *software*. At early stages of hardware development, a hardware engineer does not reach for a soldering iron. The software engineer should not reach for a compiler. Design must be accomplished first.

The first step of the development phase concentrates on design. The design process for software begins with a description of architectural and data design. That is, a modular structure is developed, interfaces are defined, and data structure is established. Design criteria are used to assess quality. This preliminary design step is reviewed for completeness and traceability to software requirements. A first-draft *Design Specification*[3] is delivered and becomes part of the software configuration.

Procedural aspects of each modular component of the software design are considered next. Each detailed procedural description is added to the *Design Specification* after review.

Coding—the generation of a program using an appropriate programming language or CASE tool—occurs after design is complete. Software engineering methodology views coding as a consequence of good design. Code

[3]Today, the *Design Specification* can be created with specialized CASE tools (e.g., Cadre Teamwork) and maintained in machine-readable form. In some cases, design documentation, called *program design language,* is embedded directly into source code files.

is reviewed for style and clarity, but should otherwise be directly traceable to a detailed design description. A source language listing for each modular component of software is the configuration deliverable for the coding step.

Verification, Release, and Maintenance Phase During the last phase in the software engineering process (Figure 5.4*c*), the software engineer tests the software to find the maximum number of errors before shipment, prepares the software for release, and then maintains the software throughout its useful life.

After source code has been generated, a series of verification and validation activities are conducted. Unit testing attempts to verify the functional performance of an individual modular component of software. Integration testing provides a means for the construction of the software architecture while at the same time testing function and interfaces. Validation testing verifies that all requirements have been met. After each of these testing steps, debugging—the diagnosis and correction of defects—may occur. A *Test Plan and Procedure* may be developed for the testing steps. Review of test documentation, test cases, and results is always conducted.

Once software testing is completed the software is almost ready for release to end users. However, before release occurs, a series of quality assurance (QA) activities are conducted to ensure that appropriate records and internal documents have been generated and cataloged, high-quality user documentation has been developed, and appropriate configuration control mechanisms have been established. The software is then distributed to end users.

As soon as software is released to end users, the software engineer's job changes. Now, the focus changes from construction to maintenance—error correction, environmental adaptation, and function enhancement. Recognition of this fact is the first step toward lessening the impact of a task that devours 50 to 70 percent of budget for many large software organizations. The tasks associated with software maintenance depend upon the type of maintenance to be performed. Modification of the software includes the entire configuration (i.e., all programs, data, and documents developed in the definition and development phases), not just code.

5.2.3 Human Factors and Human Engineering

A computer-based system almost always has a human element. A person may directly interact with hardware and software, conducting a dialog that drives the function of the system; in all cases, people are responsible for the development and maintenance of the system.

Our perception of the human element of computer-based systems has changed in recent years. Early computer-based systems forced the user to communicate in ways that were easy to implement in hardware and software (if not always easy to understand in the human context). Today, the phrase "user friendly" has taken on new meaning. Human engineering for computer-based systems is recognized as an important step in system development.

When people interact with other people, a culturally defined set of rules, cues, and responses allows the interaction to proceed smoothly. Unfortunately, the conventions for person-to-person interaction are not present when *human-computer interaction* (HCI) is attempted.

Before a system engineer can allocate function to the human element, the interaction necessary to perform function must be specified. To do this, the "components" of the human element should be understood. Among many components that comprise the human element are: human memory and knowledge representation, thinking and reasoning, visual perception, human dialog construction.

Human engineering is a multidisciplinary activity that applies knowledge derived from psychology and technology to specify and design high-quality HCI. The human engineering process encompasses the following steps:

- *Activity analysis.* Each activity that has been allocated to the human element is evaluated in the context of required interaction with other elements. An activity is subdivided into tasks that are further analyzed in later steps.
- *Semantic analysis and design.* The precise meaning of each action required of the user and produced by the machine is defined. The design of a "dialog" that communicates proper semantics is established.
- *Syntactic and lexical design.* The specific form of actions and commands is identified and represented. Then, the hardware and software implementation of each action or command is designed.
- *User environment design.* Hardware, software, and other system elements are combined to form a user environment. The environment may include physical facilities (lighting, space management, etc.) as well as the HCI itself.
- *Prototyping.* It is difficult, if not impossible, to formally specify an HCI without the use of a prototype. Prototyping enables the HCI to be evaluated from the human perspective, using active participation rather than passive evaluation. Prototyping results in evaluation and the iterative application of all the human engineering steps noted above.

A more detailed discussion of human factors and human engineering (applied to user interface design) is presented in Chapter 14.

5.2.4 Databases and Database Engineering

Not all computer-based systems make use of a database, but for those that do, this information store is often pivotal to overall function. *Database engi-*

neering (a relatively new term that encompasses database analysis, design, and implementation) is a technical discipline that is applied once the information domain of the database has been defined. Therefore, the role of the system engineer is to define the information to be contained in a database, the types of queries to be submitted for processing, the manner in which data will be accessed, and the capacity of the database. Although database engineering is a topic for serious study in its own right (e.g., see [DAT86], [IEE89]), data analysis and design are also fundamental software engineering activities, regardless of the presence of a formal database. These database engineering topics, collectively called *data design,* are discussed in Chapters 8, 9, and 10.

5.3 SYSTEM ANALYSIS

System analysis is an activity that encompasses most of the tasks that we have collectively called *computer system engineering*. Confusion sometimes occurs because the term is often used in a context that alludes only to software requirements analysis activities (see Chapters 6 through 9). For the purposes of this discussion, system analysis focuses on all system elements—not just software.

System analysis is conducted with the following objectives in mind: (1) identify the customer's need; (2) evaluate the system concept for feasibility; (3) perform economic and technical analysis; (4) allocate functions to hardware, software, people, database, and other system elements; (5) establish cost and schedule constraints; (6) create a system definition that forms the foundation for all subsequent engineering work. Both hardware and software expertise (as well as human and database engineering) are required to successfully attain the objectives listed above. Although most industry professionals recognize that time and effort expended on system analysis pay important dividends later in the system development process, three questions still arise:

- *How much effort should be expended on analysis and definition for systems and software?* Definitive guidelines for analysis effort are difficult to establish. System size and complexity, application area, end use, and contractual obligations are only a few of many variables that affect overall analysis effort. An oft-used rule of thumb is that 10 to 20 percent of all development effort should be applied to system analysis and that another 10 to 20 percent of software engineering effort should be applied to software requirements analysis.
- *Who does it?* An experienced, well-trained analyst should conduct most of the tasks. The analyst works in conjunction with management and technical staff of the customer and system developer. For very large projects, an analysis team may be formed to conduct each analysis task.

- *Why is it so difficult?* A nebulous concept must be transformed into a concrete set of tangible elements. Because communication content is exceptionally high during analysis, the opportunity for misunderstanding, omission, inconsistency, and error abounds. Finally, the perception of the system may change as the activity progresses, thereby invalidating earlier work.

5.3.1 Identification of Need

The first step of the system analysis process involves the identification of need. The analyst (system engineer) meets with the customer and the end user (if different from the customer). The customer may be a representative of an outside company, the marketing department of the analyst's company (when a product is being defined), or another technical department (when an internal system is to be developed).

Identification of need is the starting point in the evolution of a computer-based system. Figure 5.5 illustrates some of the questions that must be answered so that the analyst can properly complete this step. To begin, the analyst assists the customer in defining the goals of the system (product): What information will be produced? What information is to be provided? What functions and performance are required? The analyst makes sure to distinguish between customer "needs" (features that are critical to the system's success) and customer "wants" (features that would be nice to have but are not essential).

Once overall goals are identified, the analyst moves on to an evaluation of supplementary information: Does the technology exist to build the system? What special development and manufacturing resources will be required? What bounds have been placed on costs and schedule? If the new system is actually a product to be developed for sale to many customers, the following questions are also asked: What is the potential market for the

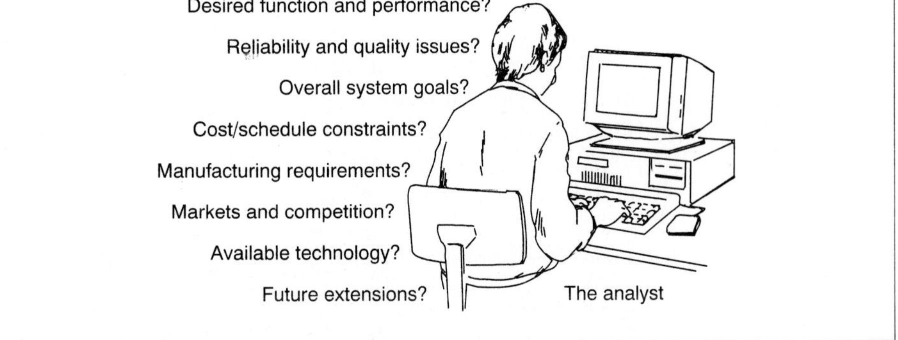
Desired function and performance?
Reliability and quality issues?
Overall system goals?
Cost/schedule constraints?
Manufacturing requirements?
Markets and competition?
Available technology?
Future extensions?
The analyst

FIGURE 5.5.
Information required by the analyst.

product? How does this product compare with competitive products? What position does this product take in the overall product line of the company?

Information gathered during the needs identification step is specified in a *System Concept Document.* The original concept document is sometimes prepared by the customer before meetings with the analyst. Invariably, customer-analyst communication results in modifications to the document.

5.3.2 Feasibility Study

All projects are feasible—given unlimited resources and infinite time! Unfortunately, the development of a computer-based system is more likely to be plagued by a scarcity of resources and difficult (if not downright unrealistic) delivery dates. It is both necessary and prudent to evaluate the feasibility of a project at the earliest possible time. Months or years of effort, thousands or millions of dollars, and untold professional embarrassment can be averted if an ill-conceived system is recognized early in the definition phase.

Feasibility and risk analysis (Chapter 4) are related in many ways. If project risk is great (for any of the reasons discussed in Chapter 4), the feasibility of producing quality software is reduced. During system engineering, however, we concentrate our attention on four primary areas of interest:

Economic feasibility. An evaluation of development cost weighed against the ultimate income or benefit derived from the developed system.

Technical feasibility. A study of function, performance, and constraints that may affect the ability to achieve an acceptable system.

Legal feasibility. A determination of any infringement, violation, or liability that could result from the development of the system.

Alternatives. An evaluation of alternative approaches to the development of the system.

A *feasibility study* is not warranted for systems in which economic justification is obvious, technical risk is low, few legal problems are expected, and no reasonable alternative exists. However, if any of the preceding conditions fails, a study should be conducted.

Economic justification is generally the "bottom-line" consideration for most systems (notable exceptions include national defense systems, systems mandated by law, and high-technology applications such as the space program). Economic justification includes a broad range of concerns that include cost-benefit analysis (discussed in the next section), long-term corporate income strategies, impact on other profit centers or products, cost of resources needed for development, and potential market growth.

Technical feasibility is frequently the most difficult area to assess at this stage of the system development process. Because objectives, functions, and performance are somewhat hazy, anything seems possible if the right assumptions are made. It is essential that the process of analysis and definition be conducted in parallel with an assessment of technical feasibility. In this way concrete specifications may be judged as they are determined.

The considerations that are normally associated with technical feasibility include:

Development risk. Can the system element be designed so that the necessary function and performance are achieved within the constraints uncovered during analysis?

Resource availability. Are competent staff available to develop the system element in question? Are other necessary resources (hardware and software) available to build the system?

Technology. Has the relevant technology progressed to a state that will support the system?

Developers of computer-based systems are optimists by nature. (Who else would be brave enough to attempt what we frequently undertake?) However, during an evaluation of technical feasibility, a cynical, if not pessimistic, attitude should prevail. Misjudgment at this stage can be disastrous.

Legal feasibility encompasses a broad range of concerns that includes contracts, liability, infringement, and myriad other traps frequently unknown to the technical staff. A discussion of legal issues and software is beyond the scope of this book. The interested reader should see Gemignani [GEM81], Harris [HAR85], or Scott [SCO89].

The degree to which alternatives are considered is often limited by cost and time constraints; however, a legitimate but "unsponsored" variation should not be buried.

The feasibility study may be documented as a separate report to upper management and included as an appendix to the *System Specification*. Although the format of a feasibility report may vary, the outline provided in Table 5.1 covers most important topics.

The feasibility study is reviewed first by project management (to assess content reliability) and by upper management (to assess project status). The study should result in a "go/no-go" decision. It should be noted that other go/no-go decisions will be made during the planning, specification, and development steps of both hardware and software engineering.

5.3.3 Economic Analysis

Among the most important information contained in a feasibility study is *cost-benefit analysis*— an assessment of the economic justification for a computer-based system project. Cost-benefit analysis delineates costs for project development and weighs them against tangible (i.e., measurable directly in dollars) and intangible benefits of a system.

TABLE 5.1

FEASIBILITY STUDY OUTLINE

I. Introduction
- **A.** Statement of the problem
- **B.** Implementation environment
- **C.** Constraints

II. Management summary and recommendations
- **A.** Important findings
- **B.** Comments
- **C.** Recommendations
- **D.** Impact

III. Alternatives
- **A.** Alternative system configurations
- **B.** Criteria used in selecting the final approach

IV. System description
- **A.** Abbreviated statement of scope
- **B.** Feasibility of allocated elements

V. Cost-benefit analysis

VI. Evaluation of technical risk

VII. Legal ramifications

VIII. Other project-specific topics

Cost-benefit analysis is complicated by criteria that vary with the characteristics of the system to be developed, the relative size of the project, and the expected return on investment desired as part of a company's strategic plan. In addition many benefits derived from computer-based systems are intangible (e.g., better design quality through iterative optimization, increased customer satisfaction through programmable control, and better business decisions through reformatted and preanalyzed sales data). Direct quantitative comparisons may be difficult to achieve.

As we noted above, analysis of benefits will differ depending on system characteristics. To illustrate, consider the benefits for management information systems [KIN78] shown in Table 5.2. Most data processing systems are developed with better information quantity, quality, timeliness, or organization as a primary objective. Therefore, the benefits noted in Table 5.2 concentrate on information access and its impact on the user environment. The benefits that might be associated with an engineering-scientific analysis program or a microprocessor-based product could differ substantially.

Benefits of a new system are always determined relative to the existing mode of operation. As an example, we consider a computer-aided design (CAD) system that will replace elements of a manual engineering design

TABLE 5.2

POSSIBLE INFORMATION SYSTEM BENEFITS*

Benefits from contributions of calculating and printing tasks
- Reduction in per unit costs of calculating and printing (CR)
- Improved accuracy in calculating tasks (ER)
- Ability to quickly change variables and values in calculation programs (IF)
- Greatly increased speed in calculating and printing (IS)

Benefits from contributions to record-keeping tasks
- Ability to "automatically" collect and store data for records (CR, IS, ER)
- More complete and systematic keeping of records (CR, ER)
- Increased capacity for record keeping in terms of space and cost (CR)
- Standardization for record keeping (CR, IS)
- Increase in amount of data that can be stored per record (CR, IS)
- Improved security in records storage (ER, CR, MC)
- Improved portability of records (IF, CR, IS)

Benefits from contributions to record-searching tasks
- Faster retrieval of records (IS)
- Improved ability to access records from large data bases (IF)
- Improved ability to change records in data bases (IF, CR)
- Ability to link sites that need search capability through telecommunications (IF, IS)
- Improved ability to create records of records accessed and by whom (ER, MC)
- Ability to audit and analyze record-searching activity (MC, ER)

Benefits from contributions to system restructuring capability
- Ability to simultaneously change entire classes of records (IS, IF, CR)
- Ability to move large files of data about (IS, IF)
- Ability to create new files by merging aspects of other files (IS, IF)

Benefits from contributions of analysis and simulation capability
- Ability to perform complex, simultaneous calculations quickly (IS, IF, ER)
- Ability to create simulations of complex phenomena to answer "what if?" questions (MC, IF)
- Ability to aggregate large amounts of data useful for planning and decision making (MC, IF)

Benefits from contributions to process and resource control
- Reduction of need for work force in process and resource control (CR)
- Improved ability to "fine tune" process such as assembly lines (CR, MC, IS, ER)
- Improved ability to maintain continuous monitoring of resources (MC, ER, IF)

*Abbreviations: CR = cost reduction or avoidance; ER = error reduction; IF = increased flexibility; IS = increased speed of activity; MC = improvement in management planning or control.
Source: King and Schrems [KIN78], p. 23. Reprinted with permission.

process. The system analyst must define measurable characteristics for the existing system (manual design) and the proposed system (CAD). Choosing time to produce a finished detailed drawing (*t-draw*) as one of the many measurable quantities, the analyst finds that a 4-to-1 reduction in *t*-draw will accrue from the CAD system. To further quantify this benefit, the following data are determined:

t-draw, average drawing time = 4 hours

d, cost per drawing-hour = \$20.00

n, number of drawings per year = 8000

p, percentage of drawing to be done on CAD system = %60

With the above data known, an estimate of yearly cost savings—the benefit—can be ascertained:

Drawing time cost savings = reduction × t-draw × n × c × p

= \$96,000 per year

Other tangible benefits from the CAD system would be treated in a similar fashion. Intangible benefits (e.g., better design quality and increased employee morale) can be assigned dollar values or used to support a go recommendation, if indicated.

Costs associated with the development of a computer-based system [KIN78] are listed in Table 5.3. The analyst can estimate each cost and then use development and on-going costs to determine a return on investment, a break-even point, and a pay-back period. The graph shown in Figure 5.6 illustrates these characteristics for the CAD system example noted above. We assume that total savings per year have been estimated to be \$96,000, total development (or purchase) cost is estimated to be \$204,000, annual costs are estimated to be \$32,000.

From the graph shown in Figure 5.6, the pay-back period requires 3.1 years. In actuality, return on investment is determined with a more detailed

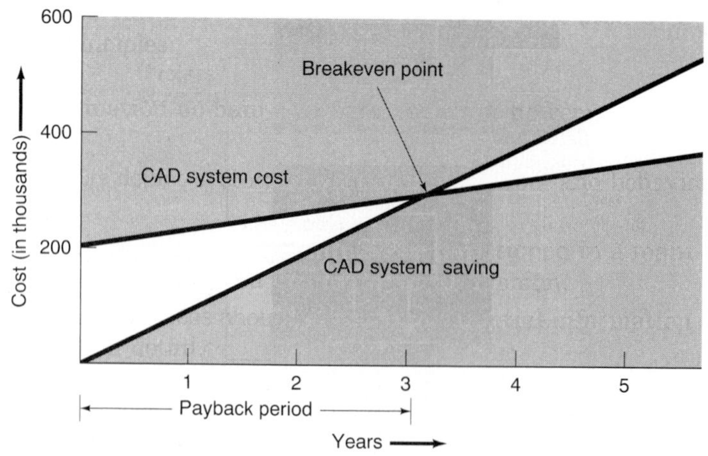

FIGURE 5.6.
Cost-benefit analysis.

TABLE 5.3

POSSIBLE INFORMATION SYSTEM COSTS

Procurement costs
- Consulting costs
- Actual equipment purchase or leave costs
- Equipment installation costs
- Costs for modifying the equipment site (air conditioning, security, etc.)
- Cost of capital
- Cost of management and staff dealing with procurement

Start-up costs
- Cost of operating system software
- Cost of communications equipment installation (telephone lines, data lines, etc.)
- Cost of start-up personnel
- Cost of personnel searches and hiring activities
- Cost of disruption to the rest of the organization
- Cost of management required to direct start-up activity

Project-related costs
- Cost of applications software purchased
- Cost of software modifications to fit local systems
- Cost of personnel, overhead, etc., from in-house application development
- Cost for training user personnel in application use
- Cost of data collection and installing data collection procedures
- Cost of preparing documentation
- Cost of development management

Ongoing costs
- System maintenance costs (hardware, software, and facilities)
- Rental costs (electricity, telephones, etc.)
- Depreciation costs on hardware
- Cost of staff involved in information systems management, operation, and planning activities

Source: King and Schrems [KIN78], p. 24. Reprinted with permission.

analysis that considers time value of money, tax consequences, and other potential uses for the investment. Taking intangible benefits into account, upper management then decides if such economic results justify the system.

Another aspect of cost-benefit analysis considers the incremental cost associated with added benefits (more or better function and performance). For computer-based systems, the incremental cost-benefit relationship can be represented as shown in Figure 5.7.

In some cases (curve AA') cost increases proportionally with benefits until some point A. After this point each additional benefit is exceedingly expensive. For example, consider a real-time polling function that has 500 milliseconds of idle time. New tasks can be added with relatively low

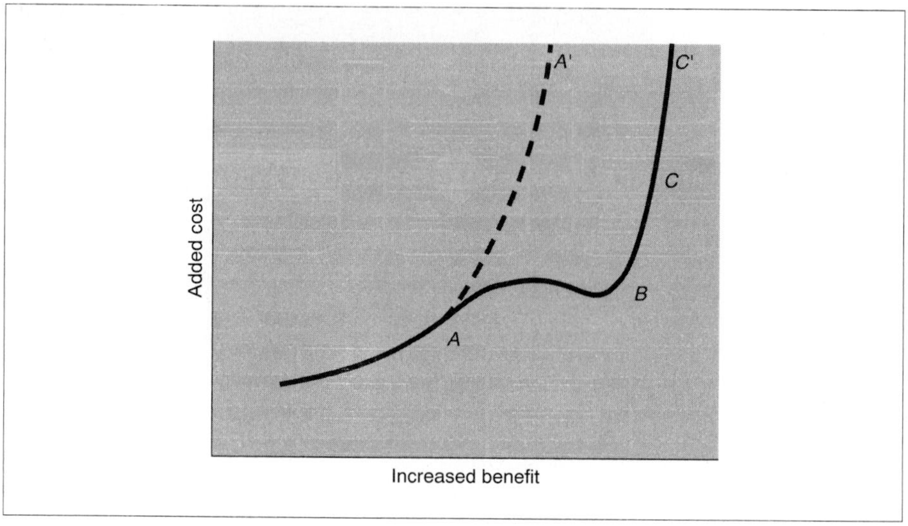

FIGURE 5.7. Incremental cost-benefit.

cost; however, if total task execution approaches 500 milliseconds, the cost to implement increases dramatically because overall performance must be improved.

In other cases (curve *ABCC'*) cost increases proportionally until *A* and then levels for added benefits (through *B*) before increasing dramatically (at *C*) for subsequent benefits. As an example, consider a single-user operating system that is enhanced incrementally to support multiple users. Once multiuser support is available, the rate of increase in cost for added multiuser functions may lessen somewhat. However, once processor capacity is reached, added features will require a more powerful processor and a large increment in cost.

The following excerpt [FRI77] may best characterize cost-benefit analysis:

> Like political rhetoric after the election, the cost-benefit analysis may be forgotten after the project implementation begins. However, it is extremely important because it has been the vehicle by which management approval has been obtained.

Only by spending the time to evaluate feasibility do we reduce the chances for extreme embarrassment (or worse) at later stages of a system project. Effort spent on a feasibility analysis that results in cancellation of a proposed project is not wasted effort.

5.3.4 Technical Analysis

During technical analysis, the analyst evaluates the technical merits of the system concept, while at the same time collecting additional information about performance, reliability, maintainability, and producibility. In some cases, this system analysis step also includes a limited amount of research and design.

Technical analysis begins with an assessment of the technical viability of the proposed system. What technologies are required to accomplish system function and performance? What new material, methods, algorithms, or processes are required and what is their development risk? How will these technology issues affect cost?

The tools available for technical analysis are derived from mathematical modeling and optimization techniques, probability and statistics, queuing theory, and control theory—to name a few sources.[4] It is important to note, however, that analytical evaluation is not always possible. Modeling (either mathematical or physical) is an effective mechanism for the technical analysis of computer-based systems. Figure 5.8 illustrates the overall flow of information for the modeling process. A model is created based on observation of the real world or approximation based on system goals. The analyst assesses model behavior and compares it to real-world or expected system behavior, gaining insight into the technical viability of the proposed system.

[4] A class of CASE tools, called *prototyping and simulation tools,* can assist greatly in technical analysis. These tools are discussed in Chapters 15 and 22.

Careful of thing to leave out

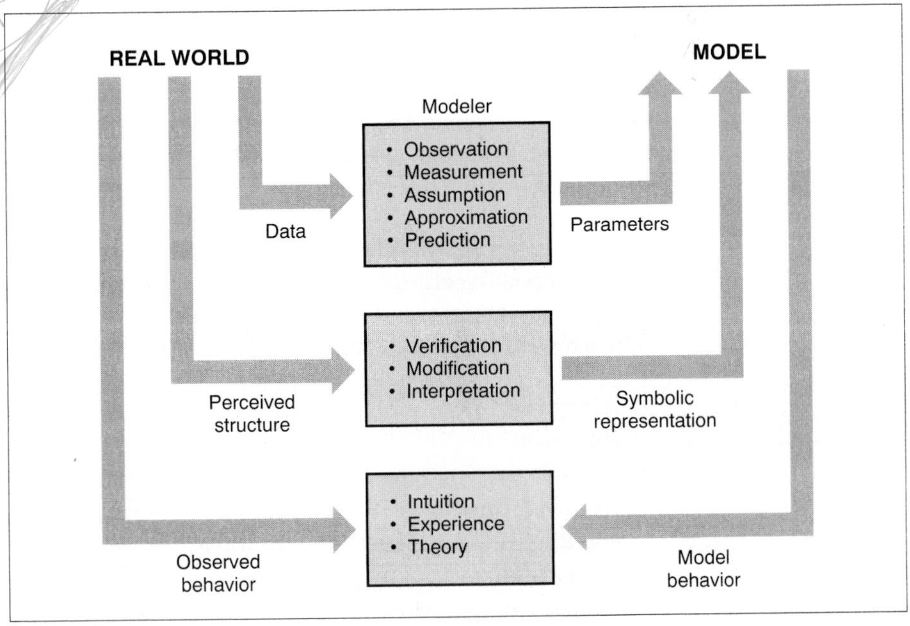

FIGURE 5.8.
System modeling.

Blanchard and Fabrycky [BLA81, p. 270] define a set of criteria for the use of models during the technical analysis of systems:

1. The model should represent the dynamics of the system configuration being evaluated in a way that is simple enough to understand and manipulate, and yet close enough to the operating reality to yield results.
2. The model should highlight those factors that are most relevant to the problem at hand, and suppress (with discretion) those that are not as important.
3. The model should be comprehensive by including *all* relevant factors and be reliable in terms of repeatability of results.
4. Model design should be simple enough to follow timely implementation in problem solving. Unless the tool can be utilized in a timely and efficient manner by the analyst or the manager, it is of little value. If the model is large and highly complex, it may be appropriate to develop a series of models where the output of one can be tied to the input of another. Also, it may be desirable to evaluate a specific element of the system independently from other elements.
5. Model design should incorporate provisions for ease of modification and/or expansion to permit the evaluation of additional factors as required. Successful model development often includes a series of trials before the overall objective is met. Initial attempts may suggest information gaps which are not immediately apparent and consequently may suggest beneficial changes.

The results obtained from technical analysis form the basis for another go/no-go decision on the system. If technical risk is severe, if models indicate that the desired function or performance cannot be achieved, if the pieces just won't fit together smoothly—it's back to the drawing board!

5.3.5 Allocation and Trade-Offs

Once the questions associated with the analysis task have been answered, alternative solutions are considered. Each system function with its requisite performance and interface characteristics is allocated to one or more system elements.

For example, the analysis of a new computer graphics system indicates that a major function is three-dimensional transformation of graphics images. An investigation of alternative solutions for the transformation function uncovers the following options:

1. All three dimension transformations are performed with the use of software.
2. "Simple" transformations (e.g., scaling, translation, rotation) are performed in hardware while "complex" transformations (e.g., perspective, shading) are performed in software.
3. All transformations are performed using a graphics processor implemented in hardware.

The overall process for the evaluation of alternative system configurations is illustrated in Figures 5.9 and 5.10 [BLA81]. Referring to Figure 5.9, each system configuration alternative is evaluated according to a set of "evaluation parameters" (trade-off criteria) that have been ordered by importance (Figure 5.10). In general, evaluation parameters are assessed with respect to economic factors (e.g., life-cycle cost). A trade-off area

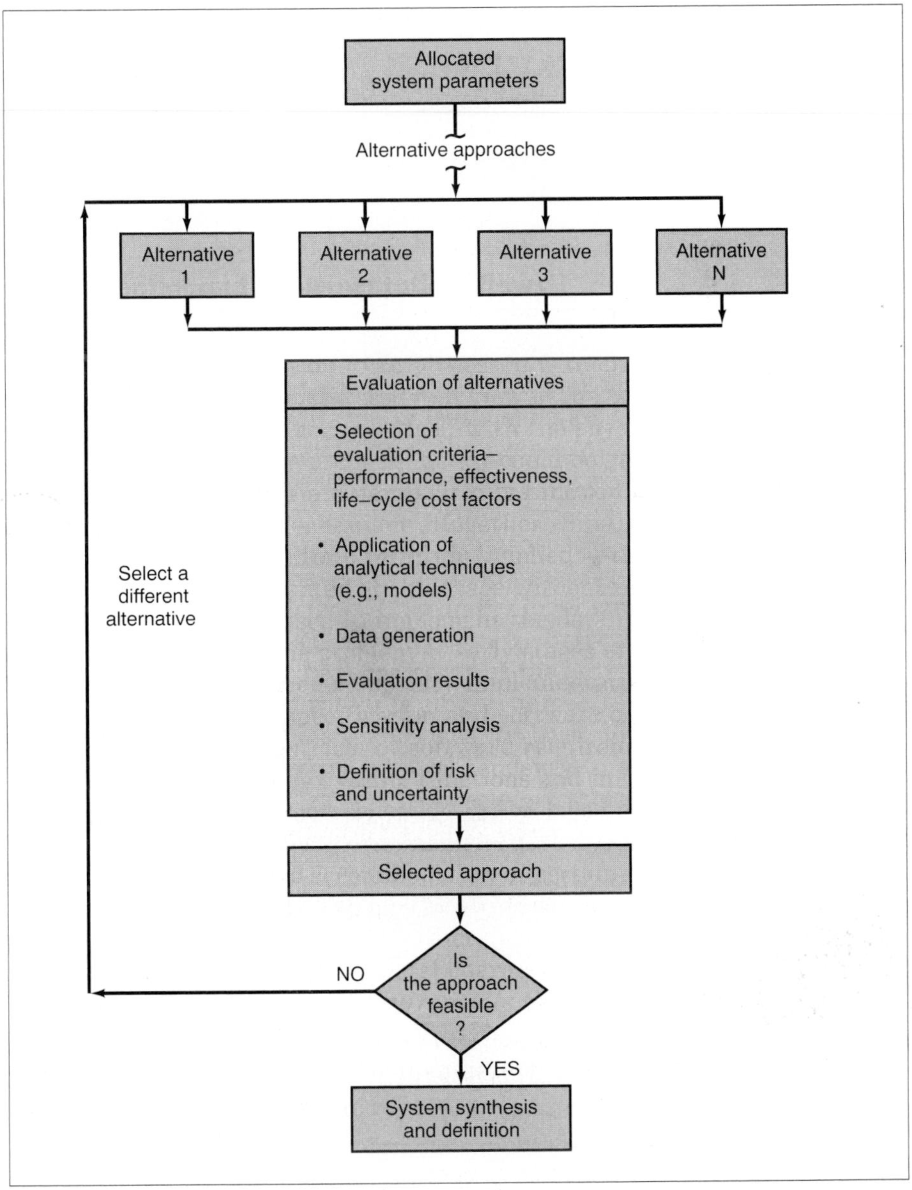

FIGURE 5.9. Evaluation of alternatives. *(Reprinted with permission of Prentice-Hall, Englewood Cliffs, NJ.)*

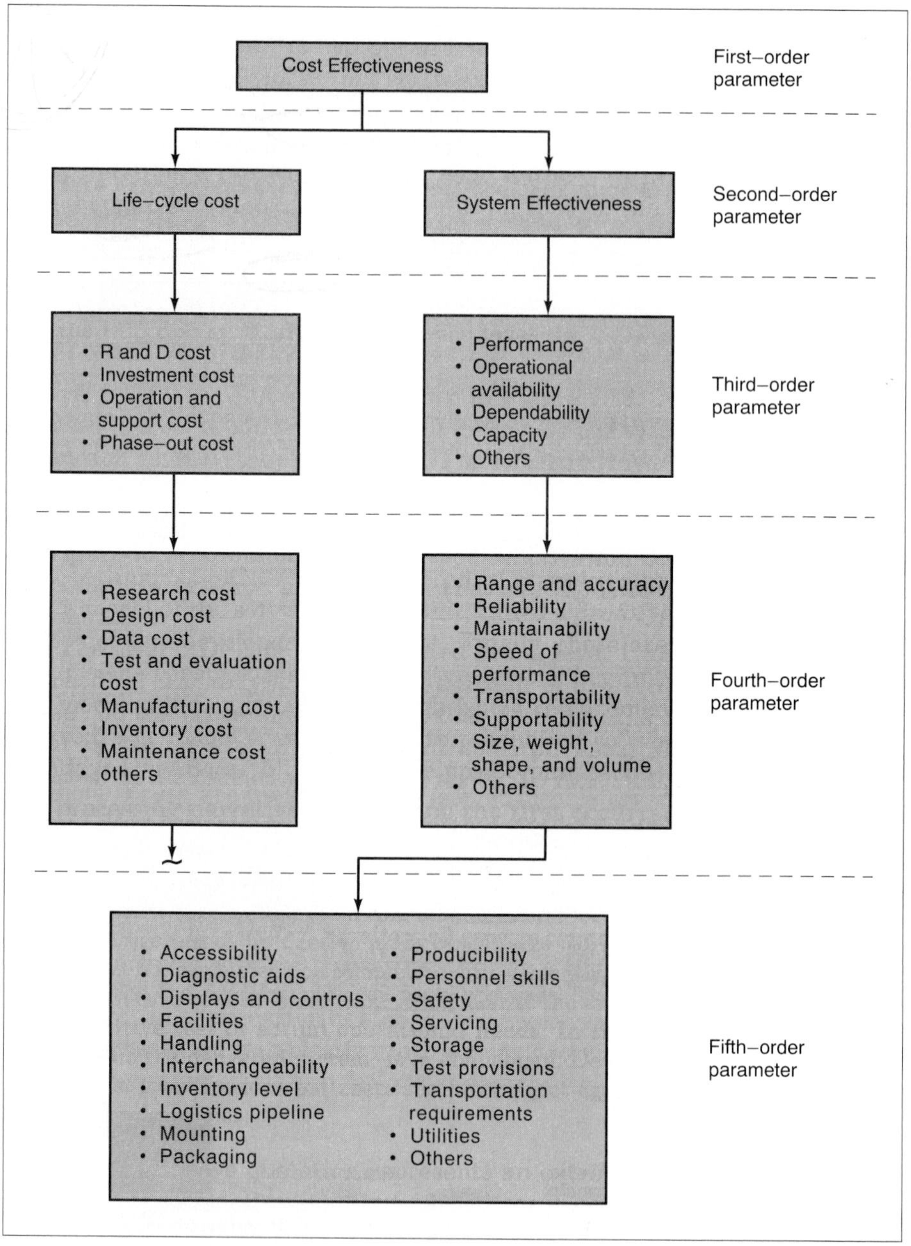

FIGURE 5.10. Order of evaluation parameters. *(Reprinted with permission of Prentice-Hall, Englewood Cliffs, NJ.)*

(Figure 5.11) is isolated when two or more system evaluation lower-order parameters (e.g., response time or display resolution) can be varied (in different allocations) and still achieve a desired higher-order parameter (e.g., cost or reliability).

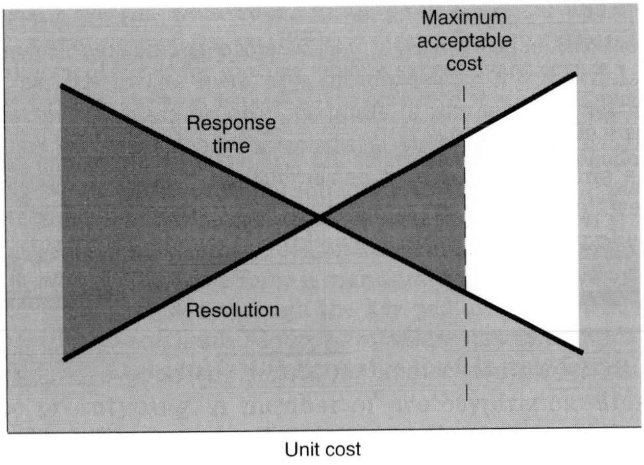

FIGURE 5.11.
Trade-off area.

5.4 MODELING THE SYSTEM ARCHITECTURE

Once the functions of a computer-based system have been allocated, the system engineer can create a model that represents the interrelationship between system elements and sets a foundation for later requirements analysis and design steps. We have already noted that every computer-based system can be modeled as an information transform using an input-processing-output architecture. Hatley and Pirbhai [HAT87] have extended this view to include two additional system features—user interface processing and maintenance and self-test processing. Although these additional features are not present for every computer-based system, they are very common, and their specification makes any system model more robust.

5.4.1 Architecture Diagrams

To develop the system model, an *architecture template* [HAT87] is used. The system engineer allocates system elements to each of five processing regions within the template: (1) user interface, (2) input, (3) system function and control, (4) output, and (5) maintenance and self-test. The format of the architecture template is shown in Figure 5.12.

Like nearly all modeling techniques used in system and software engineering, the architecture template enables the analyst to create a hierarchy of detail. An *architecture context diagram* (ACD) resides at the top level of the hierarchy.

The context diagram establishes the information boundary between the system being implemented and the environment in which the system is to

Know this and how to expand it

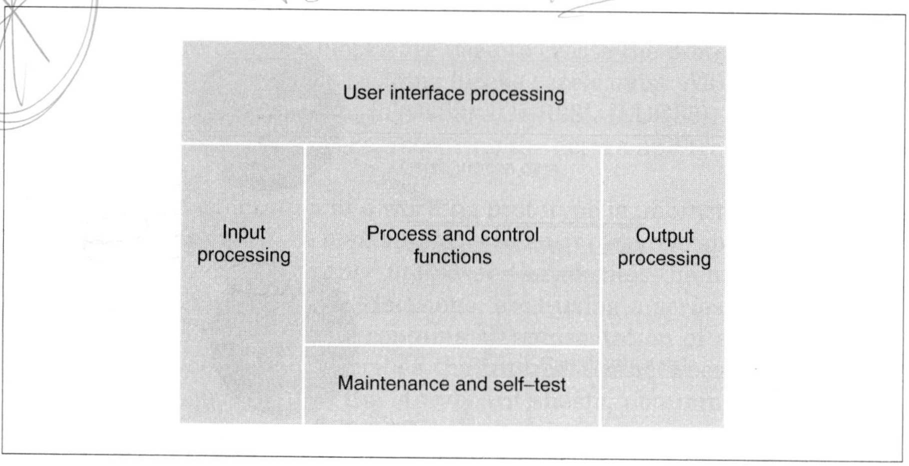

FIGURE 5.12.
Architecture
template.

operate [HAT87]. That is, the ACD defines all external producers of information used by the system, all external consumers of information created by the system, and all entities that communicate through the interface or perform maintenance and self-test.

To illustrate the use of the ACD, consider an extended version of the conveyor line sorting system discussed earlier in this chapter. The extended version makes use of a personal computer at the sorting station site. The PC executes all CLSS software, interfaces with the bar code reader to read part numbers on each box, interfaces with the conveyor line monitoring equipment to acquire conveyor line speed, stores all part numbers sorted, interacts with a sorting station operator to produce a variety of reports and diagnostics, sends control signals to the shunting hardware to sort the boxes, and communicates with a central factory automation mainframe. The ACD for CLSS (extended) is shown in Figure 5.13.

Each box shown in Figure 5.13 represents an *external entity*—that is, a producer or consumer of information from the system. For example, the **bar code reader** produces information that is input to the CLSS system. The symbol for the entire system (or at lower levels, major subsystems) is a rectangle with rounded corners. Hence, CLSS is represented in the processing and control region at the center of the ACD. The labeled arrows shown in the ACD represent information (data and control) as it moves from the external environment into the CLSS system. The external entity **bar code reader** produces input information that is labeled **bar code**. In essence, the ACD places any system into the context of its external environment.

The system engineer refines the architecture context diagram by considering the shaded rectangle in Figure 5.13 in more detail. The major subsystems that enable the conveyor line sorting system to function within the

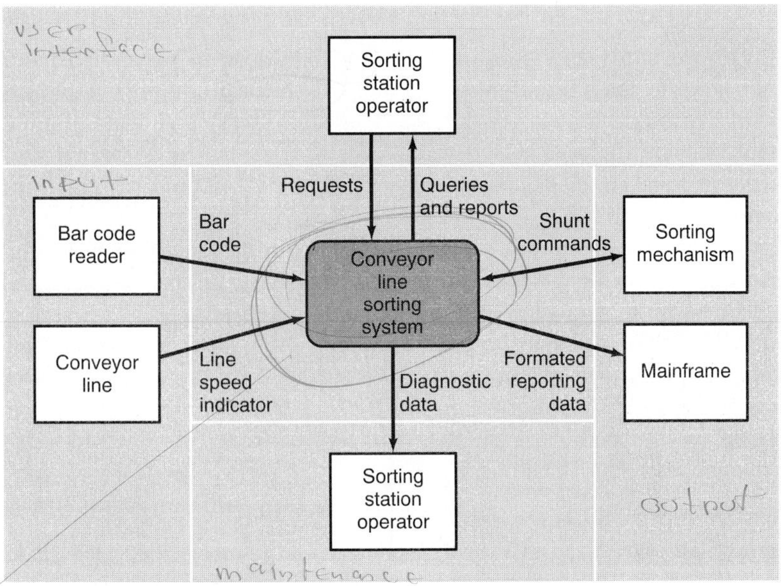

FIGURE 5.13.
Architecture context diagram for CLSS (extended).

context defined by the ACD are identified. Referring to Figure 5.14, the major subsystems[5] are defined in an *architecture flow diagram* (AFD) that is derived from the ACD. Information flow across the regions of the ACD is used to guide the system engineer in developing the AFD—a more detailed "schematic" for CLSS. The architecture flow diagram shows major subsystems and important lines of information (data and control) flow. In addition, the architecture template partitions the subsystem processing into each of the five processing regions discussed earlier. At this stage, each of the subsystems can contain one or more system elements (e.g., hardware, software, people) as allocated by the system engineer.

The initial architecture flow diagram becomes the top node of a hierarchy of AFDs. Each rounded rectangle in the original AFD can be expanded into another architecture template dedicated solely to it. This process is illustrated schematically in Figure 5.15. Each of the AFDs for the system can be used as a starting point for subsequent engineering steps for the subsystem that has been described.

[5]Hatley and Pirbhai [HAT87] call these *system modules*.

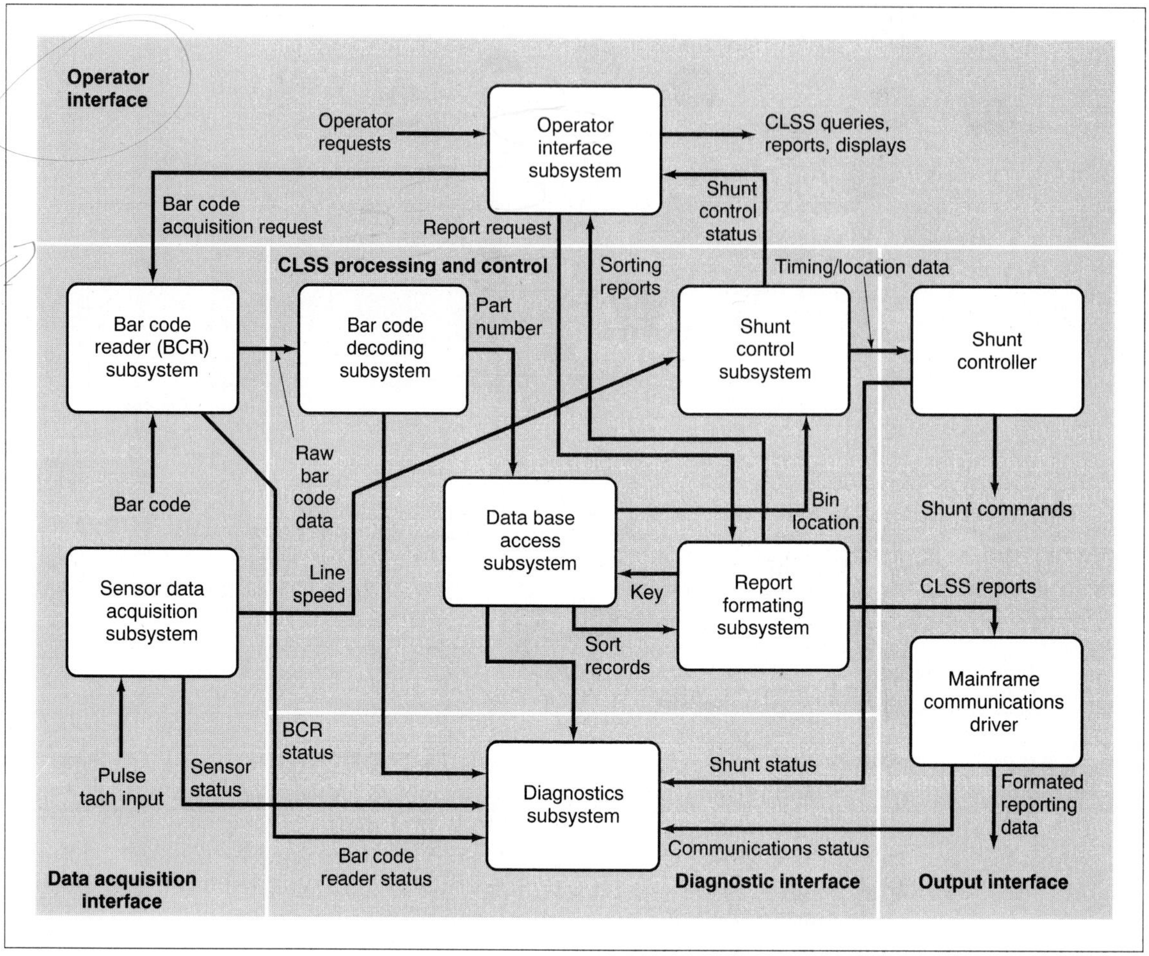

FIGURE 5.14. Architecture flow diagram for CLSS (extended).

5.4.2 Specification of the System Architecture

Subsystems and the information that flows between them can be specified (bounded) for subsequent engineering work. The *Architecture Diagram Specification*[6] (ADS) presents information about each subsystem and the information flows between subsystems. The ADS contains a description—called a *system module narrative*—for each subsystem. The system module narrative describes *what* the subsystem does, what information it processes,

[6]The ADS is an adaptation of a number of different specifications suggested by Hatley and Pirbhai [HAT87]. For simplicity, these have been combined into a single document.

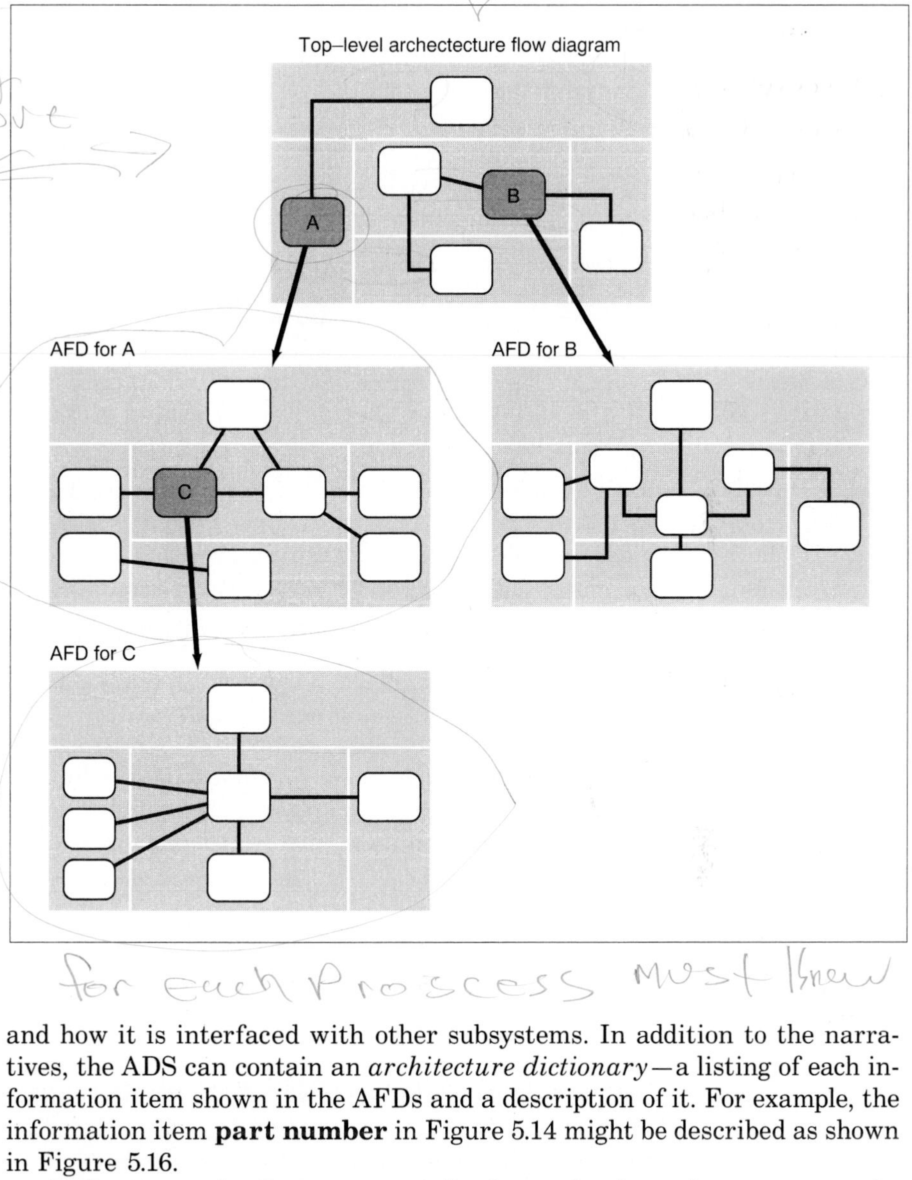

FIGURE 5.15. Building an AFD hierarchy.

and how it is interfaced with other subsystems. In addition to the narratives, the ADS can contain an *architecture dictionary*—a listing of each information item shown in the AFDs and a description of it. For example, the information item **part number** in Figure 5.14 might be described as shown in Figure 5.16.

Referring to the figure, a specialized notation is used to represent the information item description. The notation (to be described in Chapter 7) indicates that **part number** is a *composite data item*—that is, a data item composed of three other data items: **product type prefix**, **numerical identifier**, and **cost category**. In reality, each of these three data items would also have to be described in the dictionary. The type, origin, and destination entries are extracted directly from the AFD (Figure 5.14), and the communication pathway indicates the manner in which the information is

Information item name:	part number
Information item description:	= product type prefix+ numerical id+ cost category
Type (data or control):	data
Origin (subsystem or external entity):	bar code decoding subsystem
Destination (subsystem or external entity):	data base access subsystem
Communication pathway (name):	internal software interface

FIGURE 5.16. An architecture dictionary entry.

physically transferred from origin to destination. In other circumstances, the communication pathway might be defined as a bus or channel that must be implemented as part of the system's design. The architecture dictionary is a system level version of the *requirements dictionary*—an important analysis notation for software that is discussed in detail in Chapter 7.

The final entry in the architecture diagram specification is the *architecture interconnect diagram* (AID) and the corresponding *interconnect description*. The arrows shown in the AFD indicate data and control flow, without describing how the flow is effected. The AID and corresponding specification describe whether the information is transferred electronically (e.g., over a bus), optically (e.g., over a high bandwidth optical link), or mechanically (e.g., using a mechanical actuator or linkage). To develop the AID, the system engineer must make implementation decisions that are better left for design. For this reason, we postpone a discussion of interconnection issues until Chapter 15.

5.5 SYSTEM MODELING AND SIMULATION

Over two decades ago, R. M. Graham [GRA69] made a distressing comment about the way we built computer-based systems: "We build systems like the Wright brothers built airplanes—build the whole thing, push it off a cliff, let it crash, and start over again." In fact, for at least one class of system—the *reactive system*—we continue to do this today.

Many computer-based systems interact with the real world in an *reactive* fashion. That is, real-world events are monitored by the hardware and software that comprise the computer-based system, and based on these events, the system imposes control on the machines, processes, and even people who cause the events to occur. Real-time and embedded systems often fall into the reactive systems category.

Unfortunately, the developers of reactive systems sometimes struggle to make them perform properly. Until recently, it has been difficult to predict the performance, efficiency, and behavior of such systems prior to building them. In a very real sense, the construction of many real-time systems was an adventure in "flying." Surprises (most of them unpleasant) were not discovered until the system was built and "pushed off a cliff." If the system crashed due to incorrect function, inappropriate behavior, or poor performance, we picked up the pieces and started over again.

Many systems in the reactive category control machines and/or processes (e.g., commercial airliners or petroleum refineries) that must operate with an extremely high degree of reliability. If the system fails, significant economic or human loss could occur. For this reason, the approach described by Graham is both painful and dangerous.

Today, CASE tools for system modeling and simulation are being used to help to eliminate surprises when reactive, computer-based systems are built. These tools are applied during the system engineering process, while the role of hardware and software, databases, and people is being specified. The role of system modeling and simulation tools is summarized by i-Logix, Inc., a system engineering tool vendor [ILO90]:

> The understanding of a system's behavior in its environment over time is most often addressed in the design, implementation and testing phases of a project, through iterative trial and error. The *Statemate* [a modeling and simulation tool] approach provides an alternative to this costly process. It allows you to build a comprehensive model that... addresses the usual functional and data flow issues, but also covers the dynamic, behavioral aspects of a system. This model can then be tested with... tools which provide extensive mechanisms for inspecting and debugging the specification and for retrieving information from it. By testing the specification model, the systems engineer can see how the system as specified would behave if implemented. One can answer "what if" questions, following specific scenarios, checking that certain desirable situations will occur... and that other undesirable ones will not. In this sense, the system engineer can be said to be playing the role of the eventual user of the system and its environment....

Modeling and simulation tools enable a system engineer to "test drive" a specification of the system. The technical details and specialized modeling techniques that are used to enable a test drive are presented in Chapter 15.

5.6 SYSTEM SPECIFICATION

The *System Specification* is a document that serves as the foundation for hardware engineering, software engineering, database engineering, and human engineering. It describes the function and performance of a computer-based system and the constraints that will govern its development. The specification bounds each allocated system element. For example, it provides the software engineer with an indication of the role of software within the context of the system as a whole and the various subsystems described in the architecture flow diagrams. The *System Specification* also describes the information (data and control) that is input to and output from the system.

TABLE 5.4

SYSTEM SPECIFICATION OUTLINE

- **I.** Introduction
  - **A.** Scope and purpose of document
  - **B.** Overview
    - **1.** Objectives
    - **2.** Constraints
- **II.** Functional and data description
  - **A.** System architecture
    - **1.** Architecture context diagram
    - **2.** ACD description
- **III.** Subsystem descriptions
  - **A.** Architecture diagram specification for subsystem *n*
    - **1.** Architecture flow diagram
    - **2.** System module narrative
    - **3.** Performance issues
    - **4.** Design constraints
    - **5.** Allocation of system components
  - **B.** Architecture dictionary
  - **C.** Architecture interconnect diagrams and description
- **IV.** System modeling and simulation results
  - **A.** System model used for simulation
  - **B.** Simulation results
  - **C.** Special performance issues
- **V.** Project issues
  - **A.** Projected development costs
  - **B.** Projected schedule
- **VI.** Appendices

A recommended outline for the *System Specification* is presented in Table 5.4. It should be noted, however, that this is but one of many outlines that can be used to define a system description document. The actual format and content may be dictated by software or system engineering standards (e.g., DoD/STD 2167A) or local custom and preference.

5.7 SYSTEM SPECIFICATION REVIEW

Throughout system engineering there is a natural tendency to short-circuit review and move quickly into development. Managers tend to become increasingly nervous when components are not being soldered and source code is not being written. Technical people want to move into the "creative engineering tasks" as soon as possible. Don't fall prey to these attitudes!

The *system specification review* evaluates the correctness of the definition contained in the *System Specification*. The review is conducted by both the developer and the customer to ensure that (1) the scope of the project has been correctly delineated; (2) functions, performance, and interfaces have been properly defined; (3) analysis of environment and development risk justify the system; and (4) the developer and the customer have the same perception of system objectives. The system specification review is conducted in two segments. Initially, a management viewpoint is applied. Second, a technical evaluation of system elements and functions is conducted.

Key management considerations generate the following questions:

- Has a firm business need been established? Does system justification make sense?
- Does the specified environment (or market) need the system that has been described?
- What alternatives have been considered?
- What is the development risk for each system element?
- Are resources available to perform development?
- Do cost and schedule bounds make sense?

Actually, the above questions should be raised and answered regularly during the analysis task. Each should be reexamined at this stage.

The level of detail considered during the technical stage of the system review varies with the level of detail considered during the allocation task. The review should include the following issues:

- Does the functional complexity of the system agree with assessments of development risk, cost, and schedule?
- Is the allocation of functions defined in sufficient detail?
- Have interfaces among system elements and with the environment been defined in sufficient detail?
- Are performance, reliability, and maintainability issues addressed in the specification?
- Does the *System Specification* provide sufficient foundation for the hardware and software engineering steps that follow?

Parallel engineering paths begin once the system review has been completed. Hardware, human, and database elements of a system are addressed as part of their corresponding engineering processes. For the remainder of this book we shall trace the software engineering path.

5.8 SUMMARY

Computer system engineering is the first step in the evolution of a new computer-based system or product. Using the steps that we have called system analysis, the system engineer identifies the customer's needs, determines economic and technical feasibility, and allocates function and performance to software, hardware, people, and databases—the key system elements. An architectural model of the system is produced and representations of each major subsystem can be developed. Finally, the system engineer can use CASE tools to create a reactive system model that can be used as the basis for a simulation of performance and behavior. The system engineering task culminates with the creation of a *System Specification*—a document that forms the foundation for all the engineering work that follows.

System engineering demands intense communication between the customer and an analyst. The customer must understand system goals and be able to state them clearly. The analyst must know what questions to ask, what advice to give, and what research to do. If communication breaks down at this stage, the success of the entire project is in jeopardy.

REFERENCES

[ALL89] Allman, W. F., *Apprentices of Wonder,* Bantam, 1989.

[BLA81] Blanchard, B. S., and W. J. Fabrycky, *Systems Engineering and Analysis,* Prentice-Hall, 1981.

[DAT86] Date, C. J., *An Introduction to Data Base Systems,* 4th ed., Addison-Wesley, 1986.

[FRI77] Fried, L., "Performing Cost Benefit Analysis," *System-Development Management,* Auerbach Publishers, 1977.

[GEM81] Gemignani, M., *Law and the Computer,* CBI Publishing Co., 1981.

[GRA69] Graham, R. M., in *Proceedings 1969 NATO Conference on Software Engineering,* 1969.

[HAR85] Harris, T. D., *Computer Software Protection,* Prentice-Hall, 1985.

[HAT87] Hatley, D. J., and I. A. Pirbhai, *Strategies for Real-Time System Specification,* Dorset House, 1987.

[IEE89] *Database Engineering,* Vol. 7, IEEE Computer Society Press, 1989.

[ILO90] *The Statemate Approach to Complex Systems,* i-Logix, Inc., 1990.

[KIN78] King, J., and E. Schrems, "Cost Benefit Analysis in Information Systems Development and Operation," *ACM Computing Surveys,* vol. 10, no. 1, March 1978, pp. 19–34.

[RAE90] Raeth, P.G., *Expert Systems: A Software Methodology for Modern Applications,* IEEE Computer Society Press, 1990.

[SCO89] Scott, M. D., *Computer Law,* Wiley, 1989.

[WAS89] Wasserman, P. D., *Neural Computing: Theory and Practice,* Van Nostrand Reinhold, 1989.

PROBLEMS AND POINTS TO PONDER

5.1 Find as many single-word synonyms for the word system as you can. Good luck!

5.2 Build a "system of systems" similar to that shown Figure 5.2 for a large system (other than the one shown). Your hierarchy should extend down to simple system elements (hardware, software, etc.) along at least one branch of the "tree."

5.3 Attempt to draw the equivalent of Figure 5.1 for a system (preferably computer-based) with which you are familiar. Show major input and output, each system element, and the interconnectivity among elements.

5.4 A system analyst can come from one of three sources: the system developer, the customer, or some outside organization. Discuss the pros and cons that apply to each source. Describe an "ideal" analyst.

5.5 Common system elements are hardware, software, and people. What other elements are frequently encountered in computer-based systems?

5.6 Add at least five additional questions to the list developed for CLSS in Section 5.2. Come up with two additional allocations for CLSS.

5.7 Your instructor will distribute a high level description of a computer-based system.
(a) Develop a set of questions that you should ask as an analyst.
(b) Propose at least two different allocations for the system based on answers to your question provided by your instructor.
(c) In class, compare your allocation to those of fellow students.

5.8 Attempt to develop a hierarchical categorization for computer hardware. Identify each class of hardware; provide examples of actual devices in the class.

5.9 Attempt to develop a hierarchical categorization for computer software. Identify each class of software; provide examples of actual programs in the class.

5.10 We have noted the similarities of the hardware and software engineering processes. How do the phases of these processes differ?

5.11 Human engineering attempts to build "human-friendly" systems. Define "human friendly" in your own terms.

5.12 Develop a checklist for attributes to be considered when the feasibility of a system is to be evaluated. Discuss the interplay among attributes and attempt to provide a method for grading each so that a quantitative "feasibility number" may be developed.

5.13 Research the accounting techniques that are used for a detailed cost-benefit analysis of a computer-based system that will require some hardware manufacturing and assembly. Attempt to write a "cookbook" set of guidelines that a technical manager could apply.

5.14 Develop a cost-benefit analysis equivalent to that shown in Tables 5.2 and 5.3 for engineering/scientific systems. Expand the tables to encompass real-time and embedded applications.

5.15 Develop an architecture context diagram and architecture flow diagrams for the computer-based system of your choice (or one assigned by your instructor).

5.16 Write a system module narrative that would be contained in an architecture diagram specification for one or more of the subsystems defined in the AFDs developed for Problem 5.15.

5.17 Research the literature on CASE tools and write a brief paper describing how modeling and simulation tools work. Alternative: Collect literature from two or more CASE vendors that sell modeling and simulation tools and assess the similarities and differences.

5.18 Based on documents provided by your instructor, develop an abbreviated *System Specification* for one of the following computer-based systems:
(a) A low-cost, self-contained word processing system
(b) A digital scanner for a personal computer
(c) An electronic mail system
(d) A university registration system
(e) An engineering analysis system
(f) An interactive reservation system
(g) A system of local interest
Be sure to create the architecture models described in Section 5.4.

5.19 Are there characteristics of a system that cannot be established at this stage? Describe the characteristics, if any, and explain why a consideration of them must be delayed until later engineering steps.

5.20 Are there situations in which formal system specification can be abbreviated or eliminated entirely? Explain.

FURTHER READINGS

Because it is interdisciplinary, computer system engineering is a difficult subject, and therefore few really good books have been published on the topic. Books by Blanchard and Fabrycky [BLA81] and Athey (*Systematic Systems Approach,* Prentice-Hall, 1982) present the system engineering process (with a distinct engineering emphasis) and provide worthwhile guidance. The IEEE Computer Society has established a task force to develop an educational framework for computer-based system engineering. Their initial findings have been published in the *Proceedings of Computer-Based System Engineering Workshop* (IEEE, 1990).

An excellent IEEE tutorial by Thayer and Dorfman (*System and Software Requirements Engineering,* IEEE Computer Society Press, 1990) discusses the interrelationship between system and software level requirements analysis issues. A companion volume by the same authors (*Standards, Guidelines and Examples: System and Software Requirements Engineering,* IEEE Computer Society Press, 1990) presents a comprehensive discussion of standards and guidelines for analysis work.

Books by Leeson (*Systems Analysis and Design,* SRA, 1981), McMenamin and Palmer (*Essential Systems Analysis,* Yourdon Press, 1984), and Silver and Silver (*Systems Analysis and Design,* Addison-Wesley, 1989) provide useful discussions of the system analysis task as it is applied in the information systems world. Each contains case study supplements that illustrate the problems, approaches, and solutions that may be applied during system analysis. Many other textbooks have been published in the general area of system analysis and definition. Among the more recent additions to the literature:

Dickinson, B., *Developing Quality Systems,* McGraw-Hill, 1988.
Gause, D. A., and G. M. Weinberg, *Exploring Requirements,* Dorset House, 1989.
Modell, M. E., *A Professional's Guide to System Analysis,* McGraw-Hill, 1988.

For those readers actively involved in systems work or interested in a more sophisticated treatment of the topic, Gerald Weinberg's books (*An Introduction to General System Thinking,* Wiley-Interscience, 1976, and *On the Design of Stable Systems,* Wiley-Interscience, 1979) have become classics and provide an excellent discussion of "general systems thinking" that implicitly leads to a general approach to system analysis and design. More recent books by Weinberg (*General Principles of Systems Design,* Dorset House, 1988, and *Rethinking Systems Analysis and Design,* Dorset House, 1988) continue in the tradition of his earlier work.

The Auerbach series, *System Development Management* (Auerbach Publishers, updated yearly), provides an excellent treatment of system planning and definition for large-scale information systems. Auerbach's pragmatic approach will be especially useful to industry professionals.

CHAPTER 6

REQUIREMENTS ANALYSIS FUNDAMENTALS

A complete understanding of software requirements is essential to the success of a software development effort. No matter how well designed or well coded, a poorly analyzed and specified program will disappoint the user and bring grief to the developer.

The requirements analysis task is a process of discovery, refinement, modeling, and specification. The software scope, initially established by the system engineer and refined during software project planning, is refined in detail. Models of the required information and control flow, operational behavior, and data content are created. Alternative solutions are analyzed and allocated to various software elements.

Both the developer and the customer take an active role in requirements analysis and specification. The customer attempts to reformulate a sometimes nebulous concept of software function and performance into concrete detail. The developer acts as interrogator, consultant, and problem solver.

Requirements analysis and specification may appear to be a relatively simple task, but appearances are deceiving. Communication content is very high. Chances for misinterpretation or misinformation abound. Ambiguity is probable. The dilemma that confronts a software engineer may best be understood by repeating the statement of an anonymous (infamous?) customer: "I know you believe you understood what you think I said, but I am not sure you realize that what you heard is not what I meant. . . ."

6.1 REQUIREMENTS ANALYSIS

Requirements analysis is a software engineering task that bridges the gap between system level software allocation and software design (Figure 6.1). Requirements analysis enables the system engineer to specify software function and performance, indicate software's interface with other system elements, and establish design constraints that the software must meet. Requirements analysis allows the software engineer (often called the *analyst* in this role) to refine the software allocation and build models of the process, data, and behavioral domains that will be treated by software. Requirements analysis provides the software designer with a representation of information and function that can be translated to data, architectural, and procedural design. Finally, the requirements specification provides the developer and the customer with the means to assess quality once the software is built.

6.1.1 Analysis Tasks

Software requirements analysis may be divided into five areas of effort: (1) problem recognition, (2) evaluation and synthesis, (3) modeling, (4) specification, and (5) review.

Initially, the analyst studies the *System Specification* (if one exists) and the *Software Project Plan*. It is important to understand software in a system context and to review the software scope that was used to generate planning estimates. Next, communication for analysis must be established so that problem recognition is ensured. The analyst must establish contact with management and the technical staff of the user/customer organization and the software development organization. The project manager can serve as a coordinator to facilitate establishment of communication paths. The goal of the analyst is recognition of the basic problem elements as perceived by the user/customer.

Problem evaluation and solution synthesis is the next major area of effort for analysis. The analyst must evaluate the flow and content of information, define and elaborate all software functions, understand software

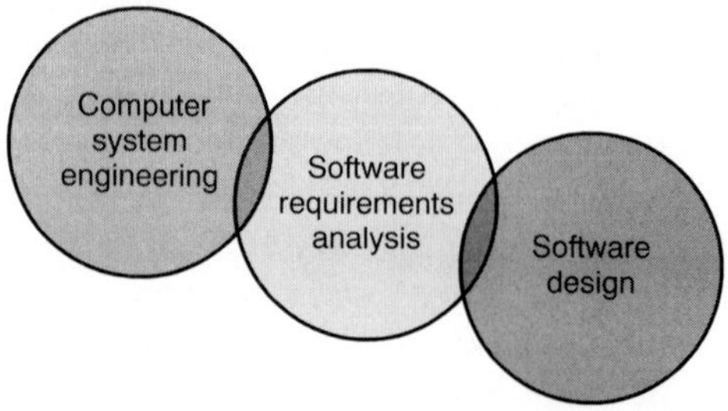

FIGURE 6.1. Overlap of the analysis task.

behavior in the context of events that affect the system, establish system interface characteristics, and uncover design constraints. Each of these tasks serves to describe the problem so that an overall approach or solution may be synthesized.

For example, an inventory control system is required for a major supplier of auto parts. The analyst finds that problems with the current manual system include (1) inability to obtain the status of a component rapidly; (2) 2- or 3-day turnaround to update a card file; (3) multiple reorders to the same vendor because there is no way to associate vendors with components, etc. Once problems have been identified, the analyst determines what information is to be produced by the new system and what data will be provided to the system. For instance, the customer desires a daily report that indicates what parts have been taken from inventory and how many similar parts remain. The customer indicates that inventory clerks will log the identification number of each part as it leaves the inventory area.

Upon evaluating current problems and desired information (input and output), the analyst begins to synthesize one or more solutions. An on-line terminal-based system will solve one set of problems, but does it fall within the scope outlined in the *Software Plan?* A database management system would seem to be required, but is the user/customer's need for associativity justified? The process of evaluation and synthesis continues until both analyst and customer feel confident that software can be adequately specified for subsequent development steps.

Throughout evaluation and solution synthesis, the analyst's primary focus is on "what", *not* "how." *What* data does the system produce and consume, *what* functions must the system perform, *what* interfaces are defined, and *what* constraints apply?

During the evaluation and solution synthesis activity, the analyst creates models of the system in an effort to better understand data and control flow, functional processing, and behavioral operation and information content. The model serves as a foundation for software design and as the basis for the creation of a specification for the software.

In Chapter 1, we noted that detailed specification may not be possible at this stage. The customer may be unsure of precisely what is required. The developer may be unsure that a specific approach will properly accomplish the desired function and performance. For these, and many other reasons, an alternative approach to requirements analysis, called *prototyping*, may be conducted. We discuss prototyping later in this chapter.

The tasks associated with analysis and specification strive to provide a representation of software that can be reviewed and approved by the customer. In an ideal world, the customer develops a *Software Requirements Specification* in its entirety. This is rarely the case in the real world. At best, the specification is developed as a joint effort between the developer and the customer.

Once basic information, functions, performance, behavior, and interfaces are described, *validation criteria* are specified to demonstrate understanding of a successful software implementation. These criteria serve as a basis for testing activities that occur later in the software engineering process. A formal requirements specification is written to define characteristics and attributes of the software. In addition, a *Preliminary User's Manual* can be drafted for cases in which a prototype has not been developed.

It may seem odd that a user's manual is developed so early in the software engineering process. After all, we are still a long way from using the program. In fact, the draft-copy user's manual forces the analyst (developer) to take a user's view of the software (particularly important in interactive systems). The manual encourages the user/customer to review the software from a human-engineering perspective and often elicits the comment: "The idea is OK, but this isn't the way I thought we'd do this." Better to uncover such comments early in the process.

Requirements analysis documents (specification and user's manual) serve as the basis for a review conducted by the customer and the developer. The requirements review (discussed in Section 6.7) almost always results in modifications to function, performance, information representations, constraints, or validation criteria. In addition, the *Software Project Plan* is reassessed to determine whether early estimates remain valid given additional knowledge obtained as part of the analysis.

6.1.2 The Analyst

Entire textbooks have been dedicated to the role and duties of the analyst. Atwood [ATW77] provides a workable job description: "...the system analyst is expected to analyze and design systems of optimum performance. That is, the analyst must produce...an output that fully meets management objectives...." The analyst is known by a variety of aliases: *system analyst, system engineer, chief system designer, programmer/analyst,* and so on. Regardless of the job title, the analyst must exhibit the following character traits:

- The ability to grasp abstract concepts, reorganize into logical divisions, and synthesize "solutions" based on each division.
- The ability to absorb pertinent facts from conflicting or confused sources.
- The ability to understand the user/customer environments.
- The ability to apply hardware and/or software system elements to the user/customer environments.
- The ability to communicate well in written and verbal form.
- The ability "to see the forest for the trees."

It is probably the last trait that separates truly outstanding analysts from the pack. Individuals who become mired in detail too early frequently lose sight of the overall software objective. Software requirements must be un-

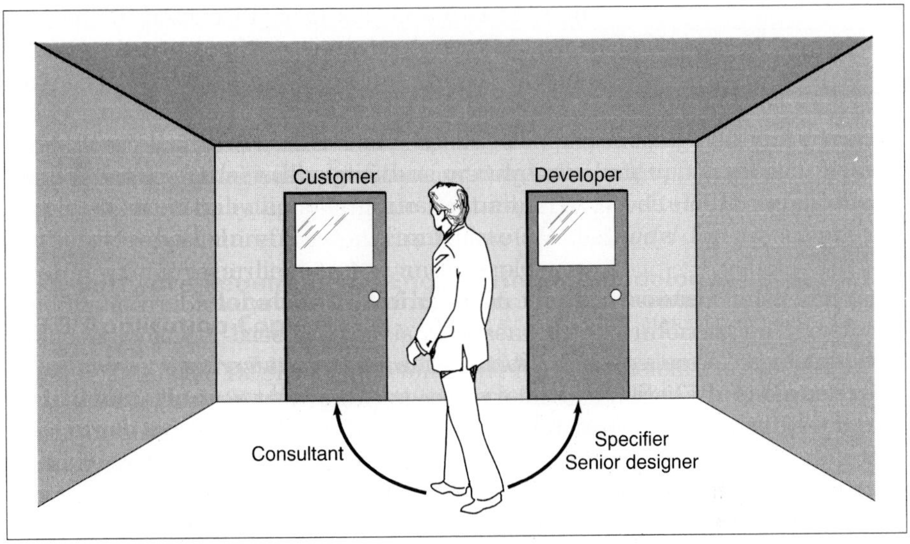

FIGURE 6.2. The role of the analyst.

covered in a "top-down" manner —major functions, interfaces, and information must be fully understood before successive layers of detail are specified.

The analyst's role is depicted in Figure 6.2. The analyst performs or coordinates each of the tasks associated with software requirements analysis (Section 6.1.1). During recognition tasks, he or she communicates with user/customer staff to ascertain characteristics of the existing environment. The analyst calls upon development staff during evaluation and synthesis tasks so that characteristics of the software are correctly defined. The analyst is generally responsible for development of a *Software Requirements Specification* and participates in all reviews.

It is important to note that the analyst must also understand each software engineering paradigm (Section 1.5) and appreciate the generic software engineering steps that are applied regardless of the paradigm that is used. Many implicit software requirements (e.g., design for maintainability) are incorporated into a requirements specification only if the analyst understands software engineering.

6.2 PROBLEM AREAS

Requirements analysis is a communication-intensive activity. When communication occurs, *noise* (e.g., misinterpretation, omission) on the communication path can cause difficulty for both analyst and customer. Among the problems that are encountered during requirements analysis are difficulties associated with acquiring pertinent information, handling problem complexity, and accommodating changes that will occur during and after analysis.

The first two analysis tasks discussed in the preceding section—problem recognition and solution evaluation and synthesis—are predicated on the successful acquisition of information. Often, customer-supplied information conflicts with other requirements stated earlier by other people, function and performance conflict with constraints imposed by other system elements, or the perception of the goals of the system changes with time. What information should be collected and how should it be represented? Who supplies the various pieces of information? What tools and techniques are available to facilitate collection of information?

As the size of a problem grows, the complexity of the analysis task also grows. Each new information item, function, or constraint may have an effect on all other elements of the software. For this reason, analysis effort grows geometrically as problem complexity increases. How can we eliminate inconsistency when specifying large systems? Is it possible to detect omissions? Can a large problem be effectively partitioned so that it becomes more manageable intellectually?

In coining "the first law of system engineering," Bersoff [BER80] said: "No matter where you are in the system life cycle, the system will change, and the desire to change it will persist throughout the life cycle." The changes alluded to in this statement are changes in requirements. Whether we talk about a system or just software, change will occur. In fact, it is likely that changes will be requested *before* we even complete the analysis task. How are changes to other system elements coordinated with software requirements? How do we assess the impact of a change on other seemingly unrelated parts of the software? How do we correct errors in specification so that side effects are not generated?

There are many causes for the problems noted above and some good answers to the resultant questions. The underlying requirements analysis problems are attributable to many causes: (1) poor communication that makes information acquisition difficult, (2) inadequate techniques and tools that result in inadequate or inaccurate specification, (3) a tendency to take short-cuts during the requirements analysis task, leading to an unstable design, and (4) a failure to consider alternatives before the software is specified. Although a software engineering approach to requirements analysis is not a panacea, application of solid communication techniques, fundamental analysis principles, and systematic analysis methods will greatly reduce the impact of the problems noted above. For the remainder of this chapter and throughout Chapters 7, 8, and 9, we discuss these techniques, principles and methods. In so doing, we shall also answer the questions that have been posed along with the statement of each problem.

6.3 COMMUNICATION TECHNIQUES

Software requirements analysis always begins with communication between two or more parties. A *customer* has a problem that may be amenable to a computer-based solution. A *developer* responds to the customer's request for help. *Communication* has begun. But as we have already noted, the road from communication to understanding is often full of potholes.

6.3.1 Initiating the Process

The most commonly used analysis technique to bridge the communication gap between the customer and developer and to get the communication process started is to conduct a preliminary meeting or interview. The first meeting between a software engineer (the analyst) and the customer can be likened to the awkwardness of a first date between two adolescents. Neither person knows what to say or ask; both are worried that what they do say will be misinterpreted; both are thinking about where it might lead (both likely have radically different expectations here); both want to get the thing over with, but at the same time, both want it to be a success.

Yet, communication must be initiated. Gause and Weinberg [GAU89] suggest that the analyst start by asking *context-free questions*—that is, a set of questions that will lead to a basic understanding of the problem, the people who want a solution, the nature of the solution that is desired, and the effectiveness of the first encounter itself. The first set of context-free questions focus on the customer, the overall goals, and benefits. For example, the analyst might ask:

- Who is behind the request for this work?
- Who will use the solution?
- What will be the economic benefit of a successful solution?
- Is there another source for the solution that you need?

The next set of questions enables the analyst to gain a better understanding of the problem and the customer to voice his or her perceptions about a solution:

- How would you characterize "good" output that would be generated by a successful solution?
- What problem(s) will this solution address?
- Can you show me (or describe) the environment in which the solution will be used?
- Are there special performance issues or constraints that will affect the way the solution is approached?

The final set of questions focus on the effectiveness of the meeting. Gause and Weinberg [GAU89] call these "meta-questions" and propose the following (abbreviated) list:

- Are you the right person to answer these questions? Are your answers "official?"
- Are my questions relevant to the problem that you have?
- Am I asking too many questions?
- Is there anyone else who can provide additional information?
- Is there anything else that I should be asking you?

These questions (and others) will help to "break the ice" and initiate the communication that is essential for successful analysis. But a question-and-answer meeting format is not an approach that has been overwhelmingly successful. In fact, the question-and-answer session should be used for the first encounter only and then be replaced by a meeting format that combines elements of problem solving, negotiation, and specification. An approach to a meeting of this type is presented in the next section.

6.3.2 Facilitated Application Specification Techniques

Customers and software engineers often have an unconscious "us and them" mind set. Rather than working as a team to identify and refine requirements, each constituency defines its own "territory" and communicates through a series of memos, formal position papers, documents, and question-and-answer sessions. History has shown that this approach doesn't work very well. Misunderstandings abound, important information is omitted, and a successful working relationship is never established.

It is with these problems in mind that a number of independent investigators have developed a team-oriented approach to requirements gathering that is applied during early stages of analysis and specification. Called *facilitated application specification technique* (FAST), this approach encourages the creation of a joint team of customers and developers who work together to identify the problem, propose elements of the solution, negotiate different approaches, and specify a preliminary set of solution requirements [ZAH90]. Today, FAST is used predominantly by the information systems community, but the technique offers potential for improved communication in applications of all kinds.

Many different approaches to FAST have been proposed.[1] Each makes use of a slightly different scenario, but all apply some variation on the following basic guidelines:

- A meeting is conducted at a neutral site and attended by both developers and customers.

[1]Two of the more popular approaches to FAST are *Joint Application Development* (JAD), developed by IBM, and *The METHOD*, developed by Performance Resources, Inc., Falls Church, VA.

- Rules for preparation and participation are established.
- An agenda is suggested that is formal enough to cover all the important points but informal enough to encourage the free flow of ideas.
- A "facilitator" (can be a customer, a developer, or an outsider) is appointed to control the meeting.
- A "definition mechanism" (can be work sheets, flip charts, wall stickers or wall board) is used.
- The goal is to identify the problem, propose elements of the solution, negotiate different approaches, and specify a preliminary set of solution requirements in an atmosphere that is conducive to the accomplishment of the goal.

To better understand the flow of events as they occur in a typical FAST meeting, we present a brief scenario that outlines the sequence of events that lead up to the meeting, occur during the meeting, and follow the meeting.

Initial meetings between the developer and customer (Section 6.3.1) occur and basic questions and answers help to establish the scope of the problem and the overall perception of a solution. Out of these initial meetings, the developer and customer write a one- or two-page "product request." A place, time, and date for a FAST meeting are selected and a *facilitator* is chosen. Attendees from both the development and customer organizations are invited to attend. The product request is distributed to all attendees before the meeting date.

While reviewing the request in the days before the meeting, each FAST attendee is asked to make a list of *objects* that are part of the environment that surrounds the system, other objects that are to be produced by the system, and objects that are used by the system to perform its functions. In addition, each attendee is asked to make another list of *operations* (processes or functions) that manipulate or interact with the objects. Finally, lists of *constraints* (e.g., cost, size, weight) and *performance criteria* (e.g., speed, accuracy) are also developed. The attendees are informed that the lists are not expected to be exhaustive, but are expected to reflect each person's perspective of the system.

As an example[2], assume that a FAST team working for a consumer products company has been provided with the following product description:

> Our research indicates that the market for home security systems is growing at a rate of 40 percent per year. We would like to enter this market by building a microprocessor-based home security system that would protect against and/or recognize a variety of undesirable "situations" such as illegal entry, fire, flood-

---

[2]This example (with extensions and variations) will be used to illustrate important software engineering methods in many of the chapters that follow. As an exercise, it would be worthwhile to conduct your own FAST meeting and develop a set of lists for it.

ing, and others. The product, tentatively called *SafeHome,* will use appropriate sensors to detect each situation, can be programmed by the homeowner, and will automatically telephone a monitoring agency when a situation is detected.

In reality, considerably more information would be provided at this stage. But even with additional information, ambiguity would be present, omissions would likely exist, and errors might occur. For now, the above "product description" will suffice.

The FAST team is comprised of representatives from marketing, software and hardware engineering, and manufacturing. An outside facilitator is to be used.

Each person on the FAST team (Figure 6.3) develops the lists described above. Objects described for *SafeHome* might include smoke detectors, window and door sensors, motion detectors, an alarm, an event (a sensor has been activated), a control panel, a display, telephone numbers, a telephone call, and so on. The list of operations might include setting the alarm, monitoring the sensors, dialing the phone, programming the control panel, reading the display (note that operations act on objects). In a similar fashion, each FAST meeting attendee will develop lists of constraints (e.g., the system must have a manufactured cost of less than $200, must be "user friendly," must interface directly to a standard phone line) and performance criteria (e.g., a sensor event should be recognized within 1 second; an event priority scheme should be implemented).

As the meeting begins, the first topic of discussion is the need and justification for the new product— everyone should agree that the product development (or acquisition) is justified. Once such agreement has been established, each participant presents his or her lists for critique and discussion. The lists can be pinned to the walls of the room using large sheets of paper, stuck to the walls using adhesive backed sheets, or written on a wall board. Ideally, each list entry should be capable of being manipulated separately so that

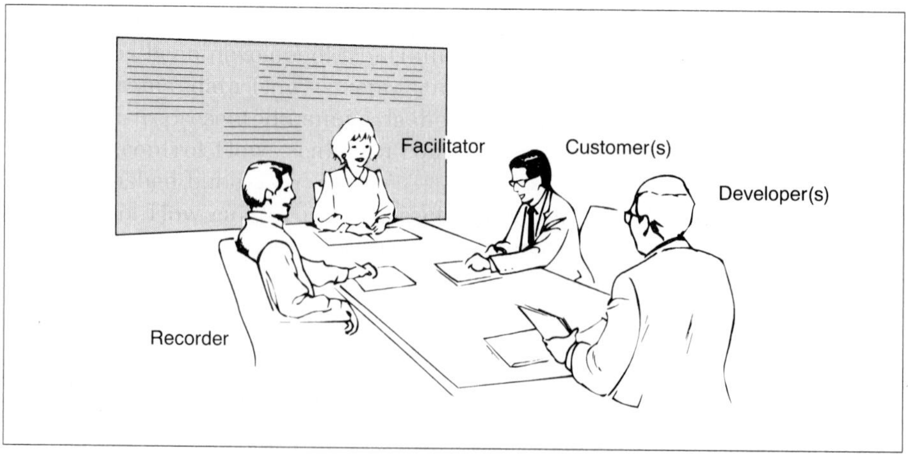

FIGURE 6.3.
The FAST meeting.

lists can be combined, entries can be deleted and additions can be made. At this stage, critique and debate are strictly prohibited.

After individual lists are presented in one topic area, a combined list is created by the group. The combined list eliminates redundant entries and adds any new ideas that have come up during the presentation, but does not delete anything. After the combined lists for all topic areas have been created, discussion—coordinated by the facilitator—ensues. Each combined list is shortened, lengthened, or reworded to properly reflect the product/system to be developed. The objective is to develop a consensus list in each topic area (objects, operations, constraints, and performance). The lists are then set aside for later action.

Once the consensus lists have been completed, the team is divided into smaller subteams; each works to develop a *mini-specification* for one or more entries on each of the lists. The mini-specification is an elaboration of the word or phrase contained on a list. For example, the mini-specification for the *SafeHome* object **control panel** might be

- Mounted on wall
- Size approximately 9 × 5 inches
- Contains standard 12 key-pad and special keys
- Contains a flat panel display of the form shown in sketch [not presented here]
- All customer interactions to occur through keys
- Used to enable and disable the system
- Software to provide interaction guidance, echoes, etc.
- Connected to all sensors

Each subteam then presents each of its mini-specs to all FAST attendees for discussion (Figure 6.4). Additions, deletions, and further elaboration are made. In some cases, the development of mini-specs will uncover new objects, operation, constraints, or performance requirements that will be added to the original lists. During all discussions, the team may raise issues that cannot be resolved during the meeting. An issues list is maintained so that these ideas will be acted on later.

After the mini-specs are completed, the FAST attendees on each subteam make a list of validation criteria for the product/system and present their list to the team. A consensus list of validation criteria is then created by everyone. Finally, one or more participants (or outsiders) is assigned the task of writing the complete draft specification using all inputs from the FAST meeting.

FAST is not a panacea for the problems encountered in early requirements gathering. But the team approach provides the benefits of many points of view, instantaneous discussion and refinement, and a concrete step toward the development of a specification.

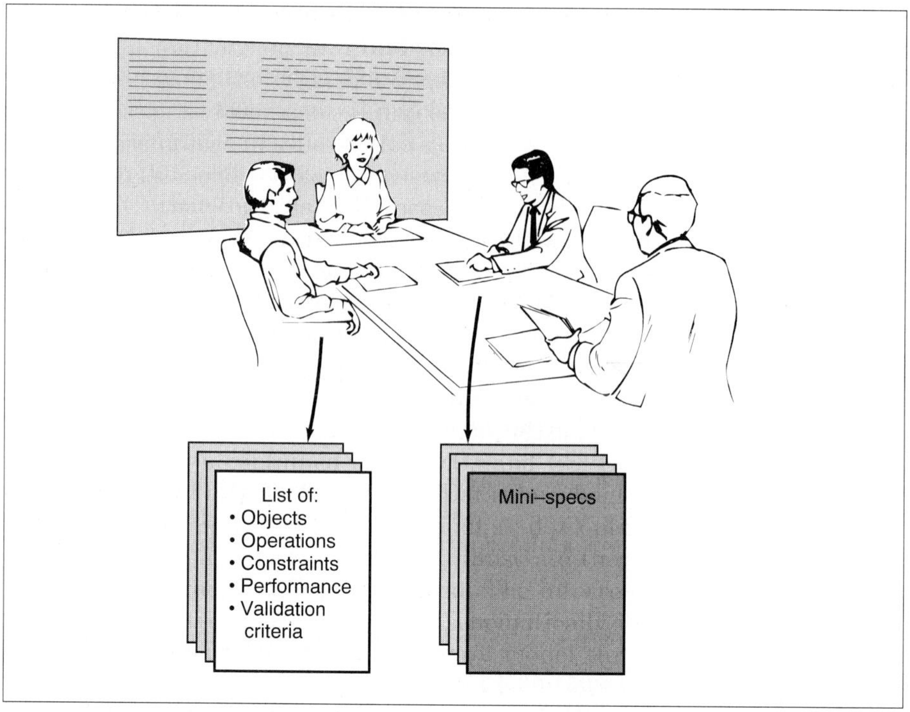

FIGURE 6.4. Output from a FAST meeting.

6.4 ANALYSIS PRINCIPLES

Over the last two decades, a number of software analysis and specification methods (discussed in Chapters 7, 8, and 9) have been developed. Investigators have identified problems and their causes, and developed rules and procedures to overcome them. Each analysis method has a unique notation and point of view. However, all analysis methods are related by a set of fundamental principles:

1. The information domain of a problem must be represented and understood.
2. Models that depict system information, function, and behavior should be developed.
3. The models (and the problem) must be partitioned in a manner that uncovers detail in a layered (or hierarchical) fashion.
4. The analysis process should move from essential information toward implementation detail.

By applying these principles, the analyst approaches a problem systematically. The information domain is examined so that function may be understood more completely. Models are used so that information can be communicated in a compact fashion. Partitioning is applied to reduce complexity. Essential and implementation views of the software are necessary to accommodate the logical constraints imposed by processing requirements and the physical constraints imposed by other system elements.

6.4.1 The Information Domain

All software applications can be collectively called *data processing*. Interestingly, this term contains a key to our understanding of software requirements. Software is built to process *data:* to transform data from one form to another, that is, to accept input, manipulate it in some way, and produce output. This fundamental statement of objective is true whether we build batch software for a payroll system or real-time embedded software to control fuel flow to an automobile engine.

It is important to note, however, that software also processes *events*. An event represents some aspect of system control and is really nothing more than boolean data—it is either on or off, true or false, there or not there. For example, a pressure sensor detects that pressure exceeds a safe value and sends an alarm signal to monitoring software. The alarm signal is an event that controls the behavior of the system. Therefore, data (numbers, characters, images, sounds, etc.) and control (events) both reside within the *information domain* of a problem.

The information domain contains three different views of the data and control as each is processed by a computer program: (1) information flow, (2) information content, and (3) information structure. To fully understand the information domain, each of these views should be considered.

Information flow represents the manner in which data and control change as each moves through a system. Referring to Figure 6.5, input is transformed to intermediate information that is then further transformed to output. Along this transformation path (or paths), additional information may be introduced from an existing *data store* (e.g., a disk file or memory buffer). The transformations that are applied to the data are functions or subfunctions that a program must perform. Data and control that move between two transformations (functions) define the interface for each function.

Information content represents the individual data and control items that comprise some larger item of information. For example, the data item, **paycheck**, is a composite of a number of important pieces of information: the payee's name, the net amount to be paid, the gross pay, deductions, and

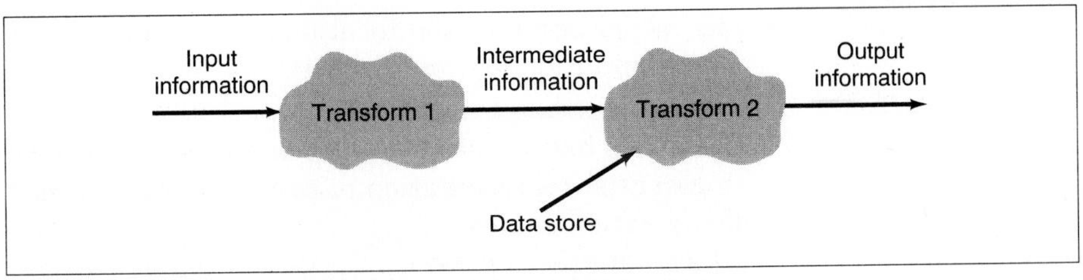

FIGURE 6.5.
Information flow.

so forth. Therefore, the *content* of **paycheck** is defined by the items that are needed to create it. Similarly, the content of a control item called **system status** might be defined by a string of bits. Each bit represents a separate item of information that indicates whether or not a particular device is on or off-line.

Information structure represents the internal organization of various data and control items. Are data or control items to be organized as an *n*-dimensional table or as a hierarchical tree structure? Within the context of the structure, what information is related to other information? Is all information contained within a single structure or are distinct structures to be used? How does information in one information structure relate to information in another structure? These questions and others are answered by an assessment of information structure. It should be noted that *data structure,* a related concept discussed later in this book, refers to the design and implementation of information structure with software.

6.4.2 Modeling

We create models to gain a better understanding of the actual entity to be built. When the entity is a physical thing (e.g., a building, a plane, a machine) we can build a model that is identical in form and shape, but smaller in scale. However, when the entity to be built is software, our model must take a different form. It must be capable of modeling the information that software transforms, the functions (and subfunctions) that enable the transformation to occur, and the behavior of the system as the transformation is taking place.

During software requirements analysis, we create models of the system to be built. The models focus on what the system must do, not on how it does it. In many cases, the models that we create make use of a graphical notation that depicts information, processing, system behavior, and other characteristics using distinct and recognizable icons. Other parts of the model may be purely textual. Descriptive information can be provided using a natural language or a specialized language for describing requirements.

Models created during requirements analysis serve a number of important roles:

- The model aids the analyst in understanding the information, function, and behavior of a system, thereby making the requirements analysis task easier and more systematic.
- The model becomes the focal point for review and, therefore, the key to a determination of completeness, consistency, and accuracy of the specification.
- The model becomes the foundation for design, providing the designer with an essential representation of software that can be "mapped" into an implementation context.

The analysis methods that are discussed in the following chapters are actually modeling methods. Although the modeling method that is used is often a matter of personal (or organizational) preference, the modeling activity is fundamental to good analysis work.

6.4.3 Partitioning

Problems are often too large and complex to be understood as a whole. For this reason, we tend to *partition* (divide) such problems into parts that can be easily understood and establish interfaces between the parts so that the overall function can be accomplished. During requirements analysis, the information, functional, and behavioral domains of software can be partitioned.

In essence, partitioning decomposes a problem into its constituent parts. Conceptually, we establish a hierarchical representation of the function or information and then partition the uppermost element by (1) exposing increasing detail by moving vertically in the hierarchy or (2) functionally decomposing the problem by moving horizontally in the hierarchy. To illustrate these partitioning approaches, let us reconsider the *SafeHome* security system described in Section 6.3. The software allocation for *SafeHome* (derived as a consequence of system engineering and FAST activities) can be stated in the following paragraphs:

> *SafeHome* software enables the homeowner to configure the security system when it is installed, monitors all sensors connected to the security system, and interacts with the homeowner through a key pad and function keys contained in the *SafeHome* control panel shown in Figure 6.6.

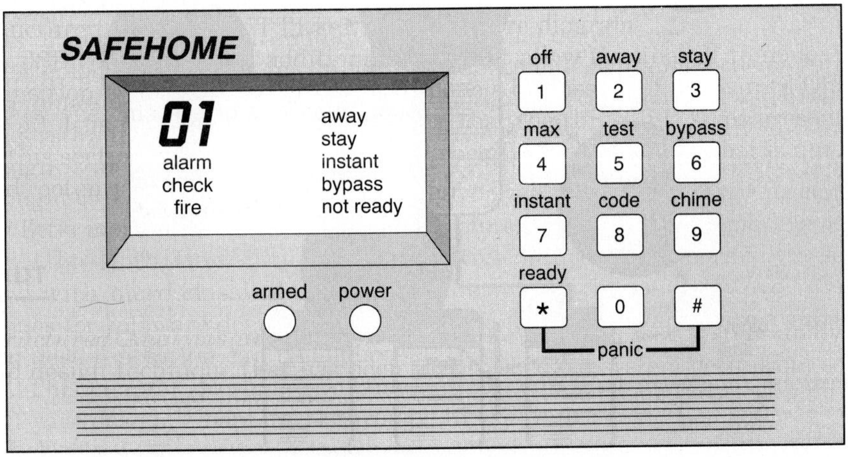

FIGURE 6.6. *SafeHome* control panel (a detailed description of control panel functions will be presented in later chapters).

During installation, the *SafeHome* control panel is used to "program" and configure the system. Each sensor is assigned a number and type, a master password is programmed for arming and disarming the system, and telephone number(s) are input for dialing when a sensor event occurs.

When a sensor event is sensed by the software, it rings an audible alarm attached to the system. After a delay time that is specified by the homeowner during system configuration activities, the software dials a telephone number of a monitoring service, provides information about the location, and reports the nature of the event that has been detected. The number will be redialed every 20 seconds until telephone connection is obtained.

All interaction with *SafeHome* is managed by a user-interaction subsystem that reads input provided through the key pad and function keys, displays prompting messages on the LCD display, displays system status information on the LCD display. Keyboard interaction takes the following form....

Requirements for *SafeHome* software may be analyzed by partitioning the information, functional, and behavioral domains of the product. To illustrate, the functional domain of the problem will be partitioned. Figure 6.7 illustrates a horizontal decomposition of *SafeHome* software. The problem is partitioned by representing constituent *SafeHome* software functions, moving horizontally in the functional hierarchy. Three major functions are noted on the first level of the hierarchy.

The subfunctions associated with a major *SafeHome* function may be examined by exposing detail vertically in the hierarchy, as illustrated in Figure 6.8. Moving downward along a single path below the function **monitor sensors,** partitioning occurs vertically to show increasing levels of functional detail.

The partitioning approach that we have applied to *SafeHome* functions can also be applied to the information domain and behavioral domain as well. In fact, partitioning of information flow and system behavior (discussed in Chapter 7) will provide additional insight into system requirements. As the problem is partitioned, interfaces between functions are derived. Data and control items that move across an interface should be restricted to inputs required to perform the stated function and outputs that are required by other functions or system elements.

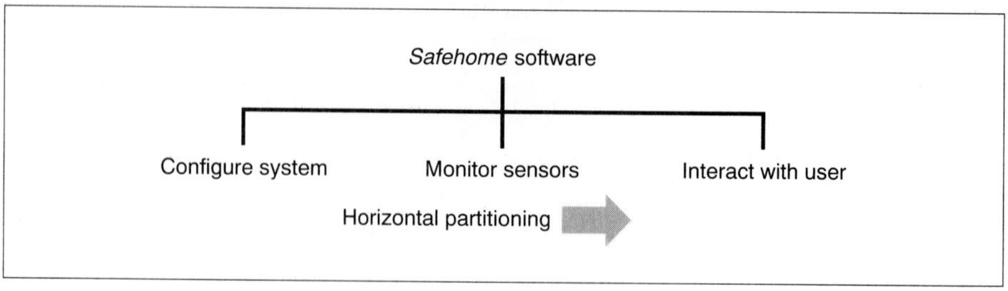

FIGURE 6.7. *SafeHome*—horizontal partitioning of function.

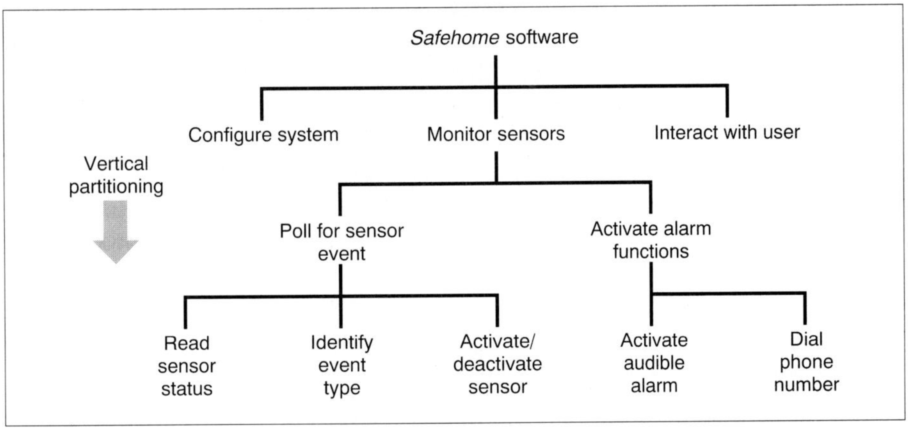

FIGURE 6.8. *SafeHome*—vertical partitioning of function.

6.4.4 Essential and Implementation Views[3]

An *essential view* of software requirements presents the functions to be accomplished and information to be processed without regard to implementation details. For example, the essential view of the *SafeHome* function **read sensor status** does not concern itself with the physical form of the data or the type of sensor that is used. In fact, it could be argued that **read status** would be a more appropriate name for this function, since it disregards details about the input mechanism altogether. Similarly, an essential *data model* of the data item **phone number** (implied in the function **dial phone number**) can be represented at this stage without regard to the underlying data structure (if any) used to implement the data item. By focusing attention on the essence of the problem at early stages of requirements analysis, we leave our options open to specify implementation details during later stages of requirements specification and software design.

The *implementation view* of software requirements presents the real-world manifestation of processing functions and information structures. In some cases, a physical representation is developed as the first step in software design. However, most computer-based systems are specified in a manner that dictates the accommodation of certain implementation details. A *SafeHome* input device is a perimeter sensor (not a watch dog, a human guard, or a booby trap). The sensor detects illegal entry by sensing a break in an electronic circuit. The general characteristics of the sensor should be noted as part of a *Software Requirements Specification*. The analyst must recognize the constraints imposed by any predefined system elements (e.g.,

[3]Many people use the terms *logical* and *physical* views to connote the same concept.

the sensor) and consider the implementation view of function and information when such a view is appropriate.

We have already noted that software requirements analysis should focus on *what* the software is to accomplish, rather than on *how* processing will be implemented. However, the implementation view should not necessarily be interpreted as a representation of *how*. Rather, an implementation model represents the current mode of operation, that is, the existing or proposed allocation for all system elements. The essential model (of function or data) is generic in the sense that realization of function is not explicitly indicated.

6.5 SOFTWARE PROTOTYPING

Analysis should be conducted regardless of the software engineering paradigm that is applied. However, the *form* that analysis takes will vary. In some cases it is possible to apply fundamental analysis principles and derive a paper specification of software from which a design can be developed. In other situations, requirements gathering (via FAST or other "brainstorming" techniques [JOR89]) is conducted, the analysis principles are applied, and a model of the software to be built, called a *prototype,* is constructed for customer and developer assessment. Finally, there are circumstances that require the construction of a prototype at the beginning of analysis, since the model is the only means through which requirements can be effectively derived. The model then evolves into production software.

Boar [BOA84, p. 5] justifies the prototyping technique in this way:

> Most currently recommended methods for defining business system requirements are designed to establish a final, complete, consistent, and correct set of requirements before the system is designed, constructed, seen or experienced by the user. Common and recurring industry experience indicates that despite the use of rigorous techniques, in many cases users still reject applications as neither correct nor complete upon completion. Consequently, expensive, time-consuming, and divisive rework is required to harmonize the original specification with the definitive test of actual operational needs. In the worst case, rather than retrofit the delivered system, it is abandoned. Developers may build and test against specifications but users accept or reject against current and actual operational realities.

Although the above quotation represents an extreme view, its fundamental argument is sound. In many (but not all) cases, the construction of a prototype, possibly coupled with systematic analysis methods, is an effective approach to software engineering.

6.5.1 A Prototyping Scenario

The prototyping paradigm for software engineering was introduced in Chapter 1. We shall expand this paradigm to indicate the individual steps in the prototyping process and the decision points that dictate how these steps are applied.

All software engineering projects begin with a request from a customer. The request can be in the form of a memo describing a problem, a report defining a set of business or product goals, a formal *Request for Proposal* (RFP) from an outside agency or company, or a *System Specification* that has allocated function and performance to software as one element of a larger computer-based system. Assuming the request for software exists in one of the forms noted above, the following steps may be applied to accomplish software prototyping.

Step 1 *Evaluate the software request and determine whether the software to be developed is a good candidate for prototyping.* Not all software is amenable to prototyping. A number of prototyping candidacy factors [BOA84] can be defined: application area, application complexity, customer characteristics, and project characteristics.

In general, any application that creates dynamic visual displays, interacts heavily with a human, or demands algorithms or combinatorial processing that must be developed in an evolutionary fashion is a candidate for prototyping. However, these application areas must be weighed against application complexity. If a candidate application (one that has the characteristics noted above) will require the development of tens of thousands of lines of code before any demonstrable function can be performed, it is likely to be too complex for prototyping. If, however, the complexity can be partitioned, it may still be possible to prototype portions of the software.

Because the customer must interact with the prototype in later steps, it is essential that (1) customer resources be committed to the evaluation and refinement of the prototype, and (2) the customer be capable of making requirements decisions in a timely fashion. Finally, the nature of the development project will have a strong bearing on the efficacy of prototyping. Is project management willing and able to work with the prototyping method? Are prototyping tools available? Do developers have experience with prototyping methods?

Step 2 *Given an acceptable candidate project, the analyst develops an abbreviated representation of the requirements.* Before construction of a prototype can begin, the analyst must represent the information domain and the functional and behavioral domains of the problem and develop a reasonable approach to partitioning. The application of these fundamental analysis principles can be accomplished through the requirements analysis methods described in Chapters 7, 8, and 9.

Step 3 *After the requirements model has been reviewed, an abbreviated design specification is created for the prototype.* Design must occur before prototyping can commence. However, design typically focuses on top-level architectural and data design issues, rather than on detailed procedural design.

Step 4 *Prototype software is created, tested, and refined.* Ideally, pre-existing software building blocks are used to create the prototype in a rapid fashion. Unfortunately, such building blocks rarely exist. Alternatively, specialized prototyping tools (e.g., [TAN89], [CER88], [LUQ88]) can be used to assist the analyst/designer in representing the design and translating it into executable form.

Even if implementation of a working prototype is impractical, the prototyping scenario can still be applied. For human-interactive applications, it is often possible to create a *paper prototype* that depicts the human-machine interaction (queries, displays, decisions, etc.) using a series of *storyboard sheets*. Each storyboard sheet contains a representation of a screen image with narrative text that describes the interaction between machine and user. The customer reviews the storyboard sheets, obtaining a user's perspective of the operation of the software. In many cases, the "paper" prototype is not paper at all, but rather a series of interactive "screens" generated using a PC or workstation-based prototyping tool.

Step 5 *Once the prototype has been tested, it is presented to the customer, who "test drives" the application and suggests modifications.* This step is the kernel of the prototyping approach. It is here that the customer can examine an implemented representation of software requirements, suggesting modifications that will make the software better meet actual needs.

Step 6 *Steps 4 and 5 are repeated iteratively until all the requirements are formalized or until the prototype has evolved into a production system.* The prototyping paradigm can be conducted with one of two objectives in mind: (1) The purpose of prototyping is to establish a set of formal requirements that may then be translated into production software through the use of software engineering methods and techniques, or (2) the purpose of prototyping is to provide a continuum that results in the evolutionary development of production software. Both approaches have merit and both create problems.

test
yes A

6.5.2 Prototyping Methods and Tools

For software prototyping to be effective, a prototype must be developed rapidly so that the customer may assess results and recommend changes. To conduct *rapid prototyping,* three generic classes of methods and tools are available: fourth-generation techniques, reusable software components, formal specification, and prototyping environments.

Fourth-Generation Techniques Fourth-generation techniques (4GTs) encompass a broad array of database query and reporting languages, program and application generators, and other very-high-level nonprocedural languages. Because 4GTs enable the software engineer to generate executable code quickly, they are ideal for rapid prototyping. Although the application domain for 4GTs is currently limited to business information systems, tools for engineering applications are beginning to emerge.

Reusable Software Components Another approach to rapid prototyping is to assemble, rather than build, the prototype by using a set of existing software components. A software component may be a data structure (or database) or a software architectural component (i.e., a program) or a procedural component (i.e., a module). In each case the software component must be designed in a manner that enables it to be reused without detailed knowledge of its internal workings.

Melding prototyping and program component reuse will work only if a library system is developed so that components that do exist can be catalogued and then retrieved. Although a number of tools have been developed to meet this need (e.g., [ARN87], [GIA91]), much work remains to be done in this area.

It should be noted that an existing software product can be used as a prototype for a "new, improved" competitive product. In a way, this is a form of reusability for software prototyping.

Formal Specification and Prototyping Environments Over the past two decades, a number of formal specification languages and tools (Chapter 9) have been developed as a replacement for natural language specification techniques. Today, developers of these formal languages are in the process of developing interactive environments [RZE85] that (1) enable an analyst to interactively create a language-based specification of a system or software, (2) invoke automated tools that translate the language-based specification into executable code, and (3) enable the customer to use the prototype executable code to refine formal requirements. Specification languages such as PSL, RSL, IORL, GYPSY, OBJ, and many others are being coupled to interactive environments in an effort to achieve an automated software engineering paradigm (Figure 6.9) [BAL83]. Although still in their early stages of development and application, such environments offer substantial hope for improved prototyping and software development productivity.

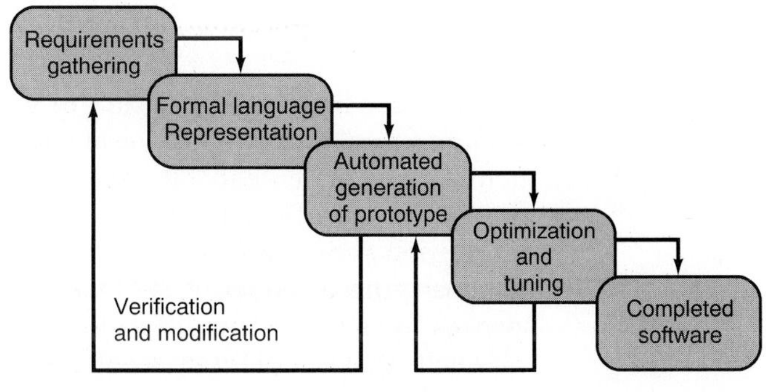

FIGURE 6.9. An automated software engineering paradigm.

6.6 SPECIFICATION

There is no doubt that the mode of specification has much to do with the quality of solution. Software engineers who have been forced to work with incomplete, inconsistent, or misleading specifications have experienced the frustration and confusion that invariably results. The quality, timeliness, and completeness of the software suffers as a consequence.

We have seen that software requirements may be analyzed in a number of different ways. Analysis techniques may lead to paper or computer-based (developed using CASE) specification that contains graphical and natural language descriptions of software requirements. Prototyping results in an *executable specification,* that is, the prototype serves as a representation of requirements. Formal specification languages lead to formal representations of requirements that may be verified or further analyzed.

6.6.1 Specification Principles

Specification, regardless of the mode through which we accomplish it, may be viewed as a representation process. Requirements are represented in a manner that ultimately leads to successful software implementation. Balzer and Goldman [BAL86] propose eight principles of good specification. Their discussion (included with permission) is reproduced below:

PRINCIPLE #1: Separate functionality from implementation.

First, by definition, a specification is a description of what is desired, rather than how it is to be realized (implemented). Specifications can adopt two quite different forms. The first form is that of mathematical functions: Given some set of input, produce a particular set of outputs. The general form of such specifications is find [a/the/all] result such that P (input), where P represents an arbitrary predicate. In such specifications, the result to be obtained has been entirely expressed in a *what* (rather than *how*) form. In part this is because the result is a mathematical function of the input (the operation has well-defined starting and stopping points) and is unaffected by any surrounding environment.

PRINCIPLE #2: A process-oriented systems specification language is required.

Consider instead a situation in which the environment is dynamic and its changes affect the behavior of some entity interacting with that environment (as in an "embedded computer system"). Its behavior cannot be expressed as a mathematical function of its input. Rather, a process-oriented description must be employed, in which the *what* specification is achieved by specifying a model of the desired behavior in terms of functional responses to various stimuli from the environment.

Such process-oriented specifications, presenting a model of system behavior, have normally been excluded from formal specification languages, but they are essential if more complex dynamic situations are to be specified. In fact, it must be recognized that in such situations both the process to be automated and the environment in which it exists must be described formally. That is, the entire system of interacting parts must be specified, rather than just one component.

PRINCIPLE #3: A specification must encompass the system of which the software is a component.

A system is composed of interacting components. Only within the context of the entire system and the interaction among its parts can the behavior of a specific component be defined. In general, a system can be modeled as a collection of passive and active objects. These objects are interrelated and over time the relationships among the objects change. These dynamic relationships provide the stimulus to which the active objects, called *agents,* respond. The responses may cause further changes and, hence, additional stimuli to which the agents might respond.

PRINCIPLE #4: A specification must encompass the environment in which the system operates.

Similarly, the environment in which the system operates and with which it interacts must be specified.

Fortunately, this merely necessitates recognizing that the environment is itself a system composed of interacting objects, both passive and active, of which the specified system is one agent. The other agents, which are by definition unalterable because they are part of the environment, limit the scope of the subsequent design and implementation. In fact, the only difference between the system and its environment is that the subsequent design and implementation effort will operate exclusively on the specification of the system. The environment specification enables the system "interface" to be specified in the same way as the system itself rather than introducing another formalism.

It should be noted that the picture of system specification presented here is that of a highly intertwined collection of agents reacting to stimuli in the environment (changes to objects) produced by those agents. Only through the coordinated actions of the agents are the goals of the system achieved. Such mutual dependence violates the principle of separability (isolation from other parts of the system and environment). But this is a *design* principle, not one of specification. Design follows specification, and is concerned with decomposing a specification into nearly separable pieces in preparation for implementation. The specification, however, must accurately portray the system and its environment as perceived by its user community in as much detail as required by the design and implementation phases. Since this level of required detail is difficult, if not impossible, to foresee in advance, specification, design, and implementation must be recognized as an interactive activity. It is therefore critical that technology exist for recovering as much of this activity as possible as the specification is elaborated and modified (during both initial development and later maintenance).

PRINCIPLE #5: A system specification must be a cognitive model.

The system specification must be a cognitive model rather than a design or implementation model. It must describe a system as perceived by its user community. The objects it manipulates must correspond to the objects of that domain; the agents must model the individuals, organizations, and equipment in that domain; and the actions they perform must model those actually occurring in the domain. Furthermore, it must be possible to incorporate into the specification the rules or laws which govern the objects of the domain. Some of these laws proscribe certain states of the system (such as "two objects cannot be at the same place at the same time"), and hence limit the behavior of the agents or indicate the need for further elaboration to prevent these states from arising. Other laws describe how objects respond when acted upon (e.g., Newton's laws of motion). These laws, which represent a "physics" of the domain, are an inherent part of the system specification.

PRINCIPLE #6: A specification must be operational.

The specification must be complete and formal enough that it can be used to determine if a proposed implementation satisfies the specification for arbitrarily chosen test cases. That is, given the results of an implementation on some arbitrarily chosen set of data, it must be possible to use the specification to validate those results. This implies that the specification, though not a complete specification of how, can act as a generator of possible behaviors among which must be the proposed implementation. Hence, in an extended sense, the specification must be operational....

PRINCIPLE #7: The system specification must be tolerant of incompleteness and augmentable.

No specification can ever be totally complete. The environment in which it exists is too complex for that. A specification is always a model—an abstraction—of some real (or envisioned) situation. Hence, it will be incomplete. Furthermore, as it is being formulated it will exist at many levels of detail. The operationality required above must not necessitate completeness. The analysis tools employed to aid specifiers and to test specifications must be capable of dealing with incompleteness. Naturally this weakens the analysis which can be performed by widening the range of acceptable behaviors which satisfy the specification, but such degradation must mirror the remaining levels of uncertainty.

PRINCIPLE #8: A specification must be localized and loosely coupled.

The previous principles deal with the specification as a static entity. This one arises from the dynamics of the specification. It must be recognized that although the main purpose of a specification is to serve as the basis for design and implementation of some system, it is not a precomposed static object, but a dynamic object which undergoes considerable modification. Such modification occurs in three main activities: formulation, when an initial specification is being created; development, when the specification is elaborated during the iterative process of design to reflect a modified environment and/or additional functional requirements.

With so much change occurring to the specification, it is critical that its content and structure be chosen to accommodate this activity. The main requirements for such accommodations are that information within the specification must be localized so that only a single piece (ideally) need be modified when information changes, and that the specification is loosely structured (coupled) so that pieces can be added or removed easily, and the structure automatically readjusted.

Although the principles espoused by Balzer and Goldman focus on the impact of specification on the definition of formal languages, their comments apply equally well to all forms of specification. However, principles must be translated into realization. In the next section we examine a set of guidelines for creating a specification of requirements.

6.6.2 Representation

Figure 6.10 is a classic example of a good specification representation. The drawing, taken from Galileo's work (circa 1638), is used to supplement text

FIGURE 6.10. Representation of specification. (*Source:* Galileo's *Discorsi e Dimonstrazioni Matematiche ubtorno a due nuove science,* Leyden, 1638. From J. D. Bernal, *Science in History,* London, Watts, 1969.)

that describes his method for the analysis of the strength of a beam. Even without the accompanying text, the diagram helps us to understand what must be done.

We have already seen that software requirements may be specified in a variety of ways. However, if requirements are committed to paper or an electronic presentation medium (and they almost always should be!) a simple set of guidelines is well worth following:

Representation format and content should be relevant to the problem. A general outline for the contents of a *Software Requirements Specification* can be developed. However, the representation forms contained within the specification are likely to vary with the application area. For example, a specification of a manufacturing automation system would use different symbology, diagrams, and language than the specification for a programming language compiler.

Information contained within the specification should be nested. Representations should reveal layers of information so that a reader can move to the level of detail that is required. Paragraph and diagram numbering schemes should indicate the level of detail that is being presented. It is sometimes worthwhile to present the same information at different levels of abstraction to aid in understanding.

Diagrams and other notational forms should be restricted in number and consistent in use. For example, the symbology shown in Figure 6.11 can be interpreted to mean at least three (and probably five or six) different things. Confusing or inconsistent notation, whether graphical or symbolic, degrades understanding and fosters errors.

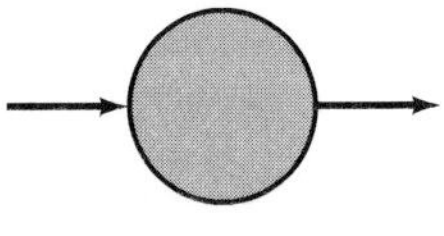

FIGURE 6.11. A symbol with multiple interpretations.

Representations should be revisable. The content of a specification will change. Ideally, CASE tools should be available to update all representations that are affected by each change.

Investigators have conducted numerous studies (e.g., [CUR85]) on human factors associated with specification. There appears to be little doubt that symbology and arrangement affect understanding. However, software engineers appear to have individual preferences for specific symbolic and diagrammatic forms. Familiarity often lies at the root of a person's preference, but other more tangible factors such as spatial arrangement, easily recognizable patterns, and degree of formality often dictate an individual's choice.

6.6.3 The *Software Requirements Specification*

The *Software Requirements Specification* is produced at the culmination of the analysis task. The function and performance allocated to software as part of system engineering are refined by establishing a complete information description, a detailed functional description, an indication of performance requirements and design constraints, appropriate validation criteria, and other data pertinent to requirements. The National Bureau of Standards, IEEE (Standard No. 830-1984), and the U.S. Department of Defense have all proposed candidate formats for software requirements specifications (as well as other software engineering documentation). For our purposes, however, the simplified outline presented in Table 6.1 may be used as a framework for the specification.

TABLE 6.1

SOFTWARE REQUIREMENTS SPECIFICATION OUTLINE

I. Introduction
- **A.** System reference
- **B.** Overall description
- **C.** Software project constraints

II. Information description
- **A.** Information flow representation
  - **1.** Data flow
  - **2.** Control flow
- **B.** Information content representation
- **C.** System interface description

III. Functional description
- **A.** Functional partitioning
- **B.** Functional description
  - **1.** Processing narrative
  - **2.** Restrictions/limitations
  - **3.** Performance requirements
  - **4.** Design constraints
  - **5.** Supporting diagrams
- **C.** Control description
  - **1.** Control specification
  - **2.** Design constraints

IV. Behavioral description
- **A.** System states
- **B.** Events and actions

V. Validation criteria
- **A.** Performance bounds
- **B.** Classes of tests
- **C.** Expected software response
- **D.** Special considerations

VI. Bibliography

VII. Appendix

The Introduction states the goals and objectives of the software, describing it in the context of the computer-based system. Actually, the Introduction may be nothing more than the software scope of the planning document.

The Information Description section provides a detailed description of the problem that the software must solve. Both information flow and structure are documented. Hardware, software, and human interfaces are described for external system elements and internal software functions.

A description of each function required to solve the problem is presented in the Functional Description section. A processing narrative is provided for each function, design constraints are stated and justified, performance characteristics are stated, and one or more diagrams are included to graphically represent the overall structure of the software and interplay among software functions and other system elements. The Behavioral Description section of the specification examines the operation of the software as a consequence of external events and internally generated control characteristics.

Validation Criteria is probably the most important and, ironically, the most often neglected section of the *Software Requirements Specification.* How do we recognize a successful implementation? What classes of tests must be conducted to validate function, performance, and constraints? We neglect this section because completing it demands a thorough understanding of software requirements—something that we often do not have at this stage. Yet, specification of validation criteria acts as an implicit review of all other requirements. It is essential that time and attention be given to this section.

Finally, the *Software Requirements Specification* includes a Bibliography and an Appendix. The Bibliography contains references to all documents that relate to the software. These include other software engineering documentation, technical references, vendor literature, and standards. The Appendix contains information that supplements the specification. Tabular data, detailed description of algorithms, charts, graphs, and other material are presented as appendices.

In many cases the *Software Requirements Specification* may be accompanied by an executable prototype (that in some cases may replace the specification), a paper prototype, or a *Preliminary User's Manual.* The *Preliminary User's Manual* presents the software as a black box. That is, heavy emphasis is placed on user input and resultant output. The manual can serve as a valuable tool for uncovering problems at the human-computer interface.

6.7 SPECIFICATION REVIEW

A review of the *Software Requirements Specification* (and/or prototype) is conducted by both software developer and customer. Because the specification forms the foundation of the development phase, extreme care should be taken in conducting the review.

The review is first conducted at a *macroscopic* level. At this level, the reviewers attempt to ensure that the specification is complete, consistent, and accurate. The following questions are addressed:

- Do stated goals and objectives for software remain consistent with system goals and objectives?
- Have important interfaces to all system elements been described?
- Is information flow and structure adequately defined for the problem domain?
- Are diagrams clear? Can each stand alone without supplementary text?
- Do major functions remain within scope and has each been adequately described?
- Is the behavior of the software consistent with the information it must process and the functions it must perform?
- Are design constraints realistic?
- What is the technological risk of development?
- Have alternative software requirements been considered?
- Have validation criteria been stated in detail? Are they adequate to describe a successful system?
- Do inconsistencies, omissions, or redundancy exist?
- Is the customer contact complete?
- Has the user reviewed the *Preliminary User's Manual* or prototype?
- How are the *Software Project Plan* estimates affected?

In order to develop answers to many of the above questions, the review may focus at a *detailed* level. Here, our concern is on the wording of the specification. We attempt to uncover problems that may be hidden within the specification content. The following guidelines for a detailed specification review are suggested:

- Be on the lookout for persuasive connectors (e.g., "certainly," "therefore," "clearly," "obviously," "it follows that") and ask "Why are they present?"
- Watch out for vague terms (e.g., "some," "sometimes," "often," "usually," "ordinarily," "most," "mostly"); ask for clarification.
- When lists are given, but not completed, be sure all items are understood. Keys to look for: "etc.," "and so forth," "and so on," "such as."
- Be sure stated ranges don't contain unstated assumptions (e.g., "Valid codes range from 10 to 100." Integer? Real? Hex?).
- Beware of vague verbs such as "handled," "rejected," "processed," "skipped," "eliminated." There are many ways they can be interpreted.
- Beware "dangling" pronouns (e.g., "The I/O module communicates with the data validation module and *its* control flag is set." Whose control flag?).

- Look for statements that imply certainty (e.g., "always," "every," "all," "none," "never"), then ask for proof.
- When a term is explicitly defined in one place, try substituting the definition for other occurrences of the term.
- When a structure is described in words, draw a picture to aid in understanding it.
- When a calculation is specified, work at least two examples.

Once the review is complete, the *Software Requirements Specification* is "signed off" by both customer and developer. The specification becomes a "contract" for software development. Changes in requirements requested after the specification is finalized will not be eliminated. But the customer should note that each after-the-fact change is an extension of software scope and therefore can increase cost and/or protract the schedule.

Even with the best review procedures in place, a number of common specification problems persist. The specification is difficult to "test" in any meaningful way, and therefore inconsistencies or omissions may pass unnoticed. During the review, changes to the specification may be recommended. It can be extremely difficult to assess the global impact of a change; that is, how does a change in one function affect requirements for other functions? Automated specification tools have been developed to help solve these problems and are discussed in Chapter 9 and later in Chapter 22.

6.8 SUMMARY

Requirements analysis is the first technical step in the software engineering process. It is at this point that a general statement of software scope is refined into a concrete specification that becomes the foundation for all software engineering activities that follow.

Analysis must focus on the information, functional, and behavioral domains of a problem. To better understand what is required, models are created, the problem is partitioned, and representations that depict the essence of requirements and, later, implementation detail are developed.

In many cases, it is not possible to completely specify a problem at an early stage. Prototyping offers an alternative approach that results in an executable model of the software from which requirements can be refined. To properly conduct prototyping, special tools and techniques are required.

The *Software Requirements Specification* is developed as a consequence of analysis. Review is essential to ensure that the developer and the customer have the same perception of the system. Unfortunately, even with the best of methods, the problem is that the problem keeps changing.

REFERENCES

[ARN87] Arnold, S. P., and S. L. Stepoway, "The Reuse System: Cataloging and Retrieval of Reusable Software," *Proceedings of COMPCON '87,* IEEE, 1987, pp. 376–379.

[ATW77] Atwood, J.W., *The Systems Analyst,* Hayden, 1977.

[BAL83] Balzer, R., T. E. Cheatham, and C. Green, "Software Technology in the 1990s: A New Paradigm," *IEEE Computer,* vol. 16, no. 11, November 1983, pp. 39–45.

[BAL86] Balzer, R., and N. Goldman, "Principles of Good Specification and their Implications for Specification Languages," in *Software Specification Techniques* (Gehani and McGetrick, eds.), Addison-Wesley, 1986, pp. 25–39.

[BER80] Bersoff, E. H., V. D. Henderson, and S.G. Siegel, *Software Configuration Management,* Prentice-Hall, 1980, p. 43.

[BOA84] Boar, B., *Application Prototyping,* Wiley-Interscience, 1984.

[CER88] Ceri, S., et al., "Software Prototyping by Relational Techniques: Experiences with Program Construction Systems," *IEEE Trans. Software Engineering,* vol. 14, no. 11, November 1988, pp. 1597–1609.

[CUR85] Curtis, B., *Human Factors in Software Development,* IEEE Computer Society Press, 1985.

[GAU89] Gause, D.C., and G. M. Weinberg, *Exploring Requirements: Quality before Design,* Dorset House, 1989.

[GIA91] Caldiera, G., and V. R. Basili, "Identifying and Qualifying Reusable Software Components," *IEEE Computer,* vol. 24, no. 2, February 1991, pp. 61–70.

[JOR89] Jordan, P.W., et al., "Software Storming: Combining Rapid Prototyping and Knowledge Engineering," *IEEE Computer,* vol. 22, no. 5, May 1989, pp. 39–50.

[LUQ88] Luqi and M. Ketabashi, "A Computer Aided Prototyping System," *IEEE Software,* vol. 5, no. 2, March 1988, pp. 66–72.

[RZE85] Rzepka, W., and Y. Ohno (eds.), "Requirements Engineering Environments," *IEEE Computer* (special issue), vol. 18, no. 4, April 1985.

[TAN89] Tanik, M. M., and R.T. Yeh (eds.), "Rapid Prototyping in Software Development," *IEEE Computer* (special issue), vol. 22, no. 5, May 1989.

[ZAH90] Zahniser, R. A., "Building Software in Groups," *American Programmer,* vol. 3, no. 7/8, July-August 1990.

PROBLEMS AND POINTS TO PONDER

6.1 Software requirements analysis is unquestionably the most communication-intensive step in the software engineering process. Why does the communication path frequently break down?

6.2 There are frequently severe political repercussions when software requirements analysis (and/or system analysis) begins. For example, workers may feel that job security is threatened by a new automated system. What causes such problems? Can the analysis task be conducted so that the political aspect is minimized?

6.3 Discuss your perceptions of the ideal training and background for a system analyst.

6.4 Throughout this chapter we refer to the "customer." Describe the customer for information systems developers, for builders of computer-based products, for systems builders. Be careful here—there may be more to this problem than you first imagine!

6.5 Develop a facilitated application specification technique "kit." The kit should include a set of guidelines for conducting a FAST meeting, materials that can be used to facilitate the creation lists, and any other items that might help in defining requirements.

6.6 Your instructor will divide the class into groups of four or six students. Half of each group will play the role of the marketing department and half will take on the role of software engineering. Your job is to define requirements for the *SafeHome* security system described in this chapter. Conduct a FAST meeting using the guidelines presented in this chapter.

6.7 Is it fair to say that a *Preliminary User's Manual* is a form of prototype? Explain your answer.

6.8 Why does a customer always react in a manner that is described by the "first law of system engineering" (Section 6.2)?

6.9 Analyze the information domain for *SafeHome*. Represent (using any notation that seems appropriate) information flow in the system, information content, and any information structure that is relevant.

6.10 Partition the functional domain for *SafeHome*. First perform horizontal partitioning; then perform vertical partitioning.

6.11 Create essential and implementation representations of the *SafeHome* system.

6.12 Build a paper prototype (or a real prototype) of *SafeHome*. Be sure to depict owner interaction and overall system function.

6.13 Try to identify software components of *SafeHome* that might be "reusable" in other products or systems. Attempt to categorize these components.

6.14 Develop a written specification for *SafeHome* using the outline provided in Table 6.1. (*Note:* Your instructor will suggest which sections to complete at this time.) Be sure to apply the questions that are described for the specification review.

6.15 How did your requirements differ from others who attempted a solution for *SafeHome?* Who built a "Chevy"—who built a "Cadillac?"

FURTHER READINGS

Requirements analysis is a communication-intensive activity. If communication fails, even the best technical approach will fall short. Worthwhile guidelines for conducting FAST meetings are presented by Gause and Weinberg [GAU89] and Zahniser [ZAH90]. The authors discuss the mechanics of effective meetings, methods for brainstorming, approaches that can be used to clarify results, and a variety of other useful issues. A book by Martin (*User Centered Requirements Analysis*, Prentice-Hall, 1988) also discusses the need for effective customer-developer communication. Additional insight into the psychology of the analysis process can be obtained from Weinberg (*Rethinking Systems Analysis and Design,* Little, Brown, 1982).

Information domain analysis is a fundamental principle of requirements analysis. The *Proceedings of the Sixth International Conference on Data Engineering* (IEEE, February 1990) presents important work in analysis methods, formal specification, and prototyping and their relationship to data engineering. Gehani and McGettrick (*Software Specification Techniques,* Addison-Wesley, 1986) have edited an important anthology of papers on software analysis topics, ranging from basic principles of specification to advanced specification and design environments. The results of more recent research can be obtained from the *Proceedings of the Sixth International Workshop on Specification and Design* (IEEE, 1990).

Boar's book on application prototyping [BOA84] and a book by Connell and Shafer (*Structured Rapid Prototyping,* Prentice-Hall, 1989) present this important analysis technique with a definite information systems flavor. However, many topics discussed by the authors are applicable across all application domains. The May 1989 special issue of *IEEE Computer* [TAN89] presents an excellent overview of developments in rapid prototyping with an emphasis on engineering applications.

The reuse of program components as an approach to software prototyping has gained a significant following over the past few years. IEEE tutorials by Freeman (*Software Reusability,* IEEE Computer Society Press, 1987) and Tracz (*Software Reuse: Emerging Technology,* IEEE Computer Society Press, 1988) present excellent coverage on this topic.

Fickas and Nagarajan ("Critiquing Software Specifications," *IEEE Software,* November 1988) present an intriguing paper that describes an expert system that can be used to review software specifications. Although their work represents a starting point only, it may be the harbinger of a future generation of CASE tools that not only enable a software engineer to create a specification, but also to critique the result.

CHAPTER 7

STRUCTURED ANALYSIS AND ITS EXTENSIONS

Structured analysis, like all software requirements analysis methods, is a model building activity. Using a notation that is unique to the structured analysis method, we create models that depict information (data and control) flow and content, we partition the system functionally and behaviorally, and we depict the essence of what must be built. Structured analysis is not a single method applied consistently by all who use it. Rather, it is an amalgam that has evolved over almost 20 years.

There is probably no other software engineering method that has generated as much interest, been tried (and often rejected and then tried again) by as many people, provoked as much criticism, and sparked as much controversy. But the method has prospered and is gaining widespread use throughout the software engineering community.

In his seminal book on the subject, Tom DeMarco [DEM79, pp. 15–16] describes structured analysis in this way:

> Looking back over the recognized problems and failings of the analysis phase, I suggest that we need to make the following additions to our set of analysis phase goals:
>
> - The products of analysis must be highly maintainable. This applies particularly to the Target Document [*Software Requirements Specification*].
> - Problems of size must be dealt with using an effective method of partitioning. The victorian novel specification is out.
> - Graphics have to be used whenever possible.
> - We have to differentiate between logical [essential] and physical [implementation] considerations....
>
> At the very least, we need...

- Something to help us partition our requirements and document that partitioning before specification....
- Some means of keeping track of and evaluating interfaces....
- New tools to describe logic and policy, something better than narrative text....

With these words, DeMarco establishes the primary goals of an analysis method that has become the most widely used in the world. In this chapter, we examine this method and its extensions.

7.1 A BRIEF HISTORY

Like many important contributions to software engineering, structured analysis was not introduced with a single landmark paper or book that was a definitive treatment of the subject. Early work in analysis modeling was begun in the late 1960s and early 1970s, but the first appearance of the structured analysis approach was as an adjunct to another important topic—"structured design." Researchers (e.g., [STE74], [YOU78]) needed a graphical notation for representing data and the processes that transformed it. These processes would ultimately be mapped into a design architecture.

The term "structured analysis" was popularized by DeMarco [DEM79]. In his book on the subject, DeMarco introduced and named the key graphical symbols that would enable an analyst to create information flow models, suggested heuristics for the use of these symbols, suggested that a *data dictionary* and *processing narratives* could be used as supplements to the information flow models, and presented numerous examples that illustrated the use of this new method. In the years that followed, variations of the structured analysis approach were suggested by Page-Jones [PAG80], Gane and Sarson [GAN82], and many others. In every instance, the method focused on information systems applications and did not provide an adequate notation to address the control and behavioral aspects of real-time engineering problems.

By the mid-1980s, the deficiencies of structured analysis (when attempts were made to apply the method to control-oriented applications) became painfully apparent. Real-time "extensions" were introduced by Ward and Mellor [WAR85] and later by Hatley and Pirbhai [HAT87]. These extensions resulted in a more robust analysis method that could be applied effectively to engineering problems. Today, attempts to develop one consistent notation have been suggested [BRU88], and modernized treatments have been published to accommodate the use of CASE tools [YOU89].

7.2 BASIC NOTATION AND ITS EXTENSIONS

Information is transformed as it *flows* through a computer-based system. The system accepts input in a variety of forms, applies hardware, software and human elements to transform input into output, and produces output in a variety of forms. Input may be a control signal transmitted by a transducer, a series of numbers typed by a human operator, a packet of information transmitted on a network link, or a voluminous data file retrieved from secondary storage. The transform(s) may comprise a single logical comparison, a complex numerical algorithm, or rule-inference approach of an expert system. Output may light a single light-emitting diode (LED) or produce a 200-page report. In effect, we can create a *flow model* for any computer-based system, regardless of size and complexity.

Structured analysis is an information flow and content modeling technique. A computer-based system is represented as an information transform, as shown in Figure 7.1. The overall function of the system is represented as a single information transform, noted as a *bubble* in the figure. One or more inputs, shown as labeled arrows, originate from external entities, represented as boxes. The input drives the transform to produce output information (also represented as labeled arrows) that is passed to other external entities. It should be noted that the model may be applied to the entire system or to the software element only. The key is to represent the information fed into and produced by the transform.

7.2.1 Data Flow Diagrams

As information moves through software, it is modified by a series of transformations. A *data flow diagram* (DFD) is a graphical technique that depicts information flow and the transforms that are applied as data move from input to output. The basic form of a data flow diagram is illustrated in Figure 7.1. The DFD is also known as a *data flow graph* or a *bubble chart*.

The data flow diagram may be used to represent a system or software at any level of abstraction. In fact, DFDs may be partitioned into levels that represent increasing information flow and functional detail. A level 0 DFD, also called a *fundamental system model* or a *context model*, represents the

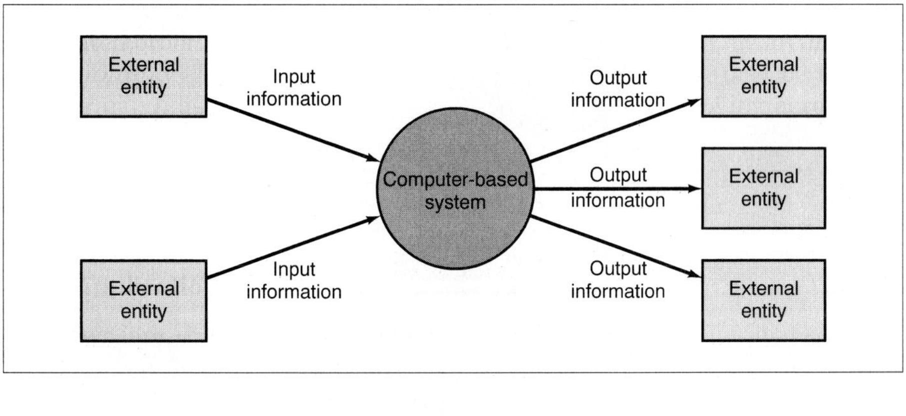

FIGURE 7.1. Information flow model.

entire software element as a single bubble with input and output data indicated by incoming and outgoing arrows, respectively. Additional processes (bubbles) and information flow paths are represented as the level 0 DFD is partitioned to reveal more detail. For example, a level 1 DFD might contain five or six bubbles with interconnecting arrows. Each of the processes represented at level 1 are subfunctions of the overall system depicted in the context model.

The basic notation[1] used to create a DFD is illustrated in Figure 7.2. A rectangle is used to represent an *external entity,* that is, a system element (e.g., hardware, a person, another program) or another system that produces information for transformation by the software or receives information produced by the software. A circle represents a *process* or *transform* that is applied to data (or control) and changes it in some way. An arrow represents one or more data items. All arrows on a data flow diagram should be labeled. The double line represents a *data store*—stored information that is used by the software. The simplicity of DFD notation is one reason why structured analysis techniques are the most widely used.

It is important to note that no explicit indication of the sequence of processing is supplied by the diagram. Procedure or sequence may be implicit in the diagram, but explicit procedural representation is generally delayed until software design.

As we noted earlier, each of the bubbles may be refined or layered to depict more detail. Figure 7.3 illustrates this concept. A fundamental model

[1]Extensions to the basic notation are discussed in Section 7.2.2.

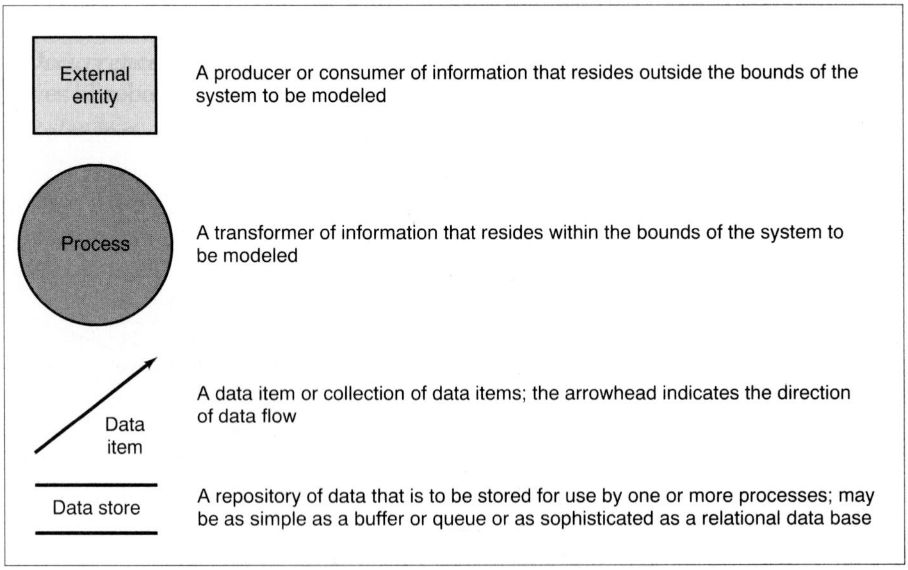

FIGURE 7.2.
Basic DFD notation.

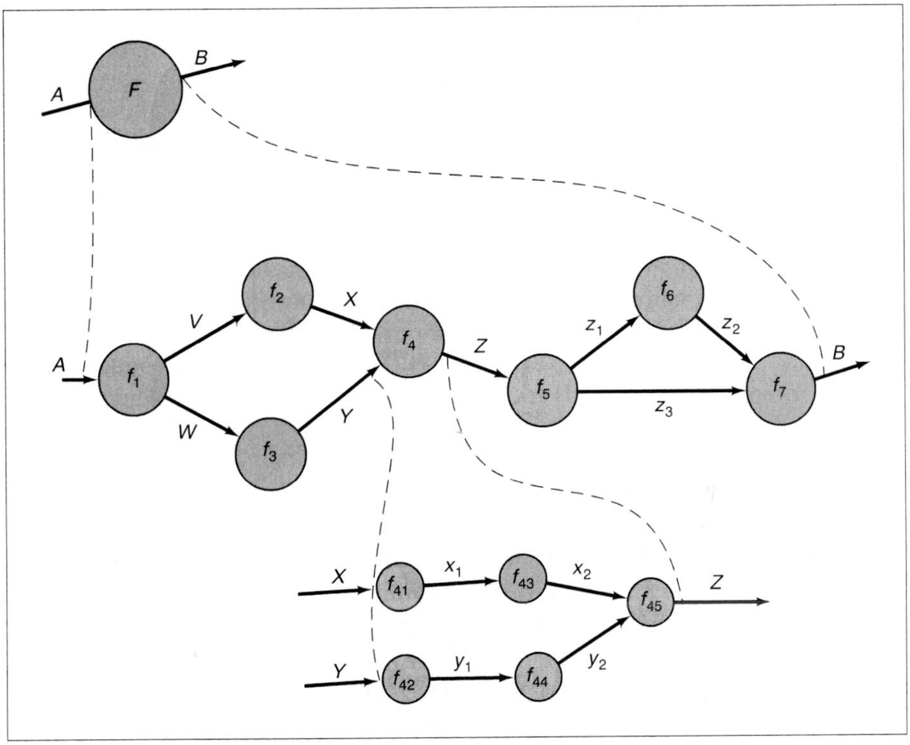

FIGURE 7.3. Information flow refinement.

for system F indicates the primary input is A and ultimate output is B. We refine the F model into transforms f_1 to f_7. Note that *information flow continuity* must be maintained, that is, input and output to each refinement must remain the same. This concept, sometimes called *balancing*, is essential for the development of consistent models. Further refinement of f_4 depicts detail in the form of transforms f_{41} to f_{45}. Again, the input (X, Y) and output (Z) remain unchanged.

The data flow diagram is a graphical tool that can be very valuable during software requirements analysis. However, the diagram can cause confusion if its function is confused with the flowchart. A data flow diagram depicts information flow without explicit representation of procedural logic (e.g., conditions or loops). It is not a flowchart with rounded edges!

The basic notation used to develop a DFD is not in itself sufficient to describe requirements for software. For example, an arrow shown in a DFD represents a data item that is input to or output from a process. A data store represents some organized collection of data. But what is the *content* of the data implied by the arrow or depicted by the store? If the arrow (or the store) represents a collection of items, what are they? These questions are answered by applying another component of the basic notation for structured analysis—the *requirements dictionary,* also called the *data dictio-*

nary. The format and use of the requirements dictionary are presented later in this chapter.

Finally, the graphical notation represented in Figure 7.2 must be augmented with descriptive text. A *processing narrative*—a paragraph that describes a process bubble—can be used to specify the processing details implied by the bubble within a DFD. The processing narrative describes the input to the bubble, the algorithm that is applied to the input, and the output that is produced. In addition, the narrative indicates restrictions and limitations imposed on the process, performance characteristics that are relevant to the process, and design constraints that may influence the way in which the process will be implemented.

7.2.2 Extensions for Real-Time Systems

Many software applications are time-dependent and process more control-oriented information than data. A detailed discussion of these real-time systems and software is reserved for Chapter 15. For now, suffice it to say that a real-time system must interact with the real world in a time frame dictated by the real world. Aircraft avionics, manufacturing process control, consumer products, and industrial instrumentation are but a few of hundreds of real-time software applications.

To accommodate the analysis of real-time software, a number of extensions to the basic notation for structured analysis have been proposed. These extensions, developed by Ward and Mellor [WAR85] and Hatley and Pirbhai [HAT87] and shown in Figures 7.4 and 7.5, enable the analyst to represent control flow and control processing as well as data flow and processing.

7.2.3 Ward and Mellor Extensions

Ward and Mellor [WAR85] extend basic structured analysis notation to accommodate the following demands imposed by a real-time system:

- Information flow that is gathered or produced on a time-continuous basis
- Control information passed throughout the system and associated control processing
- Multiple instances of the same transformation that are sometimes encountered in multitasking situations
- System states and the mechanism that causes transition between states

In a significant percentage of real-time applications, the system must monitor *time-continuous* information generated by some real-world process. For example, a real-time test monitoring system for gas turbine engines might be required to monitor turbine speed, combustor temperature,

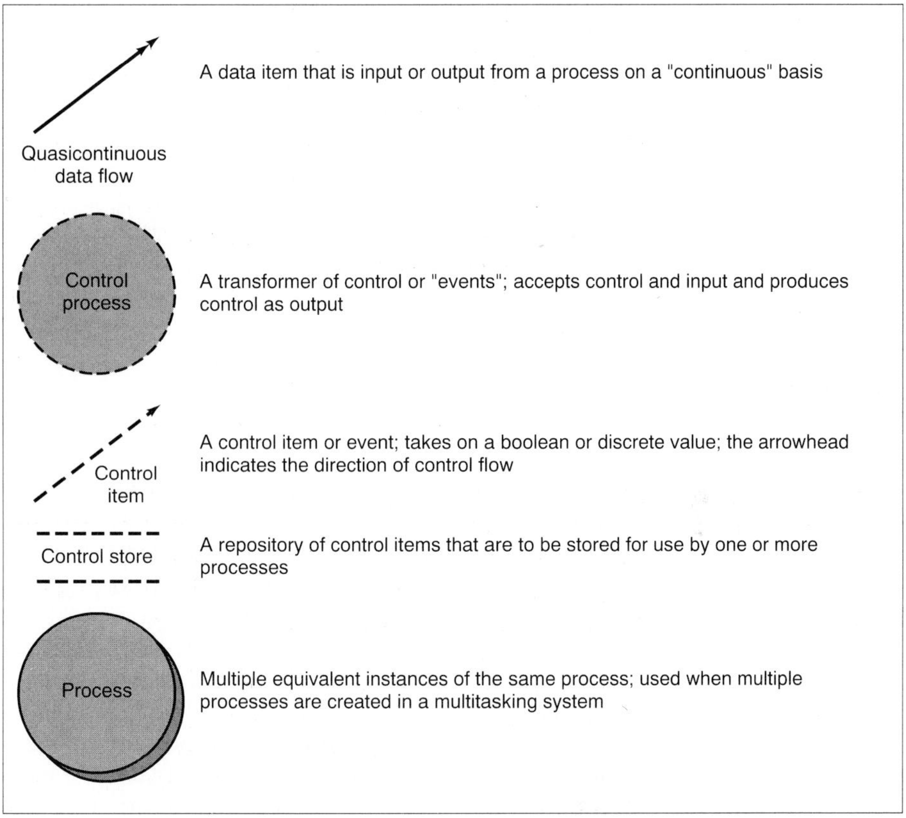

FIGURE 7.4. Extended structured analysis notation for real-time systems developed by Ward and Mellor [WAR85].

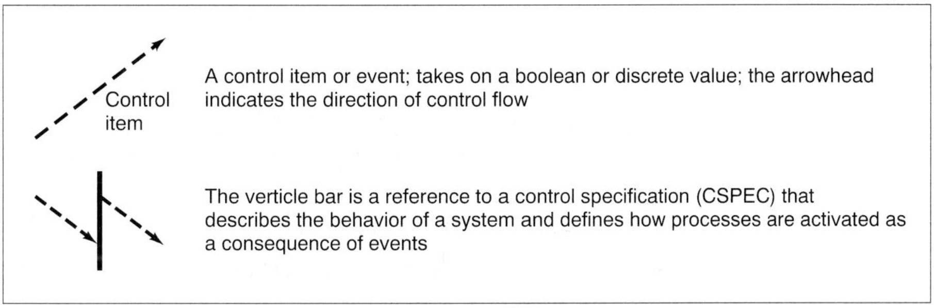

FIGURE 7.5. Extended structured analysis notation for real-time systems developed by Hatley and Pirbhai [HAT87].

and a variety of pressure probes on a continuous basis. Conventional data flow notation does not make a distinction between discrete data and time-continuous data. An extension to basic structured analysis notation, shown in Figure 7.6, provides a mechanism for representing time-continuous data flow. The double headed arrow is used to represent time-continuous flow while a single headed arrow is used to indicate discrete data flow. In the figure, **monitored temperature** is measured continuously while a single

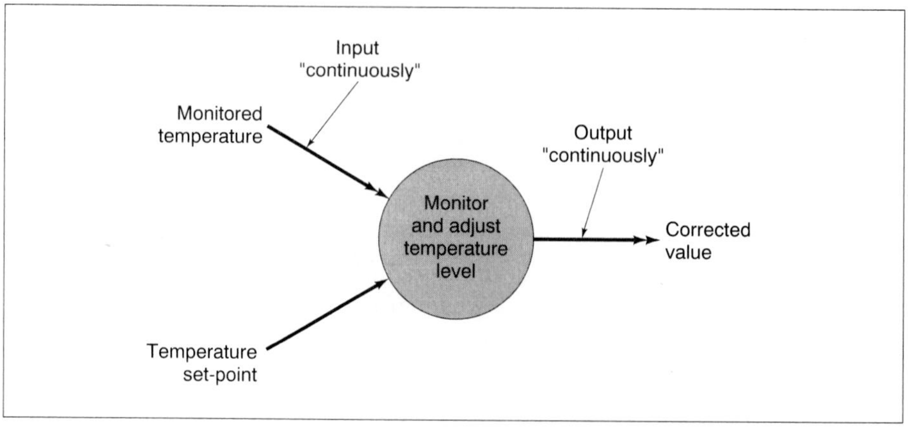

FIGURE 7.6.
Time-continuous data flow.

value for **temperature set-point** is also provided. The process shown in the figure produces a time-continuous output, **corrected value.**

The distinction between discrete and time-continuous data flow has important implications for both the system engineer and the software designer. During the creation of the system model, a system engineer will be better able to isolate those processes that may be performance-critical (it is often likely that the input and output of time-continuous data will be performance-sensitive). As the physical or implementation model is created, the designer must establish a mechanism for collection of time-continuous data. Obviously, the digital system collects data in a quasicontinuous fashion using techniques such as high-speed polling. The notation indicates where analog-to-digital hardware will be required and which transforms are likely to demand high-performance software.

In conventional data flow diagrams, control or *event flows* are not represented explicitly. In fact, the analyst is cautioned to specifically exclude the representation of control flow from the data flow diagram. This exclusion is overly restrictive when real-time applications are considered, and for this reason a specialized notation for representing event flows and control processing has been developed. Continuing the convention established for data flow diagrams, data flow is represented using a solid arrow. *Control flow,* however, is represented using a dashed or shaded arrow. A process that handles only control flows, called a *control process,* is similarly represented using a dashed bubble.

Control flow can be input directly to a conventional process or into a control process. Figure 7.7 illustrates control flow and processing as it would be represented using Ward and Mellor notation. The figure illustrates a top-level view of a data and control flow for a manufacturing cell.[2] As

[2]A manufacturing cell is used in factory automation applications. It contains computers and automated machines (e.g., robots, NC machines, specialized fixtures) and performs one discrete manufacturing operation under computer control.

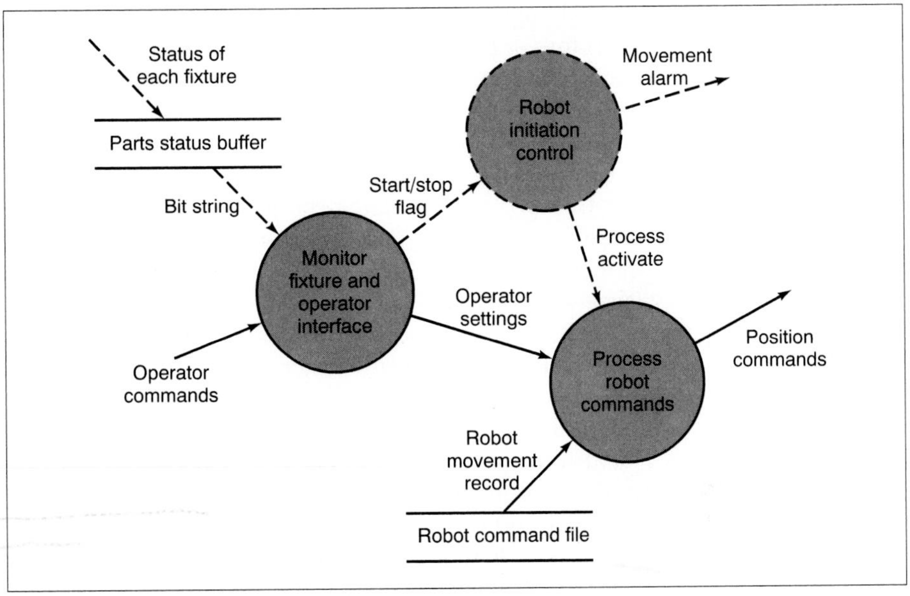

FIGURE 7.7. Data and control flows using Ward and Mellor [WAR85] notation.

components to be assembled by a robot are placed on fixtures, a status bit is set within a **parts status buffer** (a control store) that indicates the presence or absence of each component. Event information contained within the **parts status buffer** is passed as a **bit string** to a process, **monitor fixture and operator** interface. The process will read **operator commands** only when the control information, **bit string**, indicates that all fixtures contain components. An event flag, **start/stop flag**, is sent to **robot initiation control**, a control process that enables further command processing. Other data flows occur as a consequence of the **process activate** event that is sent to **process robot commands**.

In some situations multiple instances of the same control or data transformation process may occur in a real-time system. This can occur in a multitasking environment when tasks are spawned as a result of internal processing or external events. For example, a number of part status buffers may be monitored so that different robots can be signaled at the appropriate time. In addition, each robot may have its own robot control system. The Ward and Mellor notation used to represent *multiple equivalent instances* of the same process is shown in Figure 7.4.

7.2.4 Hatley and Pirbhai Extensions

The Hatley and Pirbhai [HAT87] extensions to basic structured analysis notation focus less on the creation of additional graphical symbols and more on the representation and specification of the control-oriented aspects of the software. Referring to Figure 7.5, the dashed arrow is once again used to represent control or event flow. Unlike Ward and Mellor, Hatley and

Pirbhai suggest that dashed and solid notation be represented separately. Therefore, a *control flow diagram* (CFD) is defined. The CFD contains the same processes as the DFD, but shows control flow rather than data flow. Instead of representing control processes directly within the flow model, a notational reference (a solid bar) to a *control specification* (CSPEC) is used. In essence, the solid bar can be viewed as a "window" into an "executive" (the CSPEC) that controls the processes (bubbles) represented in the DFD based on the event that is passed through the window. The CSPEC, described in detail in Section 7.3.3, is used to indicate (1) how the software behaves when an event or control signal is sensed and (2) which processes are invoked as a consequence of the occurrence of the event. A *process specification* (PSPEC) is used to describe the inner workings of a process represented in a flow diagram.

Using the notation described in Figures 7.2 and 7.5, along with additional information contained in PSPECs and CSPECs, Hatley and Pirbhai create a model of a real-time system. Data flow diagrams are used to represent data and the processes that manipulate it. Control flow diagrams show how events flow among processes and illustrate those external events that cause various processes to be activated. The interrelationship between the process and control models is shown schematically in Figure 7.8. The process model is "connected" to the control model through *data conditions*. The control model is "connected" to the process model through process activation information contained in the CSPEC.

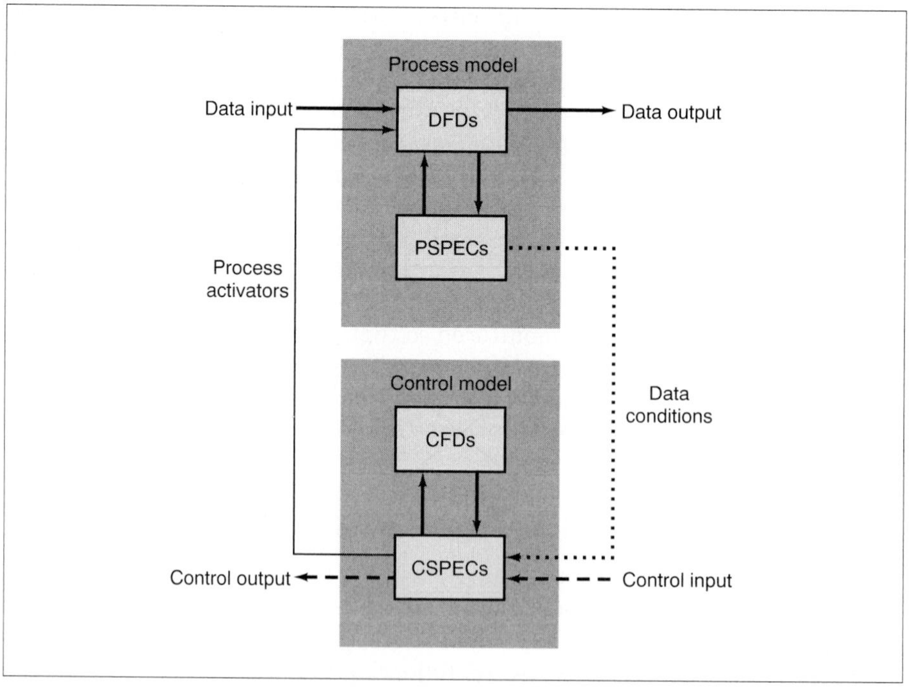

FIGURE 7.8. The relationship between data and control models [HAT87].

A data condition occurs whenever data input to a process results in a control output. This situation is illustrated in Figure 7.9, part of a flow model for an automated monitoring and control system for pressure vessels in an oil refinery. The process **check and convert pressure** implements the algorithm described in the PSPEC pseudocode shown. When the absolute tank pressure is greater than an allowable maximum, an **above pressure** event is generated. Note that when Hatley and Pirbhai notation is used, the data flow is shown as part of a DFD, while the control flow is noted separately as part of a control flow diagram. To determine what happens when this event occurs, we must check the CSPEC.

The control specification contains a number of important modeling tools. A *process activation table* (described in Section 7.3.3) is used to indicate which processes are activated by a given event that flows through the vertical bar. For example, a process activation table (PAT) for Figure 7.9 might indicate that the **above pressure** event would cause a process **reduce tank pressure** (not shown) to be invoked. In addition to the PAT, the CSPEC may contain a *state transition diagram* (STD). The STD is a behavioral model that relies on the definition of a set of *system states*. A state is any observable mode of behavior. For example, states for a monitoring and control system for pressure vessel might be: monitoring state, alarm state, pressure release state, and so on. Each of these states represent a mode of behavior of the system. A state transition diagram (described in Section 7.3.3) indicates how the system moves from state to state.

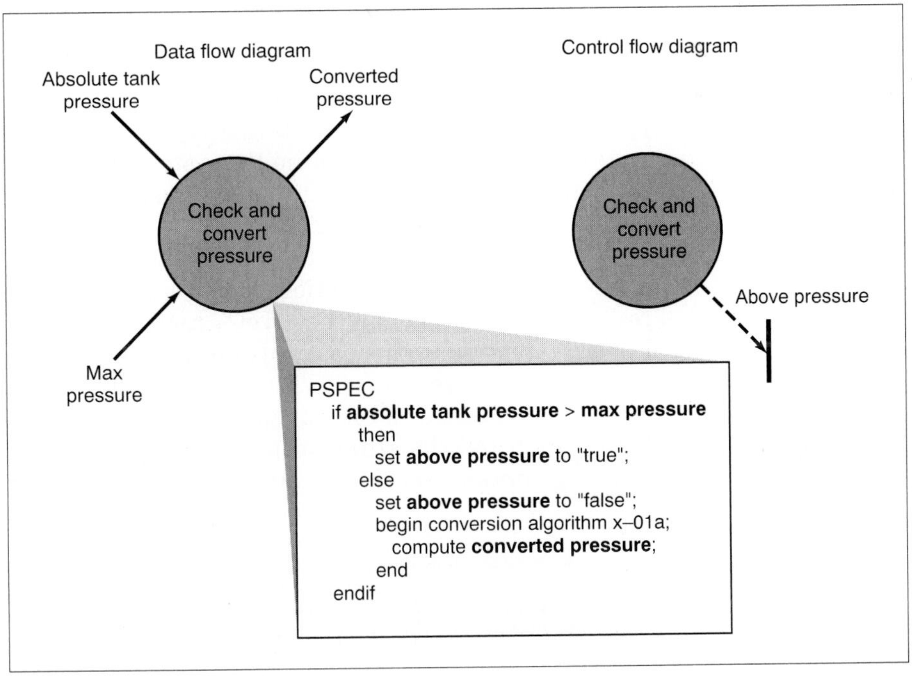

FIGURE 7.9.
Data conditions.

To illustrate the use of the Hatley and Pirbhai extensions, consider software embedded within an office photocopying machine. The photocopier performs a number of functions that are implied by the level 1 DFD shown in Figure 7.10. It should be noted that additional refinement of the data flow and definition of each data item (using a requirements dictionary) would be required.

The control flow for the photocopier software is shown in Figure 7.11. Control flows are shown entering and exiting individual processes and the CSPEC "window." For example, the **paper feed status** and **start/stop** events flow into the CSPEC bar. This implies that each of these events will cause some process represented in the CFD to be activated. If we were to examine the CSPEC internals, the **start/stop** event would be shown to activate/deactivate the **manage copying** process. Similarly, the **jammed** event (part of paper feed status) would activate **perform problem diagnosis**. It should be noted that all vertical bars within the CFD refer to the same CSPEC.

An event flow can be input directly into a process as shown with **repro fault**. However, this flow does not activate the process, but rather provides control information for the process algorithm. Data flow arrows have been dotted for illustrative purposes, but in reality they are not shown as part of a control flow diagram.

7.2.5 Behavioral Modeling

Behavioral modeling is one of the fundamental principles for all requirements analysis methods. Yet, only extended versions of structured analysis ([WAR85], [HAT87]) provide a notation for this type of modeling. The state transition diagram[3] represents the behavior of a system by depicting its states and the events that cause the system to change state. In addition, the STD indicates what actions (e.g., process activation) are taken as a consequence of a particular event.

A simplified state transition diagram for the photocopier software described in the preceding section is shown in Figure 7.12. The rectangles represent system states and the arrows represent *transitions* between states. Each arrow is labeled with a ruled expression. The top entry indicates the event(s) that causes the transition to occur. The bottom entry indicates the action that occurs as a consequence of the event. Therefore, when the paper tray is ***full*** and the ***start*** button is pressed, the system moves from the ***reading commands*** state to the ***making copies*** state. Note that states do

---

[3]Instead of a diagram, a tabular representation for state transition can also be used. For additional information, see Hatley and Pirbhai [HAT87].

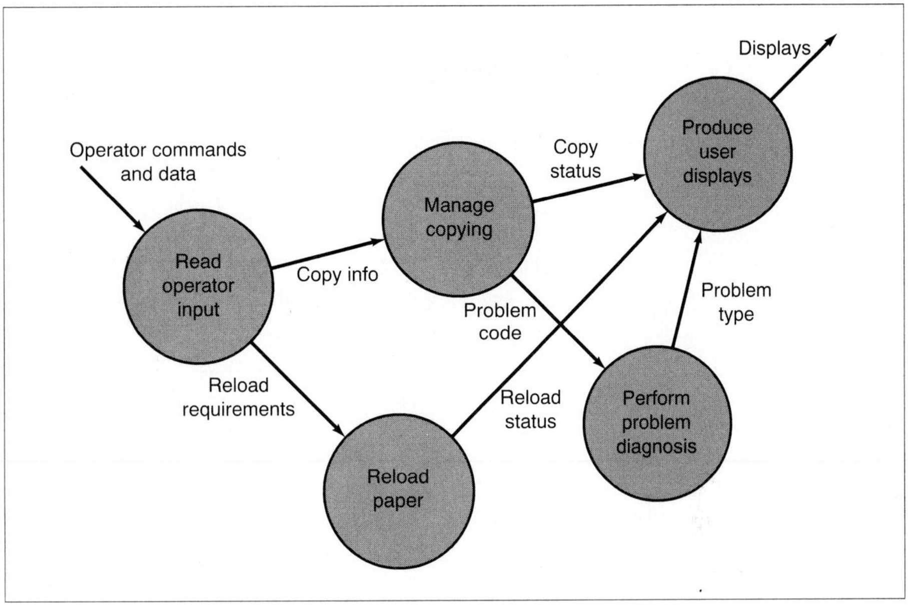

FIGURE 7.10. Level 1 DFD for photocopier software.

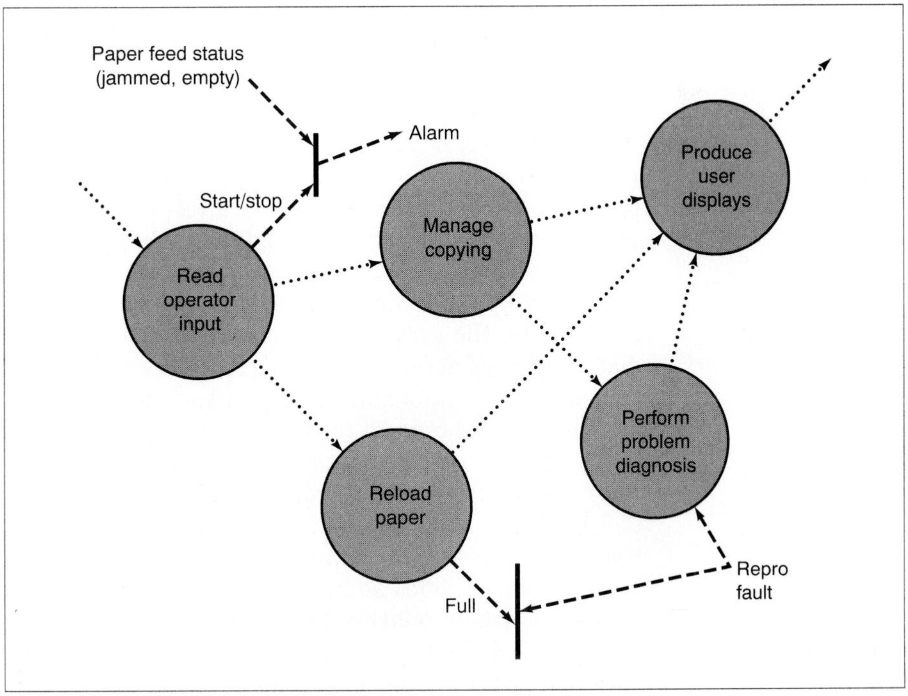

FIGURE 7.11. Level 1 CFD for photocopier software.

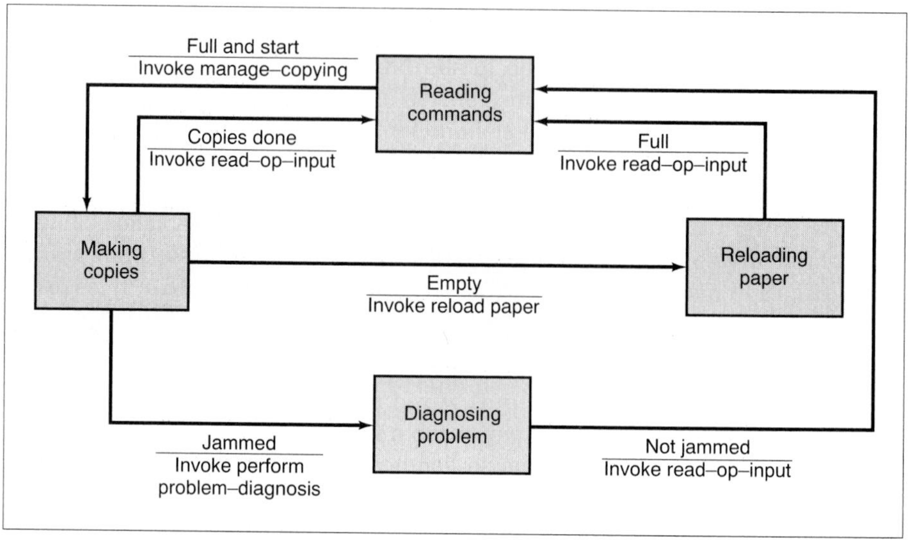

FIGURE 7.12. Simplified state transition diagram for photocopier software.

not necessarily correspond to processes on a one-to-one basis. For example, the state ***making copies*** would encompass both the **manage copying** and **produce user displays** processes shown in Figure 7.11.

7.2.6 Extensions for Data-Intensive Applications

The basic notation for structured analysis works well when relatively simple information flows through a series of processes. However, in many information systems applications (and a growing number of engineering/scientific applications), there is a need to represent the relationship between complex collections of data. To accomplish this, structured analysis notation has been extended to encompass a *data modeling* component.

Data modeling answers a set of specific questions that are relevant to any data processing application. What are the primary *data objects* to be processed by the system? What is the composition of each data object and what attributes describe the object? Where do the objects currently reside? What are the relationships between each object and other objects? What is the relationship between the objects and the processes that transform them?

To answer these questions, data modeling methods make use of the *entity-relationship* (E-R) *diagram*. The E-R diagram, described in Chapter 8, enables a software engineer to identify data objects and their relationships using a graphical notation. In the context of structured analysis, the E-R diagram provides additional insight into the detail of data stores (Figure 7.2) and their relationship to processes within the flow model. In addition, the E-R diagram complements the representation of data content contained in the requirements dictionary.

7.3 THE MECHANICS OF STRUCTURED ANALYSIS

In the previous section, we discussed basic and extended notation for structured analysis. To be used effectively in software requirements analysis, this notation must be combined with a set of heuristics that enables a software engineer to derive a good analysis model. To illustrate the use of these heuristics, an adapted version of the Hatley and Pirbhai [HAT87] extensions to the basic structured analysis notation will be used throughout the remainder of this chapter.

In the sections that follow, we examine each of the steps that should be applied to develop complete and accurate models using structured analysis. Throughout this discussion, the notation introduced in Section 7.2 will be used, and other notational forms, alluded to earlier, will be presented in some detail.

7.3.1 Creating a Data Flow Model

The data flow diagram (DFD) enables the software engineer to develop models of the information domain and functional domain at the same time. As the DFD is refined into greater levels of detail, the analyst performs an implicit functional decomposition of the system. At the same time, the DFD refinement results in a corresponding refinement of data as it moves through the processes that embody the application.

A few simple guidelines can aid immeasurably during derivation of a data flow diagram: (1) the level 0 data flow diagram should depict the software/system as a single bubble; (2) primary input and output should be carefully noted; (3) refinement should begin by isolating candidate processes, data items, and stores to be represented at the next level; (4) all arrows and bubbles should be labeled with meaningful names; (5) *information flow continuity* must be maintained from level to level; (6) one bubble at a time should be refined. There is a natural tendency to overcomplicate the data flow diagram. This occurs when the analyst attempts to show too much detail too early or represents procedural aspects of the software in lieu of information flow.

To illustrate the use of these basic guidelines, the *SafeHome* security system example, introduced in Chapter 6, will be used. A processing narrative for *SafeHome* is reproduced below:

> *SafeHome* software enables the homeowner to configure the security system when it is installed, monitors all sensors connected to the security system, and interacts with the homeowner through a key pad and function keys contained in the *SafeHome* control panel shown in Figure 6.6.
>
> During installation, the *SafeHome* control panel is used to "program" and configure the system. Each sensor is assigned a number and type, a master pass-

> word is programmed for arming and disarming the system, and telephone number(s) are input for dialing when a sensor event occurs.
>
> When a sensor event is sensed by the software, it rings an audible alarm attached to the system. After a delay time that is specified by the homeowner during system configuration activities, the software dials a telephone number of a monitoring service, provides information about the location, reporting the nature of the event that has been detected. The number will be redialed every 20 seconds until telephone connection is obtained.
>
> All interaction with *SafeHome* is managed by a user-interaction subsystem that reads input provided through the key pad and function keys, displays prompting messages on the LCD display, displays system status information on the LCD display. Keyboard interaction takes the following form. . . .

A level 0 DFD for *SafeHome* is shown in Figure 7.13. The primary external entities (boxes) produce information for use by the system and consume information generated by the system. The labeled arrows represent composite data items, that is, a data item that is actually a collection of many additional data items. For example, **user commands and data** encompasses all configuration commands, all activation/deactivation commands, all miscellaneous interactions, and all data that are input to qualify or expand a command.

The level 0 DFD is now expanded into a level 1 model. But how do we proceed? A simple, yet effective, approach is to perform a "grammatical parse" on the processing narrative that describes the context level bubble. That is, we isolate all nouns (and noun phrases) and verbs (and verb phrases) in the narrative presented above. To illustrate, we again reproduce the processing narrative, underlining the first occurrence of all nouns and italicizing the first occurrence of all verbs:

> *SafeHome* software *enables* the homeowner *to configure* the security system when it is *installed*, *monitors* all sensors connected to the security system, and *interacts* with the homeowner through a keypad and function keys *contained* in the *SafeHome* control panel shown in Figure 6.6.

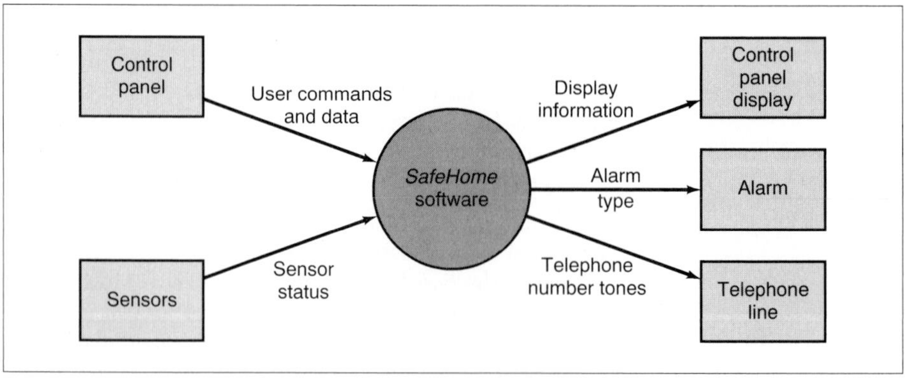

FIGURE 7.13. Context level DFD for *SafeHome*.

During installation, the *SafeHome* control panel is *used* to *"program"* and *configure* the system. Each sensor is *assigned* a number and type, a master password is programmed for *arming* and *disarming* the system, and telephone number(s) is (are) *input* for *dialing* when a sensor event occurs.

When a sensor event is *sensed* by the software, it *rings* an audible alarm attached to the system. After a delay time that is *specified* by the homeowner during system configuration activities, the software dials a telephone number of a monitoring service, *provides* information about the location, *reporting* the nature of the event that has been detected. The telephone number will be *redialed* every 20 seconds until telephone connection is *obtained*.

All interaction with *SafeHome* is *managed* by a user-interaction subsystem that *reads* input provided through the key pad and function keys, *displays* prompting messages on the LCD display, *displays* system status information on the LCD display. Keyboard interaction takes the following form....

It should be noted that nouns and verbs that are synonyms or have no direct bearing on the modeling process are omitted.

Referring to the grammatical parse, a pattern begins to emerge. All verbs are *SafeHome* processes; that is, they may ultimately be represented as bubbles in a subsequent DFD. All nouns are either external entities (boxes), data or control items (arrows), or data stores (double lines). Note further that nouns and verbs can be attached to one another (e.g., sensor is *assigned* number and type). Therefore, by performing a grammatical parse on the processing narrative for a bubble at any DFD level, we can generate much useful information about how to proceed with the refinement to the next level. Using this information, a level 1 DFD is shown in Figure 7.14. The context level process shown in Figure 7.13 has been expanded into seven processes derived from an examination of the grammatical parse. Similarly, the information flow between processes at level 1 has been derived from the parse.

It should be noted that information flow continuity is maintained between levels 0 and 1. Elaboration of the content of inputs and output at DFD levels 0 and 1 is postponed until Section 7.3.5.

The processes represented at DFD level 1 can be further refined into lower levels. For example, the process **monitor sensors** can be refined into a level 2 DFD as shown in Figure 7.15. Note once again that information flow continuity has been maintained between levels.

The refinement of DFDs continues until each bubble performs a simple function, that is, until the process represented by the bubble performs a function that would be easily implemented as a program component. In Chapter 10 we discuss a concept, called *cohesion*, that can be used to assess the simplicity of a given function. For now, we strive to refine DFDs until each bubble is "single-minded."

During requirements analysis, a software engineer may discover that certain aspects of the system "are subject to change" or "will be enhanced in the future" or are nebulously defined by the customer. Alternatively, an analyst may be working on existing software that is about to undergo modi-

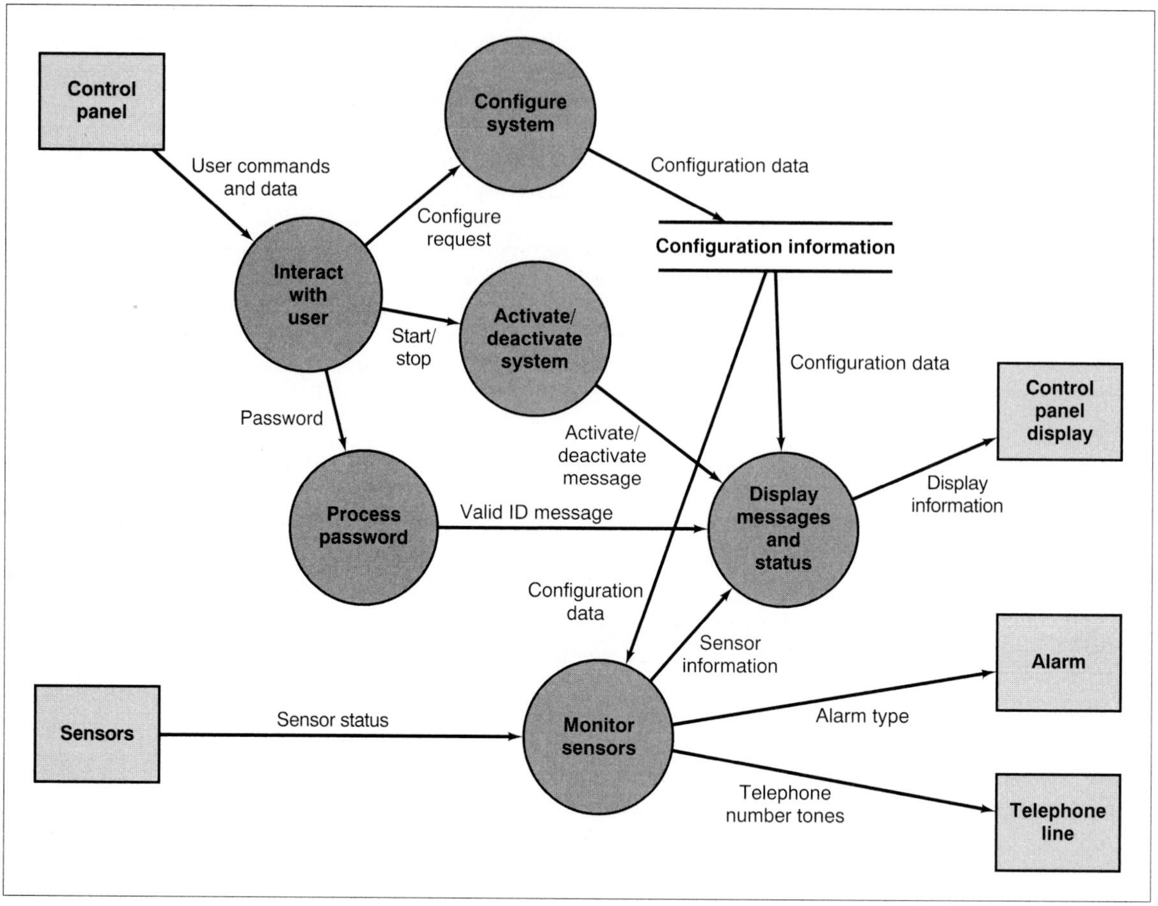

FIGURE 7.14. Level 1 DFD for *SafeHome*.

fication. In either case, the data flow diagram allows easy isolation of the *domain of change,* as shown in Figure 7.16*a* and *b*. By clearly understanding the flow of information across the domain-of-change boundary, better preparation can be made for future modification, or current modification can be conducted without upsetting other elements of the system.

7.3.2 Creating a Control Flow Model

For many types of data processing applications, data flow modeling is all that is necessary to obtain meaningful insight into software requirements. As we have already noted, however, there exists a large class of applications that are "driven" by events rather than by data, that produce control infor-

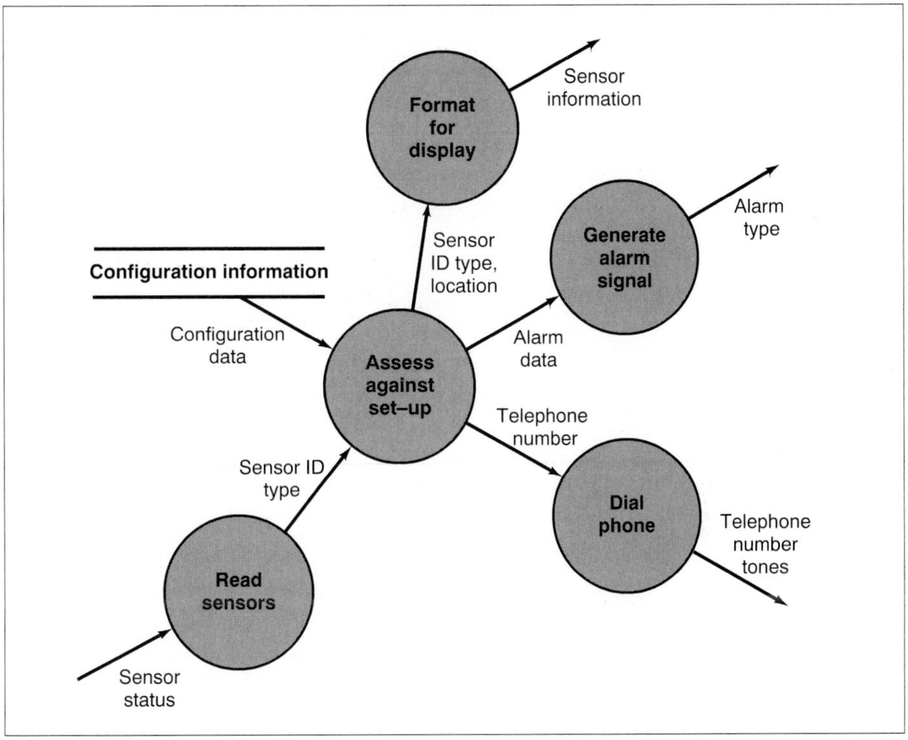

FIGURE 7.15. Level 2 DFD that refines the **monitor sensors** process.

mation rather than reports or displays, that process information with heavy concern for time and performance. Such applications require the use of control flow modeling in addition to data flow modeling.

The graphical notation required to create a control flow diagram was presented in Section 7.2.4. To review the approach for creating a CFD, a data flow model is "stripped" of all data flow arrows.[4] Events and control items (dashed arrows) are then added to the diagram and a "window" (a vertical bar) into the control specification is shown. But how are events selected?

We have already noted that an event or control item is implemented as a boolean value (e.g., *true* or *false, on* or *off,* 1 or 0) or a discrete list of conditions *(empty, jammed, full)*. To select potential candidate events, the following guidelines are suggested:

- List all sensors that are "read" by the software.
- List all interrupt conditions.

[4]For instructional clarity, the data flow arrows have been dotted and remain in the picture. In practice, they are eliminated altogether.

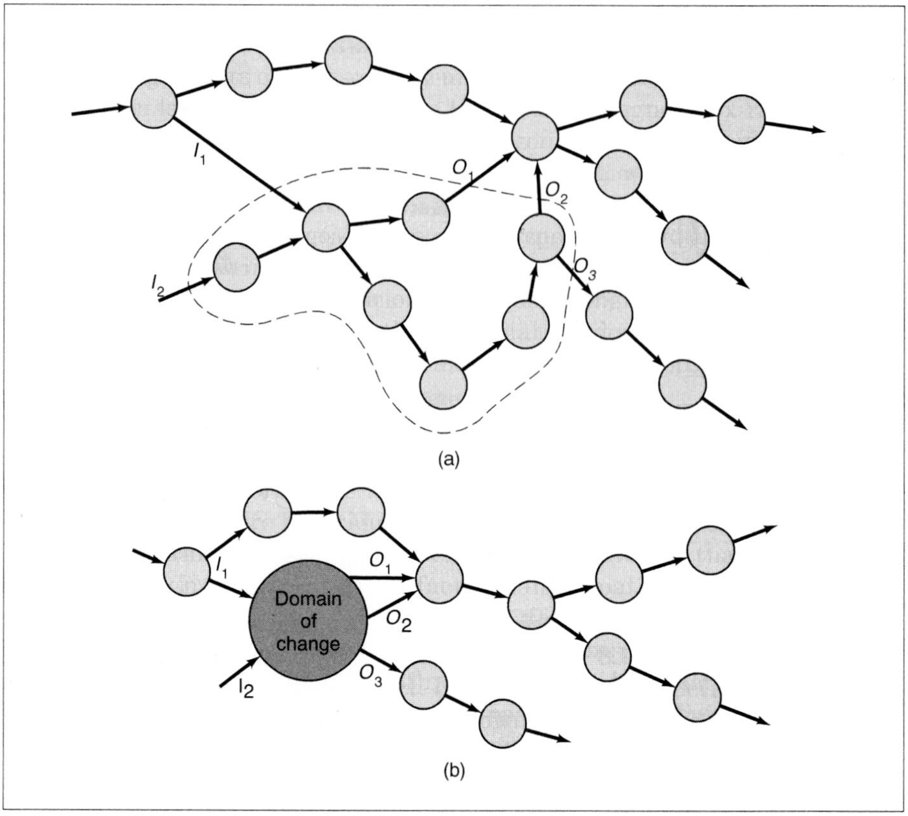

FIGURE 7.16.
Isolating the domain of change.

- List all "switches" that are actuated by the operator.
- List all data conditions.
- Recalling the noun-verb parse that was applied to the processing narrative, review all "control items" as possible CSPEC inputs/outputs.
- Describe the behavior of a system by identifying its states; identify how each state is reached and define the transitions between states.
- Focus on possible omissions—a very common error in specifying control; e.g., ask: "Is there any other way I can get to this state or exit from it?"

A level 1 CFD for *SafeHome* software is illustrated in Figure 7.17. Among the events and control items noted are **sensor event** (i.e., a sensor has been tripped), **blink flag** (a signal to blink the LCD display) and **start/stop switch** (a signal to turn the system on or off). When the event flows into the CSPEC bar from the outside world, it implies that the CSPEC will activate one or more of the processes shown in the CFD. When a control item emanates from a process and flows into the CSPEC window, control and activation of some other process or an outside entity is implied.

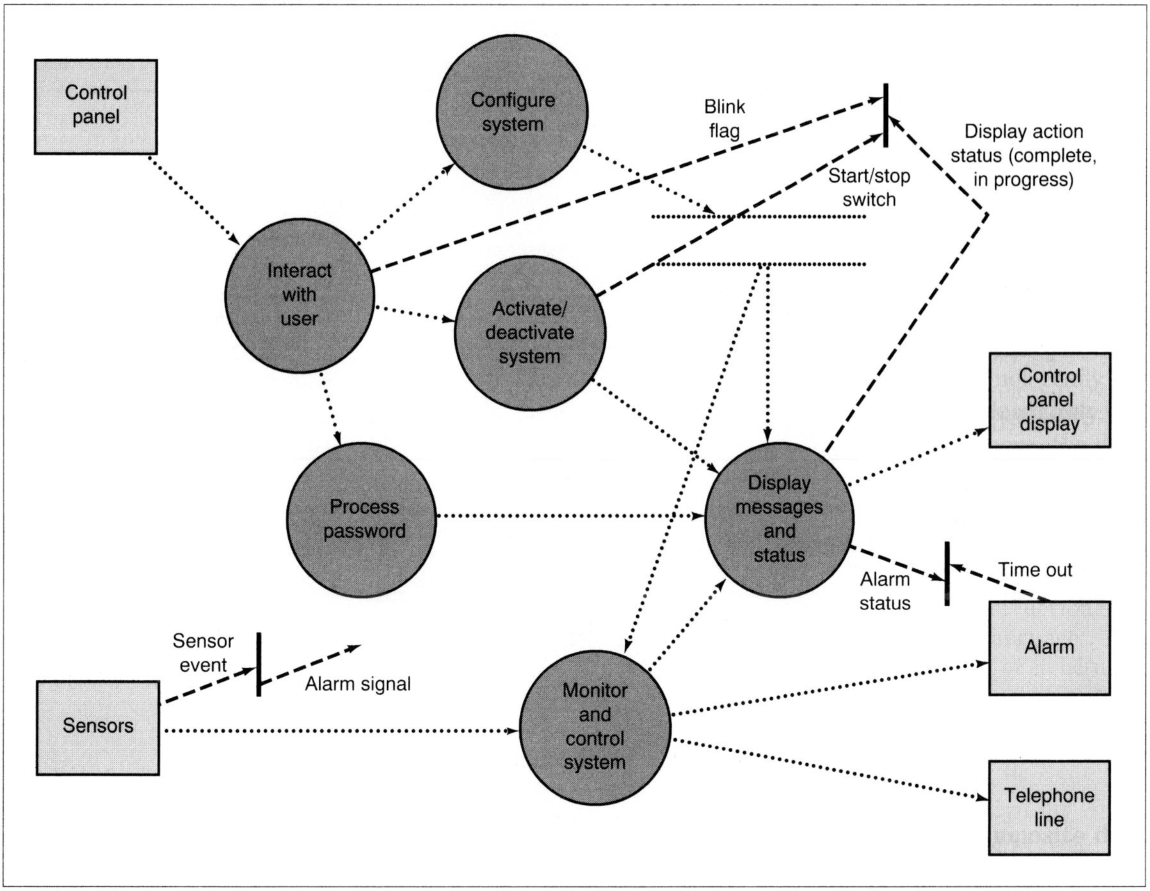

FIGURE 7.17. Level 1 CFD for *SafeHome.*

7.3.3 The Control Specification

The *control specification* (CSPEC) represents the behavior of the system (at the level from which it has been referenced) in two different ways. The CSPEC contains a state transition diagram (STD) that is a *sequential specification* of behavior. It can also contain a program activation table (PAT)—a *combinatorial specification* of behavior. The underlying attributes of the CSPEC were introduced in Section 7.2.4. It is now time to examine an example of this important modeling notation for structured analysis.

Figure 7.18 depicts a *state transition diagram* for the level 1 flow model for *SafeHome.* The labeled transition arrows indicate how the system responds to events as it traverses the four states defined at this level. By studying the STD, a software engineer can determine the behavior of the system and, more importantly, can ascertain whether there are "holes" in the specified behavior. For example, the STD (Figure 7.18) indicates that the

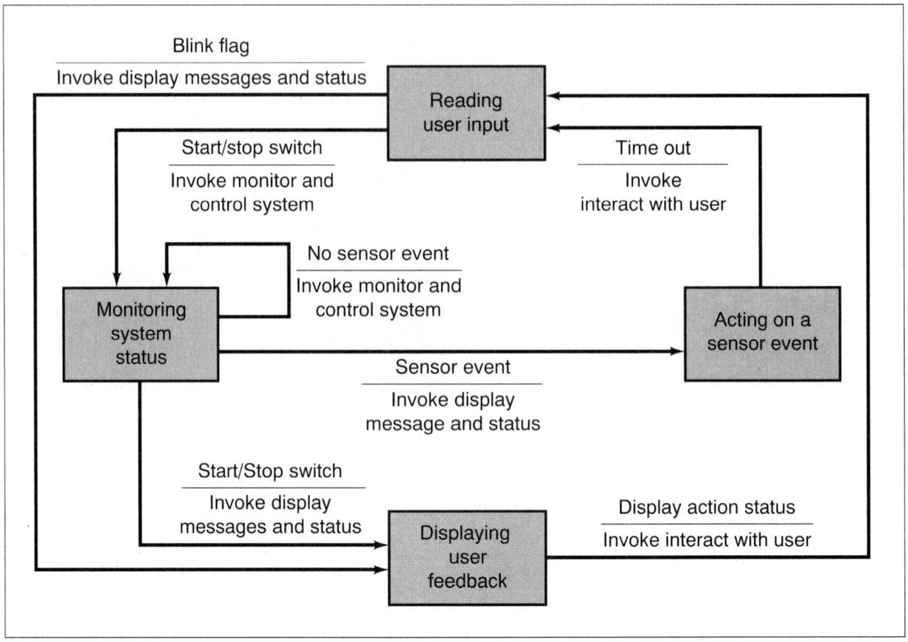

FIGURE 7.18. State transition diagram for *SafeHome*.

only transition from the ***reading user input*** state occurs when the ***start/stop switch*** is encountered and a transition to the ***monitoring system status*** state occurs. Yet, there appears to be no way, other than the occurrence of ***sensor event*** or **start/stop switch**, that will allow the system to return to ***reading user input***. This may be an error in specification and would hopefully be uncovered during review and corrected. Examine the STD to determine whether there are any other anomalies.

A somewhat different mode of behavioral representation is the *process activation table*. The PAT represents information contained in the STD in the context of processes, not states. That is, the table indicates which processes (bubbles) in the flow model will be invoked when an event occurs. The PAT can be used as a guide for a designer who must build an executive that controls the processes represented at this level. A PAT for the level 1 flow model of *SafeHome* software is shown in Figure 7.19.

The CSPEC describes the behavior of the system, but it does not give us any information about the inner working of the processes that are activated as a result of this behavior. The modeling notation that provides this information is discussed in the next section.

7.3.4 The Process Specification

The *process specification* (PSPEC) is used to describe all flow model processes that appear at the final level of refinement. The content of the process

Input events						
Sensor event	0	0	0	0	1	0
Blink flag	0	0	1	1	0	0
Start stop switch	0	1	0	0	0	0
Display action status						
Complete	0	0	0	1	0	0
In-progress	0	0	1	0	0	0
Time out	0	0	0	0	0	1
Output						
Alarm signal	0	0	0	0	0	0
Process activation						
Monitor and control system	0	1	0	0	1	1
Activate/deactivate system	0	1	0	0	0	0
Display messages and status	1	1	1	1	1	1
Interact with user	1	0	0	1	0	1

FIGURE 7.19. Process activation table for *SafeHome*.

specification can include narrative text, a *program design language* (PDL) description[5] of the process algorithm, mathematical equations, tables, diagrams, or charts. By providing a PSPEC to accompany each bubble in the flow model, the software engineer creates a "mini-spec" that can serve as a first step in the creation of the *Software Requirements Specification* and as a guide for design of the program component that will implement the process.

To illustrate the use of the PSPEC, consider a software application in which the dimensions of various geometric objects are analyzed to identify the shape of the object. Refinement of a context level data flow diagram continues until level 2 processes are derived. One of these, named **analyze triangle**, is depicted in Figure 7.20. The PSPEC for **analyze triangle** is first written as an English language narrative, as shown in the figure. If additional algorithmic detail is desired at this stage, a program design language representation (Figure 7.21) may also be included as part of the PSPEC. However, many believe that the PDL version should be postponed until design commences.

7.4 THE REQUIREMENTS DICTIONARY

An analysis of the information domain would be incomplete if only data flow were considered. Each arrow of a data flow diagram represents one or more

[5]Program design language is often used as a procedural design notation and is described in detail in Chapter 10.

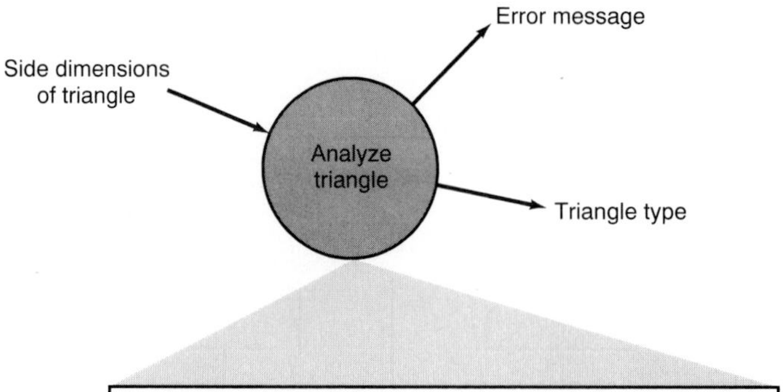

PSPEC: Processing Narrative for Analyze Triangle

The analyze-triangle process accepts values *A*, *B*, and *C* that represent the side dimensions of a triangle. The process tests the dimension values to determine whether all values are positive. If a negative value is encountered, an error message is produced. The process evaluates valid input data to determine whether the dimensions define a valid triangle and, if so, what type of triangle—equilateral, isosceles, or scalene—is implied by the dimensions. The type is output.

FIGURE 7.20. Process specification for a DFD process.

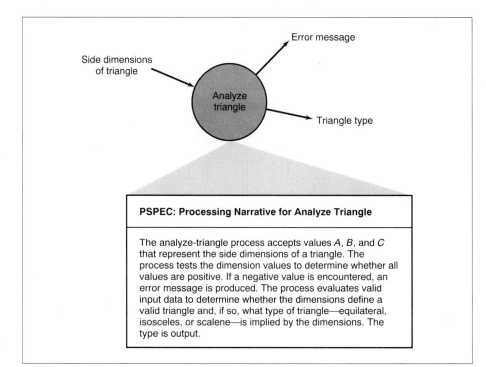

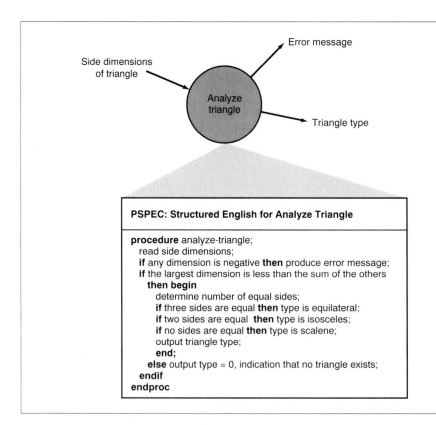

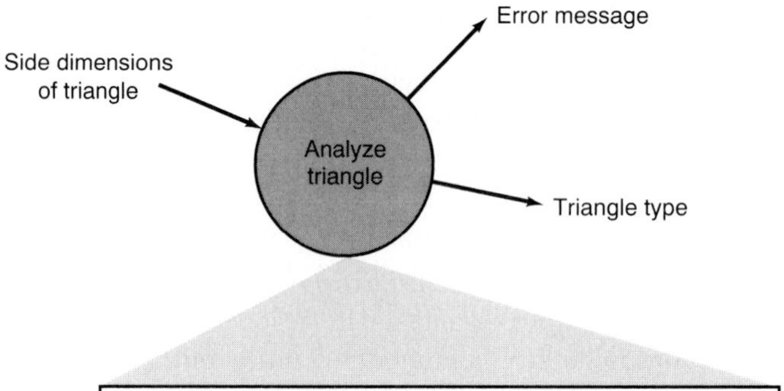

PSPEC: Structured English for Analyze Triangle

```
procedure analyze-triangle;
  read side dimensions;
  if any dimension is negative then produce error message;
  if the largest dimension is less than the sum of the others
    then begin
      determine number of equal sides;
      if three sides are equal then type is equilateral;
      if two sides are equal  then type is isosceles;
      if no sides are equal then type is scalene;
      output triangle type;
      end;
    else output type = 0, indication that no triangle exists;
  endif
endproc
```

FIGURE 7.21. Process specification using PDL for a DFD process.

items of information. Each data store is often a collection of individual data items. Each control item may be defined in terms of other control items (e.g., **display action status** shown in Figure 7.17 is composed of two control items: **complete** and **in-progress**). Even the content of an external entity may require expansion before its meaning can be explicitly defined. Therefore, some method for representing the content of each flow model component must be available to the analyst.

The *requirements dictionary* (also called the *data dictionary*) has been proposed as a quasiformal grammar for describing the content of objects defined during structured analysis. This important modeling notation has been defined in the following manner [YOU89, p. 189]:

> The data dictionary is an organized listing of all data elements that are pertinent to the system, with precise, rigorous definitions so that both user and system analyst will have a common understanding of inputs, outputs, components of stores and [even] intermediate calculations.

Today, the requirements dictionary is almost always implemented as part of a CASE "structured analysis and design tool." Although the format of dictionaries varies from tool to tool, most contain the following information:

- *Name*—the primary name of the data or control item, the data store or an external entity
- *Alias*—other names used for the first entry
- *Where used/how used*—a listing of the processes that use the data or control item and how it is used (e.g., input to the process, output from the process, as a store, as an external entity
- *Content description*—a notation for representing content
- *Supplementary information*—other information about data types, preset values (if known), restrictions, or limitation, etc.

Once a name and its aliases are entered into the requirements dictionary, consistency in naming can be enforced. That is, if an analysis team member decides to name a newly derived data item *xyz*, but *xyz* is already in the dictionary, the CASE tool supporting the dictionary posts a warning to indicate duplicate names. This improves the consistency of the analysis model and helps to reduce errors.

"Where used/how used" information is recorded automatically from the flow models. When a dictionary entry is created, the CASE tool will scan DFDs and CFDs to determine which processes use the data or control information and how it is used. Although this may appear unimportant, it is actually one of the most important benefits of the dictionary. During analysis, there is an almost continuous stream of changes. For large projects, it is often quite difficult to determine the impact of a change. Many a software engineer has asked, "Where is this data item used? What else will have to change if we modify it? What will the overall impact of the change be?" Because the requirements dictionary can be treated as a database,[6] the analyst can ask where used/how used questions, and get answers to the queries noted above.

The notation used to develop a content description, illustrated in Figure 7.22, enables the analyst to represent *composite data* in one of the three fundamental ways that it can be constructed:

1. As a *sequence* of data items
2. As a *selection* from among a set of data items
3. As a *repeated grouping* of data items

Each data item entry that is represented as part of a sequence, selection, or repetition may itself be another composite data item that needs further refinement within the dictionary.

To illustrate the use of the requirements dictionary and the content description notation shown in Figure 7.22, we return to the level 2 DFD for the **monitor system** process for *SafeHome,* shown in Figure 7.15. Referring to the figure, the data item **telephone number** is specified. But what exactly is a telephone number? It could be a seven-digit local number, a four-digit extension, or a 25-digit long-distance carrier sequence. The requirements dictionary provides us with a precise definition of **telephone number** for the DFD in question. In addition it indicates where and how

[6]In reality the requirements dictionary can be one element of a larger CASE repository. This is discussed in Chapter 23.

Data construct	Notation	Meaning
	=	is composed of
Sequence	+	and
Selection	[|]	either–or
Repetition	$\{\ \}^n$	*n* repetitions of
	( )	optional data
	* *	delimits comments

FIGURE 7.22. Content description notation for a requirements dictionary.

this data item is used and any supplementary information that is relevant to it. The requirements dictionary entry begins as follows:

name:	**telephone number**
aliases:	none
where used/how used:	**assess against set-up** (output) **dial phone** (input)

description:

telephone number = **[local extension | outside number]**

The above content description may be read: **telephone number** is composed of either a **local extension** (for use in a large factory) or an **outside number**. **Local extension** and **outside number** represent composite data and must be refined further in other content description statements. Continuing the content description:

telephone number = [local extension | outside number]
local extension = [2001 | 2002 | ... | 2999]
outside number = 9 + [local number | long distance number]
local number = prefix + access number
long distance number = (1) + area code + local number
prefix = [795 | 799 | 874 | 877]
access number = *any four number string*

The content description is expanded until all composite data items have been represented as elementary items (items that require no further expansion) or until all composite items are represented in terms that would be well known and unambiguous to all readers (e.g., **area code** is generally understood to mean a three-digit number that never starts with 0 or 1 and always has a 0 or 1 as the second digit). It is also important to note that a specification of elementary data often restricts a system. For example, the definition of **prefix** indicates that only four branch exchanges can be accessed locally.

The data dictionary defines information items unambiguously. Although we might assume that the telephone number represented by the DFD in Figure 7.15 could accommodate a 25-digit long-distance carrier access number, the requirements dictionary content description tells us that such numbers are not part of the data that may be used.

For large computer-based systems, the requirements dictionary grows rapidly in size and complexity. In fact, it is extremely difficult to maintain a dictionary manually. For this reason, CASE tools should be used.

7.5 STRUCTURED ANALYSIS AND CASE

Structured analysis was originally intended to be used as a manual descriptive technique for systems and software. Paper, plastic templates (for the graphical symbols), and a pencil were all that the analyst needed to do the job. It didn't take long, however, to recognize that the modeling notation for structured analysis can create a paperwork nightmare when large projects are to be modeled. It is difficult to relate the many different levels of flow models manually; it is challenging to associate CSPECs and PSPECs with their respective CFDs and DFDs manually; it is irritating to track and manage changes manually. For all of these reasons, CASE tools have become the preferred approach. (*Note:* For small projects, a manual approach can be used, although CASE is still preferred.)

A detailed discussion of computer-aided software engineering and CASE tools for analysis and design is presented in Chapter 22. However, a brief overview of the mechanics of using CASE in structured analysis is worthwhile at this point.

Because flow modeling is a graphical activity, DFDs and CFDs can be efficiently and aesthetically developed using CASE tools. The software engineer uses the drawing features of a CASE tool to create each flow model. A mouse, pull-down menus, multiple windows, and a pallet that contains all modeling symbols (Figures 7.2, 7.4, and/or 7.5) are the key elements of this approach.

As each flow model level is refined, the CASE tool builds an internal hierarchy so that a "parent" bubble and its "children" are automatically associated with one another. In this way, the analyst can step through the flow model, working from the context level downward toward the most detailed refinement. Using menu commands, the analyst can complete PSPECs or CSPECs for the flow model and "attach" them to the appropriate processes or CFDs. Requirements dictionary entries can also be "attached" to specific data or control arrows, stores, or entities with a series of simple mouse clicks. Once the model is created, it can be redrawn, changed, and transmitted to hardcopy with only a few commands.

7.6 SUMMARY

Structured analysis, the most widely used of requirements modeling methods, relies on the flow model as a first element of a graphical representation for a computer-based system. Using data and control flow diagrams as a basis, the analyst partitions the functions that transform flow. Next, a behavioral model is created using the state transition diagram, and a data content model is developed with a requirements dictionary. Process and control specifications provide additional elaboration of detail.

The original notation for structured analysis was developed for conventional data processing applications, but extensions now make the method applicable to real-time systems. Structured analysis is supported by an array of CASE tools that assist in the creation of each element of the model and also help to ensure consistency and correctness.

REFERENCES

[BRU88] Bruyn, W. et al., "ESML: An Extended Systems Modeling Language Based on the Data Flow Diagram," *ACM Software Engineering Notes,* vol. 13, no. 1, January 1988, pp. 58–67.

[DEM79] DeMarco, T., *Structured Analysis and System Specification,* Prentice-Hall, 1979.

[GAN82] Gane, T., and C. Sarson, *Structured Systems Analysis,* McDonnell Douglas, 1982.

[HAT87] Hatley, D. J., and I. A. Pirbhai, *Strategies for Real-Time System Specification,* Dorset House, 1987.

[PAG80] Page-Jones, M., *The Practical Guide to Structured Systems Design,* Yourdon Press, 1980.

[STE74] Stevens, W. P., G. J. Myers, and L. L. Constantine, "Structured Design," *IBM Systems Journal,* vol. 13, no. 2, 1974, pp. 115–139.

[WAR85] Ward, P. T., and S. J. Mellor, *Structured Development for Real-Time Systems* (three volumes), Yourdon Press, 1985.

[YOU78] Yourdon, E. N., and Constantine, L. L., *Structured Design,* Yourdon Press, 1978.

[YOU89] Yourdon, E. N., *Modern Structured Analysis,* Prentice-Hall, 1990.

PROBLEMS AND POINTS TO PONDER

7.1 Acquire at least three of the references discussed in Section 7.1 and write a brief paper that outlines how the perception of structured analysis has changed over time. As a concluding section, suggest ways that you think the method will change in the future.

7.2 Recalling the fundamental analysis principles discussed in Chapter 6, indicate how structured analysis accomplishes each fundamental. That is, how do DFDs, CFDs, PSPECs, CSPECs, and the requirements dictionary provide support for the four basic principles.

7.3 Discuss the difference between information flow and information structure. Are there systems in which there is no information flow? Are there systems in which there is no information structure?

7.4 Draw a context level model (level 0 DFD) for five systems with which you are familiar. The systems need not be computer-based. Using a few paragraphs for each system, describe input-processing-output for each system.

7.5 Using the systems described in Problem 7.4, refine each into a level 1 and level 2 data flow diagram. Use a grammatical parse to get yourself started. Remember to specify all information flow by labeling all arrows between bubbles. Use meaningful names for each transform.

(handwritten margin notes:)
Inputs Output
Public
Inspector
Pot Report
Someone

7.6 Select one of the systems described in Problems 7.4 and 7.5 and develop a CFD, CSPEC, PSPEC, and requirements dictionary for it. Try to make your model as complete as possible.

7.7 Does the information flow continuity concept mean that if one flow arrow appears as input at level 0, then one flow arrow must appear as input at subsequent levels? Discuss your answer.

7.8 Using the Ward and Mellor extensions described in Section 7.2.3, redraw the flow model contained in Figures 7.10 and 7.11. How will you accommodate the CSPEC that is implied in Figure 7.11? Ward and Mellor do not use this notation.

7.9 Using the Hatley and Pirbhai extensions described in Section 7.2.4, redraw the flow model contained in Figure 7.7. How will you accommodate the control process (dashed bubble) that is implied in Figure 7.7? Hatley and Pirbhai do not use this notation.

7.10 Describe an event flow in your own words.

7.11 Develop a complete flow model for the photocopier software discussed in Section 7.2.4. You may use either Ward and Mellor or Hatley and Pirbhai. Be certain to develop a detailed state transition diagram for the system.

7.12 Complete the processing narrative for _SafeHome_ software, presented in Section 7.3.1, by describing the interaction mechanics between the user and the system. Will your additional information change the flow models for _SafeHome_ presented in this chapter? If so, how?

7.13 The department of public works for a large city has decided to develop a "computerized" pot hole tracking and repair system (PHTRS). As pot holes are reported, they are assigned an identifying number and stored by street address, size (on a scale of 1 to 10), location (middle, curb, etc.), district (determined from street address), and repair priority (determined from the size of the pot hole). Work order data are associated with each pot hole and include pot hole location and size, repair crew identifying number, number of people on the crew, equipment assigned, hours applied to repair, hole status (work in progress, repaired, temporary repair, not repaired), amount of filler material used, and cost of repair (computed from hours applied, number of people, material, and equipment used). Finally, a damage file is created to hold information about reported damage due to the pot hole and includes citizen's name, address, phone number, type of damage, and dollar amount of damage. PHTRS is an on-line system; queries are to be made interactively. Use structured analysis to model the PHTRS.

7.14 Software for a personal computer-based word processing system is to be developed. Do a few hours of research on the application area and conduct a FAST meeting (Chapter 5) with your fellow students to develop requirements (your instructor will help you coordinate this). Build a requirements model of the system using structured analysis.

7.15 Software for a real-time test monitoring system for gas turbine engines is to be developed. Proceed as in Problem 7.14.

7.16 Software for a manufacturing control system for an automobile assembly plant is to be developed. Proceed as in Problem 7.14.

7.17 Software for a video game is to be developed. Proceed as in Problem 7.14.

7.18 Contact four or five vendors that sell CASE tools for structured analysis. Review their literature and write a brief paper that summarizes generic features that seem to distinguish one tool from another.

FURTHER READINGS

There are literally dozens of books that have been published on structured analysis. All cover the subject adequately but only a few do a truly excellent job. DeMarco's book [DEM79] remains a good introduction to the basic notation. Books by Dickinson (*Developing Structured Systems,* Yourdon Press, 1980), Page-Jones (*The Practical Guide to Structured Systems Design,* 2d ed., Prentice-Hall, 1988), and Mittra (*Structured Techniques of System Analysis, Design and Implementation,* Wiley-Interscience, 1988) are worthwhile references. Yourdon's most recent book on the subject [YOU89] remains the most comprehensive coverage published to date. For an engineering emphasis Ward and Mellor [WAR85] and Hatley and Pirbhai [HAT87] are the books of preference.

Many variations on structured analysis have evolved over the last decade. Cutts (*Structured Systems Analysis and Design Methodology,* Van Nostrand Reinhold, 1990) and Hares (*SSADM for the Advanced Practitioner,* Wiley, 1990) describe SSADM, a variation on structured analysis that is widely used in the United Kingdom and Europe.

The requirements dictionary has been the subject of books by Braithwaite (*Analysis, Design and Implementation of Data Dictionaries,* McGraw-Hill, 1988) and Wertz (*The Data Dictionary: Concepts and Uses,* QED Information Sciences, 1989). These books present the data dictionary in the context of database applications.

Braithwaite (*Applications Development Using CASE Tools,* Academic Press, 1990) and Schindler (*Computer-Aided Software Design,* Wiley, 1990) describe the synergy between CASE and the structured analysis method. Papers by Oman ("CASE Analysis and Design Tools," *IEEE Software,* May 1990), Sanden (*CACM,* December 1989), Manucci et al. (*IEEE Software,* November 1989) focus on current analysis and design tools, second generation CASE tools for structured analysis, and real-time modeling approaches, respectively. Useful sources of information on CASE tools for structured analysis (and all other software engineering activities) are industry newsletters such as: *CASE Outlook,* (CASE Consulting Group, Lake Oswego, OR), *CASE Strategies* (Cutter Information Corp., Arlington, MA), and *CASE Trends* (Software Productivity Group, Shrewsbury, MA).

CHAPTER 8

OBJECT-ORIENTED ANALYSIS AND DATA MODELING

As the 1980s came to a close, the "object-oriented paradigm" for software engineering began to mature into a practical and powerful approach to software development. We created designs for applications of all kinds using an object-oriented mind-set, and we implemented (coded) programs using object-oriented programming languages and techniques.[1] But requirements analysis lagged behind.

Today, *object-oriented analysis* (OOA) is making slow but steady progress as a requirements analysis method in its own right and as a complement to other analysis methods. Instead of examining a problem using the classic input-processing-output (information flow) model or a model derived exclusively from hierarchical information structures, OOA introduces a number of new concepts. These new concepts seem unusual to many people, but they are really quite natural. Coad and Yourdon [COA90, p. 1] consider this issue when they write:

> OOA—object-oriented analysis—is based upon concepts that we first learned in kindergarten: objects and attributes, classes and members, wholes and parts. Why it has taken us so long to apply these concepts to the analysis and specification of information systems is anyone's guess—perhaps we've been too busy "following the flow" during the heyday of structured analysis to consider the alternatives.

---

[1]Object-oriented design is discussed in Chapter 12 and object-oriented programming languages are presented in Chapter 16.

It is important to note that there is no universal agreement on the "concepts" that serve as a foundation for OOA. But a limited number of key ideas appear repeatedly, and it is these that we will consider in this chapter.

8.1 OBJECT-ORIENTED CONCEPTS

Any discussion of object-oriented analysis (OOA) must begin by addressing the term "object-oriented." What is an object-oriented viewpoint? Why is a method considered to be object-oriented? What is an object? There are many different opinions (e.g., [MEN90], [STR88], [BOO86]) about the correct answers to these questions. In the discussion that follows, we attempt to synthesize the most common of these.

To understand the object-oriented point of view, consider an example of a real-world object—the thing you are sitting in right now—a chair. **Chair** is a member (the term "instance" is also used) of a much larger *class* of objects that we call **furniture**. A set of generic *attributes* can be associated with every object in the class **furniture**. For example, all furniture has a **cost, dimensions, weight, location,** and **color,** among many possible attributes. These apply whether we are talking about a table or a chair, a sofa or an armoire. Because chair is a *member* of the class **furniture**, chair *inherits* all attributes defined for the class. This concept is illustrated schematically in Figure 8.1.

Once the class has been defined, the attributes can be reused when new instances of the class are created. For example, assume that we were to define a new object called **chable** (a cross between a chair and a table) that is a member of the class **furniture**. **Chable** inherits all of the attributes of **furniture**.

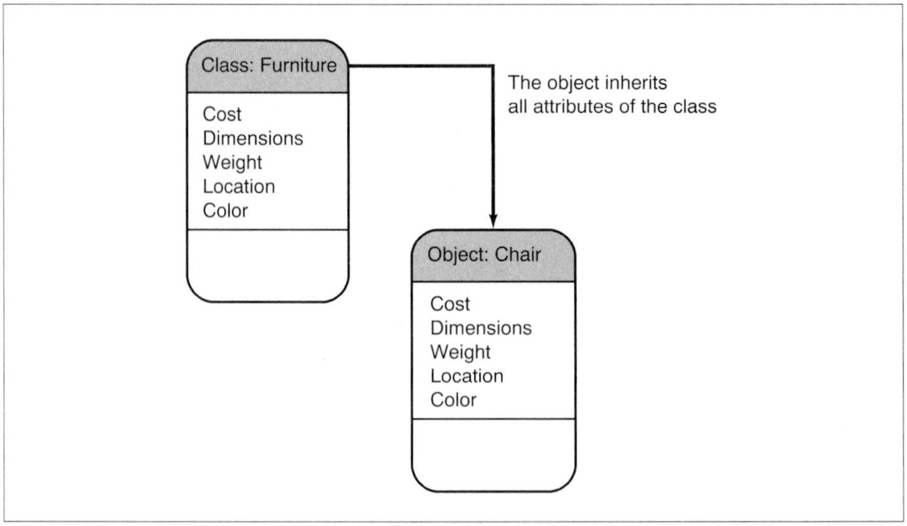

FIGURE 8.1. Inheritance from class to object.

We have attempted an anecdotal definition of a class by describing its attributes, but something is missing. Every object in the class **furniture** can be manipulated in a variety of ways. It can be bought and sold, physically modified (e.g., you can saw off a leg or paint the object purple), or moved from one place to another. Each of these *operations* (other terms are *services* or *methods*) will modify one or more attributes of the object. For example, if the attribute **location** is actually a composite date item defined (using data dictionary notation from Chapter 7) as:

location = building + floor + room

then an operation named **move** would modify one or more of the data items (**building, floor,** or **room**) that comprise the attribute **location**. To do this, **move** must have "knowledge" of these data items. The operation **move** could be used for a chair or a table, as long as both are instances of the class **furniture.** All valid operations (e.g., **buy, sell, weigh**) for the class **furniture** are "connected" to the object definition as shown in Figure 8.2 and are inherited by all instances of the class.

The object **chair** (and all objects in general) *encapsulates* data (the attribute values that define the chair), operations (the actions that are applied to change the attributes of chair), other objects (*composite objects* can be defined [EVB89]), constants (set values), and other related information. *Encapsulation* means that all of this information is packaged under one name and can be reused as one specification or program component.

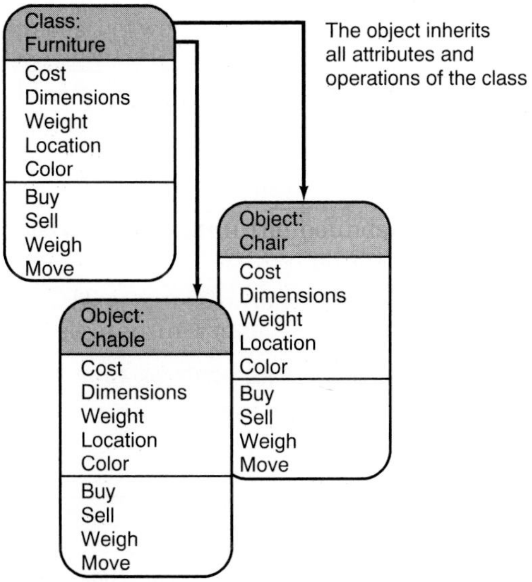

FIGURE 8.2.
Inheritance of operations from class to object.

Now that we have introduced a few basic concepts, a more formal definition of "object-oriented" will prove more meaningful. Coad and Yourdon [COA90] define the term this way:

object-oriented = objects + classification + inheritance + communication

Three of these concepts have already been introduced. We will postpone a discussion of communication until later.

8.1.1 Identifying Objects

If you look around a room, there is a set of physical objects that can be easily identified, classified, and defined (in terms of attributes and operations). But when you "look around" the problem space of a software application, the objects may be more difficult to comprehend.

We can begin to identify objects[2] by examining the problem statement or (using the terminology from the previous chapter) by performing a "grammatical parse" on the processing narrative for the system to be built. Objects are determined by underlining each noun or noun clause and entering it in a simple table. Synonyms should be noted. If the object is required to implement a solution, then it is part of the *solution space;* otherwise, if an object is necessary only to describe a solution, it is part of the *problem space.* But what should we look for once all of the nouns have been isolated?

Objects manifest themselves in one of the ways represented in Figure 8.3. Objects can be:

- *External entities* (e.g., other systems, devices, people) that produce or consume information to be used by a computer-based system
- *Things* (e.g., reports, displays, letters, signals) that are part of the information domain for the problem
- *Occurrences* or *events*[3] (e.g., a property transfer or the completion of a series of robot movements) that occur within the context of system operation
- *Roles* (e.g., manager, engineer, salesperson) played by people who interact with the system
- *Organizational units* (e.g., division, group, team) that are relevant to an application
- *Places* (e.g., manufacturing floor or loading dock) that establish the context of the problem and the overall function of the system
- *Structures* (e.g., sensors, four-wheeled vehicles, or computers) that define a class of objects or, in the extreme, related classes of objects

---

[2]In reality, OOA actually attempts to define *classes* from which objects are *instantiated.* Therefore, when we isolate potential objects, we also identify potential classes.

[3]In this context, the term "event" connotes any occurrence. It does not necessarily imply control as it did in Chapter 7.

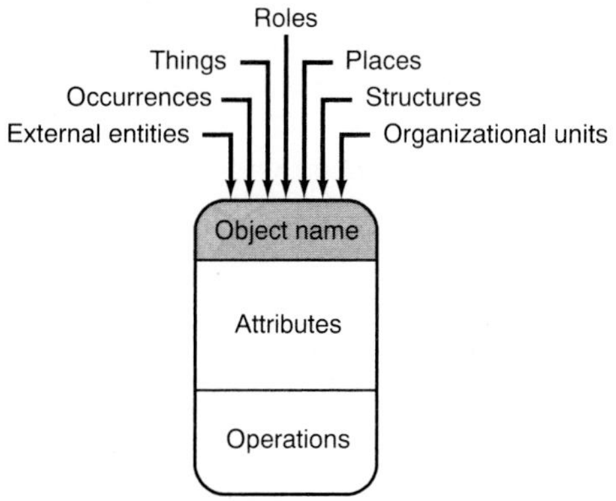

FIGURE 8.3.
Objects.

It is also important to note what objects are not. In general, an object should never have an "imperative procedural name" [CAS89]. For example, if the developers of software for a medical imaging system defined an object with the name **image inversion,** they would be making a subtle mistake. The **image** obtained from the software could, of course, be an object (it is a thing that is part of the information domain). **Inversion** of the image is an operation that is applied to the object. It is likely that inversion would be defined as an operation for the object **image**, but it would not be defined as a separate object to connote "image inversion." As Cashman [CAS89] states: "...the intent of object-orientation is to encapsulate, but still keep separate, data and operations on the data."

To illustrate how objects might be defined during the early stages of analysis, we return to the *SafeHome* security system example introduced earlier in this book. In Chapter 7, we performed a grammatical parse on a processing narrative for the *SafeHome* system. The processing narrative is reproduced below:

> *SafeHome* software enables the homeowner to configure the security system when it is installed, monitors all sensors connected to the security system, and interacts with the homeowner through a key pad and function keys contained in the *SafeHome* control panel shown in Figure 6.6.
>
> During installation, the *SafeHome* control panel is used to "program" and configure the system. Each sensor is assigned a number and type, a master password is programmed for arming and disarming the system, and telephone number(s) is (are) input for dialing when a sensor event occurs.
>
> When a sensor event is sensed by the software, it rings an audible alarm attached to the system. After a delay time that is specified by the homeowner during system configuration activities, the software dials a telephone number of a monitoring service, provides information about the location, and reports the nature of the event that has been detected. The number will be redialed every 20 seconds until telephone connection is obtained.

All interaction with *SafeHome* is managed by a user-interaction subsystem that reads input provided through the key pad and function keys, displays prompting messages on the LCD display, displays system status information on the LCD display. Keyboard interaction takes the following form....

Extracting the nouns, we can propose a number of potential objects:

Potential Object/Class	*General Classification*
homeowner	role or external entity
sensor	external entity
control panel	external entity
installation	occurrence
system (alias security system)	thing
number, type	*not objects, attributes of sensor*
master password	thing
telephone number	thing
sensor event	occurrence
audible alarm	external entity
monitoring service	organizational unit or external entity

The above list would be continued until all nouns in the processing narrative were considered. Note that we call each entry in the list a *potential* object. We must consider each further before a final decision is made.

Coad and Yourdon [COA89] suggest six selection characteristics that should be used as an analyst considers each potential object for inclusion in the analysis model:

1. *Retained information.* The potential object will be useful during analysis only if information about it must be remembered so that the system can function.
2. *Needed services.* The potential object must have a set of identifiable operations that can change the value of its attributes in some way.
3. *Multiple attributes.* During requirements analysis, the focus should be on "major" information; an object with a single attribute may, in fact, be useful during design, but is probably better represented as an attribute of another object during the analysis activity.
4. *Common attributes.* A set of attributes can be defined for the potential object and these attributes apply to all occurrences of the object.
5. *Common operations.* A set of operations can be defined for the potential object and these operations apply to all occurrences of the object.
6. *Essential requirements.* External entities that appear in the problem space and produce or consume information that is essential to the operation of any solution for the system will almost always be defined as objects in the requirements model.

To be considered a legitimate object for inclusion in the requirements model, a potential object should satisfy all (or almost all) of the above characteristics. The decision for inclusion of potential objects in the analysis model is somewhat subjective, and later evaluation may cause an object to be discarded or reinstated. However, the first step of OOA must be a definition of objects, and decisions (even subjective ones) must be made. With this in mind, we apply the selection characteristics to the list of potential *SafeHome* objects:

Potential Object/Class	*Characteristic Number that Applies*
homeowner	rejected: 1, 2 fail even though 6 applies
sensor	accepted: all apply
control panel	accepted: all apply
installation	rejected
system (alias security system)	accepted: all apply
number, type	rejected: 3 fails, attributes of sensor
master password	rejected: 3 fails
telephone number	rejected: 3 fails
sensor event	accepted: all apply
audible alarm	accepted: 2, 3, 4, 5, 6 apply
monitoring service	rejected: 1, 2 fail even though 6 applies

It should be noted that (1) the above list is not all-inclusive—additional objects would have to be added to complete the model; (2) some of the rejected potential objects will become attributes for those objects that were accepted (e.g., **number** and **type** are attributes of **sensor,** and **master password** and **telephone number** may become attributes of **system**); (3) different statements of the problem might cause different "accept" or "reject" decisions to be made (e.g., if each homeowner had his or her own password or was identified by voice print, the **homeowner** object would satisfy characteristics 1 and 2 and would have been accepted).

8.1.2 Specifying Attributes

Attributes describe an object that has been selected for inclusion in the analysis model. In essence, it is the attributes that define the object—that clarify what is meant by the object in the context of the problem space. For example, if we were to build a system that tracks baseball statistics for professional baseball players, the attributes of the object **player** would be quite different than the attributes of the same object when it is used in the context of the professional baseball pension system. In the former, attributes such as name, position, batting average, fielding percentage, years played, games played might be relevant. For the latter, some of these attributes would be meaningful, but others would be replaced by attributes like average salary, credit toward full vesting, projected monthly benefit, mailing address, etc.

To develop a meaningful set of attributes for an object, the analyst can again study the processing narrative (or statement of scope) for the problem and select those things that reasonably "belong" to the object. In addition, the following question should be answered for each object: What data items (composite and/or elementary) fully define this object in the context of the problem at hand?

To illustrate, we consider the **system** object defined for *SafeHome*. We noted earlier in the book that the homeowner can configure the security system to reflect sensor information, alarm response information, activation/deactivation information, identification information, and so forth. Using the content description notation defined for the requirements dictionary and presented in Chapter 7, we can represent these composite data items in the following manner:

sensor information =

sensor type + sensor number + alarm threshold

alarm response information =

delay time + telephone number + alarm type

activation/deactivation information =

master password + number of allowable tries + temporary password

identification information =

system ID + verification phone number + system status

Each of the data items on the right of the equal sign could be further defined to an elementary level, but for our purposes, they comprise a reasonable list of attributes for the **system** object (Figure 8.4).

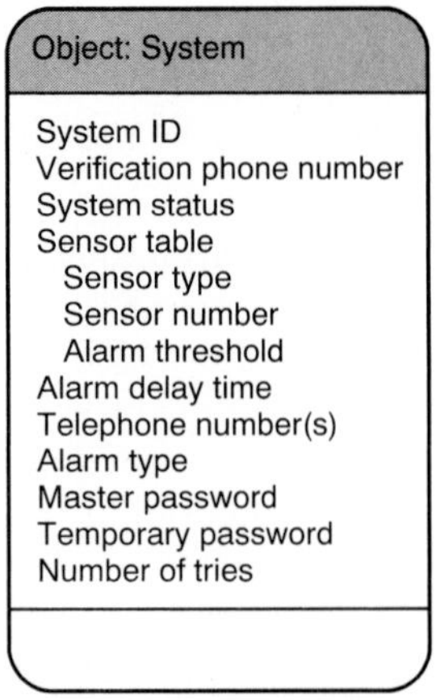

FIGURE 8.4.
The **system** object.

8.1.3 Defining Operations

An operation changes an object in some way. More specifically, it changes one or more attribute values that are contained within the object. Therefore, an operation must have "knowledge" of the nature of the object's attributes and must be implemented (see Chapter 13) in a manner that enables it to manipulate the data structures that have been derived from the attributes.

Although many different types of operations exist, they can generally be divided into three broad categories: (1) operations that *manipulate* data in some way (e.g., adding, deleting, reformatting, selecting); (2) operations that perform a *computation;* (3) operations that *monitor* an object for the occurrence of a controlling event.

As a "first cut" at deriving a set of operations for the objects of the analysis model, the analyst can again study the processing narrative (or statement of scope) for the problem and select those operations that reasonably "belong" to the object. To accomplish this, the grammatical parse is again studied and verbs are isolated. Some of these verbs will be legitimate operations and can be easily connected to a specific object. For example, from the *SafeHome* processing narrative presented earlier in this chapter, we see that "sensor is assigned a number and type" or that "a master password is programmed for arming and disarming the system." These two phrases indicate a number of things:

- That an **assign** operation is relevant for the **sensor** object
- That a **program** operation will be applied to the **system** object
- That **arm** and **disarm** are operations that apply to system (also that system status may ultimately be defined, using data dictionary notation, as system status = [armed | disarmed]).

Upon further investigation, it is likely that the operation **program** will be divided into a number of more specific suboperations required to configure the system. For example, **program** implies: specifying phone numbers, configuring system characteristics (e.g., create the sensor table, input alarm characteristics), and inputting password(s). But for now, we specify **program** as a single operation.

In addition to the grammatical parse, we can gain additional insight into other operations by considering the *communication* that occurs between objects. Objects communicate by passing messages to one another. Before continuing with the specification of operations, we explore this matter in a bit more detail.

8.1.4 Interobject Communication

Defining objects within the context of an analysis model may be enough to lay a foundation for design. But something else must be added (either during analysis or during design) so that the system can be built—a mechanism for communication must be established between objects. This mechanism is called a *message*.

The use of messages is illustrated schematically in Figure 8.5. Four objects, **A**, **B**, **C**, and **D**, communicate with one another by passing messages. For example, if object **B** required processing associated with operation **op10** of object **D**, it would send **D** a message that would take the form:

message: (destination, operation, arguments)

where "destination" defines the object (in this case, object **D**) to receive the message, "operation" refers to the operation that is to receive the message (**op10**), and "arguments" provides information that is required for the operation to be successful. As part of the execution of **op10**, object **D** may send a message to object **C** of the form:

message: (**C**, **op08**, ⟨data⟩)

C finds **op08**, performs it, and then returns control to **D**. Operation **op10** completes and control is returned to **B**.

Cox [COX86, p. 50] describes the interchange between objects in the following manner:

> An object is requested to perform one of its operations by sending it a message telling the object what to do. The receiver [object] responds to the message by first choosing the operation that implements the message name, executing this operation, and then returning control to the caller.

Messaging is important to the implementation of an object-oriented system, but it need not be considered in detail during requirements analysis. In fact, our only concern at this stage is to use the concept to help determine candidate operations for a specific object.

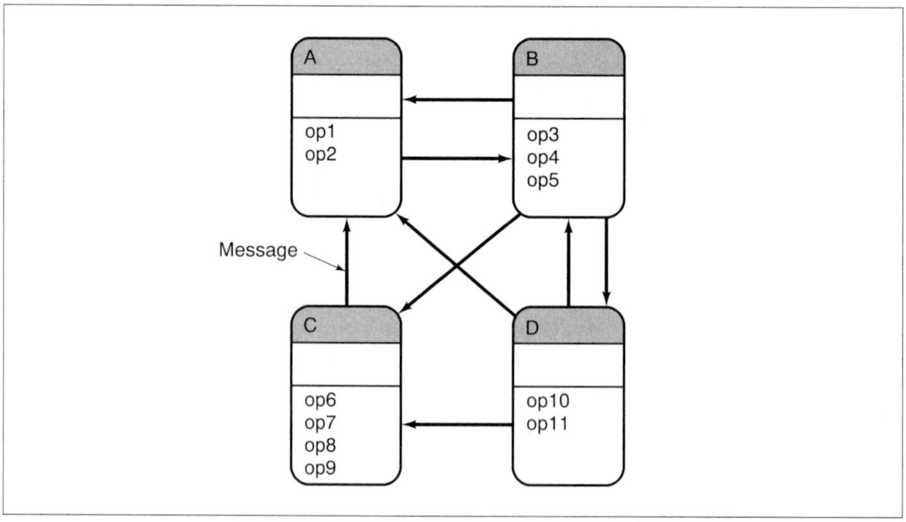

FIGURE 8.5.
Messaging.

8.1.5 Finalizing the Object Definition

The definition of operations is the last step in completing the specification of an object. In Section 8.1.3, we culled operations from a grammatical parse of the processing narrative for the system. Additional operations may be determined by considering the "life history" [COA90] of an object and the messages that are passed among objects defined for the system.

The generic life history of an object can be defined by recognizing that the object must be created, modified, manipulated, or read in other ways, and possibly deleted. For the **system** object, this can be expanded to reflect known activities that occur during its life (in this case, during the time that *SafeHome* is operational). Some of the operations can be ascertained from likely communication between objects. For example, **sensor event** will send a message to **system** to *display* the event location and number; **control panel** will send a *reset* message to update system status (an attribute); the **audible alarm** will send a *query* message; the **control panel** will send a *modify* message to change one or more attributes without reconfiguring the entire system object; **sensor event** will also send a message to *call* the phone number(s) contained in the object. Other messages can be considered and operations derived. The resulting object definition is shown in Figure 8.6.

A similar approach would be used for each of the objects defined for *SafeHome*. After attributes and operations were defined for each of the objects defined to this point, the beginnings of an OOA model can be created (Figure 8.7).

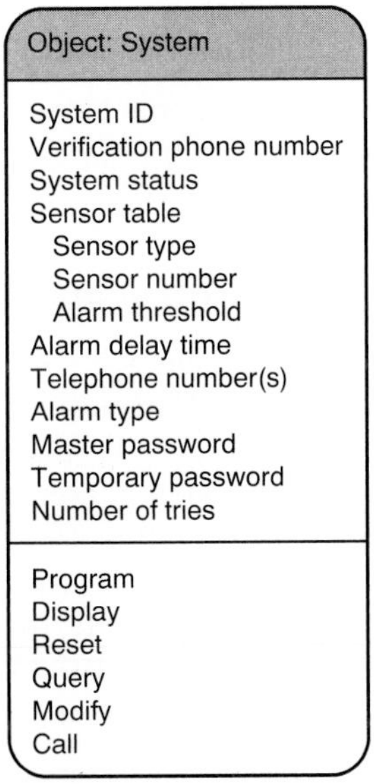

FIGURE 8.6. The system object with operations attached.

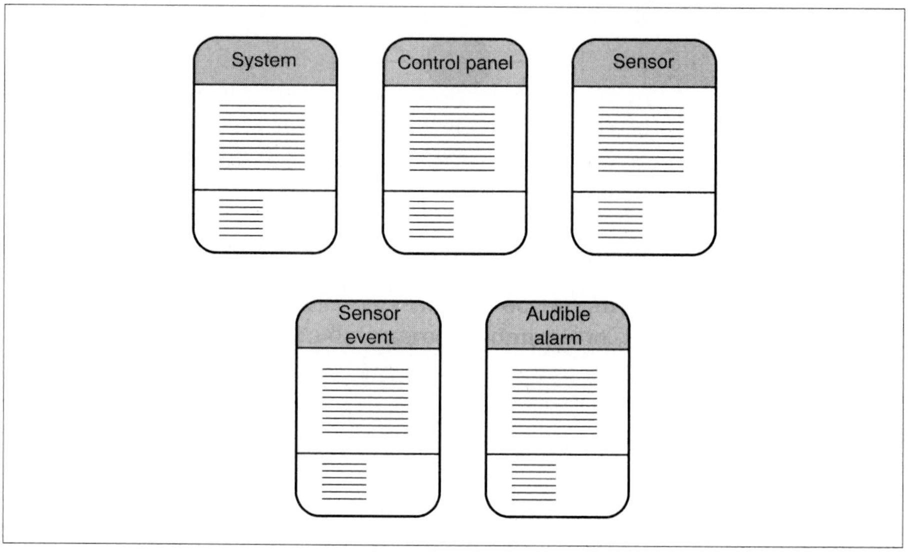

FIGURE 8.7. The beginnings of an OOA model.

8.2 OBJECT-ORIENTED ANALYSIS MODELING

A number of different modeling schemes have been suggested for OOA [COA90, EVB89, SHL88]. All make use of the object definition presented in Section 8.1, but each introduces its own notation, heuristics, and philosophy. To illustrate the OOA modeling approach, the notation adapted from Coad and Yourdon [COA90] will be used.[4]

The OOA approach proposed by Coad and Yourdon consists of five steps: (1) identifying objects; (2) identifying structures; (3) defining subjects; (4) defining attributes and instance connections; and (5) defining operations and message connections. An overview of the mechanics and notation for steps 2 through 5 is presented in the paragraphs that follow.

8.2.1 Classification and Assembly Structures

Once objects have been identified, the analyst begins to focus on *classification structure*. Each object is "considered as a generalization, then as a specialization" [COA90]. That is, the instances of an object are defined and named. To illustrate, consider the **sensor** object defined for *SafeHome* and shown in Figure 8.8. In other cases, an object represented in the initial model might actually be composed of a number of component parts that could themselves be defined as objects. Structures of this type are called

[4]Although other techniques are equally powerful, the Coad and Yourdon notation is somewhat easier to present in overview fashion.

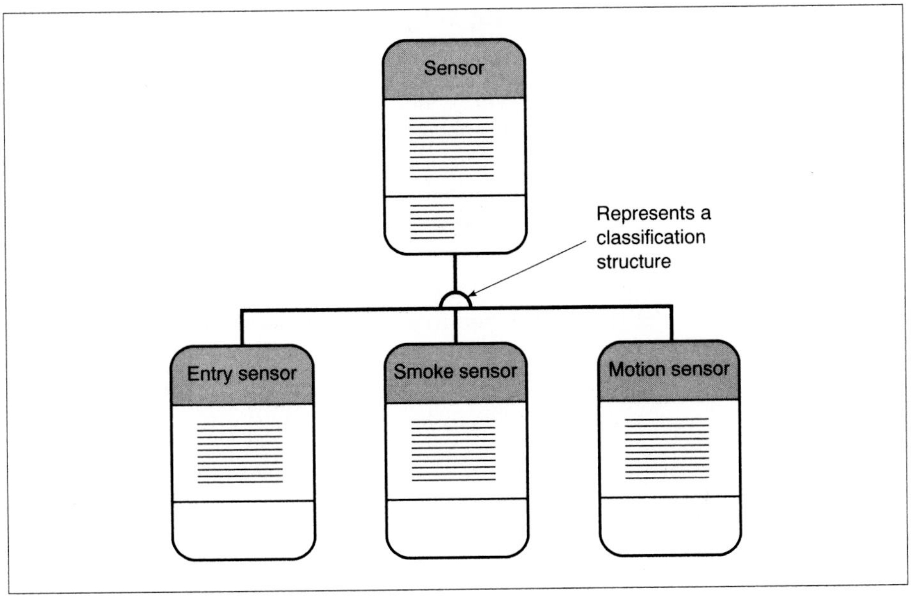

FIGURE 8.8. Classification structure notation.

assembly structures, and are defined using the notation represented in Figure 8.9. The triangle implies an assembly relationship. It should be noted that the connecting lines may be augmented with additional symbols (not shown) that are adapted from the entity-relationship modeling notation discussed later in this chapter.

Structure representation provides the analyst with a means for partitioning the requirements model. The expansion of each object provides needed detail for review and for subsequent design.

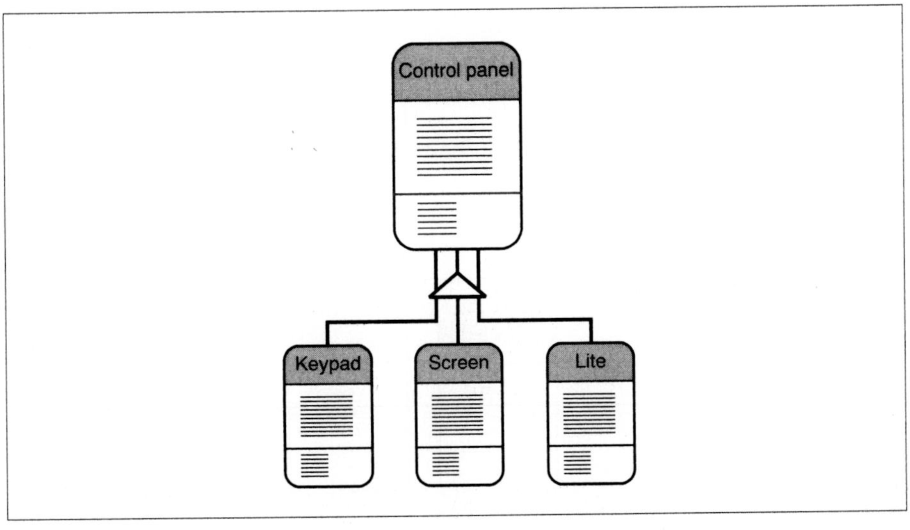

FIGURE 8.9. Assembly structure notation.

8.2.2 Defining Subjects

A real OOA model may have hundreds of objects and dozens of structures. For this reason, it is necessary to define some concise representation that is a digest of the object and structure models described above.

A *subject* is nothing more than a reference or pointer to more detail in the analysis model. For example, assume that the control panel for *Safe-Home* is considerably more complex than the one implied by Figure 8.9, containing multiple display areas, a sophisticated key arrangement, and other features. It might be modeled as an assembly structure shown in Figure 8.10. If the overall requirements model contains dozens of these structures (*Safe-Home* would not), it would be difficult to absorb the entire representation at one time. By defining a subject reference as shown in Figure 8.10, the en-

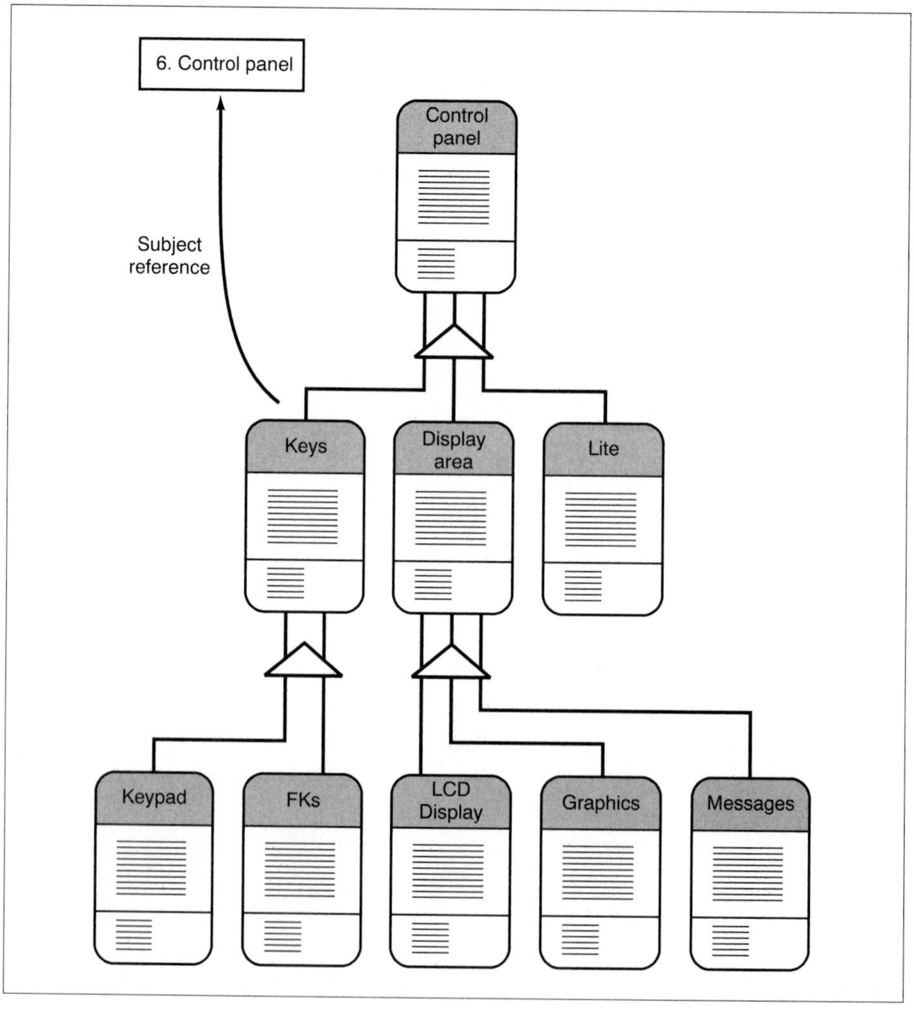

FIGURE 8.10.
Subject references.

tire structure can be referenced by a single icon (the rectangle). Subject references are generally created for any structure that has more than five or six objects.

At the most abstract level, the OOA model would contain only subject references such as those illustrated at the top of Figure 8.11. Each of the references would be expanded into a structure. Structures for the control panel and sensor object (Figures 8.9 and 8.10) are shown in the lower portion of Figure 8.11; structures for **system, sensor event,** and **audible alarm** would also be created if these objects required more than five or six classification or assembly objects.

The dotted, doubled-headed arrows shown at the top of Figure 8.11 represent communication (message) paths between objects. These are derived as a consequence of the activities described in the next section.

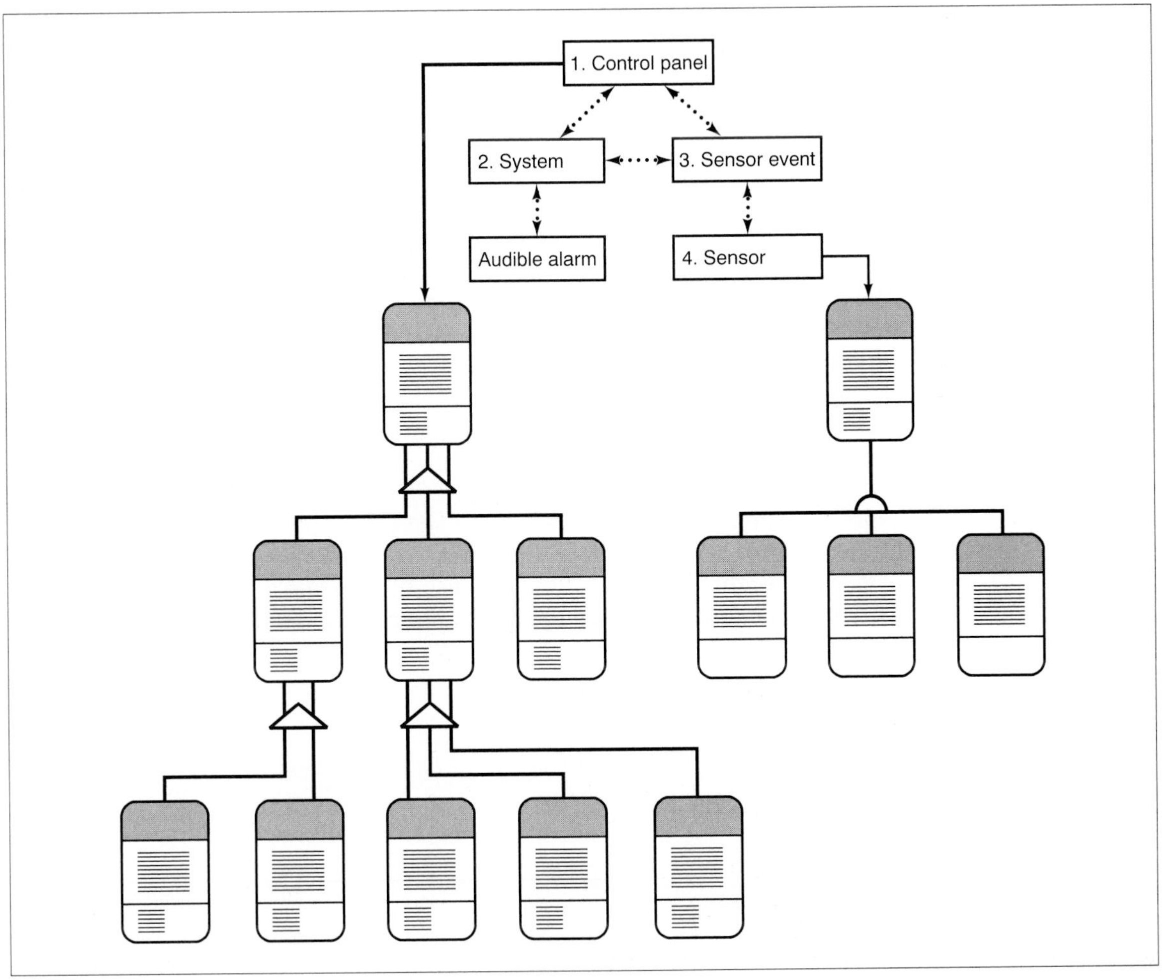

FIGURE 8.11. An OOA model with subject references.

8.2.3 Instance Connections and Message Paths

Objects do not exist in a vacuum, and for this reason, an analyst should define relationships for each object in the model. An *instance connection* is a modeling notation that defines a specific relationship between instances of an object.

For example, Figure 8.12*a* represents the first step in creation of instance connections for *SafeHome* objects. The simple lines between objects indicate that some important relationship does exist. For example, sensors can generate a sensor event and sensor events must be recognized by the system. Once the lines have been established, each end is evaluated to determine whether a single (1:1) connection exists or a multiple connection (1:many) exists. For a 1:1 connection, the line is annotated with a single bar. A 1:many connection is annotated with a three-pronged fork symbol as shown in Figure 8.12*b*. Finally, we add another vertical bar if the connection is mandatory and a circle to represent an optional connection. To illustrate, at least one and possibly many sensors can lead to a sensor event (e.g., smoke is detected or a break-in has occurred) for *SafeHome*. Yet in any particular situation, either 0 or 1 sensor events will occur.[5] This type of evaluation continues for each instance connection. The resultant representation is shown in Figure 8.12*c*.

By representing instance connections, the analyst adds still another dimension to the OOA model. Not only are the relationships between objects identified, but all important *message paths* are defined. In our discussion of Figure 8.11, we made reference to the dotted arrows that connected subject symbols. These are message paths (sometimes referred to as *message connections*); each arrow implies the interchange of messages among objects in the model. As we have already noted, messages will move along each instance connection path; therefore, message connections are derived directly from instance connections.

Like the structured analysis diagrams presented in Chapter 7, graphical representation forms the basis for the OOA model and provides an excellent foundation for the creation of a *Software Requirements Specification*. Each object represented graphically must also be described using a text-oriented format. A suggested outline for object description is shown in Table 8.1.

8.2.4 OOA and Prototyping

It is important to note that the use of OOA can lead to extremely effective prototyping and "evolutionary software engineering" techniques. The objects that are specified and ultimately implemented for a current project

---

[5]It is conceivable that multiple events will occur at exactly the same time. We assume that the system has a priority scheme and will choose the event with highest priority and latch all others.

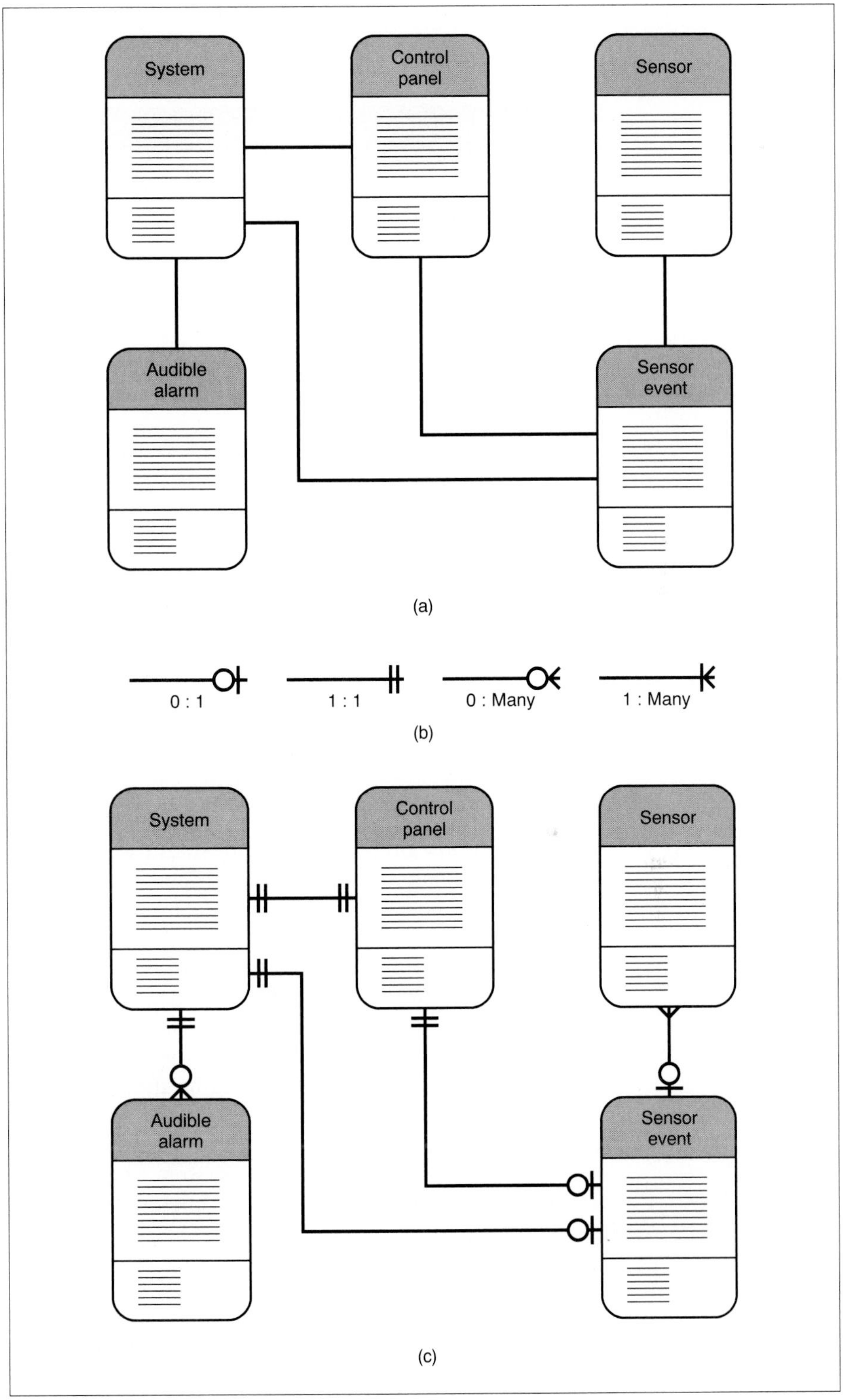

FIGURE 8.12.
(a) Establishing instance connections; (b) connection notation; (c) defining multiplicity.

TABLE 8.1

OBJECT SPECIFICATION

- **I.** Object name
- **II.** Attribute descriptions
  - **A.** Attribute name
  - **B.** Attribute content
  - **C.** Attribute data type/structure
- **III.** External input to object
- **IV.** External output from object
- **V.** Operation descriptions
  - **A.** Operation name
  - **B.** Operation interface description
  - **C.** Operation processing description
  - **D.** Performance issues
  - **E.** Restrictions and limitations
- **VI.** Instance connections
- **VII.** Message connections

can be catalogued in a library. Objects are inherently reusable [COA90, TRA88], and over time the library of reusable objects will grow. When OOA is applied to new projects, the analyst can work to specify the system using existing (implemented) objects contained in the object library rather than inventing new ones (this practice is commonplace in hardware design; system engineers specify existing integrated circuits, rather than requiring custom design). For example, the **sensor** and **sensor event** objects described for *SafeHome* could be used without change in a variety of process control and monitoring applications. Similarly, the **control panel** object would have broad application in other products.

By using existing objects during analysis, specification time is reduced substantially, and a rapid prototype of the specified system can be created and reviewed by the customer. Even more important, the prototype can evolve into a working product or system because the building blocks that created it (the objects) have already been proven in practice.

8.3 DATA MODELING

The OOA concepts presented in Sections 8.1 and 8.2 are actually extensions of an analysis technique that has been used for many years in data-intensive applications. This technique, called *data modeling* or *information modeling*, focuses solely on data (and therefore satisfies one of the fundamental analysis principles), representing a "data network" that exists for a given system. Data modeling is useful for applications in which data and the relationships that govern data are complex. Unlike the structured analysis approach, data modeling considers data independently of the processing that transforms the data.[6]

Data modeling terminology and some of its graphic notation are similar to those used for OOA. But it is important to recognize that OOA and data modeling are different approaches with a rather different point of view. Both use the term "object," but its definition is much more limited in a data modeling context. Both describe relationships between objects, but data modeling does not concern itself with how these relationships are achieved. Data modeling does exactly what its name implies—it models data—without concern for the processing that must be applied to transform the data. It is, therefore, a complementary technique that serves a specific analysis function. It must be combined with another modeling approach that considers processing issues to form a complete requirements analysis method.

Data modeling is used extensively in database applications. It provides the database analyst and designer with insight into the data and the relationships that govern data. In the context of structured analysis (Chapter 7), data modeling can be used to represent the contents of data stores and the relationships that exist among them. For example, a data item in one file structure (a data store) might be a pointer into another file structure (a different data store). Structured analysis notation provides no direct mechanism for representing this relationship. Data modeling does.

8.3.1 Data Objects, Attributes, and Relationships

When data modeling is used as a requirements analysis technique, the analyst begins by creating models for data objects. A *data object* is defined in much the same way that an object is defined for OOA. Recalling our earlier discussion of objects in Section 8.1.1, a data object can be external entities, things, occurrences or events, roles, organizational units, places, or structures. For example, a **person** or a **car** (Figure 8.13) can be viewed as a data object in the sense that either can be defined in terms of a set of attributes. Data objects are related to one another. For example, **person** can ***own*** **car**, where the relationship ***own*** connotes a specific connection between **person** and **car**. The relationships are always defined by the context of the problem that is being analyzed.

A data object does not take the same form as the object introduced earlier in this chapter. It encapsulates data *only*—there is no reference within

---

[6]Data modeling is often considered to be a *complementary* analysis approach. That is, it can be used to complement structured analysis or other methods.

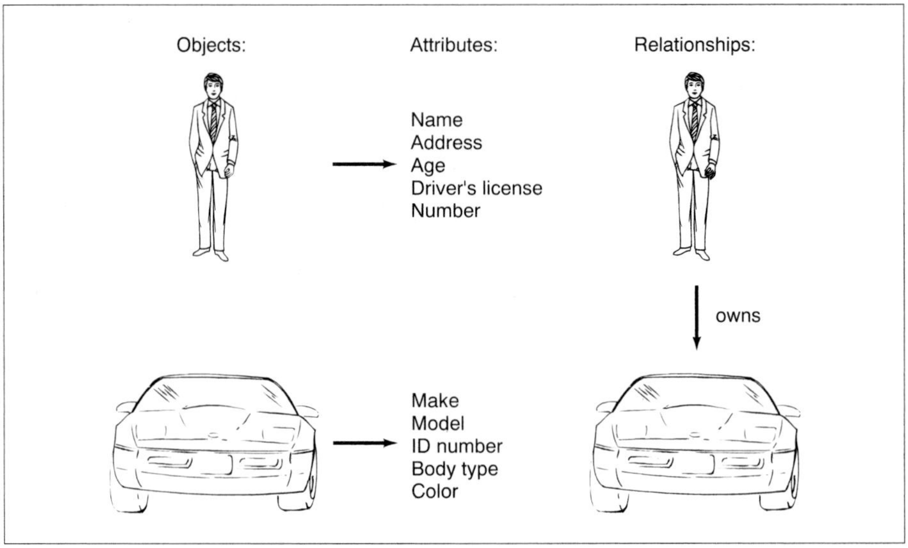

FIGURE 8.13. Data objects, attributes, and relationships.

a data object to operations that act on the data. Therefore, the data object can be represented as a table, as shown in Figure 8.14. The headings in the table reflect attributes of the object. In this case, a car is defined in terms of make, model, ID#, body type, color, and owner. The body of the table represents specific instances of the data object. For example, a Chevy Corvette is an instance of the data object **car**.

Data object attributes take on one of three different characteristics. They can be used to (1) name an instance of the data object, (2) describe the instance, or (3) make reference to another instance in another table. In addition, one or more of the attributes must be defined as an *identifier*—that is, the identifier attribute becomes a "key" when we want to find an instance of the data object. In some cases, values for the identifier(s) are unique, al-

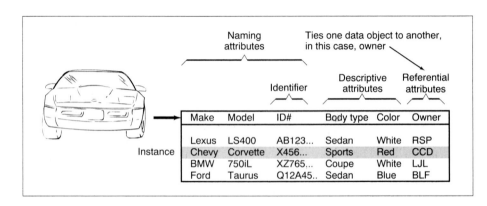

Naming attributes (Make, Model, ID#) — Identifier (ID#) — Descriptive attributes (Body type, Color) — Referential attributes (Owner) — Ties one data object to another, in this case, owner

	Make	Model	ID#	Body type	Color	Owner
	Lexus	LS400	AB123...	Sedan	White	RSP
Instance	Chevy	Corvette	X456...	Sports	Red	CCD
	BMW	750iL	XZ765...	Coupe	White	LJL
	Ford	Taurus	Q12A45..	Sedan	Blue	BLF

FIGURE 8.14. Data objects as tables.

though this is not a requirement. Referring to the data object **car**, a reasonable identifier might be the **ID#**. Attributes for data objects are determined in exactly the same way as suggested for attributes defined as part of object-oriented analysis (Section 8.1.2).

Data object tables can be "formalized" by applying a set of *normalization rules* that will result in a *relational model* for the data. Normalization rules, when applied to data object tables, result in minimum redundancy—that is, the amount of information that we need to maintain to satisfy a particular problem is minimized. These normalization rules [SHL88] can be summarized in the following manner:

1. *A given instance of a data object has one and only one value for each attribute.*
For example, this rule requires that the car table (Figure 8.14) have only one owner for each instance of car. If Chevy Corvette had two owners, the data object would have to be redesigned. Additionally, the table is assumed to have an entry for every attribute. There should be no "holes" in the table. This rule helps us define a *relation* when we use the jargon of database designers.

2. *Attributes represent elementary data items; they should contain no internal structure.*
For example, if **body type** were defined as

body type = number of doors + height + width + name

name = [coupe | sedan | sports | luxury]

we would have a violation of this rule.

To accommodate a situation in which an attribute is a composite data item, we must define the table so that each of the data components of **body type** are noted as separate attributes.

3. *When more than one attribute is used to identify a data object, be sure that descriptive and referential attributes represent "a characteristic of the entire object, and not a characteristic of something that would be identified by only part of the identifier"* [SHL88].
For example, assume that a new identifier, **dealership**, is added to the **car** table shown in Figure 8.14. If we continue our modifications to the table (the data object description) and add **dealership location** as a descriptive attribute, we have violated rule 3 because **dealership location** is an attribute of only one identifier—dealership. It is not an attribute of **ID#**, the other identifier for **car**.

If tables are designed to conform to the first three rules, then the resulting data model is said to be in *second normal form*.

4. *All nonidentifier attributes must represent some characteristic of the instance named by the identifier of the data object and describe some other attribute that is not an identifier.*

For example, if a attribute, **paint name**,[7] were added to the data object car, we would have a violation of rule 4. **Paint name** is a characteristic of **color**, not the instance of car identified by **ID#**.

8.3.2 Entity-Relationship Diagrams

The cornerstone notation for data modeling is the *entity-relationship (E-R) diagram*. A number of different writers (e.g., [MAR82], [CHE86], [ROS88]) have contributed to the development of E-R notation. All identify a set of primary components for the E-R diagram: data objects, attributes, relationships, and various type indicators. The primary purpose of the E-R diagram is to represent data objects and their relationships.

E-R diagram notation is relatively simple. Data objects are represented by labeled rectangles. Relationships are indicated with diamonds. *Connections* between data objects and relationships are established using a variety of special connection lines.

The relationship between data objects **car** and **manufacturer** would be represented as shown in Figure 8.15. One manufacturer builds one or many cars. Given the context implied by the E-R diagram, the specification of the data object **car** (data object table in Figure 8.15) would be radically different from the earlier specification (Figure 8.14). The connection lines have the same meaning as those introduced in Figure 8.12*b*.

Expanding the model, we represent an grossly oversimplified E-R diagram (Figure 8.16) of the distribution element of the automobile business. New data objects, **shipper** and **dealership** are introduced. In addition, new relationships—**transports, contracts, licenses,** and **stocks**—indicate how the data objects shown in the figure associate with one another.

[7]For example, the color red might be named "Arizona Sunset" by the manufacturer.

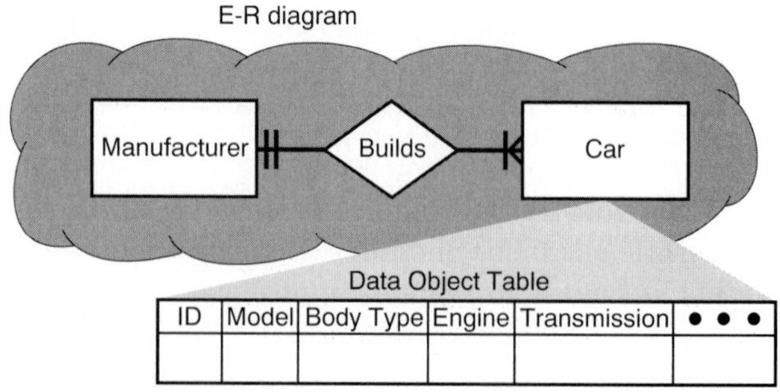

ID	Model	Body Type	Engine	Transmission	• • •

FIGURE 8.15.
A simple E-R diagram and object table.

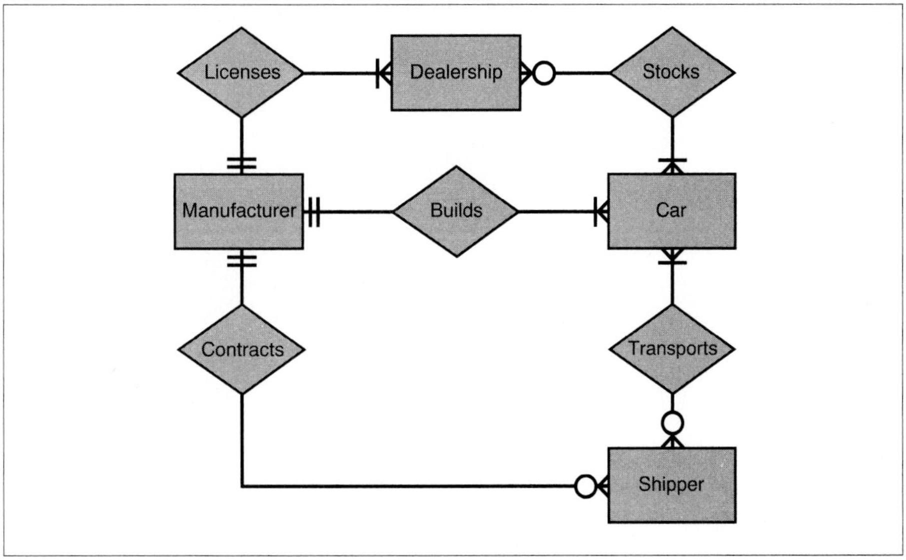

FIGURE 8.16.
An expanded E-R diagram.

Tables for each of the data objects contained in the E-R diagram would have to be developed according to the rules introduced in Section 8.3.1.

In addition to the basic E-R diagram notation introduced in Figures 8.15 and 8.16, the analyst can represent *data-object-type hierarchies*. These are analogous to the structure notation for OOA objects introduced earlier in this chapter. For example, the data object **car** can be categorized as domestic, European, or Far Eastern. The E-R notation shown in Figure 8.17 represents this categorization in the form of a hierarchy [ROS88].

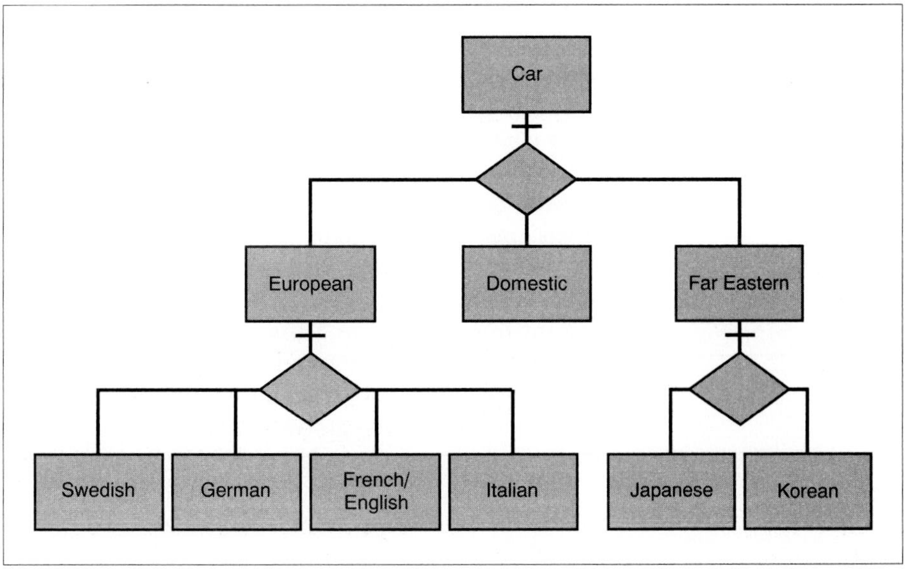

FIGURE 8.17.
Data-object-type hierarchies.

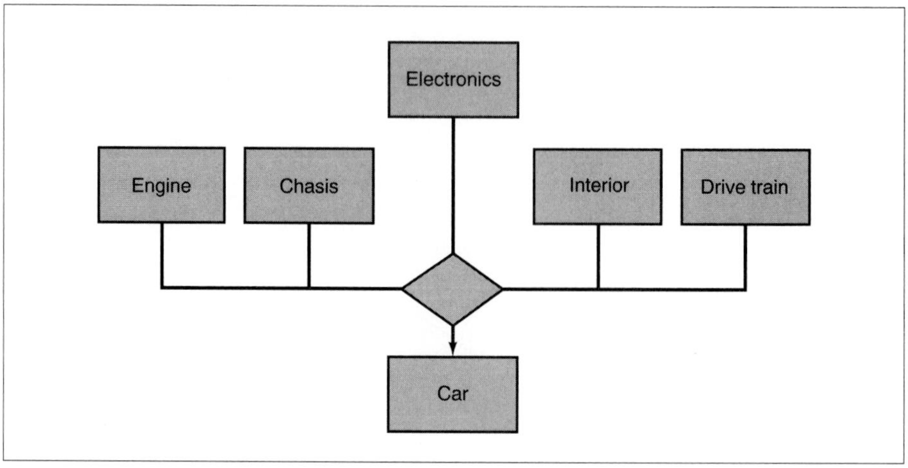

FIGURE 8.18.
Associating objects.

E-R notation provides a mechanism that represents the associativity between objects. An *associative data object* is represented as shown in Figure 8.18. In the figure, the data objects that model the individual subsystems are each associated with the data object **car**.

Data modeling and the entity-relationship diagram provide the analyst with a concise notation for examining data within the context of a data processing application. In most cases, the data modeling approach is used as an adjunct to structured analysis, but it can also be used for database design and to support any other requirements analysis method.

8.4 SUMMARY

Object-oriented methods for software requirements analysis enable the analyst to model a problem by representing classes, objects, attributes, and operations as the primary modeling components. The object-oriented viewpoint combines classification of objects, inheritance of the attributes, and communication of messages in the context of a modeling notation.

Objects model almost any identifiable aspect of the problem domain: external entities, things, occurrences, roles, organizational units, places, and structures can all be represented as objects. As importantly, objects encapsulate both data and process. Processing operations are part of the object and are initiated by passing the object a message. A class definition, once defined, forms the basis for reusability at the modeling, design, and implementation levels. New objects can be instantiated from a class.

The object-oriented analysis method provides a notation and a set of heuristics for building an OOA model. Structures, subjects, instance connections, and message paths are used to build a graphical specification of a computer-based system. The primary objective of OOA is to identify classes from which objects are instantiated.

Data modeling can be viewed as a subset of OOA. Using the entity-relationship diagram as the primary notation, data modeling focuses on the definition of data objects (objects that do *not* encapsulate processing) and the manner in which they relate to one another. Data modeling is used in data-intensive applications and can be applied as a complementary notation during structured analysis.

REFERENCES

[BOO86] Booch, G., "Object-Oriented Development," *IEEE Trans. Software Engineering,* vol. SE-12, no. 2, February 1986, pp. 211ff.

[CAS89] Cashman, M., "Object Oriented Domain Analysis," *ACM Software Engineering Notes,* vol. 14, no. 6, October 1989, p. 67.

[CHE86] Chen, P., "The Entity Relationship Model—Toward a Unified View of Data," *ACM Trans. Data Base Systems,* vol. 1, no. 1, March 1976, pp. 6–36.

[COA90] Coad, P., and E. Yourdon, *Object-Oriented Analysis,* Prentice-Hall, 1990.

[COX86] Cox, B. J., *Object-Oriented Programming,* Addison-Wesley, 1986.

[EVB89] *Object-Oriented Requirements Analysis* (course notebook), EVB Software Engineering, 1989.

[MAR82] Martin, J., *Computer Data Base Organization,* Prentice-Hall, 1982.

[MEN90] Meng, B., "Object-Oriented Programming," *MacWorld,* vol. 7, no. 1, January 1990, pp. 174–183.

[ROS88] Ross, R.G., *Entity Modeling: Techniques and Application,* Data Research Group, 1988.

[SHL88] Schlaer, S., and S. J. Mellor, *Object-Oriented Systems Analysis,* Yourdon Press, 1988.

[STR88] Stroustrup, B., "What is Object-Oriented Programming?" *IEEE Software,* vol. 5, no. 3, May 1988, pp. 10–20.

[TRA88] Tracz, W., *Software Reuse: Emerging Technology,* IEEE Computer Society Press, 1988.

PROBLEMS AND POINTS TO PONDER

8.1 The object-oriented paradigm is "hot." Articles at every level of technical sophistication have been written about it. Using the *Reader's Guide* in your library, find three current nontechnical (not published in engineering journals or magazines; PC magazines are OK) articles and write a brief paper summarizing what they have to say.

8.2 In this chapter we did not consider the case in which a new object requires an attribute or operation that is not contained in the class from which it inherited all other attributes and operations. How do you think this is handled?

8.3 Do some research and find the real answer to Problem 8.2.

8.4 Using your own words and a few examples, define the terms "class," "inheritance," and "encapsulation."

8.5 Review the objects defined for the *SafeHome* system. Are there other objects that you feel should be defined as modeling begins?

8.6 Develop a complete OOA model for the PHTRS application introduced in Problem 7.13.

8.7 Software for a personal computer-based word processing system is to be developed. Do a few hours of research on the application area and conduct a FAST meeting (Chapter 5) with your fellow students to develop requirements (your instructor will help you coordinate this). Build a requirements model of the system using OOA.

8.8 Software for a real-time test monitoring system for gas turbine engines is to be developed. Proceed as in Problem 8.7.

8.9 Software for a manufacturing control system for an automobile assembly plant is to be developed. Proceed as in Problem 8.7.

8.10 Software for a video game is to be developed. Proceed as in Problem 8.7.

8.11 Research the messaging concept in one or two technical books and write a one- or two-page paper describing how it is implemented in object-oriented systems.

8.12 Do some research on "reusability" and discuss the impact of OOA and other object-oriented methods used later in the software engineering process. Expand on the discussion of OOA and prototyping presented in Section 8.2.4.

8.13 Describe in your own words the difference between an object used in OOA and an object used during data modeling.

8.14 Develop a complete data model for the PHTRS application introduced in Problem 7.13. Use an entity relationship diagram to create the model. Be sure to represent the contents of data objects as tables and to apply the rules presented in Section 8.3.1.

8.15 Assume that you have been asked to develop an on-line course registration system (OLCRS) for your university. (This was first introduced in Problem 3.3.) Define a set of basic requirements (use FAST, if required) and then develop a data model for the system. Your instructor will indicate to what level of detail you should take this problem.

FURTHER READINGS

Some people believe that structured analysis was the analysis method of the 1980s, but that object-oriented analysis will become the method of the 1990s. In an interesting paper that attempts to bridge the gap, Ward (*IEEE Software,* March 1989) discusses "how to integrate object orientation with structured analysis and design."

There are relatively few books that have as yet been published with an exclusive emphasis on OOA. The work of Coad and Yourdon [COA90] is probably the most useful of those that are readily available. However, other books on object-oriented technology, such as Meyer (*Object-Oriented Software Construction,* 2d ed., Prentice-Hall, 1990), Booch (*Object-Oriented Design,* Benjamin-Cummings, 1990), Winblad et al. (*Object-Oriented Software,* Addison-Wesley, 1990), and Khoshaflan and Abnous (*Object-Orientation,* Wiley, 1990) provide additional insight into basic concepts, languages, databases, and user interfaces. An excellent anthology of papers on object-oriented issues has been compiled by Peterson (*Object-Oriented Computing:*

Concepts, IEEE Computer Society Press, 1987). Mullin (*Rapid Prototyping for Object-Oriented Systems,* Addison-Wesley, 1990) discusses the marriage between the prototyping paradigm and object-oriented approaches.

The *OOPSLA Conference Proceedings* (published yearly by the ACM) is dedicated to object-oriented topics and has many papers that are related to analysis issues. The *Compsac '89 Proceedings* (IEEE Computer Society Press, September 1989) has over 35 papers on object-oriented computing. A number of these deal with object-oriented databases (a topic that is beyond the scope of this book, but provides an interesting bridge to data modeling issues).

Data modeling is closely related to database design and is emphasized in books on that subject. Useful discussions of database design, data modeling, normalization, and E-R diagramming techniques may be found in

Braithwaite, K. S., *Systems Design in a Database Environment,* McGraw-Hill, 1989.

Date, C. J., *Relational Databases—Writings 1985–1989,* Addison-Wesley, 1990.

Dutka, A. F., and H. H. Hanson, *Fundamentals of Data Normalization,* Addison-Wesley, 1989.

Hogan, R., *A Practical Guide to Data Base Design,* Prentice-Hall, 1990.

Kim, W., and F. Lochovsky (eds.), *Object-Oriented Languages, Applications and Databases,* ACM Press, 1989.

Books by Barker (*Entity Relationship Modeling,* Addison-Wesley, 1990) and Ross [ROS88] present complete tutorials on E-R diagramming and provide examples developed using CASE tools. E-R modeling is one of many topics presented in books by Finkelstein (*An Introduction to Information Engineering,* Addison-Wesley, 1989) and Martin (*Information Engineering,* 3 volumes, Prentice-Hall, 1990).

CHAPTER 9

ALTERNATIVE ANALYSIS TECHNIQUES AND FORMAL METHODS

Any requirements analysis method combines a set of distinct heuristics and a unique notation to analyze information, function, and behavior for a computer-based system. Through the application of the fundamental analysis principles (Chapter 6), each method creates a model of the problem and the requirements for its solution.

Most requirements analysis methods are *information-driven*. That is, the method provides a mechanism for representing the information domain of the problem. From this representation, function and behavior are derived and other software characteristics are established.

Liskov and Berzins [LIS86] have stated:

> Every program performs some task correctly. What is of interest to computer scientists [and software engineers and their managers] is whether a program performs its intended task. To determine this, a precise and independent description of the desired program behavior is needed. Such a description is called a *specification*.

The role of requirements analysis methods is to assist the analyst in deriving "a precise and independent description" of the software element of a computer-based system.

Structured analysis (Chapter 7) and object-oriented analysis (Chapter 8) are analysis methods that represent today's mainstream and tomorrow's direction. But many other requirements analysis and modeling methods are in use. In this chapter, alternative methods for analysis modeling are discussed.

9.1 REQUIREMENTS ANALYSIS METHODS

Requirements analysis methods enable an analyst to apply fundamental analysis principles (Chapter 6) in a systematic fashion. We have already examined structured analysis and object-oriented analysis—two radically different approaches to the same problem. Yet in each of these methods, and in the methods described in this chapter,[1] there are underlying similarities and fundamental differences.

9.1.1 Common Characteristics

Requirements analysis methods have more in common than a cursory inspection might indicate. Each supports the fundamental requirements analysis principles; each creates a hierarchical representation of a system; each demands a careful consideration of external and internal interfaces; each provides a foundation for the design and implementation steps that follow; and none (with the exception of formal specification languages) focuses serious attention on the representation of constraints or validation criteria.

Although each method introduces new notation and analysis heuristics, all methods can be evaluated in the context of the following common characteristics: (1) mechanism for information domain analysis, (2) approach for functional and/or behavioral representations, (3) definition of interfaces, (4) mechanisms for problem partitioning, (5) support for abstraction, and (6) representation of essential and implementation views.

Even though information domain analysis is conducted differently with each method, common threads can be recognized. All methods address (either directly or indirectly) information flow and information content or structure. In some cases, information flow is characterized in the context of transformations (functions) that are applied to change input into output (e.g., structured analysis). Yet with other methods, content may be represented directly, but flow is implied and not explicitly modeled. Data content may be represented explicitly using a dictionary mechanism, defined in terms of a data object, or implied by first addressing the hierarchical structure of data.

Functions are typically described as information transforms or processes. Each function may be represented using specific notation (e.g., a circle, a box). A description of the function may be developed using natural language text, a pseudoprocedural language with informal syntax rules, or a formal specification language. Behavioral models range from graphical

[1]Formal analysis methods, discussed in Sections 9.6 and 9.7, represent a radical departure from other analysis methods. Yet, the fundamental principles of requirements analysis remain.

representations (e.g., the state transition diagram) to an implicit indication of behavior.

A description of interfaces is generally an outgrowth of information and function representations. Flow of data and control into and out of a specific function can be matched with information flows to other functions. Interfaces are derived from an examination of information flow. Alternatively, information flow is implied by examining messages that move about a system or "connections" that couple various subsystems.

Problem partitioning and abstraction are accomplished through a *layering* process that enables the analyst to represent the information domain and the functional domain at different levels of abstraction. In fact, even the behavioral domain can be layered.

For example, all methods enable an analyst to represent a function such as **compute all payroll taxes** and to represent and manipulate the function at this level of abstraction. In addition, all methods provide a mechanism for partitioning **compute all payroll taxes** into a set of subfunctions: **compute withholding tax, compute FICA, compute state tax,** and **compute local tax.** Each of these functions may be represented at a lower level of abstraction using a function descriptive notation (e.g., a pseudo-procedural language). Most analysis methods allow the analyst to evaluate the essential representation of a problem prior to deriving the implementation solution. In general, the same notation is used to represent both views.

9.1.2 Differences in Analysis Methods

Each method for the analysis of computer-based systems has its own point of view, its own notation, and its own approach to modeling. Although the modeling approach and notation will differ among all methods, confusion sometimes occurs because the same symbol (e.g., a square or a circle) has different meanings in different methods. In addition, each method has its own jargon and terminology.

The degree to which the method establishes a firm foundation for design differs greatly. In some cases, the analysis model can be mapped directly into a working program (using a number of transformations that are described later in this chapter). In other cases, the analysis method establishes a starting point only and the designer is left to derive the design with little help from the analysis model.

The level of CASE tools support varies greatly among the methods. Structured analysis—the most widely used method (Chapter 7)—is supported by dozens of high-quality CASE tools. But other more obscure methods may have only one rudimentary tool available.

To complicate matters even further, there are a number of different versions of many of the analysis methods presented in this and the preceding chapters. Most software engineers, however, view these as "dialects." Once the basic "language" of analysis modeling is understood, a dialect can be easily learned. Last, the degree of mathematical rigor varies significantly, with formal methods leading the pack in this characteristic.

In the sections that follow we examine a number of different analysis methods. Each has characteristics that are similar to those methods that have already been presented, and each has aspects that make it unique.

9.2 DATA STRUCTURE-ORIENTED METHODS

We have already noted that the information domain for a software problem encompasses flow, content, and structure. Data structure-oriented analysis methods represent software requirements by focusing on data structure rather than data flow. Although each data structure-oriented method has a distinct approach and notation, all have some characteristics in common: (1) each assists the analyst in identifying key *information objects* (also called *entities* or *items*) and *operations* (also called *actions* or *processes*); (2) each assumes that the structure of information is hierarchical; (3) each requires that the data structure be represented using the sequence, selection, and repetition constructs for composite data discussed in Chapter 7; and (4) each provides a set of steps for mapping a hierarchical data structure into a program structure.

Like their flow-oriented counterparts, data structure-oriented analysis methods lay the foundation for software design. In every case, an analysis method may be extended to encompass architectural and procedural design for software.

In the sections that follow, an overview of two important data structure-oriented analysis methods is presented.

9.3 DATA STRUCTURED SYSTEMS DEVELOPMENT

Data structured systems development (DSSD), also called the *Warnier-Orr methodology,* evolved from pioneering work on information domain analysis conducted by J. D. Warnier [WAR74, WAR81]. Warnier developed a notation for representing an information hierarchy using the three constructs for sequence, selection, and repetition and demonstrated that the software structure could be derived directly from the data structure.

Ken Orr [ORR77, ORR81] has extended Warnier's work to encompass a somewhat broader view of the information domain that has evolved into data structured systems development. DSSD considers information flow and functional characteristics as well as data hierarchy.

9.3.1 Warnier Diagrams

The *Warnier diagram* [WAR74] enables the analyst to represent information hierarchy in a compact manner. The information domain is analyzed and the hierarchical nature of the output is represented. To illustrate, let us consider an automated composition system used by a newspaper to prepare each day's edition. The general organization of the paper takes the following form:

FRONT SECTION
  Headline news
  National news
  Local news
EDITORIAL SECTION
  Editorials columns
  Letters to the editor
  Satirical cartoon
SECOND SECTION
  Sports news
  Business news
  Classified

The newspaper outline shown above is an information hierarchy. The Warnier diagram may be used to represent the hierarchy at any level of detail. Referring to Figure 9.1*a*, the newspaper information hierarchy is represented using Warnier notation. The brace ({) is used to differentiate levels of the information hierarchy. All names contained within a brace represent a *sequence* of information items (each item may be a composite of other items or an elementary item). The notation next to some names represents *repetition,* that is, the number of times the particular item appears in the hierarchy. For example, 1 to 3 editorials will appear in the editorial section, while a cartoon may or may not be present (appears 0 to 1 times).

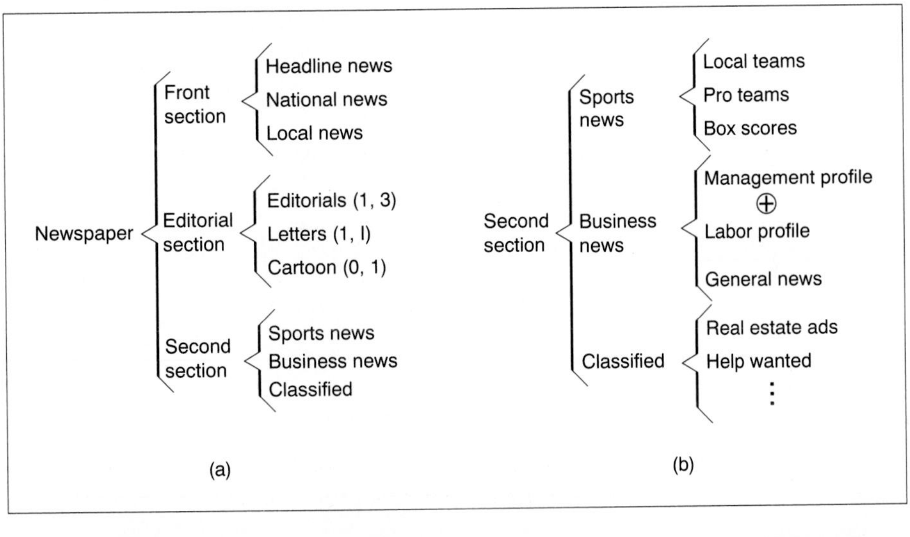

FIGURE 9.1.
(a) Warnier diagram;
(b) refined diagram.

The Warnier diagram may be used to further partition the information domain by refining composite data items. Figure 9.1*b* illustrates refinement for the second section. The *exclusive-or* symbol (⊕) indicates a conditional occurrence (**selection**) of an information item; in this case, the business news section will contain either a management profile or a labor profile, but not both.

9.3.2 The DSSD Approach

Rather than beginning analysis by examining the information hierarchy, DSSD first examines the *application context,* that is, how data moves between producers and consumers of information from the perspective of one of the producers or consumers. Next, *application functions* are assessed with a Warnier-like representation that depicts information items and the processing that must be performed on them (this is similar in concept to the data flow diagram). Finally, application results are modeled using the Warnier diagram. Using this approach, DSSD encompasses all the attributes of the information domain: data flow, content, and structure.

To illustrate DSSD notation and to provide an overview of the analysis method, we present a simple example. A mail/phone order business, called *The Software Store,* sells personal computer software. A computer-based order processing system is to be specified for the business.

To illustrate the overall flow of information for *The Software Store,* refer to the data flow diagram in Figure 9.2. (Note: The DFD is not part of

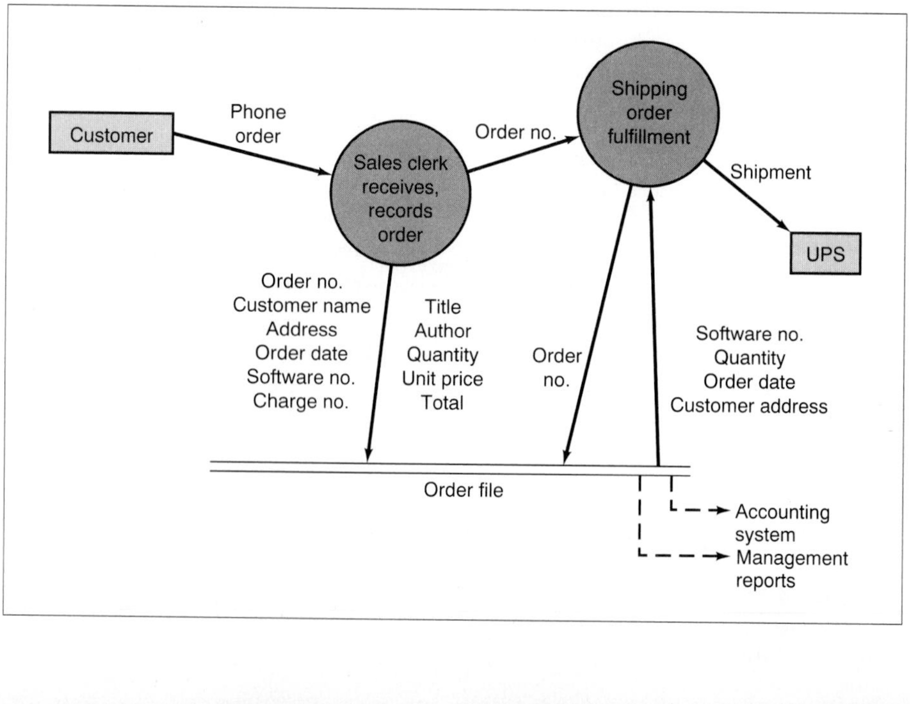

FIGURE 9.2.
The software store—an example.

the DSSD method, but has been used because it is an already familiar analysis notation.) Phone orders are received by a sales clerk who records the order and builds an order file that is comprised of the data items shown in Figure 9.2. An order number is assigned to a particular order and passed to the shipping department, which prepares the shipment using information in the order file. Other business functions (e.g., accounting) have access to the order file.

9.3.3 Application Context

To determine the DSSD *application context,* the problem must be stated in a manner that enables us to answer three questions:

1. What are the information items that must be processed?
2. Who/what are the producers and consumers of information?
3. How does each producer/consumer view information in the context of other constituencies?

DSSD proposes an *entity diagram* as a mechanism for answering these questions.

The entity diagram uses a notation that is, regrettably, very similar to the data flow diagram. However, similar symbols have different meanings. The circle in an entity diagram depicts a producer or consumer (a person, a machine, another system) of information. The five producers and consumers of information for *The Software Store* are shown in Figure 9.3*a*. An entity diagram for the **sales: order receiving** department is illustrated in Figure 9.3*b*. All interfaces between **sales: order receiving** and other constituencies are shown from the point of view of **sales: order receiving**. Entity diagrams for other producers and consumers of information could also be developed.

After each entity diagram is reviewed for correctness, a *combined entity diagram* (Figure 9.4) is created for all producers and consumers of information. Those entities that fall within the bounds of the proposed system (an automated order processing system) are indicated by identifying an *application boundary.* The detail within the application boundary may be hidden (temporarily), as illustrated in Figure 9.5. Information moving across the application boundary must be processed by the order processing system to be analyzed.

9.3.4 Application Functions

The functions that must be implemented to accomplish the automated order processing system can be discerned by examining information flow across

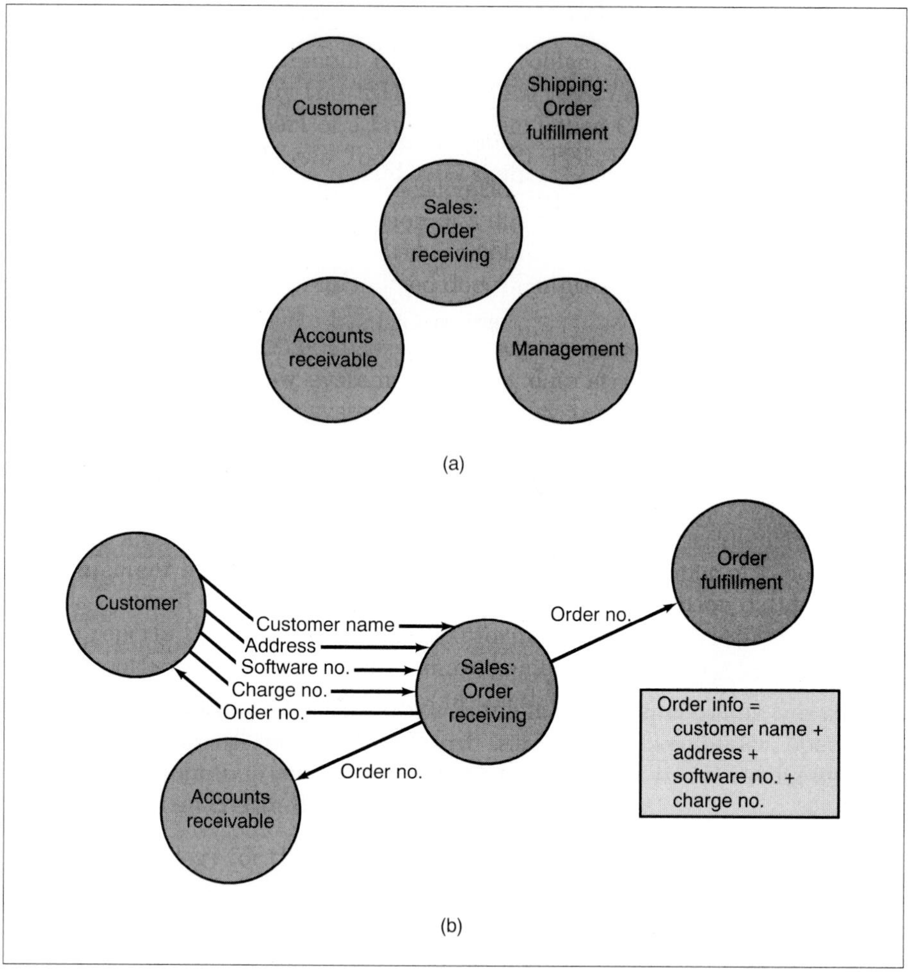

FIGURE 9.3. Entity diagrams. (a) Producers and consumers of information; (b) entity diagram for **sales: order receiving.**

the application boundary. Using Figure 9.5 as a guide, the sequence in which data items move across the boundary is noted as shown in the figure. Using a Warnier-like notation called an *assembly line diagram* (ALD), DSSD provides a mechanism for coupling information and the processes (transforms or functions) that are applied to it. Conceptually, the ALD plays the same role as the data flow diagram.

An assembly line diagram is developed by beginning with the last numbered information flow (Figure 9.5) and working backward showing the processing that derives the preceding numbered information item. An ALD for the order processing system is shown in Figure 9.6. Reading left to right, the monthly report (based on monthly data to accounting) is derived by tak-

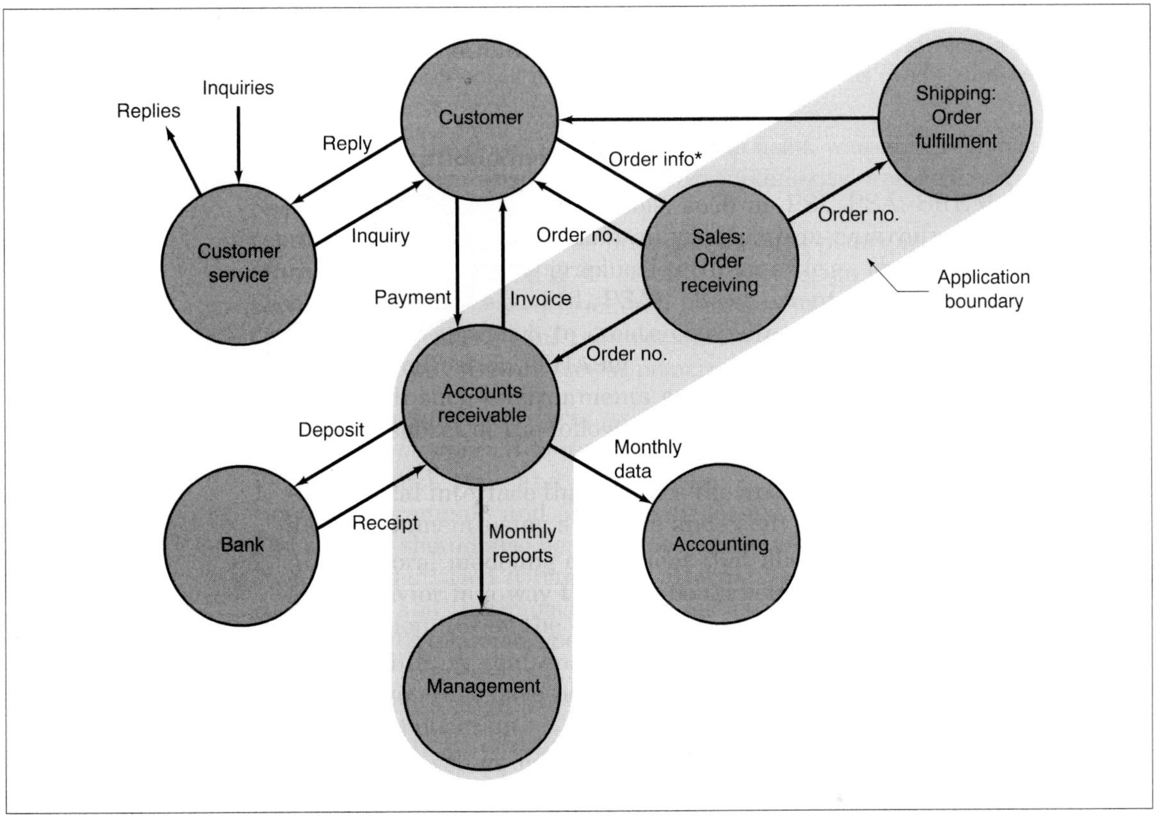

FIGURE 9.4. A combined entity diagram.

ing bank receipt information and applying a report generation process. The plus sign indicates the coupling between process and information.[2] Receipts information is derived from a bank deposit (information) and the associated function that processes the deposit, producing a receipt. A similar progression occurs until we reach **order info**, the first input in the sequence (Figure 9.5).

Each process in the ALD is refined by developing a processing narrative that addresses output, action, frequency of action, and input. A Warnier-Orr diagram, described in the next section, may be used to represent procedural details for each process.

[2]By encapsulating process and data in the same representation, it could be argued that the assembly line diagram creates an "object-oriented" model (Chapter 8) of requirements.

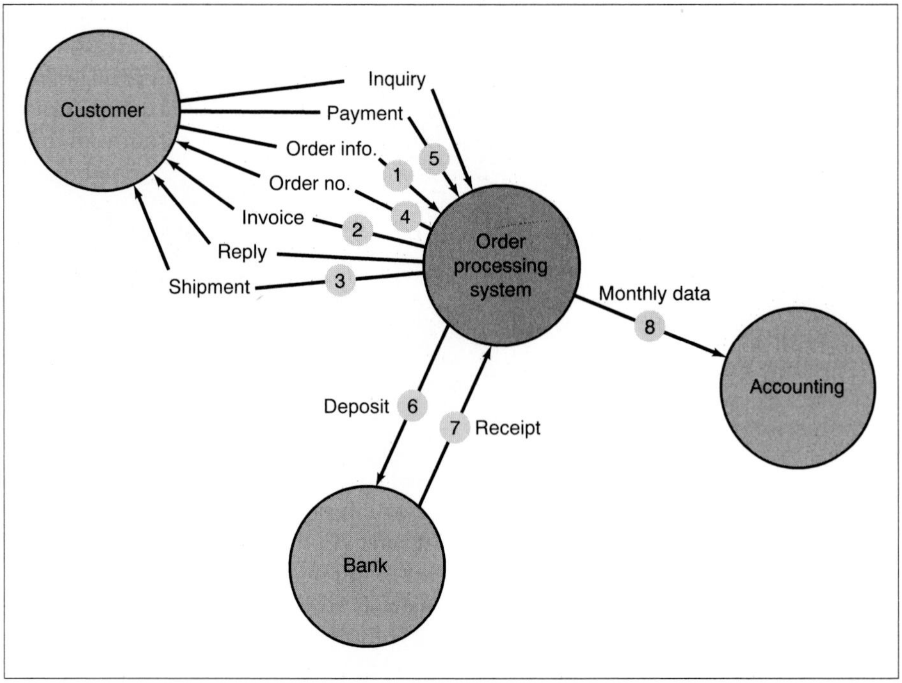

FIGURE 9.5.
An application-level entity diagram.

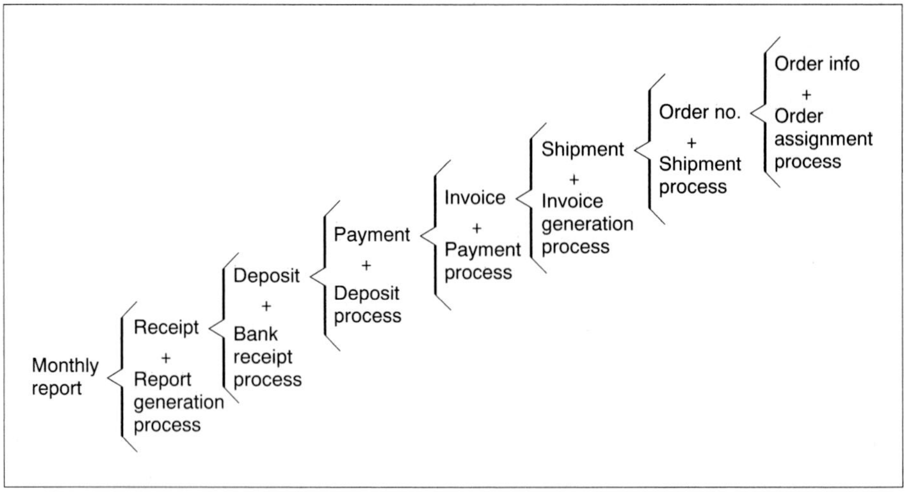

FIGURE 9.6.
Assembly line diagram.

9.3.5 Application Results

DSSD requires the analyst to build a *paper prototype* of desired output for the system. The prototype identifies primary system output and the organization of information items that comprise the output. Once a prototype has

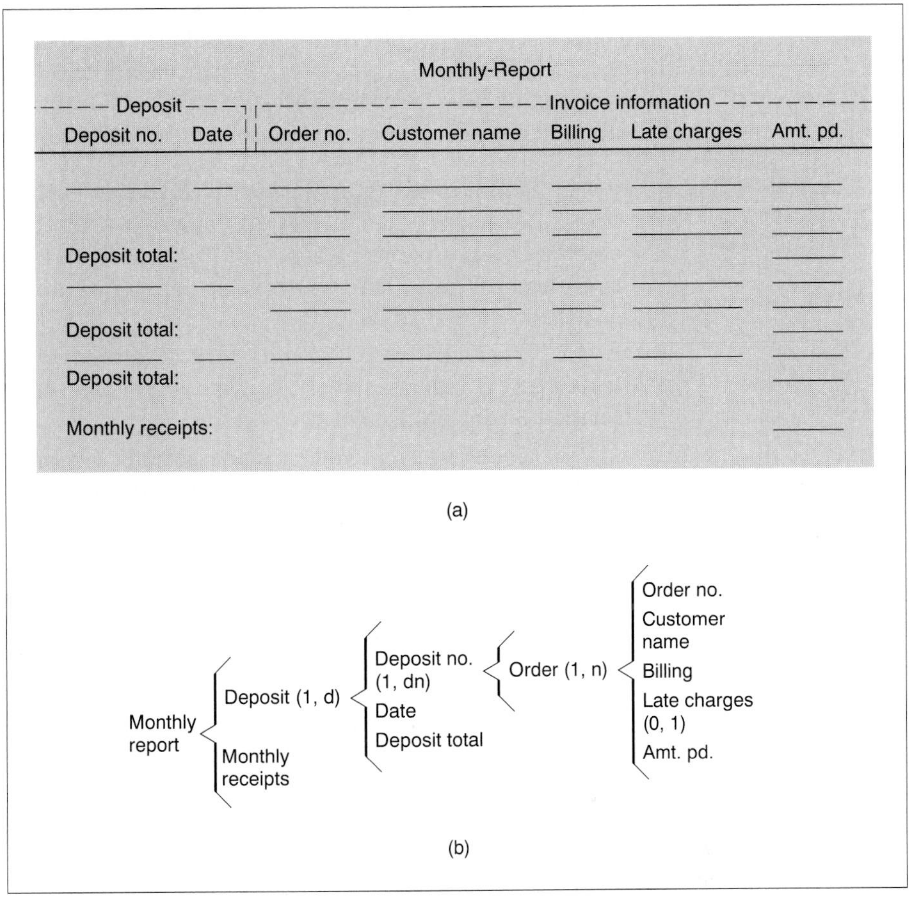

FIGURE 9.7. (a) Paper prototype; (b) Warnier-Orr diagram for application results.

been created, the information hierarchy may be modeled using a *Warnier-Orr diagram*—essentially a Warnier diagram (Section 9.3.1) with small variations in notation and format.

To illustrate the use of paper prototyping and the Warnier-Orr diagram in the derivation of application results, we consider the **monthly report** generated as output from the automated order processing system for *The Software Store*. Figure 9.7*a* shows a paper prototype for the report and Figure 9.7*b* illustrates a Warnier-Orr diagram of the corresponding information hierarchy.

9.4 JACKSON SYSTEM DEVELOPMENT

Jackson System Development (JSD) evolved out of work conducted by M. A. Jackson [JAC75, JAC83] on information domain analysis and its relationship to program and system design. Similar in some ways to Warnier's approach and DSSD, JSD focuses on models of the "real-world" information domain. In Jackson's words [JAC83]: "The developer begins by creating a model of the reality with which the system is concerned, the reality which furnishes its [the system's] subject matter...."

To conduct JSD, the analyst applies the following steps:

Entity action step. Using an approach that is quite similar to the object-oriented analysis technique described in Chapter 8, *entities* (people, objects, or organizations that a system needs to produce or use information) and *actions* (the events that occur in the real world that affect entities) are identified.

Entity structure step. Actions that affect each entity are ordered by time and represented with *Jackson diagrams* (a tree-like notation described later in this section).

Initial modeling step. Entities and actions are represented as a process model; connections between the model and the real world are defined.

Function step. Functions that correspond to defined actions are specified.

System timing step. Process scheduling characteristics are assessed and specified.

Implementation step. Hardware and software are specified as a design.

The last three steps in JSD are closely aligned with system or software design. Therefore, in this chapter we discuss only the first three steps, postponing a consideration of the remaining three until Chapter 13.

9.4.1 The Entity Action Step

The entity action step begins with a brief (usually one-paragraph) natural language statement of the problem. As an example we shall analyze requirements for a software based control system for the *university shuttle service* (USS) described below:

> A large university is spread over two campuses which are over a mile apart. To help students who must travel between campuses to get to lectures on time, the university plans to install a shuttle service. The shuttle service makes use of only one high-speed shuttle that travels over tracks between a station at each campus. Each station has a call button that students can use to request transport to the other station. When students arrive at a station, they push the call button. If the shuttle is already there, they board it and depart for the other station. If the shuttle is in transit, they must wait for it to stop at the other station, board students (if any), and return. If the shuttle is at the other station, it leaves to come and pick up the students who pushed the button. The shuttle will wait at a station until the next request for service (a button is pushed) occurs.

Entities are selected by examining all nouns in the description. After review of the above description, the following candidate entities are chosen: **univer-**

sity, campus, students, lectures, shuttle, station, and **button.** We are not directly concerned with **campus, students, lectures,** or **station**—all of these lie outside the model boundary and are rejected as possible entities. **University** is merely a collective term for both campuses, so we reject it as a possible entity. We select **shuttle** and **button**.

An action occurs at a specific point in time and is applied to an entity. Actions are selected by examining all the verbs in the description. Candidate actions are: **travels, arrive, push, board, leaves, waits.** We reject **travels** because it refers to **student** and **student** has not been selected as an entity. **Waits** is rejected because it represents a state, rather than an atomic action. We select **arrive, push,** and **leaves.**

It should be noted that by rejecting candidate entities and actions, we have bounded the scope of the system to be developed. For example, by rejecting **student**, we have precluded later enhancements such as the generation of information on how many students use the shuttle system on a given day. However, the list of entities and actions may be modified as analysis continues.

9.4.2 The Entity Structure Step

When used in the context of JSD, the *structure* of an entity describes the entity's history by considering the impact of actions over time. To represent entity structure, Jackson introduced the diagrammatic notation illustrated in Figure 9.8. Actions are applied to an entity as a sequence, as part of an either-or selection or repetitively (an iteration).

The entity structure for **shuttle** and **button** are shown in Figure 9.9*a* and *b*. In the structure diagram shown in Figure 9.9*a*, the shuttle begins and ends its history at station 1. The actions that affect the entity are arrivals and departures. The diagram indicates that the shuttle begins at station 1, spends its time moving back and forth between stations 1 and 2, and ultimately returns to station 1. We indicate that an arrival at a station is followed by a departure from the same station by representing both actions [*arrive* (*i*) and *leave* (*i*)] with the same station index *i*. Notes may accompany

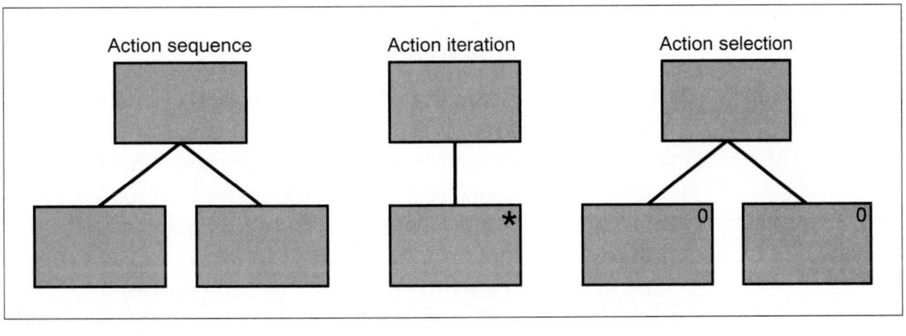

FIGURE 9.8. Structure diagram notation.

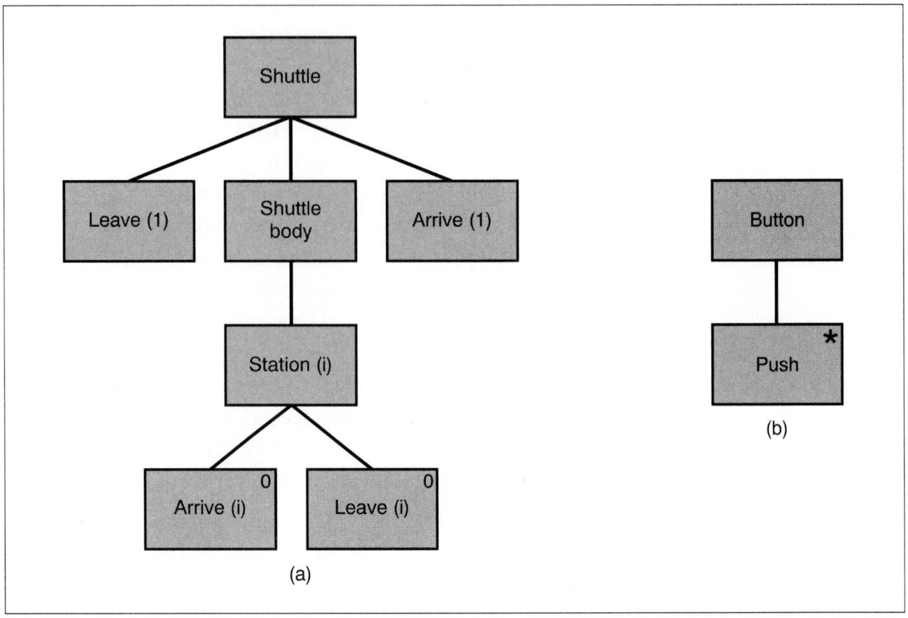

FIGURE 9.9.
(a) Structure diagram for the shuttle entity; (b) structure diagram for the button entity.

the diagram to specify constraints that cannot be represented directly with JSD notation. For example:

> The value of *i* must be 1 or 2 and, in any two successive occurrences of station, the value of *i* must change.

A single repetitive action (*push*) may be applied to the entity **button** (Figure 9.9*b*).

The structure diagram presents a *time-ordered* specification of the actions performed on or by an entity. For this reason, it is a more precise representation of the real world than a simple list of actions and entities. A structure diagram is created for each entity and may be accompanied with narrative text.

9.4.3 The Initial Model Step

The first two steps of JSD are concerned with "an abstract description of the real world" [JAC83]. Entities and actions are selected and related to each other through structure diagrams. The initial model step begins to construct a specification of the system as a model of the real world. The specification is created with a *system specification diagram* (SSD) using symbology illustrated in Figure 9.10. A *data stream connection* occurs when one process transmits a stream of information (e.g., writes records) and the other process receives the stream (e.g., reads records). Arrowheads repre-

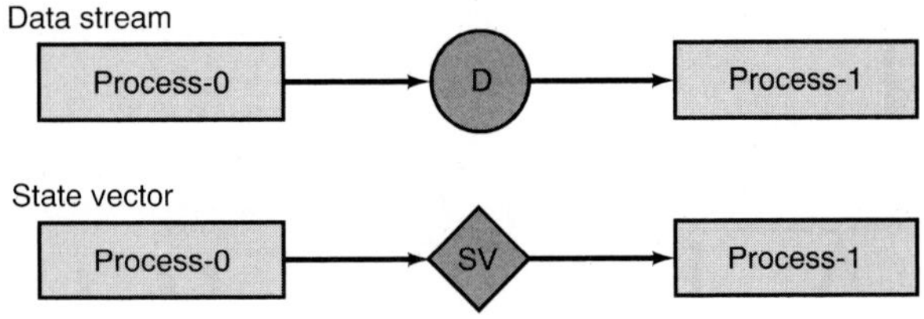

FIGURE 9.10.
SSD notation.

sent the direction of information flow, and the circle represents the data stream which is assumed to be placed in a first-in first-out (FIFO) buffer of unlimited capacity. A *state vector connection* occurs when one process directly inspects the state vector of another process. Arrowheads represent the direction of information flow, and the diamond indicates the state vector. This connection is common in process control applications in which it is necessary to check the state of some electromechanical device. By convention, the suffix 0 represents a real world process and the suffix 1 represents a system model process.

The system specification diagram for USS is illustrated in Figure 9.11. Whenever possible, it is preferable to connect model processes with real-world entities by data streams because direct correspondence between the behavior of the model and the real world is assured. In our example, the call button emits a pulse when pressed. This can be transmitted to the **button-1** process as a data stream connection. However, we shall assume that the sensors that detect arrival or departure of the shuttle do not emit a pulse, but do close an electric switch. The state of the switch (on/off) can be accessed. Hence, a state vector connection is required.

The internal details of model processes are specified using what Jackson calls *structure text*. Structure text represents the same information as structure diagrams (Figure 9.8)—sequence, selection, repetition—but does so in a textual format. The structure text for **button-1** is

```
BUTTON-1
    read BD;
    PUSH-BDY itr while BD
        PUSH;
        read DB;
    PUSH-BDY end
BUTTON-1 end
```

The structure of BUTTON-1 corresponds identically to the structure of BUTTON-0, with the addition of *read* operations that connect the real world to the system.

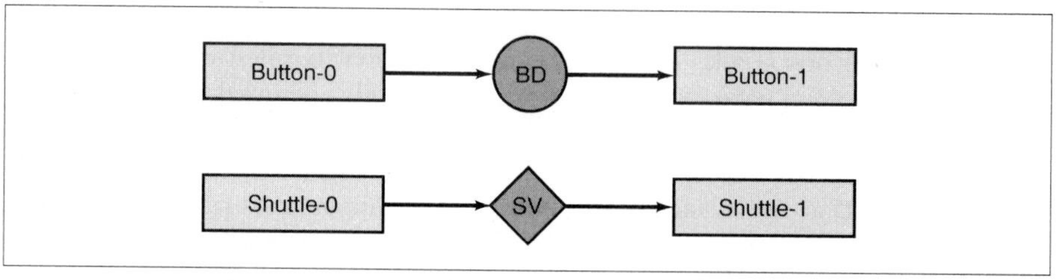

FIGURE 9.11.
An SSD for USS.

As noted earlier, the SHUTTLE-1 process cannot be connected to its real world counterpart by a data stream connection. Instead, we must interrogate the switches that are turned on/off by the arrival/departure of the shuttle at a station. The system process must inspect the real-world entity frequently enough to ensure that no actions pass undetected. This is accomplished by executing a *getsv* (get state vector) operation that obtains the state vector of the real world entity. It is likely that the system process will obtain each value of the state vector a number of times before it is changed, and the model process can be elaborated to show these "in transit" values of the state vectors. A structure text description of SHUTTLE-1 follows:

```
SHUTTLE-1 seq
    getsv SV;
    WAIT-BDY itr while WAIT1
        getsv SV;
    WAIT-BDY end
    LEAVE (1);
    TRANSIT-BDY1 itr while TRANSIT1
        getsv SV;
    TRANSIT-BDY1 end
    SHUTTLE-BDY1 itr
        STATION seq
            ARRIVE (i);
            WAIT-BDY itr while WAITi
                getsv SV;
            WAIT-BDY end
            LEAVE (i);
            TRANSIT-BDY itr while TRANSITi
                getsv SV;
            TRANSIT-BDY end
        STATION end
    SHUTTLE-BDY end
    ARRIVE (1);
SHUTTLE-1 end
```

The state values WAIT and TRANSIT represent appropriate values of the arrival and departure switch. The real-world process SHUTTLE-0 pro-

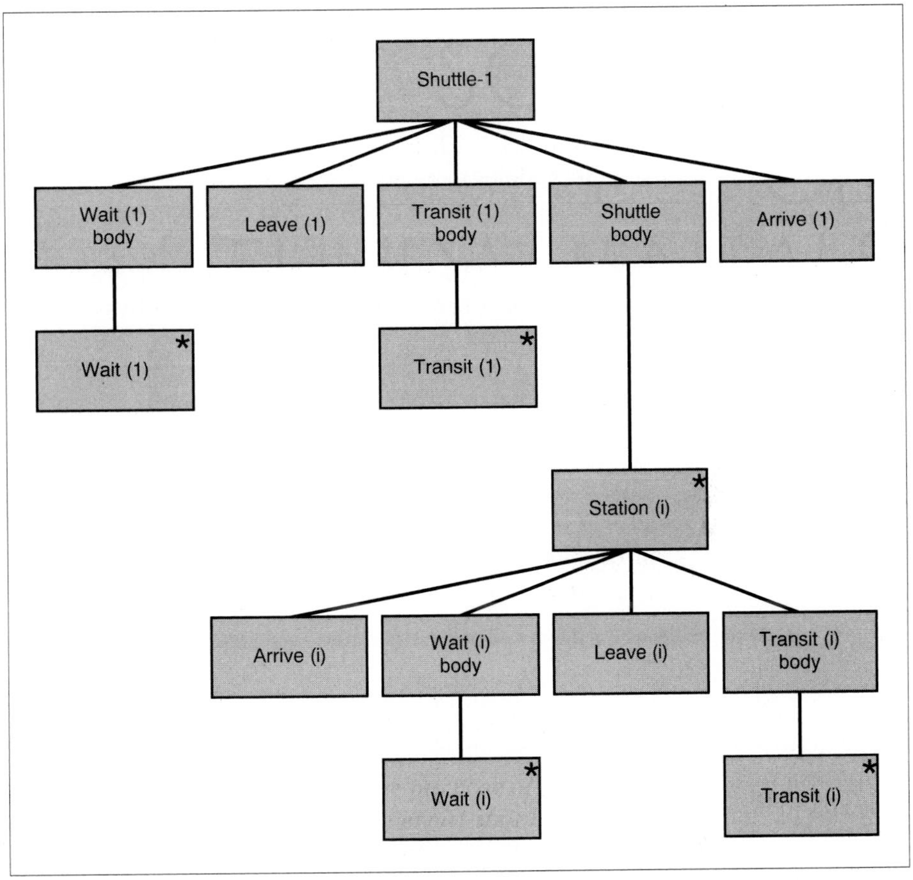

FIGURE 9.12. Structure diagram corresponding to structure text.

duces a change of state in the switch, and the system process SHUTTLE-1 executes *getsv* operations to sense this change. Figure 9.12 illustrates the structure text for SHUTTLE-1 as a structure diagram.

JSD continues with additional steps that allow the analyst to make the transition to software design. We postpone a discussion of these until Chapter 13. It is important to note, however, that the three JSD steps presented in this section provide an analysis and specification approach that is unique and, potentially, quite powerful.

9.5 SADT

Structured Analysis and Design Technique (SADT)[3] is a system analysis and design technique that has been widely used for system definition, soft-

[3]SADT is a trademark of Softech, Inc.

ware requirements analysis, and system/software design [ROS77, ROS85]. SADT consists of procedures that allow the analyst to decompose software (or system) functions; a graphical notation, the SADT *actigram* and *datagram*, that communicates the relationships of information (data and control) and function within software; and project control guidelines for applying the methodology.

Using SADT, the analyst develops a model comprised of many hierarchically defined actigrams and datagrams. A format for this notation is shown in Figure 9.13. An example of two SADT actigrams that describe a manufacturing process are depicted in Figures 9.14*a* and 9.14*b* [MAR88]. The actigram in Figure 9.14*a* is analogous to the context level model described in Chapter 7. It is expanded into a more detailed SADT model that is partially illustrated in Figure 9.14*b*. Each box within the actigram can be further refined in much the same way that a data flow diagram undergoes refinement.

The SADT methodology encompasses automated tools to support analysis procedures and a well-defined organizational harness through which the tools are applied. Reviews and milestones are specified, allowing validation of developer-customer communication. Staff responsibilities are similar to

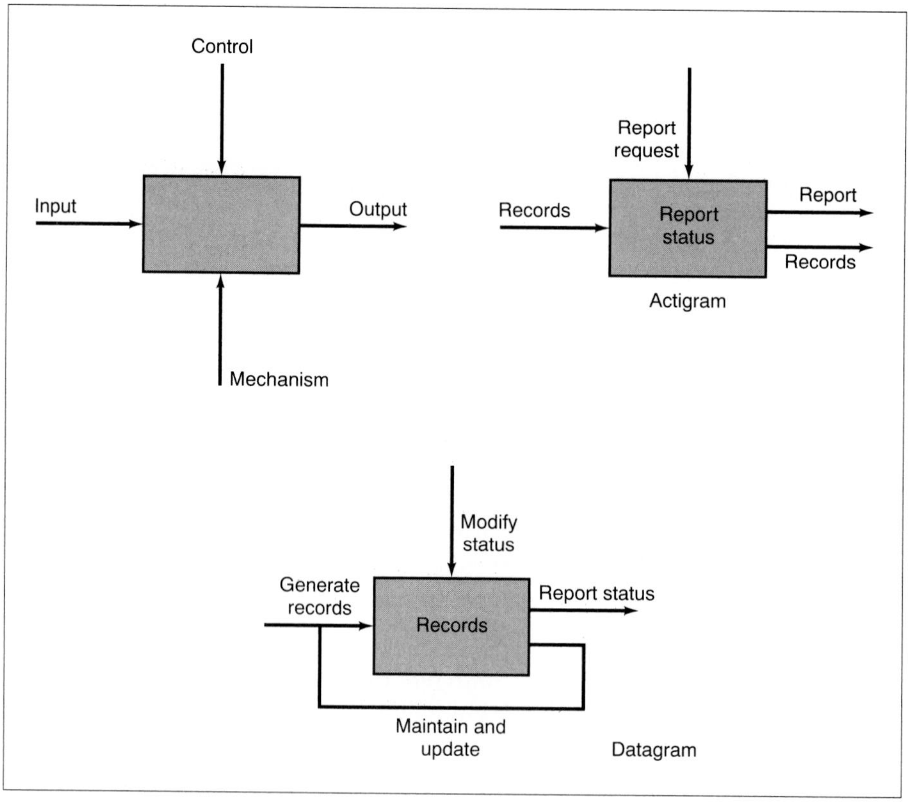

FIGURE 9.13. SADT diagrammatic notation.

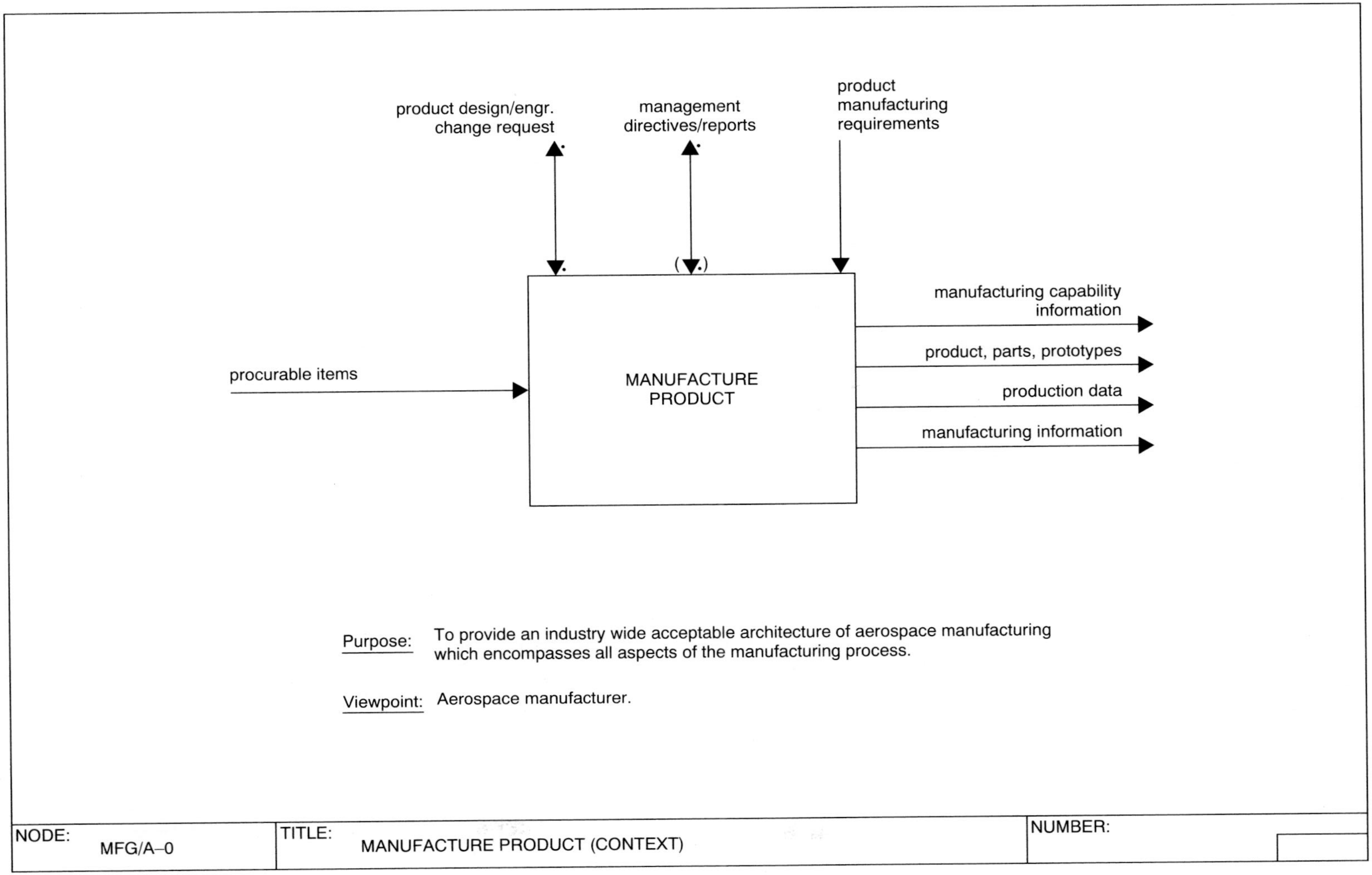

FIGURE 9.14*a*.
SADT context diagram [MAR88, p. 247]. Reproduced with permission.

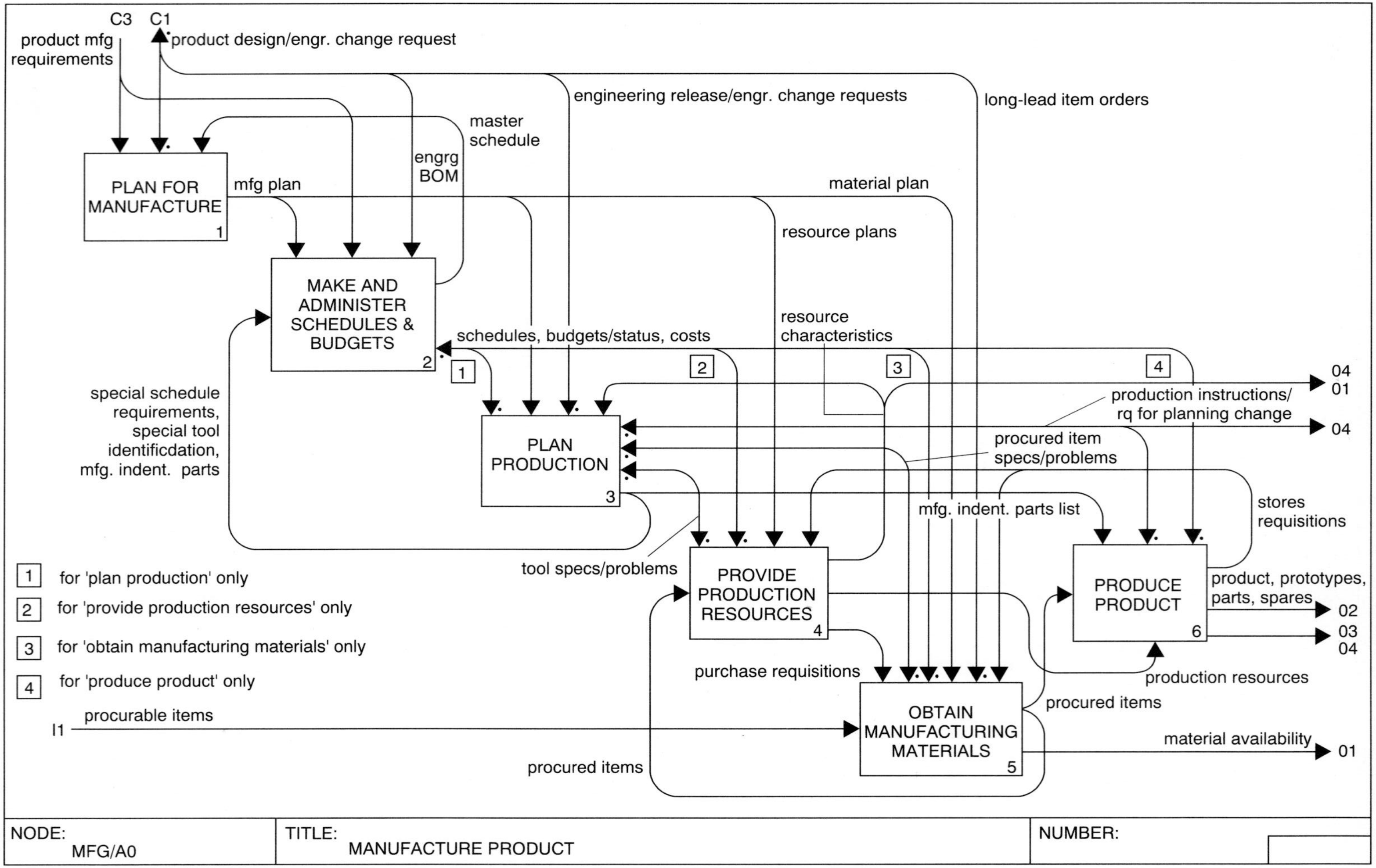

FIGURE 9.14*b*.
A refined SADT actigram [MAR88, p. 249]. Reproduced with permission.

those found for the chief programmer team (Chapter 4), stressing a team approach to analysis, design, and review.

9.6 FORMAL SPECIFICATION TECHNIQUES

Specification techniques can be categorized on a "formality" spectrum. The analysis methods that have been discussed in Chapters 7, 8, and the first part of this chapter fall at the informal end of the spectrum. A combination of diagrams, text, tables, and simple notation is used to describe and model software requirements.

We now consider the other end of the formality spectrum. Here, a specification is described using a formal syntax and semantics to specify system function and behavior. A formal specification is often mathematical in form (e.g., predicate calculus can be used as the basis for a formal specification language). In this and the section that follows, we explore formal methods for specification and examine their potential impact on software engineering in the years to come.

9.6.1 Current Status of Formal Methods

In his introductory discussion of formal methods, Anthony Hall [HAL90] states:

> Formal methods are controversial. Their advocates claim that they can revolutionize [software] development. Their detractors think they are impossibly difficult. Meanwhile, for most people, formal methods are so unfamiliar that it is difficult to judge the competing claims.

Formal methods enable a software engineer to specify, develop, and verify a computer-based system by applying a rigorous, mathematical notation. Using a *formal specification language,* a formal method provides a means for specifying a system so that consistency, completeness, and correctness can be assessed in a systematic fashion.

When formal methods are used during development, they provide a mechanism for eliminating many of the problems that we have discussed in earlier chapters. Ambiguity, incompleteness, and inconsistency can be discovered and corrected more easily—not through ad hoc review, but through the application of mathematical analysis. When formal methods are used during design, they serve as a basis for program verification and therefore enable the software engineer to discover and correct errors that might otherwise go undetected.

Part of the reason that formal methods show promise as a new approach to specification and design problems is that they make the software engineer consider a software problem in a manner that is analogous to an algebraic derivation or a proof in analytical geometry. The rigor of a mathematical description (see Section 9.6.3) forces the specifier to think more carefully about the problem at hand.

9.6.2 The Attributes of Formal Specification Languages

A formal specification language is usually composed of three primary components: (1) a *syntax* that defines the specific notation with which the specification is represented, (2) a *semantics* that helps to define a "universe of objects" [WIN90] that will be used to describe the system, and (3) a set of *relations* that defines the rules that indicate which objects properly satisfy the specification.

The syntactic domain of a formal specification language is often based on a syntax that is derived from standard set theory notation and predicate calculus.[4] For example, *variables* such as x, y, and z describe a set of objects that relate to a problem (sometimes called the *domain of discourse*) and are used in conjunction with *logic symbols* such as $\forall$, $\exists$, $\neg$, $\wedge$, $\vee$, that mean *for all, there exists, not, and,* and *or,* respectively. Although the syntax is usually symbolic, icons (e.g., graphical symbols such as boxes, arrows, and circles) can also be used, if they are unambiguous.

The semantic domain of a specification language indicates how the language represents system requirements. For example, a programming language has a set of formal semantics that enables the software developer to specify algorithms that transform input to output. A formal grammar (such as BNF) can be used to describe the syntax of the programming language. However, a programming language does not make a good specification language because it can represent only computable functions. A specification language must have a semantic domain that is broader; that is, the semantic domain of a specification language must be capable of expressing ideas such as "For all x in an infinite set A, there exists a y in an infinite set B such that the property P holds for x and y" [WIN90]. Other specification languages apply a semantic domain that enables the specification of system behavior. For example, a syntax and semantics can be developed to specify states and state transition, events and their affect on state transition, synchronization, and timing.

It is possible to use different semantic abstractions to describe the same system in different ways. We did this in a less formal fashion in Chapter 7. Data flow and corresponding processing were described using the data flow diagram, and system behavior was depicted with the state transition diagram. Both graphical notations represented the same system, but the se-

---

[4]Predicate calculus is a mathematical language for the expression of logical statements. For additional information, see Wiltala [WIL87].

mantics of the representation provided a different, but complementary, view. To illustrate this approach when formal methods are used, assume that a formal specification language is used to describe the set of events that causes a particular state to occur in a system. Another formal relation depicts all functions that occur within a given state. The intersection of these two relations provides an indication of the events that will cause specific functions to occur.

The desired properties of a formal specification—lack of ambiguity, consistency, and completeness—are the objectives of all specification methods. However, the use of formal methods results in a much higher likelihood of achieving these ideals. The formal syntax of a specification language enables requirements or design to be interpreted in only one way, eliminating ambiguity that often occurs when a natural language (e.g., English) or a graphical notation must be interpreted by a reader. The descriptive facilities of set theory and logic notation enable the clear statement of facts (requirements). To be consistent, facts stated in one place in a specification should not be contradicted in another place. Consistency is ensured by mathematically proving that initial facts can be formally mapped (using inference rules) into later statements within the specification.

Completeness is difficult to achieve, even when formal methods are used. Some aspects of a system may be left undefined as the specification is being created; other characteristics may be purposely omitted to allow designers some freedom in choosing an implementation approach; and finally, it is impossible to consider every operational scenario in a large, complex system. Things may simply be omitted by mistake.

A variety of formal specification languages are in use today. For example, the Z specification language [SPI88] enables the representation of reasonably complex programs using a notation described in Section 9.6. The Z specification language is coupled with an automated tool called a "proof assistant" that stores axioms, rules of inference, and application-oriented theorems that lead to mathematical *proof of correctness* of the specification [WOO89]. The *Vienna development method* (VDM) [JON90], *Larch* [GUT85], and *Communicating Sequential Processes* (CSP) [HOR85, MOR90] are representative of other formal specification languages that have achieved notoriety in the research community.

9.7 A FORMAL SPECIFICATION IN Z

To illustrate the practical use of a specification language, Spivey [SPI90] considers a real-time operating system kernel and represents some of its basic characteristics using the Z specification language [SPI88]. The paragraphs below and Section 9.7.1–9.7.5 have been adapted from Spivey [SPI90] with permission of the IEEE.

****

Embedded systems are commonly built around a small operating-system kernel that provides process-scheduling and interrupt-handling facilities. The following reports on a case study made using Z notation, a mathematical specification language, to specify the kernel for a diagnostic x-ray machine.

Beginning with the documentation and source code of an existing implementation, a mathematical model, expressed in Z, was constructed of the states that the kernel could occupy and the events that could take it from one state to another. The goal was a precise specification that could be used as a basis for a new implementation on different hardware.

This case study in specification had a surprising byproduct. In studying one of the kernel's operations, the potential for deadlock was discovered: The kernel would disable interrupts and enter a tight loop, vainly searching for a process ready to run.

This flaw in the kernel's design was reflected directly in a mathematical property of its specification, demonstrating how formal techniques can help avoid design errors. This help should be especially welcome in embedded systems, which are notoriously difficult to test effectively.

A conversation with the kernel designer later revealed that, for two reasons, the design error did not in fact endanger patients using the x-ray machine. Nevertheless, the error seriously affected the x-ray machine's robustness and reliability because later enhancements to the controlling software might reveal the problem with deadlock that had been hidden before.

The specification presented here has been simplified by making less use of the schema calculus, a way of structuring Z specifications. This has made the specification a little longer and more repetitive, but perhaps a little easier to follow without knowledge of Z.

9.7.1 About the Kernel

The kernel supports both background processes and interrupt handlers. There may be several background processes, and one may be marked as current. This process runs whenever no interrupts are active, and it remains current until it explicitly releases the processor; the kernel may then select another process to be current. Each background process has a ready flag, and the kernel chooses the new current process from among those with a ready flag set to true.

When interrupts are active, the kernel chooses the most urgent according to a numerical priority, and the interrupt handler for that priority runs. An interrupt may become active if it has a higher priority than those already active and it becomes inactive again when its handler signals that it has finished. A background process may become an interrupt handler by registering itself as the handler for a certain priority.

9.7.2 Documentation

Figures 9.15 and 9.16 are diagrams from the existing kernel documentation, typical of the ones used to describe kernels like this. Figure 9.15 shows the kernel data structures. Figure 9.16 shows the states that a single process may occupy and the possible transitions between them, caused either by a kernel call from the process itself or by some other event.

In a way, Figure 9.16 is a partial specification of the kernel as a set of finite-state machines, one for each process. However, it gives no explicit information about the interactions between processes—the very thing the kernel is required to manage. Also, it fails to show several possible states of a process. For example, the current background process may not be ready if it has set its own ready flag to false, but the state "current but not ready" is not shown in the diagram. Correcting this defect would require adding two

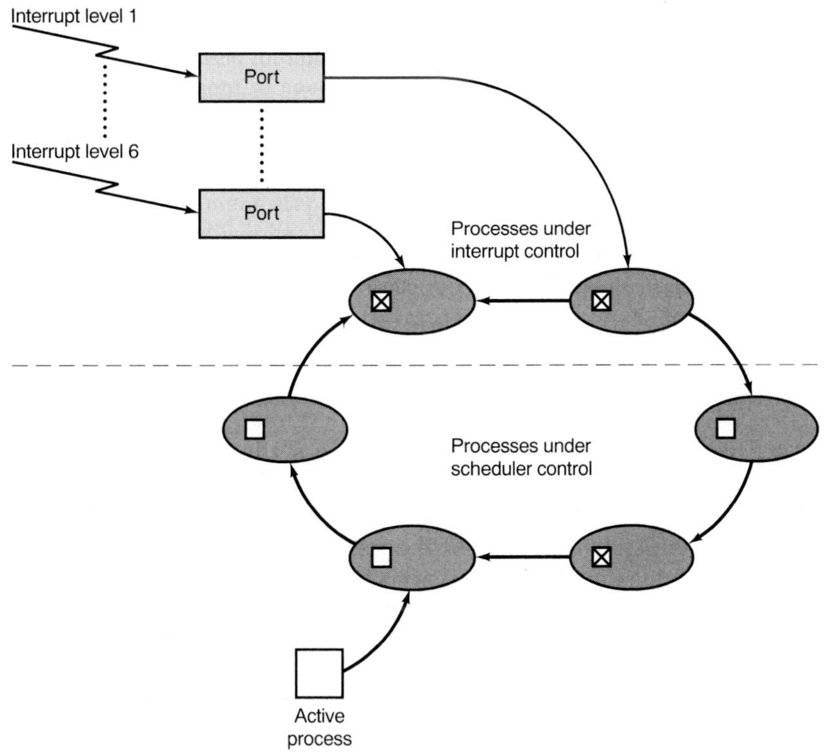

Processes, shown as ovals, are linked in a ring. The processes above the horizontal dotted line are the interrupt handlers and those below it are the background processes. The ready flag for each process is shown as a small square.

FIGURE 9.15. Data structures for OS kernel.

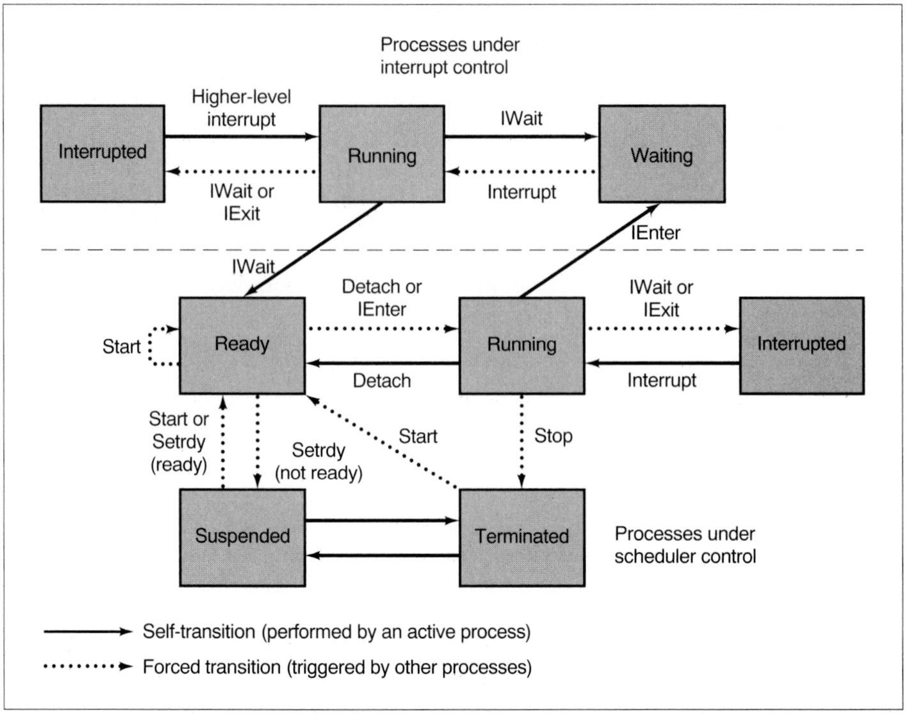

FIGURE 9.16. State transition diagram for OS kernel.

more states and seven more transitions. This highlights another deficiency of state diagrams like this: Their size tends to grow exponentially as system complexity increases.

9.7.3 Kernel States

Like most Z specifications, the kernel model begins with a description of the *state space,* the collection of variables that determine what state the kernel is in and the invariant relationships that always hold between these variables' values.

Here, the kernel state space is described in several parts, corresponding to the background processes, the interrupt handlers, and the state of the processor on which the kernel runs. Each piece is described by a *schema,* the basic unit of specification in Z. Table 9.1 describes the Z notation used in this case study.

The state space of the whole kernel is obtained by putting together these pieces and adding more invariants, among them the static policy for allocating the processor to a background process or interrupt handler. Processes are named in the kernel by *process identifiers* (PID). In the implemented kernel, these are the addresses of process-control blocks, but this detail

TABLE 9.1

SUMMARY OF Z NOTATION

Z notation is based on typed set theory and first-order logic. Z provides a construct, called a *schema*, to describe a specification's state space and operations. A schema groups variable declarations with a list of predicates that constrain the possible values of a variable. In Z, the schema *X* is defined by the form

```
——X——————————————————————
declarations
—————————————————————————
predicates
—————————————————————————
```

Global functions and constants are defined by the form

```
declarations
—————————————————————————
predicates
```

The declaration gives the type of the function or constant, while the predicate gives its value. Only those Z symbols used in Section 9.7 are included in this table.

Sets	
S: $\mathbb{P}\,X$	*S* is declared as a set of *X*'s.
$x \in S$	*x* is a member of *S*.
$x \notin S$	*x* is not a member of *S*.
$S \subseteq T$	*S* is a subset of *T*: Every member of *S* is also in *T*.
$S \cup T$	The union of *S* and *T*: It contains every member of *S* or *T* or both.
$S \cap T$	The intersection of *S* and *T*: It contains every member of both *S* and *T*.
$S \setminus T$	The difference of *S* and *T*: It contains every member of *S* except those also in *T*.
$\varnothing$	Empty set: It contains no members.
$\{x\}$	Singleton set: It contains just *x*.
$\mathbb{N}$	The set of natural numbers 0, 1, 2, ...
S: $\mathbb{F}\,X$	*S* is declared as a finite set of *X*'s.
max (*S*)	The maximum of the nonempty set of numbers *S*.
Functions	
$f: X \rightarrowtail\!\!\!\!\!+\!\!\!\!\rightarrow Y$	*f* is declared as a partial injection from *X* to *Y*.
dom *f*	The domain of *f*: The set of values *x* for which *f*(*x*) is defined.
ran *f*	The range of *f*: The set of values taken by *f*(*x*) as *x* varies over the domain of *f*.
$f \oplus \{x \mapsto y\}$	A function that agrees with *f* except that *x* is mapped to *y*.
$\{x\} \lhd f$	A function like *f*, except that *x* is removed from its domain.
Logic	
$P \wedge Q$	*P* and *Q*: It is true if both *P* and *Q* are true.
$P \Rightarrow Q$	*P* implies *Q*: It is true if either *Q* is true or *P* is false.
$\theta_{S'} = \theta_S$	No components of schema *S* change in an operation.

is irrelevant to a programmer using the kernel, so they are introduced as a basic-type PID:

$$[\mathrm{PID}]$$

This declaration introduces PID as the name of a set, without giving any information about its members. From the specification's point of view, the members are simply atomic objects.

For convenience, a fictitious process identifier, *none,* was introduced. *None* is not the name of any genuine process. When the processor is idle, the current process is *none*. The set PID_1 contains all process identifiers except *none:*

$$\begin{array}{l} none\colon \mathrm{PID} \\ \mathrm{PID}_1\colon \mathbb{P}\ \mathrm{PID} \\ \hline \mathrm{PID}_1 = \mathrm{PID} \setminus \{none\} \end{array}$$

The part of the kernel state concerned with background processes is described by this schema:

$$\begin{array}{l} \text{—— Scheduler ——} \\ background\colon \mathbb{P}\ PID_1 \\ ready\colon \mathbb{P}\ PID_1 \\ current\colon PID \\ \hline ready \subseteq background \\ current \in background \cup \{none\} \\ \hline \end{array}$$

Like all schema, this one declares some typed variables and states a relationship between them. Above the horizontal dividing line, in the *declaration* part, the three variables are declared:

- *background* is the set of processes under control of the scheduler.
- *ready* is the set of processes that may be selected for execution when the processor becomes free.
- *current* is the process selected for execution in the background.

Below the line, in the predicate part, the schema states two relationships that always hold. The set *ready* is always a subset of *background,* and *current* is either a member of *background* or the fictitious process *none.* This schema lets the current process be not *ready,* because no relationship between *current* and *ready* is specified.

This schema does not reflect the full significance of the set *ready,* but its real meaning will be shown later in the *Select* operation, where it forms the pool from which a new current process is chosen.

Interrupts are identified by their priority levels, which are small positive integers. The finite set *ILEVEL* includes all the priorities:

$$\frac{\text{ILEVEL: } \mathbb{F}\, \mathbb{N}}{0 \notin \text{ILEVEL}}$$

Zero is not one of the interrupt priority levels, but it is the priority associated with background processes.

The state space for the interrupt-handling (*IntHandler*) part of the kernel is described like this:

```
——————IntHandler——————
handler: ILEVEL >+> PID_1
enabled, active: P ILEVEL
——————————————————————
enabled ∪ active ⊆ dom handler
——————————————————————
```

This schema declares the three variables:

- *handler* is a function that associates certain priority levels with processes, the interrupt handlers for those priorities.
- *enabled* is the set of priority levels that are enabled, so an interrupt can happen at that priority.
- *active* is the set of priority levels for which an interrupt is being handled.

The predicate part of this schema says that each priority level that is either enabled or active must be associated with a handler. An interrupt may be active without being enabled if, for example, it has been disabled by the handler itself since becoming active. The declaration

$$handler\colon ILEVEL \rightarrowtail\!\!\!\!\!+\; PID_1$$

declares handler to be a partial injection. It is partial in that not every priority level need be associated with an interrupt handler and it is an injection in that no two distinct priority levels may share the same handler.

Information like this—that interrupts may be active without being enabled and that different priority levels may not share a handler—is vital to understanding how the kernel works. It is especially valuable because it is static information about what states the kernel may occupy rather than information about what happens as the system moves from state to state. Such static information is often absent from the text of the program, which consists mostly of dynamic, executable code.

The state space of the whole kernel combines the background and interrupt parts:

```
──────── Kernel ────────────────
  Scheduler
  IntHandler
────────────────────────────────
  background ∩ ran handler = ∅
────────────────────────────────
```

The declarations *Scheduler* and *IntHandler* in this schema implicitly include above the line all the declarations from those schemas and implicitly include below the line all their invariants. So the schema *Kernel* has six variables: *background, ready,* and *current* from *Scheduler,* and *handler, enabled,* and *active* for *IntHandler.*

The additional invariant has been added so that no process can be both background process and an interrupt handler at the same time.

The main job of the kernel is to control which process the processor runs and at what priority. Therefore, the *running* process and the processor *priority* have been made part of the state of the system. Here is a schema that declares them:

```
──────── CPU ────────────────
  running: PID
  priority: ILEVEL ∪ {0}
─────────────────────────────
```

This schema has an empty predicate part, so it places no restriction on the values of its variables, except that each must be a member of its type. The variable *running* takes the value *none* when no process is running.

Of course, there are many other parts of the processor state, including the contents of registers and memory, condition codes, and so on, but they are irrelevant in this context.

Because the kernel always uses the same scheduling policy to select the running process and the central processing unit (CPU) priority, this policy is another invariant of the system. It is stated in the schema *State,* which combines the kernel and CPU parts of the system state:

```
──────── State ─────────────────────────────
  Kernel
  CPU
────────────────────────────────────────────
  priority = max (active ∪ {0})
  priority = 0 ⟹ running = current
  priority > 0 ⟹ running = handler (priority)
────────────────────────────────────────────
```

If any interrupts are active, the processor *priority* is the highest priority of an active interrupt, and the processor runs the interrupt handler for that priority. Otherwise, the processor runs the current background process at priority zero.

The invariant part of this schema uniquely determines *priority* and *running* in terms of *active, current,* and *handler,* three variables of the schema *Kernel*. This fact will be exploited when the events that change the system state are described. With the description of the kernel's and processor's state space complete, the next step is to look at the operations and events that can change the state.

9.7.4 Background Processing

Some kernel operations affect only the background processing part of the state space. They start background processes, set and clear their ready flags, let them release the processor temporarily or permanently, and select a new process to run when the processor is idle.

A process enters the control of the scheduler through the operation *Start,* described by this schema:

Start

$\Delta State$
$p?: PID_1$

$p? \notin \text{ran } handler$
$background' = background \cup \{p?\}$
$ready' = ready \cup \{p?\}$
$current' = current$
$\Theta_{IntHandler'} = \Theta_{IntHandler}$

Like all schemas describing operations, this one includes the declaration $\Delta State$, which implicitly declares two copies of each variable in the state space *State,* one with a prime (′) and one without. Variables like *background* and *ready* without a prime refer to the system state before the operation has happened, and variables like *background′* and *ready′* refer to the state afterward.

The declaration $\Delta State$ also implicitly constrains these variables to obey the invariant relationships that were documented in defining the schema *State*—including the scheduling policy—so they hold both before and after the operation.

In addition to these state variables, the *Start* operation has an input *p?*, the identifier of the process to be started. By convention, inputs to operations are given names that end in a ?.

The predicate part of an operation schema lists the precondition that must be true when the operation is invoked and postcondition that must be true afterward. In this case, the precondition is explicitly stated: that the process *p?* being started must not be an interrupt handler (because that would violate the invariant that background processes are disjoint from interrupt handlers).

In general, an operation's precondition is that a final state exists that satisfies the predicates written in the schema. Part of the precondition may be implicit in the predicates that relate the initial and final states. If an operation is specified by the schema *Op*, its precondition can be calculated as

$$\exists State \cdot Op$$

If the precondition is true, the specification requires that the operation should terminate in a state satisfying the postcondition. On the other hand, if the precondition is false when the operation is invoked, the specification says nothing about what happens. The operation may fail to terminate, or the kernel may stop working completely.

For the *Start* operation, the postcondition says that the new process is added to the set of background processes and marked as ready to run. The new process does not start to run immediately, because *current* is unchanged; instead, the processor continues to run the same process as before.

The final equation in the postcondition

$$\Theta_{Inthandler'} = \Theta_{Inthandler}$$

means that the part of the state described by the schema *IntHandler* is the same after the operation as before it.

The equation in this schema determines the final values of the six variables in the kernel state space in terms of their initial values and the inputs *p?*, but they say nothing about the final values of the CPU variables *running* and *priority*. These are determined by the requirements, implicit in the declaration $\Delta State$, that the scheduling policy be obeyed after the operation has finished. Because the values of *active, handler,* and *current* do not change in the operation, neither does the CPU state.

The current background process may release the processor by calling the *Detach* operation, specified like this:

———— *Detach* ————

$\Delta State$

————————————

$running \in background$
$background' = background$
$ready' = ready$
$current' = none$
$\Theta_{IntHandler'} = \Theta_{IntHandler}$

————————————

Another kernel operation, *IExit*, lets an interrupt handler cancel its registration:

$$
\begin{array}{l}
\textit{IExit} \\
\hline
\Delta \textit{State} \\
\hline
\textit{priority} > 0 \\
\textit{background}' = \textit{background} \cup \{\textit{handler}(\textit{priority})\} \\
\textit{ready}' = \textit{ready} \cup \{\textit{handler}\ (\textit{priority})\} \\
\textit{current}' = \textit{current} \\
\textit{handler}' = \{\textit{priority}\} \lhd \textit{handler} \\
\textit{enabled}' = \textit{enabled} \setminus \{\textit{priority}\} \\
\text{active}' = \text{active} \setminus \{\textit{priority}\} \\
\hline
\end{array}
$$

Again, the processor must be running an interrupt handler. This handler leaves the interrupt-handling part of the kernel and becomes a background process again, marked as ready to run. As with *IWait,* the processor returns to the interrupt handler with the next highest priority or to the current background process. The process that called *IWait* is suspended until the scheduler selects it for execution. In this schema, the expression

$$\{\textit{priority}\} \lhd \textit{handler}$$

denotes a function identical to handler except that priority has been removed from its domain; it is an injection provided that handler is one.

Two more kernel operations, *Mask* and *Unmask,* let interrupt priorities be selectively disabled and enabled. Their specifications are like *SetReady,* so they have been omitted. The kernel specification is now complete.

9.7.6 Formal Methods—The Road Ahead

Although formal, mathematically based specification techniques are not as yet used widely in the industry, they do offer substantial advantages over less formal techniques. Liskov and Berzins [LIS86] summarize these in the following way:

> Formal specifications can be studied mathematically while informal specifications cannot. For example, a correct program can be proved to meet its specifications, or two alternative sets of specifications can be proved equivalent.... Certain forms of incompleteness or inconsistency can be detected automatically.

In addition, formal specification removes ambiguity and encourages greater rigor in the early stages of the software engineering process.

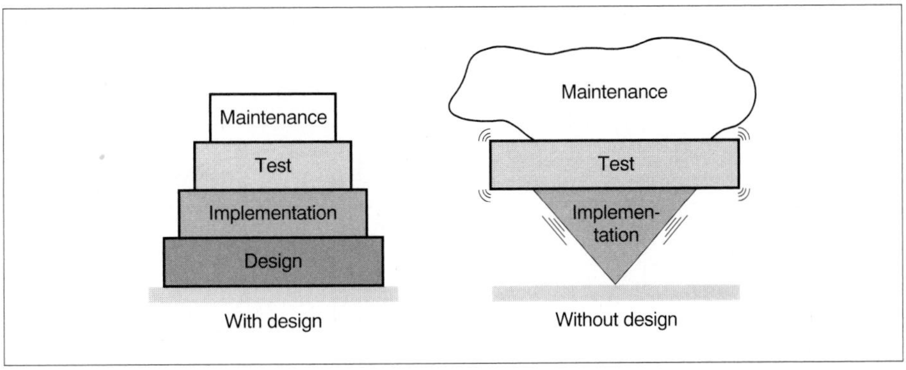

Again, this operation is described using $\Delta State$ variables before and after the operation has happened. The precondition is that the process is running a background process. The only change specified in the postcondition is that the current process changes to none, meaning that the processor is now idle. The next event will be either an interrupt or the selection of a new background process or run.

After a call to *Detach*—and after other operations described later—*current* has values *none,* indicating that no background process has been selected for execution. If no interrupts are active, the processor is idle, and the *Select* operation may happen spontaneously. It is specified like this:

$$
\begin{array}{l}
\hline
\textit{Select} \\
\Delta State \\
\hline
running = none \\
background' = background \\
ready' = ready \\
current' \in ready \\
\Theta_{IntHandler'} = \Theta_{IntHandler} \\
\hline
\end{array}
$$

Rather than a part of the interface between the kernel and an application, *Select* is an internal operation of the kernel that can happen whenever its precondition is true. The precondition is

$$running = none \land ready \neq \varnothing$$

The processor must be idle, and at least one background process must be ready to run. The first part of this precondition is stated explicitly, and the second part is implicit in the predicate

$$current' \in ready$$

The new value of *current* is selected from *ready,* but the specification does not say how the choice is made—it is nondeterministic. This nondeterminism lets the specification say exactly what programmers may rely on the kernel to do: There is no guarantee that processes will be scheduled in a particular order.

In fact, the nondeterminism is a natural consequence of the abstract view taken in the specification. Although the program that implements this specification is deterministic—if started with the ring of processes in a certain state, it will always select the same process—it appears to be nondeterministic if the *set* of processes that are ready is considered, as has been done in the specification.

However, the kernel selects the new current process, the specification says that it starts to run, because of the static scheduling policy, which determines that, after the operation, *running* is *current* and *priority* is zero.

A background process may terminate itself using the *Stop* operation:

$$
\begin{array}{l}
\text{—— } Stop \text{ ——} \\
\Delta State \\
\hline
running \in background \\
background' = background \setminus \{current\} \\
ready' = ready \setminus \{current\} \\
current' = none \\
\Theta_{IntHandler'} = \Theta_{IntHandler} \\
\hline
\end{array}
$$

For this operation to be permissible, the processor must be running a background process. This process is removed from *background* and *ready*, and the current process becomes *none*, so the next action will be to select another process.

A final operation, *SetReady*, sets or clears a process's ready flag. It has two inputs, the process identifier and a flag, which takes one of the values *set* or *clear*:

$$\mathrm{FLAG} ::= set \setminus clear$$

The *SetReady* operation is:

$$
\begin{array}{l}
\text{—— } SetReady \text{ ——} \\
\Delta State \\
p?: PID \\
flag?: FLAG \\
\hline
p? \in background \\
flag? = set \Rightarrow ready' = ready \cup \{p?\} \\
flag? = clear \Rightarrow ready' = ready \setminus \{p?\} \\
background' = background \\
current' = current \\
\Theta_{IntHandler'} = \Theta_{IntHandler} \\
\hline
\end{array}
$$

The precondition is that *p?* is a background process; according to the value of *flag?*, it is either inserted in *ready* or removed from it. The scheduling parameters do not change, so there is no change in the running process.

9.7.5 Interrupt handling

Other operations affect the kernel's interrupt-handling part. A background process may register itself as the handler for a certain priority level by calling the operation *IEnter:*

$$\begin{array}{l}
\hline
\textit{IEnter} \\
\Delta State \\
i?: ILEVEL \\
\hline
running \in background \\
background' = background \setminus \{current\} \\
ready' = ready \setminus \{current\} \\
current' = none \\
handler' = handler \oplus \{i? \mapsto current\} \\
enabled' = enabled \cup \{i?\} \\
\text{active}' = \text{active} \\
\hline
\end{array}$$

This operation may be called only by a background process. The operation removes the calling process from *background* and *ready,* and the new value of current is *none,* just as in the *Stop* operation. Also, the calling process becomes an interrupt handler for the priority level *i?*, given as an input to the operation, and that priority level becomes enabled. The expression

$$handler \oplus \{i? \mapsto current\}$$

denotes a function identical to *handler,* except that *i?* is mapped to *current.* This function is an injection, because *current,* a background process, cannot already be the handler for any other priority level. The new handler supersedes any existing handler for priority *i?*, which can never run again unless restarted with the *Start* operation.

Once a process has registered itself as an interrupt handler, the scheduler chooses a new process to run in the background, and the new interrupt handler waits for an interrupt to happen:

$$\begin{array}{l}
\hline
\textit{Interrupt} \\
\Delta State \\
i?: ILEVEL \\
\hline
i? \in enabled \wedge i? > priority \\
\theta_{Scheduler'} = \theta_{Scheduler} \\
handler' = handler \\
enabled' = enabled \\
\text{active}' = \text{active} \cup \{i?\} \\
\hline
\end{array}$$

The process hardware ensures that interrupts happen only when they are enabled and have a priority greater than the processor priority. If these conditions are satisfied, the interrupt can happen and the kernel then adds the interrupt to *active.*

The scheduling policy ensures that the associated interrupt handler starts to run. In this calculation of the processor priority, each step is justified by the comment in brackets:

$$
\begin{aligned}
& \mathit{Priority}' \\
= & \text{ [scheduling policy]} \\
& \quad \max(\mathit{active}' \cup \{0\}) \\
= & \text{ [postcondition]} \\
& \quad \max((\mathit{active} \cup \{i?\}) \cup \{0\}) \\
= & \text{ [}\cup\text{ assoc. and comm.]} \\
& \quad \max((\mathit{active} \cup \{0\}) \cup \{i?\}) \\
= & \text{ [max dist. over }\cup\text{]} \\
& \quad \max\{\max(\mathit{active} \cup \{0\}), i?\} \\
= & \text{ [scheduling policy]} \\
& \quad \max\{\mathit{priority}, i?\} \\
= & \text{ [}i? > \text{priority]} \\
& \quad i?
\end{aligned}
$$

So priority$' = i? > 0$ and the other part of the scheduling policy ensures that *running'* equals handler $(i?)$.

After the interrupt handler has finished the processing associated with the interrupt, it calls the kernel operation *IWait* and suspends itself until another interrupt arrives. *IWait* is specified as

$$
\begin{array}{|l}
\hline
\textit{IWait} \\
\Delta \mathit{State} \\
\hline
\mathit{priority} > 0 \\
\theta_{\mathit{Scheduler}'} = \theta_{\mathit{Scheduler}} \\
\mathit{handler}' = \mathit{handler} \\
\mathit{enabled}' = \mathit{enabled} \\
\text{active}' = \text{active} \setminus \{\mathit{priority}\} \\
\hline
\end{array}
$$

The precondition *priority* > 0 means that the processor must be running an interrupt handler. The current priority level is removed from *active*, and as for the *Interrupt* operation, the scheduling policy determines what happens next. If any other interrupts are active, the processor returns to the interrupt handler with the next highest priority. Otherwise, it returns to the current background process.

Another kernel operation, *IExit,* lets an interrupt handler cancel its registration:

$$
\begin{array}{l}
\textit{IExit} \\
\hline
\Delta State \\
\hline
priority > 0 \\
background' = background \cup \{handler(priority)\} \\
ready' = ready \cup \{handler\ (priority)\} \\
current' = current \\
handler' = \{priority\} \lhd handler \\
enabled' = enabled \backslash \{priority\} \\
\text{active}' = \text{active} \backslash \{priority\} \\
\hline
\end{array}
$$

Again, the processor must be running an interrupt handler. This handler leaves the interrupt-handling part of the kernel and becomes a background process again, marked as ready to run. As with *IWait,* the processor returns to the interrupt handler with the next highest priority or to the current background process. The process that called *IWait* is suspended until the scheduler selects it for execution. In this schema, the expression

$$\{priority\} \lhd handler$$

denotes a function identical to handler except that priority has been removed from its domain; it is an injection provided that handler is one.

Two more kernel operations, *Mask* and *Unmask,* let interrupt priorities be selectively disabled and enabled. Their specifications are like *SetReady,* so they have been omitted. The kernel specification is now complete.

9.7.6 Formal Methods—The Road Ahead

Although formal, mathematically based specification techniques are not as yet used widely in the industry, they do offer substantial advantages over less formal techniques. Liskov and Berzins [LIS86] summarize these in the following way:

> Formal specifications can be studied mathematically while informal specifications cannot. For example, a correct program can be proved to meet its specifications, or two alternative sets of specifications can be proved equivalent.... Certain forms of incompleteness or inconsistency can be detected automatically.

In addition, formal specification removes ambiguity and encourages greater rigor in the early stages of the software engineering process.

But problems remain. Formal specification focuses primarily on function and data. Timing, control, and behavioral aspects of a problem are more difficult to represent. In addition, there are elements of a problem (e.g., human-machine interfaces) that are better specified using graphical techniques or prototyping. Finally, specification using formal methods is difficult to learn and represents a significant "culture shock" for some software practitioners. For this reason, it is likely that formal, mathematical specification techniques will form the foundation for a future generation of CASE tools (already, some CASE tools that use formal specification languages as their foundations are in use), but the notation described above will not be widely used by software engineers.[5]

9.8 AUTOMATED TECHNIQUES FOR REQUIREMENTS ANALYSIS

Automated techniques for requirements analysis may be categorized in a number of different ways. Some "automated techniques" are nothing more than a manual method that has been complemented by an automated CASE tool. The tool automates the generation and maintenance of what was originally a stack of paper and typically makes use of a graphical notation for analysis. This class of tools produces diagrams, aids in problem partitioning, maintains a hierarchy of information about the system, and applies heuristics to uncover problems with the specification. More importantly, such tools enable the analyst to update information and track the connections between new and existing representations of the system. For example, CASE tools such as *DEC Design* (Digital Equipment Corp.), *DesignAid* (Transform Logic Corp.), *Excelerator* (Index Technology), *IEF* (Texas Instruments), *IEW* (Knowledgeware), *STP* (Interactive Development Environments) *Teamwork* (Cadre Technologies), and many others enable the analyst to generate flow diagrams and a data dictionary (Chapter 7) and maintain these in a database that can be analyzed for correctness, consistency, and completeness. In fact, the true benefit of this, and most automated requirements tools, is in the "intelligent processing" that the tool applies to the problem specification.

Another class of automated requirements analysis techniques makes use of a special notation (in most cases this is a requirements specification language) that has been explicitly designed for processing using an automated tool. Requirements are described with a specification language that combines keyword indicators with a natural language (e.g., English) narrative. The specification language is fed to a processor that produces a requirements specification and, more importantly, a set of diagnostic reports about the consistency and organization of the specification.

[5] It is important to note that others disagree. In Chapter 17, we will discuss this matter further.

In this section, we present an overview of some of the more important automated requirements analysis techniques that fall into the second category discussed above. Tools in the first category are discussed in Chapter 22. It is important to note that the techniques and tools presented below are representative. Many other tools exist, and an entirely new generation of "expert" or knowledge-based analysis tools is on the horizon.

9.8.1 Software Requirements Engineering Methodology

Software Requirements Engineering Methodology (SREM) [ALF85] is an automated requirements analysis tool that makes use of a *requirements statement language,* RSL, to describe elements, attributes, relationships, and structures. *Elements* (in SREM terminology) comprise a set of objects and concepts that are used to develop a requirements specification. *Relationships* between objects are specified as part of RSL, and *attributes* are used to modify or qualify elements. *Structures* are used to describe information flow. These RSL primitives are combined with narrative information to form the detail of a requirements specification.

The power of an automated requirements tool may be measured by the support software that has been developed to analyze the specification. SREM applies a *requirements engineering and validation system,* REVS. REVS software uses a combination of reports and computer graphics to study information flow, determine consistency in the use of information throughout the system, and simulate dynamic interrelationships among elements.

Like SADT, SREM incorporates a set of procedures that guide the analyst through the requirements step. The procedures include:

1. *Translation.* An activity that transforms initial software requirements described in a *System Specification* into a more detailed set of data descriptions and processing steps.
2. *Decomposition.* An activity that evaluates information at the interface to the software element and results in a complete set of computational (functional) requirements.
3. *Allocation.* An activity that considers alternative approaches to the requirements that have been established; trade-off studies and sensitivity analyses are conducted.
4. *Analytical feasibility demonstration.* An activity that attempts to simulate critical processing requirements to determine feasibility.

RSL is used heavily in the first two procedures and REVS is used to accomplish procedures 3 and 4.

SREM was developed for embedded computer systems. Recent extensions provide support for distributed concurrent systems.

9.8.2 PSL/PSA

PSL/PSA (Problem Statement Language/Problem Statement Analyzer) was originally developed by the ISDOS project [TEI77] at the University of Michigan and is now part of a larger system called *Computer Aided Design and Specification Analysis Tool* (CADSAT). PSL/PSA provides an analyst with capabilities that include (1) description of information systems, regardless of application area; (2) creation of a database containing descriptors for the information system; (3) addition, deletion, and modification of descriptors; and (4) production of formatted documentation and a variety of reports on the specification

The PSL model [SAY90] uses a set of keywords to define descriptors for system information flow, system structure, data structure, data derivation, system size and volume, system dynamics, system properties, and project management. CASE tools enable other representations of requirements (e.g., data flow diagrams and data dictionary) to be translated into a PSL representation.

Once a complete PSL description for the system is established, a *problem statement analyzer* is invoked. PSA produces a number of reports that include a record of all modifications made to the specification database, reference reports that present database information in varying formats, summary reports that provide project management information, and analysis reports that evaluate characteristics of the database.

9.8.3 TAGS

TAGS (Technology for the Automated Generation of Systems) was developed by Teledyne Brown Engineering [SEI85] as an automated approach for the application of system engineering methods. Like SREM and PSL/PSA, TAGS is composed of three key components: a specification language called *Input/Output Requirements Language* (IORL), a set of software tools for requirements analysis and IORL processing, and an underlying TAGS methodology.

Unlike SREM and PSL/PSA, the TAGS specification language was designed to accommodate both graphical and textual representations that are created by the analyst using an interactive tool. The highest level of IORL representation is a *schematic block diagram* (SBD). SBDs identify primary system components and the data interfaces between them. Each system component in an SBD may be refined by representing input/output relationships, timing, and other supplementary information.

The IORL specification is analyzed using a variety of software tools. These include a *diagnostic analyzer* that helps to uncover static errors (e.g., syntax errors, range violations) in the specification and a *simulation compiler* that aids in uncovering dynamic errors by simulating the system that has been modeled with IORL. The combined output of the analyzer and compiler is Ada programming language source code that is used to create the system simulation.

9.8.4 Specification Environments

Specification languages and tools, such as PSL/PSA, SREM, and TAGS, represent the first generation of *specification environments*. Today, researchers are combining graphical techniques (e.g., flow models), language-based techniques (e.g., PSL/PSA), object-oriented concepts, and even an expert system approach to create complete environments for system and software specification [THA90].

Although such environments are still in their formative stages, most will have a subset of the following characteristics:

1. A graphical interface that enables the analyst to describe the system and its environment using a concise and easily understood notation
2. A behavioral modeling component that allows the analyst to define system behavior in a way that can be translated into a formal specification (see Section 9.6) by the tools contained within the environment
3. A reuse library that enables the analyst to select from existing objects and classes that have been developed for other programs within the domain of application
4. An expert system, called an automated "specification critic," that uses domain-specific knowledge-based heuristics to assess the completeness and consistency of the specification [FIC88]
5. A prototyping facility that will generate prototype programming language source code directly from the specification model

By the turn of the century, specification environments will change the *level of abstraction* with which software engineers build computer programs. It is likely that coding, an activity that today continues to absorb the time and fancy of many software developers, will become a customization activity only. Software will be created by specifying programs using specification environments with characteristics like the ones described above. In fact, CASE tools with some of these characteristics already exist, and the race to develop a complete specification environment has begun.

9.8.5 Tools for Formal Methods

The formal methods discussed in Sections 9.6 and 9.7 will become widely integrated into the software engineering community only if automated tools are available to assist in specification and verification. Tools have been developed to automate certain elements of the specification and verification process for Z, VDM, CSP and Larch, and Gypsy, among others. *Model checking tools* enable a software engineer to build a finite state model of the system to be specified. The tool then verifies that properties defined using a formal specification language hold for each state or state transition. Algebraic manipulation tools work directly with the specification language syntax and semantics and are categorized by Wing [WIN90]:

- *Proof checking tools.* These enable the specifier to manipulate algebraic specifications as a set of rules to be proven (e.g., Affirm, Reve, Rewrite Rule Laboratory, and the Larch prover).
- *Logic manipulators.* These analyze first-order or subsets of high-order logic as it is defined with a formal specification language (e.g., FDM, HDM, HOL, LCF).

The use of automated tools for the application of formal methods is in its infancy. Many of the tools noted above have been used only in a research environment. However, it is likely that formal methods will become increasingly common as a metalanguage for CASE tools that perform analysis and specification. Although the formal descriptions may not be directly visible to the user of a CASE tool, the metalanguage will enable the tool to perform sophisticated analysis for correctness, consistency, completeness.

9.8.6 Automated Techniques—A Summary

The automated approach to requirements analysis provided by SREM, PSL/PSA, TAGS, and the requirements specification environments that have grown out of them is not a panacea, but it does provide benefits that include:

- Improved documentation quality through standardization and reporting
- Better coordination among analysts in that the database is available to all
- Easier detection of gaps, omissions, and inconsistencies through cross-reference maps and reports
- Easier tracing of the impact of modifications
- Reduction in maintenance costs for the specification

The perceptive reader will note that each of these techniques and tools has many characteristics in common. Each demands a more formal approach (either graphical or textual) to specification; each provides an automated or semiautomated mechanism for analyzing the specification; each creates a database that represents requirements in terms of system information, components, and processes; each is used to aid the analyst but must rely on information provided by the analyst and customer.

9.9 SUMMARY

Requirements analysis methods provide a systematic approach for problem analysis. Although each method has a unique set of procedures and symbology, all provide mechanisms for assessment and representation of the information domain, partitioning of the functional domain, and modeling procedures for both the physical and logical world.

DSSD and JSD are not as widely used as structured analysis, nor as "current" as OOA, but they have many things in common with these methods. More importantly, each introduces its own unique view of analysis modeling, and in some ways each is more powerful than the methods discussed in Chapters 7 and 8. These data structure-oriented methods identify information items and actions (processes) and model these according to the information hierarchy (structure) of the problem.

Formal, mathematical specification techniques provide a foundation for specification environments that may become predominant later in this decade. Using a rigorous notation, such techniques enable a software engineer to develop specifications that are unambiguous, consistent, and complete.

Language-based requirements analysis methods model a system in a more formal manner than graphical techniques, and enable automated processing to uncover inconsistency, omissions, and other errors. Today, these methods are coupled with tools that enable the analyst to create the model graphically and then automatically translate the "picture" into the language form.

We conclude our discussion of requirements analysis methods with the words of Gehani and McGettrick [GEH86]:

> There are important benefits which stem from writing specifications, i.e., stating in precise terms the intended effect of a piece of software. For then it is possible to talk about such issues as the correctness of an implementation, a measure of the consistency between that specification and the effect of the program. The range of benefits are actually wider than this: they relate to methods of programming, to possible approaches to verification and validation of programs, and even to the management and control of large software projects.

In the chapters to come, we will follow a "map" that has been created by the requirements analysis methods presented in Chapters 7, 8, and 9. If an analysis method has been applied correctly, it is likely that the road will be direct and the journey will be successful.

REFERENCES

[ALF85] Alford, M., "SREM at the Age of Eight; The Distributed Computing Design System," *IEEE Computer*, vol. 18, no. 4, April 1985, pp. 36–46.

[FIC88] Fickas, S., and P. Nagarajan, "Critiqing Software Specifications," *IEEE Software,* November 1988, pp. 37–47.

[GEH86] Gehani, N., and D. McGettrick (eds.), *Software Specification Techniques,* Addison-Wesley, 1986, p. 1.

[GUT85] Guttag, J.V., J. J. Horning, and J. M. Wing, "An Overview of the Larch Family of Specification Languages," *IEEE Software,* vol. 2, no. 5, September 1985, pp. 24–36.

[HAL90] Hall, A., "Seven Myths of Formal Methods," *IEEE Software,* September 1990, pp. 11–20.

[HOR85] Hoare, C. A. R., *Communicating Sequential Processes,* Prentice-Hall International, 1985.

[JAC75] Jackson, M. A., *Principles of Program Design,* Academic Press, 1975.

[JAC83] Jackson, M. A., *System Development,* Prentice-Hall, 1983.

[JON90] Jones, C. B., *Systematic Software Development Using VDM,* 2d ed., Prentice-Hall, 1990.

[LIS86] Liskov, B. H., and V. Berzins, "An Appraisal of Program Specifications," in *Software Specification Techniques* (N. Gehani and A.T. McGettrick, eds.), Addison-Wesley, 1986, p. 3.

[MAR88] Marca, D. A., and C. L. McGowan, *SADT—Structured Analysis and Design Technique,* McGraw-Hill, 1988.

[MOR90] Moore, A. P., "The Specification and Verified Decomposition of System Requirements Using CSP," *IEEE Trans. Software Engineering,* vol. 16, no. 9, September 1990, pp. 932–948.

[ORR77] Orr, K.T., *Structured Systems Development,* Yourdon Press, New York, 1977.

[ORR81] Orr, K.T., *Structured Requirements Definition,* Ken Orr & Associates, 1981.

[ROS77] Ross, D., and K. Schoman, "Structured Analysis for Requirements Definition," *IEEE Trans. Software Engineering,* vol. 3, no. 1, January 1977, pp. 6–15.

[ROS85] Ross, D., "Applications and Extensions of SADT," *IEEE Computer,* vol. 18, no. 4, April 1984, pp. 25–35.

[SAY90] Sayani, H. H., "PSL/PSA at the Age of Fifteen," *System and Software Requirements Engineering* (R. Thayer and M. Dorfman, eds.), IEEE Computer Society Press, 1990, pp. 403–417.

[SEI85] Sievert, G. E., and T. A. Mizell, "Specification-based Software Engineering with TAGS," *IEEE Computer,* vol. 18, no. 4, April 1985, pp. 56–65.

[SPI88] Spivey, J. M., *Understanding Z: A Specification Language and Its Formal Semantics,* Cambridge University Press, 1988.

[SPI90] Spivey, J. M., "Specifying a Real-Time Kernel," *IEEE Software,* September 1990, pp. 21–28.

[TEI77] Teichroew, D., and E. Hershey, "PSL/PSA: A Computer Aided Technique for Structured Documentation and Analysis of Information Processing Systems," *IEEE Trans. Software Engineering,* vol. 3, no. 1, January 1977, pp. 41–48.

[THA90] Thayer, R. H., and M. Dorfman, *System and Software Requirements Engineering,* IEEE Computer Society Press, 1990.

[WAR74] Warnier, J. D., *Logical Construction of Programs,* Van Nostrand Reinhold, 1974.

[WAR81] Warnier, J. D., *Logical Construction of Systems,* Van Nostrand Reinhold, 1981.

[WIL87] Wiltala, S. A., *Discrete Mathematics: A Unified Approach,* McGraw-Hill, 1987.

[WIN90] Wing, J. M., "A Specifier's Introduction to Formal Methods," *IEEE Computer,* vol. 23, no. 9, September 1990, pp. 8–24.

[WOO89] Woodcock, J. C., "Calculating Properties of Z Specifications," *ACM Software Engineering Notes,* vol. 14, no. 5, July 1989, pp. 43–54.

PROBLEMS AND POINTS TO PONDER

9.1 Recalling the fundamental analysis principles discussed in Chapter 6, indicate how DSSD accomplishes each fundamental. That is, how does DSSD notation represent the information domain, partition the problem, and build essential and implementation models of a system?

9.2 Redo Problem 9.1, but this time focus on JSD.

9.3 Using Marca and McGowan [MAR88] as a reference, redo Problem 9.1, but this time focus on SADT.

9.4 Attempt to develop a JSD model for the *SafeHome* security system that has been discussed in earlier chapters.

9.5 Use DSSD to represent PHTRS described in Problem 7.13.

9.6 Using Marca and McGowan [MAR88] as a reference, redo Problem 9.4, but this time focus on SADT.

9.7 Software for a word processing system is to be developed. Do a few hours of research on the application area and develop a list of questions that you, as an analyst, would ask a requester. Attempt to structure your questions so that major topics are addressed in a rational sequence. Represent the system using (a) DSSD, (b) JSD, or (c) SADT.

9.8 Software for a real-time test monitoring system for gas turbine engines is to be developed. Proceed as in Problem 9.7.

9.9 Software for a manufacturing control system for an automobile assembly plant is to be developed. Proceed as in Problem 9.7.

9.10 Do some research in the area of formal, mathematical specification and (a) write a paper that describes one mathematical notation in detail (be sure to use examples) or (b) develop a presentation on the subject for your class.

9.11 Using the Z notation presented in Section 9.6.3, select some part of the *SafeHome* security system described earlier and attempt to specify it with Z.

9.12 Write a paper on the latest progress in the area of automated requirements analysis tools and specification environments. Use recent conference proceedings and journal articles/papers as your primary sources of information.

FURTHER READINGS

Books by Warnier [WAR81] and Orr [ORR81] provide necessary background for an understanding of DSSD. The Jackson System Development method is described in an excellent book by Cameron (*JSP & JSD: The Jackson Approach to Software Development,* 2d ed., IEEE Computer Society Press, 1989). A complete description of the method is complemented with a set of interesting examples.

Marca and McGowen's book [MAR88] on SADT is the most comprehensive treatment of the subject that is readily available. A detailed treatment of SADT notation, accompanied by worthwhile examples, provides good insight into this analysis technique.

Formal methods represent a promising approach to software development in the latter part of this decade. In September 1990, issues of *IEEE Transactions of Software Engineering, IEEE Software,* and *IEEE Computer* were all dedicated to this important subject. In addition, books by Cohen et al. (*The Specification of Complex Systems,* Addison-Wesley, 1986), Dijkstra (*The Formal Development of Programs and Proofs,* Addison-Wesley, 1989), and Jones [JON90] offer excellent surveys of the subject. Research findings are presented in the *Proceeding of the International Workshop on Formal Methods in Software Development* (ACM, May, 1990).

Automated specification tools and formal specification languages are generating substantial interest. Gehani and McGettrick [GEH86] and Rzepka and Ohno ("Requirements Engineering Environments," *IEEE Computer,* April 1985) provide excellent surveys of early work, while conference proceedings (e.g., *Proceedings of the Fifth Workshop on Software Specification and Design,* ACM, 1989) are the source for more current information. Dromby (*Program Derivation: The Development of Programs from Specifications,* Addison-Wesley, 1989) presents a thorough treatment of the subject.

PART 3

THE DESIGN AND IMPLEMENTATION OF SOFTWARE

CHAPTER 10

SOFTWARE DESIGN FUNDAMENTALS

Design is the first step in the development phase for any engineered product or system. It may be defined as: "... *the process of applying various techniques and principles for the purpose of defining a device, a process or a system in sufficient detail to permit its physical realization.*" [TAY59]

The designer's goal is to produce a model or representation of an entity that will later be built. The process by which the model is developed combines intuition and judgment based on experience in building similar entities, a set of principles and/or heuristics that guide the way in which the model evolves, a set of criteria that enable quality to be judged, and a process of iteration that ultimately leads to a final design representation.

Computer software design, like engineering design approaches in other disciplines, changes continually as new methods, better analysis, and broader understanding evolve. Unlike mechanical or electronic design, software design is at a relatively early stage in its evolution. We have given serious thought to software design (as opposed to "programming" or "writing code") for little more than three decades. Therefore, software design methodology lacks the depth, flexibility, and quantitative nature that is normally associated with more classical engineering design disciplines. However, techniques for software design do exist, criteria for design quality are available, and design notation can be applied.

This chapter presents fundamental concepts that are applicable to all software design. Chapters 11 through 15 examine a variety of software design methods.

10.1 SOFTWARE DESIGN AND SOFTWARE ENGINEERING

Software design sits at the technical kernel of the software engineering process and is applied regardless of the development paradigm that is used. Beginning once software requirements have been analyzed and specified, software design is the first of three technical activities—*design, code,* and *test*—that are required to build and verify software. Each activity transforms information in a manner that ultimately results in validated computer software.

The flow of information during this technical phase of the software engineering process is illustrated in Figure 10.1. Software requirements, manifested by information, functional, and behavioral models, feed the design step. Using one of a number of design methods (discussed in later chapters), the design step produces a data design, an architectural design, and a procedural design. The *data design* transforms the information domain model created during analysis into the data structures that will be required to implement the software. The *architectural design* defines the relationship among major structural components of the program. The *procedural design* transforms structural components into a procedural description of the software. Source code is generated, and testing is conducted to integrate and validate the software.

Design, code, and test absorb 75 percent or more of the cost of software engineering (excluding maintenance). It is here that we make decisions that will ultimately affect the success of software implementation and, as important, the ease with which software will be maintained. These decisions are

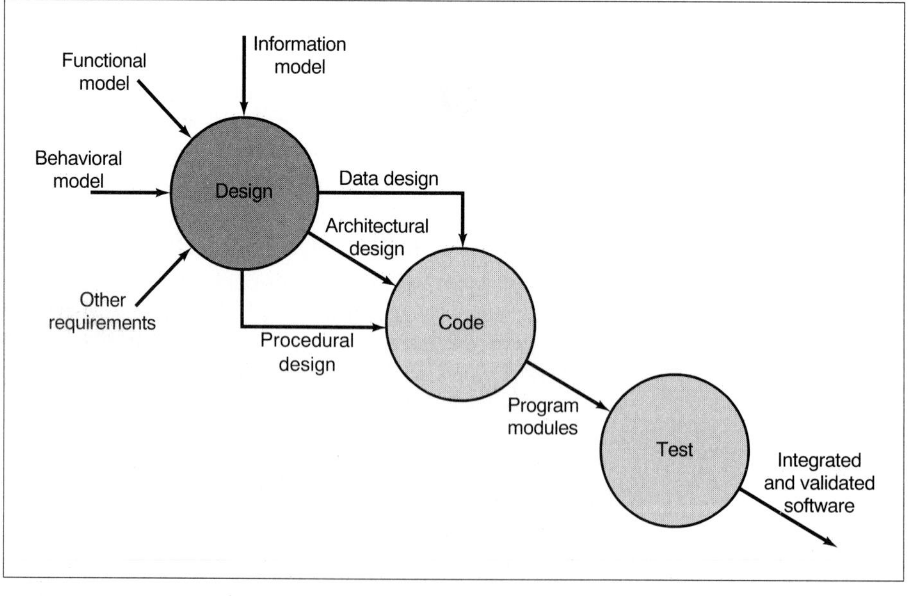

FIGURE 10.1.
Software design and software engineering.

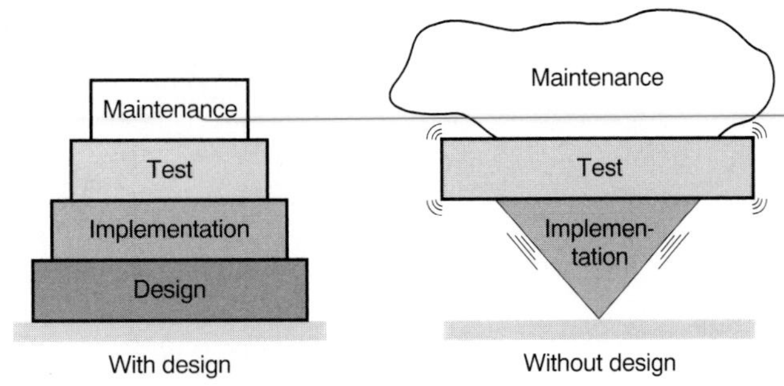

FIGURE 10.2.
The importance of design.

made during software design, making it the pivotal step in the development phase.

The importance of software design can be stated with a single word—*quality*. Design is the place where quality is fostered in software development. Design provides us with representations of software that can be assessed for quality. Design is the only way that we can accurately translate a customer's requirements into a finished software product or system. Software design serves as the foundation (Figure 10.2) for all software engineering and software maintenance steps that follow. Without design, we risk building an unstable system—one that will fail when small changes are made; one that may be difficult to test; one whose quality cannot be assessed until late in the software engineering process, when time is short and many dollars have already been spent.

10.2 THE DESIGN PROCESS

Software design is a process through which requirements are translated into a representation of software. Initially the representation depicts a holistic view of software. Subsequent refinement leads to a design representation that is very close to source code.

From a project management point of view, software design is conducted in two steps. *Preliminary design* is concerned with the transformation of requirements into data and software architecture. *Detail design* focuses on refinements to the architectural representation that lead to detailed data structure and algorithmic representations for software.

Within the context of preliminary and detail design, a number of different design activities occur. In addition to data, architectural, and procedural design, many modern applications have a distinct *interface design* activity. Interface design establishes the layout and interaction mechanisms for human-machine interaction. The relationship between the technical and management aspects of design is illustrated in Figure 10.3.

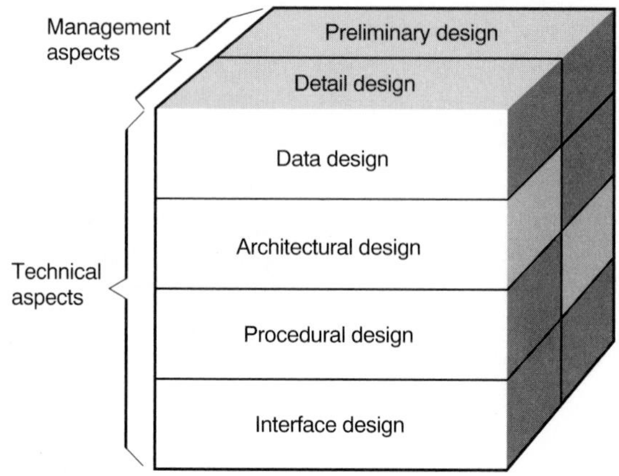

FIGURE 10.3. Relationship between technical and management aspects of design.

10.2.1 Design and Software Quality

Throughout the design process, the quality of the evolving design is assessed with a series of *formal technical reviews* or *design walkthroughs* that are described in Chapter 17. In order to evaluate the quality of a design representation, we must establish criteria for good design. Later in this chapter, we discuss design quality criteria in some detail. For the time being, we present the following guidelines:

1. A design should exhibit a hierarchical organization that makes intelligent use of control among components of software.
2. A design should be modular; that is, the software should be logically partitioned into components that perform specific functions and subfunctions.
3. A design should contain distinct and separable representation of data and procedure.
4. A design should lead to modules (e.g., subroutines or procedures) that exhibit independent functional characteristics.
5. A design should lead to interfaces that reduce the complexity of connections between modules and with the external environment.
6. A design should be derived using a repeatable method that is driven by information obtained during software requirements analysis.

The above characteristics of a good design are not achieved by chance. The software engineering design process encourages good design through the application of fundamental design principles, systematic methodology, and thorough review.

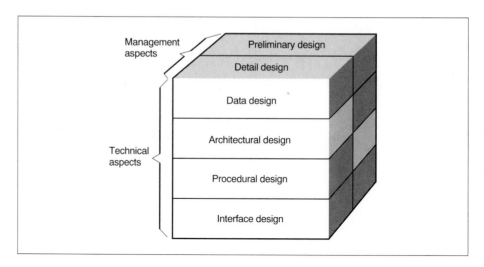

10.2.2 The Evolution of Software Design

The evolution of software design is a continuing process that has spanned the past three decades. Early design work concentrated on criteria for the development of modular programs [DEN73] and methods for refining software architecture in a top-down manner [WIR71]. Procedural aspects of design definition evolved into a philosophy called *structured programming* [DAH72, MIL72]. Later work proposed methods for the translation of data flow [STE74] or data structure [JAC75, WAR74] into a design definition. Newer design approaches [BOO83, MEY88] propose an *object-oriented* approach to design derivation.

Many design methods, growing out of the work noted above, are being applied throughout the industry. Like the analysis methods presented in the preceding chapters, each software design method introduces unique heuristics and notation, as well as a somewhat parochial view of what characterizes design quality. Yet, each of these methods (described in detail in Chapters 11 through 15) have a number of common characteristics: (1) a mechanism for the translation of information domain representation into design representation, (2) a notation for representing functional components and their interfaces, (3) heuristics for refinement and partitioning, and (4) guidelines for quality assessment.

Regardless of the design methodology that is used, a software engineer should apply a set of fundamental concepts to data, architectural and procedural design. Each of these concepts is considered in the sections that follow.

10.3 DESIGN FUNDAMENTALS

A set of fundamental software design concepts has evolved over the past three decades. Although the degree of interest in each concept has varied over the years, each has stood the test of time. Each provides the software designer with a foundation from which more sophisticated design methods can be applied. Each helps the software engineer to answer the following questions:

- What criteria can be used to partition software into individual components?
- How is function or data structure detail separated from a conceptual representation of the software?
- Are there uniform criteria that define the technical quality of a software design?

M. A. Jackson once said: "The beginning of wisdom for a computer programmer [software engineer] is to recognize the difference between getting a program to work, and getting it *right*" [JAC75]. Fundamental software design concepts provide the necessary framework for "getting it right."

10.3.1 Abstraction

When we consider a modular solution to any problem, many *levels of abstraction* can be posed. At the highest level of abstraction, a solution is stated in broad terms using the language of the problem environment. At lower levels of abstraction, a more procedural orientation is taken. Problem-oriented terminology is coupled with implementation-oriented terminology in an effort to state a solution. Finally, at the lowest level of abstraction, the solution is stated in a manner that can be directly implemented. Wasserman [WAS83] provides a useful definition:

> ...the psychological notion of "abstraction" permits one to concentrate on a problem at some level of generalization without regard to irrelevant low level details; use of abstraction also permits one to work with concepts and terms that are familiar in the problem environment without having to transform them to an unfamiliar structure....

Each step in the software engineering process is a refinement in the level of abstraction of the software solution. During system engineering, software is allocated as an element of a computer-based system. During software requirements analysis, the software solution is stated in terms "that are familiar in the problem environment." As we move from preliminary to detail design, the level of abstraction is reduced. Finally, the lowest level of abstraction is reached when source code is generated.

As we move through different levels of abstraction, we work to create procedural and data *abstractions*. A *procedural abstraction* is a named sequence of instructions that has a specific and limited function. An example of a procedural abstraction would be the word "enter" on a door. "Enter" implies a long sequence of procedural steps (e.g., walk to the door, reach out and grasp nob, turn nob and pull door, step away from opening door, etc.). A *data abstraction* is a named collection of data that describes a data object (Chapter 8). An example of a data abstraction would be "paycheck." This data object is actually a collection of many different pieces of information (e.g., payee name, gross pay amount, tax withheld, FICA, pension fund contribution, etc.). Yet, we can refer to all the data by stating the name of the data abstraction.

To illustrate software defined by three different levels of procedural abstraction, we consider the following problem: Develop software that will perform all the functions associated with a two-dimensional drafting system for low-level computer-aided design applications.

Abstraction I The software will incorporate a computer graphics interface that will enable visual communication with the draftsperson and a mouse that replaces the drafting board and square. All line and curve drawing, all geometric computations, all sectioning and auxiliary views will be performed by the CAD software.... Drawings will be stored in a drawing file that will contain all geometric, text, and supplementary design information.

At this level of abstraction, the solution is stated in terms of the problem environment.

Abstraction II

CAD software tasks:
    user interaction task;
    2-D drawing creation task;
    graphics display task;
    drawing file management task;
end.

At this level of abstraction, each of the major software tasks associated with the CAD software is noted. Terms have moved away from the problem environment but are still not implementation-specific.

Abstraction III

procedure: 2-D drawing creation;
    repeat until <drawing creation task terminates>
        do while <digitizer interaction occurs>
            digitizer interface task;
            determine drawing request:
                line: line drawing task;
                circle: circle drawing task;
                .
                .
                .
    end;
        do while <keyboard interaction occurs>
            keyboard interaction task;
            select analysis/computation:
                view: auxiliary view task;
                section: cross sectioning task;
                .
                .
                .
    end;
    .
    .
    .
    end repetition;
end procedure.

At this level of abstraction, a preliminary procedural representation exists. Terminology is now software-oriented (e.g., the use of constructs such as *do while*) and an implication of modularity begins to surface.

The concepts of *stepwise refinement* and *modularity* (discussed in later sections) are closely aligned with abstraction. As the software design evolves, each level of modules in program structure represents a refinement in the level of abstraction of the software.

Data abstraction, like procedural abstraction, enables a designer to represent a data object at varying levels of detail and, more importantly, specify a data object in the context of those operations (procedures) that can be applied to it. Continuing the CAD software example above, we could define a data object called **drawing.** The data object **drawing** connotes certain information with no further expansion, when it is considered in the context of the drafting system. The designer, however, might specify **drawing** as an *abstract data type*. That is, the internal details of **drawing** are defined:

```
TYPE drawing IS STRUCTURE DEFINED
     number IS STRING LENGTH (12);
     geometry DEFINED ...
     notes IS STRING LENGTH (256)
     BOM DEFINED ...
END drawing TYPE;
```

In the design language description above, drawing is defined in terms of its constituent parts. In this case, the data abstraction drawing is itself comprised of other data abstractions: geometry and BOM (bill of materials).

Once the type **drawing** (an abstract data type) has been defined, we can use it to describe other data objects, without reference to the internal details of **drawing**. For example, at another location in the data design, we might say:

```
blueprint IS INSTANCE OF drawing:
```

or

```
schematic IS INSTANCE OF drawing;
```

implying that **blueprint** and **schematic** take on all characteristics of **drawing** as defined above. In Chapter 8, we referred to this typing process as *instantiation*.

Once a data abstraction is defined, a set of operations that may be applied to it is also defined. For example, we might identify operations such as **erase, save, catalog,** and **copy** for the abstract data type **drawing**. By definition (literally), each of these procedures can be specified without the need to define details of **drawing** every time the procedure is invoked.

A number of programming languages (e.g., Ada, Modula, CLU) provide mechanisms for creating abstract data types. For example, the Ada *package* is a programming language mechanism that provides support for both data and procedural abstraction [HAB83]. The original abstract data type is used as a template or generic data structure from which other data structures can be *instantiated*.

Control abstraction is the third form of abstraction used in software design. Like procedural and data abstraction, control abstraction implies a program control mechanism without specifying internal details. An example of a control abstraction is the synchronization semaphore [KAI83] used to coordinate activities in an operating system. The concept of the control abstraction is discussed in Chapter 15.

10.3.2 Refinement

Stepwise refinement is an early top-down design strategy proposed by Niklaus Wirth [WIR71]. The architecture of a program is developed by successively refining levels of procedural detail. A hierarchy is developed by decomposing a macroscopic statement of function (a procedural abstraction) in a stepwise fashion until programming language statements are reached. An overview of the concept is provided by Wirth [WIR71]:

> In each step (of the refinement), one or several instructions of the given program are decomposed into more detailed instructions. This successive decomposition or refinement of specifications terminates when all instructions are expressed in terms of any underlying computer or programming language.... As tasks are refined, so the data may have to be refined, decomposed, or structured, and it is natural to refine the program and the data specifications in parallel.
>
> Every refinement step implies some design decisions. It is important that... the programmer be aware of the underlying criteria (for design decisions) and of the existence of alternative solutions....

The process of program refinement proposed by Wirth is analogous to the process of refinement and partitioning that is used during requirements analysis. The difference is in the level of detail that is considered, not the approach.

Refinement is actually a process of *elaboration*. We begin with a statement of function (or description of information) that is defined at a high level of abstraction. That is, the statement describes the function or information conceptually, but provides no information about the internal workings of the function or the internal structure of the information. Refinement causes the designer to elaborate on the original statement, providing more and more detail as each successive refinement (elaboration) occurs.

10.3.3 Modularity

The concept of modularity in computer software has been espoused for almost four decades. Software architecture (described in Section 10.3.4) embodies modularity; that is, software is divided into separately named and addressable components, called *modules,* that are integrated to satisfy problem requirements.

It has been stated that "modularity is the single attribute of software that allows a program to be intellectually manageable" [MYE78]. Monolithic software (i.e., a large program comprised of a single module) cannot be easily grasped by a reader. The number of control paths, span of reference, number of variables, and overall complexity would make understanding close to impossible. To illustrate this point, consider the following argument based on observations of human problem solving.

Let $C(x)$ be a function that defines the perceived complexity of a problem x, and $E(x)$ be a function that defines the effort (in time) required to solve a problem x. For two problems, p_1 and p_2, if

$$C(p_1) > C(p_2) \tag{10.1a}$$

it follows that

$$E(p_1) > E(p_2) \tag{10.1b}$$

As a general case, this result is intuitively obvious. It does take more time to solve a difficult problem.

Another interesting characteristic has been uncovered through experimentation in human problem solving. That is,

$$C(p_1 + p_2) > C(p_1) + C(p_2) \tag{10.2}$$

Equation (10.2) implies that the perceived complexity of a problem that combines p_1 and p_2 is greater than the perceived complexity when each problem is considered separately. Considering equation (10.2) and the condition implied by equations (10.1*a*) and (10.1*b*), it follows that

$$E(p_1 + p_2) > E(p_1) + E(p_2) \tag{10.3}$$

This leads to a "divide and conquer" conclusion—it's easier to solve a complex problem when you break it into manageable pieces. The result expressed in inequality (10.3) has important implications with regard to modularity and software. It is, in fact, an argument for modularity.

It is possible to conclude from inequality (10.3) that if we subdivide software indefinitely, the effort required to develop it will become negligibly small! Unfortunately, other forces come into play, causing this conclusion to be (sadly) invalid. Referring to Figure 10.4, the effort (cost) to develop an individual software module does decrease as the total number of modules increases. Given the same set of requirements, more modules means smaller individual size. However, as the number of modules grows, the effort (cost) associated with interfacing the modules also grows. These characteristics lead to a total cost or effort curve shown in the figure. There is a number M of modules that would result in minimum development cost, but we do not have the necessary sophistication to predict M with assurance.

The curves shown in Figure 10.4 do provide useful guidance when modularity is considered. We should modularize, but care should be taken to stay in the vicinity of M. Undermodularity or overmodularity should be avoided. But how do we know "the vicinity of M?" How modular should we make

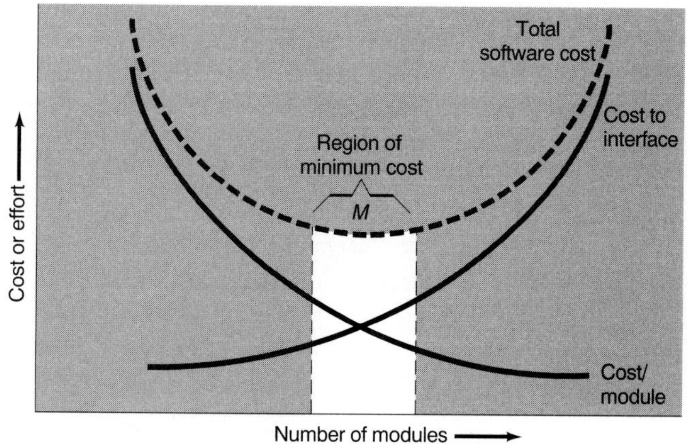

FIGURE 10.4. Modularity and software cost.

software? The size of a module will be dictated by its function and application. In Section 10.4, design measures that help determine the appropriate number of modules for software are presented.

It is important to note that a system may be designed modularly, even if its implementation must be "monolithic." There are situations (e.g., real-time software, microprocessor software) in which the relatively minimal speed and memory overhead introduced by subprograms (i.e., subroutines, procedures) are unacceptable. In such situations software can and should be designed with modularity as an overriding philosophy. Code may be developed "in-line." Although the program source code may not look modular at first glance, the philosophy has been maintained, and the program will provide the benefits of a modular system.

10.3.4 Software Architecture

Software architecture alludes to two important characteristics of a computer program: (1) the hierarchical structure of procedural components (modules) and (2) the structure of data. Software architecture is derived through a partitioning process that relates elements of a software solution to parts of a real-world problem implicitly defined during requirements analysis. The evolution of software and data structure begins with a problem definition. The solution occurs when each part of the problem is solved by one or more software elements. This process, symbolically represented in Figure 10.5, represents a transition between software requirements analysis and design.

Referring to Figure 10.6, it can be seen that a problem may be satisfied by many different candidate structures. A software design method (Chapters 11 through 15) may be used to derive structure, but because each is based

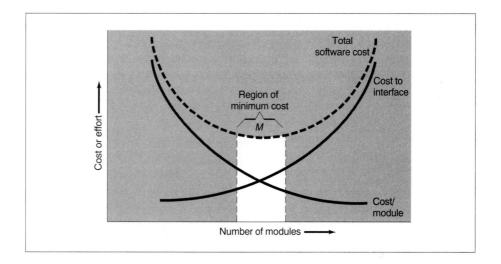

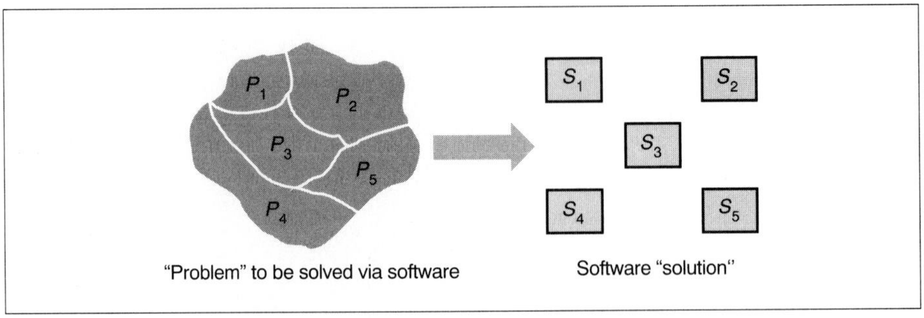

FIGURE 10.5. Evolution of structure.

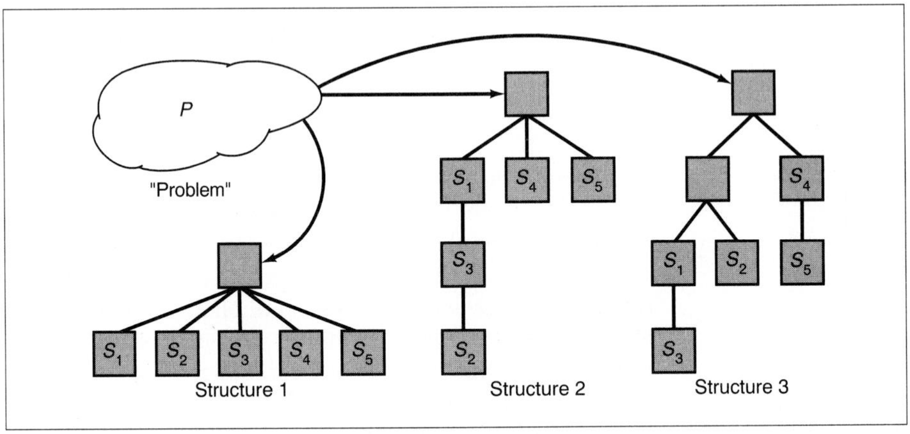

FIGURE 10.6. Different structures.

on different underlying concepts of "good" design, each design method will result in a different structure for the same set of software requirements. There is no easy answer to the question "Which is best?" We have not yet advanced to that stage of science. However, there are characteristics of a structure that can be examined to determine overall quality. We discuss these later in this chapter.

10.3.5 Control Hierarchy

Control hierarchy, also called *program structure,* represents the organization (often hierarchical) of program components (modules) and implies a hierarchy of control. It does not represent procedural aspects of software such as sequence of processes, occurrence/order of decisions, or repetition of operations.

Many different notations are used to represent control hierarchy. The most common is the tree-like diagram shown in Figure 10.7. However, other notations, such as Warnier-Orr and Jackson diagrams (Chapter 5) may also be

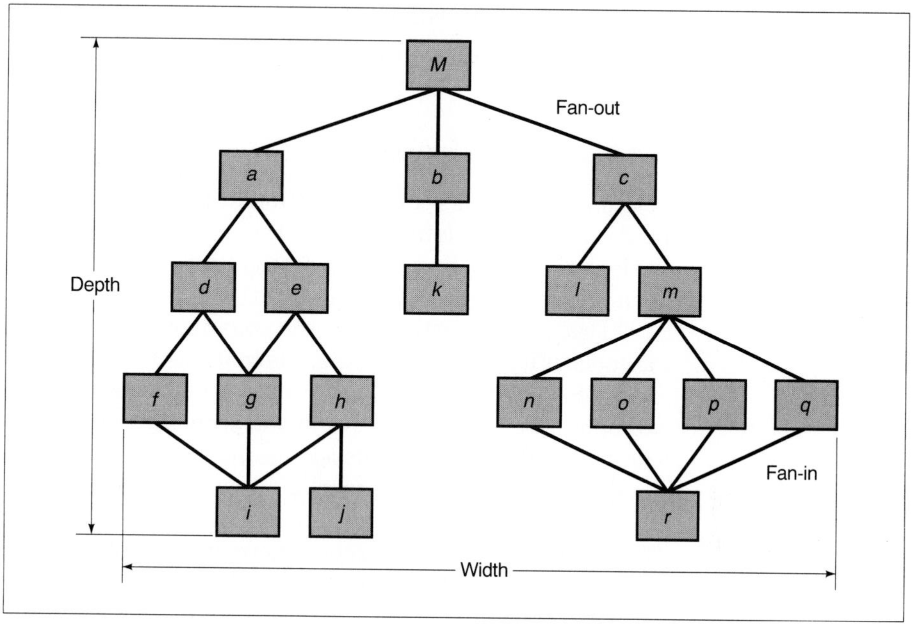

FIGURE 10.7. Structure terminology.

used with equal effectiveness.[1] In order to facilitate later discussions of structure, we define a few simple measures and terms. Referring to Figure 10.7, *depth* and *width* provide an indication of the number of levels of control and overall span of control, respectively. *Fan-out* is a measure of the number of modules that are directly controlled by another module. *Fan-in* indicates how many modules directly control a given module.

The control relationship among modules is expressed in the following way: A module that controls another module is said to be *superordinate* to it, and conversely, a module controlled by another is said to be *subordinate* to the controller [YOU79]. For example, referring to Figure 10.7, module *M* is superordinate to modules *a, b,* and *c*. Module *h* is subordinate to module *e* and is ultimately subordinate to module *M*. Width-oriented relationships (e.g., between modules *d* and *e*), although possible to express in practice, need not be defined with explicit terminology.

The control hierarchy also represents two subtly different characteristics of the software architecture: *visibility* and *connectivity* [CRO90]. Visibility indicates the set of program components that may be invoked or used as data by a given component, even when this is accomplished indirectly. For example, a module in an object-oriented system may have access to a wide array of data objects that it has inherited, but only make use of a small number of these data objects. All of the objects are visible to the module. Connectivity indicates the set of components that are directly invoked or used

[1]For object-oriented designs (Chapter 12), the concept of program structure is less obvious.

as data by a given component. For example, a module that directly causes another module to begin execution is connected to it.[2]

10.3.6 Data Structure

Data structure is a representation of the logical relationship among individual elements of data. Because the structure of information will invariably affect the final procedural design, data structure is as important as program structure to the representation of software architecture.

Data structure dictates the organization, methods of access, degree of associativity, and processing alternatives for information. Entire texts (e.g., [AHO83], [KRU84], [GAN89]) have been dedicated to these topics and a complete discussion is beyond the scope of this book. However, it is important to understand the classic methods available for organizing information and the concepts that underlie information hierarchies.

The organization and complexity of a data structure are limited only by the ingenuity of the designer. There are, however, a limited number of classic data structures that form the building blocks for more sophisticated structures. These classic data structures are illustrated in Figure 10.8.

A *scalar item* is the simplest of all data structures. As its name implies, a scalar item represents a single element of information that may be addressed by an identifier; that is, access may be achieved by specifying a single address in storage. The size and format of a scalar item may vary within bounds that are dictated by a programming language. For example, a scalar item may be a logical entity 1 bit long, an integer or floating point number that is 8 to 64 bits long, or a character string that is hundreds or thousands of bytes long.

When scalar items are organized as a list or contiguous group, a *sequential vector* is formed. Vectors are the most common of all data structures and open the door to variable indexing of information. To illustrate we consider a simple Pascal example:

```
type G = array [1..100] of integer;
. . .
procedure S (var T:G; n: integer; sum: integer)
var i: integer
begin
    sum := 0;
    for i := 1 to n do
        sum := sum + t[i]
end;
```

[2]In Chapter 12, we explore the concept of inheritance for object-oriented software. A program component can inherit control logic and/or data from another component without explicit reference in the source code. Components of this sort would be visible, but not directly connected. A structure chart (Chapter 11) indicates connectivity.

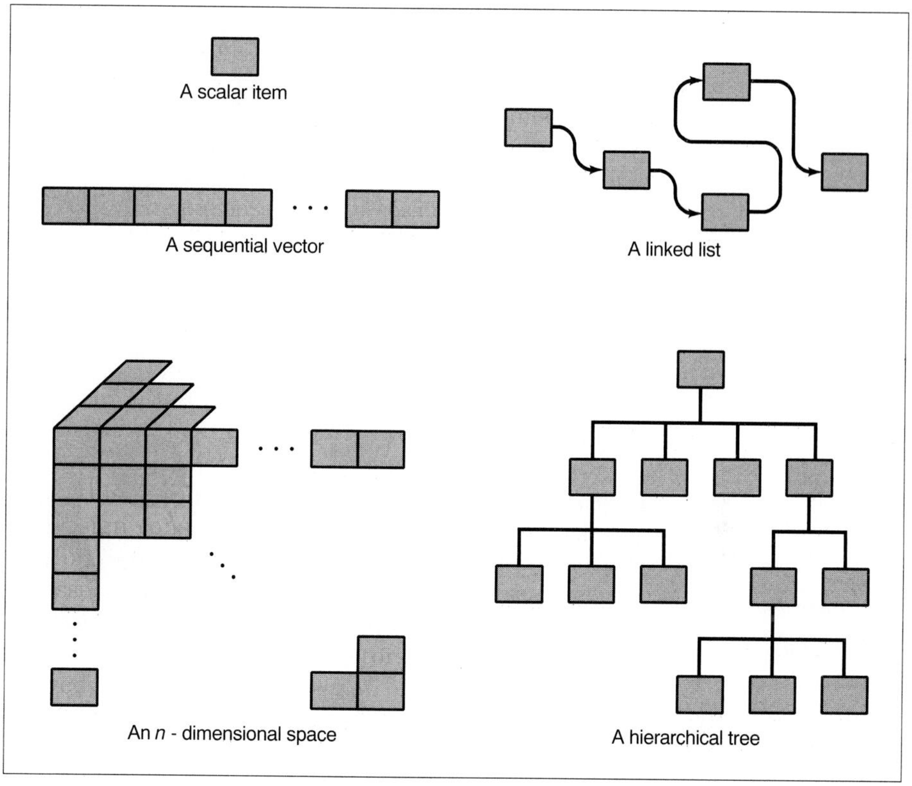

FIGURE 10.8. Classic data structures.

A sequential vector (array) of 100 scalar integer items, G, is defined. Access to each element of G is *indexed* in the procedure S so that elements of the data structure are referenced in a defined order.

When the sequential vector is extended to two, three, and ultimately an arbitrary number of dimensions, an *n-dimensional space* is created. The most common *n*-dimensional space is the two-dimensional matrix. In most programming languages, an *n*-dimensional space is called an *array.*

Items, vectors, and spaces may be organized in a variety of formats. A *linked list* is a data structure that organizes noncontiguous scalar items, vectors, or spaces in a manner (called *nodes*) that enables them to be processed as a list. Each node contains the appropriate data organization (e.g., a vector) and one or more pointers that indicate the address in storage of the next node in the list. Nodes may be added at any point in the list by redefining pointers to accommodate the new list entry.

Other data structures incorporate or are constructed using the fundamental data structures described above. For example, a *hierarchical data structure* is implemented using multilinked lists that contain scalar items, vectors, and, possibly, *n*-dimensional spaces. A hierarchical structure is commonly encountered in applications that require information categorization and associativity. Categorization implies a grouping of information by some generic category (e.g., all subcompact automobiles or all 32-bit microprocessors that are supported by the UNIX operating system).

Associativity implies the ability to associate information from different categories—e.g., find all entries in the microprocessor category that cost less that $100.00 (cost subcategory), run at 25 MHz (cycle time subcategory), and are made by U.S. vendors (vendor subcategory).

It is important to note that data structures, like program structure, can be represented at different levels of abstraction. For example, a *stack* is a conceptual model of a data structure that can be implemented as a vector or a linked list. Depending on the level of design detail, the internal workings of *stack* may or may not be specified.

10.3.7 Software Procedure

Program structure defines control hierarchy without regard to the sequence of processing and decisions. Software procedure (Figure 10.9) focuses on the processing details of each module individually. Procedure must provide a precise specification of processing, including sequence of events, exact decision points, repetitive operations, and even data organization/structure.

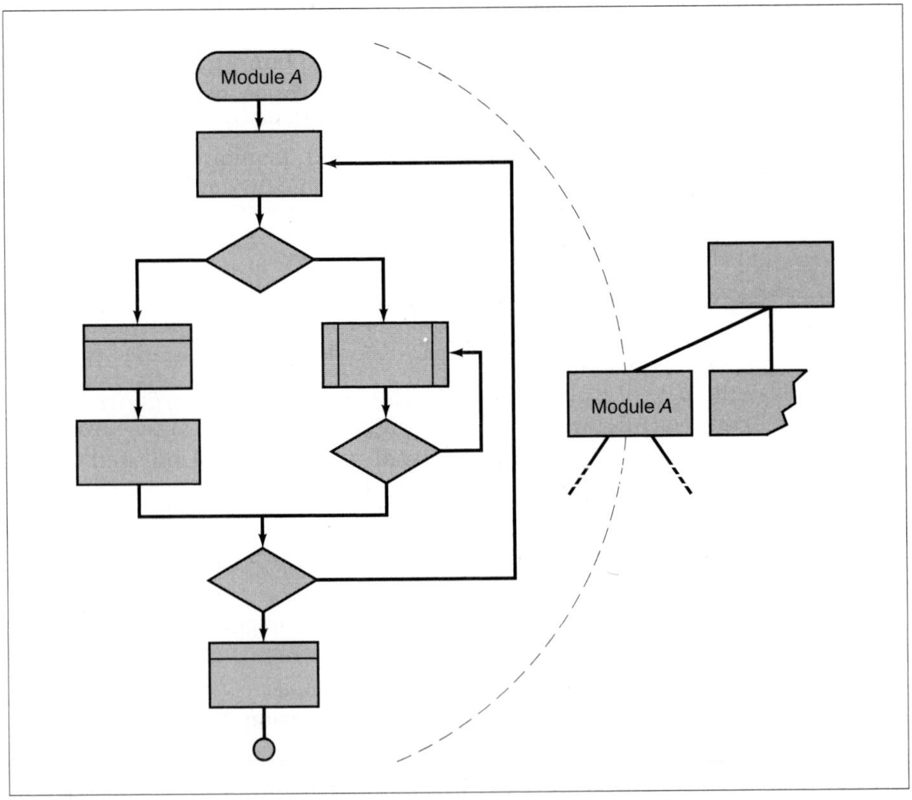

FIGURE 10.9. Procedure within a module.

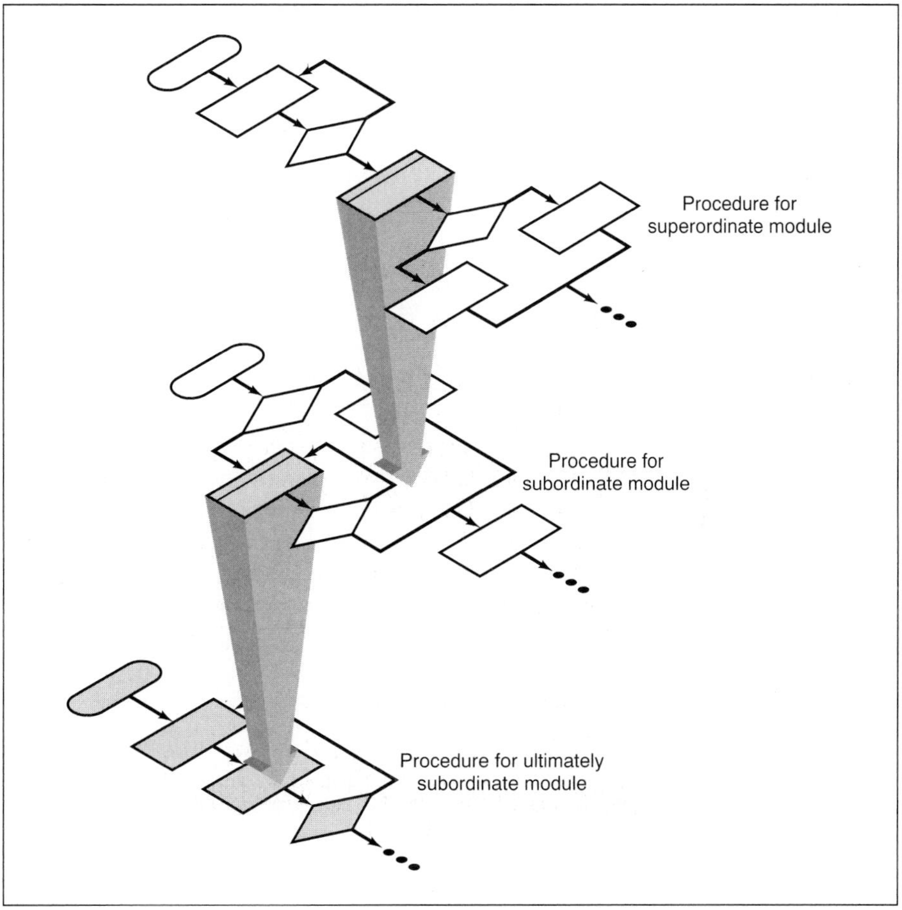

FIGURE 10.10.
Procedure is layered.

There is, of course, a relationship between structure and procedure. Processing indicated for each module must include a reference to all modules subordinate to the module being described. That is, a procedural representation of software is layered as illustrated in Figure 10.10.

10.3.8 Information Hiding

The concept of modularity leads every software designer to a fundamental question: How do we decompose a software solution to obtain the best set of modules? The principle of *information hiding* [PAR72] suggests that modules be "characterized by design decisions that (each) hides from all others." In other words, modules should be specified and designed so that information (procedure and data) contained within a module are inaccessible to other modules that have no need for such information.

Hiding implies that effective modularity can be achieved by defining a set of independent modules that communicate with one another only that information which is necessary to achieve software function. Abstraction helps to define the procedural (or informational) entities that comprise the software. Hiding defines and enforces access constraints to both procedural detail within a module and any local data structure used by the module [ROS75].

The use of information hiding as a design criterion for modular systems provides the greatest benefits when modifications are required during testing and later during software maintenance. Because most data and procedures are hidden from other parts of the software, inadvertent errors introduced during modification are less likely to propagate to other locations within the software.

10.4 EFFECTIVE MODULAR DESIGN

The design fundamentals described in the preceding section all serve to precipitate modular designs. In fact, modularity has become an accepted approach in all engineering disciplines. A modular design reduces complexity (see Section 10.3.3), facilitates change (a critical aspect of software maintainability), and results in easier implementation by encouraging parallel development of different parts of a system.

10.4.1 Module Types

Abstraction and information hiding are used to define modules within a software architecture. Both of these attributes must be translated into module operational features that are characterized by time history of incorporation, activation mechanism, and pattern of control.

Time history of incorporation refers to the time at which a module is included within a source language description of the software. For example, a module defined as a *compile time macro* is included as in-line code by the compiler via a reference made in developer supplied code. A conventional subprogram (e.g., a subroutine or procedure) is included via generation of branch and link code.

Two *activation mechanisms* are encountered. Conventionally, a module is invoked *by reference* (e.g., a "call" statement). However, in real-time applications, a module may be invoked *by interrupt;* that is, an outside event causes a discontinuity in processing that results in the passage of control to another module. Activation mechanics are important because they can affect program structure.

The *pattern of control* of a module describes the manner in which it is executed internally. Conventional modules have a single entry and exit and are executed sequentially as part of one user task. More sophisticated patterns of control are sometimes required. For example, a module may be *reentrant.* That is, a module is designed so that it does not in any way modify itself or the local addresses that it references. Therefore, the module may be used by more than one task concurrently.

Within a program structure, a module may be categorized as

- A *sequential* module that is referenced and executed without apparent interruption by the applications software
- An *incremental* module that can be interrupted prior to completion by application software and subsequently restarted at the point of interruption
- A *parallel* module that executes simultaneously with another module in concurrent multiprocessor environments

Sequential modules are most commonly encountered and are characterized by compile time macros and conventional subprograms—subroutines, functions, or procedures. Incremental modules, often called *coroutines,* maintain an entry pointer that allows the module to restart at the point of interruption. Such modules are extremely useful in interrupt-driven systems. Parallel modules, sometimes called *conroutines,* are encountered when high-speed computation (e.g., pipeline processing) demands two or more CPUs working in parallel. A typical control hierarchy may not be encountered when coroutines or conroutines are used. Such nonhierarchical or *homologous* structures require special design approaches.

Another module type is encountered in programming languages such as Modula and Ada. The Modula *module* and the Ada *package* (see Chapter 16) are program components that combine data abstractions and procedural elements in an object-oriented manner.

10.4.2 Functional Independence

The concept of *functional independence* is a direct outgrowth of modularity and the concepts of abstraction and information hiding. In landmark papers on software design Parnas [PAR72] and Wirth [WIR71] alluded to refinement techniques that enhance module independence. Later work by Stevens, Myers, and Constantine [STE74] solidified the concept. Functional independence is achieved by developing modules with "single-minded" function and an "aversion" to excessive interaction with other modules. Stated another way, we want to design software so that each module addresses a specific subfunction of requirements and has a simple interface when viewed from other parts of the program structure.

It is fair to ask why independence is important. Software with *effective modularity,* i.e., independent modules, is easier to develop because function may be compartmentalized and interfaces are simplified (consider the ramifications when development is conducted by a team). Independent modules are easier to maintain (and test) because secondary effects caused by design/code modification are limited, error propagation is reduced, and reusable modules are possible. To summarize, functional independence is a key to good design, and design is the key to software quality.

Independence is measured using two qualitative criteria: cohesion and coupling. *Cohesion* is a measure of the relative functional strength of a module. *Coupling* is a measure of the relative interdependence among modules.

10.4.3 Cohesion

Cohesion is a natural extension of the information hiding concept described in Section 10.3.8. A cohesive module performs a single task within a software procedure, requiring little interaction with procedures being performed in other parts of a program. Stated simply, a cohesive module should (ideally) do just one thing.

Cohesion may be represented as a "spectrum," as shown in Figure 10.11. We always strive for high cohesion, although the midrange of the spectrum is often acceptable. The scale for cohesion is nonlinear. That is, low-end cohesiveness is much "worse" than middle range, which is nearly as "good" as high-end cohesion. In practice, a designer need not be concerned with categorizing cohesion in a specific module. Rather, the overall concept should be understood and low levels of cohesion should be avoided when modules are designed.

To illustrate (somewhat facetiously) the low end of the spectrum, we relate the following story:

> In the late 1960s most data processing managers began to recognize the worth of modularity. Unfortunately many existing programs were monolithic, e.g., 20,000 lines of undocumented FORTRAN with one 2500 line subroutine! To bring his environment to the state of the art, a manager asked his staff to modularize such a program that underwent maintenance continuously. This was to be done "in your spare time."
>
> Under the gun, one staff member asked (innocently) the proper length for a module. "Seventy-five lines of code," came the reply. She then obtained a red pen and a ruler, measured the linear distance taken by 75 lines of source code, and drew a red line on the source listing, then another and another. Each red line indicated a module boundary. This technique is akin to developing software with coincidental cohesion!

A module that performs a set of tasks that relate to each other loosely, if at all, is termed *coincidentally cohesive*. A module that performs tasks that

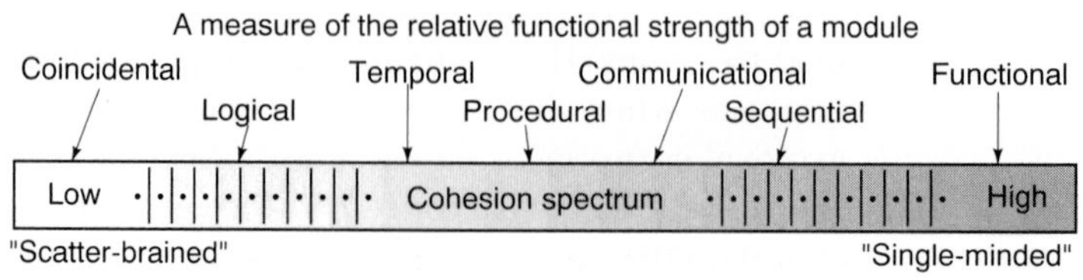

FIGURE 10.11. Cohesion.

are related logically (e.g., a module that produces all output regardless of type) is *logically cohesive*. When a module contains tasks that are related by the fact that all must be executed with the same span of time, the module exhibits *temporal cohesion*.

As an example of low cohesion, consider a module that performs error processing for an engineering analysis package. The module is called when computed data exceed prespecified bounds. It performs the following tasks: (1) computes supplementary data based on original computed data; (2) produces an error report (with graphical content) on the user's workstation; (3) performs follow-up calculations requested by the user; (4) updates a database; (5) enables menu selection for subsequent processing. Although the preceding tasks are loosely related, each is an independent functional entity that might best be performed as a separate module. Combining the functions into a single module can only serve to increase the likelihood of error propagation when a modification is made to one of the processing tasks noted above.

Moderate levels of cohesion are relatively close to one another in the degree of module independence. When the processing elements of a module are related and must be executed in a specific order, *procedural cohesion* exists. When all processing elements concentrate on one area of a data structure, *communicational cohesion* is present. High cohesion is characterized by a module that performs one distinct procedural task.

The following excerpt from Stevens et al. [STE75] provides a set of simple guidelines for establishing the degree of cohesion (called "binding" in this reference):

> A useful technique in determining whether a module is functionally bound is writing a sentence describing the function (purpose) of the module, and then examining the sentence. The following tests can be made:
>
> 1. If the sentence has to be a compound sentence, contains a comma, or contains more than one verb, the module is probably performing more than one function; therefore, it probably has sequential or communicational binding.
>
> 2. If the sentence contains words relating to time, such as "first", "next", "then", "after", "when", "start", etc., then the module probably has sequential or temporal binding.
>
> 3. If the predicate of the sentence doesn't contain a single specific object following the verb, the module is probably logically bound. For example, *Edit All Data* has logical binding: *Edit Source Statement* may have functional binding.
>
> 4. Words such as "initialize", "clean-up", etc., imply temporal binding.
>
> Functionally bound modules can always be described by way of their elements using a compound sentence. But if the above language is unavoidable while still completely describing the module's function, then the module is probably not functionally bound.

As we have already noted, it is unnecessary to determine the precise level of cohesion. Rather it is important to strive for high cohesion and recognize low cohesion so that software design can be modified to achieve greater functional independence.

10.4.4 Coupling

Coupling is a measure of interconnection among modules in a software structure. Like cohesion, coupling may be represented on a spectrum, as shown in Figure 10.12. Coupling depends on the interface complexity between modules, the point at which entry or reference is made to a module, and what data passes across the interface.

In software design, we strive for the lowest possible coupling. Simple connectivity among modules results in software that is easier to understand and less prone to a "ripple effect" [STE75] caused when errors occur at one location and propagate through a system.

Figure 10.13 provides examples of modules residing in a structure with low coupling. Modules 1 and 2 are subordinate to different modules. Each is unrelated and therefore no direct coupling occurs. Module 3 is subordinate to module 2 and is accessed via a conventional argument list through which data are passed. As long as a simple argument list is present (i.e., simple data are passed; a one-to-one correspondence of items exists), low coupling (*data coupling* on the spectrum) is exhibited in this portion of the struc-

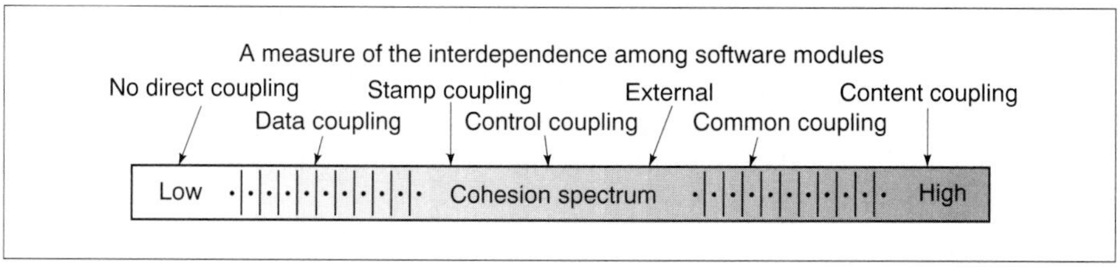

FIGURE 10.12. Coupling spectrum.

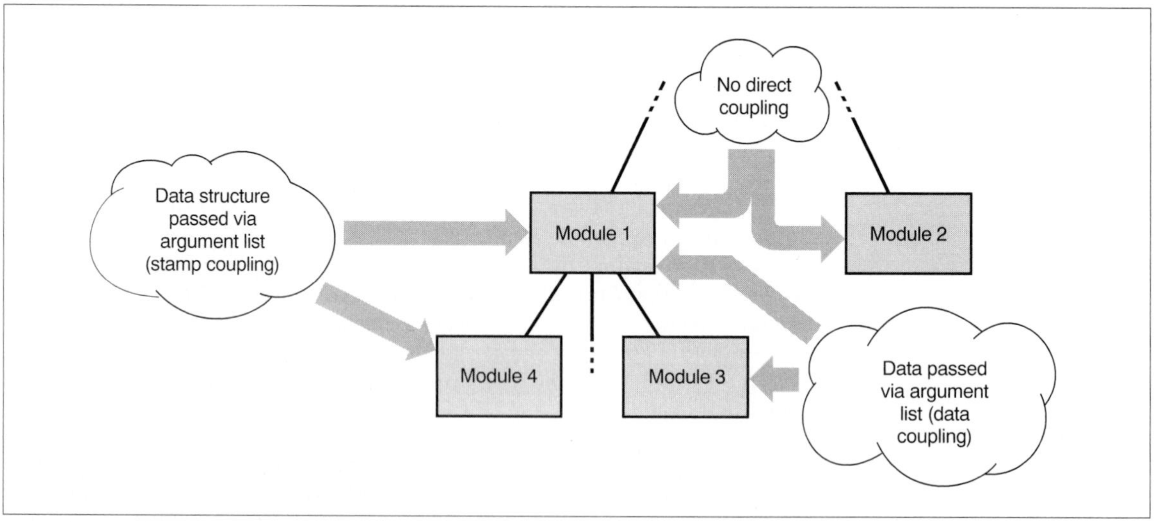

FIGURE 10.13. Low coupling.

ture. A variation of data coupling, called *stamp coupling,* is found when a portion of a data structure (rather than simple arguments) is passed via a module interface.

At moderate levels coupling is characterized by passage of control between modules. *Control coupling* is very common in most software designs and is illustrated in Figure 10.14. In its simplest form, control is passed via a "flag" on which decisions are made in a subordinate or superordinate module.

Relatively high levels of coupling occur when modules are tied to an environment external to software. For example, I/O couples a module to specific devices, formats, and communication protocols. External coupling is essential, but should be limited to a small number of modules with a structure. High coupling also occurs when a number of modules reference a global data area. *Common coupling,* as this mode is called, is shown in Figure 10.15. Modules *C, E,* and *N* each access a data item in a global data area (e.g., a disk file, FORTRAN COMMON, external data types in the C programming language). Module *C* reads the item, invoking *E* which recomputes and updates the item. Let's assume that an error occurs and *E* updates the item incorrectly. Much later in processing, module *N* reads the item, attempts to process it, and fails, causing the software to abort. The apparent cause of the abort is module *N*; the actual cause is module *E*.

Diagnosing problems in structures with considerable common coupling is time-consuming and difficult. However, this does not mean that the use of global data is necessarily "bad." It does mean that a software designer must be aware of potential consequences of common coupling and take special care to guard against them.

The highest degree of coupling, *content coupling,* occurs when one module makes use of data or control information maintained within the bound-

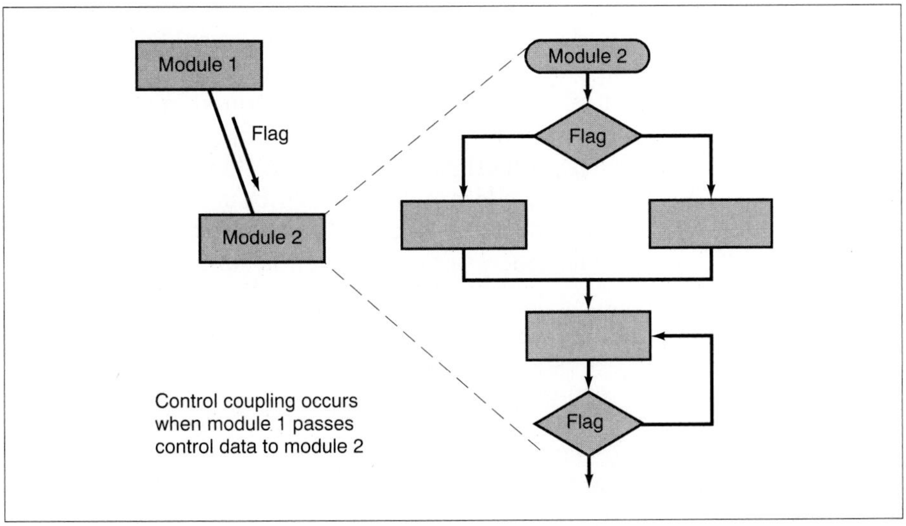

FIGURE 10.14.
Moderate coupling.

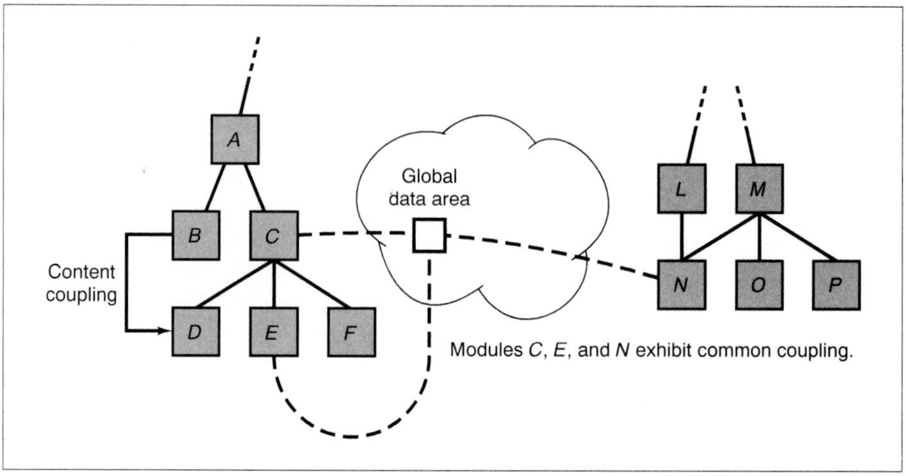

FIGURE 10.15.
High coupling.

ary of another module. Secondarily, content coupling occurs when branches are made into the middle of a module. This mode of coupling can and should be avoided.

The coupling modes discussed above occur because of design decisions made when a structure is developed. Variants of external coupling, however, may be introduced during coding. For example, compiler coupling ties source code to specific (and often nonstandard) attributes of a compiler; operating system (OS) coupling ties design and resultant code to operating system "hooks" that can create havoc when OS changes occur.

10.5 DATA DESIGN

Data design is the first (and some would say the most important) of three design activities that are conducted during software engineering. The impact of data structure on program structure and procedural complexity causes data design to have a profound influence on software quality. Each of the design methods presented in this book (Chapters 11 to 15) makes some attempt to address data design issues. The concepts of information hiding and data abstraction provide the foundation for an approach to data design.

The process of data design is summarized by Wasserman [WAS80]:

> The primary activity during data design is to select logical representations of data objects (data structures) identified during the requirements definition and specification phase. The selection process may involve algorithmic analysis of alternative structures in order to determine the most efficient design or may simply involve the use of a set of modules (a "package") that provide the desired operations upon some representation of an object.

> An important related activity during design is to identify those program modules that must operate directly upon the logical data structures. In this way the scope of effect of individual data design decisions can be constrained.

Regardless of the design techniques to be used, well-designed data can lead to better program structure, effective modularity, and reduced procedural complexity.

Wasserman [WAS80] has proposed a set of principles that may be used to specify and design data. In actuality, the design of data is often encountered as part of the requirements analysis task described in Chapters 6 through 9. Recalling that requirements analysis and design often overlap, we consider the following set of principles [WAS80] for data specification:

1. *The systematic analysis principles applied to function and behavior should also be applied to data.*
We spend much time and effort deriving, reviewing, and specifying functional requirements and preliminary design. Representations of data flow and content should also be developed and reviewed (Chapter 7), data objects should be identified (Chapter 8), alternative data organizations should be considered, and the impact of data modeling on software design should be evaluated. For example, specification of a multi-ringed linked list may nicely satisfy data requirements, but may lead to an unwieldy software design. An alternative data organization may lead to better results.

2. *All data structures and the operations to be performed on each should be identified.*
The design of an efficient data structure must take the operations to be performed on the data structure into account (e.g., see [AHO83]). For example, consider a data structure made up of a set of diverse data elements. The data structure is to be manipulated in a number of major software functions. Upon evaluation of the operation performed on the data structure, an abstract data type is defined for use in subsequent software design. Specification of the abstract data type may simplify software design considerably.

3. *A data dictionary should be established and used to define both data and program design.*
The concept of a data dictionary has been introduced in Chapter 7. A data dictionary explicitly represents the relationships among data objects and the constraints on the elements of a data structure. Algorithms that must take advantage of specific relationships can be more easily defined if a dictionary-like data specification exists.

4. *Low-level data design decisions should be deferred until late in the design process.*
A process of stepwise refinement may be used for the design of data. That is, overall data organization may be defined during requirements analysis, refined during preliminary design work, and specified in detail during the

detail design step. The top-down approach to data design provides benefits that are analogous to a top-down approach to software design—major structural attributes are designed and evaluated first so that the architecture of the data may be established.

5. *The representation of data structure should be known only to those modules that must make direct use of the data contained within the structure.* The concept of information hiding and the related concept of coupling provide important insight into the quality of a software design. Principle 5 alludes to the importance of these concepts as well as "the importance of separating the logical view of a data object from its physical view" [WAS80].

6. *A library of useful data structures and the operations that may be applied to them should be developed.*
Data structures and operations should be viewed as a resource for software design. Data structures can be designed for reusability. A library of data structure *templates* (abstract data types) can reduce both specification and design effort for data.

7. *A software design and programming language should support the specification and realization of abstract data types.*
The implementation (and corresponding design) of a sophisticated data structure can be made exceedingly difficult if no means for direct specification of the structure exists. For example, implementation (or design) of a linked list structure or a multilevel heterogeneous array would be difficult if the target programming language was FORTRAN because the language does not support direct specification of these data structures.

The principles described above form a basis for a data design approach that can be integrated into both the definition and development phase of the software engineering process. As we have noted elsewhere in this book, a clear definition of information is essential to successful software development.

10.6 ARCHITECTURAL DESIGN

The primary objective of *architectural design* is to develop a modular program structure and represent the control relationships between modules. In addition, architectural design melds program structure and data structure, defining interfaces that enable data to flow throughout the program.

To understand the importance of architecture design, we present a brief story from every day life:

> You've saved your money, purchased a beautiful piece of land, and have decided to build the house of your dreams. Having no experience in such matters, you visit a builder and explain your desires [e.g., number and size of rooms, contemporary styling, spa (of course!), cathedral ceilings, lots of glass, etc.]. The

builder listens carefully, asks a few questions, and then tells you that he'll have a design in a few weeks.

As you wait anxiously for his call, you conjure up many different (and outrageously expensive) images of your new house. What will he come up with? Finally, the phone rings and you rush to his office.

Pulling out a large manila folder, the builder spreads a diagram of the plumbing for the second floor bathroom in front of you and proceeds to explain it in great detail.

"But what about the overall design!" you say.

"Don't worry," says the builder, "we'll get to that later."

Does the builder's approach seem a bit unusual? Does our hero feel comfortable with the builder's final response? Of course not! Anyone would first want to see a sketch of the house, a floor plan, and other information that will provide an *architectural view.* Yet many software developers act like the builder in our story. They concentrate on the "plumbing" (procedural details and code) to the exclusion of the software architecture.

The design methods presented in the following chapters encourage the software engineer to concentrate on architectural design before worrying about the plumbing. Although each method has a different approach to architectural derivation, all recognize the importance of a holistic view of software.

10.7 PROCEDURAL DESIGN

Procedural design occurs after data and program structure have been established. In an ideal world, the procedural specification required to define algorithmic details would be stated in a natural language such as English. After all, members of a software development organization all speak a natural language (in theory, at least); people outside the software domain could more readily understand the specification, and no new learning would be required.

Unfortunately, there is one small problem. Procedural design must specify procedural detail unambiguously, and a lack of ambiguity in a natural language is not natural. Using a natural language, we can write a set of procedural steps in too many different ways. We frequently rely on context to get a point across. We often write as if a dialogue with the reader were possible (it isn't). For these and many other reasons, a more constrained mode for representing procedural detail must be used.

10.7.1 Structured Programming

The foundations of procedural design were formed in the early 1960s and were solidified with the work of Edsgar Dijkstra and his colleagues [BOH66, DIJ65, DIJ76]. In the late 1960s Dijkstra and others proposed the use of a set of simple logical constructs from which any program could be formed.

The constructs emphasized "maintenance of functional domain." That is, each construct had a predictable logical structure, was entered at the top, and was exited at the bottom, enabling a reader to follow procedural flow more easily.

The constructs are *sequence, condition,* and *repetition*. Sequence implements processing steps that are essential in the specification of any algorithm. Condition provides the facility for selected processing based on some logical occurrence, and repetition provides for looping. These three constructs are fundamental to *structured programming*—an important design technique in the broader field that we have learned to call software engineering.

The structured constructs were proposed to limit the procedural design of software to a small number of predictable operations. Complexity metrics (Chapter 17) indicate that the use of the structured constructs reduces program complexity and thereby enhances readability, testability, and maintainability. The use of a limited number of logical constructs also contributes to a human understanding process that psychologists call *chunking*. To understand this process, consider the way in which you are reading this page. You do not read individual letters; but rather, recognize patterns or chunks of letters that form words or phrases. The structured constructs are logical chunks that allow a reader to recognize procedural elements of a module, rather than reading the design or code line by line. Understanding is enhanced when readily recognizable logical forms are encountered.

Any program, regardless of application area or technical complexity, can be designed and implemented using only the three structured constructs. It should be noted, however, that a dogmatic use of only these constructs can sometimes cause practical difficulties. Section 10.7.2 considers this issue in further detail.

10.7.2 Graphical Design Notation

"A picture is worth a thousand words," but it's rather important to know which picture and which 1000 words. There is no question that graphical tools, such as the flowchart or box diagram, provide excellent pictorial patterns that readily depict procedural detail. However, if graphical tools are misused, the wrong picture may lead to the wrong software.

The *flowchart* is the most widely used graphical representation for procedural design. Unfortunately, it is the most widely abused method as well.

The flowchart is quite simple pictorially. A box is used to indicate a processing step. A diamond represents a logical condition and arrows show the flow of control. Figure 10.16 illustrates the three structured constructs discussed in Section 10.7.1. Sequence is represented as two processing boxes connected by a line (arrow) of control. Condition, also called *if-then-else,* is depicted as a decision diamond which if true causes *then-part* processing to occur, and if false, invokes *else-part* processing. Repetition is represented

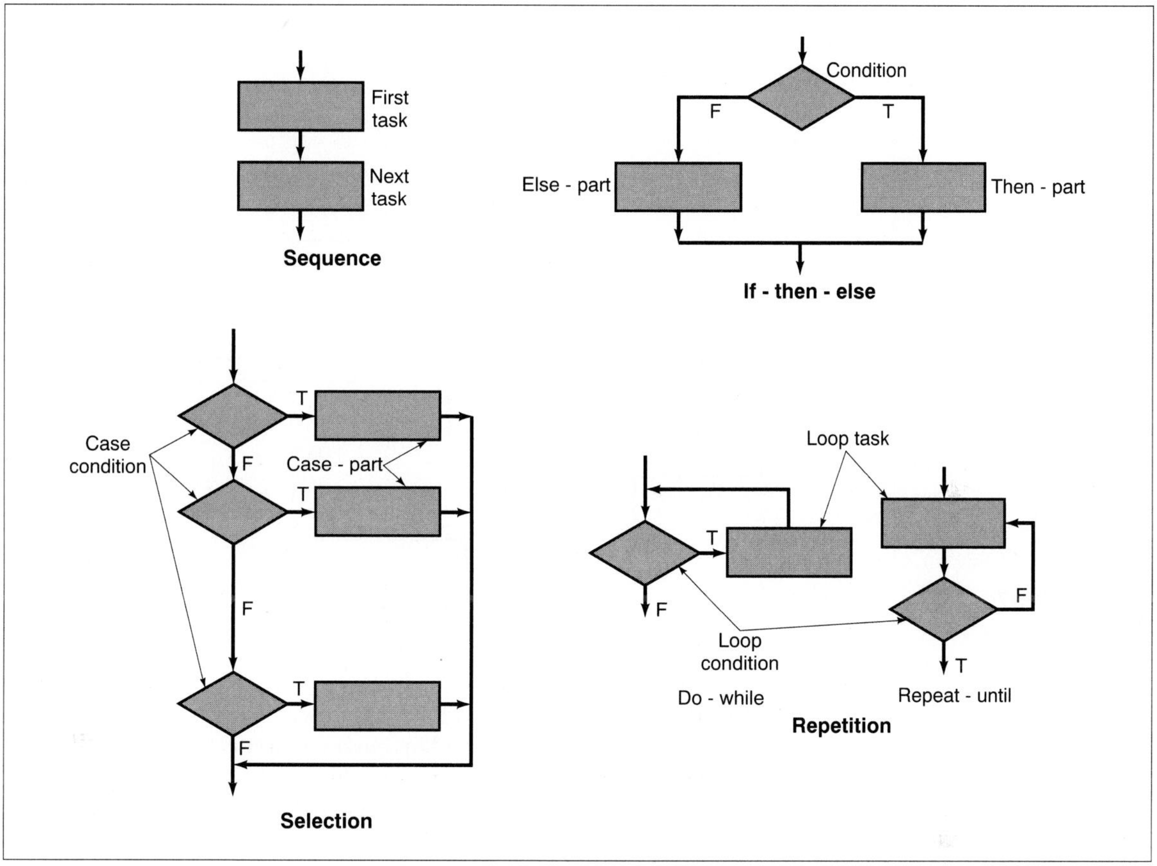

FIGURE 10.16. Flowchart constructs.

using two slightly different forms. The *do-while* tests a condition and executes a *loop task* repetitively as long as the condition holds true. A *repeat-until* executes the loop task first, then tests a condition, and repeats the task until the condition is true. The selection (or *select-case*) construct shown in the figure is actually an extension of the *if-then-else*. A parameter is tested by successive decisions until a true condition occurs and a *case part* processing path is executed.

The structured constructs may be nested within one another as shown in Figure 10.17. Referring to the figure, a *repeat-until* forms the *then-part* of an *if-then-else* (shown enclosed by the outer dashed boundary). Another *if-then-else* forms the *else-part* of the larger condition. Finally, the condition itself becomes a second block in a sequence. By nesting constructs in this manner, a complex logical schema may be developed. It should be noted that any one of the blocks in Figure 10.17 could reference another module, thereby accomplishing *procedural layering* implied by program structure.

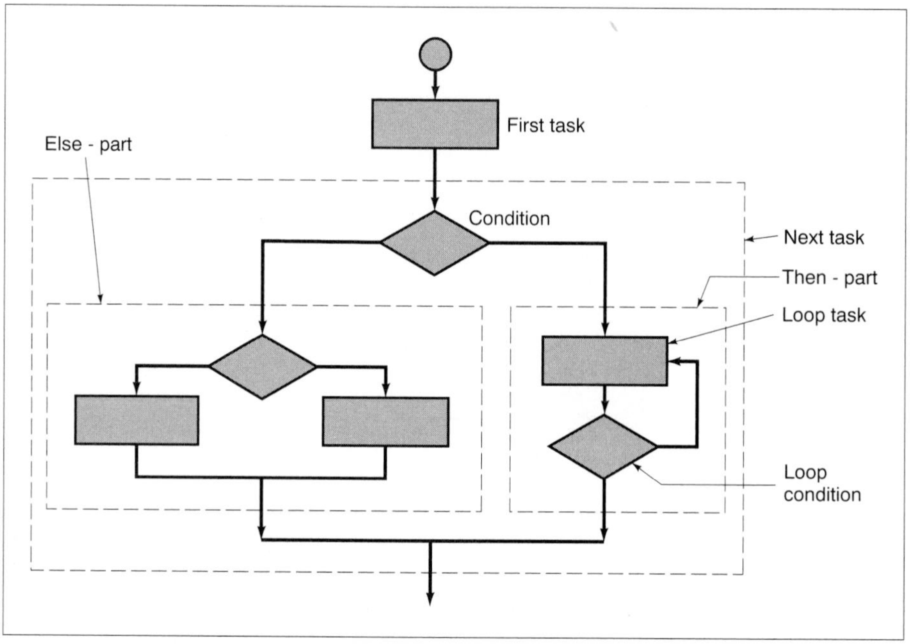

FIGURE 10.17.
Nesting constructs.

A more detailed structured flowchart is shown in Figure 10.18. As an exercise, the reader should attempt to box each construct. Upon completion of the exercise, two things will be apparent. The entire procedure is constructed using the constructs shown in Figure 10.16, and as the constructs are boxed, boundaries of the boxes never cross. That is, all constructs have a single entry and single exit.

The use of only structured constructs can at times introduce complications in logical flow. For example, assume that as part of process i (Figure 10.18) a condition z may arise that requires an immediate branch to process j. A direct branch violates the logical constructs by escaping from the functional domain of the *repeat-until* of which process i is a part. To implement the above branch without violation, tests for condition z must be added to x_7 and x_8. These tests occur repeatedly, even if the occurrence of z is rare. We have introduced additional complications and execution inefficiency.

In general, the dogmatic use of only the structured constructs can introduce inefficiency when an escape from a set of nested loops or nested conditions is required. More importantly, additional complications of all the logical tests along the path of escape can cloud program control flow, increase the possibility of error, and have a negative impact on readability and maintainability. What can we do?

The designer is left with two options: (1) The procedural representation can be redesigned so that the "escape branch" is not required at a nested location in the flow of control; (2) the structured constructs can be violated in a

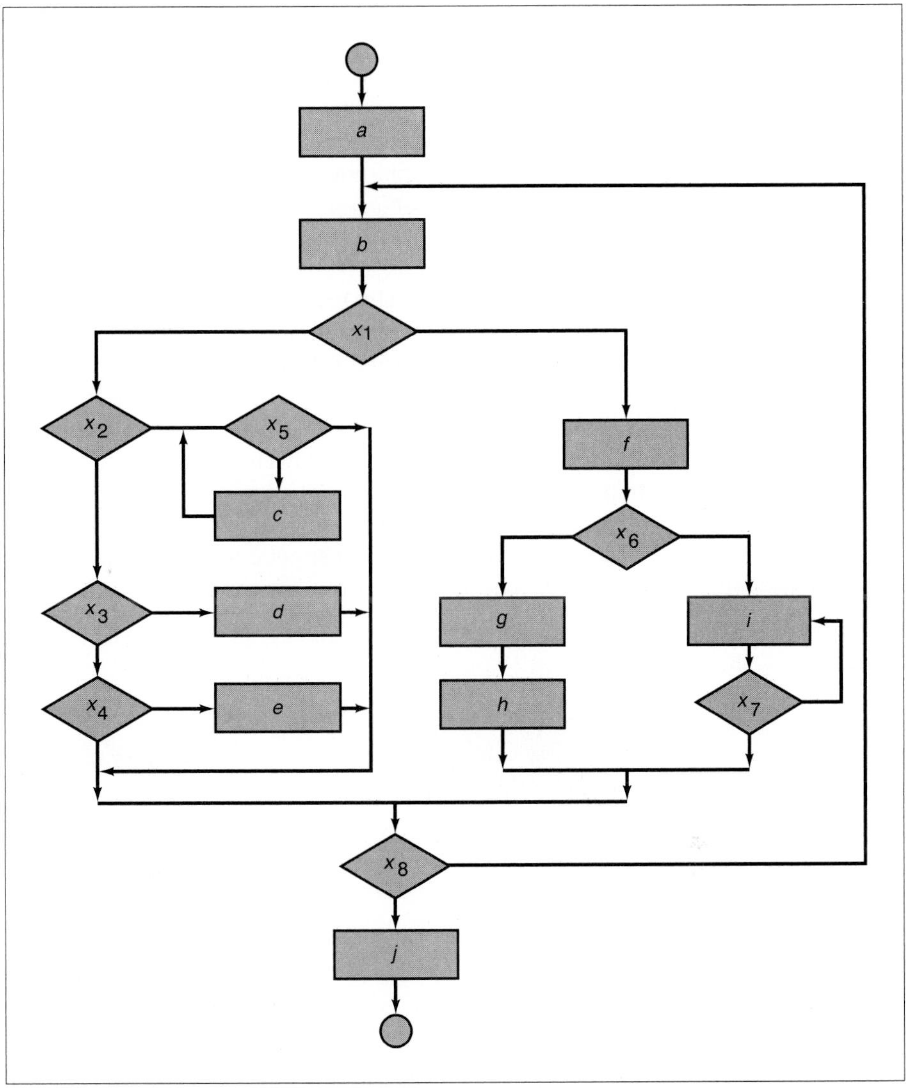

FIGURE 10.18. A structured flowchart.

controlled manner; that is, a constrained branch out of the nested flow can be designed. Option 1 is obviously the ideal approach, but option 2 can be accommodated without violating of the spirit of structured programming.

Another graphical design tool, the *box diagram,* evolved from a desire to develop a procedural design representation that would not allow violation of the structured constructs. Developed by Nassi and Shneiderman [NAS73] and extended by Chapin [CHA74], the diagrams (also called *Nassi-Shneiderman charts, N-S charts,* or *Chapin charts*) have the following characteristics: (1) *Functional domain* (that is, the scope of repetition or an *if-then-else*) is well defined and clearly visible as a pictorial representation; (2) arbitrary transfer of control is impossible; (3) the scope of local and/or global data can be easily determined; (4) recursion is easy to represent.

The graphical representation of structured constructs using the box diagram is illustrated in Figure 10.19. The fundamental element of the diagram is a box. To represent sequence, two boxes are connected bottom to top. To represent an *if-then-else,* a condition box is followed by a *then-part* and *else-part* box. Repetition is depicted with a bounding pattern that encloses the process (*do-while-part* or *repeat-until-part*) to be repeated. Finally, selection is represented using the graphical form shown at the bottom of the figure.

Like flowcharts, a box diagram is layered on multiple pages as the processing elements of a module are refined. A "call" to a subordinate module can be represented by a box with the module name enclosed by an oval.

Figure 10.20 illustrates the use of a box diagram to represent flow of control that is identical to the flowchart given in Figure 10.18. To illustrate the relative ease with which functional domain may be discerned, refer to the *repeat until* loop for condition x_8. All logical constructs contained within the loop are readily apparent because of the boundary pattern. Note that an escape from the loop can only be implemented in one way—via strict adher-

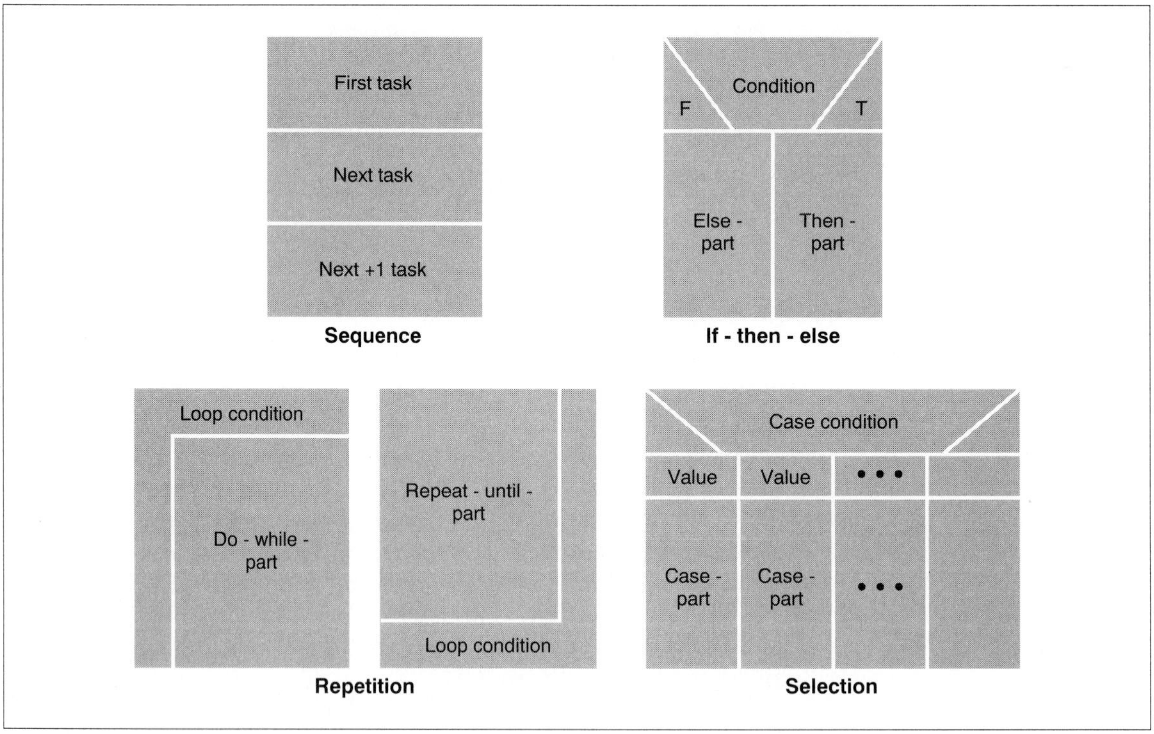

FIGURE 10.19. Box diagram constructs.

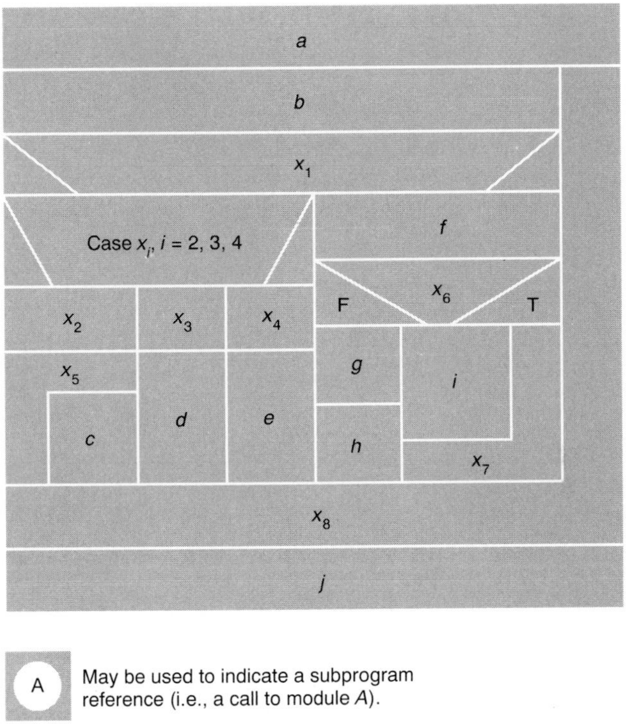

FIGURE 10.20. Box diagram.

ence to the structured constructs. In fact, there is no mechanism for violation of the constructs.

10.7.3 TABULAR DESIGN NOTATION

In many software applications, a module may be required to evaluate a complex combination of conditions and select appropriate actions based on these conditions. *Decision tables* provide a notation that translates actions and conditions (described in a processing narrative) into a tabular form. The table is difficult to misinterpret and may even be used as a machine-readable input to a *table-driven* algorithm. In a comprehensive treatment of this design tool, Ned Chapin states [HUR83, p. v]:

> Some old software tools and techniques mesh well with new tools and techniques of software engineering. Decision tables are an excellent example. Decision tables preceded software engineering by nearly a decade, but fit so well with software engineering that they might have been designed for that purpose.

Decision table organization is illustrated in Figure 10.21. Referring to the figure, double lines divide the table into four sections. The upper left-

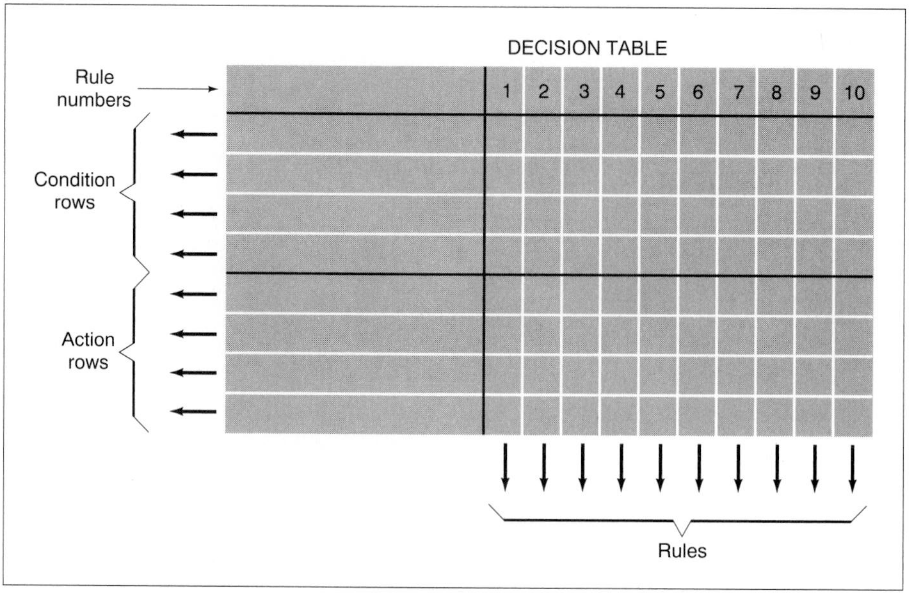

FIGURE 10.21. Decision table nomenclature.

hand section contains a list of all conditions. The lower left-hand section contains a list of all actions that are possible based on combinations of conditions. The right-hand sections form a matrix that indicates condition combinations and the corresponding actions that will occur for a specific combination. Therefore, each column of the matrix may be interpreted as a processing *rule*.

The following steps are applied to develop a decision table:

1. List all actions that can be associated with a specific procedure (or module).
2. List all conditions (or decisions made) during execution of the procedure.
3. Associate specific sets of conditions with specific actions, eliminating impossible combinations of conditions; alternatively, develop every possible permutation of conditions.
4. Define *rules* by indicating what action(s) occurs for a set of conditions.

To illustrate the use of a decision table, consider the following excerpt from a processing narrative for a public utility billing system:

> ...if the customer account is billed using a fixed-rate method, a minimum monthly charge is assessed for consumption of less than 100 kWh (kilowatt-hours). Otherwise, computer billing applies a Schedule A rate structure. However, if the account is billed using a variable-rate method, a Schedule A rate structure will apply to consumption below 100 kWh, with additional consumption billed according to Schedule B.

		1	2	3	4	5
Conditions	Fixed rate account	T	T	F	F	F
	Variable rate account	F	F	T	T	F
	Consumption < 100 KWH	T	F	T	F	
	Consumption ≥ 100 KWH	F	T	F	T	
Actions	Minimum monthly charge	X				
	Schedule A billing		X	X		
	Schedule B billing				X	
	Other treatment					X

FIGURE 10.22. Resultant decision table.

Figure 10.22 illustrates a decision table representation of the preceding narrative. Each of the five rules indicates one of five viable conditions [e.g., a "T" (true) in both fixed rate and variable rate account makes no sense in the context of this procedure]. As a general rule, the decision table can be effectively used to supplement other procedural design notation.

10.7.4 PROGRAM DESIGN LANGUAGE

Program design language (PDL), called structured English or pseudocode in earlier chapters, is "a pidgin language in that it uses the vocabulary of one language (i.e., English) and the overall syntax of another (i.e., a structured programming language)" [CAI75]. In this chapter PDL is used as a generic reference for a design language. It should be noted, however, that PDL is sometimes used to describe a specific design language developed by Caine, Farber, and Gordon [CAI75].

At first glance PDL looks like PASCAL or Ada. The difference between PDL and a real high-order programming language lies in the use of narrative text (e.g., English) embedded directly within PDL statements. Given the combined use of narrative text embedded directly into a syntactical structure, PDL cannot be compiled (at least not yet). However, PDL "processors" currently exist to translate PDL into a graphical representation (e.g., a flowchart) of design, and produce nesting maps, a design operation index, cross reference tables, and a variety of other information.

A program design language may be a simple transposition of a language such as PASCAL or may be a product purchased specifically for procedural design. Regardless of origin, a design language should have the following characteristics:

- A fixed syntax of *keywords* that provide for all structured constructs, data declaration, and modularity characteristics

- A free syntax of natural language that describes processing features
- Data declaration facilities that should include both simple (scalar, array) and complex (linked list or tree) data structures
- Subprogram definition and calling techniques that support various modes of interface description.

Today, a high-order programming language is often used as the basis for a PDL. For example, Ada-PDL is widely used in the Ada community as a design definition tool. Ada language constructs and format are "mixed" with English narrative to form the design language.

As an example PDL, we consider a design language modeled after any of the more common "structured" programming languages. A basic PDL syntax should include:

- Subprogram definition
- Interface description
- Data declaration
- Techniques for *block structuring*
- Condition constructs
- Repetition constructs
- I/O constructs

The format and semantics of the example PDL are presented in the paragraphs below.

During earlier discussions of design, we emphasized the importance of data structure on both a local (per module) and global (program-wide) scale. PDL contains a construct that enables a designer to represent both local and global data structure:

```
TYPE <variable-name> IS <qualifier-1><qualifier-2>
```

where: <variable-name> is a variable contained within a module or declared for global use among modules; <qualifier-1> indicates the specific data structure and includes keywords such as SCALAR, ARRAY, LIST, STRING, STRUCTURE; and <qualifier-2> indicates how variable names are to be used in the context of a module or program.

PDL also allows the specification of abstract data types [MOR80] that are problem-specific. For example,

```
TYPE table.1 IS INSTANCE OF symboltable
```

would be useful in the procedural design of modules for a compiler. The abstract data type symboltable would be defined in terms of other data types at some other location in the design.

Referring back to the CAD system example presented in Section 10.3.1, we can use PDL to define a **drawing** that must be globally available to many modules. A **drawing** is comprised of different data types in a specific hierarchy and is therefore characterized as a *heterogeneous structure*. Using PDL:

```
TYPE drawing IS STRUCTURE DEFINED
    number IS STRING LENGTH (12);
    geometry DEFINED
        lines: (x,y) start; (x,y) end; line.type;
        circle: (x,y) center, radius, arc.angle;
        point: (x,y);
        curve: (x[i], y[i]) for i > 2;
    notes IS STRING LENGTH (256);
    BOM DEFINED
        part.sequence IS LIST;
        part.no: STRING format aa-nnnnnn;
        pointer IS PTR;
END drawing TYPE;
```

It is important to note that the above description of **drawing** is *not* a programming language description. The designer should follow the overall syntax of the PDL but can define the constituent parts of **drawing** in whatever manner is appropriate (and informative). Obviously, the translation of PDL into programming language source code must follow a precise syntax.

The procedural elements of PDL are *block-structured*. That is, pseudocode may be defined in blocks that are executed as a single entity. A block is delimited in the following manner:

```
BEGIN <block-name>
      <pseudocode statements>;
END
```

where <blockname> may be used (but is not required) to provide a mode for subsequent reference to a block and <pseudocode statements> are a combination of all other PDL constructs. For example:

```
BEGIN <draw-line-on-graphics-terminal>
    get end-points from display list;
    scale physical end-points to screen coordinates;
    DRAW a line using screen coordinates;
END
```

The above block makes use of pseudocode statements that describe appropriate processing. The use of a specialized keyword, DRAW, illustrates the manner in which a PDL may be customized to address a specific application.

The condition construct in PDL takes a classic *if-then-else* form:

```
IF <condition-description>
    THEN <block or pseudocode statement>;
    ELSE <block or pseudocode statement>;
ENDIF
```

where <condition-description> indicates the logical decision that must be made to invoke either *then-part* or *else-part* processing. For example, the following PDL segment describes a decision sequence for a payroll system:

```
IF year.to.date.FICA < maximum
  THEN BEGIN
      calculate FICA.deduction (see formula no.30-1);
         IF (year.to.date.FICA + FICA.deduction) > maximum
            THEN set FICA.deduction = maximum − year.to.date.FICA;
            ELSE skip
         ENDIF
      END
  ELSE set FICA.deduction = 0;
ENDIF
```

Two nested IFs are shown in the PDL segment above. The *then-part* of the outer IF contains a block that combines the inner IF with pseudocode statements. ELSE skip indicates that *else-part* processing is skipped. The ENDIF is used to indicate unambiguous termination of the construct and is particularly useful when nested IFs are represented. The END following the first ENDIF terminates the block that processes FICA information.

The selection (or *select-case*) construct, actually a degenerate set of nested IFs, is represented as follows:

```
CASE OF <case-variable-name>:
      WHEN<case-condition-1>SELECT<block or pseudocode statement>;
      WHEN<case-condition-2>SELECT<block or pseudocode statement>;
         .
         .
         .
      WHEN<last-case-condition>SELECT<block or pseudocode statement>;
      DEFAULT: <default or error case: block or pseudocode statement>;
ENDCASE
```

In general, this construct tests a specific parameter, the *case variable,* against a set of conditions. Upon satisfaction of a condition, a block or individual pseudocode statement is invoked. As an example of the CASE construct in PDL, we consider a segment for system I/O processing:

```
CASE OF communication-status-bits (csb):
    WHEN csb = clear-to-send SELECT
        BEGIN
        select channel path;
        initiate message transmission;
        END
    WHEN csb = clear-to-receive SELECT initiate buffer management;
    WHEN csb = busy SELECT set queuing bit;
    DEFAULT: process csb content error;
ENDCASE
```

PDL repetition constructs include *pretest* and *posttest loops* as well as an *indexing loop:*

```
DO WHILE <condition-description>
    <block or pseudocode statement>;
ENDDO

REPEAT UNTIL <condition-description>
    <block or pseudocode statement>;
ENDREP

DO FOR <index> = <index list, expression or sequence>
    <block or pseudocode statement>;
ENDFOR
```

In addition to standard loop constructs, PDL supports two keywords, NEXT and EXIT, that enable the designer to specify constrained exits from loops. There are situations (as discussed in Section 10.7.2) in which an escape from nested loops is required. The PDL constructs EXIT and NEXT provide a constrained violation of purely structured constructs, as shown in Figure 10.23. Referring to the figure, EXIT causes a branch to the statement immediately following the repetition construct in which it is contained. NEXT causes further loop processing to be discontinued but restarts repetition on the next loop cycle. By labeling outer loops, EXIT and NEXT can be used to escape from nesting as shown by

```
ELSE NEXT loop-y
```

that causes a branch to an outer loop labeled *loop-y*.

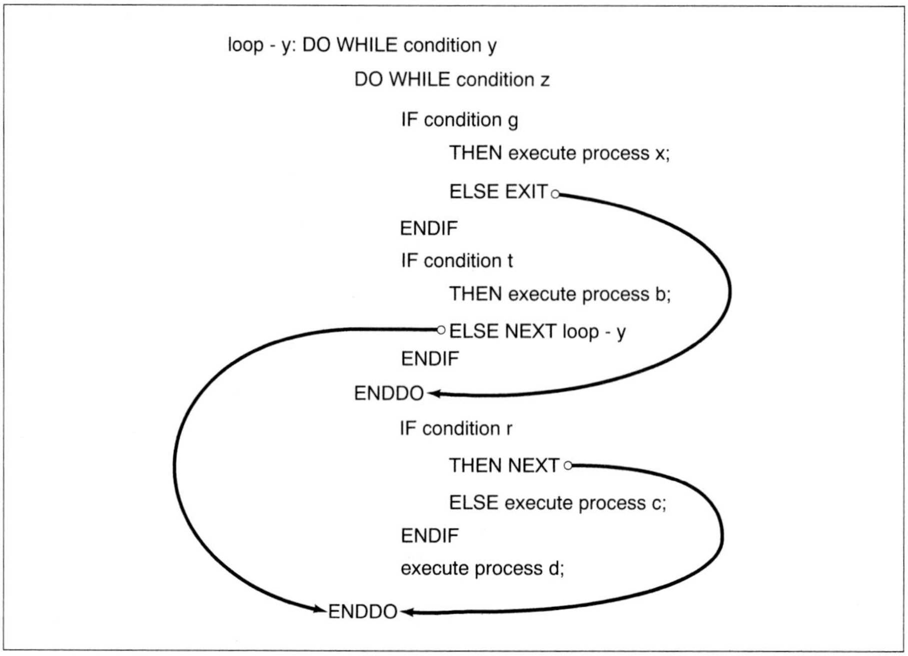

FIGURE 10.23.
"Violation" exits.

As an example of PDL repetition constructs, consider the following analysis loop that tests for the convergence of two calculated values:

```
epsilon := 1.0;
no-of-tries := 0;
DO WHILE (epsilon > 0.001 AND no-of-tries < 100)
      calculate value-1 := f(x, y, z);
      calculate value-2 := g(x, y, z);
      epsilon := ABSVAL (value-1 − value-2);
      increment no-of-tries by 1;
ENDDO
```

It should be noted that the loop condition must be defined so that escape from the loop is guaranteed. The no-of-tries counter is established for this purpose.

Subprograms and corresponding interfaces are defined using the following PDL constructs:

```
PROCEDURE <subprogram-name> <attributes>
INTERFACE <argument-list>
<blocks and/or pseudocode statements>;
END
```

where <attributes> of a subprogram describe its reference characteristics (e.g., an INTERNAL or EXTERNAL module) and other implementation (programming-language) dependent attributes (if any). INTERFACE is used to specify a module argument list that contains identifiers for all incoming and outgoing information.

Input/output specification is highly variable among design languages. Typical forms include:

```
READ/WRITE TO <device> <I/O-list>
```

or

```
ASK <query> ANSWER <response-options>
```

where <device> indicates the physical I/O device (e.g., CRT, disk, printer, tape) and <I/O list> contains variables to be transmitted. ASK-ANSWER is used for human interactive design in which a question-answer format is appropriate. For example:

```
ASK "select processing option" ANSWER "cost", "schedule";
```

I/O specification is frequently expanded to include special characteristics such as audio output or window-oriented, pull-down menu interfaces.

It should be noted that PDL can be extended to include keywords for multitasking and/or concurrent processing, interrupt handling, interprocess synchronization, and many other features. The application design for which PDL is to be used should dictate the final form for the design language.

10.7.5 A PDL Example

To illustrate the use of PDL, we present a more detailed example of a procedural design for the *SafeHome* security system software introduced in earlier chapters. The *SafeHome* system in question monitors alarms for fire, smoke, burglar, water, and temperature (e.g., furnace breaks while home owner is away during winter); produces an alarm bell; and calls a monitoring service, generating a voice-synthesized message. In the PDL that follows, we illustrate some of the important constructs that have been discussed in Section 10.7.4. Recall that PDL is not a programming language. The designer can adapt it as required without worry over syntax errors. However, the design for the monitoring software would have to be reviewed (do you see any problems?) and further refined before code could be written.

```
PROCEDURE security.monitor;
INTERFACE RETURNS system.status;
```

```
TYPE signal IS STRUCTURE DEFINED
    name IS STRING LENGTH VAR;
    address IS HEX device location;
    bound.value IS upper bound SCALAR;
    message IS STRING LENGTH VAR;
END signal TYPE;
TYPE system.status IS BIT (4);
TYPE alarm.type DEFINED
    smoke.alarm IS INSTANCE OF signal;
    fire.alarm IS INSTANCE OF signal;
    water.alarm IS INSTANCE OF signal;
    temp.alarm IS INSTANCE OF signal;
    burglar.alarm IS INSTANCE OF signal;
TYPE phone.number IS area code + 7-digit number;
    .
    .
    .
initialize all system ports and reset all hardware;
CASE OF control.panel.switches (cps):
    WHEN cps = "test" SELECT
        CALL alarm PROCEDURE WITH
            "on" for test.time in seconds;
    WHEN cps = "alarm-off" SELECT
        CALL alarm PROCEDURE WITH
            "off";
    WHEN cps = "new.bound.temp" SELECT
        CALL keypad.input PROCEDURE;
    WHEN cps = "burglar.alarm.off" SELECT
        deactivate signal [burglar.alarm];
    .
    .
    .
    DEFAULT none;
ENDCASE
REPEAT UNTIL activate.switch is turned off
    reset all signal.values and switches;
    DO FOR alarm.type = smoke, fire, water, temp, burglar;
        READ address[alarm.type] signal.value;
        IF signal.value > bound [alarm.type]
            THEN phone.message = message[alarm.type];
            set alarm.bell to "on" for alarm.timeseconds;
        PARBEGIN
            CALL alarm PROCEDURE WITH "on", alarm.time in seconds;
            CALL phone PROCEDURE WITH message [alarm.type],
            phone.number;
        ENDPAR
```

```
    ELSE skip
ENDIF
    ENDFOR
ENDREP
END security.monitor
```

Note that the designer for the security.monitor procedure has used a new construct PARBEGIN . . . ENDPAR that specifies a *parallel block*. All tasks specified within the PARBEGIN block are executed in parallel. In this case, implementation details are not considered.

Program design language is often used in conjunction with CASE design tools that in some cases overlay a graphical component on the procedural design representation. For example, the *control structure diagram* (CSD) [CRO90] can be used in conjunction with either programming language source code or PDL. The design text is augmented with graphical symbols that depict all important structured programming constructs and special language forms (e.g., the Ada task or rendezvous). CSD notation for the structured programming constructs is illustrated in Figure 10.24.

10.7.6 Comparison of Design Notation

In this chapter we have presented a number of procedural design notations. Any comparison must be predicated on the premise that any notation for procedural design, if used correctly, can be an invaluable aid in the design process; conversely, even the best notation, if poorly applied, adds little to understanding. With this thought in mind, we examine criteria that may be applied to compare design notation.

Design notation should lead to a procedural representation that is easy to understand and review. In addition, the notation should enhance "code

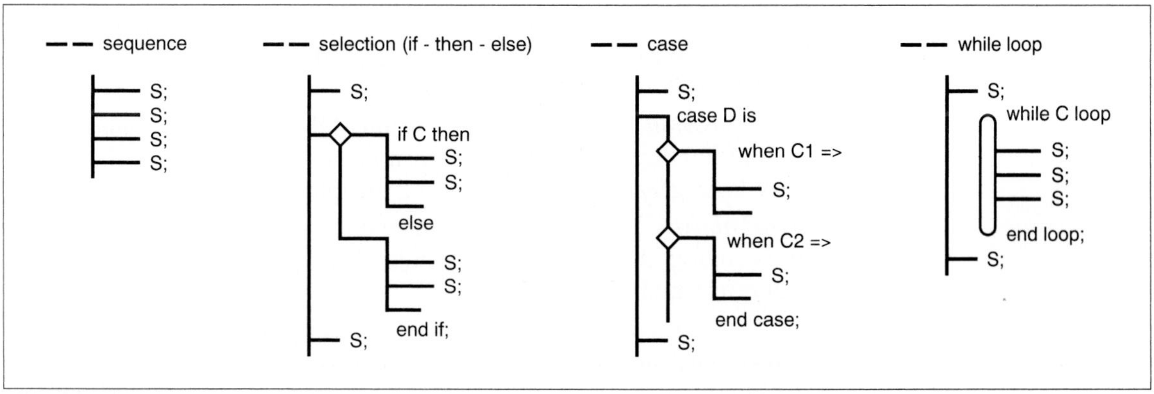

FIGURE 10.24. Control structure diagram notation.

to" ability so that code does, in fact, become a natural byproduct of design. Finally, the design representation must be easily maintainable so that design always correctly represents the program.

The following attributes of design notation have been established in the context of the general characteristics described above:

Modularity. A design notation should support the development of modular software (e.g., direct specification of procedures and block structuring) and provide a means for interface specification.

Overall simplicity. A design notation should be relatively simple to learn, relatively easy to use, and generally easy to read.

Ease of editing. The procedural design may require modification during the design step, during software testing, and, finally, during the maintenance phase of the software life cycle. The ease with which a design representation can be edited can help facilitate each of these software engineering steps.

Machine readability. Computer-aided software engineering environments are being adopted throughout the industry. A notation that can be input directly into a computer-based development system offers significant benefits.

Maintainability. Software maintenance is the most costly phase of the software life cycle. Maintenance of the software configuration nearly always means maintenance of the procedural design representation.

Structure enforcement. The benefits of a design approach that uses structured programming concepts have already been discussed. A design notation that enforces the use of only the structured constructs promotes good design practice.

Automatic processing. A detail design contains information that can be processed to give the designer new or better insights into the correctness and quality of a design. Such insight can be enhanced with reports provided via an automatic processor.

Data representation. The ability to represent local and global data is an essential element of detail design. Ideally, a design notation should represent such data directly.

Logic verification. Automatic verification of design logic is a goal that is paramount during software testing. A notation that enhances the ability to verify logic greatly improves testing adequacy.

"Code-to" ability. The software engineering step that follows procedural design is coding. A notation that may be converted easily to source code reduces effort and error.

A natural question that arises in any discussion of design notation is: What notation is really the best, given the attributes noted above? An answer to this question is admittedly subjective and is open to debate. However, it appears that program design language offers the best combination of characteristics. PDL may be embedded directly into source listings, improving documentation and making design maintenance less difficult. Editing can be accomplished with any text editor or word processing system, automatic processors already exist, and the potential for "automatic code generation" is good.

However, it does not follow that other design notation is necessarily inferior to PDL or is "not good" in specific attributes. The pictorial nature of flowcharts and box diagrams provide a perspective on control flow that many designers prefer. The precise tabular content of decision tables is an excellent tool for table-driven applications. And many other design representations (e.g., see [PET81], [SOM89]), not presented in this book, offer their own unique benefits. In the final analysis, the choice of a design notation may be more closely related to human factors [CUR85] than to technical attributes.

10.8 DESIGN DOCUMENTATION

The document outline contained in Table 10.1 can be used as a model for a *Design Specification*. Each section is comprised of numbered paragraphs that address different aspects of the design representation.

The documentation outline presents a complete design description of software. The sections of the *Design Specification* are completed as the designer refines his or her representation of the software.

The overall scope of the design effort is described in Section I (section numbers refer to *Design Specification* outline). Much of the information contained in this section is derived from the *System Specification* and other software definition phase documents. Specific references to supporting documentation are made in Section II.

Section III, the *design description,* is completed as part of the preliminary design. We have noted that design is *information-driven*—that is, the flow and/or structure of data will dictate the architecture of software. In this section, data flow diagrams or other data representations developed during requirements analysis are refined and used to derive software structure. Because information flow is available, interface descriptions may be developed for elements of the software.

Sections IV and V evolve as preliminary design moves into detail design. Modules—separately addressable elements of software such as subroutines, functions, or procedures—are initially described with an English language processing narrative. The processing narrative explains the procedural function of a module. Later, a procedural design tool is used to translate the narrative into a structured description.

TABLE 10.1

DESIGN SPECIFICATION OUTLINE

I. Scope
- **A.** System objectives
- **B.** Hardware, software, and human interfaces
- **C.** Major software functions
- **D.** Externally defined database
- **E.** Major design constraints, limitations

II. Reference documents
- **A.** Existing software documentation
- **B.** System documentation
- **C.** Vendor (hardware or software) documents
- **D.** Technical reference

III. Design description
- **A.** Data description
  - **1.** Review of data flow
  - **2.** Review of data structure
- **B.** Derived program structure
- **C.** Interfaces within structure

IV. Modules; *for each module:*
- **A.** Processing narrative
- **B.** Interface description
- **C.** Design language (or other) description
- **D.** Modules used
- **E.** Data organization
- **F.** Comments

V. File structure and global data
- **A.** External file structure
  - **1.** Logical structure
  - **2.** Logical record description
  - **3.** Access method
- **B.** Global data
- **C.** File and data cross reference

VI. Requirements cross reference (see Figure 10.25)

VII. Test provisions
- **A.** Test guidelines
- **B.** Integration strategy
- **C.** Special considerations

VIII. Packaging
- **A.** Special program overlay provisions
- **B.** Transfer considerations

IX. Special Notes

X. Appendices

A description of data organization is contained in Section V. File structures maintained on secondary storage media are described during preliminary design, global data (e.g., FORTRAN COMMON) are assigned, and a cross reference that associates individual modules to files or global data is established.

Section VI of the *Design Specification* contains a *requirements cross reference*. The purpose of this cross reference matrix (Figure 10.25) is (1) to establish that all requirements are satisfied by the software design, and (2) to indicate which modules are critical to the implementation of specific requirements.

The first stage in the development of test procedures is contained in Section VII of the design document. Once software structure and interfaces have been established, we can develop guidelines for testing of individual modules and the integration of the entire package. In some cases, a detailed specification of the test procedure occurs in parallel with design. In such cases, this section may be deleted from the *Design Specification*.

Design constraints, such as physical memory limitations or the necessity for a specialized external interface, may dictate special requirements for assembling or packaging of the software. Special considerations caused by the necessity for program overlay, virtual memory management, high-speed processing, or other factors may cause a modification in the design derived from information flow or structure. Requirements and considerations for software packaging are presented in Section VIII. Secondarily, this section describes the approach that will be used to transfer software to a customer site.

Sections IX and X of the *Design Specification* contain supplementary data. Algorithm descriptions, alternative procedures, tabular data, excerpts from other documents, and other relevant information are presented as a

Module name / Requirement paragraph	Module *A*	Module *B*	Module *C*	...	Module *Z*	
Paragraph 3.1.1	√				√	
Paragraph 3.1.2		√	√			
Paragraph 3.1.3		√				
⋮						
Paragraph 3.m.n			√		√	

FIGURE 10.25.
Requirements cross reference.

special note or as a separate appendix. It may be advisable to develop a *Preliminary Operations/Installation Manual* and include it as an appendix to the design document.

10.9 SUMMARY

Design is the technical kernel of software engineering. During design, progressive refinements of data structure, program structure, and procedural detail are developed, reviewed, and documented. Design results in representations of software that can be assessed for quality.

A number of fundamental software design concepts have been proposed over the past three decades. Modularity (in both program and data) and the concept of abstraction enable the designer to simplify and reuse software components. Refinement provides a mechanism for representing successive layers of functional detail. Program and data structure contribute to an overall view of software architecture, while procedure provides the detail necessary for algorithm implementation. Information hiding and functional independence provide heuristics for achieving effective modularity.

Software design can be viewed from either a technical or project management perspective. From the technical point of view, design is comprised of four activities: data design, architectural design, procedural design, and interface design. From the project management viewpoint, the design evolves through preliminary and detail design.

Design notation, coupled with structured programming concepts, enables the designer to represent procedural detail in a manner that facilitates translation to code. Graphical, tabular, and textual notation are available.

We conclude our discussion of design fundamentals with the words of Glenford Myers [MYE78]:

> ...we try to solve the problem by rushing through the design process so that enough time will be left at the end of the project to uncover errors that were made because we rushed through the design process....

The moral is: *Don't rush through it!* Design is worth the effort.

We have not concluded our discussion of design. In the chapters that follow, a number of important software design methods are introduced. These methods, combined with the fundamentals discussed in this chapter, form the basis for a complete view of software design.

REFERENCES

[AHO83] Aho, A.V., J. Hopcroft, and J. Ullmann, *Data Structures and Algorithms,* Addison-Wesley, 1983.

[BOH66] Bohm, C., and G. Jacopini, "Flow Diagrams, Turing Machines and Languages with only Two Formation Rules," *CACM,* vol. 9, no. 5, May 1966, pp. 366–371.

[BOO83] Booch, G., *Software Engineering with Ada,* Benjamin-Cummings, 1983.

[CAI75] Caine, S., and K. Gordon, "PDL—A Tool for Software Design," in *Proc. National Computer Conference,* AFIPS Press, 1975, pp. 271–276.

[CHA74] Chapin, N., "A New Format for Flowcharts," *Software—Practice and Experience,* vol. 4, no. 4, 1974, pp. 341–357.

[CRO90] Cross, J. H., S. V. Sheppard, and W. H. Carlisle, "Control Structure Diagrams for Ada," *Journal of Pascal, Ada and Modula-2,* September-October 1990, pp. 27–33.

[CUR85] Curtis, B., *Human Factors in Software Development,* 2d ed., IEEE Computer Society Press, 1985.

[DAH72] Dahl, O., E. Dijkstra, and C. Hoare, *Structured Programming,* Academic Press, 1972.

[DEN73] Dennis, J., "Modularity," in *Advanced Course on Software Engineering* (F. L. Bauer, ed.), Springer-Verlag, 1973, pp. 128–182.

[DIJ65] Dijkstra, E., "Programming Considered as a Human Activity," in *Proc. 1965 IFIP Congress,* North-Holland Publishing Co., 1965.

[DIJ76] Dijkstra, E., "Structured Programming," in *Software Engineering, Concepts and Techniques,* (J. Buxton et al., eds.), Van Nostrand Reinhold, 1976.

[GAN89] Gannet, G., *Handbook of Algorithms and Data Structures,* 2d ed., Addison-Wesley, 1989.

[HAB83] Haberman, N., and D. E. Perry, *Ada for Experienced Programmers,* Addison-Wesley, 1983.

[HUR83] Hurley, R. B., *Decision Tables in Software Engineering,* Van Nostrand Reinhold, 1983.

[JAC75] Jackson, M., Principles of Program Design, Academic Press, 1975.

[KAI83] Kaiser, S. H., *The Design of Operating Systems for Small Computer Systems,* Wiley-Interscience, 1983, pp. 594ff.

[KRU84] Kruse, R. L., *Data Structures and Program Design,* Prentice-Hall, 1984.

[MEY88] Meyer, B., *Object-Oriented Software Construction,* Prentice-Hall, 1988.

[MIL72] Mills, H. D., "Mathematical Foundations for Structured Programming," Technical Report FSC 71-6012, IBM Corp., Federal Systems Division, Gaithersburg, Maryland, 1972.

[MOR80] Morris, J., "Programming by Successive Refinement of Data Abstractions," *Software—Practice and Experience,* vol. 10, no. 4, April 1980, pp. 249–263.

[MYE78] Myers, G., *Composite Structured Design,* Van Nostrand, 1978.

[NAS73] Nassi, I., and B. Shneiderman, "Flowchart Techniques for Structured Programming," *SIGPLAN Notices,* ACM, August 1973.

[PAR72] Parnas, D. L., "On Criteria to be used in Decomposing Systems into Modules," *CACM,* vol. 14, no. 1, April 1972, pp. 221–227.

[PET81] Peters, L. J., *Software Design: Methods and Techniques,* Yourdon Press, 1981.

[ROS75] Ross, D., J. Goodenough, and C. Irvine, "Software Engineering: Process, Principles and Goals," *IEEE Computer,* vol. 8, no. 5, May 1975.

[SOM89] Sommerville, I., *Software Engineering,* 3d ed., Addison-Wesley, 1989.

[STE74] Stevens, W., G. Myers, and L. Constantine, "Structured Design," *IBM Systems Journal,* vol. 13, no. 2, 1974, pp. 115–139.

[TAY59] Taylor, E.S., *An Interim Report on Engineering Design,* Massachusetts Institute of Technology, 1959.

[WAR74] Warnier, J., *Logical Construction of Programs,* Van Nostrand Reinhold, 1974.

[WAS80] Wasserman, A., "Principles of Systematic Data Design and Implementation," in *Software Design Techniques* (P. Freeman and A. Wasserman, eds.), 3d ed., IEEE Computer Society Press, 1980, pp. 287–293.

[WAS83] Wasserman, A., "Information System Design Methodology," in *Software Design Techniques* (P. Freeman and A. Wasserman, eds.), 4th ed., IEEE Computer Society Press, 1983, p. 43.

[WIR71] Wirth, N., "Program Development by Stepwise Refinement," *CACM,* vol. 14, no. 4, 1971, pp. 221–227.

[YOU79] Yourdon, E., and L. Constantine, *Structured Design,* Prentice-Hall, 1979.

PROBLEMS AND POINTS TO PONDER

10.1 Do you design software when you "write" a program? What makes software design different from coding?

10.2 Apply a "stepwise refinement approach" to develop three different levels of procedural abstraction for one or more of the following programs:

(*a*) Develop a check writer that, given a numeric dollar amount, will print the amount in words that is normally required on a check.

(*b*) Iteratively solve for the roots of a transcendental equation.

(*c*) Develop a simple round-robin scheduling algorithm for an operating system.

10.3 Is there a case when inequality (10.2) may not be true? How might such a case affect the argument for modularity?

10.4 When should a modular design be implemented as monolithic software? How can this be accomplished? Is performance the only justification for the implementation of monolithic software?

10.5 Describe the concept of abstraction for software in your own words.

10.6 Develop at least five levels of abstraction for one of the following software problems:

(*a*) A full screen editor

(*b*) A three-dimensional transformation package for computer graphics applications

(*c*) A BASIC language interpreter

(*d*) A two degree-of-freedom robot controller

(*e*) Any problem mutually agreeable to you and your instructor

As the level of abstraction decreases, your focus may narrow so that at the last level (source code) only a single task need be described.

10.7 Obtain the original Parnas paper [PAR72] and summarize the software example that he uses to illustrate decomposition of a system into modules. How is information hiding used to achieve the decomposition?

10.8 Discuss the relationship between the concept of information hiding as an attribute of effective modularity and the concept of module independence.

10.9 Review some of your recent software development efforts and grade each module (on a scale of 1, low, to 7, high). Bring in samples of your best and worst work.

10.10 A number of high-level programming languages support the internal procedure as a modular construct. How does this construct affect coupling? How does it affect information hiding?

10.11 How are the concepts of coupling and software portability related? Provide examples to support your discussion.

10.12 An enormous literature has evolved on the topic of structured programming. Write a brief paper that highlights the published arguments—pro and con—about the exclusive use of structured constructs.

Problems 10.13 through 10.21 may be represented using any one (or more) of the design notations that have been presented in this chapter. Your instructor may assign a specific notation to a specific problem.

10.13 Develop a procedural design for modules that implement the following sorts: Shell-Metzner sort; heapsort; BSST (tree) sort. Refer to a book on data structures if you are unfamiliar with these sorts.

10.14 Develop a procedural design for an interactive user interface that queries for basic income tax information. Derive your own requirements and assume that all tax computations are performed by other modules.

10.15 Develop a procedural design for a garbage collection function for a variable partitioned memory management scheme. Define all the appropriate data structures in the design representation. Refer to a book on operating systems for more information.

10.16 Develop a procedural design for a program that accepts an arbitrarily long text as input and produces a list of words and their frequencies of occurrence as output.

10.17 Develop the procedural design of a program that will numerically integrate a function f in the bounds a to b.

10.18 Develop the procedural design for a generalized Turing machine that will accept a set of quadruples as program input and produce output as specified.

10.19 Develop the procedural design for a program that will solve the Towers of Hanoi problem. Many introductory books on artificial intelligence discuss this problem in some detail.

10.20 Develop a procedural design for all or major portions of an LR parser for a compiler. Refer to one or more books on compiler design.

10.21 Develop a procedural design for an encryption/decryption algorithm of your choosing.

10.22 Write a one- or two-page argument for the procedural design notation that you feel is best. Be certain that your argument addresses the criteria presented in Section 10.7.6.

FURTHER READINGS

An excellent survey of software design is contained in an anthology edited by Freeman and Wasserman (*Software Design Techniques,* 4th ed., IEEE,

1983). In addition to papers on every important aspect of design, this tutorial reprints many of the "classic" papers that have formed the basis for current trends in software design. Good discussions of software design fundamentals can be found in books by Myers [MYE78], Peters [PET81], Sommerville [SOM89], Fairley (*Software Engineering Concepts,* McGraw-Hill, 1985), and Macro (*Software Engineering: Concepts and Management,* Prentice-Hall, 1990). An excellent survey of different design notations can be found in a book by Martin and McClure (*Diagramming Techniques for Analysts and Programmers,* Prentice-Hall, 1985). Stevens (*Software Design: Concepts and Methods,* Prentice-Hall, 1990) presents a worthwhile treatment of data, architectural, and procedural design.

Mathematically rigorous treatments of computer software and design fundamentals may be found in books by Jones (*Software Development: A Rigorous Approach,* Prentice-Hall, 1980) and Wulf (*Fundamental Structures of Computer Science,* Addison-Wesley, 1981). Each of these texts helps to supply a necessary theoretical foundation for our understanding of computer software. Measures of design quality, presented from both technical and management perspectives, are considered by Card and Glass (*Measuring Software Design Quality,* Prentice-Hall, 1990).

Fundamental design concepts and what others call "programming" are so closely related that no meaningful distinction can be made. Many excellent books on computer programming (particularly recent books on PASCAL, C, and Ada—see Chapter 16 for references) contain many fine examples of good design practice. *Software Tools in Pascal* by Kernighan and Plauger (Addison-Wesley, 1981) was written with the premise that "good programming (detail design) is not learned from generalities, but by seeing... significant programs." The authors provide programming guidance and examples that are invaluable to the student and practitioner alike. The work of Linger, Mills, and Witt (*Structured Programming—Theory and Practice,* Addison-Wesley, 1979) remains a definitive treatment of the subject. The text contains a good PDL as well as detailed discussions of the ramifications of structured programming.

CHAPTER 11

DATA FLOW-ORIENTED DESIGN

Design has been described as a multistep process in which representations of data structure, program structure, and procedure are synthesized from information requirements. This description is extended by Freeman [FRE80]:

> ...design is an activity concerned with making major decisions, often of a structural nature. It shares with programming a concern for abstracting information representation and processing sequences, but the level of detail is quite different at the extremes. Design builds coherent, well planned representations of programs that concentrate on the interrelationships of parts at the higher level and the logical operations involved at the lower levels....

As we have noted in the preceding chapter, design is information-driven. Software design methods are derived from consideration of the information domain.

A data flow-oriented design method is presented in this chapter. The objective of the method is to provide a systematic approach for the derivation of program structure—a global view of software and the underpinning of architectural design.

11.1 DESIGN AND INFORMATION FLOW

The representation of information flow is one element of requirements analysis that we call *information domain analysis* (Chapter 6). Beginning with a *fundamental system model* (Chapter 7), information may be represented as a continuous flow that undergoes a series of transforms (processes) as it evolves from input to output. The *data flow diagram* (DFD) is used as a graphical tool to depict information flow. Data flow-oriented design defines a number of different mappings that transform information flow into program structure.

11.1.1 Contributors

Data flow-oriented design (often called "structured design") has its origins in earlier design concepts that stressed modularity [DEN73], top-down design [WIR71], and structured programming [DAH72, LIN79]. However, the data flow-oriented design approach extended these procedural techniques by explicitly integrating information flow into the design process. Stevens, Myers, and Constantine [STE74] were early proponents of software design based on the flow of data through a system. Early work was refined and presented in books by Myers [MYE78] and Yourdon and Constantine [YOU79]. The methods presented in this chapter are a synthesis of this material.

11.1.2 Areas of Application

Each software design methodology has strengths and weaknesses. An important selection factor for a design method is the breadth of applications to which it can be applied. Data flow-oriented design is amenable to a broad range of application areas. In fact, because all software can be represented by a data flow diagram, a design method that makes use of the diagram could theoretically be applied in every software development effort. A data flow-oriented approach to design is particularly useful when information is processed sequentially and no formal hierarchical data structure exists. For example, microprocessor control applications, complex numerical analysis procedures, process control, and many other engineering and scientific software applications fall into this category. An extension of data flow-oriented design, called *DARTS* [GOM84], adapts the approach to real-time, interrupt-driven applications and is presented in detail in Chapter 15. Data flow-oriented design techniques are also applicable in data processing applications and can be effectively applied even when hierarchical data structures do exist.

There are cases, however, in which a consideration of data flow is at best a side issue. In such applications (e.g., database systems, expert systems, object-oriented interfaces), the design methods described in Chapters 12 and 13 may be more appropriate.

11.2 DESIGN PROCESS CONSIDERATIONS

Data flow-oriented design allows a convenient transition from information representations (e.g., the data flow diagram) contained in a *Software Requirements Specification* to a design description of program structure. The transition from information flow to structure is accomplished as part of a five-step process: (1) The type of information flow is established; (2) flow boundaries are indicated; (3) the DFD is mapped into program structure; (4) the control hierarchy is defined by *factoring;* (5) the resultant structure is refined using design measures and heuristics. The information flow type is the driver for the mapping approach required in step 3. In the following paragraphs we examine two flow types.

11.2.1 Transform Flow

Recalling the fundamental system model (level 0 data flow diagram), information must enter and exit software in an "external world" form. For example, data typed on a keyboard, tones on a telephone line, and pictures on a computer graphics display are all forms of external world information. Such externalized data must be converted into an internal form for processing. The time history of data can be illustrated in Figure 11.1. Information enters the system along paths that transform external data into an internal form and are identified as *incoming flow.* At the kernel of the software, a transition occurs. Incoming data are passed through a *transform center* and

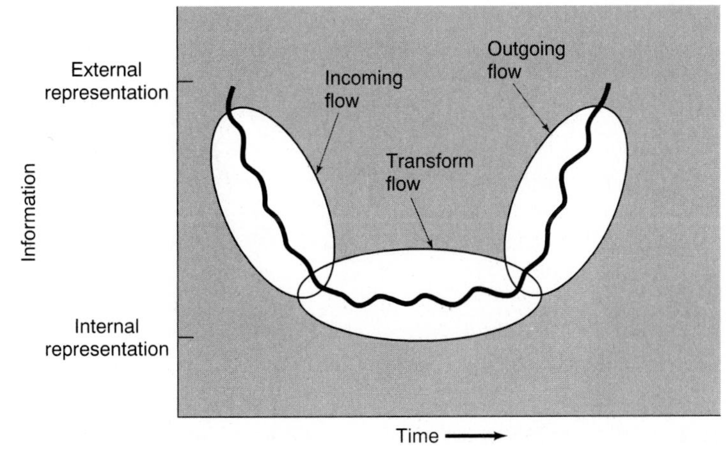

FIGURE 11.1.
Flow of information.

begin to move along paths that now lead "out" of the software. Data moving along these paths are called *outgoing flow.* The overall flow of data occurs in a sequential manner and follows one, or only a few, "straight-line" paths. When a segment of a data flow diagram exhibits these characteristics, *transform flow* is present.

11.2.2 Transaction Flow

The fundamental system model implies transform flow; therefore, it is possible to characterize all data flow in this category. However, information flow is often characterized by a single data item, called a *transaction,* that triggers other data flow along one of many paths. When a DFD takes the form shown in Figure 11.2, *transaction flow* is present.

Transaction flow is characterized by data moving along an incoming path (also called the *reception path*) that converts external world information into a transaction. The transaction is evaluated and, based on its value, flow along one of many *action paths* is initiated. The hub of information flow from which many action paths emanate is called a *transaction center.*

It should be noted that within a DFD for a large system, both transform and transaction flow may be present. For example, in a transaction-oriented flow, information flow along an action path may have transform flow characteristics.

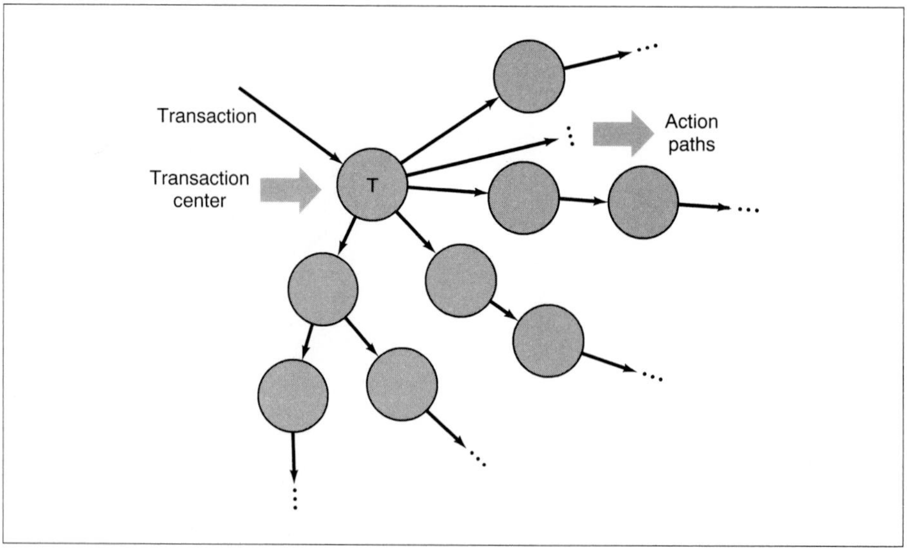

FIGURE 11.2.
Transaction flow.

11.2.3 A Process Abstract

The overall approach to data flow-oriented design is illustrated in Figure 11.3. Design begins with an evaluation of the level 2 or level 3 data flow diagram. The information flow category (i.e., transform or transaction flow) is established, and flow boundaries that delineate the transform or transaction center are defined. Based on the location of boundaries, transforms (the DFD "bubbles") are mapped into program structure as modules. The precise mapping and definition of modules is accomplished by distributing control top-down in the structure (a process called *factoring*) and applying the guidelines for effective modularity described in Chapter 10.

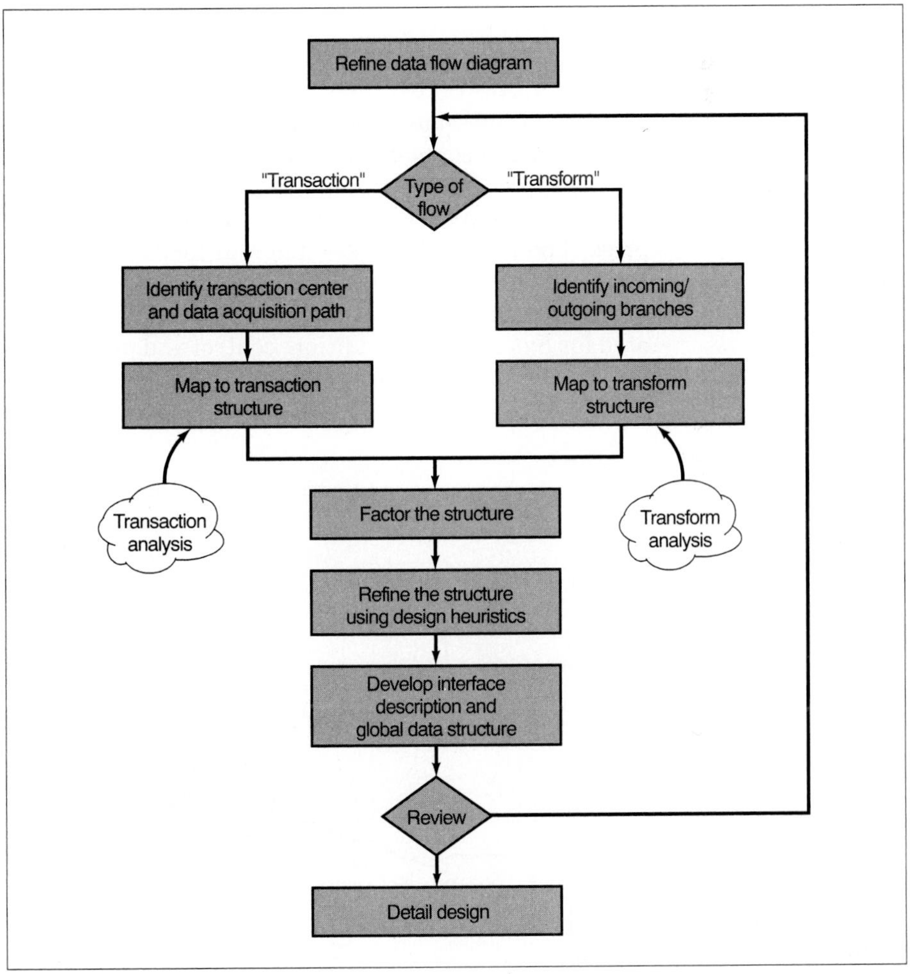

FIGURE 11.3. Data flow-oriented design.

Figure 11.3 illustrates a step-by-step approach to design. However, variation and adaptation can and do occur. Above all, software design demands human judgment that can often transcend the "rules" of a method.

11.3 TRANSFORM ANALYSIS

Transform analysis is a set of design steps that allows a DFD with transform flow characteristics to be mapped into a predefined template for program structure. In this section transform analysis is described by applying design steps to an example system—a portion of the *SafeHome* security software presented in earlier chapters.

11.3.1 An Example

The *SafeHome* security system, introduced in Chapters 6 and 7, is representative of many computer-based products and systems in use today. The product monitors the real world and reacts to changes that it encounters. It also interacts with a user through a series of typed inputs and alphanumeric displays. The level 0 data flow diagram for *SafeHome,* reproduced from Chapter 7, is shown in Figure 11.4.

During requirements analysis, more detailed flow models would be created for *SafeHome*. In addition, control and process specifications, a requirements dictionary, and various behavioral models would also be created.[1]

[1]Readers who have not read Chapters 6 and 7 are urged to do so before continuing with this chapter.

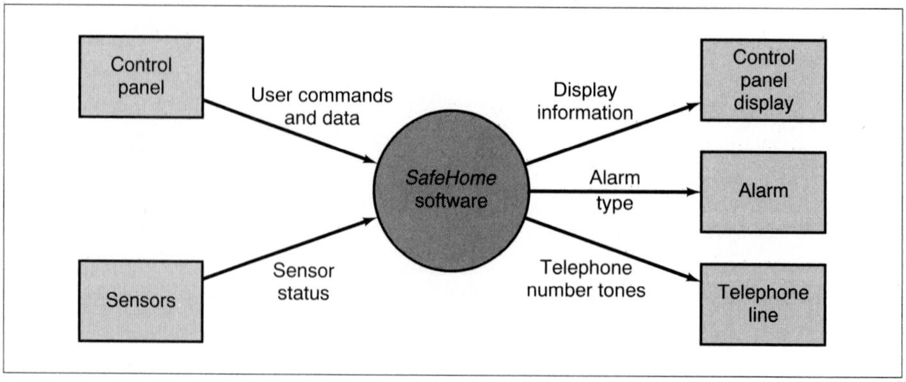

FIGURE 11.4. Context level DFD for *SafeHome*.

11.3.2 Design Steps

The above example will be used to illustrate each step in transform analysis. The steps begin with a re-evaluation of work done during requirements analysis and then move to the development of program structure.

Step 1. Review the Fundamental System Model The fundamental system model encompasses the level 0 DFD and supporting information. In actuality the design step begins with an evaluation of both the *System Specification* and the *Software Requirements Specification*. Both documents describe information flow and structure at the software interface. Figures 11.4 and 11.5 depict level 0 and level 1 data flow for the *SafeHome* software.

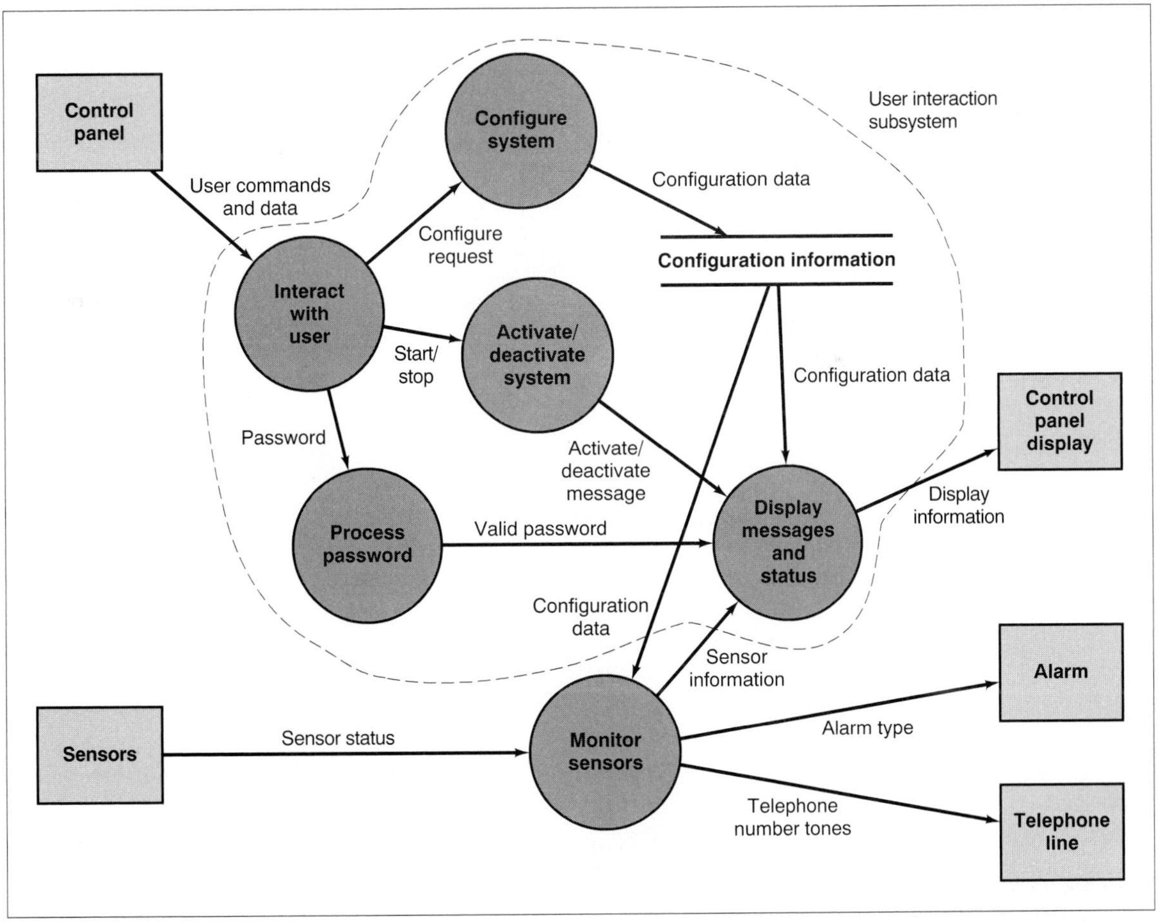

FIGURE 11.5. Level 1 DFD for *SafeHome*.

Step 2. Review and Refine Data Flow Diagrams for the Software Information obtained from analysis models contained in the *Software Requirements Specification* is refined to produce greater detail. For example, the level 1 and 2 DFDs for **monitor sensors** (Figures 11.5 and 11.6) are examined, and a level 3 data flow diagram is derived as shown in Figure 11.7. At level 3, each transform in the data flow diagram exhibits relatively high *cohesion* (Chapter 10). That is, the process implied by a transform performs a single, distinct function that can be implemented as a module in the *SafeHome* software. Therefore, the DFD in Figure 11.7 contains sufficient detail for a "first cut" at the design of program structure for the **monitor sensors** subsystem and we proceed without further refinement.

Step 3. Determine Whether the DFD Has Transform or Transaction Flow Characteristics In general, information flow within a system can always be represented as transform. However, when an obvious transaction characteristic (Figure 11.2) is encountered, a different design mapping is recommended. In this step, the designer selects a global (software-wide) flow characteristic based on the prevailing nature of the DFD. In addition, local regions of transform or transaction flow are isolated. These *subflows* can be used to refine program structure derived from a global characteristic de-

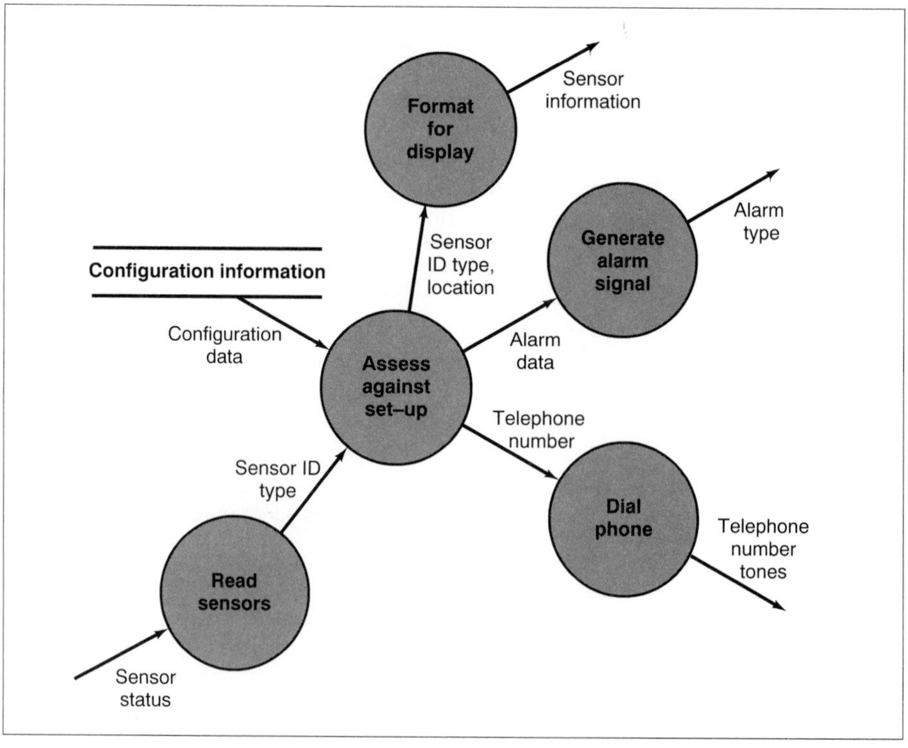

FIGURE 11.6. Level 2 DFD that refines the **Monitor Sensors** process.

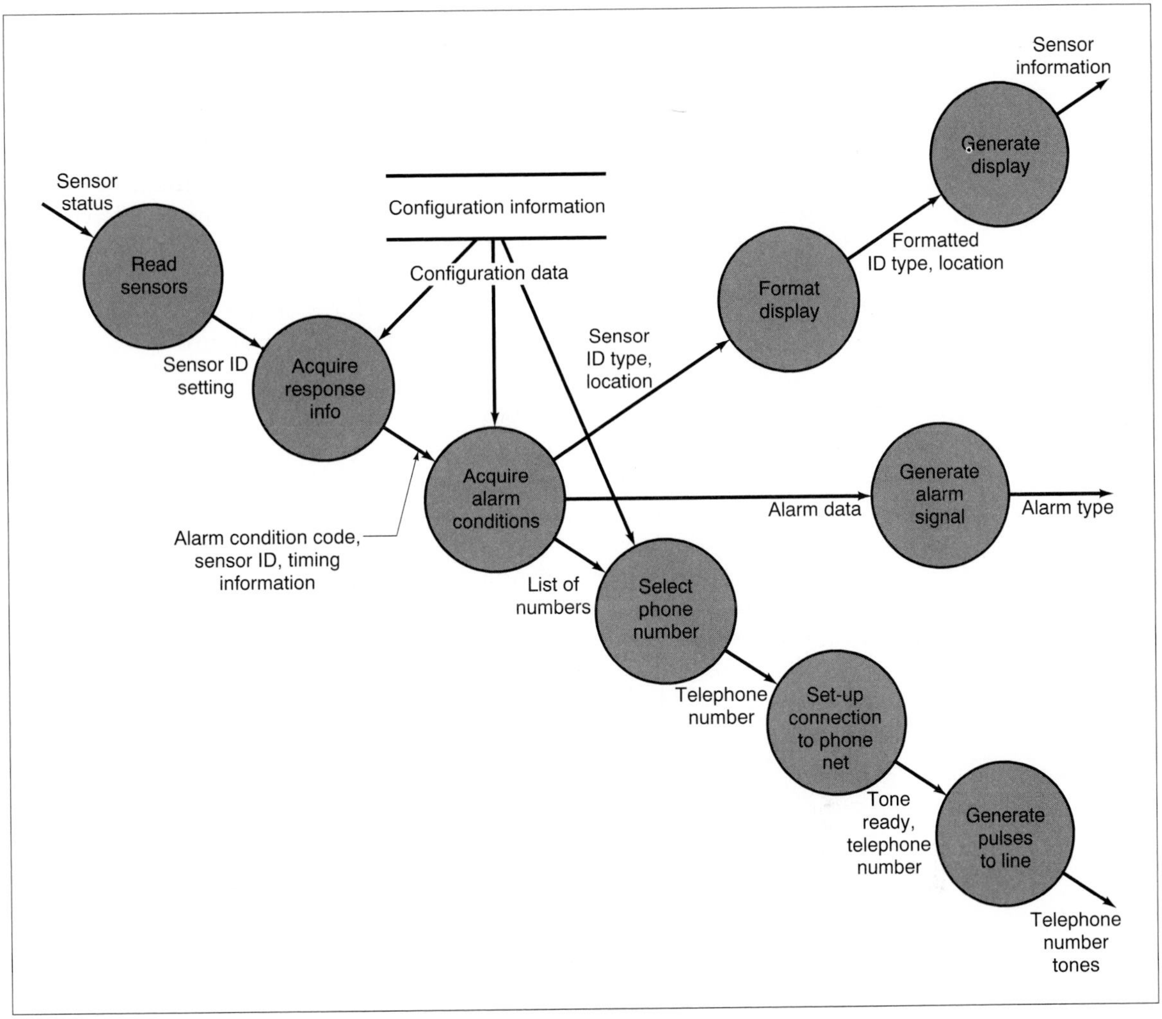

FIGURE 11.7. Level 3 DFD that refines the **Monitor Sensors** process.

scribed above. For now, we focus our attention only on the **monitor sensors** subsystem data flow depicted in Figure 11.7.

Evaluating the DFD (Figure 11.7), we see data entering the software along one incoming path and exiting along three outgoing paths. No distinct transaction center is implied (although the transform **acquire alarm conditions** could be perceived as such). Therefore, an overall transform characteristic will be assumed for information flow.

Step 4. Isolate the Transform Center by Specifying Incoming and Outgoing Flow Boundaries In the preceding section incoming flow was described as a path in which information is converted from external to internal form; outgoing flow converts from internal to external form. Incoming and outgoing flow boundaries are open to interpretation. That is, different designers may select slightly different points in the flow as boundary locations. In fact, alternative design solutions can be derived by varying the placement of flow boundaries. Although care should be taken when boundaries are selected, a variance of one bubble along a flow path will generally have little impact on the final program structure.

Flow boundaries for the example are illustrated in Figure 11.8. The transforms (bubbles) that comprise the transform center lie within the two dotted boundaries that run from top to bottom in the figure. An argument

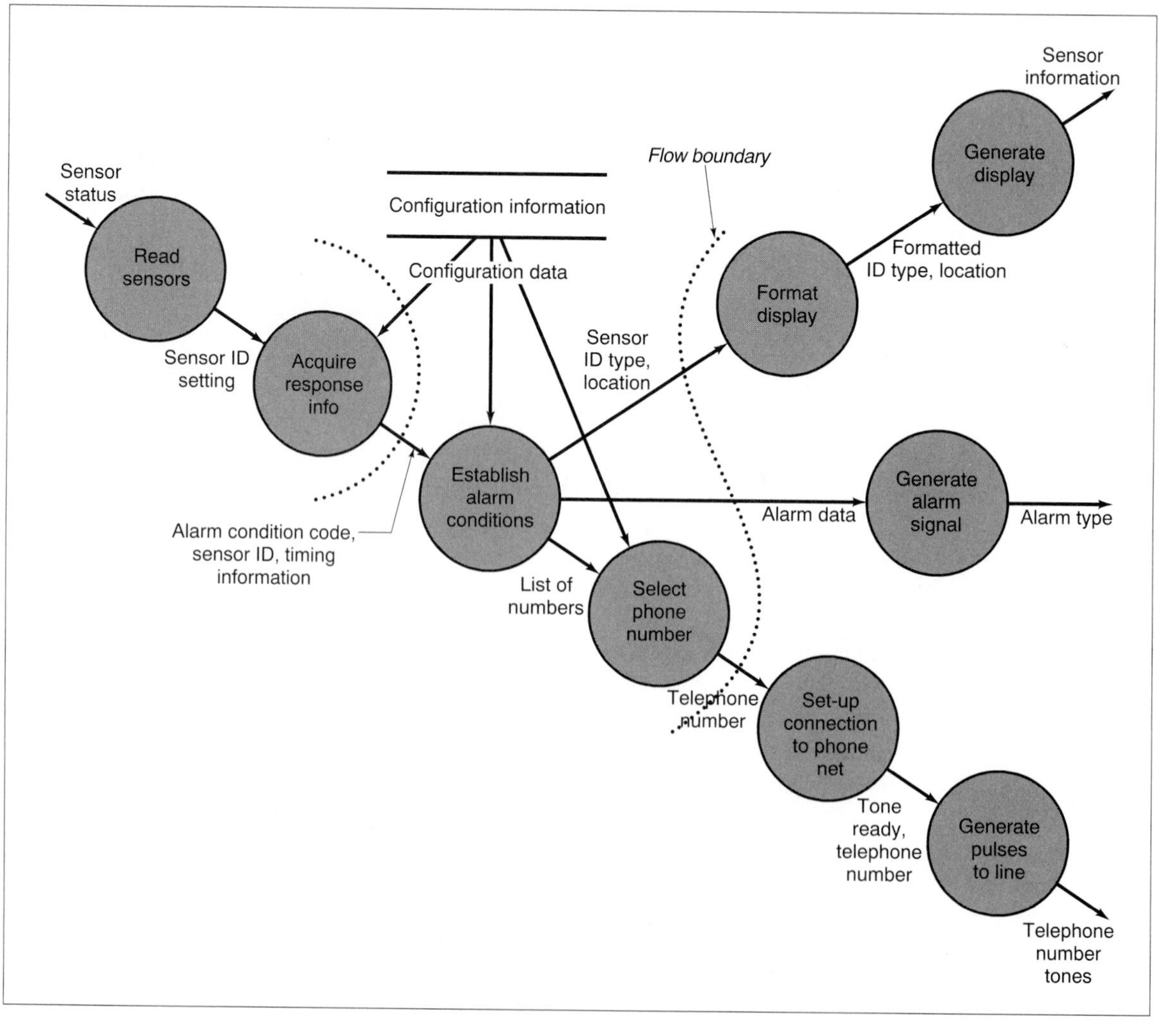

FIGURE 11.8. Specifying flow boundaries.

can be made to re-adjust a boundary (e.g., an incoming flow boundary separating **read sensors** and **acquire response info** could be proposed). The emphasis in this design step should be on selecting reasonable boundaries, rather than lengthy iteration on placement of the boundaries.

Step 5. Perform "First-Level Factoring" Program structure represents a top-down distribution of control. *Factoring* results in a program structure in which top-level modules perform decision making and low-level modules perform most input, computational, and output work. Middle-level modules perform some control and do moderate amounts of work.

When transform flow is encountered, a DFD is mapped to a specific structure that provides control for incoming, transform, and outgoing information processing. This *first-level factoring* is illustrated in Figure 11.9. A main controller resides at the top of the program structure and serves to coordinate the following subordinate control functions:

- An incoming information processing controller that coordinates the receipt of all incoming data
- A transform flow controller that supervises all operations on data in internalized form (e.g., a module that invokes various data transformation procedures)
- An outgoing information processing controller that coordinates the production of output information

Although a three-pronged structure is implied by Figure 11.9, complex flows in large systems may dictate two or more control modules for each of

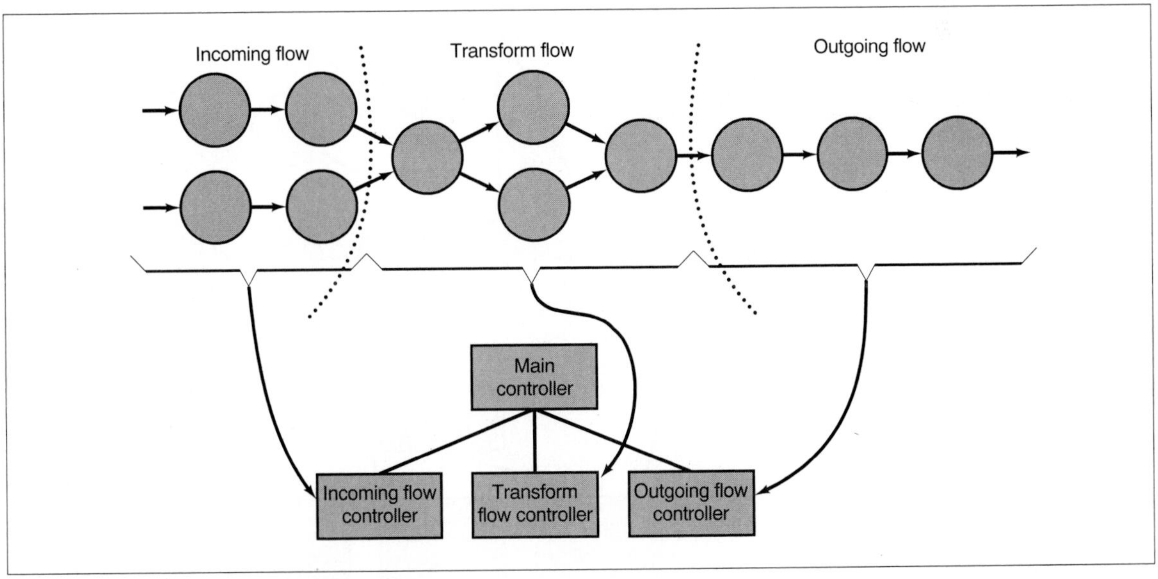

FIGURE 11.9. First-level factoring.

the generic control functions described above. The number of modules at the first level should be limited to the minimum that can accomplish control functions and still maintain good coupling and cohesion characteristics.

Continuing the **monitor sensors** subsystem for *SafeHome,* first-level factoring is illustrated as a structure in Figure 11.10. Each control module is given a name that implies the function of the subordinate modules it controls.

Step 6. Perform "Second-Level Factoring" *Second level factoring* is accomplished by mapping individual transforms (bubbles) of a DFD into appropriate modules within the program structure. Beginning at the transform center boundary, and moving outward along incoming and then outgoing paths, transforms are mapped into subordinate levels of the program structure. The general approach to second-level factoring is illustrated in Figure 11.11.

Although Figure 11.11 illustrates a one-to-one mapping between DFD transforms and software modules, different mappings frequently occur. Two or even three bubbles can be combined and represented as one module (recalling potential problems with cohesion) or a single bubble may be expanded to two or more modules. Practical considerations and measures of design quality dictate the outcome of second-level factoring.

Program structure derived from the outgoing flow paths of the DFD (Figure 11.8) is shown in Figure 11.12. A simple one-to-one mapping of bub-

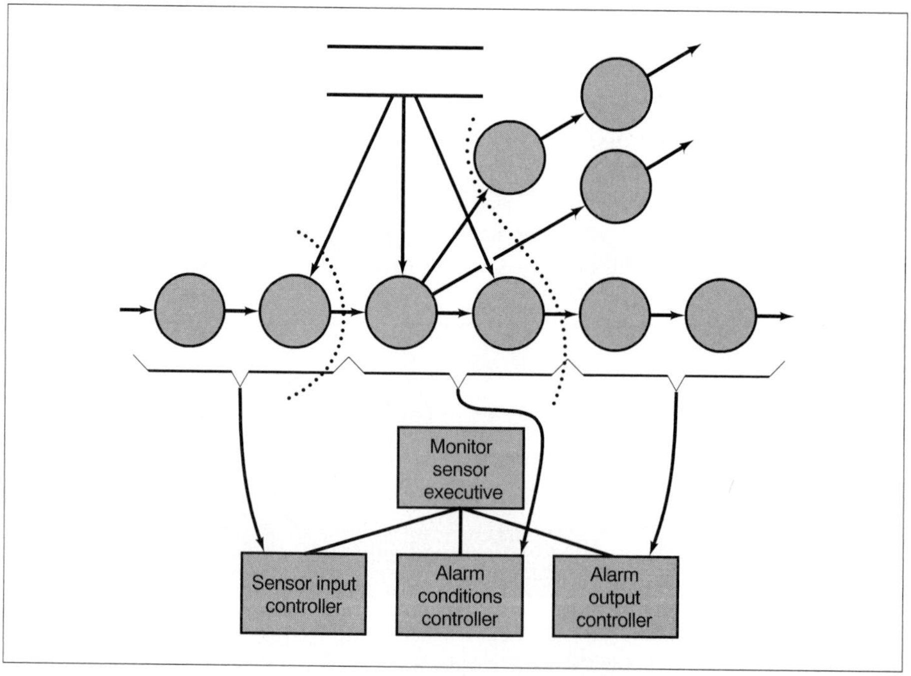

FIGURE 11.10. First-level factoring for **Monitor Sensors.**

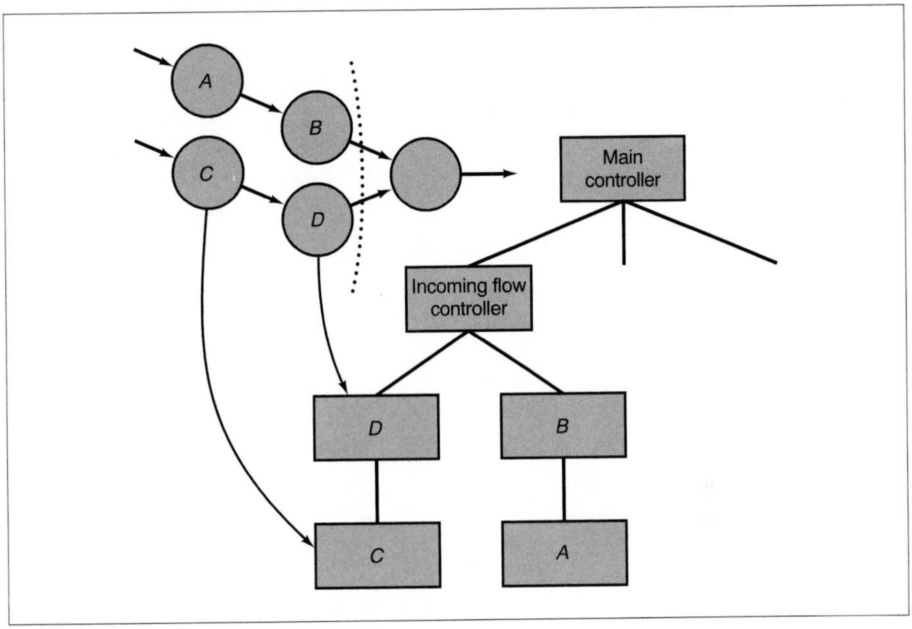

FIGURE 11.11. Second-level factoring.

bles to modules can be observed by following flow from the transform center boundary outward. Review and refinement may lead to changes in this structure, but it can serve as a "first-cut" design.

Second-level factoring for incoming flow follows in the same manner. Factoring is again accomplished by moving outward from the transform center boundary on the incoming flow side. The transform center of **monitor sensors** subsystem software is mapped somewhat differently. Each of the data conversion or calculation transforms of the transform portion of the DFD is mapped into a module subordinate to the transform controller. A completed "first-cut" program structure is shown in Figure 11.13. The program structure representation is often called a *structure chart.*

The modules mapped in the manner described above and shown in Figure 11.13 represent an initial design of the program structure. Although modules are named in a manner that implies function, a brief processing narrative (adapted from the PSPEC created during analysis modeling) should be written for each. The narrative describes

- Information that passes into and out of the module (an interface description)
- Information that is retained by a module, e.g., data stored in a local data structure
- A procedural narrative that indicates major decisions points and tasks
- A brief discussion of restrictions and special features (e.g., file I/O, hardware-dependent characteristics, special timing requirements)

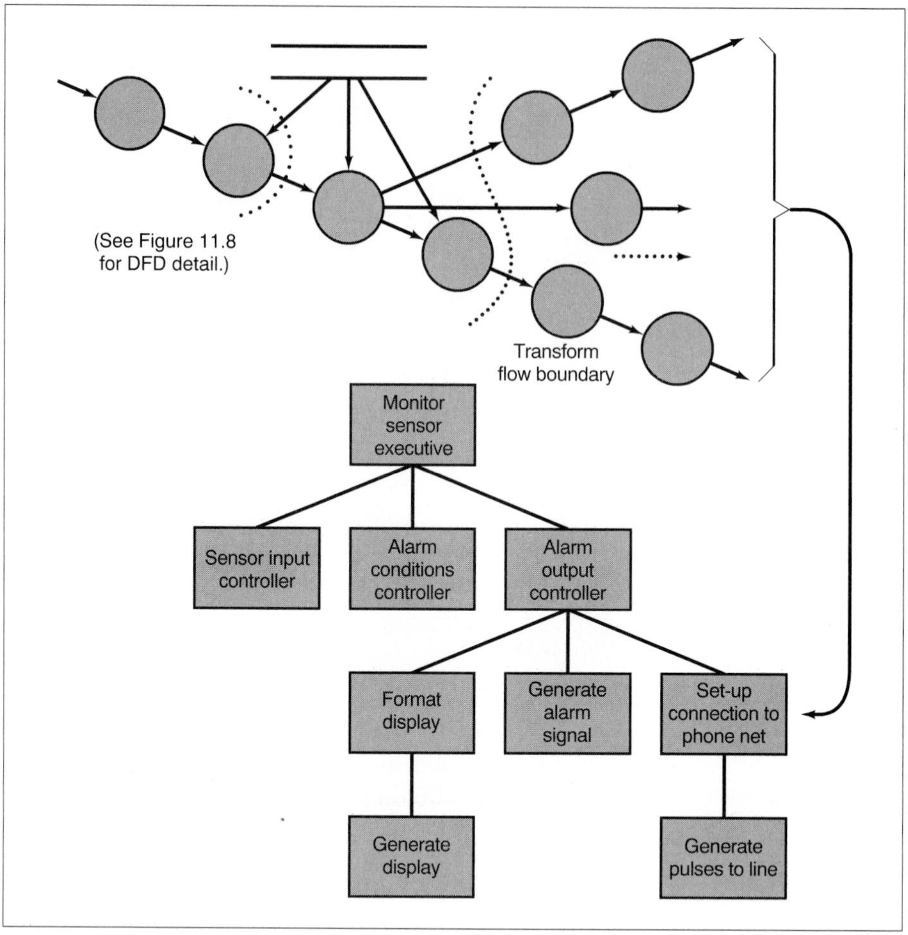

FIGURE 11.12. First-level factoring for **Monitor Sensors.**

The narrative serves as a first-generation *Design Specification*. However, further refinement and additions occur regularly during this period of design.

Step 7. Refine the "First-Cut" Program Structure Using Design Heuristics for Improved Software Quality A first-cut program structure can always be refined by applying concepts of module independence (Chapter 10). Modules are *exploded* or *imploded* to produce sensible factoring, good cohesion, minimal coupling, and, most importantly, a structure that can be implemented without difficulty, tested without confusion, and maintained without grief.

Refinements are dictated by practical considerations and common sense. There are times, for example, when the controller for incoming data flow is totally unnecessary, when some input processing is required in a

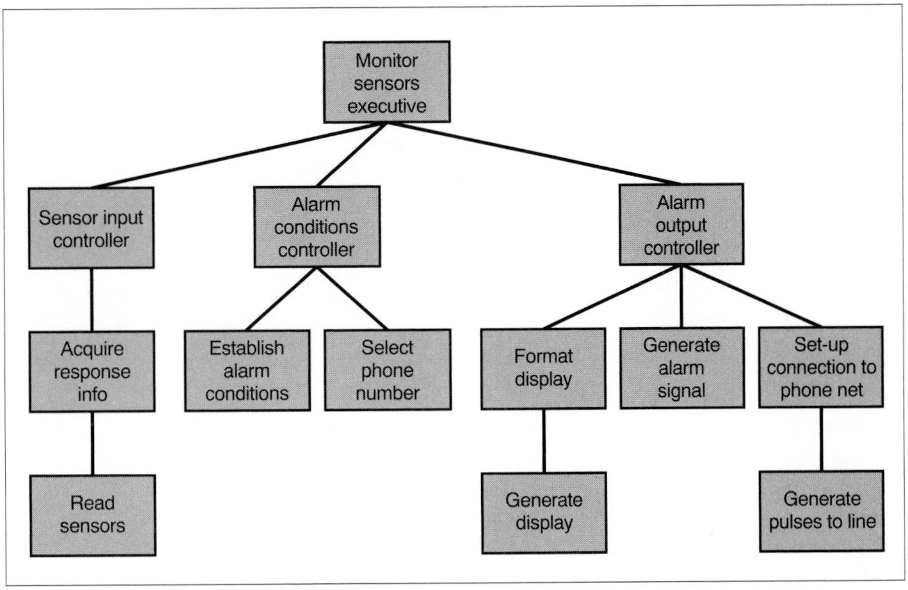

FIGURE 11.13. "First-cut" program structure (structure chart) for **Monitor Sensors.**

module that is subordinate to the transform controller, when high coupling due to global data cannot be avoided, or when optimal structural characteristics (see Section 10.6) cannot be achieved. Software requirements coupled with human judgment is the final arbiter.

Many modifications can be made to the first-cut structure developed for the *SafeHome* **monitor sensors** subsystem. Among many possibilities: (1) The incoming controller can be removed in that it is unnecessary when a single incoming flow path is to be managed; (2) the substructure generated from the transform flow can be imploded into the module **establish alarm conditions** (which will now include the processing implied by **select phone number**); the transform controller will not be needed and the small decrease in cohesion is tolerable; (3) the modules **format display** and **generate display** can be imploded (we assume that display formatting is quite simple) into a new module called **produce display.** The refined program structure for the **monitor sensors** subsystem is shown in Figure 11.14.

The objective of the preceding seven steps is to develop a global representation of software. That is, once structure is defined, we can evaluate and refine software architecture by viewing it as a whole. Modifications made at this time require little additional work, yet can have a profound impact on software quality and maintainability.

The reader should pause for a moment and consider the difference between the design approach described above and the process of "writing programs." If code is the only representation of software, the developer will have great difficulty evaluating or refining at a global or holistic level and will, in fact, have difficulty "seeing the forest for the trees."

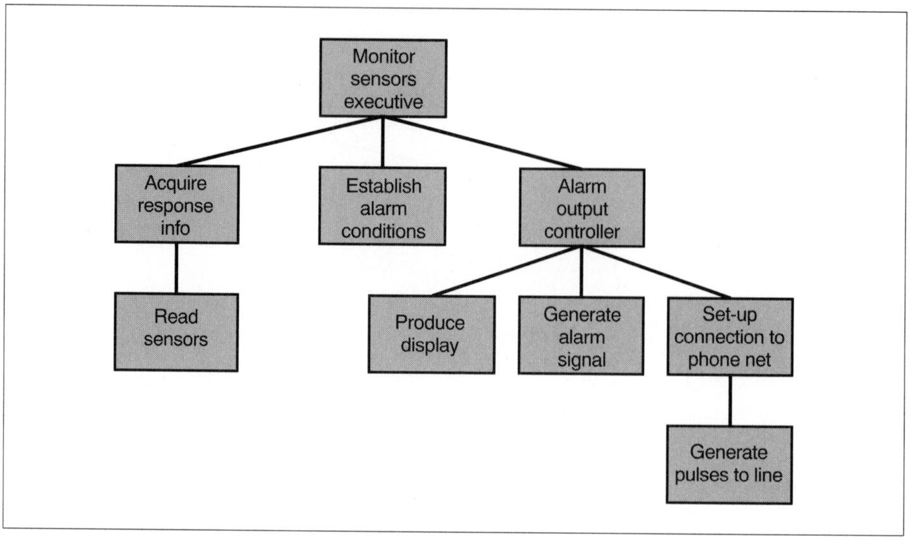

FIGURE 11.14. Refined program structure for **Monitor Sensors.**

11.4 TRANSACTION ANALYSIS

In many software applications, a single data item triggers one or a number of information flows that affect a function implied by the triggering data item. The data item, called a *transaction,* and its corresponding flow characteristics were discussed in Section 11.2.2. In this section we consider design steps used to treat transaction flow.

11.4.1 An Example

Transaction analysis will be illustrated by considering the user interaction subsystem of the *SafeHome* software. Level 1 data flow for this subsystem is shown as part of Figure 11.5. Refining the flow, a level 2 data flow diagram (a corresponding data dictionary, CSPEC, and PSPECs, would also be created) is developed and shown in Figure 11.15.

Referring to Figure 11.15, **user commands and data** flows into the system and results in additional information flow along one of three action paths. A single data item, **command type**, causes the data flow to fan outward from a hub. Therefore, the overall data flow characteristic is transaction-oriented.

It should be noted that information flow along two of the three action paths accommodates additional incoming flow (e.g., **system parameters and data** are input on the "configure" action path). Each action path flows into a single transform, **display messages and status.**

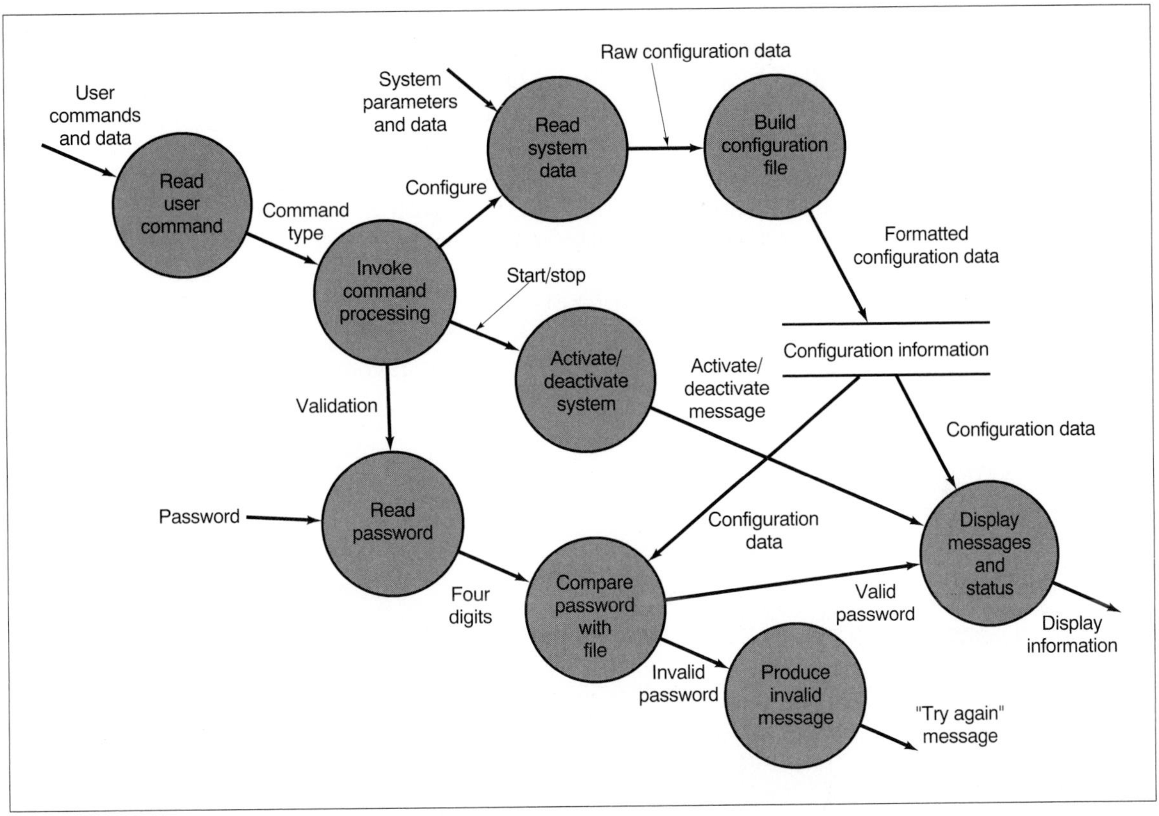

FIGURE 11.15. Level 2 DFD for user interaction subsystem.

11.4.2 Design Steps

The design steps for transaction analysis are similar and in some cases identical to the steps for transform analysis (Section 11.3). A major difference lies in the mapping of DFD to program structure.

Step 1. Review the Fundamental System Model

Step 2. Review and Refine Data Flow Diagrams for the Software

Step 3. Determine Whether the DFD Has Transform or Transaction Flow Characteristics Steps 1, 2, and 3 are identical to the corresponding steps in transform analysis. The DFD shown in Figure 11.15 has a classic transaction flow characteristic. However, flow along two of the action paths emanating from the **invoke command processing** bubble appears to have transform flow characteristics. Therefore, flow boundaries must be established for both flow types.

Step 4. Identify the Transaction Center and the Flow Characteristics Along Each of the Action Paths The location of the transaction center can be immediately discerned from the DFD. The transaction center lies at the origin of a number of action paths that flow radially from it. For the flow shown in Figure 11.15, the **invoke command processing** bubble is the transaction center.

The incoming path (i.e., the flow path along which a transaction is received) and all action paths must also be isolated. Boundaries that define a reception path and action paths are shown in Figure 11.16. Each action path must be evaluated for its individual flow characteristic. For example, the "password processing" path (shown enclosed by a shaded area in Figure 11.16) has transform characteristics. Incoming, transform, and outgoing flow are indicated with boundaries.

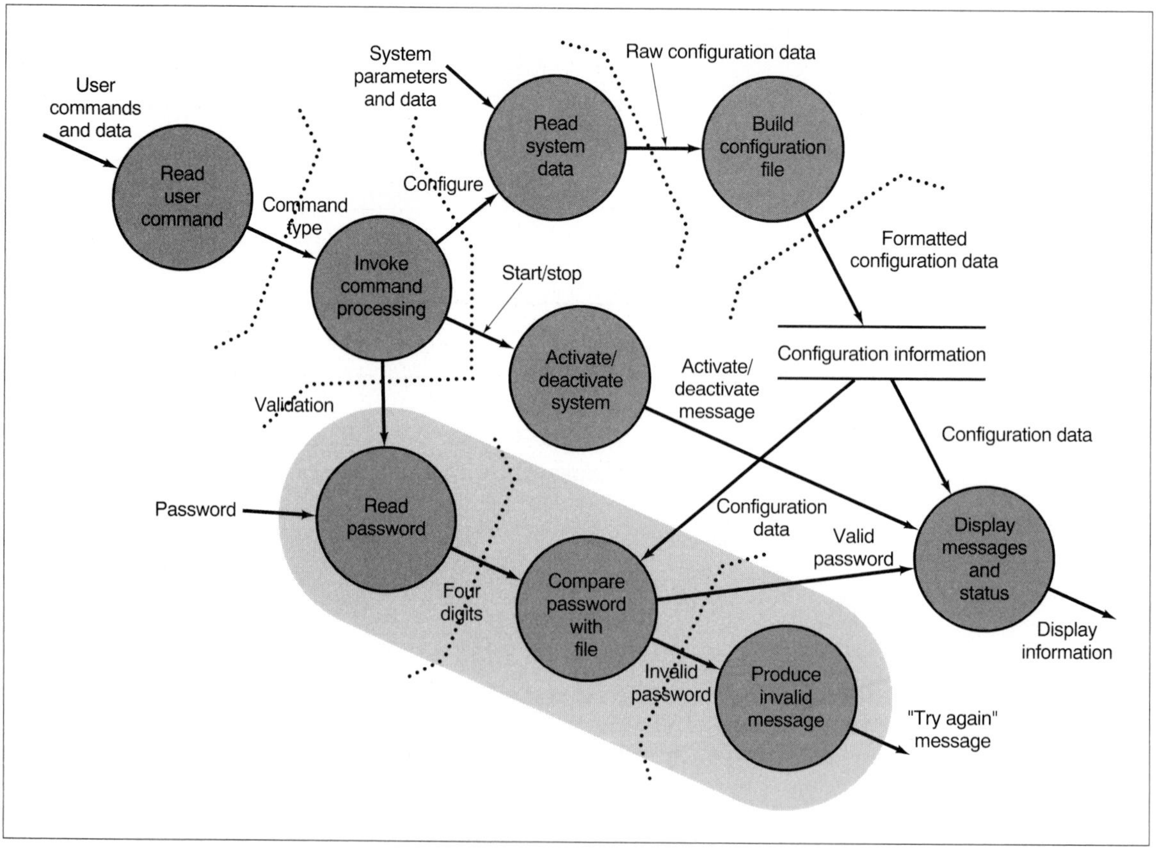

FIGURE 11.16. Establishing flow boundaries.

Step 5. Map the DFD in a Program Structure Amenable to Transaction Processing Transaction flow is mapped into a program structure that contains an incoming branch and a *dispatch branch*. Structure for the incoming branch is developed in much the same way as transform analysis. Starting at the transaction center, bubbles along the incoming path (the reception path) are mapped into modules. The structure of the dispatch branch contains a *dispatcher module* that controls all subordinate action path controllers. Each action path of the DFD is mapped to a structure that corresponds to its specific flow characteristics. This process is illustrated in Figure 11.17.

Considering the user interaction subsystem data flow, first-level factoring for step 5 is shown in Figure 11.18. The bubbles **read user command** and **activate/deactivate system** map directly into the program structure without the need for intermediate control modules. The transaction center **invoke command processing** maps directly into a dispatcher module of the same name. Controllers for system configuration and password processing are derived using the mapping shown in Figure 11.17.

Step 6. Factor and Refine the Transaction Structure and the Structure of Each Action Path Each action path of the data flow diagram has its own

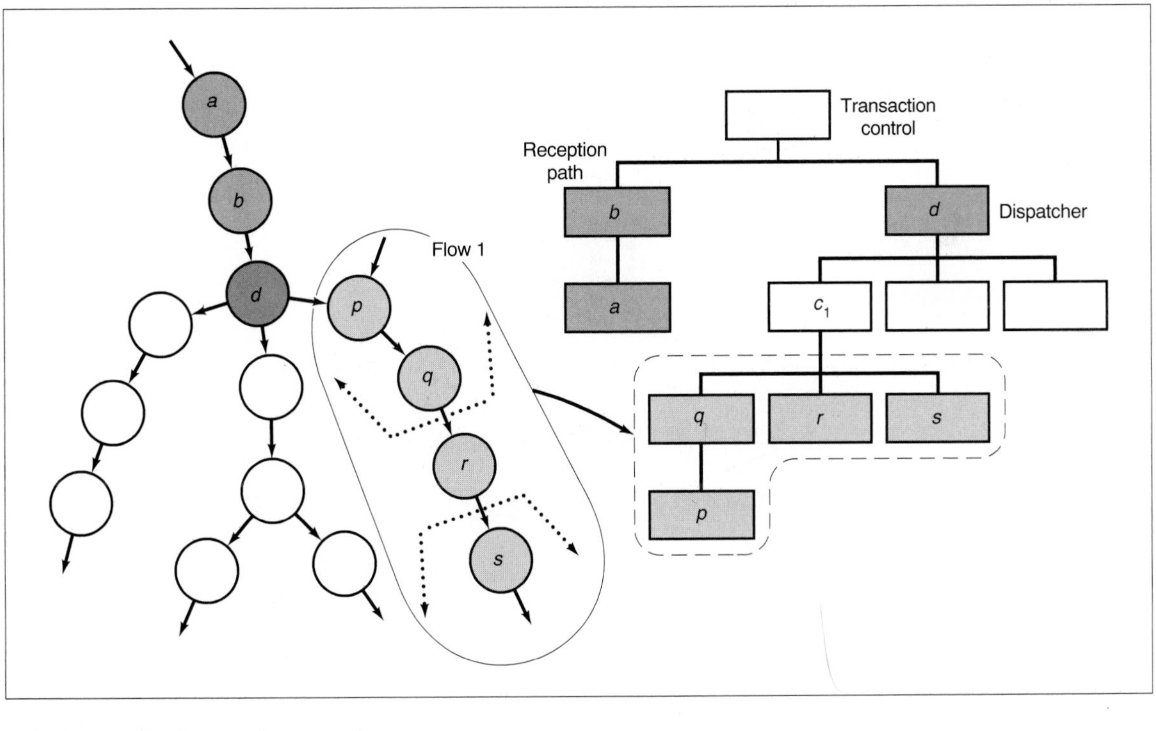

FIGURE 11.17. Transaction mapping.

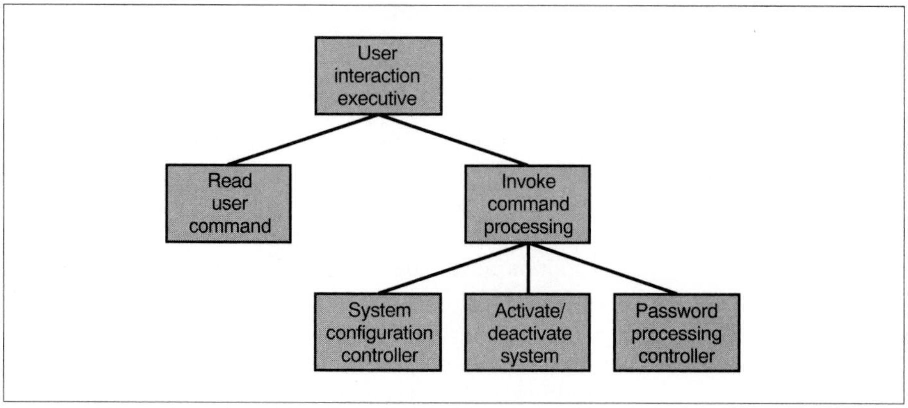

FIGURE 11.18. First-level factoring for user interaction subsystem.

information flow characteristics. We have already noted that transform or transaction flow may be encountered. The action path-related "substructure" is developed using the design steps discussed in this and the preceding section.

As an example, consider the "password processing" information flow shown (inside shaded area) in Figure 11.16. The flow exhibits classic trans-

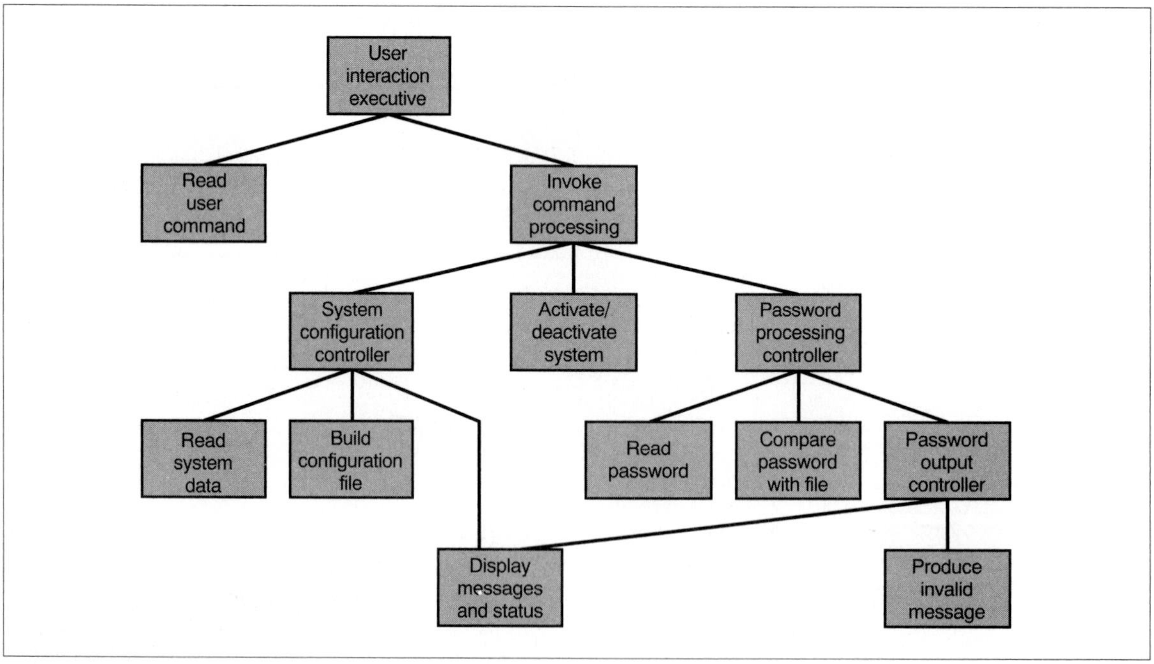

FIGURE 11.19. "First-cut" program structure for user interaction subsystem.

form characteristics. A password is input (incoming flow) and transmitted to a transform center where it is compared against stored passwords. An alarm and warning message (outgoing flow) are then produced. The "configure" path is drawn similarly using transform mapping. The resultant program structure is shown in Figure 11.19.

Step 7. Refine the "First-Cut" Program Structure Using Design Heuristics for Improved Software Quality This step for transaction analysis is identical to the corresponding step for transform analysis. In both design approaches, criteria such as module independence, practicality (efficacy of implementation and test), and maintainability must be carefully considered as structural modifications are proposed.

11.5 DESIGN HEURISTICS

Once a program structure is developed using data flow-oriented design, effective modularity can be achieved by applying the concepts introduced in Chapter 10 and manipulating the resultant structure according to a set of heuristics (guidelines) presented in this section.

I. Evaluate the "First-Cut" Program Structure to Reduce Coupling and Improve Cohesion Once program structure has been developed, modules may be *exploded* or *imploded* with an eye toward improving module independence. An exploded module becomes two or more modules in the final program structure. An imploded module is the result of combining the processing implied by two or more modules.

An exploded module often results when a common process component exists in two or more modules and can be redefined as a separate cohesive module. When high coupling is expected, modules can sometimes be imploded to reduce passage of control, reference to global data, and interface complexity.

II. Attempt to Minimize Structures with High Fan-Out; Strive for Fan-In as Depth Increases The structure shown on the left-hand side of Figure 11.20 does not make effective use of factoring. In general, a more reasonable distribution of control is shown in the right-hand structure of the figure. The structure takes an oval shape, indicating a number of layers of control and highly utilitarian modules at lower levels.

III. Keep Scope of Effect of a Module within the Scope of Control of That Module The *scope of effect* of a module m is defined as all other modules that are affected by a decision made in module m. The *scope of control* of module m is all modules that are subordinate and ultimately subordinate to module m. Figure 11.21 illustrates a violation of heuristic III and a modification that satisfies the heuristic.

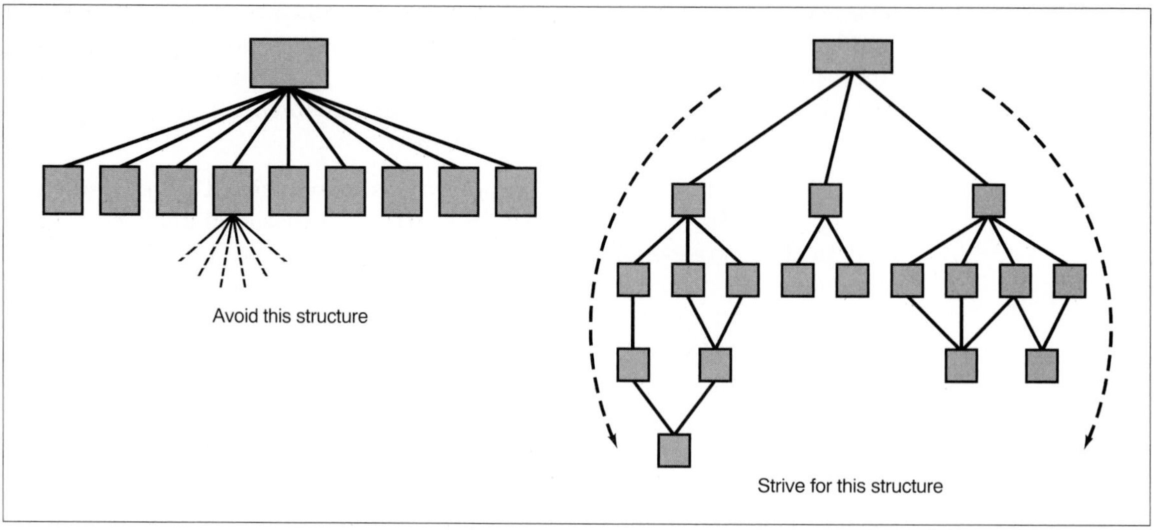

FIGURE 11.20. Fan-in and fan-out.

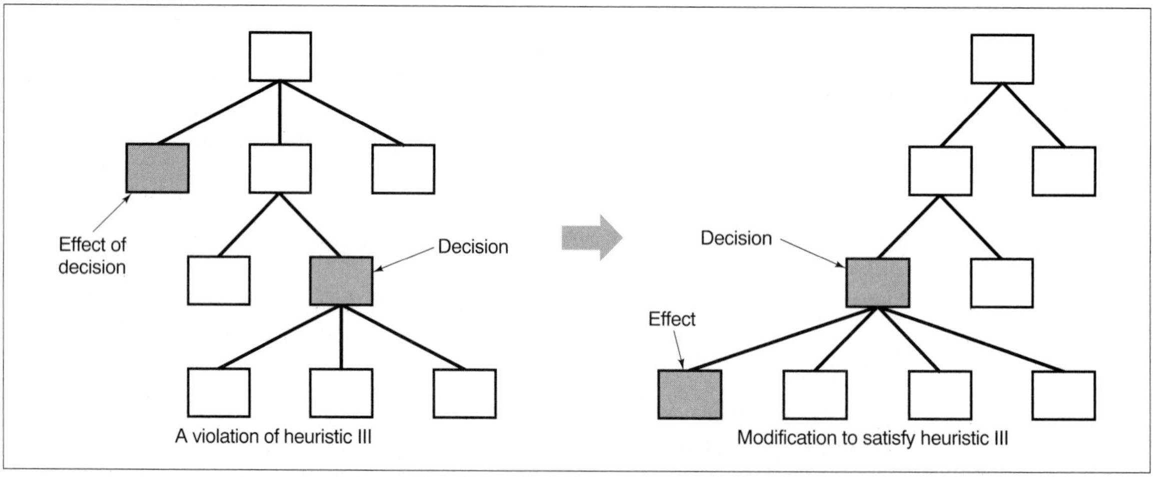

FIGURE 11.21. Scope of effect and control.

IV. Evaluate Module Interfaces to Reduce Complexity and Redundancy and Improve Consistency Module interface complexity is a prime cause of software errors. Interfaces should be designed to pass information simply and should be consistent with the function of a module. Interface inconsistency (i.e., seemingly unrelated data passed via an argument list or other technique) is an indication of low cohesion. The module in question should be re-evaluated.

V. Define Modules Whose Function Is Predictable, But Avoid Modules That Are Overly Restrictive A module is predictable when it can be treated as a "black box," that is, when the same external data will be produced regardless of internal processing details.[2] Modules that have internal "memory" can be unpredictable unless care is taken in their use.

A module that restricts processing to a single subfunction exhibits high cohesion and is viewed with favor by a designer. However, a module that arbitrarily restricts the size of a local data structure, options within control flow, or modes of external interface will invariably require maintenance to remove such restrictions.

VI. Strive for Single-Entry–Single-Exit Modules, Avoiding "Pathological Connections" This design heuristic warns against content coupling (Chapter 10). Software is easier to understand, and therefore easier to maintain when modules are entered at the top and exited at the bottom. "Pathological connection" refers to branches or references into the middle of a module.

VII. Package Software Based on Design Constraints and Portability Requirements "Packaging" alludes to the techniques used to assemble software for a specific processing environment. Design constraints sometimes dictate that a program "overlay" itself in memory. When this must occur, the design structure may have to be reorganized to group modules by degree of repetition, frequency of access, and interval between calls. In addition optional or "one-shot" modules may be separated in the structure so that they may be effectively overlaid. An excellent discussion of packaging considerations for software design is presented in Yourdon and Constantine [YOU79].

11.6 DESIGN POSTPROCESSING

Successful application of transform or transaction analysis is supplemented by additional documentation that is required as part of the architectural design. After the structure has been developed and refined, the following tasks must be completed:

- A processing narrative is developed for each module.
- An interface description is provided for each module.
- Local and global data structures are defined.
- All design restrictions/limitations are noted.
- A preliminary design review is conducted.
- "Optimization" is considered (if required and justified).

---

[2]A black box module is a *procedural abstraction* that exhibits good information hiding. See Chapter 10 for details.

A processing narrative is (ideally) an unambiguous, bounded description of processing that occurs within a module. The narrative describes processing tasks, decisions, and I/O.

The design of data structures can have a profound impact on program structure and the procedural details for each module. Techniques described in Chapters 8 and 10 can be applied to design both local and global data structures.

Restrictions and/or limitations for each module are also documented. Typical topics for discussion include restriction of data type or format, memory or timing limitations, bounding values or quantities of data structures, special cases not considered, specific characteristics of an individual module. The purpose of a restrictions/limitations section is to reduce the number of errors introduced because of "assumed" functional characteristics.

Once design documentation has been developed for all modules, a preliminary design review is conducted (see Chapter 17 for review guidelines). The review emphasizes traceability to software requirements, quality of program structure, interface descriptions, data structure descriptions, implementation and test practicality, and maintainability.

11.7 DESIGN OPTIMIZATION

Any discussion of design optimization should be prefaced with the following comment: Remember that an "optimal design" that doesn't work has questionable merit. The software designer should be concerned with developing a representation of software that will meet all functional and performance requirements and merit acceptance based on design measures and heuristics.

Refinement of program structure during the early stages of design is to be encouraged. Alternative representations may be derived, refined, and evaluated for the "best" approach. This approach to optimization is one of the true benefits derived by developing a representation of software architecture.

It is important to note that structural simplicity often reflects both elegance and efficiency. Design optimization should strive for the smallest number of modules that is consistent with effective modularity and the least complex data structure that adequately serves the information requirements.

For time-critical applications, it may be necessary to "optimize" during detailed design and, possibly, during coding. The software developer should note, however, that a relatively small percentage (typically, 10 to 20 percent) of a program often accounts for a large percentage (50 to 80 percent) of all processing time. It is not unreasonable to propose the following approach for time-critical software:

1. Develop and refine the program structure without concern for time-critical optimization.
2. Use CASE tools that simulate run-time performance to isolate areas of inefficiency.

3. During detail design, select modules that are suspected "time hogs" and carefully develop procedures (algorithms) for time efficiency.
4. Code in a high-order programming language.
5. Instrument the software to isolate modules that account for heavy processor utilization.
6. If necessary, redesign or recode in machine dependent language to improve efficiency.

This approach follows a dictum that will be further discussed in a later chapter: Get it to work, then make it fast.

11.8 SUMMARY

Data flow-oriented design is a method that uses information flow characteristics to derive program structure. A data flow diagram is mapped into the program structure using one of two mapping approaches—transform analysis or transaction analysis.

Transform analysis is applied to an information flow that exhibits distinct boundaries between incoming and outgoing data. The DFD is mapped into a structure that allocates control to input, processing, and output along three separately factored module hierarchies.

Transaction analysis is applied when a single information item causes flow to branch along one of many paths. The DFD is mapped into a structure that allocates control to a substructure that acquires and evaluates a transaction. Another substructure controls all the potential processing actions based on a transaction.

The techniques presented in this chapter lead to a preliminary design description of software. Modules are defined, interfaces are established, and data structure is developed. These design representations form the basis for all subsequent development work.

REFERENCES

[DAH72] Dahl, O., E. Dijkstra, and C. Hoare, *Structured Programming*, Academic Press, 1972.

[DEN73] Dennis, J. B., "Modularity," in *Advanced Course on Software Engineering* (F. L. Bauer, ed.), Springer-Verlag, 1973, pp. 128–182.

[FRE80] Freeman, P., "The Context of Design," in *Software Design Techniques*, 3d ed. (P. Freeman and A. Wasserman, eds.), IEEE Computer Society Press, 1980, pp. 2–4.

[GOM84] Gomaa, H., "A Software Design Method for Real Time Systems," *CACM*, vol. 27, no. 9, September 1984, pp. 938–949.

[LIN79] Linger, R.C., H.D. Mills, and B.I. Witt, *Structured Programming*, Addison-Wesley, 1979.

[MYE78] Myers, G., *Composite Structured Design,* Van Nostrand, 1978.
[STE74] Stevens, W., G. Myers, and L. Constantine, "Structured Design," *IBM Systems Journal,* vol. 13, no. 2, 1974, pp. 115–139.
[WIR71] Wirth, N., "Program Development by Stepwise Refinement," *CACM,* vol. 14, no. 4, 1971, pp. 221–227.
[YOU79] Yourdon, E., and L. Constantine, *Structured Design,* Prentice-Hall, 1979.

PROBLEMS AND POINTS TO PONDER

11.1 Write a paper that tracks the progress of software design methodologies from 1970 to the present. A starting point for reference material can be the contributors noted in Section 11.1.1.

11.2 Some designers contend that all data flow may be treated as transform-oriented. Discuss how this contention will affect the software structure that is derived when a transaction-oriented flow is treated as transform. Use an example flow to illustrate important points.

11.3 If you haven't done so, complete Problem 7.13 in Chapter 7. Use the design methods described in this chapter to develop a program structure for the PHTRS.

11.4 Propose an approach to the design of real-time software applications that makes use of data flow-oriented techniques. To begin your discussion, list problems with real-time systems (e.g., interrupt-driven) that make the direct application of data flow-oriented design somewhat unwieldy. Compare your approach to the ones proposed in Chapter 15.

11.5 Using a data flow diagram and a processing narrative, describe a computer-based system that has distinct transform flow characteristics. Define flow boundaries and map the DFD into a program structure using the technique described in Section 11.3.

11.6 Using a data flow diagram and a processing narrative, describe a computer-based system that has distinct transaction flow characteristics. Define flow boundaries and map the DFD into a program structure using the technique described in Section 11.4.

11.7 Using requirements that are derived from a classroom discussion, complete the DFDs and architectural design for the *SafeHome* example presented in Sections 11.3 and 11.4. Assess the functional independence of all the modules. Document your design.

11.8 For readers with a background in compiler design: Develop a DFD for a simple compiler; assess its overall flow characteristic, and derive a program structure using the techniques described in this chapter. Provide processing narratives for each module.

11.9 How does the concept of *recursive modules* (i.e., modules that invoke themselves) fit into the design philosophy and techniques presented in this chapter?

11.10 Using the DFD shown in Figure 11.22, apply transaction analysis to the DFD and derive a program structure. The overall flow characteristic should be assumed to be transaction flow (with transaction center at transform *c*). Flow in region I is transform; flow in region II is transaction, with transform subflows as shown; flow in region III is transform. Your program structure should

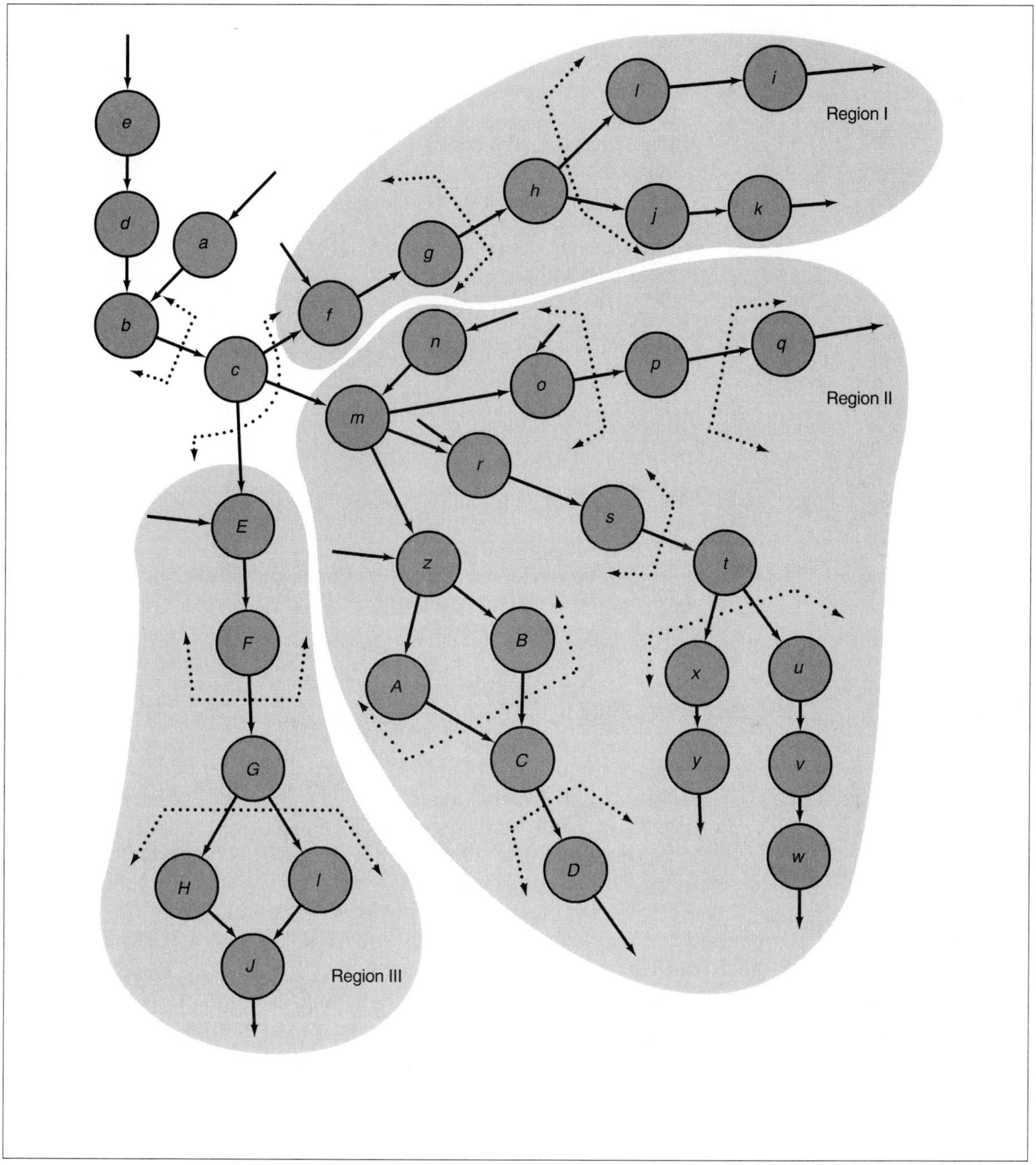

FIGURE 11.22. Problem 11.10.

have modules that correspond on a one-to-one basis with the transforms in the figure. It will be necessary to derive a number of control modules.

11.11 Discuss the relative merits and difficulties of applying data flow-oriented design in the following areas:
(*a*) Embedded microprocessor applications
(*b*) Engineering/scientific analysis
(*c*) Computer graphics
(*d*) Operating system design
(*e*) Business applications
(*f*) Database management system design
(*g*) Communications software design
(*h*) Compiler design
(*i*) Process control applications
(*j*) Artificial intelligence applications

11.12 Given a set of requirements provided by your instructor (or a set of requirements for a problem on which you are currently working), develop a complete design including all design documentation. Conduct a design review (Chapter 17) to assess the quality of your design. This problem may assigned to a team rather than to an individual.

11.13 The data flow-oriented design approach does not address (directly) a key element in the design of software. What is it?

11.14 List at least three attributes of software that sometimes require optimization and describe how a systematic design method that derives program structure can assist in such optimization.

FURTHER READINGS

Complete presentations of data flow-oriented design may be found in Myers [MYE78], Yourdon and Constantine [YOU79], Buhr (*System Design with Ada,* Prentice-Hall, 1984) and Page-Jones (*The Practical Guide to Structured Systems Design,* 2d ed., Prentice-Hall, 1988). These books are dedicated to design alone and provide comprehensive tutorials in the data flow approach. Each text contains numerous examples and all are strongly recommended for those readers who intend to actively apply the data flow method. Additional information about structured design approaches can be found in Easteal and Davies (*Software Engineering: Analysis and Design,* McGraw-Hill, 1989) and Sommerville (*Software Engineering,* 3d ed., Addison-Wesley, 1989).

CHAPTER 12

OBJECT-ORIENTED DESIGN

Object-oriented design (OOD), like other information-oriented design methodologies, creates a representation of the real-world problem domain and maps it into a solution domain that is software. Unlike other methods, OOD results in a design that interconnects data objects (data items) and processing operations in a way that modularizes information and processing rather than processing alone.

The unique nature of object-oriented design lies in its ability to build upon three important software design concepts: abstraction, information hiding, and modularity (Chapter 10). All design methods strive for software that exhibits these fundamental characteristics, but only OOD provides a mechanism that enables the designer to achieve all three without complexity or compromise.

Wiener and Sincovec [WIE84, p. 129] summarize OOD methodology in the following manner:

> No longer is it necessary for the system designer to map the problem domain into predefined data and control structures present in the implementation language. Instead, the designer may create his or her own abstract data types and functional abstractions and map the real-world domain into these programmer-created abstractions. This mapping, incidentally, may be much more natural because of the virtually unlimited range of abstract types that can be invented by the designer. Furthermore, software design becomes decoupled from the representational details of the data objects used in the system. These representational details may be changed many times without any fallout effects being induced in the overall software system.

Object-oriented analysis (Chapter 8), object-oriented design, and object-oriented programming comprise a set of software engineering activities for the construction of an object-oriented system. In Chapter 8 we examined basic definitions and explored a notation and an approach that can be used to define classes and objects. Like OOA, it is premature to call object-oriented design a mature method. However, as the popularity of the object-oriented approach continues to grow, methods for the design of object-oriented systems are mandatory.

12.1 ORIGINS OF OBJECT-ORIENTED DESIGN

Objects and operations are not new programming concepts, but object-oriented design is. In the very earliest days of computing, assembly languages enabled programmers to use machine instructions (operators) to manipulate data items (operands). The level of abstraction that was applied to the solution domain was very low.

As high order programming languages (e.g., FORTRAN, ALGOL, COBOL) appeared, objects and operations in the real-world problem space could be modeled by predefined data and control structures that were available as part of the high-order language. In general, software design (whenever it was explicitly considered) focused on representation of procedural detail using the programming language of choice. Design concepts such as stepwise refinement of function, procedural modularity, and, later, structured programming evolved.

During the 1970s, concepts such as abstraction and information hiding were introduced, and data-driven design methods emerged, but software developers still concentrated on process and its representation. At the same time, modern high-order languages (e.g., Pascal) introduced a much richer variety of data structures and types.

While conventional high-order languages (languages out of the FORTRAN and ALGOL tradition) were evolving, researchers were hard at work on a new class of simulation and prototyping languages such as SIMULA and Smalltalk. In these languages, data abstraction was emphasized and real-world problems were represented by a set of *data objects* to which a corresponding set of *operations* were attached. The use of these languages was radically different from the use of more conventional languages.

The approach that we call object-oriented design has evolved over the past 20 years. Early work in software design laid the foundation by establishing the importance of abstraction, information hiding, and modularity to software quality.

During the 1980s, the rapid evolution of the programming languages Smalltalk and Ada, followed by the explosive growth in use of object-oriented dialects of C such as C++ and Objective-C, caused increased interest in OOD. In an early discussion of methods to achieve object-oriented design, Abbott [ABB83] showed "how the analysis of the English statement of the problem and its solution can be used to guide the development of both the visible part of a useful package [a package holds both data and the procedures that operate on it] and the particular algorithm for a given problem." Booch [BOO86a] expanded upon Abbott's work and popularized the concept of object-oriented design. By the late 1980s, OOD was being used in software design applications that ranged from computer graphics animation to telecommunications. Today, many believe that object-oriented methods and programming languages will become predominant as we approach the millennium year.

12.2 OBJECT-ORIENTED DESIGN CONCEPTS

Like other design methods, OOD introduces a new set of terminology, notation, and procedures for the derivation of a software design. In this section, we review object-oriented terminology (first introduced in Chapter 8) and introduce a few additional concepts that are relevant to design.

12.2.1 Objects, Operations, and Messages

Software function is accomplished when a data structure (of varying levels of complexity) is acted upon by one or more processes according to an invocation procedure defined by a static algorithm or dynamic commands. To accomplish object-oriented design, we must establish a mechanism for (1) the representation of data structure, (2) the specification of process, and (3) the invocation procedure.

An *object* is a component of the real world that is mapped into the software domain. In the context of a computer-based system, an object is typically a producer or consumer of information or an information item. For example, typical objects might be machines, commands, files, displays, switches, signals, alphanumeric strings, or any other person, place, thing, occurrence, role, or event. When an object is mapped into its software realization, it consists of a private data structure and processes, called *operations,*[1] that may legitimately transform the data structure. Operations contain control and procedural constructs that may be invoked by a *message*—a request to the object to perform one of its operations.

Recalling the object notation introduced in Chapter 8, we represent an object as shown in Figure 12.1. The object **system** (part of the *SafeHome* security product) exhibits a private data structure and related operations.

The object also has a *shared part* that is its interface. *Messages* move across the interface and specify what operation on the object is desired, but

[1]The terms "methods" or "services" are also used.

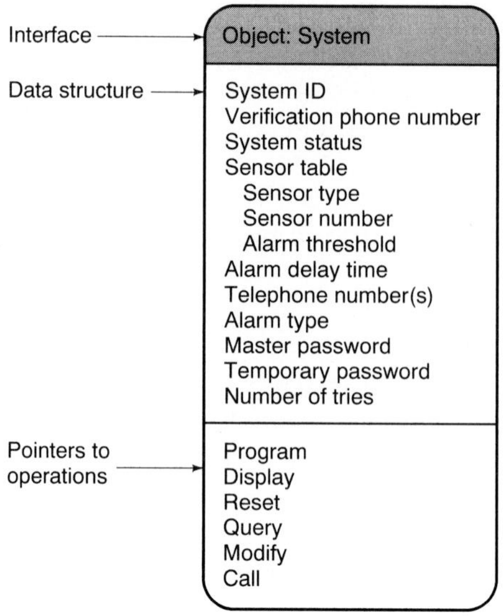

FIGURE 12.1. Representation of an object.

not *how* the operation is to be performed. The object that receives a message determines how the requested operation is to be implemented.

By defining an object with a private part and providing messages to invoke appropriate processing, we achieve *information hiding*—that is, the details of implementation are hidden from all program elements outside the object. Objects and their operation provide inherent *modularity*—that is, software elements (data and process) are grouped together with a well-defined interface mechanism (in this case, messages).

12.2.2 Design Issues

Bertrand Meyer [MEY90] suggests five criteria for judging a design method's ability to achieve modularity and relates these to object-oriented design:

- *Decomposability*—the facility with which a design method helps the designer to decompose a large problem into subproblems that are easier to solve
- *Composability*—the degree to which a design method ensures that program components (modules), once designed and built, can be reused to create other systems
- *Understandability*—the ease with which a program component can be understood without reference to other information or other modules

- *Continuity*—the ability to make small changes in a program and have these changes manifest themselves with corresponding changes in just one or a very few modules
- *Protection*—an architectural characteristic that will reduce the propagation of side effects if an error does occur in a given module

From these criteria, Meyer [MEY90] suggests that five basic design principles can be derived for modular architectures: (1) linguistic modular units; (2) few interfaces; (3) small interfaces (weak coupling); (4) explicit interfaces; (5) information hiding.

Modules are defined as *linguistic modular units* when they "correspond to syntactic units in the language used" [MEY90]. That is, the programming language to be used should be capable of supporting the modularity defined directly. For example, if the designer creates a *subroutine*, any of the more popular programming languages (e.g., FORTRAN, C, PASCAL) could implement it as a syntactic unit. But if a *package* that contains data structures and procedures and identifies them as a single unit were defined, a language such as Ada (or other object-oriented languages) would be necessary to directly represent this type of module in the language syntax.

To achieve low coupling (a design concept introduced in Chapter 10), the number of interfaces between modules should be minimized ("few interfaces") and the amount of information that moves across an interface should be minimized ("small interfaces"). Whenever modules do communicate, they should do so in an obvious and direct way ("explicit interfaces"). For example, if module *X* and module *Y* communicate through a global data area (what we have called "common coupling" in Chapter 10), they violate the principle of explicit interfaces because the communication between the modules is not obvious to an outside observer. Finally, we achieve the principle of information hiding when all the information about a module is hidden from outside access, unless that information is specifically defined as "public information."

The design criteria and principles presented in this section can be applied to any design method (e.g., we can apply them to structured design). As we will see, however, the object-oriented design method achieves each of the criteria more efficiently than other approaches and results in modular architectures that allow us to meet each of the modularity criteria most effectively.

12.2.3 Classes, Instances, and Inheritance

Many objects in the physical world have reasonably similar characteristics and perform reasonably similar operations. If we look at the manufacturing floor of a heavy equipment manufacturer, we see milling machines, drill presses, and jig borers. Although each of these objects is different, all belong to a larger *class* that is called "metal cutting tools." All objects in the metal cutting tools class have attributes in common (e.g., all use electric motors) and perform common operations (e.g., cut, start, or stop). Therefore, by categorizing a "hobber" as a member of the class metal cutting machines, we know something about its attributes and the operations it performs even if we don't know what its detailed function is.

Software realizations of real-world objects are categorized in much the same way. All objects are members of a larger class and *inherit* the private data structure and operations that have been defined for that class. Stated another way, a class is a set of objects that each has the same characteristics. An individual object is therefore an *instance* of a larger class.

Recalling the *SafeHome* security system presented in earlier chapters, we conduct an object-oriented analysis (Chapter 8) and identify candidate classes. One such class is **sensor**. From this class definition we can instantiate specific sensor objects, **entry sensor, smoke sensor,** and **motion sensor.** Using the program design language (PDL) introduced in Chapter 10,

TYPE **motion sensor** IS INSTANCE OF **sensor**;

implies *inheritance* of the attributes of **sensor**.

But what happens if inheritance isn't perfect? This situation occurs when a candidate instance of a class shares most, but not all, of the attributes of the class and requires all of the operations of the class as well as additional operations that are relevant only to the candidate member. For example, assume that a new sensor type is to be added to the *SafeHome* system. Unlike smoke, entry, and motion sensors, the new sensor is "aggressive," that is it will perform some action once an event is sensed. A **fire sensor** will alert the *SafeHome* control panel (see Chapter 8), but will also spray a fire retardant chemical into the air for a programmable period of time. To accommodate the fire sensor, we create a *subclass*—that is, the attributes and operations of the class **sensor** are inherited, but they are modified to accommodate the special characteristics of **fire sensor.** The original **sensor** class and the new subclass, called **aggressive sensor,** are shown in Figure 12.2.

The use of classes, subclasses, and inheritance is crucially important in modern software engineering. Reuse of program components (our ability to achieve *composition*) is attained by creating objects (instances) that build on existing attributes and operations inherited from a class or subclass. We only need to specify how the new object differs from the class, rather than defining all the characteristics of the new object.

Unlike other design concepts that are programming language-independent, the implementation of classes, subclasses, and objects varies with the programming language to be used. For this reason, the preceding generic discussion may require modification in the context of a specific programming language. For example, Ada implements the object as a *package* and

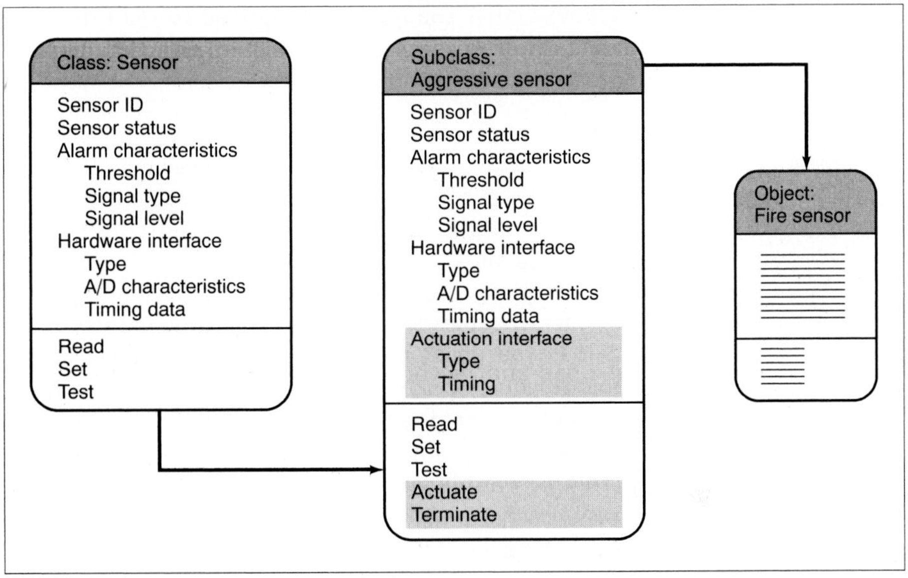

FIGURE 12.2. Illustration of the class **sensor** and subclass **aggressive sensor.**

achieves instances through the use of data abstractions and typing. The Smalltalk programming language, on the other hand, implements each of the concepts described above directly, making it a true object-oriented programming language.

12.2.4 Object Descriptions

A design description of an object (an instance of a class or subclass) can take one of two forms [GOL83]:

1. A *protocol description* that establishes the interface of an object by defining each message that the object can receive and the related operation that the object performs when it receives the message
2. An *implementation description* that shows implementation details for each operation implied by a message that is passed to an object. Implementation details include information about the object's private part, that is, internal details about the data structure and procedural details that describe operations.

The protocol description is nothing more than a set of messages and a corresponding comment for each message. For example, a portion of the protocol description for the object **motion sensor** (described earlier) might be:

MESSAGE (motion sensor) → read: RETURNS sensor ID, sensor status;

which describes the message required to read the sensor. Similarly,

MESSAGE (motion sensor) → set: SENDS sensor ID, sensor status;

sets or resets the status of the sensor.

For a large system with many messages, it is often possible to create message categories. For example, message categories for the *SafeHome* system object might include system configuring messages, monitoring messages, event messages, and so forth.

An implementation description of an object provides the internal ("hidden") details that are required for implementation but are not necessary for invocation. That is, the designer of the object must provide an implementation description and must therefore create the internal details of the object. However, another designer or implementer who uses the object or other instances of the object requires only the protocol description but not the implementation description.

An implementation description is comprised of the following information: (1) a specification of the object's name and reference to a class; (2) a specification of private data structure with an indication of data items and types; (3) a procedural description of each operation or, alternatively, pointers to such procedural descriptions. The implementation description must contain sufficient information to provide for the proper handling of all messages described in the protocol description.

Cox [COX85] characterizes the difference between the information contained in the protocol description and that contained in the implementation description in terms of "users" and "suppliers" of services. A user of the "service" provided by an object must be familiar with the protocol for invoking the service, that is, for specifying *what* is desired. The supplier of the service (the object itself) must be concerned with *how* the service is to be supplied to the user, that is, with implementation details. This concept, called *encapsulation,* is summarized as follows [COX85]:

> [An object] delivers *encapsulation,* whereby a data structure and a group of procedures for accessing it can be put into service such that the users of that capability can access it through a set of carefully documented, controlled and standardized interfaces. These encapsulated data structures, called objects, amount to active data that can be requested to *do* things by sending them messages.

12.3 OBJECT-ORIENTED DESIGN METHODS

It is sometimes difficult to make a clear distinction between object-oriented analysis (Chapter 8) and object-oriented design.[2] In essence, object-oriented

[2]Readers who have not yet read Chapter 8 in its entirety are urged to do so now.

analysis (OOA) is a classification activity. That is, a problem is analyzed in an effort to determine the classes of objects that will be applicable as a solution is developed. Object-oriented design (OOD) enables a software engineer to indicate the objects that are derived from each class and how these objects interrelate with one another. In addition, OOD should provide a notation that depicts the relationships among objects. The terminology, notation, and approach presented for OOA are equally applicable to the topics presented in this chapter.

The first attempts to describe an object-oriented design method did not surface until the early 1980s. Both Abbott [ABB83] and Booch [BOO86a] contended that OOD begins with a natural language (e.g., English) description of the solution strategy for the software realization of a real-world problem. From this description, the designer can isolate objects and operations. Later contributions by Schlaer and Mellor [SCL88] and Coad and Yourdon [COA90] introduced a more comprehensive notation to support this approach and argued that this activity is more properly characterized as analysis.

At their current stage of evolution, OOD methods combine elements of all three design categories discussed earlier in this book: data design, architectural design, and procedural design. By identifying classes and objects, data abstractions are created. By coupling operations to data, modules are specified and a structure for the software is established. By developing a mechanism for using the objects, (e.g., generating messages) interfaces are described.

Early OOD approaches [BOO86a] are typified by the following steps:

1. Define the problem.
2. Develop an informal strategy (processing narrative) for the software realization of the real-world problem domain.
3. Formalize the strategy using the following substeps:
   a. Identify objects and their attributes.
   b. Identify operations that may be applied to objects.
   c. Establish interfaces by showing the relationship between objects and operations.
   d. Decide on detailed design issues that will provide an implementation description for objects.
4. Reapply steps 2, 3, and 4 recursively.

It should be noted that all four steps (with the possible exception of step 3) are performed during software requirements analysis. Extending these activities into design, the following steps are added:

5. Refine the work done during OOA, looking for subclasses, message characteristics, and other elaboration of detail.
6. Represent the data structure(s) associated with object attributes.
7. Represent the procedural detail associated with each operation.

In the section that follows, we review the first four steps (already presented in Chapter 8) and consider the design activities associated with steps 5 through 7.

12.4 CLASS AND OBJECT DEFINITION

"Definition" is simply another term for requirements analysis. To adequately define the problem, computer system engineering should be applied to allocate function to the software element of a system. Next, software requirements analysis methods should be applied to identify the information domain and partition the problem. Obviously, OOA methods are best suited for a system that will be implemented using the object-oriented approach.

The application of requirements analysis principles and methods will enable the analyst and the designer to perform two necessary substeps [EVB86]: (1) stating the problem and (2) analyzing and clarifying known constraints. The software realization of the real-world problem, regardless of its size or complexity, should be stated in a single, grammatically correct sentence. Obviously, the level of abstraction may be very high, but a single problem statement "allows software engineers working on the project to have a single, unified, understanding of the problem." [EVB86]

To illustrate the problem definition step (and all subsequent steps), we recall the *SafeHome* processing narrative presented in Chapter 8:

> *SafeHome* software enables the homeowner to configure the security system when it is installed, monitors all sensors connected to the security system, and interacts with the homeowner through a key pad and function keys contained in the *SafeHome* control panel shown in Figure 6.6.
>
> During installation, the *SafeHome* control panel is used to "program" and configure the system. Each sensor is assigned a number and type, a master password is programmed for arming and disarming the system, and telephone number(s) is (are) input for dialing when a sensor event occurs.
>
> When a sensor event is sensed by the software, it rings an audible alarm attached to the system. After a delay time that is specified by the homeowner during system configuration activities, the software dials a telephone number of a monitoring service, provides information about the location, and reports the nature of the event that has been detected. The number will be redialed every 20 seconds until telephone connection is obtained.
>
> All interaction with *SafeHome* is managed by a user-interaction subsystem that reads input provided through the key pad and function keys, displays prompting messages on the LCD display, displays system status information on the LCD display. Keyboard interaction takes the following form. . . .

After performing a noun-verb parse and eliminating candidate objects that do not meet the criteria discussed in Section 8.1.1, the objects shown in Figure 12.3 are selected.

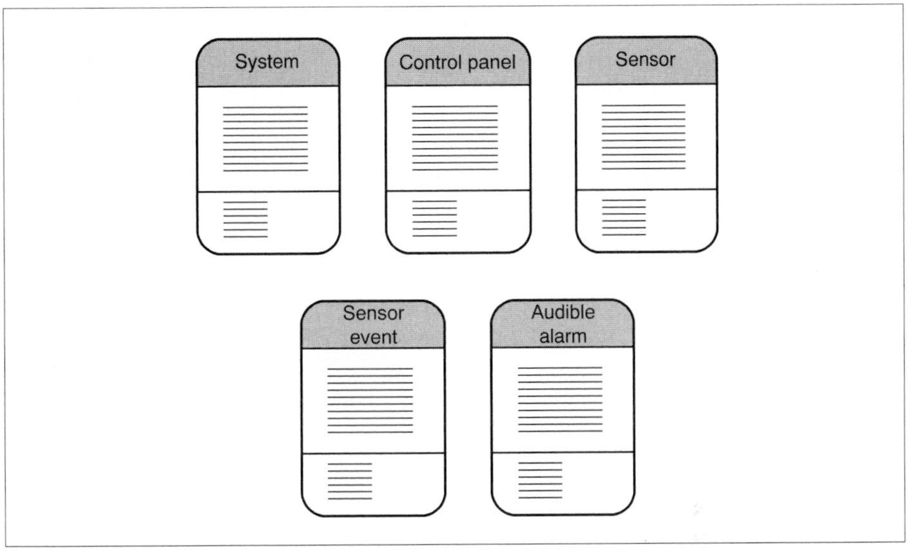

FIGURE 12.3. Objects selected at first level of refinement.

Continuing object-oriented analysis activities, the attributes and operations for each object are specified (e.g., attributes and operations for the system object as shown in Figure 12.1). In addition, objects defined at the first level of refinement may be refined further using the assembly structure notation described in Section 8.2.1 and repeated in Figure 12.4.

The identification of objects lies at the core of OOA and serves as the basis for OOD. Abbott [ABB83] provides a worthwhile discussion:

> Object orientation emphasizes the importance of precisely identifying the objects and their properties to be manipulated by a program before starting to write the details of those manipulations. Without this careful identification, it is almost impossible to be precise about the operations to be performed and their intended effects.
>
> The nouns and noun phrases in the informal strategy are good indicators of the objects and their classifications (i.e., data types) in our problem solution.

Therefore, our focus during OOA is to isolate all nouns and noun phrases contained in the processing narrative that describes what the system is to do.

A brief digression into noun categories is worthwhile at this point. A *common noun* is often the name of a class. For example, **sensor** is a common noun that describes a class of devices that are used to detect some event. *Proper nouns* are the names of specific beings or things. For example, **Ferrari F-40, Chevy Eurosport,** and **Lexus LS400** are all proper nouns or noun phrases within the class that we could call **automobile**. A *mass* or *abstract noun* is the name of a quantity, an activity, or a measure. For example, **traffic** is a mass noun that refers to a collection of proper nouns within the class implied by the common noun **automobile**.

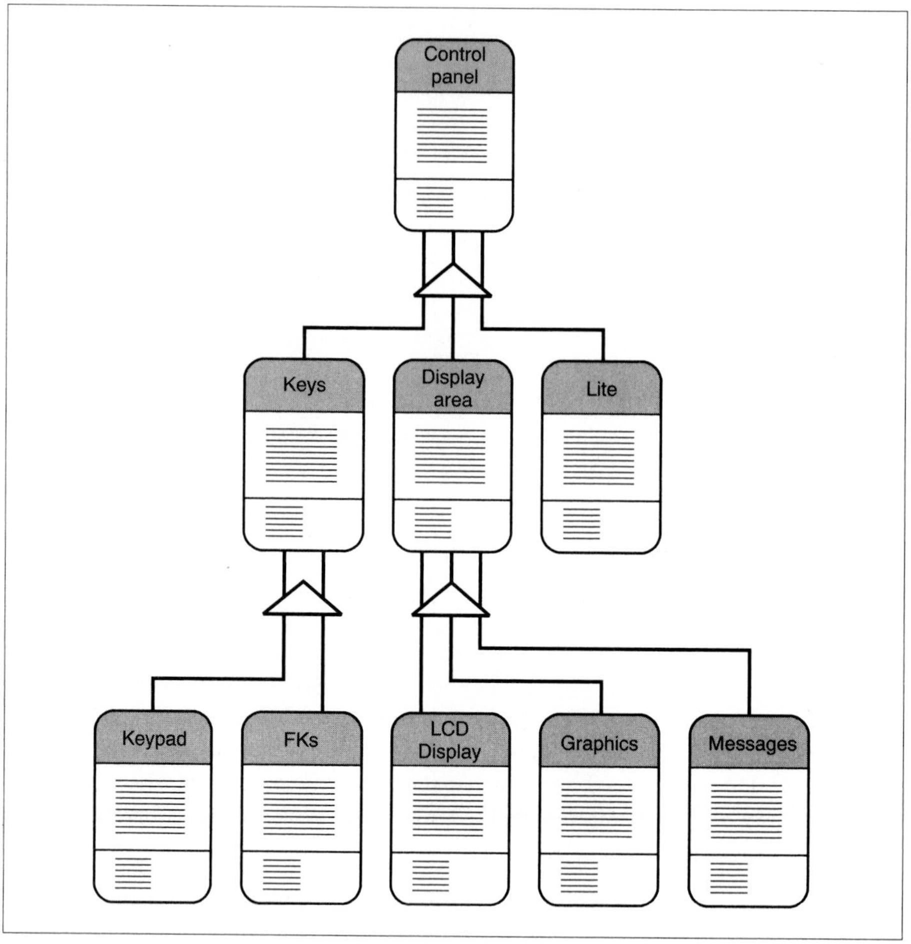

FIGURE 12.4. Refining an object using an assembly structure (Chapter 8).

This categorization can be used to help define classes, subclasses, and objects. A common noun will often represent a class of objects (a data abstraction). A proper noun will represent an instance of a class. A mass or abstract noun (including units of measurement) will serve to indicate constraining characteristics or problem specific groupings for objects or classes. It is important to note, however, that context and semantics must be used to determine noun categories. A word can be a common noun in one context, a proper noun in another, and in some cases a mass or abstract noun in a third context.

It is important to note that not all nouns and noun phrases will be of interest in the final software realization of the solution. Some objects, as already noted, will reside outside the bounds of the software solution space. Other objects, although relevant to the problem, may be redundant or extraneous when the solution is refined.

12.5 REFINING OPERATIONS

Once objects in the solution space have been identified, the designer selects the set of operations that act on the objects. Operations are identified by examining all verbs stated in the informal strategy (the processing narrative). Recalling our discussion from Chapter 8:

Although many different types of operations exist, they can generally be divided into three broad categories: (1) operations that *manipulate* data in some way (e.g., adding, deleting, reformatting, selecting); (2) operations that perform a *computation;* (3) operations that *monitor* an object for the occurrence of a controlling event.

For example, the *SafeHome* processing narrative contains the sentence fragments: "sensor is assigned a number and type" and "a master password is programmed for arming and disarming the system." These two phrases indicate a number of things:

- That an **assign** operation is relevant for the **sensor** object
- That a **program** operation will be applied to the **system** object
- That **arm** and **disarm** are operations that apply to **system**; also that system status may ultimately be defined (using data dictionary notation) as

system status = [armed | disarmed]

The operation **program** is allocated during OOA, but during OOD it will be refined into a number of more specific operations that are required to configure the system. For example, after discussions with product engineering, the analyst, and possibly the marketing department, the designer might elaborate the original processing narrative and write the following for **program**[3]:

> Program enables the *SafeHome* user to configure the system once it has been installed. The user can (1) install phone numbers; (2) define delay times for alarms; (3) build a sensor table that contains each sensor ID, its type, and location; and (4) load a master password.

Therefore, the designer has refined the single operation **program** and replaced it with the operations **install, define, build,** and **load.** Each of these new operations becomes part of the **system** object, has knowledge of the internal data structures that implement the object's attributes, and is invoked by sending the object messages of the form:

MESSAGE (system) → install: SENDS telephone number;

which implies that to provide the system with an emergency phone number, an install message will be sent to **system**.

[3]Underlining has been added to isolate verbs.

Verbs connote actions or occurrences. In the context of OOD formalization, we consider not only verbs but also *descriptive verb phrases* and *predicates* (e.g., "is equal to") as potential operations. The grammatical parse is applied recursively until each operation has been refined to its most detailed level.

12.6 PROGRAM COMPONENTS AND INTERFACES

An important aspect of software design quality is *modularity*—that is, the specification of *program components* (modules) that are combined to form a complete program. The object-oriented approach defines the object as a program component that is itself linked to other components (e.g., private data, operations). But defining objects and operations is not enough. During design, we must also identify the *interfaces* that exist between objects and the overall structure (considered in an architectural sense) of the objects.

Although a program component is a design abstraction, it should be represented in the context of the programming language with which the design is to be implemented. To accommodate OOD, the programming language to be used for implementation should be capable of creating the following program component (modeled after Ada):

```
PACKAGE program-component-name IS
      TYPE specification of data objects
            .
            .
            .
      PROC specification of related operations . . .
PRIVATE
      data structure details for objects
PACKAGE BODY program-component-name IS
      PROC operation.1 (interface description) IS
            .
            .
            .
      END
      PROC operation.n (interface description) IS
            .
            .
            .
      END
END program-component-name
```

Referring to the Ada-like PDL (program design language) shown above, a program component is specified by indicating both data objects and operations. The *specification part* of the component indicates all data objects (declared with the TYPE statement) and the operations (PROC for "procedure") that act on them. The private part (PRIVATE) of the component provides otherwise hidden details of data structure and processing. In the context of our earlier discussion, the PACKAGE is conceptually similar to objects discussed throughout this chapter.

The first program component to be identified should be the highest-level module from which all processing originates and all data structures evolve. Referring once again to the *SafeHome* example considered in preceding sections, we can define the highest-level program component as:

```
PROCEDURE SafeHome software
```

Using Figure 8.3 as a guide, the *SafeHome* software component can be coupled with a preliminary design for the following packages (objects):

```
PACKAGE system IS
    TYPE system data
    PROC install, define, build, load
    PROC display, reset, query, modify, call
    PRIVATE
        PACKAGE BODY system IS
        PRIVATE
            system.id IS STRING LENGTH (8);
            verification phone number, telephone number, . . .
            IS STRING LENGTH (8);
            sensor table DEFINED
                sensor type IS STRING LENGTH (2),
                sensor number, alarm threshold IS NUMERIC;
        PROC install RECEIVES (telephone number)
            {design detail for operation install}
        .
        .
        .
END system
PACKAGE sensor IS
    TYPE sensor data
    PROC read, set, test
    PRIVATE
        PACKAGE BODY sensor IS
        PRIVATE
            sensor.id IS STRING LENGTH (8);
            sensor status IS STRING LENGTH (8);
            alarm characteristics DEFINED
                threshold, signal type, signal level IS NUMERIC,
            hardware interface DEFINED
                type, a/d.characteristics, timing.data IS NUMERIC,
```

```
END sensor
    .
    .
    .
END SafeHome software
```

Data objects and corresponding operations are specified for each of the program components for *SafeHome* software. It should be noted that many details have not as yet been specified about the *private part* of the data objects or details of the operations. These implementation details are considered later.

Once program components have been identified, we are ready to examine the evolving design and critically assess the need for changes. It is likely that a review of the "first-cut" definition of packages will result in modifications that add new objects or return to earlier OOD steps (i.e., the informal strategy) to assess the completeness of operations that have been specified.

12.7 A NOTATION FOR OOD

In Chapter 8, we used a graphical notation for the representation of objects, operations, messages, and other structures that has been proposed by Coad and Yourdon [COA90]. This notation will also work quite well for the early stages of design. However, other notations have also been proposed and are sometimes encountered in the industry. In this section, we present a brief overview of one of these.

Booch [BOO90] proposes a notation that combines four distinct diagrams to create an object-oriented design. A *class diagram* depicts classes and their relationships. An *object diagram* represents specific objects (instances of a class) and the messages that pass among them. Classes and objects are allocated to specific software components as part of a physical design. The *module diagram,* sometimes called a *Booch diagram,* is used to illustrate these program components. Because many object-oriented systems contain a number of programs that may be executing on a set of distributed processors, Booch also suggests a notation, called a *process diagram,* that enables the designer to depict how processes are allocated to specific processors within a large system.

12.7.1 Representing Class and Object Relationships

As an alternative to the notation suggested in Chapter 8, Booch [BOO90] suggests diagrams that depict classes and objects and the relationships among them. The class diagram, illustrated in Figure 12.5, indicates the class "architecture" for a system. Inheritance is shown with an arrow symbol, and the double line connectors indicate that one class makes use of information contained within another class. The symbols at the ends of the

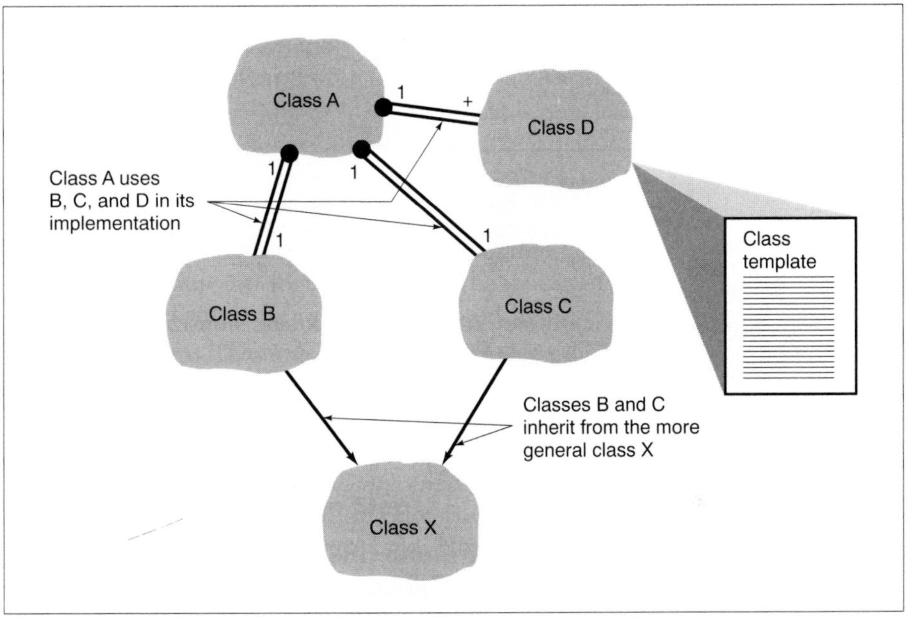

FIGURE 12.5.
Basic notation of a class diagram.

uses (double-line) notation indicate cardinality. For example, for every instance of class A in the figure, there will be one or more instances (indicated by the + sign) of class D. In addition to the class diagram itself, each class can be defined with a template that includes its name, attributes, and operations, as well as information about inheritance, parameters, and behavior. It should be noted that the class template is not actually part of the diagram, but is created as a supplement to it.

Classes are defined as part of the design of a system and exist regardless of the execution behavior of the system. Objects, however, are created and removed dynamically as a program executes. For this reason, a notation that captures the "dynamic semantics" or a "time lapse snapshot" [BOO90] of a program can be invaluable to a designer. The object diagram (Figure 12.6) depicts each instance of a class, the operations that will be applied, and the messages that are passed. The connecting line between objects is terminated by a labeled square that indicates the type of data that is contained within a message. The arrow parallel to the line indicates the type of synchronization between objects (e.g., synchronous, asynchronous, timeout). An object template is created for each object and defines the object and the messages that are passed to it.

12.7.2 Modularizing the Design

The importance of modularity in software design was discussed in Chapter 10. But how is the concept of a module defined when OOD is applied? The answer to this question leads us to a design notation that allocates classes

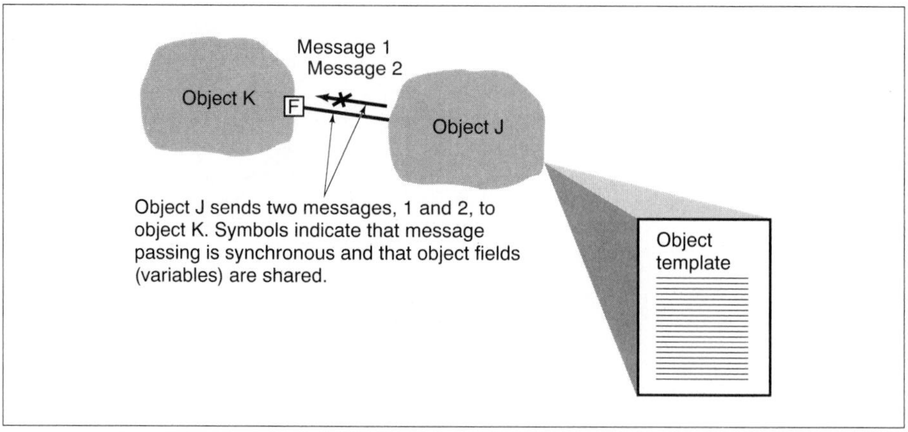

FIGURE 12.6.
Basic notation of an object diagram.

and objects to physical program components (modules) and thereby represents an implementation view of the program architecture. The module diagram represents a program component (object) as a box that can be divided into a *specification part* (visible to the outside) and a *private part* (also called a *body part*) that is hidden from the outside. At this stage, the implementation details that are part of the private part or *package body* are not yet specified. Data objects are noted by an elongated oval while operations that act on the objects are indicated by rectangles.

Figure 12.7 illustrates the use of a module diagram to represent the dependencies among program components. The connecting arrows imply dependency, that is, the package or component at the origin of the arrow depends on the package or program component at the tip of the arrow. In Figure 12.7, the highest level program component, *A*, depends on the objects and operations contained in *B*, *C*, and *D* to satisfy its function.

Software for a computer-based system is executed by one or more processors (computers) that interact with other devices through a series of defined connections. The use of object-oriented design and implementation does not alter this fact. Therefore, the process diagram (Figure 12.8) is used to indicate the processors (shaded boxes), devices (white boxes), and connections (lines) that define the hardware architecture of a system. The software processes that execute on a given processor are also noted on the diagram.

A detailed example using the notation presented in Section 12.7 is beyond the scope of this book. The interested reader should refer to Booch [BOO90], where case studies in a variety of application areas are presented.

The use of graphical notation for OOD is not essential, but it does provide an indication of relationships among classes and objects that is lacking in a PDL representation. The notation proposed by Booch can be used to represent program components at a relatively high level of abstraction. When implementation detail design commences, the graphical notation is abandoned and PDL is used as the design representation.

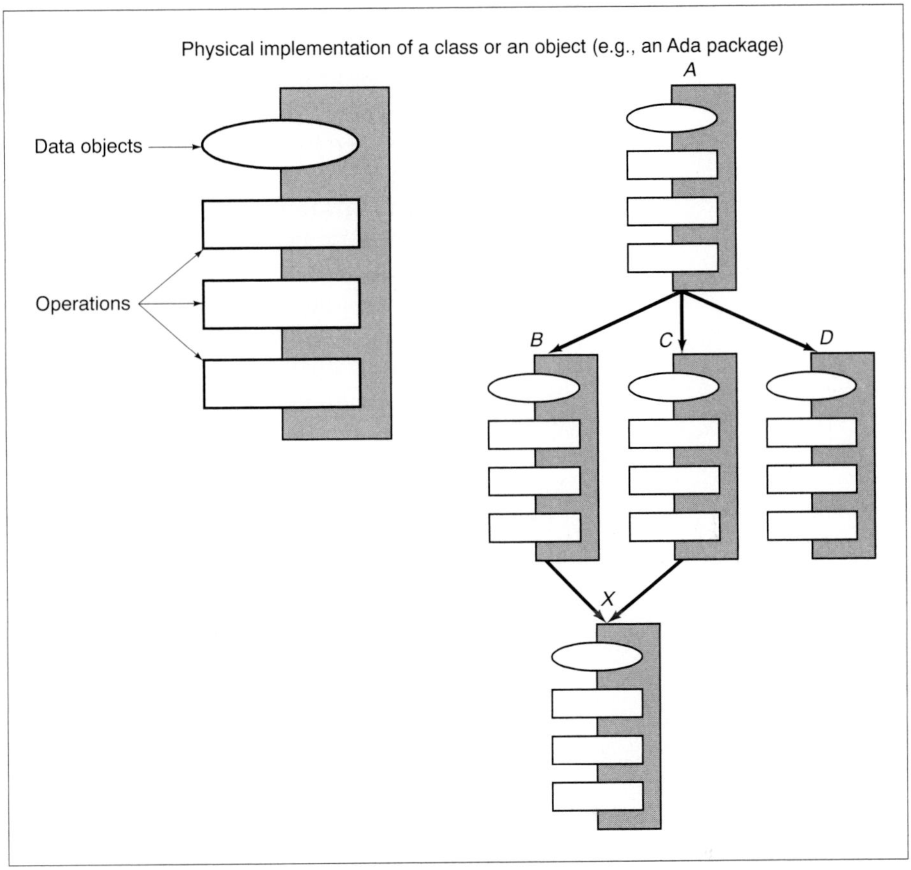

FIGURE 12.7. Basic notation for a module diagram.

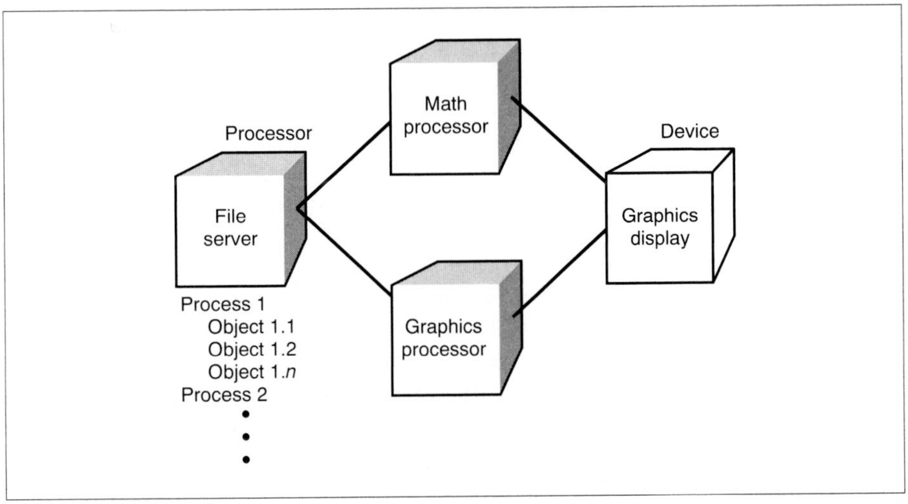

FIGURE 12.8. Basic notation for a process diagram.

12.8 IMPLEMENTATION DETAIL DESIGN

The detail design step of OOD is similar in many respects to detail design for any software design methodology. Interfaces are described in detail; data structures are refined and specified; algorithms are designed for each program unit using fundamental design concepts such as stepwise refinement and structured programming. The key difference for OOD is that the process described in the preceding sections may be applied recursively at any time. In fact, recursive definition of the solution strategy is essential to achieve a level of design and data abstraction from which implementation detail may be derived. The following guideline has been suggested [EVB86, p. 3–82] for determining when recursive application of OOD is necessary: "If the implementation of an operation will require a large (greater than 200 lines) amount of code, then one takes the stated function of the operation as the statement of a new problem and repeats the OOD process for this new problem."

The PDL design template for a package can be used as the starting point for detail design. Recalling the overall package structure:

```
PACKAGE program-component-name IS
      TYPE specification of data objects
           .
           .
           .
      PROC specification of related operations
           .
           .
           .
      PRIVATE
           data structure details for objects
PACKAGE BODY program-component-name IS
      PROC operation.i (interface description) IS
           .
           .
           .
      END
END program-component-name
```

Detail design completes all information required to fully implement the data structure and types contained in the PRIVATE portion of the package and all procedural detail contained in the PACKAGE body.

To illustrate the detail design of a program component, we reconsider the **sensor** package defined as part of the *SafeHome* example. To this point in the OOD process, **sensor** may be represented with the following package skeleton:

```
PACKAGE sensor IS
    TYPE sensor data
    PROC read, set, test
    PRIVATE
        PACKAGE BODY sensor IS
        PRIVATE
            sensor.id IS STRING LENGTH (8);
            sensor status IS STRING LENGTH (8);
            alarm characteristics DEFINED
                threshold, signal type, signal level IS NUMERIC,
            hardware interface DEFINED
                type, a/d.characteristics, timing.data IS NUMERIC,
END sensor
```

The data structures for sensor attributes have already been defined. Therefore, the first step is to define the interfaces for each of the operations attached to **sensor**:

```
PROC read (sensor.id, sensor status: OUT);
PROC set (alarm characteristics, hardware interface: IN)
PROC test (sensor.id, sensor status, alarm characteristics: OUT);
```

The next step requires stepwise refinement of each operation associated with the **sensor** package. To illustrate the refinement, we develop a processing narrative (an informal strategy) for **read**:

> When the sensor object receives a *read* message, the **read** process is invoked. The process determines the interface and signal type, polls the sensor interface, converts A/D (analog/digital) characteristics into an internal signal level, and compares the internal signal level to a threshold value. If the threshold is exceeded, the sensor status is set to "event." Otherwise, the sensor status is set to "no event." If an error is sensed while polling the sensor, the sensor status is set to "error."

Given the processing narrative, a PDL description of the read process can be developed:

```
PROC read (sensor.id, sensor.status: OUT);
    raw.signal IS BIT STRING
    IF (hardware.interface.type = "s" &
            alarm.characteristics.signal.type = "B")
```

```
        THEN
              GET (sensor, exception: sensor status : =  error) raw.signal;
              CONVERT raw.signal TO internal.signal.level;
              IF internal.signal.level > threshold
                 THEN sensor status : = "event";
                 ELSE sensor status : = "no event";
              ENDIF
        ELSE {processing for other types of s interfaces would be specified}
        ENDIF
        RETURN sensor.id, sensor status;
END read
```

The PDL representation of the **read** operation can be translated into the appropriate implementation language. The functions GET and CONVERT are assumed to be available as part of a run-time library.

12.9 AN ALTERNATIVE OBJECT-ORIENTED DESIGN STRATEGY

The object-oriented design method presented in Sections 12.3 to 12.8 is oriented toward software development in programming languages such as Ada. The method does not explicitly address a number of important object-oriented concepts (e.g., inheritance, messages) that can serve to make OOD even more powerful. This section describes an alternative approach to OOD that has evolved from software development in programming languages such as Smalltalk—languages that directly support abstraction, inheritance, messages, and all other OOD concepts.

William Lorensen [LOR86] has done an excellent job of summarizing an alternative approach to OOD. The remainder of this section (reproduced with the permission of General Electric Co., Corporate Research and Development Center) contains an adapted excerpt from his discussion of object-oriented design.

12.9.1 Design Steps

The OOD approach described in this section is appropriate for preliminary design. The primary objective is to define and characterize abstractions in a manner that results in a definition of all important objects, methods (operations), and messages. Lorensen [LOR86] suggests the following approach:

1. *Identify the data abstractions for each subsystem.*
These data abstractions are the classes for the system. Working from the requirements document, the abstraction process should be performed top-down when possible, although many times the abstractions are mentioned

explicitly in the requirements. Often the classes correspond to physical objects within the system being modeled. If this is not the case, the use of analogies, drawn from the designer's experience on past system designs, is helpful. This is, by far, the most difficult step in the design process and the selection of these abstractions influences the entire system architecture.

2. *Identify the attributes for each abstraction.*
The attributes become the instance variables (methods for manipulating data) for each class. Many times, if the classes correspond to physical objects, the required instance variables are obvious. Other instance variables may be required to respond to requests from other objects in the system. Defer the specification of the data structures containing the attributes until the detail design stage.

3. *Identify the operations for each abstraction.*
The operations are the methods (or procedures) for each class. Some methods access and update instance variables, while others execute operations singular to the class. Do not specify the details of the methods' implementations now, only the functionalities. If the new abstraction inherits from another class, inspect the methods of that class to see if any need to be overridden by the new class. Defer the internal design of methods until the detail design stage, where more conventional design techniques can be used.

4. *Identify the communication between objects.*
This step defines the messages that objects send to each other. Here, define a correspondence between the methods and the messages that invoke the methods. Even if an object-oriented implementation is not planned, messages help the design team to communicate and can be used in the next step to write scenarios. The design team decides on this protocol with consistency in message naming as a primary consideration.

5. *Test the design with scenarios.*
Scenarios, consisting of messages to objects, test the designer's ability to match the system's requirements specification.

6. *Apply inheritance where appropriate.*
If the data abstraction process in step 1 is performed top-down, introduce inheritance there. However, if abstractions are created bottom-up (often because the requirements directly name the abstractions), apply inheritance here, before going to another level of abstraction. The goal is to reuse as much of the data and/or methods that have already been designed as possible. At this step, common data and operations often surface and these common instances variables and methods can be combined into a new class. This class may or may not have meaning as an object by itself. Its sole purpose is to collect common instance variables and methods; it is called an *abstract class.*

12.9.2 A Design Example

As an example of the OOD method described above, we consider a simple CAD tool to view and manipulate a variety of primitives in two dimensions. This CAD tool has the following requirements, described in a narrative form:

> The tool allows users to create and manipulate two-dimensional polygons, splines, and conics on a color graphics device. Using a graphics input device such as a mouse, the user can move, rotate, scale, and color the primitives.

This is, indeed, a vague requirements definition, but it contains enough information for us to begin the design process. Here we'll concentrate on the design of conic support. A conic is a second order implicit curve of the form

$$ax^2 + bxy + cy^2 + dx + ey + f = 0$$

Conics embrace circles, ellipses, hyperbolas, and parabolas.

First Pass

1. *Identify the data abstractions for each subsystem.*
Abstractions for geometric systems are particularly easy to derive. The requirements say that the tool will have three different primitives, but first we look for things that are common to all primitives. Our initial class hierarchy is shown in Figure 12.9*a*. The highest class in the diagram is called the **geometric object,** performing functions that are appropriate to all classes. The **primitive** class is an abstract class, acting as a place holder for data and methods that can be used by classes lower in the hierarchy.

2. *Identify the attributes for each abstraction.*
At least one attribute of all primitives is obvious, color. If we think about geometric objects in general, other attributes come into mind such as position, orientation, texture, scale, opacity, etc. We know from the requirements that the user will move, scale, and rotate the primitives, so position, scale factors, and orientation are appropriate instance variables.

3. *Identify the operations for each abstraction.*
Requirements documents often explicitly mention operations. Here, our tool requirements specify **create, move, scale,** and **rotate** operations. We'll also

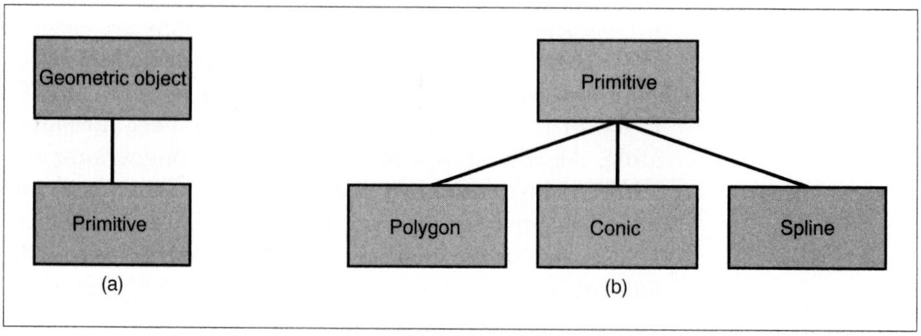

FIGURE 12.9.
(a) Initial class hierarchy; (b) second level of abstraction.

need methods to access instance variables. A summary of the methods for primitives follows:

create_primitive	creates a primitive
set_position	sets x, y position
get_position	gets x, y position
add_position	increments the x, y position
set_orientation	sets angle of rotation
get_orientation	gets angle of rotation
add_orientation	increments angle of rotation
set_scale	sets x, y scale factor
get_scale	gets the x, y scale factor
add_scale	increments the x, y scale factor
set_color	sets the color
get_color	gets the color

4. *Identify the communication between objects.*
Now we can specify the interobject protocol by associating messages with the methods defined above:

new!	create_primitive
position=	set_position
position?	get_position
position+	add_position
orientation=	set_orientation
orientation?	get_orientation
orientation+	add_orientation
scale=	set_scale
scale?	get_scale
scale+	add_scale
color=	set_color
color?	get_color

5. *Test the design with scenarios.*
We match the requirements with simple scenarios that show how each requirement will be met:

Create a primitive:	primitive new! name=aPrimitive
Move:	aPrimitive position = (1,2)
Rotate:	aPrimitive orientation = 30
Scale:	aPrimitive scale = (10,1)
Set color:	aPrimitive = (1,0,0)

6. *Apply inheritance where appropriate.*
Since we only have one level of inheritance so far, we skip this step for now.

Second Pass

Now we repeat the six steps again to add further abstractions.

1. *Identify the data abstractions for each subsystem.*
The polygons, conics, and splines are types of primitives. This level of abstraction is shown in Figure 12.9*b*.

2. *Identify the attributes for each abstraction.*
Here we'll go through the remaining steps for the conic only. Six coefficients specify **conic** and become instance variables.

3. *Identify the operations for each abstraction.*
We add new operations to set and retrieve the six coefficients:

set_coefficients	sets the coefficients
get_coefficients	gets the coefficients

Also, since **conic** has different data structure than **primitive,** we need a method to create a conic:

create_conic	create a conic

4. *Identify the communication between objects.*

new!	create_conic
coefficients =	set_coefficients
coefficients?	get_coefficients

5. *Test the design with scenarios.*

Create a conic:	Conic new! name = aConic
Modify a conic:	aConic coefficients = (1,0,3,2,5,3,0)
Move:	aConic position = (1,2)
Rotate:	aConic orientation = 30
Scale:	aConic scale = (10,1)
Set color:	aConic color = (1,0,0)

6. *Apply inheritance where appropriate.*
No inheritance since we're proceeding in a top-down mode.

Third Pass

One more pass through the design will complete the process for now.

1. *Identify the data abstractions for each subsystem.*
Six coefficients specify a conic, but this is not a convenient way for users to specify shape. We note, however, that circles and ellipses have parameters that a user can easily specify, either numerically or graphically. As long as we're at it, we might as well add hyperbolas and parabolas, so we introduce a new level of abstraction in Figure 12.10.

2. *Identify the attributes for each abstraction.*
Here we'll go through the remaining steps for **circle.** An additional attribute of a circle is its radius.

3. *Identify the operations for each abstraction.*

set_radius	gets the radius of the circle
get_radius	gets the radius of the circle

The circle is a restriction of a conic, so we provide a creation method that maintains the restriction.

create_circle	create a circle

Since **circle** inherits methods from **conic,** we must look at the conic's methods to see if there are any we need to override. For example, in the conic equation, the circle has some of the coefficients set to zero. If we let **circle** inherit the set_coefficients method from **conic,** we might create what

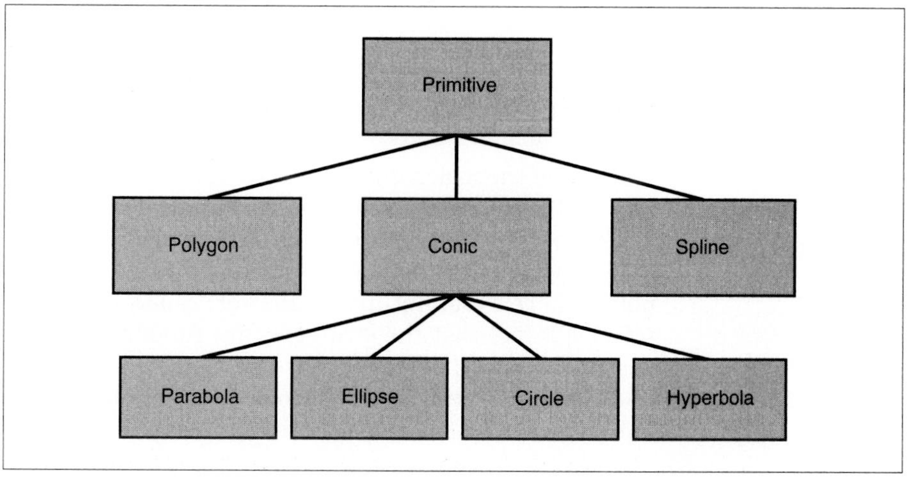

FIGURE 12.10. Third level of abstraction.

we think is a circle but is actually a general conic. We need to override the conic's set_coefficients method. The conic's get_coefficients method is still valid however.

set_coefficients	set conic coefficients for a circle

4. *Identify the communication between objects.*

new!	create_circle
radius =	set_radius
radius ?	get_radius
set_coefficients	set_coefficients

5. *Test the design with scenarios.*

Create a circle:	Circle new! name = aCircle
Modify a conic:	aCircle radius = 10
Move:	aCircle position = (1,2)
Rotate:	aCircle orientation = 30
Scale:	aCircle scale = (10,1)
Set color:	aCircle color = (1,0,0)

6. *Apply inheritance where appropriate.*
After we repeat the steps for an ellipse, we realize that a circle is a specialization of an ellipse. Although this seems obvious in this example, many times in a design it is only after we have designed some classes that we come to such a realization.

12.10 INTEGRATING OOD WITH STRUCTURED ANALYSIS AND STRUCTURED DESIGN

Because of the widespread use of structured analysis (SA) and structured design (SD) (Chapters 7 and 11, respectively) and the intense interest in object-oriented approaches, a natural question arises: Can these two analysis and design strategies be integrated to form a common approach? At this point, there is no definitive answer. Some investigators (e.g., [BOO86b], [MEY90]) feel that the strategies are fundamentally different, while others (e.g., [WAR89], [LOY90]) believe that elements of each method can be used to develop a comprehensive model of a problem. In this section, the overlap between SA/SD and OOA/OOD is explored briefly, and an attempt is made to indicate situations in which the techniques may be able to peacefully coexist.[4]

The key elements of SA/SD are the flow model, the data dictionary, the control specification, the process specification, and the entity relationship (E-R) diagram for data modeling (see Section 8.3). At first examination, it would seem that the data flow diagram would provide good connectivity between SA and OOA/OOD. The data elements—flows (arrows) and stores (double lines)—and processes ("bubbles") would seem to provide an approximate model of objects and operations, respectively. But this is not the case.

Recall that object orientation creates a representation of the *real-world* problem domain and maps it into a solution domain that is software. For this reason, the SA/SD representations that depict real-world elements of the problem will provide a better bridge to OOA/OOD. External entities (boxes) that are represented as producers and consumers of data flow are possible candidate objects. The data objects defined as part of an E-R diagram are also candidates for objects. It is true that lower-level DFDs may provide an indication of the attributes of some objects and the processes shown in these diagrams will provide an indication of the operations that are applied to the objects. But the DFD does not depict the system from an object-oriented viewpoint.

The control specification (CSPEC) provides a behavioral model that may help the designer better understand messaging within the object-oriented model. Finally, the entity-relationship diagram can help to isolate candidate classes and subclasses and the relationships between them.

Ward [WAR89] describes a mapping between SA/SD for real-time systems and object-oriented design. A data abstraction (a class) can be represented "as a disembodied transformation with its inputs and outputs; it is *not* instantiated by being incorporated into the flow model... such a transformation could be built with reuse in mind by including data and transformation suitable for many application domains [in which the data abstraction appears]." In essence, Ward suggests that a class or subclass can be represented as a lone bubble. Flows into and out of the bubble still represent data flow, but imply operations that are attached to the class. To instantiate an object, the lone bubble is included within the context of the flow model. For example, a **sensor** class can be modeled as a data abstraction (using an E-R diagram) and represented by a lone ("disembodied") bubble. An object within the **sensor** class could be instantiated (e.g., **smoke sensor**) within a specific flow model by including a **smoke sensor** bubble in the DFD.

An object-oriented structured design (OOSD) notation that encompasses elements of the structure chart (Chapter 11) and the Booch diagram

[4]For new projects, it is probably best to choose one method (OOA/OOD is an attractive choice) and stick with it. Mixing the methods on a single problem is less than ideal.

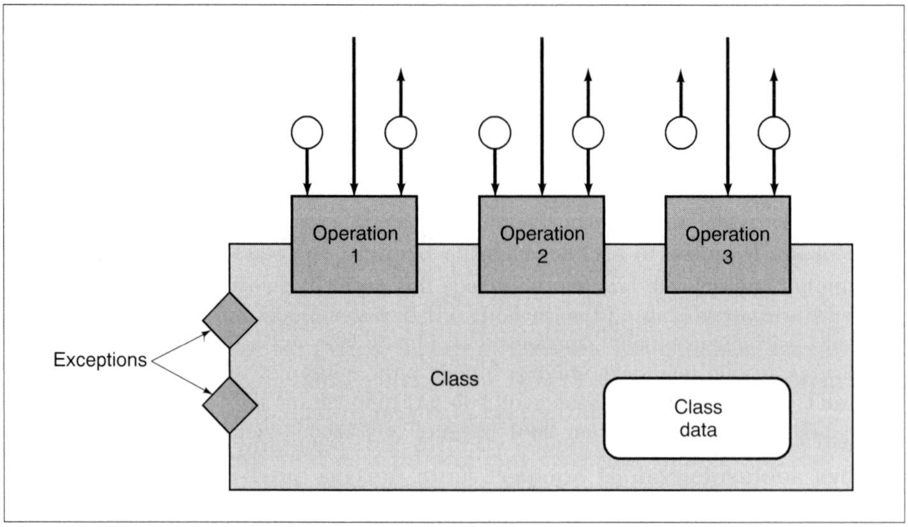

FIGURE 12.11.
OOSD notation.

as well as class definition and inheritance principles has been suggested by Wasserman et al. [WAS90]. The authors suggest a notation that takes the form shown in Figure 12.11. The large rectangle is used to define a class that makes use of operations denoted by boxes that overlap the rectangle.[5] A "parameter passing notation" (the small circles with arrows emanating from them) that is sometimes used in the definition of structure charts is used to show input and output data from the operations. The heavy arrows indicate coupling between modules in a program structure and the diamonds indicate *exception conditions* that require "special-case" processing.

Some investigators contend that "there is no fundamental opposition between SA/SD and OOD" [WAR89], while others (the "purists") believe that objected-oriented methods and the structured design approach are mutually exclusive (and that OOD is far superior). Only time will tell whether these worthwhile design methods go their separate ways or develop a long-lasting marriage.

12.11 SUMMARY

Object-oriented design creates a model of the real world that can be realized in software. Objects provide a mechanism for representing the information domain, while operations describe the processing that is associated with the

[5]This is only one of a number of symbols suggested for OOSD. The interested reader should refer to Wasserman et al. [WAS90].

information domain. Messages (an interfacing mechanism) provide the means by which operations are invoked. The unique characteristic of OOA/OOD is that objects "know" what operations may be applied to them. This knowledge is achieved by combining data and procedural abstractions in a single program component (called an *object* or a *package*).

OOA/OOD has evolved as a result of a new class of object-oriented programming languages such as Smalltalk, C++, Objective-C, CLU, Ada, Modula, and others. Consequently, object-oriented design representations are more prone than others to have a programming language dependency.

OOA/OOD methodology consists of a three-step approach that requires the designer to state the problem, define an informal solution strategy, and formalize the strategy by identifying objects and operations, specifying interfaces, and providing implementation details for data and procedural abstractions. The role of OOD is to take the basic classes and objects defined as part of OOA and refine them with additional design detail. Designs are represented using one of a number of graphical notations and a program design language.

Object-oriented design represents a unique approach for software engineers. To quote Tom Love [LOV85]:

> The roots of software problems may lie in the most traditional terms for describing our industry—data processing. We have been taught that data and processing are two distinct "things" which are somehow fundamental to our business. That partitioning may be far more detrimental than we realize.

OOD provides us with a means for breaking down the "partitions" between data and process. In doing so, software quality can be improved.

REFERENCES

[ABB83] Abbott, R. J., "Program Design by Informal English Descriptions," *CACM*, vol. 26, no. 11, November 1983, pp. 882–894.

[BOO86a] Booch, G., *Software Engineering with Ada*, 2d ed., Benjamin-Cummings, 1986.

[BOO86b] Booch, G., "Object-Oriented Development," *IEEE Trans. Software Engineering*, vol. SE-12, no. 2, February 1986, pp. 211–221.

[BOO90] Booch, G., *Object-Oriented Design*, Benjamin-Cummings, 1990.

[COA90] Coad, P., and E. Yourdon, *Object-Oriented Analysis*, Prentice-Hall, 1990.

[COX85] Cox, B., "Software ICs and Objective-C," *UnixWorld*, Spring 1985.

[EVB86] *Object-Oriented Design Handbook*, EVB Software Engineering, 1986.

[GOL83] Goldberg, A., and D. Robson, *Smalltalk-80: The Language and Its Implementation*, Addison-Wesley, 1983.

[LOR86] Lorensen, W., "Object-Oriented Design," *CED Software Engineering Guidelines*, General Electric Co., 1986.

[LOV85] Love, T., *Message-Object Programming: Experiences with Commercial Systems*, Productivity Products International, 1985.

[LOY90] Loy, P. H., Comparisons of O-O and Structured Development, *ACM Software Engineering Notes,* vol. 15, no. 1, January 1990, pp. 44–47.

[MEY90] Meyer, Bertrand, *Object-Oriented Software Construction,* 2d ed., Prentice-Hall, 1988.

[SHL88] Shlaer, S. and S. J. Mellor, *Object-Oriented Systems Analysis,* Yourdon Press, 1988.

[WAR89] Ward, P. T., "How to Integrate Object Orientation with Structured Analysis and Design," *IEEE Software,* March 1989, pp. 74–82.

[WAS90] Wasserman, A. I., P. A. Pircher, and R. J. Muller, "The Object-Oriented Design Notation for Software Design Representation," *IEEE Computer,* vol. 23, no. 3, March 1990, pp. 50–63.

[WIE84] Wiener, R., and R. Sincovec, *Software Engineering with Modula-2 and Ada,* Wiley, 1984.

PROBLEMS AND POINTS TO PONDER

12.1 From your everyday experience, select five classes of objects and provide at least five instantiations of objects for each class. Define the attributes for each class and the operations that apply to it.

12.2 Do some research on object-oriented programming languages (e.g., Smalltalk or Eiffel) and explain why a programming language such as FORTRAN would not be suited to object-oriented applications.

12.3 For students with a knowledge of the C programming language: It is possible to implement the object-oriented design in native C. Do some research and explain how this can be done.

12.4 For students with a knowledge of the C programming language: Explain how C++ or Objective C differs from native C.

12.5 OOD tends to be programming language-dependent. Why?

12.6 Apply OOD techniques to the *SafeHome* system described earlier in this book.

12.7 Apply OOD techniques to the PHTRS system described in Problem 7.13.

12.8 Describe a video game and apply OOD methods to represent its design.

12.9 You are responsible for the development of an electronic mail (E-mail) system to be implemented on a PC network. The E-mail system will enable users to create letters to be mailed to another user, distribution, or a specific address list. Letters can be read, copied, stored, etc. The E-mail system will make use of existing word processing capability to create letters. Using this description as a starting point, derive a set of requirements and apply OOD techniques to create a top level design of the E-mail system.

12.10 A small island nation has decided to build an air traffic control (ATC) system for its one airport. The system is specified as follows:

> All aircraft landing at the airport must have a transponder that transmits aircraft type and flight data in high-density packed format to the ATC ground station. The ATC ground station can query an aircraft for specific information. When the ATC ground station receives data, it is unpacked and stored in an aircraft database. A computer graphics display is created from the stored information and displayed for

an air traffic controller. The display is updated every 10 seconds. All information is analyzed to determine if "dangerous situations" are present. The air traffic controller can query the database for specific information about any plane displayed on the screen.

Using OOD, create a design for the ATC system. Do not attempt to implement or use it!

12.11 Using Booch [BOO86a] as a guide, develop a detailed representation of the ATC system (Problem 12.10) using Booch diagrams.

12.12 Using your library as a source, get a copy of Wasserman, Pircher, and Muller [WAS90] and use the OOSD notation to model any one of the systems developed in Problems 12.6 through 12.11.

FURTHER READINGS

The object-oriented design literature is expanding rapidly. Books by Goldberg and Robson [GOL83], Booch [BOO86a], Cox (*Object Oriented Programming*, Addison-Wesley, 1986), Meyer [MEY90], Winblad, Edwards, and King (*Object-Oriented Software*, Addison-Wesley, 1990), Mullin (*Object-Oriented Program Design*, Addison-Wesley, 1989), Wirf-Brock et al. (*Designing Object-Oriented Software*, Prentice-Hall, 1990), and Rumbaugh et al. (*Object-Oriented Modeling and Design*, Prentice-Hall, 1991) are recommended for those who intend to pursue OOD more fully. Booch [BOO90] presents a useful treatment of OOD concepts, introduces an effective method for object-oriented design, and provides an extensive bibliography. A special edition of the *Communications of the ACM* (September 1990) is dedicated to object-oriented design and surveys research directions.

Not everyone is enthusiastic about the potential of OOD. In a scathing attack on the technology ("Are the Emperor's New Clothes Object-Oriented," *Dr. Dobb's Journal*, December 1989), Scott Guthery questions the run-time performance of object-oriented programs and the lack of hard data supporting current claims of reusability. He also voices other legitimate concerns about the efficacy of the approach.

Literally dozens of books have been published on object-oriented programming languages. Among many are two volumes by Pinson and Weiner (*Object-Oriented Programming and Smalltalk* and *Object-Oriented Programming and C++*, Addison-Wesley, 1988). Books by Keene (*Object-Oriented Programming in Common Lisp*, Addison-Wesley, 1988) and Pohl (*C++ for C Programmers*, Addison-Wesley, 1989) are also worth examining.

Object-oriented software development is quite common for personal computer applications. Smucker (*Object-Oriented Programming for the Macintosh*, Heyden Book Co., 1988) describes one approach for the Apple Macintosh. The *Journal of Object-Oriented Programming* (published approximately six times per year) is an excellent source of current information.

In addition to the OOD approaches that have been summarized in this chapter, the interested reader should explore Hierarchical Object-Oriented Design (HOOD), a technique developed by the European Space Agency (*HOOD Reference Manual,* Issue 3.0, September 1989) and a technique proposed by Buhr (*System Design with Ada,* Prentice-Hall, 1984).

CHAPTER 13

DATA-ORIENTED DESIGN METHODS

The intimate relationship between programs and data can be traced to the origins of computing. The original concept behind the stored program computer is that programs can be viewed as data and data interpreted as programs. The structure of information, called *data structure,* has been shown to have an important impact on the complexity and efficiency of algorithms designed to process information.

As software design methods have evolved, one school of thought holds that:

> The identification of the inherent data structure (for a computer-based system) is vital, and the structure of data (input and output) can be used to derive the structure (and some details) of a program [PET77]

In many areas of application, a distinct, hierarchical information structure exists. Input data, internally stored information (i.e., a database), and output data may each have a unique structure. Data structure-oriented design makes use of these structures as a foundation for development of software.

13.1 DESIGN AND DATA STRUCTURE

Data structure affects the design of both structural and procedural aspects of software. Repetitive data are always processed with software that has control facilities for repetition; alternative data (i.e., information that may or may not be present) precipitate software with conditional processing elements; a hierarchical data organization frequently has a remarkable resemblance to the program structure of the software that uses the data. In fact, the structure of information is an excellent predictor of program structure.

Data structure-oriented design transforms a representation of data structure into a representation of software. Like data flow-oriented techniques (Chapter 11), developers of data structure-oriented design have defined a set of "mapping" procedures that use information (data) structure as a guide.

13.1.1 Contributors

The origins of data structure-oriented design can be found in technical discussions on the "fundamentals of data structures" (e.g., [TRE76]), computer algorithms [HOR78], the structure of control and data [WUL81], and the concept of data abstractions [GUT77]. More pragmatic treatments of software design and its relationship to data structure have been proposed by Jackson [JAC75, JAC83], Warnier [WAR74, WAR81] and Orr [ORR81, HAN83].

Jackson structured programming (JSP), a widely used software design method, takes the view that "paralleling the structure of input data and output (report) data will ensure a quality design" [JAC75]. More recent extensions to the methodology, called *Jackson system development* [CAM89], focus on the identification of information entities and the actions that are applied to them and are quite similar in some respects to the object-oriented design approach described in Chapter 12. Jackson emphasizes practicality, developing pragmatic techniques to transform data to program structure.

Logical construction of programs (LCP), developed by J. D. Warnier [WAR74], provides a rigorous method for software design. Drawing upon the relationship between data structure and procedural structure, Warnier develops a set of techniques that accomplish a mapping from input/output data structure to a detailed procedural representation of software.

Data structured systems development (DSSD), also called the *Warnier-Orr methodology* [ORR81, HAN83], is an extension of LCP and adds strong analysis as well as design capabilities. The DSSD approach provides a notation and procedures for deriving data structure, program structure, and detailed procedural design of program components (modules). In addition, DSSD provides a notation that enables the designer to examine data flow between sources and receivers of information and through processes that transform information.

A technique called *logical construction of software* [CHA80] is representative of a synthesis of both data flow- and data structure-oriented design approaches. The developers of the method contend that "logical design can be described explicitly if the software is viewed as a system of data sets and data transforms" [CHA80].

13.1.2 Areas of Application

Data structure-oriented design may be successfully applied in applications that have a well-defined, hierarchical structure of information. Typical examples include:

- *Business information system applications.* Input and output have a distinct structure (e.g., input files, output reports); the use of a hierarchical database is common.
- *Systems applications.* The data structure for operating systems is comprised of many tables, files, and lists that have a well-defined structure.
- *CAD/CAE/CIM applications.* Computer-aided design, engineering, and manufacturing systems require sophisticated data structures for information storage, translation, and processing.

In addition, applications from the engineering/scientific domain, computer-aided instruction, combinatorial problem solving, and many other areas may be amenable to data structure-oriented design.

13.1.3 Data Structure versus Data Flow Techniques

Before considering differences between data structure- and data flow-oriented design, it is important to note that both begin with analysis steps that lay the foundation for subsequent design steps; both are information-driven; both attempt to transform information into a software representation; both are based on separately derived concepts of "good" design.

Data structure-oriented design does not make explicit use of a data flow diagram. Therefore, transform and transaction flow classifications have little relevance to the data structure-oriented design method. More importantly, the ultimate objective of data structure-oriented methods is to produce a procedural description of the software. The concept of program modular structure is not explicitly considered. Modules are considered byproducts of procedure, and a philosophy of module independence is given little emphasis.

Data structure-oriented design makes use of a hierarchical diagram to represent information structure. Therefore, the emphasis during software requirements analysis must be placed on these modes of representation.

13.1.4 Data Structure versus Object-Oriented Design

Because both data structure-oriented design and object-oriented design focus on real-world objects and their manifestations in a software-based system, there are important similarities between the two design methods. Like the comparison between data structure- and data flow-oriented methods, data structure-oriented design and OOD are both information-driven; both use a representation of data as a basis for developing a representation of the program; both have their own (independently derived) concept of a "good" design. The data hierarchy (used in data structure-oriented methods) is similar to the class hierarchy used in OOD. Both apply data abstractions and each considers the operations that transform the data to be secondary to the data items themselves.

The primary difference between OOD and data structure-oriented design methods is in the definition of an *object*. In OOD, an object encapsulates both data and process. Data structure-oriented design methods take the more conventional route—an object (data object) is data only. Although there is no direct representation of inheritance, messaging, or encapsulation in data structure-oriented design methods, these concepts do manifest themselves subtly in the design heuristics described in this chapter.

13.2 DESIGN PROCESS CONSIDERATIONS

Software requirements analysis remains the foundation for data structure-oriented design. The description of the information domain (data structure, content, and flow) contained in the *Software Requirements Specification* foreshadows software architecture to be developed during design. Each design method provides a set of "rules" that enable the designer to transform data structure into a representation of software.

Each data structure-oriented method has its own set of rules. However, the following design tasks are always conducted: (1) data structure characteristics are evaluated; (2) data is represented in terms of elementary forms such as sequence, selection, and repetition; (3) data structure representation is mapped into a control hierarchy for software; (4) software hierarchy is refined using guidelines defined as part of a method; (5) a procedural description of software is ultimately developed.

A clean division between the architectural and procedural design steps (as they have been described as part of the software design process) is not as evident in data structure-oriented methods. Jackson, Warnier, and Orr move quickly to a procedural representation.

13.3 JACKSON SYSTEM DEVELOPMENT

Like most software design methods, Jackson system development (JSD) is actually a continuum of technical steps that support software analysis and design. In Chapter 9 the analysis-oriented steps of JSD were presented.[1] To conduct JSD, the analyst and designer perform the following steps:

- *Entity action step.* Using an approach that is quite similar to the object-oriented analysis technique described in Chapter 8, *entities* (people, objects, or organizations that a system needs to produce or use information) and *actions* (the events that occur in the real world that affect entities) are identified.
- *Entity structure step.* Actions that affect each entity are ordered by time and represented with *Jackson diagrams* (a tree-like notation reintroduced later in this section).
- *Initial model step.* Entities and actions are represented as a process model; connections between the model and the real world are defined.
- *Function step.* Functions that correspond to defined actions are specified.
- *System timing step.* Process scheduling characteristics are assessed and specified.
- *Implementation step.* Hardware and software are specified as a design.

The first three steps in JSD have been described in Section 9.4. To summarize, the *entity action step* begins with a brief English language statement of a problem from which entities (nouns) and actions (verbs) are chosen. Only those entities and actions that have a direct relationship to the software solution are chosen for further evaluation.

The *entity structure step* creates a Jackson diagram that describes a time-ordered specification of the actions performed on or by an entity. The Jackson diagram, depicted in Figure 13.1 (for the university shuttle service or USS example introduced in Section 9.4), is created for each entity (**shuttle** and **button** entities in the case of Figure 13.1) and is often accompanied by narrative text.

The *initial model step* begins the construction of a specification of a system as a model of the real world. The specification is created with a *system specification diagram* (SSD) using symbology that is illustrated in Figure 13.2. A *data stream connection* occurs when one process transmits a stream of information (e.g., writes records) and the other process receives the stream (e.g., reads records). Arrowheads represent the direction of information flow, while the circle represents the data stream which is assumed to be placed in a FIFO buffer of unlimited capacity. A *state vector connection* occurs when one process directly inspects the state vector of another process. Arrowheads represent the direction of information flow and the diamond indicates the state vector. This connection is common in process

[1]The reader is urged to review Section 9.4 before continuing with this section.

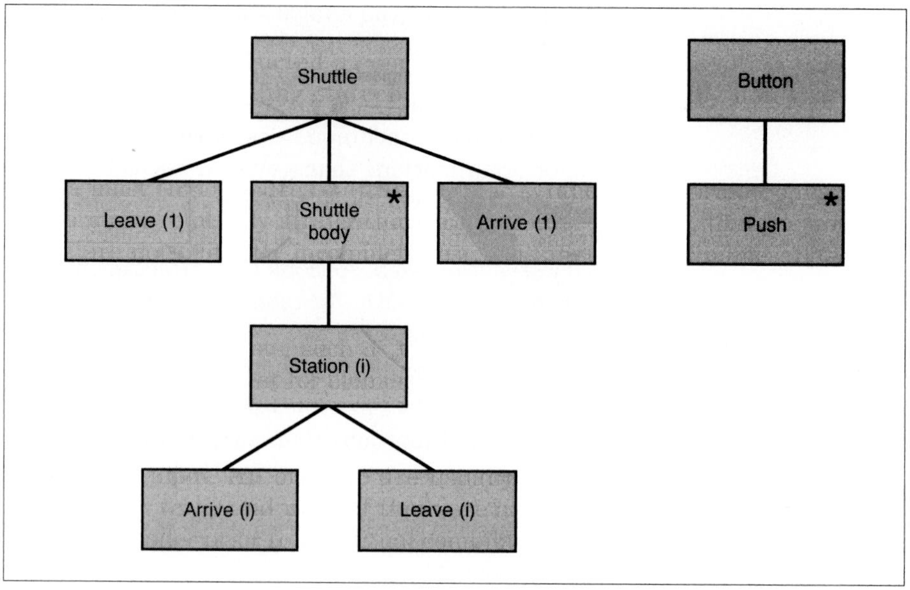

FIGURE 13.1.
Jackson structure diagram.

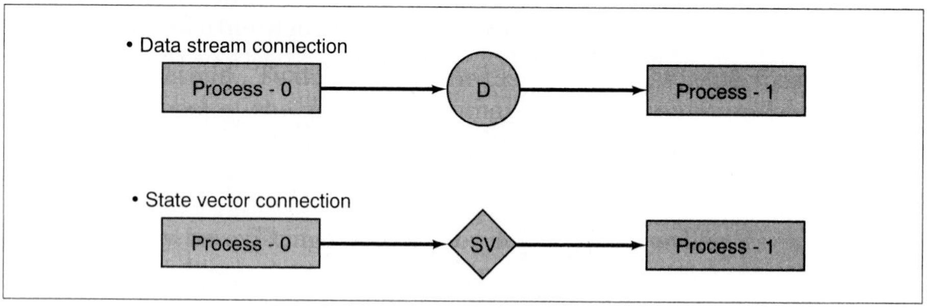

FIGURE 13.2.
SSD notation.

control applications in which it is necessary to check the state of some electromechanical device. By convention, the suffix 0 represents a real-world process and the suffix 1 represents a system model process.

13.3.1 JSD Design Steps

In order to discuss design steps for Jackson system development, we continue the university shuttle service example presented in Section 9.4. Reproducing the problem statement:

> A large university is spread over two campuses which are over a mile apart. To help students who must travel between campuses to get to lectures on time, the university plans to install a shuttle service.

> The shuttle service makes use of only one high-speed shuttle that travels over tracks between a station at each campus. Each station has a call button that students can use to request transport to the other station. When students arrive at a station, they push the call button. If the shuttle is already there, they board it and depart for the other station. If the shuttle is in transit, they must wait for it to stop at the other station, board students (if any), and return. If the shuttle is at the other station, it leaves to come and pick up the students who pushed the button. The shuttle will wait at a station until the next request for service (a button is pushed) occurs.

Entities are selected by examining all nouns in the description. After review, the following candidate entities are chosen: **university, campus, students, lectures, shuttle, station, button.** We are not directly concerned with **campus**, **lectures, students,** or **stations**—all of these lie outside the model boundary and are rejected as possible entities. **University** is merely a collective term for both campuses, so we reject it as a possible entity. We select **shuttle** and **button**. Using a similar analysis, we select **arrive, push,** and **leave** as actions that affect **shuttle** and **button**.

The Jackson structure diagram for **shuttle** and **button** is shown in Figure 13.1. The system specification diagram for USS is illustrated in Figure 13.3. Finally, the initial model step for USS is conducted as described in the following discussion [reproduced from Section 9.4.3].

Whenever possible, we prefer to connect model processes with real-world entities by data streams because a direct correspondence between the behavior of the model and the real world is assured. In our example, the call button emits a pulse when pressed. This can be transmitted to the **button-1** process as a data stream connection. However, we shall assume that the sensors that detect arrival or departure of the shuttle do not emit a pulse, but do close an electric switch. The state of the switch (on/off) can be accessed. Hence, a state vector connection is required.

The internal details of model processes are specified using what Jackson calls *structure text.* Structure text represents the same information as structure diagrams (Figure 13.4)—sequence, selection, repetition—but does so in a textual format. The structure text for **button-1** is

```
BUTTON-1
    read BD;
        PUSH-BDY itr while BD
            PUSH;
            read DB;
        PUSH-BDY end
BUTTON-1 end
```

The structure of BUTTON-1 corresponds identically to the structure of BUTTON-0, with the addition of **read** operations that connect the real world to the system.

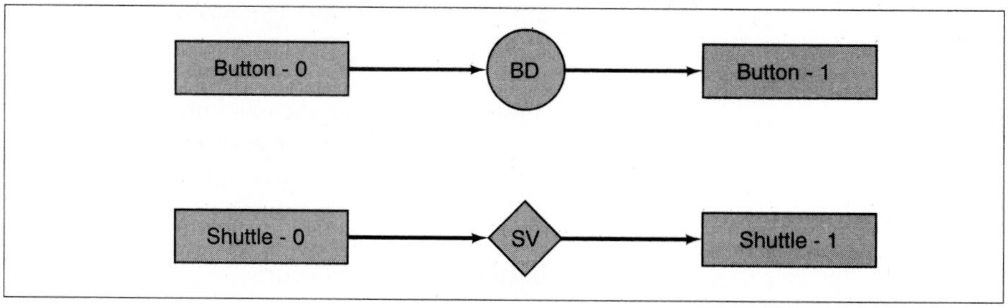

FIGURE 13.3. An SSD for USS.

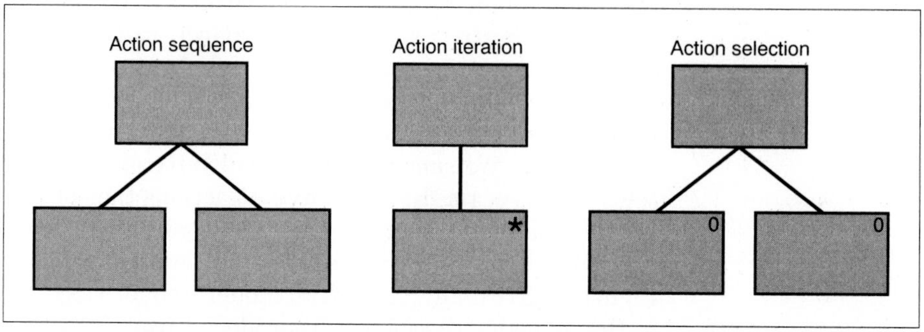

FIGURE 13.4. Structure diagram notation.

As noted earlier, the SHUTTLE-1 process cannot be connected to its real-world counterpart by a data stream connection. Instead, we must interrogate the switches that are turned on/off by the arrival/departure of the shuttle at a station. The system process must inspect the real-world entity frequently enough to ensure that no actions pass undetected. This is accomplished by executing a **getsv** (get state vector) operation that obtains the state vector of the real-world entity. It is likely that the system process will obtain each value of the state vector a number of times before it is changed, and the model process can be elaborated to show these "in transit" values of the state vectors. A structure text description of SHUTTLE-1 follows:

```
SHUTTLE-1 seq
    getsv SV;
    WAIT-BDY itr while WAIT1
        getsv SV;
    WAIT-BDY end
    LEAVE (1);
    TRANSIT-BDY1 itr while TRANSIT1
        getsv SV;
    TRANSIT-BDY1 end
    SHUTTLE-BDY1 itr
        STATION seq
            ARRIVE (i);
```

```
                WAIT-BDY itr while WAITi
                    getsv SV;
                WAIT-BDY end
                LEAVE (i);
                TRANSIT-BDY itr while TRANSITi
                    getsv SV;
                TRANSIT-BDY end
            STATION end
        SHUTTLE-BDY end
        ARRIVE (1);
    SHUTTLE-1 end
```

The state values WAIT and TRANSIT represent appropriate values of the arrival and departure switch. The real-world process SHUTTLE-0 produces a change of state in the switch, and the system process SHUTTLE-1 executes **getsv** operations to sense this change. Figure 13.5*a* illustrates the structure text for SHUTTLE-1 as a structure diagram.

13.3.2 The Function Step

The purpose of the JSD function step is to expand the system specification diagram by connecting newly defined function processes to the model processes by data or vector streams. JSD recognizes three kinds of functions:

Embedded functions. This function is achieved by allocating (write) operations to a model process structure text.
Imposed functions. This function inspects the state vector of the model process and produces output results.
Interactive functions. This function inspects the state vector of the model process, writes a data stream to affect the actions of the model process, and includes operations to write results.

The outputs of the function processes are system outputs and may be reports, commands to hardware devices, or any other outgoing information.

To illustrate the function step, we consider the USS example and examine the model of the shuttle. In the shuttle, there is a light panel that is used to indicate arrival at the station by lighting a display message. The lamps are switched on/off by the lamp commands LON(i) and LOFF(i). A function must be embedded into the shuttle process model to write a command to lamp(i) when the shuttle arrives at station(i); another command must be generated to switch lamp(i) off when the shuttle leaves station(i). Thus, as the shuttle travels between stations, it outputs a data stream consisting of lamp commands. The SSD that represents this situation is shown in Figure 13.5*b*.

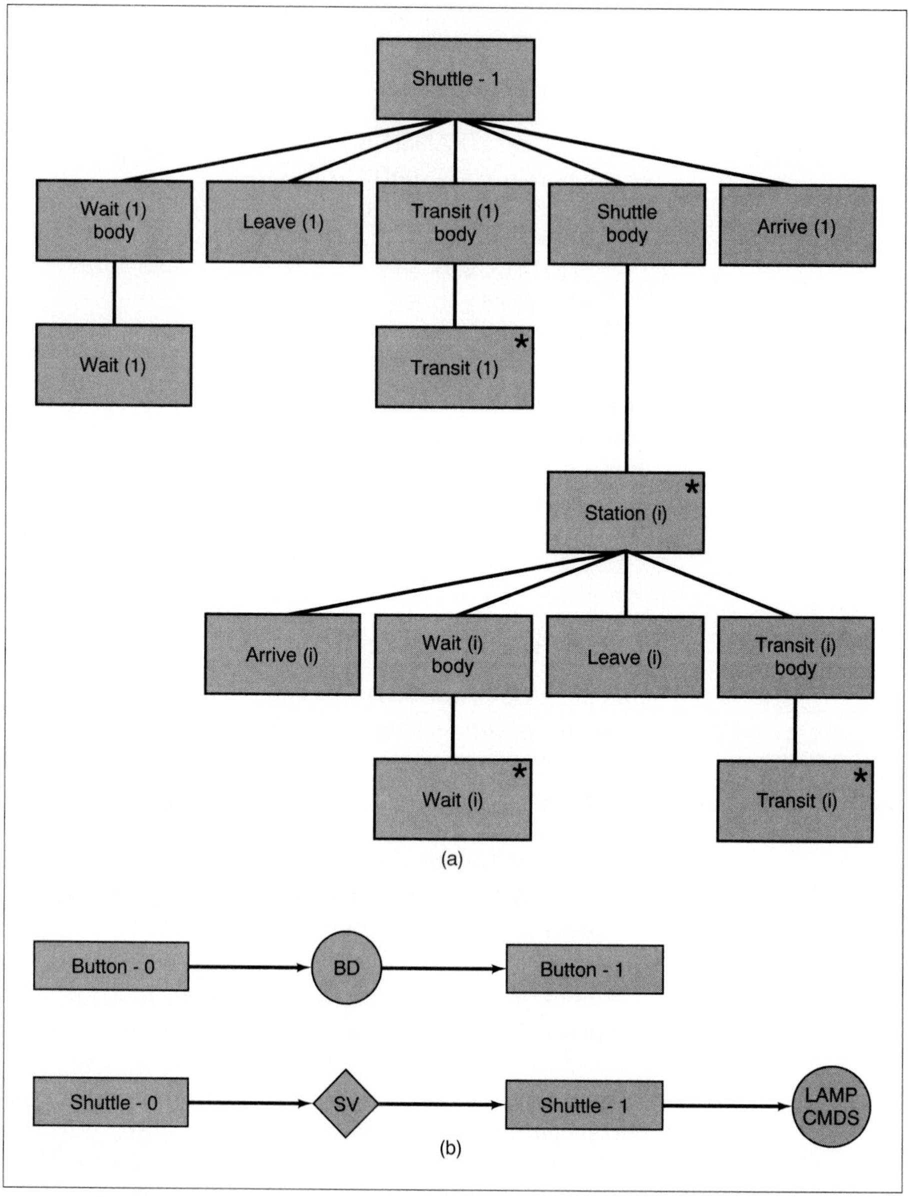

FIGURE 13.5.
(a) Structure diagram corresponding to structure text;
(b) updated SSD.

To implement the lamp commands, the structure text for SHUTTLE-1 is modified as follows:

```
SHUTTLE-1 seq
    LON(1);
    getsv SV;
```

```
    WAIT-BDY itr while WAIT1
        getsv SV;
    WAIT-BDY end
    LOFF(1);
    LEAVE (1);
    TRANSIT-BDY1 itr while TRANSIT1
        getsv SV;
    TRANSIT-BDY1 end
    SHUTTLE-BDY1 itr
        STATION seq
            ARRIVE (i);
            LON(i);
            WAIT-BDY itr while WAITi
                getsv SV;
            WAIT-BDY end
            LOFF(i);
            LEAVE (i);
            TRANSIT-BDY itr while TRANSITi
                getsv SV;
            TRANSIT-BDY end
        STATION end
    SHUTTLE-BDY end
    ARRIVE (1);
SHUTTLE-1 end
```

Referring to the structure text above, a command is issued to switch on the message display announcing station 1 on the panel. This occurs at the start of the shuttle's life, before it leaves station 1 for the first time. Each time the sensors indicate arrival at a station, the appropriate lamp is lit and, when the shuttle leaves, the lamp is turned off.

A second function is to produce motor commands, START and STOP, that will control the movement of the shuttle. These commands are to be issued under the following conditions:

STOP—when sensors indicate arrival at a station

START—when a button is pushed (the first time) to request the shuttle, and the shuttle is waiting at one of the stations

The need to issue the STOP command is determined solely by the shuttle's arrival at a station. However, the timing of the START command is affected by both the buttons and the shuttle. Therefore, we introduce a function process called **mcontrol** that acts on data it receives from the shuttle-1 and button processes and issues START and STOP commands.

The connection between the shuttle-1 process and **mcontrol** will be by data stream S1D. This means that the shuttle-1 process cannot miss the arrival of the shuttle, as may occur if the state vector were periodically inspected.

The structure text for the SHUTTLE-1 process is reproduced once more, this time amended for lamp and motor control:

```
SHUTTLE-1 seq
    LON(1)
    getsv SV;
    WAIT-BDY itr while WAIT1
         getsv SV;
    WAIT-BDY end
    LOFF(1);
    LEAVE (1);
    TRANSIT-BDY1 itr while TRANSIT1
         getsv SV;
    TRANSIT-BDY1 end
    SHUTTLE-BDY1 itr
         STATION seq
             ARRIVE (i);
             write arrive to S1D;
             LON(i);
             WAIT-BDY itr while WAITi
                  getsv SV;
             WAIT-BDY end
             LOFF(i);
             LEAVE (i);
             TRANSIT-BDY itr while TRANSITi
                  getsv SV;
             TRANSIT-BDY end
         STATION end
    SHUTTLE-BDY end
    ARRIVE (1);
    write arrive to S1D;
SHUTTLE-1 end
```

It is necessary to ensure that the SHUTTLE-1 process executes getsv SV operations, and that **mcontrol** reads its arrival records with sufficient frequency to stop the shuttle in time. Timing constraints, scheduling, and implementation are considered in JSD steps that follow.

To complete the USS example, we return to the model for the button entity. The original model, **button-1**, is an accurate statement of button actions, but it is now necessary to distinguish between the first push that requests a journey, and subsequent pushes before the journey actually starts. A new level-2 process, **button-2**, is described to accommodate these requirements and is depicted with a Jackson structure diagram in Figure 13.6. A function process inspects the state vector of **button-2** to determine whether there is an outstanding request for a journey. The **mcontrol** function informs **button-2** when a request has been serviced, i.e., when the shuttle has

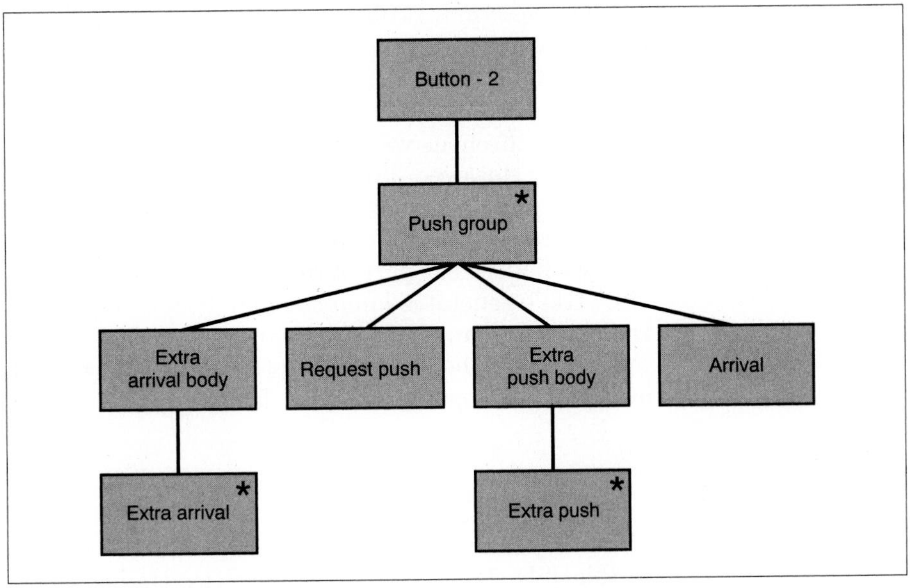

FIGURE 13.6. University shuttle service—function step.

arrived at the station where the request was made. It does this by passing the arrival records it receives from SHUTTLE-1. Thus, an interactive function for the **button-2** process is defined.

Structure text for the **button-2** process follows:

```
BUTTON-2 seq
    request : = no;
    read MBD and B1D;
    BUTTON-BDY itr
        PUSH-GROUP seq
            EXTRA-AR-BDY itr while (ARRIVAL)
                read MBD and B1D;
            EXTRA-AR-BDY end
            RQ-PUSH seq
                request : = yes;
                read MBD and B1D;
            RQ-PUSH end
            EXTRA-RQ-PUSH itr while
                read MBD and B1D;
            EXTRA-RQ-PUSH end
            ARRIVAL seq
                request : = no;
                read MBD and B1D;
            ARRIVAL end
        PUSH-GROUP end
    BUTTON-BDY end
BUTTON-2 end
```

The input to BUTTON-2 consists of two data streams, merged in a manner that is termed a *rough merge*. A rough merge occurs when the reading process simply accepts the next record that occurs in a data stream. Therefore, the order in which records are processed is dependent on two potentially asynchronous writing processes. For this example, the rough merge is sufficient. However, JSD provides other types of merging that would introduce less indeterminacy into the system [JAC83].

Figure 13.7 shows a system specification diagram that reflects all the changes imposed as part of the function step. An embedded function within SHUTTLE-1 generates lamp commands, and a new function process, **mcontrol**, imposes an interactive function on BUTTON-2 and produces motor commands for the shuttle. The structure of the **mcontrol** process is derived by examining input and output data structures (Sections 13.3.4 and 13.3.5).

13.3.3 System Timing Step

In this JSD step, the designer specifies timing constraints imposed on the system. The earlier design steps produce a system composed of sequential processes that communicate by data streams and direct inspection of state vectors. The relative scheduling of the processing is indeterminate.

One mechanism that can be used to synchronize processes is the *time grain marker* (TGM). The TGM is a data record that indicates the occur-

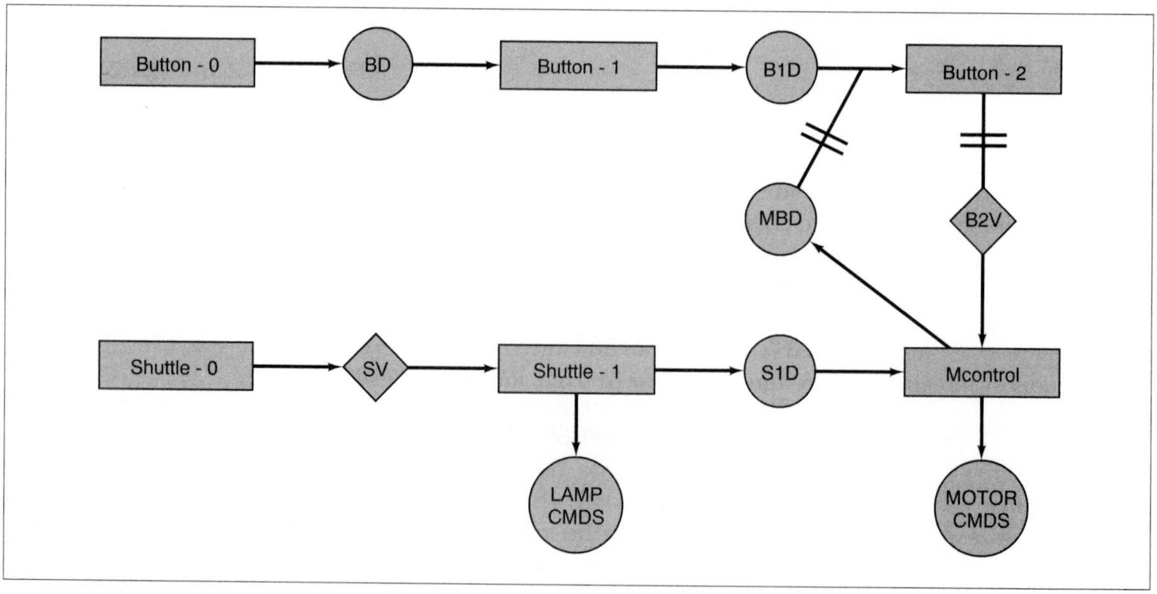

FIGURE 13.7. SSD, extended for functions 1 and 2.

rence of a particular interval of time and can be used to enable the passage of time to affect the actions of a process.

The timing constraints for the university shuttle service example might include:

1. The time within which the STOP command must be issued, based on the shuttle forward speed and braking power
2. The response times for switching the panel lamps on/off

For the USS example, there is no need to introduce any special synchronization mechanism. To some extent, the interchange of data has already imposed some degree of synchronization.

13.3.4 The Implementation Step

The implementation step of JSD draws on earlier work [JAC75] to derive the remaining program or process structure from the problem data structure. In this and the following section, an overview of the Jackson's program design approach, called *Jackson structured programming* (JSP), is presented. The mappings associated with this approach are the reason that this design methodology has been categorized as data structure-oriented.

The essence of the implementation step may be stated by paraphrasing Jackson: "Problems should be decomposed into hierarchical structures of parts that may be represented by three structural forms." The "structural forms" that Jackson alludes to are sequence, condition, and repetition—in actuality, *procedural constructs* (in the terminology of this book) that are the foundation of the structured programming philosophy (Chapter 10).

Data structure notation is a variation of the Jackson structure diagram and is illustrated in Figure 13.8. Referring to the figure, a collection of data, A, is comprised of multiple occurrences (denoted by *) of data substructure B. B includes multiple occurrences of C and another substructure D that contains either data item E or F (alternative data are denoted by an 0). Jackson's block diagrammatic representation of the information hierarchy may be applied to input, output, or database structures with equal facility.

As a more concrete example of this notation, we consider software to be developed for a credit card accounting system (grossly simplified), shown in Figure 13.9. A **payment-file**, containing customer numbers (CNO), payment date (Date), and amount paid (Amt), is to be reconciled with a customer master file that contains CNO and the outstanding balance. The payment file is presorted in customer number groupings (CNO-GROUP) so that all payments by an individual are contained within a single record. The data structure for both files, described in Jackson notation, is shown in the figure.

An output report format for the credit card accounting system and the resultant data structure diagram is shown in Figure 13.10. The report im-

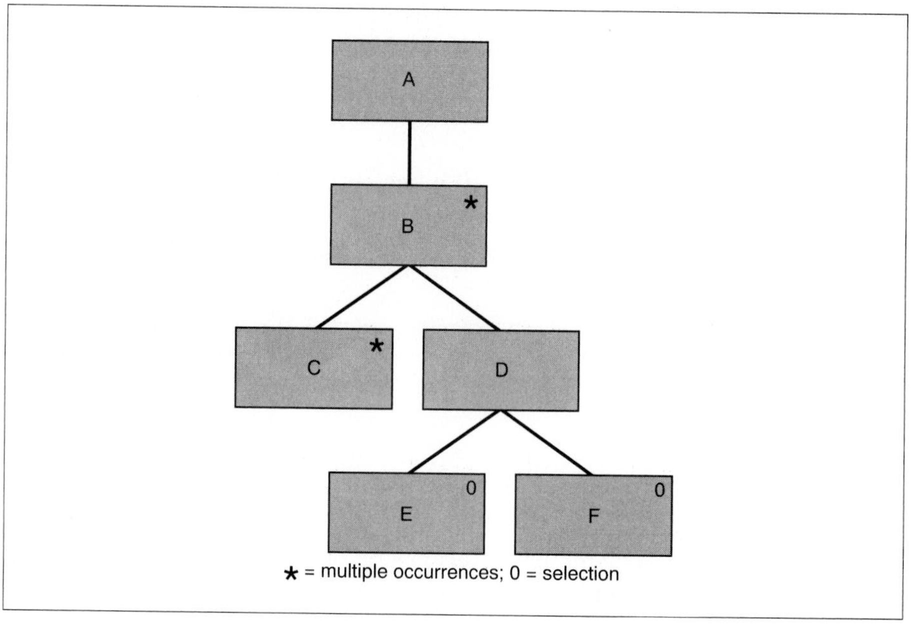

FIGURE 13.8. Data structure notation.

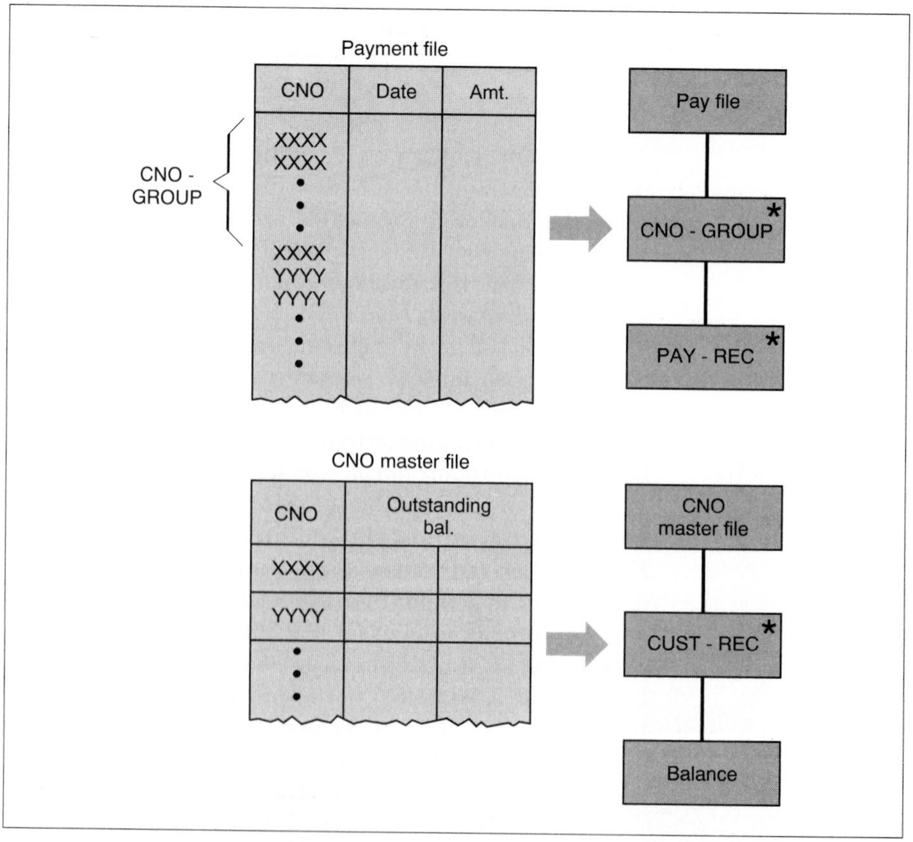

FIGURE 13.9. Credit card billing system.

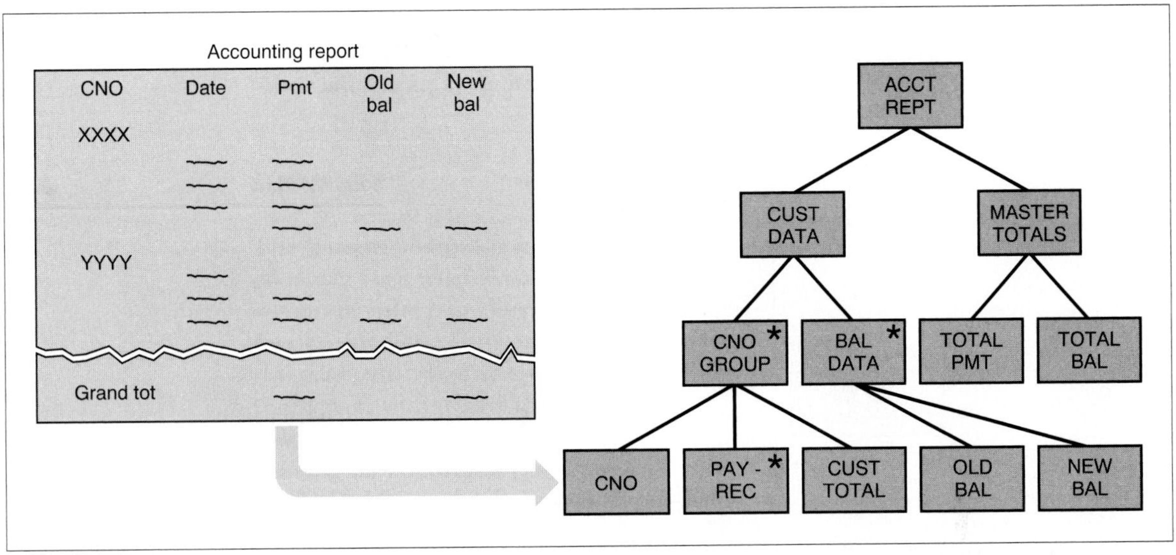

FIGURE 13.10. System output.

plies a hierarchy that includes customer data (CUST-DATA) and master totals. Substructures indicate information contained with the hierarchy.

13.3.5 Procedural Representation

A procedural representation of a program or process is derived directly from the organization of its hierarchical data structure. The data structure shown in Figure 13.10 results in the derivation of the program structure shown in Figure 13.11. Using the program structure as a guide, the structure text can be developed. To illustrate, the structure text for the PROCESS-CUST-DATA (process customer data) branch of Figure 13.11 is shown below:

```
PROCESS-CUST-DATA seq
    open PAY-FILE;
    open C-M-F;
    PROCESS CNO-GROUP iter until eof:PAY-FILE;
        read PAY-FILE;
        PROCESS-CNO {read C-M-F, finds old balance}
        PROCESS-PAY-REC iter until end: CNO-GROUP;
            write report line;
            compute total payments;
            read PAY-FILE;
        end PROCESS-PAY-REC
        COMPUTE-CUST-TOTAL;
```

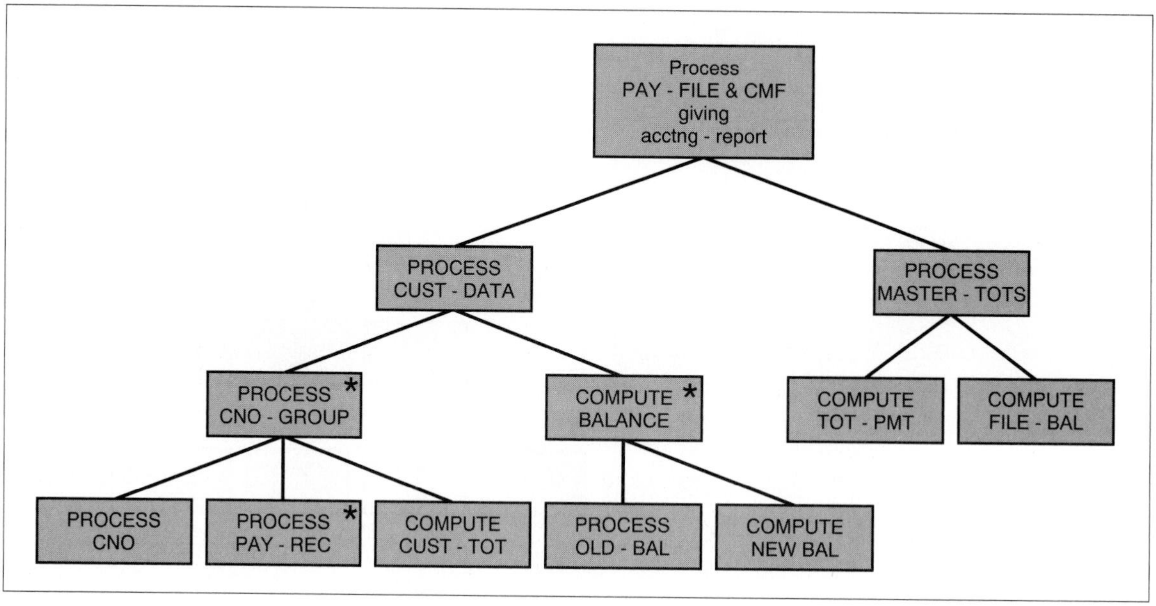

FIGURE 13.11. Resultant program structure.

```
                COMPUTE-BALANCE seq
                    PROCESS-OLD-BAL;
                    COMPUTE-NEW-BAL;
                    write report line;
                end COMPUTE-BALANCE
            end PROCESS-CNO-GROUP
        end PROCESS-CUST-DATA
```

Jackson's methodology supports a number of supplementary techniques that broaden its applicability and enrich the overall design approach. A complete discussion of each of these techniques can be found in books by Jackson ([JAC75], [JAC83]) and Cameron [CAM89].

13.4 DATA STRUCTURED SYSTEMS DEVELOPMENT

Data structured systems development (DSSD) extends the basic concepts developed by Warnier [WAR81] into a comprehensive methodology for the analysis and design of computer-based systems. In Chapter 9, the analysis-oriented steps of DSSD were presented.[2]

[2]The reader is urged to review Section 9.3 before continuing with this section.

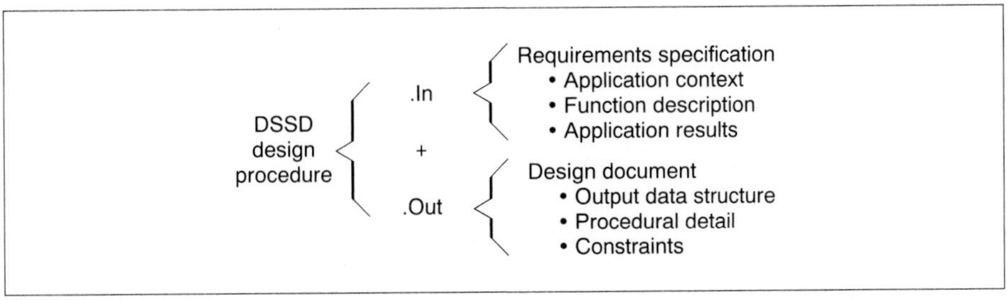

FIGURE 13.12. DSSD design procedure.

The DSSD design procedure is described using Warnier diagram notation in Figure 13.12. Input to the DSSD design procedure is requirements analysis information that includes the application context, function description, and application results (see Section 9.3). The diagrams and data contained in these representations are used as the foundation for DSSD logical and physical design. The logical design focuses on outputs, interfaces, and the procedural design of software. The physical design evolves from the logical design and focuses on the "packaging" of the software to best achieve the desired performance, maintainability, and other design constraints imposed by the system environment.

13.4.1 A Simplified Design Approach

The logical design process can be divided into two activities: the derivation of *logical output structure* (LOS) and the resultant definition of *logical process structure* (LPS). A simplified approach [HAN83] has been proposed for the derivation of LOS. In this approach, the data items that are part of the information domain of a problem are organized hierarchically in much the same way that Jackson approaches design. A four-step process is applied to derive LOS:

1. The problem statement or related requirements information is evaluated and all distinct data items (called *atoms*) that cannot be subdivided further are listed.
2. The frequency of occurrence of each atom is specified.
3. Data items that can be subdivided (called *universals*) are evaluated.
4. A diagrammatic representation of LOS is developed.

To illustrate the four-step process described above, we introduce a brief example. A "Daily Machine Tool Usage Report" (Figure 13.13) is generated as part of a large automated manufacturing information system. The simplified DSSD design approach will be used to derive LOS and LPS.

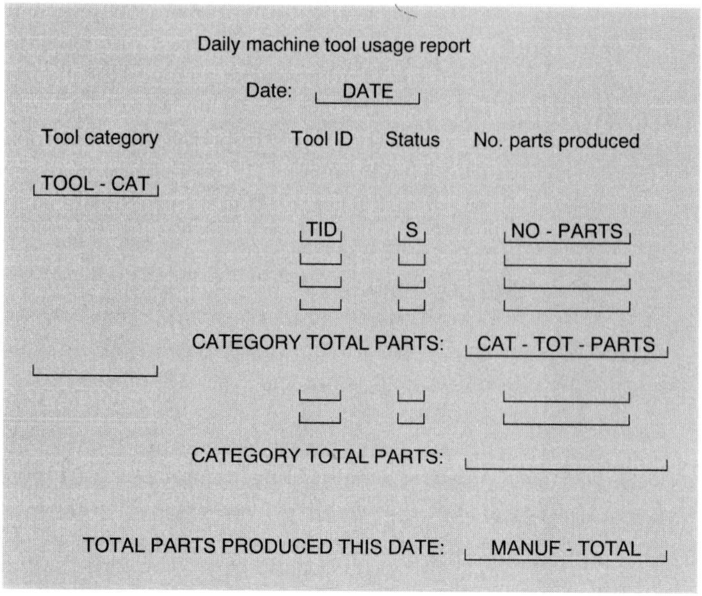

FIGURE 13.13. Report prototype.

13.4.2 Derivation of Logical Output Structure

The logical output structure is a hierarchical representation of data items that comprise output from a computer-based system. The first step in the derivation of LOS is to isolate all atoms (data items that cannot be subdivided). This can be accomplished by reviewing the problem statement or, in the case of the tool usage report example, examining the format of the prototype report (Figure 13.13) itself. Next, the frequency of occurrence of each atom should be noted as shown in Figure 13.14.

Once all atoms and their frequencies have been defined, the designer begins an examination of *universals*. Universals are data items or categories[3] that are comprised of other universals and atoms. For our example, universals would be: **report** (occurs a single time), **tools-category** (occurs *t* times per report), and **tool-id** (occurs *s* times per tool-category).

Using information contained in Figure 13.14 and collected as part of universal analysis, a Warnier-Orr diagram (Section 9.3) for the "Daily Machine Tool Usage Report" can be developed (Figure 13.15).

---

[3]In earlier chapters, these have been called "composite data items."

Data Element (Atom)	Frequency	Details
HEADING	1 / report	Daily machine tool usage report
DATE	1 / report	
COLUMN - HEAD	1 / report	Tool category, Tool ID, ...
TOOL - CAT	1 / tool category	
TID	1 / tool - id	
S	1 / tool - id	
NO PARTS	1 / tool - id	
SUBTOTOAL - HEAD	1 / tool category	Category total parts
CAT - TOT - PARTS	1 / tool category	
TOTAL - HEAD	1 / report	Total parts produced this date
MANUF - TOTAL	1 / report	

FIGURE 13.14. Atoms and frequencies.

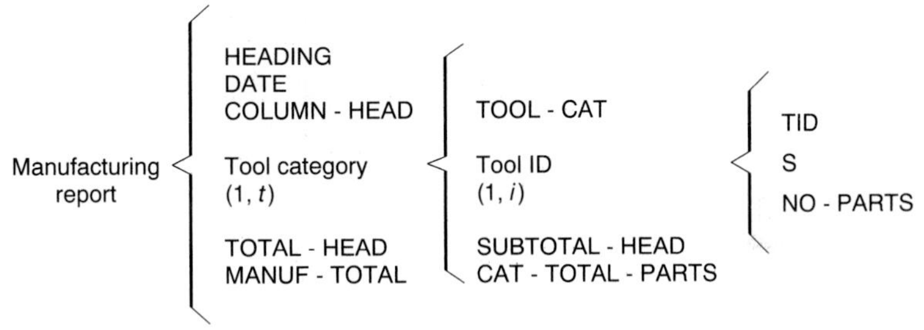

FIGURE 13.15. Warnier-Orr notation for LOS.

13.4.3 Derivation of Logical Process Structure

The logical process structure is a procedural representation of software that is required to process the corresponding LOS. Each universal data item becomes a *repetition* construct to which processing instructions are added. The following steps are conducted to derive LPS:

1. All atoms are stripped from the Warnier-Orr diagram for LOS.
2. BEGIN and END delimiters are added to all universals (repetitions).

If steps 1 and 2 are applied to our example, a diagram of the form shown in Figure 13.16 results. Continuing with the steps for derivation of LPS:

3. All initialization and termination instructions or processes are defined.
4. All computational or nonnumeric processing is specified.

Applying steps 3 and 4 results in an expanded Warnier-Orr diagram shown in Figure 13.17. Continuing:

5. All output instructions and processes are specified.
6. All input instructions and processes are specified.

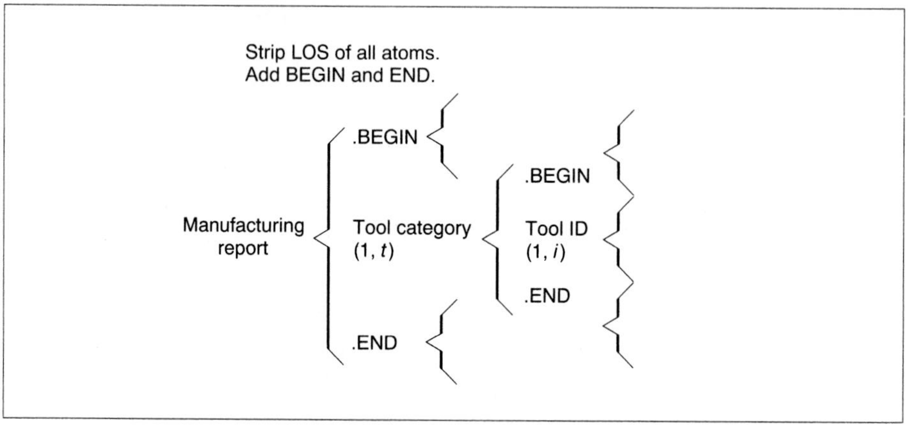

FIGURE 13.16. Transforming LOS to LPS.

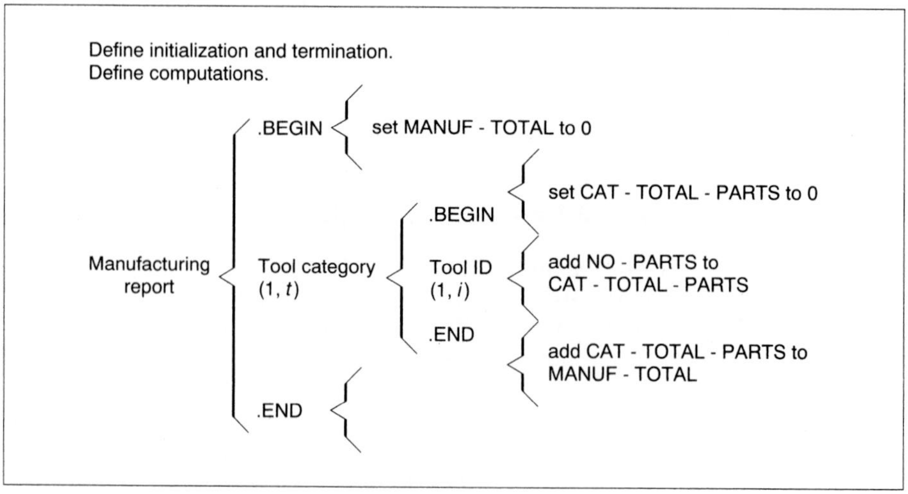

FIGURE 13.17. Deriving LPS.

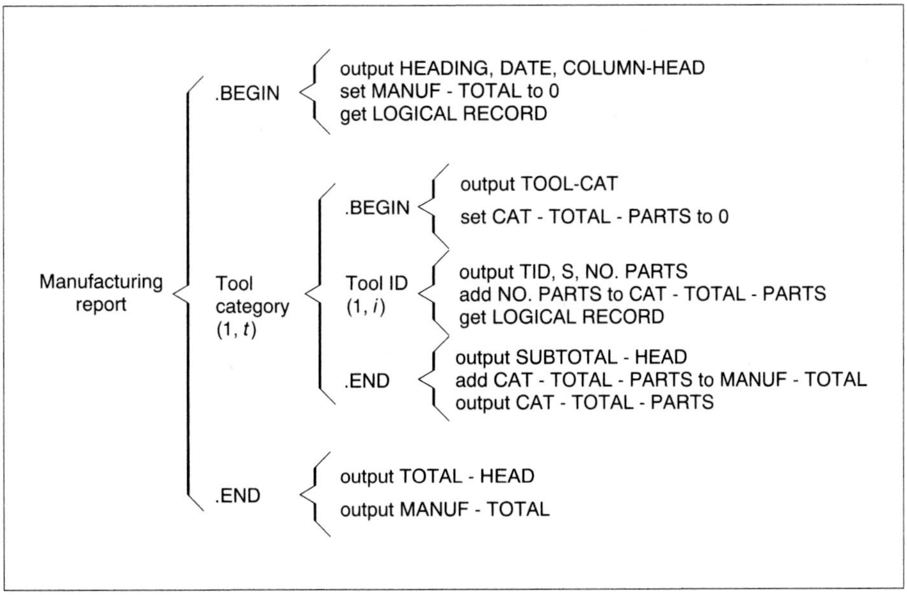

FIGURE 13.18.
Complete LPS.

Application of steps 5 and 6 completes the specification of LPS and is shown for the example in Figure 13.18.

13.4.4 Complex Process Logic

In many cases, the procedural nature of a LPS is considerably more complicated than the example presented in the preceding sections. DSSD provides a notation for handling computational and conditional processing—*complex process logic*.

To illustrate the use of complex process logic, we consider a different example:

> A mail order business computes total amount payable on orders by adding the costs of all the items ordered to the shipping cost, and subtracting any discounts. Shipping cost is determined from the following table:

Distance, mi	Weight, lb	Fee Schedule
<= 100	<= 50	0.01 × distance × weight
<= 100	+ 50	1.10 × weight
+ 100	<= 50	0.02 × distance × weight
+ 100	+ 50	2.35 × weight

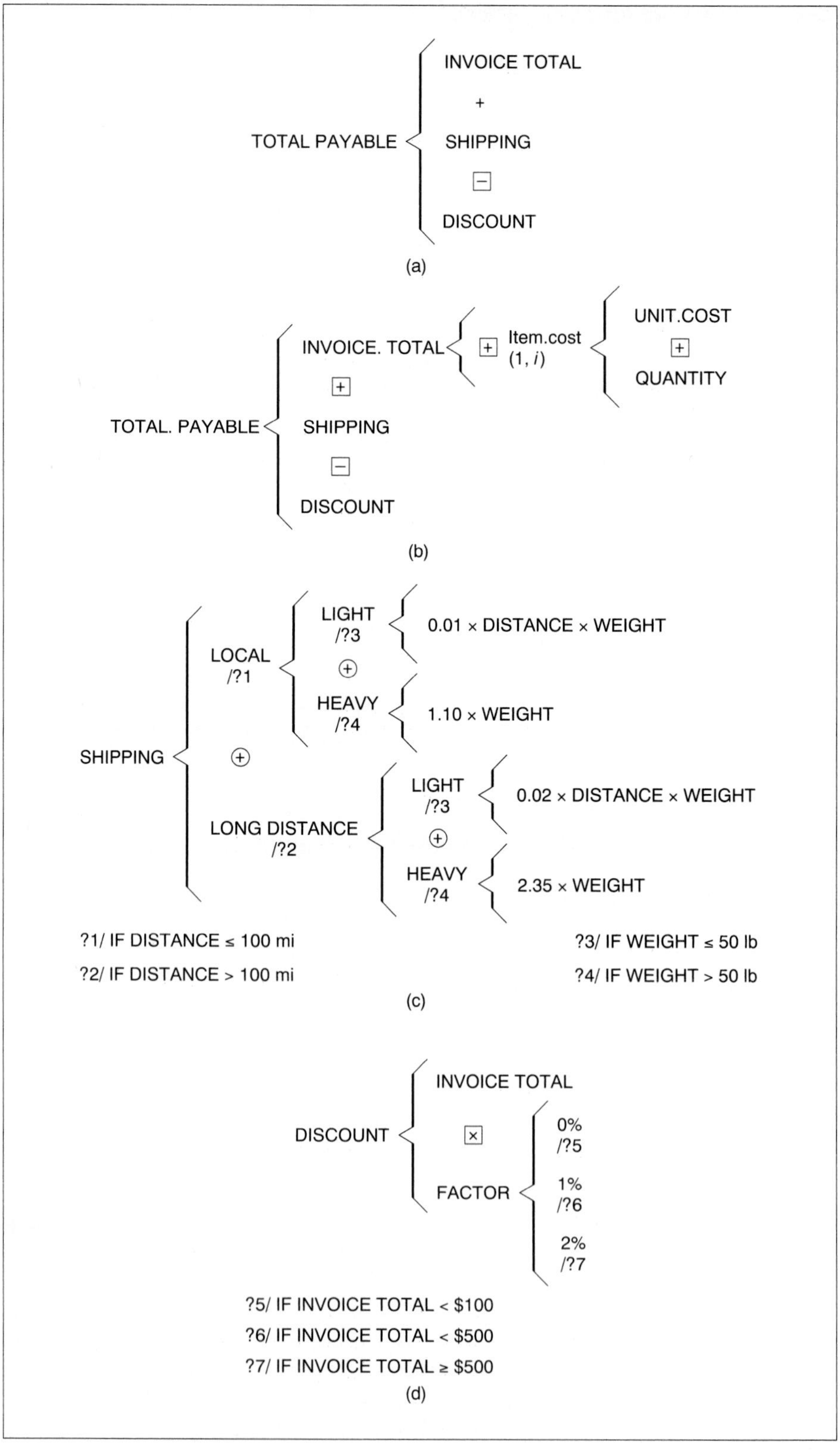

FIGURE 13.19. Process logic. (a) First level; (b) second level; (c) third level; (d) third level.

The discount is determined based on the total invoice amount according to the following schedule:

Invoice total, $	Discount factor, %
< 100	0
< 500	1
>= 500	2

The processing required to model the computation of the total amount payable is shown in Figure 13.19. Arithmetic operators are represented in boxes to distinguish them from logical operators. It should be noted, however, that arithmetic operators may be specified without boxes when it is unlikely that confusion might occur. A footnote symbol, /?*n*, where *n* is the footnote number, is used to qualify certain specified processing.

In addition to procedures for complex process logic, DSSD also provides techniques for handling situations in which the logical output structure and a corresponding physical output structure have different hierarchical characteristics. A *melding* process [HAN83] enables the design to handle these *structure clashes*.

DSSD, like Jackson system development, offers a complete methodology for software analysis and design. Because each of these data structure-oriented methods provides a mechanism for derivation of detailed procedural design, each is amenable to automatic source code generation.

13.5 SUMMARY

Data structure-oriented design, like all major software design methods, focuses on the information domain. However, rather than concentrating on data flow, data structure-oriented methods use information structure as the driver for derivation of design.

Two important design methods—Jackson system development and data structured system development—have been presented in this chapter. Both are remarkably similar in many respects, but each approaches the software design process from a somewhat different point of view. Jackson has introduced a set of preliminary notation that has little to do with data structure, concentrating instead on process modeling and control. Process design and implementation continue to depend on data structure representation. Orr (DSSD) incorporates subtle elements of data flow techniques (during analysis) and adapts from both LCP/LCS (see [WAR74], [WAR81]) and (to a lesser extent) JSD for his design procedures.

Orr [ORR81] provides a worthwhile summary for all design methods presented in this chapter (and throughout this book):

> Bad systems are complex, hard to change, hardware and software dependent and monolithic. Moreover, they are large, costly and time-consuming to develop.
>
> Unfortunately, knowing what a bad system looks like does not necessarily provide a clear guide for developing a good one. Over the last twenty years, many methodologies were developed that aimed at avoiding the creation of bad systems, but not until the 1970s did approaches appear that defined what a good system should look like.

Each of the data structure-oriented design methods presented in this chapter were "children" of the 1970s. Each introduces important ideas about the nature of good design and specific methods for achieving it. As these methods have matured, their singular focus on data structure has been broadened as our understanding of "what a good system should look like" evolves.

REFERENCES

[CAM89] Cameron, J., *JSP & JSD: The Jackson Approach to Software Development,* 2d ed., IEEE Computer Society Press, 1989.

[CHA80] Chand, D. R., and S. B. Yadav, "Logical Construction of Software," *CACM,* vol. 23, no. 10, October 1980, pp. 546–555.

[GUT77] Guttag, J., "Abstract Data Types and the Development of Data Structures," CACM, vol. 20, no. 6, June 1977, pp. 396–404.

[HAN83] Hansen, K., *Data Structured Program Design,* Ken Orr & Associates, 1983.

[HOR78] Horowitz, E., and S. Sahni, *Fundamentals of Computer Algorithms,* Computer Science Press, 1978.

[JAC75] Jackson, M., *Principles of Program Design,* Academic Press, 1975.

[JAC83] Jackson, M., *System Development,* Prentice-Hall, 1983.

[ORR81] Orr, K., *Structured Requirements Definition,* Ken Orr & Associates, 1981.

[PET77] Peters, L. J., and L. L. Tripp, "Comparing Software Design Methodologies," *Datamation,* November 1977.

[TRE76] Tremblay, J. P., and P.G. Sorenson, *An Introduction to Data Structures with Applications,* McGraw-Hill, 1976.

[WAR74] Warnier, J. D., *Logical Construction of Programs,* Van Nostrand Reinhold, 1974.

[WAR81] Warnier, J. D., *Logical Construction of Systems,* Van Nostrand Reinhold, 1981.

[WUL81] Wulf, W., et al., *Fundamental Structures of Computer Science,* Addison-Wesley, 1981.

PROBLEMS AND POINTS TO PONDER

13.1 In this chapter we have introduced two important design techniques. Using the references as a guide, do some research and construct a table that indicates similarities and differences between the methods. Comparison criteria should include representation of data, methods for representing procedural design, special notation and features, and so forth.

13.2 You have been asked to design inventory control software for an auto dealership that markets both new and used cars. Among other items, the system should maintain a list of each car on the lot, its year of manufacture, date of purchase, amount paid, wholesale value, asking price, condition, and repair cost. The car dealer can get any of this information on-line and generate reports that categorize cars by maker, by age, by cost or asking price, and so on. Expanding upon these requirements, provide a complete description of a data structure that will support the inventory system.

13.3 Apply one of the design techniques presented in this chapter to the auto inventory data structure described in Problem 13.2. It will be necessary to review Chapter 9 and first apply the analysis "front-end" before you move into design.

13.4 You have been hired to develop a microprocessor-based controller for a state-of-the-art elevator system for a high-rise office building. The elevators (there are *n* of them) must respond to rider commands for service. Commands include (1) buttons pressed outside the elevator on each floor of the building; (2) buttons pressed inside the elevator to indicate a destination floor; (3) an emergency command (generated by the fire detection system) that returns all elevators to the ground floor and disables the system. The controller must generate door open and close commands and coordinate elevators so that only one idle elevator moves to respond to a request for service. Using these comments as a starting point, derive additional requirements and develop a design for the system using JSD.

13.5 Explain how modules are defined as part of the Jackson design method. Can program structure and procedure be separated using Jackson's approach?

13.6 Recalling the *SafeHome* security system introduced in earlier chapters, apply JSD and DSSD analysis and design techniques to model software for the system.

13.7 Apply JSD to the PHTRS system described in Problem 7.13. Derive requirements and develop a design.

13.8 Apply DSSD to the PHTRS system described in Problem 7.13. Derive requirements and develop a design.

13.9 Given a set of requirements provided by your instructor or the requirements of a project on which you are currently working, apply the JSD approach and attempt to derive a procedural design. Use a structure text to define the procedure.

13.10 A word processor produces an output file that contains formatting information for document production. All the documents contain header information that includes margin specification, line spacing, font selection, etc. The text file may (or may not) contain other margin modification information; it always contains paragraph indicators, end of text block indicators, and other text specific commands.

Use the DSSD approach to define the output data structure and the resultant program procedural organization for document production software. Optionally, continue development by developing a detailed organization using a known word processing system as a guide.

13.11 Search the literature for comparisons of software design methods and write a short paper summarizing the criteria for comparison and the recommendations of the authors.

13.12 A major class project: Define full specifications and develop an "automated design tool" that would assist in the application of a data structure-oriented design technique. The tool should be interactive, should mechanize some or all of the design mappings, and should provide graphical output as well as other reports that might help the designer assess his/her design. The tool should also support "hooks" for analysis tools and programming languages.

FURTHER READINGS

Books by Jackson [JAC83], Warnier [WAR81], Hansen [HAN83], and Cameron [CAM89] are required reading for those who are interested in data structure-oriented design. King and Pardoe (*Program Design Using JSP,* Wiley, 1985) provides a worthwhile summary of Jackson's program design approach that can be used to complement [JAC83] and [CAM89].

A complete survey of data structure-oriented design would not be complete without reference to design techniques for databases and database management systems. Worthwhile papers are reprinted in *Software Design Techniques, Software Design Strategies,* and *Data Base Engineering*—all IEEE tutorials.

CHAPTER 14

USER INTERFACE DESIGN

In the preface to his book on user interface design, Ben Shneiderman [SHN87, p. v] states:

> Frustration and anxiety are part of daily life for many users of computerized information systems. They struggle to learn command language or menu selection systems that are supposed to help them do their job. Some people encounter such serious cases of computer shock, terminal terror, or network neurosis that they avoid using computerized systems.

The problems to which Shneiderman alludes are real. We have all encountered "interfaces" that are hard to learn, difficult to use, confusing, unforgiving, and, in many cases, totally frustrating. Yet, someone spent time and energy building each of these interfaces, and it is likely that the builder did not create these problems purposely.

In this Chapter we consider user interface design—a topic that has become increasingly important as computer use grows. We encounter "intelligent" interfaces when we use a photocopier, a microwave oven, a word processor, or a computer-aided design system. From the point of view of the user, it is the interface that enables a pilot to fly a modern aircraft, a radiologist to interpret the output from a CAT scanner, a banker to transfer millions of dollars across continents. The interface is in many ways the "packaging" for computer software. If it is easy to learn, simple to use, straightforward, and forgiving, the user will be inclined to make good use of what is inside. If it has none of these characteristics, problems will invariably arise.

In earlier chapters we have discussed design as it relates to software internals. Although crucially important to overall software quality, the "design" considered in Chapters 10 to 13 (and again in Chapter 15) is in many ways hidden from the end user. Interface design is different. If it is very good, the user will fall into a natural rhythm of interaction. He or she may even forget that communication is being conducted with a machine. But if it is bad, the user will know it immediately and will not be pleased with the "unfriendly" mode of interaction.

User interface design has as much to do with the study of people as it does with technology issues. Who is the user? How does the user learn to interact with a new computer-based system? How does the user interpret information produced by the system? What will the user expect of the system? These are only a few of the many questions that must be asked and answered as part of user interface design.

14.1 HUMAN FACTORS

When we consider a software-based interactive system, the phrase "human factors" takes on a number of different meanings. At a fundamental level, we should understand visual perception, the cognitive psychology of reading, human memory, deductive and inductive reasoning. At another level, we should understand the user and his or her behavior. Finally, we must understand the tasks that the software-based system performs for the user and the tasks that are demanded of the user as part of human-computer interaction.

The user interface is the mechanism through which a dialogue between the program and the human is established. If human factors have been taken into account, the dialogue will be smooth and a rhythm will be established between the user and the program. If human factors have been ignored, the system will almost always be viewed as "unfriendly."

14.1.1 Fundamentals of Human Perception

A human being perceives the world through a sensory system that is reasonably well understood. When a human-computer interface (HCI) is considered, the visual, tactile and auditory senses predominate. These enable the user of a computer-based system to perceive information, store it in (human) memory, and process it using inductive or deductive reasoning.

The neurophysiology of sensory perception is beyond the scope of this book. An excellent discussion of relevant topics, developed with specific reference to HCI, is provided by Monk [MON84]. To provide a basic first-level understanding of human factors and their relationship to user interface design, a brief overview is presented in this section.

Most HCI is accomplished through a visual medium (e.g., printed reports or graphics, CRT or flat panel displays). The eye and brain work together to receive and interpret visual information based on size, shape, color, orientation, movement, and other characteristics. Visual communication has a "parallel" quality. Many discrete information items are presented simultaneously for the human to absorb. Proper specification of visual communication is a key element of a "user-friendly" interface.

Although there is a definite trend toward pictorial (graphical) communication in HCI design, much visual information is still presented in textual form. Reading—the process of extracting information from text—is a pivotal activity in most interfaces. The human must decode visual patterns and retrieve the meaning of words or phrases. The speed of this process is controlled by an eye movement pattern that scans the text using high-speed, jerking motions called *saccades* [MON84]. The text size, font type, text line length, capitalization, location, and color all affect the ease with which information extraction occurs.

As information is extracted from the interface, it must be stored for later recall and use. In addition, the user may have to remember commands, operating sequences, alternatives, error situations, and other arcane data. All of this information is stored in human memory—an extremely complex system that is currently believed to be comprised of *short-term memory* (STM) and *long-term memory* (LTM) [KLA80]. Sensory input (visual, auditory, tactile) is placed in a "buffer" and then stored in STM where it can be reused immediately. The buffer's size and the length of time during which reuse can occur are limited. Knowledge is maintained in LTM and forms the basis for our learned response when an HCI is used. Both semantic and syntactic information (knowledge) are stored in LTM. If the system engineer specifies a human-computer interface that makes undue demands on STM and/or LTM, the performance of the human element of the system will be degraded.

Most people do not apply formal inductive or deductive reasoning when confronted with a problem. Rather, we apply a set of heuristics (guidelines, rules, and strategies) based on our understanding of similar problems (see [GIL82], [ALL89]). In fact, the heuristics that we use tend to be domain-specific. That is, an identical problem, encountered in entirely different contexts, might be solved by applying different heuristics. An HCI should be specified in a manner that enables the human to develop heuristics for interaction. In general, these heuristics should remain consistent across different interaction domains.

14.1.2 Human Skill Level and Behavior

In addition to the basic elements of human perception, it is important to note individual skill level differences, personality variations, and behavioral distinctions among users of a computer-based system. An interface that is entirely acceptable for a degreed engineer might be completely inadequate for an unskilled worker. An interface used by two individuals with the same education and background, but entirely different personalities, might seem "friendly" to one and "unfriendly" to the other.

The skill level of the end user will have a significant impact on the ability to extract meaningful information from the HCI, respond efficiently to tasks that are demanded by the interaction, and effectively apply heuristics that create a rhythm of interaction. In most cases, context- or domain-specific knowledge is more important than overall education or intelligence. For example, a mechanic who uses a computer-based automotive diagnostic system understands the problem domain and can interact effectively through an interface specifically designed to accommodate users with a mechanic's background. This same interface might confuse a physician—even though the physician has considerably more formal education and may, in fact, be more comfortable with computers.

Every computer user has a unique personality. In most cases, an individual's personality is closely coupled with his or her cognitive style. Therefore, the ideal HCI would be designed to accommodate for differences in personality or, alternatively, would be designed to accommodate for a "typical" personality among a class of end users. Shneiderman [SHN87] delineates the following psychological scales: risk taking/risk avoidance, internal/external locus of control, reflective/impulsive, convergent/divergent, high/low anxiety, high/low tolerance for stress, high/low tolerance for ambiguity, field dependence/independence, assertive/passive, high/low motivation, high/low compulsiveness, left/right brain orientation. There is relatively little empirical data that will help HCI designers to create an interface that accommodates a specific personality type. However, there is little question that certain interfaces will be more readily accepted by users with one type of personality than by users with another.

The proliferation of computer-based systems has spawned a phenomenon called "technofright" [KNE85]—an irrational fear of high-technology products and systems. As we broaden our understanding of the human element in computer-based systems and specify HCI in ways that accommodate human needs, it is likely that the level of technofright will be greatly reduced.

14.1.3 Tasks and Human Factors

An interactive computer-based system rarely enables a user to do something entirely new. In most cases, the system is built to automate (and thereby improve) certain tasks that were previously performed by hand or using some other approach. Ideally, the new technology enables a user to perform tasks better, faster, more efficiently, more accurately, or less expensively. But the underlying tasks remain the same, and an HCI must provide the end user with a facile, natural environment for conducting these tasks.

Although the tasks for each application differ, an overall categorization is possible. Whether we consider the "old ways" of doing things or a new approach that uses an interactive computer-based system, the following generic tasks [RUB88] are almost always performed:

Communication tasks. Activities that enable information to be transferred from producer to consumer.

Dialogue tasks. Activities that enable the user to direct and control interaction with the computer-based system.

Cognitive tasks. Activities that are performed once information has been obtained; activities associated with the function of the system.

Control tasks. Activities that allow the user to control information and cognition and order the process through which other generic tasks occur.

To develop specific instances of these generic tasks, a user interface design technique, called *task analysis and modeling,* is used. We discuss this in a later section.

14.2 STYLES OF HUMAN-COMPUTER INTERACTION

The styles of human-computer interaction run a gamut of options that are closely tied to the historical evolution of computers (and related interactive devices) and to HCI trends. As hardware has become more sophisticated, options for interaction style have grown. Yet in many instances, modern computer-based systems still make use of interaction styles that were originally designed for hardware environments that have been obsolete for 20 years.

In the early days of computing (before graphical displays, the mouse, high-speed workstations, and the like) the only realistic mode of human-computer interaction was the *command and query interface.* Communication was purely textual and was driven via commands and responses to system-generated queries. The user might communicate with the system by specifying a command such as:

```
> run progr1.exe/debug= 'on'/out=p1/in=t1/alloc=1000K
* RUN ALLOCATION TO BE QUEUED? >> yes
* AUTOMATIC CHECKPOINTING INTERVAL? >> 5
```

Although such arcane command and query strings were concise, they were also error-prone, very unforgiving (if an error was made), and relatively difficult to learn.

A variation (and often an improvement) on the command and query interface is the *simple menu* interface. Here, a list of options is presented to the user and the appropriate decision is selected via some typed code:

```
Choose program option that is desired:
    1 = input data manually
    2 = input data from existing data file
    3 = perform simplified analysis
    4 = perform detailed analysis
    5 = produce tabular output
    6 = produce graphical output
    7 = other options classes
Select option ? __
```

The simple menu provides the user with an overall context and is less error-prone than the command line format, but it can be tedious to use. For example, option 7 in the above example implies that additional options (menus) can be acquired. Yet the user cannot go directly to another option, but must work through each menu level until the desired option is reached. This can be frustrating and inefficient.

As hardware became more sophisticated and software engineers learned more about human factors and their impact on interface design, the modern *window-oriented, point and pick interface* evolved.[1] The concept of the *desk top* had arrived. Illustrated schematically in Figure 14.1, this "third-generation" interface provided the user with a number of important benefits:

1. Different types of information can be displayed simultaneously, enabling the user to switch context (e.g., writing source code in one window; examining output results in another; writing an update to a processing narrative in a third) without losing visual connection with other work. Windows enable the user to perform many communication and cognitive tasks (Section 14.1.3) without frustration.
2. Many different interactive tasks are available through a *pull-down menu* scheme. Such menus enable the user to perform control and dialog tasks in a facile manner.
3. The use of graphical icons, pull-down menus, buttons, and scrolling techniques reduce the amount of typing. This can increase the interaction efficiency of those who are not expert typists and can make the computer accessible to users who are keyboard-phobic.

The current HCI generation couples all of the attributes of third-generation interfaces with hypertext [NIE90] and multitasking—the ability

---

[1]These interfaces are sometimes referred to as "WIMP" (windows, icons, menus, and pointing devices) interfaces. There are likely some reactionary hackers who see great significance in this acronym!

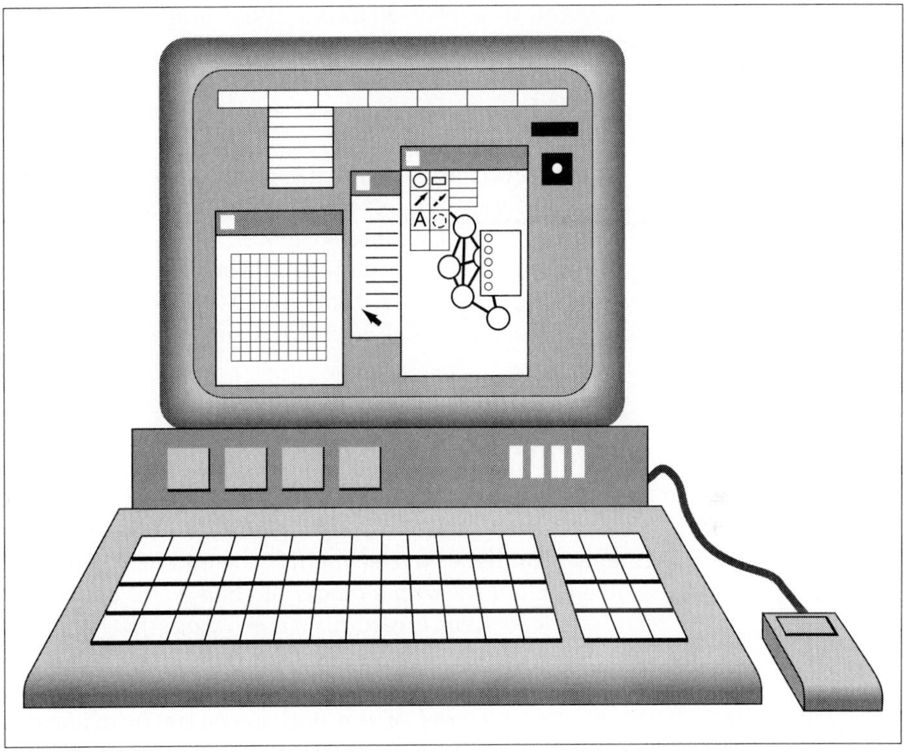

FIGURE 14.1. Window, icon, menus, pointing interface.

to perform a number of different tasks simultaneously (from the user's point of view). Therefore, an author using a desk-top publishing system could invoke spell checking of a lengthy chapter, while at the same time doing a database look-up of references on a new topic and typing text for a new chapter. While all of this was happening, the author's workstation would perform background tasks such as monitoring electronic mail and/or maintaining a daily appointments calendar with alarms to indicate an approaching commitment. These fourth-generation interfaces are currently available on many workstations and PCs.

Each of the interfaces that has been described above is encountered across every application area. There is no doubt that the trend is toward multitasking, window-oriented, point and pick interfaces. But a word of caution is necessary. Third- and fourth-generation interfaces do make HCI easier and more friendly, but only if careful design of the interface is conducted.

14.3 HUMAN-COMPUTER INTERFACE DESIGN

Human-computer interface design is one element of a larger topic that we have learned to call *software design*. The software design methods that we considered in earlier chapters make pragmatic use of data flow, real-world objects, or data structure and introduce a modeling notation for representing the design. Design methods for HCI are not widely used, although both language-based and graphical specification techniques for user interfaces do exist [MYE89].

The overall process for designing a user interface begins with the creation of different models of system function (as perceived from the outside). The human- and computer-oriented tasks that are required to achieve system function are then delineated, design issues that apply to all interface designs are considered, tools are used to prototype and ultimately implement the design model, and the result is evaluated for quality.

14.3.1 Interface Design Models

Four different models come into play when an HCI is to be designed. The software engineer creates a *design model;* a human engineer (or the software engineer) establishes a *user model,* the end user develops a mental image that is often called the *user's model* or the *system perception,* and the implementers of the system create a *system image* [RUB88]. Unfortunately, each of these models may differ significantly. The role of interface design is to reconcile these differences and derive a consistent representation of the interface.

A *design model* of the entire system incorporates data, architectural, and procedural representations of the software (Chapter 10). The requirements specification may establish certain constraints that help to define the user of the system, but the interface design is often only incidental to the design model.[2]

The *user model* depicts the profile of end users of the system. To build an effective user interface, "all design should begin with an understanding of the intended users, including profiles of their age, sex, physical abilities, education, cultural or ethnic background, motivation, goals and personality" [SHN87]. In addition, users can be categorized as:

- *Novices*—no syntactic knowledge[3] of the system and little semantic knowledge[4] of the application or computer usage in general

---

[2]Of course, this is not as it should be. For interactive systems, the interface design is as important as the data, architectural or procedural design.

[3]In this context *syntactic knowledge* refers to the mechanics of interaction required to use the interface effectively.

[4]*Semantic knowledge* refers to an underlying sense of the application—an understanding of the functions that are performed, the meaning of input and output, and the goals and objectives of the system.

- *Knowledgeable, intermittent users*—reasonable semantic knowledge of the application, but relatively low recall of syntactic information necessary to use the interface
- *Knowledgeable, frequent users*—good semantic and syntactic knowledge that often leads to the "power-user syndrome," that is, individuals who look for short cuts and abbreviated modes of interaction

The *system perception* (user's model) is the image of the system that an end user carries in his or her head. For example, if the user of a particular word processor were asked to describe its operation, the system perception would guide the response. The accuracy of the description will depend upon the user's profile (e.g., novices would provide a sketchy response at best) and overall familiarity with software in the application domain. A user who understands word processors fully, but has only worked with the specific word processor once, might actually be able to provide a more complete description of its function than the novice who has spent weeks trying to learn the system.

The *system image* combines the outward manifestation of the computer-based system (the look and feel of the interface), with all the supporting information (books, manuals, video tapes) that describes system syntax and semantics. When the system image and the system perception are coincident, users generally feel comfortable with the software and use it effectively. To accomplish this "melding" of the models, the design model must have been developed to accommodate the information contained in the user model, and the system image must accurately reflect syntactic and semantic information about the interface. The interrelationship among the models is shown in Figure 14.2.

The models described in this section are "abstractions of what the user is doing or thinks he is doing or what somebody else thinks he ought to be doing when he uses an interactive system" [MON84]. In essence, these models enable the interface designer to satisfy a key element of the most important principle of user interface design: Know the user, know the tasks.

14.3.2 Task Analysis and Modeling

In earlier chapters, we discussed *stepwise elaboration* (also called *functional decomposition* or *stepwise refinement*) as a mechanism for refining the processing tasks that are required for software to accomplish some desired function. We also considered object-oriented analysis as a modeling approach for computer-based systems. *Task analysis* is also performed using either elaborative or object-oriented approaches that are analogous to those we have already discussed, but task analysis is applied to human activities.

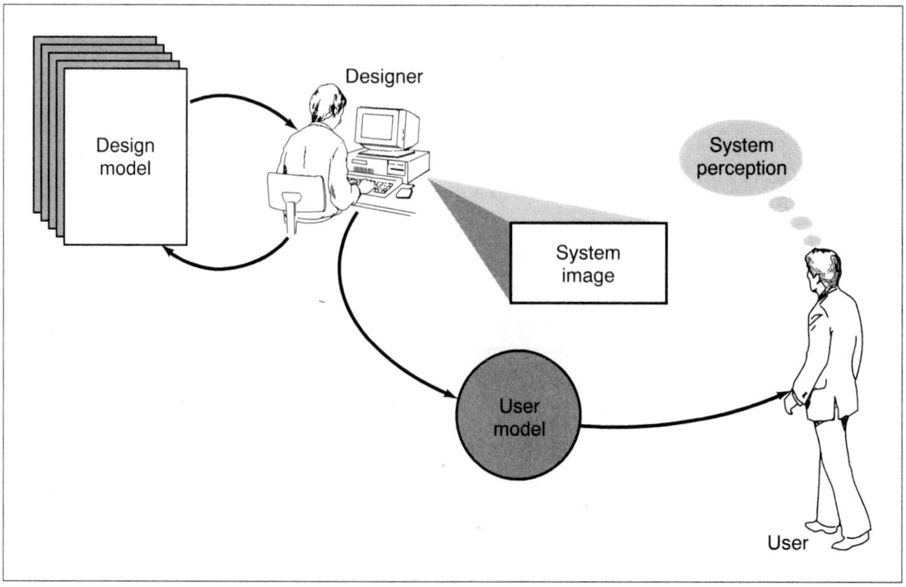

FIGURE 14.2.
Relating interface design models.

Task analysis can be applied in two ways. As we have already noted, an interactive, computer-based system is often used to replace a manual or semimanual activity. To understand the tasks that must be performed to accomplish the goal of the activity, a human engineer[5] must understand the tasks that humans currently perform (when using a manual approach) and then map these into a similar (but not necessarily identical) set of tasks that are implemented in the context of the HCI. Alternatively, the human engineer can study an existing specification for a computer-based solution and derive a set of user tasks that will accommodate the user model, the design model, and the system perception.

Regardless of the overall approach to task analysis, the human engineer must first define and classify tasks. We have already noted that one approach is stepwise elaboration. For example, assume that a small software company wants to build a computer-aided design system explicitly for interior designers. By observing a designer at work, the engineer notices that interior design is comprised of a number of major activities: furniture layout, fabric and material selection, wall and window covering selection, presentation (to the customer), costing, and shopping. Each of these major tasks can be elaborated into subtasks. For example, furniture layout can be refined into the following tasks: (1) draw floor plan based on room dimensions; (2) place windows and doors at appropriate locations; (3) use furniture

[5]In many cases the activities described in this section are performed by a software engineer. Hopefully, the individual has had some training in human engineering and user interface design.

templates to draw scaled furniture outlines on floor plan; (4) move furniture outlines to get best placement; (5) label all furniture outlines; (6) draw dimensions to show location; (7) draw perspective view for customer. A similar approach could be used for each of the other major tasks.

Subtasks 1 to 7 can each be refined further. Subtasks 1 to 6 will be performed by manipulating information and performing actions with the user interface. On the other hand, subtask 7 can be performed automatically in software and will result in little direct user interaction. The design model of the interface should accommodate each of these tasks in a way that is consistent with the user model (what is the profile of a "typical" interior designer) and system perception (what does the interior designer expect from an automated system).

An alternative approach to task analysis takes an object-oriented point of view. The human engineer observes the physical objects that are used by the interior designer and the actions that are applied to each object. For example, **furniture template** would be an object in this approach to task analysis. The interior design would *select* the appropriate template, *move* it to a *position* on the floor plan, *trace* the furniture outline, and so forth. The design model for the interface would not provide a literal implementation for each of these actions, but it would define user tasks that accomplish the end result (drawing furniture outlines on the floor plan).

Once each task or action has been defined, interface design begins. The first steps in the interface design process [NOR86] can be accomplished using the following approach:

1. Establish the goals and intentions for the task.
2. Map each goal/intention to a sequence of specific actions.
3. Specify the action sequence as it will be executed at the interface level.
4. Indicate the state of the system, i.e., what does the interface look like at the time that an action in the sequence is performed?
5. Define control mechanisms, i.e., the devices and actions available to the user to alter the system state.
6. Show how control mechanisms affect the state of the system.
7. Indicate how the user interprets the state of the system from information provided through the interface.

14.3.3 Design Issues

As the design of a user interface evolves, four common design issues almost always surface: system response time, user help facilities, error information handling, and command labeling. Unfortunately, many designers do not address these issues until relatively late in the design process (sometimes the first inkling of a problem doesn't occur until an operational prototype is available). Unnecessary iteration, project delays, and customer frustration almost always result. It is far better to establish each as a design issue to be considered at the beginning of software design, when changes are easy and costs are low.

System response time is *the* primary complaint for many interactive systems (particularly time-sharing applications that make use of a centralized mainframe computer). In general, system response time is measured from the point at which the user performs some control action (e.g., hits the return key or clicks a mouse) until the software responds with the desired output or action.

System response time has two important characteristics: *length* and *variability.* If the length of system response is too long, user frustration and stress are the inevitable results. However, a very brief response time can also be detrimental if the user is being paced by the interface. A rapid response may force the user to rush and therefore make mistakes.

"Variability" refers to the deviation from average response time, and in many ways it is the more important of the response time characteristics. Low variability enables the user to establish a rhythm, even if response time is relatively long. For example, a 1-second response to a command is preferable to a response that varies from 0.1 to 2.5 seconds. In the latter case, the user is always kept off balance, always kept wondering whether something "different" has occurred behind the scenes.

Almost every user of an interactive, computer-based system requires help now and then. In some cases, a simple question addressed to a knowledgeable colleague can do the trick. In others, detailed research in a multivolume set of "user manuals" may be the only option. In many cases, however, modern interactive systems provide on-line help facilities that enable a user to get a question answered or resolve a problem without leaving the interface.

Two different types of help facilities are encountered: *integrated* and *add-on* [RUB88]. An *integrated help facility* is designed into the software from the beginning. It is often context-sensitive, enabling the user to select from those topics that are relevant to the actions currently being performed. Obviously, this reduces the time required for the user to obtain help and increases the "friendliness" of the interface. An *add-on help facility* is added to the software after the system has been built. In many ways, it is really an on-line user's manual with limited query capability. The user may have to search through a list of hundreds of topics to find the appropriate guidance, often making many false starts and receiving much irrelevant information. There is little doubt that the integrated help facility is preferable to the add-on approach.

A number of design issues [RUB88] must be addressed when a help facility is considered:

- Will help be available for all system functions and at all times during system interaction? Options include: help only for a subset of all functions and actions; help for all functions.

- How will the user request help? Options include: a help menu; a special function key; a HELP command.
- How will help be represented? Options include: a separate window; a reference to a printed document (less than ideal); a one- or two-line suggestion produced in a fixed screen location.
- How will the user return to normal interaction? Options include: a return button displayed on the screen; a function key or control sequence.
- How will help information be structured? Options include: a "flat" structure in which all information is accessed through a keyword; a layered hierarchy of information that provides increasing detail as the user proceeds into the structure; the use of hypertext.

Error messages and warnings are "bad news" delivered to users of interactive systems when something has gone awry. At their worst, error messages and warnings impart useless or misleading information and serve only to increase user frustration. There are few computer users who have not encountered an error of the form:

SEVERE SYSTEM FAILURE -- 14A

Somewhere, an explanation for error 14A must exist; otherwise, why would the designers have added the identification? Yet, the error message provides no real indication of what is wrong or where to look to get additional information. An error message presented in the manner shown above does nothing to assuage user anxiety or to help correct the problem.

In general, every error message or warning produced by an interactive system should have the following characteristics:

- The message should describe the problem in jargon that the user can understand.
- The message should provide constructive advice for recovering from the error.
- The message should indicate any negative consequences of the error (e.g., potentially corrupted data files) so that the user can check to ensure that they have not occurred (or correct them if they have).
- The message should be accompanied by an audible or visual cue. That is, a beep might be generated to accompany the display of the message, or the message might flash momentarily or be displayed in a color that is easily recognizable as the "error color."
- The message should be "nonjudgmental." That is, the wording should never place blame on the user.

Because no one really likes bad news, few users will like an error message no matter how well designed. But an effective error message philosophy can do much to improve the quality of an interactive system and will significantly reduce user frustration when problems do occur.

The typed command was once the most common mode of interaction between user and system software and was commonly used for applications of every type. Today, the use of window-oriented, point and pick interfaces has reduced reliance on typed commands, but many power-users continue to prefer a command-oriented mode of interaction. In many situations, the user can be provided with an option—software functions can be selected from a static or pull-down menu or invoked through some keyboard command sequence.

A number of design issues arise when commands are provided as a mode of interaction:

- Will every menu option have a corresponding command?
- What form will commands take? Options include: a control sequence (e.g., ^P); function keys; a typed word.
- How difficult will it be to learn and remember the commands? What can be done if a command is forgotten (see discussion of help earlier in this section)?
- Can commands be customized or abbreviated by the user?

In a growing number of applications, interface designers provide a *command macro facility* that allows the user to store a sequence of commonly used commands under a user-defined name. Instead of typing each command individually (and repetitively), the command macro is typed and all commands implied by it are executed in sequence.

In an ideal setting, conventions for command usage should be established across all applications.[6] It is confusing and often error-prone for a user to type (^ D) when a graphics object is to be duplicated in one application and (^ D) when a graphics object is to be deleted in another. The potential for error is obvious.

14.3.4 Implementation Tools

The process of user interface design is iterative. That is, a design model is created, implemented as a prototype,[7] examined by users (who fit the user model described earlier), and modified based on their comments. To accommodate this iterative design approach, a broad class of interface design and

---

[6]Much of the success of the Apple Macintosh computer can be attributed to the consistency of its interface across many applications developed by many different vendors. In general, a "save" command for a Macintosh wordprocessor is identical to the "save" command for a drawing tool.

[7]It should be noted that in some cases (e.g., aircraft cockpit displays) the first step might be to simulate the interface on a display device rather than prototyping it using hardware.

prototyping tools has evolved. Called *user-interface toolkits* or u *development systems* (UIDS), these tools provide modules or facilitate creation of windows, menus, device interaction, erro ssages, commands, and many other elements of an interactive environment.

Using prepackaged software that can be used directly by the designer and implementer or a user interface, a UIDS provides built-in mechanisms [MYE89] for:

- Managing input devices (such as the mouse or keyboard)
- Validating user input
- Handling errors and displaying error messages
- Providing feedback (e.g., automatic input echo)
- Providing help and prompts
- Handling windows and fields, scrolling within windows
- Establishing connections between application software and the interface
- Insulating the application from interface management functions
- Allowing the user to customize the interface.

The functions described above can be implemented using either a language-based or graphical approach. Tools in each of these categories are described in more detail in Chapter 22.

14.3.5 Design Evaluation

Once an operational user interface prototype has been created, it must be evaluated to determine whether it meets the needs of the user. Evaluation can span a formality spectrum that ranges from an informal "test drive" in which a user provides impromptu feedback to formally designed studies that use statistical methods for the evaluation of questionnaires completed by a population of end users.

The user interface evaluation cycle takes the form shown in Figure 14.3. After the preliminary design has been completed, a first-level prototype is created. The prototype is evaluated by the user, who provides the designer with direct comments about the efficacy of the interface. In addition, if formal evaluation techniques are used (e.g., questionnaires, rating sheets), the designer may extract information from this information (e.g., 80 percent of all users did not like the mechanism for saving data files). Design modifications are made based on user input and the next level prototype is created. The evaluation cycle continues until no further modifications to the interface design are necessary. But is it possible to evaluate the quality of a user interface before a prototype is built? If potential problems can be uncovered and corrected early, the number of loops through the evaluation cycle will be reduced and development time for the prototype will shorten.

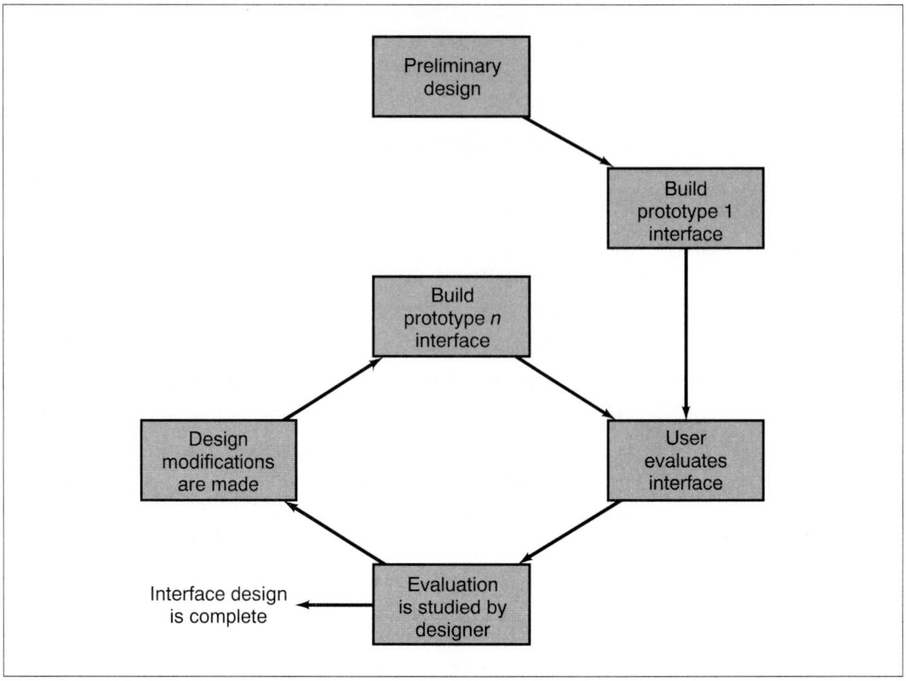

FIGURE 14.3.
The interface design evaluation cycle.

If a design model of the interface has been created, a number of evaluation criteria [MOR81] can be applied during early design reviews:

1. The length and complexity of the written specification of the system and its interface provide an indication of the amount of learning required by users of the system.
2. The number of commands specified and the average number of arguments per command provide an indication of interaction time and the overall efficiency of the system.
3. The number of actions, commands, and system states (Section 14.3.2) indicated by the design model indicate the *memory load* on users of the system.
4. Interface style, help facilities, and error-handling protocol provide a general indication of the complexity of the interface and the degree to which it will be accepted by the user.

Once the first prototype is built, the designer can collect a variety of qualitative and quantitative data that will assist in evaluating the interface. To collect qualitative data, questionnaires can be distributed to users of the prototype. Questions can be (1) simple yes/no response, (2) numeric response,

(3) scaled (subjective) response, or (4) percentage (subjective) response. Examples are:

1. Were the commands easy to remember? yes/no
2. How many different commands did you use?
3. How easy was it to learn basic system operations? (scale 1 to 5)
4. Compared to other interfaces you've used, how would this rate? top 1%, top 10%, top 25%, top 50%, bottom 50%

If quantitative data are desired, a form of time study analysis can be conducted. Users are observed during interaction and data such as the number of tasks correctly completed over a standard time period; the frequency of command use; the sequence of commands; the time spent "looking" at the display; the number of errors, types of error, and error recovery time; the time spent using help; and the number of help references per standard time period are collected and used as a guide for interface modification.

A complete discussion of user interface evaluation methods is beyond the scope of this book. For further information, see Lea [LEA88].

14.4 INTERFACE DESIGN GUIDELINES

The design of user interfaces draws heavily on the experience of the designer and on anecdotal experience presented in hundreds of technical papers and dozens of books. Many sources in the literature (e.g., [DUM88]) present a set of HCI design guidelines that will result in a "friendly," efficient interface. In this section, some of the more important HCI design guidelines are presented.

Three categories of HCI design guidelines are suggested: general interaction, information display, and data input.

14.4.1 General Interaction

Guidelines for general interaction often cross the boundary into information display, data entry, and overall system control. They are, therefore, all-encompassing and are ignored at great risk. The following guidelines focus on general interaction:

Be consistent. Use a consistent format for menu selection, command input, data display, and the myriad other functions that occur in an HCI.

Offer meaningful feedback. Provide the user with visual and auditory feedback to ensure that two-way communication (between user and interface) is established.

Ask for verification of any non-trivial destructive action. If a user requests the deletion of a file, indicates that substantial information is to be overwritten, or asks for the termination of a program, an "Are you sure...?" message should appear.

Permit easy reversal of most actions. UNDO or REVERSE functions have saved tens of thousands of end users from millions of hours of frustration. Reversal should be available in every interactive application.

Reduce the amount of information that must be memorized in between actions. The user should not be expected to remember a list of numbers or names so that he or she can reuse them in a subsequent function. Memory load should be minimized.

Seek efficiency in dialogue, motion, and thought. Keystrokes should be minimized, the distance a mouse must travel between picks should be considered in designing screen layout, and the user should rarely encounter a situation where he or she asks, "Now what does this mean?"

Forgive mistakes. The system should protect itself from user errors that might cause it to fail.

Categorize activities by function and organize screen geography accordingly. One of the key benefits of the pull-down menu is the ability to organize commands by type. In essence, the designer should strive for "cohesive" placement of commands and actions.

Provide help facilities that are context-sensitive. See Section 14.3.3.

Use simple action verbs or short verb phrases to name commands. A lengthy command name is more difficult to recognize and recall. It may also take up unnecessary space in menu lists.

14.4.2 Information Display

If information presented by the HCI is incomplete, ambiguous, or unintelligible, the application will fail to satisfy the needs of a user. Information is "displayed" in many different ways: with text, pictures, and sound; by placement, motion and size; using color, resolution; and even by omission. The following guidelines focus on information display:

Display only that information that is relevant to the current context. The user should not have to wade through extraneous data, menus, and graphics to obtain information relevant to a specific system function.

Don't bury the user with data—use a presentation format that enables rapid assimilation of information. Graphs or charts should replace voluminous tables.

Use consistent labels, standard abbreviations, and predictable colors. The meaning of a display should be obvious without reference to some outside source of information.

Allow the user to maintain visual context. If computer graphics displays are scaled up and down, the original image should be displayed constantly (in reduced form at the corner of the display) so that the user understands the relative location of the portion of the image that is currently being viewed.

Produce meaningful error messages. See Section 14.3.3.

Use upper- and lowercase, indentation, and text grouping to aid in understanding. Much of the information imparted by an HCI is textual, yet the layout and form of the text has a significant impact on the ease with which information is assimilated by the user.

Use windows (if available) to compartmentalize different types of information. Windows enable the user to "keep" many different types of information within easy reach.

Use "analog" displays to represent information that is more easily assimilated with this form of representation. For example, a display of holding tank pressure in an oil refinery would have little impact if a numeric representation were used. However, if a thermometer-like display were used, vertical motion and color changes could be used to indicate dangerous pressure conditions. This would provide the user with both absolute and relative information.

Consider the available geography of the display screen and use it efficiently. When multiple windows are to be used, space should be available to show at least some portion of each. In addition, screen size (a system engineering issue) should be selected to accommodate the type of application that is to be implemented.

14.4.3 Data Input

Much of the user's time is spent picking commands, typing data, and otherwise providing system input. In many applications, the keyboard remains the primary input medium, but the mouse, digitizer, and even voice recognition systems are rapidly becoming effective alternatives. The following guidelines focus on data input:

Minimize the number of input actions required of the user. Above all reduce the amount of typing that is required. This can be accomplished by using the mouse to select from predefined sets of input; using a "sliding scale" to specify input data across a range of values; using "macros" that enable a single keystroke to be transformed into a more complex collection of input data.

Maintain consistency between information display and data input. The visual characteristics of the display (e.g., text size, color, placement) should be carried over to the input domain.

Allow the user to customize input. An expert user might decide to create custom commands or dispense with some types of warning messages and action verification. The HCI should allow this.

Interaction should be flexible but also tuned to the user's preferred mode of input. The user model will assist in determining which mode of input is preferred. A clerical worker might be very happy with keyboard input, while a manager might be more comfortable using a point and pick device such as a mouse.

Deactivate commands that are inappropriate in the context of current actions. This protects the user from attempting some action that could result in an error.

Let the user control the interactive flow. The user should be able to jump unnecessary actions, change the order of required actions (when possible in the context of an application), and recover from error conditions without exiting from the program.

Provide help to assist with all input actions. See Section 14.3.3.

Eliminate "mickey mouse" input. Do not require the user to specify units for engineering input (unless there may be ambiguity). Do not require the user to type .00 for whole number dollar amounts, do provide default values whenever possible, and never require the user to enter information that can be acquired automatically or computed within the program.

14.5 INTERFACE STANDARDS

Most builders of modern software applications strive to implement window-oriented point and pick interfaces. Yet the creation of such interfaces is no easy task. For this reason, user interface standards are being adopted throughout the industry. Interface standardization benefits both the developer and the user of an HCI.

The developer can reuse existing (or prepackaged) HCI modules and objects, thereby creating the interface more rapidly and with significantly higher quality. UIDS tools (see Section 14.3.4) can be used to create a user interface prototype in a fraction of the time required to build the interface software from scratch.

The user becomes familiar with the layout and rhythm of the HCI and therefore learns any new application that uses the same interface standard much more rapidly. After a time, the use of the interface becomes intuitive, and, therefore, far more productive for the end user.

Although a number of competing interface standards are in development, the most commonly used standard is the *X Window System* [YOU90]. The X Window System defines a syntax and semantics for HCI design and provides tools for the creation of displays, windows, and graphics as well as a protocol for resource handling, device interactions, and event handling. A number of variations and extensions of the X Window System standard have been developed and are used on PCs and workstations under UNIX and other operating systems.

14.6 SUMMARY

The human-computer interface, commonly called the "user interface," is the doorway into an interactive software application. The design of human-computer interfaces demands an understanding of human factors and interface technology. Human perception, the skill level and behavioral profile of the user, and the overall tasks that the user must conduct are all factors in the design of an interface. In addition, the style of the interface, the available hardware and software technology, and the application itself all have a bearing on the final result.

HCI design encompasses the creation of four different types of models: the design model, the user model, the system perception, and the system image. Each represents the interface from a different perspective and each is used during the design process. To develop a successful interface, all must eventually coalesce into one representation of the system.

The HCI design process begins with task modeling, an analysis and design activity that defines user tasks and actions using either an elaborative or an object-oriented approach. Design issues such as response time, command structure, error handling, and help facilities are considered and a design model for the system is refined. A variety of implementation tools is used to build a prototype for evaluation by the user. A set of generic design guidelines governs general interaction, information display, and data entry.

REFERENCES

[ALL89] Allman, W. F., *Apprentices of Wonder,* Bantam, 1989.

[DUM88] Dumas, J. S., *Designing User Interfaces for Software,* Prentice-Hall, 1988.

[GIL82] Gilhooly, K. J., *Thinking: Directed, Undirected and Creative,* Academic Press, 1982.

[KLA80] Klatzky, R. L., *Human Memory,* 2d ed., W. H. Freeman & Co., 1980.

[KNE85] Kneale, D., "Coping with Technofright," Technology in the Workplace, *The Wall Street Journal,* September 16, 1985, p. 98.

[LEA88] Lea, M., "Evaluating User Interface Designs," in *User Interface Design for Computer Systems,* (T. Rubin, ed.) Halstead Press (Wiley), 1988.

[MON84] Monk, A. (ed.), *Fundamentals of Human-Computer Interaction,* Academic Press, 1984.

[MOR81] Moran, T. P., "The Command Language Grammar: A Representation for the User Interface of Interactive Computer Systems," *International Journal of Man-Machine Studies,* vol. 15, pp. 3–50.

[MYE89] Myers, B. A., "User Interface Tools: Introduction and Survey," *IEEE Software,* January 1989, p. 15–23.

[NIE90] Nielsen, J., *Hypertext and Hypermedia,* Academic Press, 1990.

[NOR86] Norman, D. A., "Cognitive Engineering," in *User Centered Systems Design,* Lawrence Earlbaum Associates, 1986.

[RUB88] Rubin, T., *User Interface Design for Computer Systems,* Halstead Press (Wiley), 1988.

[SHN87] Shneiderman, B., *Designing the User Interface,* Addison-Wesley, 1987.

[YOU90] Young, D. A., *Introduction to the X Window System,* Prentice-Hall, 1990.

PROBLEMS AND POINTS TO PONDER

14.1 Describe the worst interface that you have ever worked with and critique it relative to the concepts introduced in this chapter.

14.2 Describe the best interface that you have ever worked with and critique it relative to the concepts introduced in this chapter.

14.3 Write a five- to seven-page paper (with references) on any one of the elements of human perception presented in Section 14.1.1.

14.4 Review the psychological scales suggested by Shneiderman [SHN87] and presented in Section 14.2.2. Select three factors (e.g., high/low anxiety) from the list and, considering each factor individually, explain how you would design an interface to accommodate users at both ends of the scale.

14.5 Describe at least three applications that would be amenable to each style of HCI introduced in Section 14.2. Can you think of situations in which a window-oriented, point and pick interface would not be appropriate?

14.6 Do some research on Hypertext and describe how it might be used effectively in HCI design.

14.7 Consider one of the following interactive applications:
(a) A desk-top publishing system
(b) A computer-aided design system
(c) An interior design system (as described in Section 14.3.2)
(d) An automated course registration system for a university
(e) A library management system
(f) A next-generation polling booth for elections
(g) A home banking system
(h) An interactive application assigned by your instructor
Develop a design model, a user model, a system image, and a system perception for any one of the above systems.

14.8 Perform a detailed task analysis for any one of the systems listed in Problem 14.7. Use either an elaborative or an object-oriented approach.

14.9 Continuing Problem 14.8, apply the seven-step interface design process described at the end of Section 14.3.2.

14.10 Describe your approach to user help facilities for the design model and task analysis you have performed as part of Problems 14.7 and 14.8.

14.11 Provide a few examples that illustrate why response time variability can be a issue.

14.12 Develop an approach that would automatically integrate error messages and a user help facility. That is, the system would automatically recognize the error type and provide a help window with suggestions for correcting it. Perform a reasonably complete software design that considers appropriate data structures and algorithms.

14.13 Write a paper that describes one UIDS tool. See Further Readings for suggested sources of information.

14.14 Develop an interface evaluation questionnaire that contains 20 generic questions that would apply to most interfaces. Have 10 classmates complete the questionnaire for an interactive system that you all use. Summarize the results and report them to your class.

14.15 Attempt to add at least five additional design guidelines to each category discussed in Section 14.4.

14.16 Write a short paper that describes the X Window System. Be sure to cover tools that are used to support the standard.

FURTHER READINGS

The literature on human-computer interfaces and human factors has expanded dramatically over the past decade. Books by Rubin [RUB88], Monk [MON84], Shneiderman [SHN87], and Thimbley (*The User Interface Design Book,* Addison-Wesley, 1989) provide worthwhile treatments of the subject. Books by Rubinstein and Hersh (*The Human Factor,* Digital Press, 1984), Dumas [DUM88], Helander (*Handbook of Human-Computer Interaction,* Elsevier Science Publishers, 1988) and Laurel (*The Art of Human-Computer Interface Design,* Addison-Wesley, 1990) each contain worthwhile lists of interface design guidelines.

A special issue of *IEEE Software* (January 1989) is dedicated to user interfaces and contains nine excellent papers on the subject. One of those papers [MYE89] contains a comprehensive bibliography (30 references) on user interface toolkits and user interface development systems. A special issue of the *Bell Systems Technical Journal* (vol. 62, no. 6, July-August 1983) is dedicated to human factors and contains interesting discussions of human factors and UNIX. The *International Journal of Man-Machine Systems* and the *Proceedings of the Human Factors Society* provide up-to-date papers and articles on a broad range of HCI topics. The annual *SIGCHI Proceedings* (the ACM Special Interest Group on Computers and Human Interaction) is an excellent source of worthwhile information. An anthology of important papers has been edited by Nielsen (*Coordinating User Interfaces for Consistency,* Academic Press, 1989). The use of HCI in process control is described by Gilmore et al. (*The User-Computer Interface in Process Control,* Academic Press, 1989).

Interest in interface standards has increased dramatically as high-powered PCs and workstations have become more widely used. Books by

Young (*The X Window System,* Prentice-Hall, 1990) and Mikes (*X Window System Technical Reference,* Addison-Wesley, 1990) provide worthwhile coverage of various standards approaches and the development tools required to implement them. However, a paper by Grudin ("The Case Against User Interface Consistency," *CACM,* vol. 32, no. 10, October 1989) provides a provocative counterpoint. Gruden argues that interface consistency is difficult to achieve, and even when it is attained, it is often at the expense of other characteristics that might make the HCI more beneficial to the end user.

CHAPTER 15

REAL-TIME DESIGN

The design of *real-time* computing systems is the most challenging and complex task that can be undertaken by a software engineer. By its very nature, software for real-time systems makes demands on analysis, design, and testing techniques that are unknown in other application areas.

Real-time software is highly coupled to the external world. That is, real-time software must respond to the problem domain (the real world) in a time frame dictated by the problem domain. Because real-time software must operate under rigorous performance constraints, software design is often driven by hardware as well as software architecture, operating system characteristics as well as application requirements, programming language vagaries as well as design issues.

In his book on real-time software, Robert Glass [GLA83, p. 1] provides a useful introduction to the subject of real-time systems:

> The digital computer is becoming ever more present in the daily lives of all of us. Computers allow our watches to play games as well as tell time, optimize the gas mileage of our latest generation cars, and sequence our appliances.... [In industry, computers control machines, coordinate processes, and increasingly, replace manual skills and human recognition with automated systems and artificial intelligence.]
>
> All these computing interactions—be they helpful or intrusive—are examples of real-time computing. The computer is controlling something that interacts with reality on a timely basis. In fact, timing is the essence of the interaction.... An unresponsive real-time system may be worse than no system at all.

No more than a decade ago, real-time software development was considered a black art, applied by anointed wizards who guarded their closed world with jealousy. Today, there just are not enough wizards to go around! Yet, there is no question that the engineering of real-time software requires special skills. In this chapter we examine real-time software and discuss at least some of the skills that are required to build it.

15.1 SYSTEM CONSIDERATIONS

Like any computer-based system, a real-time system must integrate hardware, software, human, and database elements to properly achieve a set of functional and performance requirements. In Chapter 5, we examined the allocation task for computer-based systems, indicating that the system engineer must allocate function and performance among the system elements. The problem for real-time systems is proper allocation. Real-time performance is often as important as function, yet allocation decisions that relate to performance are often difficult to make with assurance. Can a processing algorithm meet severe timing constraints, or should we build special hardware to do the job? Can an off-the-shelf operating system meet our need for efficient interrupt handling, multitasking, and communication, or should we build a custom executive? Can specified hardware coupled with proposed software meet performance criteria? These, and many other questions, must be answered by the real-time system engineer.

A comprehensive discussion of all elements of real time systems is beyond the scope of this book. Among a number of good sources of information are Foster [FOS81], Mellichamp [MEL83], and Savitsky [SAV85]. However, it is important that we understand each of the elements of a real-time system before focusing on software analysis and design issues.

"Real-Time Systems" [HIN83] appeared in the Special Series on System Integration published in *Electronic Design* magazine. The article considers real-time issues from a system point of view and serves as a worthwhile introduction to other topics in this chapter. Major excerpts (edited to conform to the format and style of this book) from the article are presented in the next section.

15.2 REAL-TIME SYSTEMS[1]

Real-time systems generate some action in response to external events. To accomplish this function, they perform high-speed data acquisition and control under severe time and reliability constraints. Because these con-

[1]Based on an article, "Real-Time Systems," by H. J. Hinden and W. B. Rausch-Hinden [HIN83]. Reproduced with permission of *Electronic Design* and Heyden Publishing.

straints are so stringent, real-time systems are frequently dedicated to a single application.

For many years, the major consumer of real-time systems was the military. Today, however, significant decreases in hardware costs make it possible for most companies to afford real-time systems (and products) for diverse applications that include process control, industrial automation, medical and scientific research, computer graphics, local and wide-area communications, aerospace systems, computer-aided testing, and a vast array of industrial instrumentation.

15.2.1 Integration and Performance Issues

Putting together a real-time system presents the system engineer with difficult hardware and software decisions. [The allocation issues associated with hardware for real-time systems are beyond the scope of this book (see Savitsky [SAV85] for additional information)]. Once the software element has been allocated, detailed software requirements are established and a fundamental software design must be developed. Among many real-time design concerns are coordination between the real-time tasks, processing of system interrupts, I/O handling to ensure that no data are lost, specifying the system's internal and external timing constraints, and ensuring the accuracy of its database.

Each real-time design concern for software must be applied in the context of system *performance*. In most cases, the performance of a real-time system is measured as one or more time-related characteristics, but other measures such as fault-tolerance may also be used.

Some real-time systems are designed for applications in which only the response time or the data transfer rate is critical. Other real-time applications require optimization of both parameters under peak loading conditions. What's more, real-time systems must handle their peak loads while performing a number of simultaneous tasks.

Since the performance of a real-time system is determined primarily by the system response time and its data transfer rate, it is important to understand these two parameters. System *response time* is the time within which a system must detect an internal or external event and respond with an action. Often, event detection and response generation are simple. It is the processing of the information about the event to determine the appropriate response that may involve complex, time-consuming algorithms.

Among the key parameters that affect the response time are *context switching* and *interrupt latency*. Context switching involves the time and overhead to switch among tasks, and interrupt latency is the time lag before the switch is actually possible. Other parameters that affect response time are the speed of computation and of access to mass storage.

The *data transfer rate* indicates how fast serial or parallel, as well as analog or digital, data must be moved into or out of the system. Hardware vendors often quote timing and capacity values for performance characteristics. However, hardware specifications for performance are usually measured in isolation and are often of little value in determining overall real-time system performance. Therefore, I/O device performance, bus latency, buffer size, disk performance, and a host of other factors, although important, are only part of the story of real-time system design.

Real-time systems are often required to process a continuous stream of incoming data. Design must assure that data are not missed. In addition, a real-time system must respond to events that are asynchronous. Therefore, the arrival sequence and data volume cannot be easily predicted in advance.

Although all software applications must be reliable, real-time systems make special demands on reliability, restart, and fault recovery. Because the real world is being monitored and controlled, loss of monitoring or control (or both) is intolerable in many circumstances (e.g., an air traffic control system). Consequently, real-time systems contain restart and fault-recovery mechanisms and frequently have built-in redundancy to ensure backup.

The need for reliability, however, has spurred an on-going debate about whether *on-line* systems, such as airline reservation systems and automatic bank tellers, also qualify as real-time. On the one hand, such on-line systems must respond to external interrupts within prescribed response times on the order of 1 second. On the other hand, nothing catastrophic occurs if an on-line system fails to meet response requirements; instead, only system degradation results.

15.2.2 Interrupt Handling

One characteristic that serves to distinguish real-time systems from any other type is *interrupt handling*. A real-time system must respond to external stimulae—*interrupts*—in a time frame dictated by the external world. Because multiple stimuli (interrupts) are often present, priorities and priority interrupts must be established. In other words, the most important task must always be serviced within predefined time constraints regardless of other events.

Interrupt handling entails not only storing information so that the computer can correctly restart the interrupted task, but also avoiding deadlocks and endless loops. The overall approach to interrupt handling is illustrated in Figure 15.1. Normal processing flow is "interrupted" by an event that is detected by processor hardware. An *event* is any occurrence that requires immediate service and may be generated by either hardware or software. The state of the interrupted program is saved (i.e., all register contents, control blocks, etc., are saved) and control is passed to an interrupt service routine that branches to appropriate software for handling the interrupt. Upon completion of interrupt servicing, the state of the machine is restored and normal processing flow continues.

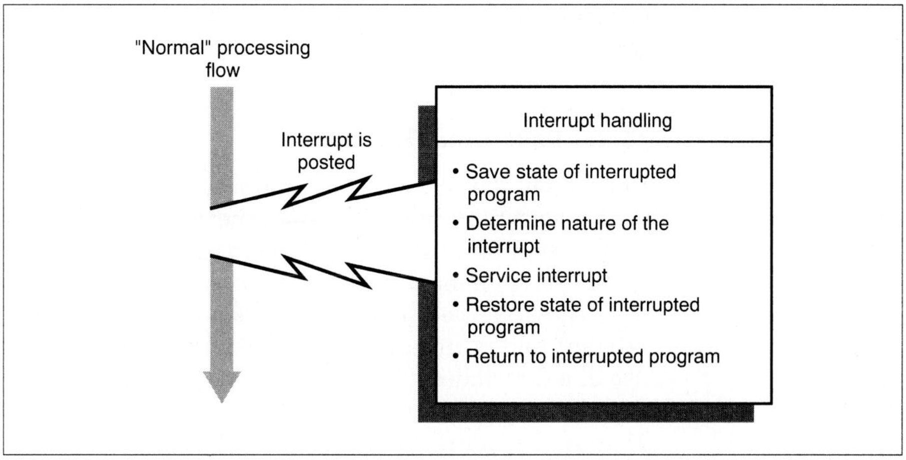

FIGURE 15.1.
Interrupts.

In many situations, interrupt servicing for one event may itself be interrupted by another, higher-priority event. Interrupt priority levels (Figure 15.2) may be established. If a lower-priority process is accidentally allowed to interrupt a higher-priority one, it may be difficult to restart the processes in the right order and an endless loop may result.

To handle interrupts and still meet the system time constraints, many real-time operating systems make dynamic calculations to determine whether the system goals can be met. These dynamic calculations are based on the average frequency of occurrence of events, the amount of time it takes to service them (if they can be serviced), and the routines that can interrupt them and temporarily prevent their servicing.

If the dynamic calculations show that it is impossible to handle the events that can occur in the system and still meet the time constraints, the system must decide on a scheme of action. One possible scheme involves

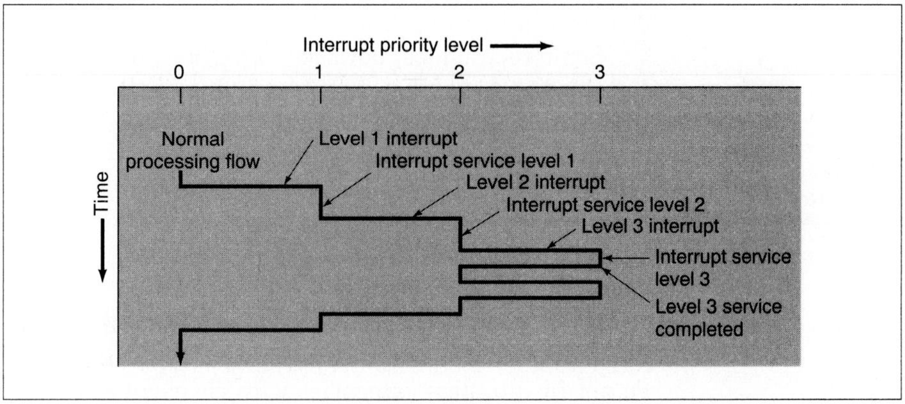

FIGURE 15.2.
Interrupt priority.

buffering the data so that it can be processed quickly when the system is ready.

15.2.3 Real-Time Databases

Like many data-processing systems, real-time systems often are coupled with a database management function. However, *distributed databases* would seem to be a preferred approach in real-time systems because multitasking is commonplace and data are often processed in parallel. If the database is distributed, individual tasks can access their data faster and more reliably, and with fewer bottlenecks than with a centralized database. The use of a distributed database for real-time applications divides input/output "traffic" and shortens queues of tasks waiting for access to a database. Moreover, a failure of one database will rarely cause the failure of the entire system, if redundancy is built in.

The performance efficiencies achieved through the use of a distributed database must be weighed against potential problems associated with data partitioning and replication. Although data redundancy improves response time by providing multiple information sources, replication requirements for distributed files also produces logistical and overhead problems, since all the file copies must be updated. In addition, the use of distributed databases introduces the problem of *concurrency control*. Concurrency control involves synchronizing the databases so that all copies have the correct, identical information free for access.

The conventional approach to concurrency control is based on what are known as *locking* and *time stamps*. At regular intervals, the following tasks are initiated: (1) The database is "locked" so that concurrency control is assured; no I/O is permitted; (2) updating occurs as required; (3) the database is unlocked; (4) files are validated to ensure that all updates have been correctly made; (5) the completed update is acknowledged. All locking tasks are monitored by a master clock (i.e., time stamps). The delays involved in these procedures, as well as the problems of avoiding inconsistent updates and deadlock, mitigate against the widespread use of distributed databases.

Some techniques, however, have been developed to speed updating and to solve the concurrency problem. One of these, called the *exclusive-writer protocol*, maintains the consistency of replicated files by allowing only a single, exclusive writing task to update a file. It therefore eliminates the high overhead of locking or time-stamp procedures.

15.2.4 Real-Time Operating Systems

Choosing a real-time operating system (RTOS) for a specific application is no easy chore. Some operating system classifications are possible, but most do not fit into neat categories with clear-cut advantages and disadvantages.

Instead, there is considerable overlap in capabilities, target systems, and other features.

Some real-time operating systems are applicable to a broad range of system configurations, while others are geared to a particular microprocessor, regardless of the surrounding electronic environment. RTOSs achieve their capabilities through a combination of software features and (increasingly) a variety of microcoded capabilities implemented in hardware.

Today, two broad classes of operating systems are used for real-time work: (1) dedicated RTOSs designed exclusively for real-time applications and (2) general-purpose operating systems that have been enhanced to provide real-time capability. The use of a *real-time executive* makes real-time performance feasible for a general-purpose operating system. Behaving like application software, the executive performs a number of operating system functions—particularly those that affect real-time performance—faster and more efficiently than the general-purpose operating system.

All operating systems must have a priority scheduling mechanism, but an RTOS must provide a *priority mechanism* that allows high-priority interrupts to take precedence over less important ones. Moreover, because interrupts occur in response to asynchronous, nonrecurring events, they must be serviced without first taking time to swap in a program from disk storage. Consequently, to guarantee the required response time, a real-time operating system must have a mechanism for *memory locking*—that is, locking at least some programs in main memory so that swapping overhead is avoided.

To determine which kind of real-time operating system best matches an application, measures of RTOS quality can be defined and evaluated. Context switching time and interrupt latency (discussed earlier) determine interrupt-handling capability, the most important aspect of a real-time system. Context switching time is the time the operating system takes to store the state of the computer and the contents of the registers so that it can return to a processing task after servicing the interrupt.

Interrupt latency, the maximum time lag before the system gets around to switching a task, occurs because in an operating system there are often non-re-entrant or critical processing paths that must be completed before an interrupt can be processed.

The length of these paths (the number of instructions) before the system can service an interrupt indicates the worst-case time lag. The worst case occurs if a high-priority interrupt is generated immediately after the system enters a critical path between an interrupt and interrupt service. If the time is too long, the system may miss an unrecoverable piece of data. It is important that the designer know the time lag so that the system can compensate for it.

Many operating systems perform multitasking [WOO90], or concurrent processing, another major requirement for real-time systems. But to be viable for real-time operation, the system overhead must be low in terms of switching time and memory space used.

15.2.5 Real-Time Languages

Because of the special requirements for performance and reliability demanded of real-time systems, the choice of a programming language is important. Many general-purpose programming languages (e.g., C, FORTRAN, Modula-2) can be used effectively for real-time applications. However, a class of so-called "real-time languages" (e.g., Ada, Jovial, HAL/S, Chill, and others) is often used in specialized military and communications applications. (We shall discuss the general characteristics of some of these languages in Chapter 16.)

A combination of characteristics makes a real-time language different from a general-purpose language. These include the multitasking capability, constructs to directly implement real-time functions, and modern programming features that help ensure program correctness.

A programming language that directly supports multitasking is important because a real-time system must respond to asynchronous events occurring simultaneously. Although many RTOSs provide multitasking capabilities, embedded real-time software often exists without an operating system. Instead, embedded applications are written in a language that provides sufficient run-time support for real-time program execution. Run-time support requires less memory than an operating system, and it can be tailored to an application, thus increasing performance.

A real-time system that has been designed to accommodate multiple tasks must also accommodate intertask synchronization [KAI83]. A programming language that directly supports synchronization primitives such as SCHEDULE, SIGNAL, and WAIT greatly simplifies the translation from design to code. The SCHEDULE command schedules a process based on time or an event; SIGNAL and WAIT commands manipulate a special flag, called a *semaphore,* that enables concurrent tasks to be synchronized.

Finally, features that facilitate reliable programming are necessary because real-time programs are frequently large and complex. These features include modular programming, strongly enforced data typing, and a host of other control and data definition constructs.

15.2.6 Task Synchronization and Communication

A multitasking system must furnish a mechanism for the tasks to pass information to each other as well as to ensure their synchronization. For these functions, operating systems and languages with run-time support commonly use queuing semaphores, mailboxes, or message systems. Semaphores supply synchronization and signaling but contain no information. Messages are similar to semaphores except that they carry the associated information. Mailboxes, on the other hand, do not signal information but instead contain it.

Queuing semaphores are software primitives that help manage traffic. They provide a method of directing several queues—for example, queues of tasks waiting for resources, database access, and devices, as well as queues of the resources and devices. The semaphores coordinate (synchronize) the waiting tasks with whatever they are waiting for without letting tasks or resources interfere with each other.

In a real-time system, semaphores are commonly used to implement and manage *mailboxes*. Mailboxes are temporary storage places (also called *message pools* or *buffers*) for messages sent from one process to another. One process produces a piece of information, puts it in the mailbox, and then signals a consuming process that there is a piece of information in the mailbox for it to use.

Some approaches to real-time operating systems or run-time support systems view mailboxes as the most efficient way to implement communications between processes. Some real-time operating systems furnish a place to send and receive pointers to mailbox data. This eliminates the need to transfer all of the data—thus saving time and overhead.

A third approach to communication and synchronization among processes is a message system. With a message system, one process sends a message to another. The latter is then automatically activated by the run-time support system or operating system to process the message. Such a system incurs overhead because it transfers the actual information, but it provides greater flexibility and ease of use.

15.3 ANALYSIS AND SIMULATION OF REAL-TIME SYSTEMS

In the preceding section, a set of dynamic attributes were discussed that cannot be divorced from the functional requirements of a real-time system:

- Interrupt handling and context switching
- Response time
- Data transfer rate and throughput
- Resource allocation and priority handling
- Task synchronization and intertask communication

Each of these performance attributes can be specified, but it is extremely difficult to verify whether system elements will achieve the desired response, system resources will be sufficient to satisfy computational requirements, or processing algorithms will execute with sufficient speed.

The analysis of real-time systems requires modeling and simulation that enable the system engineer to assess "timing and sizing" issues. Although a number of analysis techniques have been proposed in the literature (e.g., [LIU90], [WIL90], and [ZUC89]), it is fair to state that analytical approaches for the analysis and design of real-time systems are still in their infancy.

15.3.1 Mathematical Tools for Real-Time System Analysis

A set of mathematical tools that enable the system engineer to model real-time system elements and assess timing and sizing issues has been proposed by Thomas McCabe [MCC85]. Based loosely on data flow analysis techniques (Chapter 7), McCabe's approach enables the analyst to model both hardware and software elements of a real-time system; represent control in a probabilistic manner; apply network analysis, queuing and graph theory, and a Markovian mathematical model [GRO85] to derive system timing and resource sizing. Unfortunately, the mathematics involved is beyond the grasp of many readers of this book, making a detailed explication of McCabe's work difficult. However, an overview of the technique will provide a worthwhile example of one analytical approach to the engineering of real-time systems.

McCabe's real-time analysis technique is predicated on a data flow model of the real-time system. However, rather than using a DFD in the conventional manner, McCabe [MCC85] contends that the transforms (bubbles) of a DFD can be represented as process states of a Markov chain (a probabilistic queuing model) and the data flows themselves represent transitions between the process states. The analyst can assign transitional probabilities to each data flow path. Referring to Figure 15.3, a value

$$0 < p_{ij} \leq 1.0$$

may be specified for each flow path, where p_{ij} represents the probability that flow will occur between process i and process j. The processes correspond to information transforms (bubbles) in the DFD.

Each process in the DFD-like model can be given a "unit cost" that represents the estimated (or actual) execution time required to perform its function and an "entrance value" that depicts the number of system interrupts corresponding to the process. The model is then analyzed using a set of mathematical tools that compute (1) the expected number of visits to a process; (2) the time spent in the system when processing begins at a specific process; (3) the total time spent in the system.

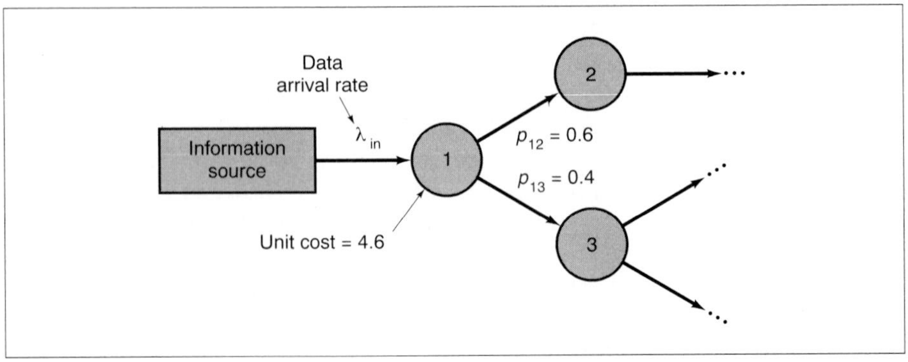

FIGURE 15.3. DFDs as a queuing network model.

To illustrate the McCabe technique on a realistic example, we consider a DFD for an electronic countermeasures system shown in Figure 15.4. The data flow diagram takes the standard form, but data flow identification has been replaced by p_{ij}. A queue network model is derived from the DFD and is shown in Figure 15.5. The lambda values (λ_i) correspond to the arrival rates (arrivals per second) at each process. Depending on the type of queue encountered, the analyst must determine statistical information such as the mean service rate (mean run-time per process), variance of service rate, variance of arrival rate, and so forth.

The arrival rates for each process are determined using the flow path probabilities p_{ij} and the arrival rate into the system, λ_{in}. A set of flow balance equations are derived and solved simultaneously to compute the flow through each process. For the example shown in Figure 15.5, the following flow balance equations result [MCC85]:

$$\lambda_1 = \lambda_{\text{in}} + \lambda_4$$

$$\lambda_2 = p_{12}\lambda_1$$

$$\lambda_3 = p_{13}\lambda_1 + p_{23}\lambda_2$$

$$\lambda_4 = p_{64}\lambda_6$$

$$\lambda_5 = p_{25}\lambda_2 + \lambda_3$$

$$\lambda_6 = \lambda_5$$

$$\lambda_7 = p_{67}\lambda_6$$

For the p_{ij} shown and an arrival rate $\lambda_{\text{in}} = 5$ arrivals per second, the above equations can be solved [MCC85] to yield:

$$\lambda_1 = 8.3$$

$$\lambda_5 = 8.3$$

$$\lambda_2 = 5.8$$

$$\lambda_6 = 8.3$$

$$\lambda_3 = 5.4$$

$$\lambda_7 = 5.0$$

$$\lambda_4 = 3.3$$

Once the arrival rates have been computed, standard queuing theory can be used to compute system timing. Each subsystem (a queue Q and a server S) may be evaluated using formulae that correspond to the queue type. For $(m/m/1)$ queues [KLI75]:

Utilization: $\rho = \lambda/\mu$

Expected queue length: $N_q = \rho^2/(1 - \rho)$

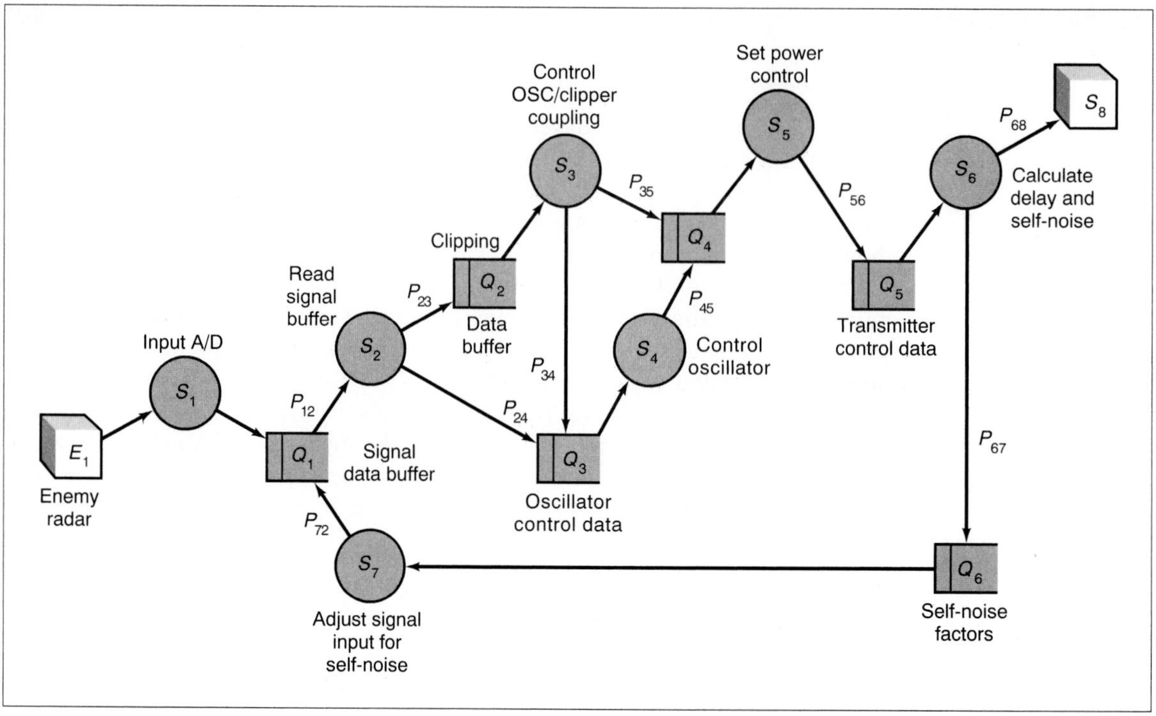

FIGURE 15.4. Example DFD (modified) for a real-time analysis. (*With permission of McCabe & Associates.*)

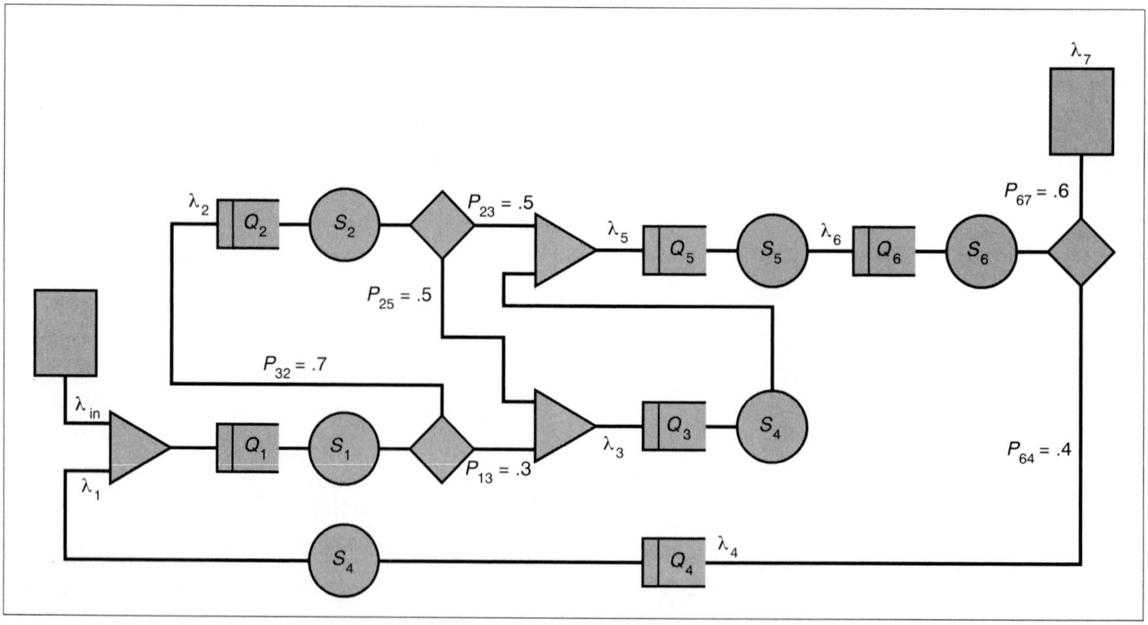

FIGURE 15.5. Queuing network model derived from flow diagram. (*With permission of McCabe & Associates.*)

Expected number in subsystem: $N_s = \rho_1/(1 - \rho)$
Expected time in queue: $T_q = \lambda/\mu(\mu - \lambda)$
Expected time in subsystem: $T_s = 1/(\mu - \lambda)$

where μ is completion rate (completions/second). Applying standard queuing network reduction rules, illustrated in Figure 15.6, the original queuing network (Figure 15.5) derived from the data flow diagram (Figure 15.4) can be simplified by applying the steps shown in Figure 15.7. The total time spent in the system is then computed to be 2.37 seconds.

Obviously, the accuracy of McCabe's analysis approach is only as good as estimates for flow probability, arrival rate, and completion rate. However, significant benefits can be achieved by taking a more analytical view of real-time systems during analysis. To quote McCabe [MCC85]:

> By changing such variables as arrival rates, interrupt rates, splitting probabilities, priority structure, queue discipline, configurations, requirements, physical implementation and variances we can easily show the program manager what affect it will have on the system at hand. These iterative methodologies are necessary to fill a void in real-time specification modeling.

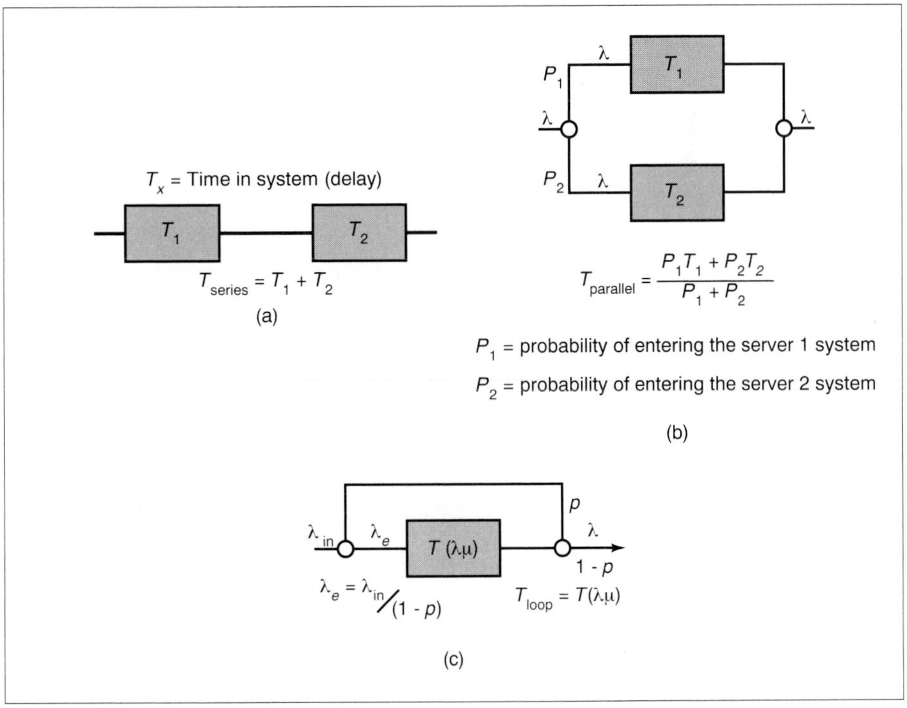

FIGURE 15.6.
Queuing network reduction rules.

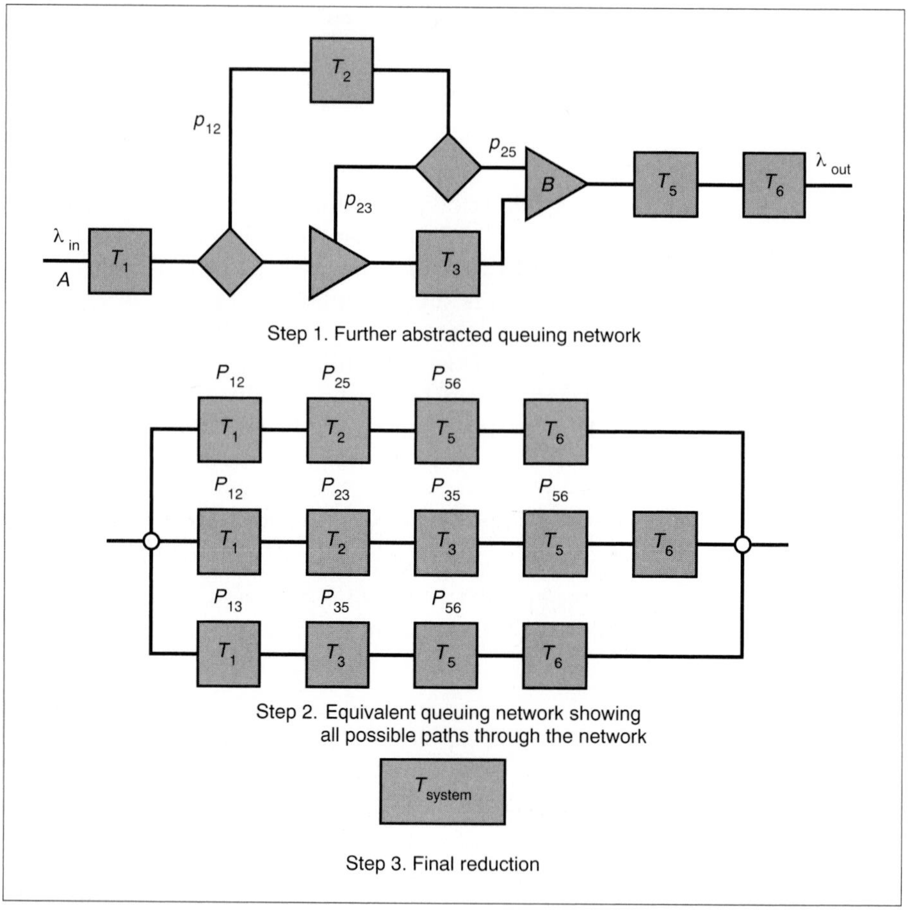

FIGURE 15.7. Simplifying the queuing network.

15.3.2 Simulation and Modeling Techniques for Real-Time Systems

Mathematical analysis of a real-time system represents one approach that can be used to understand projected performance. However, a growing number of real-time software developers use simulation and modeling tools that not only analyze a system's performance, but also enable the software engineer to build a prototype, execute it, and thereby gain an understanding of a system's behavior.

The overall rationale behind simulation and modeling for real-time systems is discussed by i-Logix (a company that develops tools for systems engineers) [ILO89]:

> The understanding of a system's behavior in its environment over time is most often addressed in the design, implementation and testing phases of a project, through iterative trial and error. The Statemate [a system engineering tool for simulation and modeling] approach provides an alternative to this costly

process. It allows you to build a comprehensive system model that is accurate enough to be relied on and clear enough to be useful. The model addresses the usual functional and flow issues, but also covers the dynamic, behavioral aspects of a system. This model can then be tested with the Statemate analysis and retrieval tools, which provide extensive mechanisms for inspecting and debugging the specification and retrieving information from it. By testing the implementation model, the system engineer can see how the system as specified would behave if implemented.

The Statemate approach [HAR90] makes use of a notation that combines three different views of a system: the *activity-chart, module-chart,* and *statechart.* In the paragraphs that follow, the Statemate approach to real-time system simulation and modeling is described.[2]

The Conceptual View

Functional issues are treated using *activities* that represent the processing capabilities of the system. Dealing with a customer's confirmation request in an airline reservation system is an example of an activity, as is updating the aircraft's position in an avionics system. Activities can be nested, forming a hierarchy that constitutes a functional decomposition of the system. Items of information, such as the distance to a target or a customer's name, will typically flow between activities, and might also be kept in data stores. This functional view of a system is captured with *activity-charts,* which are similar to conventional data flow diagrams.

Dynamic behavioral issues, commonly referred to as *control aspects,* are treated using *statecharts.* Here, states (or modes) can be nested and linked in a number of ways to represent sequential or concurrent behavior. An avionics mission computer, for example, could be in one of three states: air-to-air, air-to-ground, or navigation. At the same time it must be in the state of either automatic or manual flight control. Transitions between states are typically triggered by events, which may be qualified by conditions. Flipping a certain switch on the throttle, for example, is an event that will cause a transition from the navigate state to the air-to-ground state, but only on condition that the aircraft has air-to-ground ammunition available. As a simple example, consider the digital watch shown in Figure 15.8. The statechart for the watch is shown in Figure 15.9.

These two views of a system are integrated in the following way. Associated with each level of an activity-chart, there will usually be a statechart, called a *control activity,* whose role is to control the activities and data flows of that level (this is similar in some ways to the relationship between flow models and CSPEC described in Chapter 7). A statechart is able to exercise control over the activities. For example, it can instruct activities to

---

[2]The text that follows has been adapted from [ILO89] which describes Statemate® and is used with the permission of i-Logix Inc.

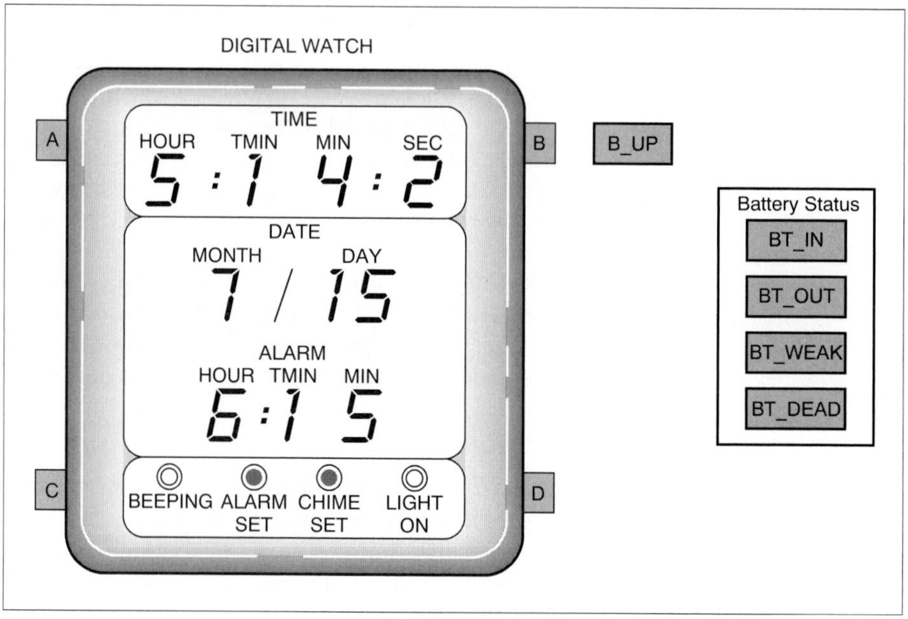

FIGURE 15.8. Digital watch prototype. (*Courtesy I-Logix.*)

start and stop and to suspend and resume their work. It is able to change the values of variables, and thus to influence the processing carried out by the activities. It is also able to send signals to other activities and thus cause them to change their own behavior. In addition to being able to generate actions, a controlling statechart is able to sense such actions being carried out by other statecharts. For example, if one statechart starts an activity or increments the value of a variable, another can sense that event and use it, say, to trigger a transition.

It is important to realize that activity-charts and statecharts are strongly linked, but they are not different representations of the same thing. Activity-charts on their own are incomplete as a model of the system, since they do not address behavior. Statecharts are also incomplete, since without activities they have nothing to control. Together, a detailed activity-chart and its controlling statecharts provide the conceptual model. The activity-chart is the backbone of the model; its decomposition of the capabilities of the system is the dominant hierarchy of the specification, while its controlling statecharts are the driving force behind the system's behavior.

The Physical View

A specification that uses activity-charts and statecharts in the form of a conceptual model is an excellent foundation, but it is not a real system. What is missing is a means for describing the system from a physical (implementation) perspective, and a means to be sure that the system is implemented in a way that is true to that specification. An important part of this

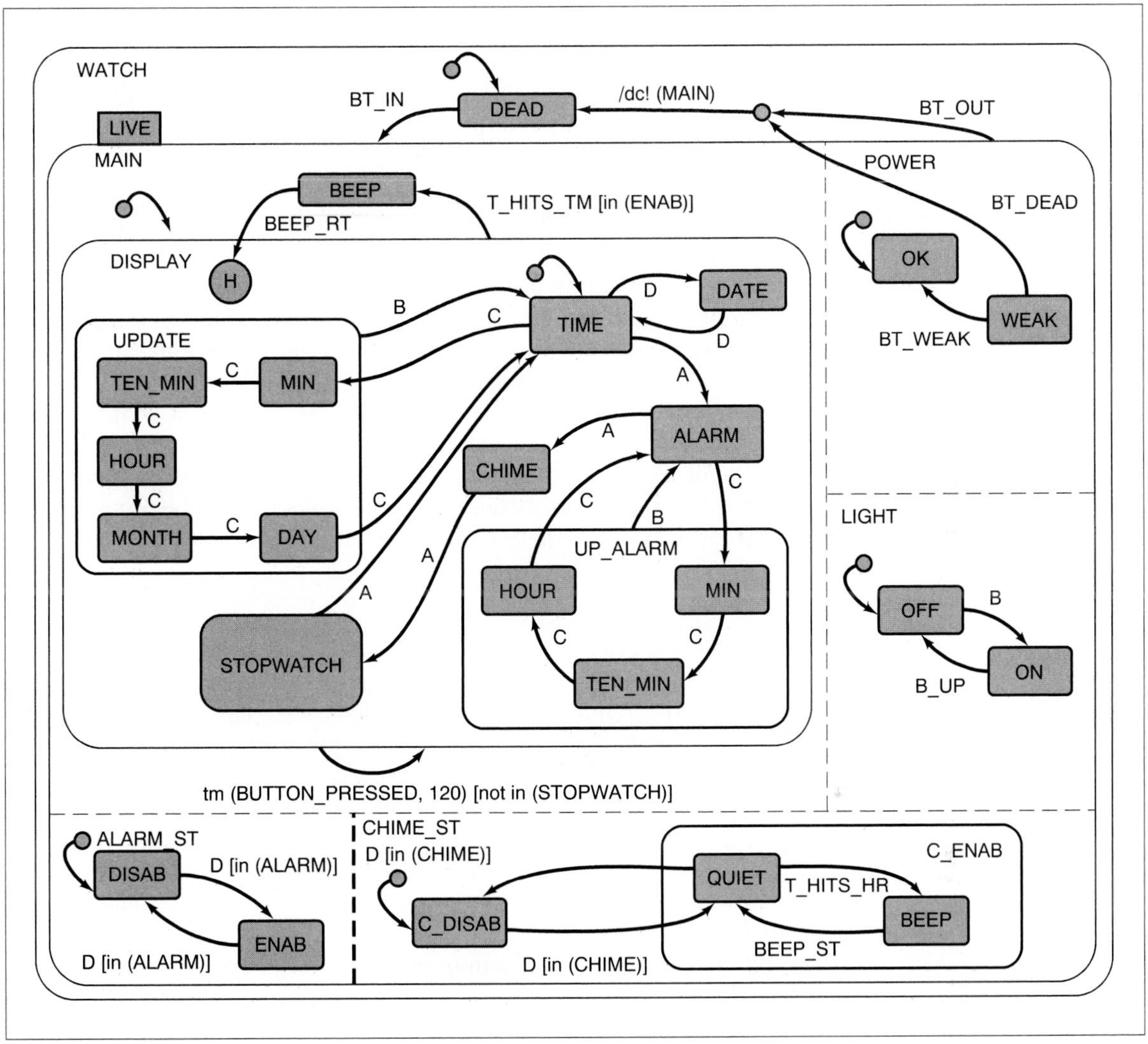

FIGURE 15.9. Statechart for digital watch. (*Courtesy I-Logix.*)

is describing the physical decomposition of the system and its relationship to the conceptual model.

The physical aspects are treated in Statemate using the language of *module-charts*. The terms "physical" and "module" are used generically to denote components of a system, whether hardware, software, or hybrid. Like activities in an activity-chart, modules are arranged in a hierarchy to show the decomposition of a system into its components and subcomponents. Modules are connected by flow lines, which one can think of as being the carriers of information between modules.

Analysis and Simulation

Once we have constructed a conceptual model, consisting of an activity-chart and its controlling statecharts, it can be thoroughly analyzed and tested. The model might describe the entire system, down to the lowest level of detail, or it might be only a partial specification.

We must first be sure that the model is syntactically correct. This gives rise to many relatively straightforward tests: for example, that the various charts are not blatantly incomplete (e.g., missing labels or names, dangling arrows); that the definitions of nongraphical elements, such as events and conditions, employ legal operations only, and so on. Syntax checking also involves more subtle tests, such as the correctness of inputs and outputs. An example of this is a test for elements that are used in the statechart but are neither input nor affected internally, such as a power-on event that is meant to cause a transition in the statechart but is not defined in the activity-chart as an input. All of these are usually referred to as *consistency* and *completeness tests,* and most of them are analogous to the checking carried out by a compiler prior to the actual compilation of a programming language.

Running Scenarios

A syntactically correct model accurately describes some system. However, it might not be the system we had in mind. In fact, the system described might be seriously flawed—syntactic correctness does not guarantee correctness of function or behavior. The real objective of analyzing the model is to find out whether it truly describes the system that we want. The analysis should enable us to learn more about the model that has been constructed, to examine how a system based on it would behave, and to verify that it indeed meets expectations. This requires a modeling language with more than a formal syntax. It requires that the system used to create the model recognize formal semantics as well.

If the model is based on a formal semantics, the system engineer can execute the model. The engineer can create and run a *scenario* that allows her or him to "press buttons" and observe the behavior of the model before the system is actually built. For example, to exercise a model of an automated teller machine (ATM) the following steps would occur: (1) A conceptual model is created; (2) the engineer plays the role of the customer and the bank computer, generating events such as insertion of a bank card, buttons being pressed, and new balance information arriving; (3) the reaction of the system to these events is monitored; (4) inconsistencies in behavior are noted; (5) the conceptual model is modified to reflect proper behavior; (6) iteration occurs until the system that is desired evolves.

The system engineer runs scenarios and views the system's response graphically. "Active" elements of the model (e.g., states that the system is in at the moment and activities that are active) are highlighted graphically, and the dynamic execution results in an animated representation of the model. The execution of a scenario simulates the system running in real time, and keeps track of time-dependent information. At any point during the execution, the engineer can ask to see the status of any other, nongraphical, element, such as the value of a variable or a condition.

Programming Simulations

A scenario enables the system engineer to exercise the model interactively. At times, however, more extensive simulation may be desirable. Performance under random conditions in both typical and atypical situations may need to be assessed. For situations in which a more extensive simulation of a real-time model is desired, Simulation Control Language (SCL) enables the engineer to retain general control over how the executions proceed, but at the same time exploits the power of the tool to take over many of the details.

One of the simplest things that can de done with SCL is to read lists of events from a batch file. This means that lengthy scenarios or parts of them can be prepared in advance and executed automatically. These can be observed by the system engineer. Alternatively, the system engineer can program with SCL to set breakpoints and to monitor certain variables, states, or conditions. For example, running a simulation of an avionics system, the engineer might ask the SCL program to stop whenever the radar locks on target and switch to interactive mode. Once "lock-on" is recognized, the engineer takes over interactively, so that this state can be examined in more detail.

The use of scenarios and simulations also enables the engineer to gather meaningful statistics about the operation of the system that is to be built. For example, we might want to know how many times, in a typical flight of the aircraft, the radar loses a locked-on target. Since it might be difficult for the engineer to put together a single, all-encompassing flight scenario, a programmed simulation can be developed using the accumulated results from other scenarios to obtain average-case statistics. A simulation control program generates random events according to predefined probabilities. Thus, events that occur very rarely (say, seat ejection in a fighter aircraft) can be assigned very low probabilities, while others are assigned higher probabilities, and the random selection of events thus becomes realistic. In order to be able to gather the desired statistics, we insert appropriate breakpoints in the SCL program.

Automatic Translation into Code

Once the system model has been built, it can be translated in its entirety into executable code using a prototyping function. Activity-charts and their controlling statecharts can be translated into a high-level programming language, such as Ada or C. Today, the primary use of the resulting code is to observe a system perform under circumstances that are as close to the real world as possible. For example, the prototype code can be executed in a full-fledged simulator of the target environment or in the final environment itself. The code produced by such CASE tools should be considered to be "prototypical." It is not production or final code. Consequently, it might not always reflect accurate real-time performance of the intended system. Nevertheless, it is useful for testing the system's performance in close to real circumstances.

15.4 DESIGN METHODS

The design of real-time software must incorporate all of the fundamental concepts (Chapter 10) associated with high-quality software. In addition, real-time software poses a set of unique problems for the designer:

- Representation of interrupts and context switching
- Concurrency as manifested by multitasking and multiprocessing
- Intertask communication and synchronization
- Wide variations in data and communication rates
- Representation of timing constraints
- Asynchronous processing
- Necessary and unavoidable coupling with operating systems, hardware, and other external system elements

Over the past two decades, a number of real-time software design methods have been proposed to grapple with some or all of the problems noted above. Some design methods extend one of the three classes of design methodology already discussed in this book (e.g., data flow [WAR85], data structure [JAC83], or object-oriented [BOO87] methodologies). Others introduce an entirely separate approach, using finite state machine models or message passing systems [WIT85], Petri nets [VID83], or a specialized language [STE84] as a basis. For the remainder of this chapter, we consider an example of a representative method.

15.5 A DATA FLOW-ORIENTED DESIGN METHOD

Data flow-oriented design methods (Chapter 11) are the most widely used in the industry. Yet the mapping techniques applied to the data flow diagram do not adequately support all of the real-time design problems noted earlier in this chapter.[3]

[3]It should be noted that the extensions to structured analysis notation presented in Chapter 7 can be used effectively to model the information requirements as well as the function and behavior of a real-time system.

Hassan Gomaa [GOM84] has developed extensions to data flow representations that provide the mechanics for real-time software design. Gomaa's approach, called *Design Method for Real-Time Systems* (DARTS), allows real-time system designers to adapt data flow techniques to the special needs of real-time applications. The following sections are adapted from Gomaa's work.

15.5.1 Requirements of a Real-Time Systems Design Method

Data flow-oriented design techniques (discussed in detail in Chapter 11) provide a worthwhile foundation for real-time design. Data flow diagrams depict information flow between system functions (or tasks) and mapping techniques enable the designer to derive a program structure from data flow characteristics. Design quality measures such as modularity and functional independence (Chapter 10) are reinforced with data flow-oriented methods.

The DARTS real-time software design method builds on the notation and approach for data flow-oriented design of conventional software. To support real-time design, data flow methods must be extended by providing (1) a mechanism for representing task communication and synchronization, (2) a notation for representing state dependency, and (3) an approach that "connects" conventional data flow methods to the real-time world.

Because most real-time systems spawn multiple tasks that either share a single processor or execute simultaneously on distributed processors, mechanisms must be available to synchronize tasks and provide communication between tasks. Synchronization occurs through *mutual exclusion* or *cross stimulation*. Mutual exclusion is applied when two tasks may access a shared data area at the same time. Semaphores are used to *exclude* one task from accessing the data while another is using (reading or writing) the same data. Cross stimulation is implemented when one task signals another (waiting) task that it has completed some activity and the signaled task may proceed.

Task communication occurs when one task must transmit information to another task. *Message communication* [HAN73] is a common communication approach. When a *producer task* sends a message to a *consumer task*, and then waits for a response from the consumer task, communication is termed *closely coupled*. When producer and consumer tasks continue processing at their own rates and use a message queue to buffer messages, communication is termed *loosely coupled*.

To implement message communication, Gomaa [GOM84] describes three different approaches:

1. A real-time operating system may provide intertask communication primitives (e.g., [KUN85]).
2. Task communication mechanisms may be implemented within the context of a programming language (e.g., Ada).

3. A special communication handler may be created, using synchronization primitives provided by the operating system [SIM79].

The DARTS approach provides a notation that supports both closely and loosely coupled communication.

15.5.2 DARTS

The DARTS design method begins with the application of fundamental software analysis principles (i.e., information domain analysis, problem partitioning) applied in the context of data flow notation. Data flow diagrams are created, a corresponding data dictionary is defined, and interfaces between major system functions (transforms) are established (see Chapters 7 and 11).

Gomaa [GOM84] describes the DARTS approach in the following manner:

> The DARTS design method can be thought of as extending the Structured Analysis/Structured Design method by providing an approach for structuring the system into tasks as well as a mechanism for defining the interfaces between tasks. In this sense, it draws on the experience gained in concurrent processing. As with other design methods, DARTS is intended to be iterative.

Once the flow model and a data dictionary have been created, the system must be examined from a different point of view. DFDs do not depict the asynchronous and concurrent tasks that implement the data flow. Therefore, we need an approach that identifies real-time system tasks in the context of system functions (transforms) drawn on a DFD. Transforms are grouped into real-time tasks. Data flow between newly defined tasks defines intertask communication requirements. Gomaa [GOM84] notes the following criteria for determining whether DFD transforms should be defined as separate tasks or grouped with other transforms into a single task:

Dependency on I/O. Depending on input or output, a transform is often constrained to run at a speed dictated by the speed of the I/O device with which it is interacting. In this case, the transform needs to be a separate task.

Time-critical functions. A time-critical function needs to run as a high priority and therefore needs to be a separate task.

Computational requirements. A computationally intensive function (or set of functions) can run as a lower-priority task-consuming spare CPU cycles.

Functional cohesion. Transforms that perform a set of closely related functions can be grouped together into a task. Since the data traffic between these functions may be high, having them as separate tasks will increase system overhead, whereas implementing each function as a separate module within the same task ensures functional cohesion both at the module and task levels.

Temporal cohesion. Certain transforms perform functions that are carried out at the same time. These functions may be grouped into a task so that they are executed each time the task receives a stimulus.

Periodic execution. A transform that needs to be executed periodically can be structured as a separate task that is activated at regular intervals.

Once tasks have been defined, DARTS provides a mechanism for communication handling between tasks by defining two classes of "task interface modules" [GOM84]: *task communication modules* (TCMs) and *task synchronization modules* (TSMs). A TCM is spawned by a communicating task and uses operating system synchronization primitives to assure proper access to data. TCMs are divided into two categories:

Message communication modules (MCMs) that support message communication and implement appropriate mechanisms for managing a message queue (for loosely coupled communication) and synchronization primitives (for closely coupled communication). DARTS notation for intertask communication that is implemented by an MCM is illustrated in Figure 15.10*a*.

Information hiding modules (IHMs) that provide access to a data pool or data store. The IHM implements the data structure as well as the access methods that enable other tasks to gain access to the data structure. Figure 15.10*b* illustrates DARTS notation for communication implemented by an IHM.

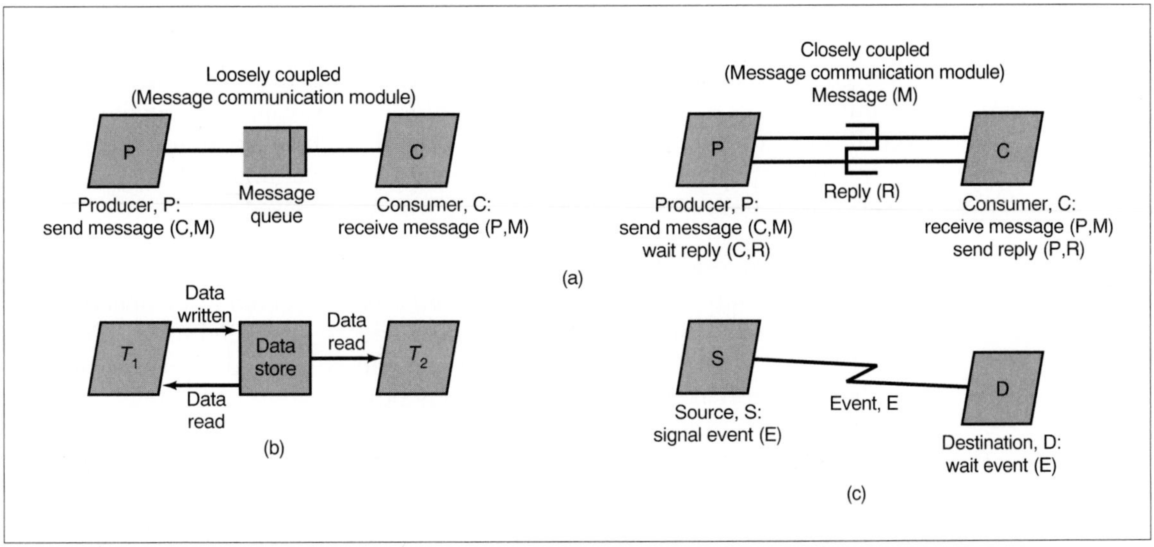

FIGURE 15.10. (*a*) Message communication; (*b*) information hiding module; (*c*) task synchronization.

When control, rather than data, is to be passed between tasks, the task synchronization module comes into play. One task may signal another that an event has occurred, or a task may wait for such a signal. The DARTS notation for task synchronization is shown in Figure 15.10*c*. A TSM may be viewed as a "supervisory module" that manages control and coordination as events occur.

15.5.3 Task Design

A real-time system task is a program that may be designed using conventional methods. That is, a task may be viewed as a sequential process implemented with a hierarchically organized program structure. Each module in the program structure may be designed using the structured programming philosophy.

Therefore, the DFD that represents data flow within a task boundary may be mapped into a program structure using conventional transform or transaction mapping techniques (Chapter 11). However, for real-time systems, control is dependent on both the input provided to the task and the current state of the system (i.e., on what has happened to place the system in its current state of operation). For this reason, control is *state-dependent.*

Gomaa [GOM84] suggests a mechanism for handling this situation that he calls a *state transition manager* (STM) The STM is an implementation of the process activation table discussed in Chapter 7. The STM is aware of the current state of the system and uses a state transition table to guide processing.

15.5.4 Example of the DARTS Design Method

As an abbreviated example of the DARTS method, we consider the top-level design of software for an air traffic control system (ATCS) illustrated in Figure 15.11. An ATCS must acquire information from transponders of aircraft within its control area. Transponder data must be analyzed to determine aircraft identification type, bearing, altitude, and so forth. Data are placed in a database from which displays are created for air traffic controllers. Controllers can query the database for supporting information.

The system must operate under extremely rigid performance and reliability constraints: (1) data acquisition *must* be conducted at prespecified intervals; (2) analysis *must* be performed within specified execution time constraints; (3) the database *must* be updated at defined intervals; (4) controller interaction should not impede any other system functions.

The DARTS approach begins with the derivation of level 0 and 1 data flow diagrams (Figures 15.12 and 15.13). In addition, the analyst creates corresponding CFDs and CSPECs, a state transition diagram to represent system behavior, PSPECs, and a data dictionary (described in Chapter 7, but not shown in this example). The DFDs make no explicit reference to the

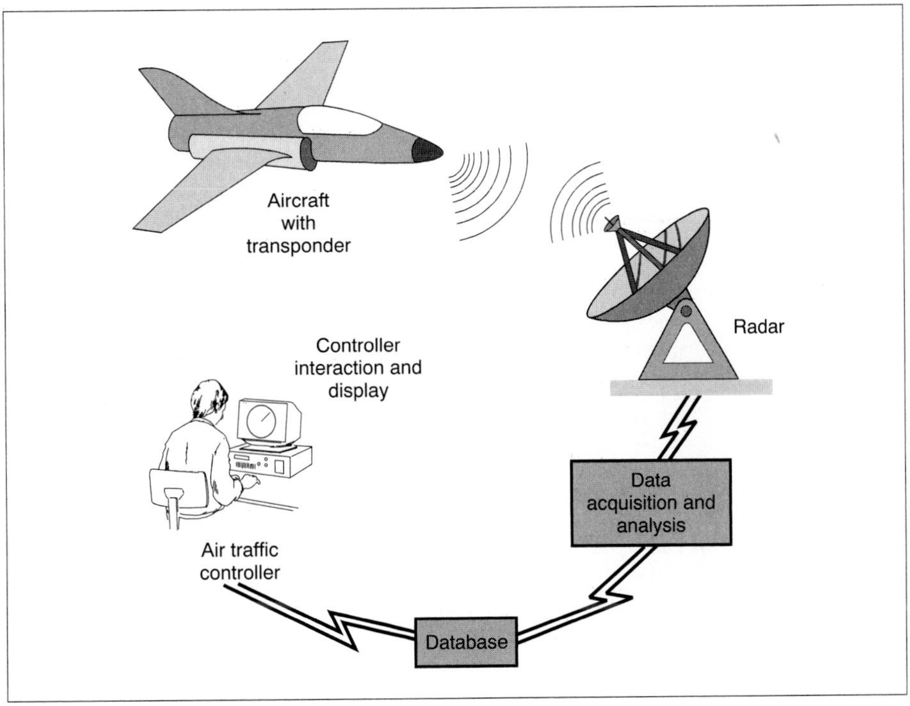

FIGURE 15.11.
Air traffic control system.

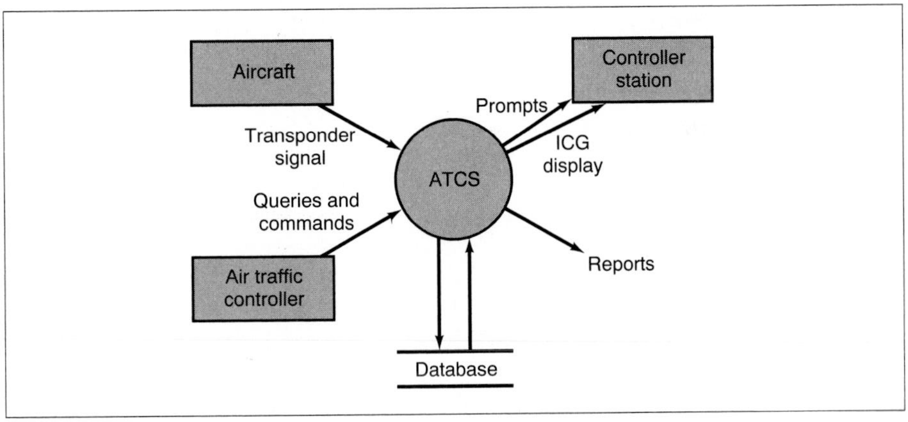

FIGURE 15.12.
ATCS: Level 0 DFD.

real-time nature of ATCS or to the different tasks that are required to implement ATCS.

Examining the level 1 DFD and applying the task definition criteria discussed in Section 15.5.2, a set of system tasks may be defined:

- Data acquisition task
- Data analysis task

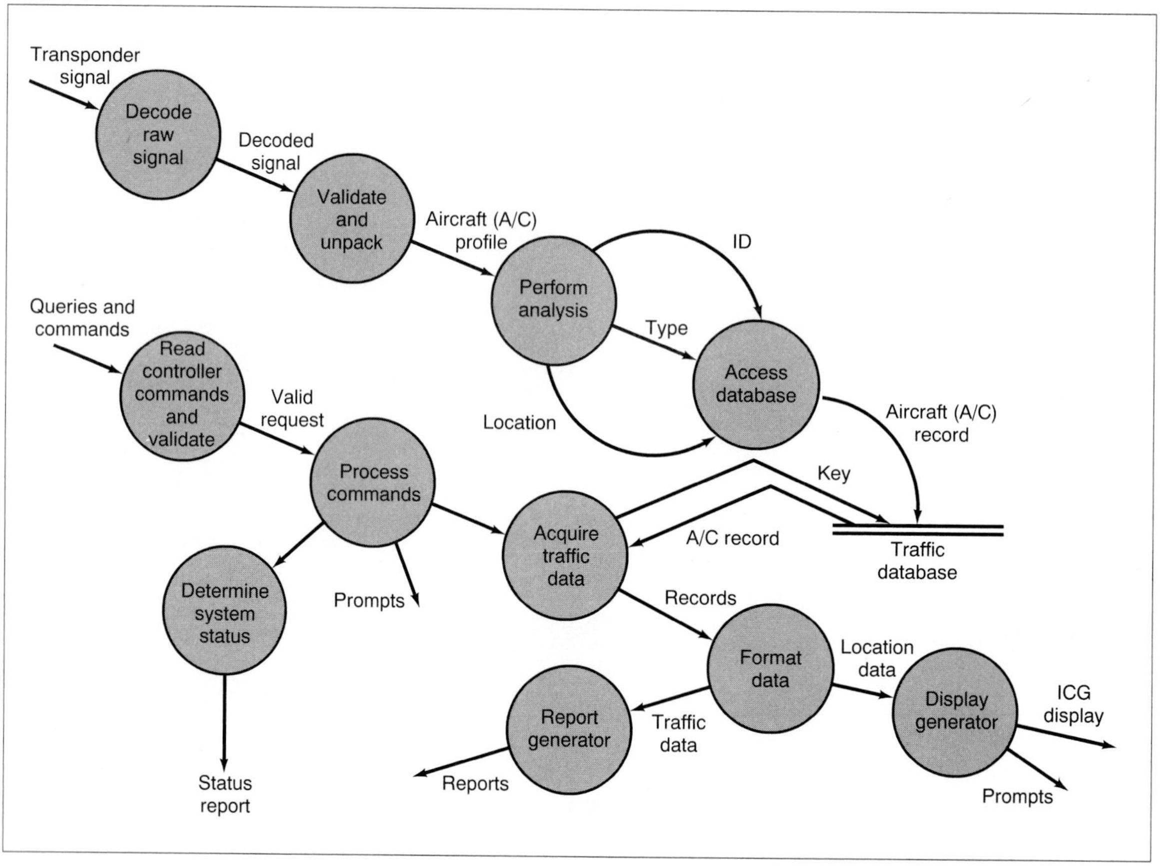

FIGURE 15.13. ATCS: Level 1 DFD.

- Database I/O task
- Display task
- Air traffic controller interaction task

It should be noted that each of these tasks may be further subdivided into other concurrent tasks. For our purposes, however, further refinement is not attempted.

A CSPEC containing a state transition diagram (or table) is created to illustrate the events that cause the system to move from one state to the next. In the ATCS example, system states correspond to real-time tasks. Referring to Figure 15.14, the data acquisition state continues receiving transponder data until (1) an internal clock (timer) signals that analysis and database I/O must be conducted or (2) the buffer containing "raw aircraft profile" data files is filled. In either case, control is transferred to the data analysis state, which continues until interrupted by a timer to return con-

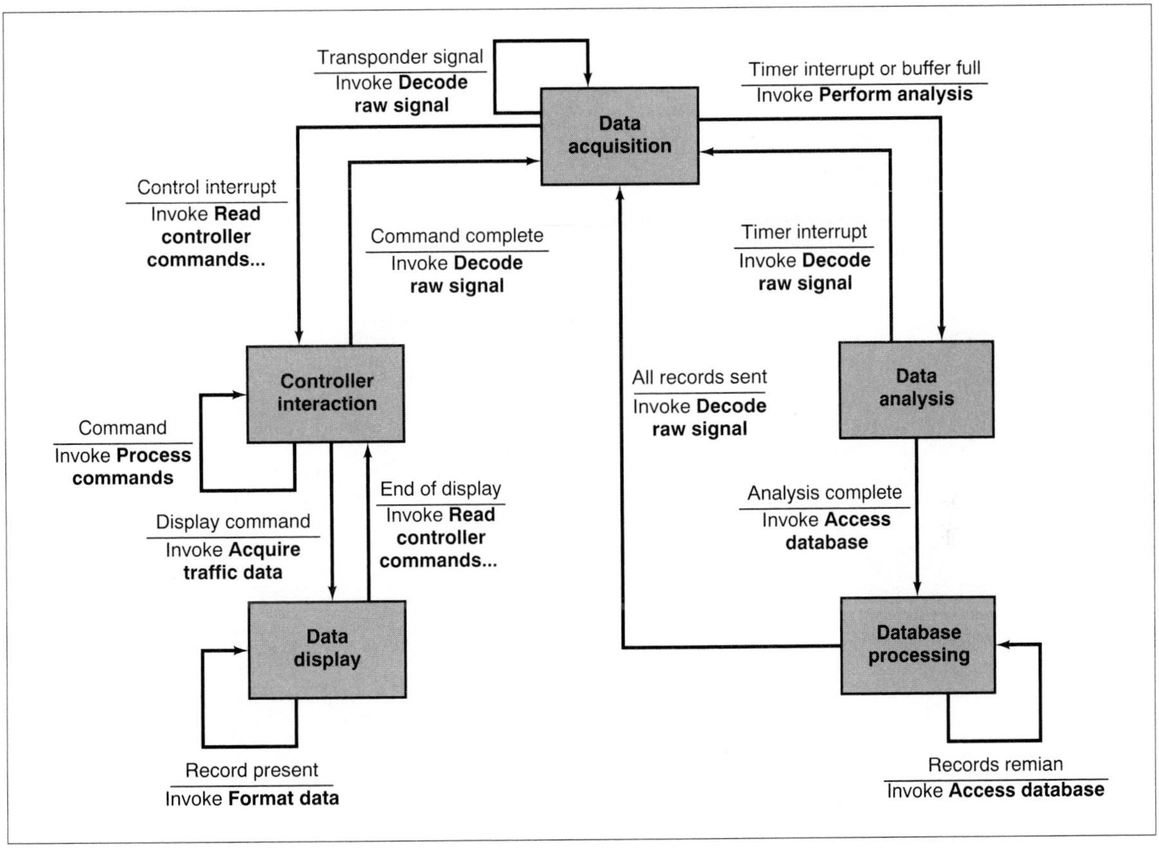

FIGURE 15.14. ATCS: simplified state diagram (see Chapter 9 for details on notation.)

trol to the acquisition task or until data analysis is complete. In the latter case, control is passed to the database I/O state which receives a data stream from the analysis task and produces logical records for the database. Controller interaction and data display (Figure 15.14) occur concurrently, with state transition illustrated as shown.

Returning to the level 1 DFD for ATCS, the real-time tasks are superimposed on the data flow, using shaded areas to delineate tasks (Figure 15.15). Finally, the notation depicted in Figure 15.10 is used to create a representation of control and communication between tasks (Figure 15.16).

Level 2 DFDs may be created for each of the tasks depicted in Figure 15.16. These DFDs may then be mapped into a program structure using transform or transaction mappings. The modules defined within the program structure for each task may be designed using conventional methods.

The DARTS approach extends data flow notation by enabling the designer to define tasks and represent intertask communication and concurrency. In addition, the use of task interface modules (TCMs and TSMs)

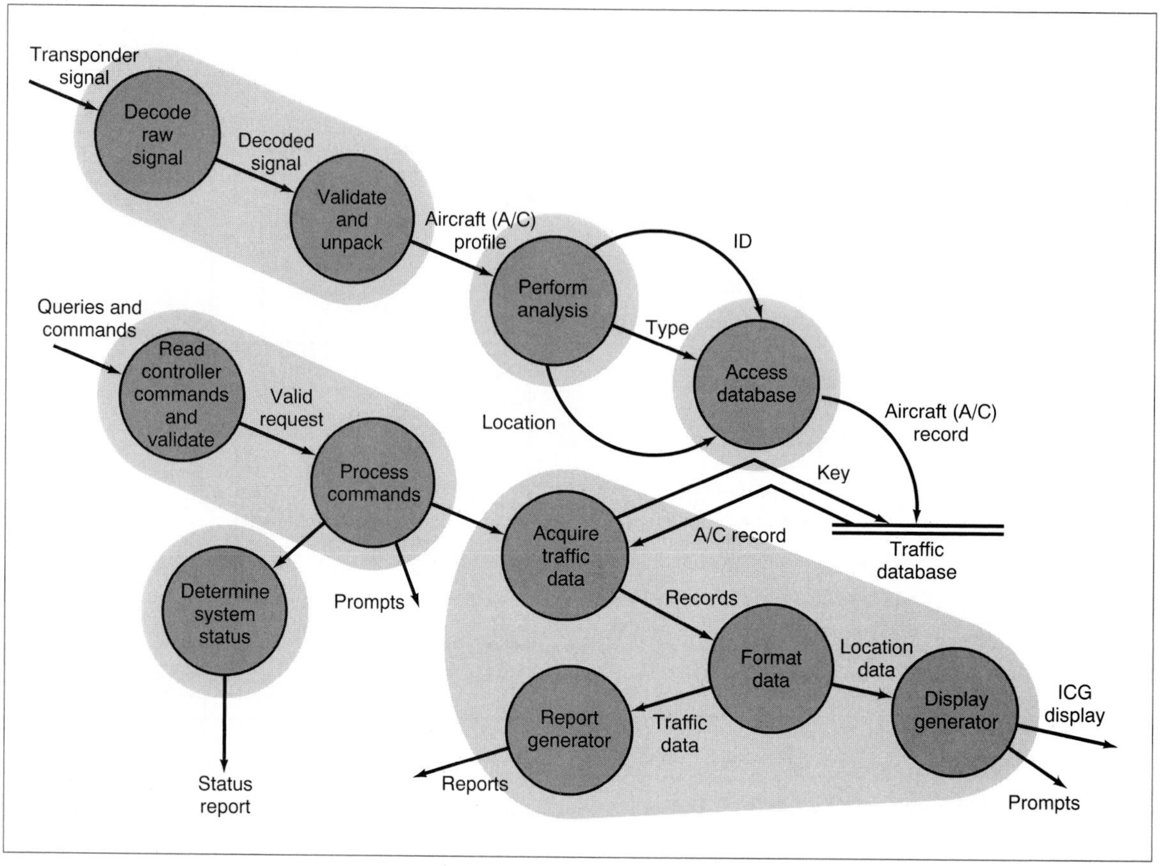

FIGURE 15.15. Superimposing tasks.

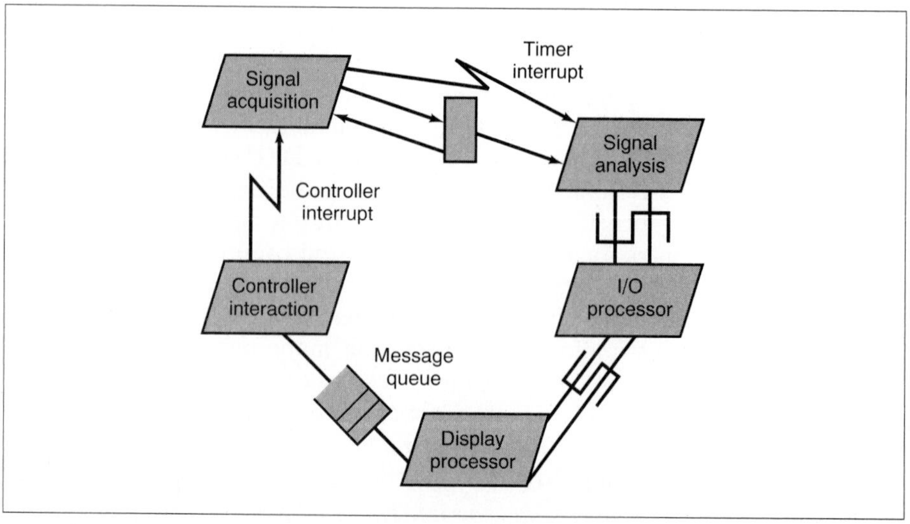

FIGURE 15.16. Representing control and communication.

provides a means for implementing the communication and synchronization activities. Those readers who desire further information should refer to Gomaa [GOM84].

15.6 SUMMARY

The design of real-time software encompasses all aspects of conventional software design while at the same time introducing a new set of design criteria and concerns. Because real-time software must respond to real-world events in a time frame dictated by those events, all classes of design (architectural, procedural, and data design) become more complex.

It is difficult, and often impractical, to divorce software design from larger system-oriented issues. Because real-time software is either clock- or event-driven, the designer must consider the function and performance of the hardware and software. Interrupt processing and data transfer rate, distributed databases and operating systems, specialized programming languages and synchronization methods are just some of the concerns of the real-time system designer.

The analysis of real-time systems encompasses mathematical modeling and simulation. Queuing and network models enable the system engineer to assess overall response time, processing rate, and other timing and sizing issues. Formal analysis tools provide a mechanism for real-time system simulation.

Software design for real-time systems can be predicated on a conventional design methodology. For example, the DARTS approach extends data flow-oriented design by providing a notation and approach that addresses real-time system characteristics.

Software design for real-time systems remains a challenge. Progress has been made; methods do exist, but a realistic assessment of the state-of-the-art suggests much remains to be done.

REFERENCES

[BOO87] Booch, G., *Software Engineering with Ada,* 2d ed., Benjamin-Cummings, 1987.

[FOS81] Foster, C.C., *Real Time Programming—Neglected Topics,* Addison-Wesley, 1981.

[GLA83] Glass, R. L., *Real-Time Software,* Prentice-Hall, 1983.

[GOM84] Gomaa, H., "A Software Design Method for Real Time Systems," *CACM,* vol. 27, no. 9, September 1984, pp. 938–949.

[GRO85] Gross, D., and C. M. Harris, *Fundamentals of Queuing Theory,* 2d ed., Wiley, 1985.

[HAN73] Brinch Hansen, P., "Concurrent Programming Concepts," *Computing Surveys,* vol. 5, no. 4, December 1973, pp. 223–245.

[HIN83] Hinden, H. J., and W. B. Rauch-Hinden, "Real-Time Systems," *Electronic Design,* January 6, 1983, pp. 288–311.

[HAR90] Harel, D., et al., "STATEMATE: A Working Environment for the Development of Complex Reactive Systems," *IEEE Trans. Software Engineering,* vol. 16, no. 3, April 1990, pp. 403–414.

[ILO89] *The Statemate Approach to Complex Systems,* I-Logix Inc., 1989.

[JAC83] Jackson, M., *System Development,* Van Nostrand Reinhold, 1983.

[KAI83] Kaiser, S. H., *The Design of Operating Systems for Small Computer Systems,* Wiley-Interscience, 1983.

[KLI75] Kleinrock, L., *Queueing Systems, Volume 1: Theory,* Wiley, 1975.

[KUN85] Kung, A., and R. Kung, "GALAXY: A Distributed Real-Time Operating System Supporting High Availability," *Proc. Real-Time Systems Symposium,* IEEE, December 1985, pp. 79–87.

[LIU90] Liu, L.Y., and R. K. Shyamasundar, "Static Analysis of Real-Time Distributed Systems," *IEEE Trans. Software Engineering,* vol. 16, no. 3, April 1990, pp. 373–388.

[MCC85] McCabe, T. J., et al., "Structured Real-Time Analysis and Design," *COMPSAC-85,* IEEE, October 1985, pp. 40–51.

[MEL83] Mellichamp, D. A. (editor), *Real Time Computing,* Van Nostrand Reinhold, 1983.

[SAV85] Savitsky, S., *Real-Time Microprocessor Systems,* Van Nostrand Reinhold, 1985.

[SIM79] Simpson, H. R., and K. L. Jackson, "Process Synchronization in Mascot," *The Computer Journal,* vol. 22, no. 4, 1979.

[STE84] Steusloff, H. U., "Advanced Real-Time Languages for Distributed Industrial Process Control," *Computer,* vol. 17, no. 2, February 1984, pp. 37–46.

[VID83] Vidondo, F., "GALILEO: Design Language for Real-Time Systems," *Proc. ITT Conf. on Programming Productivity and Quality,* ITT Corporation, June 1983, pp. 198–210.

[WAR85] Ward, P.T., and S. J. Mellor, *Structured Development for Real-Time Systems,* 3 volumes, Yourdon Press, 1985, 1986.

[WIL90] Wilson, R.G., and B. H. Krogh, "Petri Net Tools for the Specification and Analysis of Discrete Controllers," *IEEE Trans. Software Engineering,* vol. 16, no. 1, January 1990, pp. 39–50.

[WIT85] Witt, B. I., "Communicating Modules: A Software Design Model for Concurrent Distributed Systems," *IEEE Computer,* vol. 18, no. 1, January 1985, pp. 67–77.

[WOO90] Wood, M., and T. Barrett, "A Real-Time Primer," *Embedded Systems Programming,* vol. 3, no. 2, February 1990, pp. 20–28.

[ZUC89] Zucconi, L., "Techniques and Experiences in Capturing Requirements for Real-Time Systems," *ACM Software Engineering Notes,* vol. 14, no. 6, October 1989, pp. 51–55.

PROBLEMS AND POINTS TO PONDER

15.1 List five examples of computer-based real-time systems. Indicate what "stimuli" feed the system and what devices or situations the system controls or monitors.

15.2 Obtain information on a commercial real-time operating system (RTOS) and write a short paper that presents a discussion of RTOS internals. What special features are present, how are interrupts handled, and how does the RTOS affect task synchronization?

15.3 Write a brief comparison of the real-time constructs in the programming languages Ada and Modula-2. Do these constructs provide distinct benefits over other languages such as C or PASCAL?

15.4 Provide three examples in which semaphores would be an appropriate task synchronization mechanism.

15.5 The analysis technique for real-time systems presented in Section 15.3 assumes a knowledge of queuing models. Do some research using the references indicated and:

(*a*) Describe how Figure 15.5 was derived from Figure 15.4.

(*b*) Show how the flow balance equations are derived from Figure 15.5.

15.6 For those readers who are familiar with queuing models and Markov analysis: Making appropriate assumptions about arrival rates and service times, attempt to apply McCabe's real-time analysis method [MCC85] to the air traffic control system described in Section 15.5.4.

15.7 Get information on one or more formal analysis tools for real-time systems (Section 15.3.2). Write a paper that outlines its (their) use in the specification and design of a real-time system.

15.8 Using the DARTS approach presented in Section 15.5.2, develop a design representation for the *SafeHome* security system described earlier in this book.

FURTHER READINGS

Hatley and Pirbhai (*Strategies for Real-Time System Specification,* Dorset House, 1987) and Ward and Mellor (*Structured Development for Real-Time Systems,* Yourdon Press, 1986) are the most widely used books for the analysis and design of real-time systems. Both suggest extensions to conventional structured analysis that were discussed in Chapter 7.

Books by Glass [GLA83] and Mellichamp [MEL83], although somewhat dated, are useful sources of information on real-time software and its design. Leigh (*Real-Time Software Design for Small Systems,* Wiley, 1988) focuses on real-time issues for small, microprocessor-based systems and embedded products. Stankovic and Ramamritham (*Hard Real-Time Systems,* IEEE Computer Society Press, 1988) have edited an excellent tutorial on real-time systems which contains 17 papers on real-time operating systems and many others on analysis, design, and implementation techniques. Booch [BOO87] provides useful guidance for real-time system development in Ada. Burns and Welling (*Real-Time Systems and Their Programming Languages,* Addison-Wesley, 1990) introduce a number of design-related issues in their discussion of modern programming languages for real-time systems. A book by Levi and Agrawala (*Real-Time System Design,* McGraw-Hill, 1990) is one of the first texts to address real-time system issues from an object-oriented point of view. Heath (*Real-Time Software Techniques,* Van Nostrand Reinhold, 1991) focuses on implementation issues for the design and development of real-time machine control software. Cooling (*Software Design for Real-Time Systems*, Van Nostrand Reinhold, 1991), considers the application of formal specification methods for time-dependent applications.

The monthly industry magazine, *Embedded Systems Programming*, (Miller Freeman Publications, San Francisco) contains useful tutorials and surveys of current methods and languages for real-time embedded software. The *Proceedings of the Real-Time Systems Symposium* (IEEE, held annually) is an excellent source of information on current research.

CHAPTER 16

PROGRAMMING LANGUAGES AND CODING

All the software engineering steps that have been presented to this point are directed toward a final objective: to translate representations of software into a form that can be "understood" by the computer. We have (finally) reached the coding step—a process that transforms design into a programming language. Gerald Weinberg [WEI71] expressed the true meaning of coding when he wrote: "...when we talk to our computers, unhappily, we are usually speaking in different tongues...."

Most readers of this book may live to see the day when the above quotation is proved incorrect. Requests for computer processing services may be coded (or spoken) in a natural language, such as English. Already, a set of so-called *fourth-generation techniques* is changing our understanding of the term "programming language." Rather than coding, developers of some classes of management information systems (and limited areas of engineering and scientific applications) can now describe desired results, rather than desired procedure, in a *nonprocedural language.* Conventional programming language source code is then automatically generated.

However, the vast majority of software applications still reside beyond the reach of fourth-generation approaches. For the time being, we code using artificial languages such as Ada, FORTRAN, PASCAL, C, COBOL, or assembler language.

When considered as a step in the software engineering process, coding is viewed as a natural consequence of design. However, programming language characteristics and coding style can profoundly affect software quality and maintainability. This chapter does not aspire to teach the reader to code.

Rather, topics associated with programming languages and coding are presented in the broader context of software engineering.

16.1 THE TRANSLATION PROCESS

The coding step translates a detail design representation of software into a programming language realization. The translation process continues when a compiler accepts *source code* as input and produces machine-dependent *object code* as output. Compiler output is further translated into *machine code*—the actual instructions that drive microcoded logic in the central processing unit.

The initial translation step—from detail design to programming language—is a primary concern in the software engineering context. "Noise" can enter the translation process in many ways. Improper interpretation of a detail design specification can lead to erroneous source code [SHE81]. Programming language complexity or restrictions can lead to convoluted source code that is difficult to test and maintain. More subtly, characteristics of a programming language can influence the way we think, propagating unnecessarily limited software designs and data structures.

For example, a design directed at a target FORTRAN 77 implementation would be less likely to select a linked list data structure, because FORTRAN 77 does not directly support such a structure. If the target language were C or PASCAL (both languages provide direct support for linked lists), the linked list would be a more feasible alternative.

Language characteristics have an impact on the quality and efficiency of translation. In the next section, we evaluate language characteristics by considering two different views of programming languages.

16.2 PROGRAMMING LANGUAGE CHARACTERISTICS

Programming languages are vehicles for communication between humans and computers. The coding process—communication via a programming language—is a human activity. As such, the psychological characteristics of a language have an important impact on the quality of communication. The coding process may also be viewed as one step in the software engineering process. The engineering characteristics of a language have an important impact on the success of a software development project. Finally, technical characteristics of a language can influence the quality of design (recall that practicality often dictates that detail design be directed toward a specific programming language). Therefore, technical characteristics can affect both human and software engineering concerns.

16.2.1 A Psychological View

In his book *Software Psychology,* Ben Shneiderman [SHN80] observed that the role of the software psychologist is to "focus on human concerns such as ease of use, simplicity in learning, improved reliability, reduced error frequency and enhanced user satisfaction, while maintaining an awareness of machine efficiency, software capacity, and hardware constraints." Even though automated tools (CASE) provide substantial assistance, software engineering remains an intensely human activity. We still have much to learn about the human aspects of computer-based system development.

Another software psychologist, Gerald Weinberg [WEI71], relates a story that bears repeating (in paraphrased form) when we consider characteristics of programming languages:

> It is impossible to begin a discussion of psychological principles of programming language design without recalling the story of "The Genius Tailor." It seems that a man had gone to the tailor to have a suit made cheaply, but when the suit was finished and he went to try it on, it didn't fit him at all.
>
> Complaining that the jacket was too big in back, the right arm was too long, one pant leg was too short and three buttons were missing, the man was justifiably upset.
>
> "No problem," said the tailor, "just hunch your back, bend your arm, walk with a limp, and stick your fingers through the button holes and you'll look just fine!"
>
> The man contorted his body to fit the suit and feeling duped by the tailor, he left. He had not walked one block when he was approached by a stranger.
>
> "Who made that suit for you?" asked the stranger. "I'm in the market for a new suit myself."
>
> Surprised, but pleased at the compliment, the man pointed out the tailor's shop.
>
> "Well, thanks very much," said the stranger, hurrying off. "I do believe I'll go to that tailor for my suit. Why, he must be a genius to fit a cripple like you!"

Weinberg suggests that we could extend this parable to a story of the genius programming language designer. The designers of programming languages often make us contort our approach to a problem so that the approach will fit the constraints imposed by a specific programming language. Because human factors are critically important in programming language design, the psychological characteristics of a language have a strong bearing on the success of design to code translation and implementation.

A number of psychological characteristics [WEI71] occur as a result of programming language design. Although these characteristics are not measurable in any quantifiable way, we recognize their manifestation in all programming languages. We discuss each characteristic briefly in the paragraphs that follow.

Uniformity indicates the degree to which a language uses consistent notation, applies seemingly arbitrary restrictions, and supports syntactic or semantic exceptions to the rule. For example, FORTRAN uses the parentheses as delimiter for array indices, as a modifier for arithmetic precedence, and as a delimiter for a subprogram argument list (to name a few!). This multiuse notation has led to more than a few subtle errors.

Ambiguity in a programming language is perceived by the programmer. A compiler will always interpret a statement in one way, but the human reader may interpret the statement differently. Here lies psychological ambiguity. For example, psychological ambiguity arises when arithmetic precedence is not obvious:

```
X = X1/X2*X3
```

One reader of the source code might interpret the above as $X = (X_1/X_2)*X_3$ while another reader might "see" $X = X_1/(X_2*X_3)$. Another potential source of ambiguity is the nonstandard use of identifiers that have default data types. For example, in FORTRAN an identifier KDELTA would be assumed (by default) to have *integer* characteristics. However, an explicit declaration, REAL KDELTA, could cause confusion due to psychological ambiguity.

A lack of uniformity and the occurrence of psychological ambiguity normally occur together. If a programming language exhibits the negative aspects of these characteristics, source code is less readable and translation from design is more error-prone.

Compactness of a programming language is an indication of the amount of code-oriented information that must be recalled from human memory. Among the language attributes that measure compactness are:

- The degree to which a language supports the structured constructs (Chapter 10) and logical "chunking"
- The kinds of keywords and abbreviations that may be used
- The variety of data types and default characteristics
- The number of arithmetic and logical operators
- The number of built-in functions.

APL is an exceptionally compact programming language. Its powerful and concise operators allow relatively little code to accomplish significant arithmetic and logical procedures. Unfortunately, the compactness of APL also makes the language difficult to read and understand, and can lead to poor uniformity (e.g., the use of *monadic* and *dyadic* forms for the same operator symbol).

The characteristics of human memory have a strong impact on the way in which we use language. Human memory and recognition may be divided into *synesthetic* and *sequential* domains [KLA80]. Synesthetic memory allows us to remember and recognize things as a whole. For example, we recognize a human face instantly; we do not consciously evaluate each of its distinct parts prior to recognition. Sequential memory provides a means for recalling the next element in a sequence (e.g., the next line in a song, given the preceding lines). Each of these memory characteristics affect programming language characteristics that are called locality and linearity.

Locality is the synesthetic characteristic of a programming language. Locality is enhanced when statements may be combined into *blocks,* when the structured constructs may be implemented directly, and when design and resultant code are highly modular and cohesive (Chapter 10). A language characteristic that supports or encourages exception handling (e.g., ON-condition processing in PL/1 or ERR = in extended versions of FORTRAN) violates locality.

Linearity is a psychological characteristic that is closely associated with the concept of maintenance of functional domain. That is, human perception is facilitated when a linear sequence of logical operations is encountered. Extensive branching (and, to some extent, large loops) violates the linearity of processing. Again, direct implementation of the structured constructs aids programming language linearity.

Our ability to learn a new programming language is affected by *tradition*. A software engineer with a background in FORTRAN or ALGOL would have little difficulty learning PL/1, PASCAL, or C. The latter languages have a tradition established by the former. Constructs are similar, form is compatible, and a sense of programming language "format" is maintained. However, if the same individual were required to learn APL , LISP, or Smalltalk, tradition would be broken and time on the learning curve would be longer.

Tradition also affects the degree of innovation during the design of a new programming language. Although new languages are proposed frequently, new language forms evolve slowly. For example, PASCAL is a close relative of ALGOL. However, a major innovation in the PASCAL language [JEN74] is an implementation of user-defined data types, a form that does not exist in earlier languages tied to PASCAL by tradition. Ada, a language that has also grown out of the ALGOL-PASCAL tradition, extends beyond both languages with a wide variety of innovative structures and typing.

The psychological characteristics of programming languages have an important bearing on our ability to learn, apply, and maintain them. In summary, a programming language colors the way we think about programs and inherently limits the way in which we communicate with a computer. Whether this is good or bad remains an open question.

16.2.2 A Syntactic/Semantic Model

Shneiderman [SHN80] has developed a *syntactic-semantic model* of the programming process that has relevance in a consideration of the coding step. When a programmer applies software engineering methods (e.g., requirements analysis, design) that are programming language-independent, semantic knowledge is tapped. Syntactic knowledge, on the other hand, is language-dependent, concentrating on the characteristics of a specific language.

Of these knowledge types, semantic knowledge is the more difficult to acquire and the more intellectually demanding to apply. All software engineering steps that precede coding make heavy use of semantic knowledge. The coding step applies syntactic knowledge that is "arbitrary and instructional" and learned by rote [SHN80]. When a new programming language is learned, new syntactic information is added to memory. Potential confusion may occur when the syntax of a new programming language is similar but not equivalent to the syntax of another language. It should be noted, however, that a new programming language can serve to force the software engineer to learn new semantic information as well. For example, the Ada programming language has caused many software engineers to rethink their approach to the design and implementation of software-based systems.

When arguments about the compelling need to "generate code" arise, the listener should realize that many problems associated with computer software have not been caused by a lack of syntactic knowledge. The problem lies in the scope of our semantic knowledge and our ability to apply it. The goal of software engineering is to expand the knowledge of the semantics of software development.

16.2.3 An Engineering View

A software engineering view of programming language characteristics focuses on the needs of a specific software development project. Although esoteric requirements for source code may be derived, a general set of engineering characteristics can be established: (1) ease of design to code translation, (2) compiler efficiency, (3) source code portability, (4) availability of development tools, and (5) maintainability.

The coding step begins after a detail design has been defined, reviewed, and modified, if necessary. In theory, source code generation from a detail design specification should be straightforward. *Ease of design to code translation* provides an indication of how closely a programming language mirrors a design representation. As we discussed in Section 16.1, a language that directly implements the structured constructs, sophisticated data structures, specialized I/O, bit manipulation capabilities, and object-oriented constructs will make translation from design to source code much easier (if these attributes are specified in the design).

Although rapid advances in processor speed and memory density have begun to mitigate the need for "superefficient code," many applications still require fast, "tight" (low memory requirement) programs. An on-going criticism of high-level language compilers is directed at an inability to produce fast, tight, executable code. Languages with optimizing compilers may be attractive if software performance is a critical requirement.

Source code portability is a programming language characteristic that may be interpreted in three different ways:

1. Source code may be transported from processor to processor and compiler to compiler with little or no modification.
2. Source code remains unchanged even when its environment changes (e.g., a new version of an operating system is installed).
3. Source code may be integrated into different software packages with little or no modification required because of programming language characteristics.

Of the three interpretations of portability, the first is by far the most common. Standardization (by the International Standards Organization—ISO—and/or the American National Standards Institute—ANSI) continues to be a major impetus for improvement of programming language portability. Unfortunately, most compiler designers succumb to a compelling urge to provide "better" but nonstandard features for a standardized language. If portability is a critical requirement, source code must be restricted to the ISO or ANSI standard, even if other features exist.

Availability of development tools can shorten the time required to generate source code and can improve the quality of the code. Many programming languages may be acquired with a suite of tools that include debugging compilers, source code formatting aids, built-in editing facilities, tools for source code control, extensive subprogram libraries in a variety of application areas, browsers, cross-compilers for microprocessor development, macroprocessor capabilities, reverse engineering tools, and others. In fact, the concept of a good "software development environment" (e.g., [BAR84], [BEN89]) that includes both conventional and automated tools has been recognized as a key contributor to successful software engineering.

Maintainability of source code is critically important for all nontrivial software development efforts. Maintenance cannot be accomplished until software is understood. Earlier elements of the software configuration (i.e., design documentation) provide a foundation for understanding, but ultimately source code must be read and modified according to changes in design. Ease of design to code translation is an important element in source code maintainability. In addition, self-documenting characteristics of a language (e.g., allowable length of identifiers, labeling format, data type/structure definition) have a strong influence on maintainability.

16.2.4 Choosing a Language

The choice of a programming language for a specific project must take into account both engineering and psychological characteristics. However, the problem associated with choice may be moot if only one language is available or dictated by a requester. Meek [MEE80, p. 37] suggests a general philosophy when a programming language must be chosen:

> ...the art of choosing a language is to start with the problem, decide what its requirements are, and their relative importance, since it will probably be impossible to satisfy them all equally well (with a single language)...available languages should be measured against a list of requirements....

Among the criteria that are applied during an evaluation of available languages are (1) general application area, (2) algorithmic and computational complexity, (3) environment in which software will execute, (4) performance considerations, (5) data structure complexity, (6) knowledge of software development staff, and (7) availability of a good compiler or cross-compiler. Applications area of a project is a criterion that is applied most often during language selection. As we noted in Chapter 1, a number of major software application areas have evolved and de facto standard languages may be selected for each.

C is often the language of choice for the development of systems software, while languages such as Ada, C, and Modula-2 (along with FORTRAN and assembly language) are encountered in real-time applications. COBOL is the language for business applications, but the increasing use of fourth-generation languages has displaced it from its preeminent position. In the engineering/scientific area, FORTRAN remains the predominant language (although ALGOL, PL/1, PASCAL, and C have wide usage). Embedded software applications make use of the same languages applied in systems and real-time applications. The predominant language for personal computer users remains BASIC, but that language is rarely used by the developers of personal computer software products—more likely choices are PASCAL or C. Artificial intelligence applications make use of languages such as LISP, PROLOG, or OPS5, although other more conventional programming languages are used as well.

The rush toward object-oriented software development across most application domains has spawned many new languages and conventional language dialects. The most widely used object-oriented programming languages are Smalltalk, C++, and Objective-C. But languages such as Eiffel, Object-PASCAL, Flavors and many others are also used by growing numbers of software engineers.

The proliferation of "new and better" programming languages continues. Although many of these languages are attractive, it is sometimes better to choose a "weaker" (old) language that has solid documentation and support software, is familiar to everyone on the software development team, and has been successfully applied in the past. However, new languages should be thoroughly evaluated and the transition from old to new should occur, recognizing the psychological resistance to change that is encountered in all organizations.

16.2.5 Programming Languages and Software Engineering

Regardless of the software engineering paradigm, programming language will have impact on project planning, analysis, design, coding, testing, and maintenance. But the role of a programming language must be kept in perspective. Languages do provide the means for human-to-machine translation; however, the quality of the end result is more closely tied to the software engineering activities that precede and follow coding.

During project planning, a consideration of the technical characteristics of a programming language is rarely undertaken. However, planning for support tools associated with resource definition may require that a specific compiler (and associated software) or programming environment be specified. Cost and schedule estimation may require learning-curve adjustments because of staff inexperience with a language.

Once software requirements have been established,[1] the technical characteristics of candidate programming languages become more important. If complex data structures are required, languages with sophisticated data structure support (e.g., PASCAL and others) would merit careful evaluation. If high-performance, real-time capability is paramount, a language designed for real-time application (e.g., Ada) or memory-speed efficiency (e.g., C) might be specified. If many output reports and heavy file manipulation are specified, languages like COBOL or RPG might fit the bill. Ideally, software requirements should precipitate the selection of a language that best fits the processing to be accomplished. In practice, however, a language is often selected because "it's the only one we have running on our computer!"

The quality of a software design is established in a manner that is independent of programming language characteristics (a notable exception is object-oriented design, Chapter 12). However, language attributes do play a role in the quality of an implemented design and affect (both consciously and unconsciously) the way that design is specified.

In Chapter 10 we discussed a number of qualitative and quantitative measures of good design. The concepts of modularity and module independence were emphasized. Technical characteristics of many programming languages can affect these design concepts during the implementation of the design. To illustrate, consider the following examples:

> *Modularity* is supported by nearly all modern programming languages. COBOL, for example, supports a hierarchy of functions that integrates various levels of procedural abstraction (Chapter 10) with the modularity concept. The hierarchy consists of divisions, sections, paragraphs, sen-

---

[1]It is important to note that the language to be used for implementation can dictate the requirements analysis method that is chosen. For example, the use of an object-oriented language such as C++ might lead an analyst to choose OOA (Chapter 8) as the requirements analysis method. The converse is, of course, also true.

tences, and finally words. Each of these terms has a precise meaning in the language and helps to emphasize a modular implementation.

Module independence can be enhanced or subverted by language characteristics. For example, the Ada *package* supports the concept of information hiding while the use of internal procedures in PL/1 can lead to extensive global data that increase module coupling.

Data design (discussed in Chapters 8 and 10) can also be influenced by language characteristics. Programming languages such as Ada, C++, and Smalltalk support the concept of *abstract data types*—an important tool in data design and specification. Other more common languages, such as PASCAL, allow the definition of user-defined data types and the direct implementation of linked lists and other data structures. These features provide the designer with greater latitude during the preliminary and detail design steps.

In some cases, design requirements can only be satisfied when a language has special characteristics. Per Brinch-Hansen [HAN78] describes a set of language characteristics essential for implementation of a design that specifies distributed processes that are executing concurrently and must communicate and coordinate with one another. Languages such as concurrent PASCAL, Ada, or Modula-2 can be used to satisfy such designs.

The effect of programming language characteristics on the steps that comprise software testing is difficult to assess. Languages that directly support the structured constructs tend to reduce the cyclomatic complexity (Chapter 17) of a program, thereby making it somewhat easier to test. Languages that support the specification of external subprograms and procedures (e.g., FORTRAN) make integration testing much less error-prone. On the other hand, some technical characteristics of a language can impede testing. For example, block structuring in ALGOL can be specified in a manner that causes the loss of intermediate data when exit from a block occurs, thereby making the status of a program more difficult to assess.

Like testing, the effect of programming language characteristics on software maintenance is not fully understood. There is no question, however, that technical characteristics that enhance code readability and reduce complexity are important for effective maintenance. Further discussion of software maintenance is postponed until Chapter 20.

16.3 PROGRAMMING LANGUAGE FUNDAMENTALS

The technical characteristics of programming languages span an enormous number of topics that range from theoretical (e.g., formal language theory and specification) to pragmatic (e.g., functional comparisons of specific languages). In this section, a brief discussion of programming language fundamentals is presented. For more detailed discussions of programming language technology, the reader should reference Pratt [PRA84] or Sebesta [SEB89].

For the purposes of our discussion, programming language fundamentals will be presented within the context of four broad topics: data typing, subprogram mechanisms, control structures, and support for object-oriented approaches. All programming languages can be characterized with respect to these topics and the overall quality of a specific programming language can be judged with regard to the strengths and weakness related to each topic.

16.3.1 Data Types and Data Typing

Today, the merits of a modern programming language are judged by more than the syntax and breadth of its procedural constructs. *Data typing,* and the specific data types supported by a programming language, are an important aspect of language quality.

Pratt [PRA84] describes data types and data typing as "...a class of data objects together with a set of operations for creating and manipulating them." A data object inherits a set of fundamental attributes of the data type to which it belongs. A data object can take on a value that resides within the range of legitimate values for the data type and can be manipulated by operations that apply to the data type.

Simple data types span a wide range that includes *numeric* types (e.g., integer, complex, floating-point numbers), *enumeration* types (e.g., user-defined data types found in PASCAL), *boolean* types (e.g., true or false), and *string* types (e.g., alphanumeric data). More complex data types encompass data structures that run the gamut of simple one-dimensional arrays (vectors) to list structures to complex heterogeneous arrays and records.

The operations that may be performed on a particular data type and the manner in which different types may be manipulated in the same statement is controlled by *type checking* implemented within the programming language compiler or interpreter. Fairley [FAI85] defines five levels of type checking that are commonly encountered in programming languages:

Level 0: typeless
Level 1: automatic type coercion
Level 2: mixed mode
Level 3: pseudostrong type checking
Level 4: strong type checking

Typeless programming languages have no explicit means for data typing and, therefore, do not enforce type checking. Languages[2] such as BASIC, APL, LISP, and even COBOL fall into this category. Although each language does enable the user to define data structures, the representation of data contained within each data object is predefined.

---

[2]References to programming languages in this chapter assume "typical" or ANSI standard implementations. It is entirely possible that other versions of a language may exhibit characteristics that contradict our discussion.

Automatic-type coercion is a type checking mechanism that allows the programmer to mix different data types, but then converts operands of incompatible types, thus allowing requested operations to occur. For example, PL/1 assigns a numeric value of 0 to the boolean value *false* and a numeric value of 1 to the boolean value *true*. Hence arithmetic operations (normally applied to numeric data types) can be applied to boolean data types in PL/1.

Mixed mode-type conversion is similar in many respects to automatic-type coercion. Different data types within the same type category (e.g., two different numeric types) are converted to a single target type so that a specified operation can occur. FORTRAN's mixed-mode arithmetic (a feature that is best avoided) enables integer and real numbers to be used in a single programming language statement.

Strong-type checking occurs in programming languages that will only permit operations to be performed on data objects that are of the same prespecified data type. Operators, operands, and subprogram (module) interfaces are checked for type compatibility at compile time, at load time, and at run time. Ada compilers perform strong-type checking.

Pseudostrong-type checking has all of the characteristics of strong-type checking but is implemented in a manner that provides one or more loopholes [FAI85]. For example, although PASCAL checks interface compatibility within a single compiled program, it does not do so for separately compiled procedures (modules)—hence, there is a loophole in the enforcement of strong-type checking.

16.3.2 Subprograms

A *subprogram* is a separately compilable program component that contains a data and control structure. Throughout this book, we have referred to a *module* as a generic manifestation of a subprogram. Depending on the programming language, a subprogram may be called a subroutine, a procedure, a function, or any of a number of specialized names. Regardless of its name, the subprogram exhibits a set of generic characteristics: (1) a specification section that includes its name and interface description; (2) an implementation section that includes data and control structure; (3) an *activation mechanism* that enables the subprogram to be invoked from elsewhere in the program.

In conventional programming languages, each subprogram is an entity in itself, operating on data in a manner that is dictated by a larger program's control structure. In object-oriented programming languages, the classic view of the subprogram is replaced with the *object*.

16.3.3 Control Structures

At a fundamental level, all modern programming languages enable the programmer to represent sequence, condition, and repetition—the structured programming logical constructs. Most modern languages provide a syntax for direct specification of *if-then-else, do-while,* and *repeat-until* (as well as *case*). Other languages, such as LISP and APL, require the programmer to emulate the constructs within the syntax bounds of the language.

In addition to the basic procedural constructs of structured programming, other control structures may be present. *Recursion* creates a second activation of a subprogram during the first activation. That is, the subprogram invokes or activates itself as part of the defined procedure. *Concurrency* provides support for the creation of multiple tasks, the synchronization of tasks, and general communication between tasks. This language feature is invaluable when real-time or systems applications are undertaken. *Exception handling* is a programming language feature that traps user-defined or system error conditions and passes control to an exception handler for processing.

16.3.4 Support for Object-Oriented Approaches

In theory, the creation of objects and the construction of object-oriented software can be accomplished using any conventional programming language (e.g., C or PASCAL). But in practice, support for object-oriented approaches should be built directly into the programming language that will be used to implement an object-oriented design.

The fundamental concepts that underlie object-oriented programming were presented in Chapters 8 and 12. In addition to the features discussed in Sections 16.3.1 through 16.3.3, an object-oriented programming language should provide direct support for class definitions, inheritance, encapsulation, and messaging. In addition to these basic object-oriented constructs, many object-oriented languages implement additional features, such as multiple inheritance and polymorphism (different objects can receive messages with the same name).

The definition of classes is basic to an object-oriented approach. An object-oriented programming language defines a class name and specifies the private and public components of the class. To illustrate the general form of the object-oriented constructs, we use C++. A class, called **counter**, can be defined in the following manner [WEI88]:

```
class counter
{
   private:
      unsigned int value;
   public:
      counter ( );
      void increment ( );
      void decrement ( );
      unsigned int access_value ( );
};
```

A new class can be derived from the basic class definition in the following manner:

```
class special_counter : public counter
{
   a copy of the private data of counter
   private:
      data private to special_counter
      ...
};
```

Objects derived from the class special_counter can use all methods defined for the "parent class" counter. The definition of a class encapsulates data abstractions and the program components (methods) that operate on them. In C++, messages are sent to an object (an instantiation of a class) using the form

```
object_name.message (arguments);
```

where object_name identifies the object and message (arguments) describes the message to be sent to it.

The implementation details and the terminology for class definitions, inheritance, encapsulation, and messaging will vary from language to language. For example, the Smalltalk programming language [PIN88] defines a class using the following form:

- *Definition*—identifies the class
- *Private data*—attributes whose values are private to individual instances of the class
- *Shared data*—attributes whose values are shared by all instances of the class
- *Pool data*—attributes whose values are shared across multiple classes
- *Instance methods*—the procedures that implement messages that can be sent to an instance of a class
- *Class methods*—the procedures that implement messages that can be sent to a class (e.g., initialize shared data)

Although these terms differ from the C++ definition, the fundamental concept of the class remains unchanged. Similarly, inheritance, encapsulation, and messaging are implemented with a different syntax, but the same fundamental semantics. Each construct will be available in any language that is truly object-oriented.

16.4 LANGUAGE CLASSES

There are hundreds of programming languages that have been applied at one time or another to serious software development efforts. Even a detailed discussion of the five most common languages is beyond the scope of this book. The reader is referred to Pratt [PRA84] and Sebesta [SEB89] for thorough surveys and comparisons of the most common programming languages. In this section, four generations of programming languages are described and representative languages from each generation are discussed.

Any categorization of programming languages is open to debate. In many cases, one language might legitimately reside in more than one category. For the purposes of this book, we develop a set of language generations that correspond roughly to the historical evolution of programming languages. Figure 16.1 illustrates this categorization.

16.4.1 First-Generation Languages

The first language generation harkens back to the days of machine-level coding. Yet, some work with first-generation languages continues to this date. Machine code and its more human-readable equivalent—assembler language—represent the first language generation. These machine-dependent languages exhibit the lowest level of abstraction with which a program can be represented.

There are as many assembler languages as there are processor architectures with custom instruction sets. From a software engineering viewpoint,

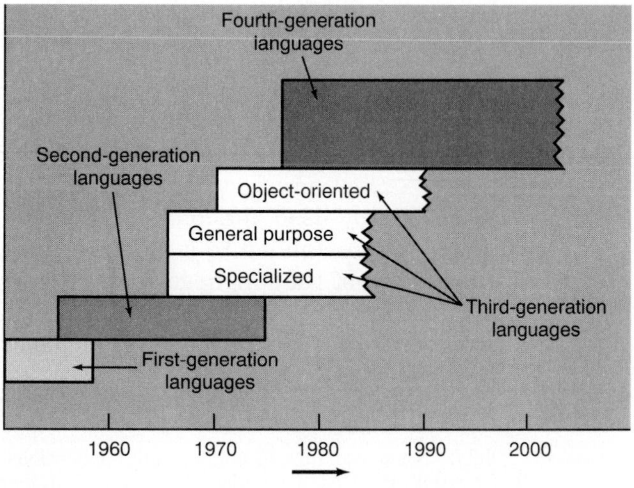

FIGURE 16.1. Programming language generations.

such languages should be used only when a high-order language cannot meet requirements or is not supported.

16.4.2 Second-Generation Languages

Second-generation languages were developed in the late 1950s and early 1960s and serve as the foundation for all modern (third-generation) programming languages. Second-generation languages are characterized by broad usage, enormous software libraries, and the widest familiarity and acceptance. There is little debate that FORTRAN, COBOL, ALGOL, and (to some extent) BASIC are foundation languages by virtue of their maturity and acceptance.

FORTRAN has withstood 30 years of criticism to remain the premier programming language in engineering/scientific work.[3] The original standardized version of FORTRAN (called "FORTRAN-66") provided a powerful tool for computational problem solving, but lacked direct support of the structured constructs, had poor data typing, could not easily support string handling, and had many other deficiencies. The newer ANSI standard (called "FORTRAN-77") and the forthcoming standard correct some of the deficiencies found in earlier versions of the language. In many cases FORTRAN has been force-fit into application areas for which it was never designed and much of the criticism of the language has been somewhat unfair. For number crunching applications, FORTRAN remains the language of choice, but for system, real-time, or embedded product software applications, other languages provide compelling advantages.

COBOL, like FORTRAN, has reached maturity and is the accepted "standard" language for commercial data processing applications. Although the language is sometimes criticized for a lack of compactness, it has excellent data definition capabilities, is largely self-documenting, and provides support for a wide range of procedural techniques relevant to business data processing.

ALGOL is the forerunner of many third-generation languages and offers an extremely rich repertoire of procedural and data typing constructs. ALGOL has been used extensively in Europe, but has found little support (with the exception of academic environments) in the United States. The most commonly used version of the language, correctly termed "ALGOL-60," has been extended to a more powerful implementation, ALGOL-68. Both versions of the language support the notion of block structuring, dynamic storage allocation, recursion, and other characteristics that have had a strong influence on the modern languages that have followed.

---

[3]FORTRAN's dominance in engineering applications is starting to wain. Ada, C, and, to a lesser extent, PASCAL are replacing FORTRAN in many application domains. However, FORTRAN will be used widely well into the twenty-first century.

BASIC is a language that was originally designed to teach programming in a time-sharing mode. The language was moving toward obsolescence in the early 1970s, but has experienced a rebirth with the advent of personal computer systems. There are hundreds of versions of BASIC, making it difficult to discuss the benefits and deficiencies of the language.

16.4.3 Third-Generation Languages

Third-generation languages (also called *modern* or *structured programming languages*) are characterized by strong procedural and data structuring capabilities. The languages in this class can be divided into three broad categories, *general-purpose high-order languages, object-oriented high-order languages,* and *specialized languages*. All general-purpose and object-oriented high-order languages exhibit the technical characteristics discussed in Section 16.3. Specialized languages, on the other hand, have been designed to satisfy special requirements and have a syntax and form that are often unique.

General-Purpose High-Order Languages The earliest general-purpose high-order language (also a foundation language), ALGOL, served as a model for other languages in this category. Its descendents, PL/1, PASCAL, Modula-2, C, and Ada are being adopted as languages with the potential for broad spectrum applications (i.e., for use in engineering/scientific, embedded products, commercial, and/or systems application areas).

PL/1 might more properly be categorized as a 2.5-generation language. It was the first true broad-spectrum language, developed with a wide range of features that enable it to be used in many different application areas. PL/1 provides support for conventional engineering/scientific and business applications while at the same time enabling specification of sophisticated data structures, multitasking, complex I/O, list processing, and many other features. Subsets of the language have been developed to teach programming (PL/C), for use in microprocessor applications (PL/M), and for systems programming (PL/S).

PASCAL is a modern programming language that was developed in the early 1970s as a language for teaching modern techniques (e.g., structured programming) in software development. Since its introduction, PASCAL has found growing support from a broad audience of software developers and is used widely for engineering/scientific applications and systems programming (the language has been called "the FORTRAN of the 1980s"). PASCAL is a direct descendent of ALGOL and contains many of the same features: block structuring, strong data typing, direct support for recursion, and other complementary features. It has been implemented on computers of all sizes.

Modula-2 is an evolutionary outgrowth of PASCAL and (some would say) a possible alternative to the Ada programming language. Modula-2 couples direct implementation of design features such as information hiding, abstraction, and strong data typing with control structures to support recursion and concurrency. To date, the use of Modula-2 for industry applications has been limited.

The C programming language was originally developed as a language for operating system implementers. The UNIX operating system is implemented in C. Today, however, a vast array of software products, embedded applications, and systems software has been built using the C language. C was developed for the sophisticated software engineer and contains powerful features that give it considerable flexibility. These same features can also create problems. Cox [COX85] provides a poetic description of the language:

> One of my favorite hobbies is green wood working. A project begins not in the lumber yard with Kiln dried wood, but in the forest. A straight-grained oak tree is cut down, and worked into rustic furniture with an awe-inspiring assortment of antique tools. . . .
>
> The tools of this hobby have a lot in common with the tools I use as a programmer. For example, the adze is a heavy blade on a four foot handle (like a hoe). It is a specialized tool, whose primary function is smoothing the rough surfaces of a split log. It is swung double-handed, standing astraddle the work. The razor sharp blade removes six-inch slabs of solid oak with a single blow, scant inches from unprotected feet and legs!
>
> I love that adze the way I love the C language. It is not a tool for fools and children. But in the hands of a skilled craftsman, it is capable of powerful, yet delicate work. Its potential for grave harm is so obvious that the danger provides the only safety mechanism; a healthy respect for what careless use can do!

Like other languages in this category, C supports sophisticated data structures and has reasonable typing characteristics, makes extensive use of pointers, and has a rich set of operators for computation and data manipulation. In addition, it enables the programmer to "get close to the machine" by providing assembly language-like features.

Ada was originally developed as a new standard language for embedded real-time computer systems to be developed for the U.S. Department of Defense. Today, the language is used widely in both defense and nondefense applications. Pascal-like in structure and notation (but far more powerful and complex), Ada supports a rich set of features that include multitasking, interrupt handling, intertask synchronization, and communication as well as a set of unique features such as the Ada *package*. Ada has created and continues to generate much controversy. Adherents praise its rich language structure and the focus on the Ada environment for software engineering rather than language-related esoterica. Opponents worry about the complexity of the language, the current inefficiency of operational compilers, and the long learning curve. It appears, however, that the benefits of the language will win out and that Ada may well dominate some application domains during the 1990s.

Object-Oriented Languages Object-oriented programming languages enable a software engineer to implement analysis and design models created using OOA and OOD (Chapters 8 and 12). These languages have characteristics described in Section 16.4.3.

Although dozens of object-oriented languages have been introduced over the past decade, only a few have gained any significant foothold in the marketplace: dialects of C (e.g., C++, Objective-C), Smalltalk, and Eiffel. Smalltalk, a "foundation" object-oriented language, was originally developed in the early 1970s to explore object-oriented concepts. Today, versions of Smalltalk are available on computers of all types, although the use of the language for the development of products and industry quality systems is limited. Object-oriented dialects of C have gained widespread use throughout the UNIX community and with many first-time developers of object-oriented systems. Building on the strengths of C, object-oriented dialects enable a smooth transition from this widely used, general-purpose, high-order language. Eiffel [MEY88] is one of a number of "new" object-oriented languages that are robust enough for industry application. Like C dialects and Smalltalk, Eiffel provides direct support for class definitions, inheritance, encapsulation, and messaging.

Specialized Languages Specialized languages are characterized by unusual syntactic forms that have been especially designed for a distinct application. Hundreds of specialized languages are in use today. In general, such languages have a much smaller user base than general-purpose languages. Among the languages that have found application within the software engineering community are LISP, PROLOG, APL, and FORTH.

LISP is a language that is especially suited to symbol manipulation and the list processing encountered in combinatorial problems. Used almost exclusively by the artificial intelligence community, the language is particularly well suited to theorem proving, tree searches, and other problem-solving activities. Subprograms are implemented as functions that make heavy use of recursion. Because each LISP function is a standalone entity, reusability can be achieved by creating libraries of primitive functions. In recent years, LISP has been used to develop a wide array of expert systems and expert system "compilers." LISP makes it relatively easy to specify facts, rules, and the corresponding inferences (implemented as LISP functions) that are required for knowledge-based systems.

PROLOG is another programming language that has found widespread use in the construction of expert systems. Like LISP, PROLOG provides features that support knowledge representation. Within the language, a uniform data structure, called the *term,* is used to construct all data and all programs. Each program consists of a set of clauses that represent facts, rules, and inferences. Both LISP and PROLOG are especially amenable to problems that treat objects and their relationships. For this reason, some people refer to LISP and PROLOG as object-oriented languages. In addition, the object-oriented nature of LISP and PROLOG enables each to be applied within the context of the prototyping paradigm for software engineering.

APL is an extremely concise and powerful language for array and vector manipulation. The language contains little support for structured constructs or data typing. APL does provide a rich set of computational operators and has gained a small but avid following for mathematical problem solving.

FORTH is a language designed for microprocessor software development. The language supports the definition of user-defined functions [implemented with post-fix (reverse-Polish) notation] that are executed in a stack-oriented manner for speed and memory efficiency.

From a software engineering standpoint, specialized languages provide both advantages and disadvantages. Because a specialized language has been designed to address a specific application, the translation of requirements to design to code implementation can be facilitated. On the other hand, most specialized languages are far less portable and often less maintainable than general-purpose languages.

16.4.4 Fourth-Generation Languages

Throughout the history of software development, we have attempted to generate computer programs at higher and higher levels of abstraction. First-generation programming languages worked at the machine instruction set level, the lowest possible level of abstraction. Second- and third-generation programming languages have raised the level at which we represent computer programs, but distinct and completely detailed algorithmic procedures still have to be specified. Over the past decade, *fourth-generation languages* (4GLs) have raised the level of abstraction still higher.

Fourth-generation languages, like all artificial languages, contain a distinct syntax for control and data structure representation. A 4GL, however, represents these structures at a higher level of abstraction by eliminating the need to specify algorithmic detail. For example, the statement:

COMPUTE NET-PRESENT-VALUE AND RETURN-ON-INVESTMENT FOR EXPENDITURES #5 AND #9.

is typical of a 4GL statement. The 4GL system "knows" how to compute the desired financial data and does so without requiring the software developer to specify the appropriate algorithms. It should be apparent that the "knowledge" described above is *domain-specific*. That is, the same 4GL would undoubtedly choke on:

COMPUTE THE ROOTS OF TRANSCENDENTAL EQUATION #3 AND APPLY THEM TO THE PHYSICAL MODEL.

although another 4GL, designed specifically for the application domain implied above, might do the job nicely.

Fourth-generation languages combine *procedural* and *nonprocedural* characteristics. That is, the language enables the user to specify conditions and corresponding actions (the procedural component) while at the same time encouraging the user to indicate the desired outcome (the nonprocedural component) and then applying its domain-specific knowledge to fill in the procedural details.

Martin ([MAR85], [MAR86]) presents a comprehensive discussion of 4GLs and develops the following broad categories.

Query Languages To date, the vast majority of 4GLs have been developed for use in conjunction with database applications. Such query languages enable the user to manipulate information contained in a pre-existing database in a sophisticated manner. Some query languages require a complex syntax that is no simpler (and in some cases, worse) than a third-generation language. For example [MAR85]:

```
list by region (87.act.sep.sales)
sum (87.est.sep.sales), (sum (sum (87.act.sep.sales)
```

However, other query languages available today offer a natural language interface that allows the user to state [INT86]:

For the eastern and western regions, how did actual sales for last
month compare with forecasts?

Needless to say, the second approach would be favored by most users.

Program Generators Program generators represent another, somewhat more sophisticated, class of 4GLs. Rather than relying on a predefined database as its point of focus, a program generator enables the user to create complete third-generation language programs using (many claim) an order-of-magnitude fewer statements. These *very-high-level programming languages* make heavy use of procedural and data abstractions (Chapter 10). Unfortunately for those working in the engineered products and systems domain, most program generators available today focus exclusively on business information systems applications and generate programs in COBOL. However, a new generation of CASE tools enables a software engineer to model an engineering application graphically and then generate C or Ada source code from the graphical model.

Other 4GLS Although query languages and application generators are the most common 4GLs, other categories exist. *Decision support languages* enable "nonprogrammers" to perform a variety of *what-if* analyses that range from simple two-dimensional spreadsheet models to sophisticated statistical or operations research modeling systems. *Prototyping languages* have been developed to assist in creating prototypes by facilitating the creation of user interfaces and dialogs and providing a means for data modeling. *Formal specification languages* (discussed in Chapter 9) can be considered to be

4GLs when such languages produce machine-executable software. Finally, tools used in a personal computer environment (e.g., spreadsheets, database systems, Macintosh Hypercard) enable the user to "program" at a higher level of abstraction than previously available.

16.5 CODING STYLE

After source code is generated, the function of a module should be apparent without reference to a design specification. In other words, code must be understandable. Coding style encompasses a coding philosophy that stresses simplicity and clarity. In their landmark text on the subject, Kernighan and Plauger [KER78, p. 9] state:

> Writing a computer program eventually boils down to writing a sequence of statements in the language at hand. How each of those statements is expressed determines in large measure the intelligibility of the whole....

The elements of style include internal (source code level) documentation, methods for data declaration, an approach to statement construction, and techniques for I/O. In the sections that follow, we consider each of these topics.

16.5.1 Code Documentation

Internal documentation of source code begins with the selection of identifier (variables and labels) names, continues with the placement and composition of commenting, and concludes with the visual organization of the program.

The selection of meaningful identifier names is crucial to understanding. Languages that limit variable names or labels to only a few characters inherently obscure meaning. Consider the following three statements:

```
D=V*T
DIST= HORVEL*TIME
DISTANCE= HORIZONTAL.VELOCITY * TIME.TRAVELED.IN.SECS;
```

The BASIC language expression is undeniably concise, but the meaning of D = V*T is unclear unless the reader has prior information. The FORTRAN expression provides more information, but the meaning of DIST and HORVEL could be misinterpreted. The ALGOL statement leaves little doubt regarding the meaning of the calculation. These statements illustrate the way in which identifiers may be chosen to help document code.

It can be argued that "wordy" expressions (like the ALGOL statement above) obscure logical flow and make modification difficult. Obviously, common sense must be applied when identifiers are selected. Unnecessarily long identifiers do indeed provide a potential for error (not to mention a backache from sitting long hours typing at a workstation). Studies [SHN80] indicate, however, that even for small programs meaningful identifiers improve comprehension. In terms of the syntactic/semantic model discussed in Section 16.2.2, meaningful names "simplify the conversion from program syntax to internal semantic structure" [SHN80].

The ability to express natural language comments as part of a source code listing is provided by all general-purpose programming languages. However, certain questions arise:

- How many comments are "enough"?
- Where should the comments be placed?
- Do comments obscure logic flow?
- Can comments mislead the reader?
- Are comments "unmaintainable," and therefore unreliable?

There are few definitive answers to the above questions. But one thing is clear: *Software must contain internal documentation.* Comments provide the developer with one means of communicating with other readers of the source code. Comments can provide a clear guide to understanding during the last phase of software engineering—maintenance.

There are many guidelines that have been proposed for commenting. Prologue comments and functional comments are two categories that require somewhat different approaches. *Prologue comments* should appear at the beginning of every module. The format for such comments is:

1. A statement of purpose that indicates the function of the module
2. An interface description that includes
  a. a sample "calling sequence"
  b. a description of all arguments
  c. a list of all subordinate modules
3. A discussion of pertinent data such as important variables and their use restrictions and limitations, and other important information
4. A development history that includes
  a. the name of the module designer (author)
  b. the name of the reviewer (auditor) and date
  c. modification dates and description

An example of prologue comments is given in Figure 16.2.

Descriptive comments are embedded within the body of source code and are used to describe processing functions. A primary guideline for such commenting is expressed by VanTassel [VAN78]: "comments should provide

```
TITLE:          SUBROUTINE NGON

PURPOSE:        THE PURPOSE OF TO CONTROL THE DRAWING OF NGONS.

SAMPLE CALL:    CALL NGON (KNOW, IX, IY, KN)

INPUTS:              KROW      = IS THE LINE ON THE TABLE WHERE THE
                                 NEXT LINE OF OUTPUT WILL BE PRINTED.
                     IX        = X-COORDINATE OF THE LEFT END OF THE
                                 BOTTOM SEGMENT
                     IY        = Y-COORDINATE OF THE LEFT END OF THE
                                 BOTTOM SEGMENT
                     KN        = IS THE NUMBER OF THE LAST NGON

OUTPUTS:             KROW      = IS THE INCREMENTED ROW COUNTER
                     KN        = IS THE INCREMENTED NGON COUNTER

SUBROUTINES REFERENCED:        1.) DBNGON
                               2.) ALPHA
                               3.) ROWCOL

PERTINENT DATA:

      KROW IS CHECKED TO SEE IF THE TABLE IS FULL.
      IF IT IS THEN REPNT IS CALLED TO REFRESH THE SCREEN
      AND PUT UP A NEW TABLET. THENGON COUNTER (KN) IS
      INCREMENTED AND THE POINTER ARRAY PO IS WRITTEN
      TO THE DISPLAY FILE.

      A PROMPT IS THEN ISSUED FOR THE NUMBER OF
      SIDES AND THE ORIENTATION OF THE NGON WITH
      RESPECT TO THE X-AXIS. THE ARRAY 'NG' IS LOADED
      AND WRITTEN TO THE OBJECT FILE.

      THEN ROUTINE DBNGON DOES THE ACTUAL DRAWING.
      IT REQUIRES THE NUMBER OF SIDES, THE LENGTH OF A
      SIDE, THE ORIENTATION, AND THE COORDINATES OF THE
      STARTING POINT AND IPEN.

AUTHOR:     M. WRIGHT
AUDITOR:    D. CURRIE
DATE:       2/15/90
MODIFICATIONS:
      11/29/90  D.C.
      CHANGES MADE TO ALLOW TABLES TO BE BUILT FOR REPNT.
      1/7/91  R.P.S.
      ADD ERROR CHECKING COMMON 'SPECIAL' AND ERROR HANDLING.
```

FIGURE 16.2. Code documentation.

something extra, not just paraphrase the code." In addition, descriptive comments should

- Describe blocks of code, rather than commenting every line.
- Use blank lines or indentation so that comments can be readily distinguished from code.
- Be correct; an incorrect or misleading comment is worse than no comment at all.

With proper identifier mnemonics and good commenting, adequate internal documentation is assured.

When a detailed procedural design is represented using a program design language (Chapter 10), design documentation can be embedded directly into the source listing as comment statements. This technique is particularly useful when implementation is to be done in assembler language and helps to ensure that both code and design will be maintained when changes are made to either.

The form of the source code as it appears on the listing is an important contributor to readability. Source code indentation indicates logical constructs and blocks of code by indenting from the left margin so that these attributes are visually offset. Like commenting, the best approach to indentation is open to debate. Manual indentation can become complicated as code modification occurs, and experiments [SHN80] indicate that only a marginal improvement in understanding accrues. Probably the best approach is to use an automatic code formatter (a CASE tool) that will properly indent source code. By eliminating the burden of indentation from the coder, form may be improved with relatively little effort.

16.5.2 Data Declaration

The complexity and organization of data structure are defined during the design step. The style of data declaration is established when code is generated. A number of relatively simple guidelines can be established to make data more understandable and maintenance simpler.

The order of data declarations should be standardized even if the programming language has no mandatory requirements. For example, declaration ordering for a FORTRAN module might be:

1. All explicit declarations (for high quality, all variables should be declared)

   INTEGER, REAL, DOUBLE PRECISION, . . .

2. All global data blocks

   COMMON/block-name/. . .

3. All local arrays

   DIMENSION array names and dimensions

4. All file declarations

   DEFINE FILE, OPEN, CLOSE

Ordering makes attributes easier to find, expediting testing, debugging, and maintenance.

When multiple variable names are declared with a single statement, an alphabetical ordering of names is worthwhile. Similarly, labeled global data (e.g., FORTRAN common blocks) should be ordered alphabetically.

If a complex data structure is prescribed by design, commenting should be used to explain peculiarities inherent in a programming language implementation. For example, a linked list data structure in C or a user-defined data type in PASCAL might require supplementary documentation contained in comments.

16.5.3 Statement Construction

The construction of software logical flow is established during design. The construction of individual statements, however, is part of the coding step. Statement construction should abide by one overriding rule: Each statement should be simple and direct; code should not be convoluted to effect efficiency.

Many programming languages allow multiple statements per line. The space saving aspects of this feature are hardly justified by the poor readability that results. Consider the following two code segments:

```
DO I = 1 TO N-1; T = I; DO J = I + 1 TO N; F A(J) < A(T) THEN DO T=J;
END;
IF T <> I THEN DO H=A(T); A(T)=A(I); A(I)=T; END; END;
```

The loop structure and conditional operations contained in the above segment are masked by the multistatement-per-line construction. Reorganizing the form of the code:

```
DO I = 1 TO N-1;
    T = I;
    DO J = I+1 TO N;
        IF A(J) < A(T) THEN DO
            T=J;
        END;
    IF T <> I THEN DO
        H=A(T);
        A(T)=A(I);
        A(I)=T;
        END;
    END;
```

Here, simple statement construction and indentation illuminates the logical and functional characteristics of the segment. Individual source code statements can be simplified by

- Avoiding the use of complicated conditional tests
- Eliminating tests on negative conditions
- Avoiding heavy nesting of loops or conditions
- Using parentheses to clarify logical or arithmetic expressions
- Using spacing and/or readability symbols to clarify statement content
- Using only ANSI standard features
- Thinking: Could I understand this if I was not the person who coded it?

Each of the above guidelines strives to "keep it simple."

16.5.4 Input/Output

The style of input and output is established during software requirements analysis and design, not coding. However, the manner in which I/O is implemented can be the determining characteristic for system acceptance by a user community. Input and output style will vary with the degree of human interaction. For batch-oriented I/O, logical input organization, meaningful input/output error checking, good I/O error recovery, and rational output report formats are desirable characteristics. For interactive I/O, a simple, guided input scheme, extensive error checking and recovery, human-engineered output, and consistency of I/O format become primary concerns.[4]

Regardless of the batch or interactive nature of software, a number of I/O style guidelines should be considered during design and coding:

- Validate all input data.
- Check the plausibility of important combinations of input items.
- Keep the input format simple.
- Use end-of-data indicators, rather than requiring a user to specify "number-of-items."
- Label interactive input requests, specifying available choices or bounding values.
- Keep the input format uniform when a programming language has stringent formatting requirements.
- Label all output and design all reports.

The style of I/O is affected by many other characteristics such as I/O devices (e.g., terminal or workstation type, computer graphics device, mouse, etc.), user sophistication, and communication environment.

---

[4]See Chapter 14 for additional guidelines on the design of human-computer interfaces.

16.6 EFFICIENCY

In well-engineered systems, there is a natural tendency to use critical resources efficiently. Processor cycles and memory locations are often viewed as critical resources, and the coding step is seen as the last point where microseconds or bits can be squeezed out of the software. Although efficiency is a commendable goal, three maxims should be stated before we discuss the topic further. First, efficiency is a *performance requirement* and should, therefore, be established during software requirements analysis. Software should be as efficient as is required, not as efficient as is humanly possible. Second, efficiency is improved with good design. Third, code efficiency and code simplicity go hand in hand. In general, don't sacrifice clarity, readability, or correctness for nonessential improvements in efficiency.

16.6.1 Code Efficiency

The efficiency of source code is directly tied to the efficiency of algorithms defined during detail design. However, coding style can have an effect on execution speed and memory requirement. The following set of guidelines can always be applied when detail design is translated into code:

- Simplify arithmetic and logical expressions before committing to code.
- Carefully evaluate nested loops to determine if statements or expressions can be moved outside.
- When possible, avoid the use of multi-dimensional arrays.
- When possible, avoid the use of pointers and complex lists.
- Use "fast" arithmetic operations.
- Don't mix data types, even if the language allows it.
- Use integer arithmetic and boolean expressions, whenever possible.

Many compilers have optimizing features that automatically generate efficient code by collapsing repetitive expressions, performing loop evaluation, using fast arithmetic, and applying other efficiency-related algorithms. For applications in which efficiency is paramount, such compilers are an indispensable coding tool.

16.6.2 Memory Efficiency

Memory restrictions in the large machine ("mainframe") and workstation world are largely a thing of the past. Low-cost memory provides a large physical address space and virtual memory management provides application software with an enormous logical address space. Memory efficiency for such environments cannot be equated to minimum memory used. Rather, memory efficiency must take into account the "paging" characteristics of an operating system. In general, code locality or maintenance of functional domain via the structured constructs is an excellent method for reducing paging and thereby increasing efficiency.

Memory restrictions in the embedded microprocessor world are a very real concern, although low-cost, high-density memory is evolving rapidly. If minimal memory is demanded by system requirements (e.g., a high-volume, low-cost product), high-order language compilers must be carefully evaluated for memory compression feature, or, as a last resort, assembler language may have to be used.

Unlike many other system characteristics that must be traded against one another, techniques for execution time efficiency can sometimes lead to memory efficiency. For example, limiting the use of three- or four-dimensional arrays results in simple element access algorithms that are fast and short. Again, the key to memory efficiency is "keep it simple."

16.6.3 Input/Output Efficiency

Two classes of I/O should be considered when efficiency is discussed: I/O directed at a human or I/O directed to another device (e.g., a disk or another computer). Input supplied by a user and output produced for a user are efficient when the information can be supplied or understood with an economy of intellectual effort.

Efficiency of I/O to other hardware is an extremely complicated topic and is beyond the scope of this book. From the coding (and detail design) standpoint, however, a few simple guidelines that improve I/O efficiency can be stated:

- The number of I/O requests should be minimized.
- All I/O should be buffered to reduce communication overhead.
- For secondary memory (e.g., disk), the simplest acceptable access method should be selected and used.
- I/O to secondary memory devices should be blocked.
- I/O to terminals and printers should recognize features of the device that could improve quality or speed.
- Remember that "superefficient" I/O is worthless if it can't be understood.

As we noted earlier in this chapter, I/O design establishes style and ultimately dictates efficiency. The guidelines presented above are applicable to both design and coding steps of the software engineering process.

16.7 SUMMARY

The coding step of software engineering is a process of translation. Detail design is translated into a programming language that is ultimately (and automatically) transformed into machine-executable instructions. Psychological and technical characteristics of a programming language affect the ease of translation from design and the effort required to test and maintain software. These characteristics may be applied to programming languages that fall into one of four language generations.

Style is an important attribute of source code and can determine the intelligibility of a program. The elements of style include internal documentation, methods for data declaration, procedures for statement construction, and I/O coding techniques. In all cases, simplicity and clarity are key characteristics. An offshoot of coding style is the execution time and/or memory efficiency that are achieved. Although efficiency can be an extremely important requirement, we should remember that an "efficient" program that is unintelligible has questionable value.

Coding lies at the kernel of the software engineering process. Critically important steps have preceded coding, relegating it to a somewhat mechanistic translation of a detail design specification. Equally important steps follow coding, and it is a discussion of these steps and related topics that constitute the next part of this book.

REFERENCES

[BAR84] Barstow, D. R., H. E. Shobe, and E. Sandewall, *Interactive Programming Environments,* McGraw-Hill, 1984.

[BEN89] Bennett, K. H., *Software Engineering Environments,* Halsted Press (Wiley), 1989.

[COX85] Cox, B., *Software ICs and Objective C,* Productivity Products International (now StepStone, Inc.), 1985.

[FAI85] Fairley, R. E., *Software Engineering Concepts,* McGraw-Hill, 1985.

[HAN78] Brinch-Hansen, P., "Distributed Processes: A Concurrent Programming Concept," *CACM,* vol. 21, no. 11, November 1978.

[INT86] *Intellect System Documentation,* Artificial Intelligence Corporation, Waltham, MA, 1986.

[JEN74] Jensen, K., and N. Wirth, *Pascal User Manual and Report,* Springer-Verlag, 1974.

[KER78] Kernighan, B., and P. Plauger, *The Elements of Programming Style,* 2d ed., McGraw-Hill, 1978.

[KLA80] Klatzky, R., *Human Memory,* 2d ed., W. H. Freeman and Co., 1980.

[LED81] Ledgard, H., and M. Marcotty, *The Programming Language Landscape,* SRA, 1981.

[MEE80] Meek, B., and P. Heath (eds.), *Guide to Good Programming,* Halsted Press (Wiley), 1980.

[MAR85] Martin, J., *Fourth Generation Languages,* volume 1, Prentice-Hall, 1985.

[MAR86] Martin, J., and J. Leben, *Fourth Generation Languages,* volume 2, Prentice-Hall, 1986.

[MEY88] Meyer, B., *Object-Oriented Software Construction,* Prentice-Hall, 1988.

[PIN88] Pinson, L. J., and R. S. Weiner, *An Introduction to Object-Oriented Programming and Smalltalk,* Addison-Wesley, 1988.

[PRA84] Pratt, T., *Programming Languages,* 2d ed., Prentice-Hall, 1984.

[SEB89] Sebesta, R.W., *Concepts of Programming Languages,* Addison-Wesley, 1989.

[SHE81] Shepard, S., E. Kruesi, and B. Curtis, "The Effects of Symbology and Spatial Arrangement on the Comprehension of Software Specifications," *Proc. 5th Intl. Conf. Software Engineering,* IEEE, San Diego, March 1981, pp. 207–214.

[SHN80] Shneiderman, B., *Software Psychology,* Winthrop Publishers, 1980.

[VAN78] VanTassel, D., *Program Style, Design, Efficiency, Debugging and Testing,* 2d ed., Prentice-Hall, 1978.

[WEI71] Weinberg, G., *The Psychology of Computer Programming,* Van Nostrand, 1971.

[WEI88] Weiner, R. S., and L. J. Pinson, *An Introduction to Object-Oriented Programming and C++,* Addison-Wesley, 1988.

PROBLEMS AND POINTS TO PONDER

16.1 Do some research on natural language processing (a book by Harris entitled *Natural Language* is a good starting point) and write a position paper on the probability of natural language programming.

16.2 Much of the work in software psychology has centered on the characteristics of programming languages and their effects on the coding task. Write a paper that presents some of the more current work in this area.

16.3 Select one or more programming languages and provide examples of each of the psychological characteristics (e.g., uniformity, ambiguity, etc.) discussed in Section 16.2.

16.4 Select the one programming language that you feel best satisfies the software engineering traits that are discussed in Section 16.2.3. Would your choice change if the technical characteristics of the language were also considered?

16.5 Select one of the third-generation languages discussed in Section 16.4.3. Prepare a brief summary of important language characteristics and write a small program that illustrates the language syntax.

16.6 Select any specialized language and prepare a summary of its important characteristics and special features. Write a small program that illustrates its language syntax.

16.7 Select any object-oriented language and prepare a summary of its important characteristics and special features. Write a small program that illustrates its language syntax.

16.8 Select any fourth-generation language (see [MAR85]) and prepare a summary of its important characteristics and special features. Write a small "program" that illustrates its language syntax.

16.9 Expert systems applications are one of a number of specialized application areas. Research the LISP and PROLOG languages and summarize their strengths and weaknesses in this application area. How are the languages similar? How do they differ?

16.10 Ada is a programming language with a wide variety of features. How is Ada different from programming languages such as PASCAL or C? In providing your answer, focus on the three fundamental characteristics discussed in Section 16.3.

16.11 Ada has been the source of much controversy over the last few years. Summarize the arguments (pro and con) that have been presented in the literature.

16.12 List by priority those style guidelines that you feel are most important. Justify your selection. Are these guidelines language-dependent, i.e., do some languages obviate the need for a particular guideline?

16.13 through 16.21 Code and attempt to implement the procedural designs for the correspondingly numbered problems in Chapter 10. You may use the programming language of your choice, but remember the style and clarity guidelines discussed in this chapter.

FURTHER READINGS

Programming languages are fundamental to an understanding of computer science and should be understood individually and in relationship to one another. Books by Sebesta [SEB89], Pratt [PRA84], and Ledgard and Marcotty [LED81] satisfy both requirements nicely. A book by Smedema et al. (*The Programming Languages Pascal, Modula, CHILL and Ada,* Prentice-Hall, 1983) presents a thumbnail sketch of these important programming languages.

The *Elements of Programming Style* [KER78] remains *must* reading for all individuals who intend to generate source code. The authors have provided an extensive, annotated set of rules for coding (and design) that are well worth heeding. In addition Jon Bentley (*Programming Pearls,* Addison-Wesley, 1986; *More Programming Pearls,* Addison-Wesley, 1988) presents a worthwhile collection of style guidelines and clever language solutions to common programming problems. Books by Weiler (*The Programmers Craft,* Reston, 1983), Liffick (*The Software Development Source Book,* Addison-Wesley, 1985), and Ledgard (*Professional Software: Programming Concepts,* Addison-Wesley, 1987) provide additional information about style.

There is no "best" textbook that can be chosen from the hundreds that have been written about languages within any one of the language classes that we have discussed. The following list contains a representative sample of source material for many of the programming languages discussed in this chapter:

FORTRAN: Ellis, M., *A Structured Approach to FORTRAN 77 Programming,* Addison-Wesley, 1989.

COBOL: Johnson, B. M., and M. Ruwe, *Professional Programming in COBOL,* Prentice-Hall, 1990.

ALGOL: Brailsford, D., and Walker, A., *Introductory ALGOL-68 Programming,* Wiley, 1979.

BASIC: Pearson, O. R., *Programming with Basic,* McGraw-Hill, 1986.

PL/1: Tremblay, J. P., et al., *Structured PL/1 (PL/C) Programming,* McGraw-Hill, 1980.

PASCAL: Mallozzi, J.S., *Program Design in Pascal,* McGraw-Hill, 1989.
C: Hutchison, R., and S. B. Just, *Programming Using the C Language,* McGraw-Hill, 1988.
C++: Lippman, S. B., *A C++ Primer,* Addison-Wesley, 1989.
Ada: Cohen, N. H., *Ada as a Second Language,* McGraw-Hill, 1986.
Modula-2: Eisenbach, S., and C. Sadler, *Program Design with Modula-2,* Addison-Wesley, 1989.
LISP: Anderson, J. R., et al., *Essential Lisp,* Addison-Wesley, 1987.
OPS5: Sherman, P. D., and J.C. Martin, *An OPS5 Primer,* Prentice-Hall, 1990.
Prolog: Clocksin, W., and C. Mellish, *Programming in Prolog,* 2d ed., Springer-Verlag, 1984.
Smalltalk: Goldberg, A., and D. Robson, *Smalltalk-80,* Addison-Wesley, 1983.
FORTH: Katzen, H., *Invitation to FORTH,* Petrocelli, 1981.

An introduction to formal language theory can be found in *Jewels of Formal Language Theory* (A. Salomaa, Computer Science Press, 1981) and Meyer (*Introduction to the Theory of Programming Languages,* Prentice-Hall, 1988). These books survey morphic representations, formal syntax specification, DOL languages, and many other topics. An equally rigorous treatment of language formalism can also be found in Dijkstra and Feijen (*A Method of Programming,* Addison-Wesley, 1988).

PART 4

ENSURING, VERIFYING, AND MAINTAINING SOFTWARE INTEGRITY

CHAPTER 17

SOFTWARE QUALITY ASSURANCE

All of the methods, tools, and procedures described in this book work toward a single goal: *to produce high-quality software*. Yet many readers will be challenged by the question: What is software quality?

Philip Crosby [CRO79], in his landmark book on quality, discusses this situation:

> The problem of quality management is not what people don't know about it. The problem is what they think they do know....
>
> In this regard, quality has much in common with sex. Everybody is for it. (Under certain conditions, of course.) Everyone feels they understand it. (Even though they wouldn't want to explain it.) Everyone thinks execution is only a matter of following natural inclinations. (After all, we do get along somehow.) And, of course, most people feel that problems in these areas are caused by other people. (If only *they* would take the time to do things right.)

The placement of this chapter might lead a reader to infer that software quality assurance is something you begin to worry about after code has been generated. Nothing could be further from the truth! *Software quality assurance* (SQA) is an "umbrella activity" that is applied throughout the software engineering process. SQA encompasses (1) analysis, design, coding and testing methods and tools; (2) formal technical reviews that are applied during each software engineering step; (3) a multitiered testing strategy; (4) control of software documentation and the changes made to it; (5) a procedure to assure compliance with software development standards (when applicable); and (6) measurement and reporting mechanisms.

In this chapter, we shall examine the meaning of the elusive term "software quality," and discuss the procedures and measures that help to ensure that quality is a natural outcome of software engineering.

17.1 SOFTWARE QUALITY AND SOFTWARE QUALITY ASSURANCE

Even the most jaded software developers will agree that high-quality software is an important goal. But how do we define quality? A wag once said, "Every program does something right, it just may not be the thing that we want it to do."

There have been many definitions of software quality proposed in the literature. For our purposes, software quality is defined as:

> Conformance to explicitly stated functional and performance requirements, explicitly documented development standards, and implicit characteristics that are expected of all professionally developed software.

There is little question that the above definition could be modified or extended. In fact, a definitive definition of software quality could be debated endlessly. For the purposes of this book, the above definition serves to emphasize three important points:

1. Software requirements are the foundation from which *quality* is measured. Lack of conformance to requirements is lack of quality.
2. Specified standards define a set of development criteria that guide the manner in which software is engineered. If the criteria are not followed, lack of quality will almost surely result.
3. There is a set of *implicit requirements* that often goes unmentioned (e.g., the desire for good maintainability). If software conforms to its explicit requirements, but fails to meet implicit requirements, software quality is suspect.

Software quality is a complex mix of factors that will vary across different applications and the customers who request them. In the sections that follow, software quality factors are identified and the human activities required to achieve them are described.

17.1.1 Software Quality Factors

The factors that affect software quality can be categorized in two broad groups: (1) factors that can be directly measured (e.g., errors/KLOC/unit-time) and (2) factors that can be measured only indirectly (e.g., usability or maintainability). In each case *measurement* must occur. We must compare the software (documents, programs, and data) to some *datum* and arrive at an indication of quality.

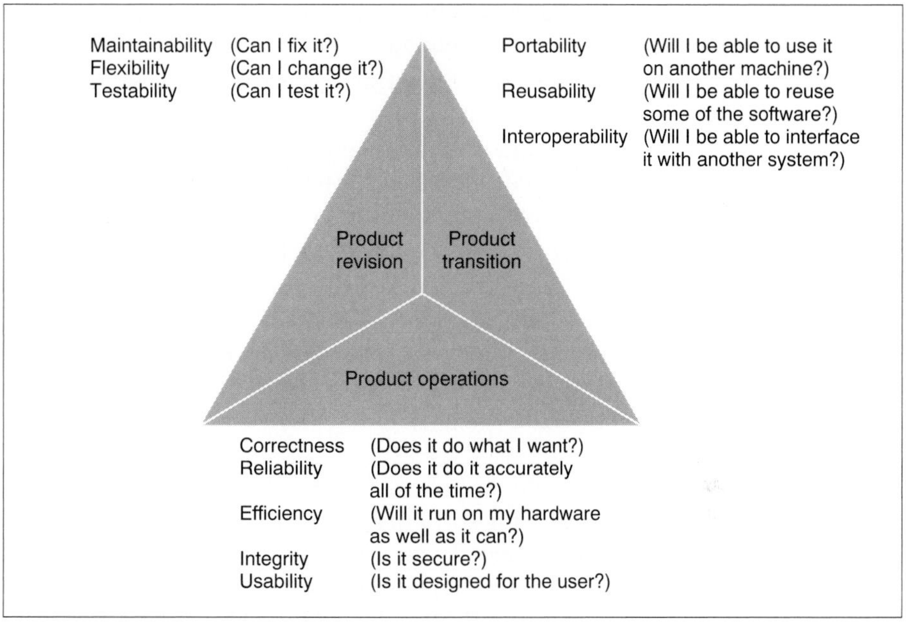
Maintainability (Can I fix it?)
Flexibility (Can I change it?)
Testability (Can I test it?)
Portability (Will I be able to use it on another machine?)
Reusability (Will I be able to reuse some of the software?)
Interoperability (Will I be able to interface it with another system?)
Product revision
Product transition
Product operations
Correctness (Does it do what I want?)
Reliability (Does it do it accurately all of the time?)
Efficiency (Will it run on my hardware as well as it can?)
Integrity (Is it secure?)
Usability (Is it designed for the user?)

FIGURE 17.1.
McCall's software quality factors.

McCall and his colleagues [MCC77] have proposed a useful categorization of factors that affect software quality. These *software quality factors,* shown in Figure 17.1, focus on three important aspects of a software product: its operational characteristics, its ability to undergo change, and its adaptability to new environments.

Referring to the factors noted in Figure 17.1, McCall provides the following descriptions:

> *Correctness.* The extent to which a program satisfies its specification and fulfills the customer's mission objectives.
>
> *Reliability.* The extent to which a program can be expected to perform its intended function with required precision. [It should be noted that other, more complete, definitions of reliability have been proposed (see Section 17.6).]
>
> *Efficiency.* The amount of computing resources and code required by a program to perform its function.
>
> *Integrity.* The extent to which access to software or data by unauthorized persons can be controlled.
>
> *Usability.* The effort required to learn, operate, prepare input, and interpret output of a program.
>
> *Maintainability.* The effort required to locate and fix an error in a program. [This is a very limited definition (see Chapter 20).]
>
> *Flexibility.* The effort required to modify an operational program.

Testability. The effort required to test a program to ensure that it performs its intended function.

Portability. The effort required to transfer the program from one hardware and/or software system environment to another.

Reusability. The extent to which a program (or parts of a program) can be reused in other applications—related to the packaging and scope of the functions that the program performs.

Interoperability. The effort required to couple one system to another.

It is difficult, and in some cases impossible, to develop direct measures of the above quality factors. Therefore, a set of metrics are defined and used to develop expressions for each of the factors according to the following relationship:

$$F_q = c_1 \times m_1 + c_2 \times m_2 + \cdots + c_n \times m_n$$

where F_q is a software quality factor, c_n are regression coefficients, and m_n are metrics that affect the quality factor. Unfortunately, many of the metrics defined by McCall can only be measured subjectively. The metrics may be in the form of a checklist that is used to "grade" specific attributes of the software [CAV78]. The grading scheme proposed by McCall is a 0 (low) to 10 (high) scale. The following metrics are used in the grading scheme:

Auditability. The ease with which conformance to standards can be checked.

Accuracy. The precision of computations and control.

Communication commonality. The degree to which standard interfaces, protocols, and bandwidths are used.

Completeness. The degree to which full implementation of required function has been achieved.

Conciseness. The compactness of the program in terms of lines of code.

Consistency. The use of uniform design and documentation techniques throughout the software development project.

Data commonality. The use of standard data structures and types throughout the program.

Error tolerance. The damage that occurs when the program encounters an error.

Execution efficiency. The run-time performance of a program.

Expandability. The degree to which architectural, data, or procedural design can be extended.

Generality. The breadth of potential application of program components.

Hardware independence. The degree to which the software is decoupled from the hardware on which it operates.

Instrumentation. The degree to which the program monitors its own operation and identifies errors that do occur.

Modularity. The functional independence (Chapter 10) of program components.

Operability. The ease of operation of a program.

Security. The availability of mechanisms that control or protect programs and data.

Self-documentation. The degree to which the source code provides meaningful documentation.

Simplicity. The degree to which a program can be understood without difficulty.

Software system independence. The degree to which the program is independent of nonstandard programming language features, operating system characteristics, and other environmental constraints.

Traceability. The ability to trace a design representation or actual program component back to requirements.

Training. The degree to which the software assists in enabling new users to apply the system.

The relationship between software quality factors and the metrics listed above is shown in Table 17.1. It should be noted that the weight given to each metric is dependent on local products and concerns.

The quality factors described by McCall and his colleagues [MCC77] represent one of a number of suggested "checklists" for software quality. Hewlett-Packard [GRA87] has developed a set of software quality factors that has been given the acronym *FURPS*—for functionality, usability, reliability, performance, and supportability. The FURPS quality factors draw liberally from earlier work, defining the following attributes for each of the five major factors:

- *Functionality* is assessed by evaluating the feature set and capabilities of the program, the generality of the functions that are delivered, and the security of the overall system.
- *Usability* is assessed by considering human factors (Chapter 14), overall aesthetics, consistency, and documentation.
- *Reliability* is evaluated by measuring the frequency and severity of failure, the accuracy of output results, the mean time between failure (MTBF), the ability to recover from failure, and the predictability of the program.
- *Performance* is measured by evaluating processing speed, response time, resource consumption, throughput, and efficiency.
- *Supportability* combines the ability to extend the program (extensibility), adaptability, and serviceability (these three attributes represent a more common term—*maintainability*), in addition to testability, compatibility,

TABLE 17.1

QUALITY FACTORS AND METRICS

Quality factor \ Software quality metric	Correctness	Reliability	Efficiency	Integrity	Maintainability	Flexibility	Testability	Portability	Reusability	Interoperability	Usability
Auditability				x			x				
Accuracy		x									
Communication commonality										x	
Completeness	x										
Complexity		x				x	x				
Concision			x		x	x					
Consistency	x	x			x	x					
Data commonality										x	
Error tolerance		x									
Execution efficiency			x								
Expandability						x					
Generality						x		x	x	x	
Hardware Indep.								x	x		
Instrumentation				x	x		x				
Modularity		x			x	x	x	x	x	x	
Operability			x								x
Security				x							
Self documentation					x	x	x	x	x		
Simplicity		x			x	x	x				
System Indep.								x	x		
Traceability	x										
Training											x

(Adapted from Arthur, L. A., *Measuring Programmer Productivity and Software Quality,* Wiley-Interscience, 1985.)

configurability [the ability to organize and control elements of the software configuration (Chapter 21)], the ease with which a system can be installed, and the ease with which problems can be localized.

The FURPS quality factors and attributes described above can be used to establish quality metrics for each step in the software engineering process. Grady and Caswell [GRA87] suggest a matrix (Figure 17.2) to guide in the collection of simple FURPS measurements.

17.1.2 Software Quality Assurance

Quality assurance is an essential activity for any business that produces products to be used by others. Prior to the twentieth century, quality assurance was the sole responsibility of the craftsperson who built a product. The first formal quality assurance and control function was introduced at Bell Labs in 1916 and spread rapidly throughout the manufacturing world. Today, every company has mechanisms to ensure quality in its products. In fact, explicit statements of a company's concern for quality have become a marketing ploy during the past decade.

The history of quality assurance in software development parallels the history of quality in hardware manufacturing. During the early days of computing (1950s and 1960s), quality was the sole responsibility of the programmer. Standards for quality assurance for software were introduced in military contract software development during the 1970s and have spread rapidly into software development in the commercial world [IEE89].

Software quality assurance (SQA) is a "planned and systematic pattern of actions" [SCH87] that are required to ensure quality in software. The scope of quality assurance responsibility might best be characterized by paraphrasing a once-popular automobile commercial: "Quality is Job #1." The implication for software is that many different constituencies in an organization have software quality assurance responsibility—software engineers, project managers, customers, salespeople, and the individuals who serve within an SQA group.

The SQA group serves as the customer's in-house representative. That is, the people who perform SQA must look at the software from the customer's point of view. Does the software adequately meet the quality factors noted in Section 17.1.1? Has software development been conducted according to pre-established standards? Have technical disciplines properly performed their roles as part of the SQA activity? The SQA group attempts to answer these and other questions to ensure that software quality is maintained.

17.1.3 SQA Activities

Software quality assurance is comprised of a variety of tasks associated with seven major activities: (1) application of technical methods, (2) con-

	Investigation/ Specifications	Design	Implementation	Testing	Support
F	# target users to review spec or prototype % grade on report card from user % features competitive with other products # interfaces with existing products	% spec included in design # changes to spec due to design requirement # users to review change if needed	% designs included in code # code changes due to omissions discovered % features removed (reviewed by original target user)	% features tested at alpha sites % user documentation tested against product # target alpha customers	# Known Problem Reports sales act. reports (esp. lost sales) user surveys internal HP user surveys
U	# target users to review spec or prototype % grade on documentation plan by target user % grade on usability of prototype	% grade of design as compared to objectives # changes to prototype manuals after review	% grade by other lab user % grade by product marketing, documentation % original users to review any change	# changes to product after alpha test % grade from usability lab testing % grade by test sites	# User misunderstandings
R	# omissions noted in reviews of objectives (reliability goals) # changes to project plan, test plan after review	# changes to design after review due to error % grade of design as compared to objectives	% code changed due to reliability errors discovered in reviews % code covered by test cases # defects/KNCSS during module testing	MTTF (MTBF) % hrs reliability testing # defects/1K hrs # defects total defect rate before release ckpoints	# Known Problem Reports # defects/KNCSS
P	# changes to objectives after review % grade on objectives by target user % grade on objective by product managers	% product to be modeled defined modeled environment	performance tests achieve % of modeled expectations % of code tested with targeted → performance suite (module)	achieve performance goal with regard to environment(s) tested (system)	
S	# changes to support objectives after review by field & CPE	# design changes by CPE & field # diagnostic/recovery changes by CPE & field input	MTTR objective (time) → MTTC objective (time) → time to train tester, use of documentation		same

FIGURE 17.2.
FURPS metrics for software quality. (*Reproduced with permission of Prentice-Hall.*)

duct of formal technical reviews, (3) software testing, (4) enforcement of standards, (5) control of change, (6) measurement, and (7) record keeping and reporting.

Software quality is designed into a product or system. It is not imposed after the fact. For this reason, SQA actually begins with the set of *technical methods and tools* that help the analyst to achieve a high-quality specification and the designer to develop a high-quality design. Measures of specification and design quality have already been discussed in this book (e.g., see Chapters 6 and 10).

Once a specification (or prototype) and design have been created, each must be assessed for quality. The central activity that accomplishes quality assessment is the *formal technical review.* The formal technical review (FTR) is a stylized meeting conducted by technical staff with the sole purpose of uncovering quality problems. In many situations, reviews have been found to be as effective as testing in uncovering defects in software. Reviews are discussed in Section 17.2.

Software testing combines a multistep strategy with a series of test case design methods that help ensure effective error detection. Many software developers use software testing as a quality assurance "safety net." That is, developers assume that thorough testing will uncover most errors, thereby mitigating the need for other SQA activities. Unfortunately, testing, even when performed well, is not as effective as we might like for all classes of errors [JON81]. Software testing is discussed in detail in Chapters 18 and 19.

The degree to which formal *standards and procedures* are applied to the software engineering process varies from company to company. In many cases, standards are dictated by customers or regulatory mandate. In other situations standards are self-imposed. If formal (written) standards do exist, an SQA activity must be established to ensure that they are being followed. An assessment of compliance to standards may be conducted by software developers as part of a formal technical review or, in situations where independent verification of compliance is required, the SQA group may conduct its own *audit.*

A major threat to software quality comes from a seemingly benign source: *changes.* Every change to software has the potential for introducing error or creating side effects that propagate errors. The *change control* process (an activity that is part of software configuration management, Chapter 21) contributes directly to software quality by formalizing requests for change, evaluating the nature of change, and controlling the impact of change. Change control is applied during software development and later, during the software maintenance phase.

Measurement is an activity that is integral to any engineering discipline. An important objective of SQA is to track software quality and assess the impact of methodological and procedural changes on improved software quality. To accomplish this, *software metrics* must be collected. Software metrics encompasses a broad array of technical and management-oriented measures and is discussed in Section 17.4.[1]

Record keeping and recording for software quality assurance provide procedures for the collection and dissemination of SQA information. The results of reviews, audits, change control, testing, and other SQA activities must become part of the historical record for a project and should be disseminated to the development staff on a need-to-know basis. For example, the results of each formal technical review for a procedural design are recorded and can be placed in a "folder" that contains all technical and SQA information about a module.

17.2 SOFTWARE REVIEWS

Software reviews are a "filter" for the software engineering process. That is, reviews are applied at various points during software development and serve to uncover defects that can then be removed. Software reviews serve to "purify" the software engineering activities that we have called analysis, design, and coding. Freedman and Weinberg [FRE90, p. 7] discuss the need for reviews this way:

> Technical work needs reviewing for the same reason that pencils need erasers: *To err is human.* The second reason we need technical reviews is that although people are good at catching some of their own errors, large classes of errors escape the originator more easily than they escape anyone else. The review process is, therefore, the answer to the prayer of Robert Burns:
>
> O wad some power the giftie give us
> to see ourselves as other see us
>
> A review—any review—is a way of using the diversity of a group of people to:
>
> 1. Point out needed improvements in the product of a single person or team;
> 2. Confirm those parts of a product in which improvement is either not desired or not needed;
> 3. Achieve technical work of more *uniform,* or at least more *predictable,* quality than can be achieved without reviews, in order to make technical work more *manageable.*

There are many different types of reviews that can be conducted as part of software engineering. Each has its place. An informal meeting around the coffee machine is a form of review, if technical problems are discussed.

---

[1]An earlier discussion of software metrics in Chapter 2 focused primarily on measures that are relevant for project planning and management. It might, however, be worthwhile to review Chapter 2 in conjunction with Section 17.4.

A formal presentation of software design to an audience of customers, management, and technical staff is a form of review. In this book, however, we focus on the formal technical review—sometimes called a *walkthrough*. A formal technical review is an effective filter from a quality assurance standpoint. Conducted by software engineers (and others) for software engineers, the FTR is an effective means for improving software quality.

17.2.1 Cost Impact of Software Defects

The obvious benefit of formal technical reviews is the early discovery of *software defects* so that each defect may be corrected prior to the next step in the software engineering process. For example, a number of industry studies (TRW, Nippon Electric, Mitre Corp., among others) indicate that design activities introduce between 50 and 65 percent of all errors (defects) during the development phase of the software engineering process. However, formal review techniques have been shown to be up to 75 percent effective [JON86] in uncovering design flaws. By detecting and removing a large percentage of these errors, the review process substantially reduces the cost of subsequent steps in the development and maintenance phases.

To illustrate the cost impact of early error detection, we consider a series of relative costs that are based on actual cost data collected for large software projects [IBM81]. Assume that an error uncovered during design will cost 1.0 monetary unit to correct. Relative to this cost, the same error uncovered just before testing commences will cost 6.5 units; during testing 15 units; and after release, between 60 and 100 units.

17.2.2 Defect Amplification and Removal

A *defect amplification model* [IBM81] can be used to illustrate the generation and detection of errors during the preliminary design, detail design, and coding steps of the software engineering process. The model is illustrated schematically in Figure 17.3. A box represents a software development step.

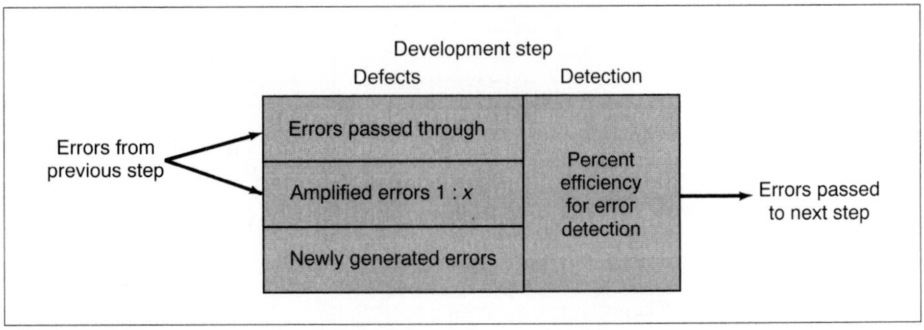

FIGURE 17.3. Defect amplification model.

During the step, errors may be inadvertently generated. Review may fail to uncover newly generated errors and errors from previous steps, resulting in some number of errors that are passed through. In some cases, errors passed through from previous steps are amplified (amplification factor x) by current work. The box subdivisions represent each of these characteristics and the percent efficiency for detecting errors, a function of the thoroughness of review.

Figure 17.4 illustrates a hypothetical example of defect amplification for a software development process in which no reviews are conducted. Referring to the figure, each test step is assumed to uncover and correct 50 percent of all incoming errors without introducing any new errors (an optimistic assumption). Ten preliminary design defects are amplified to 94 errors before testing commences. Twelve latent defects are released to the field. Figure 17.5 considers the same conditions except that design and code reviews are conducted as part of each development step. In this case, 10 initial preliminary design errors are amplified to 24 errors before testing commences. Only three latent defects exist. Recalling the relative costs associated with the discovery and correction of errors, overall cost (with and without review for our hypothetical example) can be established. Referring to Table 17.2 it can be seen that the total cost for development and maintenance when reviews are conducted is 783 cost units. When no reviews are conducted, the total cost is 2177 units—nearly three times more costly.

To conduct reviews, a developer must expend time, effort, and money. However, the results of the preceding example leave little doubt that we have

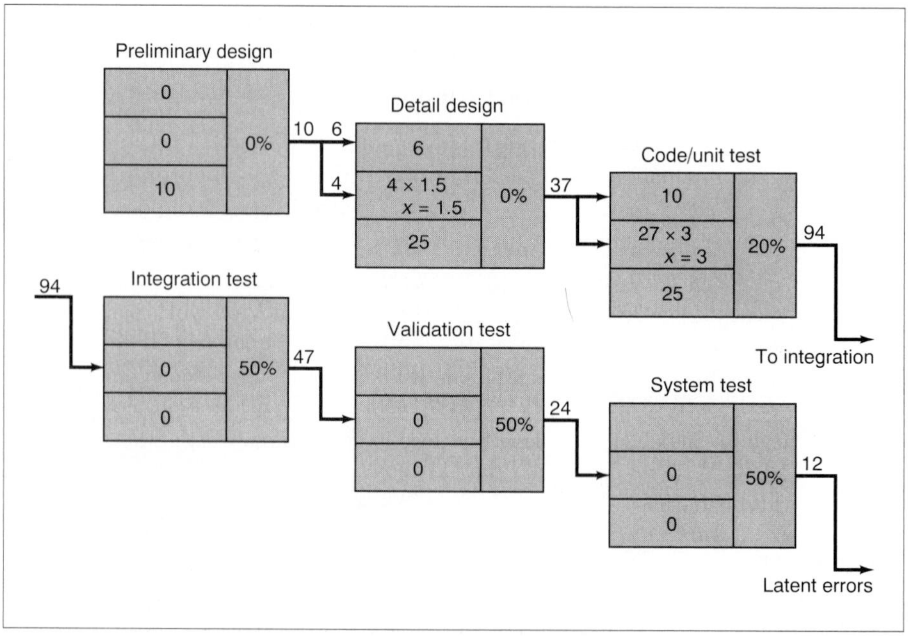

FIGURE 17.4. Defect amplification—no reviews.

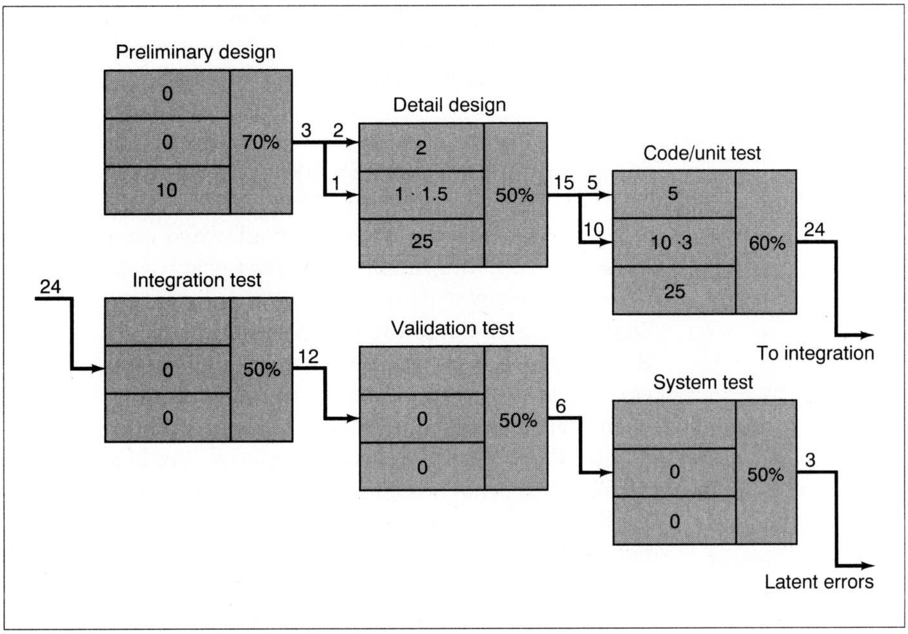

FIGURE 17.5. Defect amplification—reviews conducted.

TABLE 17.2

DEVELOPMENT COST COMPARISON

Errors found	Number	Cost unit	Total
	Reviews conducted		
During design	22	1.5	33
Before test	36	6.5	234
During test	15	15	315
After release	3	67	201
			783
	No reviews conducted		
Before test	22	6.5	143
During test	82	15	1230
After release	12	67	804
			2177

encountered a "pay now or pay much more later" situation. Formal technical reviews (for design and other technical activities) provide a demonstrable cost benefit. They should be conducted.

17.3 FORMAL TECHNICAL REVIEWS

A formal technical review is a software quality assurance activity that is performed by software engineering practitioners. The objectives of the FTR are (1) to uncover errors in function, logic, or implementation for any representation of the software, (2) to verify that the software under review meets its requirements, (3) to ensure that the software has been represented according to predefined standards, (4) to achieve software that is developed in a uniform manner, and (5) to make projects more manageable. In addition, the FTR serves as a training ground, enabling junior engineers to observe different approaches to software analysis, design, and implementation. The FTR also serves to promote backup and continuity because a number of people become familiar with parts of the software that they may not have otherwise seen.

The FTR is actually a class of reviews that include *walkthroughs, inspections, round-robin reviews,* and other small group technical assessments of software. Each FTR is conducted as a meeting and will be successful only if it is properly planned, controlled, and attended. In the paragraphs that follow, guidelines similar to those for a *walkthrough* [FRE90, YOU89] are presented as a representative formal technical review.

17.3.1 The Review Meeting

Regardless of the FTR format that is chosen, every review meeting should abide by the following constraints:

- Between three and five people (typically) should be involved in the review.
- Advance preparation should occur but should require no more than 2 hours of work for each person.
- The duration of the review meeting should be less than 2 hours.

Given the above constraints, it should be obvious that an FTR focuses on a specific (and small) part of the overall software. For example, rather than attempting to review an entire design, walkthroughs are conducted for each module or small group of modules. By narrowing the focus, the FTR has a higher likelihood of uncovering errors.

The focus of the FTR is on a *product*—a component of the software (e.g., a portion of a requirements specification, a detailed module design, a source code listing for a module). The individual who has developed the product—the *producer*—informs the project leader that the product is complete and that a review is required. The project leader contacts a *review leader* who evaluates the product for readiness, generates copies of product materials and distributes them to two or three *reviewers* for advance preparation. Each reviewer is expected to spend between 1 and 2 hours reviewing the product, making notes, and otherwise becoming familiar with the work. Concurrently, the review leader also reviews the product and establishes an agenda for the review meeting, which is typically scheduled for the next day.

The review meeting is attended by the review leader, all reviewers, and the producer. One of the reviewers takes on the role of the *recorder,* that is, the individual who records (in writing) all important issues raised during the review. The FTR begins with a discussion of the agenda and a brief introduction by the producer. The producer then proceeds to "walk through" the product, explaining the material, while the reviewers raise issues based on their advance preparation. When valid problems or errors are discovered, the recorder notes each.

At the end of the review, all attendees of the FTR must decide whether to (1) accept the product without further modification, (2) reject the product due to severe errors (once corrected, another review must be performed), or (3) accept the product provisionally (minor errors have been encountered and must be corrected, but no additional review will be required). The decision made, all FTR attendees complete a *sign-off,* indicating their participation in the review and their concurrence with the review team's findings.

17.3.2 Review Reporting and Record Keeping

During the FTR, a reviewer (the recorder) actively records all issues that have been raised. These are summarized at the end of the review meeting and a *review issues list* is produced. In addition, a simple *review summary report* is completed. A review summary report answers three questions:

1. What was reviewed?
2. Who reviewed it?
3. What were the findings and conclusions?

The review summary report takes the form illustrated in Figure 17.6*a*. In general, this single page form (with possible attachments) becomes part of the project historical record and may be distributed to the project leader and other interested parties.

The review issues list serves two purposes: (1) to identify problem areas within the product and (2) to serve as an *action item* checklist that guides the producer as corrections are made. An issues list that corresponds to the summary report is shown in Figure 17.6*b*.

It is important to establish a follow-up procedure to ensure that items on the issues list have been properly corrected. Unless this is done, it is possible that the issues raised can "fall between the cracks."

Technical Review Summary Report

Review Identification:

Project: NC Real-Time Controller Review Number: D-004
Date: 11 July 86 Location: Bldg. 4, Room 3 Time: 10:00 AM

Product Identification:

Material Reviewed: Detailed Design - Modules for motion control

Producer: Alan Frederick

Brief Description: Three modules for x, y, z axis motion control

Material Reviewed: (note each item separately)
1. Detailed design descriptions: modules XMOTION, YMOTION, ZMOTION
2. PDL for modules

Review Team: (indicate leader and recorder)

	Name	Signature:
1.	R. S. Pressman (Leader)	Roger S. Pressman
2.	A. D. Dickerson (Recorder)	A. Dickerson
3.	P. W. Brotherton	Paul W. Brotherton
4.	M. Lambert	M. Lambert
5.		

Product Appraisal:

Accepted: as is ( ) with minor modification (√)
Not Accepted: major revision ( ) minor revision ( )
Review Not Completed: (explanation follows)

Supplementary material attached:

Issues list (√) Annotated Produce Materials (√)
Other (describe)

FIGURE 17.6a. Technical review summary report.

17.3.3 Review Guidelines

Guidelines for the conduct of formal technical reviews must be established in advance, distributed to all reviewers, agreed upon, and then followed. A review that is uncontrolled can often be worse that no review at all.

The following represents a minimum set of guidelines for formal technical reviews:

1. *Review the product, not the producer.*
An FTR involves people and egos. Conducted properly, the FTR should leave all participants with a warm feeling of accomplishment. Conducted improperly, the FTR can take on the aura of an inquisition. Errors should be pointed

Review Number: D-004
Date of Review: 07-11-86
Review leader: R.S. Pressman Recorder: A.D. Dickerson

Issues List

1. Prologues for module YMOTION, ZMOTION are not consistent with design standards. Purpose of the module should be explicitly stated (reference is not acceptable) and data item declaration must be specified.

2. Loop counter for interpolation in X, Y, Z axes increments one time too many for step motor control. Review team recommends a recheck of stepping motor specifications and correction (as required) of the loop counter STEP.MOTOR.CTR.

3. Typo in reference to current X position, X.POSITION. in modules XMOTION and ZMOTION. See marked PDL for specifics.

4. PDL pseudo code statement must be expanded. The pseudo code statement: "Converge on proper control position as in XMOTION" contained in modules YMOTION and ZMOTION should be expanded to specifics for Y and Z motion control.

5. Review team recommends a modification to the "position comparator" algorithm to improve run time performance. Necessary modifications are noted in annotated PDL. Designer has reservations about the modification and will analyze potential impact before implementing change.

FIGURE 17.6*b*.
Review issues list.

out gently; the tone of the meeting should be loose and constructive; the intent should not be to embarrass or belittle. The review leader should conduct the review meeting to ensure that the proper tone and attitude are maintained and should immediately halt a review that has gotten out of control.

2. *Set an agenda and maintain it.*
One of the key maladies of meetings of all types is *drift*. An FTR must be kept on track and on schedule. The review leader is chartered with the responsibility for maintaining the meeting schedule and should not be afraid to nudge people when drift sets in.

3. *Limit debate and rebuttal.*
When an issue is raised by a reviewer, there may not be universal agreement on its impact. Rather than spending time debating the question, the issue should be recorded for further discussion off-line.

4. *Enunciate problem areas, but don't attempt to solve every problem noted.*
A review is not a problem-solving session. The solution of a problem can often be accomplished by the producer alone or with the help of only one other individual. Problem solving should be postponed until after the review meeting.

5. *Take written notes.*
It is sometimes a good idea for the recorder to make notes on a wall board, so that wording and prioritization can be assessed by the other reviewers as information is recorded.

6. *Limit the number of participants and insist upon advance preparation.*
Two heads are better than one, but 14 are not necessarily better than four. Keep the number of people involved to the necessary minimum. However, all review team members must prepare in advance. Written comments should be solicited by the review leader (providing an indication that the reviewer has reviewed the material).

7. *Develop a checklist for each product that is likely to be reviewed.*
A checklist helps the review leader to structure the FTR meeting and helps each reviewer to focus on important issues. Checklists should be developed for analysis, design, code, and even test documents. A set of representative review checklists is presented in Section 17.3.4.

8. *Allocate resources and time schedule for FTRs.*
For reviews to be effective, they should be scheduled as tasks during the software engineering process. In addition, time should be scheduled for the inevitable modifications that will occur as the result of an FTR.

9. *Conduct meaningful training for all reviewers.*
To be effective all review participants should receive some formal training. The training should stress both process-related issues and the human psychological side of reviews. Freedman and Weinberg [FRE90] estimate a 1-month learning curve for every 20 people who are to participate effectively in reviews.

10. *Review your early reviews.*
Debriefing can be beneficial in uncovering problems with the review process itself. The very first product to be reviewed might be the review guidelines themselves.

17.3.4 A Review Checklist

Formal technical reviews can be conducted during each step in the software engineering process. In this section, we present a brief checklist that can be used to assess products that are derived as part of software development. The checklists are not intended to be comprehensive, but rather to provide a point of departure for each review.

System Engineering The *System Specification* allocates function and performance to many system elements. Therefore, the system review involves many constituencies that may each focus on their own area of concern. Software engineering and hardware engineering groups focus on software and hardware allocation, respectively. Quality assurance assesses system-level validation requirements and field service examines the requirements for diagnostics. Once all reviews are conducted, a larger review meeting, with representatives from each constituency, is conducted to ensure early communication of concerns. The following checklist covers some of the more important areas of concern:

1. Are major functions defined in a bounded and unambiguous fashion?
2. Are interfaces between system elements defined?
3. Have performance bounds been established for the system as a whole and for each element?
4. Are design constraints established for each element?
5. Has the best alternative been selected?
6. Is the solution technologically feasible?
7. Has a mechanism for system validation and verification been established?
8. Is there consistency among all system elements?

Software Project Planning Software project planning assesses risk and develops estimates for resources, cost, and schedule based on the software allocation established as part of the system engineering activity. The review of the *Software Project Plan* establishes the degree of risk. The following checklist is applicable:

1. Is software scope unambiguously defined and bounded?
2. Is terminology clear?
3. Are resources adequate for scope?
4. Are resources readily available?
5. Have risks in all important categories been defined?
6. Is a risk management plan in place?
7. Are tasks properly defined and sequenced? Is parallelism reasonable given available resources?
8. Is the basis for cost estimation reasonable? Has the cost estimate been developed using two independent methods?
9. Have historical productivity and quality data been used?
10. Have differences in estimates been reconciled?
11. Are pre-established budgets and deadlines realistic?
12. Is the schedule consistent?

Software Requirements Analysis Reviews for software requirements analysis focus on traceability to system requirements and consistency and correctness of the analysis model. A number of FTRs are conducted for the requirements of a large system and may be augmented by reviews and the evaluation of prototypes as well as customer meetings. The following topics are considered during FTRs for analysis:

1. Is information domain analysis complete, consistent, and accurate?
2. Is problem partitioning complete?
3. Are external and internal interfaces properly defined?
4. Does the data model properly reflect data objects, their attributes, and relationships?
5. Are all requirements traceable to system level?
6. Has prototyping been conducted for the user/customer?
7. Is performance achievable within the constraints imposed by other system elements?
8. Are requirements consistent with schedule, resources, and budget?
9. Are validation criteria complete?

Software Design Reviews for software design focus on data design, architectural design, and procedural design. In general, two types of design reviews are conducted. The *preliminary design review* assesses the translation of requirements to the design of data and architecture. The second review, often called a *design walkthrough,* concentrates on the procedural correctness of algorithms as they are implemented within program modules. The following checklists are useful for each review:

For the preliminary design review:

1. Are software requirements reflected in the software architecture?
2. Is effective modularity achieved? Are modules functionally independent?
3. Is the program architecture factored?
4. Are interfaces defined for modules and external system elements?
5. Is the data structure consistent with the information domain?
6. Is the data structure consistent with software requirements?
7. Has maintainability been considered?
8. Have quality factors (Section 17.1.1) been explicitly assessed?

For the design walkthrough:

1. Does the algorithm accomplish the desired function?
2. Is the algorithm logically correct?
3. Is the interface consistent with the architectural design?
4. Is the logical complexity reasonable?
5. Have error handling and "antibugging" been specified?
6. Are local data structures properly defined?

7. Are structured programming constructs used throughout?
8. Is design detail amenable to implementation language?
9. Which are used: operating system or language-dependent features?
10. Is compound or inverse logic used?
11. Has maintainability been considered?

Coding Although coding is a mechanistic outgrowth of procedural design, errors can be introduced as the design is translated into a programming language. This is particularly true if the programming language does not directly support data and control structures represented in the design. A code walkthrough can be an effective means for uncovering these translation errors. The checklist that follows assumes that a design walkthrough has been conducted and that algorithm correctness has been established as part of the design FTRs.

1. Has the design properly been translated into code? (The results of the procedural design should be available during this review.)
2. Are there misspellings and typos?
3. Has proper use of language conventions been made?
4. Is there compliance with coding standards for language style, comments, module prologue?
5. Are there incorrect or ambiguous comments?
6. Are data types and data declaration proper?
7. Are physical constants correct?
8. Have all the items on the design walkthrough checklist been reapplied (as required)?

Software Testing Software testing is a quality assurance activity in its own right. Therefore, it may seem odd to discuss reviews for testing. However, the completeness and effectiveness of testing can be dramatically improved by critically assessing any test plans and procedures that have been created. In the next two chapters, test case design techniques and testing strategies are discussed in detail. A review of Chapters 18 and 19 is suggested prior to the consideration of the following checklists:

For the test plan:

1. Have major test phases properly been identified and sequenced?
2. Has traceability to validation criteria/requirements been established as part of software requirements analysis?
3. Are major functions demonstrated early?
4. Is the test plan consistent with the overall project plan?
5. Has a test schedule been explicitly defined?

6. Are test resources and tools identified and available?
7. Has a test record-keeping mechanism been established?
8. Have test *drivers* and *stubs* been identified and has work to develop them been scheduled?
9. Has *stress testing* for software been specified?

For the test procedure:

1. Have both white and black box tests (see Chapter 18) been specified?
2. Have all the independent logic paths been tested?
3. Have test cases been identified and listed with their expected results?
4. Is error handling to be tested?
5. Are boundary values to be tested?
6. Are timing and performance to be tested?
7. Has an acceptable variation from the expected results been specified?

In addition to the formal technical reviews and review checklists noted above, reviews (with corresponding checklists) can be conducted to assess the readiness of field service mechanisms for product software, to evaluate the completeness and effectiveness of training, to assess the quality of user and technical documentation, and to investigate the applicability and availability of software tools.

Maintenance The review checklists for software development are equally valid for the software *maintenance* phase (Chapter 20). In addition to all of the questions posed in the preceding checklists, the following special considerations should be kept in mind:

1. Have side effects associated with change been considered?
2. Has the request for change been documented, evaluated, and approved?
3. Has the change, once made, been documented and reported to all interested parties?
4. Have appropriate FTRs been conducted?
5. Has a final *acceptance review* been conducted to ensure that all software has been properly updated, tested, and replaced?

17.4 SOFTWARE QUALITY METRICS

Earlier in this chapter, a set of qualitative factors for the "measurement" of software quality were discussed (Section 17.1.1). We strive to develop precise measures for software quality and are sometimes frustrated by the subjective nature of the activity. Cavano and McCall [CAV78] discuss this situation:

> The determination of quality is a key factor in every day events—wine tasting contests, sporting events [e.g., gymnastics], talent contests, etc. In these situations, quality is judged in the most fundamental and direct manner: side by side comparison of objects under identical conditions and with predetermined concepts. The wine may be judged according to clarity, color, bouquet, taste, etc. However, this type of judgement is very subjective; to have any value at all, it must be made by an expert.
>
> Subjectivity and specialization also apply to determining software quality. To help solve this problem, a more precise definition of software quality is needed as well as a way to derive quantitative measurements of software quality for objective analysis.... Since there is no such thing as absolute knowledge, one should not expect to measure software quality exactly, for every measurement is partially imperfect. Jacob Bronowsky described this paradox of knowledge in this way: "Year by year we devise more precise instruments with which to observe nature with more fineness. And when we look at the observations we are discomfited to see that they are still fuzzy, and we feel that they are as uncertain as ever."

In this section, we examine a set of software metrics that can be applied to the quantitative assessment of software quality. In all cases, the metrics represent indirect measures, that is, we never really measure *quality* but rather some manifestation of quality. The complicating factor is the precise relationship between the variable that is measured and the quality of the software.

17.4.1 Software Quality Indices

The U.S. Air Force Systems Command [USA87] has developed a number of software quality indicators that are based on the measurable design characteristics of a computer program. Using concepts similar to those proposed in IEEE Standard 982.1-1988 [IEE89], the Air Force uses information obtained from data and architectural design to derive a *design structure quality index* (DSQI) that ranges from 0 to 1. The following values must be ascertained to compute the DSQI [CHA89]:

S_1 = the total number of modules defined in the program architecture

S_2 = the number of modules whose correct function depends on the source of data input or that produces data to be used elsewhere [in general, control modules (among others) would not be counted as part of S_2]

S_3 = the number of modules whose correct function depends on prior processing

S_4 = the number of database items (includes data objects and all attributes that define objects)

S_5 = the total number of unique database items

S_6 = the number of database segments (different records or individual objects)

S_7 = the number of modules with a single entry and exit (exception processing is not considered to be a multiple exit)

Once values S_1 through S_7 are determined for a computer program, the following intermediate values can be computed:

Program structure: D_1, where D_1 is defined as follows: If the architectural design was developed using a distinct method (e.g., data flow-oriented design or object-oriented design), then $D_1 = 1$; otherwise $D_1 = 0$.
Module independence: $D_2 = 1 - (S_2/S_1)$.
Modules not dependent on prior processing: $D_3 = 1 - (S_3/S_1)$.
Database size: $D_4 = 1 - (S_5/S_4)$.
Database compartmentalization: $D_5 = 1 - (S_6/S_4)$.
Module entrance/exit characteristic: $D_6 = 1 - (S_7/S_1)$.

With these intermediate values determined, the DSQI is computed in the following manner:

$$\text{DSQI} = \sum w_i D_i \tag{17.1}$$

where $i = 1$ to 6, w_i is the relative weighting of the importance of each of the intermediate values, and $\sum w_i = 1$ (if all D_i are weighted equally, then $w_i = 0.167$).

The value of DSQI for past designs can be determined and compared to a design that is currently under development. If the DSQI is significantly lower than average, further design work and review is indicated. Similarly, if major changes are to be made to an existing design, the effect of those changes on DSQI can be calculated.

IEEE Standard 982.1-1988 [IEE89] suggests a *software maturity index* (SMI) that provides an indication of the stability of a software product (based on changes that occur for each release of the product). The following information is determined:

M_T = the number of modules in the current release

F_c = the number of modules in the current release that have been changed

F_a = the number of modules in the current release that have been added

F_d = the number of modules from the preceding release that were deleted in the current release

The software maturity index is computed in the following manner:

$$\text{SMI} = \frac{[M_T - (F_a + F_c + F_d)]}{M_T} \tag{17.2}$$

As SMI approaches 1.0, the product begins to stabilize. SMI may also be used as a metric for planning software maintenance activities. The mean time to produce a release of a software product can be correlated with SMI, and empirical models for maintenance effort can be developed.

17.4.2 Halstead's Software Science

Halstead's theory of software science [HAL77] is "probably the best known and most thoroughly studied...composite measures of (software) complexity" [CUR80]. Software science proposes the first analytical "laws" for computer software.[2]

Software science assigns quantitative laws to the development of computer software. Halstead's theory is derived from one fundamental assumption [HAL77]: "the human brain follows a more rigid set of rules (in developing algorithms) than it has been aware of...." Software science uses a set of primitive measures that may be derived after code is generated or estimated once design is complete. These are listed below:

n_1—the number of distinct operators that appear in a program
n_2—the number of distinct operands that appear in a program
N_1—the total number of operator occurrences
N_2—the total number of operand occurrences

To illustrate how these primitive measures are obtained, refer to the simple SORT program [FIT78] shown in Figure 17.7.

Halstead uses the primitive measures to develop expressions for the overall program *length,* the potential minimum *volume* for an algorithm, the actual volume (number of bits required to specify a program), the *program level* (a measure of software complexity), the *language level* (a constant for a given language), and other features such as development effort, development time, and even the projected number of faults in the software.

Halstead shows that length N can be estimated from

$$N = n_1 \log_2 n_1 + n_2 \log_2 n_2 \tag{17.3}$$

---

[2]It should be noted that Halstead's "laws" have generated substantial controversy and that not everyone agrees that the underlying theory is correct. However, experimental verification of Halstead's findings have been made for a number of programming languages (e.g., [FEL89]).

Interchange sort program

```
      SUBROUTINE SORT (X,N)
      DIMENSION X(N)
      IF (N.LT.2) RETURN
      DO 20 I = 2,N
         DO 10 J = 1,I
         IF (X(I).GE.X(J)) GO TO 10
            SAVE = X(I)
            X(I) = X(J)
            X(J) = SAVE
   10 CONTINUE
   20 CONTINUE
      RETURN
      END
```

Operators of the interchange sort program

Operator		Count
1	End of statement	7
2	Array subscript	6
3	=	5
4	IF ( )	2
5	DO	2
6	,	2
7	End of program	1
8	.LT.	1
9	.GE.	1
n_1 = 10	GO TO 10	1
		$28 = N_1$

Operands of the interchange sort program

Operand		Count
1	X	6
2	I	5
3	J	4
4	N	2
5	2	2
6	SAVE	2
n_2 = 7	1	1
		$22 = N_2$

FIGURE 17.7. Operators and operands for a simple program. (*Source:* A. Fitzsimmons and T. Love, "A Review and Evaluation of Software Science," *ACM Computing Surveys*, vol. 10, no. 1, March 1978. Copyright 1978, Association of Computing Machinery, Inc. Reprinted with permission.)

and program volume may be defined as

$$V = N \log_2(n_1 + n_2) \tag{17.4}$$

It should be noted that V will vary with the programming language and represents the volume of information (in bits) required to specify a program. For the SORT module shown in Figure 17.7, it can be shown [FIT78] that the volume for the FORTRAN version is 204. The volume for an equivalent assembler language version would be 328. As we would suspect, it takes more effort to specify a program in assembler language.

Theoretically, a minimum volume must exist for a particular algorithm. Halstead defines a volume ratio L as the ratio of the volume of the most compact form of a program to the volume of the actual program. In actuality, L must always be less than 1. In terms of primitive measures, the volume ratio may be expressed as

$$L = \left(\frac{2}{n_1}\right) \times \left(\frac{n_2}{N_2}\right)$$

Halstead proposes that each language may be categorized by language level l, which will vary among languages. Halstead theorized that language level is constant for a given language, but other work [ZEL81] indicates that language level is a function of both the language and the programmer. The following language level values have been empirically derived for common languages:

Language	Mean/l
English prose	2.16
PL/1	1.53
ALGOL/68	2.12
FORTRAN	1.14
Assembler	0.88

It appears that language level implies a level of abstraction in the specification of procedure. High-level language allows the specification of code at a higher level of abstraction than does assembler (machine-oriented) language.

Halstead's work is amenable to experimental verification and a large body of research has been conducted to investigate software science. A discussion of this work is beyond the scope of this text, but it can be said that good agreement has been found between analytically predicted and experimental results. For further information, see Waguespack and Badlani [WAG87].

17.4.3 McCabe's Complexity Metric

A complexity measure of software proposed by Thomas McCabe ([MCC76], [MCC89]) is based on a control flow representation of a program. A *program graph,* illustrated in Figure 17.8, is used to depict control flow. Each circled letter represents a processing task (one or more source code statements); flow of control (branching) is represented with connecting arrows. (A more detailed discussion is presented in the following chapter.) For graph G in Figure 17.8, processing task a may be followed by tasks b, c, or d, depending on conditions tested as part of a. Processing task b is always followed by e, and both may be executed as part of a doubly nested loop (the curved arrows moving upward to b and a, respectively).

McCabe defines a software complexity measure that is based on the *cyclomatic complexity* of a program graph for a module. One technique (oth-

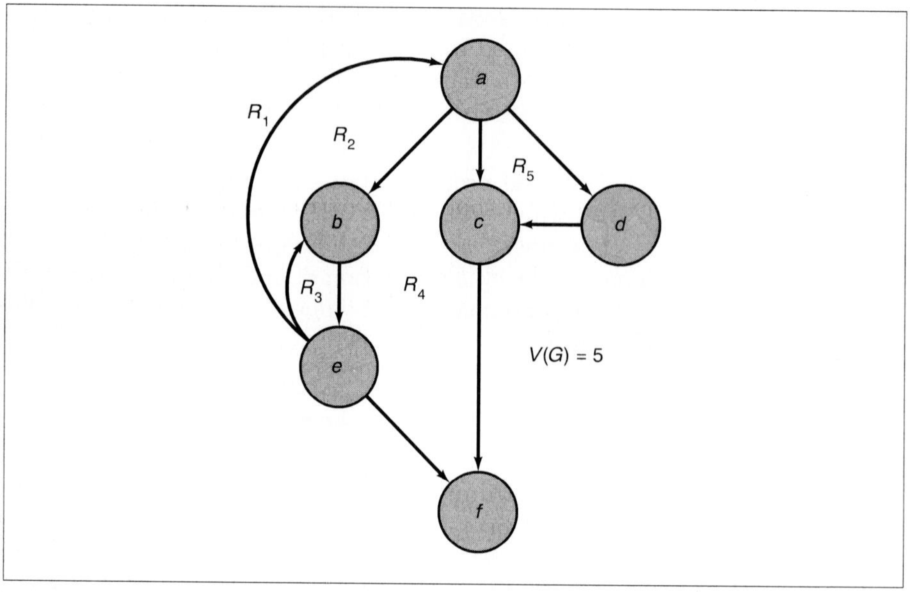

FIGURE 17.8. Control flow graph complexity.

ers are discussed in Chapter 18) that may be used to compute the cyclomatic complexity metric, $V(G)$, is to determine the number of regions in a planar graph (see McCabe [MCC76] or, for more detail, Bondy and Murty [BON76]). A *region* may be informally described as an enclosed area on the plane of the graph. The number of regions is computed by counting all bounded areas and the unbounded area outside the graph. The graph in Figure 17.8 has five regions (noted as R_1 through R_5) and thus has a cyclomatic complexity metric of $V(G) = 5$.

Because the number of regions increases with the number of decision paths and loops, the McCabe metric provides a quantitative measure of testing difficulty and an indication of ultimate reliability. Experimental studies (e.g., [GRE76], [CUR79]) indicate distinct relationships between the McCabe metric and the number of errors existing in source code, as well as the time required to find and correct such errors.

McCabe also contends that $V(G)$ may be used to provide a quantitative indication of maximum module size. Collecting data from a number of actual programming projects, he has found that $V(G) = 10$ appears to be a practical upper limit for module size. When the cyclomatic complexity of modules exceeded this number, it became extremely difficult to adequately test a module (see Chapter 18 for a discussion of test case design techniques).

17.5 FORMAL APPROACHES TO SQA

In the preceding sections, we have argued that software quality is everyone's job and that it can be achieved through competent analysis, design, coding, and testing, as well as through the application of formal technical reviews, a multitiered testing strategy, better control of software documentation, and the changes made to it, and the application of accepted software development standards. In addition, quality can be defined in terms of a broad array of quality factors and measured (indirectly) using a variety of indices and metrics.

Over the past two decades, a small, but vocal, segment of the software engineering community has argued that a more formal approach to software quality assurance is required. This approach could be an important supplement to each of the activities described above. In the sections that follow, a brief overview of "formal approaches" to SQA is presented.

17.5.1 Proof of Correctness

It can be argued that a computer program is a mathematical object [SOM89]. A rigorous syntax and semantics can be defined for every programming language, and work is underway to develop a similarly rigorous approach to the specification of software requirements (see Chapter 9). If the requirements model (specification) and the programming language can be represented in a rigorous manner, it should be possible to apply mathematical proofs of correctness to demonstrate that a program conforms exactly to its specification.

Attempts to prove programs correct are not new. Dijkstra [DIJ76] and Linger et al. [LIN79], among others, advocated proofs of program correctness and tied these to the use of structured programming concepts (Chapter 10). Although a number of different approaches to formal proof of correctness have been proposed and the mathematics that underlie most are relatively complex, the basis for the technique is actually quite simple. A program is viewed as a sequence of instructions that implements some specified function. At various points in the sequence, the designer of the program can determine (from the specification) the correct value of program variables, the proper status of control information, and other internal relationships. Therefore, at selected statements $s_1, s_2, \ldots, s_n$ in the program, the software engineer can assert that specific conditions $c_1, c_2, \ldots, c_n$ are invariably true.

To prove the program correct, the program statements between selected statements s_i and s_{i+1} must be shown to cause the asserted condition c_i to be transformed into c_{i+1}. Progressing incrementally, it can be shown that the application of the program to the input will produce the asserted output conditions at the end of the program. An analogous approach is used to demonstrate the correspondence between the formal specification and the program.

Some proponents of proof of correctness believe that the approach described above (or other variations of it) must be applied by each software engineer as she or he designs and implements individual program modules.

Others feel that the only hope for formal proofs lies in the development of automated tools that will do most of the work for the developer.

17.5.2 Statistical Quality Assurance

Statistical quality assurance reflects a growing trend throughout industry to become more quantitative about quality. For software, statistical quality assurance implies the following steps:

1. Information about software defects is collected and categorized.
2. An attempt is made to trace each defect to its underlying cause (e.g., nonconformance to specification, design error, violation of standards, poor communication with customer).
3. Using the Pareto principle (80 percent of the defects can be traced to 20 percent of all the possible causes), isolate the 20 percent (the "vital few").
4. Once the vital few causes have been identified, move to correct the problems that have caused the defects.

This relatively simple concept represents an important step toward the creation of an adaptive software engineering process in which changes are made to improve those elements of the process that introduce error.

To illustrate the process, assume that a software development organization collects information on defects for a period of 1 year. Some of the defects are uncovered as the software is being developed. Others are encountered after the software has been released to its end user. Although hundreds of different errors are uncovered, all can be tracked to one (or more) of the following causes:

- Incomplete or erroneous specification (IES)
- Misinterpretation of customer communication (MCC)
- Intentional deviation from specification (IDS)
- Violation of programming standards (VPS)
- Error in data representation (EDR)
- Inconsistent module interface (IMI)
- Error in design logic (EDL)
- Incomplete or erroneous testing (IET)
- Inaccurate or incomplete documentation (IID)
- Error in programming language translation of design (PLT)
- Ambiguous or inconsistent human-computer interface (HCI)
- Miscellaneous (MIS)

To apply statistical SQA, Table 17.3 is built. The table indicates that IES, MCC, and EDR are the vital few causes that account for 53 percent of all

TABLE 17.3

DATA COLLECTION FOR STATISTICAL SQA

	Total		Serious		Moderate		Minor	
Error	**No.**	**%**	**No.**	**%**	**No.**	**%**	**No.**	**%**
IES	205	22	34	27	68	18	103	24
MCC	156	17	12	9	68	18	76	17
IDS	48	5	1	1	24	6	23	5
VPS	25	3	0	0	15	4	10	2
EDR	130	14	26	20	68	18	36	8
IMI	58	6	9	7	18	5	31	7
EDL	45	5	14	11	12	3	19	4
IET	95	10	12	9	35	9	48	11
IID	36	4	2	2	20	5	14	3
PLT	60	6	15	12	19	5	26	6
HCI	28	3	3	2	17	4	8	2
MIS	56	6	0	0	15	4	41	9
Totals	942	100%	128	100%	379	100%	435	100%

errors. It should be noted, however, that IES, EDR, PLT, and EDL would be selected as the vital few causes if only serious errors were considered. Once the vital few causes are determined, the software development organization can begin corrective action. For example, to correct MCC, the software developer might implement facilitated application specification techniques (Chapter 6) to improve the quality of customer communication and specification. To improve EDR, the developer might acquire CASE tools for data modeling and perform more stringent data design reviews.

It is important to note that corrective action focuses primarily on the vital few. As the vital few causes are corrected, new candidates pop to the top of the stack.

In conjunction with the collection of defect information, software developers can calculate a defect index (DI) for each major step in the software engineering process. After analysis, design, coding, testing, and release, the following data are gathered:

D_i = the total number of defects uncovered during the ith step in the software engineering process

S_i = the number of serious defects

M_i = the number of moderate defects

T_i = the number of minor defects

PS = size of the product (LOC, design statements, pages of documentation) at the ith step

w_j = weighting factor for serious, moderate, and trivial defects, where $j = 1$ to 3

At each step of the software engineering process, a phase index, PI_i, is computed:

$$PI_i = w_1\left(\frac{S_i}{D_i}\right) + w_2\left(\frac{M_i}{D_i}\right) + w_2\left(\frac{T_i}{D_i}\right)$$

The defect index (DI) is computed by calculating the cumulative effect of each PI_i, weighting errors encountered later in the software engineering process more heavily than those encountered earlier:

$$\begin{aligned} DI &= \frac{\sum (i \times PI_i)}{PS} \\ &= \frac{PI_1 + 2PI_2 + 3PI_3 + \cdots + iPI_i}{PS} \end{aligned} \tag{17.5}$$

The defect index can be used in conjunction with information collected in Table 17.3 to develop an overall indication of improvement in software quality.

The application of the statistical SQA and the Pareto principle can be summarized in a single sentence: Spend your time focusing on things that really matter, but first be sure that you understand what really matters! Experienced industry practitioners agree that most really difficult defects can be traced to a relatively limited number of root causes. In fact, most practitioners have an intuitive feeling for the "real" causes of software defects, but few have spent time collecting data to support their feelings. By performing the basic steps of statistical SQA, the vital few causes for defects can be isolated and appropriate corrections can be made.

A comprehensive discussion of statistical SQA is beyond the scope of this book. See Schulmeyer and McManus [SCH87] for an overview of the subject, and Juran [JUR79] for more detailed information.

17.5.3 The Cleanroom Process

Formal program verification (correctness proofs) and statistical SQA have been combined into a technique that improves the quality of product software. Called the *cleanroom process* [CUR86] or *cleanroom software engineering*, it is described by Mills et al. [MIL87]:

> With the cleanroom process, you can engineer software under statistical quality control. As with cleanroom hardware development, the process's first

> priority is defect prevention rather than defect removal (of course, any defects not prevented should be removed). This first priority is achieved by using human mathematical verification [proofs of correctness] in place of program debugging to prepare software for system test.
>
> Its next priority is to provide valid, statistical certification of the software's quality.... The measure of quality is the mean time to failure....

Developers of the cleanroom process argue that mathematical program verification "need take no more time than debugging" and that the resultant number of defects per KLOC can be reduced substantially. For software projects (between 1000 and 50,000 LOC) developed using the cleanroom approach, 90 percent of all defects were found before the first executable tests were conducted.

To date, cleanroom software engineering has not been widely applied in the industry. Although the underlying concepts have merit, substantial changes in both the management and technical approaches to software development must be made before such techniques can work effectively. For additional information, the interested reader should see Poore et al. [POO90].

17.6 SOFTWARE RELIABILITY

There is no doubt that the reliability of a computer program is an important element of its overall quality. If a program repeatedly and frequently fails to perform, it matters little whether other software quality factors are acceptable.

Software reliability, unlike many other quality factors, can be measured directly and estimated using historical and developmental data. Software reliability is defined in statistical terms as "the probability of failure free operation of a computer program in a specified environment for a specified time." [MUS87] To illustrate, program X is estimated to have a reliability of 0.96 over eight elapsed processing hours. In other words, if program X were to be executed 100 times and require 8 hours of elapsed processing time (execution time), it is likely to operate correctly (without failure) 96 times out of 100.

Whenever software reliability is discussed, a pivotal question arises: What is meant by the term "failure"? In the context of any discussion of software quality and reliability, failure is nonconformance to software requirements. Yet, even within this definition there are gradations. Failures can be merely annoying or they can be catastrophic. One failure can be corrected within seconds while another requires weeks or even months to correct. Complicating the issue even further, the correction of one failure may in fact result in the introduction of other errors that ultimately result in other failures.

17.6.1 Measures of Reliability and Availability

Early work in software reliability attempted to extrapolate the mathematics of hardware reliability theory (e.g., [ALV64]) to the prediction of software reliability. Most hardware-related reliability models are predicated on failure due to *wear* rather than failure due to design defects. In hardware, failures due to physical wear (e.g., the affects of temperature, corrosion, shock) are more likely than a design-related failure. Unfortunately, the opposite is true for software. In fact, all software failures can be traced to design or implementation problems; wear (see Chapter 1) does not enter into the picture.

There is still debate over the relationship between key concepts in hardware reliability and their applicability to software. Although an irrefutable link has yet to be established, it is worthwhile to consider a few simple concepts that apply to both system elements.

If we consider a computer-based system, a simple measure of reliability is *mean time between failure* (MTBF), where

$$\text{MTBF} = \text{MTTF} + \text{MTTR}$$

(The acronyms MTTF and MTTR are *mean time to failure* and *mean time to repair,* respectively.)

Many researchers argument that MTBF is a far more useful measure than defects/KLOC. Stated simply, an end user is concerned with failures, not with the total error count. Because each error contained within a program does not have the same failure rate, the total error count provides little indication of the reliability of a system. For example, consider a program that has been in operation for 14 months. Many errors in this program may remain undetected for decades before they are discovered. The MTBF of such obscure errors might be 50 or even 100 years. Other errors, as yet undiscovered, might have a failure rate of 18 or 24 months. Even if every one of the first category of errors (those with long MTBF) is removed, the impact on software reliability is negligible.

In addition to a reliability measure, we must develop a measure of *availability.* Software availability is the probability that a program is operating according to requirements at a given point in time and is defined as

$$\text{Availability} = \frac{\text{MTTF}}{(\text{MTTF} + \text{MTTR})} \times 100\%$$

The MTBF reliability measure is equally sensitive to MTTF and MTTR. The availability measure is somewhat more sensitive to MTTR, an indirect measure of the maintainability of software.

17.6.2 Software Reliability Models

In a comprehensive treatment of software reliability, Musa and his colleagues [MUS87, p. 18] describe software reliability models in the following manner:

> To model software reliability one must first consider the principal factors that affect it: fault introduction, fault removal, and the environment. Fault introduction depends primarily on the characteristics of the developed code (code created or modified for the application) and development process characteristics. The most significant code characteristic is size. Development process characteristics include software engineering technologies and tools used and level of experience of personnel. Note that code can be developed to add features or to remove faults. Fault removal depends on time, operational profile, and the quality of the repair activity. The environment directly depends on the operational profile. Since some of the foregoing factors are probabilistic in nature and operate over time, software reliability models are generally formulated in terms of random processes.

Software reliability models fall into two broad categories: (1) models that predict reliability as a function of chronological (calendar) time and (2) models that predict reliability as a function of elapsed processing time (CPU execution time). Musa et al. [MUS87] suggest that software reliability models that are based on elapsed processing time (execution time) show the best overall results.

Models that have been derived from hardware reliability work make the following assumptions: (1) the debugging time between error occurrences has an exponential distribution with an error occurrence rate that is proportional to the number of remaining errors; (2) each error discovered is immediately removed, decreasing the total number of errors by one; (3) the failure rate between errors is constant [SUK78]. The validity of each of these assumptions can be questioned. For example, correction of one error may inadvertently introduce other errors into the software, invalidating the second assumption.

Another class of reliability models is based on the internal characteristics of a program and computes a predicted number of errors that exist in the software. The models, based on the quantitative relationships derived as a function of software complexity measures (Sections 17.4.2 and 17.4.3), relate specific design or code-oriented attributes of a program (e.g., number of operands and operators or the cyclomatic complexity) to "an estimate of the initial number of errors to be expected in a given program" [HAL77].

Seeding models (e.g., [KNI85]) can be used as an indication of software reliability or, more practically, as a measure of the "error detection power" of a set of test cases. A program is randomly seeded with a number of known "calibration" errors [MIL72]. The program is tested (using test cases). The probability of finding j real errors of a total population of J (an unknown) errors can be related to the probability of finding k seeded errors from all K errors embedded in the code.

Much more sophisticated stochastic models for software reliability have also been proposed (e.g., see [SHO83], [MIL85], and [MUS87]). For those readers who intend to study such models in greater detail, Iannino [IAN84] suggests a set of criteria for comparison and assessment:

Predictive validity—the ability of the model to predict future failure behavior based on data collected from the testing and operational phases

Capability—the ability of the model to generate data that can be readily applied to pragmatic industrial software development efforts

Quality of assumptions—the plausibility of the assumptions on which the mathematical foundation of the model is based and the degree of degradation of the model when the limits of those assumptions are reached

Applicability—the degree to which a reliability model can be applied across different software application domains and types

Simplicity—the degree to which collection of data to support the model is straightforward; the degree to which the mathematics and approach are intuitive; the degree to which the overall approach can be automated

A discussion of the models to which these criteria apply requires a background in statistics and probability and is better left to textbooks dedicated to software reliability. The interested reader should refer to Shooman [SHO83], Musa et al. [MUS87], and Rook [ROO90].

17.6.3 Software Safety

There has been an historical reluctance to use computers (and software) to control safety critical processes such as nuclear reactors, aircraft flight control, weapons systems, and large-scale industrial processes. Although the probability of failure of a well-engineered system is small, an undetected fault in a computer-based control or monitoring system could result in enormous economic damage or, worse, significant human injury or loss of life. But the cost and functional benefits of computer-based control and monitoring often outweigh the risk. Today, computer hardware and software are used regularly to control safety critical systems. Leveson [LEV86] discusses the impact of software in safety critical systems when she writes:

> Before software was used in safety critical systems, they were often controlled by conventional (nonprogrammable) mechanical and electronic devices. System safety techniques are designed to cope with random failures in these [nonprogrammable] systems. Human design errors are not considered since it is

assumed that all faults caused by human errors can be avoided completely or removed prior to delivery and operation.

When software is used as part of the control system, complexity can increase by an order of magnitude or more. Subtle design faults induced by human error—something that can be uncovered and eliminated in hardware-based conventional control—become much more difficult to uncover when software is used.

Software safety is a software quality assurance activity that focuses on the identification and assessment of potential hazards that may impact software negatively and cause an entire system to fail. If hazards can be identified early in the software engineering process, software design features can be specified that will either eliminate or control potential hazards.

A modeling and analysis process is conducted as part of software safety. Initially, hazards are identified and categorized by criticality and risk. For example, some of the hazards associated with a computer-based cruise control for an automobile might be:

- Causes uncontrolled acceleration that cannot be stopped
- Does not respond to depression of brake pedal (by turning off)
- Does not engage when switch is activated
- Slowly loses or gains speed

Once these system level hazards are identified, analysis techniques are used to assign severity and probability of occurrence.[3] To be effective, software must be analyzed in the context of the entire system. For example, a subtle user input error (people *are* system components) may be magnified by a software fault to produce control data that improperly position a mechanical device. If a set of external environmental conditions are met (and only if they are met), the improper position of the mechanical device will cause a disastrous failure. Analysis techniques such as fault tree analysis [VES81], real-time logic [JAN86], or petri net models [LEV87] can be used to predict the chain of events that can cause hazards and the probability that each of the events will occur to create the chain.

Fault tree analysis builds a graphical model of the sequential and concurrent combinations of events that can lead to a hazardous event or system state. Using a well-developed fault tree, it is possible to observe the consequences of a sequence of interrelated failures that occur in different system components. *Real-time logic* (RTL) builds a system model by specifying events and corresponding actions. The event-action model can be analyzed

[3]This approach is analogous to the risk analysis approach described for software project management in Chapter 4. The primary difference is the emphasis on technology issues as opposed to project-related topics.

using logic operations to test safety assertions about system components and their timing. *Petri net* models can be used to determine the faults that are most hazardous.

Once hazards are identified and analyzed, safety-related requirements can be specified for the software. That is, the specification can contain a list of undesirable events and the desired system responses to these events. The role of software in managing undesirable events is then indicated.

In an earlier section, the role of software reliability analysis was discussed. Although software reliability and software safety are closely related, it is important to understand the subtle difference between them. Software reliability uses statistical analysis to determine the likelihood that a software failure will occur. However, the occurrence of a failure does not necessarily result in a hazard or mishap. Software safety examines the ways in which failures result in conditions that can lead to a mishap. That is, failures are not considered in a vacuum, but are evaluated in the context of an entire computer-based system.

A comprehensive discussion of software safety is beyond the scope of this book. For those readers with further interest, excellent bibliographies are given by Leveson ([LEV86], [LEV91]) and Parnas et al. [PAR90].

17.7 A SOFTWARE QUALITY ASSURANCE APPROACH

Although few managers and practitioners would debate the need for software quality, many are disinterested in establishing formal SQA functions. The reasons for this seeming contradiction are many: (1) Managers are reluctant to incur the extra up-front cost; (2) practitioners feel they are already doing everything that needs to be done; (3) no one knows where to put such a function organizationally; (4) everyone wants to avoid the "red tape" that SQA is perceived to introduce into the software engineering process.

In this section, we present a brief discussion of the most important concerns for instituting software quality assurance activities. For a more detailed presentation, see Schulmeyer and McManus [SCH87], and Dunn [DUN90].

17.7.1 Examining the Need for SQA

All software development organizations have some mechanism for quality assessment. At the low end of the scale, quality is the sole responsibility of the individual who may engineer, review, and test at any comfort level. At the high end of the scale, an SQA group is chartered with the responsibility for establishing standards and procedures for achieving software quality and ensuring that each is followed. The real question for every software engineering organization is: Where on the scale do we sit?

Before formal quality assurance procedures are instituted, a software development organization should adopt software engineering procedures, methods, and tools. This methodology, when combined with an effective paradigm for software development, can do much to improve the quality of all the software produced by the organization.

The first step to be conducted as part of a concerted effort to institute software quality assurance procedures is an *SQA/SCM audit*. The current "state" of software quality assurance and software configuration management (Chapter 21) is assessed by examining the following topics:

Policies. What current policies, procedures, and standards exist for all phases of software development? Are they enforced? Is there a specific (management-supported) policy for SQA? Are policies applied to both development and maintenance activities?

Organization. Where does software engineering reside in the current organizational chart? Where does quality assurance reside?

Functional interfaces. What is the current relationship between quality assurance and SQA functions and other constituencies? How does SQA interact with the people who perform formal technical reviews, configuration management, and testing?

Once the above questions have been answered, strengths and weaknesses are identified. If the need for SQA is apparent, a careful assessment of the pros and cons is undertaken.

On the positive side, SQA offers the following benefits: (1) Software will have fewer latent defects, resulting in reduced effort and time spent during testing and maintenance; (2) higher reliability will result in greater customer satisfaction; (3) maintenance costs (a substantial percentage of *all* software costs) can be reduced; and (4) overall life cycle cost of software is reduced. As Crosby [CRO79] states: Quality is free!

On the negative side, SQA can be problematic for the following reasons: (1) It is difficult to institute in small organizations, where available resources to perform the necessary activities are not available; (2) it represents cultural change—and change is never easy; (3) it requires the expenditure of dollars that would not otherwise be explicitly budgeted to software engineering or QA.

At a fundamental level, SQA is cost-effective if

$$C_3 > C_1 + C_2$$

where C_3 is the cost of errors that occur with no SQA program, C_1 is the cost of the SQA program itself, and C_2 is the cost of errors not found by SQA activities. It is important to note, however, that a more detailed analysis must also consider reduced testing and integration costs, reduced numbers of pre-release changes, reduced maintenance costs, and improved customer satisfaction. In general, SQA evolves as part of an overall management commitment to improved quality—often called "total quality management."

17.7.2 SQA Planning and Standards

Once an organization has decided to institute SQA, a plan should be developed and standards should be acquired. The IEEE [IEE89] has developed a standard format for SQA plans that is shown in Table 17.4.

TABLE 17.4

ANSI/IEEE STANDARDS 730-1984 AND 983-1986, SOFTWARE QUALITY ASSURANCE PLAN

- **I.** Purpose of the plan
- **II.** References
- **III.** Management
  - **A.** Organization
  - **B.** Tasks
  - **C.** Responsibilities
- **IV.** Documentation
  - **A.** Purpose
  - **B.** Required software engineering documents
  - **C.** Other documents
- **V.** Standards, practices, and conventions
  - **A.** Purpose
  - **B.** Conventions
- **VI.** Reviews and audits
  - **A.** Purpose
  - **B.** Review requirements
    - **1.** Software requirements review
    - **2.** Design reviews
    - **3.** Software verification and validation reviews
    - **4.** Functional audit
    - **5.** Physical audit
    - **6.** In-process audits
    - **7.** Management reviews
- **VII.** Software configuration management
- **VIII.** Problem reporting and corrective action
- **IX.** Tools, techniques, and methodologies
- **X.** Code control
- **XI.** Media control
- **XII.** Supplier control
- **XIII.** Records collection, maintenance, and retention

TABLE 17.5

SQA STANDARDS

DOD-STD-2167A	Software engineering
DOD-STD-2168	Software quality evaluation standard
FAA-STD-018	SQA standard for the FAA
IEEE Std. 730-1984	SQA plans
IEEE Std. 983-1986	Software quality assurance planning
IEEE Std. 1028-1988	Software reviews and audits
IEEE Std. 1012-1986	Software verification and validation plans

The *SQA Plan* provides a road map for instituting software quality assurance. Table 17.5 presents a list of SQA related standards that will serve to guide the development of technical procedures for achieving software quality.

17.8 SUMMARY

Software quality assurance is an "umbrella activity" that is applied at each step in the software engineering process. SQA encompasses procedures for the effective application of methods and tools, formal technical reviews, testing strategies and techniques, procedures for change control, procedures for assuring compliance to standards, and measurement and reporting mechanisms.

SQA is complicated by the complex nature of software quality—an attribute of computer programs that is defined as "conformance to explicitly defined requirements." But when considered more generally, software quality encompasses many different product and process factors and related metrics.

Software reviews are one of the most important SQA activities. Reviews serve as a filter for the software engineering process, removing defects while they are relatively inexpensive to find and correct. The formal technical review or walkthrough is a stylized review meeting that has been shown to be extremely effective in uncovering defects.

To properly conduct software quality assurance, data about the software engineering process should be collected, evaluated, and disseminated. Software quality metrics include both direct and indirect measures of software. Some metrics are the result of subjective qualitative assessment, while others are quantitative in nature. Formal techniques such as program proofs and statistical SQA help to improve the quality of the product and process, respectively. Software reliability models extend measurements, enabling collected defect data to be extrapolated into projected failure rates and reliability. Software safety assesses the system-wide impact of software failure.

In summary, we recall the words of Dunn and Ullman [DUN82]: "software quality assurance is the mapping of the managerial precepts and design disciplines of quality assurance onto the applicable managerial and technological space of software engineering." The ability to ensure quality is the measure of a mature engineering discipline. When the mapping alluded to above is successfully accomplished, mature software engineering is the result.

REFERENCES

[ALV64] von Alvin, W. H. (ed.), *Reliability Engineering,* Prentice-Hall, 1964.

[BON76] Bondy, J., and U. Murty, *Graph Theory with Applications,* North Holland, 1976.

[CAV78] Cavano, J. P., and J. A. McCall, "A Framework for the Measurement of Software Quality," *Proc. ACM Software Quality Assurance Workshop,* November 1978, pp. 133–139.

[CHA89] Charette, R. N., *Software Engineering Risk Analysis and Management,* McGraw-Hill/Intertext, 1989.

[CRO79] Crosby, P., *Quality is Free,* McGraw-Hill, 1979.

[CUR79] Curtis, W., et al., "Measuring the Psychological Complexity of Software Maintenance Tasks with the Halstead and McCabe Metrics," *IEEE Trans. Software Engineering,* vol. 5, no. 2, March 1979, pp. 96–104.

[CUR80] Curtis, W., "Management and Experimentation in Software Engineering, *Proceedings of the IEEE,* vol. 68, no. 9, September 1980.

[CUR86] Currit, A., M. Dyer, and H. D. Mills, "Certifying the Reliability of Software," *IEEE Trans. Software Engineering,* vol. 12, no. 1, January 1986, pp. 3–11.

[DIJ76] Dijkstra, E., *A Discipline of Programming,* Prentice-Hall, 1976.

[DUN82] Dunn, R., and R. Ullman, *Quality Assurance for Computer Software,* McGraw-Hill, 1982.

[DUN90] Dunn, R., *Software Quality Assurance,* Prentice-Hall, 1990.

[FEL89] Felican, L., and G. Zalateu, "Validating Halstead's Theory for Pascal Programs," *IEEE Trans. Software Engineering,* vol. 15, no. 12, December 1989, pp. 1630–1632.

[FIT78] Fitzsimmons, A., and T. Love, "A Review and Evaluation of Software Science," *ACM Computing Surveys,* vol. 10, no. 1, March 1978, pp. 3–18.

[FRE90] Freedman, D. P., and G. M. Weinberg, *Handbook of Walkthroughs, Inspections and Technical Reviews,* 3d ed., Dorset House, 1990.

[GRA87] Grady, R. B., and D. L. Caswell, *Software Metrics: Establishing a Company-Wide Program,* Prentice-Hall, 1987.

[GRE76] Green, T. F., et al., "Program Structures, Complexity and Error Characteristics," in *Computer Software Engineering,* (J. Fox, ed.) Polytechnic Press, New York, 1976, pp. 139–154.

[HAL77] Halstead, M., *Elements of Software Science,* North Holland, 1977.

[IAN84] Iannino, A., et al., "Criteria for Software Reliability Model Comparisons," *IEEE Trans. Software Engineering,* vol. SE-10, no. 6, November 1984, pp. 687–691.

[IBM81] "Implementing Software Inspections," course notes, IBM Systems Sciences Institute, IBM Corporation, 1981.

[IEE89] *Software Engineering Standards,* 3d ed., IEEE, 1989.

[JAN86] Jahanian, F., and A. K. Mok, "Safety Analysis of Timing Properties of Real-Time Systems," *IEEE Trans. Software Engineering,* vol. SE-12, no. 9, September 1986, pp. 890–904.

[JON81] Jones, T.C., *Programming Productivity: Issues for the 80s,* IEEE Computer Society Press, 1981, pp. 13–20.

[JON86] Jones, T.C., *Programming Productivity,* McGraw-Hill, 1986.

[JUR79] Juran, J. M. et al., (eds.), *Quality Control Handbook,* 3d ed., McGraw-Hill, 1979.

[KNI85] Knight, J.C., and P. E. Ammenn, "An Experimental Evaluation of Simple Methods for Seeding Program Errors," *Proc. 8th Intl. Conf. Software Engineering,* IEEE, London, August 1985, pp. 337–342.

[LEV86] Leveson, N.G., "Software Safety: Why, What, and How," *ACM Computing Surveys,* vol. 18, no. 2, June 1986, pp. 125–163.

[LEV87] Leveson, N.G., and J. L. Stolzy, "Safety Analysis using Petri Nets," *IEEE Trans. Software Engineering,* vol. SE-13, no. 3, March 1987, pp. 386–397.

[LEV91] Leveson, N.G., "Software Safety in Embedded Computer Systems," *CACM,* vol. 34, no. 2, February 1991, pp. 34–46.

[LIN79] Linger, R., H. Mills, and B. Witt, *Structured Programming,* Addison-Wesley, 1979.

[MCC76] McCabe, T. J., "A Software Complexity Measure," *IEEE Trans. Software Engineering,* vol. 2, no. 6, December 1976, pp. 308–320.

[MCC77] McCall, J., P. Richards, and G. Walters, "Factors in Software Quality," three volumes, NTIS AD-A049-014, 015, 055, November 1977.

[MCC89] McCabe, T. J., and C.W. Butler, "Design Complexity Measurement and Testing," *CACM,* vol. 32, no. 12, December 1989, pp. 1415–1425.

[MIL72] Mills, H. D., "On the Statistical Validation of Computer Programs," FSC 72:6015, IBM Federal Systems Division, 1972.

[MIL85] Miller, D. R., and A. Sofer, "Completely Monotone Regression Estimates for Software Failure Rates," *Proc. 8th Intl. Conf. Software Engineering,* IEEE, London, August 1985, pp. 343–348.

[MIL87] Mills, H. D., M. Dyer, and R. C. Linger, "Cleanroom Software Engineering," *IEEE Software,* September 1987, pp. 19–25.

[MUS87] Musa, J. D., A. Iannino, and K. Okumoto, *Engineering and Managing Software with Reliability Measures,* McGraw-Hill, 1987.

[PAR90] Parnas, D. L., A. J. van Schouwen, and S. P. Kwan, "Evaluation of Safety Critical Software," *CACM,* vol. 33, no. 6, June 1990, pp. 636–648.

[POO90] Poore, J. H., D. Mutchler, and H. D. Mills, *Stars-Cleanroom Reliability, Cleanroom Ideas in the Stars Environment,* IBM Corp., System Integration Div., 1990.

[ROO90] Rook, J., *Software Reliability Handbook,* Elsevier, 1990.

[SCH87] Schulmeyer, G.C., and J. I. McManus (eds.), *Handbook of Software Quality Assurance,* Van Nostrand Reinhold, 1987.

[SHO83] Shooman, M., *Software Engineering,* McGraw-Hill, 1983.

[SOM89] Somerville, I., *Software Engineering,* 3d ed., Addison-Wesley, 1989.
[SUK78] Sukert, A., and A. Goel, "Error Modelling Applications in Software Quality Assurance," in *Proc. SQA Workshop,* ACM, San Diego, CA, November 1978, pp. 33–38.
[USA87] *Management Quality Insight,* AFCSP 800-14, U.S. Air Force, January 20, 1987.
[VES81] Veseley, W. E., et al., *Fault Tree Handbook,* NUREG-0492, U.S. Nuclear Regulatory Commission, January 1981.
[WAG87] Waguespack, L. J., and S. Badlani, "Software Complexity Assessment: An Introduction and Annotated Bibliography," *ACM Software Engineering Notes,* vol. 12, no. 4, October 1987, pp. 52–71.
[YOU89] Yourdon, E., *Structured Walkthroughs,* 4th ed., Yourdon Press (Prentice-Hall), 1989.
[ZEL81] Zelkowitz, M., private communication, 1981.

PROBLEMS AND POINTS TO PONDER

17.1 Although the quality factors described in Section 17.1 are interesting at a macroscopic level, how would you assess the quality of a computer program if the source listing were dumped on your desk right now? Discuss both the qualitative and the quantitative aspects of your assessment.

17.2 Is it possible to assess the quality of software if the customer keeps changing his or her mind about what it is supposed to do?

17.3 Quality, reliability, and safety are related concepts, but are fundamentally different in a number of ways. Discuss them.

17.4 Can a program be correct and still not be reliable? Explain. Can a program be correct and still not be safe? Explain.

17.5 Can a program be correct and still not exhibit good quality? Explain.

17.6 Why is there often tension between a software engineering group and an independent software quality assurance group? Is this healthy?

17.7 You have been given the responsibility for improving the quality of software across your organization. What is the first thing that you should do? What's next?

17.8 Besides counting errors, are there other countable characteristics of software that imply quality? What are they and can they be measured directly?

17.9 A formal technical review is effective only if everyone has prepared in advance. How do you recognize a review participant who has not prepared? What do you do, if you're the review leader?

17.10 Some people argue that an FTR should assess programming style as well as correctness. Is this a good idea? Why?

17.11 Develop a small software tool that will perform a Halstead analysis on a programming language source code of your choosing.

17.12 Research the literature and write a paper on the relationship of Halstead's metric and McCabe's metric on software quality (as measured by error count). Are the data compelling? Recommend guidelines for the application of these metrics.

17.13 Develop a software tool that will compute McCabe's metric (cyclomatic complexity) for a programming language module. You may choose the language.

17.14 Review Table 17.3 and select four vital few causes of serious and moderate errors. Suggest corrective actions based on information presented in other chapters.

17.15 An organization uses a five-step software engineering process in which errors are found according to the following percentage distribution:

Step	Percentage of errors found
1	20
2	15
3	15
4	40
5	10

Using Table 17.3 information and the percentage distribution above, compute the overall defect index for the organization. Assume PS = 100,000.

17.16 Research the literature on software reliability and write a paper that describes one software reliability model. Be sure to provide an example.

17.17 The MTBF concept for software is open to criticism. Can you think of a few reasons why?

17.18 Consider two safety-critical systems that are controlled by computer. List at least three hazards for each that can be directly linked to software failures.

FURTHER READINGS

Books by Crosby [CRO79] and Deming (*Out of the Crisis,* MIT Press, 1986) are excellent management-level presentations on the benefits of formal quality assurance programs. Although they do not focus on software, both books are must reading for senior managers with software development responsibilities.

Books by Dunn [DUN90], Vincent et al. (*Software Quality Assurance,* Prentice-Hall, 1988), Bryan and Seigel (*Software Product Assurance,* Elsevier, 1988), and Chow (*Software Quality Assurance: A Practical Approach,* IEEE Computer Society Press, 1985) provide detailed coverage of SQA, quality metrics, and the management issues associated with establishing an SQA function. Dunn and Ullman [DUN82] present comprehensive guidelines for planning, establishing, and conducting the SQA function.

Freedman and Weinberg [FRE90] contains a comprehensive discussion of every facet of formal technical reviews. In addition books by Yourdon [YOU89] and Hollocker (*Software Reviews and Audits Handbook,* Wiley, 1990) contain useful guidelines for conducting these worthwhile SQA activities.

Schulmeyer (*Zero Defects Software,* McGraw-Hill, 1990) discusses "quality control" for computer software. The book presents a detailed taxonomy of defects, and discusses review and inspection techniques, statistical SQA, and software testing. Dijkstra (*The Formal Development of Programs and Proofs,* Addison-Wesley, 1990) presents a mathematically rigorous treatment of proof of correctness.

Waguespack and Badlani [WAG87] present a well-researched bibliography on software complexity and related software metrics. Their paper contains well over 150 annotated references. Books by Shooman [SHO83] and Musa et al. [MUS87] contain detailed stochastic models for software reliability. Rook [ROO90] presents a comprehensive anthology that covers basic reliability concepts, models methods, and measures. Leveson (*Software Safety,* Addison-Wesley, 1990) presents an in-depth discussion of software safety concepts that should be of particular interest to developers of real-time monitoring and control and embedded systems.

CHAPTER 18

SOFTWARE TESTING TECHNIQUES

The importance of software testing and its implications with respect to software quality cannot be overemphasized. To quote Deutsch [DEU79]:

> The development of software systems involves a series of production activities where opportunities for injection of human fallibilities are enormous. Errors may begin to occur at the very inception of the process where the objectives... may be erroneously or imperfectly specified, as well as [errors that occur in] later design and development stages.... Because of human inability to perform and communicate with perfection, software development is accompanied by a quality assurance activity.

Software testing is a critical element of software quality assurance and represents the ultimate review of specification, design, and coding.

The increasing visibility of software as a system element and the attendant "costs" associated with a software failure are motivating forces for well-planned, thorough testing. It is not unusual for a software development organization to expend 40 percent of total project effort on testing. In the extreme, the testing of human-rated software (e.g., flight control, nuclear reactor monitoring) can cost three to five times as much as all other software engineering steps combined!

In this chapter, we discuss software testing fundamentals and techniques for software test case design. Software testing fundamentals define the overriding objectives for software testing. Test case design focuses on a set of techniques for the creation of test cases that meet overall testing objectives. In Chapter 19, testing strategies and software debugging are presented.

18.1 SOFTWARE TESTING FUNDAMENTALS

Testing presents an interesting anomaly for the software engineer. During earlier definition and development phases, the engineer attempts to build software from an abstract concept to a tangible implementation. Now comes testing. The engineer creates a series of test cases that are intended to "demolish" the software that has been built. In fact, testing is the one step in the software engineering process that could be viewed (psychologically, at least) as destructive rather than constructive.

Software developers are by their nature constructive people. Testing requires that the developer discard preconceived notions of the "correctness" of the software just developed and overcome a conflict of interest that occurs when errors are uncovered.

Beizer [BEI90, p. 1] describes this situation effectively when he states:

> There's a myth that if we were really good at programming, there would be no bugs to catch. If only we could really concentrate, if only everyone used structured programming, top-down design, decision tables, if programs were written in SQUISH, if we had the right silver bullets, then there would be no bugs. So goes the myth. There are bugs, the myth says, because we are bad at what we do; and if we are bad at it, we should feel guilty about it. Therefore, testing and test case design is an admission of failure, which instills a goodly dose of guilt. And the tedium of testing is just punishment for our errors. Punishment for what? For being human? Guilt for what? For failing to achieve inhuman perfection? For not distinguishing between what another programmer thinks and what he says? For failing to be telepathic? For not solving human communications problems that have been kicked around... for forty centuries?

Should testing instill guilt? Is testing really destructive? The answer to these questions is "No!" However, the objectives of testing are somewhat different than we might expect.

18.1.1 Testing Objectives

In an excellent book on software testing, Glen Myers [MYE79] states a number of rules that can serve well as testing objectives:

1. Testing is a process of executing a program with the intent of finding an error.
2. A good test case is one that has a high probability of finding an as yet undiscovered error.
3. A successful test is one that uncovers an as yet undiscovered error.

The above objectives imply a dramatic change in viewpoint. They move counter to the commonly held view that a successful test is one in which no errors are found. Our objective is to design tests that systematically uncover different classes of errors and to do so with a minimum amount of time and effort.

If testing is conducted successfully (according to the objective stated above), it will uncover errors in the software. As a secondary benefit, testing demonstrates that software functions appear to be working according to specification, that performance requirements appear to have been met. In addition, data collected as testing is conducted provide a good indication of software reliability and some indication of software quality as a whole. But there is one thing that testing cannot do:

> Testing cannot show the absence of defects, it can only show that software defects are present.

It is important to keep this (rather gloomy) statement in mind as testing is being conducted.

18.1.2 Test Information Flow

Information flow for testing follows the pattern described in Figure 18.1. Two classes of input are provided to the test process: (1) a software configuration that includes a *Software Requirements Specification*, a *Design Specification*, and source code; (2) a *test configuration* that includes a *Test Plan and Procedure*, any testing tools (Section 18.7) that are to be used, and test cases and their expected results. In actuality, the test configuration is a subset of the software configuration.

Tests are conducted and all results are evaluated. That is, test results are compared with the expected results. When erroneous data are uncov-

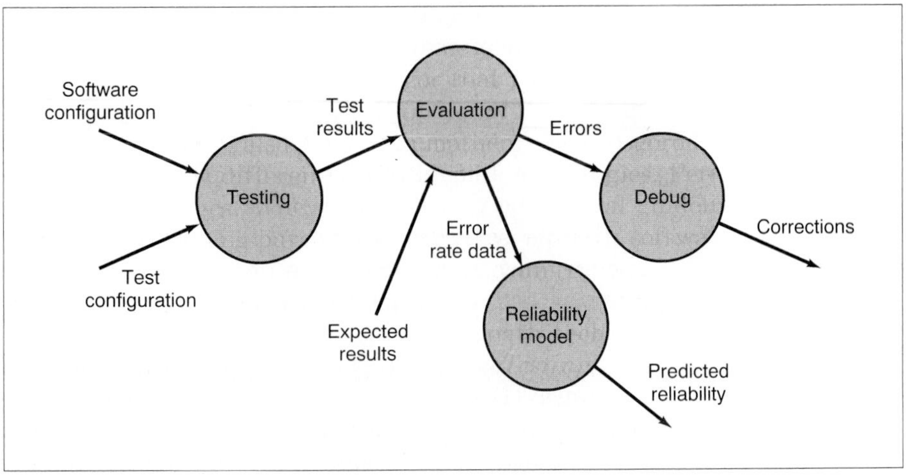

FIGURE 18.1.
Test information flow.

ered, an error is implied and debugging commences. The debugging process (discussed in Chapter 19) is the most unpredictable part of the testing process. An "error" that indicates a discrepancy of 0.01 percent between the expected and actual results can take 1 hour, 1 day, or 1 month to diagnose and correct. It is the uncertainty inherent in debugging that makes testing difficult to schedule reliably.

As test results are gathered and evaluated, a qualitative indication of software quality and reliability begins to surface. If severe errors that require design modification are encountered with regularity, software quality and reliability are suspect and further tests are indicated. If, on the other hand, software functions appear to be working properly and the errors encountered are easily correctable, one of two conclusions can be drawn: (1) Software quality and reliability are acceptable, or (2) tests are inadequate to uncover severe errors! Finally, if testing uncovers no errors there is little doubt that the test configuration was not given enough thought and that errors do lurk in the software. These defects will eventually be uncovered by the users and corrected by the developer during the maintenance phase (when cost per fix can be 60 to 100 times the cost per fix during the development phase).

The results accumulated during testing can also be evaluated in a more formal manner. Software reliability models (Chapter 17) use error-rate data to predict future occurrence of errors and, hence, reliability.

Each bubble of Figure 18.1 represents an exceedingly complex transform. Throughout the remainder of this chapter, we examine the concepts and processes that make test information flow comprehensible and test transforms understandable.

18.1.3 Test Case Design

The design of tests for software and other engineered products can be as challenging as the initial design of the product itself. Yet for reasons that we have already discussed, software engineers often treat testing as an afterthought, developing test cases that may "feel right" but have little assurance of being complete. Recalling the objectives of testing, we must design tests that have the highest likelihood of finding the most errors with a minimum amount of time and effort.

Over the past decade a rich variety of test case design methods have evolved for software. These methods provide the developer with a systematic approach to testing. More importantly, methods provide a mechanism that can help to ensure the completeness of tests and provide the highest likelihood for uncovering errors in software.

Any engineered product (and most other things) can be tested in one of two ways: (1) Knowing the specified function that a product has been designed to perform, tests can be conducted that demonstrate each function is fully operational; (2) knowing the internal workings of a product, tests can be conducted to ensure that "all the gears mesh," that is, that the internal operation of the product performs according to specification and all internal components have been adequately exercised. The first test approach is called *black box testing* and the second *white box testing*.

When computer software is considered, black box testing alludes to tests that are conducted at the software interface. Although they are designed to uncover errors, black-box tests are used to demonstrate that software functions are operational; that input is properly accepted, and output is correctly produced; that the integrity of external information (e.g., data files) is maintained. A black box test examines some aspect of a system with little regard for the internal logical structure of the software.

White box testing of software is predicated on a close examination of procedural detail. Logical paths through the software are tested by providing test cases that exercise specific sets of conditions and/or loops. The "status of the program" may be examined at various points to determine if the expected or asserted status corresponds to the actual status.

At first glance it would seem that very thorough white box testing would lead to "100 percent correct programs." All we need do is define all logical paths, develop test cases to exercise them, and evaluate the results, that is, generate test cases to exercise program logic exhaustively. Unfortunately, exhaustive testing presents certain logistical problems. For even small programs, the number of possible logical paths can be very large. For example, consider the flow chart shown in Figure 18.2. The procedural design illustrated by the flow chart might correspond to a 100-line PASCAL program with a single loop that may be executed no more than 20 times. There are approximately 10^{14} possible paths that may be executed!

To put this number in perspective, we assume that a *magic* test processor ("magic" because no such processor exists) has been developed for exhaustive testing. The processor can develop a test case, execute it, and evaluate the results in 1 millisecond. Working 24 hours a days, 365 days a year, the processor would work for 3170 years to test the program represented in Figure 18.2. This would, undeniably, cause havoc in most development schedules. Exhaustive testing is impossible for large software systems.

White box testing should not, however, be dismissed as impractical. A limited number of important logical paths can be selected and exercised. Important data structures can be probed for validity. The attributes of both black and white box testing can be combined to provide an approach that validates the software interface and selectively ensures that the internal workings of the software are correct.

18.2 WHITE BOX TESTING

White box testing is a test case design method that uses the control structure of the procedural design to derive test cases. Using white box testing methods, the software engineer can derive test cases that (1) guarantee that

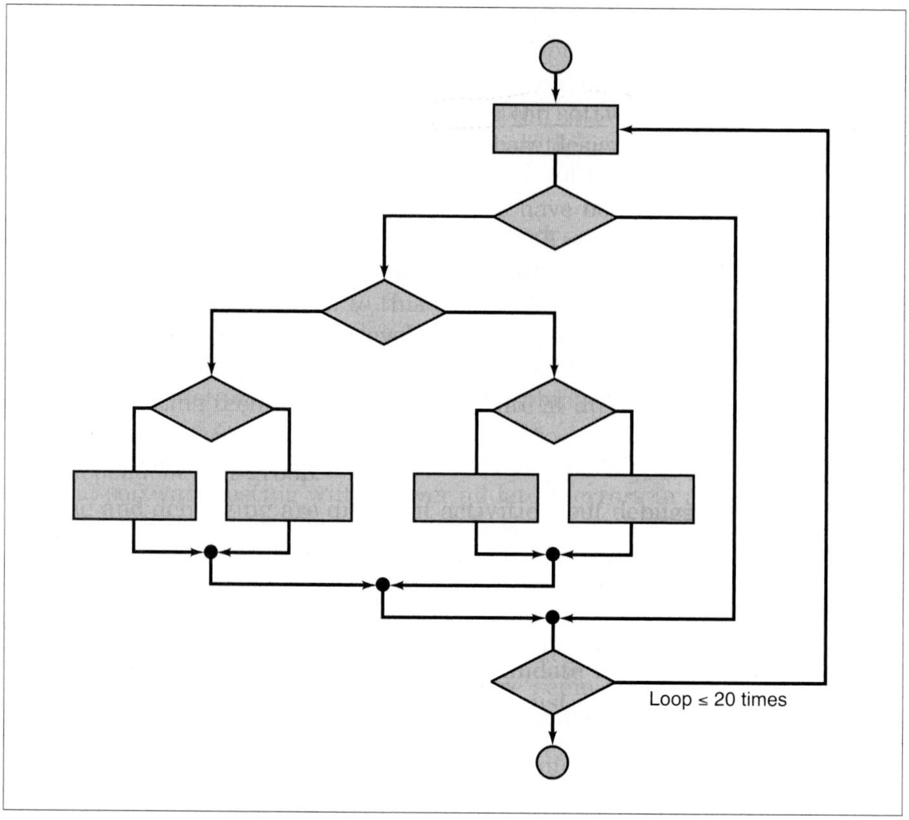

FIGURE 18.2. Problems with exhaustive testing.

all *independent paths* within a module have been exercised at least once, (2) exercise all logical decisions on their *true* and *false* sides, (3) execute all loops at their boundaries and within their operational bounds, and (4) exercise internal data structures to ensure their validity.

A reasonable question might be posed at this juncture: Why spend time and energy worrying about (and testing) logical minutiae when we might better expend effort demonstrating that program requirements have been met? Stated another way, why don't we spend all of our energies on black-box tests? The answer lies in the nature of software defects (e.g., [JON81]):

- *Logic errors and incorrect assumptions are inversely proportional to the probability that a program path will be executed.* Errors tend to creep into our work when we design and implement function, conditions, or control that are out of the mainstream. Everyday processing tends to be well understood (and well scrutinized) while "special case" processing tends to fall into the cracks.
- *We often believe that a logical path is not likely to be executed when, in fact, it may be executed on a regular basis.* The logical flow of a program is sometimes counterintuitive, meaning that our unconscious assumptions

about flow of control and data may lead us to make design errors that are uncovered only once path testing commences.

- *Typographical errors are random*. When a program is translated into programming language source code, it is likely that some typing errors will occur. Many will be uncovered by syntax checking mechanisms, but others will go undetected until testing begins. It is as likely that a typo will exist on an obscure logical path as on a mainstream path.

Each of these reasons provides an argument for conducting white box tests. Black box testing, no matter how thorough, may miss the kinds of errors noted above. As Beizer has stated [BEI90]: "Bugs lurk in corners and congregate at boundaries." White box testing is far more likely to uncover them.

18.3 BASIS PATH TESTING

Basis path testing is a white box testing technique first proposed by Tom McCabe [MCC76]. The basis path method enables the test case designer to derive a logical complexity measure of a procedural design and use this measure as a guide for defining a *basis set* of execution paths. Test cases derived to exercise the basis set are guaranteed to execute every statement in the program at least one time during testing.

18.3.1 Flow Graph Notation

Before the basis path method can be introduced, a simple notation for the representation of control flow, called a *flow graph* (or *program graph*) must be introduced.[1] The flow graph depicts logical control flow using the notation illustrated in Figure 18.3. Each structured construct (Chapter 10) has a corresponding flow graph symbol.

[1]In actuality, the basis path method can be conducted without the use of flow graphs. However, they serve as a useful tool for understanding control flow and illustrating the approach.

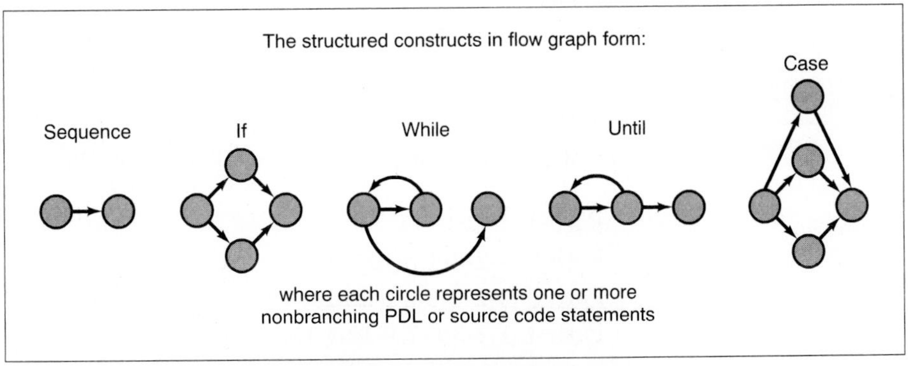

FIGURE 18.3.
Flow graph notation.

To illustrate the use of a flow graph, we consider the procedural design representation in Figure 18.4*a*. Here, a flow chart is used to depict program control structure. Figure 18.4*b* maps the flow chart into a corresponding flow graph (assuming that no compound conditions are contained in the decision diamonds of the flow chart). Referring to Figure 18.4*b*, each circle, called a flow graph *node,* represents one or more procedural statements. A sequence of process boxes and a decision diamond can map into a single node. The arrows on the flow graph, called *edges,* represent flow of control and are analogous to flow chart arrows. An edge must terminate at a node, even if the node does not represent any procedural statements (e.g, see the symbol for the *if-then-else* construct). Areas bounded by edges and nodes are called *regions.* When counting regions, we include the area outside the graph and count it as a region.

Any procedural design representation can be translated into a flow graph. In Figure 18.5, a program design language (PDL) segment and its corresponding flow graph are shown. Note that the PDL statements have been numbered and a corresponding numbering is used for the flow graph.

When compound conditions are encountered in a procedural design, the generation of a flow graph becomes slightly more complicated. A compound condition occurs when one or more Boolean operators (logical OR, AND, NAND, NOR) are present in a conditional statement. Referring to Figure 18.6, the PDL segment translates into the flow graph shown. Note that a separate node is created for each of the conditions *a* and *b* in the statement IF *a* OR *b*. Each node that contains a condition is called a *predicate node,* and is characterized by two or more edges emanating from it.

18.3.2 Cyclomatic Complexity

Cyclomatic complexity (Chapter 17) is a software metric that provides a quantitative measure of the logical complexity of a program. When used in the context of the basis path testing method, the value computed for cyclomatic complexity defines the number of *independent paths* in the *basis set* of a program and provides us with an upper bound for the number of tests that must be conducted to ensure that all statements have been executed at least once.

An independent path is any path through the program that introduces at least one new set of processing statements or a new condition. When stated in terms of a flow graph, an independent path must move along at least one edge that has not been traversed before the path is defined. For example, a set of independent paths for the flow graph illustrated in Figure 18.4*b* is

Path 1: 1-11
Path 2: 1-2-3-4-5-10-1-11
Path 3: 1-2-3-6-8-9-10-1-11
Path 4: 1-2-3-6-7-9-10-1-11

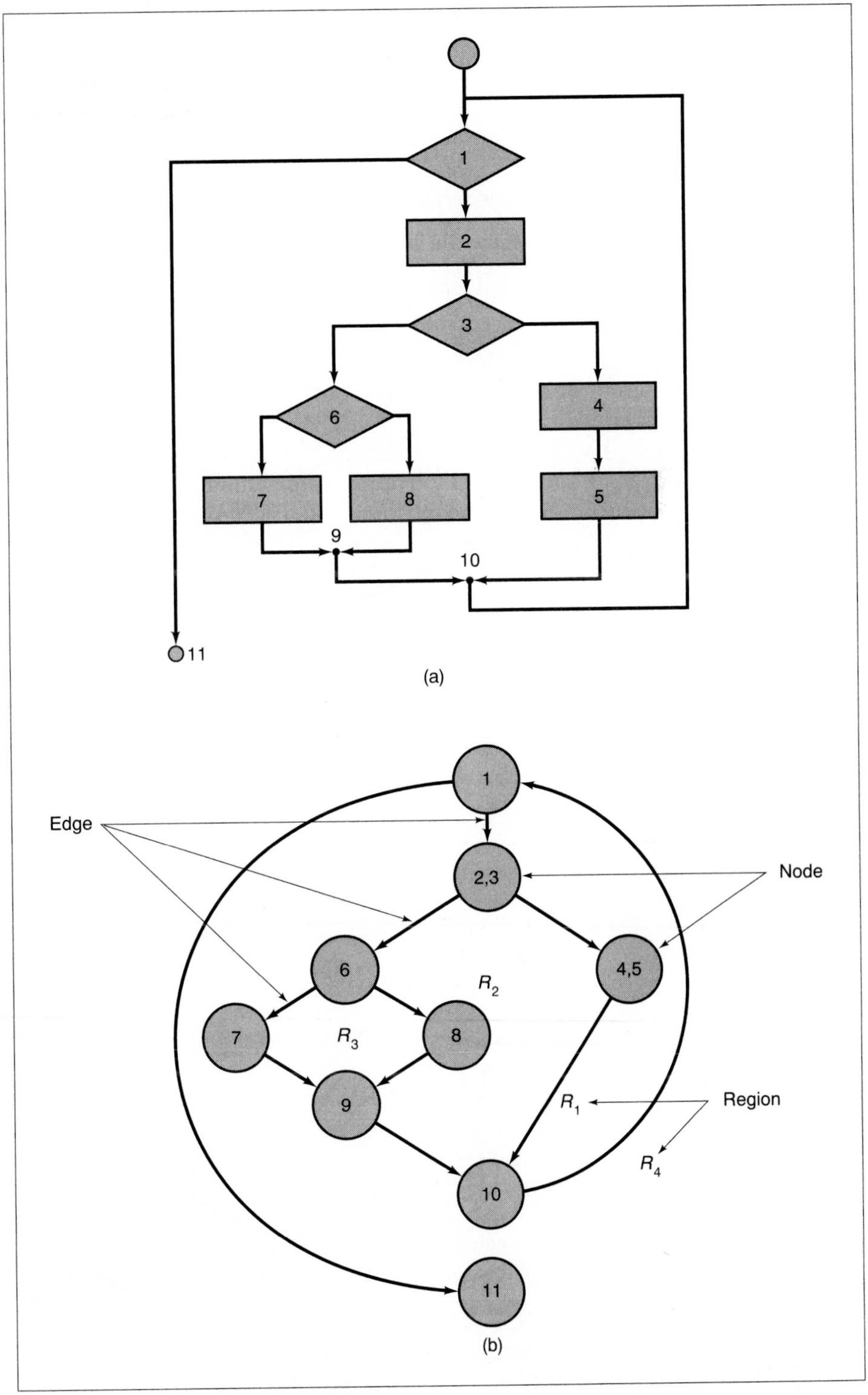

FIGURE 18.4.
(*a*) Flow chart;
(*b*) flow graph.

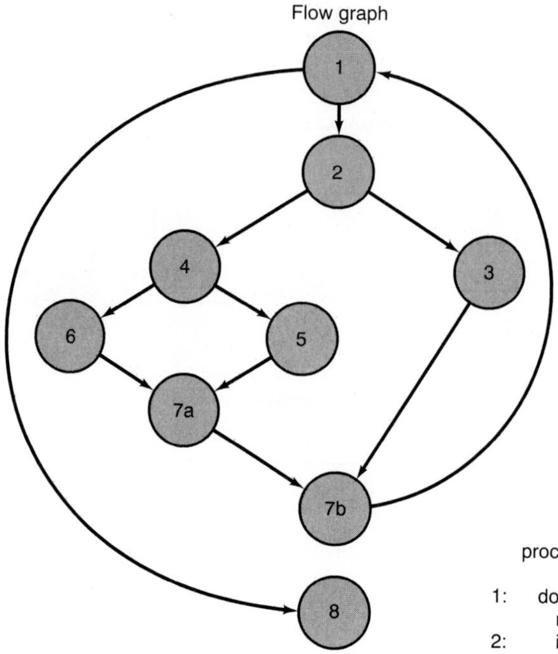

PDL

```
procedure: sort

1:    do while records remain
         read record;
2:       if record field 1 = 0
3:          then process record;
               store in buffer;
               increment counter;
4:          elseif record field 2 = 0
5:             then reset counter;
6:             else process record;
               store in file;
7a:         endif
         endif
7b:   enddo
8:    end
```

FIGURE 18.5.
Translating PDL to flow graph.

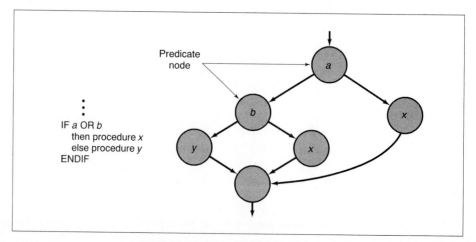

```
  ⋮
IF a OR b
   then procedure x
   else procedure y
ENDIF
```

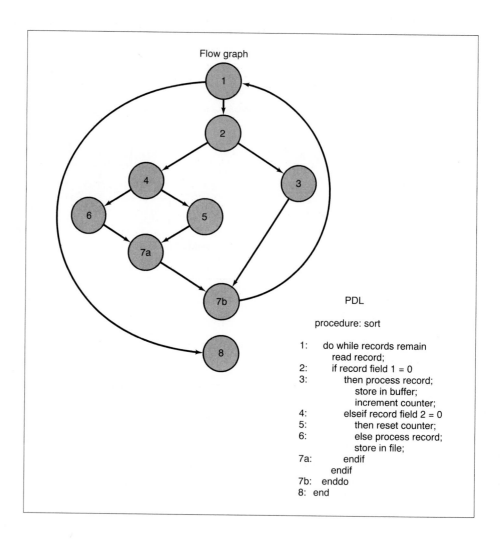

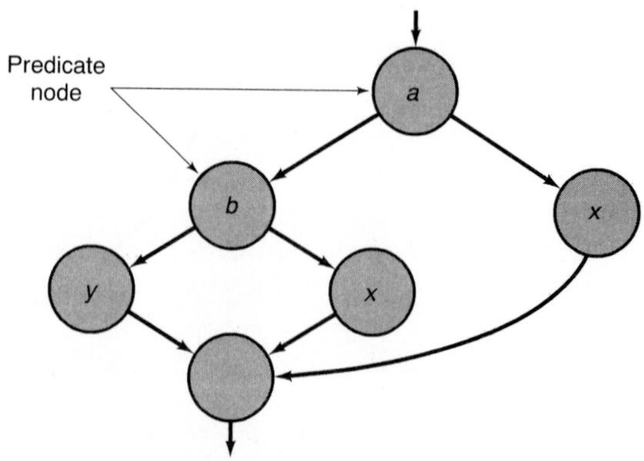

FIGURE 18.6.
Compound logic.

Note that each new path introduces a new edge. The path

1-2-3-4-5-10-1-2-3-6-8-9-10-1-11

is not considered to be an independent path because it is simply a combination of already specified paths and does not traverse any new edges.

Paths 1, 2, 3, and 4 defined above comprise a *basis set* for the flow graph shown in Figure 18.4*b*. That is, if tests can be designed to force execution of these paths (a basis set), every statement in the program will have been guaranteed to be executed at least one time and every condition will have been executed on its true and false side. It should be noted that the basis set is not unique. In fact any number of different basis sets can be derived for a given procedural design.

How do we know how many paths to look for? The computation of cyclomatic complexity provides the answer.

Cyclomatic complexity has a foundation in graph theory and provides us with an extremely useful software metric. Complexity is computed in one of three ways:

1. The number of regions of the flow graph correspond to the cyclomatic complexity.
2. Cyclomatic complexity, $V(G)$, for a flow graph G is defined as
   $$V(G) = E - N + 2$$
   where E is the number of flow graph edges and N is the number of flow graph nodes.
3. Cyclomatic complexity, $V(G)$, for a flow graph G is also defined as
   $$V(G) = P + 1$$
   where P is the number of predicate nodes contained in the flow graph G.

Referring once more to the flow graph in Figure 18.4*b*, the cyclomatic complexity can be computed using each of the algorithms noted above:

1. The flow graph has 4 regions.
2. $V(G) = 11$ edges $-$ 9 nodes $+ 2 = 4$.
3. $V(G) = 3$ predicate nodes $+ 1 = 4$.

Therefore, the cyclomatic complexity of the flow graph in Figure 18.4b is 4.

More importantly, the value for $V(G)$ provides us with an upper bound for the number of independent paths that comprise the basis set, and by implication, *an upper bound on the number of tests that must be designed and executed* to guarantee coverage of all program statements.

18.3.3 Deriving Test Cases

The basis path testing method can be applied to a detailed procedural design or to source code. In this section, we present basis path testing as a

```
PROCEDURE average;

   *  This procedure computes the average of 100 or fewer
      numbers that lie between bounding values; it also computes the
      sum and the total number valid.

   INTERFACE RETURNS average, total.input, total.valid;
   INTERFACE ACCEPTS value, minimum, maximum;

   TYPE value[1:100] IS SCALAR ARRAY;
   TYPE average, total.input, total.valid;
      minimum, maximum, sum IS SCALAR;
   TYPE i IS INTEGER;
   i = 1;
   total.input = total.valid = 0;
   sum = 0;
   DO WHILE value[ i ] < > –999 and total.input < 100
      increment total.input by 1;
      IF value[ i ] > = minimum AND value[ i ] < = maximum
            THEN increment total.valid by 1;
                  sum = sum + value[ i ]
            ELSE skip
      ENDIF
      increment i by 1;
   ENDDO
   IF total.valid > 0
      THEN average = sum / total.valid;
      ELSE average = –999;
   ENDIF
END average
```

FIGURE 18.7.
PDL for test design.

series of steps. The procedure **average**, depicted in PDL in Figure 18.7, will be used as an example to illustrate each step in the test case design method. Note that **average**, although an extremely simple algorithm, contains compound conditions and loops.

1. *Using the design or code as a foundation, draw a corresponding flow graph.*
A flow graph is created using the symbols and construction rules presented in Section 18.3.1.

Referring to the PDL for **average** in Figure 18.7, a flow graph is created by numbering those PDL statements that will be mapped into the corresponding flow graph nodes. The numbering scheme is shown in Figure 18.8 and the corresponding flow graph in Figure 18.9.

2. *Determine the cyclomatic complexity of the resultant flow graph.*
The cyclomatic complexity $V(G)$ is determined by applying the algorithms described in Section 18.3.2. It should be noted that $V(G)$ can be determined without developing a flow graph by counting all the conditional statements in the PDL [for the procedure **average**, compound conditions count as 2 (number of boolean operators plus 1)].

```
PROCEDURE average;

   * This procedure computes the average of 100 or fewer
     numbers that lie between bounding values; it also computes the
     sum and the total number valid.

  INTERFACE RETURNS average, total.input, total.valid;
  INTERFACE ACCEPTS value, minimum, maximum;

  TYPE value[1:100] IS SCALAR ARRAY;
  TYPE average, total.input, total.valid;
     minimum, maximum, sum IS SCALAR;
  TYPE i IS INTEGER;
     i = 1;
 1   total.input = total.valid = 0;            2
     sum = 0;
     DO WHILE value[ i ] < > –999 and total.input < 100   3
  4  increment total.input by 1;
     IF value[ i ] > = minimum AND value[ i ] < = maximum   6
  5        THEN increment total.valid by 1;
       7          sum = sum + value[ i ]
           ELSE skip
  8  ENDIF
     increment i by 1;
  9 ENDDO
    IF total.valid > 0  10
  11  THEN average = sum / total.valid;
  12  ELSE average = –999;
  13 ENDIF
END average
```

FIGURE 18.8.
Identifying nodes.

Referring to Figure 18.9,

$$V(G) = 6 \text{ regions}$$
$$V(G) = 18 \text{ edges} - 14 \text{ nodes} + 2 = 6$$
$$V(G) = 5 \text{ predicate nodes} + 1 = 6$$

3. *Determine a basis set of linearly independent paths.*
The value of $V(G)$ provides the number of linearly independent paths through the program control structure. In the case of procedure **average**, we expect to specify six paths:

Path 1: 1-2-10-11-13
Path 2: 1-2-10-12-13
Path 3: 1-2-3-10-11-13
Path 4: 1-2-3-4-5-8-9-2-$\cdots$
Path 5: 1-2-3-4-5-6-8-9-2-$\cdots$
Path 6: 1-2-3-4-5-6-7-8-9-2-$\cdots$

The ellipsis ($\cdots$) following paths 4, 5, and 6 indicates that any path through the remainder of the control structure is acceptable. It is often worthwhile

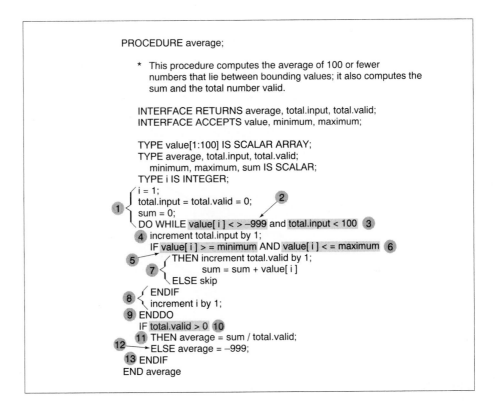

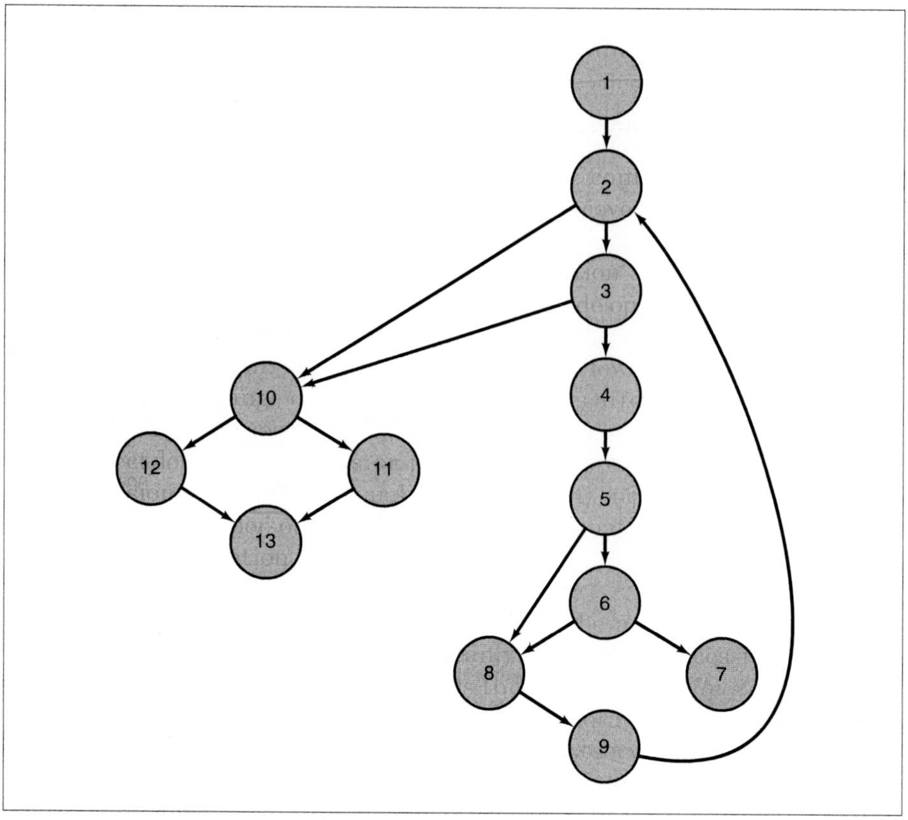

FIGURE 18.9.
Flow graph of the procedure average.

to identify predicate nodes as an aid in the derivation of test cases. In this case, nodes 2, 3, 5, 6, and 10 are predicate nodes.

4. *Prepare test cases that will force execution of each path in the basis set.* Data should be chosen so that conditions at the predicate nodes are appropriately set as each path is tested. Test cases that satisfy the basis set described above are:

Path 1 test case:
value(k) = valid input, where $k < i$ defined below
value(i) = −999 where $2 \le i \le 100$
expected results:
correct average based on k values and proper totals
Note: cannot be tested stand-alone; must be tested as part of path 4, 5, and 6 tests

Path 2 test case:
value(1) = −999
expected results:
average = −999; other totals at initial values

Path 3 test case:
attempt to process 101 or more values
first 100 values should be valid
expected results:
 same as test case 1

Path 4 test case:
value(i) = valid input where $i < 100$
value(k) < minimum where $k < i$
expected results:
 correct average based on k values and proper totals

Path 5 test case:
value(i) = valid input where $i < 100$
value(k) > maximum where $k \leq i$
expected results:
 correct average based on n values and proper totals

Path 6 test case:
value(i) = valid input where $i < 100$
expected results:
 correct average based on n values and proper totals

Each test case is executed and compared to the expected results. Once all test cases have been completed, the tester can be sure that all statements in the program have been executed at least once.

It is important to note that some independent paths (e.g., path 1 in our example) cannot be tested in stand-alone fashion. That is, the combination of data required to traverse the path cannot be achieved in the normal flow of the program. In such cases, these paths are tested as part of another path test.

18.3.4 Graph Matrices

The procedure for deriving the flow graph and determining a set of basis paths is amenable to mechanization. To develop a software tool that assists in basis path testing, a data structure, called a *graph matrix*, can be quite useful.

A graph matrix is a square matrix whose size (i.e., number of rows and columns) is equal to the number of nodes on the flow graph. Each row and column corresponds to an identified node, and matrix entries correspond to *connections* (an edge) between nodes. A simple example of a flow graph and it corresponding graph matrix [BEI90] is shown in Figure 18.10.

Referring to the figure, each node on the flow graph is identified by numbers, while each edge is identified by letters. A letter entry is made in

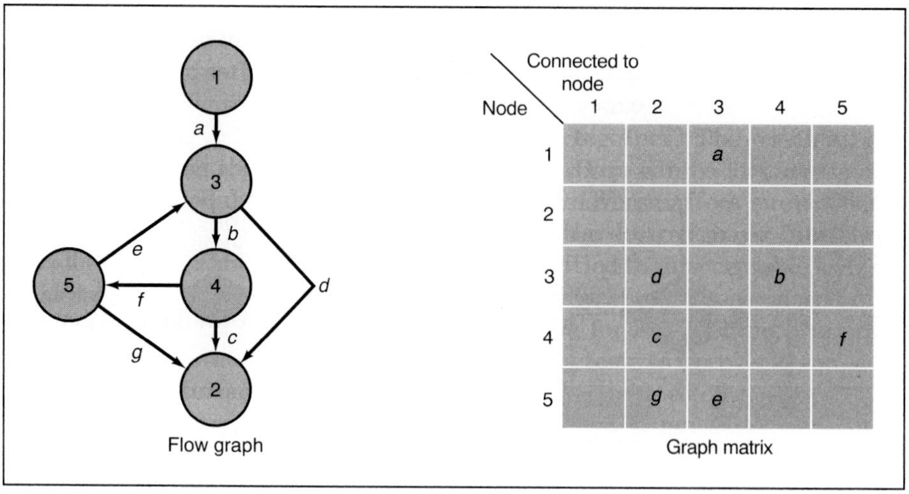

FIGURE 18.10. Flow graph and corresponding graph matrix.

the matrix to correspond to a connection between two nodes. For example, node 3 is connected to node 4 by edge *b*.

To this point, the graph matrix is nothing more than a tabular representation of a flow graph. However, by adding a *link weight* to each matrix entry, the graph matrix can become a powerful tool for evaluating program control structure during testing. The link weight provides additional information about control flow. In its simplest form, the link weight is 1 (a connection exists) or 0 (a connection does not exist). But link weights can be assigned other, more interesting properties:

- The probability that a link (edge) will be executed
- The processing time expended during traversal of a link
- The memory required during traversal of a link
- The resources required during traversal of a link

To illustrate, we use the simplest weighting to indicate connections (0 or 1). The graph matrix in Figure 18.10 is redrawn as shown in Figure 18.11. Each letter has been replaced with a 1, indicating that a connection exists (zeros have been excluded for clarity). Represented in this form, the graph matrix is called a *connection matrix*.

Referring to Figure 18.11, each row with two or more entries represents a predicate node. Therefore, performing the arithmetic shown to the right of the connection matrix provides us with still another method for determining cyclomatic complexity (Section 18.3.2).

Beizer [BEI90] provides a thorough treatment of additional mathematical algorithms that can be applied to graph matrices. Using these techniques, the analysis required to design test cases can be partially or fully automated.

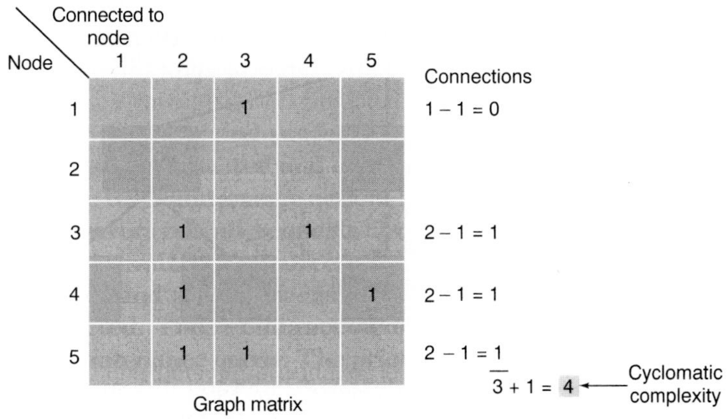

FIGURE 18.11.
Connection matrix.

18.4 CONTROL STRUCTURE TESTING

The basis path testing technique described in Section 18.3 is one of a number of techniques for *control structure testing*. Although basis path testing is simple and highly effective, it is not sufficient in itself. In this section, other variations on control structure testing are discussed. These broaden testing coverage and improve the quality of white box testing.

18.4.1 Condition Testing[2]

Condition testing is a test case design method that exercises the logical conditions contained in a program module. A *simple condition* is a boolean variable or a relational expression, possibly preceded with one NOT ($\neg$) operator. A *relational expression* takes the form

$$E_1\langle\text{relational-operator}\rangle E_2$$

where E_1 and E_2 are arithmetic expressions and ⟨relational-operator⟩ is one of the following: $<$, $\leq$, $=$, $\neq$ (nonequality), $>$, or $\geq$. A *compound condition* is composed of two or more simple conditions, boolean operators, and parentheses. We assume that boolean operators allowed in a compound condition include OR (|), AND (&), and NOT ($\neg$). A condition without relational expressions is referred to as a *boolean expression*.

Therefore, the possible types of components in a condition include a boolean operator, a boolean variable, a pair of boolean parentheses (sur-

[2]Sections 18.4.1 and 18.4.2 were adapted from Tai [TAI89] with permission of Professor K.C. Tai.

rounding a simple or compound condition), a relational operator, or an arithmetic expression.

If a condition is incorrect, then at least one component of the condition is incorrect. Thus, types of errors in a condition include the following:

- Boolean operator error (existence of incorrect/missing/extra boolean operators)
- Boolean variable error
- Boolean parenthesis error
- Relational operator error
- Arithmetic expression error

The *condition testing* method focuses on testing each condition in the program. Condition testing strategies (discussed later in this section) generally have two advantages. First, measurement of the test coverage of a condition is simple. Second, the test coverage of conditions in a program provides guidance for the generation of additional tests for the program.

The purpose of condition testing is to detect not only errors in the conditions of a program but also other errors in the program. If a test set for a program P is effective for detecting errors in the conditions contained in P, it is likely that this test set is also effective for detecting other errors in P. In addition, if a testing strategy is effective for detecting errors in a condition, then it is likely that this strategy will also be effective for detecting errors in a program.

A number of condition testing strategies have been proposed. *Branch testing* is probably the simplest condition testing strategy. For a compound condition C, the true and false branches of C and every simple condition in C need to be executed at least once [MYE79].

Domain testing [WHI80] requires three or four tests to be derived for a relational expression. For a relational expression of the form

$$E_1\langle\text{relational-operator}\rangle E_2$$

three tests are required to make the value of E_1 greater than, equal to, or less than that of E_2, respectively [HOW82]. If ⟨relational-operator⟩ is incorrect and E_1 and E_2 are correct, then these three tests guarantee the detection of the relational operator error. To detect errors in E_1 and E_2, a test that makes the value of E_1 greater or less than that of E_2 should make the difference between these two values as small as possible.

For a boolean expression with n variables, all of 2^n possible tests are required ($n > 0$). This strategy can detect boolean operator, variable, and parenthesis errors, but it is practical only if n is small.

Error-sensitive tests for boolean expressions can also be derived [FOS84, TAI87]. For a singular boolean expression (a boolean expression in which each boolean variable occurs only once) with n boolean variables ($n > 0$), we can easily generate a test set with fewer than 2^n tests such that this test set guarantees the detection of multiple boolean operator errors and is also effective for detecting other errors.

Tai [TAI89] suggests a condition testing strategy that builds on the techniques outlined above. Called *branch and relational operator testing* (BRO), the technique guarantees the detection of branch and relational operator errors in a condition provided that all boolean variables and relational operators in the condition occur only once and have no common variables.

The BRO strategy uses *condition constraints* for a condition C. A condition constraint for C with n simple conditions is defined as $(D_1, D_2, \ldots, D_n)$, where D_i $(0 < i \leq n)$ is a symbol specifying a constraint on the outcome of the ith simple condition in condition C. A condition constraint D for condition C is said to be covered by an execution of C if during this execution of C the outcome of each simple condition in C satisfies the corresponding constraint in D.

For a boolean variable B, we specify a constraint on the outcome of B that states that B must be either true (t) or false (f). Similarly, for a relational expression, the symbols $>$, $=$, and $<$ are used to specify constraints on the outcome of the expression.

As an example, consider the condition

$$C_1\text{: } B_1 \ \& \ B_2$$

where B_1 and B_2 are boolean variables. The condition constraint for C_1 is of the form (D_1, D_2), where each of D_1 and D_2 is t or f. The value (t, f) is a condition constraint for C_1 and is covered by the test that makes the value of B_1 to be true and the value of B_2 to be false. The BRO testing strategy requires that the constraint set {(t, t), (f, t), (t, f)} be covered by the executions of C_1. If C_1 is incorrect due to one or more boolean operator errors, at least one pair in the constraint set will force C_1 to fail.

As a second example, consider a condition of the form

$$C_2\text{: } B_1 \ \& \ (E_3 = E_4)$$

where B_1 is a boolean expression and E_3 and E_4 are arithmetic expressions. A condition constraint for C_2 is of the form (D_1, D_2), where each of D_1 is t or f and D_2 is $>$, $=$, or $<$. Since C_2 is the same as C_1 except that the second simple condition in C_2 is a relational expression, we can construct a constraint set for C_2 by modifying the constraint set {(t, t), (f, t), (t, f)} defined for C_1. Note that t for $(E_3 = E_4)$ implies $=$ and that f for $(E_3 = E_4)$ implies either $<$ or $>$. By replacing (t, t) and (f, t) with (t, =) and (f, =), respectively, and by replacing (t, f) with (t, <) and (t, >), the resulting constraint set for C_2 is {(t, =), (f, =), (t, <), (t, >)}. Coverage of the above constraint set will guarantee the detection of boolean and relational operator errors in C_2.

As a third example, we consider a condition of the form

$$C_3\text{: } (E_1 > E_2) \ \& \ (E_3 = E_4)$$

where E_1, E_2, E_3, and E_4 are arithmetic expressions. A condition constraint for C_3 is of the form (D_1, D_2), where each of D_1 and D_2 is $>$, $=$, or $<$. Since C_3 is the same as C_2 except that the first simple condition in C_3 is a relational expression, we can construct a constraint set for C_3 by modifying the constraint set for C_2, obtaining

$$\{(>, =), (=, =), (<, =), (>, >), (>, <)\}$$

Coverage of the above constraint set will guarantee detection of relational operator errors in C_3.

18.4.2 Data Flow Testing

The *data flow testing* method selects test paths of a program according to the locations of definitions and uses of variables in the program. A number of data flow testing strategies have been studied and compared (e.g., [FRA88], [NTA88]).

To illustrate the data flow testing approach, assume that each statement in a program is assigned a unique statement number and that each function does not modify its parameters or global variables. For a statement with S as its statement number,

$$\text{DEF}(S) = \{X \mid \text{statement } S \text{ contains a definition of } X\}$$

$$\text{USE}(S) = \{X \mid \text{statement } S \text{ contains a use of } X\}$$

If statement S is an *if* or loop statement, its DEF set is empty and its USE set is based on the condition of statement S. The definition of variable X at statement S is said to be *live* at statement S' if there exists a path from statement S to statement S' which does not contain any other definition of X.

A *definition-use chain* (or DU chain) of variable X is of the form $[X, S, S']$, where S and S' are statement numbers, X is in DEF(S) and USE(S'), and the definition of X in statement S is live at statement S'.

One simple data flow testing strategy is to require that every DU chain be covered at least once. We refer to this strategy as the *DU testing strategy*. It has been shown that DU testing does not guarantee the coverage of all the branches of a program. However, a branch is not guaranteed to be covered by DU testing only in rare situations such as *if-then-else* constructs in which the *then* part has no definition of any variable and the *else* part does not exist. In this situation, the *else* branch of the above *if* statement is not necessarily covered by DU testing.

Data flow testing strategies are useful for selecting test paths of a program containing nested *if* and loop statements. To illustrate this, consider the application of DU testing to select test paths for the PDL that follows:

```
proc x
    B1;
    do while C1
      if C2
        then
          if C4
            then B4;
            else B5;
          endif;
        else
          if C3
            then B2;
            else B3;
          endif;
      endif;
    enddo;
    B6;
end proc;
```

To apply the DU testing strategy to select test paths of the control flow diagram, we need to know the definitions and uses of the variables in each condition or block in the PDL. Assume that variable X is defined in the last statement of block $B1$, $B2$, $B3$, $B4$, and $B5$, and is used in the first statement of blocks $B2$, $B3$, $B4$, $B5$, and $B6$. The DU testing strategy requires an execution of the shortest path from each of B_i, $0 < i \leq 5$, to each of B_j, $1 < j \leq 6$. (Such testing also covers any use of variable X in conditions $C1$, $C2$, $C3$, and $C4$.) Although there are 25 DU chains of variable X, we only need five paths to cover these DU chains. The reason is that five paths are needed to cover the DU chain of X from B_i, $0 < i \leq 5$, to $B6$, and other DU chains can be covered by making these five paths contain iterations of the loop.

Note that if we apply the branch testing strategy to select test paths of the PDL noted above, we do not need any additional information. To select paths of the diagram for BRO testing, we need to know the structure of each condition or block. (After the selection of a path of a program, we need to determine whether the path is feasible for the program, i.e., whether there exists at least one input that exercises the path.)

Since the statements in a program are related to each other according to the definitions and uses of variables, the data flow testing approach is effective for error protection. However, the problems of measuring test coverage and selecting test paths for data flow testing are more difficult than the corresponding problems for condition testing.

18.4.3 Loop Testing

Loops are the cornerstone for the vast majority of all algorithms implemented in software. And yet, we often pay them little heed while conducting software testing.

Loop testing is a white box testing technique that focuses exclusively on the validity of loop constructs. Four different classes of loops [BEI90] can be defined: *simple loops, concatenated loops, nested loops,* and *unstructured loops* (Figure 18.12).

Simple Loops The following set of tests should be applied to simple loops, where n is the maximum number of allowable passes through the loop:

1. Skip the loop entirely.
2. Only one pass through the loop.

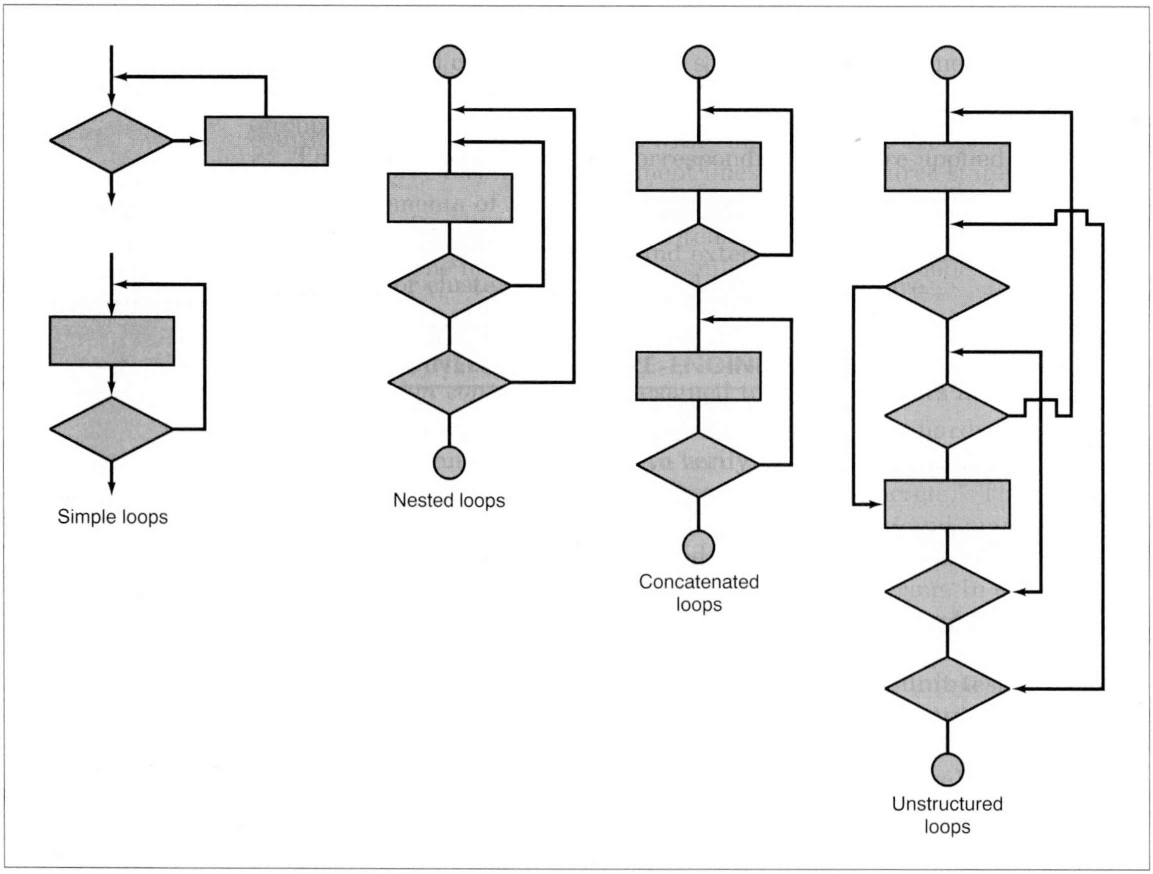

FIGURE 18.12. Loops.

3. Two passes through the loop.
4. m passes through the loop where $m < n$.
5. $n - 1, n, n + 1$ passes through the loop.

Nested Loops If we extend the test approach for simple loops to nested loops, the number of possible tests grows geometrically as the level of nesting increases. This would result in an impractical number of tests. Beizer [BEI90] suggests an approach that will help to reduce the number of tests:

1. Start at the innermost loop. Set all other loops to minimum values.
2. Conduct simple loop tests for the innermost loop while holding the outer loops at their minimum iteration parameter (e.g., loop counter) values. Add other tests for out-of-range or excluded values.
3. Work outward, conducting tests for the next loop, but keeping all other outer loops at minimum values and other nested loops to "typical" values.
4. Continue until all the loops have been tested.

Concatenated Loops Concatenated loops can be tested using the approach defined for simple loops above, if each of the loops is independent of the others. However, if two loops are concatenated and the loop counter for loop 1 is used as the initial value for loop 2, then the loops are *not* independent. When the loops are not independent, the approach applied to nested loops is recommended.

Unstructured Loops Whenever possible, this class of loops should be *redesigned* to reflect the use of the structured programming constructs (Chapter 10).

18.5 BLACK BOX TESTING

Black box testing methods focus on the functional requirements of the software. That is, black box testing enables the software engineer to derive sets of input conditions that will fully exercise all functional requirements for a program. Black box testing is *not* an alternative to white box techniques. Rather, it is a complementary approach that is likely to uncover a different class of errors than white box methods.

Black box testing attempts to find errors in the following categories: (1) incorrect or missing functions, (2) interface errors, (3) errors in data structures or external database access, (4) performance errors, and (5) initialization and termination errors.

Unlike white box testing, which is performed early in the testing process, black box testing tends to be applied during later stages of testing (see Chapter 19). Because black box testing purposely disregards control structure, attention is focused on the information domain. Tests are designed to answer the following questions:

- How is functional validity tested?
- What *classes* of input will make good test cases?
- Is the system particularly sensitive to certain input values?
- How are the boundaries of a data class isolated?
- What data rates and data volume can the system tolerate?
- What effect will specific combinations of data have on system operation?

By applying black box techniques, we derive a set of test cases that satisfy the following criteria [MYE79]: (1) test cases that reduce, by a count that is greater than 1, the number of additional test cases that must be designed to achieve reasonable testing, and (2) test cases that tell us something about the presence or absence of classes of errors, rather than an error associated only with the specific test at hand.

18.5.1 Equivalence Partitioning

Equivalence partitioning is a black box testing method that divides the input domain of a program into classes of data from which test cases can be derived. An ideal test case single-handedly uncovers a class of errors (e.g., incorrect processing of all character data) that might otherwise require many cases to be executed before the general error is observed. Equivalence partitioning strives to define a test case that uncovers classes of errors, thereby reducing the total number of test cases that must be developed.

Test case design for equivalence partitioning is based on an evaluation of equivalence classes for an *input condition*. An *equivalence class* represents a set of valid or invalid states for input conditions. Typically, an input condition is either a specific numeric value, a range of values, a set of related values, or a boolean condition. Equivalence classes may be defined according to the following guidelines:

1. If an input condition specifies a *range,* one valid and two invalid equivalence classes are defined.
2. If an input condition requires a specific *value,* one valid and two invalid equivalence classes are defined.
3. If an input condition specifies a member of a *set,* one valid and one invalid equivalence class are defined.
4. If an input condition is *boolean,* one valid and one invalid class are defined.

As an example, consider data maintained as part of an automated banking application. The user can "dial" the bank using his or her personal computer, provide a six-digit password, and follow with a series of keyword commands that trigger various banking functions. The software supplied for the banking application accepts data in the following form:

Area code—blank or three-digit number
Prefix—three-digit number not beginning with 0 or 1
Suffix—four-digit number
Password—six-digit alphanumeric value
Commands—"check," "deposit," "bill pay," etc.

The input conditions associated with each data element for the banking application can be specified as:

Area code:	input condition, *boolean*—the area code may or may not be present
	input condition, *range*—values defined between 200 and 999, with specific exceptions (e.g., no values > 905) and requirements (e.g., all area codes have a 0 or 1 as a second digit)
Prefix:	input condition, *range*—specified value > 200
Suffix:	input condition, *value*—four-digit length
Password:	input condition, *boolean*—a password may or may not be present
	input condition, *value*—six-character string
Command:	input condition, *set*—containing commands noted above

Applying the guidelines for the derivation of equivalence classes, test cases for each input domain data item could be developed and executed. Test cases are selected so that the largest number of attributes of an equivalence class are exercised at once.

18.5.2 Boundary Value Analysis

For reasons that are not completely clear, a greater number of errors tends to occur at the boundaries of the input domain than in the "center." It is for this reason that *boundary value analysis* (BVA) has been developed as a testing technique. Boundary value analysis leads to a selection of test cases that exercise bounding values.

Boundary value analysis is a test case design technique that complements equivalence partitioning. Rather than selecting any element of an equivalence class, BVA leads to the selection of test cases at the "edges" of the class. Rather than focusing solely on input conditions, BVA derives test cases from the output domain as well [MYE79].

Guidelines for BVA are similar in many respects to those provided for equivalence partitioning:

1. If an input condition specifies a *range* bounded by values *a* and *b*, test cases should be designed with values *a* and *b*, just above and just below *a* and *b*, respectively.
2. If an input condition specifies a number of values, test cases should be developed that exercise the minimum and maximum numbers. Values just above and below minimum and maximum are also tested.
3. Apply guidelines 1 and 2 to output conditions. For example, assume that a temperature versus pressure table is required as output from an engineering analysis program. Test cases should be designed to create an output report that produces the maximum (and minimum) allowable number of table entries.
4. If internal program data structures have prescribed boundaries (e.g., an array has a defined limit of 100 entries), be certain to design a test case to exercise the data structure at its boundary.

Most software engineers intuitively perform BVA to some degree. By applying the guidelines noted above, boundary testing will be more complete, thereby having a higher likelihood for error detection.

18.5.3 Cause-Effect Graphing Techniques

In far too many instances, an attempt to translate a policy or procedure specified in a natural language into a software-based algorithm leads to frustration and error. Consider the following memo (believe it or not, it's real!) published in the *Personnel Information Bulletin* for the U.S. Army Corps of Engineers. The discussion centers on the procedure for determining employee holidays. Read it and weep.

> Executive Order 10358 provided in the case of an employee whose work week varied from the normal Monday through Friday work week, that Labor Day and Thanksgiving Day each were to be observed on the next succeeding workday when the holiday fell on a day outside the employee's regular basic work week. Now, when Labor Day, Thanksgiving Day or any of the new Monday holidays are outside an employee's basic workweek, the immediately preceding workday will be his holiday when the non-workday on which the holiday falls is the second non-workday or the non-workday designated as the employee's day off in lieu of Saturday. When the non-workday on which the holiday falls is the first non-workday or the non-workday designated as the employee's day off in lieu of Sunday, the holiday observance is moved to the next succeeding workday.

There are few readers who would enthusiastically volunteer to test a computer program developed to implement the procedure described above.

Cause-effect graphing is a test case design technique that provides a concise representation of logical conditions and corresponding actions. (Under no circumstances will we attempt the memo presented above, leaving it instead to the adventurous reader.) The technique follows four steps:

1. *Causes* (input conditions) and *effects* (actions) are listed for a module and an identifier is assigned to each.
2. A cause-effect graph (described below) is developed.
3. The graph is converted to a decision table.
4. Decision table rules are converted to test cases.

A simplified version of cause-effect graph symbology is shown in Figure 18.13. The left-hand column of the figure illustrates various logical relationships between causes c_i and effects e_i. The dashed notation in the right-hand columns indicates potential constraining relationships that may apply to either causes or effects.

To illustrate the use of cause-effect graphs, we consider a variant of the utility billing example discussed in Chapter 10. Four causes are defined:

1: residential indicator
2: commercial indicator

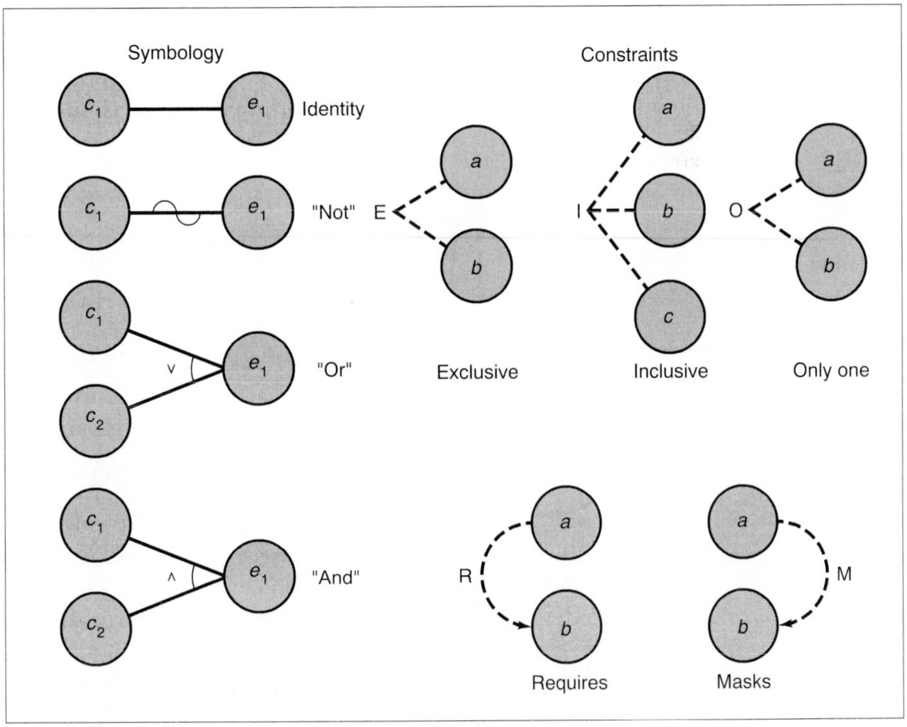

FIGURE 18.13. Cause-effect graphing.

3: peak consumption $\geq$ 100 kWh
4: off-peak consumption $\geq$ 100 kWh

Based on various combinations of causes, the following effects may be listed:

101: schedule A billing
102: schedule B billing
103: schedule C billing

A cause-effect graph for the above example is shown in Figure 18.14. Causes 1, 2, 3, and 4 are represented along the left-hand side and final effects 101, 102, and 103 along the right-hand side. Secondary causes are identified (e.g., causes 11, 12, 13, 14, ...) in the central part of the graph. From the cause-effect graph, a decision table (Figure 18.15) can be developed. Test case data are selected so that each *rule* in the table is exercised. Obviously, if a decision table has been used as a design tool, cause-effect graphing is no longer necessary.

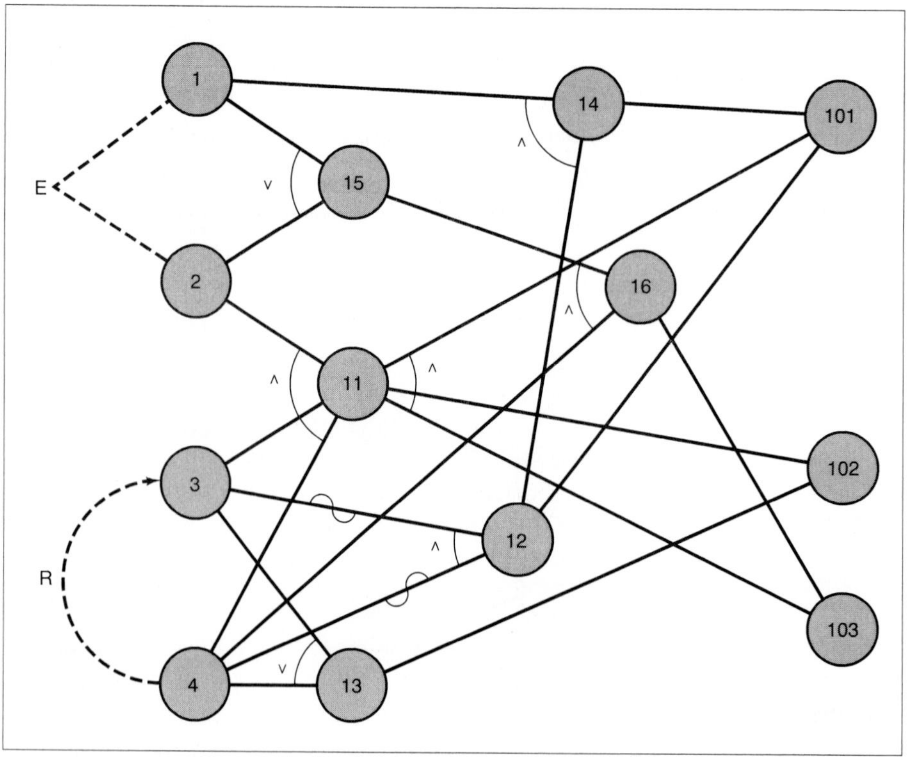

FIGURE 18.14.
Cause-effect graph.

		1	2	3	4	5	6	7	8	9
Causes	1	1							0	1
	2		1		1			1	1	0
	3	0	1	0	1	0	1	1		
	4	0	1	0	1	1	0	1	1	1
Intermediate causes	11		1		1			1		
	12	1		1						
	13					1	1			
	14	1								
	15								1	1
	16								1	1
Effects	101	1	1	1	0	0	0	0	0	0
	102	0	0	0	1	1	1	0	0	0
	103	0	0	0	0	0	0	1	1	1

FIGURE 18.15.
Decision table.

18.5.4 Comparison Testing

There are some situations (e.g., aircraft avionics, nuclear power plant control) in which the reliability of software is absolutely critical. In such applications redundant hardware *and* software are often used to minimize the possibility of error. When redundant software is developed, separate software engineering teams develop independent versions of an application using the same specification. In such situations, each version can be tested with the same test data to ensure that all provide identical output. Then all the versions are executed in parallel with a real-time comparison of results to ensure consistency.

Using lessons learned from redundant systems, researchers (e.g., [BRI87]) have suggested that independent versions of software be developed for critical applications, even when only a single version will be used in the delivered computer-based system. These independent versions form the basis of a black box testing technique called *comparison testing* or *back-to-back testing* [KNI89].

When multiple implementations of the same specification have been produced, test cases designed using other black box techniques (e.g., equivalence partitioning) are provided as input to each version of the software. If the output from each version is the same, it is assumed that all implementations are correct. If the output is different, each of the applications is investigated to determine if a defect in one or more of the versions is responsible for the difference. In most cases, the comparison of outputs can be performed by an automated tool.

Comparison testing is not foolproof. If the specification from which all versions have been developed is in error, all versions will likely reflect the error. In addition, if each of the independent versions produces identical, but incorrect, results, condition testing will fail to detect the error.

18.6 TESTING FOR REAL-TIME SYSTEMS

The special characteristics of real-time systems (Chapter 15) offer major challenges when testing is to be conducted. The time-dependent, asynchronous nature of many real-time applications adds a new and potentially difficult element to the testing mix—*time*. Not only does the test case designer have to consider white and black box test cases, but also the timing of the data and the parallelism of the tasks (processes) that handle the data. In many situations, test data provided when a real-time system is in one state will result in proper processing, while the same data provided when the system is in a different state may lead to error.

For example, the real-time software that controls a new photocopier accepts operator interrupts (i.e., the machine operator hits control keys such as RESET or DARKEN) with no error when the machine is making copies (in the "copying" state). These same operator interrupts, if input when the machine is in the "jammed" state, cause a diagnostic code indicating the location of the jam to be lost (an error).

In addition, the intimate relationship that exists between real-time software and its hardware environment can also cause testing problems. Software tests must consider the impact of hardware faults on software processing. Such faults can be extremely difficult to simulate realistically.

Comprehensive test case design methods for real-time systems have yet to evolve. However, an overall four-step strategy can be proposed:

Task testing. The first step in the testing of real-time software is to test each task independently.[3] That is, white and black box tests are designed

[3] In this context, we view a task as a separate program that accepts input and produces output. A task may be composed of many modules.

and executed for each task. Each task is executed independently during these tests. Task testing uncovers errors in logic and function, but will not uncover timing or behavioral errors.

Behavioral testing. Using system models created with CASE tools (see Section 15.3), it is possible to simulate the behavior of a real-time system and examine its behavior as a consequence of external events. These analysis activities can serve as the basis for the design of test cases that are conducted when the real-time software has been built. Using a technique that is similar to equivalence partitioning (Section 18.5.1), events (e.g., interrupts, control signals, data) are categorized for testing. For example, events for the photocopier might be user interrupts (e.g., reset counter), mechanical interrupts (e.g., paper jammed), system interrupts (e.g., toner low), and failure modes (e.g., roller overheated). Each of these events is tested individually and the behavior of the executable system is examined to detect errors that occur as a consequence of processing associated with these events. The behavior of the system model (developed during the analysis activity) and the executable software can be compared for conformance. Once each class of events has been tested, events are presented to the system in random order and with random frequency. The behavior of the software is examined to detect behavior errors.

Intertask testing. Once errors in individual tasks and in system behavior have been isolated, testing shifts to time-related errors. Asynchronous tasks that are known to communicate with one another are tested with different data rates and processing load to determine if intertask synchronization errors will occur. In addition, tasks that communicate via a message queue or data store are tested to uncover errors in the sizing of these data storage areas.

System testing. Software and hardware are integrated and a full range of system tests (Chapter 19) are conducted in an attempt to uncover errors at the software/hardware interface.

18.7 AUTOMATED TESTING TOOLS

Because software testing often accounts for as much as 40 percent of all effort expended on a software development project, tools that can reduce test time (without reducing thoroughness) are very valuable. Recognizing the potential benefits, researchers and practitioners have developed a first generation of automated test tools. Miller [MIL79] describes a number of categories for test tools:

Static analyzers. These program-analysis systems support "proving" of static allegations—weak statements about a program's structure and format.

Code auditors. These special-purpose filters are used to check the quality of software to ensure that it meets minimum coding standards.

Assertion processors. These preprocessor/postprocessor systems are employed to tell whether programmer-supplied claims, called assertions, about a program's behavior are actually met during real program executions.

Test file generators. These processors generate, and fill with predetermined values, typical input files for programs that are undergoing testing.

Test data generators. These automated analysis systems assist a user in selecting test data that make a program behave in a particular fashion.

Test verifiers. These tools measure internal test coverage, often expressed in terms that are related to the control structure of the test object, and report the coverage value to the quality assurance expert.

Test harnesses. This class of tool supports the processing of tests by making it almost painless to (1) install a candidate program in a test environment, (2) feed it input data, and (3) simulate by stubs the behavior of subsidiary (subordinate) modules.

Output comparators. This tool makes it possible to compare one set of outputs from a program with another (previously archived) set to determine the difference between them.

Dunn [DUN84] adds additional classes of automated tools to the above list:

Symbolic execution systems. This tool performs program testing using algebraic input, rather than numeric data values. The software being tested thus appears to test classes of data, rather than one specific test case. The output is algebraic and can be compared to expected results that are specified in algebraic form.

Environment simulators. This tool is a specialized computer-based system that enables the tester to model the external environment of real-time software and then simulate actual operating conditions dynamically.

Data flow analyzers. This tool tracks the flow of data through a system (similar in many respects to path analyzers) and attempts to find undefined data references, incorrect indexing, and other data-related errors.

Current usage of automated tools for software testing is growing, and it is likely that application will accelerate during the next decade. Descendents of the first-generation testing tools are likely to cause radical changes in the way we test software and thereby improve the reliability of computer-based systems.

18.8 SUMMARY

The primary objective for test case design is to derive a set of tests that has the highest likelihood for uncovering defects in the software. To accomplish this objective, two different categories of test case design techniques are used: white box testing and black box testing.

White box tests focus on the program control structure. Test cases are derived to ensure that all statements in the program have been executed at least once during testing and that all logical conditions have been exercised. Basis path testing, a white box technique, makes use of program graphs (or graph matrices) to derive the set of linearly independent tests that will ensure coverage. Condition and data flow testing further exercise program logic, and loop testing complements other white box techniques by providing a procedure for exercising loops of varying degrees of complexity.

Hetzel [HET84] describes white box testing as "testing in the small." His implication is that the white box tests that we have considered in this chapter are typically applied to small program components (e.g., modules or small groups of modules). Black box testing, on the other hand, broadens our focus and might be called "testing in the large."

Black box tests are designed to validate functional requirements without regard to the internal workings of a program. Black box testing techniques focus on the information domain of the software, deriving test cases by partitioning input and output in a manner that provides thorough test coverage. Equivalence partitioning divides the input domain into classes of data that are likely to exercise specific software function. Boundary value analysis probes the program's ability to handle data at the limits of acceptability. Cause-effect graphing is a technique that enables the tester to validate complex sets of actions and conditions.

Experienced software developers often say, "Testing never ends, it just gets transferred from you [the developer] to your customer. Every time your customer uses the program, a test is being conducted." By applying test case design, the software engineer can achieve more complete testing and thereby uncover and correct the highest number of errors before the "customer's tests" begin.

REFERENCES

[BEI90] Beizer, B., *Software Testing Techniques,* 2d ed., Van Nostrand Reinhold, 1990.

[BRI87] Brilliant, S.S., J.C. Knight, and N.G. Levenson, "The Consistent Comparison Problem in N-Version Software," *ACM Software Engineering Notes,* vol. 12, no. 1, January 1987, pp. 29–34.

[DEU79] Deutsch, M., "Verification and Validation," in *Software Engineering,* (R. Jensen and C. Tonies, eds.), Prentice-Hall, 1979, pp. 329–408.

[DUN84] Dunn, R., *Software Defect Removal,* McGraw-Hill, 1984.

[FOS84] Foster, K.A., "Sensitive Test Data for Boolean Expressions," *ACM Software Engineering Notes,* vol. 9, no. 2, April 1984, pp. 120–125.

[FRA88] Frankl, P.G., and E. J. Weyuker, "An Applicable Family of Data Flow Testing Criteria," *IEEE Trans. Software Engineering,* vol. 14, no. 10, October 1988, pp. 1483–1498.

[HET84] Hetzel, W., *The Complete Guide to Software Testing,* QED Information Sciences, 1984.

[HOW82] Howden, W. E., "Weak Mutation Testing and the Completeness of Test Cases," *IEEE Trans. Software Engineering,* vol. SE-8, no. 4, July 1982, pp. 371–379.

[JON81] Jones, T. C., *Programming Productivity: Issues for the 80s,* IEEE Computer Society Press, 1981.

[KNI89] Knight, J., and P. Ammann, "Testing Software Using Multiple Versions," Report No. 89029N, Software Productivity Consortium, Reston, Virginia, June 1989.

[MCC76] McCabe, T., "A Software Complexity Measure," *IEEE Trans. Software Engineering,* vol. 2, no. 6, December 1976, pp. 308–320.

[MIL79] Miller, E., *Automated Tools for Software Engineering,* IEEE Computer Society Press, 1979, p. 169.

[MYE79] Myers, G., *The Art of Software Testing,* Wiley, 1979.

[NTA88] Ntafos, S. C., "A Comparison of Some Structural Testing Strategies," *IEEE Trans. Software Engineering,* vol. 14, no. 6, June 1988, pp. 868–874.

[TAI87] Tai, K. C., and H. K. Su, "Test Generation for Boolean Expressions," *Proc. COMPSAC '87,* October 1987, pp. 278–283.

[TAI89] Tai, K. C., "What to Do Beyond Branch Testing," *ACM Software Engineering Notes,* vol. 14, no. 2, April 1989, p. 58–61.

[WHI80] White, L. J., and E. I. Cohen, "A Domain Strategy for Program Testing," *IEEE Trans. Software Engineering,* vol. SE-6, no. 5, May 1980, pp. 247–257.

PROBLEMS AND POINTS TO PONDER

18.1 Myers [MYE79] uses the following program as a self assessment for your ability to specify adequate testing: A program reads three integer values. The three values are interpreted as representing the lengths of the sides of a triangle. The program prints a message that states whether the triangle is scalene, isosceles, or equilateral. Develop a set of test cases that you feel will adequately test this program.

18.2 Design and implement the program (with error handling where appropriate) specified in Problem 18.1. Derive a flow graph for the program and apply basis path testing to develop test cases that will guarantee that all the statements in the program have been tested. Execute the cases and show your results.

18.3 Can you think of any additional testing objectives that are not discussed in Section 18.1.1?

18.4 Apply the basis path testing technique to any one of the programs that you have implemented in Problems 16.13 through 16.21.

18.5 Specify, design, and implement a software tool that will compute the cyclomatic complexity for the programming language of your choice. Use the graph matrix as the operative data structure in your design.

18.6 Read Beizer [BEI90] and determine how the program you have developed in Problem 18.5 can be extended to accommodate various link weights. Extend your tool to process execution probabilities or link processing times.

18.7. Use the condition testing approach described in Section 18.4.1 to design a set of test cases for the program you created in Problem 18.2.

18.8. Using the data flow testing approach described in Section 18.4.2, make a list of definition-use chains for the program you created in Problem 18.2.

18.9 Design an automated tool that will recognize loops and categorize them as indicated in Section 18.4.3.

18.10 Extend the tool described in Problem 18.9 to generate test cases for each loop category, once encountered. It will be necessary to perform this function interactively with the tester.

18.11 Give at least three examples in which black box testing might give the impression that "everything's O.K.," while white box tests might uncover an error.

18.12 Will exhaustive testing (even if it is possible for very small programs) guarantee that the program is 100 percent correct?

18.13 Using the equivalence partitioning method, derive a set of test cases for the *SafeHome* system described earlier in this book.

18.14 Using boundary value analysis, derive a set of test cases for the PHTRS system described in Chapter 7.

18.15 Using cause-effect graphing, derive a set of test cases for Executive Order 10358 described in Section 18.5.3. Good luck! For the adventurous: Attempt to design an algorithm that will implement the rules noted for the executive order.

18.16 Develop a set of guidelines for testing human-computer interfaces. Use Chapter 14 as a guide.

18.17 Suggest the types of test case design techniques that you would use to test a new compiler. Explain your selections.

18.18 Write a paper that describes a software testing tool in detail. Focus on tools that are currently applied outside purely research environments.

FURTHER READINGS

A number of excellent books are now available for those readers who desire additional information on software testing. Myers' book [MYE79] remains a classic text, covering black box techniques in considerable detail. Beizer [BEI90] provides comprehensive coverage of white box techniques, introducing a level of mathematical rigor that has often been missing in other treatments of testing. Howden (*Functional Program Testing and Analysis,* McGraw-Hill, 1987) also presents a mathematically rigorous discussion that attempts to unify different test case design strategies. Perry (*How to Test Software Packages,* Wiley, 1986) provides practical guidelines and useful checklists for testing purchased software (as well as software developed internally). Books by Hetzel [HET84] and Dunn [DUN84] provide worthwhile supplementary information.

A detailed discussion of the basis path techniques can be found in McCabe's tutorial on testing (*Structured Testing,* IEEE Computer Society Press, 1983). Glass (*Real-Time Software,* Prentice-Hall, 1983), and Levi and Agrawala (*Real-Time System Design,* McGraw-Hill, 1990) discuss specialized techniques for testing and debugging of real-time systems. A worthwhile paper by Ntafos [NTA88] provides a detailed comparison of white box techniques.

Chapters by Miller ("Software Testing Technology: An Overview") and Saib ("Formal Verification") in Van Nostrand Reinhold's *Handbook on Software Engineering* (Vick and Ramamoorthy, eds., 1984) are good summaries of these complex topics. Miller and Howden (*Software Testing and Validation Techniques,* 2d ed., IEEE Computer Society Press, 1981) have edited an excellent anthology of papers on testing.

An excellent source of information on automated tools for software testing is the *Testing Tools Reference Guide* (Software Quality Engineering, Inc., Jacksonville, Florida, updated yearly). This directory contains descriptions of over 120 testing tools, categorized by testing activity, hardware platform, and software support.

CHAPTER 19

SOFTWARE TESTING STRATEGIES

A strategy for software testing integrates software test case design techniques into a well-planned series of steps that result in the successful construction of software. As importantly, a software testing strategy provides a road map for the software developer, the quality assurance organization, and the customer—a road map that describes the steps to be conducted as part of testing, when these steps are planned and then undertaken, and how much effort, time, and resources will be required. Therefore, any testing strategy must incorporate test planning, test case design, test execution, and the resultant data collection and evaluation.

A software testing strategy should be flexible enough to promote the creativity and customization that are necessary to adequately test all large software-based systems. At the same time, the strategy must be rigid enough to promote reasonable planning and management tracking as the project progresses. Shooman [SHO83, p. 238] discusses these issues:

> In many ways, testing is an individualistic process, and the number of different types of tests varies as much as the different development approaches. For many years, our only defense against programming errors was careful design and the native intelligence of the programmer. We are now in an era in which modern design techniques [and formal technical reviews] are helping us to reduce the number of initial errors that are inherent in the code. Similarly, different test methods are beginning to cluster themselves into several distinct approaches and philosophies.

These approaches and philosophies are what we shall call *strategy*. In Chapter 18, the technology of software testing was presented. In this chapter, we focus our attention on the strategy for software testing.

19.1 A STRATEGIC APPROACH TO SOFTWARE TESTING

Testing is a set of activities that can be planned in advance and conducted systematically. For this reason a *template* for software testing—a set of steps into which we can place specific test case design techniques and testing methods—should be defined for the software engineering process.

A number of software testing strategies have been proposed in the literature. All provide the software developer with a template for testing and all have the following generic characteristics:

- Testing begins at the module level and works "outward" toward the integration of the entire computer-based system.
- Different testing techniques are appropriate at different points in time.
- Testing is conducted by the developer of the software and (for large projects) an independent test group.
- Testing and debugging are different activities, but debugging must be accommodated in any testing strategy.

A strategy for software testing must accommodate low-level tests that are necessary to verify that a small source code segment has been correctly implemented as well as high-level tests that validate major system functions against customer requirements. A strategy must provide guidance for the practitioner and a set of milestones for the manager. Because the steps of the test strategy occur at a time when deadline pressure begins to rise, progress must be measurable and problems must surface as early as possible.

19.1.1 Verification and Validation

Software testing is one element of a broader topic that is often referred to as *verification and validation* (V&V). Verification refers to the set of activities that ensure that software correctly implements a specific function. Validation refers to a different set of activities that ensure that the software that has been built is traceable to customer requirements. Boehm [BOE81] states this another way:

Verification: "Are we building the product right?"

Validation: "Are we building the right product?"

The definition of V&V encompasses many of the activities that we have referred to as software quality assurance (SQA).

Recalling the discussion of software quality in Chapter 17, the activities required to achieve it may be viewed as a set of components depicted in Figure 19.1. Software engineering methods provide the foundation from which quality is built. Analysis, design, and implementation (coding) methods act

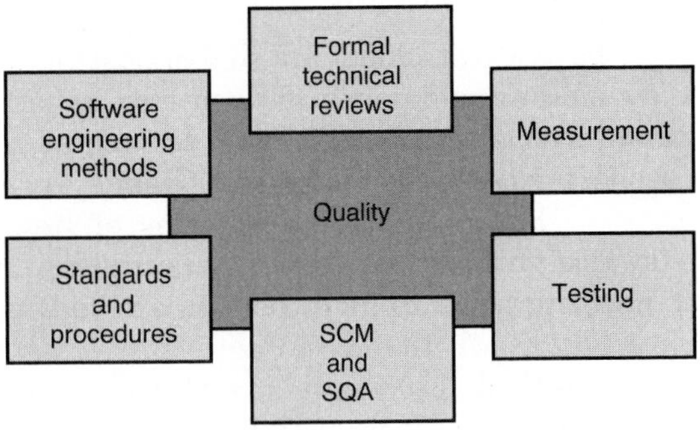

FIGURE 19.1. Achieving software quality.

to enhance quality by providing uniform techniques and predictable results. Formal technical reviews (walkthroughs) help to ensure the quality of the products produced as a consequence of each software engineering step. Throughout the process, measurement and control are applied to every element of a software configuration. Standards and procedures help to ensure uniformity and a formal SQA process enforces a "total quality philosophy."

Testing provides the last bastion from which quality can be assessed and, more pragmatically, errors can be uncovered. But testing should *not* be viewed as a safety net. As they say, "You can't test in quality. If it's not there before you begin testing, it won't be there when you're finished testing." Quality is incorporated into software throughout the process of software engineering. Proper application of methods and tools, effective formal technical reviews and solid management and measurement all lead to quality that is confirmed during testing.

Miller [MIL77] relates software testing to quality assurance by stating that "the underlying motivation of program testing is to affirm software quality with methods that can be economically and effectively applied to both large-scale and small-scale systems."

It is important to note that verification and validation encompasses a wide array of SQA activities that include formal technical reviews, quality and configuration audits, performance monitoring, simulation, feasibility study, documentation review, database review, algorithm analysis, development testing, qualification testing, and installation testing [WAL89]. Although testing plays an extremely important role in V&V, many other activities are also necessary.

19.1.2 Organizing for Software Testing

For every software project, there is an inherent conflict of interest that occurs as testing begins. The people who have built the software are now asked to test the software. This seems harmless in itself; after all, who knows the program better than its developers? Unfortunately, these same developers have a vested interest in demonstrating that the program is error-free, that it works according to customer requirements, that it will be completed on schedule and within budget. Each of these interests mitigates against finding errors throughout the testing process.

From a psychological point of view, software analysis and design (along with coding) are *constructive* tasks. The software engineer creates a computer program, its documentation, and related data structures. Like any builder, the software engineer is proud of the edifice that has been built and looks askance at anyone who attempts to tear it down. When testing commences, there is a subtle, yet definite, attempt to "break" the thing that the software engineer has built. From the point of view of the builder, testing can be considered to be (psychologically) *destructive*. So the builder treads lightly, designing and executing tests that will demonstrate that the program works, rather than uncovering errors. Unfortunately, errors will be present. And if the software engineer doesn't find them, the customer will!

There are often a number of misconceptions that can be erroneously inferred from the above discussion: (1) that the developer of software should do no testing at all; (2) that the software should be "tossed over the wall" to strangers who will test it mercilessly; (3) that testers get involved with the project only when the testing steps are about to begin. Each of these statements is incorrect.

The software developer is always responsible for testing the individual units (modules) of the program, ensuring that each performs the function for which it was designed. In many cases, the developer also conducts *integration testing*—the testing step that leads to the construction (and test) of the complete program structure. Only after the software architecture is complete does an independent test group become involved.

The role of an *independent test group* (ITG) is to remove the inherent problems associated with letting the builder test the thing that has been built. Independent testing removes the conflict of interest that may otherwise be present. After all, the personnel in the independent group team are paid to find errors.

However, the software developer doesn't turn the program over to the ITG and walk away. The developer and the ITG work closely throughout a software project to ensure that thorough tests will be conducted. While testing is conducted, the developer must be available to correct errors that are uncovered.

The ITG is part of the software development project team in the sense that it becomes involved during the specification process and stays involved (planning and specifying test procedures) throughout a large project. However, in many cases the ITG reports to the software quality assurance organization, thereby achieving a degree of independence that might not be possible if it were a part of the software development organization.

19.1.3 A Software Testing Strategy

The software engineering process may be viewed as a spiral, as illustrated in Figure 19.2. Initially, system engineering defines the role of software and leads to software requirements analysis, where the information domain, function, behavior, performance, constraints, and validation criteria for the software are established. Moving inward along the spiral, we come to design and finally to coding. To develop computer software, we spiral in along streamlines that decrease the level of abstraction on each turn.

A strategy for software testing may also be envisioned by moving outward along the spiral of Figure 19.2. *Unit testing* begins at the vortex of the spiral and concentrates on each unit of the software as implemented in the source code. Testing progresses by moving outward along the spiral to *integration testing,* where the focus is on the design and the construction of the software architecture. Taking another turn outward on the spiral, we encounter *validation testing,* where requirements established as part of software requirements analysis are validated against the software that has been constructed. Finally, we arrive at *system testing,* where the software and other system elements are tested as a whole. To test computer software, we spiral out along streamlines that broaden the scope of testing with each turn.

Considering the process from a procedural point of view, testing within the context of software engineering is actually a series of three steps that are implemented sequentially. The steps are shown in Figure 19.3. Initially, tests focus on each module individually, ensuring that it functions properly as a unit. Hence, the name *unit testing*. Unit testing makes heavy use of white box testing techniques, exercising specific paths in a module's control structure to ensure complete coverage and maximum error detection. Next, modules must be assembled or integrated to form the complete software package. *Integration testing* addresses the issues associated with the dual problems of verification and program construction. Black box test case design techniques are the most prevalent during integration, although

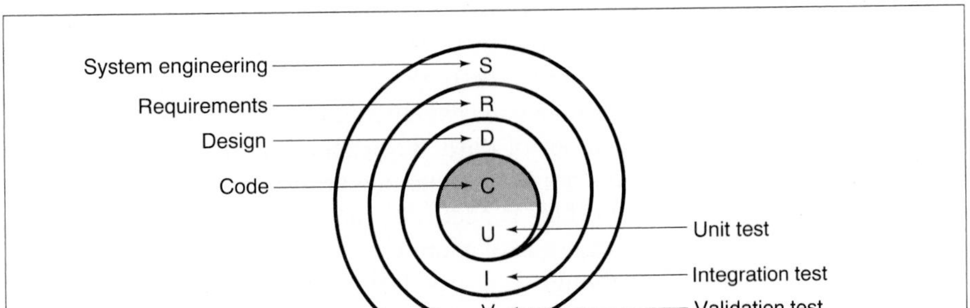

FIGURE 19.2.
Testing strategy.

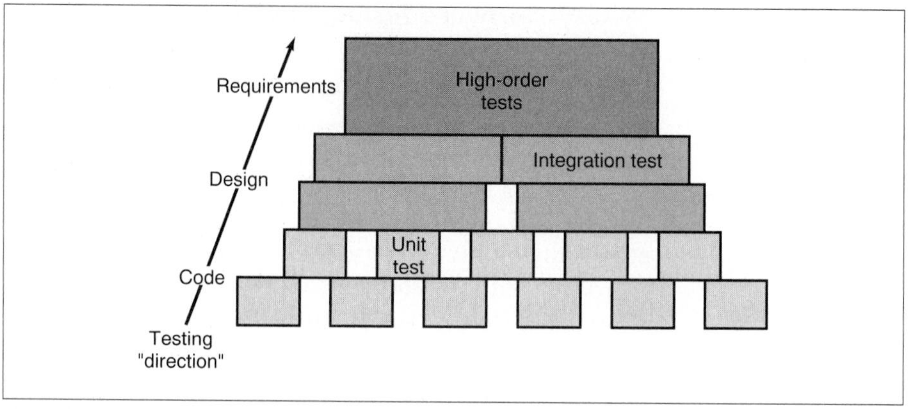

FIGURE 19.3. Software testing steps.

a limited amount of white box testing may be used to ensure coverage of major control paths. After the software has been integrated (constructed), a set of *high-order tests* are conducted. Validation criteria (established during requirements analysis) must be tested. *Validation testing* provides the final assurance that software meets all functional, behavioral, and performance requirements. Black box testing techniques are used exclusively during validation.

The last high-order testing step falls outside the boundary of software engineering and into the broader context of computer system engineering. Software, once validated, must be combined with other system elements (e.g., hardware, people, databases). *System testing* verifies that all elements mesh properly and that overall system function/performance is achieved.

19.1.4 Criteria for Completion of Testing

A classic question arises every time software testing is discussed: When are we done testing—how do we know that we've tested enough? Sadly, there is no definitive answer to this question, but there are a few pragmatic responses and early attempts at empirical guidance.

One response to the above question is: You're never done testing, the burden simply shifts from you (the developer) to your customer. Every time the customer/user executes a computer program, the program is being tested on a new set of data. This sobering fact underlines the importance of other software quality assurance activities. Another response (somewhat cynical, but nonetheless accurate) is: You're done testing when you run out of time or you run out of money.

Although few practitioners would argue with these responses, a software engineer needs more rigorous criteria for determining when sufficient testing has been conducted. Musa and Ackerman [MUS89] suggest a response that is based on statistical criteria: "No, we cannot be absolutely certain that the software will never fail, but relative to a theoretically sound and experimentally validated statistical model, we have done sufficient testing to say with 95 percent confidence that the probability of 1000 CPU hours of failure free operation in a probabilistically defined environment is at least 0.995."

Using statistical modeling and software reliability theory, models of software failures (uncovered during testing) as a function of execution time can be developed [MUS89]. A version of the failure model, called a *logarithmic Poisson execution-time model,* takes the form

$$f(t) = \left(\frac{1}{p}\right) \ln[l_0 pt + 1)] \tag{19.1}$$

where $f(t)$ = cumulative number of failures that are expected to occur once the software has been tested for a certain amount of execution time t

l_0 = the initial software *failure intensity* (failures per unit time) at the beginning of testing

p = the exponential reduction in failure intensity as errors are uncovered and repairs are made.

The instantaneous failure intensity, $l(t)$, can be derived by taking the derivative of $f(t)$:

$$l(t) = \frac{l_0}{l_0 pt + 1} \tag{19.2}$$

Using the relationship noted in equation (19.2), testers can predict the drop-off of errors as testing progresses. The actual error intensity can be plotted against the predicted curve (Figure 19.4). If the actual data gathered during

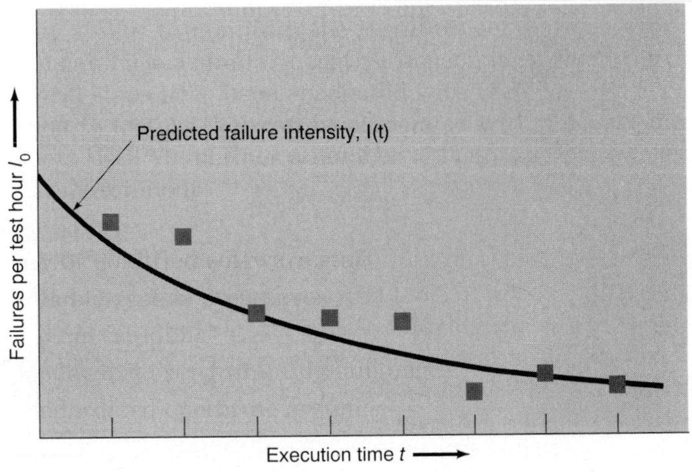

FIGURE 19.4. Failure intensity as a function of execution time. ■, Data collected during test.

testing and the logarithmic Poisson execution-time model are reasonably close to one another over a number of data points, the model can be used to predict the total testing time required to achieve an acceptably low failure intensity.

By collecting metrics during software testing and making use of existing software reliability models, it is possible to develop meaningful guidelines for answering the question: When are we done testing? There is little debate that further work remains to be done before quantitative rules for testing can be established, but the empirical approaches that currently exist are considerably better than raw intuition.

19.2 UNIT TESTING

Unit testing focuses verification effort on the smallest unit of software design—the module. Using the detail design description as a guide, important control paths are tested to uncover errors within the boundary of the module. The relative complexity of tests and the errors detected as a result is limited by the constrained scope established for unit testing. The unit test is always white box-oriented, and the step can be conducted in parallel for multiple modules.

19.2.1 Unit Test Considerations

The tests that occur as part of unit testing are illustrated schematically in Figure 19.5. The module *interface* is tested to ensure that information properly flows into and out of the program unit under test. The local *data structure* is examined to ensure that data stored temporarily maintains its integrity during all steps in an algorithm's execution. *Boundary conditions* are tested to ensure that the module operates properly at boundaries established to limit or restrict processing. All *independent paths* (basis paths)

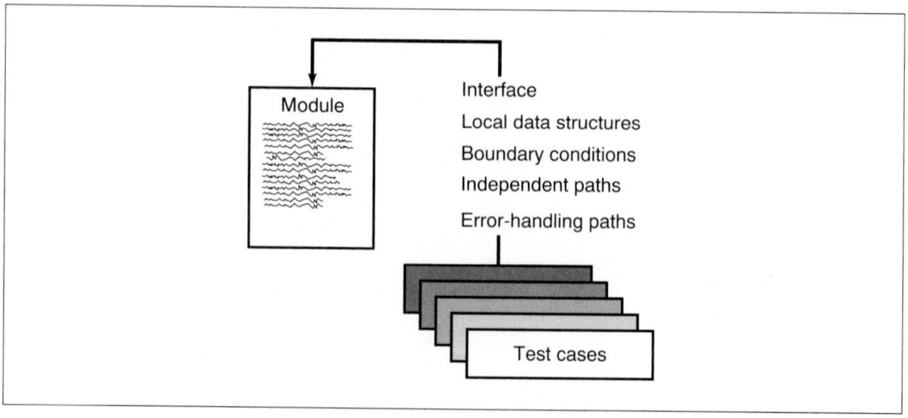

FIGURE 19.5.
Unit test.

through the control structure are exercised to ensure that all statements in a module have been executed at least once. And finally, all *error-handling paths* are tested.

Tests of data flow across a module interface are required before any other test is initiated. If data do not enter and exit properly, all other tests are moot. In his text on software testing, Myers [MYE79] proposes a checklist for interface tests:

1. Number of input parameters equal to number of arguments?
2. Parameter and argument attributes match?
3. Parameter and argument units system match?
4. Number of arguments transmitted to called modules equal to number of parameters?
5. Attributes of arguments transmitted to called modules equal to attributes of parameters?
6. Units system of arguments transmitted to called modules equal to units system of parameters?
7. Number attributes and order of arguments to built-in functions correct?
8. Any references to parameters not associated with current point of entry?
9. Input-only arguments altered?
10. Global variable definitions consistent across modules?
11. Constraints passed as arguments?

When a module performs external I/O, additional interface tests must be conducted. Again, from Myers [MYE79]:

1. File attributes correct?
2. OPEN/CLOSE statements correct?
3. Format specification matches I/O statement?
4. Buffer size matches record size?
5. Files opened before use?
6. End-of-file conditions handled?
7. I/O errors handled?
8. Any textual errors in output information?

The local data structure for a module is a common source of errors. Test cases should be designed to uncover errors in the following categories:

1. Improper or inconsistent typing
2. Erroneous initialization or default values
3. Incorrect (misspelled or truncated) variable names
4. Inconsistent data types
5. Underflow, overflow, and addressing exceptions

In addition to local data structures, the impact of global data (e.g., FORTRAN COMMON) on a module should be ascertained (if possible) during unit testing.

Selective testing of execution paths is an essential task during the unit test. Test cases should be designed to uncover errors due to erroneous computations, incorrect comparisons, or improper control flow. Basis path and loop testing are effective techniques for uncovering a broad array of path errors.

Among the more common errors in computation are (1) misunderstood or incorrect arithmetic precedence, (2) mixed-mode operations, (3) incorrect initialization, (4) precision inaccuracy, and (5) incorrect symbolic representation of an expression. Comparison and control flow are closely coupled to one another (i.e., change of flow frequently occurs after a comparison). Test cases should uncover errors such as (1) comparison of different data types, (2) incorrect logical operators or precedence, (3) expectation of equality when precision error makes equality unlikely, (4) incorrect comparison or variables, (5) improper or nonexistent loop termination, (6) failure to exit when divergent iteration is encountered, and (7) improperly modified loop variables.

Good design dictates that error conditions be anticipated and error-handling paths set up to reroute or cleanly terminate processing when an error does occur. Yourdon [YOU75] calls this approach *antibugging*.

Unfortunately, there is a tendency to incorporate error handling into software and then never test it. A true story may serve to illustrate:

> A major interactive design system was developed under contract. In one analysis module, a practical joker placed the following error-handling message after a series of conditional tests that invoked various control flow branches: ERROR! THERE IS NO WAY YOU CAN GET HERE. This "error message" was uncovered by a customer during user training!

Among the potential errors that should be tested when error handling is evaluated are

1. Error description is unintelligible.
2. Error noted does not correspond to error encountered.
3. Error condition causes system intervention prior to error handling.
4. Exception-condition processing is incorrect.
5. Error description does not provide enough information to assist in the location of the cause of the error.

Boundary testing is the last (and probably most important) task of the unit test step. Software often fails at its boundaries. That is, errors often occur when the nth element of an n-dimensional array is processed; when the ith repetition of a loop with i passes is invoked; when the maximum or minimum allowable value is encountered. Test cases that exercise data structure, control flow, and data values just below, at, and just above maxima and minima are very likely to uncover errors.

19.2.2 Unit Test Procedures

Unit testing is normally considered an adjunct to the coding step. After source level code has been developed, reviewed, and verified for correct syntax, unit test case design begins. A review of design information provides guidance for establishing test cases that are likely to uncover errors in each of the categories discussed above. Each test case should be coupled with a set of expected results.

Because a module is not a stand-alone program, *driver* and/or *stub* software must be developed for each unit test. The unit test environment is illustrated in Figure 19.6. In most applications a driver is nothing more than a "main program" that accepts test case data, passes such data to the module (to be tested), and prints the relevant results. Stubs serve to replace modules that are subordinate (called by) the module to be tested. A stub or "dummy subprogram" uses the subordinate module's interface, may do minimal data manipulation, prints verification of entry, and returns.

Drivers and stubs represent overhead. That is, both are software that must be written (formal design is not commonly applied) but that is not delivered with the final software product. If drivers and stubs are kept simple, actual overhead is relatively low. Unfortunately, many modules cannot be adequately unit-tested with "simple" overhead software. In such cases, complete testing can be postponed until the integration test step (where drivers or stubs are also used).

Unit testing is simplified when a module with high cohesion is designed. When only one function is addressed by a module, the number of test cases is reduced and errors can be more easily predicted and uncovered.

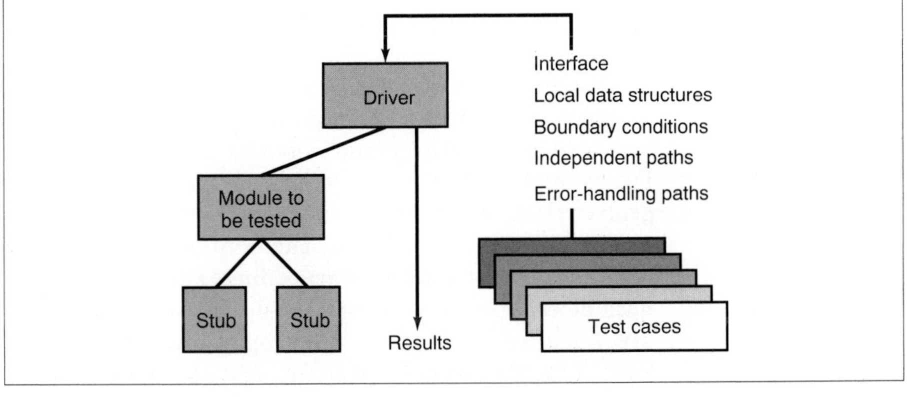

FIGURE 19.6. Unit test environment.

19.3 INTEGRATION TESTING

A neophyte in the software world might ask a seemingly legitimate question once all modules have been unit-tested: If they all work individually, why do you doubt that they'll work when we put them together? The problem, of course, is "putting them together"—interfacing. Data can be lost across an interface; one module can have an inadvertent, adverse affect on another; subfunctions, when combined, may not produce the desired major function; individually acceptable imprecision may be magnified to unacceptable levels; global data structures can present problems. Sadly, the list goes on and on.

Integration testing is a systematic technique for constructing the program structure while at the same time conducting tests to uncover errors associated with interfacing. The objective is to take unit-tested modules and build a program structure that has been dictated by design.

There is often a tendency to attempt *nonincremental integration;* that is, to construct the program using a "big bang" approach. All modules are combined in advance. The entire program is tested as a whole. And chaos usually results! A set of errors are encountered. Correction is difficult because the isolation of causes is complicated by the vast expanse of the entire program. Once these errors are corrected, new ones appear and the process continues in a seemingly endless loop.

Incremental integration is the antithesis of the big bang approach. The program is constructed and tested in small segments, where errors are easier to isolate and correct; interfaces are more likely to be tested completely, and a systematic test approach may be applied. In the sections that follow, a number of different incremental integration strategies are discussed.

19.3.1 Top-Down Integration

Top-down integration is an incremental approach to the construction of program structure. Modules are integrated by moving downward through the control hierarchy, beginning with the main control module (main program). Modules subordinate (and ultimately subordinate) to the main control module are incorporated into the structure in either a *depth-first* or *breadth-first* manner.

Referring to Figure 19.7, depth-first integration would integrate all modules on a major control path of the structure. Selection of a major path is somewhat arbitrary and depends on application-specific characteristics. For example, selecting the left-hand path, modules M_1, M_2, M_5 would be integrated first. Next, M_8 or (if necessary for proper functioning of M_2) M_6 would be integrated. Then, the central and right-hand control paths are built. Breadth-first integration incorporates all modules directly subordinate at each level, moving across the structure horizontally. From the figure, modules M_2, M_3, and M_4 (a replacement for stub S_4) would be integrated first. The next control level, M_5, M_6, etc., follows.

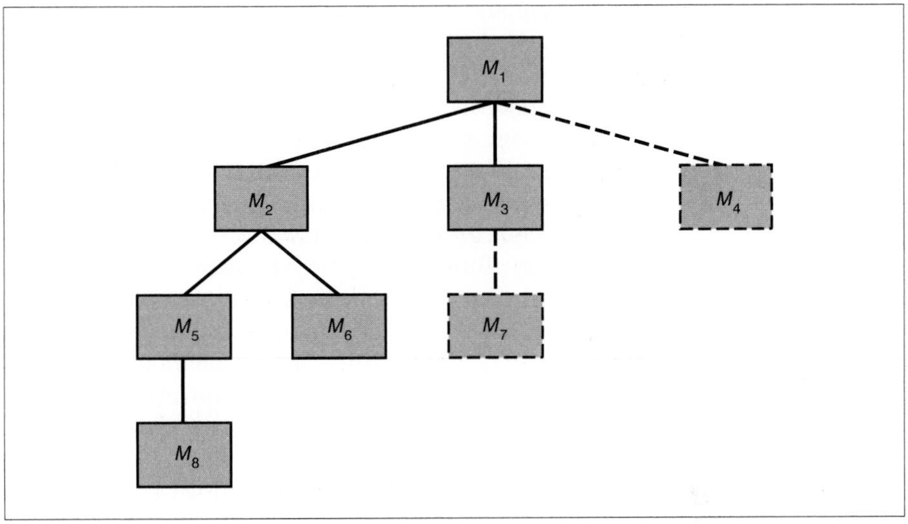

FIGURE 19.7. Top-down integration.

The integration process is performed in a series of five steps:

1. The main control module is used as a test driver and stubs are substituted for all modules directly subordinate to the main control module.
2. Depending on the integration approach selected (i.e., depth- or breadth-first), subordinate stubs are replaced one at a time with actual modules.
3. Tests are conducted as each module is integrated.
4. On the completion of each set of tests, another stub is replaced with the real module.
5. *Regression testing* (i.e., conducting all or some of the previous tests) may be conducted to ensure that new errors have not been introduced.

The process continues from step 2 until the entire program structure is built. Figure 19.7 illustrates the process. Assuming a depth-first approach and a partially completed structure, stub S_7 is the next to be replaced with module M_7. M_7 may itself have stubs that will be replaced with corresponding modules. It is important to note that at each replacement tests are conducted to verify the interface.

The top-down integration strategy verifies major control or decision points early in the test process. In a well-factored program structure, decision making occurs at upper levels in the hierarchy and is therefore encountered first. If major control problems do exist, early recognition is essential. If depth-first integration is selected, a complete function of the software may be implemented and demonstrated. For example, consider a classic transaction structure (Chapter 11) in which a complex series of interactive inputs are requested, acquired, and validated via an incoming path. The incoming path may be integrated in a top-down manner. All input processing (for subsequent transaction dispatching) may be demonstrated before other elements of the structure have been integrated. Early demonstration of functional capability is a confidence builder for both the developer and the customer.

Top-down strategy sounds relatively uncomplicated but, in practice, logistical problems can arise. The most common of these problems occurs when processing at low levels in the hierarchy is required to adequately test upper levels. *Stubs* replace low-level modules at the beginning of top-down testing; therefore, no significant data can flow upward in the program structure. The tester is left with three choices: (1) delay many tests until stubs are replaced with actual modules, (2) develop stubs that perform limited functions that simulate the actual module, and (3) integrate the software from the bottom of the hierarchy upward. Figure 19.8 illustrates typical classes of stubs, ranging from the simplest (stub A) to the most complex (stub D).

The first approach (delay tests until stubs are replaced by actual modules) causes us to lose some control over the correspondence between specific tests and the incorporation of specific modules. This can lead to difficulties in determining the cause of errors and tends to violate the highly constrained nature of the top-down approach. The second approach is workable, but can lead to significant overhead, as stubs become more and more complex. The third approach, called *bottom-up testing,* is discussed in the next section.

19.3.2 Bottom-Up Integration

Bottom-up integration testing, as its name implies, begins construction and testing with *atomic modules* (i.e., modules at the lowest levels in the program structure). Because modules are integrated from the bottom up, pro-

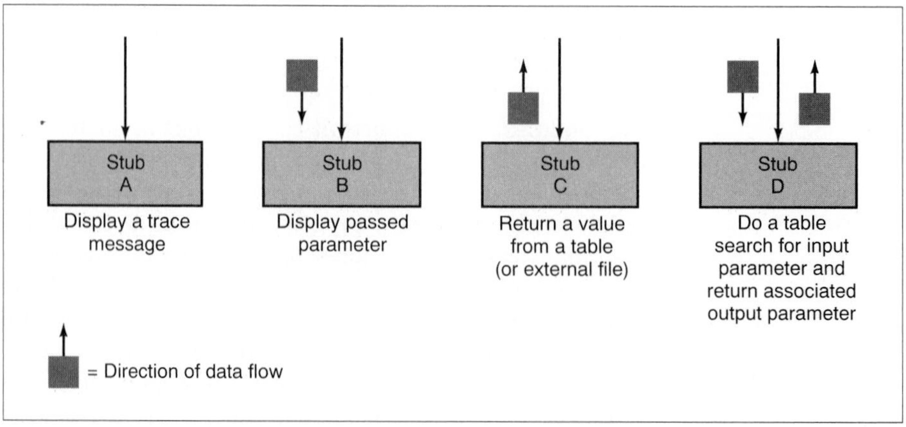

FIGURE 19.8.
Stubs.

cessing required for modules subordinate to a given level is always available and the need for stubs is eliminated.

A bottom-up integration strategy may be implemented with the following steps:

1. Low-level modules are combined into *clusters* (sometimes called *builds*) that perform a specific software subfunction.
2. A driver (a control program for testing) is written to coordinate test case input and output.
3. The cluster is tested.
4. Drivers are removed and clusters are combined moving upward in the program structure.

Integration follows the pattern illustrated in Figure 19.9. Modules are combined to form clusters 1, 2, and 3. Each of the clusters is tested using a driver (shown as a dashed block). Modules in clusters 1 and 2 are subordinate to M_a. Drivers D_1 and D_2 are removed and the clusters are interfaced

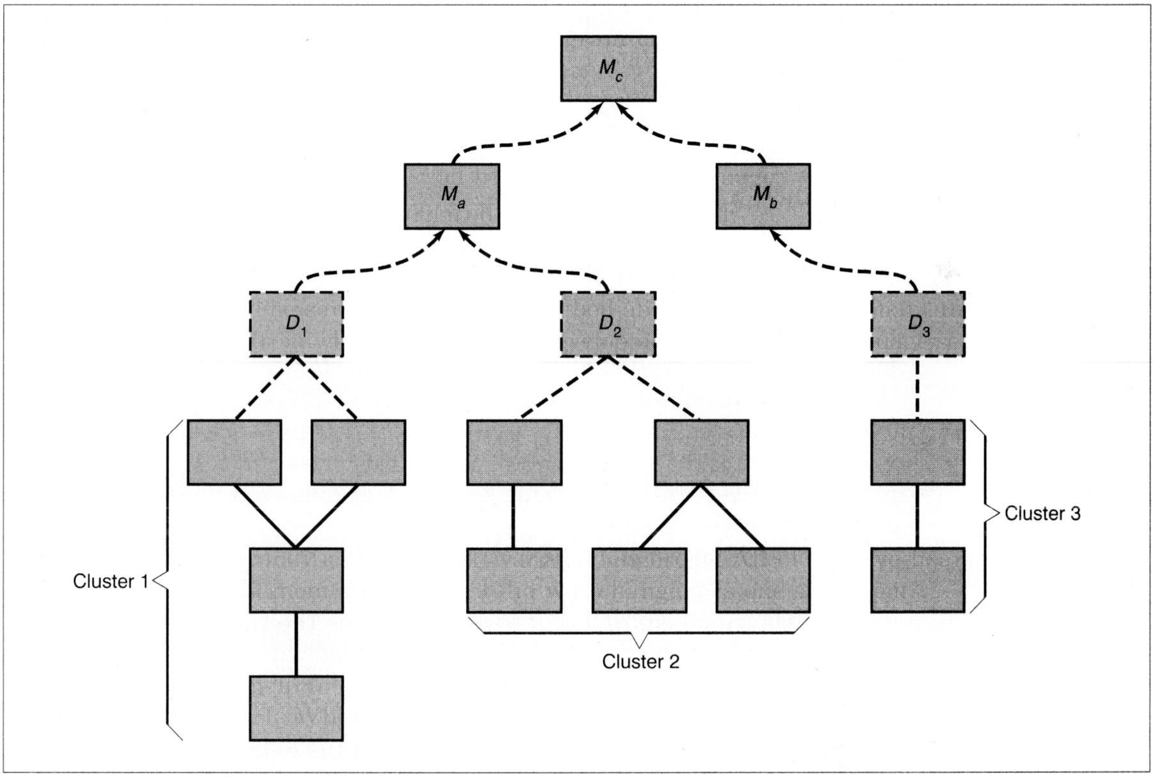

FIGURE 19.9. Bottom-up integration.

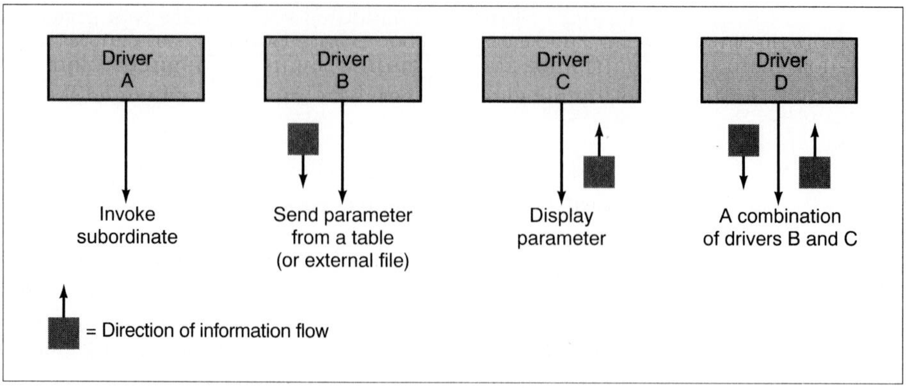

FIGURE 19.10. Drivers.

directly to M_a. Similarly, driver D_3 for cluster 3 is removed prior to integration with module M_b. Both M_a and M_b will ultimately be integrated with module M_c, and so forth. Different categories of drivers are illustrated in Figure 19.10.

As integration moves upward, the need for separate test drivers lessens. In fact, if the top two levels of program structure are integrated top down, the number of drivers can be reduced substantially and the integration of clusters is greatly simplified.

19.3.3 Comments on Integration Testing

There has been much discussion (e.g., [BEI84]) of the relative advantages and disadvantages of top-down versus bottom-up integration testing. In general, the advantages of one strategy tend to result in disadvantages for the other strategy. The major disadvantage of the top-down approach is the need for stubs and the attendant testing difficulties that can be associated with them. Problems associated with stubs may be offset by the advantage of testing major control functions early. The major disadvantage of bottom-up integration is that "the program as an entity does not exist until the last module is added" [MYE79]. This drawback is tempered by easier test case design and a lack of stubs.

The selection of an integration strategy depends upon software characteristics and, sometimes, project schedule. In general, a combined approach (sometimes called *sandwich testing*) that uses the top-down strategy for the upper levels of the program structure, coupled with a bottom-up strategy for the subordinate levels, may be the best compromise.

As integration testing is conducted, the tester should identify *critical modules*. A critical module has one or more of the following characteristics: (1) addresses several software requirements, (2) has a high level of control (resides relatively high in the program structure), (3) is complex or error-prone (cyclomatic complexity may be used as an indicator), or (4) has definite performance requirements. Critical modules should be tested as early as possible. In addition, regression tests should focus on critical module function.

19.3.4 Integration Test Documentation

An overall plan for integration of the software and a description of specific tests are documented in a *Test Specification*. The specification is a deliverable in the software engineering process and becomes part of the software configuration. Table 19.1 presents a *Test Specification* outline that may be used as a framework for this document.

Scope of testing summarizes the specific functional, performance, and internal design characteristics that are to be tested. Testing effort is

TABLE 19.1

TEST SPECIFICATION OUTLINE

- **I.** Scope of testing
- **II.** Test plan
  - **A.** Test phases and builds
  - **B.** Schedule
  - **C.** Overhead software
  - **D.** Environment and resources
- **III.** Test procedure *n*. (description of test for build *n*)
  - **A.** Order of integration
    - **1.** Purpose
    - **2.** Modules to be tested
  - **B.** Unit tests for modules in build
    - **1.** Description of tests for module *m*
    - **2.** Overhead software description
    - **3.** Expected results
  - **C.** Test environment
    - **1.** Special tools or techniques
    - **2.** Overhead software description
  - **D.** Test case data
  - **E.** Expected results for build *n*
- **IV.** Actual test results
- **V.** References
- **VI.** Appendices

bounded, criteria for completion of each test phase are described, and schedule constraints are documented.

The *Test plan* section describes the overall strategy for integration. Testing is divided into *phases* and *builds* that address specific functional and behavioral characteristics of the software. For example, integration testing for a computer graphics-oriented CAD system might be divided into the following test phases:

- User interaction (command selection; drawing creation; display representation; error processing and representation)
- Data manipulation and analysis (symbol creation; dimensioning; rotation; computation of physical properties)
- Display processing and generation (two-dimensional displays; three-dimensional displays; graphs and charts)
- Database management (access; update; integrity; performance)

Each of these phases and subphases (denoted in parentheses) delineates a broad functional category within the software and can generally be related to a specific domain of the program structure. Therefore, program builds (groups of modules) are created to correspond to each phase.

The following criteria and corresponding tests are applied for all test phases:

Interface integrity. Internal and external interfaces are tested as each module (or cluster) is incorporated into the structure.

Functional validity. Tests designed to uncover functional errors are conducted.

Information content. Tests designed to uncover errors associated with local or global data structures are conducted.

Performance. Tests designed to verify performance bounds established during software design are conducted.

These criteria and the tests associated with them are discussed in this section of the *Test Specification.*

A schedule for integration, overhead software, and related topics are also discussed as part of the *Test plan* section. Start and end dates for each phase are established and "availability windows" for unit-tested modules are defined. A brief description of overhead software (stubs and drivers) concentrates on characteristics that might require special effort. Finally, the test environment and resources are described. Unusual hardware configurations, exotic simulators, special test tools or techniques are a few of many topics that may be discussed in this section.

A detailed testing procedure that is required to accomplish the test plan is described in the *Test procedure* section. Referring back to *Test Specification* outline item II, the order of integration and corresponding tests at each integration step are described. A listing of all test cases (annotated for subsequent reference) and expected results is also included.

A history of actual test results, problems, or peculiarities is recorded in the fourth section of the *Test Specification*. Information contained in this section can be vital during software maintenance. Appropriate references and appendices are presented in the final two sections.

Like all other elements of a software configuration, the *Test Specification* format may be tailored to the local needs of a software development organization. It is important to note, however, that an integration strategy, contained in a *Test plan,* and testing details, described in a *Test procedure,* are essential ingredients and must appear.

19.4 VALIDATION TESTING

At the culmination of integration testing, software is completely assembled as a package, interfacing errors have been uncovered and corrected, and a final series of software tests—*validation testing*—may begin. Validation can be defined in many ways, but a simple (albeit harsh) definition is that validation succeeds when the software functions in a manner that can be reasonably expected by the customer. At this point a battle-hardened software developer might protest: Who or what is the arbiter of *reasonable expectations?*

Reasonable expectations are defined in the *Software Requirements Specification*—a document (Chapter 6) that describes all user-visible attributes of the software. The *Specification* contains a section called *Validation criteria*. Information contained in that section forms the basis for a validation testing approach.

19.4.1 Validation Test Criteria

Software validation is achieved through a series of black box tests that demonstrate conformity with requirements. A test plan outlines the classes of tests to be conducted and a test procedure defines specific test cases that will be used to demonstrate conformity with requirements. Both the plan and the procedure are designed to ensure that all functional requirements are satisfied, all performance requirements are achieved, documentation is correct and human-engineered, and other requirements are met (e.g., transportability, compatibility, error recovery, maintainability).

After each validation test case has been conducted, one of two possible conditions exist: (1) The function or performance characteristics conform to specification and are accepted, or (2) a deviation from specification is uncovered and a deficiency list is created. Deviation or error discovered at this stage in a project can rarely be corrected prior to scheduled completion. It is often necessary to negotiate with the customer to establish a method for resolving deficiencies.

19.4.2 Configuration Review

An important element of the validation process is a *configuration review.* The intent of the review, as illustrated in Figure 19.11, is to ensure that all the elements of the software configuration have been properly developed, are cataloged, and have the necessary detail to support the maintenance phase of the software life cycle. The configuration review, sometimes called an *audit,* is discussed in more detail in Chapter 21.

19.4.3 Alpha and Beta Testing

It is virtually impossible for a software developer to foresee how the customer will *really* use a program. Instructions for use may be misinterpreted; strange combinations of data may be regularly used; output that seemed clear to the tester may be unintelligible to a user in the field.

When custom software is built for one customer, a series of *acceptance tests* are conducted to enable the customer to validate all requirements. Conducted by the end user rather than the system developer, an acceptance test can range from an informal "test drive" to a planned and systematically executed series of tests. In fact, acceptance testing can be conducted over a period of weeks or months, thereby uncovering cumulative errors that might degrade the system over time.

If software is developed as a product to be used by many customers, it is impractical to perform formal acceptance tests with each one. Most software product builders use a process called *alpha* and *beta testing* to uncover errors that only the end user seems able to find.

The alpha test is conducted at the developer's site by a customer. The software is used in a natural setting with the developer "looking over the

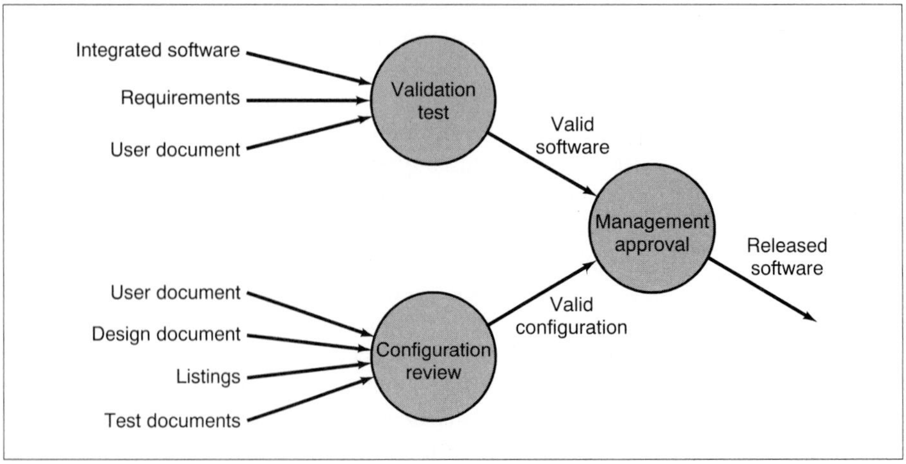

FIGURE 19.11.
Configuration review.

shoulder" of the user and recording errors and usage problems. Alpha tests are conducted in a controlled environment.

The beta test is conducted at one or more customer sites by the end user of the software. Unlike alpha testing, the developer generally is not present. Therefore, the beta test is a "live" application of the software in an environment that cannot be controlled by the developer. The customer records all the problems (real or imagined) that are encountered during beta testing and reports these to the developer at regular intervals. As a result of problems reported during beta test, the software developer makes modifications and then prepares for release of the software product to the entire customer base.

19.5 SYSTEM TESTING

At the beginning of this book, we stressed the fact that software is only one element of a larger computer-based system. Ultimately, software is incorporated with other system elements (e.g., new hardware, information), and a series of system integration and validation tests are conducted. These tests fall outside the scope of the software engineering process and are not conducted solely by the software developer. However, steps taken during software design and testing can greatly improve the probability of successful software integration in the larger system.

A classic system testing problem is "finger pointing." This occurs when a defect is uncovered, and one system element developer blames another for the problem. Rather than indulging in such nonsense, the software engineer should anticipate potential interfacing problems and (1) design error-handling paths that test all information coming from other elements of the system; (2) conduct a series of tests that simulate bad data or other potential errors at the software interface; (3) record the results of tests to use as "evidence" if finger pointing does occur; (4) participate in the planning and design of system tests to ensure that software is adequately tested.

System testing is actually a series of different tests whose primary purpose is to fully exercise the computer-based system. Although each test has a different purpose, all work should verify that all system elements have been properly integrated and perform allocated functions. In the sections that follow, we discuss the types of system tests [BEI84] that are worthwhile for software-based systems.

19.5.1 Recovery Testing

Many computer-based systems must recover from faults and resume processing within a prespecified time. In some cases, a system must be fault-tolerant, i.e., processing faults must not cause overall system function to cease. In other cases, a system failure must be corrected within a specified period of time or severe economic damage will occur.

Recovery testing is a system test that forces the software to fail in a variety of ways and verifies that recovery is properly performed. If recovery is automatic (performed by the system itself), reinitialization, checkpointing mechanisms, data recovery, and restart are each evaluated for correctness. If recovery requires human intervention, the mean time to repair is evaluated to determine whether it is within acceptable limits.

19.5.2 Security Testing

Any computer-based system that manages sensitive information or causes actions that can improperly harm (or benefit) individuals is a target for improper or illegal penetration. Penetration spans a broad range of activities: *hackers* who attempt to penetrate systems for sport; disgruntled employees who attempt to penetrate for revenge; dishonest individuals who attempt to penetrate for illicit personal gain. Denning [DEN90] presents a compendium of the modes of "attack" and the people involved.

Security testing attempts to verify that protection mechanisms built into a system will, in fact, protect it from improper penetration. To quote Beizer [BEI84]: "The system's security must, of course, be tested for invulnerability from frontal attack—but must also be tested for invulnerability from flank or rear attack."

During security testing, the tester plays the role(s) of the individual who desires to penetrate the system. Anything goes! The tester may attempt to acquire passwords through external clerical means; may attack the system with custom software designed to breakdown any defenses that have been constructed; may overwhelm the system, thereby denying service to others; may purposely cause system errors, hoping to penetrate during recovery; may browse through insecure data, hoping to find the key to system entry.

Given enough time and resources, good security testing will ultimately penetrate a system. The role of the system designer is to make penetration cost more than the value of the information that will be obtained.

19.5.3 Stress Testing

During earlier software testing steps, white box and black box techniques resulted in a thorough evaluation of normal program functions and performance. *Stress tests* are designed to confront programs with abnormal situations. In essence, the tester who performs stress testing asks: How high can we crank this up before it fails?

Stress testing executes a system in a manner that demands resources in abnormal quantity, frequency, or volume. For example, (1) special tests may be designed that generate 10 interrupts per second, when one or two is the average rate; (2) input data rates may be increased by an order of magnitude to determine how input functions will respond; (3) test cases that require maximum memory or other resources may be executed; (4) test cases that may cause thrashing in a virtual operating system are designed; (5) test cases that may cause excessive hunting for disk resident data are designed. Essentially, the tester attempts to break the program.

A variation of stress testing is a technique called *sensitivity testing*. In some situations (the most common occur in mathematical algorithms) a very small range of data contained within the bounds of valid data for a program may cause extreme and even erroneous processing or profound performance degradation. This situation, illustrated in Figure 19.12, is analogous to a singularity in a mathematical function. Sensitivity testing attempts to uncover data combinations within valid input classes that may cause instability or improper processing.

19.5.4 Performance Testing

For real-time and embedded systems, software that provides required function but does not conform to performance requirements is unacceptable. *Performance testing* is designed to test the run-time performance of software within the context of an integrated system. Performance testing occurs throughout all steps in the testing process. Even at the unit level, the performance of an individual module may be assessed as white box tests are conducted. However, it is not until all system elements are fully integrated that the true performance of a system can be ascertained.

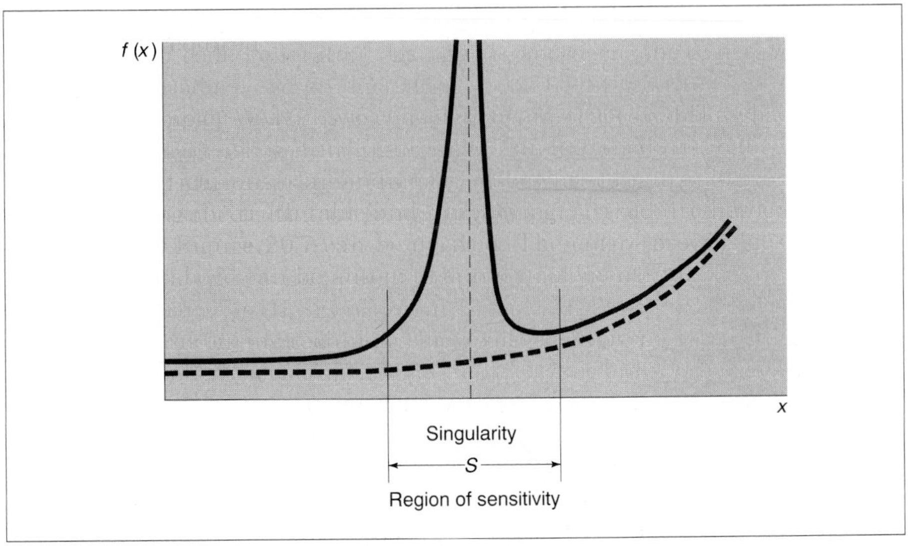

FIGURE 19.12.
Sensitivity analysis.

Performance tests are sometimes coupled with stress testing and often require both hardware and software *instrumentation*. That is, it is often necessary to measure resource utilization (e.g., processor cycles) in an exacting fashion. External instrumentation can monitor execution intervals, log events (e.g., interrupts) as they occur, and sample machine states on a regular basis. By instrumenting a system, the tester can uncover situations that lead to degradation and possible system failure.

19.6 THE ART OF DEBUGGING

Throughout Chapters 18 and 19, we have seen that software testing is a process that can be systematically planned and specified. Test case design can be conducted, a strategy can be defined, and the results can be evaluated against prescribed expectations.

Debugging occurs as a consequence of successful testing. That is, when a test case uncovers an error, debugging is the process that results in the removal of the error. Although debugging can and should be an orderly process, it is still very much an art. A software engineer, evaluating the results of a test, is often confronted with a "symptomatic" indication of a software problem. That is, the external manifestation of the error and the internal cause of the error may have no obvious relationship to one another. The poorly understood mental process that connects a symptom to a cause is debugging.

19.6.1 The Debugging Process

Debugging is *not* testing, but always occurs as a consequence of testing.[1] Referring to Figure 19.13, the debugging process begins with the execution of a test case. The results are assessed and a lack of correspondence between the expected and actual outcome is encountered. In many cases, the noncorresponding data are a symptom of an underlying cause as yet hidden. The debugging process attempts to match symptom with cause, thereby leading to error correction.

The debugging process will always have one of two outcomes: (1) The cause will be found, corrected and removed, or (2) the cause will not be found. In the latter case, the person performing debugging may suspect a cause, design a test case to help validate his or her suspicion, and work toward error correction in an iterative fashion.

[1]In making this statement, we take the broadest possible view of "testing." Not only does the developer test software prior to release, but the customer/user tests software every time it is used!

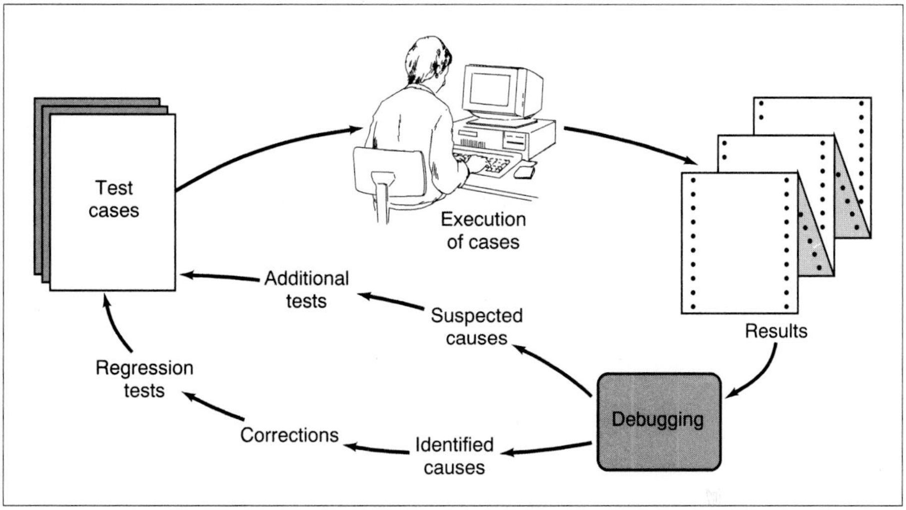

FIGURE 19.13.
Debugging.

Why is debugging so difficult? In all likelihood, human psychology (see the next section) has more to do with an answer than software technology. However, a few characteristics of bugs provide some clues:

1. The symptom and the cause may be geographically remote. That is, the symptom may appear in one part of a program, while the cause may actually be located at a site that is far removed. Highly coupled program structures (Chapter 10) exacerbate this situation.
2. The symptom may disappear (temporarily) when another error is corrected.
3. The symptom may actually be caused by nonerrors (e.g., round-off inaccuracies).
4. The symptom may be caused by a human error that is not easily traced.
5. The symptom may be a result of timing problems, rather than processing problems.
6. It may be difficult to accurately reproduce input conditions (e.g., a real-time application in which input ordering is indeterminate).
7. The symptom may be intermittent. This is particularly common in embedded systems that couple hardware and software inextricably.
8. The symptom may be due to causes that are distributed across a number of tasks running on different processors [CHE90].

During debugging, we encounter errors that range from mildly annoying (e.g., an incorrect output format) to catastrophic (e.g., the system fails, causing serious economic or physical damage). As the consequences of an error increase, the amount of pressure to find the cause also increases. Often, pressure forces a software developer to fix one error and at the same time introduce two more.

19.6.2 Psychological Considerations

Unfortunately, there appears to be some evidence that debugging prowess is an innate human trait. Some people are good at it, and others aren't. Although experimental evidence on debugging is open to many interpretations, large variances in debugging ability have been reported for software engineers with the same educational and experiential background.

Commenting on the human aspects of debugging, Shneiderman [SHN80] states:

> Debugging is one of the more frustrating parts of programming. It has elements of problem solving or brain teasers, coupled with the annoying recognition that you have made a mistake. Heightened anxiety and the unwillingness to accept the possibility of errors, increases the task difficulty. Fortunately, there is a great sigh of relief and a lessening of tension when the bug is ultimately... corrected.

Although it may be difficult to "learn" debugging, a number of approaches to the problem can be proposed. We examine these in the next section.

19.6.3 Debugging Approaches

Regardless of the approach that is taken, debugging has one overriding objective: to find and correct the cause of a software error. The objective is realized by a combination of systematic evaluation, intuition, and luck. Bradley [BRA85] describes the debugging approach in this way:

> Debugging is a straightforward application of the scientific method that has been developed over 2,500 years. The basis of debugging is to locate the problem's source [the cause] by binary partitioning, through working hypotheses that predict new values to be examined.
>
> Take a simple non-software example: A lamp in my house does not work. If nothing in the house works, the cause must be in the main circuit breaker or outside; I look around to see whether the neighborhood is blacked out. I plug the suspect lamp into a working socket and a working appliance into the suspect circuit. So goes the alternation of hypothesis and test.

In general, three categories for debugging approaches may be proposed [MYE79]:

- Brute force
- Backtracking
- Cause elimination

The *brute force* category of debugging is probably the most common and least efficient method for isolating the cause of a software error. We apply brute force debugging methods when all else fails. Using a "let the computer find the error" philosophy, memory dumps are taken, run-time traces are invoked, and the program is loaded with WRITE statements. We hope that somewhere in the morass of information that is produced we will find a clue that can lead us to the cause of an error. Although the mass of information produced may ultimately lead to success, it more frequently leads to wasted effort and time. Thought must be expended first!

Backtracking is a fairly common debugging approach that can be used successfully in small programs. Beginning at the site where a symptom has been uncovered, the source code is traced backward (manually) until the site of the cause is found. Unfortunately, as the number of source lines increases, the number of potential backward paths may become unmanageably large.

The third approach to debugging—*cause elimination*—is manifested by induction or deduction and introduces the concept of *binary partitioning*. Data related to the error occurrence are organized to isolate potential causes. A "cause hypothesis" is devised and the above data are used to prove or disprove the hypothesis. Alternatively, a list of all possible causes is developed and tests are conducted to eliminate each. If initial tests indicate that a particular cause hypothesis shows promise, the data are refined in an attempt to isolate the bug.

Each of the above debugging approaches can be supplemented with debugging tools. We can apply a wide variety of debugging compilers, dynamic debugging aids ("tracers"), automatic test case generators, memory dumps, and cross reference maps. However, tools are not a substitute for careful evaluation based on a complete software design document and clear source code.

In many ways, the debugging of computer software is like problem solving in the business world. Brown and Sampson [BRO73] have proposed a debugging approach, called "The Method," that is an adaptation of management problem solving techniques. The authors propose the development of a *specification of deviation* that describes a problem by delineating "what, when, where, and to what extent?"

Each of the above questions (what, when, where, and to what extent) is split into *is* and *is not* responses so that a clear distinction between what has occurred and what has not occurred can be made. Once information about the bug has been recorded, a cause hypothesis is developed based on distinctions observed from the *is* and *is not* responses. Debugging continues using a deductive or inductive approach described earlier in this section.

Any discussion of debugging approaches and tools is incomplete without mention of a powerful ally: other people! Weinberg's "egoless programming" concept (discussed earlier in this book) should be extended to egoless debugging as well. Each of us can recall puzzling for hours or days over a persistent bug. A colleague wanders by and in desperation we explain the problem and throw open the listing. Instantaneously (it seems), the cause of the error is uncovered. Smiling smugly, our colleague wanders off. A fresh viewpoint, unclouded by hours of frustration, can do wonders. A final maxim for debugging might be: When all else fails, get help!

Once a bug has been found, it must be corrected. But as we have already noted, the correction of a bug can introduce other errors and therefore do more harm than good. Van Vleck [VAN89] suggests three simple questions that every software engineer should ask before making the "correction" that removes the cause of a bug:

1. *Is the cause of the bug reproduced in another part of the program?* In many situations, a program defect is caused by an erroneous pattern of logic that may be reproduced elsewhere. Explicit consideration of the logical pattern may result in the discovery of other errors.
2. *What "next bug" might be introduced by the fix I'm about to make?* Before the correction is made, the source code (or better, the design) should be evaluated to assess coupling of logic and data structures. If the correction is to be made in a highly coupled section of the program, special care must be taken when any change is made.
3. *What could we have done to prevent this bug in the first place?* This question is the first step toward establishing a statistical software quality assurance approach (Chapter 17). If we correct the process as well as the product, the bug will be removed from the current program *and* may be eliminated from all future programs.

19.7 SUMMARY

Software testing accounts for the largest percentage of technical effort in the software development process. Yet we are only beginning to understand the subtleties of systematic test planning, execution, and control.

The objective of software testing is to uncover errors. To fulfill this objective, a series of test steps—unit, integration, validation, and system tests—are planned and executed. Unit and integration tests concentrate on functional verification of a module and the incorporation of modules into a program structure. Validation testing demonstrates traceability to software requirements, and system testing validates software once it has been incorporated into a larger system.

Each test step is accomplished through a series of systematic test techniques that assist in the design of test cases. With each testing step, the level of abstraction with which software is considered is broadened.

Unlike testing (a systematic, planned activity), debugging is best described as an art. Beginning with a symptomatic indication of a problem, the debugging activity must track down the cause of an error. Of the many resources available during debugging, the most valuable is the counsel of other members of the software development staff.

The requirement for higher-quality software demands a more systematic approach to testing. To quote Dunn and Ullman [DUN82]:

> What is required is an overall strategy, spanning the strategic test space, quite as deliberate in its methodology as was the systematic development on which analysis, design and code were based.

In this chapter, we have examined the "strategic test space," considering the steps that have the highest likelihood of meeting the overriding test objective: to find and remove defects in an orderly and effective manner.

REFERENCES

[BEI84] Beizer, B., *Software System Testing and Quality Assurance,* Van Nostrand Reinhold, 1984.

[BOE81] Boehm, B., *Software Engineering Economics,* Prentice-Hall, 1981, p. 37.

[BRA85] Bradley, J. H., "The Science and Art of Debugging," *Computerworld,* August 19, 1985, pp. 35–38.

[BRO73] Brown, A., and W. Sampson, *Programming Debugging,* American Elsevier, 1973.

[CHE90] Cheung, W. H., J. P. Black, and E. Manning, "A Framework for Distributed Debugging," *IEEE Software,* January 1990, pp. 106–115.

[DEN90] Denning, P. J. (ed.), *Computers Under Attack,* Addison-Wesley, 1990.

[DUN82] Dunn, R., and R. Ullman, *Quality Assurance for Computer Software,* McGraw-Hill, 1982, p. 158.

[MIL77] Miller, E., "The Philosophy of Testing," in *Program Testing Techniques,* IEEE Computer Society Press, 1977, pp. 1–3.

[MUS89] Musa, J. D., and Ackerman, A. F., "Quantifying Software Validation: When to Stop Testing?" *IEEE Software,* May 1989, pp. 19–27.

[MYE79] Myers, G., *The Art of Software Tests,* Wiley, 1979.

[SHO83] Shooman, M. L., *Software Engineering,* McGraw-Hill, 1983.

[SHN80] Shneiderman, B., *Software Psychology,* Winthrop Publishers, 1980, p. 28.

[VAN89] Van Vleck, T., "Three Questions About Each Bug You Find," *ACM Software Engineering Notes,* vol. 14, no. 5, July 1989, pp. 62–63.

[WAL89] Wallace, D. R., and R. U. Fujii, "Software Verification and Validation: An Overview," *IEEE Software,* May 1989, pp. 10–17.

[YOU75] Yourdon, E., *Techniques of Program Structure and Design,* Prentice-Hall, 1975.

PROBLEMS AND POINTS TO PONDER

19.1 Using your own words, describe the difference between verification and validation. Do both make use of test case design methods and testing strategies?

19.2 List some problems that might be associated with the creation of an independent test group. Are an ITG and an SQA group the same people?

19.3 Is it always possible to develop a strategy for testing software that uses the sequence of testing steps described in Section 19.1.3? What are possible complications that might arise for embedded systems?

19.4 If you could only select three test case design methods to apply during unit testing, what would they be and why?

19.5 Add at least three additional questions to each segment of the unit test checklist presented in Section 19.2.1.

19.6 The concept of "antibugging" (Section 19.2.1) is an extremely effective way to provide built-in debugging assistance when an error is uncovered.
(*a*) Develop a set of guidelines for antibugging.
(*b*) Discuss the advantages of using the techniques.
(*c*) Discuss the disadvantages.

19.7 Develop an integration testing strategy for any one of the systems implemented in Problems 16.13 through 16.21. Define test phases, note the order of integration, specify additional test software, and justify your order of integration. Assume that all modules have been unit-tested and are available. *Note:* It may be necessary to do a bit of design work first.

19.8 How can project scheduling affect integration testing?

19.9 Is unit testing possible or even desirable in all circumstances? Provide examples to justify your answer.

19.10 Who should perform the validation test—the software developer or the software user? Justify your answer.

19.11 Develop a complete test strategy for the *SafeHome* system discussed earlier in this book. Document it in a *Test Specification*.

19.12 As a class project, develop a *Debugging Guide* for your installation. The guide should provide language- and system-oriented hints that have been learned through the school of hard knocks! Begin with an outline of topics that will be reviewed by the class and your instructor. Publish the guide for others in your local environment.

FURTHER READINGS

A detailed discussion on testing strategies can be found in books by Evans (*Productive Software Test Management*, Wiley-Interscience, 1984), Hetzel (*The Complete Guide to Software Testing*, QED Information Sciences, 1984), Ould and Unwin (*Testing in Software Development*, Cambridge University Press, 1986), and Beizer [BEI84]. Each delineates the steps of an effective strategy, provides a set of techniques and guidelines, and suggests procedures for controlling and tracking the testing process.

For individuals that build product software, Gunther's book (*Management Methodology for Software Product Engineering*, Wiley-Interscience, 1978) remains a useful guide for the establishment and conduct of effective test strategies. In addition, Perry (*How to Test Software Packages*, Wiley, 1986) provides useful information for both the product builder and the purchaser.

Deutsch's contribution to Jensen and Tonies' book ("Verification and Validation" in *Software Engineering,* Prentice-Hall, 1979) provides a concise description of many important aspects of V&V. A special edition of *IEEE Software* (May 1989) is dedicated to V&V and presents current approaches to this important software engineering activity. Lewis (*Software Engineering,* Reston, 1983) describes a "transform theory of software verification" that may be of interest to those who desire a rigorous view of testing.

Guidelines for debugging are contained in a book by Dunn (*Software Defect Removal,* McGraw-Hill, 1984). Beizer [BEI84] presents an interesting "taxonomy of bugs" that can lead to effective methods for test planning. A comprehensive bibliography on debugging topics, containing over 240 references, has been assembled by Agrawal and Spafford ("Bibliography on Debugging and Backtracking," *ACM Software Engineering Notes,* April 1989).

CHAPTER 20

SOFTWARE MAINTENANCE

Software maintenance has been characterized [CAN72] as an "iceberg." Wishfully, we hope that what is immediately visible is all there is to it. Realistically, we know that an enormous mass of potential problems and cost lies under the surface. The maintenance of existing software can account for over 70 percent of all effort expended by a software organization. The percentage continues to rise as more software is produced. On the horizon we can foresee a "maintenance-bound" software organization that can no longer produce new software because it is expending all its available resources maintaining old software.

Uninitiated readers may ask why so much maintenance is required, and why so much effort is expended. Osborne and Chikofsky [OSB90] provide a partial answer:

> Much of the software we depend on today is on average 10 to 15 years old. Even when these programs were created using the best design and coding techniques known at the time [and most were not], they were created when program size and storage space were principal concerns. They were then migrated to new platforms, adjusted for changes in machine and operating system technology and enhanced to meet new user needs—all without enough regard to overall architecture.
>
> The result is the poorly designed structures, poor coding, poor logic, and poor documentation of the software systems we are now called on to keep running....

The ubiquitous nature of change underlies all software work. Change is inevitable when computer-based systems are built; therefore, we must develop mechanisms for evaluating, controlling, and making modifications.

Throughout this book we have discussed the software engineering process. A primary goal of this process is to improve the ease with which changes can be accommodated and reduce the amount of effort expended on maintenance. In this chapter and the chapter that follows, we discuss the specific activities that enable us to accomplish this goal.

20.1 A DEFINITION OF SOFTWARE MAINTENANCE

Upon reading the introduction to this chapter a reader may protest: "... but I don't spend 70 percent of my time fixing mistakes in the programs I develop...." Software maintenance is, of course, far more than "fixing mistakes." We may define maintenance by describing four activities that are undertaken after a program is released for use.

The first maintenance activity occurs because it is unreasonable to assume that software testing will uncover all latent errors in a large software system. During the use of any large program, errors will occur and be reported to the developer. The process that includes the diagnosis and correction of one or more errors is called *corrective maintenance.*

The second activity that contributes to a definition of maintenance occurs because of the rapid change that is encountered in every aspect of computing. New generations of hardware seem to be announced on a 24-month cycle; new operating systems, or new releases of old ones, appear regularly; peripheral equipment and other system elements are frequently upgraded or modified. The useful life of application software, on the other hand, can easily surpass 10 years, outliving the system environment for which it was originally developed. Therefore, *adaptive maintenance*—an activity that modifies software to properly interface with a changing environment—is both necessary and commonplace.

The third activity that may be applied to a definition of maintenance occurs when a software package is successful. As the software is used, recommendations for new capabilities, modifications to existing functions, and general enhancements are received from users. To satisfy requests in this category, *perfective maintenance* is performed. This activity accounts for the majority of all effort expended on software maintenance.

The fourth maintenance activity occurs when software is changed to improve future maintainability or reliability, or to provide a better basis for future enhancements. Often called *preventive maintenance,* this activity is characterized by *reverse engineering* and *re-engineering* techniques that are discussed later in this chapter.

The terms used to describe the first three maintenance activities were coined by Swanson [SWA76]. The fourth term is commonly used in the maintenance of hardware and other physical systems. It should be noted, however, that analogies between software and hardware maintenance can be misleading. As we noted in the first chapter of this book, software, unlike hardware, does not wear out, and therefore the major activity associated with hardware maintenance—replacement of worn or broken parts—simply does not apply.

Some software professionals are troubled by the inclusion of the second and third activities as part of a definition of maintenance. In actuality, the tasks that occur as part of adaptive and perfective maintenance are the same tasks that are applied during the development phase of the software engineering process. To adapt or perfect, we must determine new requirements, redesign, generate code, and test existing software. Traditionally, such tasks, when they are applied to an existing program, have been called *maintenance*.

20.2 MAINTENANCE CHARACTERISTICS

Software maintenance has until very recently been the neglected phase in the software engineering process. The literature on maintenance contains very few entries when compared to development activities. Relatively little research or production data have been gathered on the subject, and few technical approaches or "methods" have been proposed.

To understand the characteristics of software maintenance, we consider the topic from three different viewpoints:

1. The activities required to accomplish the maintenance phase and the impact of a software engineering approach (or lack thereof) on the efficacy of such activities
2. The costs associated with the maintenance phase
3. The problems that are frequently encountered when software maintenance is undertaken

In the sections that follow, the characteristics of maintenance are described from each of the perspectives listed above.

20.2.1 Structured versus Unstructured Maintenance

The flow of events that can occur as a result of a maintenance request is illustrated in Figure 20.1. If the only available element of a software configuration is source code, maintenance activity begins with a painstaking evaluation of the code, often complicated by poor internal documentation.[1] Subtle characteristics such as program structure, global data structures, system interfaces, and performance and/or design constraints are difficult to

[1]A new generation of reverse engineering tools (discussed later in this chapter) makes the evaluation of source code easier. However, these tools do not replace the need for good design documentation.

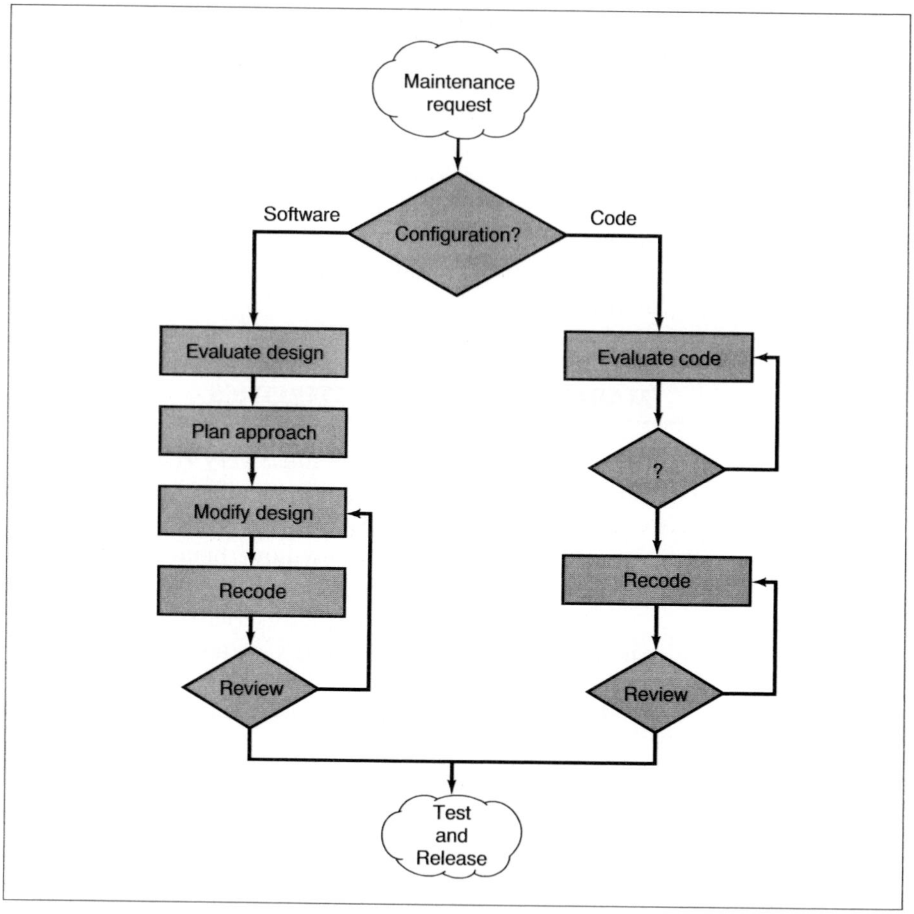

FIGURE 20.1. Structured versus unstructured maintenance.

ascertain and frequently misinterpreted. The ramifications of the changes that are ultimately made to the code are difficult to assess. Regression tests (repeating past tests to ensure that modifications have not introduced faults into previously operational software) are impossible to conduct because no record of testing exists. We are conducting *unstructured maintenance* and paying the price (in wasted effort and human frustration) that accompanies software that has not been developed using a well-defined methodology.

If a complete software configuration exists, the maintenance task begins with an evaluation of the design documentation. Important structural, performance, and interface characteristics of the software are determined. The impact of required modifications or corrections is assessed, and an approach is planned. The design is modified (using techniques identical to those discussed in earlier chapters) and reviewed. New source code is developed, regression tests are conducted using information contained in the *Test Specification,* and the software is released again.

This sequence of events constitutes *structured maintenance* and occurs as a result of earlier application of a software engineering methodology. Although the existence of a software configuration does not guarantee problem-free maintenance, the amount of wasted effort is reduced and the overall quality of a change or correction is enhanced.

20.2.2 Maintenance Cost

The cost of software maintenance has increased steadily during the past 20 years. During the 1970s, maintenance accounted for between 35 and 40 percent of the software budget for an information system organization. This number jumped to approximately 60 percent during the 1980s. If nothing is done to improve our maintenance approach, many companies will spend close to 80 percent of their software budget on maintenance by the mid-1990s.

The dollar cost of maintenance is our most obvious concern. However, other less tangible costs may ultimately be a cause for greater concern. To quote Daniel McCracken [MCC80]:

> Backlogs of new applications and major changes that measure in years are getting longer. As an industry, we can't even keep up—let alone catch up—with what our users want us to do.

McCracken alludes to the maintenance-bound organization. One intangible cost of software maintenance is development opportunity that is postponed or lost because available resources must be channeled to maintenance tasks. Other intangible costs include:

- Customer dissatisfaction when seemingly legitimate requests for repair or modification cannot be addressed in a timely manner
- Reduction in overall software quality as a result of changes that introduce latent errors in the maintained software
- Upheaval caused during development efforts when staff must be "pulled" to work on a maintenance task

The final cost of software maintenance is a dramatic decrease in productivity (measured in LOC per person-month or function points per person-month) that is encountered when the maintenance of old programs is initiated. Productivity reductions of 40:1 have been reported [BOE79]. That is, a development effort that cost $25.00 per line of code to develop might cost $1000.00 for every line of code that is maintained.

Effort expended on maintenance may be divided into productive activities (e.g., analysis and evaluation, design modification, coding) and "wheel spinning" activities (e.g., trying to understand what the code does; trying to interpret data structure, interface characteristics, performance bounds). The following expression [BEL72] provides a model of maintenance effort:

$$M = p + Ke^{(c-d)}$$

where M = total effort expended on maintenance
p = productive effort (as described above)
K = an empirical constant
c = a measure of complexity that can be attributed to a lack of good design and documentation
d = a measure of the degree of familiarity with the software.

The model described above indicates that effort (and cost) can increase exponentially if a poor software development approach (i.e., a lack of software engineering) was used, and the person or group that used the approach is not available to perform maintenance.

20.2.3 Problems

Most problems that are associated with software maintenance can be traced to deficiencies in the way software was planned and developed. The classic "pay now or pay more later" situation applies. A lack of control and discipline in software engineering development activities nearly always translates into problems during software maintenance.

Among the many classic problems [SCH87] that can be associated with software maintenance are the following:

- It is often difficult or impossible to trace the evolution of the software through many versions or releases. Changes are not adequately documented.
- It is often difficult or impossible to trace the process through which software was created.
- It is often exceptionally difficult to understand "someone else's" program. The difficulty increases as the number of elements in a software configuration decreases. If only undocumented code exists, severe problems should be expected.
- "Someone else" is often not around to explain. Mobility among software personnel is high. We cannot rely upon a personal explanation of the software by the developer when maintenance is required.
- Documentation doesn't exist or is awful. The recognition that software must be documented is a first step, but documentation must be understandable and consistent with source code to be of any value.
- Most software is not designed for change. Unless a design method accommodates change through concepts such as functional independence or object classes, modifications to software are difficult and error-prone.

- Maintenance has not been viewed as very glamorous work. Much of this perception comes from the high frustration level associated with maintenance work.

All of the problems described above can, in part, be attributed to the large number of programs currently in existence that have been developed with no thought of software engineering. A disciplined methodology should not be viewed as a panacea. However, software engineering does provide at least partial solutions to each problem associated with maintenance.

A number of technical and management issues arise as a consequence of the problems associated with software maintenance. Is it possible to develop software that is well-designed and maintainable? Can we maintain the integrity of software when it has to be modified? Are there technical and management approaches that can be successfully applied to software maintenance? These and other issues are discussed in the sections that follow.

20.3 MAINTAINABILITY

The characteristics described in the preceding section are all affected by the *maintainability* of software. Maintainability may be defined qualitatively as the ease with which software can be understood, corrected, adapted, and/or enhanced. As we have stressed throughout this book, maintainability is a key goal that guides the steps of a software engineering process.

20.3.1 Controlling Factors

The ultimate maintainability of software is affected by many factors. Inadvertent carelessness in design, coding, and testing has an obvious negative impact on our ability to maintain the resultant software. A poor software configuration can have a similar negative impact, even when the aforementioned technical steps have been conducted with care.

In addition to factors that can be associated with a development methodology, Kopetz [KOP79] defines a number of factors that are related to the development environment:

- Availability of qualified software staff
- Understandable system structure
- Ease of system handling
- Use of standardized programming languages
- Use of standardized operating systems
- Standardized structure of documentation
- Availability of test cases

- Built-in debugging facilities
- Availability of a proper computer to conduct maintenance

In addition to these factors, we might add (half facetiously): the availability of the person or group that originally developed the software.

Many of the factors stated above reflect characteristics of hardware and software resources that are used during development. For example, there is no question that the absence of high-order language compilers (necessitating the use of assembler language) has a detrimental effect on maintainability. Other factors indicate a need for the standardization of methods, resources, and approach. Possibly, the most important factor that affects maintainability is planning for maintainability. If software is viewed as a system element that will inevitably undergo change, the chances that maintainable software will be produced are likely to increase substantially.

20.3.2 Quantitative Measures

Software maintainability, like quality or reliability, is a difficult term to quantify. However, we can assess maintainability indirectly by considering attributes of the maintenance activity that can be measured. Gilb [GIL79] provides a number of *maintainability metrics* that relate to the effort expended during maintenance:

1. Problem recognition time
2. Administrative delay time
3. Maintenance tools collection time
4. Problem analysis time
5. Change specification time
6. Active correction (or modification) time
7. Local testing time
8. Global testing time
9. Maintenance review time
10. Total recovery time

Each of the above metrics can, in fact, be recorded without great difficulty. Such data can provide a manager with an indication of the efficacy of new techniques and tools.

In addition to these time-oriented measures, maintainability can be measured indirectly by considering measures of design structure (Chapter 10) and software complexity metrics (Chapter 17). A number of industry studies (e.g., [KAF87], [ROM87]) have found that logical complexity and program structure have a strong correlation to the maintainability of the resultant program.

20.3.3 Reviews

Because maintainability should be an essential characteristic of all software, we must ensure that the factors noted in Section 20.3.1 are built in during the development phase. At each level of the software engineering review process, maintainability should be considered. During requirements review, areas of future enhancement and potential revision are noted, software portability issues are discussed, and system interfaces that might impact software maintenance are considered. During design reviews, data design, architectural design, procedural design, and interface design are evaluated for ease of modification and overall design quality. Code reviews stress style and internal documentation, two factors that have an influence on maintainability. Finally, each test step can provide hints about portions of the program that may require preventive maintenance before the software is formally released.

The most formal maintenance review occurs at the conclusion of testing and is called the configuration review. Discussed in the next chapter, the configuration review ensures that all elements of the software configuration are complete, understandable, and filed for modification control.

The software maintenance task itself should be reviewed at the completion of each software project. Methods for evaluation are discussed in the next section.

20.4 MAINTENANCE TASKS

Tasks associated with software maintenance begin long before a request for maintenance is made. Initially, a maintenance organization (de facto or formal) must be established, reporting and evaluation procedures must be described, and a standardized sequence of events must be defined for each maintenance request. In addition, a record-keeping procedure for maintenance activities should be established and review and evaluation criteria defined.

20.4.1 A Maintenance Organization

As we have noted elsewhere in this book, there are almost as many organizational structures as there are software development organizations. For this reason, "recommended organizational structures" for software development and software maintenance have been avoided. In the case of maintenance, however, formal organizations rarely exist (notable exceptions are very large software developers), and maintenance is often performed on a catch-as-catch-can basis.

Although a formal maintenance organization need not be established, an informal delegation of responsibility is absolutely essential for even small

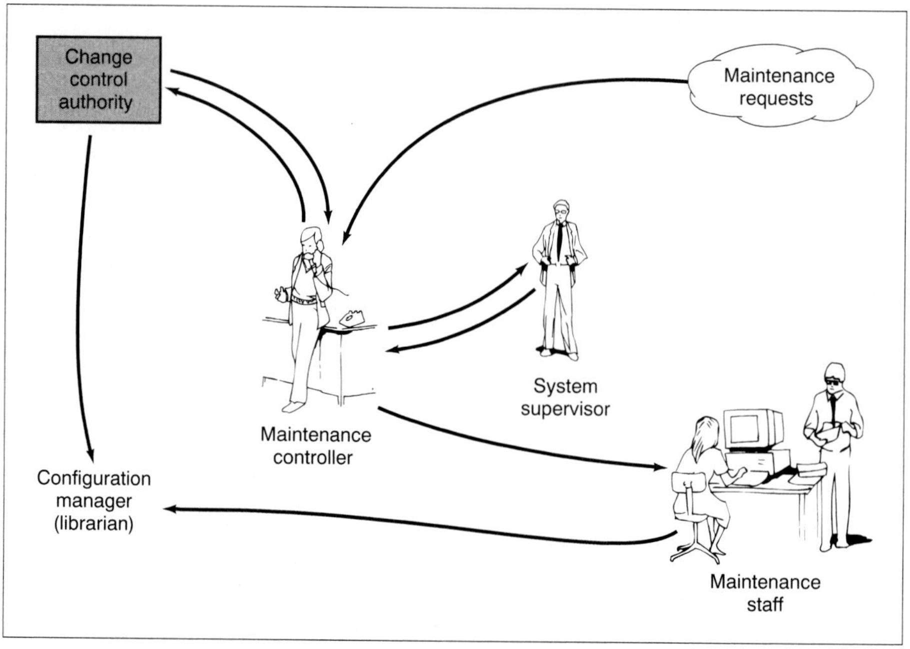

FIGURE 20.2.
Organization.

software developers. One such schema is illustrated in Figure 20.2. Maintenance requests are channeled through a *maintenance controller* who forwards each request for evaluation to a *system supervisor*. The system supervisor is a member of the technical staff who has been assigned the responsibility to become familiar with a small subset of production programs. Once an evaluation is made, a change control authority (sometimes called a *change control board*) must determine the action to be taken.

The organization suggested above reduces confusion and improves the flow of maintenance activities. Because all maintenance requests are funneled through a single individual (or group), "back door fixes" (i.e., changes that have not been sanctioned and therefore can cause confusion) are less likely to occur. Because at least one individual will always have some familiarity with a production program, requests for changes (maintenance) can be assessed more rapidly. Because specific change control[2] approval is implemented, an organization can avoid making changes that benefit one requester but negatively impact many other users.

Each of the above job titles serves to establish an area of responsibility for maintenance. The controller and change control authority may be a single person or (for large systems) a group of managers and senior technical staff. The system supervisor may have other duties, but provides a "contact" with a specific software package.

---

[2]This topic is discussed in more detail in Chapter 21.

When responsibilities are assigned prior to the start of maintenance activity, confusion is greatly reduced. More importantly, an early definition of responsibilities can temper any hard feelings that develop when a person is preemptively "pulled off" a development effort to conduct maintenance.

20.4.2 Reporting

All requests for software maintenance should be presented in a standardized manner. The software developer normally generates a *maintenance request form* (MRF), sometimes called a *software problem report,* that is completed by the user who desires a maintenance activity. If an error is encountered, a complete description of the circumstances leading to the error (including input data, listings, and other supporting material) must be included. For adaptive or perfective maintenance requests, a brief *change specification* (an abbreviated requirements specification) is submitted. The maintenance request form is evaluated as described in the preceding section.

The MRF is an externally generated document that is used as a basis for planning the maintenance task. Internally, the software organization develops a *software change report* (SCR) that indicates (1) the magnitude of effort required to satisfy an MRF, (2) the nature of modifications required, (3) the priority of the request, and (4) after-the-fact data about the modification. The SCR is submitted to a change control authority before further maintenance planning is initiated.

20.4.3 Flow of Events

The sequence of events that occurs as a result of a maintenance request are shown in Figure 20.3. The first requirement is to determine the type of maintenance that is to be conducted. In many cases, a user may view a request as an indication of software error (corrective maintenance) while a developer may view the same request as adaptation or enhancement. If a difference of opinion exists, a settlement must be negotiated.

Referring to the flow shown in Figure 20.3, a request for corrective maintenance (*error* path) begins with an evaluation of error severity. If a severe error exists (e.g., a critical system cannot function), personnel are assigned under the direction of the system supervisor and problem analysis begins immediately. For less severe errors, the request for corrective maintenance is evaluated and categorized and then scheduled in conjunction with other tasks requiring software development resources.

In some cases, an error may be so severe that normal controls for maintenance must be abandoned temporarily. Code must be modified immediately, without a corresponding evaluation for potential side effects and an appropriate updating of documentation. This *fire-fighting* mode for corrective maintenance is reserved only for "crisis" situations and should repre-

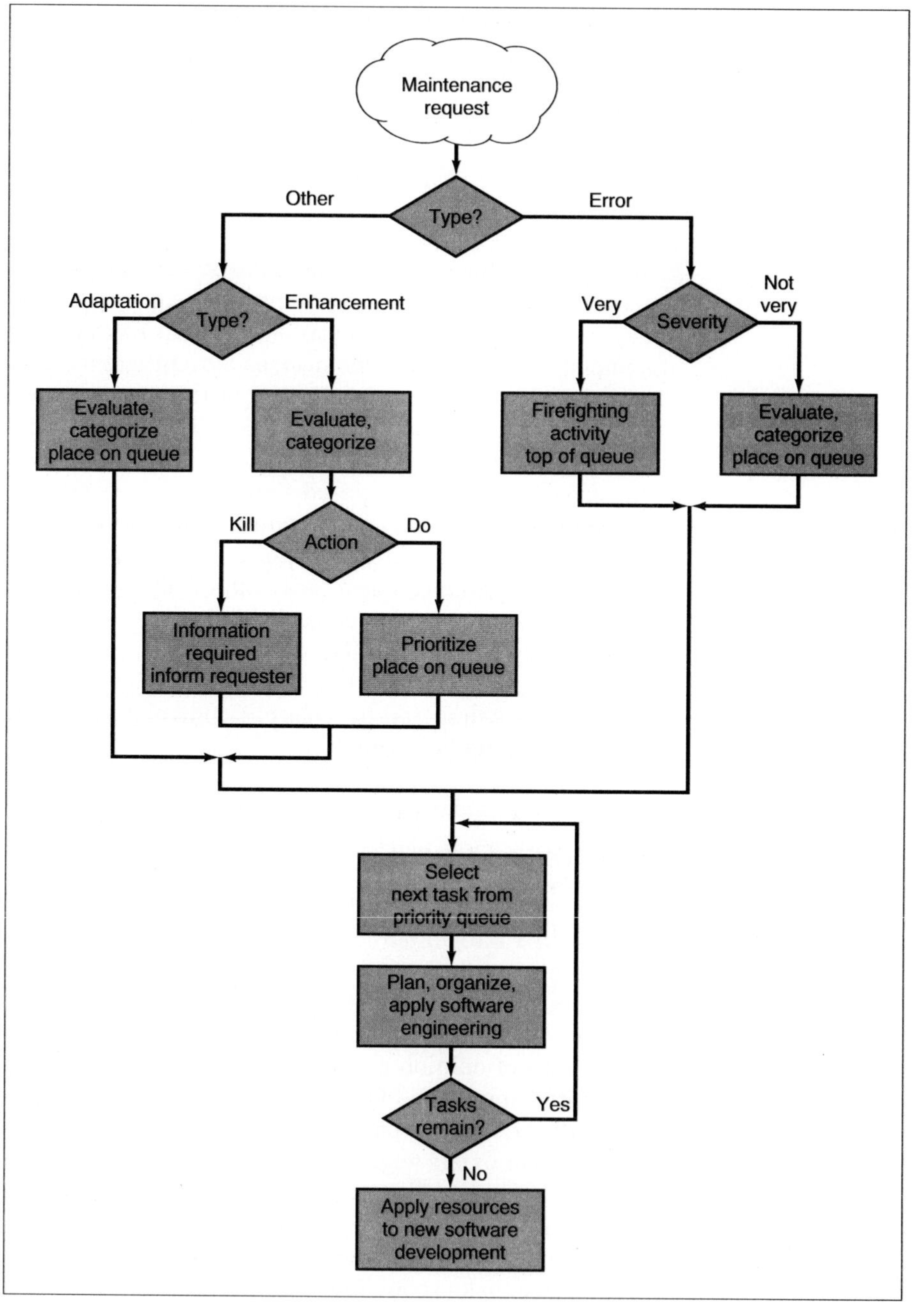

FIGURE 20.3.
Maintenance flow of events.

sent a very small percentage of all maintenance activities. It should be noted that fire fighting postpones, but does not eliminate, the need for controls and evaluation. After the crisis has been resolved, these activities must be conducted to ensure that present fixes will not propagate even more severe problems.

Requests for adaptive and perfective maintenance follow a different path. Adaptations are evaluated and categorized (prioritized) prior to being placed on a queue for maintenance action. Enhancements undergo the same evaluation. However, not all requests for enhancement are undertaken. Business strategy, available resources, the direction of current and future software products, and many other issues may cause a request for enhancement to be rejected. Those enhancements that are to be made are also placed on the maintenance queue. The priority of each request is established and the required work is scheduled as if it were another development effort (for all intents and purposes, it is). If an extremely high priority is set, work may begin immediately.

Regardless of maintenance type, the same technical tasks are conducted. These maintenance tasks include modification to software design, review, requisite code modification, unit and integration testing (including regression tests using previous test cases), validation tests, and review. In fact, software maintenance is actually software engineering applied recursively. The emphasis will shift with each maintenance type, but the overall approach remains unchanged. The final event in the maintenance flow is a review that revalidates all elements of the software configuration and ensures that the MRF has, in fact, been fulfilled.

After the software maintenance task is complete, it is often a good idea to conduct a *situation review.* In general, the review attempts to answer the following questions:

- Given the current situation, what aspects of design, code, or test could have been done differently?
- What maintenance resources should have been available, but weren't?
- What were the major (minor) stumbling blocks for this effort?
- Is preventive maintenance indicated by the types of requests being reported?

The situation review can have an important influence on the conduct of future maintenance efforts and provides feedback that is important to effective management of a software organization.

20.4.4 Record Keeping

Historically, record keeping for all phases of the software engineering process has been inadequate. Record keeping for software maintenance has been nonexistent. For this reason we are frequently unable to assess the effectiveness of maintenance techniques, incapable of determining the quality of a production program, and unwilling to determine what maintenance really costs.

The first problem encountered in maintenance record keeping is to understand what data are worth recording. Swanson [SWA76] provides a comprehensive list:

1. Program identification
2. Number of source statements
3. Number of machine code instructions
4. Programming language used
5. Program installation date
6. Number of program runs since installation
7. Number of processing failures associated with item 6
8. Program change level and identification
9. Number of source statements added by program change
10. Number of source statements deleted by program change
11. Number of person-hours spent per change
12. Program change date
13. Identification of software engineer
14. MRF identification
15. Maintenance type
16. Maintenance start and close dates
17. Cumulative number of person-hours spent on maintenance
18. Net benefits associated with maintenance performed

The above data are collected for each maintenance effort. Swanson proposes these items as the foundation of a maintenance database that can be evaluated as described in Section 20.4.5.

Other work on software maintenance metrics has focused on software characteristics that are most likely to affect frequency of maintenance and empirical models for predicting the amount of maintenance work based on other program characteristics. In a study of over 400 COBOL programs, Vessey and Weber [VES83] found that program complexity and programming style were the most significant factors in the occurrence of corrective maintenance. Using COCOMO (Chapter 3) as a basis [SCH85], the following model has been suggested as a predictor for the number of person-months, E.maint, expended on software maintenance annually:

$$\text{E.maint} = \text{ACT} * 2.4 * \text{KLOC}^{1.05}$$

where ACT is the *annual change traffic* defined as

$$\text{ACT} = \frac{\text{KLOC for a system undergoing maintenance}}{\text{CI}}$$

for CI = number of source code instructions that are modified or added during 1 year of maintenance.

Although the results of clinical studies must be applied with caution, quantitative models provide one element of management control that has been missing for software maintenance.

20.4.5 Evaluation

An evaluation of software maintenance activities is often complicated by a lack of hard data. If record keeping is initiated, a number of measures of maintenance performance may be developed. Again, from Swanson [SWA76] we present an abbreviated list of potential measures:

1. Average number of processing failures per program run
2. Total person-hours spent in each maintenance category
3. Average number of program changes made per program, per language, per maintenance type
4. Average number of person-hours spent per source statement added or deleted due to maintenance
5. Average person-hours spent per language
6. Average turnaround time for an MRF
7. Percentage of maintenance requests by type

The seven measures described above can provide a quantitative framework from which decisions on development technique, language selection, maintenance effort projections, resource allocation, and many other issues can be made. Clearly, such data can be applied to evaluate the maintenance task.

20.5 MAINTENANCE SIDE EFFECTS

Modification of software is dangerous. All of us have heard the following lament: "...but all I did was change this one statement...." Unfortunately, each time a change is introduced into a complex logical procedure, the potential for error grows. Design documentation and careful regression testing help to eliminate error, but maintenance *side effects* will be encountered.

When used in the context of software maintenance, the term "side effects" implies an error or other undesirable behavior that occurs as a result of modification. Freedman and Weinberg [FRE90] define three major categories for side effects that are discussed in the following sections.

20.5.1 Coding Side Effects

A simple change to a single statement can sometimes have disastrous results. The inadvertent (and undetected) replacement of a , with a . had near-tragic consequences when ground support software for a manned space flight failed. Although not all side effects have such dramatic consequences, change invites error and error always leads to problems.

We communicate with a machine using programming language source code. The opportunities for side effects abound. Although every code modification has the potential for introducing error, the following set of changes [FRE90] tends to be more error-prone than others:

1. A subprogram is deleted or changed.
2. A statement label is deleted or modified.
3. An identifier is deleted or modified.
4. Changes are made to improve execution performance.
5. File open or close is modified.
6. Logical operators are modified.
7. Design changes are translated into major code changes.
8. Changes are made to logical tests of boundary conditions.

Coding side effects range from nuisance errors detected and remedied during regression testing to problems that cause software failure during operation. Again, we paraphrase Murphy's law: If a change to a source statement can introduce error, it will.

20.5.2 Data Side Effects

The importance of data structure in software design was noted in Chapter 10. During maintenance, modifications are often made to individual elements of a data structure or to the structure itself. When data change, the software design may no longer fit the data and errors can occur. Data side effects occur as a result of modifications made to the software information structure.

The following changes [FRE90] in data frequently result in side effects: (1) redefinition of local and global constants, (2) redefinition of record or file formats, (3) increase or decrease in the size of an array or a higher-order data structure, (4) modification to global data, (5) reinitialization of control flags or pointers, (6) rearrangement of arguments for I/O or subprograms. Data side effects can be limited by thorough design documentation that describes data structure and provides a cross reference that associates data elements, records, files, and other structures with software modules.

20.5.3 Documentation Side Effects

Maintenance should focus on the entire software configuration and not on source code modification alone. Documentation side effects occur when changes to source code are not reflected in the design documentation or user-oriented manuals.

Whenever a change to data flow, design architecture, module procedure, or any other related characteristic is made, supporting technical documentation must be updated. Design documentation that doesn't accurately reflect the current state of the software is probably worse than no documentation at all. Side effects occur in subsequent maintenance efforts when an innocent perusal of technical documents leads to an incorrect assessment of software characteristics.

To a user, software is only as good as the documentation (both written and interactive) that describes its use. If modifications to the executable software are not reflected in user documentation, side effects are guaranteed. For example, changes in the order or format of interactive input, if not properly documented, can cause significant problems. New undocumented error messages can cause confusion; outdated tables of contents, indices, and text can cause user frustration and dissatisfaction.

Documentation side effects can be reduced substantially if the entire configuration is reviewed prior to re-release of the software. In fact, some maintenance requests may require no change to software design or source code, but indicate a lack of clarity in user documentation. In such cases the maintenance effort focuses on documentation.

20.6 MAINTAINING "ALIEN CODE"

Nearly every mature software organization must maintain programs that were developed 15 or more years ago. Such programs are sometimes called "alien code" because (1) no current member of the technical staff worked on development of the program; (2) no development methodology was applied, and therefore poor data and architectural design resulted; documentation is incomplete and a record of past changes is sketchy.

Early in this chapter we discussed the necessity for a *system supervisor*—a person that becomes familiar with a subset of production programs that may require maintenance. Familiarization with programs developed using a software engineering approach is facilitated by a complete software configuration and good design. What can be done with alien code? Yourdon [YOU75] provides a number of useful suggestions:

> 1. Study the program before you get into "emergency mode." Try to get as much background information as possible....

2. Try to become familiar with the overall flow of control of the program; ignore coding details at first. It may be very useful to draw your own structure diagram and high level flow chart, if one doesn't already exist.
3. Evaluate the reasonableness of existing documentation; insert your own comments in the (source) listing if you think they will help.
4. Make good use of cross reference listings, symbol tables and other aids generally provided by the compiler and/or assembler.
5. Make changes to the program with the greatest caution. Respect the style and formatting of the program if at all possible. Indicate on the listing itself which instructions you have changed.
6. Don't eliminate code unless you are sure it isn't used.
7. Don't try to share the use of temporary variables and working storage that already exist in the program. Insert your own variables to avoid trouble.
8. Keep detailed records (of maintenance activities and results).
9. Avoid the irrational urge to throw the program away and rewrite it. [Author's note: This "urge" is sometimes both rational and practical!]
10. Do insert error checking.

Each of the above guidelines will help in the maintenance of old programs. However, there is a class of programs with control flow that is the graphic equivalent to a bowl of spaghetti: with "modules" that are 2000 statements long, with three meaningful comment lines in 9000 source statements, with no other elements of a software configuration. Incredibly, such programs may work for years, but when maintenance is requested, the task may be untenable. In the next section we examine what can be done.

20.7 REVERSE ENGINEERING AND RE-ENGINEERING

The term "reverse engineering" has its origins in the hardware world. A company disassembles a competitive hardware product in an effort to understand its competitor's design and manufacturing "secrets." These secrets could be easily understood if the competitor's design and manufacturing specifications were obtained. But these documents are proprietary and are not available to the company doing the reverse engineering. In essence, successful reverse engineering derives one or more design and manufacturing specifications for a product by examining actual specimens of the product.

Reverse engineering for software is quite similar. In most cases, however, the program to be reverse-engineered is not a competitor's. Rather, it is the company's own work (often done many years earlier). The "secrets" to be understood are obscure because no specification was ever developed. Therefore, reverse engineering for software is the process of analyzing a program in an effort to create a representation of the program at a higher level of abstraction than source code. Reverse engineering is a process of *design recovery*. Reverse engineering tools extract data, architectural, and procedural design information from an existing program.

Re-engineering, also called *renovation* or *reclamation* [CHI90], not only recovers design information from existing software, but uses this information to alter or reconstitute the existing system in an effort to improve its overall quality. In most cases, re-engineered software reimplements the function of the existing system. But at the same time, the software developer also adds new functions and/or improves overall performance.

Because every large company (and many small ones) have millions of lines of code that are candidates for reverse engineering and/or re-engineering, it would seem that every company should undertake a massive effort to re-engineer every program in its library. Unfortunately, this is unrealistic for a number of reasons: (1) Some of these programs are used infrequently and are not likely to change, (2) reverse engineering and re-engineering tools are still in their infancy,[3] (3) therefore, these tools are capable of performing reverse engineering or re-engineering for only a limited class of applications, and (4) the cost (in effort and dollars) would be prohibitive.

To perform preventive maintenance, a software organization must select those programs that are likely to change in the near future and prepare them for that change. Reverse engineering and re-engineering are used to perform this maintenance task. In the sections that follow, we examine preventive maintenance and then discuss reverse engineering and re-engineering in more detail.

20.7.1 Preventive Maintenance

A program with control flow that is the graphic equivalent to a bowl of spaghetti—with "modules" that are 2000 statements long, with three meaningful comment lines in 9000 source statements, and with no other documentation—must be modified to accommodate changing user requirements. We have the following options:

1. We can struggle through modification after modification, "fighting" the implicit design and source code to implement the necessary changes.
2. We can attempt to understand the broader inner workings of the program in an effort to make modifications more effectively.
3. We can redesign, recode, and test those portions of the software that require modification, applying a software engineering approach to all revised segments.

---

[3]Some CASE tools in limited application domains are relatively sophisticated, but overall, reverse engineering and re-engineering tools are quite rudimentary.

4. We can completely redesign, recode, and test the program, using CASE tools (reverse engineering and re-engineering tools) to assist us in understanding the current design.

There is no single "correct" option. Circumstances may dictate the first option even if the others are more desirable.

Rather than waiting until a maintenance request is received, the development or maintenance organization selects a program that (1) will remain in use for a preselected number of years, (2) that is currently being used successfully, and (3) that is likely to undergo major modification or enhancement in the near future. Then, option 2, 3, or 4 above is applied.[4]

The preventative maintenance approach was pioneered by Miller [MIL81] under the title "structured retrofit." He defined this concept as "the application of today's methodologies to yesterday's systems to support tomorrow's requirements."

At first glance, the suggestion that we redevelop a large program when a working version already exists may seem quite extravagant. Before passing judgment, consider the following points:

1. The cost to maintain one line of source code may be 20 to 40 times the cost of the initial development of that line.
2. Redesign of the software architecture (program and/or data structure), using modern design concepts, can greatly facilitate future maintenance.
3. Because a prototype of the software already exists, development productivity should be much higher than average.
4. The user now has experience with the software. Therefore, new requirements and the direction of change can be ascertained with greater ease.
5. CASE tools for reverse engineering and re-engineering will automate some parts of the job.
6. A software configuration will exist upon the completion of preventive maintenance.

When a software development organization sells software as a product, preventive maintenance is seen in "new releases" of a program. A large in-house software developer (e.g., a business systems software development group for a large consumer products company) may have 500 to 2000 production programs within its domain of responsibility. These programs can be prioritized by importance and then reviewed as candidates for preventive maintenance.

---

[4]Before continuing, reread Section 1.1.3. If management correctly responds to the specter of an "aging software plant," preventive maintenance will likely become mandatory in many companies.

20.7.2 Elements of Reverse Engineering

Reverse engineering conjures an image of the "magic slot." We feed an unstructured, undocumented source listing into the slot and out the other end comes full documentation for the computer program. Unfortunately, the magic slot doesn't exist. Reverse engineering can extract design information from source code, but the abstraction level, the completeness of the documentation, the degree to which tools and a human analyst work together, and the directionality of the process are highly variable [CAS88].

The *abstraction level* of a reverse engineering process and the tools that are used to effect it refers to the sophistication of the design information that can be extracted from source code. Ideally, the abstraction level should be as high as possible. That is, the reverse engineering process should be capable of deriving procedural design representations (a low level of abstraction), program and data structure information (a somewhat higher level of abstraction), data and control flow models (a relatively high level of abstraction), and entity relationship models (a high level of abstraction). As the abstraction level increases, the software engineer is provided with information that will allow an easier understanding of the program.

The *completeness* of a reverse engineering process refers to the level of detail that is provided at an abstraction level. In most cases, the completeness decreases as the abstraction level increases. For example, given a source code listing, it is relatively easy to develop a complete procedural design representation. Simple data flow representations may also be derived, but it is far more difficult to develop a complete set of data flow diagrams.

Completeness improves in direct proportion to the amount of analysis performed by the person doing reverse engineering. *Interactivity* refers to the degree to which the human is "integrated" with automated tools to create an effective reverse engineering process. In most cases, as the abstraction level increases, interactivity must increase or completeness will suffer.

If the *directionality* of the reverse engineering process is one way, all information extracted from the source code is provided to the software engineer who can then use it during any maintenance activity. If directionality is two way, the information is fed to a re-engineering tool that attempts to restructure or regenerate the old program.

20.7.3 A Restructuring Technique for Re-Engineering

Re-engineering combines the analysis and design extraction features of reverse engineering with a restructuring capability for program data, architecture, and logic. Restructuring is performed to yield a design that produces the same function with higher quality (Chapter 10) than the original program.

As a simple example of restructuring, we consider Warnier's logical simplification techniques [WAR74]. These can be used to restructure "spaghetti-bowl" program logic and yield a procedural design that conforms to the structured programming philosophy (Chapter 10). To understand how restructuring can be accomplished, we must first examine the simplification technique itself. Assume that a reverse engineering tool is applied to a program that uses data items A, B, C, and D and processing actions (segments of code) V, W, X, Y, Z, and $\overline{R}$ (not R). A tabular representation of four data items, A, B, C, D, and the corresponding processing actions is generated and shown in Figure 20.4. This *truth table* indicates under what circumstances processing actions will be executed. For example, from the third row, actions V and Y will be executed when data item C is encountered. It is possible to execute V under two different sets of conditions. Applying boolean algebra, we obtain

$$V = \overline{A} \cdot \overline{B} \cdot C \cdot \overline{D} + \overline{A} \cdot \overline{B} \cdot C \cdot D + \overline{A} \cdot B \cdot C \cdot \overline{D} + \overline{A} \cdot B \cdot C \cdot D + A \cdot \overline{B} \cdot C \cdot \overline{D} + A \cdot \overline{B} \cdot C \cdot D + A \cdot B \cdot C \cdot \overline{D} + A \cdot B \cdot C \cdot D$$

where in boolean notation $\cdot$ indicates logical AND and $+$ indicates logical OR. Applying rules of logic simplification, we obtain the equations shown below:

$$\begin{aligned} V &= \overline{A} \cdot \overline{B} \cdot C(\overline{D} + D) + \overline{A} \cdot B \cdot C(\overline{D} + D) + A \cdot \overline{B} \cdot C(\overline{D} + D) \\ &\quad + A \cdot B \cdot C(\overline{D} + D) \\ &= \overline{A} \cdot \overline{B} \cdot C + \overline{A} \cdot B \cdot C + A \cdot \overline{B} \cdot C + A \cdot B \cdot C \\ &= \overline{A} \cdot C(\overline{B} + B) + A \cdot C(\overline{B} + B) \\ &= \overline{A} \cdot C + A \cdot C = C(\overline{A} + A) \\ &= C \end{aligned}$$

	DATA ABCD	V	W	X	Y	Z	$\overline{R}$
	0000						X
	0001						X
	0010	X			X		
	0011	X			X		
	0100						X
	0101						X
Complex Alternatives	0110	X				X	
	0111	X				X	
	1000						X
	1001						X
	1010	X	X	X			
	1011	X	X	X			
	1100						X
	1101						X
	1110	X	X				
	1111	X	X				

FIGURE 20.4. A truth table. *(Reprinted with permission of Van Nostrand Reinhold Company. Copyright 1974, Les Editions d'Organisation.)*

and similarly

$$X = A \cdot \overline{B} \cdot C \cdot \overline{D} + A \cdot \overline{B} \cdot C \cdot D$$
$$= A \cdot \overline{B} \cdot C(\overline{D} + D)$$
$$= A \cdot \overline{B} \cdot C$$

Therefore, V will be executed whenever C is encountered, and X will be executed when A and C are present and B is not present.

From the table in Figure 20.4, the following additional simplifications can be made for other processing actions:

$$V = C$$
$$W = C \cdot A$$
$$X = C \cdot A \cdot \overline{B}$$
$$Y = C \cdot \overline{A} \cdot \overline{B}$$
$$Z = C \cdot \overline{A} \cdot B$$
$$\overline{R} = \overline{C}$$

Logical simplification may be used as a re-engineering technique for "unstructured" software. The following steps can be applied to accomplish *restructuring:*

1. Develop a flowchart for the software.
2. Derive a boolean expression for each processing sequence.
3. Compile a truth table.
4. Reconstruct the software, using techniques described above; add modifications as required.

As an example [WAR74] we consider the unstructured flowchart and resultant truth table shown in Figures 20.5 and 20.6. Maintenance requires that the modifications ("amendments") shown in Figure 20.6 be applied. After amending the truth table and simplifying, a structured procedural design shown in Figure 20.7 can be derived. The entire process described in the four steps above can be automated and implemented using a CASE tool for re-engineering.

Other restructuring techniques have also been proposed for use with re-engineering tools. For example, Choi and Scacchi [CHO90] suggest the creation of a resource exchange diagram that maps each program module and the resources (data types, procedures, and variables) that are exchanged between it and other modules. By creating representations of resource flow, the program architecture can be restructured to achieve minimum coupling among modules.

$1 = \overline{A}$
$2 = A$
$3 = \overline{A} \cdot B$
$4 = \overline{A} \cdot \overline{B}$
$5 = \overline{A} \cdot B + A \cdot B = B$
$6 = A \cdot \overline{B}$
$7 = A \cdot \overline{B} \cdot C$
$8 = A \cdot \overline{B} \cdot C \cdot D$

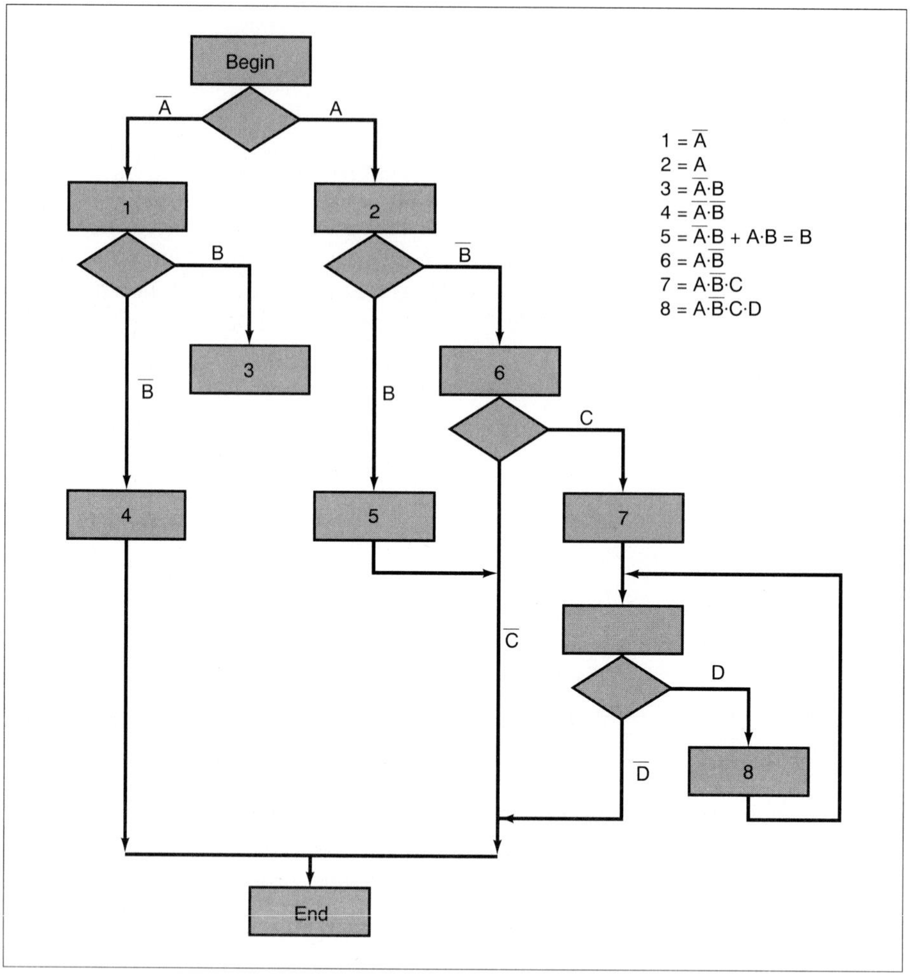

FIGURE 20.5.
An unstructured program. *(Reprinted with permission of Van Nostrand Reinhold Company. Copyright 1974, Les Editions d'Organisation.)*

20.8 SUMMARY

Maintenance, the last phase in the software engineering process, accounts for the majority of all dollars spent on computer software. As more programs are developed, a disturbing trend has emerged—the amount of effort and resources expended on software maintenance is growing. Ultimately, some software organizations may become maintenance-bound, unable to embark upon new projects because all their resources are dedicated to the maintenance of old programs.

E ABCD	1	2	3	4	5	6	7	8
0000	X			X				
0001	X			X				
0010	X			X				
0011	X			X				
0100	X		X		X			
0101	X		X		X			
0110	X		X		X			
0111	X		X		X			
1000		X				X		
1001		X				X		
1010		X				X	X	
1011		X				X	X	X
1100		X			X			
1101		X			X			
1110		X			X			
1111		X			X			

The amendments required for this program subset are the following:

- action 9 = A. This action must be executed at the end of the processing of A.
- action 10 = A·B·C·D. This action must be executed once for the group D at the end, but not at all if D contains no elements

FIGURE 20.6.
Resultant truth table. *(Reprinted with permission of Van Nostrand Reinhold Company. Copyright 1974, Les Editions d'Organisation.)*

Four types of maintenance are performed on computer software. Corrective maintenance acts to correct errors that are uncovered after the software is in use. Adaptive maintenance is applied when changes in the external environment precipitate modifications to software. Perfective maintenance incorporates enhancements that are requested by the user community. Finally, preventive maintenance improves future maintainability and reliability and provides a basis for future enhancement.

Technical and management approaches to the maintenance phase can be implemented with little upheaval. However, tasks performed during the software engineering process define maintainability and have an important impact on the success of any maintenance approach.

Reverse engineering and re-engineering tools and techniques will become a significant part of the maintenance process as the 1990s progress. Reverse engineering extracts design information from program source code when no other documentation is available. Re-engineering takes the information obtained and restructures the program to achieve higher quality and, therefore, better maintainability for the future.

The methods and techniques presented in this book have many goals, but one of the most important is to build software that is amenable to change. Fewer person-hours will be expended on each modification or maintenance request. People will be freed to develop new software that will be required in the increasingly complex systems of the twenty-first century.

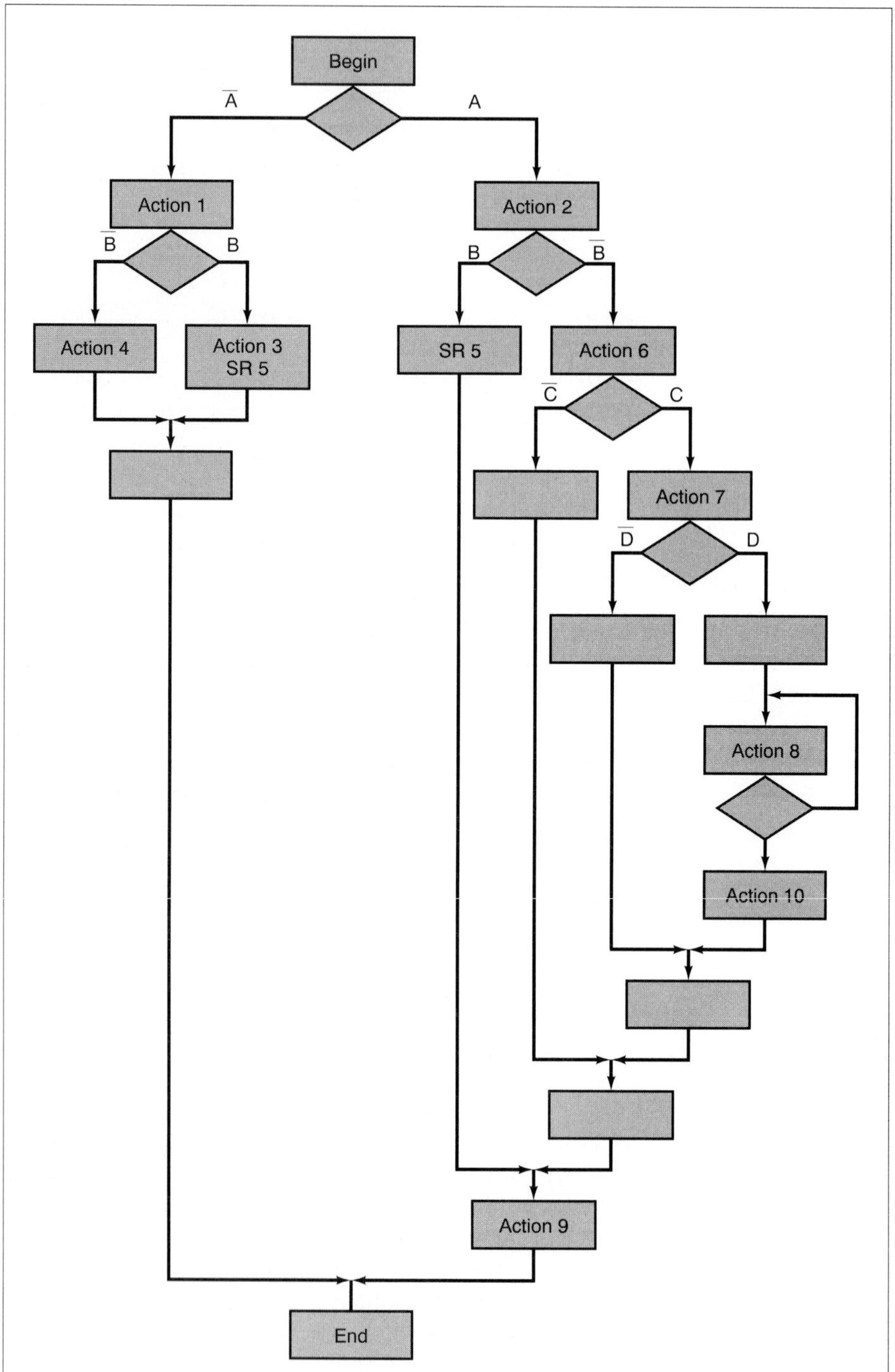

FIGURE 20.7. Amended, structured program. *(Reprinted with permission of Van Nostrand Reinhold Company. Copyright 1974, Les Editions d'Organisation.)*

REFERENCES

[BEL72] Belady, L., and M. Lehman, "An Introduction to Growth Dynamics," in *Statistical Computer Performance Evaluation* (W. Freiberger, ed.), Academic Press, 1972, pp. 503–511.

[BOE79] Boehm, B., "Software Engineering—R&D Trends and Defense Needs," in *Research Directions in Software Technology* (P. Wegner, ed.), MIT Press, 1979, pp. 44–86.

[CAN72] Canning, R., "The Maintenance 'Iceberg,'" *EDP Analyzer,* vol. 10, no. 10, October 1972.

[CAS88] "Case Tools for Reverse Engineering," *CASE Outlook,* vol. 2, no. 2, 1988, p. 1–15.

[CHI90] Chikofsky, E. J., and J. H. Cross, III, "Reverse Engineering and Design Recovery: A Taxonomy," *IEEE Software,* January 1990, pp. 13–17.

[CHO90] Choi, S.C., and W. Scacchi, "Extracting and Restructuring the Design of Large Systems," *IEEE Software,* January 1990, pp. 66–71.

[FRE90] Freedman, D. P., and G. M. Weinberg, *Handbook of Workthroughs, Inspections, and Technical Reviews,* 3d ed., Dorset House, 1990.

[GIL79] Gilb, T., "A Comment on the Definition of Reliability," *ACM Software Engineering Notes,* vol. 4, no. 3, July 1979.

[KAF87] Kafura, D., and G. R. Reddy, "The Use of Software Complexity Metrics in Software Maintenance," *IEEE Trans. Software Engineering,* vol. SE-13, no. 3, March 1987, pp. 335–343.

[KOP79] Kopetz, H., *Software Reliability.* Springer-Verlag, 1979, p. 93.

[MCC80] McCracken, D., "Software in the 80s—Perils and Promises," *Computerworld* (special edition), vol. 14, no. 38, September 17, 1980, p. 5.

[MIL81] Miller, J., in *Techniques of Program and System Maintenance* (G. Parikh, ed.), Winthrop Publishers, 1981.

[OSB90] Osborne, W. M., and E. J. Chikofsky, "Fitting Pieces to the Maintenance Puzzle," *IEEE Software,* January 1990, pp. 10–11.

[ROM87] Rombach, H. D., "A Controlled Experiment on the Impact of Software Structure on Maintainability," *IEEE Trans. Software Engineering,* vol. SE-13, no. 3, March 1987, pp. 344–354.

[SCH85] Schaefer, H., "Metrics for Optimal Maintenance Management," *Proc. Conf. Software Maintenance—1985,* IEEE, November 1985, pp. 114–119.

[SCH87] Schneidewind, N. F., "The State of Software Maintenance," *IEEE Trans. Software Engineering,* vol. SE-13, no. 3, March 1987, pp. 303–310.

[SWA76] Swanson, E. B., "The Dimensions of Maintenance," *Proc. 2nd Intl. Conf. Software Engineering,* IEEE, October 1976, pp. 492–497.

[VES83] Vessey, I., and R. Weber, "Some Factors Affecting Program Repair Maintenance," *CACM,* vol. 26, no. 2., February 1983, pp. 128–134.

[WAR74] Warnier, J. D., *Logical Construction of Programs,* Van Nostrand Reinhold, 1974.

[YOU75] Yourdon, E., *Techniques of Program Structure and Design,* Prentice-Hall, 1975, p. 24.

PROBLEMS AND POINTS TO PONDER

20.1 Your instructor will select one of the programs that everyone in the class has developed during this course. Exchange your program randomly with someone else in the class. *Do not* explain or walk through the program. Now, implement an enhancement (specified by your instructor) in the program you have received.
   (*a*) Perform all software engineering tasks, including a brief walkthrough (but not with the author of the program).
   (*b*) Keep careful track of all errors encountered during testing.
   (*c*) Discuss your experiences in class.

20.2 Attempt to develop a software rating system that could be applied to existing programs in an effort to pick candidate programs for preventive maintenance.

20.3 Are corrective maintenance and debugging the same thing? Explain your answer.

20.4 Discuss the impact of high-level languages on adaptive maintenance. Is it always possible to adapt a program?

20.5 Should maintenance costs be incorporated in the software planning step? Are they?

20.6 Will the overall duration of the software life cycle expand or contract over the next decade? Discuss this issue in class.

20.7 Team project: Develop an automated tool that will enable a manager to collect and analyze quantitative maintenance data. Use Sections 20.3.2 and 20.4.4 as sources for software requirements.

20.8 Some people believe that artificial intelligence technology will increase the abstraction level of the reverse engineering process. Do some research on this subject (i.e., the use of AI for reverse engineering) and write a brief paper that takes a stand on this point.

20.9 Why is completeness difficult to achieve as the abstraction level increases?

20.10 Why must interactivity increase if completeness is to increase?

20.11 Get product literature on three reverse engineering tools and present their characteristics in class.

20.12 Discuss the viability of a "spare parts" strategy. Consider both technical and economic issues.

20.13 For the practitioner: Relate a maintenance "horror story."

20.14 Research the literature in an attempt to find recently published papers, books, and, most importantly, quantitative data on software maintenance and reverse engineering. Write a paper on your findings.

FURTHER READINGS

The literature on software maintenance expanded significantly during the early 1980s, but few recent books have been published on the subject. Most books on maintenance rehash software engineering procedures and methods and also present some discussion of the maintenance process. Martin and McClure (*Software Maintenance,* Prentice-Hall, 1983) discuss the impact of fourth-generation techniques on the maintenance process. Parikh (*Handbook of Software Maintenance,* Wiley-Interscience, 1986) discusses software maintenance using an effective question and answer format. Glass and Noiseux (*Software Maintenance Guidebook,* Prentice-Hall, 1981) is still another worthwhile treatment of the subject. Data collected by Lientz and Swanson (*Software Maintenance Management,* Addison-Wesley, 1980) remains the most comprehensive study on maintenance published to date.

Parikh's anthology (*Techniques of Program and System Maintenance,* Winthrop Publishers, 1981) and another anthology by Parikh and Zvegintzov (*Software Maintenance,* IEEE Computer Society Press, 1983) contain collections of papers on maintenance. A special issue of the *IEEE Transactions of Software Engineering* (vol. SE-13, no. 3, March 1987) is dedicated to software maintenance and contains six excellent papers on the subject. Annual conferences on maintenance are sponsored by the ACM/IEEE, and an industry newsletter, *Software Maintenance News* (edited by N. Zvegintzov, Staten Island, NY), provides a useful forum for new ideas.

Reverse and re-engineering are extremely "hot" topics in the software engineering community, but the literature is only beginning to form. A special issue of *IEEE Software* (January 1990) is dedicated to maintenance and reverse engineering and contains a thorough treatment of the subject. *CASE Outlook, CASE Trends, CASE Strategies,* and other industry newsletters contain a continuing stream of information on reverse engineering and re-engineering tools. An issue of *Software Magazine* (May 1990) contains a listing of popular reverse engineering tools.

CHAPTER 21

SOFTWARE CONFIGURATION MANAGEMENT

Change is inevitable when computer software is built. And change increases the level of confusion among software engineers who are working on a project. Confusion arises when changes are *not* analyzed before they are made, recorded before they are implemented, reported to those with a need to know, or controlled in a manner that will improve quality and reduce error. Babich [BAB86, p. 8] discusses this when he states:

> The art of coordinating software development to minimize... confusion is called *configuration management*. Configuration management is the art of identifying, organizing, and controlling modifications to the software being built by a programming team. The goal is to maximize productivity by minimizing mistakes.

Software configuration management (SCM) is an "umbrella" activity that is applied throughout the software engineering process. Because change can occur at any time, SCM activities are developed to (1) identify change, (2) control change, (3) ensure that change is being properly implemented, and (4) report change to others who may have an interest.

It is important to make a clear distinction between software maintenance and software configuration management. Maintenance is a set of software engineering activities that occur after software has been delivered to the customer and put into operation. Software configuration management is a set of tracking and control activities that begin when a software development project begins and terminate only when the software is taken out of operation.

A primary goal of software engineering methodology is to improve the ease with which changes can be accommodated and reduce the amount of effort expended when changes must be made. In this chapter, we discuss the specific activities that enable us to manage change.

21.1 SOFTWARE CONFIGURATION MANAGEMENT

The output of the software engineering process is information that may be divided into three broad categories: (1) computer programs (both source level and executable forms), (2) documents that describe the computer programs (targeted at both technical practitioners and users), and (3) data structures (contained within the program or external to it). The items that comprise all information produced as part of the software engineering process are collectively called a *software configuration*.

As the software engineering process progresses, the number of *software configuration items* (SCIs) grows rapidly. A *System Specification* spawns a *Software Project Plan* and *Software Requirements Specification* (as well as hardware-related documents). These in turn spawn other documents to create a hierarchy of information. If each SCI simply spawned other SCIs, little confusion would result. Unfortunately, another variable enters the process—*change*. Change may occur at any time, for any reason. In fact, the *First Law of System Engineering* [BER80] states: *No matter where you are in the system life cycle, the system will change, and the desire to change it will persist throughout the life cycle.*

Software configuration management is a set of activities that have been developed to manage change throughout the software life cycle. SCM can be viewed as a software quality assurance activity that is applied during all phases of the software engineering process. In the sections that follow, we examine major SCM tasks and important concepts that help us to manage change.

21.1.1 Baselines

Change is a fact of life in software development. Customers want to modify requirements. Developers want to modify technical approach. Management wants to modify project approach. Why all this modification? The answer is really quite simple. As time passes all constituencies know more (about what they need, which approach would be best, how to get it done and still make money). This additional knowledge is the driving force behind most changes and leads to a statement of fact that is difficult for many software engineering practitioners to accept: Most changes are justified!

A *baseline* is a software configuration management concept that helps us to control change without seriously impeding justifiable change. One way to describe a baseline is through analogy:

> Consider the doors to the kitchen of a large restaurant. To eliminate collisions, one door is marked OUT and the other is marked IN. The doors have stops that allow them to be opened only in the appropriate direction.
>
> If a waiter picks up an order in the kitchen, places it on a tray, and then realizes he has selected the wrong dish, he may change to the correct dish quickly and informally before he leaves the kitchen.
>
> If, however, he leaves the kitchen, gives the customer the dish, and then is informed of his error, he must follow a set procedure: (1) look at the check to determine if an error has occurred; (2) apologize profusely; (3) return to the kitchen through the IN door; (4) explain the problem, and so forth.

A baseline is analogous to the kitchen doors in the restaurant. Before a software configuration item becomes a baseline, change may be made quickly and informally. However, once a baseline is established, we figuratively pass through a swinging one-way door. Changes can be made, but a specific, formal procedure must be applied to evaluate and verify each change.

In the context of software engineering, we define a baseline as a milestone in the development of software that is marked by the delivery of one or more software configuration items and the approval of these SCIs that is obtained through a formal technical review (Chapter 17). For example, the elements of a *Design Specification* have been documented and reviewed. Errors are found and corrected. Once all parts of the specification have been reviewed, corrected, and then approved, the *Design Specification* becomes a baseline. Further changes to the software architecture (contained in the *Design Specification*) can be made only after each has been evaluated and approved.

Although baselines can be defined at any level of detail, the most common software baselines are shown in Figure 21.1. Once an SCI becomes a baseline, it is placed in a *project database* (also called a *project library* or *software repository*). When a member of a software engineering team wants to make a modification to a baselined SCI, it is copied from the project database into the engineer's private work space. Referring to Figure 21.2, an SCI labeled B is copied from the project database into a software engineer's private workspace. A record of this activity is recorded in an accounting file. The engineer can work on B′ (the copy of the SCI) until the required changes are completed. After change control procedures have been completed (discussed later in this chapter), B′ can be used to update B. In some cases, the baselined SCI will be locked so that no one else can work on it until the change has been implemented, reviewed, and approved.

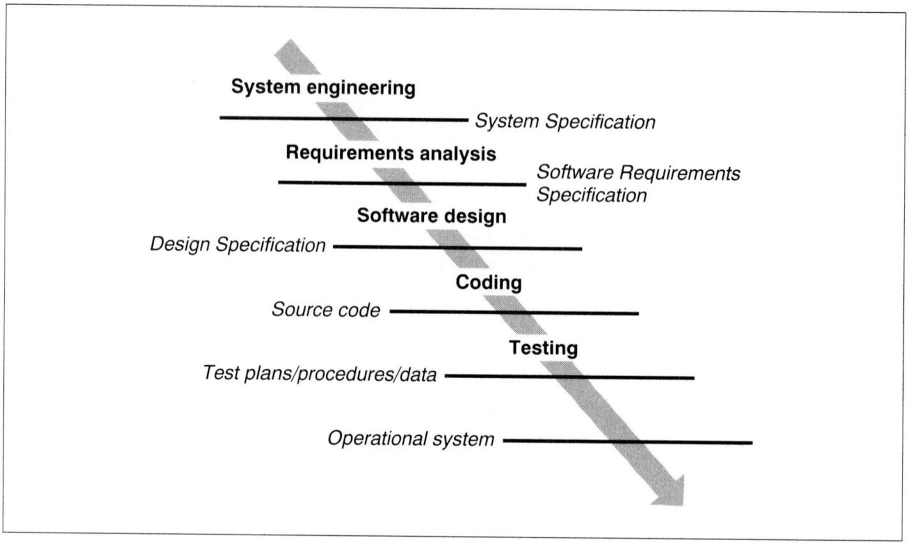

FIGURE 21.1.
Baselines.

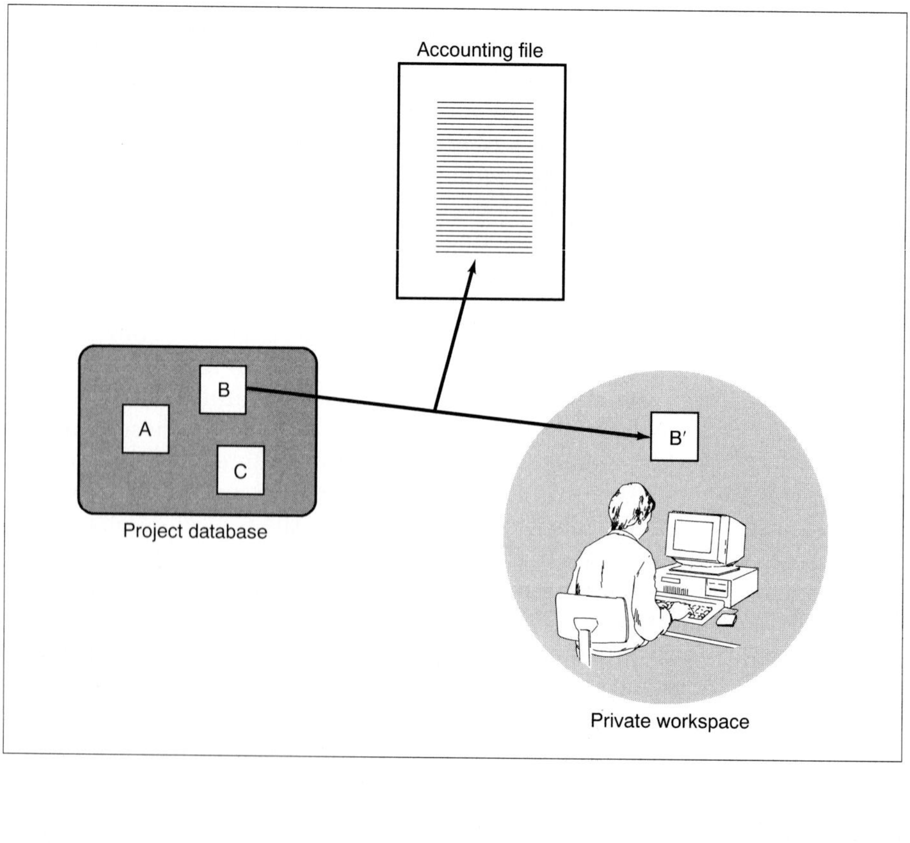

FIGURE 21.2.
Baselined SCIs and the project database.

21.1.2 Software Configuration Items

We have already defined a software configuration item as information that is created as part of the software engineering process. In the extreme, an SCI could be considered to be a single section of a large specification or one test case in a large suite of tests. More realistically, an SCI is a document, an entire suite of test cases, or a named program component (e.g., a PASCAL procedure or an Ada package).

The following SCIs become the target for configuration management techniques and form a set of baselines:

1. *System Specification*
2. *Software Project Plan*
3. **a.** *Software Requirements Specification*
   b. Executable or "paper" prototype
4. *Preliminary User Manual*
5. *Design Specification*
   a. Data design description
   b. Architectural design description
   c. Module design descriptions
   d. Interface design descriptions
   e. Object descriptions (if object-oriented techniques are used)
6. Source code listing
7. **a.** *Test Plan and Procedure*
   b. Test cases and recorded results
8. *Operation and Installation Manuals*
9. Executable program
   a. Modules—executable code
   b. Linked modules
10. Database description
    a. Schema and file structure
    b. Initial content
11. *As-Built User Manual*
12. Maintenance documents
    a. Software problem reports
    b. Maintenance requests
    c. Engineering change orders
13. Standards and procedures for software engineering

In addition to the SCIs noted above, many software engineering organizations also place software tools under configuration control. That is, specific versions of editors, compilers, and other CASE tools are "frozen" as part of the software configuration. Because these tools were used to produce documentation, source code, and data, they must be available when changes to the software configuration are to be made. Although problems are rare, it is possible that a new version of a tool (e.g., a compiler) might produce different results than the original version. For this reason, tools, like the software that they help to produce, can be baselined as part of a comprehensive configuration management process.

In reality, SCIs are organized to form *configuration objects* that may be catalogued in the project database with a single name. Recalling the discussion of data objects in Chapter 8, a configuration object has a name and attributes and is "connected" to other objects by relationships. Referring to Figure 21.3, the configuration objects, **Design Specification, data model, module N, source code,** and **Test Specification** are each defined separately. However, each of the objects is related to the others as shown by the arrows. A curved arrow indicates a compositional relation. That is, **data model** and **module N** are part of the object **Design Specification**. A double-headed straight arrow indicates an interrelationship. If a change is made to the **source code** object, an interrelationship enables a software engineer to determine what other objects (and SCIs) might be affected.[1]

[1]These relationships are discussed in Section 21.2.1 and the structure of the project database will be discussed in greater detail in Chapter 23.

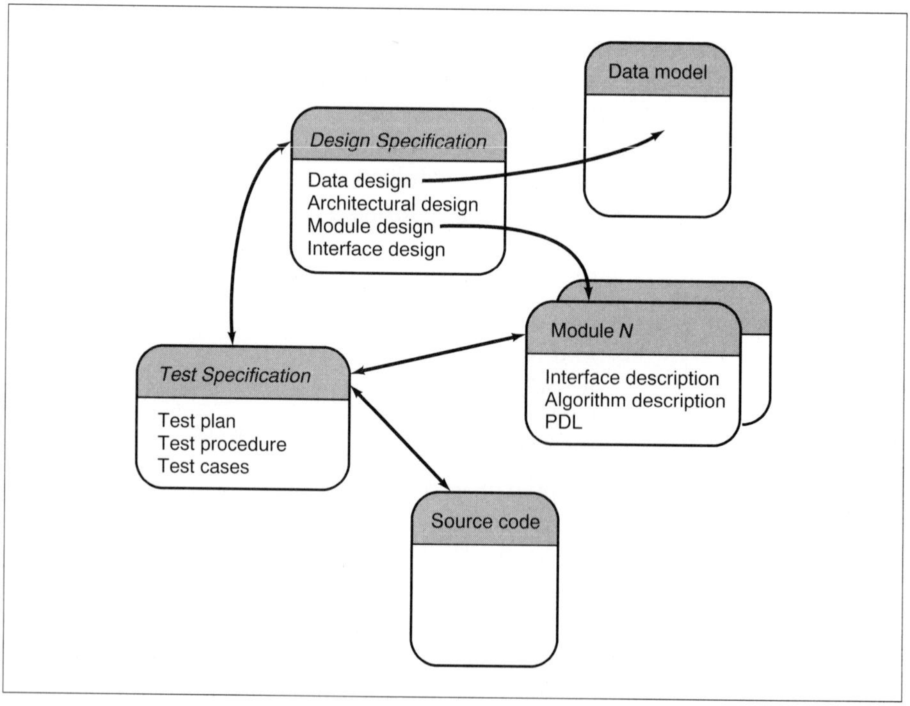

FIGURE 21.3. Configuration objects.

21.2 THE SCM PROCESS

Software configuration management is an important element of software quality assurance. Its primary responsibility is the control of change. However, SCM is also responsible for the identification of individual SCIs and various versions of the software, the auditing of the software configuration to ensure that it has been properly developed, and the reporting of all changes applied to the configuration.

Any discussion of SCM introduces a set of complex questions:

- How does an organization identify and manage the many existing versions of a program (and its documentation) in a manner that will enable changes to be accommodated efficiently?
- How does an organization control changes before and after software is released to a customer?
- Who has responsibility for approving and prioritizing changes?
- How can we ensure that changes have been made properly?
- What mechanism is used to appraise others of changes that are made?

These questions lead us to the definition of five SCM tasks: *identification, version control, change control, configuration auditing,* and *reporting.*

21.3 IDENTIFICATION OF OBJECTS IN THE SOFTWARE CONFIGURATION

To control and manage software configuration items, each must be separately named and then organized using an object-oriented approach. Two types of objects can be identified [CHO89]: *basic objects* and *composite objects.*[2] A basic object is a "unit of text" that has been created by a software engineer during analysis, design, code, or test. For example, a basic object might be a section of a requirements specification, a source listing for a module, or a suite of test cases that are used to exercise an equivalence class (see Chapter 18). A composite object is a collection of basic objects and other composite objects. Referring to Figure 21.3, **Design Specification** is a composite object. Conceptually, it can be viewed as a named (identified) list of pointers that specify basic objects such as **data model** and **module N**.

Each object has a set of distinct features that identify it uniquely: a name, a description, a list of "resources," and a "realization." The object

[2]The concept of an *aggregate object* [GUS89] has been proposed as a mechanism for representing a complete version of a software configuration.

name is a character string that identifies the object unambiguously. The object description is a list of data items that identify

- The SCI type (e.g., document, program, data) that is represented by the object
- A project identifier
- Change and/or version information

Resources are "entities that are provided, processed, referenced, or otherwise required by the object" [CHO89]. For example, data types, specific functions, or even variable names may be considered to be object resources. The realization is a pointer to the "unit of text" for a basic object and *null* for a composite object.

Configuration object identification must also consider the relationships that exist between named objects. An object can be identified as <part-of> a composite object. The relationship <part-of> defines a hierarchy of objects. For example, using the simple notation

E-R diagram 1.4 <part-of> data model;
data model <part-of> Design Specification;

we create a hierarchy of SCIs.

It is unrealistic to assume that the only relationships among objects in an object hierarchy are along direct paths of the hierarchical tree. In many cases, objects are interrelated across branches of the object hierarchy. For example, the data model is interrelated to data flow diagrams (assuming the use of structured analysis) and also interrelated to a set of test cases for a specific equivalence class. These cross-structural relationships can be represented in the following manner:

data model <interrelated> data flow model;
data model <interrelated> test case class m;

In the first case, the interrelationship is between a composite object, while the second relationship is between a composite object (**data model**) and a basic object (**test case class m**).

The interrelationships between configuration objects can be represented with a *module interconnection language* (MIL) [NAR87]. A MIL describes the interdependencies among configuration objects and enables any version of a system to be constructed automatically.

The identification scheme for software objects must recognize that objects evolve throughout the software engineering process. Before an object is baselined, it may change many times, and even after a baseline has been established, changes may be quite frequent. It is possible to create an *evolution graph* [GUS89] for any object. The evolution graph describes the change history of the object and is illustrated in Figure 21.4. Configuration object

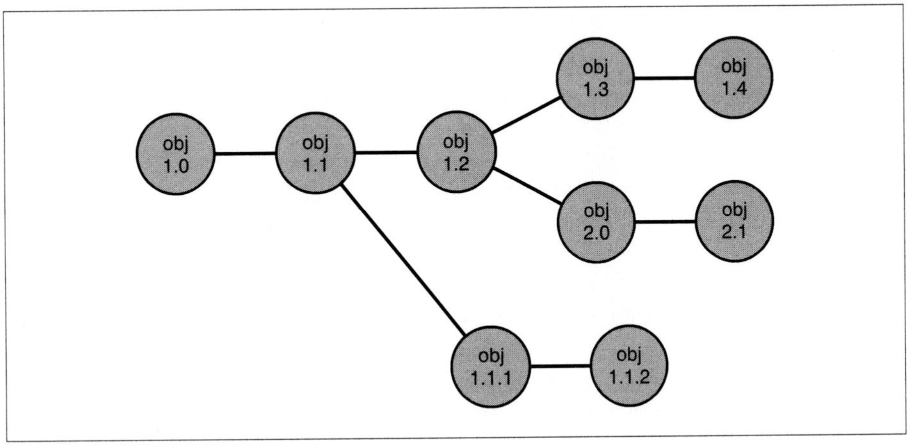

FIGURE 21.4.
Evolution graph.

1.0 undergoes revision and becomes object 1.1. Minor corrections and changes result in versions 1.1.1 and 1.1.2, which are followed by a major update that is object 1.2. The evolution of object 1.0 continues through 1.3 and 1.4, but at the same time, a major modification to the object results in a new evolutionary path, version 2.0. Both versions are currently supported.

It is possible that changes may be made to any version, but not necessarily to all versions. How does the developer reference all modules, documents, and test cases for version 1.4? How does the marketing department know what customers currently have version 2.1? How can we be sure that changes to version 2.1 source code are properly reflected in the corresponding design documentation? A key element in the answer to all of the above questions is identification.

A variety of automated tools (e.g., CCC, RCS, SCCS, CMS, NSE) has been developed to aid in identification (and other SCM) tasks. In some cases, a tool is designed to maintain full copies of only the most recent version. To achieve earlier versions (of documents or programs), changes (cataloged by the tool) are "subtracted" from the most recent version [TIC82]. This scheme makes the current configuration immediately available and other versions easily available.

21.4 VERSION CONTROL

Version control combines procedures and tools to manage different versions of configuration objects that are created during the software engineering process. Clemm [CLE89] describes version control in the context of SCM:

> Configuration management allows a user to specify alternative configurations of the software system through the selection of appropriate versions. This is supported by associating attributes with each software version, and then al-

lowing a configuration to be specified [and constructed] by describing the set of desired attributes.

The "attributes" mentioned above can be as simple as a specific version number that is attached to each object or as complex as a string of boolean variables (switches) that indicate specific types of functional changes that have been applied to the system [LIE89].

One representation of the different versions of a system is the evolution graph presented in Figure 21.4. Each node on the graph is an *aggregate object,* that is, a complete version of the software. Each version of the software is a collection of SCIs (source code, documents, data), and each version may be composed of different *variants.* To illustrate this concept, consider a version of a simple program that is composed of components 1, 2, 3, 4, and 5 (Figure 21.5).[3] Component 4 is used only when the software is implemented using color displays. Component 5 is implemented when monochrome displays are available. Therefore, two variants of the version can be defined: (1) components 1, 2, 3, and 4; (2) components 1, 2, 3, and 5.

---

[3]In this context, the term "component" refers to all composite objects and basic objects for a baselined SCI. For example, an "input" component might be constructed with six different software modules, each responsible for an input subfunction.

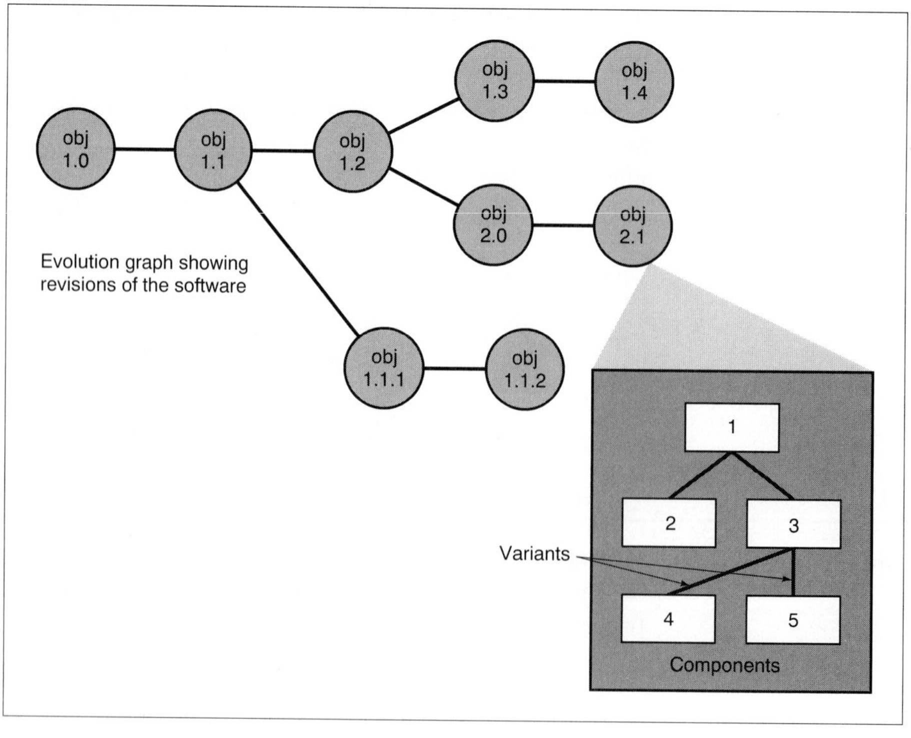

FIGURE 21.5. Versions and variants.

To construct the appropriate variant of a given version of a program, each component can be assigned an "attribute-tuple"—a list of features that will define whether the component should be used when a particular variant of a software version is to be constructed. One or more attributes is assigned for each variant. For example, a *color* attribute could be used to define which component should be included when color displays are to be supported.

Another way to conceptualize the relationship between components, variants, and versions (revisions) is to represent them as an *object pool* [REI89]. Referring to Figure 21.6, the relationship between configuration objects and components, variants, and versions can be represented as a three-dimensional space. A component is composed of a collection of objects at the same revision level. A variant is a different collection of objects at the same revision level, and therefore coexists in parallel with other variants. A new version is defined when major changes are made to one or more objects.

A number of different automated approaches to version control have been proposed over the past decade. The primary difference in approaches is the sophistication of the attributes that are used to construct specific versions and variants of a system and the mechanics of the process for construction. In early systems, such as SCCS [ROC75], attributes took on numeric values. In later systems, such as RCS [TIC82], symbolic revision keys were used. Modern systems, such as NSE or DSEE [ADA89], create version specifications that can be used to construct variants or new versions. These systems also support the baselining concept, thereby precluding uncontrolled modification (or deletion) of a particular version.

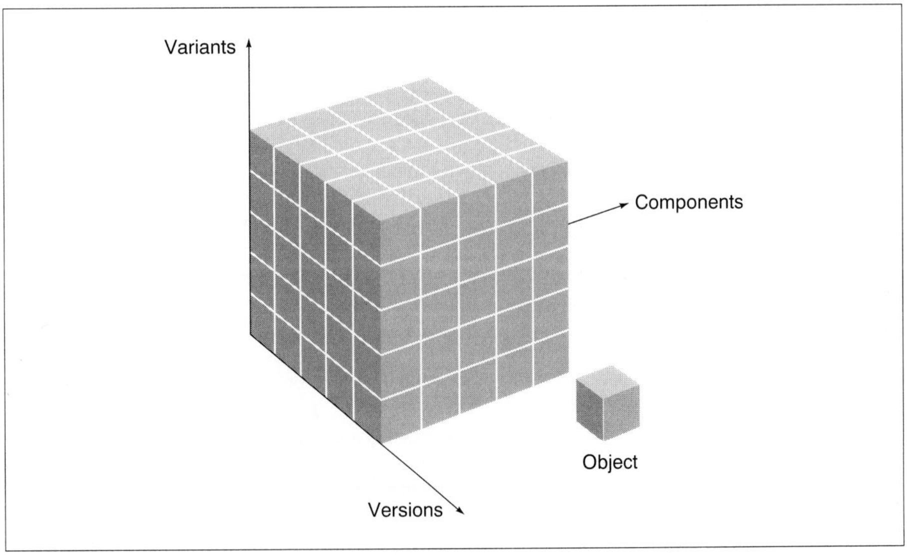

FIGURE 21.6. Object pool representation of components, variants, and versions.

21.5 CHANGE CONTROL

For a large software development effort, uncontrolled change rapidly leads to chaos. *Change control* combines human procedures and automated tools to provide a mechanism for the control of change. The change control process is illustrated schematically in Figure 21.7. A *change request*[4] is submitted and evaluated to assess technical merit, potential side effects, the

[4]Although many change requests are submitted during the software maintenance phase, we take a broader view in this discussion. A request for change can occur at any time during the software engineering process. It should be noted, however, that a change request is required only for a baselined object.

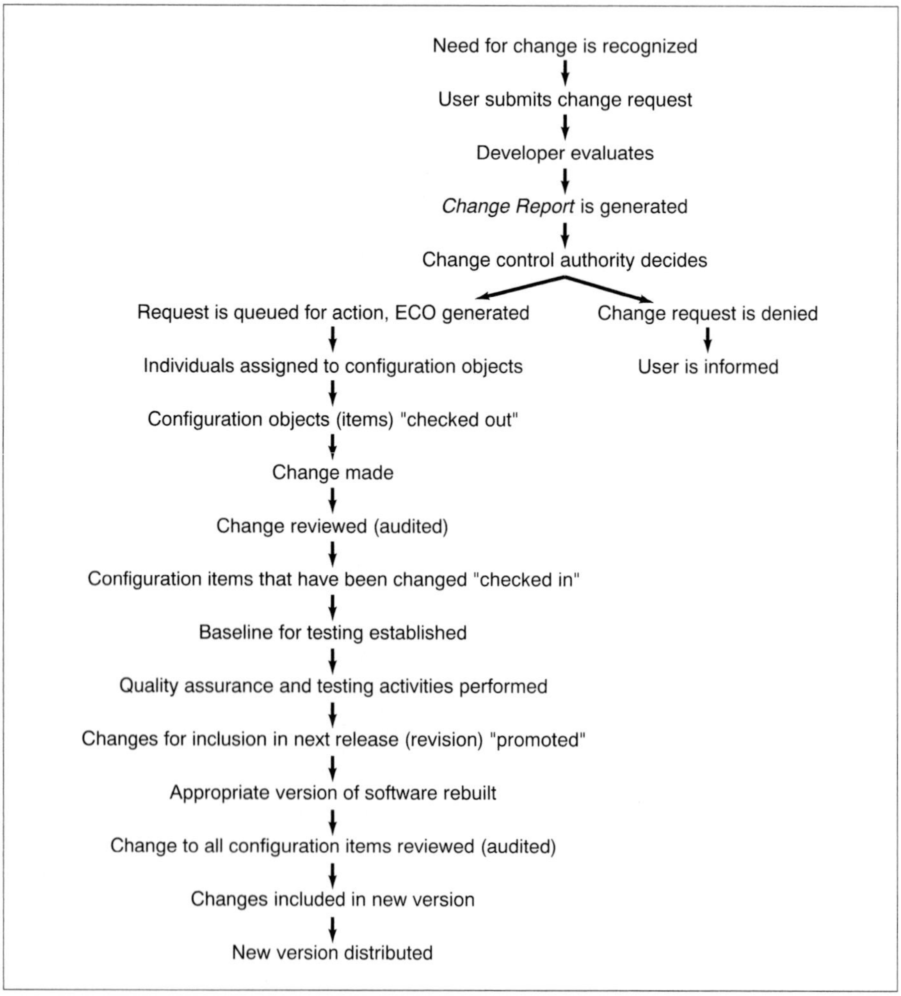

FIGURE 21.7. The change control process.

overall impact on other configuration objects and system functions, and the projected cost of the change. The results of the evaluation are presented as a *change report* that is used by a *change control authority* (CCA)—a person or group who makes a final decision on the status and priority of the change. An *engineering change order* (ECO) is generated for each approved change. The ECO describes the change to be made, the constraints that must be respected, and the criteria for review and audit. The object to be changed is "checked out" of the project database, the change is made, and appropriate SQA activities are applied. The object is then "checked in" to the database and the appropriate version control mechanisms (Section 21.4) are used to create the next version of the software.

The "check in" and "check out" process implements two important elements of change control—access control and synchronization control. *Access control* governs which software engineers have the authority to access and modify a particular configuration object. *Synchronization control* helps to ensure that parallel changes, performed by two different people, don't overwrite one another [HAR89].

Access and synchronization control flow is illustrated schematically in Figure 21.8. Based on an approved change request and ECO, a software engineer checks out a configuration object. An access control function ensures that the software engineer has the authority to check out the object, and synchronization control locks the object in the project database so that no updates can be made to it until the currently checked-out version has been replaced. Note that other copies can be checked out, but other updates cannot be made. A copy of the baselined object, called the *extracted version*,

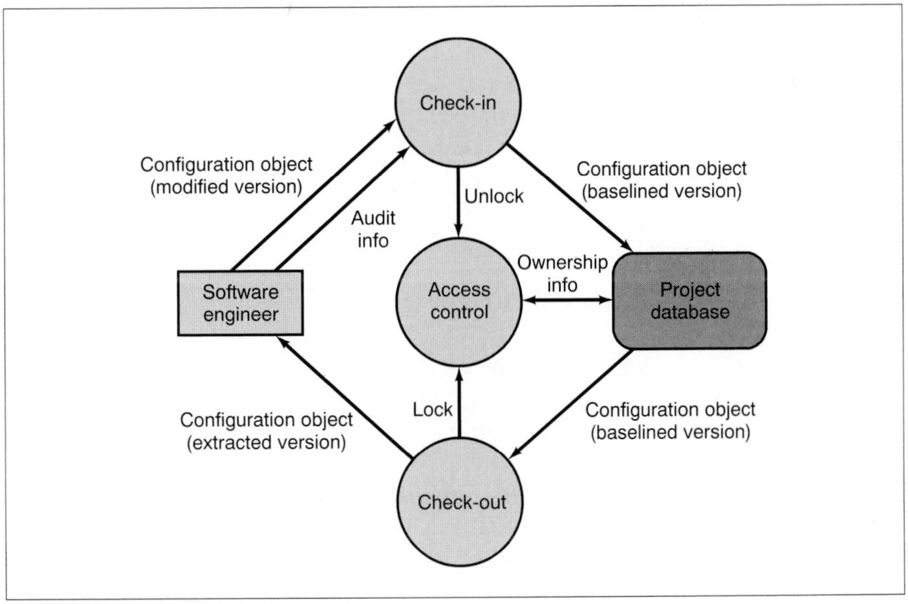

FIGURE 21.8. Access and synchronization control.

is modified by the software engineer. After appropriate SQA and testing, the modified version of the object is checked in and the new baseline object is unlocked.

Some readers may begin to feel uncomfortable with the level of bureaucracy implied by the change control process description. This feeling is not uncommon. Without proper safeguards, change control can retard progress and create unnecessary red tape. Most software developers who have change control mechanisms (unfortunately, many have none) have created a number of layers of control to help avoid the problems alluded to above.

Prior to an SCI becoming a baseline, only *informal change control* need be applied. The developer of the configuration object (SCI) in question may make whatever changes are justified by project and technical requirements (as long as the changes do not impact broader system requirements that lie outside the developer's scope of work). Once the object has undergone a formal technical review and has been approved, a baseline is created.

Once an SCI becomes a baseline, *project level change control* is implemented. Now, to make a change, the developer must gain approval from the project manager (if the change is "local") or from the CCA if the change impacts other SCIs. In some cases, formal generation of change requests, change reports, and ECOs is dispensed with. However, an assessment of each change is conducted and all changes are tracked and reviewed.

When the software product is released to customers, *formal change control* is instituted. The formal change control procedure has been outlined in Figure 20.7.

The change control authority plays an active role in the second and third layer of control. Depending on the size and character of a software project, the CCA may be comprised of one person—the project manager—or a number of people (e.g., representatives from software, hardware, database engineering, support, marketing). The role of the CCA is to take a global view, that is, to assess the impact of change beyond the SCI in question. How will the change impact hardware? How will the change impact performance? How will the change modify the customer's perception of the product? How will the change affect product quality and reliability? These and many other questions are addressed by the CCA.

21.6 CONFIGURATION AUDIT

Identification, version control, and change control help the software developer to maintain order in what would otherwise be a chaotic and fluid situation. However, even the most successful control mechanisms track a change only until an ECO is generated. How can we ensure that the change has been properly implemented? The answer is twofold: (1) *formal technical reviews* and (2) the *software configuration audit*.

The formal technical review (presented in detail in Chapter 17) focuses on the technical correctness of the configuration object that has been modified. The reviewers assess the SCI to determine its consistency with other SCIs, omissions, or potential side effects. A formal technical review should be conducted for all but the most trivial changes.

A software configuration audit complements the formal technical review by assessing a configuration object for characteristics that are generally not considered during the review. The audit asks and answers the following questions:

1. Has the change specified in the ECO been made? Have any additional modifications been incorporated?
2. Has a formal technical review been conducted to assess technical correctness?
3. Have software engineering standards been properly followed?
4. Has the change been "highlighted" in the SCI? Have the change date and change author been specified? Do the attributes of the configuration object reflect the change?
5. Have SCM procedures for noting the change, recording it, and reporting it been followed?
6. Have all related SCIs been properly updated?

In some cases, the audit questions are asked as part of a formal technical review. However, when SCM is a formal activity, the SCM audit is conducted separately by the quality assurance group.

21.7 STATUS REPORTING

Configuration status reporting (CSR) (sometimes called *status accounting*) is an SCM task that answers the following questions: (1) What happened? (2) Who did it? (3) When did it happen? (4) What else will be affected? The flow of information for configuration status reporting is tied to the tasks illustrated in Figure 21.7. Each time an SCI is assigned new or updated identification, a CSR entry is made. Each time a change is approved by the CCA (i.e., an ECO is issued), a CSR entry is made. Each time a configuration audit is conducted, the results are reported as part of the CSR task. Output from CSR may be placed in an on-line database [TAY85], so that software developers or maintainers can access change information by keyword category. In addition, an SCR report is generated on a regular basis and is intended to keep management and practitioners appraised of important changes.

Configuration status reporting plays a vital role in the success of a large software development project. When many people are involved, it is likely that "the left hand not knowing what the right hand is doing" situation will occur. Two developers may attempt to modify the same SCI with different and conflicting intentions. A software engineering team may spend months of effort building software to an obsolete hardware specification. The person who would recognize serious side effects for a proposed change is not aware that the change is being made. CSR helps to eliminate these problems by improving communication among all the people involved.

21.8 SCM STANDARDS

Over the past two decades a number of software configuration management standards have been proposed. Many early SCM standards, such as MIL-STD-483, DOD-STD-480A, and MIL-STD-1521A, focused on software developed for military applications. However, more recent ANSI/IEEE standards, such as ANSI/IEEE Standards 828-1983, 1042-1987, and 1028-1988 [IEE89], are applicable to nonmilitary software and are recommended for both large and small software engineering organizations.

21.9 SUMMARY

Software configuration management is an umbrella activity that is applied throughout the software engineering process. SCM identifies, controls, audits, and reports modifications that invariably occur while software is being developed and after it has been released to a customer. All the information produced as part of the software engineering process becomes part of a software configuration. The configuration is organized in a manner that enables the orderly control of change.

The software configuration is composed of a set of interrelated objects, also called software configuration items, that are produced as a result of some software engineering activity. In addition to documents, program, and data, the development environment that is used to create software can also be placed under configuration control.

Once a configuration object has been developed and reviewed, it becomes a baseline. Changes to a baselined object result in the creation of a new version of that object. The evolution of a program can be tracked by examining the revision history of all configuration objects. Basic and composite objects form an object pool from which variants and versions are created. Version control is the set of procedures and tools for managing the use of these objects.

Change control is a procedural activity that ensures quality and consistency as changes are made to a configuration object. The change control process begins with a change request, leads to a decision to make or reject the request for change, and culminates with a controlled update of the SCI that is to be changed.

The configuration audit is an SQA activity that helps to ensure that quality is maintained as changes are made. Status reporting provides information about each change to those with a need to know.

REFERENCES

[ADA89] Adams, E., M. Honda, and T. Miller, "Object Management in a CASE Environment," *Proc. 11th Intl. Conf. Software Engineering,* IEEE, Pittsburg, May 1989, pp. 154–163.

[BAB86] Babich, W. A., *Software Configuration Management,* Addison-Wesley, 1986.

[BER80] Bersoff, E. H., V. D. Henderson, and S.G. Siegel, *Software Configuration Management,* Prentice-Hall, 1980.

[BRY80] Bryan, W., C. Chadbourne, and S. Siegel, *Software Configuration Management,* IEEE Compter Society Press, 1980.

[CHO89] Choi, S.C., and W. Scacchi, "Assuring the Correctness of a Configured Software Description," *Proc. 2nd Intl. Workshop on Software Configuration Management,* ACM, Princeton, October 1989, pp. 66–75.

[CLE89] Clemm, G. M., "Replacing Version Control with Job Control," *Proc. 2nd Intl. Workshop on Software Configuration Management,* ACM, Princeton, October 1989, pp. 162–169.

[GUS89] Gustavsson, A., "Maintaining the Evaluation of Software Objects in an Integrated Environment," *Proc. 2nd Intl. Workshop on Software Configuration Management,* ACM, Princeton, October 1989, pp. 114–117.

[HAR89] Harter, R., "Configuration Management," *HP Professional,* vol. 3, no. 6, June 1989.

[IEE89] *Software Engineering Standards,* 3d ed., IEEE Computer Society, 1989.

[LIE89] Lie, A., et al., "Change Oriented Versioning in a Software Engineering Database," *Proc. 2nd Intl. Workshop on Software Configuration Management,* ACM, Princeton, October 1989, pp. 56–65.

[NAR87] Narayanaswamy, K., and W. Scacchi, "Maintaining Configurations of Evolving Software Systems," *IEEE Trans. Software Engineering,* vol. SE-13, no. 3, March 1987, pp. 324–334.

[REI89] Reichenberger, C., "Orthogonal Version Management," *Proc. 2nd Intl. Workshop on Software Configuration Management,* ACM, Princeton, October 1989, pp. 137–140.

[ROC75] Rochkind, M., "The Source Code Control System," *IEEE Trans. Software Engineering,* vol. SE-1, no. 4, December 1975, pp. 364–370.

[TAY85] Taylor, B., "A Database Approach to Configuration Management for Large Projects," *Proc. Conf. Software Maintenance—1985,* IEEE, November 1985, pp. 15–23.

[TIC82] Tichy, W. F., "Design, Implementation and Evaluation of a Revision Control System," *Proc. 6th Intl. Conf. Software Engineering,* IEEE, Tokyo, September 1982, pp. 58–67.

PROBLEMS AND POINTS TO PONDER

21.1 Why is the First Law of System Engineering true? How does it affect our perception of software engineering paradigms?

21.2 Discuss the reasons for baselines in your own words.

21.3 Assume that you're the manager of a small project. What baselines would you define for the project and how would you control them?

21.4 Design a project database system that would enable a software engineer to store, cross reference, trace, update, change, etc., all important software configuration items. How would the database handle different versions of the same program? Would source code be handled differently than documentation? How will two developers be precluded from making different changes to the same SCI at the same time?

21.5 Do some research on object-oriented databases and write a paper that describes how they can be used in the context of SCM.

21.6 Use an E-R model to describe the interrelationships among the SCIs (objects) listed in Section 21.1.2.

21.7 Research an existing SCM tool and describe how it implements control for versions, variants, and configuration objects in general.

21.8 The relations <part-of> and <interrelated> represent simple relationships between configuration objects. Describe five additional relationships that might be useful in the context of a project database.

21.9 Research an existing SCM tool and describe how it implements the mechanics of version control. Alternatively, read two or three of the papers referenced in this chapter and research the different data structures and referencing mechanisms that are used for version control.

21.10 Using Figure 21.7 as a guide, develop an even more detailed work breakdown for change control. Describe the role of the CCA and suggest formats for the change request, the change report, and the ECO.

21.11 Develop a checklist for use during configuration audits.

21.12 What is the difference between an SCM audit and a formal technical review? Can their functions be folded into one review? What are the pros and cons?

FURTHER READINGS

The literature on software configuration management has expanded significantly over the past few years. However, most of the recent literature is in the form of technical papers and articles. Relatively few books have been written on the subject. Bersoff et al. [BER80] and Babich [BAB86] are good introductions to the procedural elements of SCM, but for more detailed discussions of configuration management tools and control mechanisms, the interested reader must resort to conference proceeding and technical papers.

A tutorial by Bryan et al. [BRY80] is an excellent anthology of early papers on the subject. More recent work is contained in the proceedings of the First and Second International Conferences on Software Configuration management, conducted on an irregular basis by the ACM. The proceedings of the International Conference on Software Engineering and COMPSAC (both held yearly by the IEEE) are other good sources of information on configuration management.

ANSI/IEEE Standard 1042-1988 [IEE89] is an excellent tutorial on SCM, providing basic definitions, guidelines for implementing an effective process, and a thorough treatment of a wide variety of management and technical issues.

PART 5

THE ROLE OF AUTOMATION

CHAPTER 22

COMPUTER-AIDED SOFTWARE ENGINEERING

Everyone has heard the saying about the shoemaker's children: The shoemaker is so busy making shoes for others that his children don't have shoes of their own. Over the past 20 years, many software engineers have been the "shoemaker's children." Although these technical professionals have built complex systems that automate the work of others, they have used very little automation themselves. In fact, until recently software engineering was fundamentally a manual activity in which tools[1] were used only at the latter stages of the process.

Today, software engineers have finally been given their first new pair of shoes—*computer-aided software engineering* (CASE). The shoes don't come in as many varieties as we would like, are often a bit stiff and sometimes uncomfortable, don't provide enough sophistication for those who are stylish, and don't always match other garments that software developers use. But they provide an absolutely essential piece of apparel for the software developer's wardrobe, and will, over time, become more comfortable, more usable, and more adaptable to the needs of individual practitioners.

In this chapter, the technical aspects of computer-aided software engineering are discussed. CASE technologies span a wide range of topics that encompass software engineering methods and project management procedures. In earlier chapters of this book we have attempted to provide a rea-

[1]In many cases, the only tools available to the software engineer were compilers and text editors. These tools address only coding—an activity that should account for no more than 20 percent of the overall software engineering process.

sonable understanding of the underpinnings of the technology. In this chapter and the next, the focus shifts to the tools and environments that will help to automate software engineering technology.

22.1 WHAT IS CASE?[2]

In the movie *Back to the Future,* the hero, Marty McFly, travels back to 1955 in a souped-up DeLorean time machine. Marty's purpose was to change his future. Ours will be more mundane: to understand how engineering automation has evolved over the past 40 years.

In 1955, mechanical and electrical engineers worked with rudimentary hand tools: books and tables that contained the formulae and algorithms that they needed for analysis of an engineering problem; slide rules and calculators (mechanical, not electronic!) for doing the computation necessary to ensure that the product would work; pens and pencils, drafting boards, rulers, and other paraphernalia that enabled the engineer to create models of the product that was to be built. Good work was done, but it was done by hand.

A decade passed and the same engineering group began experimenting with computer-based engineering. Many staff members resisted the use of computers. "I just don't trust the results," was a common complaint. But many others jumped in with both feet. The engineering process was changing.

We jump to 1975. The formulae and algorithms that the engineer needed were embedded in a large suite of computer programs that were used to analyze a wide array of engineering problems. People trusted the results of these programs. In fact, much of their work could not be accomplished without them. Computer graphics workstations, tied to large mainframes, were in use in a few companies and had replaced the drafting board and related tools for the creation of engineering models. A bridge between engineering and manufacturing work was under construction, creating the first link between computer-aided design (CAD) and computer-aided manufacturing (CAM).

Good work continued to be done, but it was now dependent on software. Computing and engineering had been joined inextricably.

Arriving back at the present, we see computer-aided engineering (CAE), computer-aided design, and computer-integrated manufacturing (CIM, the successor to CAM) as commonplace activities in most companies. Engineering automation has not only arrived, it is an integral part of the process.

Unlike Marty McFly, mechanical and electrical engineers can't go back and change the future. But, in a way, software engineers can. They have the opportunity to mold the future of CASE by learning lessons from the evolution of CAE, CAD, and CIM.

---

[2]This section has been adapted from Pressman and Herron [PRE91].

22.1.1 A Software Engineering Workshop

The best workshops have three primary characteristics: (1) a collection of useful tools that will help in every step of building a product; (2) an organized layout that enables the tools to be found quickly and used efficiently; (3) a skilled craftsperson who understands how to use the tools in an effective manner. Software engineers now recognize that they need more and varied tools (hand tools alone just won't meet the demands of modern computer-based systems). They also need an organized and efficient workshop in which to place the tools.

The workshop for software engineering is called an *integrated project support environment* (discussed in Chapter 23) and the tool set that fills the workshop is CASE.

22.1.2 An Analogy

It is fair to state that computer-aided software engineering has the potential to become the most important technological advance in the history of software development. The key word in the preceding sentence is "potential."

Today, CASE tools add to the software engineer's tool box. CASE provides the engineer with the ability to automate manual activities and to improve engineering insight. Yet to become "the most important technological advance," CASE must do much more. It must form the building blocks of a workshop for software development.

Today, CASE is where CAD/CAE/CIM were in 1975. Individual tools are being used by some companies, usage across the industry is spreading rapidly, and serious effort is underway to integrate the individual tools to form a consistent environment.

There is little doubt that CASE will impact software engineering in substantially the same way that CAE/CAD/CIM has impacted other engineering disciplines. However, there are some important differences. During its early years of evolution CAD/CAE/CIM implemented engineering practices that had been tried and proven over the past 100 years. CASE, on the other hand, provides a set of semiautomated and automated tools that are implementing an engineering culture that is new to many companies. The difference in impact and in acceptance is profound.

CAD/CAE focuses almost exclusively on problem solving and design. It continues to struggle with a bridge to manufacturing through CIM. The primary goal of CASE (over the long haul) is to move toward the automatic generation of programs from a design-level specification. Unlike CAD/CAE, many people believe that analysis and design by themselves are not enough for CASE, but that analysis and design must ultimately lead to the direct generation of the end product—computer software. There is little doubt that this makes the challenge significantly more difficult, but the end result, if it can be effectively accomplished, may be significantly more powerful.

22.2 BUILDING BLOCKS FOR CASE

Computer-aided software engineering can be as simple as a single tool that supports a specific software engineering activity or as complex as a complete "environment" that encompasses tools, a database, people, hardware, a network, operating systems, standards, and myriad other components. In this section, an overview of the building blocks that create a CASE environment is presented. In Chapter 23, these building blocks are discussed in the context of CASE environments.

The building blocks for CASE are illustrated in Figure 22.1. Each building block forms a foundation for the next, with tools sitting at the top of the heap. It is interesting to note that the foundation for effective CASE environments has relatively little to do with software engineering tools themselves. Rather, successful environments for software engineering are built on an *environment architecture* that encompasses appropriate hardware and systems software. In addition, the environment architecture must consider the human work patterns that are applied during the software engineering process.

During the 1960s, 1970s, and 1980s, software development was a mainframe activity.[3] Terminals were linked to a central computer and each software developer shared the resources of that computer. Software tools that were available (and there were relatively few) were designed to operate in a terminal-based time-sharing environment.

Today, the trend in software development is away from the mainframe computer and toward the workstation as a software engineering platform. Individual workstations are networked so that software engineers can communicate effectively. The project database (Chapter 21) is available through

[3]Certainly, there were exceptions, but it was not until the late 1980s that workstations and PCs began to be used in significant numbers to build computer-based systems.

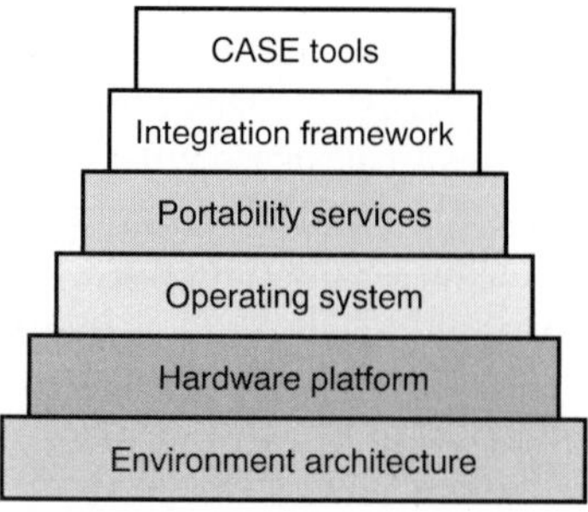

FIGURE 22.1. CASE building blocks.

a network file server that is accessible from all workstations. An operating system that supports the hardware, the network, and the tools ties the environment together.

The environment architecture, composed of the hardware platform and operating system support (including networking and database management software), lays the groundwork for CASE. But the CASE environment itself demands other building blocks. A set of *portability services* provides a bridge between CASE tools and their *integration framework* and the environment architecture. The integration framework is a collection of specialized programs that enables individual CASE tools to communicate with one another, to create a project database, and to exhibit the same look and feel to the end user (the software engineer). Portability services allow CASE tools and their integration framework to migrate across different hardware platforms and operating systems without significant adaptive maintenance.

The building blocks depicted in Figure 22.1 represent a comprehensive foundation for the integration of CASE tools. However, most CASE tools in use today have not been constructed using all of the building blocks discussed above. In fact, the majority of CASE tools are "point solutions." That is, a tool is used to assist in a particular software engineering activity (e.g., analysis modeling), but does not directly communicate with other tools, is not tied into a project database, and is not part of an *integrated CASE* (I-CASE) *environment*.[4] Although this situation is not ideal, a CASE tool can be used quite effectively, even if it is a point solution.

The relative levels of CASE integration are shown in Figure 22.2. At the low end of the integration spectrum is the *individual* (point solution) *tool*. When individual tools provide facilities for *data exchange* (most do), the integration level is improved slightly. Such tools produce output in a standard format that should be compatible with other tools that can read the format. In some cases, the builders of complementary CASE tools work together to form a *bridge* between the tools (e.g., an analysis and design tool that is coupled with a code generator). Using this approach, the synergy between the tools can produce end products that would be difficult to create using either tool separately. *Single-source integration* occurs when a single CASE tools vendor integrates a number of different tools and sells them as a package. Although this approach is quite effective, the closed architecture of most single-source environments precludes easy addition of tools from other vendors.

At the high end of the integration spectrum is the *integrated project support environment* (IPSE). Standards for each of the building blocks described above are created. CASE tools vendors use these IPSE standards to build tools that will be compatible with the IPSE and therefore compatible with one another.

---

[4]A detailed discussion of I-CASE environments is presented in Chapter 23.

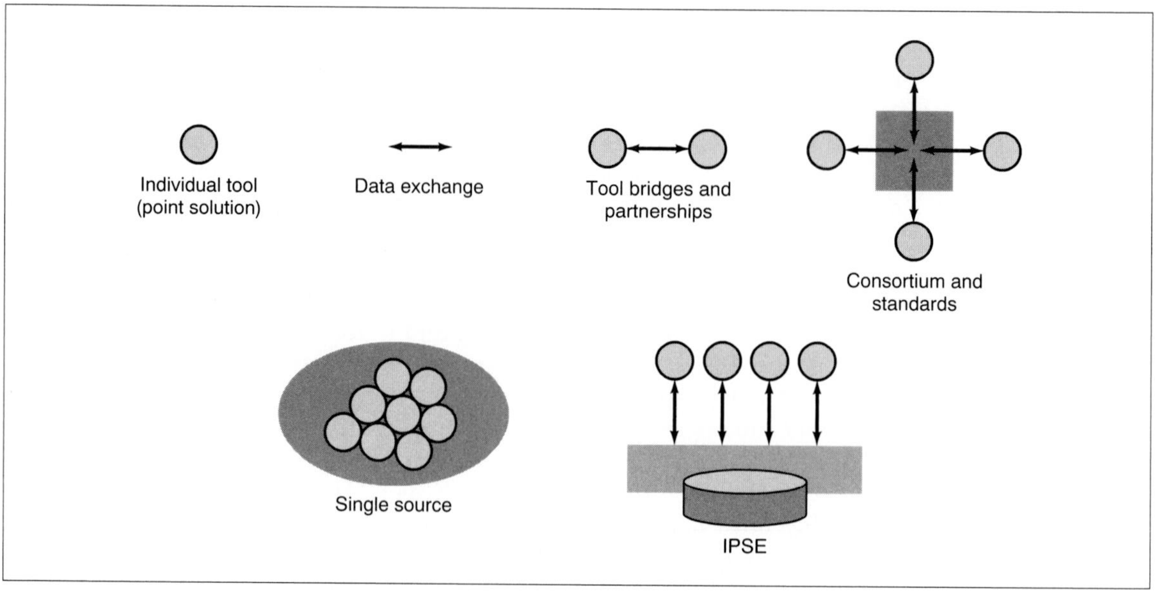

FIGURE 22.2. Integration options.

22.3 A TAXONOMY OF CASE TOOLS[5]

A number of risks are inherent whenever we attempt to categorize CASE tools. There is a subtle implication that to create an effective CASE environment one must implement all categories of tools—but this is simply not true. Confusion (or antagonism) can be created by placing a specific tool within one category when others might believe it belongs in another category. Some readers may feel that an entire category has been omitted—thereby eliminating an entire set of tools for inclusion in the overall CASE environment. In addition, simple categorization tends to be flat—that is, we do not show the hierarchical interaction of tools or the relationships among them. But even with these risks, it is necessary to create a taxonomy of CASE tools—to better understand the breadth of CASE and to better appreciate where such tools can be applied in the software engineering process.

CASE tools can be classified by function, by their role as instruments for managers or technical people, by their use in the various steps of the software engineering process, by the environment architecture (hardware and software) that supports them, or even by their origin or cost [QED89]. The taxonomy created in this book (Figure 22.3) uses function as a primary criteria.

[5]Representative tools for each category presented in the sections that follow have been listed in the Further Readings section of this chapter.

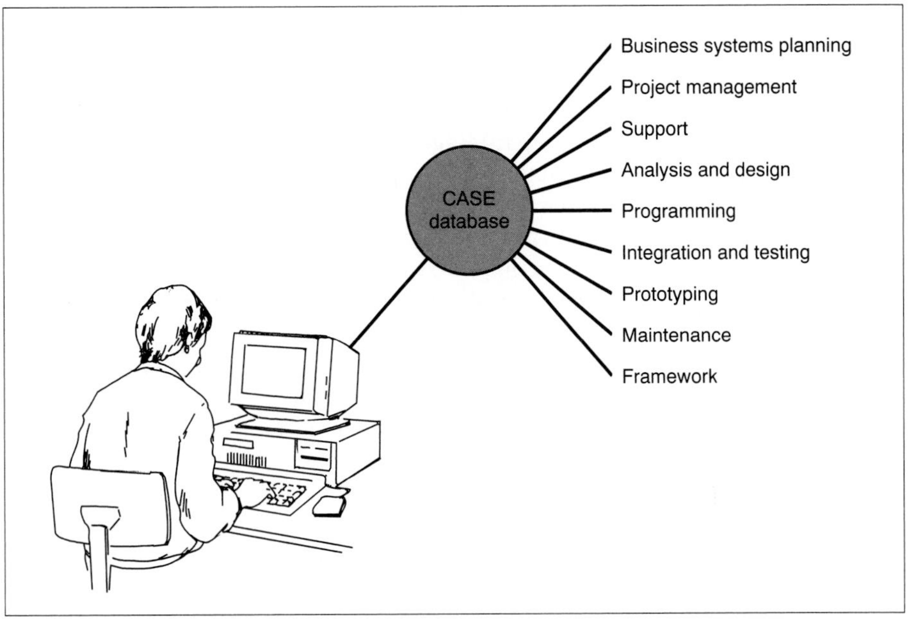

FIGURE 22.3.
A CASE taxonomy.

22.4 BUSINESS SYSTEMS PLANNING TOOLS

By modeling the strategic information requirements of an organization, *business systems planning tools* provide a "metamodel" from which specific information systems are derived. Rather than focusing on the requirements of a specific application, business information is modeled as it moves between various organizational entities within a company [MAR89]. The primary objective for tools in this category is to help improve the understanding of how information moves between the various organizational units.

It is important to note that business systems planning tools are not for every organization. They require a major commitment in resources and a major philosophical commitment by management to produce a complete model and then act upon the information derived from it. However, such tools do provide substantial insight when information systems strategies are to be constructed and when current systems and methods do not meet the needs of an organization.

22.5 PROJECT MANAGEMENT TOOLS

Many software project managers continue to estimate, control, and track software projects in much the same way that these activities were performed during the 1950s. Ironically, there is a broad array of CASE project management tools that could have a profound impact on the quality of project management for software development efforts both large and small.

Today, most CASE project management tools focus on one specific element of project management, rather than providing all-encompassing support for the management activity. By using a selected set of CASE tools, the project manager can generate useful estimates of effort, cost, and duration of a software project, define a work breakdown structure (WBS) and plan a workable project schedule, and track projects on a continuing basis. In addition the manager can use tools to collect metrics that will ultimately provide an indication of software development productivity and product quality. For those managers who have the responsibility for contract software development, CASE tools are available to trace requirements from the original customer request for proposal (RFP) to the software development work that implements these requirements in a deliverable system.

22.5.1 Project Planning Tools

Tools in this category focus on two primary areas: software project effort and cost estimation and project scheduling. Cost estimation tools enable the project manager to estimate the size of the project using an indirect measure (e.g., lines of code and function points) and describe overall project characteristics (e.g., problem complexity, staff experience, process maturity). The estimation tool then computes estimated effort, project duration, and the recommended number of people using one or more of the techniques introduced in Chapter 3. Many tools in this category allow some form of game-playing. For example, the project manager can permute the project deadline and examine its impact on overall cost.

Project scheduling tools enable the manager to define all project tasks (the work breakdown structure), create a task network (usually using graphical input), represent task interdependencies, and model the amount of parallelism possible for the project. Most tools use the critical-path scheduling method (Chapter 4) to determine the impact of slippage on delivery date.

22.5.2 Requirements Tracing Tools

When large systems are developed, things "fall into the cracks." This phrase refers to a critical problem in the development of computer-based systems—the delivered system does not fully meet customer-specified requirements. In some cases, nonconformance to requirements arises from technical difficulties. But in other situations, the requirements are missed—they simply were not addressed.

The objective of requirements tracing tools (Figure 22.4) is to provide a systematic approach to the isolation of requirements, beginning with the customer RFP or specification. The typical requirements tracing tool combines

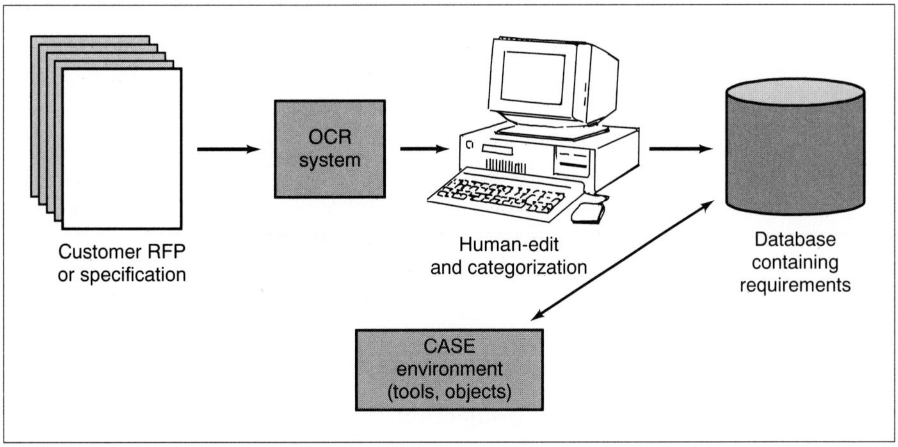

FIGURE 22.4. Requirements tracing tools.

human-interactive text evaluation, with a database management system that stores and categorizes each system requirement that is "parsed" from the original RFP or specification. The parsing of requirements can be as simple as finding every occurrence of the verb "shall" (indicative of a requirement) and then high-lighting the statement in which "shall" appears. The analyst then categorizes the requirement implied by the sentence and enters it into a database. Subsequent development work can be cross-referenced to the database so that conformance to requirements is more likely.

22.5.3 Metrics and Management Tools

Software metrics improve a manager's ability to control and coordinate the software engineering process and a practitioner's ability to improve the quality of the software that is produced. Today's metrics or measurement tools focus on process and product characteristics. Management-oriented tools capture project specific metrics (e.g., LOC/person-month, defects per function point) that provide an overall indication of productivity or quality (Chapter 2). Technically oriented tools determine technical metrics (e.g., cyclomatic complexity) that provide greater insight into the quality of design or code (Chapter 17). Many of the more advanced metrics tools maintain a database of "industry average" measures. Based on project and product characteristics provided by the user, such tools "rate" local numbers against industry averages (and past local performance) and suggest strategies for improvement.

Management tools (exclusive of project estimation and scheduling tools) assist information systems managers in prioritizing the many projects that compete for limited development resources. Using customer requirements and priorities, constraints placed on the development organization, and technical and business risks, such tools use an expert system approach to suggest the order in which a project should be undertaken.

22.6 SUPPORT TOOLS

The support tools category encompasses systems and application tools that complement the software engineering process. Tools in this broad category encompass the umbrella activities that are applicable across the entire software engineering process. They include documentation tools, systems software and networking tools, quality assurance tools, and software configuration management and database management tools (also members of framework tools category).

22.6.1 Documentation Tools

Document production and desk-top publishing tools support nearly every aspect of software engineering and represent a substantial "leverage" opportunity for all software developers. Most software development organizations spend a substantial amount of time developing documents, and in many cases the documentation process itself is quite inefficient. It is not unusual for a software engineering organization to spend as much as 20 or 30 percent of all its software development effort on documentation. For this reason, documentation tools provide an important opportunity to improve productivity.

Documentation tools are often linked to other CASE tools using a data bridge implemented by the vendor of the technical tool. For example, a number of analysis and design tools have links to one or more desk-top publishing systems, so that models and text created during analysis and design can be transmitted to a documentation tool and embedded in the specification created using the documentation tool.

22.6.2 System Software Tools

CASE is a workstation technology. Therefore, the CASE environment must accommodate high-quality network system software, electronic mail, bulletin boards, and other communication capabilities. Although the operating system of preference for most engineering workstations (and an increasing number of high-end PCs) is UNIX, the portability services provided by an IPSE may enable CASE tools to migrate to other operating systems without great frustration.

22.6.3 Quality Assurance Tools

The majority of CASE tools that claim to focus on quality assurance are actually metrics tools that audit source code to determine compliance with language standards. Other tools extract technical metrics (see Section 22.5.3) in an effort to project the quality of the software that is being built.

22.6.4 Database and SCM Tools

Database management software serves as a foundation for the establishment of a CASE database (repository) that we have called the project database (Chapter 21). Given the emphasis on configuration objects, database management tools for CASE may evolve from relational database management systems (RDMS) to object-oriented database management systems (OODMS).

Proponents claim that an OODMS [GUP91] will make configuration management easier to accomplish and argue that the object-oriented structure is a natural organization for software configuration items that combine many different types of information. Proponents for RDMS claim better performance and significantly more industry experience than OODMS and argue that the relational model can accomplish most, if not all, of the capability that can be achieved using the object-oriented model. Only time will tell which approach predominates for CASE databases.

CASE tools can assist in all five major SCM tasks—identification, version control, change control, auditing, and status accounting. The CASE database provides a mechanism for identifying each configuration item and relating it to other items; the control process discussed in Chapter 21 can be implemented with the aid of specialized tools; easy access to individual configuration items facilitate the auditing process; and CASE communication tools can greatly improve status accounting (reporting information about changes to all who need to know). Software configuration management lies at the kernel of every CASE environment. By controlling changes to the software configuration, SCM tools enforce human cognizance of each change, thereby reducing misunderstanding and improving system quality.

The use of the database, configuration management tools, and specialized "browsing" tools provides a first step toward the creation of a library for software that will encourage the reuse of software components. Although relatively little reuse has been accomplished to date, CASE offers the first real promise for achieving broader reuse of computer software components.

22.7 ANALYSIS AND DESIGN TOOLS

Analysis and design tools enable a software engineer to create a model of the system to be built. The model contains a representation of data and control flow, data content (through a definition of a requirements dictionary), process representations, control specifications, and a variety of other modeling representations. Analysis and design tools assist in the creation of the model and also in an evaluation of the model's quality. By performing consistency and validity checking on the model, analysis and design tools provide a software engineer with some degree of insight into the analysis representation and help to eliminate errors before they propagate into the design, or worse, into implementation itself.

22.7.1 SA/SD Tools

Most analysis and design tools implement the structured analysis and structured design (SA/SD) method discussed in Chapters 7 and 11. SA/SD is a modeling technique. It enables a software engineer to create progressively more complex models of a system, beginning at the requirements level and finishing with an architectural design. SA/SD combines a specific notation, analysis and design heuristics, and an analysis-to-design transformation process (a mapping) to produce workable representations of software.

22.7.2 PRO/SIM Tools

Prototyping and simulation (PRO/SIM) tools [NIC90] provide the software engineer with the ability to predict the behavior of a real-time system prior to the time that it is built. In addition, it enables the software engineer to develop mock-ups of the real-time system that allow the customer to gain insight into the function, operation, and response prior to actual implementation. There is little doubt that such capability provides distinct benefits in an area where success has been unpredictable and software development itself is something of a black art.

Most PRO/SIM tools provide the software engineer with a means for creating functional and behavioral models of a system. Tools in this category provide a means for specifying projected performance characteristics of each system element (e.g., execution speed of a hardware or software function), defining the input and output data characteristics (e.g., input data arrival rates or interrupt characteristics), and modeling the interfaces/interconnectivity among system elements.

Many PRO/SIM tools provide a code generation capability for Ada and other programming languages that will likely become considerably more sophisticated as new generations of these tools evolve. In addition, all tools in this category make use of an underlying formal or quasi-formal specification language, opening the door to more comprehensive code generation and formal verification of the system specification.

22.7.3 Interface Design and Development Tools

Even with the evolution of user interface standards (Chapter 14), the design and development of human-computer interfaces remain a challenge for software engineers. Industry studies have found that between 50 to 80 percent of all code generated for interactive applications is generated to manage and implement the human-computer interface [LEE90].

Interface design and development tools are actually a tool kit of program components such as menus, buttons, window structures, icons, scrolling mechanisms, device drivers, and so forth. However, these tool kits are being replaced by interface prototyping tools that enable the rapid on-screen creation of sophisticated user interfaces that conform to the interfacing standard (e.g., X-Windows, Motif) that has been adopted for the software.

User interface development systems (UIDS) combine individual CASE tools for human computer interaction (Chapter 14) with a program components library that enables a developer to build a human-computer interface quickly [MYE89]. A UIDS provides program components that manage input devices, validate user inputs, handle error conditions, process aborts and "undos," provide visual feedback, prompts, and help, update the display, manage application data, handle scrolling and editing, insulate the application from screen management functions, and support customization features for the end user.

22.7.4 Analysis and Design Engines

A new generation of analysis and design tools, called *analysis and design engines,* uses a rule-based architecture that enables the tool to be customized for any analysis and design method. Using these advanced CASE tools, an analysis and design method such as the SADT (Chapter 9) can be supported by building the appropriate graphical notation, entering the rules that govern the semantics of the symbology, and developing an interface that supports analysis and design using the method. In essence, analysis and design engines enable a software engineer to customize the tool to meet the needs of a specific (and possibly obscure) method. All the tools in this category support SA/SD, but they can also support JSD, DSSD, SADT, HOOD, and a variety of other methodologies.

22.8 PROGRAMMING TOOLS

The programming tools category encompasses compilers, editors, and debuggers that are available to support most conventional programming languages. In addition, object-oriented (O-O) programming environments, fourth-generation languages, application generators, and database query languages also reside within this category.

22.8.1 Conventional Coding Tools

There was a time when the only tools available to a software engineer were conventional coding tools—compilers, editors, and debuggers. Pressman and Herron [PRE91] discuss this when they state:

> There's an old saying: "When the only tool that you have is a hammer, every problem looks like a nail." Think about it. You can use a hammer to pound nails, but if it's the only tool that you have, you can also use it to pound screws (sloppy,

> but workable), bend metal (noisy, but workable), punch a hole in wood or concrete (very sloppy, but possible),.... We do the best we can by adapting the tools that we have on hand.

For almost 30 years, the only tools available to programmers were conventional coding tools and, therefore, every software engineering problem looked like a coding problem. Today, conventional tools continue to exist at the front lines of software development, but they are supported by all the other CASE tools discussed in this chapter.

22.8.2 Fourth-Generation Coding Tools

The thrust toward the representation of software applications at a higher level of abstraction has caused many developers to move headlong toward fourth-generation coding tools. Database query systems, code generators, and fourth-generation languages have changed the way in which systems are developed. There is little doubt that the end goal of CASE is automatic code generation—that is, the representation of systems at a higher level of abstraction than conventional programming languages. Ideally, such code generation tools will not only translate a system description into an operational program but also serve to help verify the correctness of the system specification so that the resulting output will conform to user requirements.

Fourth-generation languages are already used widely in information systems applications. It is not unusual to read claims such as: "Rank Xerox in the U.K.... created an application with 350,000 lines of COBOL code... yet it was created with three full-time people and one part-time person in ten weeks" [CAS89]. Although such accomplishments are possible in very limited domains of applicability, they represent a harbinger of things to come in broader application areas. We are already beginning to see the first code generation tools appear in the engineered products and systems market (most focus on Ada). As the 1990s progress, it is likely that less and less source code will be "written" manually.

Although fourth-generation languages, code generators, and application generators (e.g., database query systems) all enable a software engineer to specify a system at a high level of abstraction, each of these tools differ in important ways [FOR87]. Referring to Figure 22.5, a fourth-generation language is input directly to a 4GL interpreter. The interpreter translates the 4GL into executable code. The input to a code generator is a *procedural specification language* (PSL) (a metalanguage). The procedural specification language is then processed by one or a number of code generation modules that translates the PSL into the appropriate programming language. An application generator uses a central database or data dictionary, interactive menu-driven features, and application-specific rules to create software that addresses a narrow application domain.

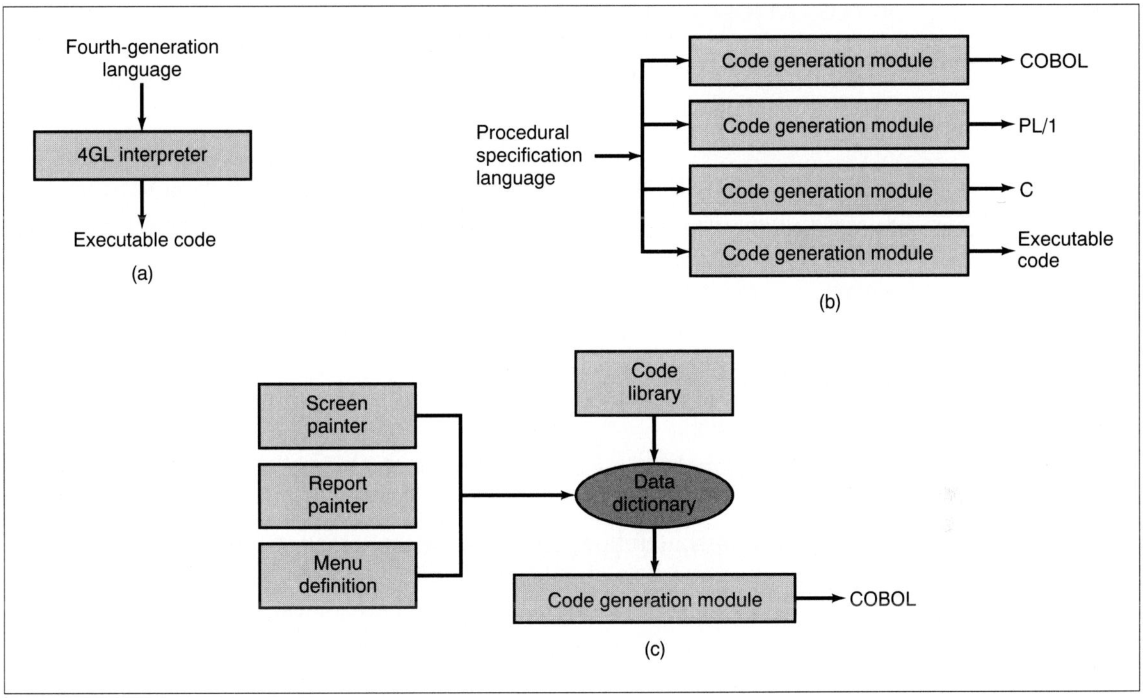

FIGURE 22.5. Fourth-generation tools. (*a*) 4 GL; (*b*) code generation; (*c*) application generator.

22.8.3 Object-Oriented Programming Tools

Object-oriented programming is one of the "hottest" technologies in software engineering. For this reason, CASE vendors are rushing new tools for object-oriented software development to the market.

Object-oriented programming environments are tied to a specific programming language (e.g., C++, Eiffel, Objective-C, or Smalltalk). A typical O-O environment incorporates third-generation interface features (mouse, windows, pull-down menus, context-sensitive operations, multitasking) with specialized functions such as the "browser"—a function that enables the software engineer to examine all objects contained in an object library[6] to determine whether any can be reused in the current application.

[6]The object library for popular object-oriented languages can contain hundreds or even thousands of reusable program components.

22.9 INTEGRATION AND TESTING TOOLS

In its directory of software testing tools, Software Quality Engineering [SQE90] defines the following testing tools categories:

- Data acquisition—tools that acquire data to be used during testing
- Static measurement—tools that analyze source code without executing test cases
- Dynamic measurement—tools that analyze source code during execution
- Simulation—tools that simulate the function of hardware or other externals
- Test management—tools that assist in the planning, development, and control of testing
- Cross-functional tools—tools that cross the bounds of the above categories

In the sections that follow, the three most widely used testing tools categories are discussed. It should be noted that many testing tools have features that span two or more of the above categories.

22.9.1 Static Analysis Tools

Static testing tools assist the software engineer in deriving test cases. Three different types of static testing tools are used in the industry: code-based testing tools, specialized testing languages, and requirements-based testing tools.

Code-based testing tools accept source code (or PDL) as input and perform a number of analyses that result in the generation of test cases. Using a description of the program input and procedural design as a guide, static testing tools derive test cases using path coverage, condition testing, and data flow criteria (Chapter 18).

Specialized testing languages (e.g., ATLAS) enable a software engineer to write detailed test specifications that describe each test case and the logistics for its execution. However, such tools do not assist the tester in designing the test cases.

Requirements-based testing tools isolate specific user requirements and suggest test cases (or classes of tests) that will exercise the requirements. To work properly, tools in this subcategory must have access to a formal specification for the software.

In most cases, static testing tools will document and catalogue tests (e.g., tests to exercise a particular type of input). They will conduct comparisons of test output to note differences between expected and actual results.

22.9.2 Dynamic Analysis Tools

Dynamic testing tools interact with an executing program, checking path coverage, testing assertions about the value of specific variables, and otherwise instrumenting the execution flow of the program. Dynamic tools can be either intrusive or nonintrusive. An *intrusive* tool changes the software to be tested by inserting probes (extra instructions) that perform the activities mentioned above. *Nonintrusive testing tools* use a separate hardware processor that runs in parallel with the processor containing the program that is being tested.

Most tools in the dynamic analysis category produce reports that indicate the number of times blocks of statements have been executed (path coverage analysis) and the average execution time for blocks of statements (performance analysis).

Another type of dynamic testing tool is sometimes called a *capture/playback tool* [POS89]. In capture mode, a capture/playback tool records all information flow at a particular point in a program's execution cycle. Often, the point of capture occurs immediately after interactive input is provided, i.e., the capture point "sits right behind the screen." Later, when the tool is placed in playback mode, the program can be restarted at the point of capture and will execute as if the original data were input to the program. Capture/playback tools are quite useful for creating regression test suites for highly interactive programs.

A dynamic testing tool can be used in conjunction with a static testing tool. The static tester is used to derive the test cases that are then monitored by the dynamic tool.

22.9.3 Test Management Tools

Test management tools are used to control and coordinate software testing for each of the major testing steps (Chapter 19). Tools in this category manage and coordinate regression testing (Chapter 19), perform comparisons that ascertain differences between actual and expected output, and conduct batch testing of programs with interactive human-computer interfaces.

In addition to the functions noted above, many test management tools also serve as generic test drivers. A test driver reads one or more test cases from a testing file, formats the test data to conform to the needs of the software under test, and then invokes the software to be tested. Testing tools in this subcategory are customized by the tester to meet specialized testing needs.

Finally, test managers sometimes work in conjunction with requirements tracing tools (Section 22.5.2) to provide requirements coverage analysis for testing. Reading each test case in sequence, the requirements coverage analyzer attempts to determine (based on information that describes the purpose of the test case) which software requirements are addressed by the test. A cross-reference matrix is often used to indicate which tests address what requirements.

22.10 PROTOTYPING TOOLS

Prototyping is a widely used software engineering paradigm (Chapter 1), and, as such, any tool that supports it can legitimately be called a prototyping tool. For this reason, many of the CASE tools discussed in this chapter can also be included in this category.

All prototyping tools reside somewhere on the implementation spectrum illustrated in Figure 22.6. At the low end of the spectrum, tools exist for the creation of a "paper prototype." An PC- or workstation-based drawing tool can create realistic screen images that can be used to illustrate system function and behavior to the customer. These images cannot be executed. *Screen painters* enable a software engineer to define screen layout rapidly for interactive applications. In some cases, a screen painter will also generate the source code to create the screens. More sophisticated CASE prototyping tools enable the creation of a data design, coupled with both screen and report layouts. Many analysis and design tools have extensions that provide a prototyping option. PRO/SIM tools (Section 22.7.2) generate skeleton Ada and C source code for engineering (real-time) applications. Finally, a variety of fourth-generation tools (Section 22.8.2) have prototyping features.

As prototyping tools evolve, it is likely that some will become *domain-specific.* That is, the tool will be designed to address a relatively narrow application area. Prototyping tools for telecommunications, aerospace applications, factory automation, and many other areas may become commonplace by the mid-1990s. Such tools will use a knowledge base that

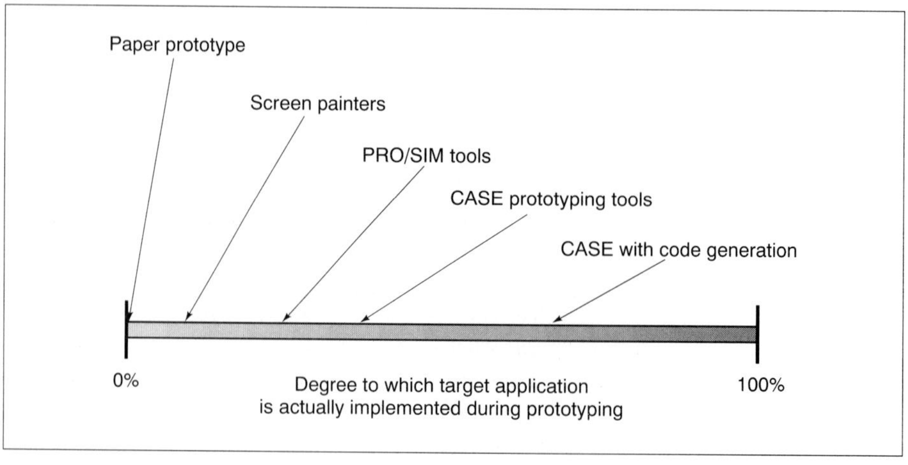

FIGURE 22.6.
Prototyping tools.

"understands" the application domain, facilitating the creation of prototype systems.

22.11 MAINTENANCE TOOLS

CASE tools for software maintenance address an activity that currently absorbs approximately 70 percent of all software related effort. The maintenance tools category can be subdivided into the following functions:

- Reverse engineering to specification tools—take source code as input and generate graphical structured analysis and design models, where-used lists, and other design information
- Code restructuring and analysis tools—analyze program syntax, generate a control flow graph, and automatically generate a structured program
- On-line system re-engineering tools—used to modify on-line database systems (e.g., convert IDMS or DB2 files into entity-relationship format)

The above tools are limited to specific programming languages (although most major languages are addressed) and require some degree of interaction with the software engineer.

Next generation reverse engineering and re-engineering tools will make much stronger use of artificial intelligence techniques, applying a knowledge base that is application domain-specific (i.e., a set of decomposition rules that will apply to all programs in a particular application area such as manufacturing control or aircraft avionics). The AI component will assist in system decomposition and reconstruction, but will still require interaction with a software engineer throughout the re-engineering cycle.

22.11.1 Reverse Engineering Tools

Reverse engineering tools (Chapter 20) perform a post-development analysis on an existing program. Like testing tools, reverse engineering tools can be categorized as *static* or *dynamic*.

A static reverse engineering tool (by far, the most common) uses program source code as input and analyzes and extracts program architecture, control structure, logical flow, data structure, and data flow. Other tools in this category apply a technique called *program slicing*. The software engineer specifies the types of program structures (data declaration, loops, other logic) that are of interest and the reverse engineering tool removes extraneous code, enabling only code of interest to be represented. *Dependency analysis tools* perform most of the functions already discussed, but, in addition, tools in this subcategory build graphical dependency maps that show the links between data structures, program components, and other user-specified program characteristics. Static reverse engineering tools have been called "code visualization" tools [OMA90]. In fact, by enabling the software engineer to "visualize" the program, such tools greatly improve the quality of changes that are made and the productivity of the people making them.

Dynamic reverse engineering tools monitor the software as it executes and use information obtained during monitoring to build a behavioral model of the program. Although such tools are relatively rare, they provide important information for software engineers who must maintain real-time software or embedded systems.

22.11.2 Re-Engineering Tools

Although re-engineering tools offer significant promise, relatively few industry quality tools are in use today. Existing re-engineering tools can be divided into two subcategories—code restructuring tools and data re-engineering tools. Code restructuring tools (Chapter 20) accept unstructured source code as input, perform the reverse engineering analysis described in Section 22.11.1, and then restructure the code to conform to modern structured programming concepts. Although such tools can be useful, they focus solely on the procedural design of a program.

Data re-engineering tools work at the other end of the design spectrum. Such tools assess data definitions or a database described in a programming language (usually COBOL) or database description language. They then translate the data description into graphical notation that can be analyzed by a software engineer. Working interactively with the re-engineering tool, the software engineer can modify the logical structure of the database, normalize the resultant files, and then automatically regenerate a new database physical design. The tools may use an expert system and knowledge base to optimize the re-engineered software for improved performance.

22.12 FRAMEWORK TOOLS

The industry trend toward I-CASE environments will continue to gain momentum during the 1990s. *Framework tools*—software tools that provide database management, configuration management, and CASE tools integration capabilities—are the first thrust in the IPSE direction.

Tools in this category exhibit functional components that support data, interface, and tools integration. Most implement an object-oriented database, with an internal tool set for establishing smooth interfaces with tools from other CASE vendors. Most framework tools provide some configuration management capability, enabling the user of the tool to control changes to all the configuration items created by all the CASE tools that are integrated with the framework tool. The key components of framework tools will be discussed in detail in Chapter 23.

22.13 CASE AND AI

A few CASE tools have limited expert system capabilities, but the vast majority of existing CASE tools make little use of artificial intelligence techniques. Most tools that do make limited use of AI employ the technology to check the graphical correctness of analysis and design models, applying design rules inherent to a particular analysis and design method to the models that have been created by the software engineer. However, the real promise of CASE-AI lies elsewhere.

Researchers are evaluating programming environments that make use of analysis and design "agents"—intelligent tools that aid in the analysis, design, and testing of computer-based systems. Rather than simply evaluating the model that a human has created, an agent will assist the software engineer in his or her problem-solving activities. Such agents must be domain-specific, accessing a knowledge base about the characteristics of a limited class of applications and being capable of using this knowledge base to guide the software engineer in analysis, design, or testing. The problem, of course, is in the definition of a knowledge base for software engineering. Although we are still a number of years away from such "agents," the future for CASE-AI is promising.

22.14 SUMMARY

Computer-aided software engineering tools span every step in the software engineering process and those umbrella activities that are applied throughout the process. CASE comprises a set of building blocks that begin at the hardware and operating system software level and end with individual tools.

In this chapter we have considered a taxonomy of CASE tools. Categories encompass both management and technical activities and span most software application areas. Each category of tool has been considered as a "point solution." In the next chapter, we consider ways in which individual tools are integrated to form an environment.

As the years pass, CASE will become part of the fabric of software engineering. Just as mechanical and electrical engineers rely on CAD/CAE/CIM for the analysis and design of high-technology products, software engineers will rely on CASE for the analysis, design, and testing of computer-based systems for the twenty-first century.

REFERENCES

[CAS89] *CASENews*, vol. 3, no. 4, April 1989, p. 1.

[FOR87] Forte, G. (ed.), "The State of Automatic Code Generation," *CASE Outlook*, vol. 1, no. 3, September 1987, pp. 1–13.

[GUP91] Gupta, R. and E. Horowitz (eds.), *Object-Oriented Databases with Applications to CASE, Networks, and VLSI CAD*, Prentice-Hall, 1991.

[LEE90] Lee, E., "User-Interface Development Tools," *IEEE Software,* May 1990, pp. 31–23.

[MAR89] Martin, J., *Information Engineering,* three volumes, Prentice-Hall, 1989.

[MYE89] Myers, B. A., "User Interface Tools: Introduction and Survey," *IEEE Software,* January 1989, pp. 15–23.

[NIC90] Nichols, K. M., "Performance Tools," *IEEE Software,* May 1990, pp. 21–23.

[OMA90] Oman, P., "Maintenance Tools," *IEEE Software,* May 1990, pp. 59–65.

[POS89] Poston, R. M., "Shopping for Software Testing Tools in 1990," *The Letter T,* Programming Environments, December 1989.

[PRE91] Pressman, R. S., and S. R. Herron, *Software Shock,* Dorset House Publishing, 1991.

[QED89] *CASE: The Potential and the Pitfalls,* QED Information Sciences, 1989.

[SQE90] *Testing Tools Reference Guide,* version 7.0, Software Quality Engineering, 1990.

PROBLEMS AND POINTS TO PONDER

22.1 Make a list of all software development tools that you use. Organize them according to the taxonomy presented in this chapter.

22.2 Research the evolution of CAD/CAM for mechanical and electrical engineering and develop a chronological time line for innovations in the field beginning in 1965. Now do the same thing for CASE, but begin your time line in 1975. Have both technologies progressed in a similar way?

22.3 What are the strengths of the "old-fashioned" software development environment architecture that made use of a mainframe and terminals? What are the disadvantages?

22.4 Using the ideas introduced in Chapter 10, how would you suggest that portability services be built?

22.5 Suggest a different taxonomy for CASE tools than the one presented in this chapter.

22.6 Review each of the tools categorized in Sections 22.4 through 22.12. Which tools would you classify as management tools? Which are technical tools? Which are umbrella tools?

22.7 Build a paper prototype for a project management tool that encompasses the categories noted in Section 22.5. Use Chapters 2, 3, and 4 for additional guidance.

22.8 Do some research on object-oriented database management systems. Discuss why OODMS would be ideal for SCM tools.

22.9 Gather product information on at least three SA/SD tools. Develop a matrix that compares their features.

22.10 Gather product information on two PRO/SIM tools. Develop a matrix that compares their features.

22.11 Gather product information on at least three fourth-generation coding tools. Develop a matrix that compares their features.

22.12 Build a paper prototype for an object-oriented programming tool that reflects the characteristics noted in Section 22.8.2. Use Chapters 8 and 12 for additional guidance.

22.13 Are there situations in which dynamic testing tools are "the only way to go?" If so, what are they?

22.14 For those readers familiar with the Apple Macintosh: Describe the features of HyperCard that make it useful as a prototyping tool. Where would you place HyperCard on the spectrum shown in Figure 22.6?

22.15 Gather product information on different maintenance tools. Develop a matrix that compares their features.

FURTHER READINGS

A number of books on CASE have been published in an effort to capitalize on the high degree of interest in the industry. Unfortunately, many suffer from one or more of the following failings: (1) The book only focuses on a narrow band of tools (e.g., analysis and design) while claiming to cover a wider categorization; (2) the book spends relatively little time on CASE and more time surveying (often poorly) the underlying methods that the tools deliver; (3) the book spends little time discussing integration issues; (4) the presentation is outdated because of an emphasis on specific CASE products.

The books that follow have avoided at least some of these failings:

Braithwaite, K. S., *Application Development Using CASE Tools,* Academic Press, 1990.

Gane, C., *Computer-Aided Software Engineering: The Methodologies, The Products and the Future,* Prentice-Hall, 1990.

Fisher, C., *CASE: Using Software Development Tools,* Wiley, 1988.

Lewis, T.G., *Computer-Aided Software Engineering,* Van Nostrand Reinhold, 1990.

McClure, C., *CASE is Software Automation,* Prentice-Hall, 1988.

Schindler, M., *Computer-Aided Software Design,* Wiley, 1990.

Towner, L. E., *CASE: Concepts and Implementation,* McGraw-Hill, 1989.

An anthology by Chikofsky (*Computer-Aided Software Engineering,* IEEE Computer Society Press, 1988) contains a useful collection of early papers on CASE and software development environments. QED Information Sciences [QED89] has done an excellent job of surveying this rapidly changing technology.

The best sources of current information on CASE tools are technical periodicals and industry newsletters. *CASE Outlook* and *CASE User* (CASE Consulting Group, Lake Oswego, OR), *The CASE Report* (Auerbach Publishers, Boston), *CASE Strategies* (Cutter Information Corporation, Arlington, MA), *CASE Trends* (Software Productivity Group, Shrewsbury, MA), and *CASEWorld* (Blum Publications, Yorktown Heights, NY) are all industry newsletters that provide in-depth analyses of new products and worthwhile tutorials on software engineering topics that affect CASE.

There are hundreds of CASE tools that fall into one or more of the categories noted in the taxonomy of CASE tools presented in this chapter. A representative sampling of tools for each category (denoted by the section number for the category) is presented in the list that follows[7]:

Section	*Tool Name*	*Vendor*
22.4	Foundation	Arthur Anderson
	Interactive Engineering Workbench	Knowledgeware
	Information Engineering Facility	Texas Instruments
22.5.1	DECPlan	Digital Equipment Corporation
	SLIM	Quantitative Software Management
	ESTIMACS	Computer Associates, Intl., Inc.
	MacProject II	Apple Computer
	Time Line	Symantec
22.5.2	RMS/PC, R-Trace	Transform Logic
	Teamwork/RQT	Cadre Technologies
22.5.3	Checkpoint	Software Productivity Research
	Expert CIO	P-Cube Corporation
22.6.1	Interleaf	Interleaf
	PageMaker	Aldus
22.6.2	UNIX and utilities	All workstation vendors
	VMS and utilities	Digital Equipment Corporation
22.6.3	Q/Auditor	Eden Systems
	Auditor	Softool Corporation
22.6.4	CCC	Softool Corporation
	EPOS	Software Products Services, Inc.
	Polytron Version Control System (PVCS)	Polytron/Sage Software
22.7.1	Teamwork	Cadre Technologies, Inc.
	Software Through Pictures	Interactive Development Environments
	Excelerator	Index Technologies
22.7.2	Statemate	I-Logix
	CardTool	Ready Systems
	ADAS	Cadre Technologies

[7]The tools presented in this list are intended to be representative and their inclusion does not imply endorsement. There are many other fine tools that have not been listed. Before selecting any CASE tool, the reader should evaluate a number of competitive products to determine the tools that best fit local needs.

22.7.3	Motif	Open Software Foundation
	Windows	Microsoft
	UIMX	Visual Edge Software, Hewlett Packard
22.7.4	Virtual Software Factory	Systematica (United Kingdom)
	DECDesign	Digital Equipment Corporation
22.8.1	Hundreds of compilers and dozens of industry quality editors and debuggers are available	
22.8.2	Netron/CAP	Netron
	Corvision	Cortex
	Transform	Transform Logic
	Meastro	Softlab
22.8.3	Objective-C	Stepstone, Inc.
	Eiffel	Interactive Software Engineering
	Smalltalk V	Digitalk
	ObjectWorks	ParcPlace Systems
	Encapsulator	Hewlett-Packard
22.9.1	BAT/ACT	McCabe Associates, Inc.
	T	Programming Environments, Inc.
22.9.2	Xray/DX	Microtec Research
	TCAT-PATH/C	Software Research
	Software Analysis Workstation	Cadre Technologies
22.9.3	DTM	Digital Equipment Corporation
	T	Programming Environments, Inc.
22.10	HyperCard	Apple Computer
	Demo II	Norton Utilities
	Focus	Information Builders
	VAX Cobol Generator	Digital Equipment Corporation
	SQL Forms, Menu, Report Writer	Oracle
	All tools listed for section 22.8.2	
22.11.1	Objective-C Browser	Stepstone
	Seela	Tuval Software Industries
	EDSA	Array Systems
	PathMap	Cadre
	HyperVue	Ten X Technology
	VIA/Center	Viasoft, Inc.

22.11.2	Bachman Re-Engineering Product Set	Bachman Information Systems
	Pathvue & Retrofit	XA Systems Corp.
22.12	Software Backplane	Atherton Technology
	AD/Cycle	IBM Corporation
	Cohesion	Digital Equipment Corporation
	DSEE	Hewlett-Packard (Apollo)
	NSE	Sun Microsystems

CHAPTER 23

INTEGRATED CASE ENVIRONMENTS

Computer-aided software engineering (CASE) is changing the industry's approach to software development. Although benefits can be derived from individual tools that address separate software engineering activities, the real power of CASE can only be achieved through *integration*. Gene Forte [FOR89a] makes this point clear when he states:

> Tool integration is among the most often discussed and debated topics in software engineering. Justly so, since no other technical or strategic issue is likely to have as much impact on the evolution of [software] technology and the CASE industry. . . .
>
> While individual CASE tools each contribute . . . , the promise of CASE really lies in the potential to integrate many tools into an integrated environment.

The benefits of *integrated CASE* (I-CASE) include (1) the smooth transfer of information (models, programs, documents, data) from one tool to another and one software engineering step to the next; (2) a reduction in the effort required to perform umbrella activities such as software configuration management, quality assurance, and document production; (3) an increase in project control that is achieved through better planning, monitoring, and communication; (4) improved coordination among staff members who are working on a large software project.

But I-CASE also poses significant challenges. Integration demands consistent representations of software engineering information, standardized interfaces between tools, a homogeneous mechanism for communication between the software engineer and each tool, and an effective approach that will enable I-CASE to move among various hardware platforms and operating systems. Although solutions to the problems implied by these challenges have been proposed, comprehensive I-CASE environments are only beginning to emerge.

In this chapter, the "integration issue" is considered in some detail.[1] It is important to remember that no single integration philosophy has been adopted throughout the industry. However, definite trends have already emerged and are evident in every effort to develop integration standards.

23.1 DEFINING INTEGRATION REQUIREMENTS

The term "integration" implies both *combination* and *closure*. I-CASE combines a variety of different tools and a variety of different information items in a way that enables the closure of communication among tools, between people, and across the software engineering process. Tools are integrated so that software engineering information is available to each tool that needs it; usage is integrated so that a common look and feel is provided for all tools; a development philosophy is integrated, implying a standardized software engineering approach that applies modern practice and proven methods.

To define "integration" in the context of the software engineering process, it is necessary to establish a set of requirements for I-CASE: An integrated CASE environment should [FOR89a]:

- Provide a mechanism for sharing software engineering information among all tools contained in the environment
- Enable a change to one item of information to be tracked to other related information items
- Provide version control and overall configuration management for all software engineering information
- Allow direct, nonsequential access to any tool contained in the environment
- Establish automated support for a procedural context for software engineering work that integrates the tools and data into a standard work breakdown structure (Chapter 4)
- Enable the users of each tool to experience a consistent look and feel at the human-computer interface
- Support communication among software engineers
- Collect both management and technical metrics that can be used to improve the process and the product

---

[1]It is recommended that those readers without a good understanding of CASE tools should first read Chapter 22.

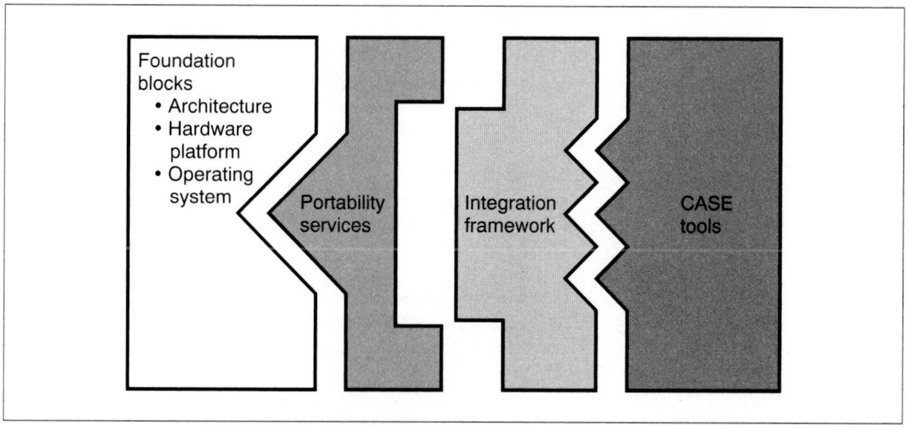

FIGURE 23.1.
Elements of I-CASE.

To achieve these requirements, each of the building blocks of a CASE architecture (Chapter 22) must fit together in a seamless fashion. Referring to Figure 23.1, the foundation building blocks—environment architecture, hardware platform, and operating system—must be "joined" through a set of portability services to an *integration framework* that achieves the requirements noted above. For the remainder of this chapter, we examine the integration framework in greater detail.

23.2 INTEGRATION OPTIONS[2]

CASE tools can be integrated in many different ways. At one end of an integration spectrum, a CASE tool is used in complete isolation. A limited number of software configuration items (documents, programs, or data) are created and manipulated by a single tool and output is in the form of hard-copy text and/or graphical documentation. In a sense, linkage to the rest of the software development environment is by paper via the developer.

In reality, few CASE tools are used in total isolation. The following integration options (Figure 23.2) are available:

Data Exchange Most tools have at least the ability to export information they gather and create in the form of an unstructured file with a published format. This enables a point-to-point data exchange (Figure 23.2*a*) between one CASE tool and some other tool, usually with a transmitting "filter" interposed. This preserves the information contained in the tool, eliminating the need to re-enter existing elements of the specification or design and preventing typographical errors from being introduced unnecessarily. Many

[2]This section has been adapted from Forte [FOR89a] with permission of CASE Consulting Group.

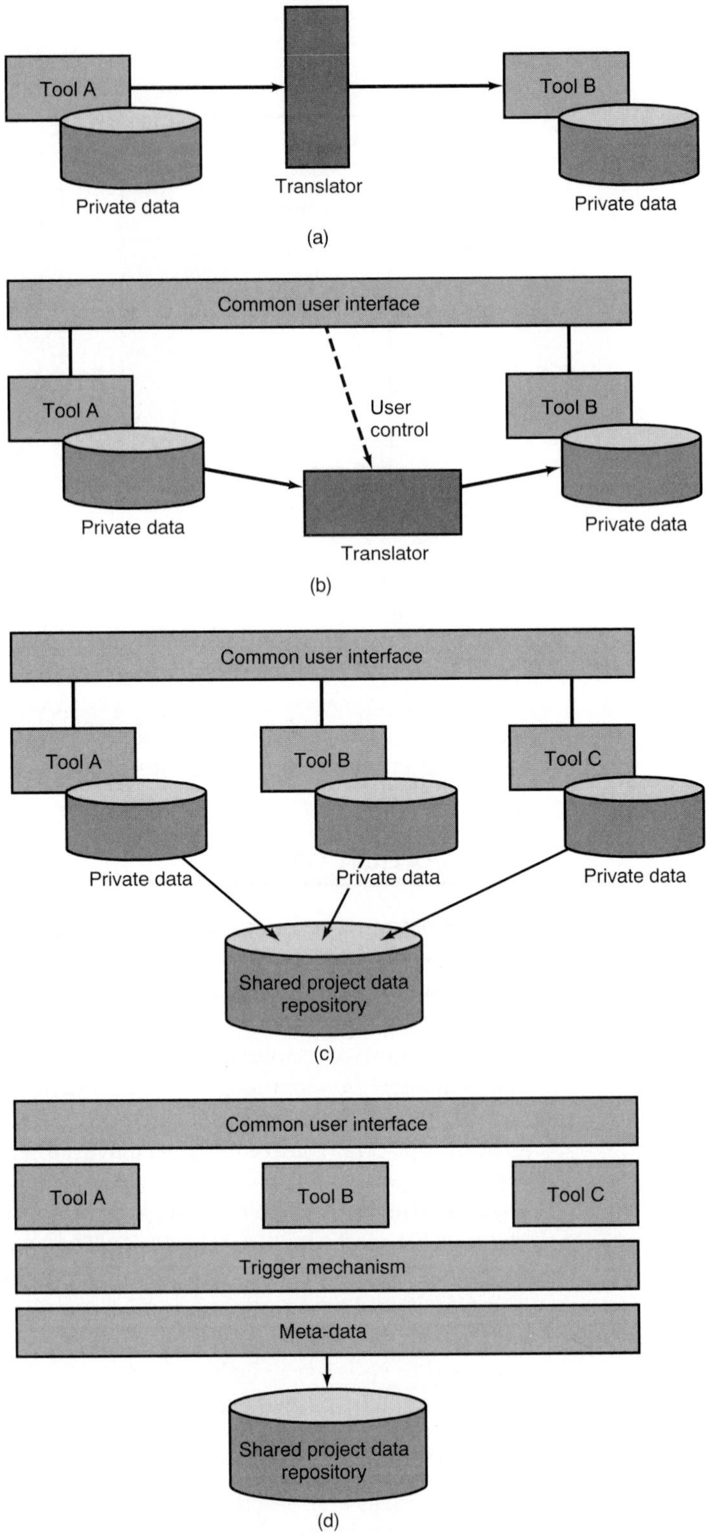

FIGURE 23.2.
Levels of CASE integration. (*a*) Data exchange; (*b*) common tool access; (*c*) data integration; (*d*) full integration.

translators have been developed through the mutual cooperation of the tool vendors involved and are available directly from them. In addition, many translators have been developed by consultants and users and are available for purchase or through "shareware" exchanges.

The drawback of the point-to-point data exchange is that usually only a portion of the data exported can be used by the receiving tool since it was not designed to be fully compatible. In addition, as the software evolves, it can become time-consuming to transfer files each time a small change is made. Versions can easily get "out of sync."

When many tools are used on a project, the number of point-to-point transfers can become unacceptably large. Finally, the transfer is normally in one direction only. There is no potential for reflecting changes in both directions, and it is difficult to make cross-document checks and maintain integrity (configuration control) of the configuration across the various tools that are used.

Common Tool Access The next level of integration is common tool access (Figure 23.2*b*), which allows the user to invoke a number of different tools in a similar manner, for example from a pull-down menu in the operating system window manager. In a multitasking environment such as UNIX or OS/2, this means a user can open several tools simultaneously, manually coordinating input to them and comparing design representations as they evolve. For example, the user might display a data flow diagram, a structure chart, a data dictionary, and a source code segment maintained by different tools. In this environment, the tool-to-tool data exchange might also be simplified by invoking the translation procedure with a simple menu or macro selection.

Common Data Management Data from a variety of tools can be maintained in a single logical database (Figure 23.2*c*), which physically may be either centralized or distributed. This simplifies the exchange of information and improves the integrity of the shared data, since each tool always has immediate access to the latest software engineering information. Access rights in a team environment can also be controlled and version management facilities may also be available, although these will be activated manually via a check-in, check-out procedure. Typically, there is a data merge function to enable developers working on different parts of an application to combine their work. If the tool set has cross-project checking capability, it can detect inconsistencies among the different developers' contributions.

Although the data from multiple tools are managed together at the common data management level, the tools have no explicit understanding of each other's internal data structures and design representation semantics. Consequently, a discrete translation step (usually invoked manually) is still required to enable one tool to use the output from another tool.

Data Sharing Tools at the data sharing level have compatible data structures and semantics and can directly use each other's data without translation. Each tool is designed to be compatible with all other tools in the data sharing environment. For this reason most data sharing occurs among tools from a single vendor or where strategic relationships between vendors have been formed to produce an integrated tool set, sometimes at the request of large customers. Unfortunately, there are few official standards in place to provide the common ground for industry-wide data sharing among CASE tools. However, de facto standards, suggested by large CASE vendors (e.g., DEC, Hewlett-Packard, IBM, or Sun), may provide the industry with some degree of coordination for data sharing.

Interoperability Tools that combine the characteristics of common access and data sharing are *interoperable*. This represents the highest level of integration among individual tools. However, there are other properties of the overall CASE environment that can be added to improve the effectiveness of the software development process.

Full Integration To achieve complete integration (Figure 23.2*d*) of the CASE environment, two additional facilities are needed: metadata management and a control facility. Metadata is information about software engineering data produced by the individual CASE tools. Metadata includes:

- Object definitions (types, attributes, representations, and valid relationships)
- Relationships and dependencies among objects of arbitrary granularity (i.e., a process on a DFD diagram, a single entity, or a subroutine code fragment)
- Software design rules (e.g., the correct ways to draw and balance a data flow diagram)
- Work flow (process) procedures (standard phases, milestones, deliverables, etc.) and events (reviews, completions, problem reports, change requests, etc.)

Often the rules and procedures portion of the metadata is defined in the form of a rule base to facilitate its modification as the software development process evolves. For example, a new design method might alter design rules for representation and change work flow process standards.

The control facility enables the individual tools to notify the rest of the environment (other tools, the metadata manager, the data manager, etc.) of significant events and to send requests for action to other tools and services via a *trigger*. For example, a design tool might notify a configuration management tool that a new version of a design document has been created and cause the configuration management tool to do a cross-document consistency check. The control facility helps to maintain the integrity of the environment and also provides a means to automate standard processes and procedures. The trigger facility might be embedded within a closed repository environment, or it might be visible to individual tools through a programmatic interface and message-passing mechanism.

23.3 THE INTEGRATION ARCHITECTURE

Using CASE tools, corresponding methods, and a procedural framework defined by the software engineering paradigm that has been selected, a pool of software engineering information is created. The integration framework facilitates transfer of information into and out of the pool. To accomplish this, the following architectural components must exist: A database must be created (to store the information); an object management system must be built (to manage changes to the information); a tools control mechanism must be constructed (to coordinate the use of CASE tools); a user interface must be available to provide a consistent pathway between actions made by the user and the tools contained in the environment. Most models (e.g., [WAS89], [FOR90]) of the integration framework represent these components as *layers*. A simple model of the framework, depicting only the components noted above, is shown in Figure 23.3.

The *user interface layer* (Figure 23.3) incorporates a standardized interface tool kit with a common presentation protocol. The *interface tool kit* contains software for human-computer interface management and a library of display objects. Both provide a consistent mechanism for communication between the interface and individual CASE tools. The most commonly used tool kit for CASE is the X-Window System [MIK90]. The *presentation protocol* is the set of guidelines that gives all CASE tools the same look and feel. Screen layout conventions, menu names and organization, icons, object names, the use of the keyboard and mouse, and the mechanism for tools access are all defined as part of the presentation protocol.

The *tools layer* incorporates a set of tools management services with the CASE tools themselves. *Tools management services* (TMS) control the behavior of tools within the environment. If multitasking is used during the

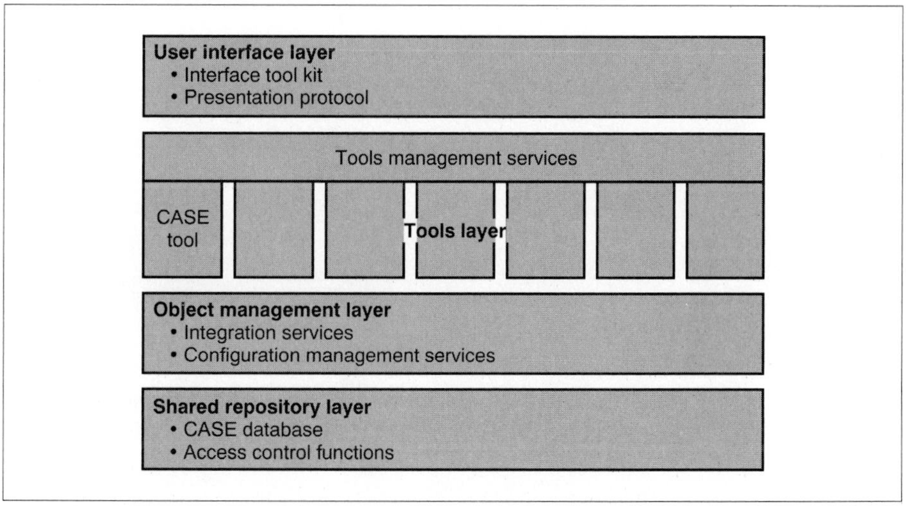

FIGURE 23.3. Architectural model for the integration framework.

execution of one or more tools, TMS perform multitask synchronization and communication, coordinates the flow of information from the repository and object management system into the tools, accomplishes security and auditing functions, and collects metrics on tool usage.

The *object management layer* (OML) performs the configuration management functions described in Chapter 21. In essence, the software in this layer of the framework architecture provides the mechanism for tools integration. Every CASE tool is "plugged into" the object management layer. Working in conjunction with the CASE repository, the OML provides *integration services*—a set of standard modules that couple tools with the repository. In addition, the OML provides configuration management services by enabling the identification of all configuration objects, performing version control, and providing support for change control, audits, and status accounting.

The *shared repository layer* is the CASE database[3] and the access control functions that enable the object management layer to interact with the database. Data integration is achieved by the object management and shared repository layers (Figure 23.4) and is discussed in greater detail later in this chapter.

23.4 TOOLS INTEGRATION

When an integrated CASE environment is considered, the mechanisms for the integration of CASE tools will be implemented differently depending on the architecture, the platform, and the philosophy of the designer of the en-

[3]In Chapter 21 we referred to the repository as the "project database."

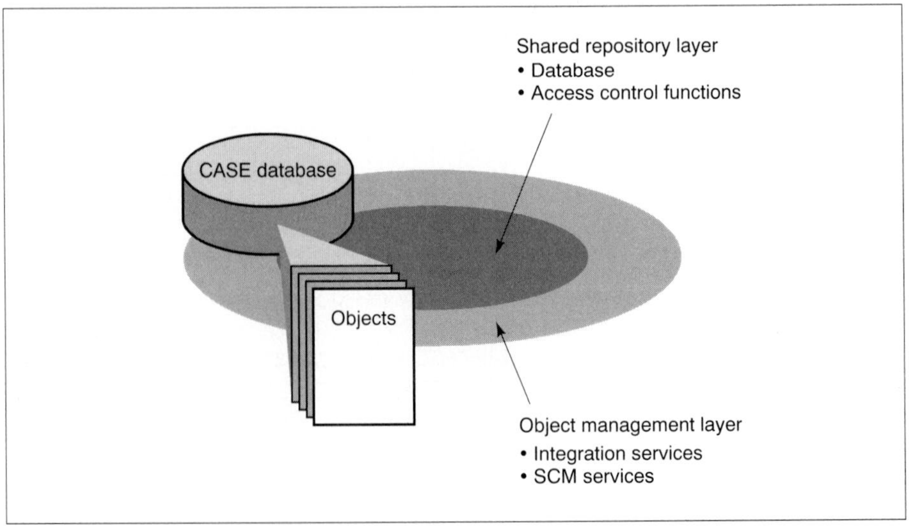

FIGURE 23.4. The layers that achieve data integration.

vironment. However, all CASE environments implement *execution mechanisms* and *communication mechanisms*. To illustrate the characteristics of these mechanisms, the Portable Common Tools Environment (PCTE) model[4]—one of a number of standards for integrated CASE environments—will be used.

Within PCTE, execution and communication mechanisms are referred to as *basic mechanisms*—functions that are defined to manipulate "entities" that exist in the software development context. Entities include both objects (e.g., data, source code, documents, devices) and the tools that operate on the objects.

Most I-CASE environments are designed to accommodate a multitasking operating system in which a number of different tools can be executing at the same time. For example, a compilation of one module can be invoked at the same time that modifications are being made to the design of another module. In addition, the completion of a task performed by one tool might lead automatically to the execution of another tool, if appropriate process activation mechanisms (triggers) are present.

Execution mechanisms provide "a uniform way to start a process from its static context regardless of whether it is an executable or interpretable program" [THO89]. In addition, these mechanisms provide features for suspending, resuming, and terminating a process. In this context a "process" can be viewed as a CASE tool.

Communication mechanisms manage interprocess communication by establishing message queues that enable different tools to communicate with one another. For example, the completion of a task performed by CASE tool *A* may result in an "event" that leads to the initiation of CASE tool *B*. To invoke *B*, an execution mechanism must be used, but to pass information from tool *A* to tool *B* requires a communication mechanism.

It should be noted that basic mechanisms use sophisticated communication and coordination capabilities that are often associated with operating system functions. The challenge for I-CASE environment developers is to implement these mechanisms in a way that decouples the environment from a specific operating system or, as a minimum, provides a layer between the environment itself and operating system internals.

Because the environment architecture for CASE is a distributed network, the mechanisms described in this section must be capable of being implemented in a networked environment. A *distribution mechanism* enables the basic mechanisms to be distributed across a network and also provides the following capabilities [THO89]: (1) network administration and supervision of all workstations connected to the network; (2) management of each network node (i.e., each workstation can be represented as an object in the repository and has as an attribute the workstation directory; (3) "transparent distribution" of execution and communication functions.

---

[4]PCTE was developed by commission of the European Communities ESPRIT program [PCT88].

23.5 DATA-TOOL AND DATA-DATA INTEGRATION

Data integration can be examined from two different points of view: (1) *Data-tool integration* considers the level of integration between CASE tools and the data that are produced by the tools (and people) throughout the software engineering process; (2) *data-data integration* examines the level of integration among the information items themselves.

In order to achieve the types of integration described above, it is necessary to define an abstraction that enables us to connect information entities (configuration objects) and provide some mechanism for establishing the relationships between these entities. This leads to an "object-oriented view" of the CASE database (Chapter 21). Elements of the software configuration (e.g., programs, documents, and data) are treated as *objects* to be manipulated as part of the software engineering process.

Once an object-oriented abstraction is established, the tool–data integration view defines *agents* (e.g., users or tools) that operate on objects (programs, documents, data). It is important to note that the operations implied by this discussion span a broad range of functionality. Operations can be as simple as a text editing process or as complex as a sophisticated software engineering method. For example, by combining the appropriate design information, it is relatively easy to create an object that we might characterize as a **design document.** The software engineer (e.g., the user of the CASE system) can operate on **design document** in a number of different ways. For instance, the software engineer can review **design document** in a purely manual fashion. Yet, the importance of the *review* operation cannot be overemphasized. The software engineer can also *edit* **design document,** *analyze* certain aspects of the architectural and or procedural design, *refine* or *elaborate* some aspects of the design, and *transmit* the design to another CASE tool that might *generate* code or provide *traceability* back to requirements. Each of the italicized terms in the preceding discussion represents an operation that can be applied to an object. Data-tool integration is accomplished as each of these operations is implemented in the I-CASE environment. It is fair to say that not all operations will be implemented as tool functions. In fact, some of the most important operations may be manual but still apply to the overall concept of integration.

Architecturally, data-tool integration was discussed in Section 23.2 and ranges from simple tool-to-tool data exchange to a complete I-CASE environment. As data-tool integration becomes more sophisticated, the complexity of the shared repository and the number of layers in the environment model must both increase.

Data-data integration can be modeled using entity-relationship techniques (Chapter 8). A configuration object (entity) is always related to one or more other configuration objects. For example, source code is related to the procedural design of a module. The module procedural design is related to the design architectural model and to one or more user requirements. The source code is also related to one or more test cases. The relationships

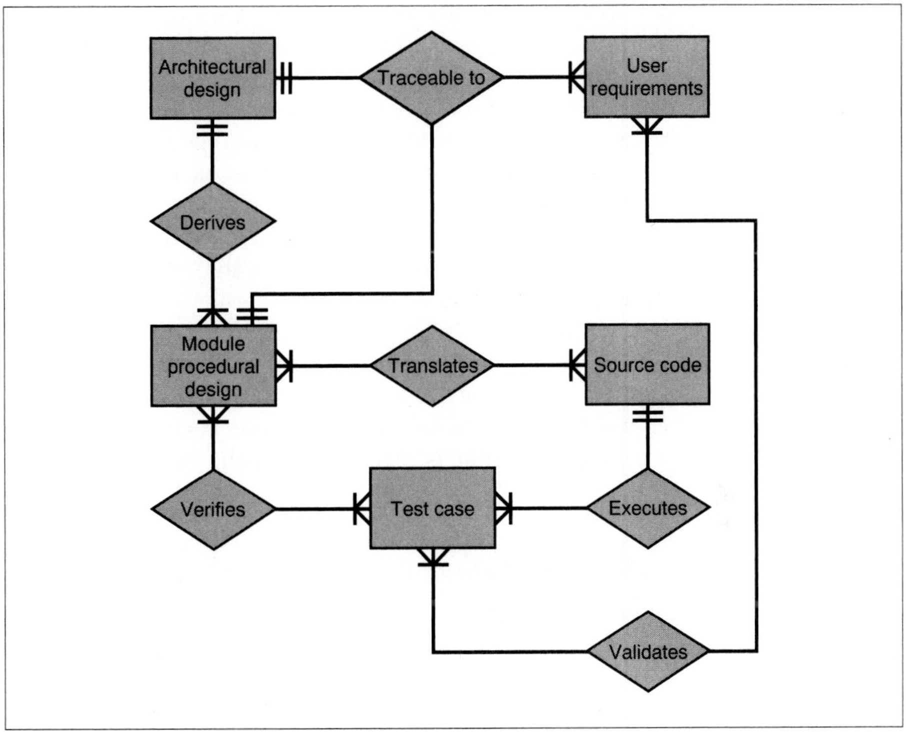

FIGURE 23.5. Simplified E-R diagram for relationships required to achieve data-data integration.

described above, as well as a few others, can be depicted as an E-R model shown in Figure 23.5. Referring to the figure, the relationships shown in the diamonds are implemented using one or more agents (CASE tools, people) and their corresponding operations.

The relationships depicted in the E-R diagram can also be used to represent different software versions. Recalling the discussion of version control in Chapter 21, the relationships defined to achieve data-data integration propagate across the evolution graph (Section 21.4) for the software. Each version maintains the same generic relationships among configuration objects.

23.6 THE CASE REPOSITORY

Webster's Dictionary [WEB74] defines the word repository as "any thing or person thought of as a center of accumulation or storage."[5] During the early

[5]Some of the other definitions of this word are equally intriguing when we consider the current state of software engineering practice: "(1) a room where things are placed for safekeeping; (2) a building for exhibiting objects; (3) a burial vault."

history of software development, the repository was indeed a person—the programmer who had to remember the location of all the information relevant to a software project; who had to recall information that was never written down and reconstruct information that had been lost. Sadly, using a person as "the center for accumulation and storage" (although it conforms to Webster's definition), does not work very well. Today, the repository is a "thing"—a database that acts as the center for both accumulation and storage of software engineering information. The role of the person (the software engineer) is to interact with the repository using CASE tools that are integrated with it.

In this book, a number of different terms are used to refer to the storage place for software engineering information: CASE database, project database, integrated project support environment (IPSE) database, and repository. Although there are subtle differences between some of these terms, all refer to the thing that is thought of as the center for accumulation and storage.

23.6.1 The Role of the Repository in I-CASE

The repository for an I-CASE environment is the set of mechanisms and data structures that achieve data-tool and data-data integration. It provides the obvious functions of a database management system,[6] but in addition, the repository performs or precipitates the following functions [FOR89b]:

- *Data integrity.* Includes a function to validate entries to the repository, ensures consistency among related objects, and automatically performs "cascading" modifications when a change to one object demands changes to objects that are related to it.
- *Information sharing.* Provides a mechanism for sharing information among multiple developers and between multiple tools, manages and controls multiuser access to data, and locks/unlock objects so that changes are not inadvertently overlaid on one another.
- *Data-tool integration.* Establishes a data model that can be accessed by all tools in the I-CASE environment, controls access to the data, and performs appropriate configuration management functions.
- *Data-data integration.* Establishes the database management system that relates data objects so that other functions can be achieved.
- *Methodology enforcement.* Defines a specific paradigm for software engineering that is implied by the E-R model of data stored in the repository; as a minimum, the relationships and objects define a set of steps that must be conducted to build the contents of the repository.

[6]Although many investigators feel that an object-oriented database management system is the correct approach, others believe that a relational DBMS can do the job adequately.

- *Document standardization.* Leads directly to a standard approach for the creation of software engineering documents by creating definitions for objects in the database.

To achieve these functions, the repository is defined in terms of a *metamodel.* The metamodel determines how information is stored in the repository, how data can be accessed by tools and viewed by software engineers, how well data security and integrity can be maintained, and how easily the existing model can be extended to accommodate new needs [WEL89].

The metamodel is the template into which software engineering information is placed. Earlier in this chapter we discussed the entity-relationship-attribute metamodel, but other more sophisticated models are also under consideration. A detailed discussion of these models is beyond the scope of this book. For further information, the interested reader should see Welke [WEL89].

23.6.2 Features and Content[7]

The features and content of the CASE repository are best understood by looking at the repository from two perspectives: what is to be stored in it and what specific services it provides. In general, the types of things to be stored in the repository include the following:

- The problem to be solved
- Information about the problem domain
- The system solution as it emerges
- Rules and instructions pertaining to the software process (methodology) being followed
- The project plan, resources, and history
- Information about the organizational context

A detailed list of types of representations, documents, and deliverables that are stored in the CASE repository is included in Table 23.1.

A robust CASE repository provides two different classes of services: (1) the same types of services that might be expected from any sophisticated database management system, and (2) services that are specific to the CASE environment.

Many repository requirements are the same as those of typical applications built on a commercial database management system. In fact, most of today's CASE repositories employ a DBMS (usually relational or object-

[7]This section has been adapted from Forte [FOR89b] with permission of CASE Consulting Group.

TABLE 23.1

CASE REPOSITORY CONTENTS [FOR89b]

Enterprise information	**Validation and verification**
Organizational structure	Test plan
Business area analyses	Test data cases
Business functions	Regression test scripts
Business rules	Test results
Process models (scenarios)	Statistical analyses
Information architecture	Software quality metrics
Application design	
Methodology rules	
Graphical representations	**Project management information**
System diagrams	Project plans
Naming standards	Work breakdown structure
Referential integrity rules	Estimates
Data structures	Schedules
Process definitions	Resource loading
Class definitions	Problem reports
Menu trees	Change requests
Performance criteria	Status reports
Timing constraints	Audit information
Screen definitions	
Report definitions	
Logic definitions	**System documentation**
Behavioral logic	Requirements documents
Algorithms	External/internal designs
Transformation rules	User manuals

Construction
- Source code
- Object code
- System build instructions
- Binary images
- Configuration dependencies
- Change information

oriented) as the basic data management technology. The standard DBMS features of a CASE repository supporting the management of software development information include:

Nonredundant data storage. The CASE repository provides a single place for the storage of all information pertinent to the development of software systems, eliminating wasteful and potentially error-prone duplication.

High-level access. The repository provides a common data access mechanism so data handling facilities do not have to be duplicated in each CASE tool.

Data independence. CASE tools and the target applications are isolated from physical storage so they are not affected when the configuration is changed.

Transaction control. The repository manages multipart interactions in a manner that maintains the integrity of the data when there are concurrent users and in the event of a system failure. This usually implies record locking, two-stage commits, transaction logging, and recovery procedures.[8]

Security. The repository provides mechanisms to control who can view and modify the information contained within it. At a minimum, the repository should enforce multilevel passwords and permission levels assigned by individual users. The repository should also provide assistance for automatic backup and restore, and archiving of selected groups of information, for example, by project or application.

Ad hoc data queries and reports. The repository allows direct access to its contents through a convenient user interface such as SQL or a forms-oriented "browser," enabling user-defined analysis beyond the standard reports provided with the CASE tool set.

Openness. Repositories usually provide a simple import/export mechanism to enable bulk loading or transfer. The interfaces are usually a flat ASCII file transfer or a standard SQL interface. Some repositories have higher-level interfaces that reflect the structure of their metamodels.

Multiuser support. A robust repository must permit multiple developers to work on an application at the same time. It must manage concurrent access to the database by multiple tools and users with access arbitration and locking at the file or record level. For environments based on networking, multiuser support also implies that the repository can interface with common networking protocols and facilities.

---

[8]A detailed discussion of these DBMS features is beyond the scope of this book. For further information refer to any good book on database management (e.g., [GUP91], [OZK90], or [FLE88]).

The CASE environment also makes special demands on the repository that go beyond what is directly available in a commercial DBMS. The special features of CASE repositories include:

Storage of sophisticated data structures. The repository must accommodate complex data types such as diagrams, documents, and files, as well as simple data elements. A repository also includes an information model (or metamodel) describing the structure, relationships, and semantics of the data stored in it. The metamodel must be extensible so that new representations and unique organizational information can be accommodated. The repository not only stores models and descriptions of the systems under development, but also associated metadata (i.e., additional information describing the software engineering data itself, such as when a particular design component was created, what its current status is, and what other components it depends upon).

Integrity enforcement. The repository information model also contains rules, or policies, describing valid business rules and other constraints and requirements on information being entered into the repository (directly or via a CASE tool). A trigger may be employed to activate the rules associated with an object whenever it is modified, making it possible to check the validity of design models in real time.

Semantic-rich tool interface. The repository information model (metamodel) contains semantics that enable a variety of tools to interpret the meaning of the data stored in the repository. For example, a data flow diagram created by a CASE tool is stored into the repository in a form based on the information model and independent of any internal representations used by the tool itself. Another CASE tool can then interpret the contents of the repository and use the information as needed for its task. Thus, the semantics stored in the repository permit data sharing among a variety of tools, as opposed to specific tool-to-tool conversions or "bridges."

Process/project management. A repository contains information not only about the software application itself, but also about the characteristics of each particular project and the organization's general process for software development (phases, tasks, and deliverables). This opens up possibilities for the automated coordination of technical development activity with the project management activity. For example, updating the status of project tasks can be done automatically or as a byproduct of using the CASE tools. Status updating can be made very easy for developers to perform without having to leave the normal development environment. Task assignment and queries can also be handled by electronic mail. Problem reports, maintenance tasks, change authorization, and repair status can be coordinated and monitored via tools accessing the repository.

The following repository features are all encompassed by software configuration management (Chapter 21). They are re-examined here to emphasize their interrelationship to I-CASE environments:

Versioning As a project progresses, many versions of individual work products will be created. The repository must be able to save all of these versions to enable the effective management of product releases and to permit developers to go back to previous versions during testing and debugging. Versioning is done with a compression algorithm to minimize storage allocation, and permits the regeneration of any previous version with some processing overhead.

The CASE repository must be able to control a wide variety of object types including text, graphics, bit maps, complex documents, and unique objects like screen and report definitions, object files, and test data and results. A mature repository tracks versions of objects with arbitrary levels of granularity; for example, a single data definition or a cluster of modules can each be tracked.

To support parallel development, the version control mechanism should permit multiple derivatives (variants) from a single predecessor. Thus a developer could be working on two possible solutions to a design problem at the same time, both generated from the same starting point.

Dependency Tracking and Change Management The repository manages a wide variety of relationships among the data elements stored in it. These include relationships between enterprise entities and processes, among the parts of an application design, between design components and the enterprise information architecture, between design elements and deliverables, and so on. Some of these relationships are merely associations, and some are dependencies or mandatory relationships. Maintaining these relationships among development objects is called *link management*.

The ability to keep track of all of these relationships is crucial to the integrity of the information stored in the repository and to the generation of deliverables based on it, and it is one of the most important contributions of the repository concept to the improvement of the software development process. Among the many functions that link management supports is the ability to identify and assess the effects of change. As designs evolve to meet new requirements, the ability to identify all objects that might be affected enables a more accurate assessment of cost, downtime, and degree of difficulty. It also helps prevent unexpected side effects that would otherwise lead to defects and system failures.

Link management helps the repository mechanism ensure that design information is correct by keeping the various portions of a design synchronized. For example, if a data flow diagram is modified, the repository can detect whether related data dictionaries, screen definitions, and code modules also require modification and can bring affected components to the developer's attention.

While CASE environments initially implemented link management at the file level, the trend is toward management at the object level, where an object can be any level of aggregation from a single data element to an application comprising many files. Such a robust implementation requires a generalized object management facility independent of the underlying file system.

Requirements Tracing A special function depending on link management is *requirements tracing*. This is the ability to track all the design components and deliverables that result from a specific requirement specification (forward tracking), as well as the ability to identify which requirement generated any given deliverable (backward tracking).

Configuration Management Another function depending on link management is configuration management. A configuration management facility works closely with the link management and versioning facilities to keep track of a series of configurations representing specific project milestones or production releases. Version management provides the needed versions, and link management keeps track of interdependencies. For example, configuration management often provides a *build* facility to automate the process of transforming design components into executable deliverables. Active link management associated with CASE design tools through the repository can ensure that all items affected by changed design representations will be properly regenerated as needed without explicit instructions from the developer. For example, a change to an E-R diagram may affect a screen definition and a database schema. Both might be automatically updated or called to the developer's attention. The configuration management facility might then initiate regeneration of the target code to reflect the change and relink the changed modules. While configuration management, automated builds, and requirements traceability are often provided by tools outside the repository, they are dependent on the repository's data and relationship management capabilities to operate effectively and without needless redundancy.

Audit Trails Related to change management is the need for an audit trail that establishes additional information about when, why, and by whom changes are made. Actually this is not a difficult requirement for a repository that has a robust information model. Information about the source of changes can be entered as attributes of specific objects in the repository. A repository trigger mechanism is helpful for prompting the developer or a tool to initiate the entry of audit information (such as the reason for a change) whenever a design element is modified.

23.6.3 Repository Standards

A number of different standards efforts are underway for I-CASE environments and the CASE repository. In some cases, a proposed standard goes beyond the definition of a repository to consider many different aspects of an integrated environment. In the United States, a number of proposed standards are competing for dominance. In Europe, a single standard has been adopted. Similarly, Japan and other far-Eastern countries have adopted a single (but different) standard for I-CASE. Each of the standards efforts is described briefly here so that the reader can gain a basic understanding of work that is underway:

Information Resource Dictionary Standard (IRDS), ANSI (X3.138-1988). The only formally approved ANSI standard presented in this section, IRDS was originally developed as a standard definition for requirements dictionaries (this standard can also be used for repositories). It focuses on the management of corporate information resources and is characterized using a multilevel metamodel. This standard helps in the creation of "bridges" between complementary tools such as analysis/design tools and code generators and in CASE tool portability across different platforms.

Atherton/DEC Tool Integration Standard (ATIS). Originally developed by Atherton Technology (a developer of framework tools) and Digital Equipment Corporation, ATIS has been adopted by the CASE Integration Standards Committee of the Software Productivity Consortium. ATIS focuses on the definition of a repository architecture and addresses SCM, tool integration, data security, and portability across platforms.

Common Ada Interface Standard (CAIS). Focusing primarily on tools for Ada software development, the CAIS standard defines interfaces between tools that will comprise the Ada development environment.

Portable Common Tools Environment (PCTE). PCTE was developed for use by the European software development community (the ESPRIT project) and has been adopted by the European Computer Manufacturer Association (ECMA). PCTE is an interface standard and architectural model for CASE. It addresses portability, concurrency control, network distribution, data architecture, and the user interface in the context of a CASE environment [THO89].

Software Industrialized Generator and Maintenance Aids (SIGMA). SIGMA is similar to PCTE in intent and scope and has been adopted in Japan and other far-Eastern countries.

Electronic Design Interchange Format (EDIF). This standard focuses on data formats for information exchange between CASE tools (and any other programs that want to exchange data). A CASE tool that produces output information in this format can easily transmit the information to other tools that accommodate input in EDIF format.

In addition to the standards introduced above, every major computer vendor has proposed "solutions" for I-CASE. A list of some of the more common frameworks follows:

- DSEE—Apollo (Hewlett-Packard)
- Cohesion—Digital Equipment Corporation
- HP-Softbench—Hewlett-Packard
- AD/Cycle—IBM
- NSE—Sun Microsystems

One or more of these integration architectures may evolve to become a de facto standard if widespread industry adoption occurs.

23.7 SUMMARY

During the software engineering process, a set of sequential tasks are coupled by a continuing flow of information. In addition, a set of "umbrella" activities occurs concurrently as one sequential task leads to the next. Each task and most activities can be assisted with the use of CASE tools. But the real benefit of the tools cannot be realized until the tools are *integrated*—until information produced with one tool can be easily used by other tools.

The I-CASE environment combines integration mechanisms for data, tools, and human-computer interaction. Data integration can be achieved through the direct exchange of information, through common file structures, by data sharing or interoperability, or through the use of a full I-CASE repository. Tools integration can be custom-designed by vendors who work together or can be achieved through management software provided as part of the repository. Human-computer integration is achieved through interface standards that are becoming increasingly common throughout the industry. An integration architecture is designed to facilitate the integration of users with tools, tools with tools, tools with data, and data with data.

The CASE repository is a relational or object-oriented database that is "the center of accumulation and storage" for software engineering information. The repository is implemented using a database management system that provides all standard features expected in a DBMS and special features required to accommodate the software engineering process. To achieve consistency in the implementation of these features, a number of CASE repository standards have been proposed.

The CASE repository has been referred to as a "software bus." Information moves through it, passing from tool to tool as the software engineering process progresses. But the repository is much more than a "bus." It is also a storage place that combines sophisticated mechanisms for integrating CASE tools, thereby improving the process through which software is developed.

REFERENCES

[GUP91] Gupta, R., and E. Horowitz (eds.), *Object-Oriented Databases with Applications,* Prentice-Hall, 1991.

[FLE88] Fleming, C., and B. von Halle, *Handbook of Relational Database Design,* Addison-Wesley, 1988.

[FOR89a] Forte, G., "In Search of the Integrated Environment," *CASE Outlook,* March/April 1989, pp. 5–12.

[FOR89b] Forte, G., "Rally Round the Repository," *CASE Outlook,* December 1989, pp. 5–27.

[FOR90] Forte, G., "Integrated CASE: A Definition," *Proc. 3rd Annual TEAMWORKERS Intl. User's Group Conference,* Cadre Technologies, Providence, RI, March 1990.

[MIK90] Mikes, S., *X Window System Technical Reference,* Addison-Wesley, 1990.

[OZK90] Ozkarahan, E. A., *Database Management: Concepts, Design and Practice,* Prentice-Hall, 1990.

[PCT88] *PCTE Functional Specification, Version 1.5,* PCTE Interface Management Board, Brussels, 1988.

[THO89] Thomas, I., "PCTE Interfaces: Supporting Tools in Software Engineering Environments," *IEEE Software,* November 1989, pp. 15–23.

[WAS90] Wasserman, A. I., "The Architecture of CASE Environments," *CASE Outlook,* March/April 1989, pp. 13–19.

[WEB74] *Webster's New World Dictionary,* second college edition, William Collins and World Publishing, 1974.

[WEL89] Welke, R. J., "Meta Systems on Meta Models," *CASE Outlook,* December 1989, pp. 35–45.

PROBLEMS AND POINTS TO PONDER

23.1 Discuss other human activities in which the integration of a set of tools has provided substantially more benefits than the use of each of the tools individually. Do not use examples from computing.

23.2 Research the CASE literature and find examples of each of the integration options discussed in Section 23.2. Write a brief paper that presents your findings.

23.3 Describe the role of a "trigger" in your own words. Discuss how a trigger might be implemented when full integration is to be used.

23.4 Select one of the I-CASE standards noted in Section 23.6.3 and get documentation about it. Using the framework architecture presented in Figure 23.3, show how the standard you have chosen maps into the framework as it is illustrated in the figure.

23.5 Discuss the differences and similarities between the tool integration mechanisms discussed in Section 23.4 and the program control mechanisms provided in most multitasking operation systems.

23.6 Expand the E-R diagram presented in Figure 23.5 to include a larger subset of software configuration objects. Refer to Chapter 8 for additional guidance in data modeling.

23.7 Describe what is meant by data-tool integration in your own words.

23.8 In a number of places in this chapter, the terms "metamodel" or "metadata" are used. Describe what these terms mean in your own words.

23.9 Can you think of additional configuration items that might be included in the repository contents shown in Table 23.1? Make a list.

23.10 How would you implement requirements tracing as part of the CASE repository?

FURTHER READINGS

Although there is great interest in I-CASE environments and the CASE repository, there are relatively few books that treat these subjects in detail. Books by Brereton (*Software Engineering Environments,* Wiley, 1988), Charette (*Software Engineering Environments,* McGraw-Hill, 1986), and Barstow, Shrobe, and Sandewall (*Interactive Programming Environments,* McGraw-Hill, 1984) present different views of the "ideal" CASE environment and provide worthwhile supplements to the information presented in this chapter. The reader who needs up-to-date information on I-CASE should refer to industry newsletters, periodicals, conference proceedings, and vendor literature.

Pomberger (*Software Engineering Tools for Professional Workstations,* Prentice-Hall, 1990) presents a series of papers that described the CASE environment developed for the experimental Lilith workstation. Some of the ideas suggested for Lilith may ultimately be incorporated into commercial products.

The industry newsletters listed in the Further Readings section of Chapter 22 are excellent sources of information on I-CASE. Articles in *IEEE Software* focus on pragmatic industry application of I-CASE while papers published in the *IEEE Transactions on Software Engineering* and the *Communications of the ACM* tend to present research directions and university-developed environments. Articles published in controlled circulation magazines such as *Datamation, Software Magazine,* and others are often superficial, but do provide an overview of popular I-CASE topics.

CASE conferences are sponsored by engineering societies, CASE vendors, and training companies. One of the best attended is "CASEWorld" (sponsored by Digital Consulting, Andover, MA, and held approximately semiannually).

All major computer companies and many of the larger CASE vendors have published reasonably detailed discussions of I-CASE. Although each has a definite bias, the generic information is worthwhile and informative.

CHAPTER 24

THE ROAD AHEAD

In the 23 chapters that have preceded this one, we have explored a process for software engineering. We have presented both management procedures and technical methods, basic principles and specialized techniques, people-oriented activities and tasks that are amenable to automation, paper and pencil notation, and CASE tools. We have argued that measurement, discipline, and an overriding focus on quality will result in software that meets the customer's needs, software that is reliable, software that is maintainable, software that is *better*. Yet, we have never promised that software engineering is a panacea.

As we move toward the dawn of a new century, software and systems technologies remain a challenge for every software professional and every company that builds computer-based systems. Max Hopper [HOP90] suggests the current state of affairs when he states:

> Because changes in information technology are becoming so rapid and unforgiving, and the consequences of falling behind are so irreversible, companies will either master the technology or die.... Think of it as a technology treadmill. Companies will have to run harder and harder just to stay in place.

Changes in software engineering technology are indeed "rapid and unforgiving," but at the same time progress is often quite slow. By the time a decision is made to adopt a new method (or a new tool), conduct the training necessary to understand its application, and introduce the technology into the software development culture, something new (and even better) has come along, and the process begins anew.

In this chapter, we examine the road ahead. Our intent is not to explore every area of research that holds promise. Nor is it to gaze into a "crystal ball" and prognosticate about the future. Rather, we will explore the scope of change and the way in which change itself will affect the software engineering process in the years ahead.

24.1 THE IMPORTANCE OF SOFTWARE—REVISITED

The importance of computer software can be stated in many ways. In Chapter 1 software was characterized as a differentiator. The function delivered by software differentiates products, systems, and services and provides competitive advantage in the marketplace. But software is more than a differentiator. The programs, documents, and data that are software help to generate the most important commodity that any individual, business, or government can acquire—information. Pressman and Herron [PRE91] describe software in the following way:

> Computer software is one of only a few key technologies that will have a significant impact on nearly every aspect of modern society during the 1990s. It is a mechanism for automating business, industry, and government, a medium for transferring new technology, a method of capturing valuable expertise for use by others, a means for differentiating one company's products from its competitors, and a window into a corporation's collective knowledge. Software is pivotal to nearly every aspect of business. But in many ways, software is also a hidden technology. We encounter software (often without realizing it) when we travel to work, make any retail purchase, stop at the bank, make a phone call, visit the doctor, or perform any of the hundreds of day-to-day activities that reflect modern life.
>
> Software is pervasive, and yet, many people in positions of responsibility have little or no real understanding of what it really is, how it's built, or what it means to the institutions that they (and it) control. More importantly, they have little appreciation of the dangers and opportunities that software offers.

It is the pervasiveness of software that leads us to a simple conclusion: Whenever a technology has a broad impact—an impact that can save lives or endanger them, build businesses or destroy them, inform government leaders or mislead them—it must be "handled with care."

24.2 THE SCOPE OF CHANGE

Change in the technologies that have an impact on computing seems to take on a progression that can be called the *5-5-5 rule*.[1] A fundamentally new

[1]The ideas for this discussion were first suggested in a presentation by Michael Horner [HOR90] of the Digital Equipment Corporation.

concept seems to move from initial idea to a mass market product in about 15 years.[2] During the first 5 years a new idea is formulated and evolves into a prototype that is used to demonstrate basic concepts. The experimental prototype is refined by scientists and engineers over the next 5 years and the first products (reflecting the new idea) are introduced during this time. The final 5 years are spent introducing the product (and its descendants) to the marketplace. By the end of 15 years (5-5-5), a new idea with technological merit can grow to encompass a multibillion dollar market (Figure 24.1). Although the 5-5-5 rule is only an approximation, the 15-year time span from initial idea to major market seems to be a reasonable scale with which we can measure the evolutionary change in the computer business.

The changes in computing over the past four decades have been driven by advances in the "hard sciences"—physics, chemistry, materials science, engineering. The 5-5-5 rule seems to work reasonably well when new technologies are derived from a basis in the hard sciences. However, during the next few decades, revolutionary advances in computing may well be driven by "soft sciences"—human psychology, neurophysiology, sociology, philosophy, and others. The gestation period for technologies derived from these disciplines is very difficult to predict.

For example, the study of human intelligence has been conducted for centuries and has resulted in only a fragmentary understanding of the psy-

[2]We assume, of course, that the idea is a good one and that sufficient resources are available to nurture it.

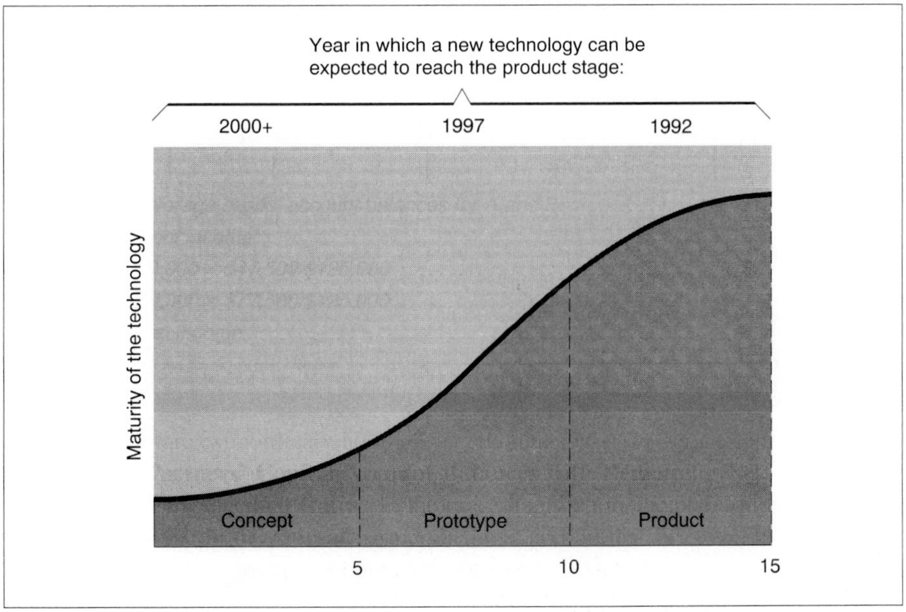

FIGURE 24.1.
The 5-5-5 rule.

chology of thought and the neurophysiology of the brain. However, significant progress has been made over the past 30 years. Information derived from the soft sciences is being used to create a new approach to software—artificial neural networks [WAS89]—that may lead to machine learning and the solution of "fuzzy" problems that have heretofore been impossible to solve using conventional computer-based systems.

The influence of the soft sciences may help mold the direction of computing research in the hard sciences. For example, the design of "future computers" may be guided more by an understanding of brain physiology than an understanding of conventional microelectronics.

The changes that will affect software engineering over the next decade will be influenced from four simultaneous directions: (1) the people who do the work, (2) the process that they apply, (3) the nature of information, and (4) the underlying computing technology. In the sections that follow, each of these components—people, the process, information, and the technology—are examined in more detail.

24.3 PEOPLE AND THE WAY THEY BUILD SYSTEMS

A dilemma faces every company that must build computer-based systems in the 1990s. The software required for high-technology systems becomes more and more complex and the size of resultant programs increases proportionally. There was a time when a program that required 100,000 lines of code was considered to be a large application. Today, the average program for a personal computer application (e.g., word processors, spreadsheets, graphics programs) is often two to three times that size. Programs built for use in industrial control, computer-aided design, information systems, electronic instrumentation, factory automation, and nearly every other "industry-capable" application often exceed 1,000,000 lines of code.[3]

The rapid growth in the size of the "average" program would present us with few problems if it weren't for one simple fact: As program size increases, the number of people who must work on the program must also increase. Experience indicates that as the number of people on a software project team increases, the overall productivity of the group may suffer. One way around this problem is to create a number of software engineering teams (Chapter 4), thereby compartmentalizing people into individual working groups. However, as the number of software engineering teams grows, communication between them becomes as difficult and time-consuming as

---

[3]With the advent of object-oriented technologies and increased reuse of program components, it is likely that the number of lines of code that must be built "from scratch" will decrease considerably over time. However, there is every indication that the overall size of programs (including reusable components) will continue to grow.

communication between individuals. Worse, communication (between individuals or teams) tends to be inefficient—that is, too much time is spent transferring too little information content and, all too often, important information "falls into the cracks."

If the software engineering community is to deal effectively with the communication dilemma, the road ahead for software engineers must include radical changes in the way individuals and teams communicate with one another. In many companies, electronic mail and bulletin boards have become commonplace as mechanisms for connecting a large number of people to an information network. The importance of these tools in the context of software engineering work cannot be overemphasized. With an effective electronic mail or bulletin board system, the problem encountered by a software engineer in New York City may be solved with the help of a colleague in Tokyo. In a very real sense, bulletin boards become knowledge repositories that allow the collective wisdom of a large group of technologists to be brought to bear on a technical problem or management issue.

As hardware and software technologies advance, the very nature of the workplace will change. The following scenario, adapted from Pressman and Herron [PRE91], provides one vision of a software engineer's work environment during the first decade of the twenty-first century:

> "Good morning," you say as you enter the office.
>
> Your workstation screen brightens, a window appears on the screen, an androgynous face appears, and a very human voice says, "Good morning. You have six voice mail messages, two facsimile transmissions, and a list of daily action items. Five development tasks are listed."
>
> The face and the voice belong to your "agent," an interface program that performs a variety of sophisticated clerical duties. It has been customized to anticipate your needs, it recognizes your voice, and it can do many things at once—like answer your phone around the clock, look up information, communicate directly with you, and perform other data processing functions. Communication with the agent can be verbal or written, but most people prefer to speak to their agents.
>
> "Show me the action items and development tasks," you say.
>
> Immediately the list of action items appears on the display and the agent begins to read the list aloud, highlighting each item as it is read.
>
> "Silence please, and hold the list," you interrupt. "While you're holding, check any of the voice mail or fax transmissions for key words."
>
> You have just asked the agent to perform an analysis of each incoming message to determine whether it contains any of a set of key words (these could be people's names, places, phone numbers, or topics that you deem as especially important). As you scan the list of action items on the screen, you see two appointments, a few telephone calls to be made, and an anniversary present to be purchased.
>
> By the time you have scanned the list of action items the agent's face has reappeared on the screen.

It's early and you're not tuned into the work day as yet. Embarrassed (but why should you be, you're communicating with a machine!), you ask, "What did I ask you to do?"

"You asked me to check any of the voice mail or fax transmissions for key words. Would you like a list?"

"Yes, but only those with reference to *changes*." A list of messages appears on your screen. You fix on one item from the list and say "Open". In less than a second, a video camera built into the workstation has tracked your eye movement at the time you said "Open" and the system has calculated which item you were looking at. You begin to read for a few moments and then stop.

"Please find all modules in the Factory Automation System that have been changed in the last month. Store the name of the modules, the source of the change, and the date and generate an action item for me to review them."

"What version of the system would you like to use?" asks the agent as a scrolling window appears.

"All," you reply.

"OK," says the agent.

While you're going through your mail the agent will have an "apprentice" perform the task you requested. That is, the agent "spawns" a task to perform configuration management functions. Within seconds, the agent returns to do your bidding. Simultaneously, the first apprentice is searching the CASE repository looking for module names.

"Can I have a word processor?" you ask the agent. A word processing program, not unlike the best that you see today, appears on the screen. You begin dictating a letter (the keyboard or a handwriting tablet can also be used). The text appears on the screen as you speak each word. While you are dictating, you think of something for the agent to do. Using a pointing device, you click on the agent's window.

"I need a source listing for module find.inventory.item. Insert it at the marker I'll note in the text of the document I was working on. Also, call Emily Harrison in system engineering and tell her that I'll be transmitting the document later today."

"OK," responds the agent. Apprentices are spawned to generate the table and make the call while you return to your dictation.

The environment implied by the above "conversation" will change the work patterns of a software engineer. Instead of using a workstation as a tool, hardware and software become an assistant, performing menial tasks, coordinating human-to-human communication, and, in some cases, applying domain-specific knowledge to enhance the engineer's ability.

If past history is any indication, it is fair to say that people themselves will not change. However, the ways in which they communicate, the environment in which they work, the methods that they use, the discipline that they apply, and, therefore, the overall culture for software development will change in significant and even profound ways. Recalling our earlier discussion of the 5-5-5 rule, some of the changes that will affect the people who do software engineering work and their current position on the 5-5-5 timeline are noted in Figure 24.2.

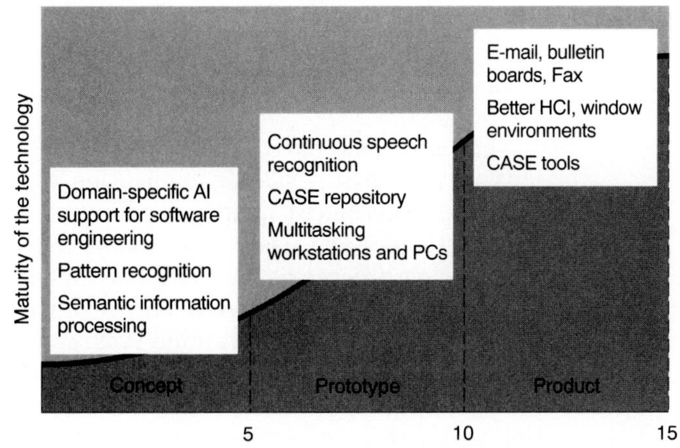

FIGURE 24.2. Influences on software engineers and their work.

24.4 THE "NEW" SOFTWARE ENGINEERING PROCESS

It is reasonable to characterize the first two decades of software engineering practice as the era of "linear thinking." Fostered by the classic life-cycle model (Chapter 1) software engineering was approached as a linear activity in which a series of sequential steps could be applied in an effort to solve complex problems. Although the sequential paradigm for software engineering work can be effective, it is not without the problems discussed in Chapter 1.

The use of the sequential software engineering paradigm will not disappear. A sequential approach will remain effective for those problems in which requirements are well defined, complexity is relatively low, and overall project and technical risks are reasonably well understood. But what about problems that don't fit into this category?

It is likely that a large segment of the software engineering community will move toward an evolutionary model for software development. The resultant software engineering paradigm (modeled after the "spiral model"), discussed in Chapter 1, represents a change from linear thinking to "iterative or evolutionary thinking."

The evolutionary model divides the software engineering space into four quadrants: management planning, formal risk analysis, engineering, and customer assessment. Recalling the discussion of the spiral model, each loop through the quadrants moves the developer closer to a completed system.

Within the engineering quadrant of the evolutionary (spiral) approach, it is likely that the road ahead will have an object-oriented orientation. The object-oriented paradigm for software development (Chapters 8 and 12) offers promise for a number of reasons:

- The derivation of reusable program components (classes) is a natural consequence of the object-oriented paradigm.

- Reuse provides immediate and compelling benefits in product quality and process productivity.
- An object-oriented viewpoint is actually a more natural way to examine complex problems.

Using a combination of object-oriented techniques and a variety of sophisticated CASE tools for application prototyping, the importance of the customer assessment quadrant will grow dramatically. In fact, it is likely that customers and users will become much more involved in the software engineering process as we move from a sequential view to an evolutionary view. By virtue of the iterative nature of the evolutionary paradigm, the customer will be forced to examine progress on a regular basis and feed back appropriate comment and concern. The additional customer involvement fostered by the evolutionary approach may lead to higher end-user satisfaction and better software quality overall.

24.5 NEW MODES FOR REPRESENTING INFORMATION

Over the past two decades, a subtle transition has occurred in the terminology that is used to describe software development work performed for the business community. Twenty years ago, the term "data processing" was the operative phrase for describing the use of computers in a business context. Today, data processing has given way to another phrase—information technology—that implies the same thing but presents a subtle shift in focus. The emphasis is not merely on processing large quantities of data, but rather on extracting meaningful information from this data. Obviously, this was always the intent, but the shift in terminology reflects a far more important shift in management philosophy.

When software applications are discussed today, the words "data" and "information" occur repeatedly. We encounter the word "knowledge" in some artificial intelligence applications, but its use is relatively rare. Virtually no one discusses "wisdom" in the context of computer software applications.

Data is raw information—collections of facts that must be processed to be meaningful. Information is derived by associating facts within a given context. Knowledge uses information obtained in one context and associates it with other information obtained in a different context. Finally, wisdom occurs when generalized principles are derived from disparate knowledge. Each of these four views of "information" is represented schematically in Figure 24.3.

To date, the vast majority of all software has been built to process data or information. Software engineers of the twenty-first century will be equally concerned with systems that process knowledge. Knowledge is two-dimensional. Information collected on a variety of related and unrelated topics is connected to form a body of fact that we call knowledge. The key is

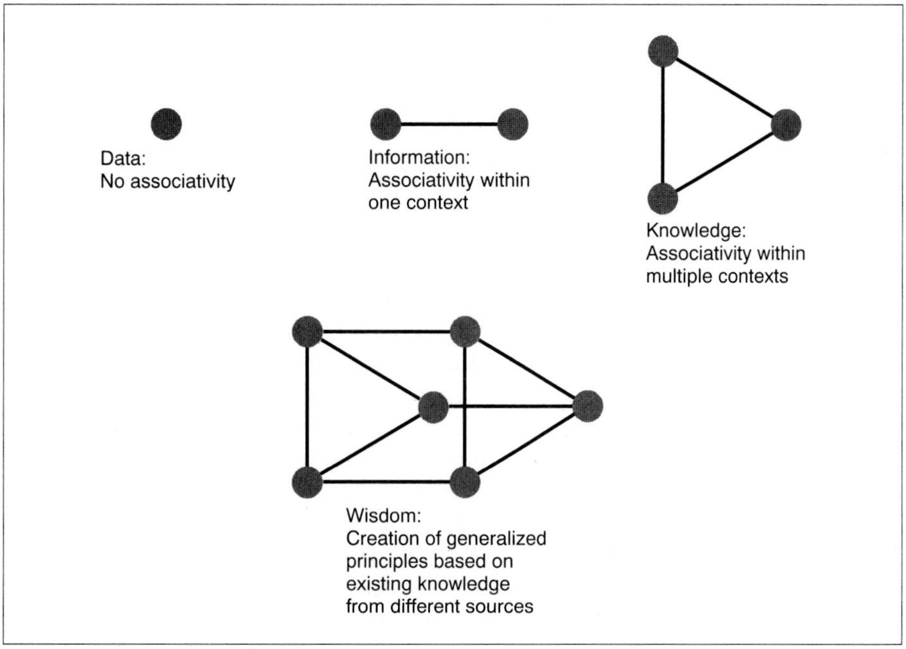

FIGURE 24.3. An "information" spectrum.

our ability to associate items of information from a variety of different sources that may not have any obvious connection to one another and combine them in a way that provides us with some distinct benefit.

To illustrate the progression from data to knowledge, consider recent census data indicating that the birthrate in 1991 in the United States was 4.1 million. This number represents a data value. Relating this piece of data with birthrates for the preceding 40 years, we can derive a useful piece of information—aging "baby boomers" of the 1950s are making a last gasp effort to have children prior to the end of their child-bearing years. This piece of information can then be connected to other seemingly unrelated pieces of information—for example, the current number of elementary school teachers who will retire during the next decade, the number of college students graduating with degrees in primary and secondary education, the pressure on politicians to hold down taxes and therefore limit pay increases for teachers.

Each of these pieces of information can be combined to formulate a representation of knowledge—there will be significant pressure on the education system in the United States in the late 1990s and this pressure will continue for over a decade. Using this knowledge, a business opportunity may emerge. There may be a significant opportunity to develop new modes of learning that are more effective and less costly than current approaches.

The road ahead for software leads toward systems that process knowledge. We have been processing data using computers for over 40 years and extracting information for over two decades. One of the most significant challenges facing the software engineering community is to build systems that take the next step along the spectrum—systems that extract knowledge from data and information in a way that is practical and beneficial.

24.6 TECHNOLOGY AS A DRIVER

The people who build and use software, the software engineering process that is applied, and the information that is produced are all affected by advances in hardware and software technology. Historically, hardware has served as the technology driver in computing. A new hardware technology provides potential. Software builders then react to customer demands in an attempt to tap the potential. Figure 24.4 applies the 5-5-5 rule in an attempt to place various hardware technologies in the overall evolutionary cycle. Placing a particular technology on the 5-5-5 curve can be difficult. For example, RISC technology has currently evolved to the product stage, but it is not yet a mature market. Hence, it has been placed in the "prototype" stage of technology maturity.

The road ahead for hardware technology is likely to progress along two parallel paths. Along one path, mature hardware technologies (CISC and RISC processors, memory, storage, and communications) will continue to evolve at a rapid pace. With greater capacity provided by traditional hardware technologies, the demands on software engineers will continue to grow.

But the real changes in hardware technology may occur along another path. The development of nontraditional hardware architectures (e.g., massively parallel machines, optical processors, neural network machines) may cause radical changes in the kind of software that we build and fundamental changes in our approach to the software engineering. Since these nontradi-

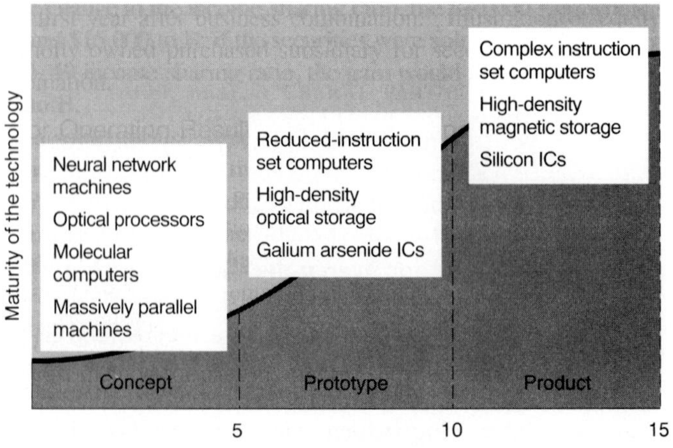

FIGURE 24.4. Changes in hardware technology.

tional approaches are in the first segment of the 15-year cycle, it is difficult to determine which will survive to maturity and even more difficult to predict how the world of software will change to accommodate them.

We have already noted that software technology tends to react to changes in hardware technology. Applying the 5-5-5 rule to software technology (Figure 24.5), the software products of today will be joined and possibly displaced by software technologies in the first and second stages of maturity. There is little doubt that the technologies shown in the prototype stage of Figure 24.5 will become extremely important as the 1990s progress. In fact, object-oriented technologies may form a bridge between artificial intelligence approaches (inherently object-oriented), conventional software applications, and database technology. In so doing, they may represent an important step toward knowledge processing as discussed in the preceding section.

The road ahead for software engineering will be driven by software technologies. As software moves more forcefully into the realm of fuzzy problems (AI, artificial neural networks, expert systems), it is likely that an evolutionary approach to software development will dominate all other paradigms. As object-oriented approaches become more prevalent, evolutionary paradigms for software engineering will be modified to accommodate program component reuse. "Foundries" that build "software ICs" may become a major new software business. In fact, as the new century dawns, the software business may begin to look very much like the hardware business of today. There may be vendors that build discrete "devices" (reusable software components), other vendors that build system components (e.g., a set of tools for human-computer interaction), and system integrators that provide solutions for the end user.

Software engineering will change—of that we can be certain. But regardless of how radical the changes are, we can be assured that quality will

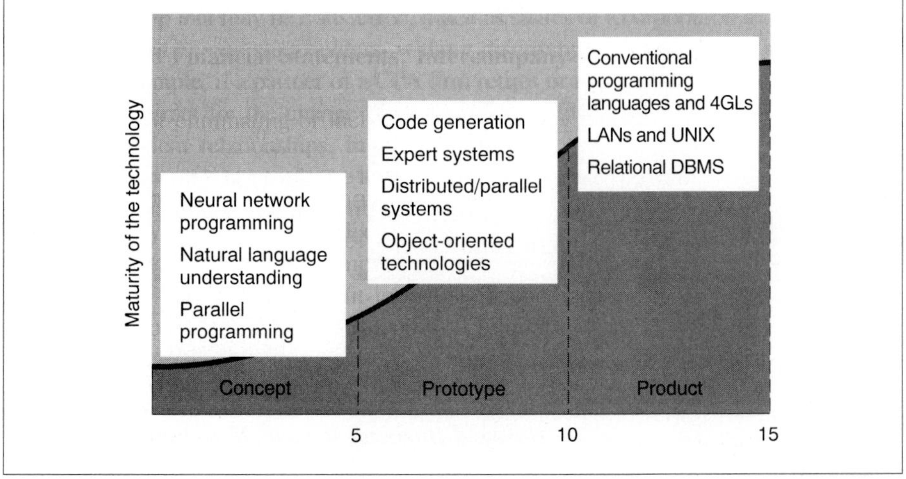

FIGURE 24.5. Changes in software technology.

never lose its importance and that effective analysis and design and competent testing will always have a place in the development of computer-based systems.

24.7 A CONCLUDING COMMENT

It is interesting, and not altogether coincidental, that the third edition of this book follows the 5-5-5 rule precisely. The preliminary "concept" (the first edition) was published in 1982; a more refined "prototype" (the second edition) was released in 1987; and the not-so-final "product" (this edition) has been introduced in 1992. Like software engineering, the content of this book has expanded and (hopefully) matured throughout the first two stages of the 5-5-5 cycle. Software engineering is now a product that is ready for a much broader market than it has currently penetrated.

An engineering approach to the development of computer software is a philosophy whose time has come. Although debate continues on the "right paradigm," the degree of automation, and the most effective methods, the underlying principles of software engineering are now accepted throughout the industry. Why then are we only recently seeing their broad adoption?

The answer, I think, lies in the difficulty of technology transition and the cultural change that accompanies it. Even though most of us appreciate the need for an engineering discipline for software, we struggle against the inertia of past practice.

To ease the transition we need many things—effective methods, powerful tools, acceptance by practitioners and support from managers, and no small dose of education and "advertising." Software engineering has not had the benefit of massive advertising, but as time passes the concept sells itself. In a way, this book is an "advertisement" for the technology.

You may not agree with every approach described in this book. Some of the techniques and opinions are controversial; others must be tuned to work well in different software development environments. It is my sincere hope, however, that *Software Engineering: A Practitioner's Approach* delineates the problems we face, demonstrates the strength of a software engineering concept, and provides a framework of methods and tools.

As we begin our approach toward the millennium year, the challenge of software remains. Let us hope that the people who meet that challenge—software engineers—will have the wisdom to develop systems that improve the human condition.

REFERENCES

[HOP90] Hopper, M. D., "Rattling SABRE, New Ways to Compete on Information," *Harvard Business Review,* May-June 1990, pp. 118–125.

[HOR90] Horner, M., "Future Directions in CASE," *Le Rendez-vous du Genie Logicial,* Centre International de Communication Avancee (CICA), Sophia Antipolis, France, May 29, 1990.
[PRE91] Pressman, R.S., and S.R. Herron, *Software Shock,* Dorset House, 1991.
[WAS89] Wasserman, P.D., *Neural Computing: Theory and Practice,* Van Nostrand Reinhold, 1989.

PROBLEMS AND POINTS TO PONDER

24.1 Get a copy of this week's major business and news magazines (e.g., *Newsweek, Time, Business Week*). List every article or news item that can be used to illustrate the importance of software.

24.2 Select three "fundamentally new ideas" that have led to major products. Draw a timeline and determine whether the 5-5-5 rule is too conservative, too optimistic, or right on target.

24.3 Add additional features to the software engineer's environment described in Section 24.3. Draw an annotated sketch that illustrates a software engineer's office in the year 2005.

24.4 Review the discussion of the spiral model in Chapter 1. Do some research and collect recent papers on the subject. Summarize the strengths and weaknesses of evolutionary paradigms based on experiences outlined in the papers.

24.5 Attempt to develop an example that begins with the collection of raw data and leads to acquisition of information, then knowledge, and finally, wisdom.

24.6 Select any one of the hardware technologies represented at the concept level in Figure 24.4 and write a two- or three-page paper that presents an overview of the technology. Present the paper to your class.

24.7 Select any one of the software technologies represented at the concept level in Figure 24.5 and write a two- or three-page paper that presents an overview of the technology. Present the paper to your class.

FURTHER READINGS

Books that discuss the road ahead for software and computing span a vast array of technical, scientific, economic, political, and social issues. Naisbitt and Aburdene (*Megatrends 2000,* William Morrow & Co., 1990) provide an intriguing picture of changes in each of these arenas as we move toward the twenty-first century. Rich and Waters (*The Programmer's Apprentice,* Addison-Wesley, 1990) present one view of "what to expect in the future of software development."

Within the more narrow context of computing and software, Allman (*Apprentices of Wonder,* Bantam Books, 1989) describes the potential impact of artificial neural networks—a book that suggests radical changes in what we will mean when the word "software" is used. Stoll (*The Cuckoo's Egg,* Doubleday, 1989) presents a fascinating look into the world of computer networks, hackers, and computer security—topics that are of significant importance as we become an integrated "electronic community."

Alvin Toffler (*Powershift,* Bantam Publishers, 1990) finishes the trilogy that began with *Future Shock* by discussing the disintegration of well-established power structures that is occurring throughout the world—a shift in power that he attributes directly to software and the information it produces.

INDEX